EXPERIMENTAL
ORGANIC CHEMISTRY

CW01653690

EXPERIMENTAL ORGANIC CHEMISTRY

Standard and Microscale

LAURENCE M. HARWOOD
BSc, MSc, PhD (Manch), MA (Oxon), CChem, FRSC
Department of Chemistry, University of Reading

CHRISTOPHER J. MOODY
BSc (Lond), PhD (L'pool), DSc (Lond), CChem, FRSC
School of Chemistry, University of Exeter

JONATHAN M. PERCY
BSc (Lond), PhD (Cantab)
School of Chemistry, University of Birmingham

Second Edition

Wiley India Pvt. Ltd.

Experimental Organic Chemistry
Standard and Microscale

Authorized reprint by Wiley India Pvt. Ltd, 4435-36/7, Ansari Road, Daryaganj, New Delhi – 110002.

Copyright © 1989, 1999 by Blackwell Science Ltd, a Blackwell Publishing company.
All rights reserved.

No part of this book, including interior design, cover design, and icons, may be reproduced or transmitted in any form except with the permission of the publisher.

Limit of Liability/ Disclaimer of Warranty: The publisher and the author make no representations or warranties with respect to the accuracy or completeness of the contents of this work and specifically disclaim all warranties, including without limitation warranties of fitness for a particular purpose. No warranty may be created or extended by sales or promotional materials. The advice and strategies contained herein may not be suitable for every situation. This work is sold with the understanding that the publisher is not engaged in rendering legal, accounting, or other professional services. If professional assistance is required, the services of a competent professional person should be sought. Neither the publisher nor the author shall be liable for damages arising herefrom. The fact that an organization or Website is referred to in this work as a citation and/or a potential source of further information does not mean that the author or the publisher endorses the information the organization or Website may provide or recommendations it may make. Further, readers should be aware that Internet Websites listed in this work may have changed or disappeared between when this work was written and when it is read.

TRADEMARKS: Wiley and the Wiley logo are trademarks or registered trademarks of John Wiley & Sons, Ltd., and/or its affiliates, in the United States and other countries, and may not be used without written permission. All other trademarks are the property of their respective owners. Wiley Publishing Inc., is not associated with any product or vendor mentioned in this book.

Wiley also publishes its books in a variety of electronic formats. Some content that appears in print may not be available in electronic books.

This edition is authorized for sale in the Indian Sub-continent only.

Reprint: 2011

Printed at: *Radha Offset, Delhi*

ISBN : 978-81-265-3044-1

Contents

Preface to the Second Edition

This book grew out of our conviction that highly developed practical skills, as well as a thorough grasp of theory, are the hallmark of an organic chemist and that chemistry is illustrated more vividly by experiment than from a book or lecture course, when the facts can seem abstract and sterile. Our aim therefore, was to produce a book containing safe, interesting experiments of varying complexity, together with all the associated technical instruction, which could be used in a variety of courses from the elementary to the advanced.

With the goal of enthusing people we have attempted to design experiments which are more than just recipes for preparing a particular compound, or manipulative exercises. Rather, we have attempted to wrap each experiment around some important reaction, an interesting mechanism, or an underlying principle; without forgetting the practical skills to be acquired along the way. Within the constant and overriding demands for safety, the range of experiments has been chosen to illustrate as many techniques and cover as much organic chemistry as possible, in order to link up with lecture courses, and provide depth and relevance to the whole teaching programme.

As with most practical texts, the book is divided into two main sections; the former surveying aspects of safety, apparatus, purification and analytical techniques, and the recording and retrieval of data; the latter containing the experimental procedures and appendices. In keeping with our aim of covering a range of procedures commonly used in the research laboratory, the first section involves a progression, from the basic apparatus and techniques required in the initial stages of a teaching course to the level of sophistication demanded at research level work. For instance, along with the more traditional descriptions, such as setting up a reduced pressure distillation or using a vacuum desiccator, are directions for analysis by gas chromatography, transferral of air-sensitive liquids by syringe, and the handling of pressurized gases. In line with current trends, the second edition contains additional sections covering the specific apparatus and techniques associated with microscale manipulations, which have found favour in many teaching laboratories due to the economy of working at reduced scale and the concomitant reduction in associated hazards and disposal of waste. Selected experiments in the second section have been chosen to exemplify this approach and are presented as both 'standard' and 'microscale' procedures. For this reason, Jonathan Percy has joined the team and has been responsible for preparing these aspects of the second edition.

As this is a practical book, greater emphasis has usually been placed on describing the practical aspects of the techniques, with any theoretical treatment being supported by cross-referencing to other works. However, space has been devoted to both the theoretical and practical aspects of spectroscopic analysis, and we make no apologies for this in light of the crucial role played by such analytical techniques. We have retained the contribution on NMR spectroscopy made by Dr Andy Derome but are deeply saddened to record his tragic and untimely death in 1991, aged 33.

Despite the emphasis on spectroscopy, the book does not ignore the more traditional elements of qualitative analysis as, although such methods have now been largely superseded by spectroscopic methods of analysis, they are invaluable for developing small-scale manipulation techniques as well as fostering an appreciation of physical and chemical properties of different classes of compound.

The second section of the book, containing the experimental procedures, has been further subdivided into chapters covering functional group interconversions, carbon–carbon bond-forming reactions, and projects. Within the first two subdivisions, we have attempted to include examples of most of the important reaction types at varying levels of experimental difficulty, so that a concerted series of experiments might be designed that is tailored to the specific teaching needs of a class or an individual student. Thus, for example, in the chapter on functional group interconversions, there is a series of experiments on reduction reactions and these range in difficulty from a simple ketone reduction with sodium borohydride to an advanced level experiment that uses an alkali metal in liquid ammonia. Likewise, in the chapter on carbon–carbon bond-forming reactions, you will find experiments involving simple carbonyl condensation reactions, progressing through to examples of modern enolate chemistry. Indeed, it is our hope that the experiments in these two chapters will come to be recognized as 'standard procedures' for carrying out, say, a lithium aluminium hydride reduction, a chromium (VI) oxidation, or a Wittig reaction. The final chapter contains experiments which are loosely described as projects. These experiments include natural product extractions, multi-stage syntheses, and physical organic investigations. We particularly wanted this chapter to reflect not only synthetic work, but also fundamental investigative work on the properties of organic compounds and on the mechanisms of organic reactions. As well as duplicating selected procedures in microscale in the second edition, several experiments from the first edition which have been judged to be less easily repeated or unduly duplicative have been deleted, while other new procedures have been included to reflect recent developments in organic chemistry.

Safety in the laboratory was always the paramount consideration when choosing an experiment, and we have attempted to minimize potential hazards by avoiding toxic materials wherever possible and by highlighting in the text any possible hazards at appropriate points of the procedure. In addition, the scale of each standard experimental procedure has been kept as small as is commensurate with the level of difficulty, to minimize any adverse consequences of an accident, in addition to lessening disposal problems and cost.

Within this consideration, the experiments have been chosen for their reproducibility and educational content. To this end the experiments have been independently assessed by chemists from around the world. Each experiment is preceded by a general discussion, outlining the aims and salient features of the investigation, and is followed by a series of problems designed to emphasize the points raised in the experiment. To make the greatest use of time available in the teaching laboratory and encourage forward planning, apparatus, instruments and chemicals required in the experiment are listed at the beginning of the procedure; together with an estimation of the amount of time necessary to complete the experiment. Wherever possible, extended periods of reflux or stirring have been avoided and long experiments have been designed so that they have clear break points at roughly 3 h intervals, indicated as margin notes in the procedure. The degree of difficulty of each experiment is also indicated:

1 = introductory level experiments requiring little previous experience;
2 = longer experiments with the emphasis on developing basic experimental techniques;
3 = experiments using more complex techniques and spectroscopic analysis;
4 = research level.

However, it must be remembered that the time and level assessments are only subjective guidelines and should not be taken as absolute. The use of spectroscopic analysis in level 3 and 4 experiments for characterization of materials reflects the overwhelming importance of these techniques in organic chemistry. However, it is not necessary to have access to spectrometers to carry out these experiments, as IR and NMR spectra of most of the compounds prepared are contained in the Aldrich Libraries of IR and NMR data. References to these, together with data on yields and melting points, useful hints and checkers' comments for each experiment, and guidelines for answers to all of the problems, are contained in an accompanying manual which is available to instructors from the publisher, free of charge.

It was not our intention to provide an exhaustive series of tables of these data in this book, as we felt it desirable to encourage the use of the chemical literature and other sources of data instead of providing all information necessary. Nevertheless, we have brought together some data in appendices at the back of the book (hazards, purification and properties of solvents, spectroscopic data) which we felt were liable to be of greatest use both to students working for their first degree as well as research chemists.

Finally we would like to acknowledge certain individuals whose help has been fundamental in the production of this book. Special thanks go to Dr Neil Isaacs of the University of Reading who provided us with a series of experiments for inclusion, particularly those having a physical organic slant, and the late Dr Andy Derome for the section on NMR spectroscopy. We would like to thank Professor Charles Rees of Imperial College for his involvement with the project from the beginning and his encouragement to take it on in the first place. Mr Peter Heath and Dr Simon Tyler kindly recorded the NMR and IR spectra which are reproduced in the experimental section of the book. Dr Jeffrey Seeman, Philip Morris Research, and Dr Jeremy Evans and Dr Guy Casy, University of Oxford, spent much spare time on the first edition and provided us with many valuable comments. We also reiterate our gratitude to those who checked the original experimental procedures or who subsequently suggested valuable modifications. In addition, we thank members of our research groups who checked the new procedures and the microscale variants in the second edition—these are the sort of enthusiastic organic chemists we hope this book will be instrumental in producing.

On the book production side we would like to thank Anne Stanford for her help and efforts in making this second edition a reality, and Nick Parsons, whose hard work on the first edition made the second edition so much easier to produce.

Laurence Harwood
Department of Chemistry
University of Reading
Whiteknights
Reading RG6 6AD

Jonathan Percy
School of Chemistry
University of Birmingham
Edgbaston
Birmingham B15 2TT

Chris Moody
School of Chemistry
University of Exeter
Stocker Road
Exeter EX4 4QD

PART 1
LABORATORY PRACTICE

Chapter 1 Safety in the Chemical Laboratory

The chemistry laboratory is a dangerous environment in which to work. The dangers are often unavoidable since chemists regularly have to use hazardous materials. However, with sensible precautions the laboratory is probably no more dangerous than your home, be it house or apartment, which, if you stop to think about it, also abounds with hazardous materials and equipment—household bleach, pharmaceutical products, herbicides and insecticides, natural or bottled gas, kitchen knives, diverse electrical equipment, the list goes on and on—all of which are taken for granted. In the same way that you learn to cope with the hazards of everyday life, so you learn good laboratory practice, which goes a long way to minimize the dangers of organic chemistry.

The experiments in this book have been carefully chosen to exclude or restrict the use of exceptionally hazardous materials, whilst still highlighting and exemplifying the major reactions and transformations of organic chemistry. However, most chemicals are harmful in some respect, and the particular hazards associated with the materials for each experiment are clearly stated; **these warnings should not be ignored**. Unfortunately it has not been possible to exclude totally the use of some chemicals, such as chloroform, which are described as 'cancer suspect agents', but if handled correctly with proper regard for the potential hazard, there is no reason why such compounds cannot be used in the organic laboratory. Ultimately, laboratory safety lies with the individual; *you* are responsible for carrying out the experiment in a safe manner without endangering yourself or other people, and therefore it is *your* responsibility to learn and observe the essential safety rules of the chemical laboratory.

1.1 Essential rules for laboratory safety

The essential rules for laboratory safety can be expressed under two simple headings: **ALWAYS** and **NEVER**.

Most of these rules are common sense and need no further explanation. Indeed if asked to name the single most important factor which contributes towards safety in the laboratory, the answer is simple: common sense.

ALWAYS
- familiarize yourself with the laboratory safety procedures
- wear eye protection
- dress sensibly
- wash your hands before leaving the laboratory
- read the instructions carefully before starting any experiment
- check that the apparatus is assembled correctly
- handle all chemicals with great care
- keep your working area tidy
- attend to spills immediately
- ask your instructor if in doubt

NEVER
- eat or drink in the laboratory
- smoke in the laboratory
- inhale, taste or sniff chemicals
- fool around or distract your neighbours
- run in the laboratory
- work alone
- carry out unauthorized experiments

Laboratory safety procedures

Your laboratory will have certain safety procedures with which you must be familiar. Some of these procedures are legal requirements; others will have been laid down by the department. Make sure you know where all the exits to the laboratory are, in the event of an evacuation because of fire or other incident. Make sure that you know the precise location of fire extinguishers, fire blankets, sand buckets, safety showers, and eye-wash stations. Make sure you know what type the fire extinguishers are, and how to operate them, especially how to remove the safety pin.

Eye protection

You must wear eye protection at all times in the laboratory. Even if you are just writing in your notebook, your neighbour may be handling corrosive chemicals. Eyes are particularly vulnerable to damage from sharp objects such as broken glass, and from chemicals, and therefore must always be protected to prevent permanent damage. Protection should be in the form of approved safety goggles or safety glasses. Ordinary prescription glasses do not provide adequate protection, since they do not have side shields, and may not have shatter-proof lenses. If you are going to do a lot of laboratory work, it is probably worth getting a pair of safety glasses fitted with prescription lenses. Alternatively, wear goggles over your normal glasses for full protection.

Contact lenses

Contact lenses are often forbidden in chemical laboratories, because in the event of an accident, chemicals can get under the lens and damage the eye before the lens can be removed. Even if contact lenses are permitted, then you must wear well-fitting goggles for protection. Inform your instructor, the laboratory staff and your neighbours that you are wearing contact lenses so that they know what to do in case of accident. Although no experiments in this book require them, full face shields should be worn for particularly hazardous operations. If a chemical does get into the eye, you must take swift action. The appropriate action is discussed on p. 13.

Dress

Dress sensibly in the laboratory. The laboratory is no place to wear your best clothes, since however careful you are, small splashes of organic chemicals or acids are inevitable. For this reason, shorts or short skirts are unsuitable for laboratory work and are forbidden in many institutions. A laboratory coat should always be worn, and loose fitting sleeves which might catch on flasks, etc. should be rolled back. Long hair is an additional hazard, and should always be tied back. Proper shoes should be worn; there may be pieces of broken glass on the laboratory floor, and sandals do not provide adequate protection from glass or from chemical spills.

Equipment and apparatus

Never attempt to use any equipment or apparatus unless you fully understand its function. This is particularly true of items such as vacuum pumps, rotary evaporators and cylinders of compressed gas, where misuse can lead to the damage of expensive equipment, your experiment being ruined or, most serious of all, an accident. Remember the golden rule:

If in doubt, ask.

Before assembling the apparatus for your experiment, check that the glassware is free from cracks and 'stars'. Always check the apparatus is properly clamped and supported and correctly assembled *before* adding any chemicals. Again, if in any doubt as to how to assemble the apparatus, ask.

Handling chemicals

Chemicals are hazardous because of their toxic, corrosive, flammable or explosive properties. Examples of the various categories of hazardous chemicals are given in the next section, but all chemicals should always be handled with great care. The major hazard in the organic laboratory is fire. Most organic compounds will burn when exposed to an open flame, and many, particularly solvents, which are often present in large quantities in the laboratory, are highly flammable. A serious solvent fire can raise the temperature of the laboratory to well over 100°C within minutes of it starting. Good laboratory practice really demands that there should be no open flames in the organic laboratory. Steam baths, heating mantles and hotplates should be used wherever possible to heat reaction mixtures and solvents. In many laboratories, the Bunsen burner is still the main source of heat, and therefore a strict code of practice is needed to prevent serious fires. **Never** light a burner before checking that there are no flammable liquids in open containers in the vicinity. Conversely **never** transfer a flammable liquid without checking that there are no open flames in the vicinity. The correct use of burners is discussed in more detail in Chapter 2. Remember that solvent vapour is heavier than air and will therefore travel along bench tops and down into sinks and drains; never pour flammable solvents down the sink.

Always check for flammable solvents before lighting a burner

Never pour flammable solvents down the sink

Avoid inhaling the vapours from organic compounds at all times and whenever possible use a reliable fume hood. The use of a good fume hood is essential for operations involving particularly toxic materials and for reactions that evolve irritating or toxic vapours.

Wear gloves when handling corrosive chemicals

Avoid skin contact with chemicals at all times. This is particularly important when handling corrosive acids and chemicals that are easily absorbed through the skin. It is best to wear disposable plastic gloves for routine laboratory operations; this minimizes the risk of chemicals coming into contact with the skin, but you must always be alert to the risk of seepage under the glove which will exacerbate the dangers due to the material being held in close contact with the skin. The risk is also reduced by good housekeeping, ensuring that your bench and areas around the balance are kept clean and tidy. When highly corrosive or toxic chemicals are being handled, thin disposable gloves are inadequate and thick protective gloves must be worn. However, remember to remove gloves before leaving the laboratory; do not contaminate door handles and other surfaces with soiled gloves.

Spills

All chemical spills should be cleared up immediately. Always wear gloves when dealing with a spill. Solids can be swept up and put in an appropriate waste container. Liquids are more difficult to deal with. Spilled acids must be neutralized with solid sodium bicarbonate or sodium carbonate, and alkalis must be neutralized with sodium bisulfate. Neutral liquids can be absorbed with sand or paper towels, although the use of sand is strongly advised, since paper towels are not appropriate for certain spills. If the spilled liquid is very volatile, it is often best to clear the area, extinguish all lighted burners and let the liquid evaporate. When highly toxic chemicals are spilt, alert your neighbours, inform your instructor, ventilate and clear the area immediately.

1.2 Hazardous chemicals

One of the fundamental rules of laboratory safety requires you to read the instructions before starting any experiment. The experimental procedures in this book contain clear warnings about the hazards associated with any particular material or operation. The properties of chemicals are given as a simple one word hazard warning—**flammable**, **explosive**, **oxidizer**, **corrosive**, **toxic**, **cancer suspect agent**, **irritant**, **lachrymator**—although some chemicals may fall into more than one hazard category. These warnings are similar to the warnings that are given on reagent bottles, although these are often accompanied by a symbol or sign. These symbols are usually the standard hazard signs required by the regulatory authorities. For instance, in the United States, the Department of Transportation is the responsible body, and in Europe there is an EU directive about warning signs. The hazard labels are usually square or diamond shaped, and consist of a pictorial warning together with appropriate words. Some examples of the commonly used symbols are shown in Fig. 1.1, and examples of each type of hazardous chemical are given below. In addition, Appendix 1 (p. 670) lists about 100 commonly encountered laboratory solvents, chemicals and reagents with a summary of their hazardous properties.

Flammable reagents

Always follow the general guidelines (pp. 5–6) when handling flammable reagents, **continually checking that there are no open flames in the vicinity**.

Solvents constitute the major flammable material in the organic laboratory. The following organic solvents are all commonly used and are highly flammable: hydrocarbons such as *hexane*, *light petroleum* (*petroleum ether*), *benzene*, *toluene*; alcohols such as *ethanol* and *methanol*; esters such as *ethyl acetate*; ketones such as *acetone*.

Ethers require a special mention because of their tendency to form explosive peroxides on exposure to air and light. *Diethyl ether* and *tetrahydrofuran* are particularly prone to this and should be handled with great care. In addi-

Fig. 1.1 Common hazard warning signs.

tion, diethyl ether has a very low flash point and has a considerable narcotic effect.

Carbon disulfide is so flammable that even the heat from a steam bath can ignite it. The use of this solvent should be avoided at all times.

Additionally some gases, notably *hydrogen*, are highly flammable, as are some solids, particularly finely divided metals such as *magnesium* and *transition-metal catalysts*. Some solids such as *sodium* and *lithium aluminium hydride* are described as flammable because they liberate hydrogen on reaction with water.

Explosive reagents

Some chemicals constitute explosion hazards because they undergo explosive reactions with water or other common substances. The alkali metals are common examples: *sodium metal* reacts violently with water; *potassium metal* reacts explosively with water.

Other compounds contain the seeds of their own destruction. This usually means that the molecule contains a lot of oxygen and/or nitrogen atoms, and can therefore undergo internal redox reactions, or eliminate a stable molecule such as N_2. Such compounds are often highly shock sensitive and constitute a considerable explosion hazard particularly when dry. Examples include *polynitro compounds*, *picric acid*, *metal acetylides*, *azides*, *diazo compounds*, *peroxides* and *perchlorate salts*. These are avoided in procedures described in this book.

If you have to use potentially explosive reagents, wear a face mask, work on the smallest scale possible and work behind a shatter-proof screen. Never do so without consulting an instructor and alert others before commencing the procedure.

Oxidizers

Oxidizers are an additional hazard in the chemical laboratory, since they can cause fires simply by coming into contact with combustible material such as paper.

Nitric and *sulfuric acids*, as well as being highly corrosive, are both powerful oxidizers.

Reagents such as *bleach*, *ozone*, *hydrogen peroxide*, *peracids*, *chromium (VI) oxide* and *potassium permanganate* are all powerful oxidizers.

Corrosive reagents

Always wear appropriate protective gloves when handling corrosive reagents. Spills on the skin should be washed off immediately with copious amounts of water.

The following acids are particularly corrosive: *sulfuric*, *hydrochloric*, *hydrobromic*, *phosphoric* and *nitric*, as are organic acids such as *carboxylic acids* and *sulfonic acids*.

Phenol is a particularly hazardous chemical and causes severe burns, as well as being extremely toxic and rapidly absorbed through the skin.

Alkalis such as *sodium hydroxide*, *potassium hydroxide* and, to a lesser extent, *sodium carbonate* are also extremely corrosive as are *ammonia*, *ammonium hydroxide* and organic bases such as *triethylamine* and *pyrrolidine*.

Bromine is an extremely unpleasant chemical. It causes severe burns to the skin and eyes, and must be handled in a hood. In addition, its high density and volatility make it almost impossible to transfer with a pipette without spills.

Thionyl chloride, *oxalyl chloride*, *aluminium chloride* and other reagents which can generate HCl by reaction with water are also corrosive and cause severe irritation to the respiratory system.

Harmful and toxic reagents

Always handle toxic chemicals in the hood

The distinction between *harmful* and *toxic* is one of degree; most organic compounds can be loosely described as harmful, but many are much worse than that, and are therefore classified as toxic. Commonly encountered compounds that are particularly toxic and therefore must always be handled in a hood include: *aniline*, *benzene*, *bromine*, *dimethyl sulfate*, *chloroform*, *hexane*, *hydrogen sulfide*, *iodomethane*, *mercury salts*, *methanol*, *nitrobenzene*, *phenol*, *phenylhydrazine*, *potassium cyanide* and *sodium cyanide*. You must always be aware of the difference between *acute* and *chronic* toxicity. The effects of acute toxicity are usually recognizable more-or-less immediately (for example, inhalation of ammonia) and appropriate remedial action can be taken promptly. Chronic effects are much more pernicious, exerting their influence during long periods of exposure and generally only manifesting their effects when irrecoverable long-term damage has been caused. Many compounds are classed as *cancer suspect agents* for instance. This need not negate their use in the laboratory but does require particularly stringent precautions to avoid exposure and these compounds must always be handled in an efficient hood.

When using the fume hood, make sure that the glass front is pulled well down. This ensures sufficient air flow to prevent the escape of toxic fumes. As a general rule, never start any experiment involving a highly toxic chemical until you have read and understood the instructions and safety information, fully appreciate the nature of the hazard, and know what to do in the event of an accident.

Cancer suspect agents

The exposure of healthy cells to certain chemicals (carcinogens) is known to result in tumour formation. The period between the exposure and the appearance of tumours in people can be several years, and therefore the dangers are not immediately apparent. The utmost care is required when handling such chemicals. In this book we follow the current practice of labelling such reagents as **cancer suspect agents**. This means that the chemical is either known to cause tumours in people or in animals, or is strongly suspected of doing so.

The following compounds or compound types should be treated as cancer suspect agents: biological alkylating agents such as *iodomethane*, *epoxides* and *dimethyl sulfate*; *formaldehyde*; *hexane*; *benzene*; aromatic amines such as *2-naphthylamine* and *benzidine*; polynuclear aromatic hydrocarbons (PAHs) such as *benzpyrene*; hydrazines in general, *hydrazine* itself and *phenylhydrazine*; *nitrosamines*; *azo compounds*; *chromium (VI) compounds*; chlorinated hydrocarbons such as carbon tetrachloride; *chloroform* and *vinyl chloride*; *thiourea* and *semicarbazide hydrochloride*.

Irritants and lachrymators

Many organic compounds are extremely irritating to the eyes, skin and respiratory system. To minimize the chance of exposure to the reagent or its vapours, the following chemicals should always be handled in a hood: *benzylic* and *allylic halides*, α-halocarbonyl compounds such as *ethyl bromoacetate*, *isocyanates*, *thionyl chloride* and *acid chlorides*.

Some organic compounds, as well as being irritants, also have a particularly penetrating or unpleasant odour. These are usually indicated by the word **stench**, and examples include *pyridine*, *phenylacetic acid*, *dimethyl sulfide* and many other sulfur-containing compounds, *butyric acid* and *indole*. Again these chemicals should be confined to a well-ventilated hood.

1.3 Disposal of hazardous waste

Waste disposal is one of the major environmental problems of modern society and the safe disposal of potentially hazardous chemical waste places a great burden of responsibility on those in charge of laboratories. It is important that everyone who works in the organic laboratory appreciates the problems and exercises their individual responsibility to their fellow citizens and to the environment by not disposing of chemical waste in a thoughtless manner. In addition to statutory legal requirements, each laboratory will have its own rules and procedures for the disposal of chemical waste; we can only offer general advice and suggest some guidelines. More information about disposal methods can be found in the works mentioned at the end of this chapter.

Think before disposing of any chemical waste

Solid waste

Solid waste from a typical organic laboratory comprises such things as spent drying agents and chromatographic supports, used filter papers, discarded capillaries from the melting point apparatus and broken glass. Common sense is the guiding principle in deciding how to dispose of such waste. Unless the solid is toxic or finely divided (e.g. chromatographic silica, see p. 179) it can be placed in an appropriate container for non-hazardous waste. Filter papers can be disposed of in this way unless of course they are contaminated with toxic chemicals. Toxic waste should be placed in special appropriately labelled containers. It is the responsibility of your laboratory staff and your instructor to provide these containers and see that they are clearly labelled: it is *your* responsibility to use them. Some toxic chemicals need special treatment to render them less toxic before disposal. This often involves oxidation, but your instructor will advise you when this is necessary.

Broken glass, discarded capillaries and other 'sharp' items should be kept separate from general waste and should be placed in an appropriately labelled glass or sharps bin. Chromatography silica should be transferred to polythene bags in a fume hood after removal of excess solvent, moistened with water and the bags sealed for later disposal.

Water-soluble waste

It is very tempting to pour water-soluble laboratory waste down the sink and into the public sewer system. It then becomes a problem for someone else, namely the water authority. This is bad practice. The only waste that can safely be poured down the sink is non-toxic, neutral, non-odorous, water-soluble material such as discarded water layers from aqueous–organic extractions. The waste should be washed down with plenty of water, and strongly acidic or alkaline solutions should be neutralized before disposal. Any chemical that might react even with dilute acid or alkali should never be disposed of down the sink. For safety's sake, if there is any doubt, do not dispose of material down the sink.

Never pour solvents down the sink

Organic solvents

Organic solvents are the major disposal problem in the organic laboratory. They are usually water immiscible and highly flammable, and often accumulate very quickly in a busy laboratory. Waste solvent should be poured into appropriately labelled containers, never down the sink. The containers are then removed from the laboratory for subsequent disposal of the solvents by burning. There should be two waste solvent containers—one for hydrocarbons and other non-chlorinated solvents and one for chlorinated solvents. Chlorinated solvents have to be handled differently during the combustion process since they generate hydrogen chloride. It is therefore very important that you do not mix the two types of waste solvent. If the waste container is full, ask the laboratory staff or your instructor for an empty one; do not be tempted to use the sink as an easily available receptacle.

Never mix chlorinated and non-chlorinated solvents

1.4 Accident procedures

In the event of a laboratory accident, it is important that you know what to do. Prompt action is always necessary, whatever the incident. **Tell your instructor immediately**, or if you are incapacitated or otherwise occupied in dealing with the incident, ensure that someone else informs the instructor. It is the instructor's responsibility to organize and coordinate any action required.

Fire

For anything but the smallest fire, the laboratory should be cleared. Do not panic, but shout loudly to your colleagues to leave the laboratory. If you hear the order, do not become inquisitive: **get out**.

Burning chemicals

The most likely contenders for chemical fires are organic solvents. If the fire is confined to a small vessel such as a beaker, it can usually be contained by simply placing a large gauze or a bigger beaker over the vessel. Sand is also very useful for extinguishing small fires, and laboratories are often equipped with sand buckets for this purpose. Remove all other flammable chemicals from the vicinity, and extinguish any burners. Since most flammable solvents are less dense than water, **water must never be used to try to extinguish a solvent fire**; it will have the effect of spreading the fire rather than putting it out. For larger fires, a fire extinguisher is needed; a carbon dioxide or dry chemical type should be used. However, the use of fire extinguishers is best left to your instructor or other experienced person; incorrect use can cause the fire to spread. If the fire cannot be quickly brought under control using extinguishers, a general fire alarm should be sounded, the fire services summoned and the building evacuated.

Burning clothing

If your clothes are on fire, shout for help. Lie down on the floor and roll over to attempt to extinguish the flames. Do not attempt to get to the safety shower unless it is very near.

If a colleague's clothes catch fire, your prompt action may save his or her life. Prevent the person from running towards the shower; running increases the air supply to the fire and fans the flames. Wrap the person in a fire blanket or make them roll on the floor. Knock them over if necessary; a few bruises are better than burns. If a fire blanket is not immediately to hand, use towels or wet paper towels, or douse the victim with water. **Never use a fire extinguisher on a person**. If the safety shower is nearby then use it. Once you are sure the fire is out, make the person lie still, keep them warm and **send for qualified medical assistance**. Do not attempt to remove clothing from anyone who has suffered burns unless it is obstructing airways.

Burns

Minor heat burns from hot flasks, steam baths and the like are fairly common events in the organic laboratory. Usually the only treatment such minor burns require is to be held under cold running water for 10–15 min. Persons with more extensive heat burns need immediate medical attention.

Any chemical that is spilled on the skin should be washed off immediately with copious amounts of running water; the affected area should be flushed for at least 15 min. If chemicals are spilled over a large area of the body, use the safety shower. It is important to get to the shower quickly, and wash yourself or the affected person with large volumes of water. Any contaminated clothing should be removed, so that the skin can be thoroughly washed. **Obtain immediate medical attention**.

Chemicals in the eye

If chemicals get into the eye, time is of the essence, since the sooner the chemical is washed out, the less the damage. The eye must be flushed with copious amounts of water for at least 15 min using an eye-wash fountain or eye-wash bottle, or by holding the injured person on the floor and pouring water into the eye. You will have to hold the eye open with your fingers to wash behind the lids. **Always obtain prompt medical attention, no matter how slight the injury might seem**.

Cuts

Minor cuts from broken glass are a constant potential hazard when working in the chemistry laboratory. The cut should be flushed thoroughly with running water for at least 10 min to ensure that any chemicals or tiny pieces of glass are removed. Minor cuts should stop bleeding very quickly and can be covered with an appropriate bandage or sticking plaster. If the bleeding does not stop, obtain medical attention.

Major cuts, that is when blood is actually spurting from the wound, are much more serious. The injured person must be kept quiet and made to lie down with the wounded area raised slightly. A pad should be placed directly over the wound and firm pressure should be applied. **Do not apply a tourniquet**. The person should be kept warm. **Prompt medical assistance is essential**; an ambulance and doctor should be summoned immediately.

Poisoning

No simple general advice can be offered. **Obtain medical attention immediately**.

Further reading

Appendix 1 (p. 670) deals with the hazardous properties of some commonly encountered laboratory chemicals. However, there are a number of texts which deal with laboratory safety practices in general and with the specific properties of, and disposal of, hazardous chemicals. These texts are written by safety experts and give far more detail than is possible in this book. If in doubt, consult the experts.

Prudent Practices in the Laboratory for Handling and Disposal of Chemicals, National Research Council, National Academy Press, Washington DC, 1995.

L. Bretherick, *Bretherick's Handbook of Reactive Chemical Hazards*, Butterworth, London, 1990.

A.J. Collins and S.G. Luxon (eds) *Safe Use of Solvents*, Academic Press, New York, 1982.

M.J. Lefevre, *First Aid Manual for Chemical Accidents*, Dowden, Hutchinson & Ross, Stroudsberg, PA, 1980.

R.E. Lenga (ed.) *Sigma-Aldrich Library of Chemical Safety Data*, 2nd edn, 1988.

R.J. Lewis, *Hazardous Chemicals Desk Reference*, 4th edn, Van Nostrand Reinhold, New York, 1997.

G. Lunn and E.B. Sansone, *Destruction of Hazardous Chemicals in the Laboratory*, 2nd edn, Wiley & Sons, New York, 1994.

D.A. Pipitone, *Safe Storage of Laboratory Chemicals*, 2nd edn, Wiley & Sons, New York, 1991.

N.I. Sax and R.J. Lewis, *Sax's Dangerous Properties of Industrial Materials*, 9th edn, Van Nostrand Reinhold, New York, 1996.

Chapter 2 Glassware and Equipment in the Laboratory

In this chapter we will consider some of the standard pieces of glassware and equipment that you will use in the laboratory. The emphasis will be on descriptive detail (Chapter 3 is largely concerned with experimental techniques and assembly of apparatus), although the operation of equipment such as oil immersion rotary pumps will be dealt with here.

Broadly speaking, equipment can be divided into two categories—that which is communal and that which is personal. Cost is usually the factor which decides the category into which an item falls, although no hard and fast rules apply and any distinction is purely arbitrary. A further arbitrary division within each category might be made by dividing equipment into that which is glassware and that which is non-glassware. Glassware is fragile and so there is much more potential for breakage within this subdivision—particularly with personal glassware. Communal glass apparatus, such as rotary evaporators, tend to be built fairly ruggedly.

Adhering to the procedures described in this and the next chapter will result in safe working and should help to minimize breakages which are costly, not only in financial terms, but also in popularity.

Remember the golden rule for working in a laboratory:

If in doubt, ask.

Never plunge headlong into a strange procedure without first verifying the safe and correct way of carrying it out. Breaking a piece of apparatus is bad enough; injuring yourself—or somebody else—is a far worse consequence of carrying on regardless. *Never* rely simply on the advice of your neighbour; you must always get instruction from a qualified individual. *Never* be frightened of pestering and upsetting instructors; that is the job for which they are paid. In any event, the surest way to annoy an instructor is to break an expensive piece of equipment or cause an injury!

On entering the organic laboratory for the first time, the first job, of course, is to familiarize yourself with the laboratory safety procedures and with the location of fire extinguishers, safety showers, fire exits and so on. The second job, however, is to check out the equipment, both personal equipment stored in your bench or locker and communal equipment. Personal equipment can be divided into glass and non-glass (hardware), and your locker will contain a set of such items. Obviously there is no such thing as a standard set of equipment, since each laboratory provides what is deemed necessary for the courses that are taught therein, but our set (see Figs 2.1–2.4) is fairly typical for classes dealing with standard-scale laboratory procedures. Apparatus specifically designed for use in microscale experiments will be dealt with in the corresponding sections.

2.1 Glass equipment

Glass equipment can be divided into that with ground glass joints and that without. For convenience and ease of use, standard-taper ground glass joint equipment is strongly recommended. Apparatus for a range of organic experiments can be quickly and easily assembled from relatively few basic items. Standard-taper joints (₸) are designated by numbers which refer to the diameter and length of the joint (in mm): for example, 14/20, 14/23, 19/22, 19/26 and 24/29. As the name implies, standard-taper joints are fully interchangeable with those of the same size.

Standard-taper ground glass joint equipment is expensive, but with careful handling is no more fragile than any other glassware. The only problem is with the joints themselves, and when assembling the apparatus it is usually better not to use grease. The only laboratory operations which require the use of grease on the ground glass joints of the apparatus are vacuum distillations using oil pumps for pressures lower than about 5 mmHg, and reactions involving hot sodium or potassium hydroxide solutions which will attack the glass. If grease is used it should be applied sparingly; a very thin smear around the joint is all that is required. Hydrocarbon-based greases are easier to remove from glassware than silicone greases. The misuse of grease can cause ground glass joints to become stuck or 'frozen'. Occasionally this happens anyway, and, of course, unless the joint can be unfrozen and the pieces of apparatus separated, the equipment becomes useless. As with many things, prevention is better than cure, and the best way to prevent frozen ground glass joints is to disassemble the apparatus as soon as it is finished with. Wipe the joints clean, checking that they are completely free of chemicals. Never leave assembled dirty apparatus lying around the laboratory. If, despite precautions, ground glass joints do become tightly frozen, it may be possible to loosen them by squirting a few drops of acetone (or other solvent) around the top of the joint. Capillary action may be enough to suck some solvent into the joint and loosen it. If this simple trick does not work, the joint may be loosened by gentle tapping, or failing that, by heating it in a flame. However, these techniques must be left to an expert. If you are unfortunate enough to break a piece of equipment that has a standard-taper ground glass joint, do not throw all the broken glass in the glass bin, but keep the ground glass joint (the expensive bit!) since your glass-blower may be able to utilize it. Some items of equip-

Care! Flammable solvent

ment, such as addition and separatory funnels, possess stopcocks. These may be ground glass or Teflon® and should be handled carefully to prevent the stopcock 'freezing' in the barrel. The correct use of separatory funnels is discussed in more detail on pp. 110–117.

A typical set of standard-taper glassware is shown in Fig. 2.1, and consists of:

- *round-bottomed flasks* for reactions, distillations;
- *three-neck flasks* for more complicated reaction set-ups (two-neck flasks are also available);
- *addition funnel* for adding liquids to reaction mixtures (may be cylindrical or pear-shaped);
- *separatory funnel* for extractions and reaction work-up;
- *condenser* for refluxing reaction mixtures, distillations;
- *air condenser* for high boiling liquids (can also be packed and used as a fractionating column);
- *drying tube* for filling with a drying agent and attaching to the apparatus to reduce the ingress of water;
- *stoppers*;
- *reduction/expansion adapters* for connecting equipment with different-sized joints;
- *still head* for distillation;
- *Claisen adapter* for distillation or converting a simple round-bottomed flask to a two-neck flask;
- *distillation adapter* for distillation;
- *vacuum distillation adapter* for distillation under reduced pressure;
- *take off adapter* for attaching to tubing;
- *thermometer/tubing adapter* for inserting thermometer or glass tube into apparatus.

Glass equipment with and without ground glass joints is available in small sizes. However, there are certain drawbacks in simply using small-scale versions of equipment with standard-taper ground glass joints, because the joint size becomes large with respect to the volume of the reaction and vapour path lengths increase proportionally. One obvious solution is to use the hemispherical ground glass joints which usually involve a smaller area of surface contact between male and female components, but most commercial microscale kits solve this problem by either replacing the male/female glass joint with a polytetrafluoroethylene (PTFE) ferrule, or alternatively, by securing the joint with a threaded closure and a *greaseless* 'O'-ring compression seal. An extensive range of the latter type of glassware is offered by several commercial suppliers. The equipment is robust and offers reasonable resistance to corrosion while resembling closely in appearance the more familiar macroscale ground glass equipment (Claisen adapters, reflux condensers, vacuum distillation adapters, etc.). The fragility of small reaction flasks is offset by the use of

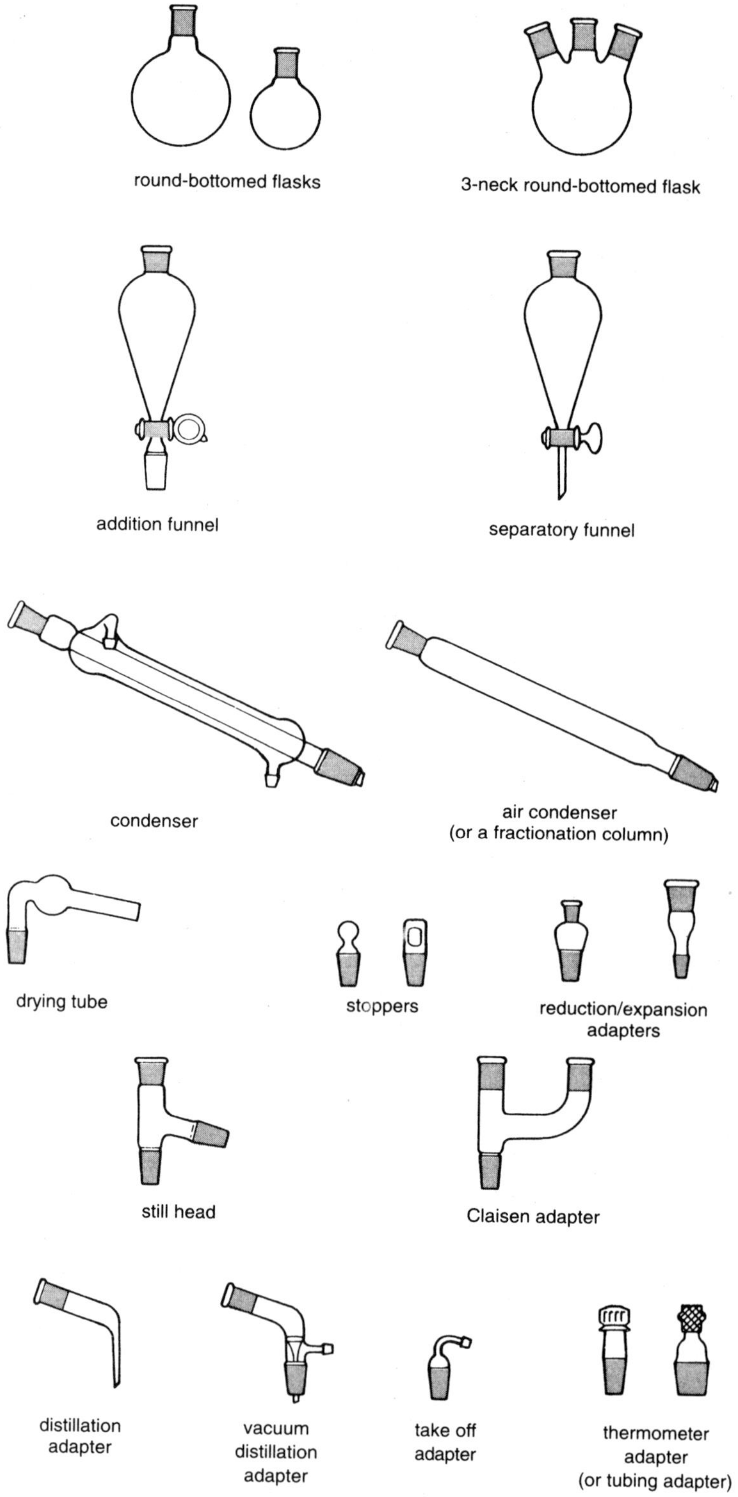

Fig. 2.1 Glass equipment with standard-taper ground glass joints.

thick-based tapered reaction vials (Fig. 2.2). Special microscale distillation equipment is also available (see pp. 154–159).

A typical set of microscale glassware would include:

- *reaction vials and round-bottomed flasks* for reactions, distillations;
- *jacketed condenser* for refluxing mixtures, distillations;

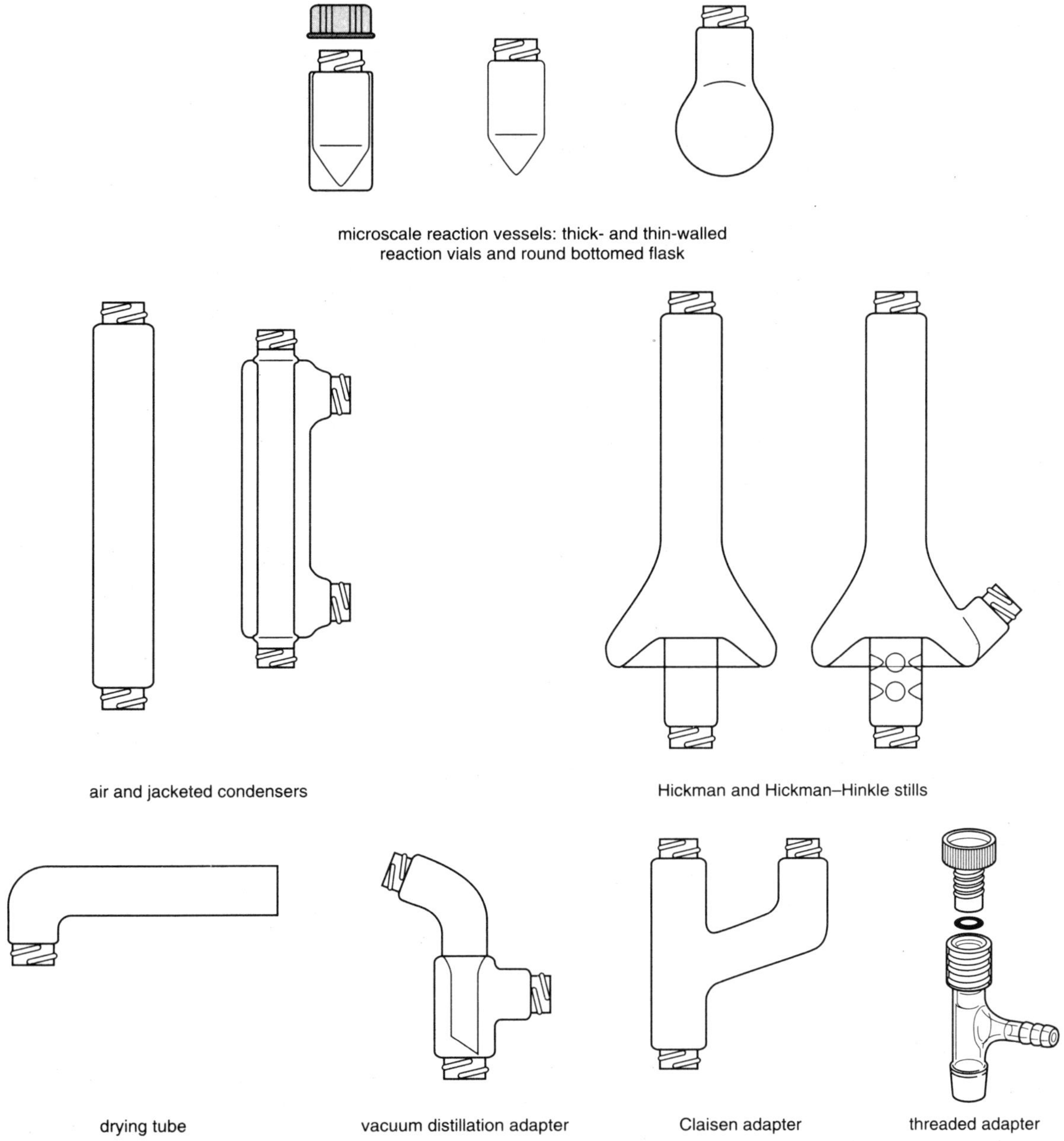

Fig. 2.2 Microscale glass equipment.

- *air condenser* for high boiling liquids;
- *Hickman and Hickman–Hinkle* stills for distillation;
- *drying tube* for filling with a drying agent and attaching to the apparatus to reduce ingress of water;
- *vacuum distillation adapter* for distillation under reduced pressure;
- *Claisen adapter* for converting a single-neck reaction vial to a two-neck reaction vessel;
- *threaded adapter* for attaching a tubing connection to a reaction vial.

Non-graduated standard scale glassware without ground glass joints is much less expensive. A typical set might contain some of the items shown in Fig. 2.3:

- *beakers* for temporary storage or transfer of materials, reactions;
- *Erlenmeyer flasks* for recrystallization, collecting solutions after extraction (versions with ground glass joints are also available);
- *funnel* for transfer of liquids, filtration;
- *powder funnel* for transfer of solids;
- *stemless funnel* for hot filtration;
- *filter flask* (Büchner flask) for suction filtration;
- *Büchner funnel* for suction filtration;
- *Hirsch funnel* for suction filtration of small quantities;
- *Pasteur pipette* for transfer of smaller quantities of liquid;
- *graduated cylinders* for measuring liquids by volume;
- *graduated pipettes* for accurate measurement of liquids.

Check for cracks and 'stars'

When checking out the glassware in your bench, examine each piece carefully for cracks and 'star-cracks'. Star-cracks are often caused by two round-bottomed flasks impacting on each other, for example if a drawer full of flasks is opened too rapidly, so care should be taken to ensure round-bottomed flasks are not touching when stored. Any damaged equipment should be replaced from the stockroom. Try and get into the habit of checking glass equipment each time you use it. This is especially important for flasks; you certainly want to avoid a cracked flask breaking half-way through a reaction or distillation.

Cleaning and drying glassware

Good laboratory practice requires that organic reactions are carried out in clean glassware. Unless the reaction is being carried out in aqueous solution, the glassware should also be dry, since many organic chemistry experiments are ruined by the presence of water.

Glassware can usually be cleaned with water and either industrial detergent or a mild scouring powder using an appropriate brush. Make sure that you clean all the inside of the piece, and that you rinse it thoroughly with water afterwards. The final rinse should be with distilled or deionized water, and the glassware should be left upside down on a drying rack or on absorbent paper to dry. The glassware can be dried more quickly by placing it in a drying

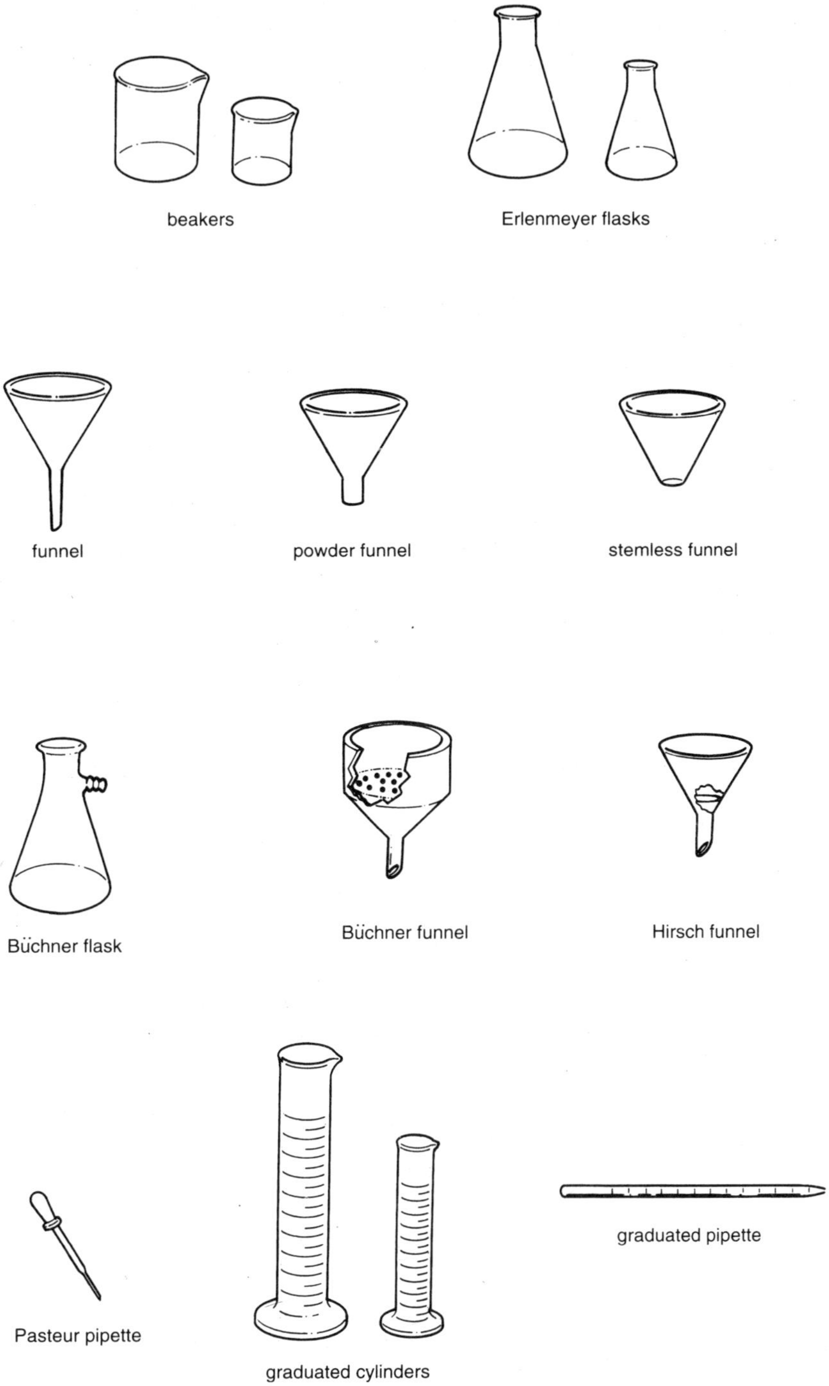

Fig. 2.3 Other glass equipment.

oven, and this is essential if it is to be used for a reaction involving air- or moisture-sensitive reagents. For *complete* drying, glass should be left in an oven at 125°C for at least 12 h (see also p. 81).

The drying process can also be speeded up by rinsing the wet glassware with acetone. Acetone is freely miscible with water, and rinsing a wet flask with 5–10 mL of washing acetone (*not* reagent grade acetone) removes the water. The acetone should be drained into the waste acetone bottle, not thrown down the sink. The remaining acetone in the flask evaporates quickly in the air, but the drying can be speeded up by drawing a stream of air through the flask. To do this, connect a *clean* piece of glass tube to the water aspirator via thick-walled tubing, turn on the suction and place the tube in the flask. Never use the compressed air line to dry equipment; the line is usually contaminated with dirt and oil from the compressor, and this will be transferred to your glassware. Alternatively the flask can be dried with hot air using a hot-air blower of the 'hair dryer' type (pp. 30–32), but **remember that acetone is flammable**. Indeed many laboratories do not permit the use of acetone for cleaning purposes because of the additional fire hazard, possible toxicity problems associated with long-term exposure and, of course, expense.

Use acetone sparingly for cleaning flasks. Check for flames in the vicinity. Acetone is flammable

Do not use compressed air line to dry glassware

Glassware that is heavily contaminated with 'black tars' or other polymeric deposits will not normally respond to washing with water and detergent as the organic polymer is insoluble in water. Large amounts of tar material can often be scraped out with a spatula, but the remaining material usually has to be dissolved out with an organic solvent. Acetone is usually used since it is a good solvent for most organic materials, although vigorous scrubbing and/or prolonged soaking may be necessary in stubborn cases. The dirty acetone should be poured into the waste container; many laboratories attempt to segregate washing acetone that has only been used to rinse water from a flask, and therefore can be reused, from dirty acetone that has been used to wash out tars. Always check that you are draining your acetone into the correct waste container.

Some books recommend the use of powerful oxidizing mixtures, such as sulfuric/nitric acids and chromic acid, as a last resort technique for cleaning dirty glassware. **This practice should be strongly discouraged from the safety point of view as the mixtures used are all highly corrosive and some are potentially explosive.**

Cleaning and drying glassware is an unavoidable chore in the organic laboratory, but it is part of the job. However, it can be made much easier by following one simple rule: *clean up as you go along*. By cleaning glassware as soon as you have finished with it, you know exactly what was in it and how to deal with it, and freshly dirtied glass is much easier to clean than dried out tars and gums. There are plenty of periods during the laboratory class when you are waiting for a reaction to warm up or cool down, for a crystallization to finish and so on. Make use of such times to clean, rinse and dry your freshly dirtied glassware. It is thoroughly bad practice to put dirty glassware back into

Clean up as you go

your locker at the end of the day, and it will certainly waste a lot more of your time in the subsequent laboratory period. Deposits are much more difficult to remove once they have dried onto the glassware.

2.2 Hardware

Your locker will also contain non-glass equipment such as that shown in Fig. 2.4. Many of these items, often known as hardware, are indispensable to experimental organic chemistry. A typical set will contain:

- *metal stands* for supporting apparatus;
- *clamps and holders* for supporting apparatus (the clamp jaws should be covered with a strip of cork or with a small piece of flexible tubing to prevent metal–glass contact);
- *metal rings* for supporting separatory funnels;
- *cork rings* for round-bottomed flasks;

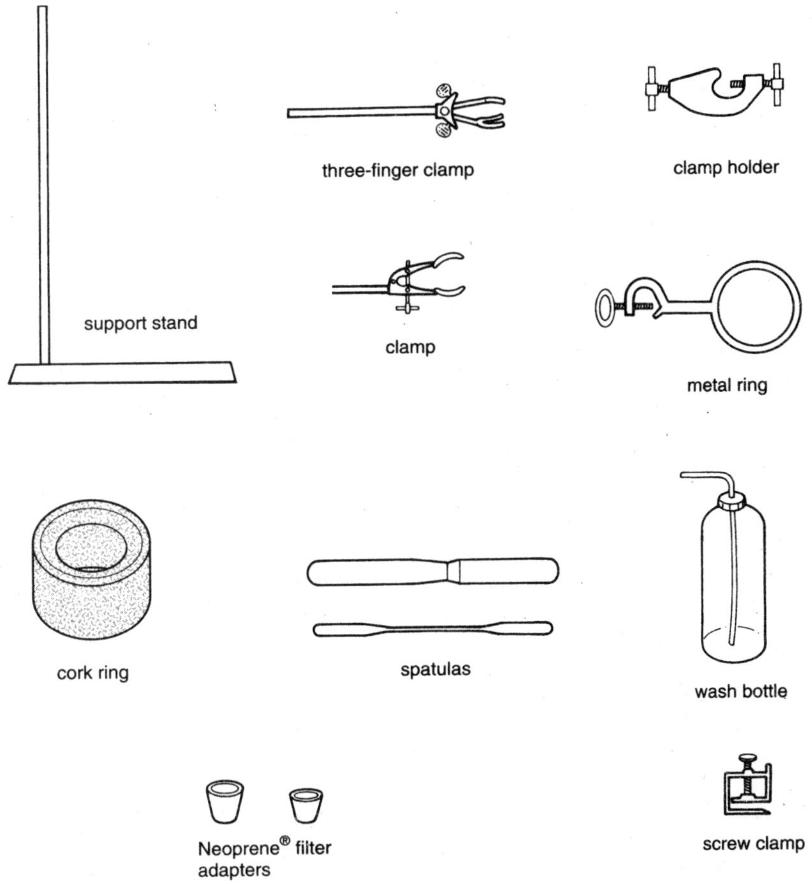

Fig. 2.4 Laboratory hardware.

- *spatulas* for the transfer of solids;
- *wash bottle* for dispensing water or wash acetone;
- *Neoprene® adapters* for suction filtration;
- *pinch/screw clamps* for restricting flexible tubing.

The items which require special mention are stands, clamps and clamp holders, which are essential items for supporting your glass apparatus during reactions, as well as safety screens for protection during reduced pressure distillations and other potentially hazardous laboratory operations.

Chemical apparatus should always be securely clamped and fixed to a stable support.

The metal stand is the most commonly used form of stable support since it is freely movable, but its heavy base ensures that in proper use it is sufficiently stable. The only practical alternative to such stands is the purpose-built laboratory frame, a square or rectangular network of horizontal and vertical rods firmly fixed to the bench and/or wall, but this is usually only found in research laboratories. The correct use of support stands requires that the clamped apparatus is always directly over the base of the stand as shown in Fig. 2.5(a). The alternative arrangement is highly unstable and potentially dangerous. Similarly there are right and wrong ways of using clamp holders and clamps with only one movable jaw. Clamp holders should be arranged so that the open slot for the clamp faces upwards (Fig. 2.5b), and when in the horizontal position, clamps should be fixed so that the fixed non-moving jaw is underneath (Fig. 2.5c).

Most complete microscale assemblies are very light; minimal clamping is required, usually at the neck of the main reaction vial. Additional clamping of condensers and adaptors is neither necessary nor recommended. Small clamps, compatible in jaw gape with the microscale reaction vials, are readily available and most effective.

Safety screens made of toughened glass or plastic should be used whenever you are carrying out reduced pressure distillations or experiments in which there is some risk of an explosion. If in doubt, ask an instructor. In addition, any operations in the hood should always be carried out with the toughened glass front pulled down, leaving just sufficient space at the bottom to permit access to the apparatus. This serves the dual purpose of protecting the face and top half of the body in the event of an explosion and permitting the hood extraction system to work most efficiently. The front of the hood should never be pushed all the way up as, in this position, it is not possible for the extractor fan to maintain the inrush of air necessary to contain noxious vapours. With the front pulled down, you will also get into the habit of not leaning over the apparatus when working. Leaning into the hood is very bad practice, negating all of the reasons for operating in the hood in the first place. It is attention to details like these which make for good laboratory practice and characterize the good experimentalist.

Do not lean into the hood

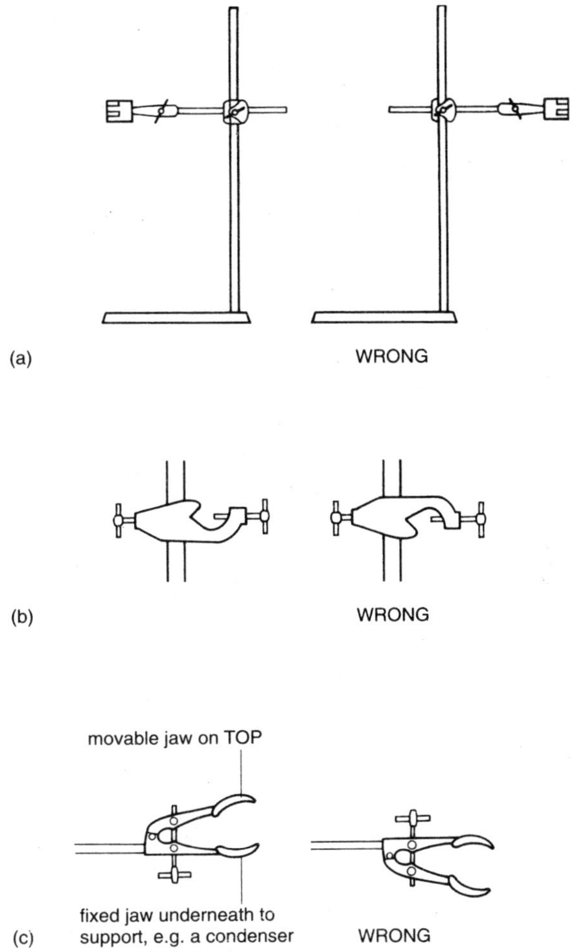

Fig. 2.5 Right and wrong ways of using support stands, clamp holders and clamps.

2.3

Heating

Working in the laboratory, it will not be long before it will be necessary to heat a reaction mixture or distil a product. Several methods of heating are commonly encountered in the laboratory, but the ready flammability of a wide range of organic solvents, coupled with their volatility, always requires vigilance when heating. Open flames pose an obvious hazard in this respect, but the hot metal surfaces of hotplates and the possibility of sparking with electrical apparatus can also give rise to dangerous situations. Whilst flames are visible, it is impossible to gauge the temperature of a metal surface simply by looking at it, so take particular care when working with hotplates.

Burners

Although the most straightforward means of applying heat, burners should normally only be used for heating aqueous solutions in open vessels. They are also useful for distillation and reflux procedures involving high boiling point materials, but in these instances care must be taken to ensure that no flammable vapours come into contact with the flame.

Always ckeck for flammable solvents before lighting a burner

Never use a burner to heat flammable solvents in an open container, or if flammable solvents are being used in the vicinity.

Burners come in two basic forms, both of which are variants on the same design. The *Bunsen burner* (Fig. 2.6a) is useful for heating aqueous solutions in flat-bottomed vessels supported on a wire gauze. The size of the flame is usually too large to permit good control during distillation and, for such procedures, it is preferable to use a *microburner* (Fig. 2.6b) which produces a smaller flame. Various designs of these burners burn natural gas or coal gas and produce a hot (blue) flame by allowing the introduction of air at the base of the barrel. The air supply is controlled by moving an adjustable collar around the inlet hole and some designs permit control of the gas supply by use of a needle valve. When not in use burners must be extinguished but, if heating is interrupted temporarily, the air inlet should be closed to give a slightly luminous, more visible flame.

Always use a wire gauze between the glass vessel and the burner flame

When heating flat-bottomed vessels or round-bottomed flasks with a burner, a wire gauze should be placed between the vessel and the flame, with the vessel resting on it. This serves both as a support and as a means of dispersing the heat. This lowers the risk of cracking the container and stops the formation of 'hot spots' and the ever attendant 'bumping' when localized overheating occurs.

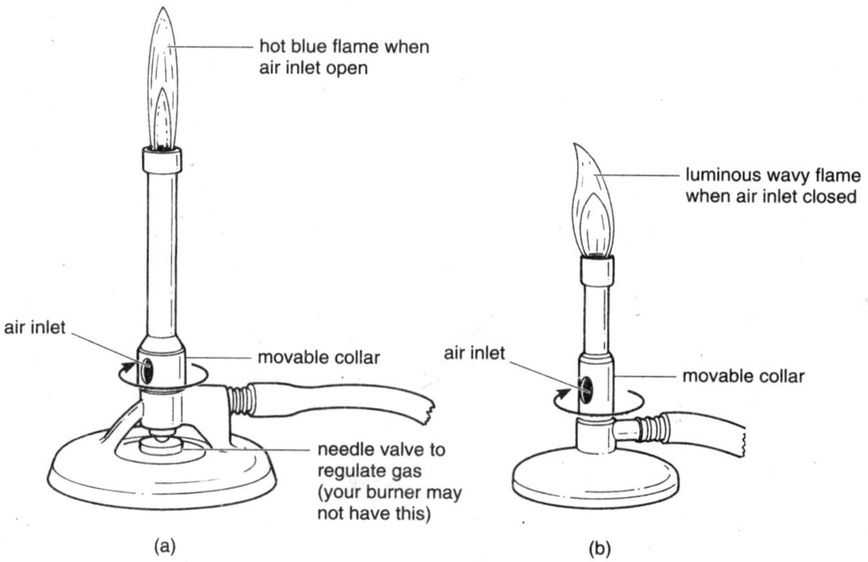

Fig. 2.6 (a) Bunsen burner; (b) microburner.

Pear-shaped distilling flasks may be heated directly without the need for a gauze, but it is recommended that microburners be used for such distillations. The burner should always be held in the hand and moved continuously over the surface of the flask below the level of the liquid in order to avoid hot-spot formation. It makes much more sense to move the burner to the apparatus than vice versa. When commencing the distillation, it is a good idea to start heating around the top edge of the liquid, moving the flame all of the time, and slowly work down the body of the flask. Heating at the bottom initially seems to be more liable to produce bumping, even when boiling stones have been added.

Keep the flame moving over the flask

Heating baths

Water and steam baths

Electrically heated water baths and steam baths are convenient means of heating liquids up to 100°C, although water condensing on and running into the vessel being heated can be a problem. This is particularly true if it is necessary to ensure anhydrous conditions within the reaction. Although the risk of fire is lowest with steam baths, you should be aware that carbon disulfide, which possesses an autoignition temperature of around 100°C, is still a potential fire hazard. In fact, carbon disulfide is so toxic and such a fire hazard that its use in the laboratory as a solvent should be avoided at all costs.

Heating with steam can be accomplished by suspending the vessel above the surface of a boiling water bath, or the laboratory may be equipped with a supply of superheated steam. With piped steam it will take a few minutes after turning on the steam source before the system clears itself of water and produces live steam. Set up your apparatus before turning on the system as everything will be too hot to handle afterwards.

Be careful with steam

You must always respect steam which, due to its high latent heat of condensation, can inflict rather nasty burns.

Steam and water baths are the heating methods of choice for carrying out recrystallizations with volatile solvents. The baths are normally equipped with a series of overlapping concentric rings, which can be removed to give the right size of support for the particular vessel being heated. Flat-bottomed vessels should sit firmly on the bath without any wobbling (Fig. 2.7a). Round-bottomed flasks should have between one-third and one-half of the surface of the flask immersed in the bath with a minimal gap between the flask and the support ring (Fig. 2.7b).

Oil baths and their relatives

Electrically heated baths are frequently used in the laboratory due to the wide temperature ranges possible with different heat-transmitting media (for example, polyethylene glycol, silicone oil, Wood's metal; see Table 3.1, p. 106).

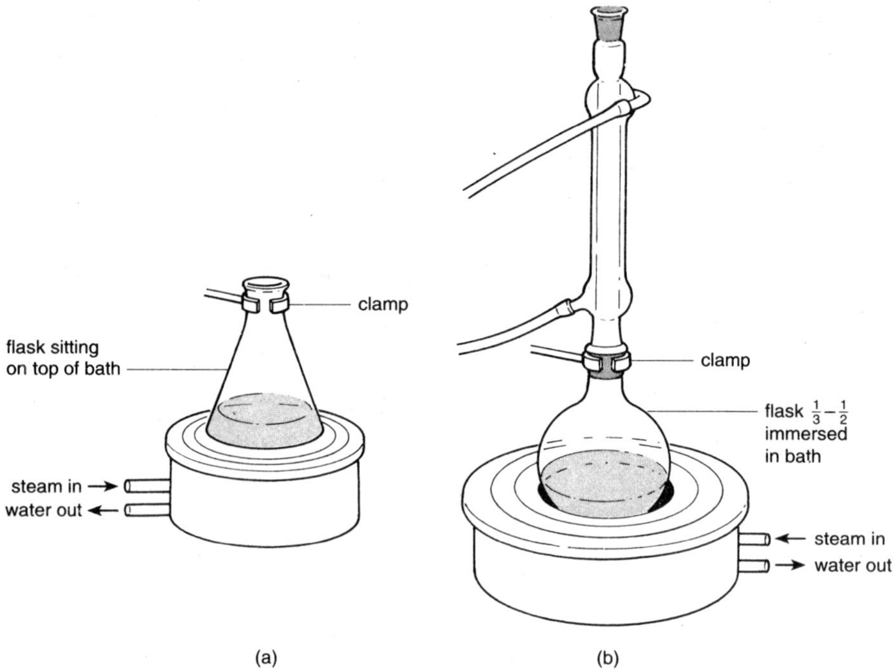

Fig. 2.7 (a) Heating an Erlenmeyer flask on a steam bath; (b) heating a reflux set-up on a steam bath.

The bath can be heated on a hotplate (see Fig. 2.10) and determination of the bath temperature is possible using a thermometer. Alternatively some hotplates are equipped with thermostatic temperature control.

Although particularly amenable to a wide range of heating demands in the laboratory, oil baths do possess several drawbacks. One disadvantage is the thermal inertia of the oil bath, which can cause temperature overshoot, although this can be minimized by choosing an oil bath that is not excessively large compared with the flask being heated. The container cannot be made of ferrous material if it is desired to stir the mixture magnetically, but at the same time it is advisable to avoid glass containers such as beakers or crystallizing dishes due to the danger of breaking a glass vessel full of hot oil. Another minor irritation associated with oil baths stems from the mess and cleaning problems that result with flasks that have been suspended in silicone oil. This can be overcome by using polyethylene glycol for the heat-transmitting medium, as this is water soluble, but this has the drawback of a limited heating range before decomposition commences. Alternatively, it is possible to use sand baths or powdered graphite baths to overcome this problem although it is less easy to control temperature gradients within the heating medium. Wood's metal baths pose their own particular problems as the alloy is solid at room temperature and thermometers and flasks must always

Use an oil bath size compatible with the size of the vessel to be heated

Remove flasks and thermometers from Wood's metal baths whilst hot—care!

Use oil baths in the hood

be removed before the bath is allowed to solidify. Heating the baths to a temperature higher than the decomposition temperature of the fluid will result in evolution of vapours which at the least are unpleasant, but are also likely to be toxic. Oil baths should always be used in the hood for this reason. Silicone oil has the greatest thermal stability and is preferable to paraffin-based oils although it is much more expensive. Proprietary oils used for culinary purposes must not be used in the laboratory (see Table 3.1, p. 106). By far the biggest problem with oil baths is the danger of spattering if an oil bath becomes contaminated with water and is then heated over 100°C. This is extremely dangerous and any oil bath which is suspected of containing water should be changed immediately. Heating baths must be examined before use and the fluid should be changed regularly, disposing of the old oil in containers specifically available for such waste.

Never use oil baths which have been contaminated with water

Electric heating mantles

Heating mantles provide a convenient means of heating mixtures under reflux although their use for distillations is to be discouraged.

Mantles are designed only for heating round-bottomed flasks and must never be used for heating any other type of vessel.

Never use a mantle which is too small or too large for the flask being heated

The mantle consists of an electrical resistance wire wound within a hemispherical woven glass jacket. Each mantle is designed specifically to accept a flask of a particular size which should sit snugly in the cavity, touching the jacket at all points with no exposed heating areas. The mantle may be housed in a casing for greater protection, but all designs are particularly vulnerable to spillages of liquids. The construction of mantles can lead to the surface being abraded with constant use and this can lay bare the wires within the heating element. Any mantle suspected of having been damaged must first be verified and, if necessary, repaired by a qualified electrician before use.

Never use any mantle which you suspect to have had any liquid spilled on it or which has a frayed appearance

Most new mantles have their own heating control, but, if not, the mantle should be connected to a variable heating controller and never directly into the mains power supply. Owing to their high heat capacity, mantles tend to heat up rather slowly and are particularly prone to overshoot the desired temperature substantially. Always allow for the possibility of removing the heating quickly if it appears that a reaction is getting out of hand due to overheating. The best way to achieve this is to clamp the apparatus at such a height that the mantle can be brought up to it or removed from it on a laboratory jack (Fig. 2.8).

Use a laboratory jack to support heating mantles

Stirrer hotplates

Stirrer hotplates are designed for heating flat-bottomed vessels, such as Erlenmeyer flasks or beakers, for which they are ideal as long as the liquid being heated is not flammable (Fig. 2.9). The built-in magnetic stirrer permits

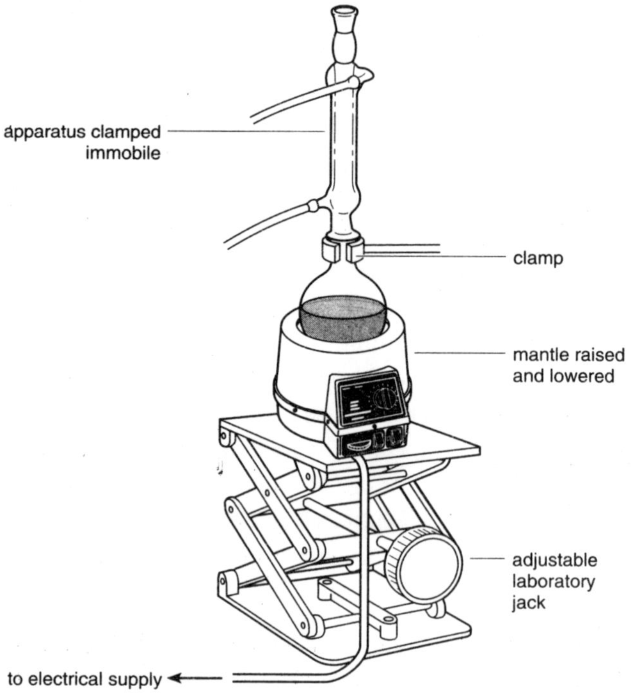

Fig. 2.8 Assembly for reflux using a mantle.

efficient agitation of non-viscous solvents by adding an appropriately sized magnetic stirrer bar to the liquid in the container (see Fig. 2.9, p. 31).

Although round-bottomed flasks cannot be heated using a hotplate alone, due to the very small contact surface between flask and hotplate, this problem can be overcome by immersing the flask in a flat-bottomed oil bath. With such an arrangement, stirrer hotplates are very useful for heating under reflux with simultaneous stirring (Fig. 2.10).

Always check that a hotplate is cool before attempting to move it

The flat exposed surface of the hotplate, designed for transferring heat rapidly, makes it extremely dangerous when hot. It is good practice whenever you have finished using a hotplate to place a beaker of cold water onto the hot surface. This will have the dual effect of cooling down the surface and alerting others to the potential danger—a hot hotplate seems very much like a cold hotplate until someone puts a hand on it.

The hot-air gun

Hot-air guns are particularly useful as a source of heat that can be directed fairly precisely in much the same manner as a burner flame. Commercial hot-air guns (Fig. 2.11a) are capable of achieving high temperatures near to the nozzle and can be useful alternatives to Bunsen burners for distillations.

The guns are able to produce a stream of heated air, usually at two rates of heat output, as well as cold air. After the gun has been used, it should not be

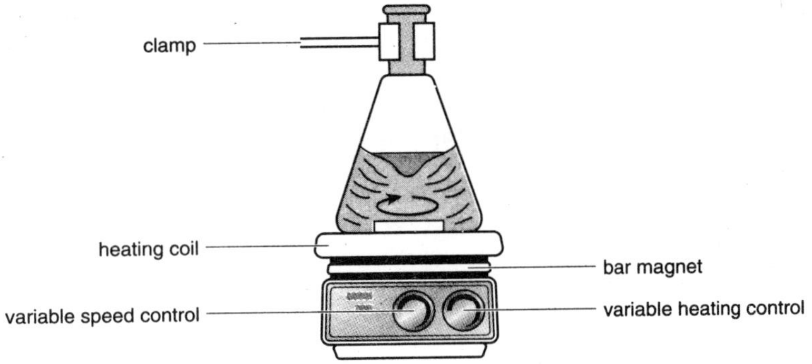

Fig. 2.9 A stirrer hotplate.

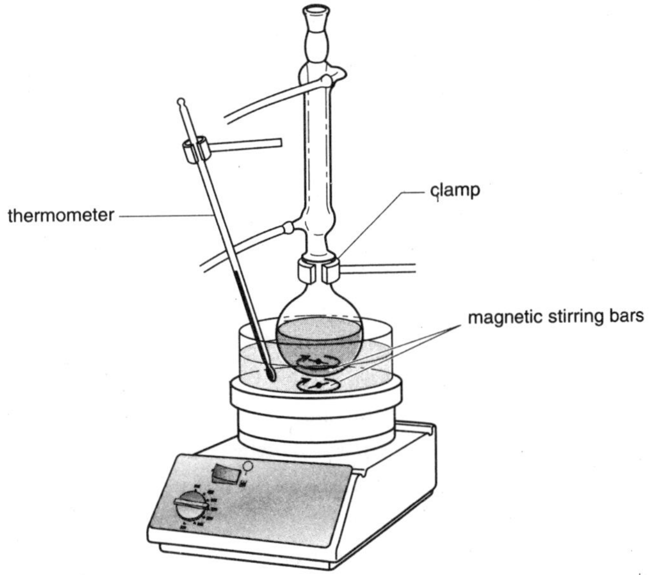

Fig. 2.10 Using a stirrer hotplate with an oil bath to heat a round-bottomed flask.

placed directly onto the bench, as the nozzle remains very hot for some period of time. It is recommended that the gun be placed in a support ring 'holster' with the cold air stream passing for a few minutes before switching it off completely (Fig. 2.11b). Do not forget that the hot nozzle can ignite solvents as well as causing nasty burns.

Heat guns are particularly useful for rapid removal of moisture from apparatus for reactions in which dry, but not absolutely anhydrous, conditions are required. Another use is for heating thin layer chromatography (TLC) plates to visualize the components when using visualizing agents which require heat as part of the development procedure (see pp. 169–170).

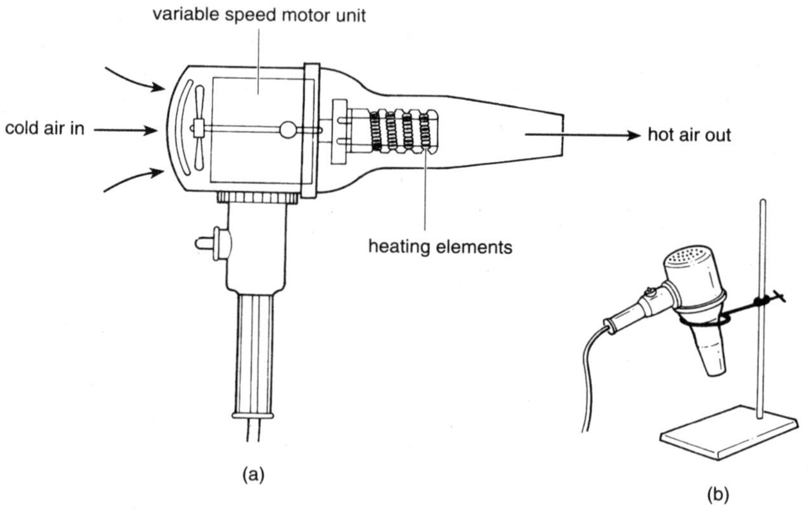

Fig. 2.11 (a) A commercial hot-air gun; (b) after use the hot-air gun should be allowed to cool in a support ring.

In all instances, it must be remembered that any form of hot-air gun poses the usual fire hazards associated with any piece of electrical equipment which may cause sparks on making or breaking contact.

Heating microscale reactions

Thermal transfer is rapid in microscale glassware and sand baths can be used for reflux and distillation. Sand is easy to clean up if spilled and cannot be splashed, and neither can it be caused to smoke or ignite. A glass crystallizing dish containing sand can be reused many times with no deterioration, though regular checking for chemical contamination is recommended. Aluminium blocks which can be used on top of conventional stirrer hotplates are also available; the blocks are bored with holes which match the external diameters of the tapered reaction vials (Fig. 2.12). Thermal transfer is efficient and stirring occurs as normal.

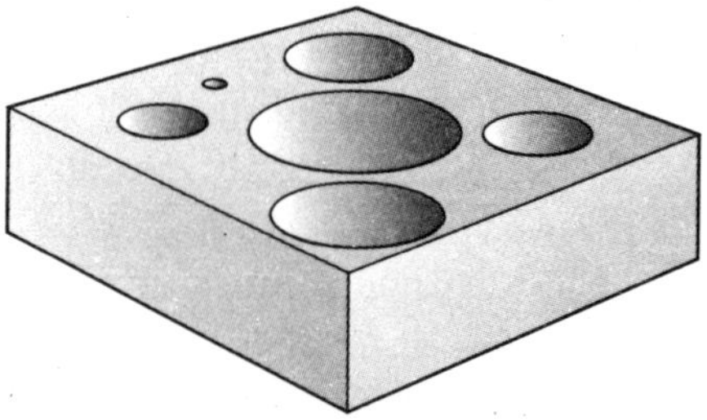

Fig. 2.12 Aluminium heating block, drilled to accommodate thick-walled reaction vials and thermometer.

When rapid heating is required, the use of an electric hot-air gun may be advantageous.

2.4 Stirring

The methods for stirring reactions are described on pp. 92–95 and so in this section it is sufficient to describe the main types of equipment. There are three main ways that mixtures can be agitated—by hand, with a magnetic stirrer, and with a mechanical stirrer; only the last two require any particularly sophisticated equipment! Remember that homogeneous solutions do not in general require any stirring after the initial mixing. The exceptions to this rule are reactions which are carried out at low temperatures (for instance, reactions involving alkyl lithium reagents or diisobutylaluminium hydride) and, in such cases, agitation is required for heat dispersal rather than for mixing of reagents.

Magnetic stirrers

Magnetic stirring (see Fig. 3.20a, p. 93) is the method of choice if an extended period of continuous agitation is required, since it is easy to set up the apparatus, particularly for small-scale set-ups or closed systems. The main drawback to the technique is that it cannot cope with viscous solutions or reactions which contain a lot of suspended solid. In addition, volumes of liquid much greater than 1 L are not stirred efficiently throughout their whole bulk. The magnetic stirrer may also be equipped with a hotplate, and these combined stirrer hotplates are particularly versatile pieces of apparatus. In general, the larger the volume of material to be stirred, the more powerful the motor needed and the longer the magnetic stirrer bar required.

Stirrer bars come in various designs and dimensions; a selection of bars, approximately 10, 20 and 30 mm (or 0.5 and 1 inch) long, of the variety which possesses a collar around the mid-section (Fig. 2.13a), will be suitable for most occasions. For reactions in the larger volume round-bottomed flasks, heavy duty football-shaped (American or rugby—depending upon which side of the Atlantic you live!) bar magnets (Fig. 2.13b) are excellent, but these can be liable to break any delicate pieces of glassware that get in their way.

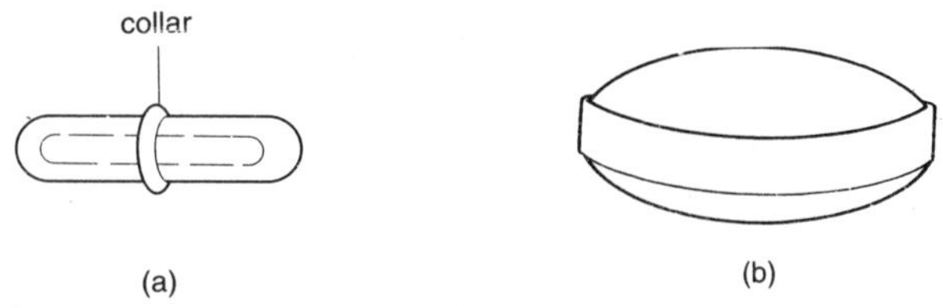

Fig. 2.13 Useful shapes of Teflon®-coated bar magnet.

Although bar magnets can be obtained with all sorts of different coatings, only Teflon®-coated stirrers are universally useful—and even these go black when used for stirring reactions involving alkali metals in liquid ammonia. This discolouration does not affect the efficiency of the stirrer, at least in the short term.

Mechanical stirrers

Mechanical stirrers need firm support

Larger scale reactions or viscous mixtures require the greater power of an external motor unit turning a stirrer blade. It is highly advantageous for the motor to possess a variable speed control and a typical model is shown in Fig. 2.14. These units are rather heavy and so it is necessary to support them firmly.

Use a stirrer guide

The stirrer is most simply attached to the motor by a flexible connection made out of a short length of pressure tubing. However, when stirring open vessels (see Fig. 3.20b, p. 93), the flexibility of this connection necessitates the use of a stirrer guide (such as a partially closed clamp) half-way down the stirrer shaft to prevent undue lateral motion ('whip'). With closed systems, such as when stirring refluxing reaction mixtures, a solvent- and air-tight adapter is required. A simple adapter, sometimes called a *Kyrides seal*, can be constructed from a tubing adapter fitted with a short length of flexible tubing which forms a sleeve around the shaft of the stirrer (Fig. 2.15a). The point of contact between the stirrer and the flexible tube is lubricated with a little sili-

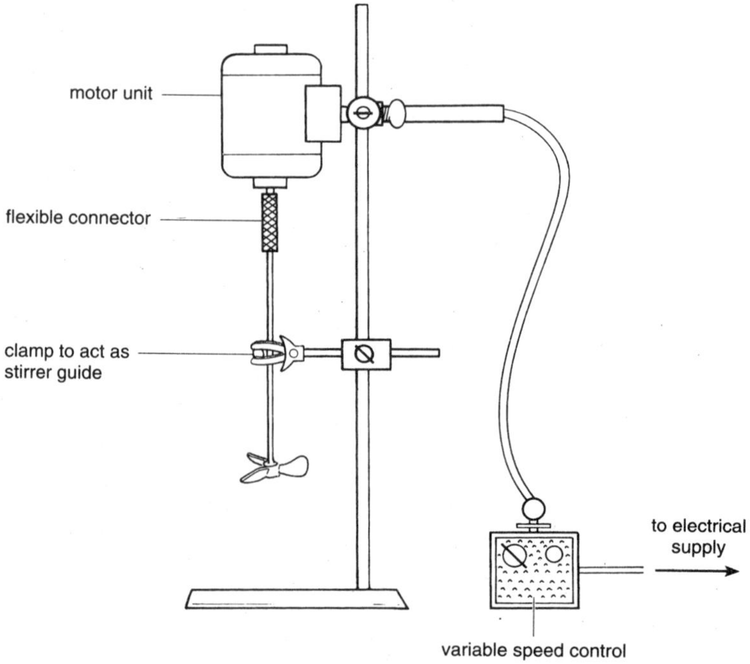

Fig. 2.14 Typical mechanical stirrer.

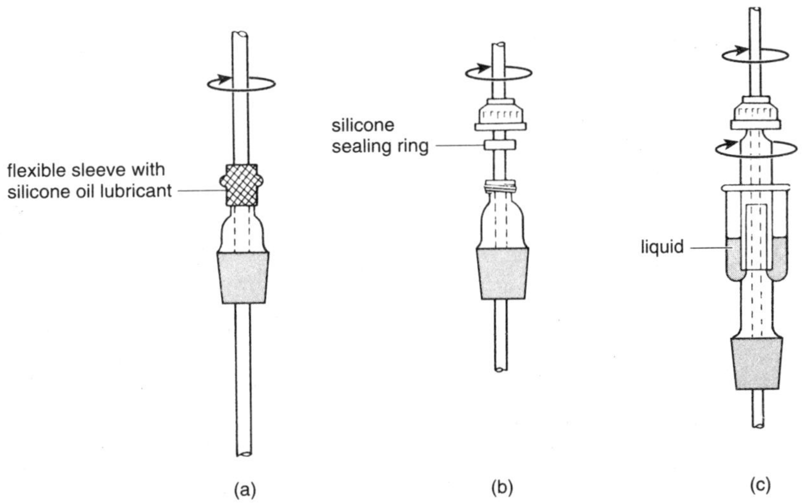

Fig. 2.15 Stirrer guides for closed systems: (a) Kyrides seal; (b) screw-cap adapter (exploded view); (c) fluid-sealed stirrer.

cone grease, and a carefully prepared seal of this type will permit stirring under water aspirator vacuum (*ca.* 20 mm). A screw-cap adapter, commonly used to hold thermometers, can also be used to good effect if a little lubrication is applied to the silicone sealing ring and the plastic screw-cap is not tightened to its fullest extent (Fig. 2.15b). Mercury-sealed stirrer guides (Fig. 2.15c) have lost favour due to their tendency to splash highly toxic mercury metal everywhere when used at high speeds. In addition, although the arrangement does permit a good air-tight seal, it cannot be used with systems under vacuum. If such an adapter is used, it is preferable to use silicone oil in the place of mercury.

The stirrer rods may be made of glass, metal or Teflon® and the paddle or blade arrangements come in a bewildering array of forms. Teflon® is the material of choice for construction of the whole stirrer as this will not break when placed under stress (when dropped on the floor for instance), and neither is it likely to break the flask in which it is being used. Normally, however, the propeller-type stirrer (Fig. 2.16a), which is useful for stirring open containers with wide mouths, is commercially available constructed from metal. A glass or Teflon® stirrer, possessing a movable Teflon® blade (Fig. 2.16b), is a very simple and robust design that is suitable for use with vessels possessing restricted openings. In addition, the Teflon® blade possesses a curved edge, making it ideal for efficient stirring in round-bottomed flasks.

Stirring on the microscale

Magnetic stirrer bars (also known as beads, fleas or followers) are available in very small sizes in a number of patterns; spherical stirrers can be used in the smallest tubes, while the more usual parallel or bullet forms are suitable for

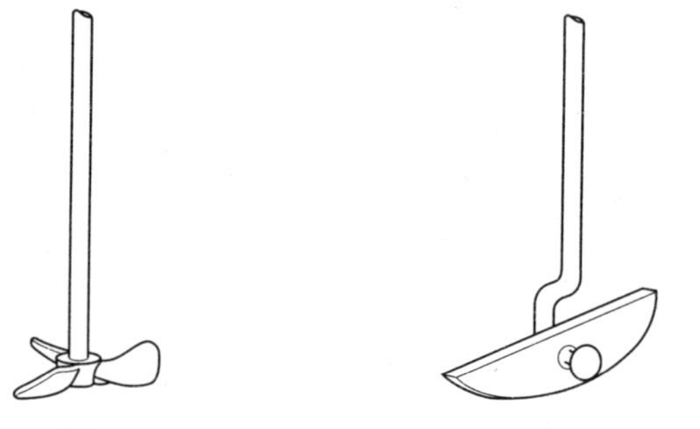

Fig. 2.16 Two useful types of stirrer: (a) propeller design for use in open vessels; (b) movable Teflon® blade for use with tapered-joint glassware.

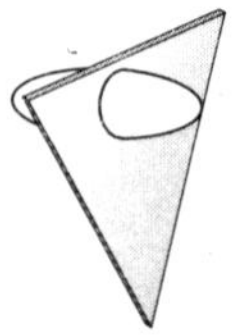

Fig. 2.17 Triangular spin vane for magnetic stirring in conical reaction vials.

use in small round-bottomed flasks or test tubes. Triangular spin vanes (Fig. 2.17) can be obtained to fit the the tapered portion of the conical reaction vials sold in most of the commercial microscale kits; when using this combination of glassware and stirrer bead, it is important to centre the apparatus accurately on the magnetic stirrer or stirrer hotplate or the vane will not revolve smoothly. High torque stirring is very difficult on the microscale; manual stirring using a glass rod probably represents the most cost-effective solution to stirring very viscous media.

2.5 Vacuum pumps

The common procedures which call for reduced pressure in the organic chemistry laboratory are filtration with suction (pp. 77–79) and reduced pressure distillation (pp. 152–155). The former technique, which simply requires a source of suction, is adequately served by use of a water aspirator, although the reduced pressures which can be achieved with this simple apparatus (*ca.* 10–20 mmHg) are frequently sufficient for use with reduced pressure distillations. Alternatively, reduced pressures of this magnitude can be attained using a diaphragm pump. However, very high boiling materials, or purifications involving sublimations, require recourse to a vacuum of 0.1–1.0 mmHg which is provided by an oil immersion rotary vacuum pump. An even higher vacuum is achieved by using a mercury vapour diffusion pump in series with a double

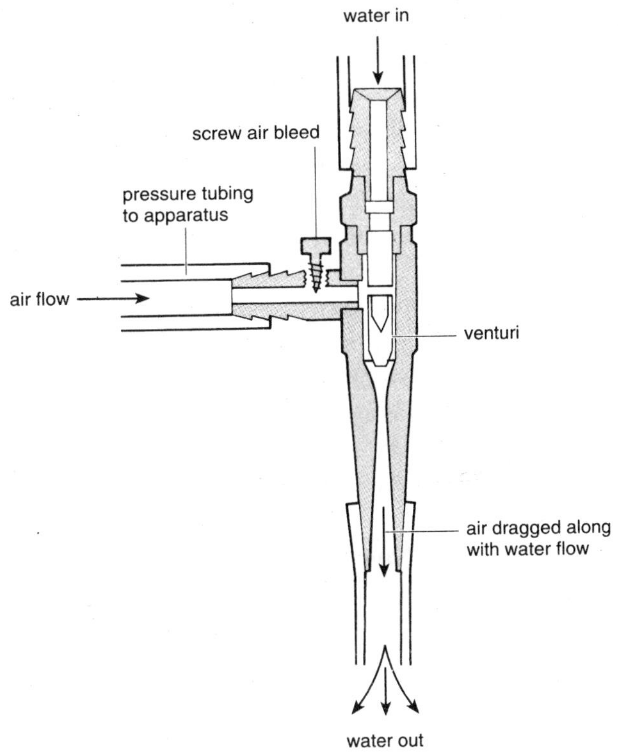

Fig. 2.18 Schematic diagram of a water aspirator.

action rotary oil pump, but such conditions are required only rarely in the laboratory and will not be discussed here. It should not be forgotten, however, that mass-spectrometric analysis would be impossible without the ability to achieve reduced pressures in the region of 10^{-6} mmHg.

Water aspirators

Water aspirators are made of glass, metal or plastic (Fig. 2.18) and operate on the Venturi effect in which the pressure in a rapidly moving gas is lower than that in a stationary one. The aspirator is designed such that the water rushing through the aspirator drags air along with it and thus generates the region of low pressure.

The theoretical maximum vacuum attainable with such an apparatus is equal to the vapour pressure of the water passing through it and is therefore dependent on the temperature of the water source. In practice, the working pressure is usually some 5–10 mmHg higher than the minimum due to leaks. Anything lower than about 30 mmHg should be acceptable in a teaching laboratory. Unfortunately, water aspirators do not work efficiently at high altitudes and alternative methods have to be found in these circumstances.

The major disadvantage with a water aspirator is that the pressure generated depends on the speed with which the water passes through it and that, in turn, is directly affected by the water pressure. In a busy teaching laboratory, the use of a large number of water aspirators at the same time places great demands upon the water supply and may be too much for it to cope with efficiently. The result is that the pressure generated by aspirators around the laboratory is liable to be variable depending on their position in the line. The tendency for the vacuum generated by any individual aspirator to vary over a period of time as the water pressure changes can have deleterious effects in reduced pressure distillations where boiling points are very sensitive to pressure variations within the system. The worst situation occurs with an abrupt drop in the water pressure (for instance when your neighbour turns on his aspirator) as this leads to 'suck-back'. In this case the vacuum generated by the aspirator suddenly cannot cope and water floods into the apparatus—a very sad sight indeed, but one which can be avoided by interposing a trap between the aspirator and apparatus (Fig. 2.19).

Using a water aspirator

Always use aspirators with the water full on

Whereas the flow of water passing through a condenser does not need to be more than a gentle trickle, *water aspirators must never be used with the water at less than full blast.* (Why do students always seem to get this one the wrong way round?) With the water turned on full, check that the air bleed screw on the side arm is open (as these little screws have a tendency to become stuck or get lost from communal apparatus, some aspirators do not have them, but an

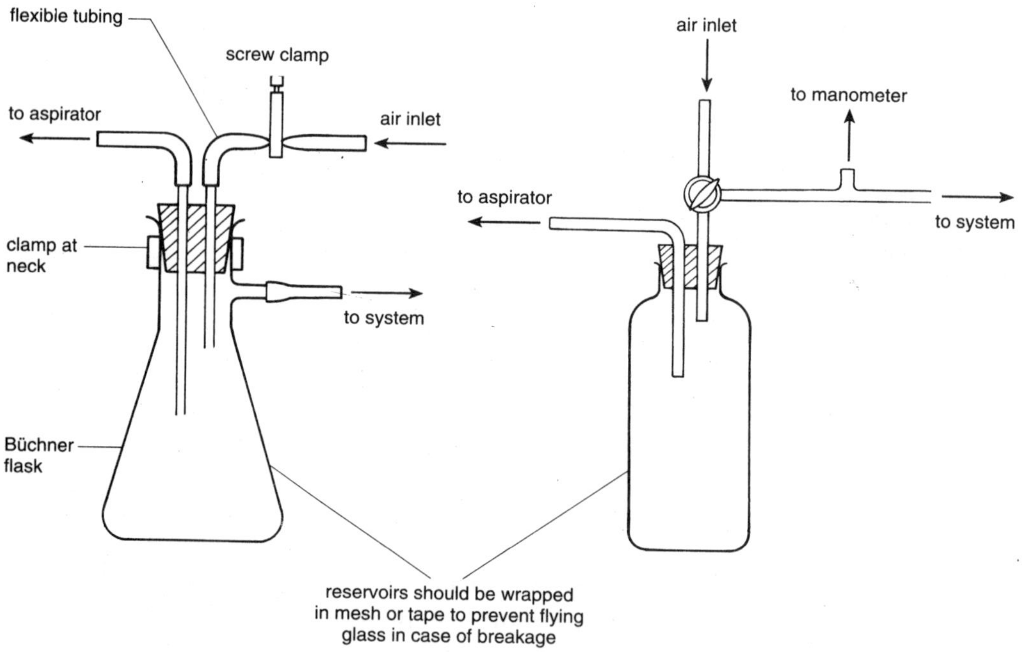

Fig. 2.19 Typical examples of water traps suitable for use with water aspirators.

additional stopcock attached to the water trap will serve the same purpose) and then attach the pressure tubing to the apparatus to be evacuated. Close the air bleed (or stopcock on the water trap) and observe the pressure drop on the manometer. For vacuum filtrations, the actual quality of the vacuum is largely unimportant but, of course, it will be necessary to note and regulate this pressure if you are carrying out a vacuum distillation.

Never turn off the water aspirator before releasing the vacuum

The critical stage in working with water aspirators comes when the vacuum is to be released. It is imperative that the water supply to the aspirator *remains on until the pressure within the system has been allowed to return to that of the atmosphere*. If you do not observe this simple procedure, the inevitable result will be a suck-back of water into the apparatus.

With suction filtration it is frequently sufficient simply to remove the pressure tubing from the side arm of the receiving vessel before turning off the tap, although this lazy practice runs the risk of spillage when the tubing is suddenly removed and air rushes into the receiver. The correct procedure for both reduced pressure filtration and distillation involves the unscrewing of the air bleed on the side arm of the aspirator (or opening the stopcock on the water trap) until the manometer registers a steady increase in pressure within the system, or the tone of the water rushing through the aspirator changes abruptly. Do not continue to unscrew the air bleed, otherwise the screw will drop out and be lost for ever down the sink. It is always good practice when carrying out reduced pressure distillations to allow the residue in the distilling flask to cool down to near room temperature before admitting air, particularly if the flask has been heated strongly during distillation.

Water traps

Always use a water trap between the aspirator and your apparatus

The danger of water sucking back into the apparatus when a sudden drop in water pressure occurs, is a constant problem when working with water aspirators. To safeguard against this, a water trap must always be included between the aspirator and the apparatus. Two simple examples are shown in Fig. 2.19; the optional modifications might include the attachment of a manometer or a means of introducing air into the system. The latter is necessary when the aspirator does not possess an air bleed, but even when one is present, using the stopcock on the water trap avoids leaning over the bench to the sink or losing the air bleed screw. As the trap simply acts as a dead space between the apparatus and the aspirator, which fills up with water on suck-back, it must be large enough to cope with this and should be no less than 1 L in volume.

Oil immersion rotary vacuum pumps

Frequently, vacuum distillations demand a better vacuum than that which can be achieved using a water aspirator, either because a lower pressure is needed, or because that produced by the aspirator is too erratic. In these instances an oil immersion rotary pump is ideal. Unfortunately, with the lower pressures comes increased complexity of operation of the pump and there are several extremely important rules that must be observed when using such equipment. Whilst the instructions given here should be generally applicable, always check the precise operation of your particular piece of apparatus with an instructor before use.

As well as the pump itself, the set-up will have a series of important pieces of ancillary equipment essential for the protection of the pump, achievement of the highest vacuum possible and measurement of the pressure within the system. All of these accessories will be connected by a rather complicated set of glass and flexible tubing, but the general arrangement will look something like that depicted in Fig. 2.20.

The pump is mounted firmly on its base on the bench top, or more conveniently, on a trolley which can be moved to wherever it is desired to carry out the distillation (such as in the hood). It is supplied with two connecting tubes made of thick-walled tubing. One (the 'downstream' side) is the exhaust tube and should always be led into a hood, whilst the 'upstream' tube leads eventually to the apparatus to be evacuated. It is what occurs on the upstream side of the pump which is crucially important.

The basic construction of the pump involves a rotor which is concentric with the motor drive shaft but which is mounted eccentrically within a cylinder (Fig. 2.21). In the commonly encountered 'internal vane' design, the rotor is fitted with one ('single action') or two ('double action') pairs of blades which bear tightly against the walls of the cylinder. Double action pumps are

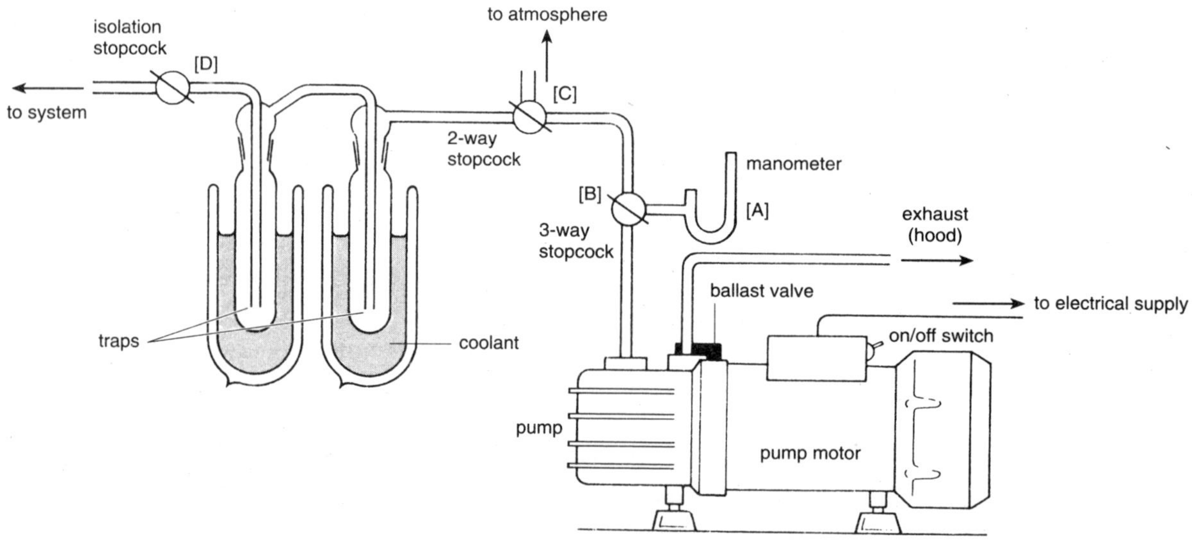

Fig. 2.20 Schematic diagram representing the typical arrangement of a rotary vacuum pump.

capable of attaining a higher vacuum and the internal vane design is preferred because of its quiet operation.

On turning, the rotor blades cut off pockets of gas and sweep them through the pump to be exhausted via an oil-sealed non-return valve. A thin film of oil within the cylinder maintains a seal between the blades and the cylinder wall. The very close tolerances between the rotor blades and the cylinder mean that the pumps are very susceptible to damage by solid particles or corrosive gases.

Never draw air through a rotary vacuum pump

Under normal circumstances, the pump must never be allowed to work whilst open to the atmosphere for two very important reasons. Firstly, drawing air continuously through the oil in the pump will cause water vapour to be trapped in the oil. This reduces the vacuum that can be achieved due to the vapour pressure of the contaminating water and might cause the pump to seize. Abuse of the pump in this way will necessitate frequent oil changes and other more extensive repairs. However, a second more important reason is the possibility of condensing liquid oxygen in the cold traps if liquid nitrogen is being used as the coolant.

The potentially lethal consequences of combining liquid oxygen and organic material cannot be overemphasized and this situation must be avoided at all costs.

One of the authors (LMH) clearly remembers the sensation he experienced when, after carrying out a reduced pressure distillation in his first week of postgraduate research, he succeeded in half filling a cold trap with liquid oxygen by forgetting to remove the nitrogen Dewar flask for 25 min after opening up the apparatus to the atmosphere. Do not learn this particular lesson the hard way. Unlike the author, you may never get a second chance to get things right.

Pressure measurement

Whilst the order of attachment of the accessories may vary, in Fig. 2.20 the

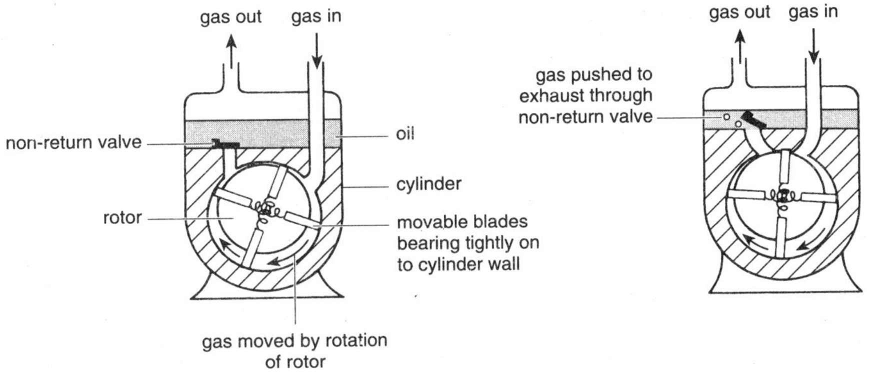

Fig. 2.21 The 'internal vane' double action oil immersion rotary pump.

nearest attachment to the pump is the manometer (A), attached by a three-way stopcock (B). The design of manometer usually found on most rotary vacuum pumps is a compact variant of a McLeod gauge which allows accurate measurement of pressures between 0.05 and 10 mmHg. Its correct use is described more fully in p. 48. but it must always be kept in the horizontal position when not being used to measure pressure. The three-way stopcock is designed to permit isolation of either the pump, the manometer or the distillation apparatus at any one time, or to allow all three to be interconnected. One design for such a stopcock is shown in Fig. 2.22.

Air-leak stopcocks

The next attachment, which should be found between the pump and the cold traps, is a two-way stopcock (Fig. 2.20 [C]). This allows for both isolation of the pump from the apparatus and also entry of air. Its positioning here is important for safety reasons, as the system must never be arranged such that the pump can draw air through the cold traps if it is left switched on with this stop-

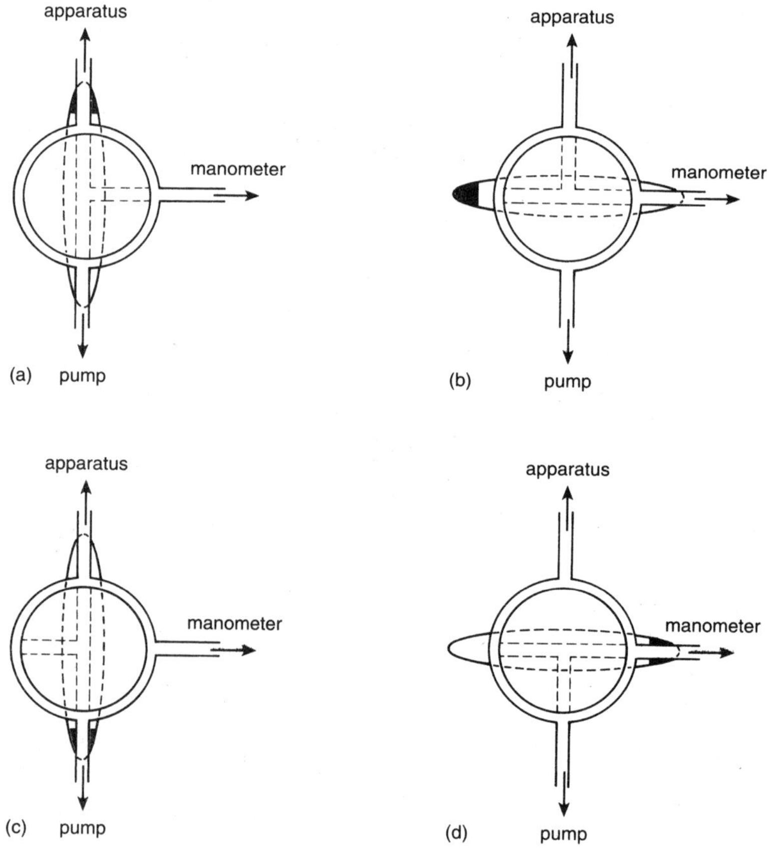

Fig. 2.22 Positions of the three-way stopcock: (a) pump, manometer and apparatus connected; (b) pump isolated; (c) manometer isolated; (d) apparatus isolated.

cock open to the atmosphere. A typical design uses a double-bored key as shown in Figure 2.23.

Cold traps

Cold traps must always be used to protect the pump

Organic vapours must not be allowed to pass through the oil of the pump as these will be trapped in the oil and will very rapidly reduce the capacity of the pump to produce a vacuum. To protect the pump, it is necessary to place two cold traps between the distillation apparatus and the pump to condense out any vapours which pass through the receiver flask. Two forms of trap are commonly found on such systems and are used for cooling with a solid CO_2–acetone slush bath (*ca.* –78°C) or liquid nitrogen (–196°C). However, neither cooling system is really ideal and care must be taken when using either of them to avoid splashes on the skin as unpleasant cold burns can result. The apparatus shown in Fig. 2.24(a) is particularly suited for use with a slush bath as fresh pieces of solid CO_2 can be added easily. That shown in Fig. 2.24(b) is better used with liquid nitrogen, as the Dewar flask containing the coolant can be removed before permitting air into the system at the completion of distillation. The drawback to the use of the slush bath is its relatively low condensing efficiency compared with liquid nitrogen. Nonetheless, its use is recommended, at least for the type of pump found in the teaching laboratory, as there is a very significant hazard associated with the use of liquid nitrogen which will cause liquid oxygen (bp –183°C) to condense in the cold traps if air is allowed into them.

Never, never draw air through a liquid nitrogen cold trap!

All mixtures of liquid oxygen and organic materials are dangerously explosive. If using liquid nitrogen as the coolant in the cold traps, NEVER permit air to enter the system. The Dewar vessel containing the liquid nitrogen must not be placed around the trap until immediately before turning on the pump and must be removed before releasing the vacuum in the system. Always wear insulating gloves when handling liquid nitrogen.

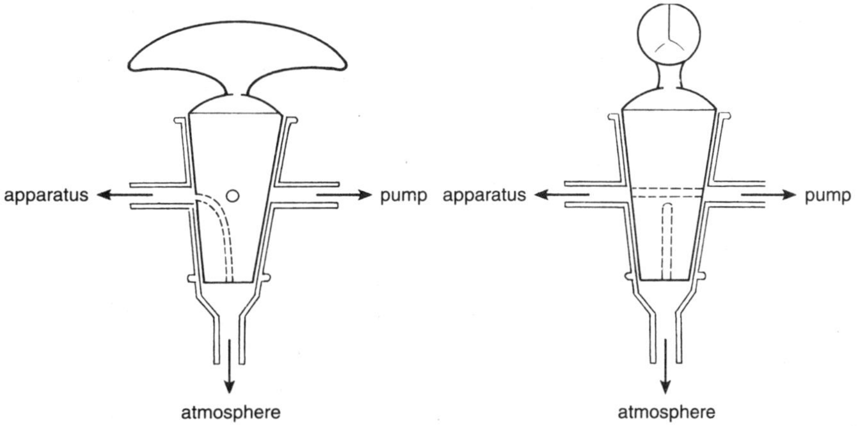

Fig. 2.23 A double-bored key two-way stopcock.

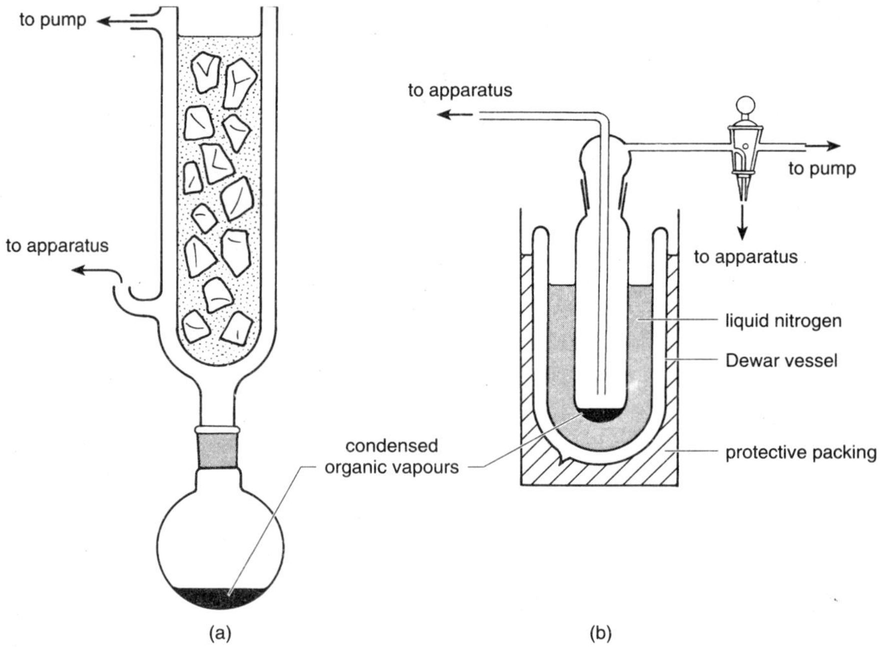

Fig. 2.24 (a) Solid CO_2–acetone trap; (b) liquid nitrogen trap.

Isolation stopcocks

The system should be equipped with a standard stopcock (Fig. 2.20 [D]) at its extremity in order to isolate the pump unit from either the atmosphere or the distillation apparatus.

Operation of the rotary vacuum pump

The procedures detailed below attempt to cover the general points and potential hazards associated with the use of rotary vacuum pumps. Nonetheless, it is imperative to consult an instructor before commencing to use the apparatus, particularly for the first time. It is quite possible that accepted procedures in your laboratory may differ from those outlined here, which are for general guidance only. In such circumstances, you must always follow the rules laid down by your laboratory.

Evacuating the system

Before using a rotary pump to evacuate the distillation apparatus, it is essential to have ensured that only minimal quantities of volatiles are present in the sample by connecting the system to a water aspirator for several minutes. The cold traps on the rotary pump will condense out small amounts of volatile materials, but it is unsafe to permit quantities of material to accumulate as there is a potential risk of explosion when reintroducing air into the traps at the end of the distillation.

Isolate the pump from the distilling apparatus by closing stopcock D, from

Wear insulating gloves when handling liquid nitrogen or solid CO_2

the atmosphere by closing stopcock C and from the manometer by closing stopcock B, with the stopcock positions such as to allow the cold traps to be evacuated (refer to Fig. 2.20). Do not add any coolant at this stage, but if using solid CO_2–acetone, the traps may be one-third filled with acetone (Fig. 2.24a). Turn on the pump and immediately add the solid CO_2 or liquid nitrogen to the trap, being careful to avoid splashing the coolant onto yourself. The few seconds of pumping without coolant in the isolated traps will do the pump no harm, but will ensure that the air-filled traps are not surrounded by liquid nitrogen. (Although this is irrelevant with solid CO_2–acetone, it is a good idea to develop the habit of doing things this way whatever the coolant.) After about 1 min, check the quality of the vacuum using the manometer, returning the manometer to its horizontal position after obtaining the reading. If the pump is pulling a satisfactory vacuum (at least 1.0 mmHg and probably better), *slowly* open stopcock D to evacuate the apparatus (**safety screen!**). Allow several minutes for residual volatile solvents in the sample to be removed and for the system to stabilize, then recheck the vacuum with the manometer. When satisfied that an acceptable stable vacuum has been established, the distillation may be commenced. Remember to check the pressure periodically during the distillation and make sure that the traps do not need additional coolant (generally unnecessary unless the distillation is protracted).

Always use a safety screen when carrying out reduced pressure distillations

Releasing the vacuum

At the end of the distillation, close stopcock D to isolate the apparatus from the pump and wait until the distilling flask has cooled down. Ensure the manometer is in its horizontal position and then turn stopcock C such that the traps are isolated but the pump is open to the atmosphere. You will hear the air rushing in through the outlet. Turn off the pump without delay, as drawing air through the oil in the pump for extended periods of time will cause a degradation of its performance. However, you must never switch off the pump when the line is still under vacuum, as oil from the pump will be sucked back into the line ruining the whole unit. If liquid nitrogen is being used as the coolant, the Dewar flasks should be removed without delay. Turn the two-way tap to allow air into the traps and dismantle them carefully (**wear gloves—they are very cold**). Place the collecting tubes or flasks in a hood ready for disposal of any condensed material (some of which may be toxic—consult an instructor) at a later stage. Finally, *slowly* open stopcock D to allow air to enter the apparatus. Always make sure that the traps have been cleaned, dried and any coolant removed after use.

Do not switch off the pump whilst it is still connected to the vacuum

Ballasting the pump

A common cause of poor performance with rotary vacuum pumps is the presence of occluded gases and solvent vapour within the sealant oil. Even with careful use, this cannot be totally avoided and it is usually necessary to carry

Report poor pump performance immediately to the person responsible

out an oil change at regular intervals of 6 months to a year depending on the treatment the pump has had. The life of the oil and the performance of the pump can be increased by degassing the oil at regular periods; a process referred to as *gas ballasting*. The ballast valve is designed to protect the oil from condensation of liquids by allowing a small amount of air to bleed continuously into the pump. This obviously reduces the performance of the pump, and it is more common practice to use the pump with the ballast valve closed and compensate for this by ballasting for an equivalent period of time after the experiment. In the laboratory it is convenient to ballast a pump overnight after every 8 h of use.

To ballast a pump, isolate the vacuum side of the pump from the atmosphere and open the ballast valve fully—no cold traps are necessary. Lead the exhaust pipe into the hood to remove any potentially toxic fumes and turn on the pump. If this procedure is carried out regularly, the pump will continue to operate satisfactorily for long periods of time, perhaps requiring topping up with a little fresh oil occasionally.

2.6 Manometers

The type of manometer used depends on the vacuum being generated and hence on whether a water aspirator or a rotary oil immersion pump is being used. Manometers for use with water aspirators need to be able to measure pressures in the range 5–200 mmHg to an accuracy of ±1 mmHg, whereas the type of manometer used with oil pumps normally has a range of 0.01–10 mmHg.

Manometers for use with water aspirators

The simplest form of manometer consists of a glass U-tube with one arm about 1 m long and one somewhat shorter. The long arm is mounted vertically against a 1 m ruler with the open end dipping into a mercury reservoir. The other arm is attached to a water trap (Fig. 2.25a). The height of the mercury column in the tube is subtracted from the prevailing atmospheric pressure. The scale may be movable so that the zero can be placed in line with the reservoir liquid level, enabling the height of mercury to be measured directly. Owing to the necessary length of the glass tube, this type of manometer has a tendency to be both unstable and fragile and also requires rather a large mercury reservoir. Breakages and spillages of highly toxic mercury metal are a common occurrence with such apparatus. Despite this, the simplicity of construction means that these unsatisfactory and inaccurate manometers are frequently found in laboratories.

Far more robust and accurate manometers work on the principle of a short U-tube sealed at one end and filled with mercury. This arrangement has the additional advantages of requiring less mercury and permitting easier reading

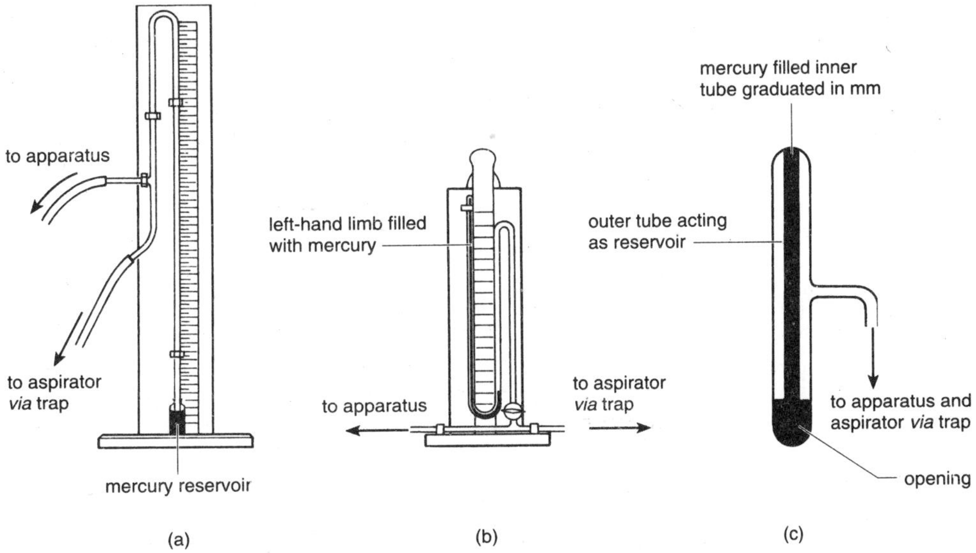

Fig. 2.25 Simple manometers for use with water aspirators (not to scale).

of the reduced pressure. The vacuum range covered is usually 0–100 mmHg with an accuracy of ±0.5 mmHg, and this is adequate for just about all requirements when distilling using a water aspirator vacuum. There are two common designs of manometer which work on this principle. The simple U-tube (Fig. 2.25b) has a tendency to accumulate air in the closed end of the tube over a period of time and is slightly less compact than the design using two concentric tubes (Fig. 2.25c). This latter piece of apparatus has an inner graduated tube filled with mercury which possesses a small outlet at its lower end. The outer tube acts as the mercury reservoir as well as the second arm of the U-tube.

With either arrangement the reduced pressure within the system is obtained by reading the difference in the mercury levels between the two halves of the manometer.

Do not release the vacuum too abruptly

A serious disadvantage common to both designs is the danger of breakage if air is allowed to re-enter the system too quickly. This allows the mercury to rush back into the tube where it may strike the sealed end with such force that it breaks the glass. All manometers should be used in conjunction with a water trap to avoid contamination with water in the event of a suck-back.

Manometers for use with rotary vacuum pumps

Keep the gauge horizontal unless taking pressure readings

There is one design of manometer which is particularly suitable for the accurate measurement of pressures in the range 0.1–10 mmHg. This is a variant of the McLeod gauge. When not being used for pressure measurement it is held horizontally and the mercury is kept in the reservoir (Fig. 2.26a). To read

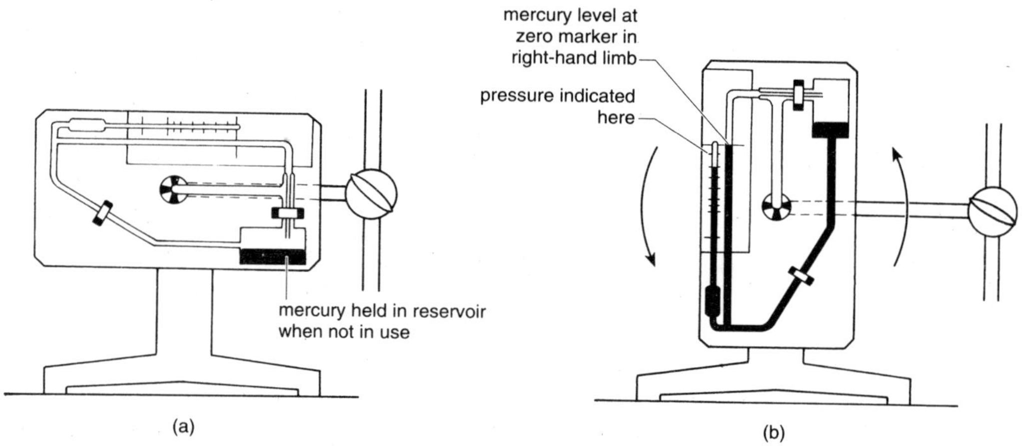

Fig. 2.26 The McLeod gauge for measuring pressures accurately below 10 mmHg: (a) apparatus horizontal when not in use; (b) apparatus vertical when taking pressure readings. (Adapted and redrawn by kind permission of W. Edwards & Co. Ltd, Crawley, UK.)

the pressure within the system, the gauge is rotated to the vertical when the mercury enters the two arms. The gauge is tilted such that the meniscus of the mercury in the right-hand arm touches the zero and the pressure is read off from the left-hand arm (Fig. 2.26b). The gauge must always be returned to the horizontal after use and the mercury allowed to drain into the reservoir. If this is not done, there is the danger of mercury rushing forcefully to the sealed end of the tube, on release of the vacuum, and breaking the glass.

2.7 Pressure regulation

More often than not, you will find that the boiling-point information that is available is quoted for a pressure different to that produced by your equipment. There is little you can do if the quoted pressure is lower than that which can be achieved in your case, although it is worth checking for leaks and examining the thickness of the capillary if one is being used. If the pressure cannot be reduced any further by these means, you will need to estimate the likely boiling point with the help of a pressure–temperature nomograph (see Fig. 3.52, p. 153). If the quoted pressure is higher, then you have the option of regulating the internal pressure within your system to correspond. The various devices to do this in conjunction with rotary vacuum pumps are rather complicated and beyond the scope of this book. However, a simple needle valve with a fine control dial (Fig. 2.27) can be used in conjunction with a water aspirator to provide steady pressures higher than those being produced by the aspirator.

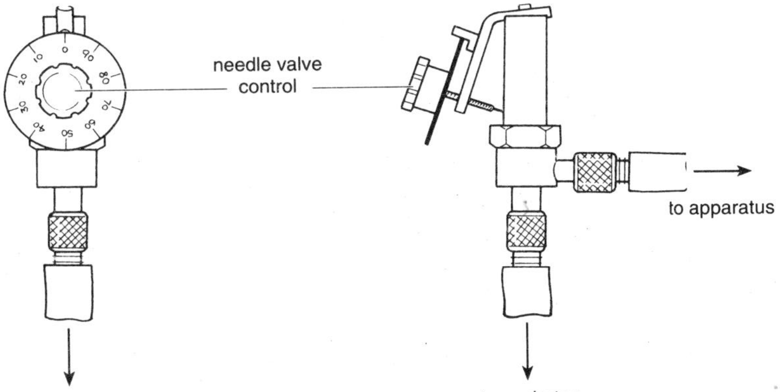

Fig. 2.27 Needle valve for controlling pressure in conjunction with a water aspirator.

2.8

The rotary evaporator

This piece of apparatus, usually communal in the teaching laboratory, is designed for the rapid removal of large quantities of volatile solvent at reduced pressure from solutions, leaving behind a relatively involatile component. Rotary evaporation finds greatest use for removing extraction and chromatography solvents used in the isolation and purification of reaction products. The principle of operation which distinguishes the apparatus from that used for ordinary reduced pressure distillation is the fact that the distillation flask is rotated during the removal of solvent. This performs the two important functions of reducing the risk of bumping (which accompanies all reduced pressure distillations), and increasing the rate of removal of solvent by spreading the contents around the walls of the flask in a thin film, with a consequent increase in the ratio of surface area to volume of solution.

A wide range of designs is available commercially for a variety of specific uses, but a basic model most commonly encountered in the teaching laboratory is depicted in Fig. 2.28.

The apparatus

The *evaporating flask*, which may be pear-shaped or any round-bottomed flask possessing a standard-taper joint, is connected to a glass sleeve (*vapour duct*) which passes through a seal permitting a vacuum to be maintained, but at the same time allowing rotation. The vapour duct leads solvent vapour from the flask onto a spiral condenser and the condensed solvent is collected in a round-bottomed *receiver flask*, connected by means of a hemispherical glass joint. The motor unit for rotating the flask is housed above the point of the seal and the rate of rotation may be varied. The water aspirator is attached through the condenser outer jacket and the application and removal of the vacuum is

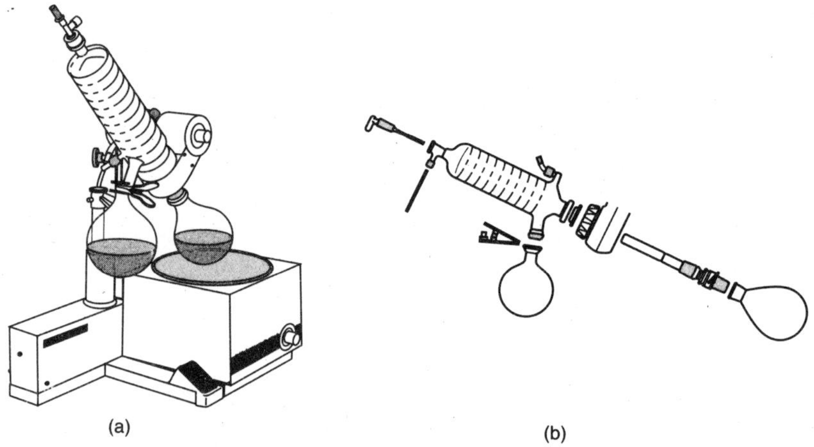

Fig. 2.28 (a) Typical example of a rotary evaporator; (b) exploded view of glassware showing vapour duct.

controlled by using the stopcock at the end of the condenser. This stopcock may be fitted with a long flexible tube which passes the length of the condenser into the evaporating flask to permit introduction of additional solution without releasing the vacuum and interrupting the evaporation.

The whole unit is mounted on a stand, of which several models exist, all designed to permit easy vertical movement of the rotary evaporator for introduction of the evaporating flask into a heating bath. The clamping system also provides for adjustment of the inclination of the rotary evaporator. The most convenient angle is somewhere around 45° from the vertical but this should not normally require adjustment.

Report poor rotary evaporator pressures immediately to the person responsible

Regular maintenance of the rotating seal is necessary to produce a reliable vacuum. Failure of this seal will result in poor and variable pressures, but any corrective work should be left to others after first ensuring that it is the seal and not the water aspirator which is the cause of the trouble. To do this, isolate the rotary evaporator and examine the pressure developed by the water aspirator. The only components which you will need to remove in the ordinary course of events are the evaporating and receiving flasks, for filling and emptying.

Always use clips to hold flasks on the rotary evaporator

During evaporation, the reduced pressure within the system will tend to hold the distilling flask firmly in place. However, **never rely on a combination of friction and vacuum to hold the evaporating flask onto the rotary evaporator**—the additional precaution of using a clip for the flask must be followed (the hemispherical joint on the receiver flask makes such a clip an absolute necessity). The sight of a flask bobbing upside-down in a hot water bath is only too common in the teaching laboratory where water pressure

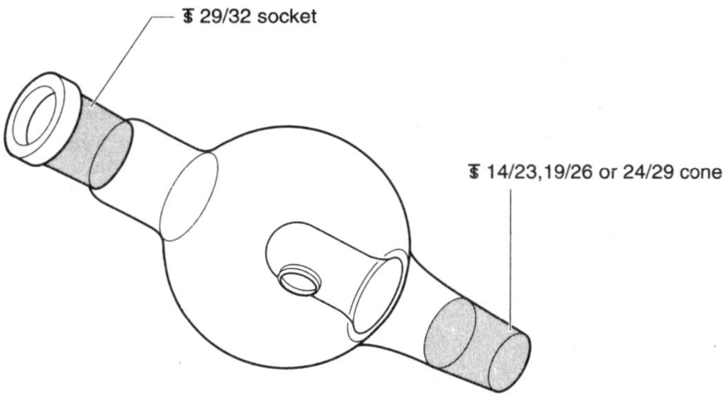

Fig. 2.29 A typical splash trap for use with a rotary evaporator.

fluctuations (and hence the quality of the water aspirator vacuum) are liable to occur.

If a standard round-bottomed flask is being used as the evaporating flask, it is likely that an expansion adapter will be necessary to attach the flask to the cone of the vapour duct. A very useful piece of apparatus for use with rotary evaporators—particularly communal ones—is a splash adapter which is placed between the evaporating flask and the vapour duct (Fig. 2.29). This acts as an expansion adapter, and at the same time prevents your sample contaminating the vapour duct by bumping up into it and also stops refluxing solvent or a bumping solution washing down somebody else's prior contamination into your sample. You should get into the habit of cleaning the splash trap before and after use with acetone from a wash bottle.

Splash traps reduce the risk of contamination

Correct use of the rotary evaporator

Ensure that the receiving flask is empty of solvent and that water is passing through the condenser coils at a slow but steady rate. Turn on the water aspirator to its fullest extent and then attach the evaporating flask (with adapter if required) to the vapour duct, using a clip to ensure that the flask stays in place. Support the flask lightly with the hand, commence slow rotation and then close the stopcock at the end of the condenser. When the manometer indicates a significant reduction of pressure within the system (if no manometer is attached to the apparatus, listen for a marked change in tone of the sound made by the water rushing from the aspirator) it is safe to remove your hand and regulate the speed of rotation to spread the solvent out around the flask without causing it to splash. If the mixture commences to boil uncontrollably, *temporarily* open the stopcock at the top of the condenser to allow entry of air and then reclose the stopcock. Once the evaporation from the solution has stabilized, the evaporating flask may be introduced into a bath of warm water if desired. However, be ready to remove the flask immediately there is any

Keep the flask supported until the system is under vacuum

Heat cautiously

indication that the mixture is beginning to boil too vigorously. The majority of common solvents such as ether or light petroleum have boiling points well below room temperature at the reduced pressures possible using this system, so you must exercise great care when heating the evaporating flask. With the more volatile solvents it is advisable to place the flask in a cold water bath at the outset and then allow the bath to warm up slowly during the course of solvent removal. The last traces of solvent are difficult to remove from samples, particularly the kinds of gummy materials which are often isolated from reactions, and so it is necessary to leave the residue on the rotary evaporator for at least 5 min after the last of any solvent has been seen running into the receiver.

Continuous evaporation of large quantities of solution

If the volume of solvent you wish to remove is inconveniently large for the size of the evaporating flask you are using (which should never be filled to more than about one-quarter of its volume), it is possible to introduce additional solution if the stopcock at the top of the condenser is fitted with a length of tubing which reaches into the evaporating flask. Simply attach a length of glass tubing to the external connector on the stopcock and dip this into the extra solution you wish to add (Fig. 2.30). Opening the stopcock carefully will cause solution to be drawn into the evaporating flask by the reduced pressure within the rotary evaporator and the solvent removal can continue after closure of the stopcock.

Do not leave your solvent in the receiver flask and check that the vapour duct is clean

When you are satisfied that all of the solvent has been removed from your sample, stop the flask rotating and raise it from the heating bath. If you reverse the order of these operations you will get wet with spray from the flask! Open the stopcock to allow air into the system, **supporting the flask with your hand**, remove the flask and turn off the aspirator and condenser water. Empty the contents of the receiver flask into the container designated for used solvents (**not down the sink!**) and check that you have left no material adhering to the

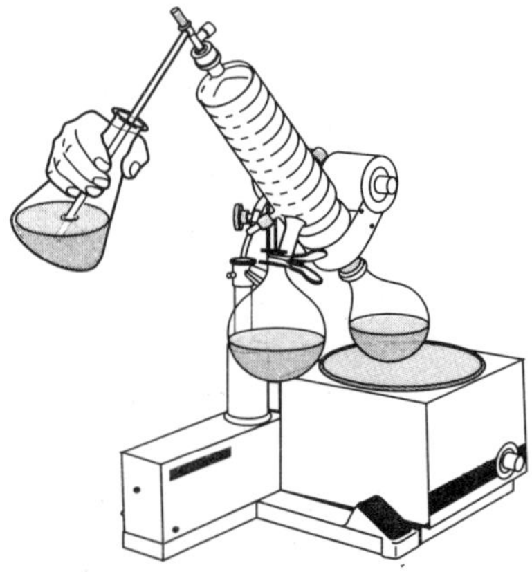

Fig. 2.30 The procedure for continuous solvent removal using a rotary evaporator.

inside of the vapour duct as this will not only reduce your yield, but also contaminate the next user's sample.

Sample concentration on the microscale

Sample concentration can be achieved with containment. For small (*ca.* 1 mL or less) volumes of solution, the solvent can be simply blown off by allowing a fine stream of nitrogen gas to pass over the surface of the solution in a hood (Fig. 2.31a). The tube containing the solution should not be allowed to cool, or condensation will occur in the tube, wetting the sample. Clamping the tube in a bath of warm water or in a warm sand bath will prevent this. This method should not be used in the open laboratory—this technique is unsuitable there because of the release of solvent vapour. Instead, the use of a water aspirator or vacuum pump is recommended (Fig. 2.31b). For small volumes, attach a Pasteur pipette via flexible tubing to the water pump and position the pipette tip close to (but not under) the surface of the solution. Warming the tube will volatilize the solvent and the aspirator will draw the vapour away, at the same time avoiding condensation of atmospheric moisture. The same technique can

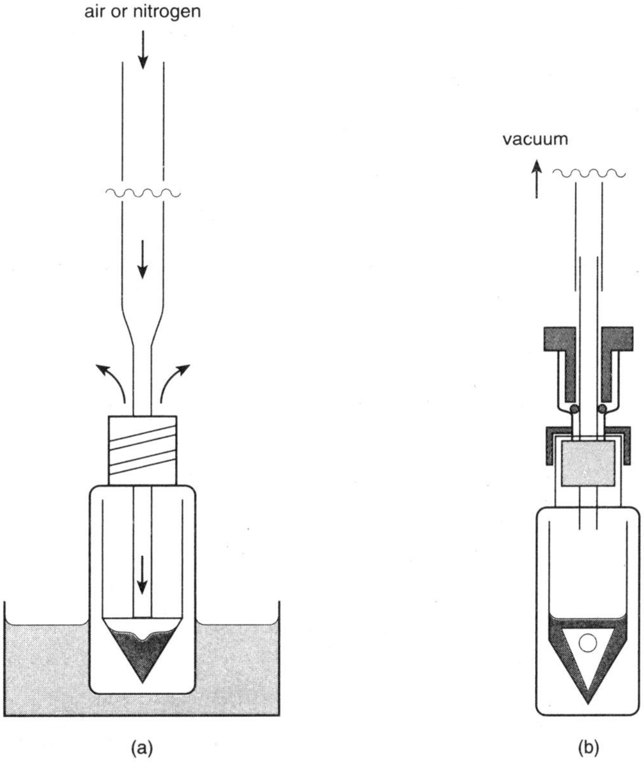

Fig. 2.31 Small quantities of solvent can be removed by blowing a stream of air or nitrogen over the surface of the solution with gentle warming, or using an aspirator, in which case the solution is stirred to prevent bumping.

be used if water aspirators have been replaced by mechanical vacuum pumps, though these should be protected by placing traps between the experiment and the pump (see p. 43–44). If a solid product (and subsequent recrystallization) is anticipated, concentration into a Craig tube directly will minimize losses.

2.9 Catalytic hydrogenation

Catalytic hydrogenation is a particularly useful means of reducing alkenes and alkynes (see Experiments 25 and 26). Frequently it is necessary to avoid over-reduction, for instance in the Lindlar catalyzed reduction of alkynes to alkenes, or if it is desired to reduce selectively only one unsaturated site within the molecule as in Experiment 26. In such instances it is necessary to use a gas burette system which enables the volume of gas taken up to be measured at atmospheric pressure and at the same time permits a certain amount of overpressure (up to about 0.5 atm) to be applied to the reaction mixture. An example of such an arrangement is shown schematically in Fig. 2.32.

Hydrogenations at higher pressures (2–400 atm) require very specialized apparatus to enable safe working due to the highly explosive nature of hydrogen, especially when under pressure. These are beyond the scope of this book but, whatever the pressure and whatever the quantity of hydrogen being used, all naked flames must be extinguished.

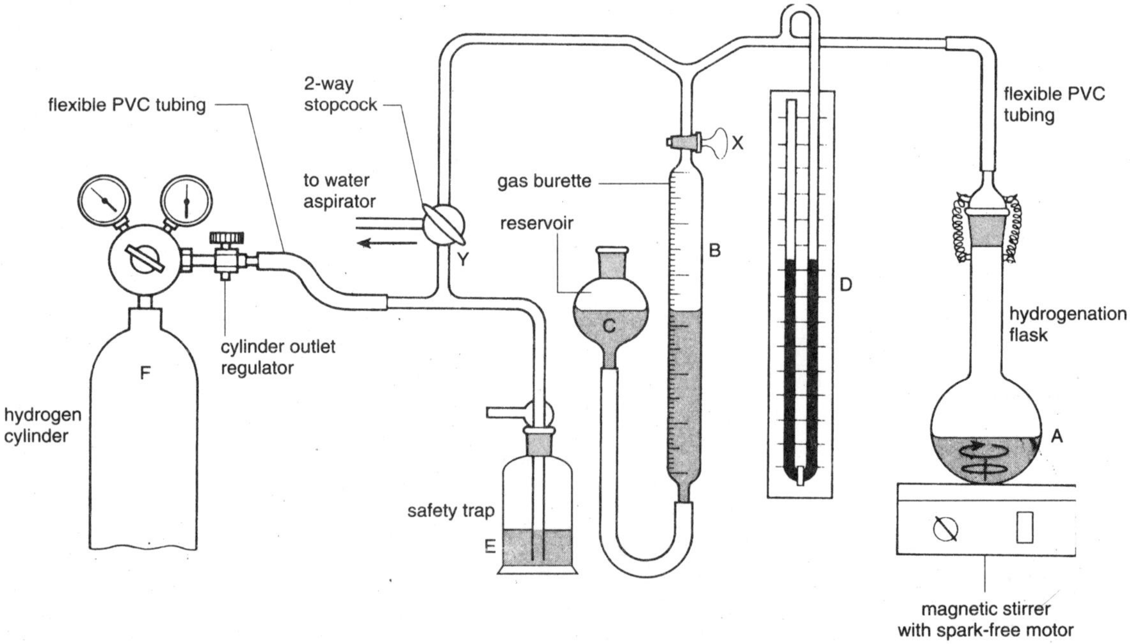

Fig. 2.32 Schematic of low pressure hydrogenation apparatus.

Whenever working with hydrogen, there must be no naked flames in the laboratory. Any electrical apparatus in the vicinity must be spark-proof.

The hydrogenation burette

The essential features of the apparatus are the hydrogenation flask (Fig. 2.32A), linked by a flexible connection to a gas burette (B) and reservoir (C). The size of the burette, usually between 2 L and 100 mL, depends on the scale of the reaction to be carried out and whether the liquid used to fill the system is water or mercury. The hydrogen pressure over the reaction mixture is controlled by adjusting the height of the reservoir. Higher internal pressures are possible using mercury in the reservoir, but this becomes impractical for larger burette volumes due to the weight of mercury necessary. If water is used, it is common practice to dissolve a few crystals of copper(II) sulfate in it to discourage algal growth and to help visualize the meniscus. Attached to the system is a manometer (D) and a pressure release safety trap (E). Hydrogen is obtained at about 1 atm pressure via a regulator valve from a pressurized cylinder (F) (see pp. 64–68). All flexible tubing used to carry hydrogen must be impermeable and is best composed of clear PVC. It should be tightly wired onto the apparatus.

Hydrogenation procedure

In carrying out any procedure involving hydrogen, two rules must be observed at all times.

Never allow naked flames in the vicinity when hydrogen is being used. Avoid the formation of air–hydrogen mixtures.

The warning about flames and hydrogen cannot be repeated too often and this is particularly important if the experiment is being carried out in a busy teaching laboratory with lots of people all doing different things. It is far better for the apparatus to be kept in a separate room specifically designed for hydrogenations.

Care! Some catalysts are pyrophoric

No flames when hydrogen is being used!

Fill the burette with water or mercury by opening stopcock X and raising the reservoir C until the liquid level in the burette reaches the stopcock; then close stopcock X and lower the reservoir to its former level. Place the sample to be hydrogenated in flask A, with a magnetic stirrer bar, and dissolve it in the specified volume of reaction solvent. Add the catalyst to the mixture, ensuring that none adheres to the sides of the flask by washing the walls with a little solvent from a pipette. Connect the flask to the system and secure the tubing adapter to the flask with metal springs or elastic bands. Turn the two-way stopcock Y to connect the system to the water aspirator and evacuate until no further movement registers on the manometer. Open the hydrogen supply at the cylinder and regulate the reduction valve on the cylinder adapter to give a working pressure of 2–3 psi (about 0.2 atm—see pp. 67–68). Turn the cylinder stopcock Z carefully and observe the gas bubbling through the pressure release trap E. Connect the evacuated system to the hydrogen cylinder, turning stopcock Y slowly, and observe the fall in the mercury level of the manometer as hydrogen is drawn in. Once again, connect the system to the aspirator, evacuate until the manometer shows a steady vacuum, and then reintroduce hydrogen. Repeat this cycle of charging and evacuation at least three more times to ensure that all of the air originally in the system has been flushed out.

Air–hydrogen mixtures are very likely to inflame if they come into contact with the catalyst.

After the fifth cycle, open the burette stopcock X and allow it to fill with hydrogen to the desired level, lowering the reservoir if necessary. Turn stopcock Y to isolate the system and shut off the aspirator and hydrogen cylinder. To obtain the initial volume reading, place the system at atmospheric pressure by moving the reservoir up or down to equalize the mercury levels in the manometer, and read off the volume in the burette. Knowing the amount of sample to be hydrogenated, the prevailing atmospheric pressure and room temperature, the amount of hydrogen uptake desired can be calculated. Raise the reservoir to develop an over-pressure of hydrogen within the system (registered on the manometer), stirring the contents of the reaction flask. Frequently, hydrogenation reactions are agitated by shaking which also serves to increase the contact area of the reaction mixture with the hydrogen atmosphere. If shaking instead of stirring, you must use a long-necked hydrogenation flask in order to avoid solution entering the PVC tubing. Periodically lower the reservoir to bring the system back to atmospheric pressure and measure the amount of hydrogen taken up on the burette. This is usually fairly rapid initially but slows down as the reaction reaches completion. The apparent uptake is often slightly greater than that calculated and may never quite stop as it is very difficult to eliminate all leaks of hydrogen within the apparatus. In addition, even small amounts of catalyst can adsorb appreciable amounts of hydrogen and, for accurate small-scale work, it is necessary to presaturate the catalyst with hydrogen. This is a rather tricky procedure, however, and should only be carried out by those with experience of hydrogenations. Certainly there will be no need to do this in the hydrogenation experiments within this book.

All electrical apparatus must be spark-proof

When the hydrogenation is complete the system must be evacuated again and the excess hydrogen must be removed before permitting re-entry of air to avoid spontaneous combustion of the air–hydrogen mixture on the catalyst surface. After assiduously filling the apparatus, many people forget this part of the procedure, with dangerously spectacular results. The reaction mixture may then be filtered with suction to remove the catalyst and the catalyst placed in the residues bottle for recycling. This filtration must always be carried out using a glass sinter funnel and care should be taken not to draw air through the dry catalyst as many are pyrophoric.

Do not draw air over the catalyst

Hydrogenation on the microscale

For microscale use, generation of hydrogen gas becomes practicable; remember that 1 mmol of gas will occupy 22.4 mL at standard temperature and pressure. The gas can be generated in a small flask or tube by the action of sulfuric acid on zinc metal, conveyed through fine polypropylene tubing and collected in an inverted measuring cylinder or microscale burette and used subsequently. The advantage of this type of procedure is the availability of equipment for multiple use; clearly the hazard associated with the use of a flammable gas still exists and utmost care must be taken to avoid contact between the gas and naked flames. The Brown procedure represents a useful *in situ* alternative. Platinum(IV) chloride is reduced by sodium borohydride in the presence of decolourizing charcoal to generate a reactive supported catalyst. Hydrogen gas is generated *in situ* by exposure of sodium borohydride to acid, and retained in the reaction by a pipette bulb, wired on to the reaction vessel.

Further reading

H.C. Brown and C.A. Brown, *J. Am. Chem. Soc.*, 1962, **84**, 1495.
P.N. Rylander, *Hydrogenation Methods*, Academic Press. Orlando, FL, 1985.

2.10 Ozonolysis

The cleavage of double bonds using ozone, followed by either a reductive or oxidative work-up to yield carbonyl-containing fragments is an important procedure in synthetic work (see Experiment 73), as well as in structure-determination studies when characterization of the fragments may be easier than the original alkene. The great advantage of ozone is its selectivity; hydroxyl groups, for instance, remain untouched by this reagent.

Ozone (O_3) is obtained by passing oxygen between two electrodes which have a high voltage electrical discharge between them. Commercial ozonizers can provide oxygen enriched with up to about 10% ozone by regulation of the operating voltage and the oxygen throughput, and yield around 0.1 mol h^{-1} of ozone. It is possible to estimate the production rate of the ozonizer by passing the ozone stream through a solution of potassium iodide in 50% aqueous acetic acid for a measured period and then determining the liberated iodine titrimetrically. However, many commercial instruments have reliable calibration charts and, in any case, it is usually sufficient to monitor the progress of the reaction by TLC and adjust the ozone production rate accordingly.

The operation simply involves passing dry oxygen over the charged plates at a predetermined rate, although the exact procedural details vary with each instrument and you must consult an instructor before attempting to use the ozonizer.

Remember that the instrument contains a very high voltage (7000–10 000 V) when in operation. Ozone is highly toxic and experiments must always be carried out in the hood. In addition, the intermediate ozonides must never be isolated as they are potentially explosive compounds. An appropriate work-up must always be carried out before attempting to isolate your product.

The apparatus

Ozone is toxic—HOOD!

A typical arrangement is shown in Fig. 2.33 and essentially consists of an oxygen supply, the ozonizer, a trap and the reaction vessel. Some means of testing the effluent gas for the presence of ozone may also be used to check for completion of reaction. The oxygen supply comes from a cylinder and that part of the apparatus which delivers or contains ozone (from the ozonizer outlet onwards) must be contained in an efficient hood.

Ozonolysis procedure

The substrate is dissolved in an inert solvent, commonly dichloromethane or cyclohexane, in a flask arranged for stirring at reduced temperature (Fig. 2.33) and fitted with a sintered inlet tube and a means of venting the ozone. The sintered inlet tube disperses the incoming stream of gas, increasing its surface area and hence the rate of absorption of the ozone. The ozonolysis is carried

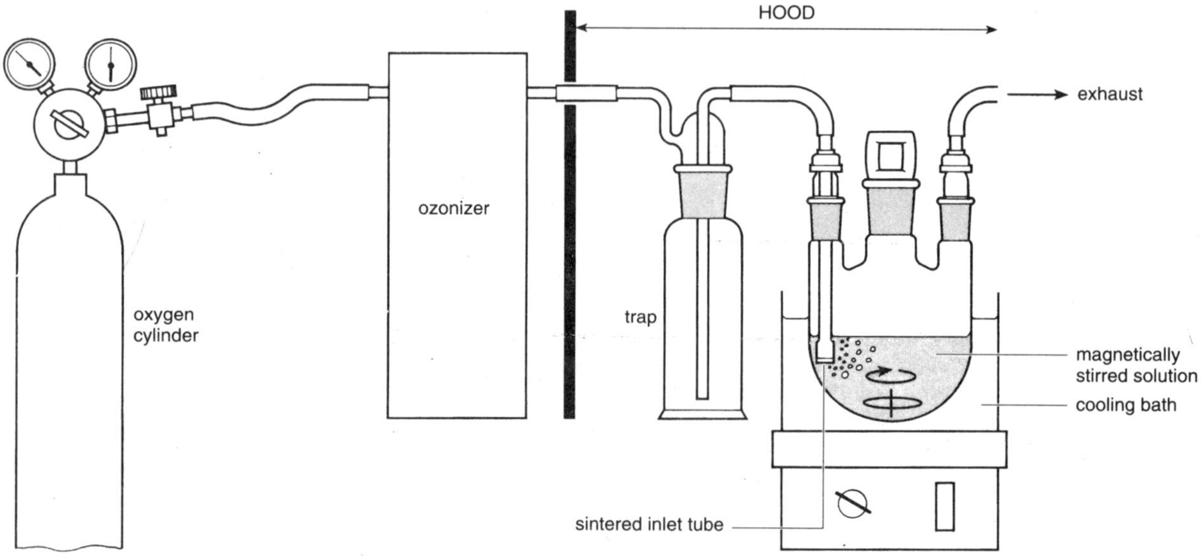

Fig. 2.33 Typical arrangement of apparatus for ozonolysis.

out with external cooling of the reaction mixture using an ice bath or a solid CO_2–acetone bath (–78°C). The progress of the reaction may be monitored by TLC, observing the disappearance of starting material, or the effluent gas may be checked for ozone using moist starch-iodide paper which turns blue-black if ozone is present in the effluent gas. Simple observation of the reaction mixture should give a good indication when excess ozone is present, as solutions of ozone are pale blue. If the passage of gas is too rapid for all of the ozone to be absorbed, a positive blue-black colouration may be obtained with the starch-iodide paper before the reaction is complete and so it is always a good idea to check by TLC before moving to the next stage of the experiment.

Ozone is highly toxic and irritates the lungs. Extreme care must be exercised when removing samples from the reaction flask for TLC analysis.

The ozonide contained in solution must be decomposed either by reduction or oxidation before any isolation work can be carried out.

Ozonides are potentially explosive and must never be isolated.

A particularly convenient reductive work-up procedure involves treating the reaction mixture with excess dimethyl sulfide which is immediately oxidized to dimethyl sulfoxide. However, dimethyl sulfide possesses a repulsive odour of rotten cabbage and its use in a crowded teaching laboratory might not be very popular! Reduction with zinc in acetic acid or triphenylphosphine present slightly more involved, but much more socially acceptable, alternatives. Use of sodium borohydride permits reductive decomposition of the ozonide with further reduction of the carbonyl fragments to alcohols. Alternatively the ozonide may be hydrolyzed, but in this instance the hydrogen peroxide produced oxidizes aldehyde groups to carboxylic acids. To ensure complete oxidation, excess hydrogen peroxide should be added to the reaction mixture in such instances. Details of these procedures may be found in the publications listed below.

Further reading

For a procedure for reductive work-up of ozonolysis reactions using catalytic hydrogenation, see: B.S. Furniss, A.J. Hannaford, P.W.G. Smith and A.R. Tatchell, *Vogel's Textbook of Practical Organic Chemistry*, 5th edn, Longman, London, 1989, p. 106.

J. March, *Advanced Organic Chemistry*, 4th edn, Wiley & Sons, New York, 1992, p. 1177.

V.N. Odinokov and G.A. Tolstikov, *Ozonolysis—a Modern Method in the Chemistry of Olefins* [*Russ. Chem. Rev.* (Engl. trans.), 1981, **50**, 636] and references cited therein.

2.11 Irradiation

The commonest way of increasing the rate of chemical reactions is to supply additional energy in the form of heat. Electromagnetic radiation in the ultraviolet (UV) region is also useful in synthetic organic chemistry, and serves not only as an energy source, but may also alter the course of the chemical reaction ('thermally forbidden–photochemically allowed' processes). The only requirement is for the incident light to possess a wavelength which can be absorbed either by the substrate (*direct photolysis*) or by an added molecule which can transfer its energy to the substrate molecule (*sensitized photolysis*).

In favourable climates, sunlight is a convenient source of radiant energy with wavelengths down to 320 nm suitable for carrying out a wide range of chemical reactions. However, this option is not open to all laboratories and, additionally, a wide range of photochemical transformations require higher energy light with wavelengths down to 220 nm. Mercury arc lamps are the most convenient sources of radiant energy in the organic chemistry laboratory. There are three types available—*low, medium* and *high pressure* mercury arc lamps, which differ in the range of wavelengths and intensity of the light they produce. The low and medium pressure types are those most commonly used in photochemical synthetic work. Commonly, low pressure lamps, operating at roughly 10^{-3} mmHg, emit light particularly rich in the 254 nm wavelength, together with some at 184 nm which can be filtered out. However, other low pressure lamps are available which emit at 300 nm and 350 nm. Medium pressure lamps, with internal vapour pressures of 1–10 atm, produce a range of wavelengths between 200 and 1400 nm with intensity maxima at 313, 366, 436 and 546 nm. High pressure lamps effectively give an intense continuum between 220 and 1400 nm, being particularly rich in the visible region. Both medium and high pressure lamps produce a great deal of heat during use and so relatively elaborate cooling arrangements are necessary when using these.

Low pressure lamps give out minimal heat and the main requirement of the apparatus is containment and focusing of the light onto the sample. Attention must be paid to the container in which the sample is held, as Pyrex® glass—the usual medium for laboratory glassware—is opaque to light below 300 nm. Reactions requiring shorter wavelength light must be carried out in quartz vessels and these are very expensive items. Great care must be taken when using them, not only against breakage, but also against touching with the hands as this leaves UV opaque deposits.

The light may come from an external source shining onto the reaction vessel or the apparatus may be designed such that the lamp is totally surrounded by solution. A Rayonet® reactor is frequently used with low pressure lamps for external irradiation. The silvered interior, together with rotation of the reaction vessels on a 'carousel', permits efficient and even irradiation of samples, whilst the low level of heat generated is removed by a fan. Medium pressure lamps are usually used as internal irradiation sources. In this arrangement, efficient heat removal is assured by enclosing the light source in a water jacket.

Both the intensity and the wavelengths of the emissions from all mercury vapour lamps make the light produced intensely hazardous to eyesight as well as having deleterious effects on the skin. Special eye protection against UV light and gloves must be worn at all times when working with mercury lamps. All photochemical reactors must be thoroughly covered in order not to permit the escape of light and, wherever possible, experiments should be carried out in a specifically designated blacked-out hood. Never commence a photochemical reaction in the teaching laboratory without first consulting an instructor to check the apparatus.

The Rayonet® photochemical reactor

The reactor container consists of an enamelled housing which contains the reaction chamber, together with the ancillary equipment for supplying power to the lamps, the fan and the carousel (Fig. 2.34). All electrical controls are on an external console to permit control of operation without the necessity for access to the interior. The internal walls of the reaction chamber are silvered and the lamps are aligned vertically around the outside walls. The sample tubes are held in a rotating holder (the carousel), and the combination of sample rotation together with the internal silvering, permits even illumination of a series of sample tubes in the same reactor.

Use of the reactor is straightforward, but special eye protection must be worn at all times during the operation. Switch on the cooling fan and load the samples into the carousel which is then set in motion. Close the apparatus, using aluminium foil to block off any small gaps which may permit leakage of

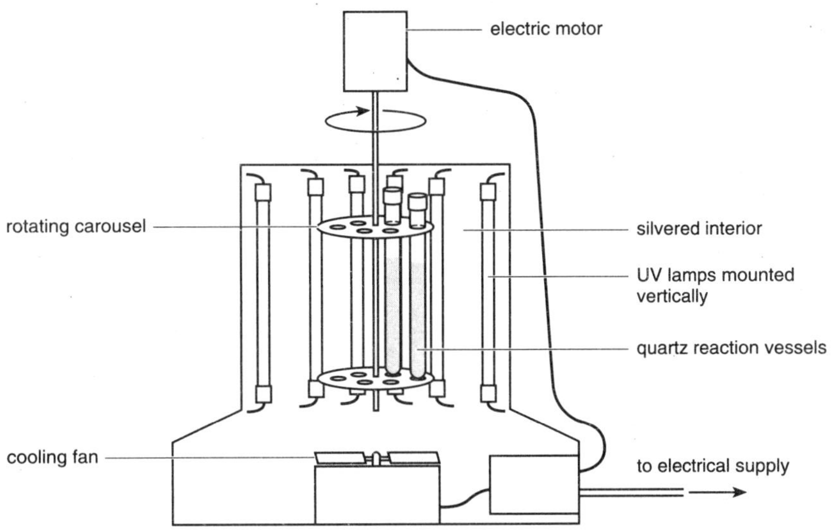

Fig. 2.34 Schematic diagram of a Rayonet® photochemical reactor.

Eye protection—UV light is hazardous

UV light, and turn on the lamps. The reaction progress may be monitored by TLC but the whole power supply to the machine must be disconnected before opening the reaction chamber to avoid any chance of accidental exposure to UV light when the protective covers are removed.

To prepare the sample, dissolve the substrate in an appropriate solvent and place the solution in quartz tubes. Take care not to contaminate the walls of the tubes with grease from the hands and fill each tube no more than two-thirds full. Stopper the tubes with serum caps and degas the solution. Do this by connecting a long needle to a nitrogen supply and pass this to the bottom of the solution. Pierce the septum with a second short needle, making sure that this does not touch the liquid in the tube, and pass nitrogen through the solution for 10 min (Fig. 2.35).

Degas samples before irradiation

Internal irradiation with a medium pressure mercury vapour lamp

The apparatus used is shown schematically in Fig. 2.36. It consists of the lamp, which is fitted into a sleeve made up of two quartz jackets. These are fitted with inlet and outlet tubes to permit the passage of coolant water. The areas of the jackets surrounding the region of the lamp which emits the light are made of particularly optically pure quartz. The same arrangement can be made of

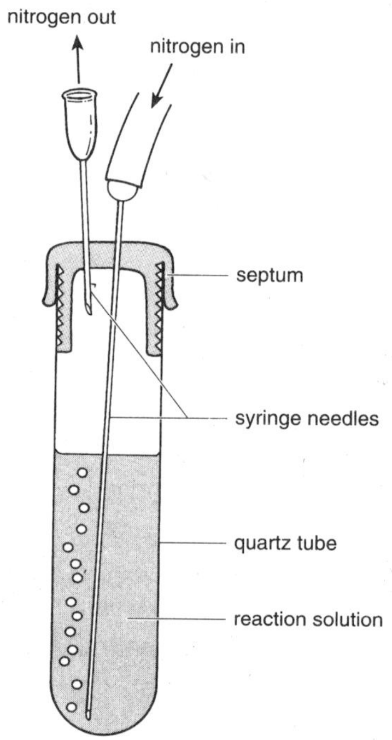

Fig. 2.35 Arrangement for degassing a sample before irradiation in a Rayonet® reactor.

Pyrex® in place of quartz when all wavelengths below 300 nm are filtered out before reaching the reaction solution. The lamp and jacket assembly is then fitted into the reaction vessel which may be a 1 L three-necked flask or a smaller two-necked vessel depending on the volume of the solution being irradiated.

Before irradiation commences, the solution should be degassed by bubbling nitrogen through it in a vigorous stream for at least 20 min—longer with larger solution volumes. The whole apparatus must be encased in a light-proof container and special eye protection must be worn before illuminating the lamp. Any leakage of light from the container must be blocked using aluminium foil. Depending on the reaction being carried out, reaction times vary from a few hours to several days and monitoring by TLC, observing all of the necessary precautions, is recommended.

Eye protection—UV light is hazardous

Microscale apparatus suitable for immersion photochemistry, which accomodates a low pressure mercury lamp and allows the photo-irradiation of 5 to 15 mL of solution, is available.

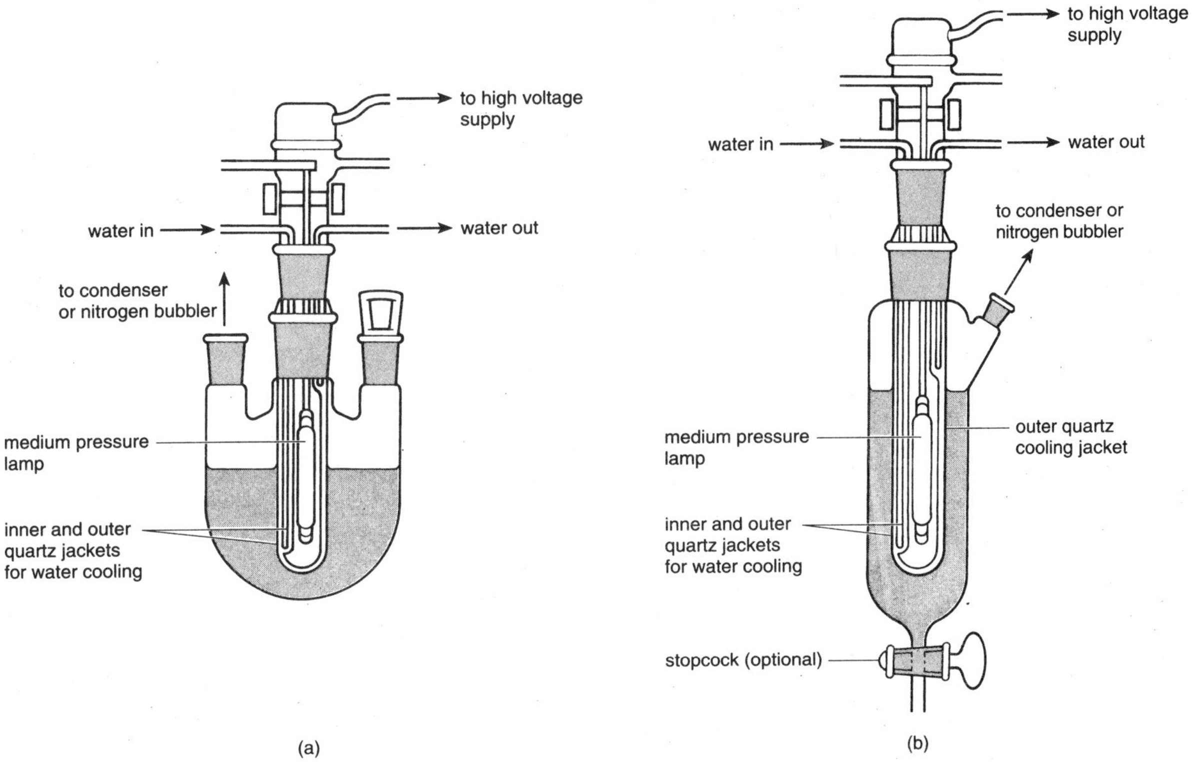

Fig. 2.36 Apparatus for internal medium pressure irradiation: (a) set-up with 1 L reaction vessel; (b) container for smaller quantities of reaction solution.

Further reading

J.D. Coyle, *Introduction to Organic Photochemistry*, Wiley, New York, 1986.
J.H. Penn and R.D. Orr, *J. Chem. Ed.*, 1989, **66**, 86–88.

2.12 Compressed gases

Whilst procedures do exist for generating some gases such as hydrogen chloride in the laboratory, it is always preferable to use gas from a cylinder. It is much more convenient to obtain the gas directly from a cylinder; the purity is more assured and the dangers associated with intermittent supply are removed. Nevertheless, pressurized gas cylinders introduce their own particular hazards and correct handling procedures must be observed at all times. The main areas of concern stem from the high pressure of the gas contained within the cylinder and the weight of the cylinder, although many gases are available in small 'lecture bottle' cylinders which are much easier to handle. It is also imperative to use the correct design of pressure regulator for the particular gas being delivered. All cylinders require a pressure-regulating device to permit controlled release of gas, but certain gases—for instance oxygen, flammable gases or corrosive gases—require a special design of pressure regulator. To minimize this problem, each specialized regulator is fitted using an adapter which is only suitable for use with the specified cylinder type.

Safe handling of gas cylinders

Gas pressure

Cylinders of gases such as hydrogen, nitrogen, oxygen and argon, which are commonly used by organic chemists, are usually supplied in cylinders at up to 200 atm pressure. The cylinders are designed to withstand rough treatment and it is extremely unlikely that any damage will be done to them in the normal course of events. Nonetheless, the cylinders should be treated with respect and, wherever possible, the valve assembly of the cylinder should be protected with a cap. This is the most vulnerable part of the cylinder and if it is broken off, for instance if the cylinder is dropped, the cylinder will be propelled with extreme force by the escaping gas and will destroy anything in its path. Any cylinder which is suspected to have been damaged, particularly around the valve, by an impact, fire or exposure to corrosive materials, must be reported immediately to the supplier.

The very real danger presented by the possibility of cylinders exploding in a fire has led to legislation in many countries banning the storage of pressurized cylinders inside laboratories. This arrangement should be followed whenever possible even where it is not mandatory.

Size and weight of cylinders

Cylinders must always be secured to a firm support and not left free-standing

Whilst very variable, a common size for laboratory cylinders is about 1.6 m in height with a gross weight of anything between 70 and 85 kg. Consequently, these are heavy and unwieldy objects which are easy to topple over if left free-standing. A cylinder of these dimensions can easily break or crush limbs and cause severe internal injury to anyone caught in the path of its fall. This very real danger must be minimized by attaching the cylinders securely to a wall or a laboratory bench with a chain or stout canvas belt (Fig. 2.37). This procedure *must* be followed for any storage even if the period is only temporary.

Cylinders must always be transported using an appropriate trolley; a two-wheeled trolley designed for this, including chains to secure the cylinder during transport, as shown in Fig. 2.38. Cylinders should not be moved by rolling along the ground or by tilting at an angle and rolling along one end whilst gripping the valve. Both procedures leave too much room for personal injury.

On transferral, the trolley should be moved as close as possible to the cylinder. Unchain the cylinder from its wall support and carefully edge it into

Fig. 2.37 Cylinders must always be strapped to a wall or a sturdy bench.

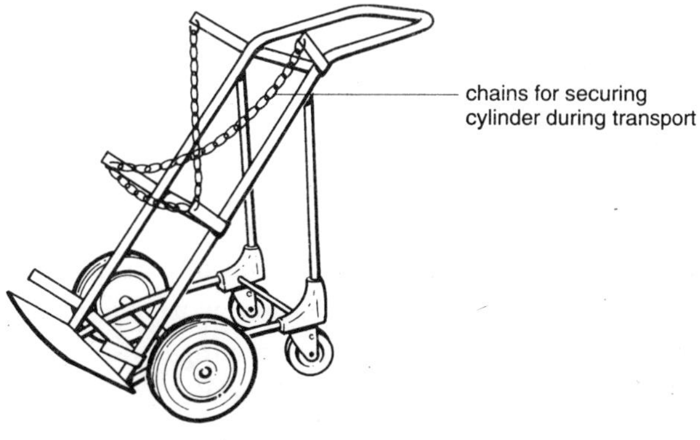

Fig. 2.38 A suitable trolley for transferring cylinders.

the trolley using both hands. Immediately rechain the cylinder to the trolley and transfer the cylinder to the desired place. Unload the cylinder from the trolley and fix it securely in its new position. This procedure is awkward and heavy work, and it is recommended that even the strongest people work in pairs. One should hold the trolley steady during the transfer and the other should move the cylinder. If the cylinder begins to topple out of control it should be allowed to fall, as severe injury can result from attempting to halt its fall.

Identification of contents

It is, of course, essential that the contents of all cylinders be correctly identified. All cylinders have labels bearing the names of the contents and details about hazards and degree of purity connected with the contents. However, labels can be lost or destroyed, so, as an additional precaution, the cylinders are painted with a colour code to indicate the gas contained within. Unfortunately, what seems to be an excellent idea in principle has led to a very confused situation as different countries have adopted different codes. In the USA no standard coding system has been adopted, although the EU has now addressed this issue and EU-approved colour codes are described in European Standard EN1089-3: 1997. However, even within Europe, code variations remain in some member states. In case of doubt, the relevant supplier's catalogue should be consulted and any further queries about identification should be addressed directly to the supplier.

Cylinders containing liquefied gas

Some cylinders containing liquefied gas are designed to deliver either the liquid or the gas as desired. This is usually the case for ammonia and chlorine which are fitted with *goose neck* withdrawal tubes capable of removing gas when the cylinder is held vertically and liquid when it is held horizontally (Fig. 2.39). Such cylinders should be supported in a specially designed cradle and must be chained in the vertical position when not in use. When using liquid ammonia for dissolving metal reductions such as the Birch reduction (see Experiment 27) it is recommended that the ammonia be obtained as a gas with the cylinder vertical and condensed into the receiver flask using a dry-ice acetone condenser (see Fig. 3.30, p. 104). Otherwise particles of ferrous material may be carried into the reaction and catalyze the formation of sodamide.

Wear protection against splashes of cold liquid

Keep a respirator to hand

Quite apart from the corrosive and toxic nature of these gases, severe burns will result from splashing the cold liquid on the skin and suitable protective clothing must be worn when dispensing any liquid from a cylinder. Needless to say, the receiving vessel must be in an efficient hood and the correct type of respirator should also be readily to hand in case of spillage in the open laboratory or the valve jamming open.

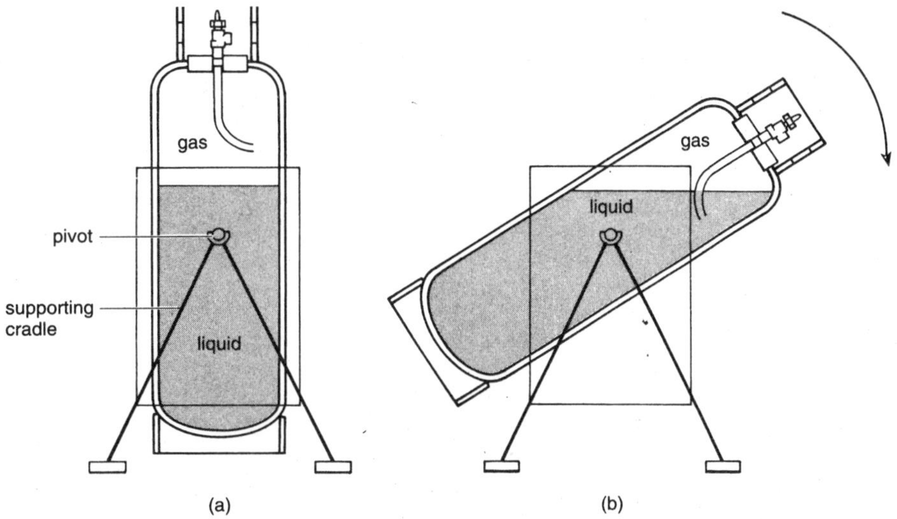

Fig. 2.39 Systems for delivery of liquid or gas from cylinders using a gooseneck adapter arrangement: (a) cylinder vertical, gas delivered; (b) cylinder tilted, liquid delivered.

The diaphragm regulator

The controlled release of gas from within the cylinder requires a pressure reduction regulator to deliver the highly compressed gas at steady flow rates and pressures which may be varied from about 0.1 to 2 atm. The regulator is attached to the cylinder by a threaded bullet adapter which fits tightly into the socket of the cylinder valve (Fig. 2.40). Regulators for use with cylinders containing flammable gases are equipped with flash arrestors to stop any combustion entering the cylinder. These regulators have fittings with left-hand threads and this is indicated by a groove cut into the edges of the hexagonal nut.

The pressure drop is achieved using a diaphragm regulator and this may be a single- or double-stage arrangement. Single-stage regulators are less expensive, but do not maintain as steady an outlet pressure as double-stage regulators. In systems where it is necessary to have a very stable gas delivery, such as in vapour phase chromatography carrier gas supplies, the double-stage regulator is necessary, but for the majority of operations requiring an inert atmosphere, a single-stage regulator is adequate. The regulator is equipped with two pressure gauges, one to indicate the cylinder pressure (A) and one to indicate the pressure on the outlet side (B) (Fig. 2.40). The outlet pressure is controlled by turning the large screw controller (C). Clockwise movement causes an increase in outlet pressure and anticlockwise movement a corresponding decrease. The regulator is also fitted with an outlet tap (D) and a bursting valve (E) as an emergency pressure release valve.

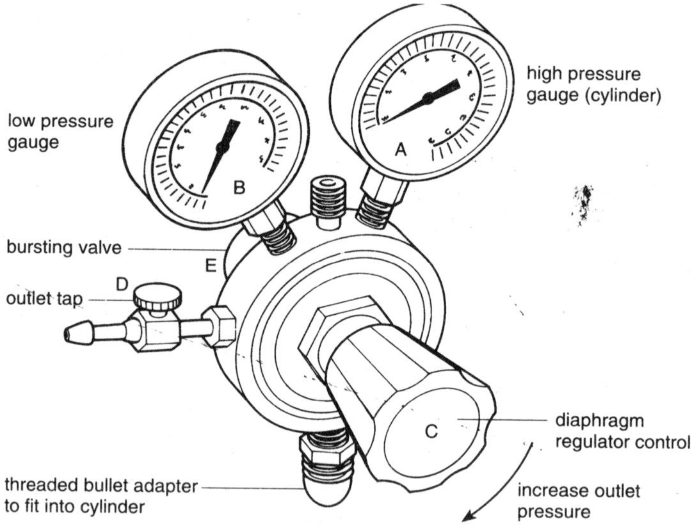

Fig. 2.40 The diaphragm pressure regulator.

Attaching the pressure regulator to the cylinder

All traces of dust and grease must be removed from the socket to permit a gas-tight seal between the cylinder valve and regulator. However, this is particularly important in the case of oxygen cylinders because oil residues are liable to explode on contact with compressed oxygen. Fitting requires firm tightening to achieve a gas-tight seal and care should be taken to ensure that the adapter is firmly in place before opening the cylinder valve, otherwise the escaping gas may eject the regulator with great force.

Check for leaks at the regulator–cylinder connection

The outlet valve should be closed and the diaphragm regulator should be turned fully anticlockwise in order to close the valve completely. On opening the cylinder valve with a square-shaped key, the cylinder pressure should register immediately on the high pressure gauge, whilst the low pressure gauge should show no movement. Slight leaks can be detected by listening for escaping gas and by applying a weak soap solution around the joints. If all appears sound, the outlet pressure may be adjusted by turning the diaphragm regulator clockwise until the desired pressure registers on the outlet pressure gauge and opening the outlet valve permits delivery of the gas.

Further reading

For full details on safe working practice with compressed gases, see: *Handbook of Compressed Gases*, 3rd edn, Van Nostrand Reinhold, New York, 1990; W. Braker and A.L. Mossman, *Compressed Gas Association, Matheson Gas Data Book*, 6th edn, Matheson, Lyndhurst, 1980; *Safe under Pressure*, BOC, 1997; European Standard EN1089-3, 1997.

Chapter 3

Organic Reactions: from Starting Materials to Pure Organic Product

Experimental organic chemistry is all about carrying out organic reactions, converting one compound into another in a safe and efficient manner. The route from starting materials to pure organic products involves a number of discrete operations which can be summarized as follows:

- Assembling suitable apparatus in which to carry out the reaction.
- Dispensing, measuring and transferring the correct quantities of starting materials, reagents and solvents for the reaction.
- Running the reaction under defined conditions, controlling, as appropriate, rates of addition of reagents, rate of stirring and, importantly, the reaction temperature. In addition, it is often necessary to follow the progress of the reaction by some means.
- Isolation of your product or products from the reaction mixture at the end of the reaction. This isolation procedure is often referred to as the reaction *work-up*.
- Purification of the product.
- Analysis of the product (Chapters 4 and 5).

This chapter explains how the first five steps of these processes can be safely and efficiently carried out, for standard and microscale processes, and ideally should be read and understood before attempting any of the experiments in Part 2 of this book. All of the basic techniques of the organic laboratory are included here, and this chapter serves as a reference for the experimental procedures that are encountered in Part 2.

3.1 Handling chemicals

Safe handling of chemicals

Check labels for hazard warnings

When handling any chemical, safety is of paramount importance. Before starting any experiment in organic chemistry, you should familiarize yourself with the properties of the chemicals and solvents that you will be using. As explained in Chapter 1, the general properties of a chemical are usually indicated on the container by a written warning or by use of standard hazard warning symbols. Get into the habit of looking at the labels on reagent bottles, and take note of any warnings given. So, before setting up any organic experiment, check the experimental procedure for warnings about chemicals, and **think**!! The mental check-list goes something like this:

- Are any of the reagents or solvents particularly corrosive? If so, wear adequate hand protection.
- Are any of the reagents or solvents particularly flammable with very low flash points? If so, check that there are no naked flames in the vicinity.
- Are any of the reagents or solvents particularly toxic or unpleasant smelling? If so, they will need to be dispensed and used in a fume hood.
- Are any of the reagents or solvents highly air or moisture sensitive? If so, special handling techniques will be required (pp. 83–89).

Always check for lighted burners before using flammable materials

Always take the utmost care when transporting chemicals around the laboratory from the stockroom or storage shelves to your bench or hood. Remember to check that the top of the reagent container is securely fastened before moving it. Large (2.5 L) solvent bottles are most safely transported in wire or basket bottle carriers.

Use bottle carriers!

Remember, if in any doubt about how to handle a given compound, ask!!

Measuring and transferring chemicals

For a successful organic chemistry experiment it is important to use defined amounts of starting materials and reagents. It is very rare that you can get away with using approximate quantities. Therefore, unless your instructor suggests that the *scale* of an experiment be changed, the amounts of chemicals given in the experimental procedures in Part 2 should be strictly adhered to. If the experimental protocol requires the use of 1.2 g of reagent, **do not** use 2.4 g in the assumption that the reaction will take half the time or give twice the yield. This is a mistaken and possibly dangerous assumption.

Do not alter the scale of a reaction without consulting an instructor

Solids

The correct amount of solid for a chemical reaction is always given by weight. Therefore, setting up your experiment requires the weighing of one or more reagents, and, or course, the final product. Careful weighing is a time-consuming process because widely differing densities of solid materials make estimation of weight very difficult. Even with experience, 'weighing by eye' is notoriously inaccurate. The accuracy of weighing required depends on the *scale* of the reaction; if the reaction is being carried out on a millimolar scale, typically 100–300 mg, then weighing to the nearest milligram is required. On the other hand, for most of the larger scale reactions described in this book, weighing to the nearest 0.1 g will usually suffice, and in cases where the amount of reagent is not critical, to the nearest 1 g. Therefore you should always use a balance that is appropriate for the accuracy of weighing required. There are a vast number of balances on the market, ranging from analytical balances that weigh to the nearest 0.01 mg, requiring totally draught- and vibration-free conditions, to simple scale pan balances. Some typical examples

Use the right balance

are shown in Fig. 3.1. Modern electronic single pan balances are by far the most convenient to use, since they have digital read-out and electronic zero facilities, making preweighing of containers unnecessary. Whichever type of balance is available in your laboratory or balance room, the first thing to do is to familiarize yourself with its operation.

Use a small container to weigh small quantities

For convenience it is often better, although not essential, to weigh chemicals into a suitable container, and subsequently transfer the chemical to the reaction flask or addition funnel. However, it is important to use an appropriate container for weighing out your sample. For example, do not use a large flask or beaker weighing more than 200 g to weigh out 0.1 g of solid. Even with modern electronic balances, this is bad practice, since you are dealing with small differences between large numbers. Rather use a small sample vial (which can be capped if necessary), or, if the solid is not air or moisture sensitive, or hygroscopic, it may be weighed out onto special weighing paper which has a smooth glossy surface. Use a micro-spatula, normal spatula or lab spoon—the choice depends on the amount of solid—to transfer the chemical from its bottle or container to the weighing vessel, although utmost care should be taken to avoid spills during the transfer. It is particularly important when using accurate balances (the type with doors as in Fig. 3.1a), that no transfers are made *inside* the weighing compartment. Spills of chemicals may seriously damage the balance mechanism.

Wipe up spills immediately

Occasionally it may be necessary, because of the properties of the chemical, for the weighing operation to be carried out inside a hood. Laboratories with plenty of hood space often have a balance permanently located in a hood for such occasions, otherwise a balance will have to be transported. However, accurate weighing on an open pan balance is difficult in a hood because the balance is adversely affected by the hood draught.

Unless you have weighed your solid starting material or reagent directly into the reaction vessel, the chemical has to be transferred from the weighing

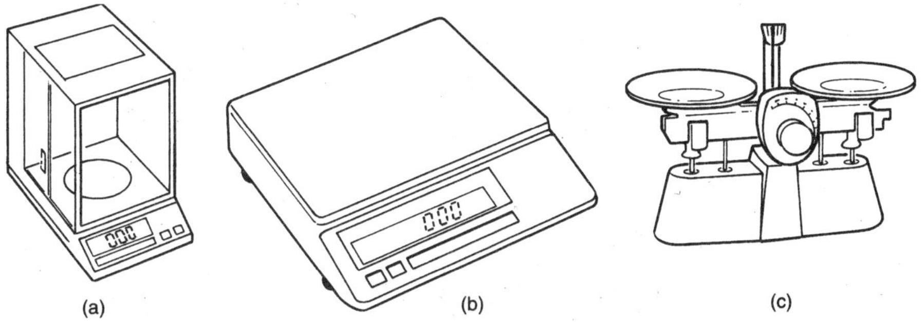

Fig. 3.1 Some typical examples of modern balances (not to scale): (a) electronic four-figure balance (weighs to nearest 0.1 mg with maximum of *ca.* 100 g); (b) single pan electronic balance (weighs to nearest 0.01 g with maximum of *ca.* 300 g); (c) scale pan type balance (weighs to nearest 1 g with a maximum of *ca.* 2000 g).

paper or container to the reaction vessel. A convenient way to do this is to use a creased filter paper or weighing paper as shown in Fig. 3.2. Place the solid on the paper, hold the paper over the vessel, and carefully scrape the solid into the vessel using a spatula. With care, this is a quick and easy technique. For transferring larger amounts of solids it is much better to use a wide bore (>2 cm) funnel (often called a powder funnel, see Fig. 2.3). These are available with standard-tapered glass joints so that they can fit directly into the reaction flask.

Treat low melting solids as liquids

Transferring and weighing low melting (<30°C) solids can present special difficulties, since they have a great tendency to become liquid during the operation. If the chemical persists in melting, it is often best to treat it as a liquid, although you may have to warm it gently. However, do not attempt such transfers using narrow bore Pasteur pipettes, since the substance is sure to re-solidify in the pipette!

Liquids

Measure liquids by volume

Liquids can be measured by weight or by volume, but it is usually easier to measure by volume. The main exceptions to this are liquid products from reactions which have to be weighed to determine the yield of the reaction. Many experimental procedures give the quantities of liquid reagents required as a volume in millilitres. If, however, the quantity is given by weight in grams, then the required volume can easily be calculated, provided that you know the density of the liquid (often quoted on the reagent bottle or in the supplier's catalogue), using the formula:

$$\text{Volume}\left(\text{in mL}\right) = \frac{\text{Weight}\left(\text{in g}\right)}{\text{Density}\left(\text{in g mL}^{-1}\right)}$$

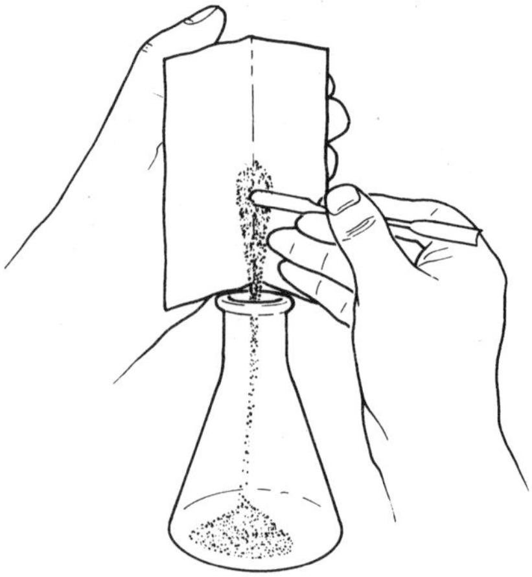

Fig. 3.2 Transferring solids with the aid of a creased paper.

There are various vessels available for measuring the volume of liquids: beakers and Erlenmeyer flasks, which have approximate volumes marked on their sides, graduated cylinders, graduated pipettes, and syringes, all of which can be obtained in several standard sizes. Again the choice of equipment depends very much on the accuracy of measurement required. For rough work, for example when *ca.* 60 mL of a solvent is required for an extraction, then a graduated beaker or Erlenmeyer flask will suffice. When a little more accuracy is needed, it is better to use a graduated cylinder. Always choose one of appropriate size; do not attempt to measure 7 mL in a 100 mL cylinder, use a 10 mL or 25 mL cylinder. If care is taken it is possible to pour liquids from a reagent bottle into a measuring cylinder, but always use a funnel to minimize the chance of spills. However, never attempt to pour a small amount of liquid, say 5 mL, from a wide-necked 2.5 L bottle into a 10 mL cylinder. Use a Pasteur pipette to transfer the liquid, although always ensure that the pipette is clean, otherwise you run the risk of contaminating the entire reagent/solvent bottle. This is particularly important when transferring deuterated nuclear magnetic resonance (NMR) solvents, as contamination from other hydrogen-containing solvents must be rigorously avoided (see Chapter 5). Smaller volumes of liquids are best measured in a graduated pipette. These are available in a range of sizes, typically from 0.1 to 10 mL, and if used carefully are very accurate. Always use a pipette filler; smaller pipettes can be filled with a simple PVC teat (as used for a Pasteur pipette), but larger ones require a special filler. Whatever the liquid, never be tempted to suck it into the pipette by mouth; even if the liquid is non-toxic, you risk ingesting chemicals from a dirty pipette. Syringes are also useful for measuring small quantities of liquids quickly and accurately, and for certain air- and moisture-sensitive liquids, the use of a syringe is essential. This technique is dealt with specifically on pp. 83–89.

Do not contaminate the reagent bottle. Use a clean Pasteur pipette

Never pipette by mouth

Having measured out your liquid reagent or starting material it needs to be transferred from the measuring vessel to the reaction flask or addition funnel. Liquids measured in a graduated pipette or syringe can simply be run in; the last drop must not be forced out because such apparatus is calibrated to take account of the 'dead space'. Slightly larger volumes of liquid may be poured from a small cylinder or transferred by Pasteur pipette. In the latter case it is probably worth rinsing out the pipette with a small amount of the same solvent that is being used for the reaction. Large volumes of liquid are simply poured, but remember it is always better to use a funnel to avoid spills. One technique which also helps to prevent spills is to pour the liquid down a glass rod as shown in Fig. 3.3.

Always use a funnel

Mechanical losses of material are extremely undesirable on the standard scale; however, on the microscale, where very small (sub-millimolar) quantities are involved, they are disastrous. The unnecessary spreading of material over the glass surface should therefore be avoided wherever possible. Liquids are rarely poured and transfers should be made using pipettes or syringes.

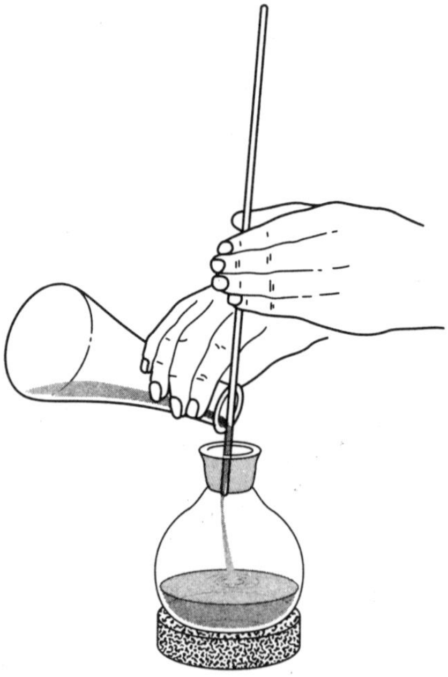

Fig. 3.3 The use of a glass rod to help in pouring liquids.

Pasteur pipettes are useful for transferring larger quantities of solutions or reagents (*ca.* 0.5 mL); drawing out the pipette in a hot flame reduces the cross-section of the aperture and makes the transfer of smaller quantities of material easier to control. Small graduated pipettes can be useful but adjustable pipettes which use disposable polypropylene tips can be used accurately and rapidly for transferring volumes from 10 μL to 1 mL. Syringes can also be used for this range of volumes though the smaller (microlitre) syringes are expensive and block easily. Disposable syringes which are available with 10 μL graduations are useful; they can be weighed accurately before and after reagent transfer to a reaction so the amount of material delivered is known precisely. Some caution is necessary because the material of the syringe may be softened or dissolved by certain solvents; testing before use is recommended.

Filtration

There are few experiments in organic chemistry that do not involve at least one filtration step. Filtration of a suspension to remove insoluble solids is a fundamental technique of preparative chemistry and is achieved by allowing the liquid to pass through a porous barrier, such as filter paper or sintered glass, whereby the solid remains on the barrier. In many cases, gravity alone is sufficient force for the liquid to pass through the porous barrier; this is referred to as *gravity filtration*. However, many organic solids are bulky, and filter slowly under gravity alone. In these cases the process is speeded up considerably by using the *suction* or *vacuum filtration* technique, in which a partial vacuum is applied to the filter flask (which must be thick-walled), and hence air pressure on the surface of the liquid in the filter funnel forces it through the porous barrier.

The choice of which filtration technique to use depends on what you are trying to achieve, but, *in general*, the following rule applies:

Gravity or suction for filtration?

If you want the filtered liquid (filtrate) use gravity filtration.
If you want the solid material use suction filtration.

Thus, if you are trying to remove small amounts of unwanted insoluble impurities, say, from a solution, gravity filtration using a folded (fluted) filter paper is often better. This is particularly so for *hot filtration*. If you need to remove larger amounts of unwanted solids, such as a spent drying agent for example, then you can still filter by gravity, although it may be considerably faster to filter by suction. In cases where you want to collect a solid material, such as a precipitated or recrystallized product, it is much better to use suction filtration.

The filtration of very small volumes of solution and the collection of small quantities of solid by filtration present special problems. These are discussed on pp. 79 and 137–138.

Gravity filtration

Gravity filtration is a simple technique only requiring a filter funnel, a piece of filter paper and a vessel, usually an Erlenmeyer, for collecting the filtrate. Glass funnels are available in several sizes, and may or may not have a stem; stemless funnels are particularly useful for hot filtration. Always use the correct size of filter paper for the filter funnel; after folding, the filter paper should always be below the rim of the glass funnel. As a rough guide, use the size of filter paper whose diameter is about 1 cm less than twice the diameter of the funnel. For example, for a funnel with a diameter of 6 cm use a filter paper with a diameter of 11 cm.

Use the right size of filter paper

The purpose of folding or fluting the filter paper is to speed the filtration by decreasing the area of contact between the paper and the funnel. Everyone develops their own way of fluting a filter paper, but one way is shown in Fig. 3.4. Start by folding the paper in half, then in half again, and then crease each

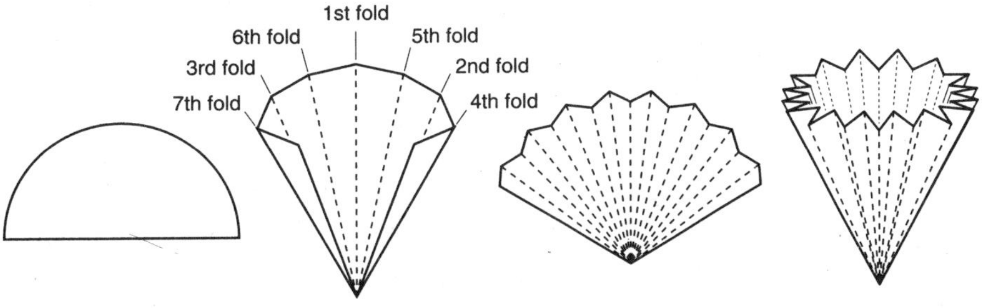

Fig. 3.4 How to flute a filter paper.

quarter into four more sections with alternate folds in opposite directions. Pull the paper into a half circle and arrange it into a pleated fan, ensuring that each fold is in the opposite direction to the previous one. Pull the sides apart and place the paper into the funnel.

Always support the glassware

Always support the filter funnel in a metal ring or clamp (Fig. 3.5). It is very tempting to place the funnel directly into the filter flask with no additional support; this is bad practice since the whole assembly is top heavy and is easily knocked over. The solution to be filtered is then simply poured into the filter paper cone, and the filtrate is collected.

Hot filtration

A useful variation on gravity filtration is *hot filtration*. This is particularly important when carrying out crystallizations (pp. 131–140), when having dissolved the material in a suitable hot solvent, you need to filter it to remove insoluble impurities. The filtration has to be carried out whilst the solution is *hot*, before the material crystallizes out of the cooling solution, and has to be conducted under gravity. Attempting to filter hot solutions by suction will

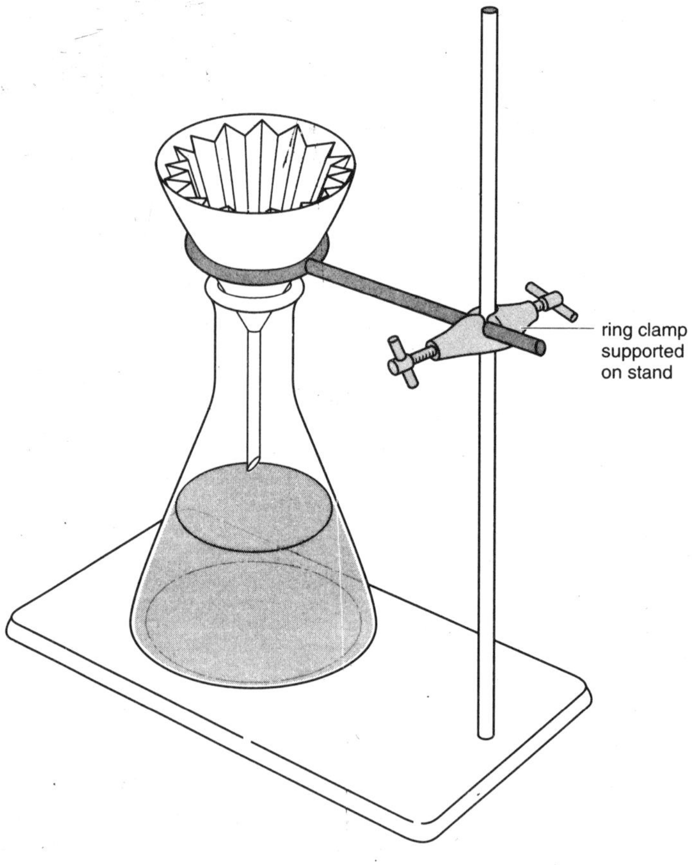

Fig. 3.5 Gravity filtration.

result in the hot filtrate boiling under the reduced pressure and in possible loss of material due to frothing. The aim of hot filtration is to complete the operation before the material starts to crystallize. For this reason, always use a stemless funnel to prevent crystallization occurring in the stem and the consequent blocking of the filter. It often helps to pre-heat the glass filter funnel before commencing the filtration and to keep the bulk of the solution to be filtered hot by pouring only small amounts of it into the filter at once. When pouring hot solutions, always use adequate hand protection; wear heat-resistant gloves or hold the hot flask in a towel.

One useful technique that considerably aids the filtration of hot solutions by keeping the funnel hot is shown in Fig. 3.6. Before commencing the filtration add a few millilitres of the same solvent to the Erlenmeyer filter flask and then heat the flask on a hotplate or steam bath. **A steam bath must be used if the solvent is flammable.** Allow the solvent to boil gently. The hot vapour will keep the funnel hot and prevent crystallization occurring in the filter. The technique necessarily generates solvent vapour, which may, of course, be flammable or toxic. In this case use a hood.

Suction filtration

Always support the filter flask

Carrying out a filtration using suction is faster than using gravity alone, but requires some additional equipment. Since the technique relies on producing a partial vacuum in the receiving flask, a thick-walled filter flask with a side arm, often called a Büchner flask, must be used, although smaller quantities can be filtered using a Hirsch tube. The flask should be securely clamped and attached to the source of the vacuum by thick-walled, flexible pressure tubing. Such tubing is heavy and will almost certainly cause unsupported flasks to topple over. The source of vacuum in the organic laboratory is almost invariably the water aspirator and the filter flask should be protected against suck-

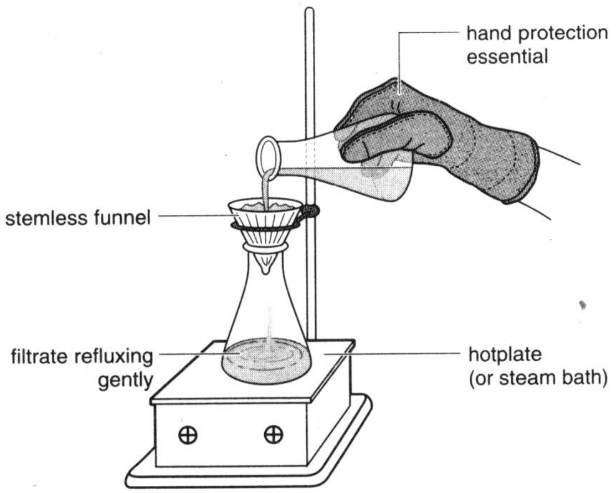

Fig. 3.6 Filtration of a hot solution.

back of water by a suitable trap (see p. 38). The most useful design of trap incorporates a valve for controlling and releasing the vacuum (see Figs. 2.19 and 3.7). Different types of funnel are also used in suction filtration; the usual types are the so-called Büchner and Hirsch funnels. The Hirsch funnel with its sloping sides is particularly suited to the collection of smaller amounts of solids. Both funnels contain a flat perforated plate or filter disk at the bottom, which is covered with a piece of filter paper. Always use a filter paper of the correct diameter. Never attempt to use a larger piece and turn up the edges; if the paper is too large, trim it to size with scissors. Finally, in order to ensure an adequate seal between the filter funnel and the flask, the funnel is placed on top of the flask through a Neoprene® filter adapter. The completed assembly for suction filtration using a Büchner or Hirsch funnel is shown in Fig. 3.7.

Use the right size of filter paper with Büchner and Hirsch funnels

Wet filter paper with solvent first

Before starting the filtration, wet the filter paper with a little solvent—the same solvent as that used in the solution that is about to be filtered. Turn on the water aspirator *gently*, and ensure that the dampened paper is sucked down flat over the perforated filter disk. Pour the mixture to be filtered onto the centre of the filter paper, and slowly increase the suction. The partial vacuum in the filter flask results in rapid filtration. With very volatile solvents, do not apply too strong a vacuum, otherwise the filtrate will boil under the reduced pressure.

When all the liquid has been sucked through, release the vacuum. Wash the collected solid with a little cold clean solvent and re-apply gentle suction. Do not wash solids under strong suction because the solvent passes through too quickly. Another advantage of suction filtration is that continuation of the suction for a few extra minutes results in fairly effective drying of the solid. To make this drying as effective as possible, press the solid flat onto the filter plate

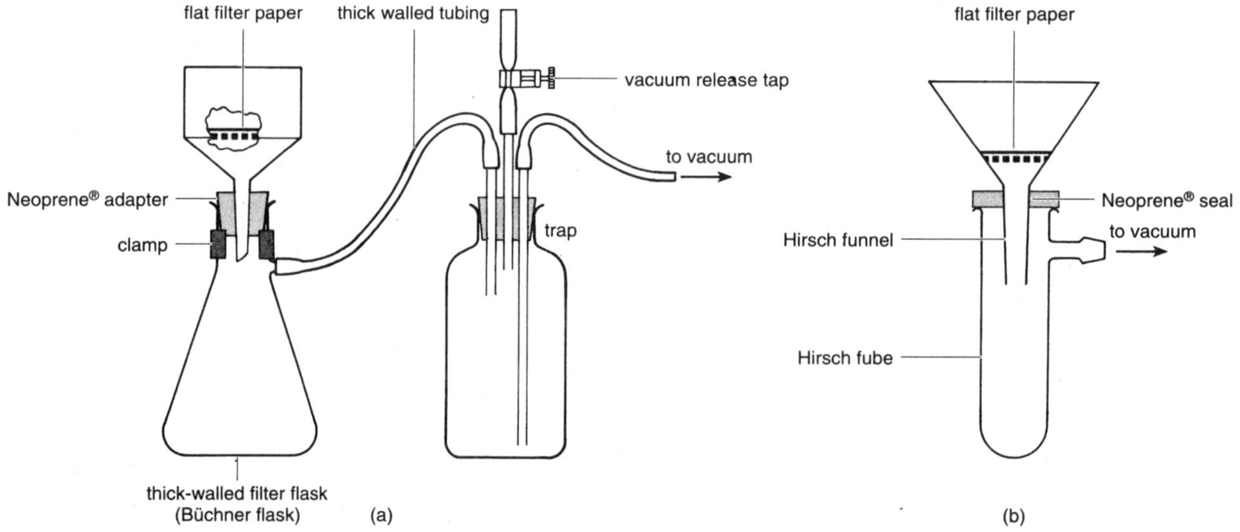

Fig. 3.7 Suction filtration using (a) a Büchner funnel or (b) a Hirsch funnel for smaller quantities.

Suck solid as dry as possible

Release vacuum before turning off aspirator

using a clean glass stopper, and then maintain the suction to remove the last traces of solvent, sucking the solid as dry as possible. This process, which involves drawing large volumes of air through the solid, is a quick way of drying solids, although it should not be used for compounds which are air or moisture sensitive. More rigorous ways of drying solids are discussed on pp. 140–143. After completion of the suction filtration, always release the vacuum and disconnect the flexible tubing from the filter flask **before** turning off the water aspirator.

An alternative to filter paper as a porous barrier is sintered glass. A variety of filter funnels containing sintered glass disks of varying size and porosity is commercially available (Fig. 3.8). These make excellent, although more expensive, alternatives to a Büchner funnel plus filter paper. In the simplest form, a sintered glass filter funnel has a stem for use with a Neoprene® adapter and filter flask as above. More sophisticated versions have a standard-tapered ground glass joint with a built-in side arm for attaching to the aspirator. These can be used for filtering directly into a standard-tapered joint round-bottomed flask, ready for subsequent evaporation or reaction.

Filtration on the microscale

Losses are incurred easily during the collection of small quantities of solids by filtration. Craig tubes are ideal (see pp. 137–138) and Hirsch funnels are available in very small sizes (5–10 mm bed size). When the filtrate is required, columns of filter agent (Celite®, Hyflo® or silica gel) can be packed into short (1 cm) columns in Pasteur pipettes (Fig. 3.9) or small chromatography columns or syringe barrels and the suspension can be forced through under pressure applied using the pipette teat. It is usually necessary to wet the filter bed with solvent to ensure that the filtrate is not held up and lost. Subsequent washing of the filter bed with small (*ca.* 0.1 mL) portions of solvent is also recommended.

Air- and moisture-sensitive compounds: syringe techniques

When working in the organic laboratory, you will eventually come across a

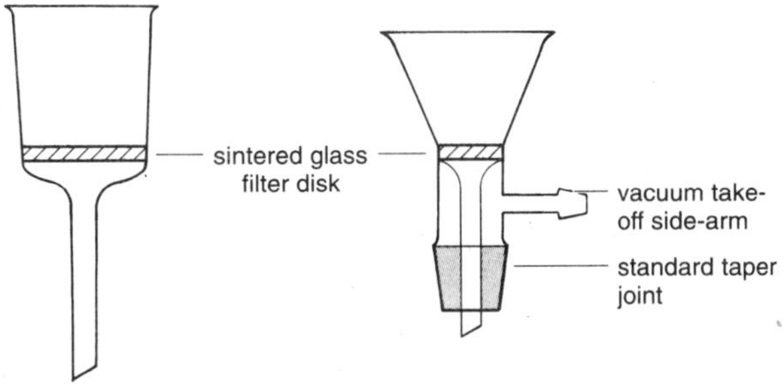

Fig. 3.8 Some typical sintered glass filter funnels.

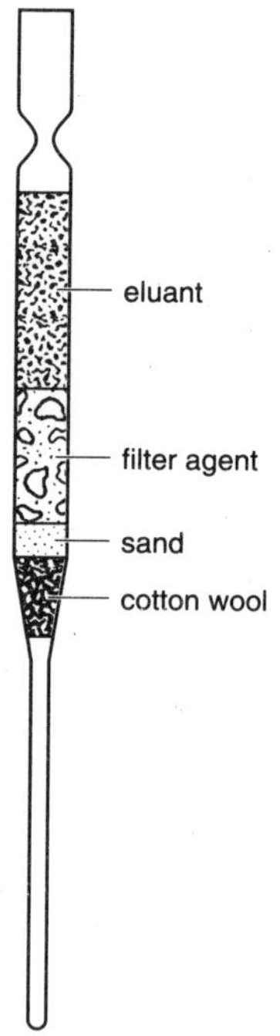

Fig. 3.9 A filtration column can be made in a Pasteur pipette plugged with glass or cotton wool, covered with a thin layer of sand which supports the filter agent (Celite®, Hyflo® or silica gel).

reagent which is described as moisture sensitive or air sensitive. Depending on the degree of this sensitivity, the reagent will need special handling, which may just simply involve bubbling dry nitrogen through the reaction mixture to maintain an inert atmosphere. At the other extreme, it may be necessary to work in a purpose-built 'dry box' under conditions which rigorously exclude air and moisture down to the last traces. However, for the experiments encountered in this book, this very specialized handling is not necessary. Rather, we attempt to describe briefly how conventional tapered glass joint apparatus, with a few additional items, can be used to handle moderately air- and moisture-sensitive reagents. A detailed treatment of such techniques is outside the scope of this book, but for those who want more details, various specialist texts are available (references on p. 91).

Air-sensitive materials are compounds which decompose on reaction with atmospheric oxygen, water or carbon dioxide. Other compounds are *pyrophoric*, that is they catch fire in air. Provided that the decomposition is *stoichiometric*, handling these compounds presents no special problems. Compounds which decompose on exposure to *catalytic* amounts of oxygen, etc. are much more difficult to deal with, and are very much the province of specialist research laboratories. The sort of reagents that you will encounter which might, depending on their precise reactivity, require some special handling are:

- alkali metals, e.g. Li, Na, K;
- metal hydrides, e.g. NaH, CaH_2;
- hydride reducing agents, e.g. $LiAlH_4$, diborane (tetrahydrofuran solution);
- organometallics, e.g. Grignards, BuLi (hexane solution);
- strong bases, e.g. $NaNH_2$;
- Lewis acids, e.g. $BF_3{\cdot}Et_2O$, $TiCl_4$;
- powerful electrophiles, e.g. acid chlorides, anhydrides.

Reactions involving air-sensitive reagents can be carried out in thoroughly dried conventional glass apparatus, but do require some extra equipment, the most important of which is a source of an inert atmosphere. In addition, a supply of syringes, needles and septa will be needed. However, when working with air-sensitive reagents, several essential points have to be borne in mind, and many quite basic operations—measuring and transferring for example—have to be carried out much more carefully than usual. The essential ingredients for success are:

- drying the apparatus thoroughly;
- drying the solvents thoroughly;
- providing an inert atmosphere;
- dispensing and transferring the reagents carefully;
- running and working-up the reaction carefully.

Drying the apparatus

Dry glassware thoroughly

Check for flammable solvents before lighting a burner

It is important to ensure that your glassware is properly dry. Although glass may look completely dry, there is usually an invisible film of moisture on it, which must be driven off. This is best achieved by heating the apparatus in a drying oven, but thorough drying takes longer than most people think. For example, if the oven temperature is 125°C, then the apparatus should be left in the oven overnight. At the higher temperature of 140°C, thorough drying still takes at least 4h. Any Teflon® (PTFE) parts such as stopcocks should be removed prior to drying, since Teflon® softens at these temperatures. After drying, the apparatus should be rapidly assembled whilst still hot (**use heat-resistant gloves**) and should be allowed to cool under an inert atmosphere. Alternatively, glass apparatus may be assembled cold and dried by flaming the outside with a Bunsen burner whilst passing a stream of inert gas through the apparatus. Do check, however, that flames are allowed in your laboratory before using this technique and take care if you have any Teflon® stopcocks or polypropylene septa in the apparatus.

Drying the solvents

Pure, dry and deoxygenated solvents are essential when working with air-sensitive reagents. The purification and drying of organic solvents is discussed in detail in several texts (references on p. 91), and methods for the more common solvents are given in Appendix 2 (p. 677). Solvents are best when freshly distilled, and although your laboratory may keep a supply of distilled

Rigorously dry solvents must be prepared immediately before use

Solvents stills must be supervised

solvents, when solvent dryness is essential for the success of a reaction, there is no substitute for distilling it yourself immediately before it is required; then you *know* how good it is (or is not). If there is a regular need for a particular solvent in your working area, then it is possible that a special solvent still will have been set up. Provided that this is regularly supervised, it can be left running, so that aliquots of pure, dry solvent can be withdrawn as required. When absolute dryness is less crucial, bottles of solvent which have been pre-dried by standing over an appropriate drying agent are often available. For example, diethyl ether is often dried by standing it in its bottle over sodium wire ('sodium-dried ether'). However, although this may well be dry enough for many purposes such as standard Grignard reactions, it should not be considered as rigorously dry.

Providing an inert atmosphere

The single major difference between working with air-sensitive reagents and 'normal' reagents is the need for an inert atmosphere. The source of this inert atmosphere is a gas cylinder which, depending on the arrangement in your laboratory, may be fixed to the bench or on a mobile trolley (see pp. 64–68). Alternatively your bench or hood may be equipped with a purpose-built inert gas line, although this is only likely in research laboratories. The most commonly used inert gas is nitrogen, which is relatively cheap, and is available in a range of purities. For most purposes, high purity grades of nitrogen, which contain no more than *ca.* 5 ppm of water and oxygen, are adequate. In cases where nitrogen is insufficiently inert, for example with reactions involving lithium metal, argon should be used. Although argon is more expensive than nitrogen, it does have advantages in that, as well as being more inert, it gives better 'blanket' protection than nitrogen since it is heavier than air and diffuses more slowly. Provided that there is no severe air turbulence, an argon-filled flask can be opened briefly and the inert atmosphere maintained if you are careful.

Do not attempt further purification of inert gases

Use shortest possible tubing

It is always better to use higher grade gases, and not to carry out further purification. Invariably, attempts to remove water or oxygen by passing the gas through various potions in a 'drying train' introduces *more* contamination than it removes, through the extra glassware, joints and tubing involved. On the question of tubing, always use the shortest possible length of flexible tubing between the inert gas supply and your apparatus. Ensure that the tubing is dry, although do not attempt to dry it in an oven!

The exit from the apparatus should be protected by a gas bubbler filled with a little mineral oil. The bubbler serves both to monitor the flow of inert gas through your apparatus and to prevent back diffusion of air. Common types of bubbler are shown in Fig. 3.10, and should always be used for reactions involving highly air-sensitive reagents. Guard tubes containing a drying agent such as calcium chloride remove little water and no oxygen, and hence should not be used in situations where exclusion of moisture is essential. Some

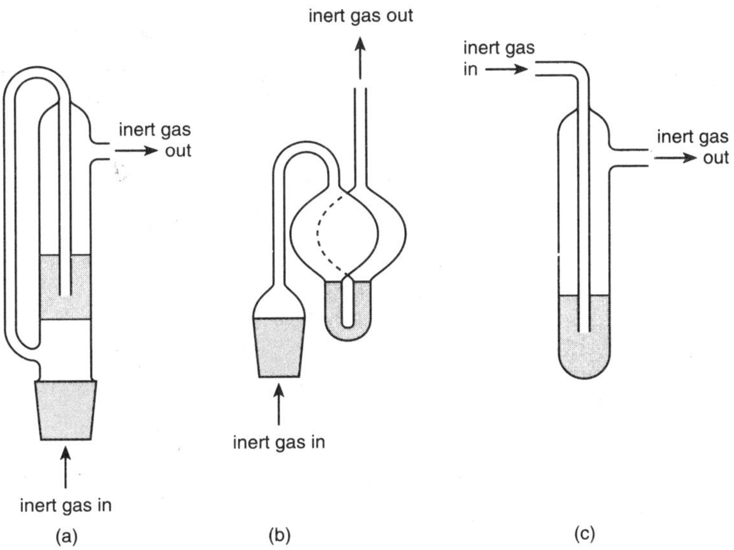

Fig. 3.10 Some typical gas bubblers for use with inert gases.

sort of bubbler should also be used in the gas supply line itself to act as a monitoring device and, more importantly, a safety device so that the system is not completely sealed (Fig. 3.10c).

Balloons only provide a temporary inert atmosphere

If an inert atmosphere is only needed for a short time, say less than 20–30 min, a balloon inflated with the inert gas may be used. The most convenient way of using a balloon is with a two-way stopcock (Fig. 3.11), which allows for evacuation of the apparatus and the filling of the balloon with inert gas. However, be warned: atmospheric oxygen, water or carbon dioxide can diffuse through a balloon skin at a surprising rate, even against a pressure of inert gas. Therefore do not think that the comforting sight of a nitrogen balloon atop your apparatus provides total protection from the atmosphere. Nevertheless, it is a quick and easy way to provide a relatively inert atmosphere for a short time, and is considerably better than nothing at all.

Dispensing and transferring air-sensitive reagents

Liquid air-sensitive reagents are best dispensed and transferred by syringe, and therefore a discussion of basic syringe techniques is called for. Syringes are ideally suited for the transfer of up to *ca.* 20 mL of liquid, and are available in a range of sizes with different needle lengths. Gas-tight syringes with 'locked' (Luer lock) type needles are the best (Fig. 3.12). As with other glassware used for air-sensitive reagents, syringes and needles should be thoroughly dried in an oven before use; but take care always to remove the needle and plunger from the syringe assembly before drying. After drying, allow the syringe to cool in a desiccator, where dry syringes can also be stored.

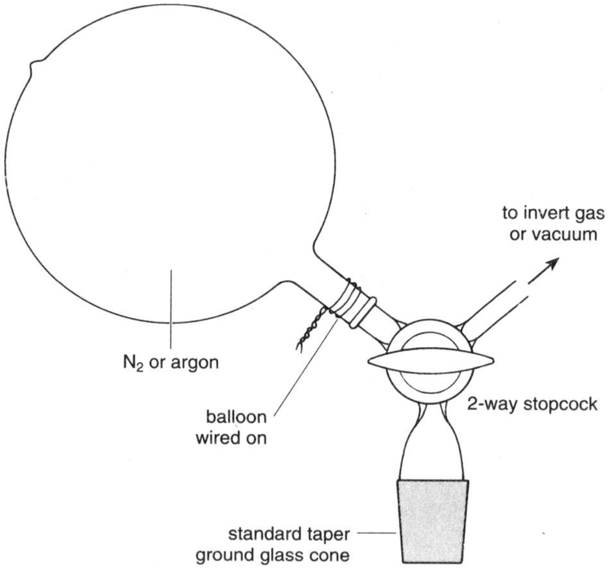

Fig. 3.11 Use of a balloon to provide a temporary inert atmosphere.

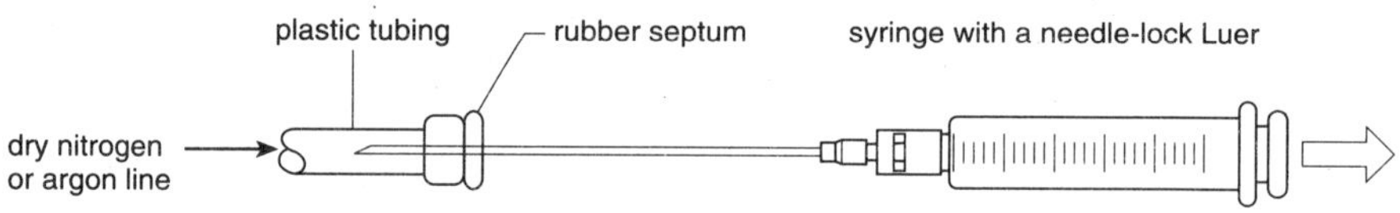

Fig. 3.12 Flushing a syringe with inert gas from the line.

Air-sensitive reagents are often sold as stock solutions in an inert solvent; butyl-lithium, for example, is sold in hexane solution in a range of concentrations. Nowadays, these solutions are sold in bottles which have special tops, to make the subsequent transfer of reagent much easier. An example of such a bottle is shown in Fig. 3.13, and is based on the Sure/Seal® system of the Aldrich Chemical Company. The metal crown cap has a small hole which allows a syringe to be inserted through it. After withdrawing the syringe needle, the hole in the crown cap liner often self-seals, but even if it does not, the lined plastic cap, when screwed down, will ensure that the bottle remains air tight.

If your air-sensitive reagent has been supplied in a normal bottle with a simple screw cap, then it must be fitted with a septum so that the reagent can be withdrawn by syringe. A quick and easy way to do this is to open the bottle under an inverted funnel attached to the inert gas supply (Fig. 3.14a). This provides a 'blanket' of inert gas to protect the reagent whilst the cap is **quickly** removed and a septum inserted. Check that you have the correct sized septum to hand **before** opening the bottle. Better protection for an open reagent bottle is provided by a polythene bag attached to the inert gas supply

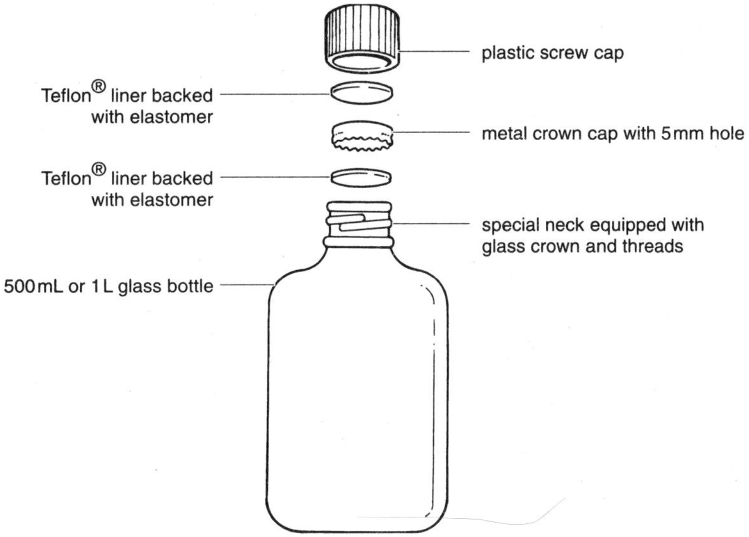

Fig. 3.13 Air-sensitive reagent bottle fitted with special seal and cap (adapted from the Aldrich Sure/Seal® system).

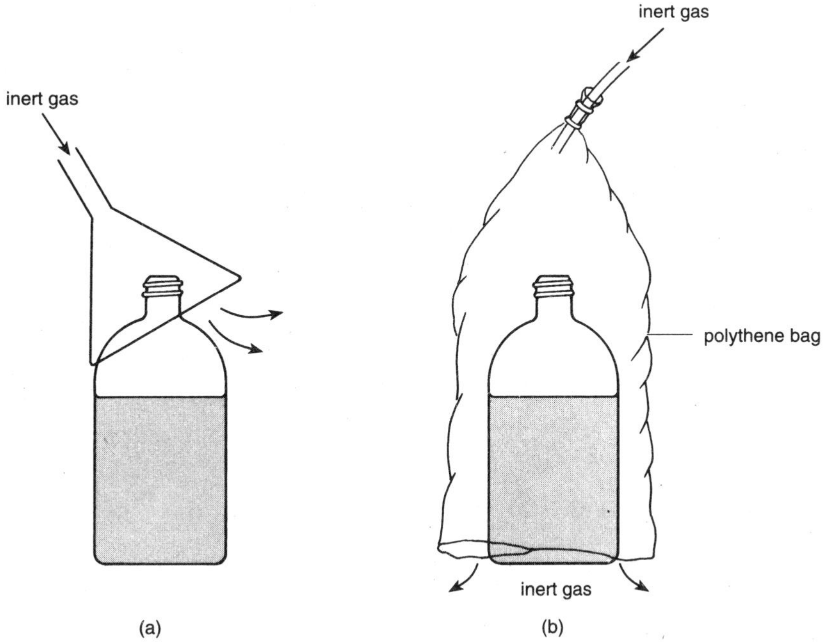

Fig. 3.14 Two ways to open a reagent bottle under an inert atmosphere.

(Fig. 3.14b). The septum should be tight fitting, and after puncturing with a needle, can be sealed by covering with paraffin wax sealing film.

When withdrawing air-sensitive reagents from stock bottles by syringe, the following general procedure should be used.

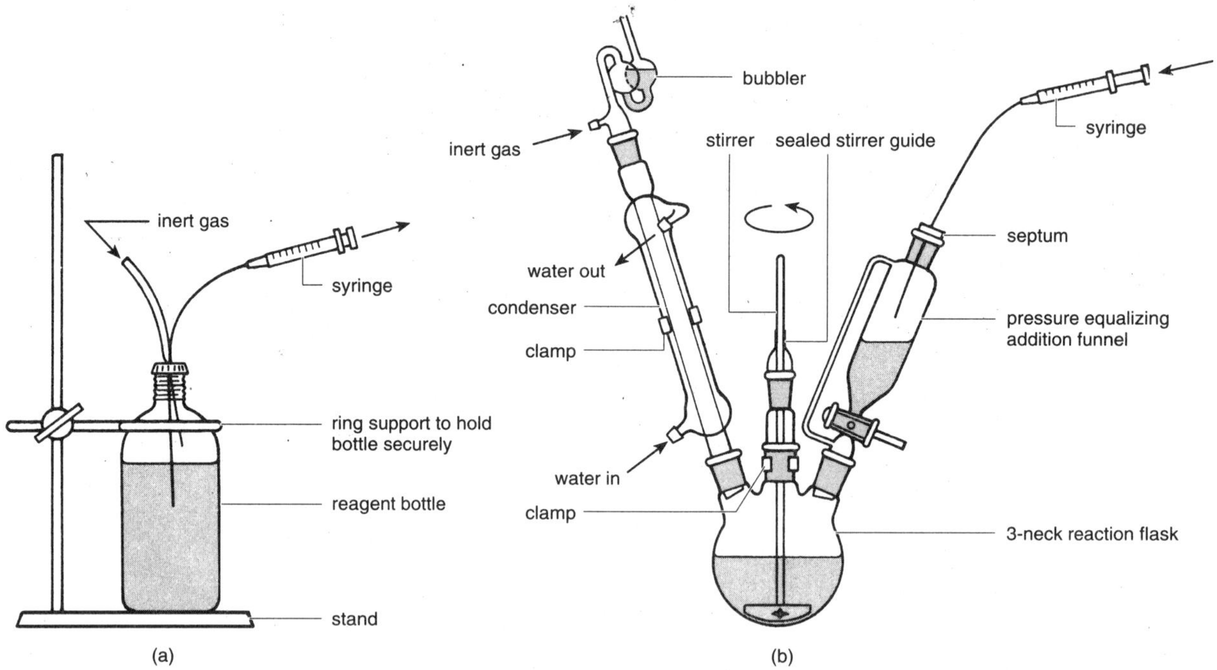

Fig. 3.15 (a) Withdrawing an air-sensitive reagent by syringe; (b) transferring the reagent to an addition funnel (see also Fig. 3.22).

1 Make sure your apparatus is clean, dry and assembled correctly for carrying out the reaction under an inert atmosphere. The neck of the vessel (reaction flask or addition funnel) that is to receive the air-sensitive reagent should be equipped with a septum. Some typical assemblies are shown in Figs 3.15(b), 3.16 and 3.22.

Always support the reagent bottle

2 Support the bottle of air-sensitive reagent in a ring clamp (Fig. 3.15a). This is very important; knocking over such a bottle would be potentially disastrous.
3 Insert a needle attached to an inert gas line through the seal or septum on the reagent bottle, and ensure a slight positive pressure of gas. This is to maintain an inert atmosphere in the bottle during and after the withdrawal of reagent. To prevent over-pressurizing the bottle, you must have a bubbler device in the inert gas line.
4 Flush your syringe with inert gas (Fig. 3.12).
5 Insert the syringe needle through the bottle seal, and fill the syringe to the desired level by slowly withdrawing the plunger, or **better**, by allowing the positive pressure of inert gas to push the plunger back (Fig. 3.15a).
6 Withdraw the syringe, and complete the transfer of reagent to reaction vessel or addition funnel as quickly as possible by puncturing the septum as shown in Fig. 3.15(b).

When larger volumes (greater than 20 mL) of air-sensitive reagents have to be transferred, syringes become unwieldy, and it is much better to use the

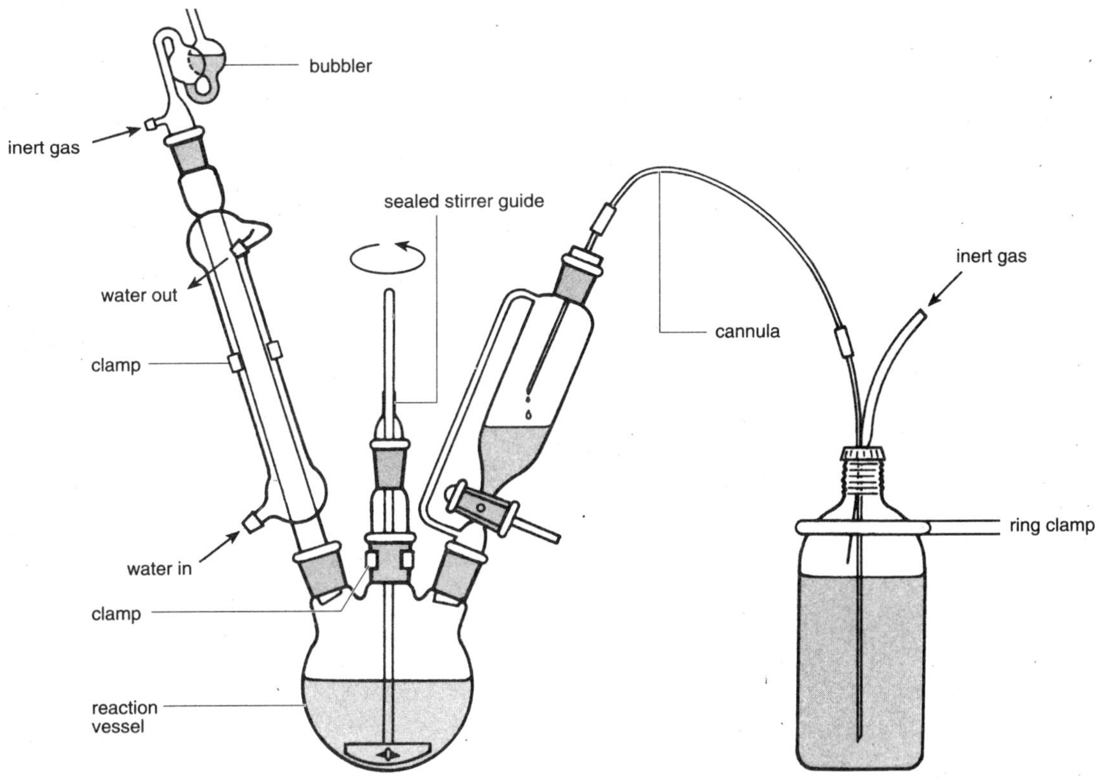

Fig. 3.16 Transfer of air-sensitive reagents using the double-ended needle technique.

Use a double-ended needle to transfer larger amounts of air-sensitive liquids

double-ended needle (or cannula) technique (Fig. 3.16). Support the reagent bottle, and as before insert a needle attached to the inert gas line through the bottle seal. Insert a pre-dried, long, flexible double-ended needle through the bottle seal **into the head space above the liquid**. This causes the inert gas to flush through the needle. Insert the other end of the needle through a septum into the receiving vessel or flask and, finally, push the end in the reagent bottle below the surface of the liquid. The positive pressure of inert gas forces the reagent from the bottle, through the needle, and into your vessel. When using this technique, the volume of liquid transferred has to be measured by using a pre-calibrated receiving vessel. When the required volume has been transferred, immediately withdraw the needle from the liquid in the reagent bottle to the head space. Remove the other end of the needle from the reaction vessel before removing the needle from the reagent bottle completely.

Clean syringes immediately

All syringes and needles must be cleaned **immediately** after use. If this is not done, needles will become blocked and plungers will stick in the syringe barrel because of oxidation and/or hydrolysis of the reagent. The cleaning should be carried out carefully; do not simply wash with water in the sink since many air-sensitive reagents react vigorously with water. The complete syringe

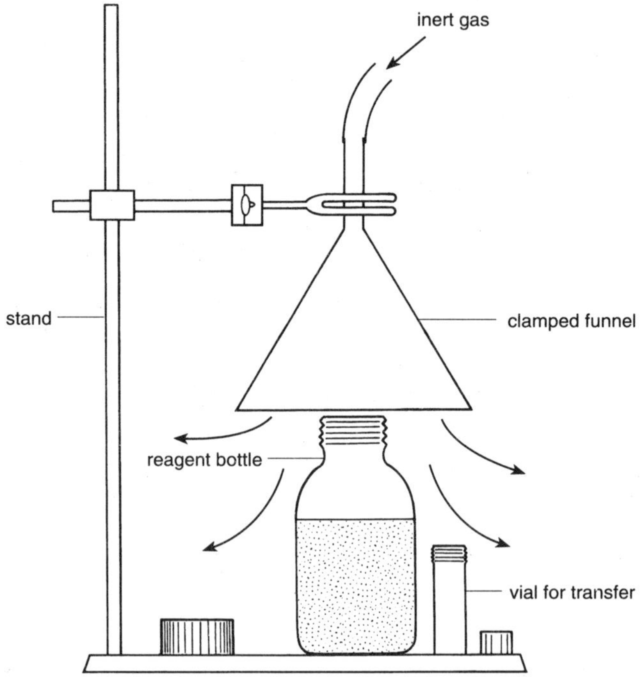

Fig. 3.17 Transferring solids under an inert gas blanket.

and needle assembly is best cleaned by rinsing out the last traces of reagent with a few millilitres of the solvent that has been used for the reaction. The rinsings can then be **cautiously** added to a beaker of cold water in the hood without incident. After two such rinses, the syringe and needle can be washed out with water in the normal way. Any stubborn inorganic residues formed by hydrolysis of the reagent may have to be washed out with dilute acid or alkali before final rinsing with water and thorough drying. Double-tipped needles, which will only contain traces of the reagent, can be washed in the sink immediately after use.

Air-sensitive solids

Solid reagents which are only moderately air and moisture sensitive can be handled fairly easily under an inert gas blanket provided by an inverted funnel attached to the gas line (Fig. 3.17). You must not use such a high pressure/flow rate of gas that the solid is blown all over the bench. This technique can be used to transfer solids from a reagent bottle to a sealable container for weighing, for example, or from a container to a reaction flask which can be sealed subsequently.

If your experimental procedure requires the addition of an air-sensitive solid in several portions, the best method is to transfer the reagent in a single portion, under an inert gas blanket, to a solid addition tube with a tapered glass joint. This is fitted to the reaction flask in the normal way, and portions of solid can be introduced into the flask by turning and gently tapping the tube (Fig. 3.18).

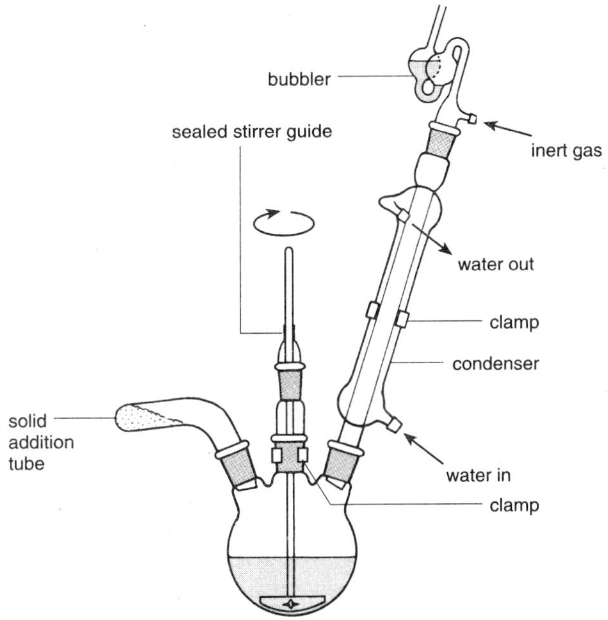

Fig. 3.18 Reaction flask fitted with solid addition tube, overhead stirrer and condenser.

However, although you should be aware of the above techniques, not many solids are sufficiently air sensitive to require very special treatment. Although several solids may react violently with liquid water, lithium aluminium hydride for example, these can usually be handled in air without undue problems from atmospheric moisture.

The provision of an inert atmosphere using a balloon and a cut-down syringe barrel is particularly attractive on the microscale; a typical method for the attachment of the balloon is shown in Fig. 3.19. A short (*ca.* 2 cm) collar of thick-walled flexible tubing is pushed over the top portion of the cut-down barrel of a disposable syringe and used as a mount for a balloon which is secured in place with an elastic band. Gas is delivered to the reaction via a disposable syringe needle.

Running the reaction

Reactions involving air-sensitive reagents include the same basic stirring, heating and cooling techniques as any other reaction. The only difference is that the apparatus has to be modified so that the reaction can be carried out under an inert atmosphere. This usually means that a two- or three-necked flask is used in place of a simple single-necked round-bottomed flask, or alternatively a single-necked flask is used fitted with a Claisen, or similar, adapter. Typical apparatus set-ups for reactions requiring an inert atmosphere are discussed in more detail in the next section.

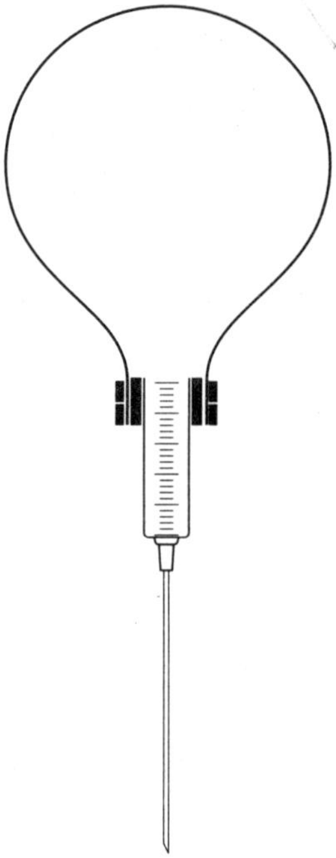

Fig. 3.19 For small-scale reactions, a balloon filled with inert gas connected to a cut-down syringe barrel via a short (*ca.* 2 cm) collar of pressure tubing and secured with an elastic band can be used to provide an inert atmosphere. Gas is introduced into the reaction vessel via a syringe needle.

Take extreme care when quenching reactions involving air or moisture sensitive reagents

At the end of the reaction, care must be taken to destroy any remaining air- or moisture-sensitive reagent that is likely to react vigorously with water, before carrying out the normal aqueous work-up (pp. 109–118). No general method can be given for this; the procedure used depends on what reagent or reagents have been involved in your reaction. Therefore an element of common sense is required at this stage, although the experimental procedures given in Part 2 of this book give precise details of what to do in specific instances.

Although the reaction might involve reagents which are air and/or moisture sensitive, the products from your reaction are very unlikely to be so air or moisture sensitive that special techniques are required **after** the reaction is over. Hence work-up and purification under air-free conditions are not normally necessary. Nevertheless, operations such as extraction, filtration, distillation and recrystallization can all be carried out under an inert atmosphere, although these techniques belong in the research laboratory rather than the teaching laboratory.

Further reading

G.B. Gill and D.A. Whiting, Guidelines for handling air sensitive compounds. *Aldrichimica Acta*, 1986, **19**, 31.

A.J. Gordon and R.J. Ford, *The Chemist's Companion. A Handbook of Practical Data, Techniques and References*, Wiley & Sons, New York, 1973.
G.W. Kramer, A.B. Levy, M.M. Midland and H.C. Brown, *Organic Syntheses via Boranes, Laboratory Operations*, Chapter 9. Wiley & Sons, New York, 1975.
C.F. Lane and G.W. Kramer, Handling air sensitive reagents. *Aldrichimica Acta*, 1977, **10**, 11.
D.D. Perrin and W.L.F. Armarego, *Purification of Laboratory Chemicals*, 4th edn, Elsevier, New York, 1996.
J.A. Riddick and W.B. Bunger, *Organic Solvents: Physical Properties and Methods of Purification*, 4th edn, Wiley & Sons, New York, 1986.
D.F. Shriver, *The Manipulation of Air Sensitive Compounds*, McGraw-Hill, New York, 1969.

In addition, many chemical companies issue technical bulletins with information about the packing and handling of their air-sensitive compounds and provision of such information is a legal requirement in many countries.

3.2 The reaction

Assembling the apparatus

Organic reactions should always be carried out in apparatus that is suitable for the task in hand. The correct choice of apparatus will allow you to combine the reactants in the right order at the right rate, stir the mixture if necessary, control the reaction temperature and, if required, exclude moisture and/or maintain an inert atmosphere. The apparatus required for an organic reaction can vary greatly in its complexity, ranging from a simple test tube or beaker in which two chemicals are mixed and heated, to a set-up involving a multi-necked flask equipped with stirrer, addition funnel, thermometer and condenser. The experimental procedures in Part 2 of this book will usually tell you what sort of apparatus to use for the reaction, with cross-reference to the basic assemblies which are detailed here.

Unless the reaction is very simple and needs just a test tube or beaker, a combination of two or more pieces of glassware will be required. It is assumed that you have access to standard-tapered joint glassware similar to the basic set described in Chapter 2. The key components are round-bottomed flasks (in various sizes), a two- or three-neck flask (if these are not available, a single-neck flask fitted with a Claisen adapter may be used), addition funnels, condensers and various adapters for fitting things like a thermometer or a gas inlet. These basic components, together with stands and clamps, can be combined in several ways to construct a range of apparatus suitable for carrying out most organic reactions. However, rather than discuss several possible permutations and combinations of glassware, we have chosen to illustrate just a few apparatus assemblies that, in our opinion, will cover most eventualities. The operations covered by these assemblies are listed below, with optional additional features given in parentheses.

- stirring a reaction mixture;
- stirring with addition (with temperature measurement);

- stirring with addition under an inert atmosphere (at low temperature);
- heating a reaction mixture (with exclusion of moisture or under an inert atmosphere);
- heating a reaction mixture with stirring;
- heating a reaction mixture with addition (with stirring);
- heating a reaction mixture with addition (liquid or solid) and stirring under an inert atmosphere;
- refluxing a reaction mixture with continuous removal of water;
- addition of gases;
- reactions in liquid ammonia.

Detailed diagrams are given for the apparatus assemblies, and in case certain pieces of glassware are not available in your laboratory, alternatives may be suggested in the text. **Whatever the apparatus, it must be adequately supported with clamps.** This is very important, since the consequences of an unsupported glass apparatus toppling over are potentially disastrous. In each of the diagrams, the recommended clamping points are clearly indicated. Ignore them at your peril!

All of the apparatus shown in pp. 94–99 (except Fig. 3.26) can be constructed from commercial microscale glassware and used in the same way.

Stirring

Most chemical reaction mixtures need stirring to mix the reagents and to aid heat transfer. In open vessels, this stirring can be done by hand using a glass rod, but it soon becomes very tedious. Likewise, efficient mixing can be achieved by swirling the reaction vessel, but again this becomes very tedious after a short while. Therefore, when constant stirring is needed for a sustained period, a stirrer motor should be used.

As described in Chapter 2, stirrer motors are of two basic types: magnetic stirrers and mechanical (or overhead) stirrers. Magnetic stirrers are easy to use, and have the advantage that they are often combined with a hotplate. A simple set-up for stirring a reaction mixture in an Erlenmeyer flask containing a magnetic stirrer bar is shown in Fig. 3.20(a). An important point to note is that, even though the flask might seem quite stable, it should be secured in a clamp. If not, the vibration of the stirrer motor may cause the flask to 'wander' towards the edge of the stirrer plate, when, at the very least, the magnetic stirrer bar will stop going round because it is so far off-centre. At worst, the unsupported flask will fall off the stirrer plate.

Magnetic stirrers are used for a range of applications, but they do have their limitations. If the liquid is very viscous, or if the reaction mixture is heterogeneous with a large amount of suspended solid, then the magnetic stirrer motor, with its relatively low torque, will not cope. In these cases a mechanical (or overhead) stirrer should be used. The higher torque motor coupled to a paddle through a stirrer shaft will usually cope with most situations where more powerful stirring is required. Mechanical stirrers should

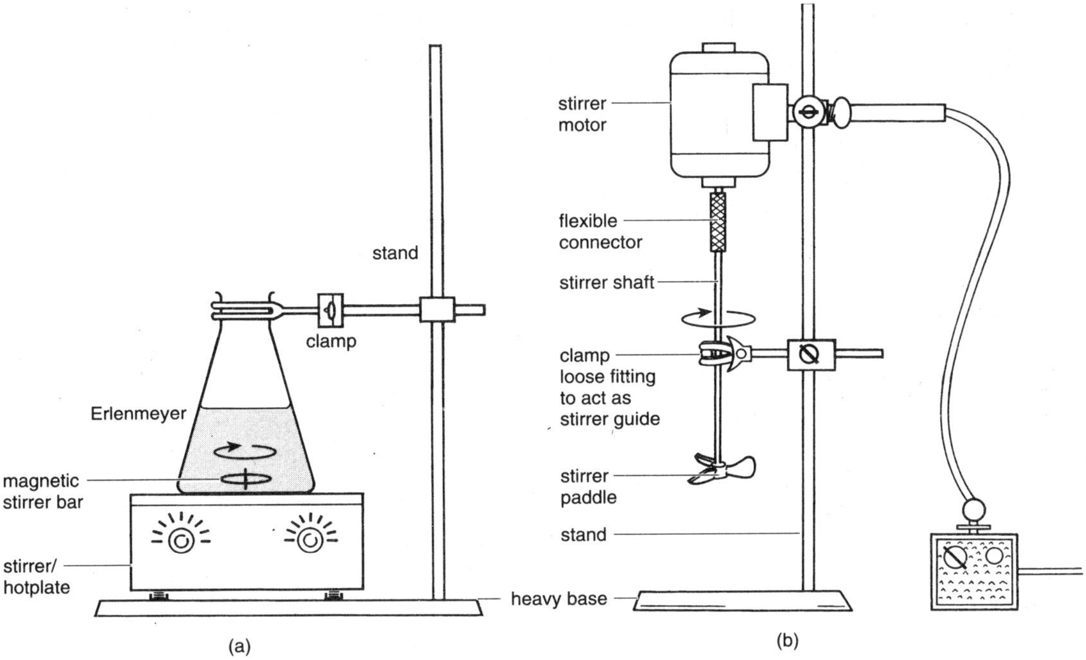

Fig. 3.20 (a) Stirring a reaction mixture in an Erlenmeyer flask with a magnetic stirrer; (b) stirring a reaction mixture with a mechanical overhead stirrer.

also be used when very rapid stirring of a two-phase system is needed. A set-up involving a mechanical stirrer is shown in Fig. 3.20(b). If the reaction mixture is contained in a beaker, care should be taken not to use too fast a stirring rate causing the liquid to spill out of the beaker. When using overhead stirrers, it is vital to provide adequate support from clamps. The whole assembly is top heavy so a stand with a heavy base should be used. A loosely tightened clamp can also be used just above the beaker to act as a stirrer guide.

Stirring with addition

You will frequently encounter experimental procedures which require you to add one reagent to a stirred solution of another, often with some sort of temperature control. Magnetic stirrers are ideally suited for such situations, and two typical set-ups are shown in Fig. 3.21. Both incorporate a thermometer to measure the reaction temperature during the addition, but if temperature control is unimportant, the thermometer can be omitted. The first set-up (Fig. 3.21a) uses a single-neck round-bottomed flask fitted with a Claisen adapter, into which are placed a thermometer in an adapter and a pressure equalizing addition funnel. An addition funnel fitted with a pressure equalizing side arm must be used in this case since there is no other outlet to the system. If a pressure equalizing addition funnel is not available, then a normal addition funnel may be used, but the thermometer must be fitted through an adapter with a

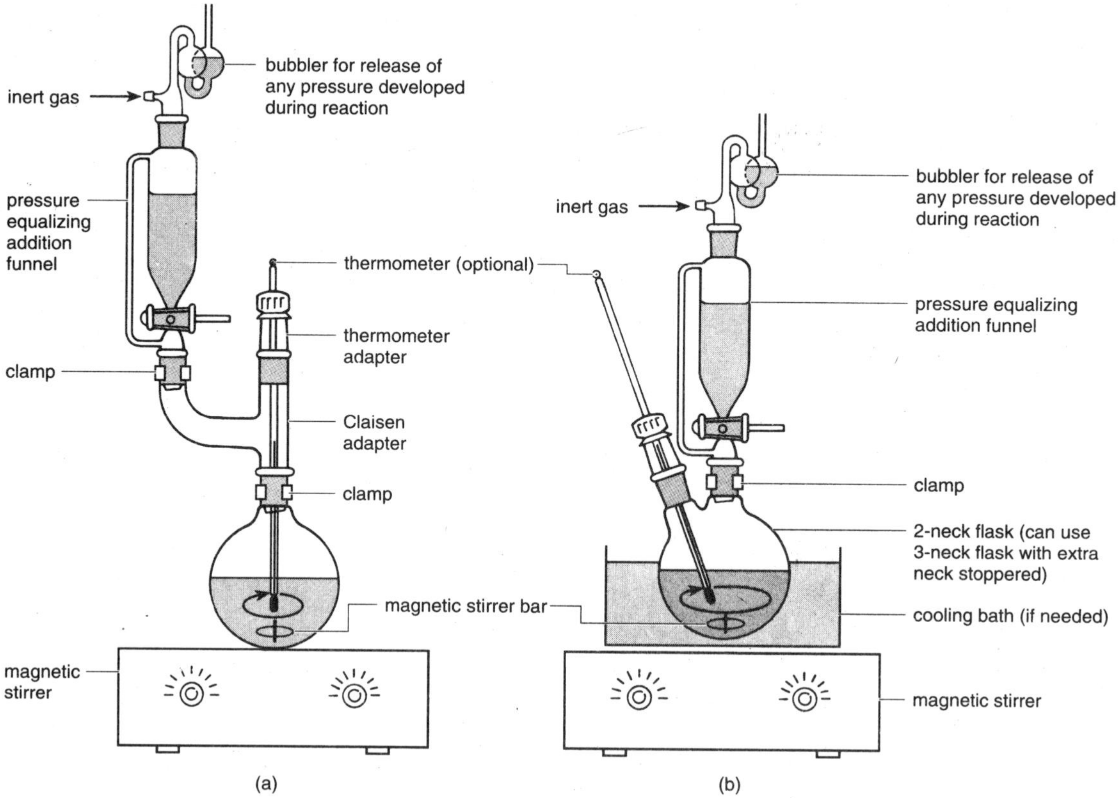

Fig. 3.21 (a) Stirring with addition using a single-neck flask with a Claisen adapter; (b) stirring with addition using a two-neck flask.

side arm outlet. To measure the temperature of your reaction mixture the thermometer bulb should be completely immersed in the liquid. Since stirring causes a vortex, the thermometer might have to be set a little lower once the stirrer has been started. However, **do not** set the thermometer so low that the bulb is hit by the magnetic stirrer bar. Thermometer bulbs will not stand this sort of treatment, and careless assembly of the apparatus in this way will surely lead to the unwanted introduction of mercury or ethanol (depending on the thermometer) into your reaction mixture. Note the need for two clamps for adequate support; the addition funnel is off-centre so must be clamped.

The second assembly (Fig. 3.21b) uses a two-neck flask fitted with a thermometer and a pressure equalizing addition funnel. One advantage of using a two-necked flask is that only one clamp is needed, the addition funnel being directly over the clamp on the flask. If a two-neck flask is not available, then obviously a three-neck flask may be used, with the third neck stoppered. Alternatively the third neck may be left open or protected by a guard (drying) tube, thereby obviating the need for the addition funnel with the pressure equalizing arm; a simple addition funnel may be used instead. This assembly also allows the use of a cold bath (see pp. 105–108) to control the reaction temperature during the addition.

Stirring with addition under an inert atmosphere

Some organic reactions need to be run under an inert atmosphere because of the sensitivity of the starting material or reagent to moisture or air. Air- and moisture-sensitive compounds have already been discussed on pp. 79–89, along with details of how to dispense and transfer them. Reactions involving such reagents can be carried out in conventional apparatus provided it is modified to allow for the provision of an inert atmosphere. This usually means attaching the reaction vessel to a supply of inert gas (nitrogen or argon). One fairly common laboratory operation using air-sensitive reagents involves the addition of a solution of the reagent by syringe to a stirred solution of starting material, which is often maintained at low temperature under the inert atmosphere. A typical apparatus for such an operation is shown in Fig. 3.22. A three-neck flask is essential. The securely clamped flask is equipped with a septum, gas bubbler, and thermometer fitted through a thermometer adapter and side arm adapter attached to the inert gas line. Flush the flask with inert gas and introduce the solution of starting material in a **dry** solvent. Maintain the flow of inert gas and, if required, cool the reaction flask in the cooling bath (pp. 105–108). It is important to maintain a fairly rapid flow of inert gas during the cooling process, since the resulting drop in pressure in the flask will cause the mineral oil from the bubbler to be sucked back into your reaction vessel if insufficient back pressure of inert gas is provided. Once the temperature in the flask has fully equilibrated, the flow of inert gas can be reduced to a trickle as monitored by the bubbler. Start the magnetic stirrer, and then add the air-sensitive reagent by syringe through the septum.

Most microscale kits supply vial closures consisting of PTFE-lined elastomer disks which reseal following puncture by a syringe needle so reagent addition can be achieved without using pressure equalizing dropping funnels. An inert atmosphere can be provided using a balloon of nitrogen or argon connected to the apparatus via a syringe needle, a cut-down plastic syringe barrel and a short length of pressure tubing (see Fig. 3.19), or by using one of the threaded tubing adaptors available commercially.

Heating

Since the rate of a chemical reaction is increased by an increase in temperature, many organic reactions are run at elevated temperatures so that they are complete within a convenient time scale. However, the desire to complete the reaction quickly should be tempered by the need to keep side reactions, the rate of which are usually increased even more by heating, to a minimum. Some reactions generate their own heat, that is they are *exothermic*, and in these cases some degree of temperature control is necessary (pp. 105–108).

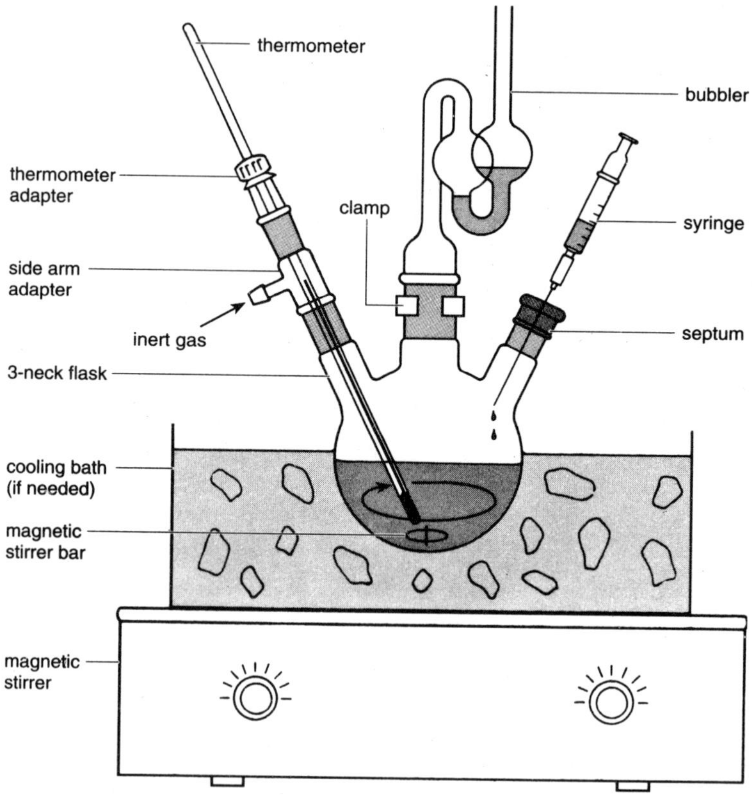

Fig. 3.22 Stirring under an inert atmosphere with addition of an air-sensitive reagent at low temperature.

However, most reactions that are run at elevated temperatures have to be carried out in apparatus that can be heated by some means, and the common sources of heat in the organic laboratory are discussed on pp. 25–33.

The most common way of conducting an organic reaction at a fixed elevated temperature is to carry it out in a boiling solvent in an apparatus equipped with a condenser, so that the solvent vapour condenses and returns to the reaction vessel. This procedure is known as *heating under reflux* or, more simply, as *refluxing*. The reaction temperature is the same as the boiling point of the solvent. It is easy to find a solvent with a suitable boiling point, but remember that the solvent should be inert and should not interfere in the reaction. Some typical arrangements for carrying out reactions in refluxing solvents are shown in Fig. 3.23. The first (Fig. 3.23a) uses a round-bottomed flask fitted with a standard water condenser, **both** of which should be clamped as shown. Always remember to add some boiling stones (anti-bumping granules) to ensure smooth boiling **before** placing the flask in the heat source. Addition of boiling stones to a liquid that is already hot and near its boiling point usually results in instant very rapid boiling. Although it may be spectacular as the solvent shoots out of the top of the condenser, as well as being

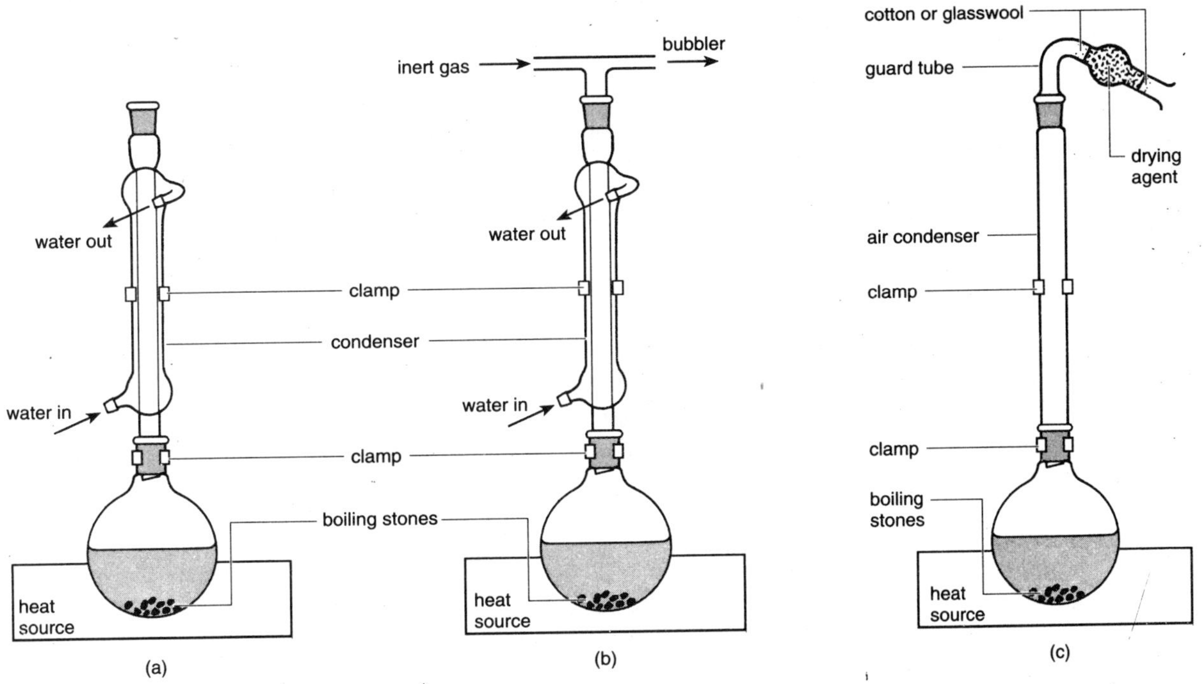

Fig. 3.23 Heating a reaction mixture under reflux: (a) with a normal water condenser; (b) under an inert atmosphere; (c) with an air condenser and drying tube.

extremely dangerous, it is annoying to have to set up your reaction again. Finally, place the flask in the heat source (heating mantle, heating bath, steam bath, etc.) and note when the solvent starts to reflux.

The second assembly (Fig. 3.23b) incorporates a minor modification so that the reflux can be carried out under an inert atmosphere. The top of the water condenser is fitted with an adapter to which the inert gas line is attached. Remove the condenser from the flask, flush it with inert gas, replace it and reduce the gas flow to a steady trickle as monitored by a bubbler. If the reaction mixture needs to be heated for only a short period (less than 30 min), then a balloon can be attached to the top of the condenser to provide a temporary inert atmosphere (see Fig. 3.11). Remember that if it is essential to exclude atmospheric moisture, then an inert gas should always be used in preference to a guard (drying) tube. The only situation where a drying tube can be used is when the reaction uses a solvent that has a boiling point greater than 140–150°C. With such high boiling solvents it is extremely unlikely that any water vapour could get into your reaction mixture. In these cases, the apparatus should also be modified to use an *air condenser* rather than a water condenser (Fig. 3.23c), although if an air condenser is not available, a normal condenser that has been drained clear of water can be used in its place.

Heating with stirring

The best way to heat a *stirred* reaction mixture is to use a magnetic stirrer hotplate and a heating bath as shown in Fig. 3.24. With modern stirrer hotplates, the temperature of the heating bath can be maintained within a very narrow range, and hence the reaction temperature can be closely controlled. Remember though that the temperature *inside* the reaction flask will be a few degrees less than that of the bath. If it is important to know the precise temperature of the reaction mixture, the apparatus will have to be modified to incorporate a thermometer in the flask. If the reaction mixture is very viscous or heterogeneous, then mechanical overhead stirring will be needed; this is discussed in the following section.

Heating with addition

Another common organic laboratory operation involves the addition of a reagent to a heated or refluxing solution of starting material. It may be that the heat of reaction causes the mixture to reflux, or that an external heat source is used, but in either case a reflux condenser is needed. Two typical assemblies are shown in Fig. 3.25 using: (a) a two-neck flask, and (b) a single-neck flask fitted with a Claisen adapter. The apparatus in Fig. 3.25(a) can be used to add a reagent to a refluxing solution in the two-neck flask. The reaction mixture is kept at reflux by heating the flask in an appropriate heat source. Figure 3.25(b) illustrates a variation which allows the reaction mixture to be stirred during the addition. Either a single-neck flask fitted with a

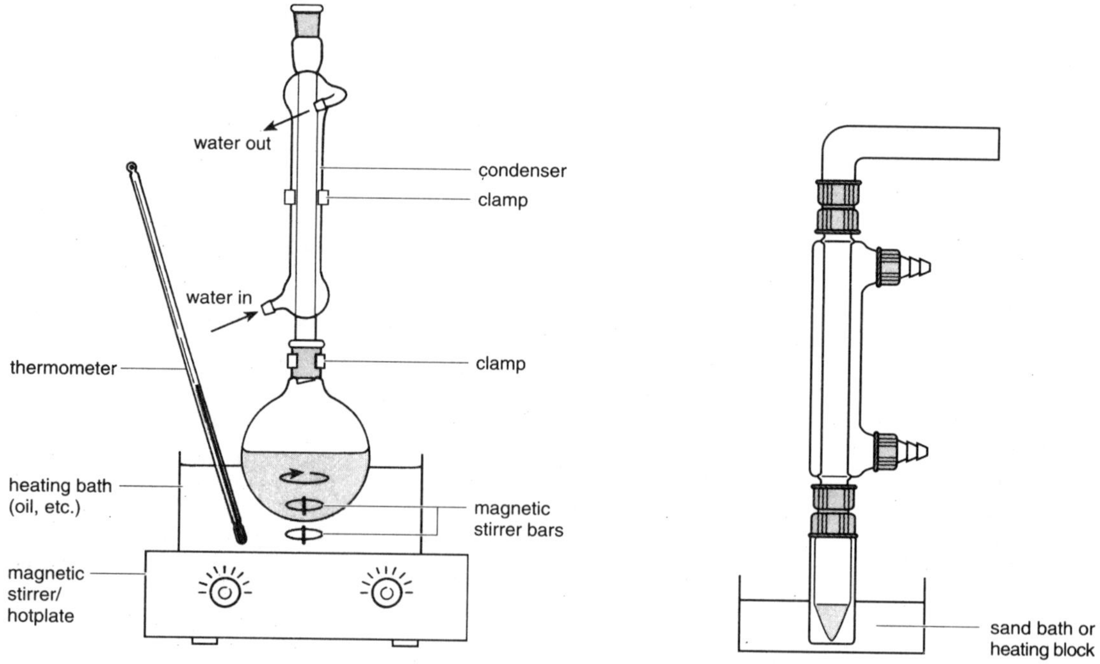

Fig. 3.24 (a) Heating a reaction mixture with magnetic stirring. (b) Heating a reaction with magnetic stirring on the microscale.

Claisen adapter (as shown) or a two-neck flask is used, and is fitted with the addition funnel and reflux condenser. The reaction mixture is stirred and heated to the required temperature in a heating bath on a magnetic stirrer hotplate.

If the reaction mixture requires stirring and heating during the addition of a reagent, but is very viscous or heterogeneous, then mechanical overhead stirring will be needed. The apparatus for this is shown in Fig. 3.26, and requires a three-neck flask fitted with addition funnel and reflux condenser, and, in the centre neck, a sealed stirrer guide through which the stirrer shaft passes. It is important that the stirrer adapter is sealed to prevent the escape of solvent vapour (see Fig. 2.15).

Heating and stirring with addition under an inert atmosphere

An apparatus for carrying out the addition of an air-sensitive solution to a stirred (and cooled) reaction mixture under an inert atmosphere is illustrated in Fig. 3.22. In some cases such reaction mixtures may require heating at a later stage, and therefore the apparatus needs modifying to include a reflux

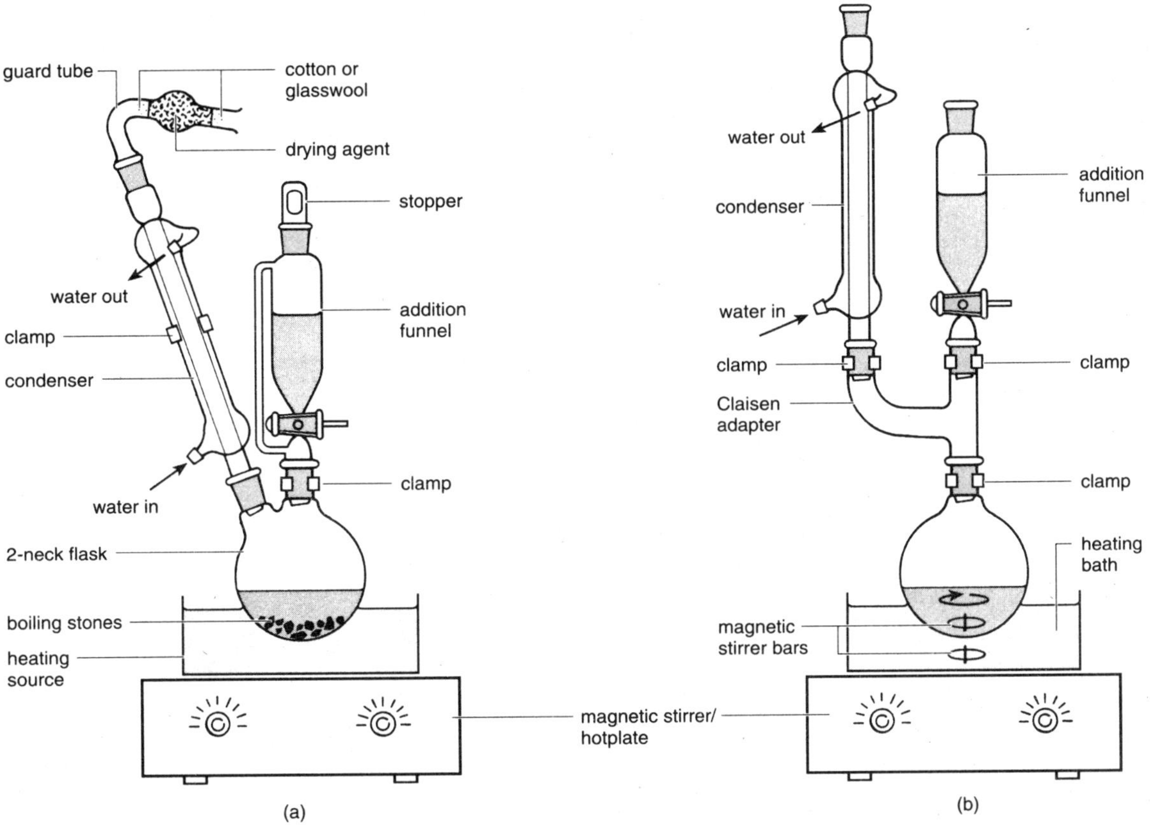

Fig. 3.25 (a) Heating a reaction mixture to reflux during the addition of a reagent; (b) heating a stirred reaction mixture during the addition of a reagent.

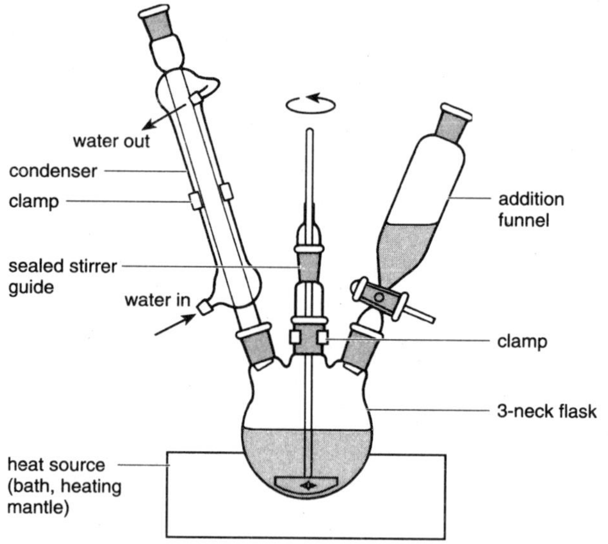

Fig. 3.26 Heating and overhead stirring of a reaction mixture during the addition of a reagent.

condenser. One simple modification of the apparatus shown in Fig. 3.22 would involve replacing the septum and syringe with an addition funnel, and incorporating a condenser in the central neck of the flask between the flask and the bubbler. If magnetic stirring is inappropriate, then overhead stirring may be used, provided that a well-sealed stirrer is employed. A typical assembly is shown in Fig. 3.15(b). If your reaction involves the addition of an air-sensitive solid reagent, then the apparatus shown in Fig. 3.18 should be used.

Continuous removal of water

Several organic transformations involve an overall loss of water, that is, a dehydration step. Examples include the formation of an ester from an acid and an alcohol and condensation reactions of carbonyl compounds. Since many of these reactions are reversible, success is dependent on removing the water from the reaction mixture as it is formed, to displace the equilibrium. One way of doing this is to use a drying agent or dehydrating reagent in the reaction flask itself, and in certain cases this is highly successful. Another way is to take advantage of the fact that water readily forms *azeotropes* with some organic solvents, and if the reaction is conducted in such a solvent at reflux, then the vapour will contain a certain percentage of water vapour as well. For example, the azeotrope formed between water and toluene boils at 85°C (lower than both pure liquids) and the vapour contains about 80% toluene and 20% water. All that is required is an apparatus which can separate the water from the vapour and return the condensed solvent vapour to the reaction flask. A purpose-designed water separator, known as a *Dean and Stark trap* (or separator), that accomplishes this task is shown in Fig. 3.27. This par-

For a further discussion of azeotropes, see pp. 214–216

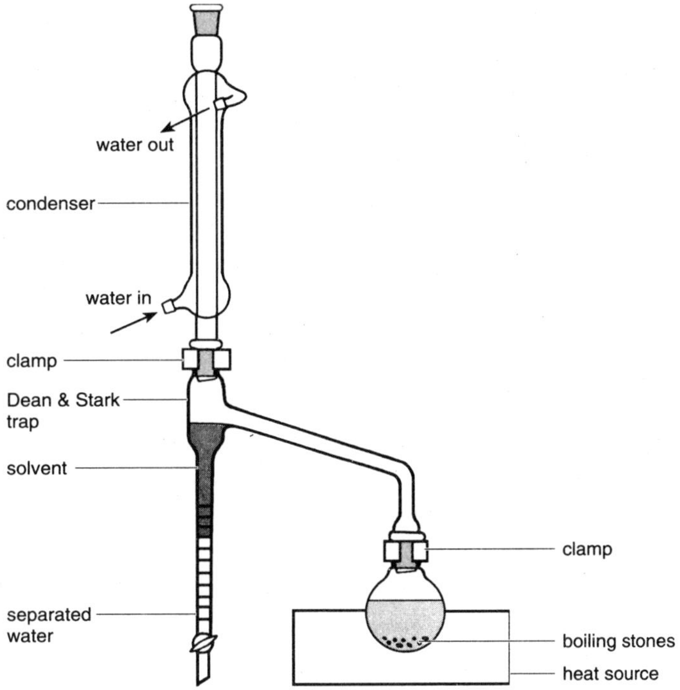

Fig. 3.27 Apparatus for continuous removal of water from a reaction mixture using a Dean and Stark water separator (trap).

ticular apparatus can only be used with solvents that are *less dense* than water, but fortunately many common organic solvents are. The complete assembly involves a round-bottomed reaction flask, which is connected to the Dean and Stark trap, on top of which is a reflux condenser. The whole apparatus should be adequately clamped, and then the flask placed on a heat source. As the reaction proceeds in the solvent, the water that is formed is carried up the trap as the azeotrope with the solvent vapour. The vapour should condense well up the condenser and to achieve this it may be necessary to prevent the heat loss from the Dean and Stark apparatus by lagging it with aluminium foil. The solvent–water azeotrope condenses and the condensed liquids fall back into the lower half of the trap. In the condensed phase, the heavier water sinks to the bottom of the trap to be retained, whilst the lighter organic solvent flows back into the reaction flask. The trap is usually graduated so that the volume of water removed from the reaction mixture can be measured. A stopcock is normally incorporated at the bottom of the trap so that if a large amount of water is formed and fills the trap, it can be run off.

Addition of gases

Very occasionally you will encounter an experiment in which one of the starting materials or reagents is a gas. The gas is added to a reaction mixture through a glass tube that dips into the solution or liquid in the reaction flask. A typical experimental set-up is shown in Fig. 3.28. The most important thing to note is that the gas supply, usually a cylinder, and the reaction vessel must be isolated from each other by two empty safety bottles. A third bottle containing a drying or purifying agent may be incorporated in between the safety bottles if necessary, although if you are using a high purity grade gas, further purification or drying is usually detrimental since it often introduces more impurities than it removes. The gas inlet tube is fitted to the flask through a thermometer adapter in a Claisen adapter, the other neck of which carries the reflux condenser. The inlet tube itself is usually a simple wide bore glass tube, although occasionally a special tube that has a small sintered glass disk at the end is used. It is particularly important to use a wide bore tube when the gas is very soluble in the reaction solvent (the solubility may cause the solvent to be sucked up the tube), or when the product of reaction of the gas with the solution is a solid (which may block the tube).

The most difficult aspect of using gaseous reagents is measuring the amount you need to use. In some cases this does not matter, for example, when a solution *saturated* with hydrogen chloride is required. In other cases, for example with a chlorination reaction, it is important to know how much chlorine is used. If the reaction is done on a large scale, then the uptake can be

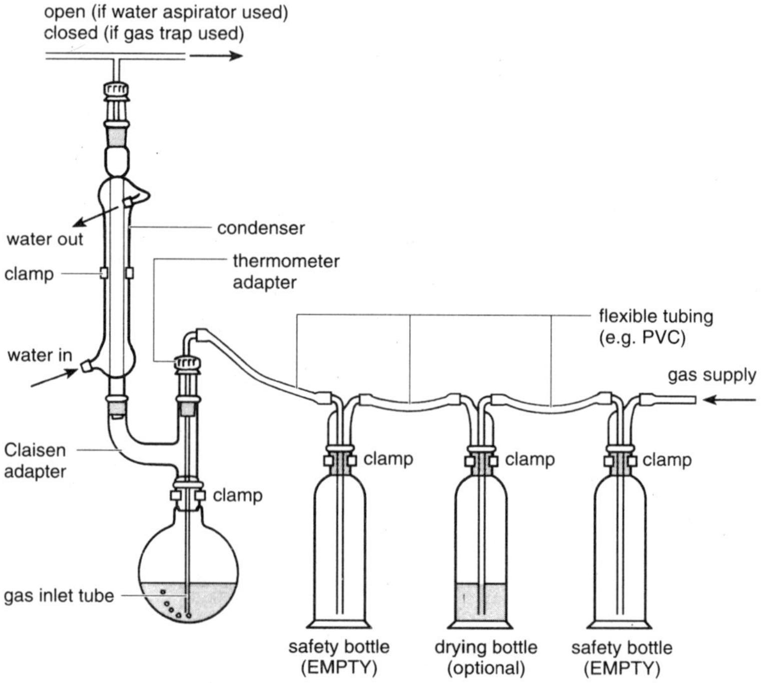

Fig. 3.28 Bubbling a gas through a reaction mixture.

measured by weighing the reaction flask or small gas cylinder before and after the reaction. Otherwise it may be possible to use a flow meter to measure the gas. The most reliable method is to condense the gas in a cold trap and measure the amount of liquid; however, you need to know the density of the liquid gas at the cold bath temperature. The liquid gas is then simply allowed to evaporate into the reaction mixture. Obviously this technique can only be used with gases that are not too low boiling.

Inevitably some gas will not dissolve in, or react with, the solution in the reaction flask and will therefore escape up the condenser. It is very important that arrangements are made to deal with this; two methods are discussed below.

Toxic effluent gases must be 'scrubbed'

If the gas that you are using is particularly irritating or toxic (and most of them are), the reaction should be carried out in an efficient hood. However, it is still important that the gas should be trapped or scrubbed **before** being vented to the hood. If the gas is water soluble, one way to do this is to attach a T-piece to the top of the condenser, leave one end open and connect the other end to a tube that is attached to the water aspirator. A more reliable method, shown in Fig. 3.29, leads the gas to a beaker of water through a tube connected to an inverted funnel, which just dips below the surface of the water. An inverted funnel must be used to prevent suck-back of the water as the gas dissolves. This method also allows you to replace water with a slightly more efficient trapping/scrubbing solution. For example, acidic gases (HCl, SO_2, etc.) can be scrubbed through dilute sodium hydroxide solution, basic gases (NH_3, $MeNH_2$, etc.) through dilute sulfuric acid, and sulfurous gases (H_2S, MeSH, etc.) through an oxidizing solution such as hypochlorite (bleach).

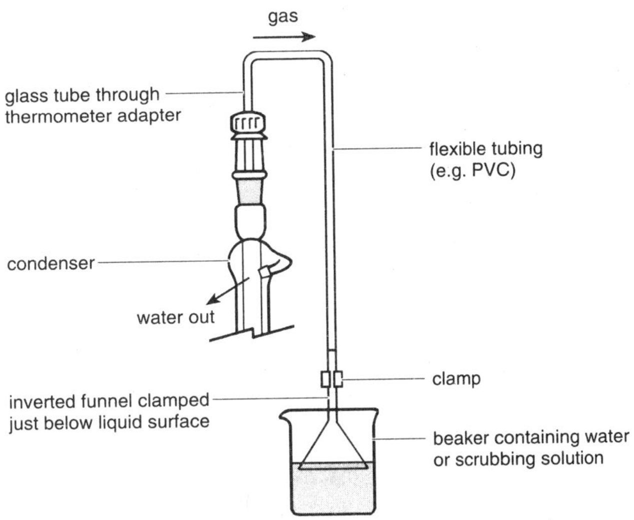

Fig. 3.29 Absorbing effluent gas from a reaction mixture by trapping/scrubbing in aqueous solution.

Gases which are not soluble in water or which cannot be scrubbed by acids, bases or oxidants present a greater problem, and are beyond the scope of this book.

Reactions in liquid ammonia

Liquid ammonia, which boils at −33°C, is a good solvent for many substances, both organic and inorganic, and is therefore an excellent medium for certain reactions, particularly those involving alkali metals. Solutions of alkali metals in liquid ammonia are blue-black in colour due to the presence of solvated electrons, and hence these solutions are powerful reducing systems.

Although not difficult to carry out, reactions in liquid ammonia do require some precautions. A standard procedure which uses a special low temperature condenser is describe below. Experiments 27 and 47 illustrate the use of alkali metal–liquid ammonia reductions.

Before starting the reaction it is a good idea to mark your reaction flask with a line that indicates the required volume of liquid ammonia. Oven dry the apparatus, set up the hot glassware in an efficient hood, as shown in Fig. 3.30 and allow it to cool under a stream of dry nitrogen. For large-scale reactions it is better to use a mechanical overhead stirrer fitted through a sealed stirrer guide. If the reaction is to be carried out with the liquid ammonia refluxing, i.e. at −33°C, then insulate the flask with a bowl of cork chips. If the reaction is to be carried out at a lower temperature, for example at −78°C, then place the flask in an appropriate cooling bath. Fill the low temperature

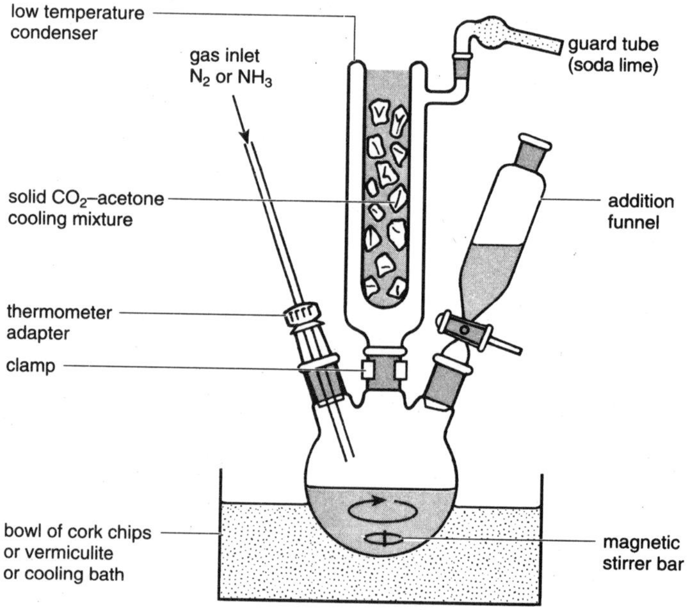

Fig. 3.30 Reaction in liquid ammonia.

condenser with a mixture of solid CO_2 and acetone. Remove the nitrogen supply and connect the flask to an ammonia cylinder via a soda lime drying tube and two empty bottles to protect against suck-back (see Fig. 3.28). Then carefully open the cylinder valve. Liquid ammonia will start to condense from the low temperature condenser. Maintain the ammonia flow until sufficient liquid ammonia for your reaction has condensed. Do not be tempted to introduce liquid ammonia directly from the cylinder as this may introduce ferrous impurities which catalyze the conversion of the dissolved sodium into sodamide. Disconnect the ammonia supply from the flask, replace the ammonia inlet with a stopper or, if required, a nitrogen inlet, and you are ready to start the reaction. Solids, for example sodium metal, can be carefully added to the reaction flask through an open neck by quickly removing the addition funnel. Solutions of reactants are simply run in from the addition funnel, although the rate of addition should not be so fast as to cause the liquid ammonia to boil too vigorously.

Microscale low temperature condensers are now available commercially.

Temperature control

Organic reactions are usually carried out at a fixed constant temperature. It is important to be able to control the temperature of a reaction mixture for the following reasons.

- The *rate* of reaction is dependent on temperature, and a fairly narrow temperature range is required if the reaction is to proceed at a desirable rate.
- The rates of side reactions increase with increasing temperature.
- Some reactions are *exothermic*, and may run out of control.

The easiest way to conduct an organic reaction at a fixed elevated temperature is to carry it out in a boiling solvent under reflux (see pp. 96–100). However, the use of refluxing solvents is not always appropriate. For example, many reactions such as SN2 displacements proceed best in dipolar aprotic solvents such as dimethyl formamide (DMF) or dimethyl sulfoxide (DMSO). These solvents decompose at reflux temperatures, and if the reaction is inconveniently slow at room temperature, then an intermediate temperature of, for example, 60 or 80°C may be needed. In this case, the reaction flask should be heated in an appropriate liquid heating bath. In fact, in all situations where fairly precise constant temperature control is needed, electrically heated liquid baths are undoubtedly the best. The heating bath can be any suitably sized metal container—glass dishes are best avoided—which is then heated electrically, either on a hotplate or with an immersion heater. The degree of temperature control is dependent on the heating system, but modern hotplates with in-built controls and immersion heaters attached to voltage regulators are fairly accurate (see pp. 29–30).

Electrically heated liquid baths are best for precise temperature control

The choice of liquid for the heating bath depends on several factors: temperature required, toxicity, flammability, expense and ease of handling—particularly removing it from your glassware. Clearly the bath medium should be fluid, should not be too viscous at the temperature required, and should have a boiling point at least 20–30°C above that temperature. Some materials that are commonly used as heating bath fluids are listed in Table 3.1. Whatever the fluid, do not fill the bath too full. Remember the level will rise when the reaction flask is immersed in the bath.

When a reaction generates its own heat, special precautions are necessary. Indeed the control of highly exothermic reactions is quite a problem, since as the temperature rises, the rate of reaction increases and, hence, the rate of heat evolution increases. If the heat cannot be efficiently removed, the reaction temperature will increase further, and the reaction will proceed faster and faster until it blows out of the reaction vessel.

Exothermic reactions

Exothermic reactions can be controlled in two ways: by the slow addition of reagent to the reaction mixture, at such a rate that the mixture is maintained at the required temperature, or by external cooling. The first method is usually satisfactory, but there is always the danger of inadvertently adding too much reagent too quickly. With too much reagent in the reaction mixture, the exotherm may be uncontrollable. One way to avoid this is by careful monitoring of the reaction temperature. If the reaction is 'well behaved' and under control, the temperature of the mixture should rise when the reagent is added, and then start to decrease when the addition is stopped.

Controlled addition

External cooling—have the cold bath ready

However, despite taking precautions such as controlling the rate of addition, it is often necessary to use external cooling. Always get the cold bath ready **before** you start the reaction. With a suitable cold bath to hand, it is easy

Table 3.1 Heating bath fluids.

Material	Usable range (°C)	Comment
Water	0–80	Ideal within its narrow range
Ethylene glycol	0–150	Cheap. **Flammable. Low flash point**
Paraffin oil (mineral oil)	0–150	**Flammable**, produces acrid smoke above 150°C
Polyethylene glycol 400	0–250	Water soluble
Silicone oil	0–250	Much better than paraffin oil, but expensive
Glycerol	0–260	Water soluble
Wood's metal (alloy of Bi, Pb, Sn, Cd)	70–350	Solid below 70°C, but good for high temperatures. **Toxic**
Sand	50–350	Poor thermal conductivity causes problems in temperature control

to moderate a reaction by immersing the reaction vessel in the bath until the temperature of the reaction mixture is reduced.

Cold baths are also needed when a reaction has to be run below room temperature. The most suitable container for a cold bath is a straight-sided dish—a glass crystallizing dish will do, although it is breakable. If the dish is used for cold baths that are required for long periods at a temperature of less than –20°C, some sort of insulation should be used; this is conveniently done by placing the dish inside a slightly larger one and filling the gap with insulating material such as cotton wool or cork chips. For extended periods of low temperature work, a Dewar flask should be used. The cooling mixture in a cold bath is based on one of the three coolants that are routinely available in a chemistry laboratory: ice, solid CO_2 (often called dry ice, DriKold® or Cardice®) or liquid nitrogen. For temperatures down to about –20°C, an ice–salt freezing mixture may be used. This is made by mixing an inorganic salt with crushed ice in the correct ratio (Table 3.2). Although it is theoretically possible to attain temperatures as low as –40°C with such freezing mixtures, the baths are fairly inefficient and short-lived.

Use hand protection for handling low temperature baths

For more effective and lower temperature cooling, cold baths based on solid CO_2 in conjunction with an organic solvent are used. Solid CO_2 baths are made by adding small pieces of solid CO_2 to the organic solvent until a slight excess of solid CO_2 coated with frozen solvent is visible. The low temperature can only be maintained by periodic topping up with the coolant. Some commonly used cooling bath systems are given in Table 3.3, of these the acetone/CO_2 system (–78°C) is best known.

Table 3.2 Ice–salt mixtures.

Salt	Ratio (salt : ice)	Lowest temperature (approx.) (°C)
$CaCl_2 \cdot 6H_2O$	1 : 2.5	–10
NH_4Cl	1 : 4	–15
NaCl	1 : 3	–20
$CaCl_2 \cdot 6H_2O$	1 : 0.8	–40

Table 3.3 Solid CO_2 cooling baths.

Solvent	Temperature (approx.) (°C)
Ethylene glycol	–15
Acetonitrile **(toxic)**	–40
Chloroform **(toxic)**	–60
Acetone	–78

Remember that most solvents are flammable and some are toxic and baths made from them should be used in a hood.

Always use an ethanol-based low temperature thermometer when measuring low temperatures; mercury freezes at –39°C.

Further reading

For further useful information on heating and cooling baths, see: A.J. Gordon and R.J. Ford, *The Chemist's Companion. A Handbook of Practical Data, Techniques and References*, Wiley & Sons, New York, 1973.

Following the progress of a reaction

All the experimental procedures in Part 2 include an indication of how long the reaction will take to go to completion. For example, you will be told that one reaction mixture should be heated under reflux for 2h, and another stirred at room temperature for 20min. However, this is a slightly false situation, since in many cases you will not know *exactly* how long a reaction will take. Therefore it is much more 'scientific' to monitor the progress of the reaction yourself. In research laboratories where new reactions are being carried out, it is essential to follow their progress. In the teaching laboratory, even if not expected to monitor the reaction in detail, the good chemist always observes and makes notes of any changes that occur, such as colour changes, gas evolution, solid precipitation and so on. Careful observation is the keystone of experimental science.

Observe!

Nowadays, chromatography is used almost universally to follow the progress of an organic reaction. Modern chromatographic analytical techniques require very little material. Therefore it is easy to withdraw small aliquots from the reaction mixture at appropriate intervals, and analyze them by one or more chromatographic techniques. In some cases it may be necessary to 'quench' the small sample of reaction mixture before carrying out the analysis. This usually means adding it to a few drops of water, which will effectively stop the reaction. This is best done in a small sample vial. Place a few drops of water in the vial, add a drop or two of the reaction mixture, followed by a few drops of an organic solvent such as diethyl ether, shake the vial and withdraw a sample from the *organic* layer—the top one in this case—for analysis. Compare the reaction mixture sample with the starting material and an authentic sample of the expected product if one is available. The chromatographic analysis is carried out using the most appropriate technique for the compounds involved, although thin layer chromatography (TLC) is the most widely used method. Since chromatography is also used extensively for the *purification* of organic compounds, for completeness and in order to avoid repetition, chromatographic techniques will be discussed in detail later in the section on purification (pp. 160–203).

Use TLC for following reactions; see also pp. 165–175

However, chromatography is not the only way to follow the progress of an organic reaction, and many other methods can be used. For example, simple colour changes will often suffice to tell you when a reaction is complete, particularly if the starting material is coloured and the product is not. In reactions involving acids or alkalis as reagents, the consumption of the reagent can be easily followed by monitoring the pH of the reaction mixture, or by withdrawing aliquots and titrating them. Titration can also be used to follow the progress of oxidation reactions. An aliquot of reaction mixture containing the oxidizing agent is withdrawn and added to potassium iodide solution; the oxidant liberates iodine, which is titrated in the normal way using thiosulfate solution. Hence the consumption of oxidant is monitored. The list of possibilities is endless, and it is up to you, the organic chemist, to use your ingenuity to devise the most suitable method for your particular experiment.

Reaction work-up (isolation of the product)

When your organic chemical reaction is over, the product has to be isolated from the reaction mixture. The *work-up*, by which this procedure is usually known, simply refers to the *isolation* of the product from the reaction mixture, free from solvent and spent reagents, and does not imply any *purification*. Purification of the organic reaction product is carried out subsequently, and will be discussed in detail later. The choice of work-up procedure should always take into account the properties of the required product.

- *Volatility*: do not evaporate your product along with the reaction solvent.
- *Polarity*: your organic product may be water soluble; aqueous extraction may not be appropriate.
- *Chemical reactivity*: towards water, acid and base; aqueous extraction may not be appropriate.
- *Thermal stability*: distillation may be inappropriate.
- *Air sensitivity*: special handling may be required.

With the above provisos in mind, most organic reaction mixtures can be worked-up according to a single general scheme as shown in Fig. 3.31. When the product is a liquid, you may be able to isolate it by *fractional distillation* of the whole reaction mixture, although careful distillation is needed to separate the product from the reaction solvent and other volatiles. The liquid product will usually need further purification by redistillation. Just occasionally you will be lucky, and the product of your reaction will separate or crystallize from the reaction mixture as a solid. Work-up in this case simply consists of collecting the product by suction filtration. Unless the product is to be used directly in a subsequent reaction, it will usually need to be purified further, by recrystallization, for example.

However, in most cases, the work-up will involve the addition of water or ice-water to the reaction mixture. Again you may be lucky and a solid product may separate at this stage, but it is more likely that the product will have to be isolated from the aqueous mixture by *extraction* with an organic solvent such as diethyl ether or dichloromethane. The extraction is carried out in a

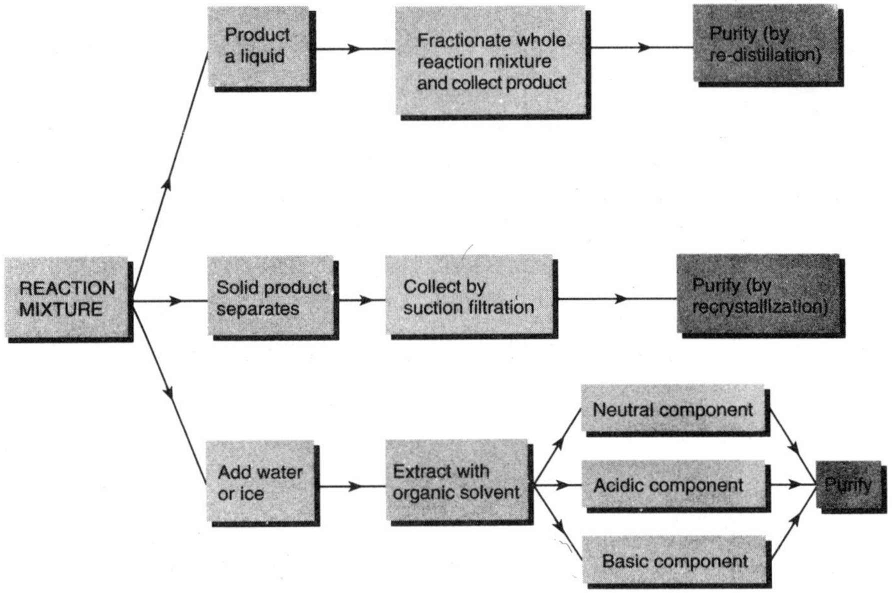

Fig. 3.31 General scheme for reaction work-up.

separatory funnel, and by carrying out multiple extractions, in combination with appropriate washes, a solution of the product in an organic solvent is isolated. The work-up can be modified at this stage to include extraction with aqueous acid or base, thereby facilitating the isolation of neutral, acidic and basic products. In either case, work-up is completed by drying the organic solution (Table 3.5, p. 127), and evaporating the solvent on the rotary evaporator (pp. 49–53) to give the crude product.

Detailed discussion of protocols for aqueous organic extractions, including the purification of neutral, acidic and basic components by extraction, is deferred until the following section (pp. 118–129). However, since you may encounter a separatory funnel for the first time during the work-up of your first organic reaction, some comments about the correct use of separatory funnels are appropriate at this point.

How to use a separatory funnel

The separatory funnel is the most commonly used piece of apparatus for carrying out routine extractions in organic chemistry. However, it is also one of the most mishandled pieces of apparatus in the organic laboratory. The correct handling of a separatory funnel requires attention to detail in all phases of the extraction and separation process. With experience, the correct manipulations should become automatic, and everyone eventually develops their own technique. Nevertheless, there are certain ground rules which should **always** be obeyed.

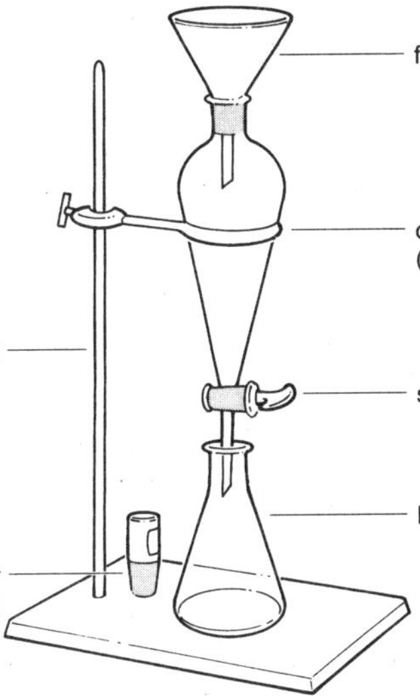

Fig. 3.32 A separatory funnel ready for use.

Preparing the separatory funnel

Grease lightly!

Do not grease Teflon®

Support the funnel in a ring stand

A separatory funnel is usually made of thin glass and therefore should be handled carefully. The most important part of it is the stopcock, which will be either glass or Teflon®. Glass stopcocks should be *lightly* greased before the funnel is used. Use just enough grease so that the stopcock turns easily; too much grease might clog the hole in the stopcock or contaminate the organic solution. Teflon® stopcocks are better because, owing to their low coefficient of friction, they do not need greasing. However, Teflon® is fairly soft and will deform with heat or pressure. With the stopcock in place, support the separatory funnel in a metal ring clamped to a stable stand. Ideally the ring support should be plastic coated to prevent metal–glass contact and to reduce the chance of cracking or breaking the funnel. If a coated ring is not available, the metal should be covered with some pieces of Neoprene® tubing which have been cut into short lengths and split lengthways. Get into the habit of placing an Erlenmeyer flask or beaker under the separatory funnel as soon as you have put it in its ring support. This is vital when the separatory funnel contains liquid, as it will catch any leaks from the stopcock. The complete set-up, which is ready for use, is shown in Fig. 3.32.

Check that a well-fitting stopper for the tapered glass joint at the neck of the separatory funnel is available. Opinion is divided as to whether the glass stopper should be greased or not. A *lightly* greased stopper will certainly be easier to remove, but you run the risk of introducing contamination from the grease, particularly if the organic solvent 'creeps' up the tapered joint. Wetting an *ungreased* stopper with water often prevents this solvent creep.

Transferring liquids to the separatory funnel

With the stopcock closed (**check!**), and the funnel adequately supported with an empty flask underneath it, pour the mixture to be extracted and the extraction solvent into the separatory funnel, using a long-stemmed glass funnel to minimize the chance of spillage. Remember to allow sufficient space in the funnel to mix the liquids. As a general rule, never fill the separatory funnel more than two-thirds full. If there is a large volume of liquid to extract, and a sufficiently large separatory funnel is not available, the extraction will have to be carried out in batches.

Never fill a separate funnel more than two-thirds full

Shaking out

To carry out an efficient extraction, the aqueous and organic layers have to be thoroughly mixed. This is achieved by swirling and shaking the separatory funnel. After adding the liquids to the funnel, and *before* inserting the stopper, it is a good idea initially to swirl the separatory funnel gently. Hold the funnel round the top, lift it just clear of the supporting ring and swirl it *gently*. This swirling causes some preliminary mixing of the layers, and is particularly important when aqueous carbonate or bicarbonate is being used to extract or neutralize acidic components. Carbon dioxide will be evolved, and the preliminary mixing will reduce the problems from excessive pressure building up during the extraction process. After swirling, return the separatory funnel to its support and insert the stopper.

CO_2 is evolved during extractions using aqueous carbonate and bicarbonate solutions. Guard against pressure build-up in the funnel

More vigorous swirling and shaking is required to mix the layers thoroughly, and to do this the separatory funnel has to be held in the hands clear of its support. Everyone develops their own technique for holding a separatory funnel, and one method is shown in Fig. 3.33(a). Whatever the exact grip on the funnel, the important points to note are as follows.

- Hold the funnel in *both* hands.
- Hold the body of the funnel in one hand and keep one finger over the stopper at all times.

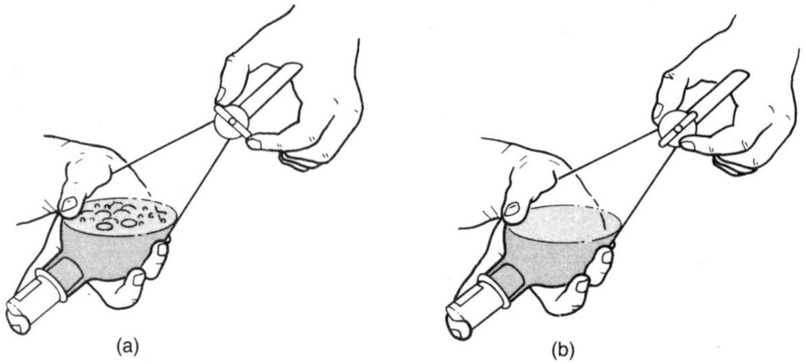

Fig. 3.33 (a) Holding a separatory funnel during shaking; (b) holding a separatory funnel during venting. **Always point the stem away from others during venting.**

- Hold the funnel around the stopcock with the other hand, so that the stopcock is kept in place and, more importantly, so that you can open and close the stopcock quickly with your fingers.
- If in doubt, practise your grip on an *empty* separatory funnel.

To carry out the extraction, lift the separatory funnel clear of its support, adjust your grip and invert the funnel. Immediately open the stopcock to release any pressure build-up as shown in Fig. 3.33(b). Most organic solvents are fairly volatile and their vapour pressure causes build-up of pressure in the funnel. For this reason, never attempt to extract hot solutions; the greatly increased vapour pressure may cause the solvent to blow out of the funnel. Similarly, as mentioned above, pressure release is very important when doing extractions with carbonate or bicarbonate solutions, which may generate carbon dioxide. **When venting a funnel, never point the stem towards your neighbours or towards yourself.** Always aim it well away from others, preferably into a hood. After the first venting, close the stopcock, swirl the inverted funnel for a few seconds, and then vent it again. If excessive pressure build-up is evident, repeat the swirling–venting process until pressure build-up diminishes. Then, and only then, shake the funnel. Opinions vary as to the duration of shaking required to establish equilibrium between the liquids, but 20 vigorous shakes (10–20 s) are thought to be adequate. Vent the funnel at least once during the shaking process. Beware of shaking too vigorously, however, as this may encourage the formation of *emulsions* (see pp. 115–116). At the end of the shaking, vent the funnel again, make sure that the stopcock is closed and return the separatory funnel to its support stand. Immediately place an empty Erlenmeyer flask under the funnel and then allow the funnel to stand until the layers separate.

Never extract hot solutions

Point stem away from others

Remember—invert, vent, swirl, vent, shake, vent

Separating the layers

All being well, the organic and aqueous solutions will separate into two easily visible layers in the separatory funnel. (If not, see the section on 'troubleshooting' below.) Remove the stopper, and if any organic material is stuck to the side of it, rinse this back into the funnel with a few drops of the extraction solvent from a Pasteur pipette. Do not do this if the stopper has been greased! Before running off the lower layer through the stopcock, you must be sure which layer is which. Often you may be able to tell just by the relative volumes of the two layers, or by the fact that the organic extraction solvent is much denser or less dense than water. However, the presence of dissolved inorganic and organic material can dramatically alter the densities of the aqueous and organic layers respectively, and therefore it might not be obvious which layer is which. In this case, add a few drops of water to the separatory funnel, and see which layer it goes into. With a clear interface between the layers, run off the lower layer through the stopcock. Hold the funnel as shown in Fig. 3.34 to ensure that the stopcock does not fall out, and arrange the funnel so that the tip of the stem touches the side of the Erlenmeyer flask; this reduces splashing.

Make sure which layer is which

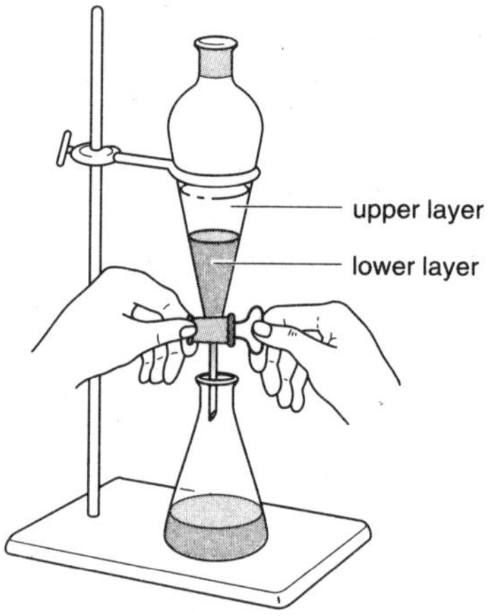

Fig. 3.34 Holding a separatory funnel whilst draining the lower layer.

Do not let a vortex form

Open the stopcock *gently*; do not allow the liquid to run out too quickly as this will cause a vortex to form which will drag some of the upper layer through as well. When the lower layer is almost drained, close the stopcock, and gently swirl the separatory funnel to knock down any drops of liquid that are clinging to the glass. Open the stopcock *slowly* and carefully run off the remaining lower layer into the flask. Close the stopcock and gently tap the funnel stem to dislodge the last drops into the Erlenmeyer. Label the Erlenmeyer flask *immediately*. The upper layer remaining in the separatory funnel should be poured out through the neck of the funnel into a clean Erlenmeyer, which should also be labelled immediately. The upper layer is poured from the funnel, rather than run out through the stopcock, to avoid contamination of the upper layer by the traces of material from the lower layer remaining in the stem and stopcock.

Label all solutions immediately

Keep everything

Always keep both solutions until you have isolated your organic product. Even experienced chemists sometimes discard the wrong layer, or discard an aqueous solution which has been incompletely extracted. It is always best to play safe, and never discard anything until you are absolutely sure that you do not need it.

Finally, wash out the separatory funnel as soon as you have finished with it. It is particularly important to remove and clean the stopcock; this will prevent it from sticking when the funnel is not in use. In fact it is better to store the funnel separately from the stopcock.

Trouble shooting

Occasionally things do not go according to plan when using separatory funnels. Some of the most commonly encountered problems are discussed below, along with some suggested remedies.

Mixture is so dark that interface is not visible

Occasionally the mixture in the separatory funnel is so dark in colour that you cannot see the interface between the two layers. If so, hold the separatory funnel up to the light, or place a small desk lamp or reading lamp directly behind it. With a brighter light source you may be able to see the interface. If that fails, start to run off the liquid *slowly* from the stopcock, and observe the flow of liquid carefully. It is usually possible to detect the changeover from water to organic solvent, or vice versa, by the change in flow properties due to differences in surface tension and viscosity.

Mixture is clear but interface is not visible

Even when the mixture is clear, the interface between the layers may not be visible. This happens when the two layers have very similar refractive indices, so that they look the same. The trick in this case is to add a pinch of powdered charcoal to the separatory funnel. This will float on top of the denser liquid, and hence the interface will be clearly marked.

Only a single layer is visible

This usually happens when the original reaction mixture, before work-up, contains large amounts of water-miscible solvents such as ethanol or tetrahydrofuran. Such solvents dissolve in water and the extraction solvent equally well, and hence a single homogeneous layer is formed in the separatory funnel. Although this can sometimes be encouraged to form two layers by adding more water and more extraction solvent, or by adding saturated sodium chloride solution, the problem is easily avoided by concentrating the original reaction mixture by evaporating the offending solvent **before** attempting aqueous work-up.

Insoluble material is visible at the interface

This is a very common problem, and in most extractions some insoluble material collects at the interface between the two layers. It is usually impossible to separate the layers without taking some of this solid into one or both of them. However, this is nothing to worry about, since the required liquid will always be processed further, and hence the insoluble impurity can be removed by filtration at a later stage.

Emulsions

Emulsions form when droplets of one solution become suspended in another, and the suspension will not separate by gravity. When this occurs in a separatory funnel, it can cause big problems. Sometimes the emulsion clears if the funnel is left undisturbed for a few minutes, and then two distinct layers will separate out. Unfortunately, most emulsions are more persistent. With such

Preventing emulsions

persistent emulsions, prevention is better than cure. Emulsions usually form in extractions involving basic solutions such as sodium hydroxide or sodium carbonate. Traces of long chain fatty acids are converted into their sodium salts, and the resulting 'soap' is a very effective emulsifying agent. Vigorous shaking also encourages the emulsification process, so in extractions involving basic components, the separatory funnel should be swirled rather than shaken, although obviously equilibrium between the liquids is reached much more slowly. In addition, if appropriate, using a weaker base such as sodium bicarbonate might help to prevent the formation of an emulsion. The tendency to form emulsions increases as electrolytes are removed from the mixture, so adding sodium chloride to the aqueous layer may prevent an emulsion. The addition of sodium chloride also has the effect of reducing the solubility of organic material in water, and of increasing the density of the aqueous layer. This latter effect may be important if the emulsion is due to the aqueous and organic solutions having very similar densities. On this basis, you can also adjust the density of the organic layer by adding pentane to reduce it, or dichloromethane to increase it. In addition, certain solvents are more likely to form emulsions than others. Benzene is particularly prone to emulsions, and is best avoided, although its toxicity generally precludes its use in any event. Chlorinated solvents (chloroform and dichloromethane) also have a tendency to form emulsions. If an emulsion still forms despite the precautions, it has to be broken up before an efficient extraction can be achieved. One plan of action is as follows.

Breaking emulsions

- Allow the separatory funnel to stand with periodic *gentle* swirling.
- Add some saturated sodium chloride solution to the emulsion.
- Add a few drops of ethanol to the emulsion.
- Filter the whole mixture by suction; emulsions are stabilized by suspended solid, and filtration removes the solid. The same effect can be achieved by *centrifugation*.
- Transfer the mixture to an Erlenmeyer flask, and allow it to stand overnight or longer.

One of these will usually work, but you do need patience!

No product is isolated after evaporation of the organic layer

After separating the organic layer, you will usually dry the solution (pp. 127, 130–131) and then evaporate the solvent on the rotary evaporator to isolate your product. Occasionally you will be left with little or no product at this stage. This is not as disastrous as it would seem *provided that you have kept the aqueous layer* from the original work-up. What it means is that your product is sufficiently polar to have some water solubility, and therefore has been poorly extracted by the organic solvent. The first thing to do in this situation is to return the aqueous layer to the separatory funnel, and to re-extract it with a more polar organic solvent. Common extraction solvents in order of increasing polarity are: hydrocarbons (light petroleum, hexane), toluene, diethyl ether, dichloromethane, ethyl acetate. More polar solvents such as acetone or

For a further discussion of extraction solvents, see pp. 121–122

ethanol are water miscible; n-butanol, however, is largely water immiscible and can be used as a polar extraction solvent. However, it does dissolve some water, and is high boiling and hence difficult to remove from your organic product. A simple way to decrease the solubility of an organic compound in water is to add solid sodium chloride to the aqueous layer. This technique is known as *salting out* the organic compound, and is discussed further in the next section (p. 120).

Microscale solvent extraction and phase separation

Using separatory funnels on the microscale is impracticable; however, efficient extraction and phase separation can be accomplished using a Pasteur pipette and a sample tube, tapered vial, or test tube. Tapered vials are particularly suitable for this purpose because the taper allows efficient removal of the lower layer (Fig. 3.35).

Assuming a reaction has been performed in a tapered vial *in a solvent less dense than water*, open the vial and add the required quantity (typically less than 1 mL) of aqueous quench or wash solution. Use the Pasteur pipette to mix the layers, by repeatedly and rapidly filling the pipette with the entire contents (aqueous and organic) of the vial, and expelling them again. The mixture can then be allowed to settle. To remove the lower aqueous layer, insert the tip of the pipette to the bottom of the taper and slowly fill the pipette, watching

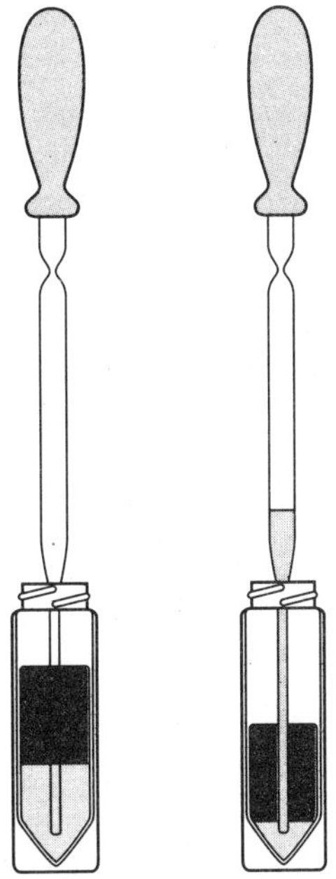

Fig. 3.35 On the microscale, the Pasteur pipette and tapered reaction vial (or tube) replace the separatory funnel. The phases are mixed intimately within the pipette; after phase separation the lower layer can be removed carefully.

the position of the meniscus carefully. The washings can be discarded and the process repeated as required.

If solvent extraction of an aqueous medium is required, transfer can be minimized using an extraction solvent that is more dense than water, such as dichloromethane. The extracts can then be combined in a second vial for washing.

Removing the upper layer efficiently is obviously more difficult because of the difference between the surface area of the meniscus and the cross-section of the pipette tip, so lower layer removal is recommended wherever possible.

3.3 Purification of organic compounds

Having worked up the reaction mixture, you will have isolated your organic product. Chemists usually refer to this as the *crude product* indicating that, in most cases, the compound will need to be purified further. To be able to purify an organic compound by separating the impurities, we have to rely on the desired compound having different properties to the impurities and we might take advantage of differences in solubility, volatility, polarity, shape and functional groups present. For example, crystallization relies on the differences in solubility between the desired compound and the impurities, whereas distillation exploits differences in volatility. Adsorption chromatography separates and purifies compounds according to their adsorption to the chromatographic material, which to a good approximation is related to the polarity of the compounds. More advanced techniques such as electrophoresis and gel filtration, which are beyond the scope of this book, separate compounds by differences in molecular charge and size, respectively. Indeed with the advent of sophisticated instruments and analytical techniques, separation science is a whole subject in itself nowadays. Our concern is merely to cover the major purification techniques that are relevant to the organic laboratory, with emphasis on the practicalities of the technique, rather than on the underlying theory. The following sections deal with the purification techniques of organic chemistry and cover extraction, crystallization, distillation and chromatography in various forms.

Extraction

Historically, extraction is one of the oldest of all chemical operations, and one which is used in everyday life. The simple act of making a cup of tea or coffee involves the extraction of various components responsible for flavour, odour and colour from tea leaves or ground coffee beans by hot water.

Extraction in the chemical sense means 'pulling out' a compound from one phase to another, usually from a liquid or a solid to another liquid. In the organic laboratory, the most common process involves the extraction of an organic compound from one liquid phase to another. The two liquid phases are usually an aqueous solution and an organic solvent, and the technique is known as *liquid–liquid extraction* or, more commonly, as *extraction*.

A simple extraction is often used in the work-up of an organic reaction mixture (see pp. 110–118), but extraction can also be used to *separate* and *purify* organic compounds. Extraction is particularly useful in the separation of acidic and basic components from an organic mixture by their reaction with dilute aqueous base or acid as appropriate. Since this relies on an acid–based chemical reaction, the technique is often called *chemically active extraction*. Whatever extraction protocol is being used, most extraction operations in the organic laboratory are carried out in *separatory funnels*, the use of which has already been discussed in the proceding section.

Aqueous–organic extraction

Before going into the experimental procedures for extracting compounds, we need to consider some of the physical chemistry theory behind the technique. When an organic compound, X, is placed in a separatory funnel with two *immiscible* liquids, such as water and dichloromethane, some of the compound will dissolve in the water and some in the dichloromethane. (We assume that X does not react with either liquid.) In more technical language, the compound is said to *partition* or distribute itself between the two liquids, and the exact amount of X in each phase clearly depends on its relative solubility in water and dichloromethane. The ratio of *concentrations* of X in each phase is known as the *partition coefficient* or *distribution coefficient* and is a constant (K) defined as

$$K = \frac{\text{Concentration in dichloromethane}}{\text{Concentration in water}}$$

which, to a rough approximation, is the same as the ratio of *solubilities* of X in dichloromethane and water measured separately.

$$K \approx \frac{\text{Solubility in dichloromethane}}{\text{Solubility in water}}$$

To illustrate this, assume that the solubility of X in dichloromethane is 35 g per 100 mL and in water is 5 g per 100 mL *at the same temperature*. Hence, the partition coefficient, K, is *approximately* given by

$$K = \frac{35\,\text{g}/100\,\text{mL}}{5\,\text{g}/100\,\text{mL}} = 7$$

Both solubilities are measured in the same units, and therefore the partition coefficient is dimensionless.

Now that we know the partition coefficient for this particular system, we can work out how much of compound X we can extract from water using dichloromethane. Suppose we have 100 mL of water containing 5 g of compound X and we are going to extract it with 100 mL of dichloromethane. How much of X will we extract? After shaking the separatory funnel until equilibrium between the two liquids is reached, assume that the amount extracted into the organic dichloromethane phase (100 mL) is x g. The amount of X remaining in the water (100 mL) is therefore $(5-x)$ g. Since

$$K = \frac{\text{Concentration in dichloromethane}}{\text{Concentration in water}}$$

we have

$$7 = \frac{x\,\text{g}/100\,\text{mL}}{(5-x)\,\text{g}/100\,\text{mL}}$$

and hence $x = 4.375$ g.

Therefore we can extract 4.375 g of X from 100 mL water using 100 mL of dichloromethane; the remaining 0.635 g of X will remain in the water. The process has been reasonably efficient in that we have extracted 87.5% of the compound. However, we can do better, even without using more dichloromethane. How? By dividing our 100 mL of extraction solvent dichloromethane into two 50 mL portions, and by carrying out the extraction of the water solution twice using 50 mL of fresh dichloromethane for each extraction. Calculating as before, you will find that the first extraction gives 3.889 g X, leaving 1.111 g in the water, which on the second extraction will give 0.864 g of X in the dichloromethane phase. Hence a total of 4.753 g, or 95%, of X has now been extracted.

Two or three smaller extractions are more efficient than one large one

The important conclusion from this exercise in the theory of extraction is that it is more efficient to carry out two small extractions with organic solvent than one large one. A greater number of even smaller extractions would be more efficient still, and as a general rule, provided that the partition coefficient is greater than 4 (which it is for many organic compounds in many two-phase water–solvent systems), a double or triple extraction will remove most of the organic compound from the water.

Water-soluble compounds

If the organic compound is *more* soluble in water than in the organic solvent, the partition coefficient is less than 1, and very little compound will be extracted simply by shaking up the two liquids. However, the partition coefficient of the organic compound can be changed by adding an inorganic salt, such as sodium chloride, to the aqueous solution. The theory is that the organic compound will be less soluble in sodium chloride solution than in water itself, and therefore the partition coefficient between the organic solvent and aqueous solution will now have a higher value, and the extraction into the organic solvent will be more efficient. Fortunately this theory is borne out in practice, and simply adding solid sodium chloride to your separatory funnel can dramatically improve the extraction of water-soluble organic compounds into an organic solvent. The technique is known as *salting out*, and was briefly referred to in the previous section.

Salting out

Very occasionally you will come across an organic compound that cannot be efficiently extracted from aqueous solution. Even after salting out, the partition coefficient is still too low, and only small amounts can be extracted by each portion of organic solvent. Obviously one could carry on shaking the aqueous solution with several small portions of organic solvent, extracting, say, 2–5% of the material each time, but this is clearly going to be a long and tedious process. If you find yourself in this situation, the way out is to use a *continuous extraction* apparatus in place of your separatory funnel. A detailed discussion of continuous extraction is beyond the scope of this book, but basically the apparatus is arranged so that organic solvent continually circulates through the aqueous solution extracting a small amount of material each time, before being recycled. The extraction can run for several hours until sufficient material is obtained in the organic solvent. There are two basic designs of apparatus: one for use with solvents that are lighter than water and the other for use with solvents that are more dense than water. You are unlikely to need such an apparatus in the teaching laboratory, but if you do have serious problems in extracting your organic material from water, the apparatus may be available. Ask your instructor.

Continuous extraction

Choice of extraction solvent

In the discussion above, we looked at a typical organic extraction process which used dichloromethane as the organic solvent to extract an aqueous solution. Although water is almost always one of the liquids in the liquid–liquid extraction process, the choice of organic solvent is quite wide. Dichloromethane is, in fact, an excellent choice, because it fulfils all the main requirements for an extraction solvent: immiscibility with water, different density to water, good solubility characteristics, stability and volatility so that it can easily be removed from the organic compound by evaporation. Ideally an extraction solvent should also be non-toxic and non-flammable, but these two criteria are less easy to meet. Extraction solvents fall into two groups: those which are less dense than water and those which are more dense. Commonly used extraction solvents which fall in the first group include diethyl ether (the most common extraction solvent of all), ethyl acetate and hydrocarbons, such as light petroleum, or pentane, or toluene. Dichloromethane is the commonly used extraction solvent which is denser than water but it does have a greater tendency to form emulsions than the non-chlorinated solvents. The properties of some common extraction solvents, listed in order of increasing dielectric constant, are given in Table 3.4. Of these, diethyl ether and dichloromethane find the widest use in the organic laboratory.

Acid–base–neutral extraction

We have already mentioned the fact that *chemically active extraction* can be used in the purification of organic compounds by separating acidic, basic and

Table 3.4 Some common extraction solvents.

Solvent	Dielectric* constant	Bp (°C)	Density ($g\,mL^{-1}$)†	Flammability‡	Toxicity‡	Suitability
Pentane	1.8	36.1	0.63	+++	+	Poor solvent for polar compounds; easily dried
Toluene	2.4	110.6	0.87	++	+	Prone to emulsions
Diethyl ether	4.3	34.6	0.71	+++	+	Good general extraction solvent, especially for oxygen-containing compounds; dissolves up to 1.5% water. **Prone to peroxide formation on storage**
Ethyl acetate	6.0	77.1	0.89	+++	+	Good for polar compounds; absorbs a large amount of water
Dichloromethane	8.9	39.7	1.31	Non-flammable	++	Good general extraction solvent; easily dried, but slight tendency to emulsify
1-Butanol	17.5	117.7	0.81	++	+	'Last resort' for extraction of very polar compounds; dissolves up to 20% water

* Although the dielectric constant (ε) gives some indication of the polarity of a solvent, it does not always reflect a solvent's ability to dissolve polar organic compounds.
† Water = 1.0, saturated sodium chloride solution = 1.2.
‡ + = least flammable/toxic, +++ = most flammable/toxic.

neutral components, and we now provide flow-charts and protocols for carrying out such extractions.

Separation according to acidity

The idea is that organic compounds, be they the required product or some by-product or other impurity, can be separated according to their acidity. Organic acids such as sulfonic and carboxylic acids are easily converted into their sodium salts, which are usually water soluble, by reaction with sodium bicarbonate. Weaker organic acids such as phenols require a stronger base such as sodium hydroxide. Conversely organic bases such as amines are converted into water-soluble hydrochloride salts by reaction with hydrochloric acid. The overall plan for the separation of an organic mixture into acidic, basic and neutral components is shown in outline in Fig. 3.36, and is discussed in more detail below.

To carry out the extraction procedure, you will require a selection of aqueous acidic and basic solutions. A well-equipped organic laboratory

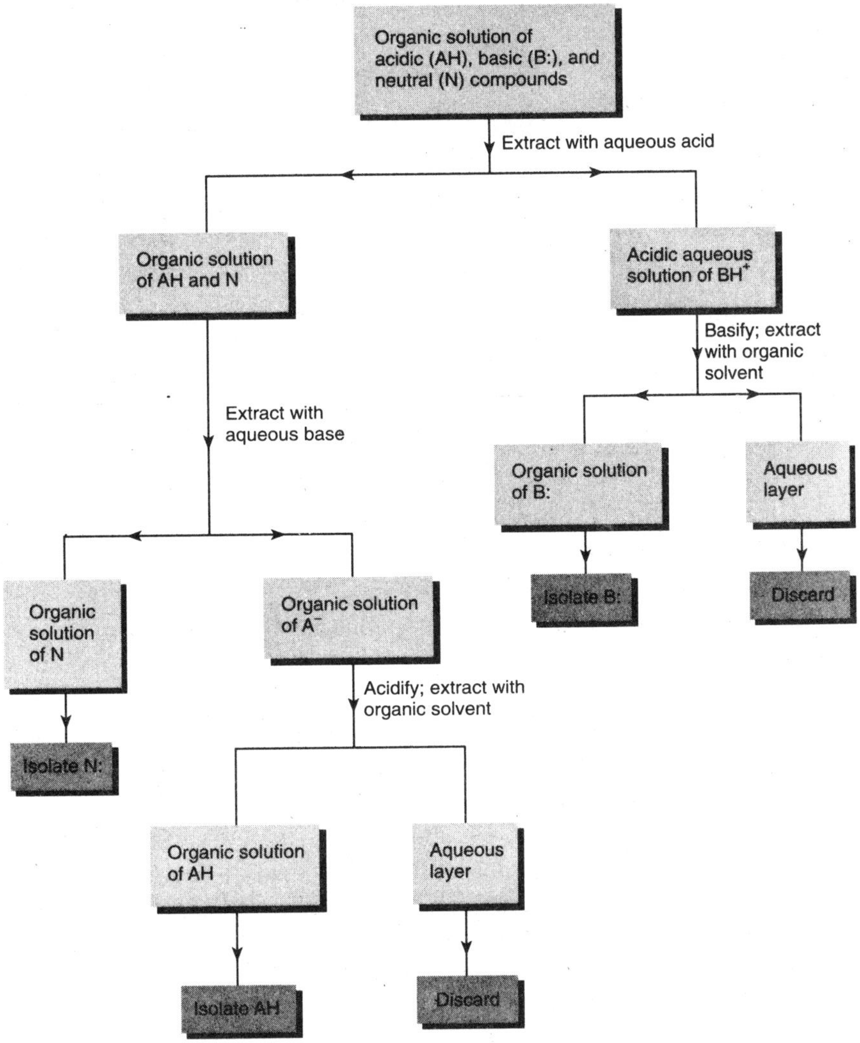

Fig. 3.36 General outline for the separation of acidic (AH), basic (B:) and neutral (N) components of a mixture.

should have these already made up, but you may have to prepare your own solutions. What you need are:

- saturated sodium bicarbonate solution (contains about 96 g L^{-1}; *ca.* 1 M);
- 2 M sodium hydroxide solution (contains 80 g L^{-1});
- 2 M hydrochloric acid (contains 200 mL concentrated acid L^{-1});
- saturated sodium chloride solution (contains about 360 g L^{-1}).

The extraction is carried out in a separatory funnel using the techniques already described, according to one of the following protocols. You will normally know the properties of the required organic product, i.e. whether it is acidic, basic or neutral, and therefore it is usually obvious which extraction protocol to follow. Remember, just as with a reaction work-up, never discard

Do not discard anything until you are sure you do not need it

any aqueous or organic layer from an extraction until you are sure it does not contain any of your organic product.

Isolation and purification of a neutral organic compound

The general scheme for the isolation and purification of a neutral organic compound is given in Fig. 3.37. The scheme starts with an organic solution containing the required neutral product together with some impurities. This solution may have been obtained by simply dissolving up the impure material or, more likely, will be the result of the work-up of your reaction mixture. As will become apparent, it is much better to use a solvent such as diethyl ether that is less dense than water for this extraction protocol. The scheme is self-explanatory, and involves successive extractions (washes) to remove acidic and basic impurities. After each extraction your neutral organic compound will remain in the organic layer, and therefore it is much more convenient if the aqueous solution to be run off and *eventually* discarded is the *lower* layer in your separatory funnel. Hence the preferred use of a solvent that is less dense than water for these extractions. After running off the first aqueous wash from the funnel, the next aqueous solution can be added directly to the organic layer remaining in the funnel. At the end of the extraction procedure you will be left with an organic solution containing the neutral component. The water wash removes traces of the previous acidic wash, but it is always a good idea to follow this with a final wash (extraction) with saturated sodium chloride solution, particularly if diethyl ether is the organic solvent involved, because, believe it or not, this extraction actually *dries* the organic layer! Diethyl ether, although largely immiscible with water, does dissolve 1.5% water by weight at room temperature. However, diethyl ether will not dissolve sodium chloride solution, and therefore if a diethyl ether solution containing dissolved water is washed with saturated sodium chloride solution, water is transferred from the diethyl ether to the aqueous layer. Strange, but true! The final traces of water are removed from the organic solution by drying over an appropriate drying agent (p. 126). After filtration (pp. 74–79) of the spent drying agent, the required neutral organic compound is recovered from the filtrate by evaporation of the solvent on the rotary evaporator.

Isolation and purification of an acidic organic compound

The extraction protocol for the isolation and purification of an acidic organic compound is shown in outline in Fig. 3.38. Again the overall procedure is self-explanatory, and the only thing you need to decide is which aqueous base to use in the first extraction. The choice depends on the properties of the acidic compound that you are trying to isolate and purify. Strong organic acids such as carboxylic and sulfonic acids can usually be extracted with saturated sodium bicarbonate solution, but weaker acids such as phenols can only be extracted with stronger bases such as sodium carbonate or sodium hydroxide. If you do not know the precise acidity of the compound, play safe, and use

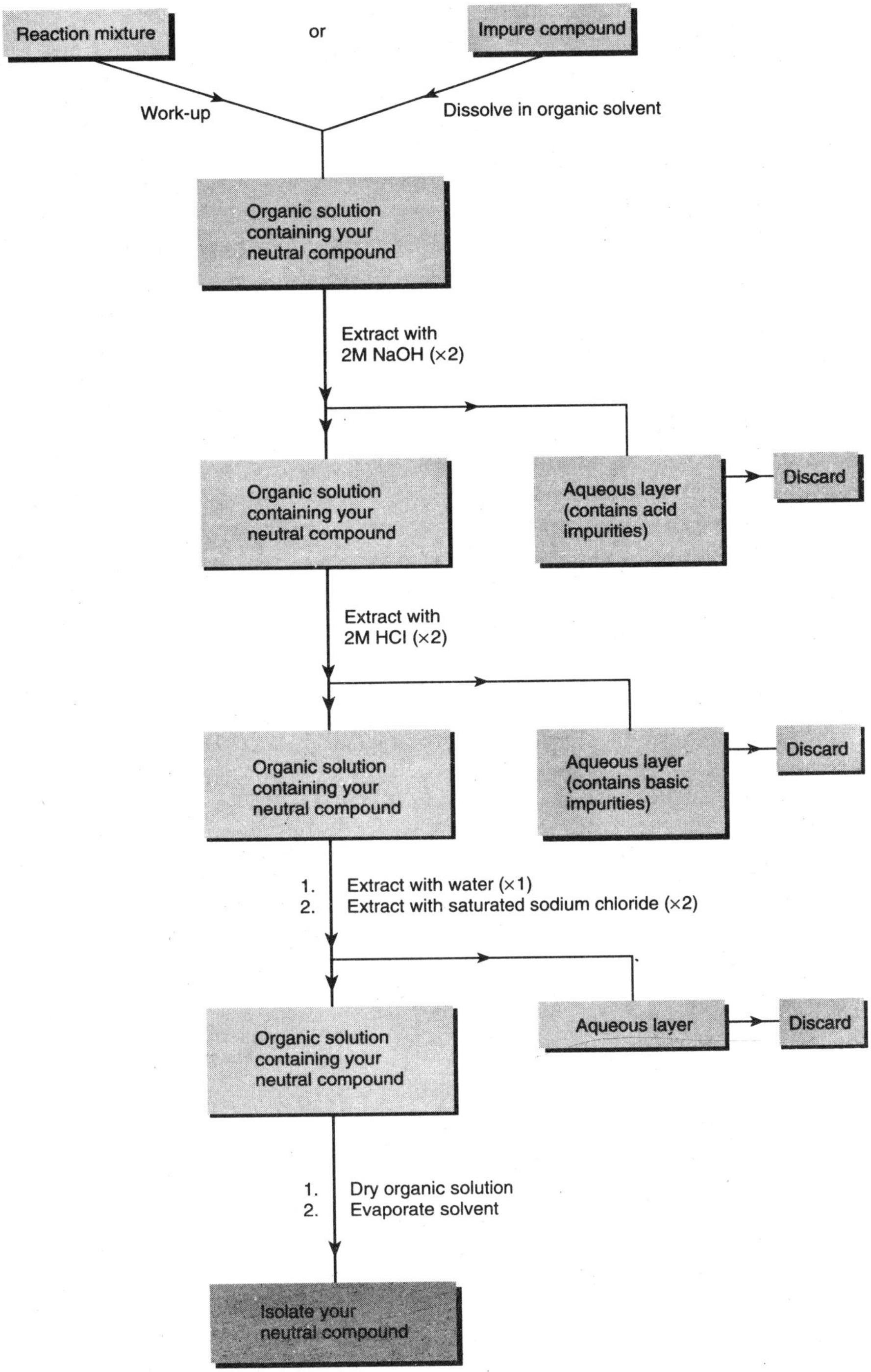

Fig. 3.37 Extraction protocol for the isolation and purification of a neutral organic compound.

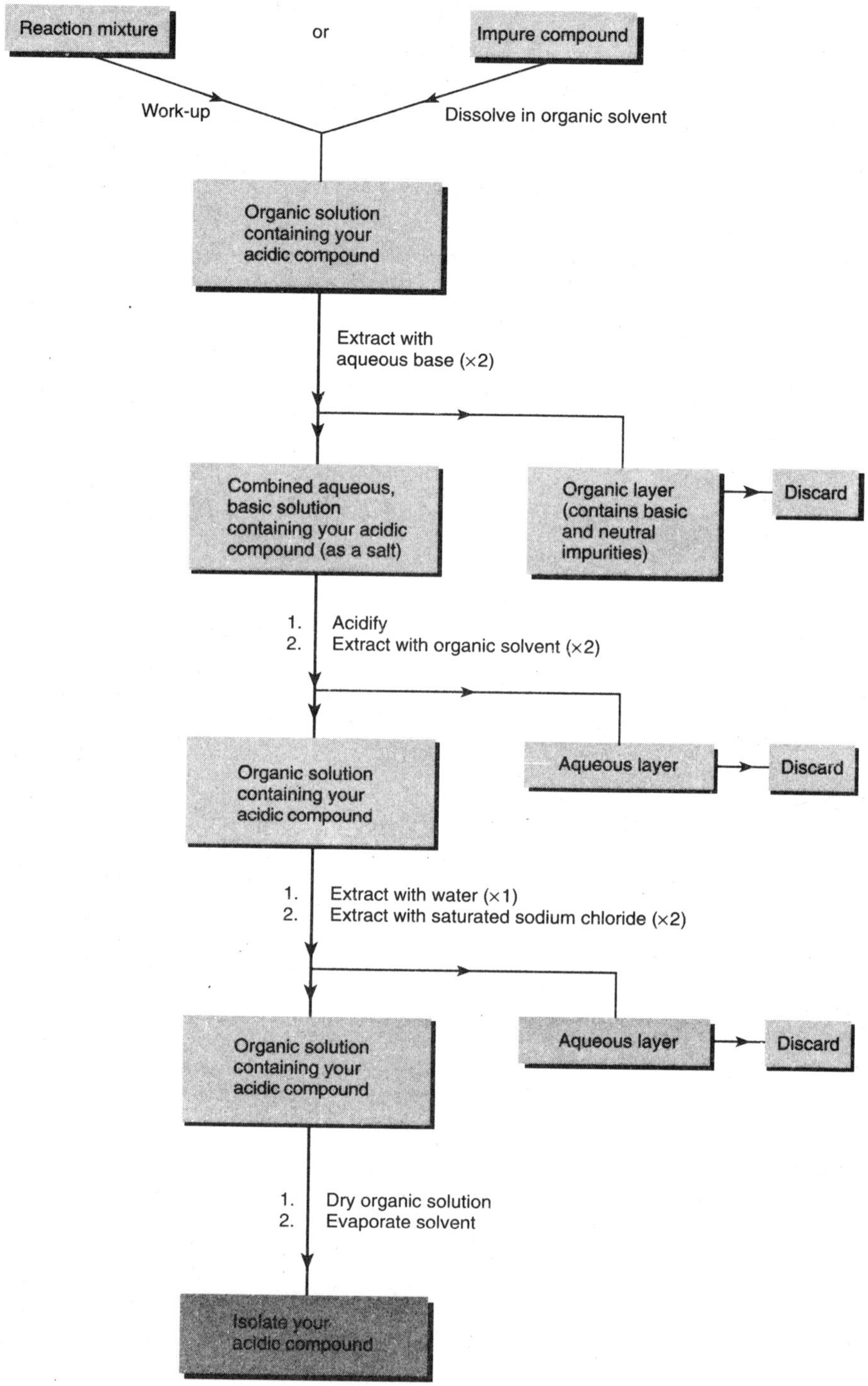

Fig. 3.38 Extraction protocol for the isolation and purification of an acidic organic compound.

sodium hydroxide solution to extract it. The acidic compound is recovered from the aqueous basic layer by making the solution strongly acidic, and then extracting it with an organic solvent. The acidification is usually done by adding 2 M hydrochloric acid until the pH reaches 1–2, but if this will result in a large increase in volume, then it is better to add concentrated acid *dropwise*. Remember that the heat of the acid–base reaction will cause the aqueous solution to become quite hot. The solution should be cooled in an ice bath before extracting it. Never attempt to extract hot solutions. At the end of the extraction procedure, you will need to dry the final organic solution over an appropriate drying agent; not all drying agents are suitable for acidic compounds (see Table 3.5).

Take care when neutralizing solutions—heat evolved! Do not attempt to extract hot aqueous solutions

Isolation and purification of a basic organic compound

Basic organic compounds can be isolated and purified by using the extraction protocol shown in Fig. 3.39. The procedure is very similar to those discussed above, but obvious changes are needed as you are trying to isolate a basic compound. The basic compound is recovered from the acidic water layer by basification and extraction. Again at the very end of the process, the choice of

Table 3.5 Some common drying agents for organic solutions.*

Drying agent	Capacity†	Speed	Efficiency	Applicability
Calcium chloride	High, 90%	Slow	Poor	Use only for hydrocarbons or halides; reacts with most oxygen- and nitrogen-containing compounds; may contain CaO (basic)
Calcium sulfate (Drierite®)	Low, 7%	Very fast	Very good	Generally useful; neutral
Magnesium sulfate	High, 100%	Fast	Good	Excellent general purpose drying agent; a weak Lewis acid; should not be used for *very* acid-sensitive compounds
Molecular sieves	Moderate, 20%	Fast	Good	When freshly activated, excellent for removing most of the water, but solutions should be predried with a higher capacity agent first
Potassium carbonate	Quite high	Quite fast	Quite good	Basic; reacts with acidic compounds; good for oxygen- and nitrogen-containing compounds
Sodium sulfate	High, 75%	Slow	Poor	Mild, generally useful, but less efficient than $MgSO_4$

* These agents are for drying organic solutions, not for drying organic solvents. The drying of organic solvents is an entirely separate problem (see Appendix 2, p. 677).
† The number indicates the amount of water, as a percentage of its own weight, that a drying agent can take up.

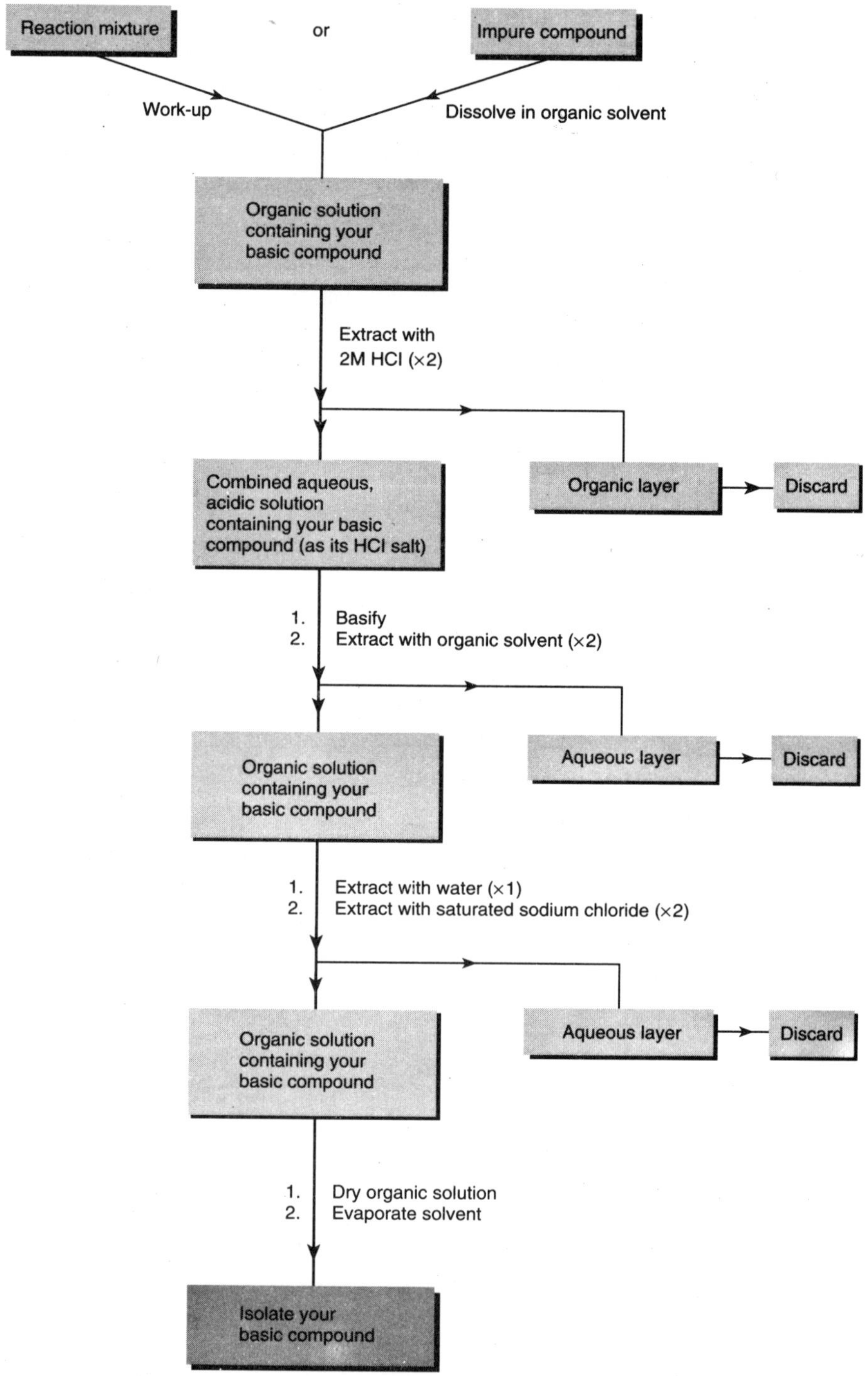

Fig. 3.39 Extraction protocol for the isolation and purification of a basic organic compound.

drying agent for the organic solution is important. Basic compounds, particularly amines, cannot be dried over certain drying agents. The choice of drying agent for organic solutions is discussed in more detail in pp. 127, 130–131.

Extraction of solids

Solids can also be extracted with organic solvents. One very simple way of doing this is to place the solid in an Erlenmeyer flask, cover the solid with the organic solvent and allow the flask to stand with occasional swirling. The organic compound that you are interested in will be slowly leached out of the solid. The unwanted solid can then be removed from the organic solution containing your compound simply by filtration. However, this is a fairly inefficient technique, although the efficiency of the extraction can be improved by using hot solvents. A much more efficient way to extract solids is to use a *Soxhlet* apparatus (Fig. 3.40). In this, the solid to be extracted is packed into a special 'thimble' made of thick filter paper. The thimble is placed in the apparatus as shown, and the whole Soxhlet extractor is placed on top of a well-supported round-bottomed flask containing the organic solvent. A reflux condenser is placed on top of the Soxhlet extractor. The flask is heated using a water or steam bath (for flammable solvents) or some form of electrical heating, so that the solvent boils. Solvent vapour passes up the large diameter outer tube of the apparatus, and condensed solvent then drips down

Soxhlet extraction

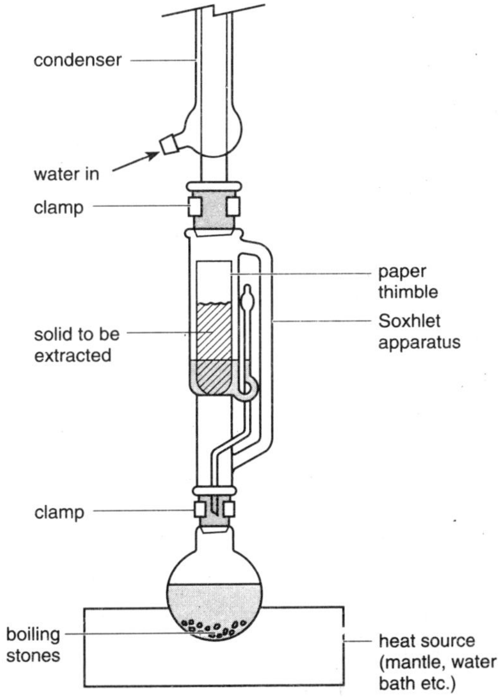

Fig. 3.40 Soxhlet apparatus for the extraction of solids.

through the thimble containing the solid. Material is extracted out of the solid into the hot solvent. When the solution level reaches the top of the siphon tube, the solution siphons automatically through the narrow tube, and returns to the flask, where the extracted material accumulates. The process is efficient, since the same batch of solvent is repeatedly recycled through the solid. If the extraction is run for prolonged periods it is possible to extract materials that are only very slightly soluble in organic solvents. The technique is often used for the extraction of natural products from biological materials such as crushed leaves or seeds, and this particular application is illustrated in Experiment 69.

Further reading

For further detailed discussion of extraction procedures in organic chemistry, see: L.C. Craig and D. Craig, *Extraction and Distribution, Techniques of Organic Chemistry*, Vol. III (ed. by A. Weissberger), Wiley (Interscience), New York, 1950.

Solution drying

After completing the isolation or purification of an organic compound by some form of extraction, or after completing the work-up of your reaction mixture, you are left with an organic solution containing your required compound. Since the organic solution has been extracted or washed with aqueous solutions, it will undoubtedly contain some water. Although, as discussed above, the amount of water can sometimes be reduced by washing the organic solution with saturated sodium chloride solution, the last traces of water have to be removed by treatment with a drying agent. Common drying agents are anhydrous inorganic salts which readily take up water to become hydrated. At the end of the drying process, the hydrated salt is removed from the organic solution by filtration.

The complete procedure is as follows. At the end of the extraction, pour the final organic solution out of the separatory funnel into an Erlenmeyer flask as described on p. 114. Add the solid drying agent and swirl the flask. If the drying agent immediately lumps together add some more. Allow the flask to stand, with occasional swirling, for 5–20 min. The time depends on the speed with which the drying agent takes up water (Table 3.5), but you can usually tell when an excess of *anhydrous* drying agent, such as magnesium sulfate (the most commonly used agent), is present by simply swirling the flask. The *anhydrous* salt forms a cloudy suspension that settles quite slowly; the effect is often described as a 'snow storm'. If, on the other hand, only *hydrated* agent is present, the suspension settles very quickly, since the hydrated salt is usually much denser. In this case add some more drying agent. When the solution is deemed to be dry, remove the spent drying agent by filtration (pp. 74–79) and recover the organic compound from the filtrate by evaporation of the solvent on a rotary evaporator (pp. 49–53).

How to tell when the solution is dry

The most important factor in drying organic solutions is the choice of drying agent. Ideally the solid drying agent should be totally insoluble in organic solvents, inert to a wide range of organic compounds (including solvents), and able to take up water quickly and efficiently to give a hydrated form which is an easily filterable solid. The most commonly used drying agents are listed in Table 3.5, which gives information on their *capacity* (how much water they can take up), *speed* (rate of water uptake), *efficiency* (how dry they leave the solution) and *applicability* (suitability for different classes of compound). Clearly the choice will depend on a number of factors, the most crucial of which is the nature of the organic compound that is dissolved in the solvent, and that is ultimately to be isolated. As a good general purpose drying agent, magnesium sulfate finds the widest use.

It is important to note that drying agents that are suitable for drying *organic solutions* are not usually appropriate for drying *organic solvents* for use with moisture-sensitive compounds (see pp. 79–89). The drying of organic solvents is an entirely separate problem that is referred to on pp. 81–82, and dealt with specifically in Appendix 2 (p. 677).

Solution drying on the microscale

Effective drying can be achieved in a plugged Pasteur pipette. Push a small plug of cotton or glass wool into the top of the constriction of a Pasteur pipette (see Fig. 3.9). Do not pack the plug too tightly; however, it should not simply wash through when solvent is loaded into the pipette. Solid drying agent can then be loaded into the wider section of the pipette to a depth of 1–2 cm. Using a second Pasteur pipette, wet the column evenly with clean extraction solvent, then load the solution to be dried onto the drying agent and use gentle pressure to push the solution through the bed of adsorbent. Simply fitting a teat to the top of the pipette and expelling the air will achieve sufficient pressure. Take care not to allow air back into the teat while it is still attached to the column as this will probably disrupt the filter bed, contaminating your sample. Some commercial microscale kits contain small chromatography columns which can also be used for this purpose, though a pipette is quite adequate.

Crystallization

The simplest and most effective technique for the purification of solid organic compounds is crystallization. Crystalline compounds are easy to handle, their purity is readily assessed (Chapter 4) and they are often easier to identify than liquids or oils. Crystals can be obtained in one of three ways: from the melted solid on cooling, by sublimation (pp. 159–160) or from a supersaturated solution. The last method is by far the most common in the organic laboratory.

Crystallization of organic compounds

A general flow-chart for the purification of an organic compound by *crystallization* is shown in Fig. 3.41. The process involves five stages: dissolution, filtration, crystallization, collection of the crystals, and drying the crystals. The

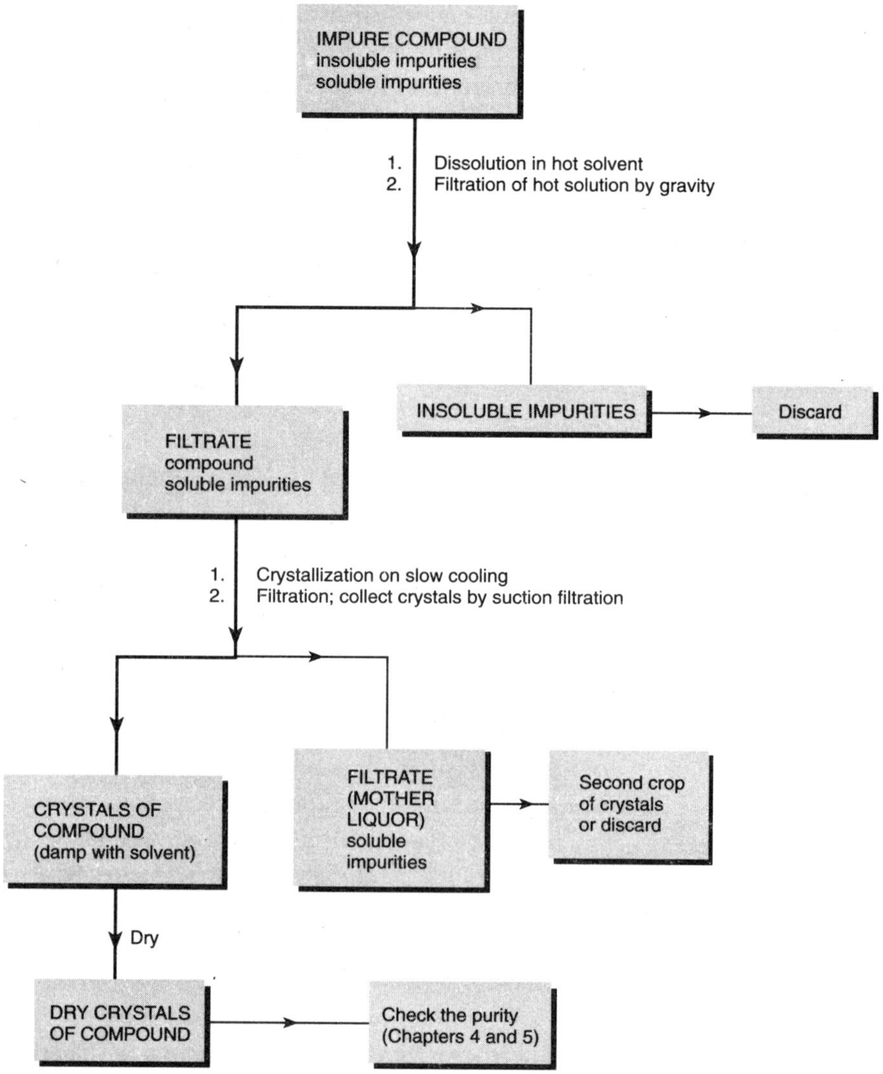

Fig. 3.41 Plan for purification of an organic compound by crystallization.

purity of the crystals can then be determined (Chapters 4 and 5), and if necessary further purification by *recrystallization* can be carried out. Before discussing each of the stages in the process in detail, we should briefly consider how crystallization succeeds in purifying compounds at all.

How crystallization works

The technique involves dissolving the impure solid in the minimum volume of a hot solvent and filtering to remove insoluble impurities. The resulting hot saturated solution of the compound, together with any soluble impurities, is set aside to cool slowly, whereupon crystals of pure compound will separate from solution. The solution remaining after crystallization is usually known as the *mother liquor*. Why are the crystals pure? The process of crystallization is an equilibrium: molecules in solution are in equilibrium with those in the crystal lattice. Since a crystal lattice is highly ordered, other different molecules, such as impurities, will be excluded from the lattice and will return to the solution. Therefore only molecules of the required compound are retained in the crystal lattice and the impurities will remain in solution. For a crystallization to be successful, *the solution must be allowed to cool slowly*, so that the crystals are formed slowly, and the equilibrium process which excludes the impurities is allowed to operate. If a solution is cooled rapidly, impurity molecules will be trapped or included in the rapidly growing crystal lattice. This rapid formation of solid material from solution is *precipitation*, and is not the same as crystallization.

Slow cooling

At this stage it should be pointed out that crystallization does not always work. Substances which are grossly impure will often refuse to crystallize, and in these cases some preliminary purification by another technique, such as extraction (pp. 118–130) or chromatography (pp. 160–203), may be necessary.

Dissolution

The first problem is to dissolve the impure substance in a suitable solvent. The ideal solvent for a crystallization should not react with the compound, should be fairly volatile so that it is easy to remove from the crystals, should have a boiling point that is lower than the melting point of the compound to be crystallized, should be non-toxic and non-flammable, but most important of all, the compound should be very soluble in hot solvent and insoluble in cold solvent. In many cases, particularly when crystallizing known compounds, you will know what solvent to use because the literature or your laboratory text will tell you. In other cases, you will have to decide what solvent to use. Choosing a solvent for crystallization is not always easy, but organic chemists tend to follow the rule that 'like dissolves like'. So, for the crystallization of non-polar substances such as hydrocarbons, use a non-polar solvent such as pentane or light petroleum. Compounds containing polar groups such as OH are best crystallized from polar OH-containing solvents such as ethanol. Indeed polar solvents are often preferred for other compounds because they tend to give better crystals. Some suggestions for crystallization solvents for the most common classes of organic compound, arranged in order of increasing polarity, are given in Table 3.6.

Like dissolves like

If the crystallization solvent is not known for certain, do not commit all your solid and attempt to dissolve it up. Rather, carry out some preliminary solubility tests. To do this, place a small quantity of the solid (*ca.* 20 mg or the amount that fits on the tip of a micro-spatula) in a small test tube—an ignition tube or a 10 × 75 mm test tube is ideal—and add a few drops of solvent to the tube. If the substance dissolves easily in cold solvent, try again with a different solvent. If the substance is insoluble in cold solvent, warm the tube on a steam or water bath, and if the substance remains insoluble, add more solvent with continued heating. If the compound still refuses to dissolve, try again with a

Test the solubility

Use a hood if the solvent is toxic

Use a steam bath for heating flammable solvents

Table 3.6 Suggested solvents for crystallization.

Class of compound	Suggested solvents
Hydrocarbons	Light petroleum, pentane, cyclohexane, toluene
Ethers	Diethyl ether, dichloromethane
Halides	Dichloromethane
Carbonyl compounds	Ethyl acetate, acetone
Alcohols, acids	Ethanol
Salts	Water

different solvent. Once you have found a solvent that dissolves the compound when hot, you need to check that the solid will separate again on cooling. Place the tube in a beaker of ice-water, and leave it to stand for a minute or two. If a solid forms on cooling, the solvent is probably suitable for crystallization of the bulk material. With experience, these preliminary solubility tests can be carried out quickly, and provide a satisfactory guide to the choice of crystallization solvent.

Always keep a seed crystal

Once you have found a suitable solvent, you are ready to dissolve up the solid for crystallization. Before doing so, it is a good idea to weigh the solid, if you have not already done so, so that the recovery of material from the crystallization process can be determined. If the substance is already crystalline, do not dissolve all of it. Always retain a few crystals in case they are needed for seeding purposes (see p. 136). Large crystals are often difficult to dissolve, and should be ground up before adding the crystallization solvent.

Mixed solvents for crystallization

If a suitable crystallization solvent cannot be found, then you may have to use a *mixed solvent system*. A mixed solvent system is a pair of miscible solvents, chosen so that one of them (the good solvent) dissolves the compound readily, and the other (the poor solvent) does not. For example, many moderately polar organic compounds are soluble in diethyl ether, but not in light petroleum, and therefore a mixture of the two solvents may be suitable for crystallization. There are two schools of thought on how to carry out a crystallization using mixed solvents. One method is to dissolve the solid in the minimum volume of hot good solvent, add the poor solvent dropwise until the solution starts to become slightly turbid or cloudy, and then set the solution aside to crystallize. The second method is to suspend the solid in hot poor solvent, and then add the good solvent dropwise with continued heating until the solid *just* dissolves; then set the solution aside as before. Typical mixed solvent systems that often work quite well include diethyl ether–light petroleum, dichloromethane–light petroleum, diethyl ether–acetone and ethanol–water. If possible choose a system in which the good solvent is the lower boiling solvent. One final word of warning: the use of mixed solvents often encourages *oiling out* (see p. 136), and therefore crystallization from a single solvent is preferred.

Filtration

Once your compound is in solution in a hot solvent, the solution should be filtered to remove any insoluble material. This material may be an insoluble impurity or by-product or may simply be pieces of extraneous material such as dust, glass or paper. The solution should be filtered under gravity through a fluted filter paper into an Erlenmeyer flask using the technique described on pp. 75–77.

Use hand protection for hot filtration

In some cases the solution of your organic compound will be strongly coloured by impurities. This is not a problem, provided that the coloured impurities remain in solution. However, occasionally they are adsorbed by the crystals as they form, to give an impure, coloured product. Luckily the fact that such impurity molecules are easily adsorbed can be used to remove them from solution. This process is usually known as *decolourization*, and involves treating the hot solution with activated charcoal, often known as decolourizing carbon or under the trade name Norit®. To decolourize a solution add a small quantity of activated charcoal, usually about 2% by weight of the sample, to the hot, but not boiling, solution. If the solution is at or close to its boiling point, the addition of the finely divided charcoal will cause it to boil over. Continue to heat the solution containing the charcoal for about 5–10 min with occasional swirling or stirring. By this time the impurity molecules responsible for the colour should have been adsorbed by the charcoal, and filtration of the mixture should give a decolourized solution of the organic compound. The filtration can be carried out under gravity through a fluted filter paper, although a second filtration may be necessary to remove all the fine particles of charcoal.

Decolourization

Use a steam bath for heating flammable solvents

Crystallization and what to do if no crystals are formed

Having filtered your hot solution into an Erlenmeyer flask, cover the flask with a watch glass to prevent contamination by atmospheric dust, and then set it aside so that the solution can cool slowly. The rate of cooling determines the size of the crystals, rapid cooling favouring the formation of a lot of small crystals, and slow cooling encouraging the growth of fewer, but much larger, crystals. A convenient compromise between speed of crystallization and crystal quality is to allow the hot solution to cool to room temperature by placing the flask on a surface such as glass or cork that does not conduct the heat away too quickly. The *rate* of crystallization is usually greatest at about 50°C below the melting point of the substance, and maximum formation of crystals occurs at about 100°C below the melting point. Once the crystals have formed, it is usually a good idea to cool the solution from room temperature to about 0°C by placing the Erlenmeyer in an ice bath. This will ensure that the maximum amount of crystals are obtained. It is not usually good practice to cool the solution below 0°C, unless there are special problems in getting crystals to form in the first place (see p. 136), because this results in condensation of water vapour into the solution unless special precautions are taken.

What do you do when no crystallization occurs after cooling the solution to room temperature? You should attempt to induce crystallization by one of the following methods. Add a seed crystal which was saved from the original material before dissolution. This will provide a nucleus on which other crystals can grow. If this fails, try scratching the side of the flask with a glass rod. This is thought to produce micro-fragments of glass which then serve as nuclei to induce crystallization. If this fails, try cooling the flask in an acetone–solid CO_2 bath (see p. 107), and then scratch the side of the flask as the solution warms up to room temperature. If the substance still refuses to crystallize, it probably means that you have too much solvent; the excess solvent should be boiled off (**hood—check for flames in the vicinity**), and the reduced volume of solution should be set aside again until crystallization occurs.

Seeding

Scratching

Cooling

Remove solvents in a hood and check for flames first

The final problem that may be encountered in crystallization is the separation of the substance as an oil rather than as crystals. This is known as *oiling out*, and usually occurs when the compound is very impure or when it has a melting point that is lower than the boiling point of the solvent. Even if the oil eventually solidifies, the compound will not be pure, and the material should be redissolved by heating the solution. You may need to add a little more solvent at this stage, or more good solvent if mixed solvents are being used. Indeed, crystallization from a slightly more dilute solution may prevent oiling out. Slower cooling also favours the formation of crystals rather than oils. If the compound completely refuses to crystallize, the chances are that it is too impure, and it should be purified by some other means such as chromatography.

Oiling out

Collecting the crystals

After crystallization the crystals are separated from the *mother liquor* by suction filtration, a technique which has already been discussed in detail on pp. 77–79. After filtration, the crystals should be washed with a little fresh solvent. Remember that if the crystallization has been performed using mixed solvents, the wash solvent should be the same mixture.

The mother liquor from the crystallization (which is now the filtrate) may still contain a significant quantity of your organic product. In this case a second batch of crystals, known as the *second crop*, can often be obtained by concentrating the mother liquor by boiling off some of the solvent (**hood—check for flames in the vicinity)** and then allowing the solution to cool and crystallize as before. However, be warned, the second crop is usually less pure than the first simply because the impurities were concentrated in the mother liquor during the first crystallization. Do not combine the two crops of crystals until you have checked the purity of each batch.

Remove solvents in a hood and check for flames first

Second crop will be less pure

Drying the crystals

After filtration and washing, the crystals should be dried to constant weight. Techniques for drying solids are discussed on pp. 140–143.

Special crystallization techniques

Crystallization of very small quantities

When the amount of material to be crystallized is less than about 100 mg, the normal techniques of crystallization are inappropriate because of the losses of material that would occur, particularly during filtration. To crystallize small quantities (10–100 mg) of organic compounds, place the solid in a *very small* test tube, and dissolve it up in the minimum volume of hot solvent in the usual way. It is impossible to filter very small volumes of solution using the normal technique, so another method is needed. One way is to put a small plug of cotton wool in the tip of a Pasteur pipette and then slowly draw the hot solution through the cotton wool into the pipette (Fig. 3.42a). The cotton wool will retain all but the finest of insoluble impurities. Quickly remove the wool from the end of the pipette using a pair of tweezers, and then release the hot solution from the pipette into the *pre-weighed* vessel where it will be allowed to crystallize. To avoid spills, it is safer to hold the Pasteur pipette over the crystallization vessel whilst removing the cotton wool. The mother liquor should be removed using a Pasteur pipette, taking care not to suck up any crystals (Fig. 3.42b). A small amount of wash solvent can be added, and can then be removed by pipette. The damp crystals should be dried in the same tube by placing it in a suitable drying apparatus (see Fig. 3.44).

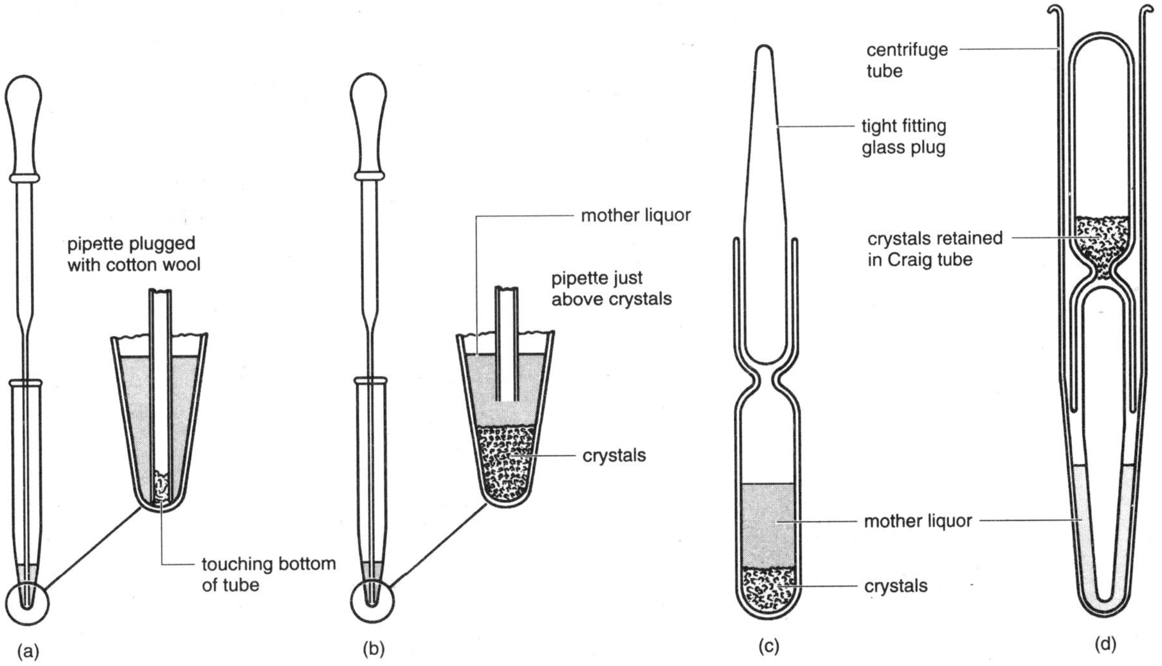

Fig. 3.42 (a) Using a Pasteur pipette and cotton wool for filtration; (b) removing the mother liquor with a Pasteur pipette; (c) Craig tube before centrifugation; (d) Craig tube after centrifugation.

The ideal vessels for the crystallization of small quantities of material are small conical-bottomed centrifuge tubes or tubes specially designed for the purpose known as *Craig tubes*. The idea is to minimize the number of transfers and to avoid having to collect the crystals by filtration. Craig tubes (Fig. 3.42c,d) are designed so that the mother liquor from the crystallization can be removed by *centrifugation*. The hot filtrate is transferred to the Craig tube as described above, and the crystallization is allowed to proceed. When crystallization is complete, insert the well-fitting glass 'plug' of the Craig tube, place an empty inverted centrifuge tube over the Craig tube, and invert the whole, making sure that the two parts of the Craig tube do not separate. Place the tube in the centrifuge, make sure the centrifuge is balanced, and spin for 20–30 s. The centrifugation will force the mother liquor past the glass plug, but the crystals will be retained by the plug (Fig. 3.42d). The Craig tube plus crystals is then placed in a suitable drying apparatus to dry the crystals.

Craig tubes

Always balance the centrifuge rotor arm with another centrifuge tube containing enough water to make the weights equal

When the crystals are dry, the crystallization tube can be weighed, and provided that the empty weight was recorded, the weight of crystals can be determined. The crystals can be removed from the tube by inverting it over a piece of filter or weighing paper, and gently tapping it.

Fractional crystallization

Fractional crystallization is a rather special technique for separating two compounds by repeated crystallization. Although chromatography has largely supplanted fractional crystallization as a separation method, the technique still has its uses, particularly in the resolution of racemic acids or bases by separation of their crystalline diastereomeric salts formed by reaction with optically active bases or acids, respectively. A schematic plan for a fractional crystallization is shown in Fig. 3.43. The first crystallization gives crystals (C_1) and mother liquor (ML_1). These are separated in the normal way, and the crys-

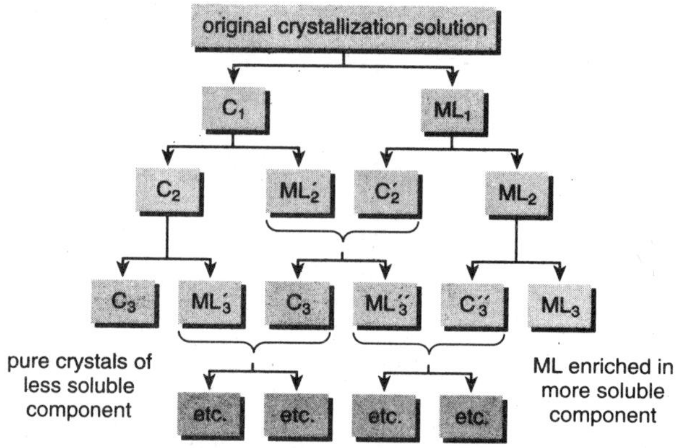

Fig. 3.43 Schematic plan for fractional crystallization.

tals are recrystallized to give crystals C_2 and mother liquor ML'_2. The first mother liquor is evaporated to dryness, and the residue is redissolved and crystallized to give crystals C'_2 and mother liquor ML_2. The crystals C'_2 are combined with ML'_2, the solvent is evaporated, and the residue is crystallized further. As the scheme unfolds, pure crystals of the less soluble component are obtained and the mother liquor becomes enriched in the more soluble component. In practice it is fairly easy to obtain a pure, less soluble component after two or three crystallizations, but the more soluble component may require further purification by some other technique.

Crystals for X-ray crystallography

Good crystals are an essential requirement if the material is to be submitted for X-ray structure analysis. Therefore the growth of X-ray quality crystals is a special skill requiring considerable patience. The simplest technique is to allow the solvent to evaporate very slowly from the crystallization flask. In practice this means leaving the open flask to stand at room temperature, **in a hood if the solvent is toxic**, whilst the solvent slowly evaporates.

Allow toxic solvents to evaporate in a hood

An alternative technique for the crystallization of compounds for X-ray analysis relies on *slow diffusion* between two different solvents. In this variant on mixed solvent crystallization, it is essential that the 'good' solvent is more dense than the 'poor' solvent. Dissolve the compound in a small volume of good solvent, such as dichloromethane, in a small sample vial, the narrower the better. *Carefully* run in an equal volume of poor solvent, such as light petroleum, on top of the first solvent, stopper the vial, and set it aside. It is essential that all of this is done very carefully so that the two solvents do not mix and the interface remains clearly visible. Over the next few hours or days, diffusion between the layers will occur, and, all being well, crystals will form at the interface. This process, although rather slow, encourages the formation of good quality crystals.

A new technique for crystallizing organic compounds that give poor quality crystals or that give crystals in only small amounts in *co-crystallization* with triphenylphosphine oxide. Triphenylphosphine oxide itself gives high quality crystals, and this property is apparently carried over to the complexes it forms with a range of other organic molecules. Triphenylphosphine oxide forms complexes with most organic molecules that contain an active hydrogen (OH, NH), the complex being stabilized by hydrogen bonding to the phosphoryl P=O. The crystalline complexes are formed by dissolving equimolar amounts of your compound and triphenylphosphine oxide in toluene, and allowing the toluene to evaporate slowly. The crystals are collected in the usual way, washed quickly with a little acetone followed by light petroleum, and then dried in air. One final word of caution: having obtained beautiful crystals by this technique, do check that they are not simply triphenylphosphine oxide itself before giving them to your X-ray crystallographer!

Further reading

For further discussion of growing crystals for X-ray analysis, see: P.G. Jones, *Chem. Br.*, 1981, **17**, 222.

The co-crystallization technique was reported by: M.C. Etter and P.W. Baures, *J. Am. Chem. Soc.*, 1988, **110**, 639.

J. Hulliger, Chemistry and crystal growth, *Angew. Chem. Int. Edn.*, 1994, **33**, 143–162.

Drying solids

Suck the solid dry on the filter

When an organic solid has been obtained by filtration of a reaction mixture, or when crystals have been obtained from a crystallization, the organic compound must be thoroughly dried before it can be weighed or analyzed or used in the next step of a reaction sequence. As described on p. 79, some preliminary drying can be carried out whilst the sample is still on the filter paper in the Büchner funnel. Press the filtered solid down onto the filter paper, and continue the suction for about 5 min. In this way the solid can be sucked fairly dry.

Another simple technique for drying solids is called *air drying*. Spread the crystals or solid out on a watch glass or large piece of filter paper, and allow them to dry in the air. However, air drying is slow, especially if water or some other high boiling solvent has been used.

Never heat compounds to their melting point to dry them

The *rate* of drying can be increased by increasing the rate of solvent evaporation from the solid. The simplest way to do this is to place the sample in an oven where it can be heated. Before doing this, however, you need to have a rough idea of the melting point of the compound. Organic compounds should never be heated to their melting point to dry them; for safety it is best to set the oven at about 30–50°C *below* the melting point of the compound. **Compounds that are thermally unstable should not be dried by heating.**

Drying pistols

Another way to increase the rate of evaporation of solvent from solids is to place the sample in an apparatus that can be evacuated by attaching it to a water aspirator or vacuum pump. Low boiling solvents are removed quickly under reduced pressure, and the drying process is reasonably efficient. The process is more efficient still if the sample is heated under reduced pressure, but you should take care that your compound will not *sublime* under these conditions. *Vacuum ovens* are useful for drying large quantities of solid materials, but for normal laboratory-scale working (200 mg to 5 g), a purpose designed *drying pistol* should be used. There are two basic types of drying pistol: the *Abderhalden* type (Fig. 3.44a) and the electrically heated type (Fig. 3.44b). Both consist of a horizontal chamber (in two parts, joined with a large diameter tapered glass joint) which can be evacuated through the stopcock. The sample to be dried is placed in a vial, which is introduced into the apparatus through the middle joint. It is a good idea to wrap a piece of copper wire around the sample vial to act as a 'handle' and to facilitate the eventual removal of the vial from the apparatus. In the Abderhalden design, the evacuated chamber is heated by hot solvent vapour from the refluxing solvent in the

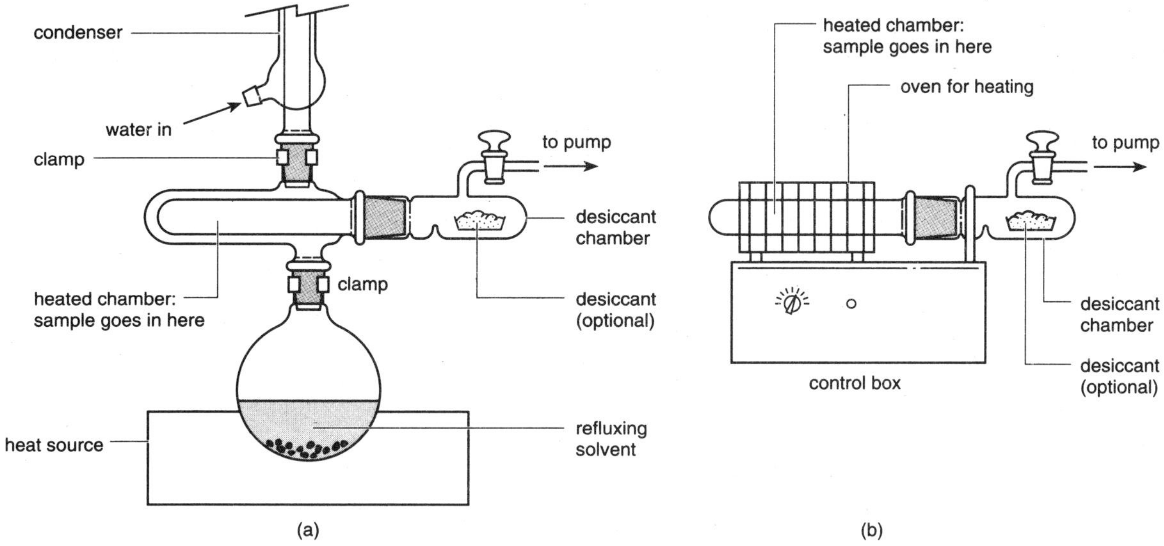

Fig. 3.44 (a) Abderhalden drying pistol; (b) electrically heated drying pistol.

round-bottomed flask below the apparatus. A condenser should be attached to the top of the apparatus. The degree of heating of the sample is controlled by the boiling point of the solvent used. The electrically heated design is more adaptable in that heating is provided by an outer glass furnace containing heating coils, which can be set to the desired temperature. Both designs incorporate a *desiccant* chamber in the unheated region of the tube.

Desiccants or *drying agents* are not normally needed when drying solids that are wet with organic solvents, but they are very useful when removing water from organic solids. Water removal at room temperature is carried out in a *desiccator* (Fig. 3.45), and the drying agent, such as anhydrous calcium chloride, is placed in the bottom of the desiccator. The sample to be dried is placed on a watch glass on the shelf above. When the cover is in place and the system is closed, the drying agent 'soaks up' the water from the atmosphere in the desiccator as the water evaporates from the solid. The drying process can be speeded up by evacuating the desiccator, and many desiccators are fitted with a vacuum take-off stopcock. For safety, an evacuated desiccator should be surrounded by a wire mesh cage, to prevent injury from flying glass should an implosion occur. Desiccants can also be used in drying pistols; the desiccant is placed in a tube or 'boat' in the unheated part of the apparatus as indicated in Fig. 3.44.

Put a safety cage around an evacuated desiccator

Drying agents that are commonly used in desiccators (Table 3.7) are: calcium chloride, calcium sulfate (Drierite®), potassium hydroxide, phosphorus pentoxide and concentrated sulfuric acid. Obviously great care should be taken when using some of these highly corrosive materials, and the use of concentrated sulfuric acid is best avoided. Check that the desiccant is fresh and

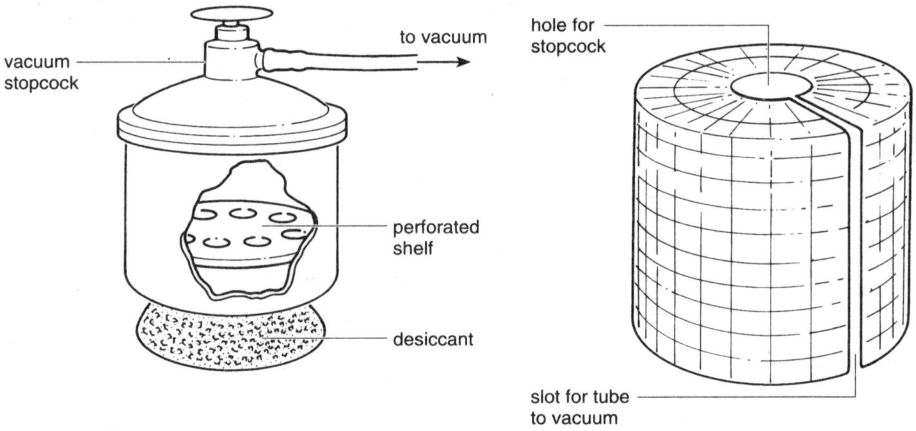

Fig. 3.45 Vacuum desiccator (with mesh safety cage).

Table 3.7 Common drying agents for use in desiccators.

Solvent to be removed	Desiccant
H_2O	$CaCl_2$, $CaSO_4$, silica gel, solid KOH, P_2O_5, H_2SO_4 (concentrated)
MeOH, EtOH	$CaCl_2$
Hydrocarbons, halogenated solvents	Freshly cut shavings of paraffin wax
CH_3CO_2H, aqueous HCl	Solid KOH + silica gel (kept separately)
Aqueous NH_3	H_2SO_4 (concentrated)

active. Phosphorus pentoxide is very efficient when new because it actually reacts with the water, but rapidly forms a glassy coating which markedly reduces its capacity to react with water.

The sample to be dried should be broken up on a suitably sized watch glass or petri dish to give it as large a surface area as possible, before placing it in the desiccator and evacuating the system. It is advisable to include a water trap (see Fig. 2.19, p. 38) between the water aspirator and the desiccator to prevent flooding in case of suck-back. At all times whilst under vacuum, the desiccator *must* be kept under its protective cover. At the end of the drying period, the vacuum can be released in a controlled manner by holding a filter paper to the inlet tube with the index finger and opening the stopcock. On removing the finger, air is sucked in gently through the filter paper holding it in place until the inside of the desiccator reaches atmospheric pressure, allowing the filter paper to fall off. The sample may now be removed safely. If such a precaution is not taken, the violent inrush of air will spread the sample all around the interior of the desiccator.

Release vacuum slowly

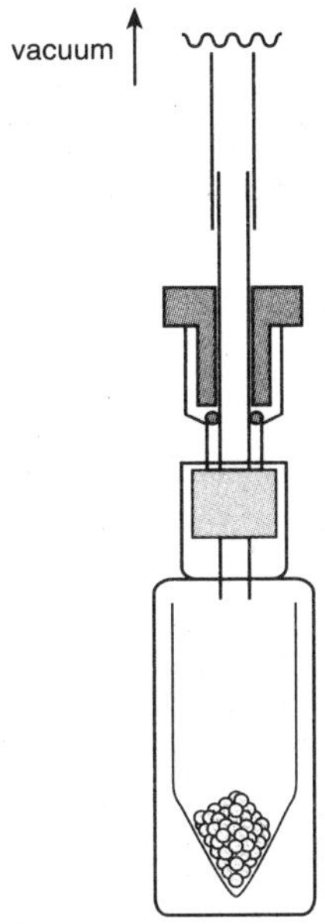

Fig. 3.46 Improvised microscale drying pistol; the vacuum connection is provided using a short length of glass tubing and a commercial threaded adapter.

A drying pistol can be improvised for drying small quantities of solid using an aspirator, a tapered or threaded reaction vial and a threaded adapter. Figure 3.46 shows a typical set-up; gentle warming of the vial in a sand or water bath can be used to increase the rate of solvent evaporation.

Distillation

The history of distillation goes back to about the second century BC when the still was invented at the school of alchemists in Alexandria for 'refining powders'. However, it was not until the twelfth century AD that the art of distillation was rediscovered as a way of producing alcoholic liquor that was much stronger than wine or beer. By the thirteenth century, distillation of alcoholic beverages (spirits) was well established. Indeed the word *alcohol* derives from the Arabic *al-koh'l*, the word for the refined powders obtained from the original stills of Alexandria.

In the organic laboratory, distillation is one of the main techniques for purifying volatile liquids. It involves vapourizing the material by heating it, and subsequently condensing the vapour back to a liquid, the *distillate*. There are various ways in which a distillation can be carried out, but in practice the choice of distillation procedure depends on the properties of the liquid that you are trying to purify and on the properties of the impurities that you are trying to separate. This section deals with the most common distillation techniques: *simple distillation, fractional distillation, distillation under reduced pressure, short path and microscale distillation and steam distillation.* In

Types of distillation

addition, *sublimation*, the purification of a solid by conversion to the vapour phase and condensation back to a solid, without going through a liquid phase, is also covered. As in other sections, the main aim is to concentrate on the practical application of the techniques, and hence a detailed discussion of the theory of distillation is inappropriate. Nevertheless, a brief consideration of the theoretical aspects of distillation is warranted.

Theoretical aspects

The *vapour pressure* of a liquid increases with temperature, and the point at which the vapour pressure equals the pressure above the liquid is defined as the *boiling point*. Pure liquids which do not decompose on heating have a sharp well-defined boiling point, although the boiling point will vary considerably with changes in pressure. A further discussion of boiling points is included on pp. 213–218, but from a practical viewpoint, if a reasonably pure liquid is distilled, the temperature of the vapour increases until it reaches the boiling point of the liquid. At this point the liquid and vapour are in thermal equilibrium with each other, and the distillation will proceed at a reasonably constant temperature. However, since we are using distillation to purify our organic compound, we are, by definition, distilling a mixture. The mixture may consist of 95% of the compound we require, together with 5% of unknown impurities, or it may be a mixture containing 50% product and 50% starting material. Whatever the situation, we need to consider the implications of the distillation of mixtures of volatile liquids.

The underlying principles of the distillation of mixtures of miscible liquids are embodied in two laws of physical chemistry: Dalton's law and Raoult's law. *Dalton's law of partial pressures* states that the total pressure of a gas, or vapour pressure of a liquid (P), is the sum of the *partial pressures* of its individual components A and B (P_A and P_B). So

Dalton's law

$$P = P_A + P_B$$

Raoult's law states that, at a given temperature and pressure, the partial vapour pressure of a compound in a mixture (P_A) is equal to the vapour pressure of the pure compound (P_A^{pure}) multiplied by its *mole fraction* (X_A) in the mixture:

Raoult's law

$$P_A = P_A^{pure} \times X_A$$

Hence, from both laws, the total vapour pressure of a liquid mixture is dependent on the vapour pressures of the pure components and their mole fractions in the mixture.

Dalton's law and Raoult's law are mathematical expressions of what happens during a distillation, and they describe the changes in the compositions of the boiling liquid and the vapour (and hence the distillate) with temperature as the distillation proceeds. Plots of vapour composition and liquid composition versus temperature can therefore be made. They are usually combined onto a single diagram known as a *phase diagram* or, sometimes, as a boiling point–composition diagram. An example is shown in Fig. 3.47. This figure shows the distillation of a two-component mixture of miscible liquids with: (a) markedly different boiling points (broken line), and (b) similar boiling points (full line). But what does it mean in terms of the *practical* aspects of distillation?

Assume that we start with a 1 : 1 mixture of the two miscible components A and B (component A having the lower boiling point) which we are to separate by simple distillation. At the start of the distillation when the liquid starts to boil, the composition of the liquid is 50 mol% of each component, and the composition of the vapour is determined by drawing a horizontal line from the liquid line to the vapour line. In the first instance, where the components have widely differing boiling points (broken line), the vapour consists of almost pure A. When most of the more volatile A has been removed from the vapour by condensation, further heating will cause a rise in temperature to the boiling point of component B. Hence the two liquids are easily separated in a *single* distillation. In practical terms this will usually be possible if the vapour pressure of the more volatile liquid is at least 10 times that of the other liquid. Translated into boiling points, this means that it is usually possible to separate, almost completely, liquids which differ in their boiling points by at least 80°C.

If the boiling points are closer (full line), the composition of the vapour as the liquid starts to boil is about 85% A and 15% B. Hence pure A cannot be obtained in a single distillation. Clearly the material containing 85% A could be subsequently redistilled to give purer A, which could be redistilled again and again until pure material was obtained. Such a series of single distillations would be extremely time consuming and tedious, so obviously an alternative

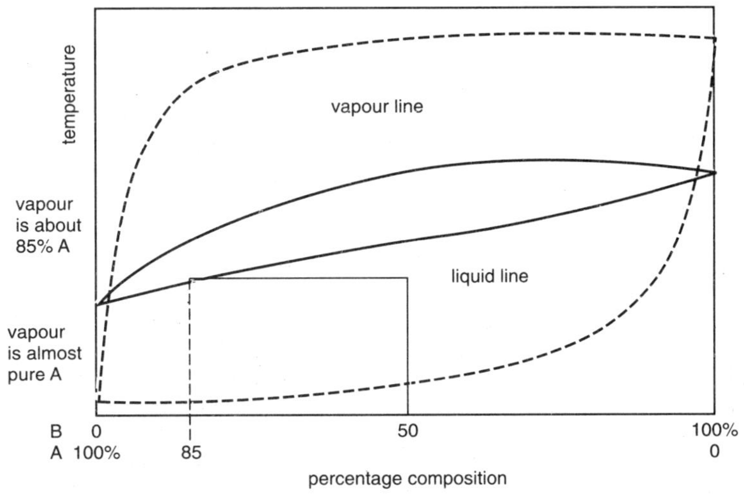

Fig. 3.47 Simple phase diagram for distillation of a two-component mixture (- - -: components with markedly different bp; —: components with similar bp).

method is needed in this situation. *Fractional distillation* is such a method, and is discussed in more detail on pp. 148–152.

Azeotropes

Many two-component mixtures do not follow Raoult's law, and therefore do not give idealized phase diagrams. Some mixtures, particularly those in which one of the components contains a hydroxyl (OH) group, distil at a constant boiling point and with constant composition. In this case the liquids are said to form an *azeotrope* or *azeotropic mixture*, a phenomenon which is discussed in more detail on pp. 214–216. Azeotropic mixtures cannot be separated by distillation.

Simple distillation

Scale

To carry out a simple distillation, set up the apparatus as shown in Fig. 3.48. The apparatus consists of a round-bottomed distillation flask (often referred to as the 'pot'), a still head, and a condenser equipped with a receiver adapter attached to the *preweighed* receiving flask. **Make sure that the apparatus is adequately supported with clamps.** The size of glassware used for the apparatus should be dictated by the *scale* of the distillation, but many laboratory operations are on the 10–100 g scale. Occasionally it will be necessary to distil smaller quantities (2–10 g), and therefore smaller glassware should be used. Glassware with size Ŧ 10 tapered joints is convenient for this purpose. For yet smaller scale distillations (50 mg to 2 g), the *short path distillation* techniques (see pp. 154–155, 158–159) should be used. Whatever the scale, always use a distillation flask that is at least 1.5 times the volume of sample.

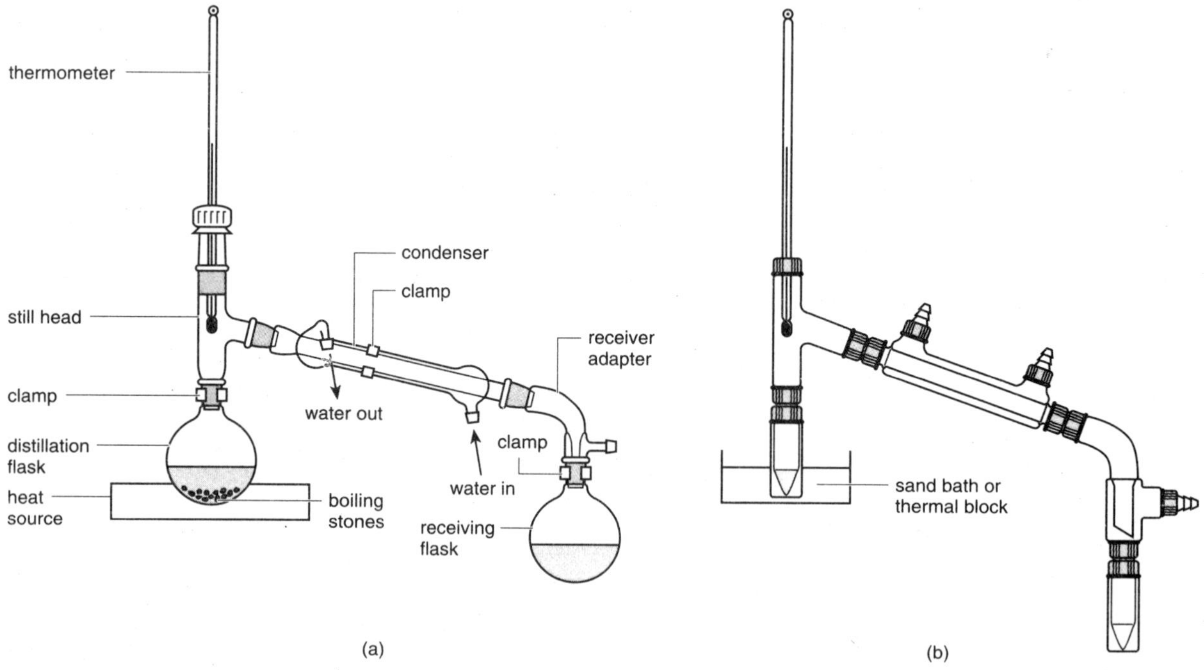

Fig. 3.48 (a) Apparatus for simple distillation. (b) Microscale distillation.

Transfer the liquid to be distilled to the distillation flask using a funnel through the neck of the still head, and add some boiling stones (anti-bumping granules) to the flask to ensure smooth boiling without 'bumping'. Fit the thermometer adapter and set the thermometer at such a height that it measures the temperature of the vapour passing over the angle of the still head, not the liquid condensing back into the flask. Heat the distillation flask in an appropriate heat source, the choice of which is influenced by both the nature and boiling point of the liquid. A water or steam bath should always be used for low boiling (less than 85°C) flammable liquids. For higher boiling liquids, an electrically heated oil bath is best. Mantles are less controllable and should only be used for the distillation of solvents. Burners are best avoided. When the liquid starts to boil, collect the condensed vapours in one or more portions, or *fractions*, in the receiving flask.

Heating

For the reasons outlined above, simple distillation can only be used to separate components that differ in boiling point by at least 80°C. More commonly, however, it is used to purify volatile components that are already fairly pure, by separating them from high boiling impurities, for example. If the liquid is relatively pure, a small amount of distillate containing the lower boiling impurities will be collected whilst the temperature at the still head is still rising; this is known as the *fore-run*. As soon as the still head temperature reaches a constant value, the main fraction can be collected, and the distillation can be continued until the bulk of the liquid has been obtained. The higher boiling impurities will remain as the residue in the distillation flask. Never attempt to distil the liquid to dryness; always leave a residue in the distillation flask. Distillation to dryness is potentially very dangerous since it involves strong heating of the material. The nature of any high boiling impurity would not be known, and hence heating it could result in a thermal decomposition reaction which may be violent.

Simple distillation will completely separate liquids that differ in boiling point by about 80°C

Never distil to dryness

If the simple distillation is being used to separate two components with widely differing boiling points, you should keep a close watch on the still head temperature. As soon as most of the more volatile compound has been collected, the temperature will start to rise, and the receiving flask should be removed, and replaced with a preweighed empty one. Collect the distillate in the second flask as long as the temperature continues to rise. This distillate will contain *both* components (*mixed fractions*), but should only account for a small fraction of the total volume. When the still head temperature becomes constant again, change the receiving flask for another preweighed empty one and collect the second component. Finally, weigh all the receiving flasks to determine the weight of each fraction. The results of a simple distillation should be recorded in a table as shown in Table 3.8.

Distilling solvents

One very common use of the simple distillation technique is in the purification of organic solvents. These are supplied in a relatively pure form which is

Table 3.8 Reporting the results of a distillation.

	bp (°C)	Weight (g)
Amount of sample to distil: 12.5 g		
Fore-run	45–88	0.5
Component A	88–90	4.8
Mixed fractions	90–180	0.9
Component B	180–183	4.2
Residue		*ca.* 2.0

adequate for most purposes, but occasionally need to be purified by distillation. For certain reactions, particularly those involving moisture-sensitive substrates, it is essential that the solvent be purified before use. In this case the purpose of distillation, as well as removing the small amounts of low and high boiling impurities, is to remove any water from the solvent. To this end a *drying agent* is often added to the distillation flask, and the solvent is said to be distilled *from* the drying agent. A list of suitable drying agents for particular solvents is given in Appendix 2 (p. 677).

If there is a regular need for distilled solvent, then it is more convenient and efficient to set up a special solvent still. An example of such a solvent still is shown in Fig. 3.49. It consists of a large distillation flask, connected to a reflux condenser via a piece of glassware which can simply be a pressure equalizing funnel modified by the inclusion of a second stopcock. Since the production of very dry solvents usually requires the exclusion of (moist) air from the apparatus, the still is fitted so that it can be operated under an inert atmosphere. With stopcock A open the solvent simply refluxes over the drying agent. When stopcock A is closed the solvent vapour passes up the narrow tube, condenses, and dry solvent collects in the central piece of the apparatus, which for convenience is often graduated. When the required volume of solvent has been collected, it can be run off, directly into the reaction flask if necessary, through stopcock B. Alternatively, smaller volumes of up to 50 mL may be drawn off by syringe through a side port closed with a septum. For safety reasons solvent stills must be closely monitored in case the water supply should fail or in case the liquid in the distillation flask should get too close to dryness.

Solvent stills must be supervised

Fractional distillation

As we have seen above, the main problem with simple distillation is that it is ineffective in the separation of compounds whose boiling points differ by less than about 80°C. One way around this problem is to carry out repeated simple redistillations until the material is adequately pure, but this is prohibitively time consuming. In practice one uses the technique of *fractional distillation*. The apparatus (Fig. 3.50) for fractional distillation only differs from that for

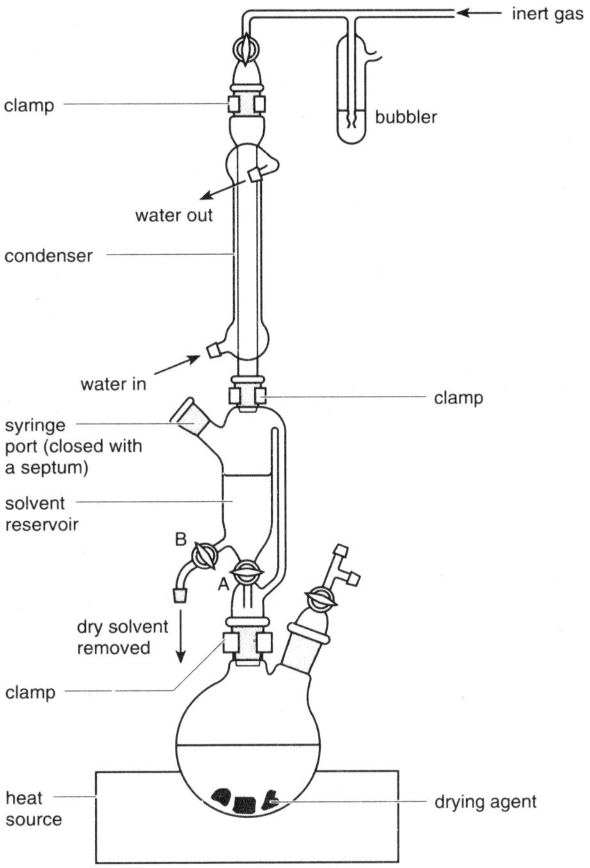

Fig. 3.49 Solvent still.

The fractionating column should be vertical and may need to be insulated

simple distillation in that a *fractionating column* (see below) is inserted between the distillation flask and the still head. The fractionating column should be perfectly vertical, and it may need to be insulated to prevent undue heat loss. The simplest way to do this is to wrap the column with aluminium foil, shiny side inwards. Since the intention is to collect separate fractions of distillate, a modified receiver adapter is often used at the end of the condenser. These receivers come in various shapes and styles and have rather pictorial names such as 'cows', 'pigs' or 'spiders'. One type is shown in Fig. 3.50, but they all serve the same purpose: to allow you to change over the receiving flask to collect another fraction of distillate simply by rotating the adapter without the need to remove the previous flask. The results of a fractional distillation should be reported in a table as shown for simple distillation, and should include the boiling point and weight of each fraction.

How does fractional distillation work? As the vapour from the distillation flask passes up through the fractionating column, it condenses on the column packing and revapourizes continuously. Each revapourization of the conden-

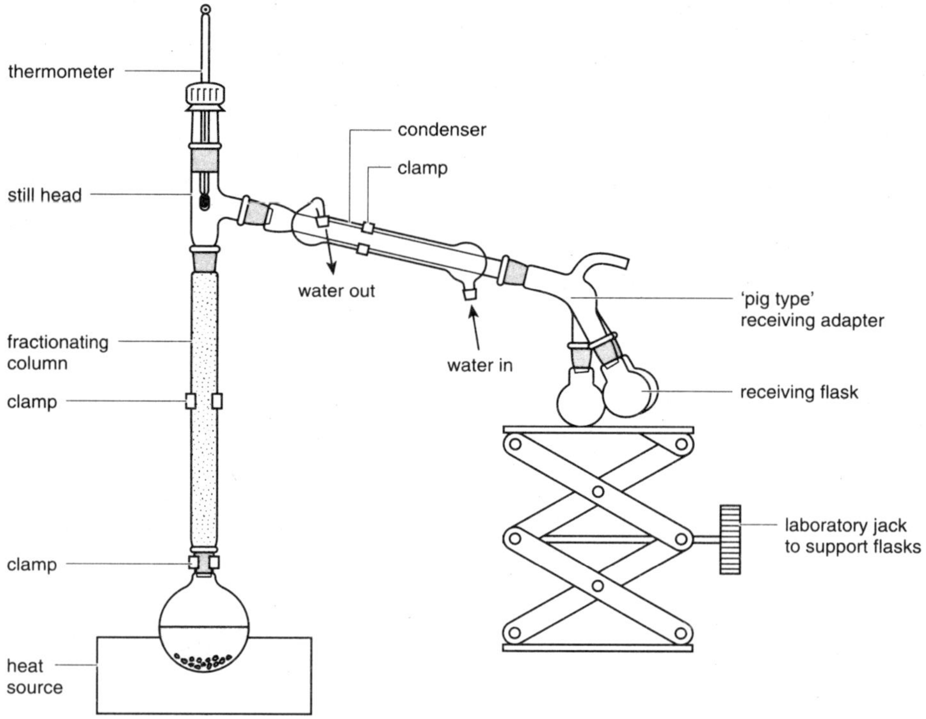

Fig. 3.50 Apparatus for fractional distillation.

sate is equivalent to a simple distillation, and therefore each of these 'separate distillations' leads to a condensate that is successively richer in the more volatile component. All being well, by the time the vapour reaches the still head, the continuous process of condensation and revapourization will have resulted in the vapour, and hence the collected distillate, being substantially enriched in the lower boiling compound. With an efficient fractionating column, the distillate may even consist of *pure* material—the ideal situation.

There are various designs of fractionating column in use in the organic laboratory; some examples are shown in Fig. 3.51. They all contain a surface on which the condensation and revapourization process can occur. This surface varies from the glass projections on the side of the Vigreux column, to the 'spiral' of the Widmer column, and columns packed with glass beads or metal turnings. The efficiency of a fractionating column depends on both its *length* and its *packing* and for columns of the same length, the efficiency is increased by increasing the *surface area* and *heat conductivity* of the packing. Hence for simple fractionating columns the efficiency increases in the order: Vigreux column, column packed with glass beads, column packed with metal turnings.

Column efficiency

Theoretical plates

In more precise terms, the efficiency of a column is expressed in *theoretical plates*, where one theoretical plate is the column that is equivalent to a single simple distillation. Therefore a column with n theoretical plates is equivalent

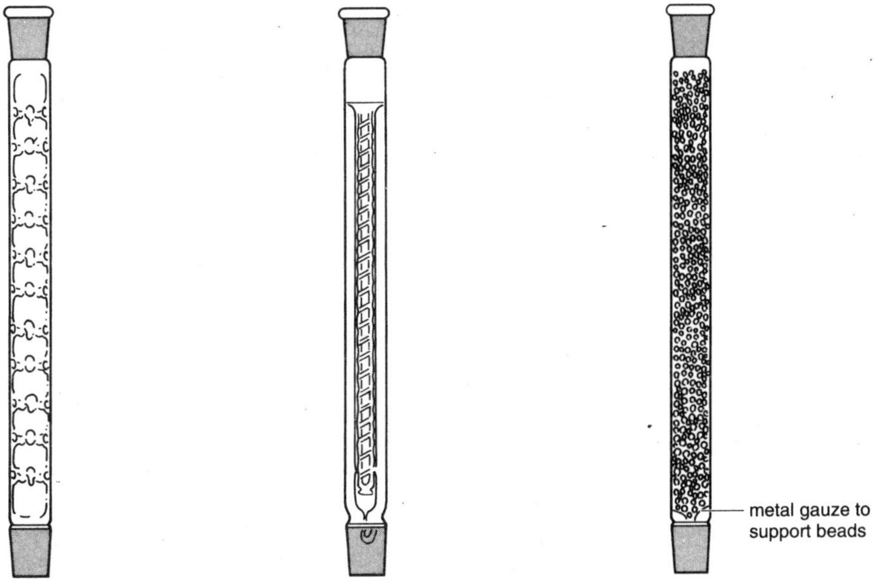

Fig. 3.51 Some types of fractionating columns: (a) Vigreux; (b) Widmer; (c) column packed with glass beads.

to carrying out *n* distillations, and one can reformulate Raoult's law to account for the *n*-fold distillation. Without going into detail, the mathematics show that for a 1 : 1 mixture of compounds having a difference in vapour pressure of a factor of 3 (which represents a difference in boiling point of about 20–30°C) a fractionating column of at least three theoretical plates would be required to obtain the more volatile compound with a purity of at least 95%. In practice most laboratory fractionating columns vary from two to 15 theoretical plates. For example, a column packed with glass beads and of about 25–30 cm length will have an efficiency of about 8–10 theoretical plates, and will adequately separate compounds with boiling points as close as 20°C.

Fractional distillation can completely separate compounds that differ in bp by about 20°C

Two other factors to consider are the *throughput* and *hold-up* of the column. The throughput is the maximum volume of liquid that can be boiled up through the column per minute whilst still maintaining the all important condensation–revapourization equilibrium process within the column. For speed of operation, a high throughput is desirable. Column hold-up is the amount of liquid that is retained on the column packing when the distillation is stopped. Columns with very high surface area packings have a high hold-up and retain a substantial volume of liquid. Hence, although they are highly efficient, they are inappropriate for the fractional distillation of small quantities where loss of sample is unacceptable.

Efficiency vs hold-up

The ultimate form of fractionating column is the *spinning band column* which will separate compounds having boiling point differences of as little as

0.5°C. However, spinning band distillation requires expensive specialized apparatus that is not routinely available, and is therefore beyond the scope of this book.

Distillation under reduced pressure

Since a liquid boils when its vapour pressure equals the pressure above it, you can reduce the boiling point of a liquid by reducing the pressure under which it is distilled. This technique is known as *distillation under reduced pressure* or more simply as *vacuum distillation*. Distillation under reduced pressure is necessary when the liquid has an inconveniently high boiling point, or when the compound is likely to decompose at elevated temperatures. Unfortunately many organic compounds do undergo significant decomposition at high temperatures, and therefore it is usually recommended that the distillation be carried out under reduced pressure if the normal boiling point is greater than about 150°C.

Water aspirator reduces bp by about 100°C

Vacuum pump reduces bp by about 150°C

The first thing to decide before carrying out a reduced pressure distillation is what reduction in pressure is required. As a general guide, halving the pressure will only reduce the boiling point by about 20°C. On the other hand, using a water aspirator vacuum of about 10–20 mmHg will reduce the boiling point by about 100°C, and using a vacuum pump, which will operate down to about 0.1 mmHg pressure, will reduce the boiling point by about 150°C. A slightly more accurate estimate of the boiling point of a liquid at reduced pressure can be obtained from a *nomograph* as shown in Fig. 3.52.

Check for star-cracks

Preventing bumping

Use a fine capillary to stop bumping during vacuum distillation

Two sets of apparatus for distillation under reduced pressure are shown in Fig. 3.53. Both set-ups require the use of suitable flasks that will withstand being evacuated; the flasks should be checked for star-cracks before use. A vacuum take-off receiver adapter is required for connecting the apparatus to the source of vacuum. Some pressure-measuring device should be incorporated between the apparatus and the vacuum source. The first set-up (Fig. 3.53a) uses a Claisen adapter and still head and a simple vacuum receiver adapter, whilst the second set-up (Fig. 3.53b) illustrates the use of a Claisen still head and a 'pig' type receiver adapter. The apparatus should be assembled using special vacuum grease to seal all joints—normal stopcock grease is not suitable for use under vacuum—and should then be tested for leaks by applying the vacuum *before* the sample is introduced into the distillation flask. Just as with simple distillation, you need to ensure that the liquid boils smoothly without bumping. However, boiling stones do not function under vacuum, and therefore an alternative method is needed. The only reliable way to ensure smooth boiling during a reduced pressure distillation is to use a *very fine capillary* to introduce a thin stream of air bubbles to the boiling liquid as shown in Fig. 3.53(b). It is stressed that the capillary must be very fine, so that, even under vacuum, only a thin stream of bubbles is drawn through the liquid. Obviously if the organic compound is likely to oxidize with air under these conditions, the capillary can be connected to a nitrogen supply instead. Use of

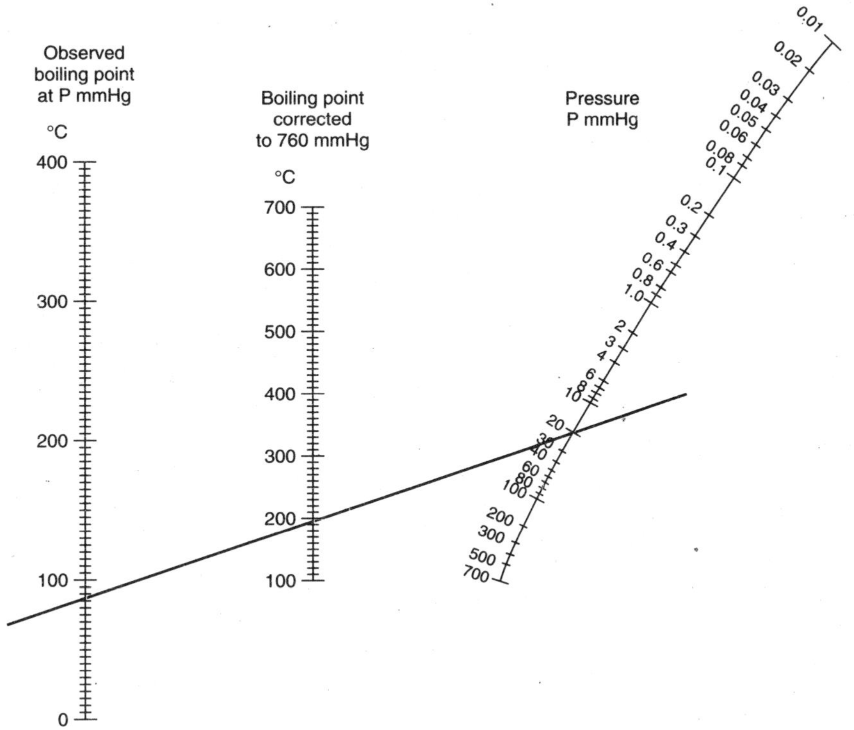

Fig. 3.52 Nomograph for estimating the boiling point of a liquid at a particular pressure. The graph connects the boiling point at atmospheric pressure (760 mmHg) to that at reduced pressure, and a line connecting points on two of the scales intersects the third scale. For example, if the boiling point at 760 mmHg is 200°C, the intercept shows that the boiling point at 20 mmHg pressure is about 90°C.

a fine capillary works well, although it may be tricky to set up properly. A simpler technique which works in most cases is to put a small magnetic stirrer bar in the distillation flask, and stir the liquid rapidly whilst heating it under reduced pressure (Fig. 3.53a). The rapid agitation usually ensures smooth boiling. A less satisfactory method which sometimes works is to put some glass wool in the distillation pot to fill up some of the space above the liquid.

Allow to cool before releasing vacuum

Fractions of distillate are collected in the normal way; remember to record the boiling point *and* the pressure. As with simple distillation, the distillation must not be allowed to proceed to dryness. At the end of the distillation, remove the heat source, and allow the apparatus to cool to room temperature before releasing the vacuum. If you arc using a water aspirator, remember to take the usual precautions to prevent water sucking back into your apparatus.

Fractional distillation can also be carried out under reduced pressure. The apparatus shown in Fig. 3.53 should be modified to include a fractionating column.

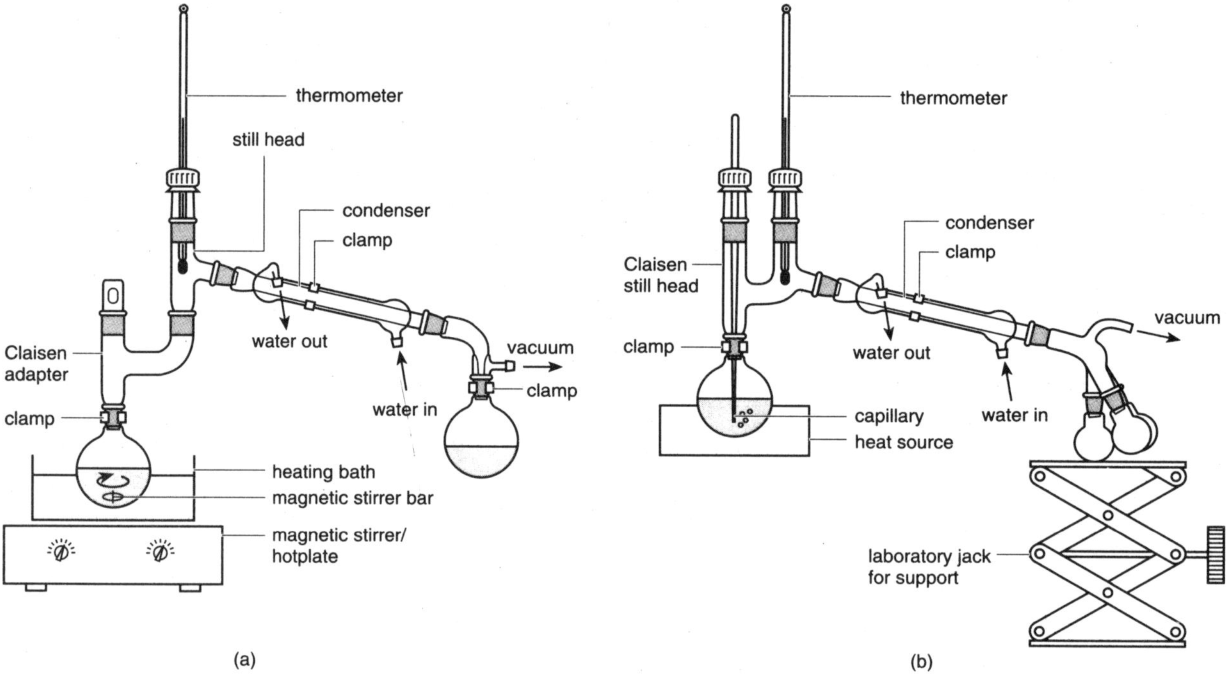

Fig. 3.53 Apparatus for distillation under reduced pressure.

Short path distillation

One particularly useful technique for the vacuum distillation of small quantities of material in the range 50 mg to 2 g is *short path distillation*. The material to be distilled is placed in a small bulb which is connected to two other small bulbs and to a short tube which can be connected to a vacuum. The complete assembly of bulbs is shown in Fig. 3.54(a). The assembly is then placed in a special oven with just the first bulb in the heated zone as shown in Fig. 3.54(b). The bulb is heated and the assembly is rotated to prevent bumping of the liquid. Sophisticated ovens incorporate a small electric motor to rotate the bulbs. Older versions simply heat the sample, and leave the chemist to rotate the tube by hand. As the distillation proceeds, the liquid distils from one bulb to another. This is only a short distance, hence the name of the technique. This type of distillation is also referred to as *bulb to bulb distillation* or *Kugelrohr distillation* from the German *Kugel* = bulb, *Rohr* = tube. If necessary, the material can be redistilled immediately by moving the second bulb into the heated zone and allowing the liquid to distil into the third bulb. For very volatile liquids, it may be necessary to cool the receiving bulb with solid CO_2 held in a suitable container; a Neoprene® filter adapter wired onto the apparatus is ideal.

Since the distillation path is so short, no separation of volatile compounds can be achieved with this technique. Nevertheless it is an excellent technique, and finds widespread use in the purification of small quantities of liquids

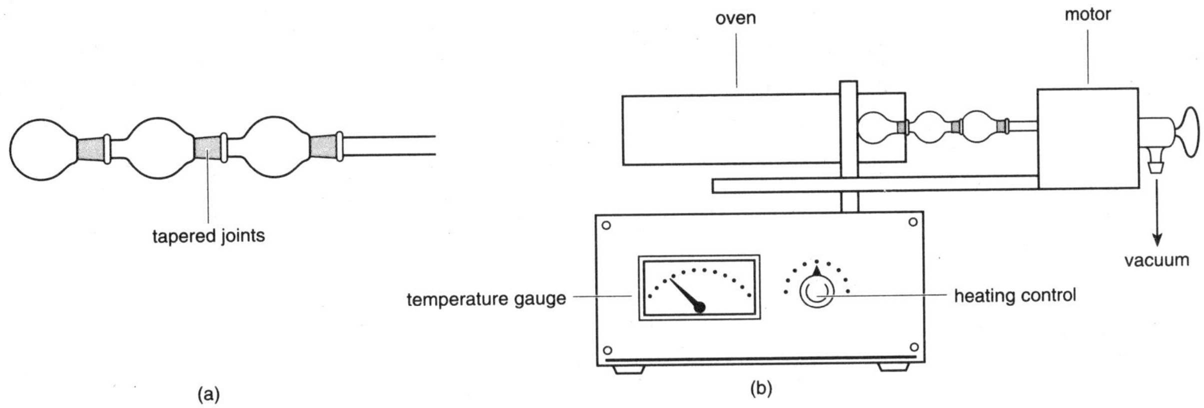

Fig. 3.54 (a) Bulb-to-bulb assembly for short path distillation; (b) special oven for short path distillation.

containing involatile impurities. It is generally much more convenient than setting up a proper vacuum distillation apparatus using small glassware. Since short path distillation provides no means of measuring the precise boiling point of the liquids, the *oven* temperature is often quoted as a useful guide.

Steam distillation

Steam distillation is a useful technique for the distillation of an immiscible mixture of an organic compound and water (steam). Immiscible mixtures do not distil in the same way as miscible liquids, since each exerts its own vapour pressure *independently* of the other. Therefore the total vapour pressure is the sum of the vapour pressures of the pure individual components. (Remember that for miscible liquids it is the *partial vapour pressure* that is important.) Therefore when the sum of the individual vapour pressures equals external (atmospheric) pressure the mixture will boil at a *lower temperature* than either of the pure liquids. Hence co-distillation of an immiscible mixture of an organic compound plus water will result in the distillation of the organic compound below 100°C, even though its boiling point may be well in excess of 100°C. For example, an immiscible mixture of water and octane (boiling point = 126°C) boils at about 90°C at atmospheric pressure (760 mmHg). We can calculate the relative amounts of water and octane in the vapour phase, and hence the distillate, as follows. From tables we ascertain that the vapour pressure of water at 90°C is about 525 mmHg, and since, by definition, for immiscible liquids

$$(\text{Vapour pressure})_{\text{total}} = (\text{Vapour pressure})_{\text{water}} + (\text{Vapour pressure})_{\text{octane}}$$

we have

$$760 = 525 + (\text{Vapour pressure})_{\text{octane}}$$

Therefore, the vapour pressure of the octane is 235 mmHg. Since, for immiscible liquids, the amount (in moles) of each component in the vapour phase is directly proportional to their individual vapour pressures, we have

$$\frac{235}{525} = \frac{\text{No. of moles of octane}}{\text{No. of moles of water}}$$

and therefore the vapour, and hence the distillate, contains 235/525 = 0.448 mole octane per mole of water. Translated into weights, the distillate will contain 51 g octane per 18 g water, or about 75% octane by weight. Hence steam distillation is a very efficient way of distilling octane at a temperature that is about 35°C below its boiling point. Not surprisingly, the technique has found wide application in the distillation of substances which cannot be purified by normal distillation.

There are two ways of carrying out a steam distillation. The 'correct' method is to pass steam into the liquid in the distillation flask, which is heated as well. The water and compound co-distil, condense in the condenser, and are collected in the normal way. A normal still head and Claisen adapter can be used as shown in Fig. 3.55(a), but specially designed still heads, splash heads or swan necks as they are called, may be available in your laboratory. These have the advantage of preventing the liquid frothing and bumping over into the condenser. Provided that sufficient water and organic compound are present in the pot, the still head temperature will remain constant during a steam distillation. You will be able to tell when all the organic compound has distilled

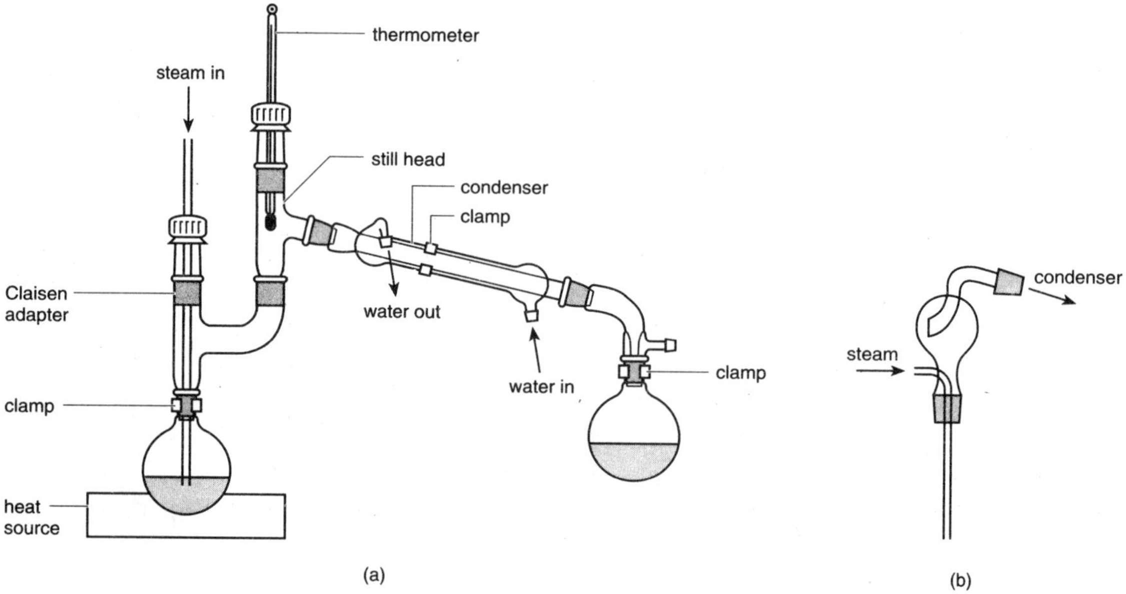

Fig. 3.55 (a) Apparatus for steam distillation; (b) a still head for steam distillation.

by observing the distillate. When only water is distilling, the distillate in the condenser will look clear with no oily drops evident. When the distillation is completed, you have to separate the immiscible organic product from the water in the distillate. This is easily done by transferring the mixture to a separatory funnel, and separating the layers in the usual way. If the organic layer is very small in volume compared with the water layer, it is much easier to *extract* the organic compound with diethyl ether, for example. The organic layer is then separated and dried over a suitable drying agent in the normal way.

Steam can cause nasty burns

Well-equipped laboratories will have steam on tap, and therefore all you have to do is connect the steam supply to your apparatus. Keep the connecting tubes as short as possible. If there is no steam supply, a simple steam-generation apparatus can be set up as shown in Fig. 3.56(a). The steam-generating flask can be heated electrically in a mantle, or, if appropriate, using a burner. Whatever the source of steam it will contain variable amounts of condensed water, and therefore it is a good idea to incorporate a device for removing some of this water before it is transferred to the distillation flask. If this is not done, the volume of liquid in the distillation flask becomes unreasonably large. A simple way to do this is to place a separatory funnel in the steam line as shown in Fig. 3.56(b); water collects in the funnel and can be run off from time to time. Alternatively, a simple water trap can be assembled from standard glassware. One excellent design for such a trap has been described by Dr Rudolph Goetz of Michigan State University (*J. Chem. Educ.*, 1983, **60**, 424).

The 'easy' way to carry out steam distillation is simply to place a mixture of the organic compound and water in the distillation flask, and carry out a simple distillation in the usual way. The water and organic compound will co-distil in just the same way as if steam were passed into the flask. Clearly this procedure is much easier to set up, and requires a simple distillation apparatus

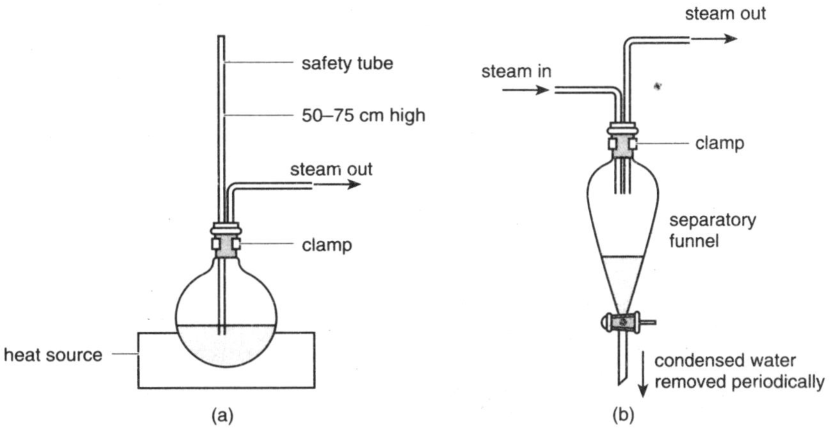

Fig. 3.56 (a) Apparatus for generating steam; (b) removing water from wet steam. Keep connecting tubes short.

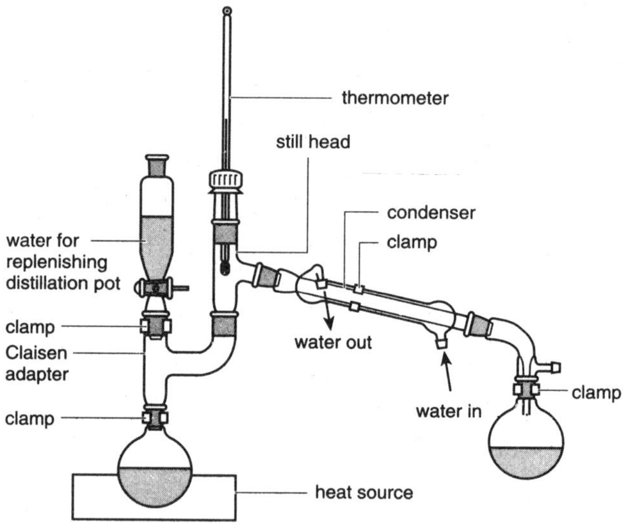

Fig. 3.57 Alternative apparatus for steam distillation.

as shown in Fig. 3.57. Since the water in the distillation flask is not continuously being replaced by steam as it distils out, an addition funnel containing water is placed on the still head so that the water can be replenished from time to time.

Microscale distillation

All of the apparatus for simple distillation described in Figs 3.48–3.57 can be assembled on the semi-microscale using commercial glassware kits. However, separation by distillation is less convincing on the microscale (<1 mL). Even the separation of volatile materials from involatile impurities is less than straightforward because of the difficulties inherent in condensing efficiently small quantities of vapour, and minimizing the ensuing losses. Kugelrohr distillation represents the method of choice, though more economical methods have been proposed. The Hickman still is a popular alternative and the item may be found in most of the commercial microscale glassware ranges. A typical set-up features the still clamped between a reaction vial and a reflux condenser (Fig. 3.58a), but the amount of dead space is considerable and much of the distillate may be in the vapour phase at once. Vapour condenses above the still and runs down inside the wall collecting in the flange or skirt, from where it can be collected by pipette. Alternatively, direct cooling of the Hickman still can be considered. A collar can be constructed around the still using aluminium foil; this retains small chips of solid CO_2, providing a cold surface upon which vapour can condense (Fig. 3.58b). Heating can be provided using a hot sand bath, small Bunsen flame or electric hot air blower.

In the research laboratory purification would be attempted by preparative

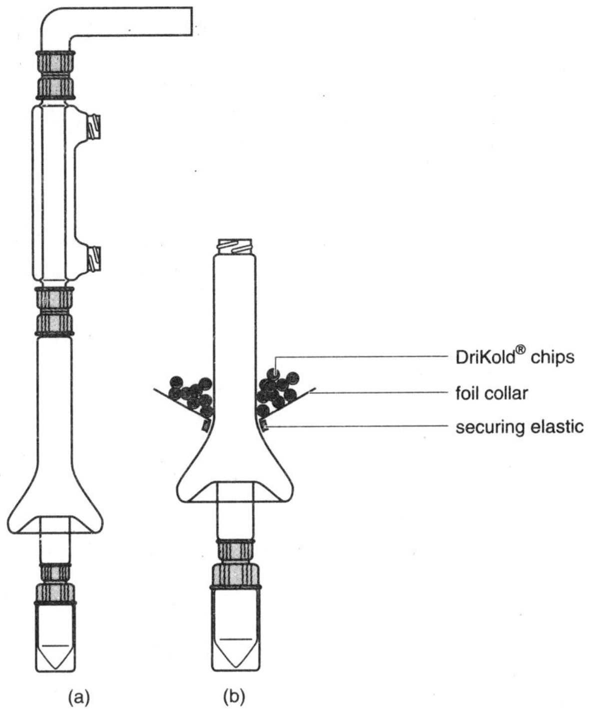

Fig. 3.58 Distillation using a Hickman still and reflux condenser (a). Alternatively, a collar made from aluminium foil may be placed around the Hickman still and secured with an elastic band (b). The collar will retain chips of solid CO_2 (DriKold®), providing a cold surface upon which vapour can condense, and a short path length so that losses of volatiles are minimized.

gas chromatography or some alternative chromatographic technique, depending on the volatility of the product.

Sublimation

Sublimation is closely related to distillation. A solid is converted into a vapour, without going through a liquid phase, which is then recondensed on a cold surface in a purified state. Not many solids sublime easily, since they usually have a very low vapour pressure. However, some solids do have an unusually high vapour pressure because of their molecular structure which results in rather weak intermolecular attractions in the solid state. The major factor that contributes to weak intermolecular forces is molecular shape, and many compounds that sublime easily have a spherical or cylindrical shape which is not ideal for strong intermolecular attraction. Hence such compounds with high vapour pressure can be purified by sublimation, provided that the impurities have a much lower vapour pressure. Just as with distillation, the rate of sublimation can be dramatically increased by heating the sample under reduced pressure, and therefore the sublimation apparatus

Spherical and cylindrical shaped molecules sublime most easily

should allow for this. The sample should never be heated to its melting point however.

A typical purpose-built apparatus for sublimation, known as a *sublimator*, is shown in Fig. 3.59(a). Essentially it is a wide glass tube with a take-off for connection to a vacuum, into which is fitted a smaller diameter tube with water inlet and outlets. The sample to be sublimed is placed in the bottom of the outer tube and heated, under vacuum if necessary. The vapour recondenses on the cold surface, often known as a *cold finger*. The apparatus is designed so that the gap between the sample and the cold finger is small. When the sublimation is complete—it is usually a fairly slow process—the cold finger can be removed carefully, and the purified solid scraped off.

If a purpose-built sublimator is not available, one can easily be improvised from standard laboratory glassware. One such design based on a Büchner filter flask is shown in Fig. 3.59(b). Variations are possible; all you need is a cold surface above the sample which is contained in a vessel that can be heated, and, if necessary, evacuated.

Chromatography

The term chromatography is derived from the fact that this technique was first used to separate pigments (Greek *chroma* = colour, *graphein* = write), but the

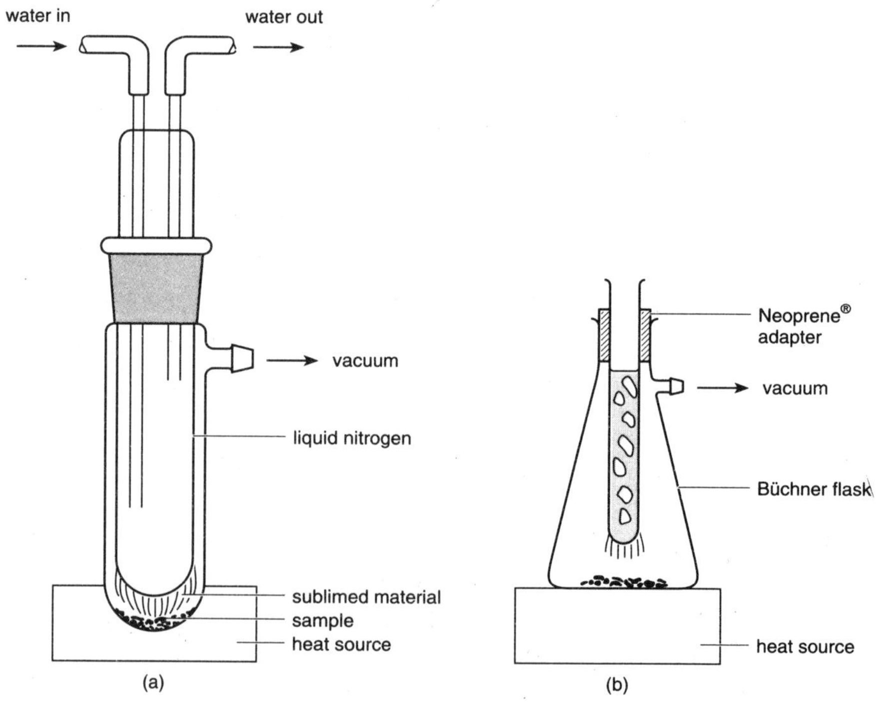

Fig. 3.59 Apparatus for sublimation using: (a) a purpose-built sublimator; (b) an improvised sublimator.

procedure, in its various modifications, is applicable to almost any chemical separation problem and is by no means confined to coloured compounds. The initial development of the methodology is ascribed to the Russian chemist Mikhail Tswett, who separated leaf extracts by percolation through a column packed with chalk. Since this pioneering work at the turn of the century, two Nobel Prizes have been awarded for work in the field of chromatography, such is its importance. The Swede, A. Tiselius, was awarded a Nobel Prize in 1948 in recognition of his contribution to work on electrophoresis and adsorption analysis and the Britons, A.J.P. Martin and R.L.M. Synge, were jointly awarded the Prize in 1952 for their work on partition chromatography.

Whatever the precise experimental procedure, all of the techniques depend upon the differential distribution of various components of a mixture between two phases—the *mobile phase* and the *stationary phase*. The mobile phase may be either a liquid or a gas and the stationary phase either a solid or liquid. Various combinations of these components give the main types of chromatographic techniques (Table 3.9).

There is insufficient space in this book to do justice to the detailed theory and practice of all of these techniques—and neither is that the aim. Instead, we will simply discuss some of the practical aspects of the particular variants of adsorption chromatography and vapour phase chromatography which will be used in the experimental section and which are of most general use in the organic research laboratory. There are many specialist books which concentrate on some or all of the techniques mentioned, and those who wish to read more on the subject should look at some of the references listed at the ends of the sections.

Table 3.9 Main chromatographic techniques.

Stationary phase	Mobile phase	Technique (substances separated)
Solid	Liquid	Adsorption chromatography (wide range of aliphatic and aromatic molecules) Reverse phase chromatography (polar organic molecules) Gel permeation chromatography (macromolecules) Ion exchange chromatography (charged molecules, amino acids)
Liquid	Liquid	Partition chromatography (thermally and acid labile organic molecules)
Liquid	Gas	Gas–liquid chromatography (volatile organic molecules)

Adsorption chromatography—a general introduction

The techniques we are going to consider in this section and which will be used in the experimental section can be categorized into *thin layer chromatography* (TLC) and *column chromatography*. The division is justified by the fact that the first technique is used almost totally for analysis, whereas the second lends itself more to preparative separations. Within the second division we will consider three techniques that are commonly useful in the laboratory—*gravity*, *'flash'* and *'dry flash'* column chromatography. To learn about other important techniques such as *preparative thin layer chromatography, dry column chromatography, ion exchange chromatography* and *gel permeation chromatography* the interested student is recommended to consult the specialist references. Let us now consider the main requirements for carrying out any type of adsorption chromatography and introduce some basic terms and principles.

The support or stationary phase

The *stationary phase* or *adsorbant* is a porous solid capable of retaining both solvents and solutes. Many different materials fill these particular requirements, but the two which enjoy most universal use are silica (SiO_2) and alumina (Al_2O_3) in highly purified and finely powdered form. Both may be supplied with a fluorescent substance (zinc sulfide) which is useful for visualizing compounds on TLC plates. This will be discussed on pp. 168–170, but, for the moment, it is sufficient to know that any grade of silica or alumina possessing the figures 254 or F_{254} will give a green fluorescence when observed under 254 nm wavelength light. Some grades of adsorbant, specifically meant for the preparation of TLC plates, where the adsorbant has to cling to a glass plate, also have the prefix G. This indicates that they contain about 15% of gypsum ($CaSO_4$, 'plaster of Paris') which acts as a binder and serves to stabilize the TLC plate. Those supports lacking this binder often have the letter H after any coding. The size and regularity of the particle diameter is very important for chromatography supports and is also indicated. The type of adsorbants most useful for standard column chromatography have particle sizes between 0.08 and 0.20 mm, whereas TLC adsorbants are much finer, and (with the exception of the technique of 'dry flash' chromatography) should not be used for column chromatography as they will pack too tightly and block solvent flow. Silica for 'flash' chromatography has a particularly regular particle size, and shows almost liquid properties at times. Thus, for example, a label bearing the description 'silica gel GF_{254}' tells us immediately that this is TLC silica possessing a fluorescer, whereas 'silica gel 60H' tells us that we are looking at an adsorbant designed for column chromatography.

Care should be exercised in handling the finer grades of silica as these are readily dispersed into the atmosphere and inhaled, and may cause respiratory

problems in the long term. Such materials should always be handled in a hood and the use of a face mask is highly recommended.

The *activity* or degree to which the support holds onto adsorbed materials is dependent to some extent on the degree of moisture contained within it. The less moisture contained, the 'stickier' or more retentive the adsorbant and the higher its activity. Most silica gel is used directly from the container for column chromatography when it usually contains about 10–20% water, but TLC plates, after having been prepared from a water slurry of silica, require activation by heating to 150°C for several hours before use to drive off excess moisture. Commercially prepared TLC plates do not require this activation, however, and can be used directly. In contrast, alumina is commonly supplied as its most active form, possessing very little water. This is usually too retentive for most practical purposes and is deactivated by thoroughly mixing with a specific amount of water. The activity of such alumina is usually measured on the Brockmann scale as shown in Table 3.10, and activity grades II and III are commonly used for column chromatography.

Whilst there are many other kinds of chromatography support, these are the only two that will be used in the experimental sections.

Elution solvents

The chromatography column or plate, loaded with the material to be separated, is developed by allowing solvent to percolate through the solid adsorbant (*elution*) either by the action of gravity, pressure or capillarity. Eluting solvents of various polarities have differing abilities to displace any solute from the active sites on the support onto which the material has been adsorbed. Generally, the more polar the solvent, the more efficiently it can compete for the active sites and the more quickly the solute will move down a column or up a TLC plate. This property of solvents has been somewhat quantified by listing them in order of their ability to displace solutes from adsorbants. Such *eluotropic series* are useful as guides as to what sort of solvent or combination of solvents will be required for a particular separation. What is frequently forgotten, however, is that such a series only holds good for one particular solid support. For reference purposes two eluotropic series, for silica and alumina, are listed in Table 3.11. In the table, the absolute positions within each series do not translate across from one support to another. In

Table 3.10 Brockmann scale for chromatograph alumina activity grades.

Activity grade	I	II	III	IV	V
Water added (%)	0	3	6	10	15

Table 3.11 Eluotropic series.

	Silica	Alumina
Least polar	Cyclohexane	Pentane
	Pentane	Cyclohexane
	Toluene	Toluene
	Diethyl ether	Diethyl ether
	Ethyl acetate	Ethyl acetate
	Acetic acid	Methanol
Most polar	Methanol	Acetic acid

other words, although cyclohexane on silica is less polar than pentane on silica, this does not mean that it has exactly the same effect as pentane on alumina. In the experimental section, you will often see the term 'light petroleum' used; this refers to a petroleum fraction that consists largely of a mixture of pentanes and can be considered to have similar eluant properties to pentane itself.

Never forget to use only distilled solvents for preparative chromatography. The large quantity of solvent used compared with the amount of material to be purified means that even small amounts of impurity present in the solvent will be concentrated in the chromatographed sample which might end up being less pure than at the outset. This is particularly important for light petroleum which always contains significant amounts of high boiling residues and these will remain in your sample if you use the solvent straight from the bottle. In addition, do not forget that most chromatography solvents are volatile and flammable and many (particularly halogenated solvents) are toxic.

Avoid all flames in the vicinity of a chromatography experiment and carry out such work in a hood wherever possible.

The aim in any chromatographic technique is to use a combination of support and solvents which causes the different components of a mixture to be eluted at different rates from the support and hence effects a separation. This deceptively simple statement hides a multitude of pitfalls and difficulties. The procedures described here will permit beginners to apply the rudiments of the techniques, but there is no substitute for experience and practice in approaching new separation problems.

Further reading

For some general references to chromatographic techniques, see:

A. Braithwaite, C.B.F. Rice and F.J. Smith, *Chromatographic Methods*, 5th edn, Chapman & Hall, London, 1996; C.F. Poole and S.A. Schuette, *Contemporary Practice of Chromatography*, Elsevier, New York, 1984.

Thin layer chromatography

The TLC plate

Thin layer chromatography is largely an analytical technique used for determining the purity of materials and also for preliminary identification purposes. The results obtained using TLC can be translated to column chromatography using the same adsorbant and so TLC is also useful for determining the best solvent system for preparative separations of mixtures. As the name suggests, the adsorbant is supported as a thin coating on a flat surface which may be a glass plate or, more conveniently, a sheet of aluminium or plastic. The most useful size of plate for TLC analysis is one of about 8 × 2.5 cm which permits two or three samples to be spotted onto the *baseline* (a line marked about 1 cm from one end of the plate) and has sufficient length to give the best resolution in a convenient amount of time. Microscope slides are ideal for the in-house preparation of TLC plates, whereas commercial plates are usually purchased in 20 × 20 cm or 10 × 20 cm sizes and should be cut down to size for economy of time and finances. For this reason the aluminium- or plastic-backed sheets are the most convenient; cutting is best carried out with a guillotine to avoid crumbling the delicate adsorbant layer.

Micro-pipettes

In order to perform a TLC analysis it is necessary to introduce a small quantity of your material onto a TLC plate before developing it. The material is conveniently loaded as a solution using a micro-pipette. To prepare these micro-pipettes (Fig. 3.60), heat the middle of a melting point tube in a small

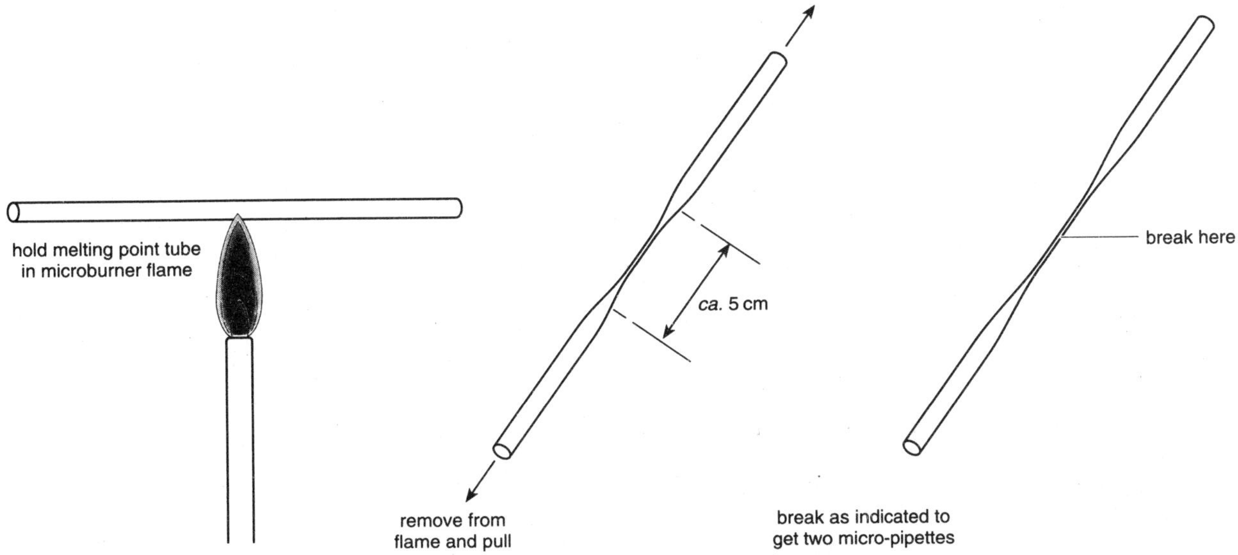

Fig. 3.60 Making micro-pipettes for spotting TLC plates.

Always be careful with flames in the open laboratory

Care! Micro-pipettes are sharp

microburner flame until the tube softens and the flame becomes yellow (1 or 2 s). Then remove the hot tube from the flame and *quickly* pull the two halves about 5 cm apart. Allow the tube to cool and break it in half at the mid-point of the thin section to produce two micro-pipettes. These are useful items and it is best to prepare them in batches of 20 or so at a time. Practice makes perfect and in a short time you should be able to prepare uniformly sized pipettes; however even the odd shaped ones you produce initially are usually serviceable.

Spotting the plate with sample

First, make a solution of a small quantity of your sample in the least polar solvent in which it is readily soluble. Dip the narrow end of the micro-pipette into the solution of your material which will cause some to rise into the tube by capillary action. Then touch the loaded pipette *lightly* onto the silica surface at a point marked on a baseline drawn across one end of the plate about 1 cm from the end. This will cause some of the liquid in the pipette to be drawn onto the adsorbant, forming a visible ring of solvent. Blow gently on the plate to dry the spot and repeat the procedure, trying all the time to keep the baseline spot as small as possible. By this means, as much sample as is judged necessary can be spotted onto the plate. Only experience will enable you to tell when this is so—too little and you will not be able to see any spots on visualizing the plate, too much and the plate will be overloaded and all resolution will be lost. One way around this problem is to make three separate spottings on the baseline, the first with only a small amount of solution, the second with about three times as much, and the third with three times as much again. In this way you are likely to get at least one spotting with the correct amount of material (Fig. 3.61).

The most accurate results are obtained using just enough sample to visualize the spots after development. Remember that TLC is an extremely sensitive procedure and it is very easy to overload the plates.

The developing tank

There are various commercially available chromatography tanks, but for analytical TLC as commonly used in research, it is easiest and cheapest to make one using a 250 mL beaker—preferably a tall form without a spout, although this is not critically important—with a lid made from a petri dish or a watch glass (Fig. 3.62). Wide-mouthed screw cap bottles may also be used, but those with plastic lids which tend not to like the developing solvents should be ruled out! The inside of the container is lined with filter papers to aid in saturating the atmosphere with solvent vapour. However, a gap in the lining should be left in order to be able to see when the plate has been fully developed. Sufficient developing solvent is placed into this tank to wet the filter papers thoroughly and to leave about 0.5 cm of solvent in the bottom. It is important that the level of this solvent does not reach the level of the sample spotted

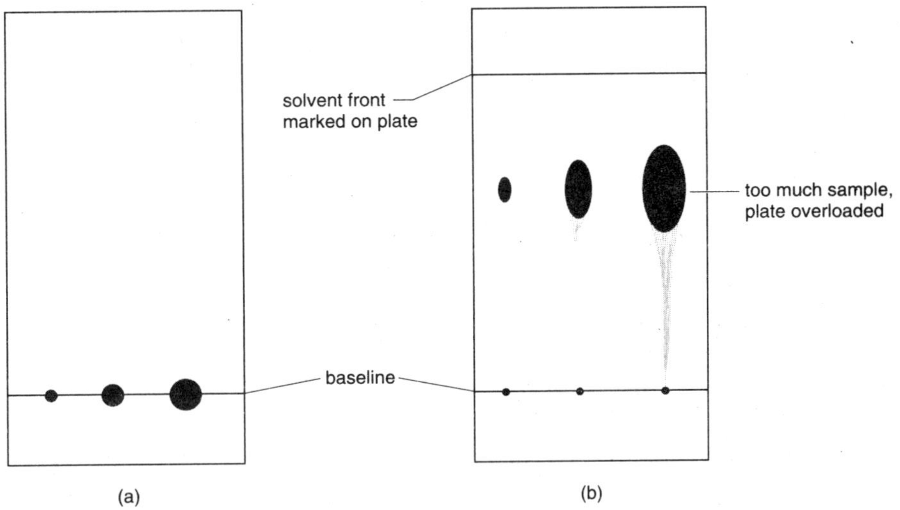

Fig. 3.61 A TLC plate spotted with three different amounts of sample: (a) before development; (b) after development.

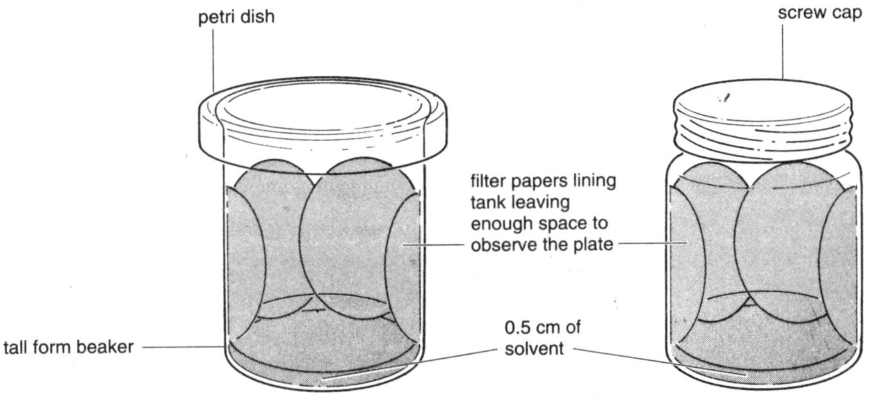

Fig. 3.62 Simple developing tanks for TLC analysis.

onto the baseline of the plate, otherwise the material will simply be dissolved off the plate instead of being carried up it by the rising solvent.

Use tweezers to transfer TLC plates

Developing the plate

With the sample spotted onto the plate and the TLC tank charged with solvent it is time to carry out the analysis. Place the TLC plate *carefully* into the tank (making sure that it is the correct way round with the baseline at the bottom) and allow the *back* of the plate to lean against the sides of the container at a slight angle from the vertical. The baseline must be above the level of the solvent in the bottom of the container (Fig. 3.63). Allow the solvent front to rise in a horizontal straight line up the plate by virtue of capillary

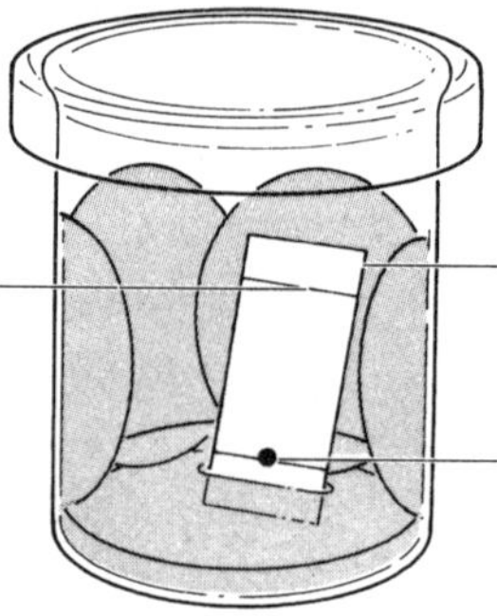

Fig. 3.63 Developing a TLC plate.

Avoid breathing solvent fumes at all times during the operation

action until it reaches about 1 cm from the top. If the solvent front is not straight the analysis must be repeated on a new plate after checking that the filter papers lining the tank have been thoroughly wetted with solvent and are not in contact with the adsorbant at the edges of the TLC plate. Finally, *carefully* remove the plate, mark the solvent front and allow the solvent to evaporate off in the hood.

Visualizing the developed plate

Unless the material being analyzed is coloured it will be necessary to treat the plate in some way in order to see the spots and measure the distance they have travelled. There are numerous *visualizing agents* for TLC plates, but by far the most useful means of analysis uses a combination of observation under UV light and staining with iodine vapour.

The great advantage of UV light is that it is normally non-destructive to the compounds on the plate and the analysis can be carried out without waiting for the spots to develop. However, UV light is particularly hazardous and can blind or cause unpleasant burns of the skin.

Great care must always be taken when working with UV light. Eye protection must always be worn and you must never look directly at the light source. As the wavelengths used for visualizing TLC are also damaging to the skin it is recommended that gloves should also be used.

Wear special eye protection when working with UV light

Light of 356 nm wavelength causes most aromatic molecules, or molecules possessing extended conjugation, to give out a bright purple fluorescence against a dark background. Of course, the drawback here is that not all molecules possess such chromophores and this is where the zinc sulfide fluorescer contained in some TLC adsorbants comes in very useful. When viewed under 254 nm wavelength light, the zinc sulfide in the adsorbant will fluoresce green, except where there is an eluted substance which quenches this fluorescence, giving a dark spot. Consequently, a TLC plate possessing fluorescer will show a series of dark spots on a bright-green background when viewed under

254 nm UV light. If an aromatic solvent such as toluene has been used in the elution, it is essential to dry the plate thoroughly, otherwise the residues will mask any products present. The positions of all spots which can be visualized with either wavelength of light should be noted by drawing around them lightly with a pencil.

The plate is now ready for staining with iodine. An iodine chamber can be made in the same way as the TLC tank, using a 250 mL tall-form beaker, with a petri dish as a lid, into which a few crystals of iodine are placed. Iodine vapour is toxic and the developing tank must be stored in a fume hood. Standing the plate in such a tank for about 30 min reveals the presence of any eluted compounds by the appearance of dark brown spots on a light brown background. Most compounds stain up within minutes but some may take several hours. However, it is worthwhile observing the plate at intervals, particularly the first few minutes, as some compounds (notably alcohols, acids and other halides) frequently give a negative stain initially. In these cases the white spot which first appears against the light brown background is due to the iodine actually reacting with the substance on the plate and being removed from the region. The limit of detection using iodine staining is about 50 μg of organic compound.

Iodine vapour is toxic

Some other useful staining systems are listed in Table 3.12 and others can be found by referring to the *Chemist's Companion*. Most other systems are applied to the plate in the form of a spray and staining is usually encouraged by heating. Consequently, such procedures are messy and there is a real danger of inhalation of the spray. A designated area in a hood should be set aside for such practices. Only sufficient spray should be applied to moisten the plate evenly. Alternatively, a less messy procedure is to dip the plate in the visualizing system. After dipping, the excess reagent is shaken off, and the plate allowed to dry. It must also be remembered that plastic-backed TLC plates are unsuitable for visualization procedures which involve strong heating. Likewise, aluminium-backed TLC plates should not be left for long periods in an iodine tank as the metal is attacked by the halogen, giving a dark brown deliquescent mess.

Always spray TLC plates in a hood. Many systems are corrosive

Retention factor (R_f)

A useful measurement that can be made from the developed TLC plate is the relation between the distance moved by the compound spot and the distance moved by the eluting solvent; this is the *retention factor* of the particular compound and is commonly simply referred to as its R_f (Fig. 3.64).

$$R_f = \frac{\text{Distance moved by the product spot}}{\text{Distance moved by the solvent front}}$$

Compounds which move a long way up the plate will have R_f values approaching unity, whereas those which do not move very far will have R_f values near zero. Although in theory any compound should always give the same R_f

Table 3.12 Some useful staining systems.

Staining system	Compounds visualized	Observation
Ammonia vapour	Phenols	Variously coloured spots (some coloured compounds may change colour)
5% $(NH_4)_6Mo_7O_{24}$ + 0.2% $Ce(SO_4)_2$ in 5% H_2SO_4, followed by heating to 150°C	General use	Deep-blue spots, often useful when other reagents fail
50% H_2SO_4, followed by heating to 150°C. **Corrosive**	General use	Black spots, often useful when other reagents fail
1% aqueous $FeCl_3$	Phenols and enolizable compounds	Variously coloured spots
HCl vapour	Aromatic amines	Variously coloured spots (some coloured compounds may change colour)
0.3% ninhydrin in n-BuOH with 3% AcOH, followed by heating to 125°C for 10 min	Amino acids and amines	Blue spots
0.5% 2,4-dinitrophenylhydrazine in 2 M HCl	Aldehydes and ketones	Red and yellow spots
0.5 g vanillin, 0.5 mL H_2SO_4, 9 mL EtOH	General use	Variously coloured spots
0.5% aqueous $PdCl_2$ with a few drops of concentrated HCl	Sulfur- and selenium-containing compounds	Red and yellow spots

value under given chromatographic conditions (adsorbant, eluant, temperature), it is virtually impossible to standardize the activity of the support on TLC plates. However, although rigorous application of R_f values from one analysis to another is ruled out, such values are useful to anyone following a procedure, particularly if developed in conjunction with a standard material, as they indicate the likely region to look for material on a TLC plate.

Comparisons with authentic materials and resolving close running materials
If authentic material is available, identity is best demonstrated by the technique of *double spotting*. As the unknown material is usually too precious to permit mixing some of it with another material, the preferred procedure involves spotting roughly equal amounts of the unknown and the authentic materials onto exactly the same place on the baseline (using different micropipettes of course). Usually the pure unknown and authentic materials are

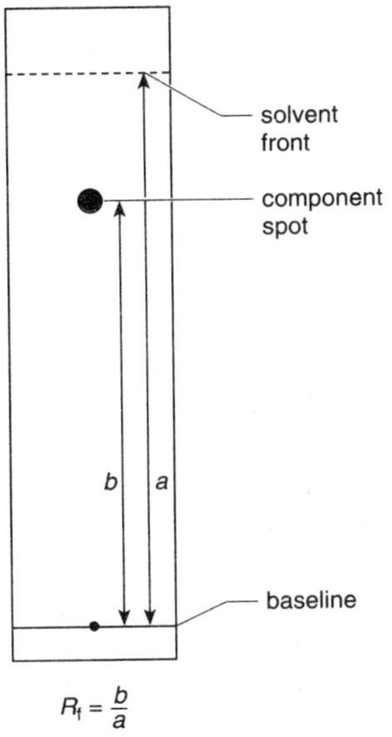

Fig. 3.64 Determination of the retention factor.

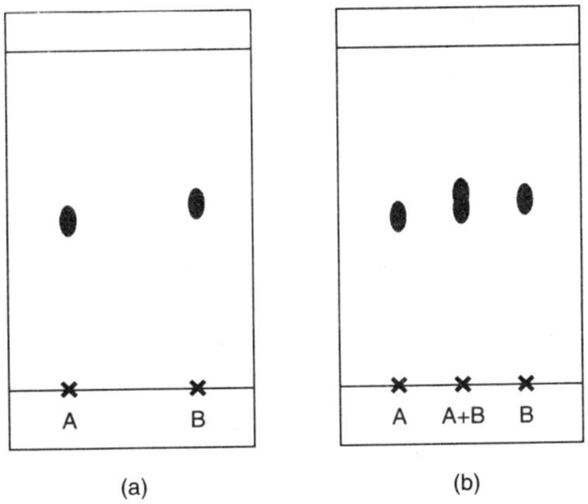

Fig. 3.65 (a) Two compounds having similar R_f values may be indistinguishable, even when run on the same TLC plate. (b) Double spotting shows the typical 'figure of eight' appearance of the two closely running but different compounds.

also run on the same plate, either side of the mixed spot. Any slight difference in R_f between the two materials will cause the mixed spot to appear as a 'figure of eight' (Fig. 3.65). If the mixed spot does not show any elongation, corroborative evidence for identity should be obtained by repeating the double spotting procedure using a different solvent system.

Such analysis can be made even more sensitive by carrying out *two-dimensional chromatography*. This involves spotting the sample at 1 cm from both edges at one corner of a square chromatography plate and carrying out

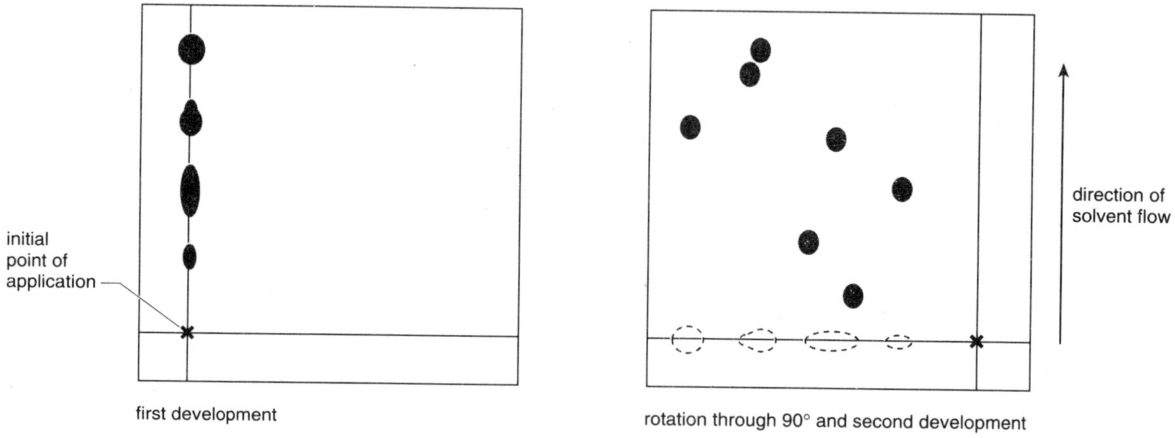

Fig. 3.66 Stages in the development of a two-dimensional chromatogram.

the first development as normal (Fig. 3.66). After the initial development, the plate is turned through 90°, with the eluted components at the bottom of the plate, and is redeveloped with a second solvent system running at right angles to the direction of the first development. This combines the advantages of analyzing the sample with two different solvent systems with the additional resolution afforded by developing the plate in two directions and provides for extremely sensitive differentiation.

An additional use of two-dimensional TLC analysis is to see whether or not the observation of several spots on TLC analysis is a result of a sample being a true mixture, or simply a consequence of decomposition on the plate, as often occurs when trying to analyze acid-sensitive compounds on silica. To check for this, spot the sample onto the corner of the plate and run it as normal in a solvent system chosen to give a good spread of the spots. Then mark the solvent front, turn the plate through 90° as before and repeat the process in the same solvent system (Fig. 3.67). If, on visualizing the plate, some of the spots (usually ill defined) do not appear on a diagonal line running from the baseline spot to the junction of the two solvent fronts, these components of the sample are not stable to the TLC conditions.

The technique of *multiple elution*, another means of separating closely running materials, is used only with preparative TLC (and then only *in extremis* when an examination of other solvent systems has not led to improved separation) as the resolving power of analytical plates is usually so high as to make recourse to this technique unnecessary. The technique simply involves developing the TLC plate using a solvent system in which the highest running component has $R_f < 0.3$ (preferably *ca.* $R_f = 0.1$), allowing the plate to dry partially and then repeating this procedure until adequate separation is achieved or the highest running spot has travelled two-thirds the distance of the plate (Fig. 3.68). Continuing any further or using a solvent system in which

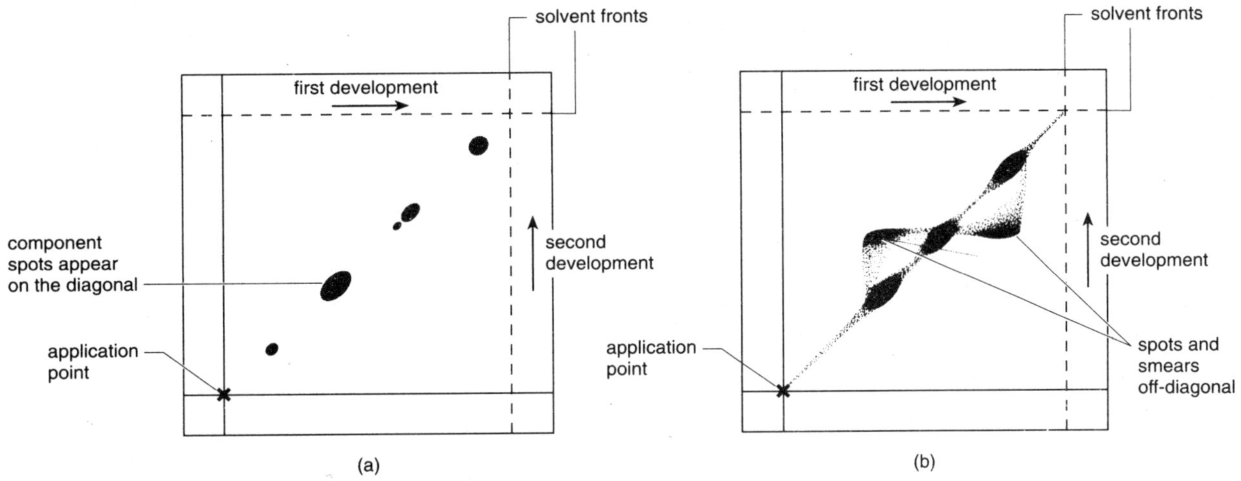

Fig. 3.67 (a) Two-dimensional thin layer chromatogram of a mixture of stable components; (b) two-dimensional chromatogram in which decomposition is occurring.

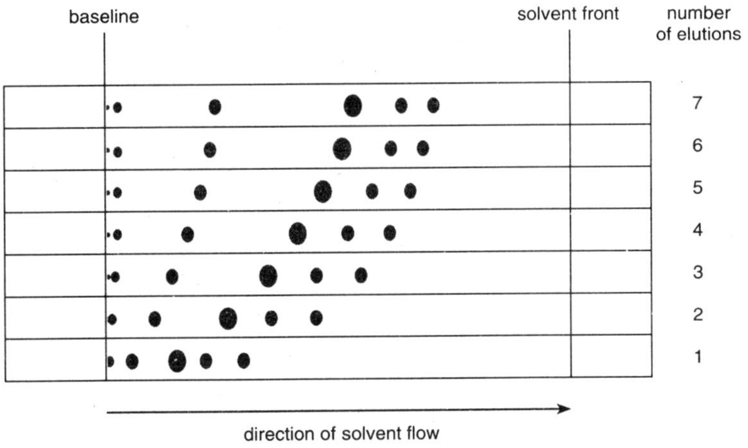

Fig. 3.68 Progress of multiple elution of a mixture of closely running components (note that, with the later elutions, the higher running spots begin to approach each other again).

the spots have R_f values higher than 0.3 actually causes the spots to run together rather than to separate. In the repeat elutions, the solvent front begins to elute the more polar material before it has reached the higher running material and this becomes the overriding effect if the developing system is too polar or the spots are too far apart.

Streaks, crescents and other strangely shaped spots

Whilst a developed TLC plate which shows a long streak instead of a clear round spot is liable to indicate that the sample is a complex mess, there are other less depressing reasons for such effects. Overloading the plate is one common reason for loss of resolution in TLC. This is usually easy to recognize if the analysis has been carried out using three spots of different amounts of material (see Fig. 3.61), as the resolution should be seen to improve with the more dilute sample. Low solubility in the eluting system is another possible cause, although if the precaution has been taken of loading the substance dissolved in the least polar solvent possible, this should not be the case.

Nonetheless, in the absence of overloading or solubility problems, some compounds still result in a smeared spot or one with the appearance of an upward pointing crescent. Such compounds are frequently those possessing strongly acidic or basic functional groups, such as amines and carboxylic acids, which cling very tenaciously to the active sites of the adsorbant (Fig. 3.69a). Much clearer TLC plates with well-defined round spots can normally be obtained with such materials if a few drops of concentrated ammonia (for amines) or formic acid (for carboxylic acids) are added to the eluting solvent.

Sometimes the spots may appear as downward pointing crescents. The most likely cause of this is careless spotting, which causes the adsorbant layer to become detached at the point of application (Fig. 3.69b). Consequently the component flows up around this blemish, carried by the rising solvent. This may also cause a visible dip in the middle of the solvent front as it rises up the plate. Flattening and doubling of spots are a consequence of using a polar solvent to apply the compound to the plate, giving a ring of sample on the baseline instead of a spot (Fig. 3.69c).

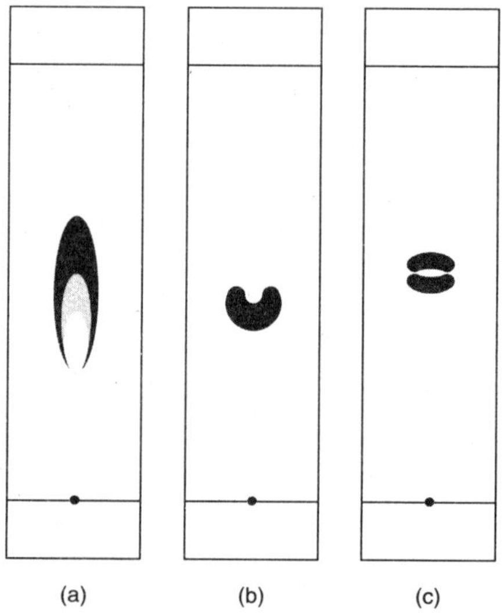

Fig. 3.69 Commonly encountered strangely shaped TLC spots from pure materials: (a) substance contains strongly acidic or basic groups; (b) adsorbant surface disturbed on application; (c) compound applied as solution in very polar solvent.

If after all this you fail to obtain a nice round spot, you have just experienced the typical TLC analysis of a failed reaction, with its one streak R_f 0–1. Tough luck!

Further reading

Among the many works giving details on the theory and practice of thin layer chromatography, see: J.C. Touchstone, *Practice of Thin Layer Chromatography*, 3rd edn, Wiley & Sons, New York, 1992; B. Fried and J. Sherma, *Handbook of Thin Layer Chromatography*, 2nd edn, Marcel Dekker, New York, 1996.

For details of adsorbants, solvent systems, visualizing agents and a lot of other very useful practical information for chromatography, see: A.J. Gordon and R.A. Ford, *The Chemist's Companion. A Handbook of Practical Data, Techniques and References*, Wiley & Sons, New York, 1972, pp. 369–407.

Gravity column chromatography

This technique, until relatively recently, was the workhorse for preparative chromatographic separation in the research laboratory. The advent of faster and (sometimes) more efficient variants has led to a decline in its use, with workers often opting for 'flash' column chromatography when a simple gravity column would be sufficient. The advantages of the gravity percolation technique are that it requires little in the way of special equipment and gives good results with a relatively low level of experimental expertise. Although slower than 'flash' or 'dry flash' column chromatography, it is possible to carry out percolation column chromatography in conjunction with other work as the amount of supervision required is much less than that for the other techniques. In addition, a percolation column requires only the most basic grades of chromatographic adsorbants, making it the most economic of the chromatographic techniques—a not inconsiderable point where large numbers of people are working, or large quantities of material need to be separated. As percolation chromatography is the progenitor to all other techniques and as it requires the lowest level of practical expertise, it is the ideal system for a newcomer to column chromatography. The aspects on pp. 160–164, dealing with stationary phases and eluting solvents, should be read before continuing with the sections on column chromatography.

The equipment

The standard apparatus for running a gravity column is shown in Fig. 3.70. The column can be simply a length of wide bore glass tubing, tapered at one end and closed with a length of flexible tubing with a screw clip. However, it is more convenient to use a column possessing a stopcock (a burette will often suffice, Fig. 3.70a). The column may possess the added sophistication of a ground glass socket for holding a solvent reservoir, or a fine porosity sintered glass disk above the stopcock to support the adsorbant (Fig. 3.70b), but these are not absolute requirements. The best stopcocks are those possessing Teflon® keys as these do not require any greasing. If the column is fitted

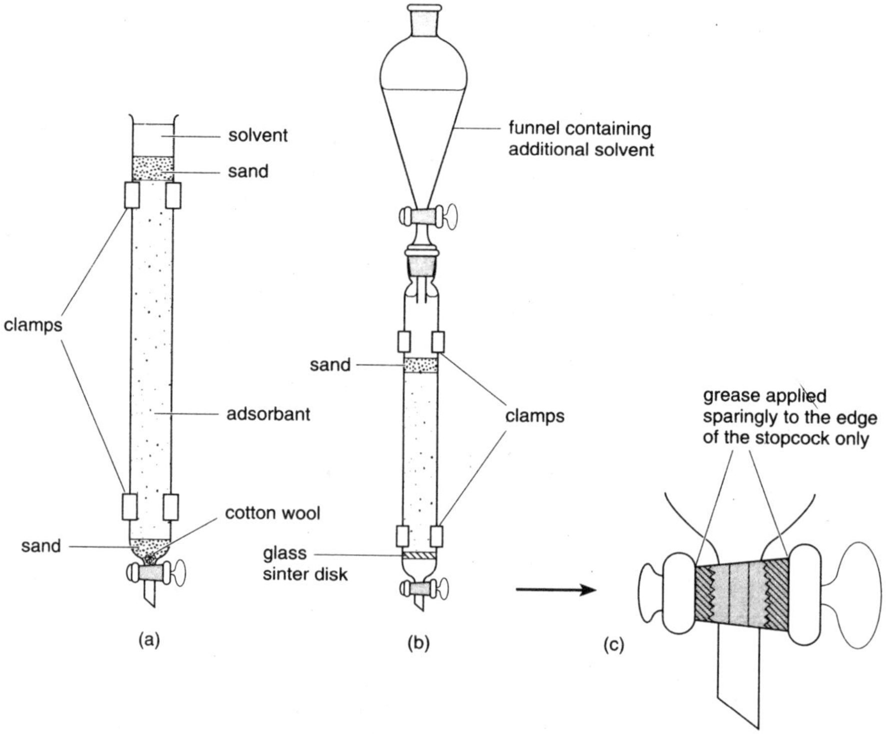

Fig. 3.70 Common arrangements for percolation column chromatography.

Use only the absolute minimum of grease on the stopcock and do not apply it close to the bore of the key

with an all glass stopcock, some greasing will be necessary, but it is pointless carrying out a chromatographic separation if your material ends up full of grease from the stopcock! It is preferable to use a silicone-based grease, wiping a very small amount onto the outer edges of the key (Fig. 3.70c) and then immediately wiping the key clean with a paper tissue. No excess grease should be visible. If the column does not possess a glass sinter above the stopcock, a small wad of cotton wool should be pushed firmly into the tapered end of the column (columns in frequent use normally have a resident plug of cotton wool). The cotton wool must not fit so tightly that solvent is unable to flow through the column. Before adding adsorbant, such columns require the addition of about 1 cm of fine sand, as cotton wool alone is not sufficient to retain the finer adsorbants; however, this is not necessary for columns possessing a sinter disk. The solvent reservoir is usually an addition funnel fitted into the ground glass socket or clamped above the column. The simplest collection system is a series of test tubes arranged in racks which can be pushed under the column at intervals. It is a good idea to number each tube, otherwise the result of prolonged chromatography can be a bewildering array of tubes in some obscure order which was forgotten long ago.

Choosing the solvent system

Before proceeding with the separation, you will need to have determined the best solvent system for separating the components of the mixture by TLC analysis. Realistically you will need a difference in R_f of about 0.3 between two components to stand a chance of obtaining an efficient separation using a gravity column. However, TLC adsorbant particle sizes (for silica and alumina) tend to be finer (and more retentive) than the same adsorbants when used for gravity column chromatography. Thus it is often advantageous to use a solvent combination for developing the column that is less polar than the optimum TLC solvent system. For instance, if the best TLC solvent system uses 1:1 light petroleum–diethyl ether, a suitable system for developing a column might have a 3:2 composition of light petroleum–diethyl ether.

Packing the column

The *wet packing* technique described here is so named because the adsorbant is added as a slurry in the eluting solvent. Columns may also be dry packed, but this procedure is much more likely to lead to cracking of the column due to the solvent boiling on admixture with the adsorbant.

Weigh out between 25 and 50 times the weight of adsorbant as you have crude sample for separation, using the higher weight ratio for more difficult separations or when separating less than 100 mg of sample. The size of column should be chosen such that about two-thirds of its length will be eventually packed with slurry and this may be estimated as follows:

Silica $$l = \frac{6w}{d^2}$$

Alumina $$l = \frac{2w}{d^2}$$

where w = weight of adsorbant (g), l = length of column (cm) and d = internal column diameter (cm).

For example, 50 g of silica would ideally require a column of 3 cm in diameter and 35–40 cm in length. The same weight of alumina would be better used in a column of 2 cm in diameter and 25 cm in length. A 15:1–10:1 ratio of diameter to length is about the right proportion for a percolation column.

Mixing the adsorbant and solvents usually results in the liberation of a large amount of heat of hydration which is often enough to cause volatile solvents, such as diethyl ether, to boil. The mixing should therefore be carried out in a beaker of sufficient volume such that it is only one-quarter full with the dry adsorbant. In a hood add the solvent mixture with stirring until a free running slurry is obtained and then allow this to cool, stirring at intervals to remove all bubbles that may be trapped within it.

Care! Carry out slurry preparations in the hood

It is important that no air enters the packed column as this causes cracking

Do not allow air into the column

of the slurry and results in the formation of channels through which the eluant will flow with no component separation.

Whilst the slurry is cooling to room temperature, fill the column to about one-third of its height with the eluting solvent mixture and run half of this through the stopcock, tapping the column gently to dislodge any trapped air bubbles (a short length of heavy duty flexible tubing is ideal for tapping the column). This operation is particularly important if you are using a column plugged with sand and cotton wool as the sand traps lots of air. Insert a filter funnel with a wide bore stem into the mouth of the column—a powder funnel is fine if it will fit. Stir up the slurry in the beaker (which by now will have settled out) to an even consistency and pour it in a steady stream into the funnel, stopping when the column is almost full. Place the beaker containing the remaining slurry underneath the column, remove the funnel, open the stopcock and allow the solvent to run into the beaker tapping the column gently as you do so. This will cause the slurry in the column to compact, dislodging any stray air bubbles. Only solvent should pass into the beaker. If any solid passes through, it will be necessary to dismantle the column, plug more firmly with cotton wool and start again. When the solvent level in the column is about 1 cm above the adsorbant layer, close the stopcock, stir up the slurry in the beaker and pour more of it into the column. Repeat the process until all of the adsorbant in the beaker has been transferred to the column. Finally, tap the column until the adsorbant surface settles no further, run out the remaining solvent to within 3 cm of the adsorbant and then carefully add a 1 cm layer of fine sand to the surface of the adsorbant to stabilize it. Your column is now ready for use.

Do not allow the column to run dry

At no time must the adsorbant in the column be permitted to run dry. If this happens, the column should be dismantled and repacked immediately.

Loading the sample

The aim of this part of the exercise is to introduce your mixture onto the top of the adsorbant column in as tight a band as possible; this requires care in minimizing the volume of solvent used to carry out the transfer. Dissolve your sample in the minimum possible volume of your elution mixture or, better still, in the least polar solvent used in the mixture if the sample is readily soluble in this. Open the column stopcock, allowing the solvent level to reach to almost the surface of the sand without touching it and then close the stopcock. Add your solution carefully to the surface of the sand using a long pipette, taking care not to disturb the protective layer. Open the stopcock and allow the level to reach the sand layer again. Rinse out the sample container with a small amount of solvent, transfer this to the column in the same manner and repeat this procedure until all of your sample has been transferred to the top of the column. This should take about four additions. Finally, add about 3 cm of eluting solvent and allow this level to drain down to just above the layer of the sand. With the sample now introduced onto the silica,

Add the solution slowly to the column

the column can be fitted with the addition funnel and filled carefully with the eluting solvent.

Eluting the column

The column is developed by allowing the eluting mixture to percolate through at a gentle rate. For most separations the maximum flow rate should not exceed 1 drop every 2 s and for difficult separations the rate should be much slower. Only experience will enable you to judge what is the correct rate for your particular problem. Fractions are collected at regular intervals; again there are no general guidelines to indicate the size of fractions, although the more difficult separations require smaller fraction sizes. Each fraction should be monitored by TLC at intervals of every five fractions or so in order to follow the progress of elution of the products. This information will help with decisions regarding flow rate and fraction size. Figure 3.71 shows the complete TLC analysis of the fractions resulting from a successful column.

Columns, once started, should ideally be finished without a break, although they may be stopped for short intervals—over lunch, for instance. Sometimes it can be possible to leave a tightly stoppered column overnight in a cool place at constant temperature. However, do not expect great things the next day as, even if the column has not cracked up, lateral diffusion of the bands will have been occurring all the time to undo your good work.

All fractions containing homogeneous material can be combined and the solvent can be removed on the rotary evaporator to furnish the purified product.

Disposal of the adsorbant

The used adsorbant must be disposed of carefully as the problems of inhalation of the powder are now worsened by the fact that it now contains adsorbed materials which have not been eluted from the column, but which may be

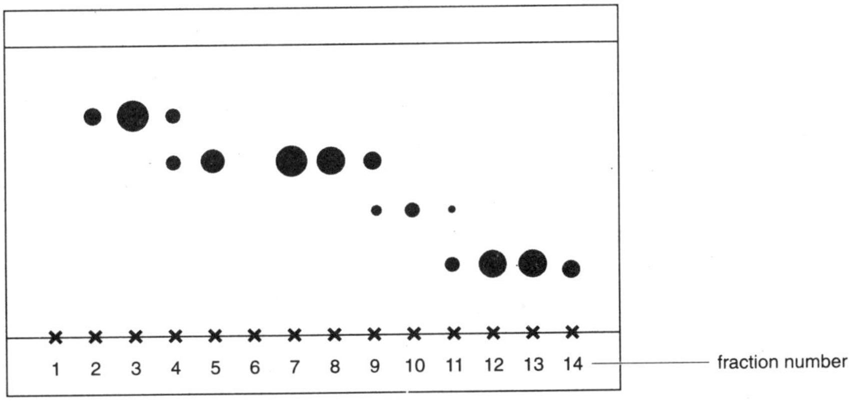

Fig. 3.71 Typical analysis by TLC of the fractions from a successful percolation column.

Take care when disposing of used chromatography adsorbant

highly toxic. The best way to empty the column is to allow the excess solvent to run out and then attach the stopcock outlet to a water aspirator in a hood to remove most of the solvent. The free running powder should be tipped carefully in a hood into a container specifically designated for chromatography residues and damped down by addition of some water.

Never dispose of chromatography residues into open bins.

'Flash' column chromatography

A more efficient preparative variant of column chromatography is that of *medium pressure chromatography*. In this technique the solvent is pushed through the column under pressure, and this faster elution rate, together with the use of a very regular fine particle adsorbant, enables an improved level of resolution to be achieved. However, the technique does require a certain amount of specialized equipment and this has tended to limit its acceptance.

In 1978 the American chemist W. Clark Still and his co-workers published a paper describing a hybrid technique between the medium pressure technique and a short column technique previously described by Rigby and Hunt in 1967. In this procedure, now simply known to chemists everywhere as 'flash' chromatography, the solvent is pushed through a relatively short column of high quality chromatography silica using gas pressure. As the pressures involved are only moderate, the technique requires very little in the way of special apparatus. Its advantages are the speed with which once tedious column chromatography can be carried out (hence the name), simplicity of operation and improved separation, particularly with larger sample sizes. Clean separation of components having R_f differences of 0.15 are possible in about 15 min and with a little more care and practice, R_f differences down to 0.1 present few problems.

Almost overnight, gravity column chromatography disappeared from research laboratories, to be replaced by 'flash' chromatography—whether the separation problem warranted it or not—and the technique is now universally used. The details below have been taken from the original paper describing the technique and, once the gravity column technique has been mastered, the transition to 'flash' chromatography should present no difficulties.

The equipment

In essence, the apparatus is the same as that used for gravity chromatography, with the additional requirement of a regulating device attached to the head of the column for controlling gas pressure, and hence elution flow rate. However, the recommended column shape is somewhat fatter than that which would be used for gravity chromatography of the same quantity of material, and has a flattened rather than a tapered bottom (Fig. 3.72). A sintered disk above the stopcock for containing the adsorbant is not recommended, as using cotton wool topped with a little sand significantly reduces the dead space at the exit

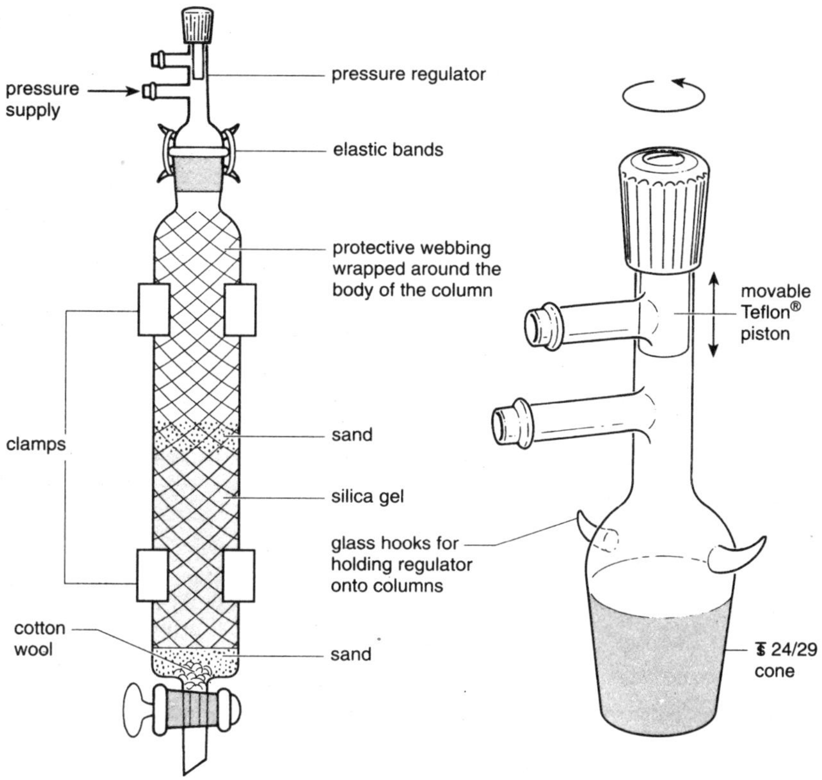

Fig. 3.72 Apparatus for 'flash' chromatography.

side of the column where remixing can occur. The top of the column may be modified to form an inbuilt solvent reservoir but this is not necessary as there is usually sufficient head space in the packed column to hold a useful quantity of solvent. The flow controller consists of a standard-taper cone fitted with a glass/Teflon® needle valve regulator which is adjustable by means of a screw thread (Fig. 3.72). All of this apparatus is commercially available but its construction poses no greater problems for a glass-blower than a standard chromatography column. As the column will be used under pressure, the glass should be thicker than normal.

Enclose flash columns in tape or webbing

The column must be wrapped in plastic webbing or adhesive tape to prevent flying glass in case of explosion when in use, and the pressure regulator must not be wired onto the column.

Before use, all equipment must be carefully checked for cracks or chips. The columns should be stored upright in racks designed for this purpose to stop the columns rolling about and banging into each other.

The adsorbant and solvent systems

The adsorbant used for separations is a high quality grade of silica with a very

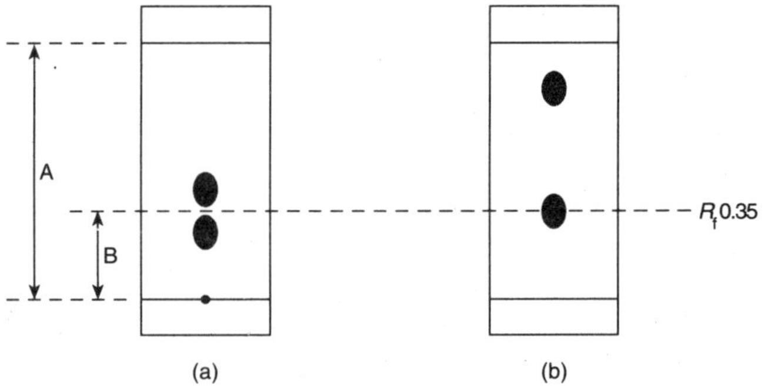

Fig. 3.73 Analytical TLC analyses of various component mixtures developed with the correct solvent combination for 'flash' chromatographic separation: (a) closely running components; (b) widely separated components.

uniform particle size of 40–63 μm. The fineness and regularity of this silica permits better packing and more efficient separations, but also leads to problems in handling the dry powder which has a tendency to disperse in the air.

Wear a face mask when handling flash silica. Handle in the hood

Flash silica must always be handled in the hood and it is recommended that a face mask is worn during transfers of this material in order to avoid accidental inhalation of any airborne powder.

The tighter packing possible with this adsorbant causes the flow rate of higher viscosity solvents to be impaired below the optimum flow rate. Wherever possible it is recommended that combinations of the following low viscosity solvents be used: light petroleum, dichloromethane, ethyl acetate or acetone. A solvent system should be chosen which gives the maximum separation of components with the desired component having an R_f value of 0.35. If the isolation of several closely running components is desired, then the solvent combination should be chosen such that the mid-point of the spots has an R_f value of 0.35. If the aim is to separate more widely separated components, the system in which the most polar material has an R_f value of 0.35 is the best choice (Fig. 3.73).

Packing the column

'Flash' chromatography columns are most simply filled using the technique of *dry packing*. The size of column and suggested fraction volumes depend on the quantity of material to be purified, and the ease of separation. Guidelines are listed in Table 3.13.

Always pack 'flash' columns in the hood

With the column in a hood, place a 0.5 cm layer of fine sand over the cotton wool plug and pour in the silica to a depth of 15 cm (for separating components with R_f differences approaching 0.1 it may be advisable to increase this depth by up to 25 cm—but no longer). Hold the column vertically and tap it

Table 3.13 Guideline size and volume parameters for 'flash' chromatography.

Sample weight (mg)		Column diameter	Suggested fraction volume
$\Delta R_f > 0.2$	$\Delta R_f < 0.2$	(mm)	(mL)
100	40	10	5
400	160	20	10
900	360	30	20
1600	600	40	30
2500	1000	50	50

For details of use of gas cylinders, see pp. 64–68

Care! Pressure

Do not allow air to enter the column

carefully on a wooden surface to compact the silica which is then covered with another 0.5 cm layer of sand to protect the adsorbant surface. With the stop-cock open, *and a collection vessel underneath*, introduce the chosen solvent system carefully (in the initial stages it is preferable to use a long pipette and to allow the solvent to run down the side of the column) until the head space is almost full. Attach the flow controller to a source of compressed gas (nitrogen cylinder, compressed air or a small air pump) *with the needle valve completely open* and hold it by hand on the top of the column. Force the solvent through the column using gas pressure by opening the compressed gas supply *slightly*, and then *carefully but firmly* closing the exit port on the flow controller with the forefinger. This will cause a certain amount of compaction of the silica and heat of hydration will also be produced in the initial stages. The pressure must be maintained until all of the adsorbant has been eluted with solvent, with displacement of the air, and the column has cooled down. If this procedure is not followed the column of adsorbant will crack up and will be useless. The heating effect is greatest with the larger columns containing the most silica and it is as well to practice making up a smaller size of column initially. Maintain the head pressure until the remainder of the solvent has passed through the column and the solvent surface is just above the sand layer; gently release the pressure and close the stopcock.

Loading the sample and eluting the column

Load the sample onto the column in the minimum quantity of the eluting system following the method described on p. 178 for percolation column loading. Pressure can be used to introduce the solution onto the column as described above. When all of your sample is on the silica and the head space has been topped up with solvent the column is ready to be eluted.

Before commencing the elution, make sure you have sufficient racks of test tubes readily to hand. You certainly will not have time to start arranging things during chromatography; the solvent passes through the column very quickly! Whilst the elution can be stopped during development, for instance to replenish the solvent reservoir, there is always a risk of the column cracking up on release of pressure and so it is as well to minimize such stoppages. Cracking frequently results from releasing excess pressure too quickly; always release the pressure slowly using the needle valve.

Release pressure slowly

With the needle value fully open, attach the flow controller to the column with an elastic band. Open the stopcock on the column and then *carefully* close the needle valve until the solvent flows fairly rapidly through the column. This gives you both hands free for changing fractions but you must take care not to allow the pressure within the column to build up too high.

Never close the stopcock whilst the column is under pressure and do not close the needle valve fully

In general the solvent surface should descend at a rate of about 5 cm min^{-1} down the cylindrical body of the column for all sizes of columns. For those columns with spherical reservoirs when such a guideline is of no use, this translates into the following flow rates:

Column diameter (mm)	10	20	30	40	50
Flow rate (mL min^{-1})	4	16	35	60	100

There will be no time to follow the progress of elution during this procedure and only experience will enable you to judge when the desired component has been eluted from the column. It is always a good idea, however, to analyze all of your fractions at any stage when it proves necessary to add more solvent.

Disposal of the silica

Dispose of the silica carefully

You must exercise extreme care when emptying the used adsorbant due to its great tendency to disperse into the atmosphere when dry. The procedure described on pp. 179–180 describes a safe way to carry out this disposal, but always check for any additional rules that may be in force in the laboratory.

Further reading

B.J. Hunt and W. Rigby, *Chem. Ind. (London)*, 1967, 1868.
W.C. Still, M. Khan and A. Mitra, *J. Org. Chem.*, 1978, **43**, 2923.
D.F. Taber, *J. Org. Chem.*, 1982, **47**, 1351.

'Dry flash' column chromatography

This technique combines the speed and separation of 'flash' chromatography with use of the cheaper TLC grade silica, simple operation and absence of special apparatus requirements. In 'dry flash' column chromatography, the silica column is eluted by suction instead of using top pressure, removing the risk of bursting glassware. Additionally the column is eluted by adding predetermined volumes of solvent and is run dry before addition of the next fraction.

These features make the procedure readily adaptable to *gradient elution* and this is in fact the preferred way of developing such columns. As its name suggests, gradient elution involves developing a column with progressively more polar combinations of eluting solvent. This can confer very real time advantages for the removal of polar compounds from a column in the latter stages of a separation, without losing the separation qualities of a relatively non-polar eluting system at the beginning for the less polar components.

Do not forget that this is the *only* instance when you should allow air to get into a chromatography column during development. In fact the whole procedure appears to fly in the face of all of the principles of classic chromatography, but it can give results at least as good as the standard flash technique at much reduced cost. It is particularly useful for the separation of enormous (in chromatographic terms at least!) quantities of material—up to 50 g—although such columns should not be attempted by the inexperienced. This technique has been the subject of a certain degree of quantification by one of the authors (LMH) but has been in fairly general use in various laboratories for a long time.

The equipment

The apparatus needed is simply that for filtration under reduced pressure using a cylindrical porosity 3 sinter funnel attached to a round-bottomed flask by means of a cone and socket adapter with a side arm for attachment to a water aspirator (Fig. 3.74). The amount of sample to be purified determines the size of sinter funnel to use and the volume of fractions to collect. Suggested guidelines are shown in Table 3.14.

Choosing the solvent system

The eluting solvent system used should be that in which the desired component has an R_f value of 0.5 by TLC analysis. Although no solvent is particularly disfavoured for this technique, various combinations of hexane, diethyl ether, ethyl acetate and methanol are adequate for the majority of separations. As the system is under reduced pressure, some of the solvent collected will evaporate and may cool the receiving vessel to such an extent that

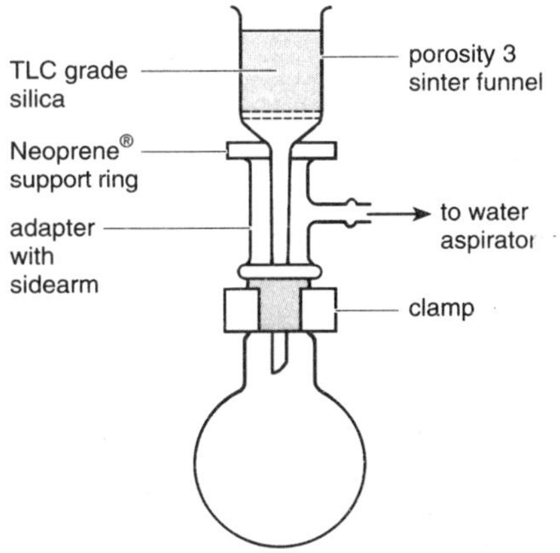

Fig. 3.74 Apparatus for 'dry flash' column chromatography.

Table 3.14 Guideline size and volume parameters for 'dry flash' chromatography.

Sinter diameter (mm)	Weight of silica (g)	Sample weight	Fraction volume (mL)
30	15	15–500 mg	10–15
40	30	500 mg–3 g	15–30
70	100	2–15 g	20–50

atmospheric moisture condenses on the apparatus. This does not affect the efficiency of the separation but, if the chromatography is prolonged, some water may find its way into the collected fractions. Use of the less volatile heptane instead of light petroleum helps somewhat in this respect.

Packing the column

Use TLC grade silica for dry flash chromatography

The silica used for this type of chromatography is TLC grade silica without the gypsum binder. This is cheaper than the silica sold for use in flash chromatography which, in any case, is too free flowing for use in these dry columns. The weight of silica recommended for each size of funnel is sufficient to leave a head space at the top of the funnel for loading solvent when the column has been packed and compacted under suction. The silica may be weighed out as indicated in the table, but it is easier just to fill the funnel to the brim with lightly packed silica. Application of suction causes the silica to compact, leaving the head space for solvent addition. During this initial compaction there is a tendency, particularly with the larger sized columns, for the silica to shrink away from the sides of the funnel or to form cracks which may remain unseen in the body of the adsorbant. To ensure good packing, press down firmly on the surface with a glass stopper, particularly at the edges, using a grinding motion. Do not worry about the state of the adsorbant surface as this can be flattened off easily when finished by repeated gentle tapping around the sides of the funnel with a spatula.

Handle silica in the hood

When satisfied that the column has been thoroughly compacted, pre-elute the column with the least polar component of the elution system. If the packing has been carried out properly, the solvent front will be seen descending in a straight, horizontal line. Keep the silica surface covered with solvent during the pre-elution, until solvent passes into the receiving flask, and then allow the silica to be sucked dry. Remember to check the back as well as the front of the column for any irregularities. If a regular solvent front is not obtained, simply suck the column dry, recompact it and repeat the pre-elution procedure. There is no excuse for attempting a separation with an improperly packed column. Note that the surface of the compacted silica is relatively stable on addition of solvent and does not require any protective layer of sand.

The column must be compacted evenly before attempting the separation

Loading the sample and eluting the column

Dissolve your sample in the minimum possible volume of pre-elution solvent and apply it evenly to the surface of the silica with the column under suction. Rinse the sample container and add the washings to the column until all of the sample has been transferred. If the sample does not dissolve easily in the pre-elution solvent, dissolve it in the least polar combination of the elution solvents in which it is readily soluble.

Commence gradient elution with the same solvent combination as was used to load the sample onto the column, following the guidelines in the table for the size of fraction to use (use the smaller volumes for more difficult separations). Allow the column to be sucked dry and transfer the first fraction to a test tube or any other convenient receptacle, rinsing both the flask and the stem of the funnel. Whilst the column is being sucked dry, prepare the next fraction, increasing the quantity of the more polar component by about 5%. Repeat the elution procedure. Continue the gradient elution in this manner until eluting with the pure, more polar component alone, and then continue with this as necessary. It is often advantageous to interrupt the gradient elution temporarily when the desired component is eluting from the column and continue with the same solvent mixture for a few fractions.

The progress of the separation should be followed by TLC analysis of the fractions. However, as a rough guide, the desired product is usually eluted from the column when the gradient elution reaches that solvent mixture in which the material would have an R_f value of 0.5 on TLC. When quantities of material of more than about 100 mg are purified, elution of product from the column is often indicated by frothing on the underside of the sinter. If the product is a solid, it may crystallize out in the stem of the funnel or the receiving flask, particularly with separations of larger quantities of material. Be sure to rinse thoroughly both the flask and the funnel stem between fractions, and check that the solid does not obstruct elution from the column.

The typically low degree of lateral diffusion of the product bands with this technique usually means that pure compounds elute in relatively few fractions, reducing the number of cross-contaminated fractions. The material recovery from the column should be excellent if the crude sample does not contain polymeric material.

Disposal of the silica

After the elution is complete, suck the silica dry and then transfer it to the silica residues bin. Generally a sharp tap with the funnel held upside down will cause the whole of the adsorbant to fall out as a single plug of material. As always, care should be taken not to produce large quantities of silica dust in the atmosphere of the laboratory.

Take care with the disposal of used silica

Further reading

L.M. Harwood, *Aldrichimica Acta*, 1985, **18**, 25.

For a technique using TLC grade silica and a combination of suction and head pressure to elute the column, see: Z. Zsótér, T. Eszenyi and T. Tímár, *J. Org. Chem.*, 1994, **59**, 672

High performance liquid chromatography

It would need a series of books to attempt to do justice to the whole range of chromatographic separation techniques. In this chapter, we have simply attempted to deal with the practical aspects of those techniques which are commonly encountered in the laboratory, or which are used in the experiments described in Part 2 of this book. Nonetheless, it would not be proper to leave this section on adsorption chromatography without at least a cursory mention of the ultimate application of this branch of chromatography—high performance (or pressure) liquid chromatography.

As one interpretation of the acronym HPLC suggests, this highly efficient technique once again uses solvent under pressure to elute the column. Although generally used as an analytical system, larger capacity columns having almost as good resolving power can be used in preparative systems. These systems are commercially available and the fine details vary from model to model but the general features are shown diagrammatically in Fig. 3.75. The general arrangement and operation bears more than a passing resemblance to gas chromatography (pp. 191–203), but HPLC is the more powerful analytical technique as it permits analysis of non-volatile and thermally labile compounds. However, development of the technique had to await the technology for preparing the specialized stationary phases so crucial for success.

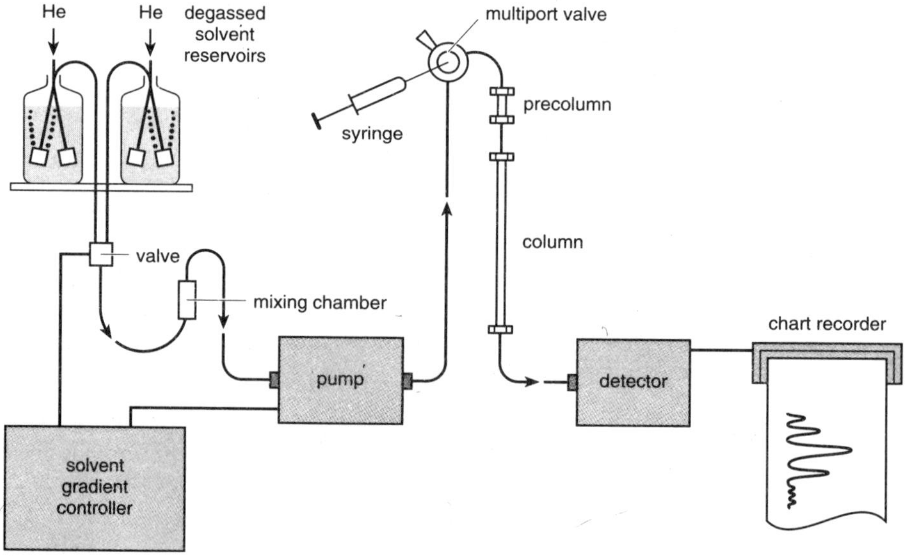

Fig. 3.75 Schematic of a typical HPLC set-up with low pressure solvent mixing.

The equipment

The column is a stainless steel tube packed with a special stationary phase consisting of extremely fine, regularly sized, spherical particles with a very high ratio of surface area to mass, usually in the range 200–300 $m^2 g^{-1}$. Owing to the small size of the particles, typically 5–10 μm in diameter, any solvent contained in the matrix of each particle is close to the external solvent and equilibration can take place readily. It is this which makes HPLC much more efficient than column chromatography using supports, in which the much larger particles have deep interstices predominantly filled with stagnant, non-equilibrating solvent. The technique may use a standard adsorption column or a *reversed phase* column. In reverse phase chromatography a highly polar solvent system is used for elution. Under such conditions polar compounds prefer to stay in the mobile phase and are eluted before non-polar materials which have a greater affinity for the stationary phase—the reverse of usual adsorption systems. Another very exciting development uses stationary phases in which the surface has been covalently linked to a chiral material. Such *chiral bonded phase supports* permit the analytical separation of enantiomers, and the potential for such chiral columns seems boundless.

These customized stationary phases are expensive, but the columns are designed to be reusable, and so the set-up always possesses a pre-column filter to remove particulate or polymeric matter before it contaminates the main column. Typically, analytical columns are 10–25 cm long with an internal diameter of 4–6 mm and may be surrounded by a thermostatted bath for extremely accurate work. Owing to the small size of the column the 'dead space' in the connections between the outlet and the detector must be kept to an absolute minimum in order to avoid remixing of components after elution from the column.

As a consequence of the highly packed nature of the stationary phase in these columns, pressures of anything up to 7000 psi are necessary to force the eluting solvent along the column. The pump must be capable of maintaining a constant flow of solvent with no pressure surges and it must also be constructed of material which can withstand a wide range of organic solvents. The pump is also designed to permit the precise choice of a particular rate from a wide range of flow rates.

The solvents used for HPLC must be highly pure, contain no solid matter and will require degassing immediately before use by sonification or by displacement of dissolved gases with helium. Any formation of air bubbles within the system totally upsets the pressure maintenance. Elution may be with a single solvent or a mixture of solvents when the process is described as *isochratic*, or the composition of the eluting system can be varied with time to permit *gradient elution*. The mixing of solvents for gradient elution may be carried out either at the low pressure side of the system, before the pump, or in the high pressure part. Both arrangements have their advantages and disadvantages and both require microprocessor control.

Samples for analysis are introduced onto the column by injection through a multiport valve which permits precise, repeatable sample loading with minimal disturbance of solvent flow. Basically, a solution of the sample is injected into an isolated, fixed volume loop of tubing which, on turning the valve, becomes part of the solvent delivery system. Sample in excess of that required to fill the loop is led to waste (Fig. 3.76). So-called *external loop* injection ports permit variation of the volume of sample introduced into the column.

The normal means of detecting the eluted components is by using a UV detector placed close to the outlet from the column. This permits continuous, instantaneous monitoring of the effluent from the column with the results being transmitted to a chart recorder; but this, of course, rules out the use of any solvent which has even a weak absorption in the UV region to be analyzed and imposes stringent purity requirements on all solvents. The most convenient type of detector is one which can be varied to monitor any specific wavelength desired. Common practice involves the simultaneous analysis of two different wavelengths as the impurities may possess different chromophores to the component of interest and may pass undetected if just one wavelength is observed. An alternative, but less frequently encountered means of monitoring column output, is to measure the refractive index of the eluant and to compare this with the pure solvent system. Perhaps the ultimate in separation–analysis techniques involves the coupling of the HPLC output to a mass spectrometer (pp. 373–378). This technique of *LC/MS* combines the ability to separate very complex mixtures with the extreme analytical sensitivity of mass spectrometry. The major problem with the technique has been the development of an interface between the liquid eluant from the column and the very low pressure within the mass spectrometer which will permit the selective introduction of the separated components and removal of the undesirable carrier solvents. It is perhaps worth reflecting on the extreme cost and sophistication of this arrangement, compared with the basic percolation column set-up, to appreciate the enormous advances which have been made in separation and analytical technology.

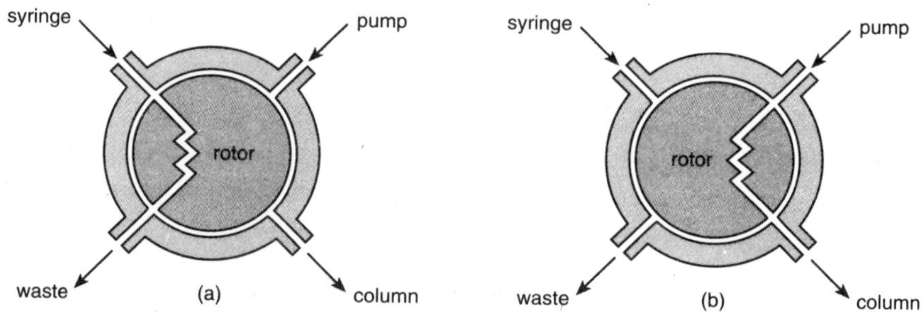

Fig. 3.76 Schematic diagram of the operation of an internal loop injection port for HPLC: (a) injection of sample; (b) introduction onto column.

Practical points for HPLC use

Every individual item of equipment used in HPLC is both delicate and expensive, and extreme care must be taken by anyone using such a set-up—that is if they want the chance to use it on future occasions! The most important 'do nots' are the following.

- Never start work on an HPLC set-up without first obtaining permission from the person responsible for its upkeep and giving instructions on its correct use.
- Do not be tempted to rush the degassing of the solvents; a few minutes skipped here will invariably cause several hours of extra work once air bubbles have got into the system. Check the solvent reservoir periodically and do not allow it to run dry.
- Never forget to use a pre-column filter and always check the age of the filter presently in use. If in doubt, clean the filter and put in fresh adsorbant. If at all possible, carry out a preliminary clean-up on your sample before the analysis—a simple filtration through a Pasteur pipette filled with a little TLC silica will be sufficient.
- Do not force the pump to work at very high rates of eluant flow. This will cause the stationary phase to compact and the resultant increase in back pressure can result in leaking joints or damage to the pump. When increasing flow rates, do so slowly, or the instantaneous back pressure developed might also damage the pump.
- If in doubt about anything, ask the person in charge for direction. Do not attempt to find out by trial and error as mistakes in HPLC are always costly in time, money and popularity.

Further reading

A. Braithwaite, C.B.F. Rice and F.J. Smith, *Chromatographic Methods*, 5th edn, Chapman & Hall, London, 1996.

P.R. Brown and A. Weston, *HPLC and CE: Principles and Practice*, Academic Press, London, 1997.

C.K. Lim (ed.) *HPLC of Small Molecules—a Practical Approach*, IRL Press, Oxford, 1986.

C.F. Simpson (ed.) *Practical High Performance Liquid Chromatography*, Heyden & Son, London, 1976.

Gas chromatography (gas–liquid chromatography)

Usually referred to as GC or GLC, gas chromatography is widely used in the resolution of mixtures of volatile compounds (or volatile derivatives if the parent compounds are insufficiently volatile) which may differ in boiling point by only a fraction of a degree. It is predominantly used as an analytical technique but, in its preparative form, provides an excellent alternative to fractional distillation for up to tens of grams of material.

It is probably easiest to think of GC as a hybrid between chromatography and distillation. The sample to be analyzed is volatilized and swept by a stream of *carrier gas* through a heated column containing an absorbant support impregnated with an involatile liquid which acts as the *stationary phase* (Fig. 3.77). *Packed column GC* is carried out using columns made of stainless steel or glass tubing, usually between 2 and 6 m in length with inside diameters of about 3–5 mm. In order to fit inside the heating oven, the columns are coiled. As with all other types of chromatography using packed columns, the packing resists any flow through it and so limits the length of column (and hence degree of separation) that can be used. *Capillary column GC*, in which the stationary phase is bonded to the walls of a long capillary tube, permits far greater selectivity. The reduced resistance to flow along such columns enables lengths of up to 50 m to be used with phenomenal increases in resolving power.

As in chromatography, the components of the mixture partition between the stationary phase and the carrier gas due to a combination of volatility and the degree with which they interact with the stationary phase. The separated components are then eluted from the column and pass over a detector. The lapsed time between injection onto the column and the exit of a particular component is referred to as the *retention time* and, just like the R_f of a compound in TLC, is diagnostically useful for a given column and set of conditions. To continue the analogy between adsorption chromatography and GC, increasing the rate of flow of carrier gas is equivalent to increasing the rate of elution of a chromatography column. Raising the oven temperature surrounding the column increases the rate of elution in GC in the same way as using a more polar solvent in column chromatography. The direct equivalent of gradient elution is called *temperature programming* in which the oven temperature may be increased during the analysis to accelerate the rate of elution of the less mobile components of a mixture. Increasing the amount of stationary phase loaded onto the solid support has the same effect on retention

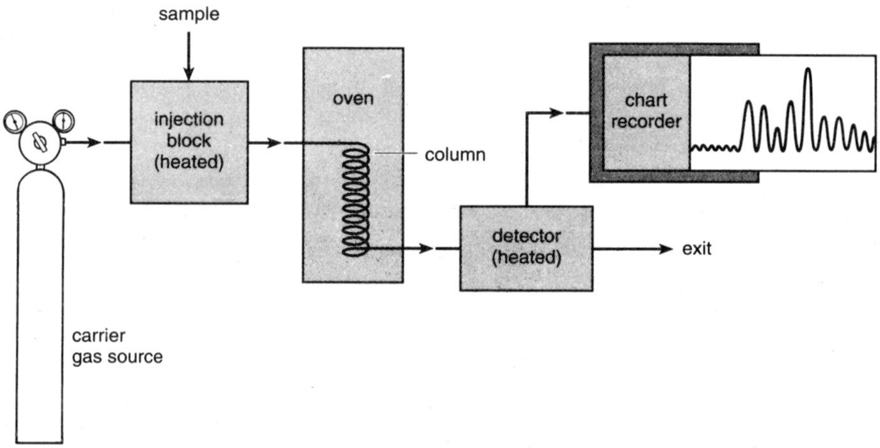

Fig. 3.77 Schematic diagram of the set-up for GC analysis.

of components as using a more active grade of adsorbant in column chromatography.

The carrier gas

The carrier gas is required to be inert to the column material and components of the sample. Depending on the detector, nitrogen, hydrogen, helium or argon may be used. In the case of flame ionization detectors, where the sample issuing from the column is burnt, the carrier gas is a mixture of hydrogen and air or nitrogen. Alternatively, on some machines fitted with flame ionization detectors, the hydrogen and air are introduced at the exit of the column just before the detector. Helium, with its low viscosity, is generally the carrier gas of choice for capillary columns. Flow rates must be controlled rigorously if retention time measurements are to have any meaning.

Packed columns and supports

The column consists of a length of glass or stainless steel tubing, coiled into several turns for convenience. The internal diameter varies from 3 to 5 mm and the length is usually between 2 and 6 m. Generally, separation efficiency increases with length and decreases with diameter, but at the same time, the greater resistance to flow in the longer columns demands a wider bore tube. The tube is filled with a porous support whose role is to absorb the stationary phase and present as large a surface area as possible. As might be expected, better efficiency of separation is obtained with supports consisting of small regularly sized particles. However, working against this is the greater pressure drop which occurs down the column when these more closely packed materials are used. The usual types of support are made from firebrick-derived materials (Chromosorb P) which are most suitable for use with non-polar hydrocarbon materials, or diatomaceous earth (Chromosorb W) which are better for use with molecules containing active hydrogens such as acids, amines and alcohols. These supports are first impregnated with the stationary phase and are then packed evenly into the column.

Stationary phase in packed column GC

As with solid–liquid chromatography, the stationary phase plays a very important role and hundreds of stationary phases have been developed in response to specific separation problems. The prime requirements are that a stationary phase should be thermally stable, unreactive and involatile over the working range of the column. All stationary phases can be classified as either *polar* or *non-polar*. Non-polar phases separate components largely on the basis of their differing boiling points, whereas polar phases may also impose dipole–dipole interactions in varying degrees on the compounds passing over them. In deciding which type of phase to use for a particular separation problem, it is helpful to remember that non-polar compounds are most suited to non-polar situations and vice versa. Another important consideration is the maximum temperature at which the stationary phase can be used before it starts to become volatile. Operating at higher temperatures will cause the stationary phase to begin to detach from the support, resulting in *stripping* and degradation of the column and swamping of the detector system. A brief list of commonly used stationary phases is given in Table 3.15 but for more comprehensive listings the reader is referred to the appropriate sections in *The Chemist's Companion* or the wide range of commercial literature available.

Capillary columns

The development of capillary columns has largely eliminated the limitations of packed column GC associated with pressure drop along the column. As

Table 3.15 Commonly used stationary phases for GC.

Stationary phase (type)	Property	Maximum operating temperature (°C)	Applications
Squalane (hydrocarbon)	Non-polar	150	General, halocarbons, hydrocarbons
Apiezon (hydrocarbon)	Non-polar	280(L), 200(M), 200(N)	General, hydrocarbons
SE-30 (methylsilicone)	Non-polar	350	Non-polar, high molecular weight compounds, silylated derivatives
OV-1, OV-101 (dimethylsilicone)	Non-polar	300–350	Non-polar, high molecular weight compounds
Carbowax® 20 M (polyglycol)	Polar	225	Low molecular weight, polar compounds
PEGA (polyethyleneglycol adipate)	Polar	180	Low molecular weight, polar compounds
DEGS (diethyleneglycol succinate)	Polar	190	Low molecular weight, polar compounds
OV-17 (50:50 dimethylsilicone: diphenylsilicone)	Intermediate	350	Low molecular weight, polar compounds, high molecular weight hydrocarbons
DC-550 (silicone oil)	Intermediate	275	Low molecular weight, polar compounds, high molecular weight hydrocarbons

their name suggests, these columns—first proposed by M.J.E. Golay—consist of a fine bore tube, usually made of silica with an internal diameter of less than 0.5 mm, the walls of which are coated with the stationary phase. As the unfilled centre permits relatively free passage of gas, there is a markedly reduced pressure drop down such columns, and lengths of 25–50 m are usual. The resolution efficiency of these columns (often referred to as the number of *theoretical plates* by analogy with distillation) is greatly superior to that of packed columns. Capillary columns possessing 500 000 theoretical plates are not uncommon as opposed to the absolute maximum of about 20 000 for packed columns. Other salient features of capillary columns compared with the equivalent packed columns may be listed as follows.

- Smaller sample sizes are necessary.
- Limits of detection are the same as packed columns, although less material is used due to the sharpness of the peaks.
- Elution times for equivalent resolutions are up to 10 times shorter.
- Column temperatures are usually about 20°C lower than those required for the corresponding packed columns.
- Almost any sample mixture can be separated using one of four stationary phases: OV-101, SE-30 (non-polar samples), OV-17 (medium polarity samples) and Carbowax® 20 M (polar samples).

The stationary phase may be deposited either as a thin film directly onto the internal wall of the tube, or adsorbed onto a support which is applied to the tube. In the case of *bonded phase capillary columns* the stationary phase is further stabilized by being covalently linked to the support. The mechanical properties of the silica when drawn out into a capillary, particularly when coated with a protective resin, result in a flexible, resilient column which can be crumpled in the hand without breaking or deforming (practise this trick at your peril, however, these columns are expensive!).

The oven

Very stringent demands are placed on the functioning of the oven as the temperature of the column has a direct effect on the retention times of the components. The oven must be capable of maintaining an accurate temperature in a range from slightly above ambient temperature to about 300°C. In addition, the temperature throughout the whole volume of the oven must be constant so that the total column length is at the same temperature. For this reason an internal fan is fitted to circulate air. The heater must also be able to produce accurate, reproducible heating rates of anything up to 40°C min^{-1} and, at the same time, the walls of the oven must have minimal heat capacity in order to keep temperature overshoot to an absolute minimum. This feature is particularly important in stepped temperature programmes, when an initial phase of temperature increase is followed by a period of steady temperature, before proceeding with a second temperature increase.

Detector and response factors

Various types of detector are used, but the most commonly encountered is the *flame ionization detector*. As the name suggests, the gas issuing from the column is burnt and the ions in the flame are detected and translated into an electric current. When a compound is eluted from the column, this causes an increase in the production of ions, with a corresponding increase in the current sent to the chart recorder. It is tempting to measure the areas under the peaks which make up the GC trace and conclude that these reflect the relative quantities of material present in the original mixture. Unfortunately, different compounds give rise to different amounts of ions when they burn, so this assumption cannot be made. Compounds containing sulfur, for instance, are notoriously poorly detected by flame ionization detectors. To quantify GC traces it is necessary to standardize the peak area due to a known quantity of each component against an internal standard in order to obtain the *response factor* in each case. This is a time-consuming exercise which may not always be possible to carry out if authentic materials are not available. However, to a first order of approximation, it may be assumed that isomers or compounds of the same structural type will have closely similar response factors and relative peak areas can be compared. That this is not really a valid assumption can be seen from the following flame ionization detector response factors for some straight-chain primary alcohols relative to ethanol:

Comparing peak areas in GC traces is not a reliable method of determining relative quantities of components

Alcohol	Ethanol	Propanol	Butanol	Pentanol
Response factor	1.00	1.41	1.63	1.97

If an automatic integrator is not available, treatment of the peaks as if they are triangles is usually permissible if the baseline is flat. An alternative method is to photocopy the trace (with enlargement if possible) and cut out and weigh the various peaks on an analytical balance.

Sample preparation

The sample should be made up as a solution in dichloromethane, toluene, or acetone to a concentration of 1–2 mg mL^{-1}. The solution must be free of any particulate matter which could block the syringe. Obviously the sample should be volatile enough to permit analysis by GC, but if not, it may be possible to convert it to a suitably volatile derivative.

Derivatization of involatile or polar compounds

As well as increasing the volatility of components to be analyzed, derivatization might also help if excessive 'tailing' of the peaks is observed—often the case with compounds capable of hydrogen bonding. By far the commonest derivatization technique is to silylate any free acid, alcohol or amine groups. Many reagents have been developed for this but the most reactive are doubly silylated derivatives of amides. Both BSTFA (*N*,*O*-bis(trimethylsilyl)trifluoroacetamide) and BSA (*N*,*O*-bis(trimethylsilyl)acetamide) trimethylsilylate alcohols, acids or amines rapidly and quantitatively.

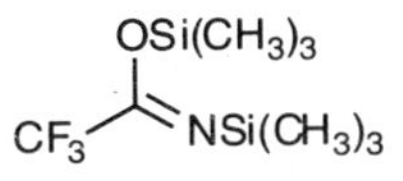

BSTFA

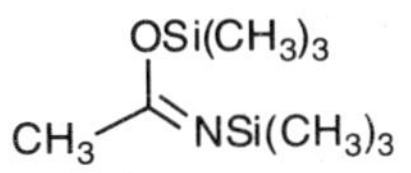

BSA

To carry out such a derivatization before analysis, dissolve a small quantity of the sample (1–2 mg) in 4 drops of dry pyridine contained in a 2 mL screw cap vial and add excess of the silylating reagent (*ca.* 20 μL). After 15 min at room temperature, the mixture can be diluted to 1 mL with the requisite solvent and the solution injected directly onto the column.

Alkylation and acylation are other commonly used derivatization techniques, but usually they have no advantage over silylation.

Introducing the sample onto the column

Samples are introduced onto the column via the injection port (Fig. 3.78) which consists of an adapter over the inlet end of the column carrying a septum which is pierced using a microlitre syringe containing a solution of the sample.

Treat GC syringes with great care

Syringes for GC analysis are high precision instruments designed to deliver (as opposed to just containing) exact amounts of liquid in microlitre quantities. With this aim, the dead space in the bore of the needle is minimized by a fine wire which runs from the tip of the plunger to the tip of the needle when the plunger is fully depressed. This fine wire is very easily damaged if the plunger is withdrawn too far from the barrel and will require expensive repair work.

Never dismantle the microlitre syringe and take care not to bend or kink the needle

Some syringes may be fitted with a device which only permits the plunger to be pulled back a certain distance (Fig. 3.79a). If not, it is recommended that

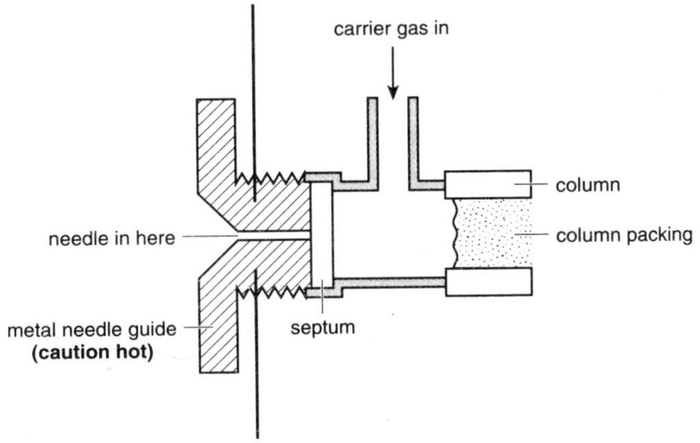

Fig. 3.78 Cross-section through a GC injection port.

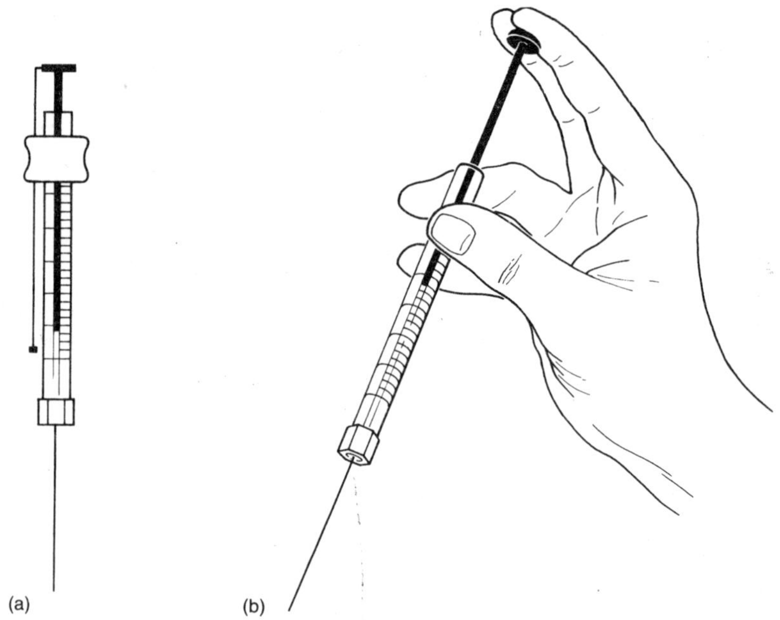

Fig. 3.79 (a) A typical syringe for GC analysis with a fitting for limiting plunger withdrawal; (b) technique for holding the syringe with one hand during rinsing and filling.

you hold the syringe in one hand only when rinsing and filling it. To do this, grasp the barrel of the syringe between the thumb and third and fourth fingers and hold the plunger with the index and forefingers (Fig. 3.79b). In this way, it is possible to take up the sample, but it is not possible to pull the plunger out too far. After a little practice, this technique soon becomes second nature.

Keep the syringe thoroughly clean at all times

As the syringe cannot be dismantled in the normal course of events, it must be thoroughly cleaned whenever it is used, *both before and after use*. Rinse the syringe out initially at least 10 times in pure sample solvent, by filling to its maximum volume and then expressing the contents of the barrel as a tiny drop of liquid. Similarly rinse out the syringe with your dissolved sample, but on the final filling, push the plunger down to the volume required for analysis (between 0.5 and 5 μL, and usually 1 μL). Now, *holding the syringe with both hands* (Fig. 3.80) push the needle slowly through the septum of the inlet port *without injecting the sample*, until the syringe barrel almost touches the metal surround of the port. *Perform this operation slowly, otherwise you will bend the needle and ruin the syringe.* The wire running the length of the needle ensures that no liquid resides in that region of the syringe, subsequently boiling off onto the column before the main body of the sample can be injected.

Take care not to burn your hands on the metal of the injection port which will be at a temperature close to that of the oven

In one smooth movement, quickly push the plunger fully into the barrel, make a mark on the chart recorder to show the actual point of introduction of the sample, and then withdraw the syringe. *Immediately rinse out the syringe 10 times with pure solvent.*

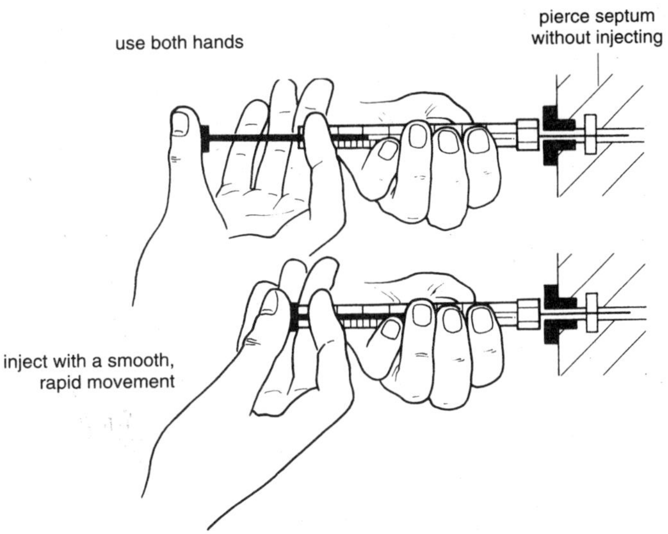

Fig. 3.80 Injecting the sample onto the column.

Your sample is now on the column and you are waiting impatiently to see the result of the analysis on the chart recorder. If things are working well, you might hope to see a trace looking something like Fig. 3.81—the peaks will be even sharper if you are using a capillary column. Knowing the rate at which the chart recorder paper is moving permits the retention time for each peak to be read off directly from the horizontal axis.

Common problems

Unfortunately, there are many reasons why you might not see anything like the trace in Fig. 3.81 and a few common problems are mentioned here.

No peaks visible or only very small peaks. If no peaks appear at all, check the recorder is connected up correctly and switched on. If all appears correct, either you have not injected enough sample or, more likely, the sensitivity of the detector is not high enough. This is controlled using the *attenuator*, which perversely enough, gives higher detection sensitivities when at lower settings. The most sensitive setting is 1 and the infinity position cuts out any response altogether. Normally you should operate between positions 4 and 64 on the attenuator.

Some or all peaks off scale. Do not worry about the first peak being off scale—this is the solvent peak—but all the other peaks should be on scale if you wish to measure peak areas. Either you are injecting too much sample, or you have the attenuator set at too sensitive a position. It is usually simple to differentiate between these possibilities as concentrated samples tend to give read-outs

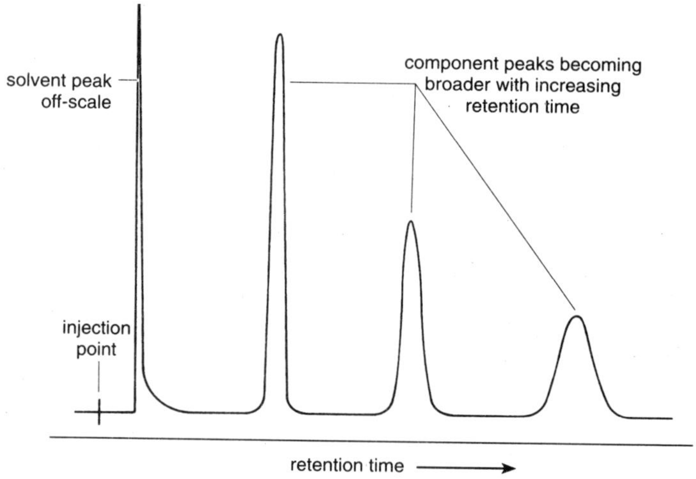

Fig. 3.81 Idealized GC trace of a sample mixture.

with a very smooth baseline, whereas high sensitivity attenuator settings result in a noisy baseline.

Irregularly shaped peaks. The ideal shape of the peaks should be gaussian or nearly so; the pen should rise and descend smoothly and symmetrically when drawing out the peak. If the peak shows noticeable tailing (Fig. 3.82a), this is often evidence that you have a mismatch between the sample being analyzed and the column stationary phase and support. This might be remedied by silylating the sample to remove any hydrogen-bonding groups, or it may be easier to opt for a less polar column. If the leading edge of the peak rises sluggishly and erratically, followed by a rapid drop at the trailing edge, giving a broad peak with a 'shark's fin' effect (Fig. 3.82b), this is a sure sign of column overload and much less sample should be injected. Owing to lateral diffusion which occurs in any chromatographic process, it is natural that some peak broadening, with consequent loss of peak height, will occur with later eluting components. When long retention times lead to the peaks becoming indistinguishable from the baseline then use of temperature programming is called for (Fig. 3.83).

Baseline drift. A baseline which drifts upward, particularly during the latter stages of a temperature programme, indicates that the stationary phase is beginning to 'strip' from the column. Lower oven temperatures are necessary to avoid ruining the column.

Appearance of spurious peaks. Remember that impurities do not count as spurious peaks! However, if the trace shows broad peaks which crop up at unpredictable intervals, this is a sign that the previous users have contami-

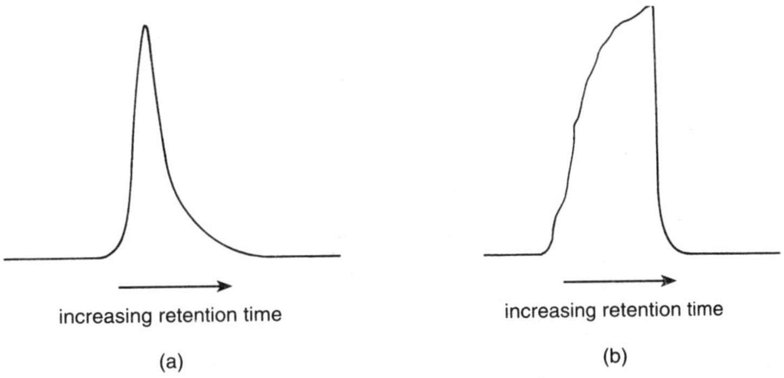

Fig. 3.82 Typical irregularities in peak shapes: (a) tailing peaks; (b) shark's fin peaks.

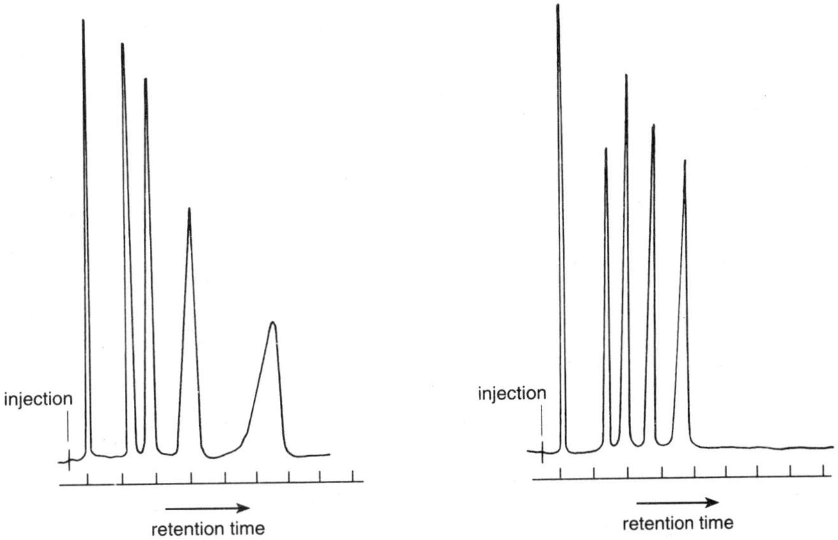

Fig. 3.83 Typical packed column GC traces: (a) isothermal conditions; (b) same sample analyzed with temperature programming—passage of the later components is speeded up by increasing the oven temperature.

nated the column with polymeric material, or that the person immediately prior to you has not allowed all the components to elute off the column before shutting it down. As some molecules take an exceedingly long time to be eluted from the column, the person who has just used the column may not be to blame. Report the state of the column to the person responsible for the apparatus—do not attempt to remonstrate with anyone yourself! After a day's use, it is usual to 'bake out' the column. This involves heating the oven overnight to near the maximum working temperature of the column with the carrier gas flowing through it.

The appearance of erratic, sharp spikes on the trace is usually caused by electrical interference from some other piece of apparatus; these spikes do not usually interfere with your result. Do not attempt to find the source of interference by switching off any electrical instruments in the vicinity!

Variable retention times. If repeated injections do not give very close retention times for the eluted peaks, something is likely to be wrong with the supply of carrier gas. If the retention times increase, it is probable that the gas supply is running out and needs renewing. If the times vary erratically, check the state of the septum in the injection port, which is liable to be leaking.

Variable peak areas. If repeated injections show wild variations in the heights of the peaks on the trace, do not blame the apparatus as this is almost certainly due to poor injection technique. Either you are not taking up the same amount of sample each time, or you are not injecting all of it onto the column. It is useless having the apparatus in perfect condition if your technique does not give repeatable results. This only comes with practice and care.

Co-injection as an indication of identity

In order to compare an unknown compound with a sample of authentic material to see if they have identical retention times, it is necessary to carry out simultaneous analysis of the unknown and the authentic material. Preparing a mixed solution of the two materials requires some care to ensure that neither component predominates by too much. If one component of the mixture is present in a large excess over the other, its peak will totally dominate the trace and will swamp any shoulder due to a closely running component. This will give the impression that the two compounds are identical. Often the components are too precious to sacrifice to a potentially mixed solution. In this case each should be dissolved separately to give solutions of roughly equal concentrations. An equal volume of each should be removed using the microlitre syringe for simultaneous injection onto the column.

Remember that, whilst the appearance of a double peak on co-injection tells you that the two components are definitely different, the observation of a single peak only *indicates* identity. Other supportive evidence must be found as the unavoidable peak broadening which occurs with packed columns means that two different compounds might have overlapping peaks.

Further reading

A. Braithwaite, C.B.F. Rice and F.J. Smith, *Chromatographic Methods*, 5th edn, Chapman & Hall, London, 1996, Chapter 5.

For the proposal of the potential of capillary columns, see: M.J.E. Golay, *Gas Chromatography* (ed. R.P.W. Scott), Butterworths, London, 1958, p. 36.

For texts dealing with capillary GC, see: W. Jennings, *Gas Chromatography with Glass Capillary Columns*, 2nd edn, Academic Press, London, 1980; D.W. Grant, *Capillary Gas Chromatography*, Wiley & Sons, New York, 1996.

For texts dealing with gas chromatography, see: A.J. Gordon and R.A. Ford, *The Chemist's Companion. A Handbook of Practical Data, Techniques and References*, Wiley & Sons,

New York, 1973; G. Schonburg, *Gas Chromatography*, VCH, 1990; P. Baugh, *Gas Chromatography*, IRL Press, Oxford, 1993; I.A. Fowlis, *Gas Chromatography*, 2nd edn, Wiley & Sons, New York, 1995; W. Jennings, E. Mittlefehldt and P. Stemple, *Analytical Gas Chromatography*, 2nd edn, Academic Press, London, 1997.

For further details of preparing derivatives for GC analysis, see: K. Blau and J.M. Halket (eds) *Handbook of Derivatives for Chromatography*, 2nd edn, Wiley & Sons, New York, 1993; D.R. Knapp, *Handbook of Analytical Derivatization Reactions*, Wiley & Sons, New York, 1979.

Chapter 4 Qualitative Analysis of Organic Compounds

4.1 Purity

Why bother to analyze compounds?

All scientists observe systems, make observations and draw conclusions from their results. It is this protocol which, if rigorously adhered to in the laboratory, is most likely to turn a chance observation into an important discovery. However, before any meaningful results can be obtained, the scientist must know for certain exactly what is under scrutiny, otherwise any results obtained are simply a worthless jumble of irreproducible facts. Organic chemists are no exception to this general situation and, as the systems usually under study in the laboratory are chemical substances, the worker must ensure at the outset the nature of the material under investigation, and whether it is indeed a single substance or a mixture of components.

All this may seem obvious, but the regularity with which students commence analyzing an unknown before actually ensuring the purity of their sample makes this reminder very necessary. Nobody would dream of undertaking an analysis of the active constituents contained in the extract of some obscure species of tropical plant without first making a thorough examination of the complexity of the extract. Likewise, the fact that a sample has been taken from a bottle on a shelf is no assurance of purity or even that the substance is what the label says it is! Quite apart from the contrived machinations of academics devising unknown mixtures for analysis in the teaching laboratory, labelling mistakes occur only too frequently; particularly in samples which have been relabelled or repackaged after purchase. Additionally, it must be remembered that most organic chemicals degrade on storage and, whilst the age of the sample might be known, its stability under the specific conditions of storage is impossible to estimate. Consequently, even commercial samples, apparently pristine in their original wrapping, should always be checked for purity before use. Too frequently this apparently self-evident precaution is overlooked by even the most experienced research chemists—often to their downfall. The least important consequences of such poor technique are erroneous results, lowered yields or wasted laboratory time; the potential for disaster is only too obvious.

It might be argued that, with the introduction of sensitive, non-destructive spectroscopic techniques (Chapter 5), there is little need for new generations of chemists to learn the art of qualitative analysis. However, apart from the practical requirements in the research laboratory which may or may not be equipped with the latest elaborate piece of spectroscopic hardware, there are other reasons for learning these techniques which apply specifically to anyone wishing to become a worthwhile chemist. The identification of an unknown compound encapsulates the events which occur during any scientific investigation, no matter how short or how grand. The cyclic sequence of test–observe–propose/extrapolate–verify/disprove teaches us good scientific practice, and if a certain amount of inspired guesswork occurs, that only mirrors the serendipity which takes place in research a good deal more frequently than most would care to admit!

The techniques required to test for functional groups and to prepare derivatives provide the student with excellent training in the various manipulative techniques of small-scale experimental work that will be required later on in the teaching and research laboratory. In addition to this, as the characterization of functional groups depends on their specific features of structure and reactivity, qualitative analysis allows us to see at first hand the chemical consequences of the presence of a particular moiety in a molecule and contributes to the general understanding that separates the good practical chemist from the nondescript. It is for these profound pedagogical reasons that the descriptions of analytical techniques precede the preparative experiments in this book.

This chapter is broken down into sections covering criteria of purity and qualitative analysis. Although frequently spectroscopic analysis alone can provide the full structure of an unknown substance, the prudent chemist will nonetheless carry out some confirmatory chemical tests to check the presence of the proposed functionalities.

Laboratory safety

It is most important when analyzing an unknown compound never to forget that its properties as well as its chemical identity are unknown. 'Safety first' is always the motto in the laboratory and never more so than when handling unidentified materials which may be toxic, corrosive, flammable or explosive.

Care is paramount when carrying out analyses on unknown materials which must always be treated as potentially hazardous to health.

Remember that the absence of known toxic effects for a chemical can never constitute an absolute assurance of its safety (the perennial problem of the pharmaceutical industry where legislation appears to demand this) and some compounds possess hazardous properties, such as carcinogenicity, which may not manifest themselves in any obvious way until many years later when it is too late.

Criteria of purity

The ancient alchemists believed that all matter was made up of various combinations of four components—earth, air, fire and water. As far as the organic chemist is concerned, the vast majority of the compounds handled regularly in the laboratory are either solid or liquid, and the physical properties relating to these two states (melting point, boiling point, refractive index) are frequently used as indications of the purity of a compound. Another physical property which holds if the molecule is optically active is the degree by which a solution of the substance will rotate plane polarized light under standard conditions ($[\alpha]_D$). We will consider the practical aspects of determining these parameters in the first part of this chapter.

Analytical techniques which have already been dealt with in Chapter 3, which depend on a combination of physical properties of the compound (polarity, volatility, solubility, shape, functional groups present), are the chromatographic techniques, particularly thin layer chromatography (TLC, see pp. 165–175) and gas chromatography (GC, see pp. 191–203). These techniques, relying as they do on the interplay of a whole range of properties, are highly selective and permit distinction between very similar substances. In addition, they use very little material and (particularly in the case of TLC) are very quick and easy to use, giving reliable results within minutes.

There is also an analysis which is still regarded as the touchstone for purity of organic substances—quantitative elemental microanalysis. This technique is a measure of the bulk contents of a sample but suffers from the disadvantages of requiring expensive specialized apparatus and highly skilled operators, which certainly puts it outside the realm of the teaching laboratory. However, it is probably the fact that it is outside the scope of the ability of most chemists to microanalyze their own samples that is its strong point. In a world where the pressure for success grows daily, microanalysis is a technique in which the second person carrying out the analysis acts effectively as an independent witness, verifying the validity of the results claimed by the first.

Melting point

The melting point of a solid substance can give an indication of its degree of purity and can also assist greatly in its identification. Whilst not always strictly true, it is considered that a sharp melting point range (<2°C) between the first appearance of drops of liquid within the sample to the disappearance of the last trace of solid constitutes good evidence for believing a substance to be pure. Rarely, however, a mixture might give a sharp melting point if the components are present in the exact proportions to form a *eutectic mixture* (see below).

Conversely a broad melting point, whilst strong evidence for lack of purity, can result if a pure substance decomposes on heating, thus introducing impurities. Darkening of the sample or evolution of a gas is an indication that this is occurring. Dissolution of the compound in residual or occluded recrystallization solvent will also give what appears to be a broad melting point and is a commonly encountered situation in the teaching laboratory!

Melting point range

To explain why impure compounds have a broad melting point range let us consider a hypothetical phase diagram of a mixture containing two components having different melting points (A = 90°C, B = 110°C) (Fig. 4.1).

In the phase diagram, the mixture corresponding to 70% A and 30% B has the lowest melting point (74°C—the *eutectic temperature*). A mixture of A and B having exactly this composition would appear to have a sharp melting point at this reduced temperature. However, suppose that A is an impurity in B and is present to the extent of 5%. Melting will first occur at 74°C and the liquid formed will have the eutectic composition containing 70% A—in other words much higher than in the original mixture containing only 5% A. The mixture will continue to melt at 74°C until all of the impurity A is in the liquid phase. The total amount of material which will have melted at this point is

$$A + B = 5\% + (30/70 \times 5)\%$$
$$= 7.1\%$$

This initial melting would probably not be visible to the naked eye, and at this stage the remaining solid, representing 92.9% of the original mixture, consists totally of B. As the temperature rises the remaining solid begins to melt, adding to the amount of B in the liquid until the first drop is observed—let us say that this occurs when 30% of the mixture has melted. At this point the melt will contain five parts of A and 25 parts of B (approximately 17% A, 83% B). From the phase diagram it can be seen that the melting point of a mixture containing 83% B would be roughly 104°C and this would be recorded as the start

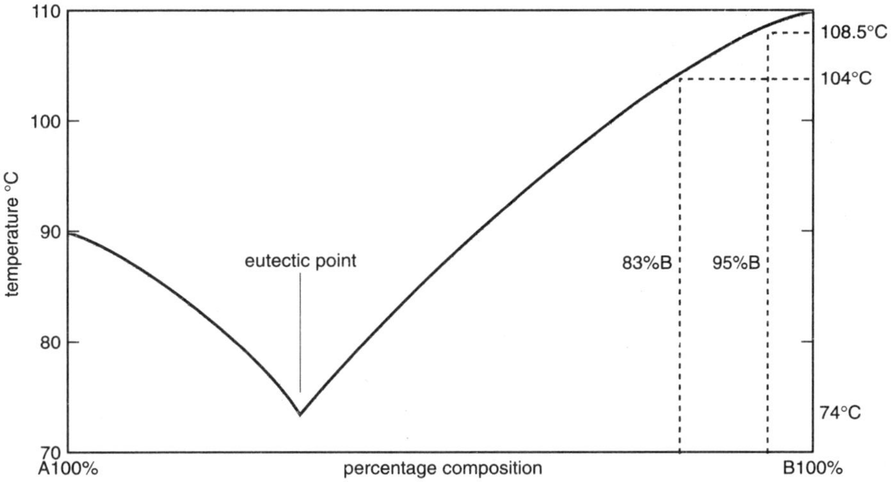

Fig. 4.1 Simple phase diagram for a two-component mixture.

of melting. As the temperature rises, B will continue to melt according to the phase diagram until the last crystal of B melts to give a liquid containing 95% B and 5% A (the original composition). This will occur at approximately 108.5°C. The melting point range would thus be recorded as 104.0–108.5°C; broader and depressed compared with that of pure B.

Mixed melting point as a means of preliminary identification

The melting point of a pure substance can be used to provide an indication of its possible structure by comparing the melting point obtained with those contained in data tables. Usually, some knowledge of the chemical reactivity of the unknown is also to hand and it is frequently possible to narrow the field to one or two prime candidates having similar melting points. The assignment may be verified or disproved by making an intimate mixture of the unknown with a pure sample of the proposed material in approximately equal proportions and recording the melting point of this mixture. If the substances are identical then the melting point will be unchanged. However, if they are different the melting point of the mixture will be depressed compared with that of the unknown as the introduction of the impurity lowers and broadens the melting point range. This technique is particularly handy when several possible candidate compounds have quoted melting points within one or two degrees of the observed value (for example benzoic acid, 121°C, and succinic anhydride, 120°C).

Experimental procedures for recording melting points

Capillary tube method

Familiarize yourself with the apparatus in your laboratory

Care! Hot surfaces

At its simplest, this consists of placing a small amount of the substance, contained in a capillary tube, into a heating bath with a means of measuring the temperature of the bath. Various refinements are possible and numerous commercial systems are available which may use an electrically heated oil bath or metal block as the heat transmission medium (Fig. 4.2).

Care! Always check for solvents or flammable materials

However, before the melting point can be measured, it is necessary to introduce your sample into the capillary tube. Commercial melting point tubes are available in which one end has been presealed, but it is more usual to utilize a simple open-ended capillary and seal it oneself—*before* introducing the sample, of course! The tube should be sealed by just touching the hot (blue) flame of a microburner with the tube pointing slightly upwards to prevent the flow and condensation into the body of the tube of any water vapour driven off by the heating (Fig. 4.3). Care should be taken not to permit a globule of glass to develop on the sealed end as this may prevent the introduction of the tube through any preset hole in a commercial apparatus and may also slow down heat transfer to the solid.

Make sure that the sample is dry and has been ground to a fine powder. Press the open end of the cooled melting point tube into a small pile of the

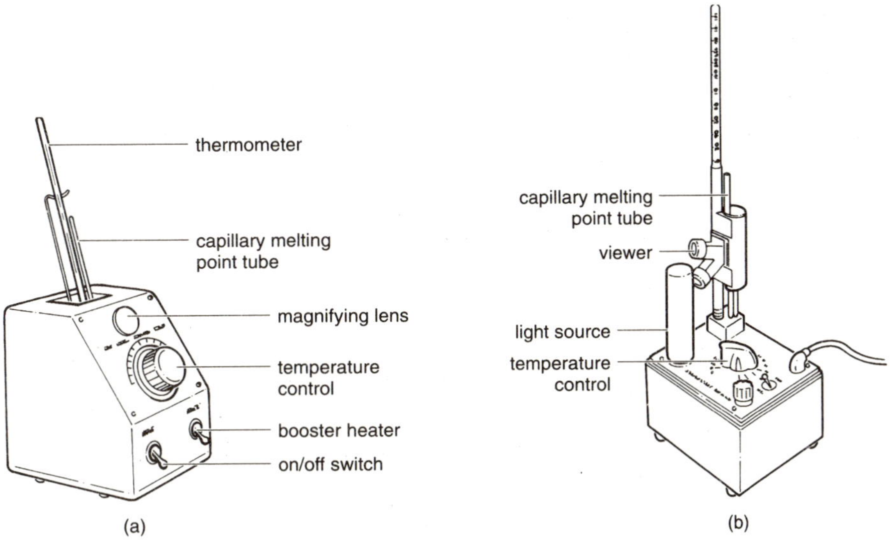

Fig. 4.2 Examples of apparatus used for capillary tube melting point determination.

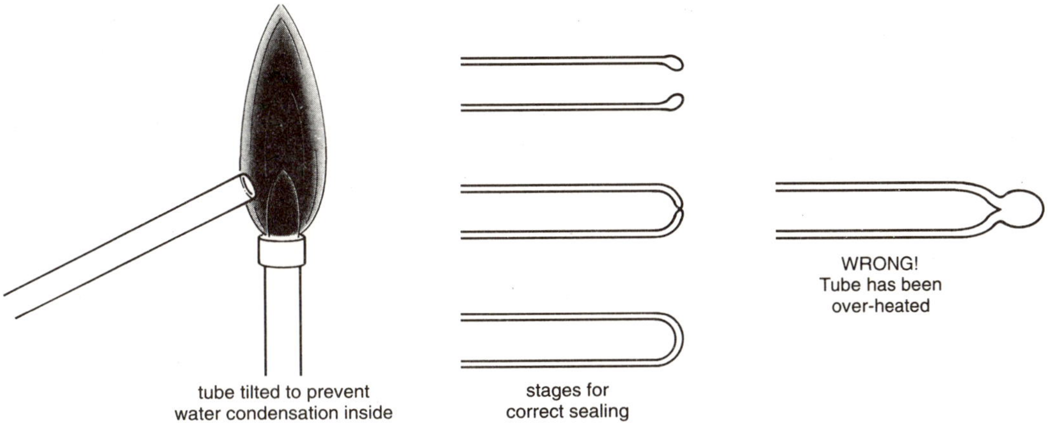

Fig. 4.3 Sealing a melting point capillary tube.

sample on a clean glass surface, such as a watch glass, causing a plug of the material to become wedged into the mouth of the tube. To move this to the sealed end, stand a length of glass tubing about 50 cm long on the bench and drop the tube, sealed end first, down it. The force of impact on the bench will not be sufficient to break the melting point tube, but it will cause the solid to be transferred to the sealed end. Repeat this procedure until about 3 mm of the tube has been packed with sample.

An alternative procedure for moving your sample to the sealed end of the capillary involves rubbing the tube with a rough surface, such as the milled edge of a coin or the serrated edge of a glass file, when the vibrations shake the sample to the bottom.

On attempting to record a melting point, it may be observed that the solid sublimes before melting (indicated by a ring of solid appearing at the point where the tube leaves the heating medium). In this instance, it may be possible to obtain a melting point by using a closed capillary prepared by sealing the open end after introduction of the sample. Needless to say, as this will involve the development of pressure within the tube, such a procedure must never be carried out in anything larger than the standard capillary tube where the relative thickness of the glass compared with the internal volume permits safe operation.

Always increase the temperature slowly near the expected melting point

As it is assumed that the temperature of the medium equates with that of the sample under investigation, it follows that the sample must be held close to the point of measurement and adequate heat distribution must be assured within the transmission medium. All commercial apparatus is designed to meet these criteria, but none of the features will be of any use if the temperature is increased too rapidly, as the sample must be allowed to come to equilibrium with its surroundings. It is usually acceptable (indeed necessary with thermally unstable compounds) to approach rapidly to within 20°C of the expected melting point and to then slow down the rate of heating such that the temperature is increased at no more than 2°C each minute—the slower the better. Some pieces of apparatus have built-in booster heaters for this purpose. It is best to be aware that the temperature of the heating bath will normally continue to rise at a relatively rapid rate for some time after the heating has been reduced owing to residual heat within the heating element. Therefore it may be necessary to slow down the heating some way below the expected melting point. The best practice (particularly if, as is usually the case, the melting point is unknown) is to carry out an initial rapid but approximate determination, followed by an accurate determination in which the melting point is approached slowly from about 20°C below the value expected.

It is necessary to observe the sample carefully before the melting point and note faithfully any changes in appearance (for example darkening) and the temperature at which they occur. This is normally made easier by the positioning of a magnifying lens in the apparatus. Above all, it is necessary not to fall prey to any preconceived ideas, but to record all of your observations objectively. This maxim always applies in the laboratory, but it appears that waiting for a substance to melt brings out the worst in some people—do not be impatient!

The first sign that your sample is about to melt is usually a contraction in volume of the sample, which may result in it pulling away from the walls of the tube, although no liquid will be visible at this stage. This phenomenon is referred to as *sintering* and the temperature at which this occurs should be noted. The first droplet of liquid should then be visible within a few degrees of the sintering point and this is considered to be the commencement of melting. The completion of melting is taken to be the point at which the last crystal disappears. These two readings constitute the melting point range (Fig. 4.4).

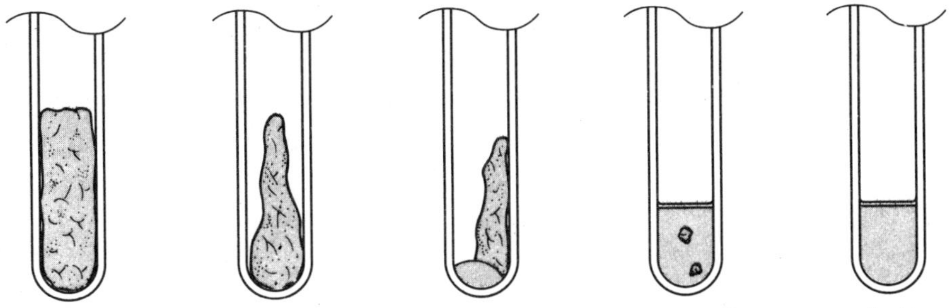

Fig. 4.4 Typical sample changes in the region of its melting point.

As soon as your sample has melted and the three readings and other observations have been noted, the apparatus should be allowed to cool and the sample should be disposed of carefully, as directed by the laboratory for disposal of sharp materials. In otherwise clean and tidy laboratories, there is frequently a mess of discarded capillary tubes around the communal melting point apparatus. This is not only slovenly, but potentially hazardous should a worker be cut accidently.

Always clean up your mess after you

Heated block method

This general heading covers two very different pieces of commercial apparatus which may be encountered. One permits rapid approximate determination of melting points (for example, to obtain an initial approximate melting point, or to enable instructors to check on students' claims!), and the other permits very accurate readings on small amounts of sample.

In the first case, the apparatus consists essentially of a metallic strip which is heated by an electric current in such a way that a temperature gradient is set up. Along the strip is a pointer which can be moved along a calibrated temperature scale (Fig. 4.5a). A small amount of compound is sprinkled onto that area of the plate corresponding to a temperature close to, but lower than, the suspected melting point of the sample. This is then spread along the plate using the pointer until a transition from solid to liquid is observed, enabling a melting point to be read off from the scale. Of course, such an apparatus can only give very approximate values, as the solid–liquid transition is often difficult to detect with precision and, more importantly, the actual temperature at any point on the metal strip depends on the temperature of the room and the absence of draughts. It is also generally forgotten that the apparatus requires time to come to equilibration (about 30 min). Nonetheless, many instructors have found that merely switching on such an apparatus will convince an adamant student that the recorded melting point might require checking!

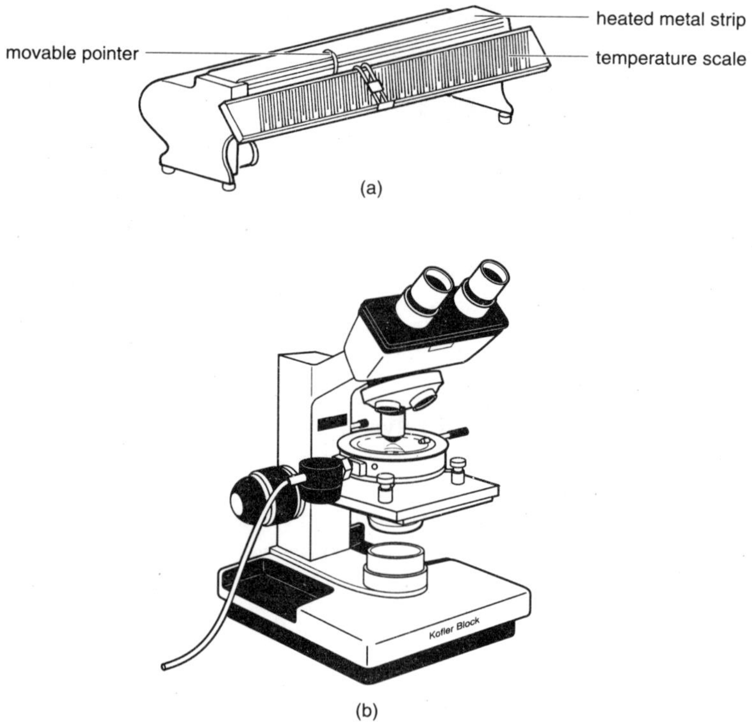

Fig. 4.5 (a) Kofler hotbench. (b) Koflerblock and viewing microscope.

Care! Hot surfaces

At all times treat such apparatus with care, as the exposed metal surface is very hot. Cleaning such apparatus between samples is problematical, and is best carried out carefully using a paper tissue held with tongs, with a much more thorough cleaning at the end of the laboratory session after the apparatus has been unplugged and allowed to cool down.

Do not contaminate the cover slips used for holding the sample

The more precise systems, of which the Kofler block apparatus (Fig. 4.5b) is an example, utilizes a very small amount of sample sandwiched between two microscope cover slips in intimate contact with a heated metal block. The sample is observed through a magnifying lens or microscope which permits very detailed observation of the beginning and end of the melting. Sintering will not be obvious in such a sample and the onset of melting can be rapid and unexpected. Draughts must be avoided and, in the case of the Kofler apparatus, a glass plate may be supplied to cover the heating block. Kofler blocks are provided with a microscope for viewing the sample. The microscope must always be focused by first lowering the tip down to the glass cover and then moving upwards. Ignoring this precaution will result in repeated, costly breakages of the glass cover. Great care must be exercised in the handling of the microscope cover slips as a deposition of grease from the hands will constitute a considerable impurity with regard to the amount of sample used. It is important to use as little sample as possible (preferably one crystal) and to press the two cover slips tightly together. If this is not done some of the sample will be in contact with the glass and some will not, with the consequence that a broad melting point range may be observed. Extra care must be taken with the thermometers used in such pieces of apparatus as they are extremely expensive.

Calibration of the melting point apparatus—the 'corrected melting point'

It stands to reason that, for a quoted melting point to have any scientific value, it must be a reproducible value regardless of the apparatus with which it has been measured. Unfortunately we do not live in such an ideal world and different pieces of apparatus, particularly thermometers, may lead to measurements which vary to some extent. Frequently organic chemists are willing to accept small discrepancies of, say 1°C, from a quoted literature value if the melting range is sharp, and the word 'uncorrected' may often be seen applied to melting point data in research literature. To correct any particular apparatus involves the determination of the melting points of a number of standard samples on the apparatus and the preparation of a calibration graph across its working temperature range. Corrected melting points can then be obtained from the graph, which is special to the apparatus, its environment and its component parts—a broken thermometer, for instance, will necessitate a new calibration graph. As poor technique (for instance heating the sample too quickly) can have a much larger effect on the measurement of a melting point than any inbuilt errors of the apparatus, it is not likely that you will be expected to correct your values in the teaching laboratory. In any case, the probable identity of an unknown is always best checked by a mixed melting point rather than by simply comparing with literature values. Nonetheless, you should be aware of the practice of correcting melting points.

Boiling point

Pure liquids which distil without decomposition will possess a sharp, constant boiling point, and will leave no residue on distillation to dryness. However, this property is very susceptible to fluctuations in atmospheric pressure and consequently an experimental determination of a boiling point may differ by several degrees from that reported in the literature. Indeed, as already discussed, the lowering of the boiling point of a substance with pressure is frequently used to advantage in the laboratory in reduced pressure distillation of thermolabile or high boiling compounds and in the removal of solvents using a rotary evaporator.

The effects of impurities on the boiling point of a liquid depend on the nature of the impurity and may commonly lead to a sharp boiling point. Therefore, it is dangerous to interpret a sharp, steady boiling point as evidence of purity in a liquid sample. As an obvious example, an involatile impurity leaves the boiling point of the distilling liquid unaffected (although the pot temperature will be higher than that of the boiling point of the pure liquid and the contaminant will remain as a residue after distillation). Unfortunately, the relationship between the temperatures of the liquid in the pot and the distilling vapour is not a reliable indication of the presence of impurities owing to the ease with which superheating can occur during a distillation.

The effects of volatile impurities on the boiling point of a mixture can vary depending on the nature and proportion of the volatile components present, but are generally manifested in one of three ways.

- The boiling point rises steadily over a certain boiling range.
- The boiling point appears to rise in a series of definite steps with detectable steady temperatures at intervals.
- The whole mixture boils at one steady temperature.

The second effect is really just an extreme case of the first and both can be illustrated by considering the phase diagram for the distillation of an ideal two-component solution as depicted in Fig. 3.47 and discussed on pp. 144–146.

It is rarely the case experimentally that a single distillation is sufficient to separate two components to an acceptable degree of purity; however, the use of a *fractionating column* can permit efficient separation of materials having boiling points as close as 20°C (pp. 148–152). The more efficient *spinning band* columns will permit separations of components having boiling point differences of as little as 0.5°C, but these are costly, highly specialized pieces of apparatus. The techniques for carrying out simple and fractional distillation are discussed in Chapter 3.

Azeotropes or constant boiling point mixtures

In some instances the components of a mixture form a constant boiling mixture which has a fixed composition and sharp boiling point (referred to as an *azeotrope*) and, in such a case, simple distillation is not sufficient to obtain the two liquid components of the mixture in pure form. Two types of azeotrope exist, namely the *minimum boiling azeotrope* and the *maximum boiling azeotrope*. These phenomena are common in both inorganic and organic systems, but it is usually the case that one of the components possesses a hydroxyl group. Examples of such azeotropes include the following:

- *Minimum boiling azeotropes*:
  95.6% ethanol/4.4% water (78.2°C/760 mmHg),
  60.5% benzene/39.5% methanol (58.3°C/760 mmHg).
- *Maximum boiling azeotropes*:
  79.8% water/20.2% hydrogen chloride (108.6°C/760 mmHg),
  77.5% formic acid/22.5% water (107.1°C/760 mmHg).

The forms of the phase diagrams corresponding to systems which yield minimum and maximum boiling azeotropic mixtures are shown diagrammatically in Fig. 4.6.

As can be seen from the diagram of the minimum boiling point azeotropic system, all other component mixtures boil at a higher temperature than the azeotropic composition, and so the azeotrope will always be the first to distil and will continue to do so until one of the components is exhausted.

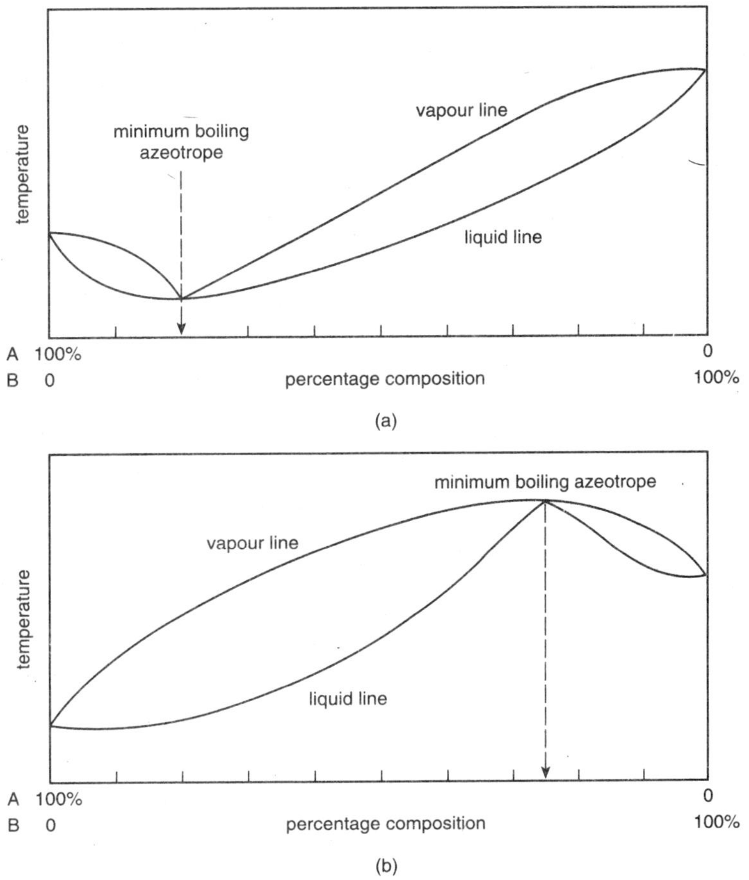

Fig. 4.6 Phase diagrams for a binary mixture forming (a) a minimum boiling point azeotrope; (b) a maximum boiling point azeotrope.

In the case of the maximum boiling point azeotropic system, attempted distillation will result in the initial removal of that component which is present in excess of the azeotropic composition. When the residue in the pot eventually reaches the azeotropic composition this mixture distils.

Azeotropes are frequently, but not always, a nuisance to the chemist—some can be quite useful. Water and benzene or toluene form minimum boiling azeotropes which can be used for removing water from systems (91.1% benzene/8.9% water has bp 69.4°C/760 mmHg; 79.8% toluene/20.2% water has bp 85.0°C/760 mmHg). The Dean and Stark apparatus (Fig. 3.27) has been designed to utilize these properties and provides an ingenious method of continuously removing water that is produced in equilibrating reactions, such as ketalization and enamine formation, in order to drive them to completion. The apparatus takes account of the facts that the azeotropes contain more water than will actually dissolve in the organic solvent at room temperature, and that water is denser than either benzene or toluene. The azeotrope compositions show that toluene is the more efficient for removing water and this, coupled with the high toxicity of benzene, makes toluene the solvent of choice for procedures involving azeotropic removal of water (albeit that its higher boiling point can sometimes be troublesome with sensitive materials).

More complex azeotropic mixtures exist and have also found use. For instance, anhydrous or 'absolute' ethanol used to be obtained by adding benzene to ethanol and removing the initial minimum boiling *ternary azeotrope* (three-component constant boiling mixture) consisting of 7.4% water, 18.5% ethanol and 74.1% benzene. Such alcohol contains traces of residual benzene which render it totally unsuitable for human consumption and also preclude its use as a solvent for UV spectroscopy.

Boiling point determination

If sufficient quantities of material are available, the boiling point can be determined by simple distillation, recording the still head temperature. Although this will frequently be the case, such a procedure is not applicable for boiling point determinations of limited quantities of compound and for such instances the following approach is recommended. *Do not forget, however, that any boiling point is meaningless if quoted without the pressure under which the determination has been carried out.*

See pp. 146–159 for distillation techniques

Microscale determination of boiling point

The boiling point of smaller quantities of liquid may be determined using the following technique. Seal a 5 cm length of 4 mm inside diameter thin-walled glass tubing at one end to make a small test tube and attach it to a thermometer with tape or an elastic band such that the sealed end of the tube is level with the bulb of the thermometer. Similarly seal the end of a melting point tube, cut the tube about 2 cm from the sealed end and place this, *open end first*, inside the first tube. Immerse the thermometer and attached tubes in an oil bath provided with means for heating and stirring, making sure that the elastic band does not touch the oil. Finally, using a pipette, introduce the liquid whose boiling point is to be determined to a depth of about 1 cm (Fig. 4.7).

Heat the oil bath with stirring and observe the tip of the inner tube carefully. Initially, a slow, erratic stream of air bubbles will be seen to leave the tube as the air inside warms up and expands, but this will eventually be replaced by a steady rapid stream of bubbles as the liquid reaches its boiling point. At this point, stop the heating but leave the sample in the oil bath, the temperature of which will continue to rise for a short while, depending on the rate of heating and the actual temperature of the bath. As the temperature begins to fall, examine the tube closely and record the temperature at which the stream of bubbles stops and liquid just begins to rise up within the inner capillary tube—this is the boiling point of the liquid. After allowing the bath to cool to about 20°C below the recorded boiling point, a second 2 cm sealed melting point

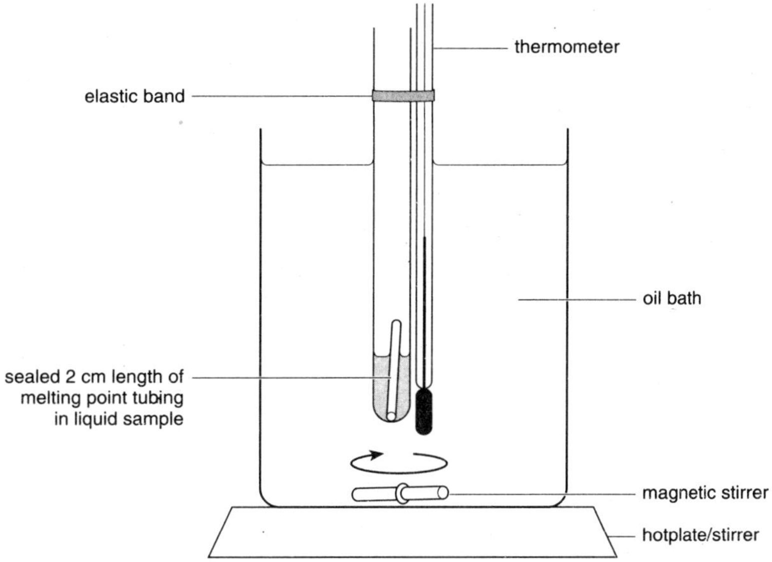

Fig. 4.7 Microscale determination of boiling point.

Always note the pressure when recording boiling points

tube can be introduced into the liquid, and the procedure repeated using the new tube to obtain a confirmatory value. *Remember to record the prevailing atmospheric pressure when determining the boiling point.*

It is worthwhile considering how this experiment works. Initially, the heating bath causes the vapour pressure above the surface of the liquid to increase, resulting in the slow, erratic evolution of air and the gradual replacement of the air within the capillary with solvent vapour. Eventually the heating bath exceeds the boiling point of the liquid, which boils, causing the constant rapid stream of bubbles to be observed. When the bath is allowed to cool down to the boiling point of the liquid, the vapour pressure within the capillary becomes equal to ambient pressure and the liquid commences rising up the tube. Therefore the whole experiment is a very clever application of the fact that liquids boil when their vapour pressure equals that of the prevailing pressure above the liquid surface.

Quoting bath temperatures in short path distillations

The microscale boiling point described above is very neat, but the chances are that you will never actually use it, except perhaps as a laboratory exercise when being introduced to experimental techniques! The truth is that chemists are no different from the rest of the world in having an aversion to doing any more than the absolute minimum, and this certainly applies to determining the boiling points of small quantities of samples. What you will see frequently reported in the literature are bath temperature boiling points for materials which have been purified by short path distillation (see pp. 154–155). This is, of course, a measurement of the pot temperature and the boiling point of the compound cannot be derived from it. Nonetheless, this value is of use to others who may be following the procedure and so is a valid piece of information. However, it must always be borne in mind that the actual boiling point of the compound is somewhat lower than the reported bath temperature, particularly if the experiment is being carried out on a scale which permits a more standard distillation procedure where the still head temperature can be observed. In several experiments described in this book you will find the bath temperature has been quoted if a short path distillation is to be used to purify the product.

Refractive index

Another characteristic physical property of a liquid which can be used as a diagnostic feature is its refractive index. Quoting refractive indices is rapidly falling into disuse as a means of contributory evidence for purity or identity in the face of more sophisticated methods of spectroscopic analysis. It is not the aim of this book to enter into the debate as to whether the loss of such a practice is to be lamented or not! However, we must all be aware of falling into the trap of relying on increasingly sophisticated instrumentation and losing contact with the basic physical properties of compounds, as it is such awareness and 'feel' that make a good experimentalist. Certainly, refractive index determination should be part of every practical training programme—even if the technique may never be used very frequently in later life.

Refractive indices are conveniently determined using an *Abbé refractometer*, and are always quoted as n_D^t, where the subscript relates to the wavelength of the light used for the analysis (standardized to the D line of sodium at 589.3 nm) and the superscript refers to the temperature at which the determination was made (often standardized to 20°C although it is frequently sufficient to measure at room temperature as long as the temperature is stated). The great advantage of the Abbé refractometer is that it can operate using ordinary white light. The instrument gives a reading corrected to 589.3 nm and can compensate for dispersion effects resulting from the fact that the incident light is not monochromatic. It is not necessary to go into the details behind the operation of the refractometer, but as it relies critically on the quality and alignment of the prism faces on which the liquid sample is placed, *great care must always be taken not to mark or scratch the prisms and to clean the faces with soft paper tissue or cotton wool before and immediately after use*. This is another one of those cases where instant, official unpopularity will result from a moment's carelessness in the laboratory.

Take care of the prism surfaces

Using the Abbé refractometer

To determine the refractive index of your sample it is first necessary to deposit a thin film of the liquid between the prism surfaces in intimate contact with them. Expose the two prism surfaces by opening the clip and allowing the bottom prism in its mounting to swing down (Fig. 4.8a). Clean both surfaces

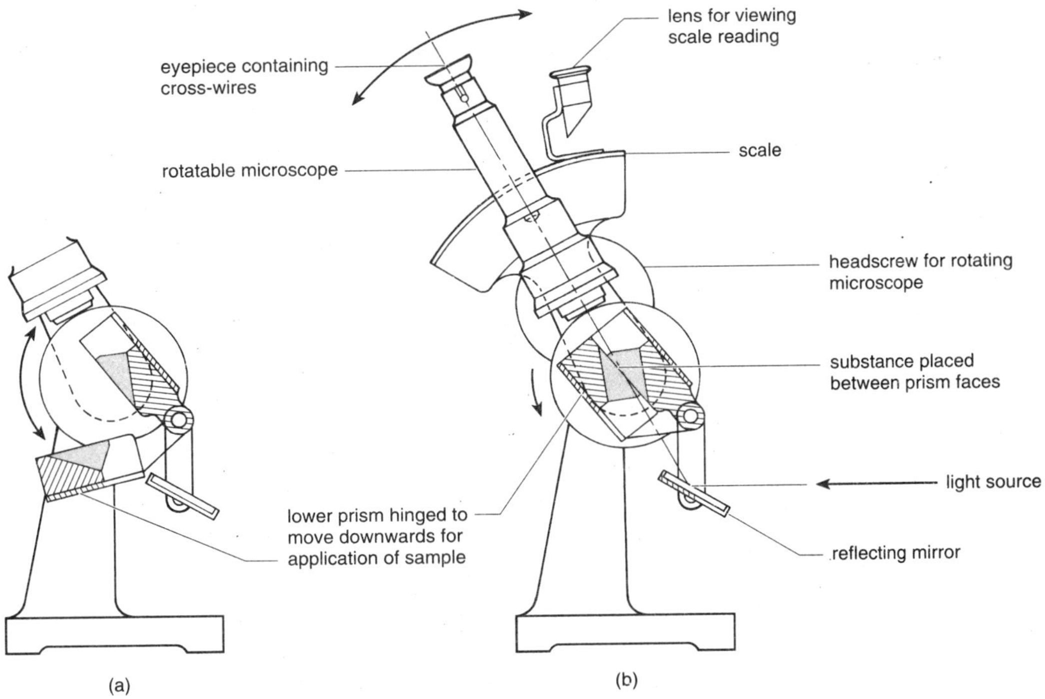

Fig. 4.8 The Abbé refractometer. (Redrawn by kind permission of Cambridge Instruments, Cambridge, UK.)

Always clean the apparatus thoroughly before and after use.

Take care with flammable solvents

thoroughly using tissue or cotton wool soaked in acetone (**flammable solvent**), held in a pair of solvent-resistant plastic tweezers. This avoids recontaminating the surfaces with grease from the hands. *Never use metal tweezers* which will scratch the surfaces if protruding through the soaked pad. Dry the surfaces thoroughly with a second pad, looking for the disappearance of interference patterns due to the presence of very thin layers of residual solvent. Dip a fire-glazed glass rod (or better a Teflon® rod) into your sample and touch the small amount of liquid adhering to the tip onto the ground glass surface of the bottom prism (*never the top prism*). It may be necessary to repeat this once or twice in order to transfer enough sample such that the prism surfaces will be completely covered when the apparatus is closed. When sufficient sample has been transferred, clamp the prisms together again. *Do not* give in to the temptation to smear out the sample over the prism surface with the glass rod as this will inevitably lead to scratching; the liquid will be spread out by the action of bringing the prisms together. As the prisms come very closely together, only a small amount of sample is necessary. One final word of warning: the tempting looking tubes which project from the prism housings are for thermostatically regulating the temperature of the sample if so desired and should *not* be used to introduce your sample!

Next it is necessary to focus on the set of cross-wires which are visible on looking down the eyepiece (or perhaps not, depending on the eyesight of the previous user). Do this by moving the eyepiece up and down carefully with a rotating motion, and when satisfied, turn the mirror under the microscope stage to get the best illumination from a suitably placed light source. Rotate the prism housing by means of the large knurled head screw at the side of the apparatus until the field appears partly light and partly dark in which the boundary may possess a more or less coloured fringe (Fig. 4.9a). Adjust the milled ring at the base of the microscope in order to get a sharp boundary, lacking any colour, between light and dark (Fig. 4.9b), and finally set the boundary exactly on the intersection of the cross-wires. It is the sharpness of this boundary which is affected by the optical quality of the prism surfaces; scratched or worn prisms make for a diffuse boundary. If insufficient sample has been placed on the prism it may be impossible to see any light–dark boundary, or the boundary may be visible in only part of the field of view (Fig. 4.9c). This situation can be simply rectified by putting some more sample onto the bottom prism as described above. The refractive index of the liquid can now be read off the scale using the magnifying eyepiece and the temperature at which the measurement was made must also be noted. The scale is normally divided to the third decimal place and the fourth decimal place can be obtained by estimation. Finally, open the prism box, clean the sufaces thoroughly with solvent, dry them carefully and close the box again, ready for the next person to use the refractometer.

Specific rotation

Substances having molecular dissymmetry are termed *chiral* and, if *resolved* into *enantiomers*, they possess the property of rotating the plane of plane polarized light as it passes through them. Such molecules are said to be *optically active*. The commonest cause of optical activity is the presence of an asymmetric carbon atom within the molecule but other structural features such as helicity (helicenes, *E*-cycloalkenes), orthogonality (biphenyls, allenes, spiranes) and extended tetrahedra (adamantanes possessing four different

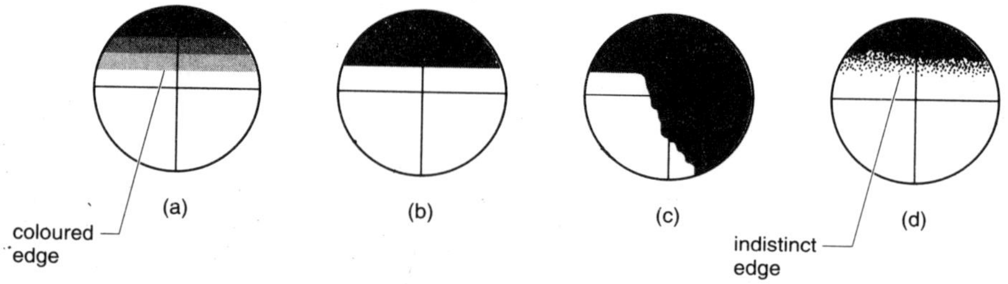

Fig. 4.9 Appearance of the field of view using an Abbé refractometer: (a) before compensation for dispersion effects; (b) after compensation for dispersion effects; (c) insufficient sample on prism surfaces; (d) using an instrument with poor quality optical surfaces.

bridgehead substituents) also result in molecular dissymmetry leading to the potential for optical activity. As optical activity is an integral part of living systems and much of organic chemistry is involved with the isolation, study and synthesis of natural products, the organic chemist will usually need to measure an optical rotation at some stage.

The instrument used to measure optical rotation is called a *polarimeter*, and the principle of its operation is easy to understand. Plane polarized light is obtained by passing light from a sodium lamp (commonly measurements are made using the 589.3 nm D line of sodium) through a *polarizer*. This light is then passed through the sample, either as the neat liquid or in solution, which causes the polarization plane to be rotated to some extent depending on the optical activity of the sample. Nowadays, polarimeters are automatic and give this α value as a digital read-out and this permits the *specific rotation* of the sample to be calculated using the following formula

$$[\alpha]_D^t = \frac{100\alpha}{l\,c}$$

where $[\alpha]_D^t$ is the specific rotation at t°C, α is the number of degrees through which the incident beam has been rotated, l is the length of the sample tube in *decimetres* (1 dm = 10 cm, usually tubes are 1 dm long to make the calculation very easy) and c is the concentration of the sample in g per 100 mL.

The specific rotation of a neat liquid is given by the following expression

$$[\alpha]_D^t = \frac{\alpha}{l\,d}$$

where d is the density of the sample. By convention the specific rotation is quoted as a dimensionless figure. The units are $°cm^2\,g^{-1}$; *not* degrees as is often seen in the literature!

When quoting the specific rotation of a sample, it is necessary to give the concentration of the solution and the solvent used as well as the temperature at which the measurement was made, as all of these factors affect the value obtained. For example, the specific rotation of an enantiomer of menthol might be quoted as: $[\alpha]_D^{20} = +49.2$ ($c = 5$, EtOH). The + sign before the value indicates that the plane of the incident light has been rotated in a *clockwise* manner and such substances are said to be *dextrorotatory* and given the prefix *d*-. The above sample is therefore *d*-menthol; its enantiomer is termed *laevorotatory*, indicated by the prefix *l*-. All of this can get rather confusing, not only because of the rather strange units used in the expressions for deriving $[\alpha]_D$, but also because the prefixes L- and D- are used to describe the absolute configuration of the highest numbered asymmetric carbon atom in sugars and the absolute configuration at the α-position of amino acids. Remember that *l*- and *d*- refer to a physical property—the ability of a compound to rotate plane polarized light—and L- and D- refer to molecular structure.

Automatic polarimeters are costly and delicate and you must seek instruction on the use of the particular instrument in your laboratory before attempting to use it alone. It is first necessary to zero the instrument with the solvent-filled cell in place and then a series of readings is taken with the same cell containing the sample. The sets of readings are averaged to give the value for the rotation. Remember that it is imperative to use the same cell for all measurements and that the cell should always be inserted the same way round into the polarimeter. There is frequently a good deal of oscillation of the last figure on the digital read-out, particularly with dilute samples or with those which are turbid. The average of the extremes of these oscillations should be taken.

It is the degree of care in preparing the sample that determines whether a reliable result will be obtained or not. It goes without saying that the sample must be made up accurately (usually a concentration of 2–5 g per 100 mL is about the right region to aim for) in a graduated flask. A 10 mL flask is normally convenient, as this results in an acceptable compromise between obtaining sufficient accuracy in the measurements and not requiring too much sample (which should be recovered afterwards in any event). The solution, when made up, must be totally free of suspended particles otherwise the dispersion of the polarimeter beam will make it difficult to obtain an accurate reading.

Cloudy solutions are no good for optical rotation measurements

A common type of sample cell used is an accurate tube of 1 dm (10 cm) in length closed at each end with optically flat glass plates and fitted with a central opening for filling (Fig. 4.10a). Such cells usually have a nominal capacity of 5 mL, but it will be necessary to make up more solution than this of course. Variations on this pattern include cells which are multiples of the standard 1 dm length, narrow bore micro-cells requiring only about 1 mL of solution (useful when limited quantities of material are available) which may be jacketed to permit measurements at a standard temperature (Fig. 4.10b).

Filling the cell demands a fair measure of care. It is imperative to avoid any air bubbles in the tube and, whilst this is not difficult with the centre-filled tubes, the narrow bore tubes, with openings at either end, sometimes encourage stubborn bubbles to cling to the inner walls. In such instances gently rocking the tube usually does the trick, and it is as well to do this under all cir-

All air bubbles must be removed from the sample

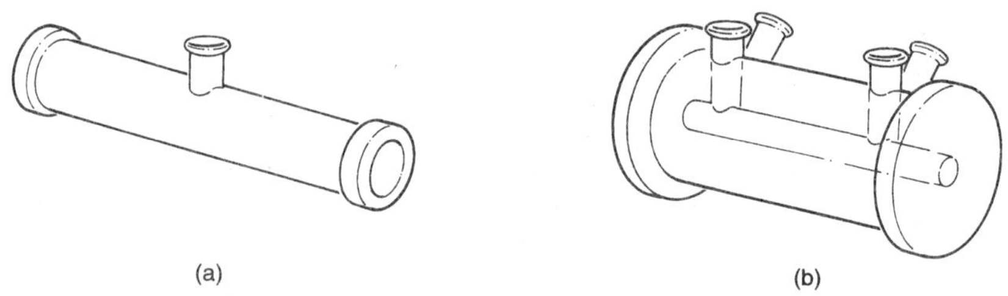

Fig. 4.10 (a) Standard polarimeter sample cell; (b) jacketed cell.

cumstances in order to remove any rogue bubbles. At all times avoid touching the end plates of the tube—the grease on your hands is optically active and will also result in dispersion of the beam.

When the measurement has been made, the sample should be recovered and the cell should be washed thoroughly in solvent and dried with a stream of nitrogen from a cylinder. Do not use compressed air lines to dry the cells as these are full of oil and grit and the tube will end up dirtier than at the outset.

Never dry apparatus using compressed air

One final word of warning is required regarding the values of specific rotation. Publications concerned with methods of enantioselective synthesis of optically active molecules often quote a specific rotation for a compound which is higher than that previously reported in the literature, implying this to be evidence of the higher optical purity of their product. Whilst this may well be true, traces of impurities having high specific rotations of the same sign as the major product will have dramatic effects on the $[\alpha]_D$ value of the bulk sample. Analysis by specific rotation alone is insufficient; there must always be additional confirmatory evidence of the homogeneity of the sample before such values can be meaningful.

Just because your $[\alpha]_D$ is higher does not necessarily mean your product is purer

Further reading

For discussions of the structural basis of optical activity in organic molecules, see: E.L. Eliel, S.H. Wilen and L.N. Mander *Stereochemistry of Carbon Compounds*, Wiley & Sons, New York, 1994, Chapters 3–8, 11, 13, 14.

J. March *Advanced Organic Chemistry*, 4th edn, Wiley & Sons, London, 1994, Chapter 4.

Chromatography: the problems of purity and identity versus homogeneity and a few hints

The practical aspects of carrying out chromatographic purification and analysis have been dealt with already in pp. 160–203. In this section we will address a little bit of philosophy and look at a few additional practical tricks.

The vexed problems of absolute proof of purity and identity using chromatography

How can a chemist *prove* that their compound is pure or that their compound is *identical* with an authentic sample? The straight answer is that demonstration of purity or identity to any degree of certainty is not possible using a single chromatographic analytical technique because such an analysis can only be considered to give meaningful information if more than one component is detected. If more than one spot is visible on the TLC plate or more than one peak is recorded on the GC trace then we do indeed have irrefutable evidence of contamination. However, a single spot on a TLC plate or a single peak on a GC trace, whilst an *indication* of purity (or identity in the case of a mixed analysis), can never in itself constitute *proof* of purity, as the *absence* of additional spots is a *negative result*. It can always be argued that the impurities have all eluted coincidentally to the same degree in the analysis system and that the observation of only one component is simply a consequence of the failure of the system to resolve the various constituents. Here we will consider briefly the sort of things the chemist can try in chromatographic analysis to increase the odds of being correct in assuming purity or identity.

Variation of TLC solvent systems or GC temperature programmes

If TLC analysis of a compound still indicates homogeneity when carried out using a second solvent system, or if GC analysis still shows only one peak on changing the temperature programme, this is stronger support for the conclusion that the compound is indeed pure. The counter-argument now depends on the constituents coincidentally having the same mobilities under two different analysis systems—a much less likely proposition.

A simple procedure which often works with TLC analysis is to carry out one analysis using an appropriate mixture of non-halogenated solvents to give an R_f value of approximately 0.5 (hexane, ether, ethyl acetate, methanol, for instance) and a second analysis with one of the components replaced by a halogenated solvent (for example, dichloromethane or chloroform for diethyl ether). It seems that, if two compounds have coincidentally identical R_f values in one such system, they may often be separated in the other. Of course, this will not work in every case, but it is quite a good first try and it is often useful to bear this in mind. To demonstrate identity when an authentic sample is available, it is necessary to carry out TLC analysis on mixtures of the authentic and unknown solutions, as even running two samples side by side on the same plate does not permit a sufficient degree of distinction (see Fig. 3.65). If the unknown is too precious to permit mixing some of it with another material, the two solutions can be spotted onto exactly the same point on the TLC plate (using different micro-pipettes of course) (see Fig. 3.65). Such analysis can be made even more sensitive by carrying it out as two-dimensional chromatography (see Fig. 3.66).

In GC analysis, the equivalent variation to changing eluting solvents can be considered to be changing the temperature programme. Again, substituting for a particular temperature programme, with a steady oven temperature set at the mid-point of the programme (or vice versa), sometimes has the desired effect. For purposes of attempting to demonstrate identity, it is necessary to carry out co-injection of the unknown and the authentic material. As before, if you do not want to mix the unknown with the authentic, a permissible technique involves taking up some of the unknown solution in the syringe, followed by a **very small** bubble of air (air destroys stationary phases) and then some of the authentic solution. In between taking up the two samples the needle should be wiped on a tissue; this and the small bubble of air minimize any cross-contamination.

Variation of stationary phases

Thin layer chromatography is frequently carried out on silica which is a relatively acidic support. Use of alumina-coated plates, in which the support is alkaline, often produces surprising variations in mobility (see solvent eluotropic series for both silica and alumina, (Table 3.11, p. 164). There are other frequently used TLC supports, but silica and alumina are probably the most useful for the organic chemist concerned with non-zwitterionic aliphatic and aromatic molecules.

The same principle applies to GC and, although it is rather a nuisance to have to change columns on a single machine, it is usually the case that several machines will be available, having complementary columns. If cast away on a desert island and able to take only two packed columns for GC analysis, the chemist would probably choose a column containing a relatively polar stationary phase such as polyethylene glycol adipate (PEGA) or Carbowax®, and a non-polar stationary phase such as SE-30 or OV-101. As a very simplistic approximation, non-polar stationary phases tend to separate molecules on the basis of their relative volatility, whereas the more polar stationary phases superimpose dipole–dipole interactions onto the volatility effect.

Capillary columns (pp. 194–195) are now frequently used as they possess a much larger number of theoretical plates than the equivalent packed columns and will sometimes resolve single broad peaks into a distressing number of components!

Use of different visualizing agents in TLC

Different visualizing systems often show very different colour reactions with different functional groups and so even compounds which co-elute may be distinguished from one another. The actual systems which are often used are discussed more fully in Table 3.12 (p. 170).

Conclusion

In the preceding sections of this chapter, we have looked at various criteria of purity which depend on the physical properties of the materials under study. In isolation, any one of these techniques will not permit the chemist to say with certainty anything about the purity or identity of any compound being studied; however, combinations of techniques do lend support to any provisional conclusions. The advantages of such techniques are that they are relatively rapid in execution and the apparatus required is usually readily to hand in the laboratory. Their main disadvantage is that, for *identification* purposes, it is necessary to have available an authentic sample, or data on the authentic material, before any conclusions can be made. Therefore the greatest use for these techniques is in permitting estimations of likely purity—or more correctly, any lack of it. In the next chapter we will consider the various techniques of spectroscopic analysis and how these can be used, usually in combination, to determine the structures of materials without any prior knowledge, except perhaps their provenance and probable degree of purity. Spectroscopic analysis requires much more expensive apparatus but, without doubt, the accuracy, sensitivity and non-destructive nature of these techniques have been the main reasons for the massive strides which have been made in research in organic chemistry over the last four or five decades.

4.2 Determining structure using chemical methods

The above discussion of the merits of spectroscopic analysis might have convinced you that there is never any need to carry out chemical analysis; do not allow yourself to be lulled into this false conclusion! Whilst it is true that modern structure determination relies very heavily on spectroscopic studies, increasingly with the more direct expedient of X-ray crystallographic analysis for the more complex materials, this does not remove the need for confirmatory chemical evidence. In addition, the derivatization procedures, designed specifically for forming highly crystalline compounds, are ideal for use in conjunction with X-ray work if the unknown itself is not crystalline.

It cannot be stressed strongly enough that the processes and logic involved in the chemical determination of the structure of an unknown provide the perfect chemical training. In essence, chemical analysis involves the use of degradative techniques to produce simpler and more readily analyzed compounds from an unknown. Its success therefore hinges on the ability to work with small quantities of material, and the accurate observation and interpretation of the results obtained. The development of these practical and theoretical skills provides the cornerstone for any chemical training.

The investigation of an unknown can be divided into four main stages.

- Preliminary observation of general physical characteristics of the material.
- Estimation of purity—with purification if necessary—and determination of the physical constants (melting or boiling point and refractive index).
- Identification of the elements and key functional groups present within the structure.
- Tentative proposal of candidate structures on the basis of the results from the first three stages and confirmation of identity by degradation or derivatization to furnish recognizable structures.

The classic means of carrying out these steps involves relatively small-scale work, with milligrams of material being used for each test. This approach will be described in the first part of this section. However, many of the degradative and derivatization reactions can be carried out on the microscale using analysis by TLC. The process of carrying out *in situ* chemical reactions on TLC plates (reaction thin layer chromatography, RTLC), which requires extremely small quantities of material, will be described in the latter part of this section. Needless to say, TLC can also be used for purity analysis of the original unknown and is also suited for the purification of small quantities of material.

Qualitative analysis

The procedures described in the following pages should be applied to any unknown and, on the basis of the results obtained, other confirmatory tests should be carried out. No rigid guidelines can be laid down here and the success of the analysis relies totally on the initiative and ability of the investigator—you. Negative results are as important in directing you to the correct conclusion as positive results.

NOTE: never forget that any unknown material has potentially dangerous properties and should be treated with all the precautions required for toxic and flammable materials.

Preliminary observation of general physical characteristics

Whilst the more specific physical properties of melting point or boiling point and refractive index will be crucial for the final identification of your material, the simple observation as to whether the material is solid or liquid is an important first guide for likely candidate structures.

Treat all unknown compounds with caution

Many procedures suggest that the odour (even the taste in some older texts!) of the compound should be noted. **This practice is strongly discouraged due to the likely toxicity of the unknown.** Many materials have disagreeable odours at the very least and many are intensely lachrymatory or worse. Any advantage from the minimal information obtained in this manner is heavily offset by the risks involved. Whilst any odour noticeable during handling should not be ignored, smelling the sample must be avoided.

Never sniff chemicals

Care! Check for flammable solvents

Heat a very small amount of the material on the tip of a spatula in a microburner flame. A luminous, sooty flame indicates that the compound possesses a high degree of unsaturation and may be aromatic, whereas a less coloured or blue flame indicates an aliphatic compound. Halogenated or highly oxygenated compounds often burn with difficulty or not at all. A residue remaining after burning is indicative of a metal salt and additional evidence for this can be obtained by testing the pH of the moistened residue—metal salt residues are often alkaline.

Solubility in distilled water is an indication that the compound either has a low molecular weight (particularly if a liquid) or possesses hydrophilic groups such as $-CO_2H$, NH_2 or $-OH$. Most monofunctional compounds with up to five carbon atoms show noticeable water solubility. A few crystals or a drop of liquid should be added to 0.5 mL of distilled water in a small test tube. Dissolution to give an acidic solution (pH 2–4) is evidence that the unknown is a carboxylic or a sulfonic acid. Compounds such as phenols are too weakly acidic to be detected in this manner. An alkaline solution (pH 10–12) indicates an aliphatic amine but, once again, heterocyclic bases such as pyridine and most aromatic amines are difficult to spot by this method.

Take care with corrosive reagents

If the compound is insoluble in distilled water, it should be similarly tested for solubility in aqueous acids and bases. Solubility in saturated sodium bicarbonate solution indicates the presence of a carboxylic or sulfonic acid, whereas insolubility in this weakly basic reagent but solubility in 2 M sodium hydroxide is evidence for a phenol or enolic material such as a 1,3-diketone. An intensification or appearance of colour on dissolution in the base often indicates that the material is aromatic. Solubility in 2 M hydrochloric acid is evidence for an amino compound or a heteroaromatic base. Any change in colour—often becoming weaker—can point to the presence of an aromatic amine. Any unknown insoluble in all of the reagents so far should also be checked for solubility in concentrated sulfuric acid (**take care!**). Most oxygenated and unsaturated aliphatic materials are soluble, whereas alkanes and unactivated aromatic compounds are insoluble. This can be a particularly useful piece of information. The general solubility behaviour of common classes of organic compounds is shown schematically in Fig. 4.11.

Take care with flammable solvents

The solubility of the material in some common organic solvents should also be examined to obtain an impression of its likely polarity. Light petroleum, dichloromethane, ethyl acetate and ethanol provide a representative range of solvents. Each test is easily carried out using 5–10 mg of the unknown in 0.5 mL of solvent and solubility in both cold and hot solvent should be examined. This information will be very helpful in deciding on the choice of solvent for recrystallization for solid unknowns (see pp. 131–140).

Purification and determination of physical constants

For a full discussion of purification by crystallization and distillation, see the appropriate sections in Chapter 3

There is no point in analyzing impure material and so the very next thing you must do is to purify your material to homogeneity. Most organic compounds degrade to some extent on storage and so it is always good practice to carry out preliminary purification before proceeding with the analysis. (In the research situation, extensive purification will normally have been necessary to obtain the compound in the first place.) Any brown colouration in your sample is usually an indication that some degradation has occurred and this should disappear on purification. However, colours which persist after purification indicate the presence of chromophoric groups in the molecule, most commonly associated with aromatic structures.

If the material is a solid it should be recrystallized to constant melting point and the melting point of the purified material should be noted. Impure low melting solids may appear as a mixture of crystals and liquid and should be purified by low temperature recrystallization. Liquids should be distilled using the standard distillation procedure if sufficient material is available, or a

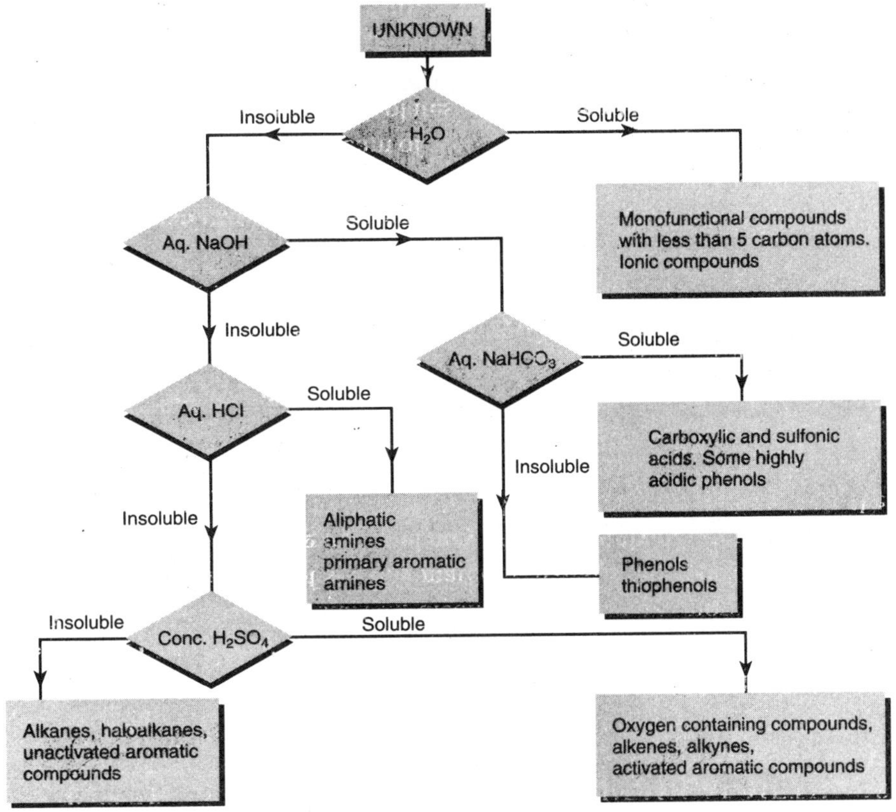

Fig. 4.11 Solubility behaviour of common classes of organic compounds.

short path or microscale distillation apparatus if not. If the material decomposes on attempted distillation at atmospheric pressure (indicated by extensive darkening or evolution of fumes) it will require reduced pressure distillation. If only a small amount of material is available, an accurate boiling point can be determined using the small-scale procedure previously described (pp. 216–217). In addition, the refractive indices of pure liquids should be measured routinely.

At the completion of these two phases of observations, you should have some impression of the overall properties of your unknown—its degree of unsaturation, whether it is acidic, neutral or basic, and an idea of its polarity. In addition, you will have the specific information relating to its physical constants for confirmatory evidence in the final analysis. The next stage is to determine the elemental constitution and the types of functional group present in the molecule.

Qualitative determination of elemental composition

In addition to the usual elements of carbon, hydrogen and oxygen, commonly encountered elements in organic molecules are nitrogen, sulfur, phosphorus and halogens. These may be detected using the *Lassaigne fusion* technique where the unknown is heated with metallic sodium, or by *Middleton's fusion* using sodium carbonate and zinc in place of sodium. Middleton's method is the less hazardous, being more suitable for use in crowded teaching laboratories, and it is also considered to be superior to Lassaigne fusion for the analysis of volatile compounds. The disadvantage of Middleton's method is that very pure zinc powder is required if spurious positive results for sulfur and halogens are not to be obtained. A blank test should always be carried out on the stock material when it is first prepared.

In both methods analysis is based on the conversion of the heteroatoms to inorganic salts such as cyanide, sulfide or halide.

Determination of nitrogen, sulfur, phosphorus and halogens by Lassaigne sodium fusion

NOTE: ***owing to its potentially hazardous nature, the fusion operation should be carried out behind a safety screen in a hood designated for this procedure. No other work should be allowed to take place in the same hood during the fusion and it is recommended that gloves be worn for this operation. The analyses should also be carried out in a hood although, at this stage, individuals may share the same hood.***

The analysis may involve the evolution of small amounts of hydrogen cyanide and hydrogen sulfide. It should be borne in mind that the toxicity of hydrogen sulfide is about the same order of magnitude as that of hydrogen cyanide. Fortunately, its repulsive smell serves as adequate warning of its presence. For both reasons, detecting hydrogen sulfide by its odour—although at times unavoidable—is not recommended.

Equipment	safety screen, microburner, test tube holder, 6 × soda glass test tubes 5 cm × 1 cm, evaporating basin, crucible tongs, 10 cm × 10 cm wire gauze, tripod; apparatus for filtration		
Materials			
unknown sample			
sodium metal		4 mm cube	**flammable, corrosive**
iron (II) sulfate			
aqueous sulfuric acid (5%)			**corrosive**
aqueous disodium pentacyanonitrosyl ferrate (0.1%) (sodium nitroprusside, sodium nitroferricyanide)*			**toxic**
aqueous nitric acid (5%)			**corrosive**
aqueous silver nitrate solution (5%)*			**corrosive**

Continued

Box cont.

chlorine water* (an equivalent reagent may be prepared from 10% aqueous NaOCl, acidified with one-fifth of its volume of 10% aqueous HCl)	**corrosive**
ammonia solution (conc. *ca.* 30%)	**corrosive, toxic, lachrymator**
ammonium molybdate reagent* (prepared by dissolving 4.5 g $(NH_4)_2MoO_4$ in 4 mL concentrated ammonia solution, adding 12 g NH_4NO_3 and diluting the mixture to 100 mL)	**toxic, irritant**
zirconium–alizarin red S paper* (for the preparation of this paper see the section in part 4 on fluorine detection)	

The reagents marked (*) are most conveniently prepared as stock solutions on the day of the experiment

Procedure

1. *Sodium fusion*

HOOD
SAFETY SCREEN

Place about 20 mg of your sample in the bottom of a small soda glass test tube, using a pipette for liquid samples to ensure that no sample is smeared on the upper part of the tube. Add 10 mL of distilled water to an evaporating basin, and place this in the hood behind the safety screen. Using a test tube holder which supports the tube firmly (crucible tongs allow the tube to rock and are not suitable), introduce a piece of sodium about the size of a small pea—roughly a 4 mm cube—into the mouth of the test tube,[1] without allowing it to come into contact with the substance at the bottom. With the safety screen in place and the front of the fume hood pulled well down, heat the sodium gently over a small microburner flame until it melts and runs down into the sample. There may be a very vigorous reaction when the molten sodium touches the sample, particularly if halogens are present. Heat the tube gently for 1 min, and then heat more strongly until the bottom 2 cm of the tube glows red hot. Holding the gauze with tongs in your free hand, drop the red-hot tube into the water in the evaporating basin and immediately place the gauze on top.[1] (The tube will shatter on contact with the water, releasing any unreacted sodium, and the gauze stops the loss of any material.) Allow any excess sodium to react and when the reaction has subsided, place the evaporating basin on the gauze on a tripod and boil the solution for 2 min. Filter the solution whilst hot,[2] to remove the broken glass and charred material, and pour an equal quantity of the colourless, alkaline filtrate into five test tubes.

[1] *Care!*

[2] *See Fig. 3.6*

2. *Sulfur*

Add 2 mL of the disodium pentacyanonitrosyl ferrate stock solution to one of the test tubes. A purple colouration which fades slowly on standing indicates sulfur is present. If a stock solution is not available, dissolve a small crystal of the reagent in 2 mL of distilled water and add this to your sample.

3. *Nitrogen*

Add *ca.* 200 mg of iron (II) sulfate to the second test tube, heat the solution to boiling and add sufficient dilute sulfuric acid to dissolve any precipitate and make the solution acid. The formation of a deep blue precipitate or colouration (Prussian blue) indicates the presence of nitrogen. If the colour of the mixture makes it impossible to tell if any blue colouration has been formed, filter the mixture, washing the filter paper with distilled water, and examine the residue for the blue colouration.

4. *Halogens*

To the third test tube, add sufficient nitric acid to render the solution acidic and boil the mixture until its volume has been halved. (The heating has the effect of removing any HCN or H_2S if cyanides or sulfides are present which would interfere with this test. It may be omitted if nitrogen and sulfur have been shown to be absent.) Add 1 mL of the silver nitrate solution to this mixture. The observation of a white or yellowish precipitate indicates the presence of halogen. To identify the halogen present, add chlorine water dropwise to the fourth tube with gentle shaking. The appearance of a brown colouration indicates bromine or iodine. In the latter case, addition of excess chlorine water will cause the brown colouration to disappear as the iodine is further oxidized to iodate. Confirmation may be obtained by adding concentrated ammonia solution to the third tube containing the precipitate. Total dissolution is indicative of iodine; by the process of elimination, a sample which gives a white precipitate with silver nitrate, but no colouration on treatment with chlorine water, must contain chlorine. In addition the white precipitate will be unaffected by the ammonia solution.

Fluorine is not frequently encountered in undergraduate qualitative analyses due to the toxicity of many compounds which contain it. Fluorine will not be detected by the standard tests for halogens and, if it is desired to test for its presence, the following additional procedure should be carried out.

Acidify *ca.* 2 mL of the filtrate with glacial acetic acid, reduce the volume of the solution to one-half by boiling, and spot the resultant mixture onto zirconium–alizarin red S paper. The appearance of a yellow spot on the red paper is a positive result indicating the presence of fluorine, although the presence of phosphate or sulfate ions in the filtrate can interfere with this result.

The zirconium–alizarin red S paper can be prepared by dipping filter paper sequentially into 5% aqueous zirconium nitrate, 5% aqueous hydrochloric acid and 2% aqueous alizarin red S solution (sodium alizarin sulfonate), followed by drying in air.

5. *Phosphorus*

Acidify the sample in the fifth test tube with dilute nitric acid and boil the mixture for 2 min. Add an equal volume of the ammonium molybdate solution, warm the mixture to *ca.* 40–50°C and allow to stand. The formation of a yellow precipitate indicates the presence of phosphorus.

Determination of nitrogen, sulfur and halogens by sodium carbonate–zinc fusion (Middleton's method)

In this method nitrogen and halogens are converted to sodium cyanide and sodium halides, respectively, and these are detected in the same manner as in the Lassaigne fusion. Any sulfur present is converted to zinc sulfide which is decomposed with dilute acid and the H_2S liberated is detected with lead acetate paper. Although less hazardous than the Lassaigne fusion, the analysis must be carried out in the hood.

Equipment (as for the Lassaigne fusion)	
Materials	
unknown sample	
zinc powder–sodium carbonate mixture	
aqueous lead (II) acetate (5%)	**cancer suspect agent, toxic**
reagents for nitrogen and halogen analysis as used in the Lassaigne fusion	
It is recommended that the zinc powder–sodium carbonate mixture be prepared as a stock reagent by grinding intimately together 25 g of anhydrous sodium carbonate and 50 g of high purity grade zinc powder. This quantity is sufficient for about a dozen experiments and a blank test should be carried out on the reagent to confirm the absence of halogens and sulfur	

Procedure

1. *Fusion*

HOOD

In a test tube mix your unknown (*ca.* 100 mg) with sufficient of the zinc–sodium carbonate reagent to fill the tube to a depth of 1 cm. Without further mixing, top up with a further 2 cm of the reagent. Place about 10 mL of water in the evaporating dish to receive the hot tube after fusion and place this behind the safety screen. With the tube held horizontally, gently heat the reagent nearest the open end of the tube and slowly increase the rate of heating until this region becomes red hot. Gradually permit the heating to extend the length of the tube until the whole mass is at red heat. **Too rapid heating at this stage may cause vigorous evolution of gases and the ejection of red-hot solid from the tube. Stop heating temporarily if this appears likely.** Finally, heat the tube in the vertical position for 2 min and then drop it into the water contained in the evaporating dish.[1] Boil the contents of the dish

[1]*Care!*

[2] *See Fig. 3.6*

for 2 min and then filter the hot mixture.[2] Retain the residue (which will be required for the sulfur test) and split the filtrate equally into three test tubes.

2. *Nitrogen*

Test the filtrate in one of the tubes in the same manner as described in the Lassaigne fusion.

3. *Halogens*

Test the other two tubes for halogens in the same manner as described in the Lassaigne fusion.

4. *Sulfur*

Wash out the evaporating dish and return the residue in the filter paper to it. Add about 10 mL of 5% hydrochloric acid to the residue and cover the evaporating dish with a filter paper moistened with the lead acetate solution. The formation of a brown stain on the paper indicates the presence of sulfur in the original sample. ■

Other investigations

With the information from these three stages of analysis to hand, you are now in a position to make preliminary proposals as to the nature of your unknown. When looking for candidate structures on the basis of the melting point or boiling point you have recorded for your unknown, it is necessary to include for consideration compounds which have values within 5°C of that which you have obtained.

Frequently, at this stage you will be required to report your preliminary findings and proposals to an instructor in order to avoid wasting time following erroneous conclusions. You may also at this stage be able to obtain or study spectroscopic data (IR, NMR, MS) associated with your unknown in order to corroborate your findings and direct your thinking (Chapter 5). Even the most basic spectroscopic examination will be of great help at this stage; for instance, examination of the IR spectrum of a suspected alcohol or ketone will immediately support or disprove your initial proposal.

For the sake of this exercise, however, it will be assumed that you do not have access to any spectroscopic data and are relying solely on chemical evidence. Whatever your situation, it is now necessary to pinpoint the actual compound from your list of candidate structures. This will involve the preparation of at least two derivatives and, obviously, the type of functional group present (alcohol, ketone, amine, etc.) will dictate the type of derivative to prepare. However, you should bear in mind that the particular derivatives chosen ought to have melting points that enable clear differentiation between other possible structures within that series.

Functional group identification

Your unknown will probably possess functionality which will place it in one or more of the classes of compounds listed in Table 4.1. Except in the teaching laboratory, it is rare for an unknown to possess just one functional group and you must always be aware of the possibility that more than one functional group may be present. Although the classification in Table 4.1 only holds for monofunctional compounds, the sequence of analysis described here can be applied to any unknown.

From the experimental results so far, you will have a general idea about the types of functional groups present in your unknown. Firstly, it is necessary to confirm the presence of these functional groups; then crystalline derivatives can be prepared to identify the actual substance by comparison of melting points with literature values. The ideal derivative should be simply and quickly prepared by a high yielding, unambiguous route and should also be easily purified and identified. As these manipulations are normally carried out on relatively small amounts of material, this requires a solid derivative with a sharp and definite melting point, preferably between 50 and 250°C. In this work, you would be well advised not to jump to premature conclusions about the likely identity of your compound. Always prepare one derivative and check that its properties agree with those expected before leaping into the preparation of the second confirmatory derivative. Much student time is wasted in qualitative analysis by attempting to prepare two unsuitable derivatives at the same time.

The tests performed so far will have enabled you to pinpoint fairly accurately any class of compound showing acidic or basic properties, and the choice of which confirmatory tests to carry out and which derivatives to prepare should be easy. This situation also holds for neutral compounds containing a halogen or nitrogen. However, neutral compounds lacking nitrogen, sulfur, phosphorus or a halogen require further investigation. The order of the confirmatory tests for these functional groups is very important and should not be varied. It follows a logical sequence of events, with each test building on the results of the previous ones. The testing order follows the reactivity of the functional groups, with the most reactive groups being checked for first. Consequently, *positive results with the later tests in the sequence will be meaningful only if the earlier tests have proved negative*, as the more reactive functionalities will interfere to give spurious positive results.

Neutral compounds in which nitrogen, halogens, sulfur and phosphorus are absent

Aldehydes and ketones

Both classes of compounds will give crystalline derivatives called *hydrazones* when reacted with 2,4-dinitrophenylhydrazine. If the crystalline product is yellow, this indicates a saturated carbonyl compound; an orange precipitate

Table 4.1 Common classes of monofunctional organic compounds.

Neutral compounds	Acidic compounds	Basic compounds
C, H, O compounds	*C, H, O compounds*	*C, H, N compounds*
Aldehydes	Carboxylic acids	Amines
Ketones	Anhydrides	Nitrogen heterocycles
Esters	Phenols (weakly acidic)	
Alcohols		*C, H, N, halogen compounds*
Ethers	*C, H, O, halogen compounds*	
	Acyl halides	Quaternary ammonium salts
C, H compounds		
Alkenes	*C, H, S compounds*	
Alkynes	Aryl thiols (weakly acidic)*	
Arenes		
Alkanes	*C, H, S, O compounds*	
	Sulfonic acids	
C, H, halogen compounds		
Halides		
C, H, N, O compounds		
Nitro compounds		
Amides		
C, H, N compounds		
Nitriles		
C, H, S compounds		
Thioethers*		
Thiols*		
C, H, O, S compounds		
Sulfoxides		
Sulfones		
C, H, P compounds		
Phosphines*		
C, H, O, P compounds		
Phosphonates		
Phosphites*		

* These compounds are generally unsuitable for use in the teaching laboratory for reasons of odour or toxicity.

indicates an α,β-unsaturated system and a red precipitate indicates an aromatic ketone or aldehyde.

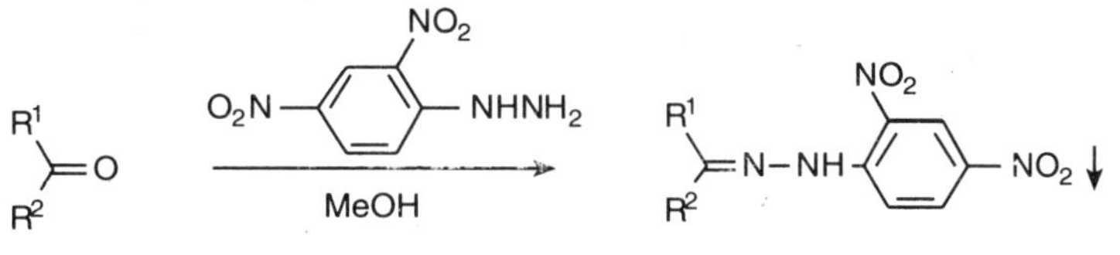

yellow, orange or red precipitate

If this test is positive, differentiation between ketones and aldehydes is possible due to the fact that aldehydes are oxidized to carboxylic acids under mild conditions, whereas ketones are not. Systems used for this differentiation include chromic acid oxidation and *Tollen's*, *Fehling's* and *Benedict's* reagents; only the Tollen's procedure will be described here.

$$RCHO \xrightarrow{2Ag(NH_3)_2OH} RCO_2NH_4 + 3NH_3 + H_2O + Ag\downarrow$$

black precipitate
or
silver mirror

If you suspect that your unknown is a methyl ketone, confirmatory evidence for this can be obtained by carrying out the *iodoform reaction*. A note of caution is necessary here, however. Alcohols which can be oxidized to methyl ketones will also give a positive result in the iodoform reaction, and so the iodoform reaction must only be applied after confirmation of the presence of a carbonyl group.

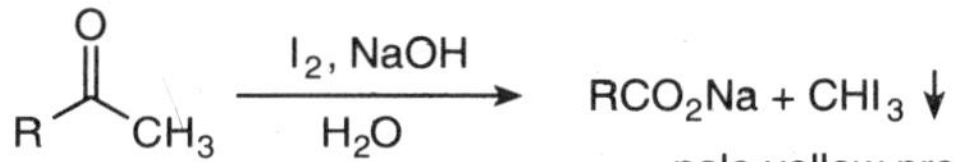

pale yellow precipitate

2,4-Dinitrophenylhydrazone formation (Brady's test)

To the unknown (2–3 drops of liquid or *ca.* 50 mg of solid) dissolved in a few drops of methanol, add 1 mL of Brady's reagent* and shake. If no precipitate is formed, boil the mixture for 1 min and cool in ice. The appearance of a yellow, orange or red precipitate of the 2,4-dinitrophenylhydrazone indicates the presence of a carbonyl compound.

Differentiation between aldehydes and ketones (Tollen's test)

To the unknown (2–3 drops of liquid or *ca.* 50 mg of solid) add 0.5 mL of freshly prepared Tollen's reagent.† The formation of a black precipitate or a

* *Brady's reagent.* This is best prepared as a stock solution by dissolving 2,4-dinitrophenylhydrazine (1.0 g) in concentrated sulfuric acid (5 mL), adding this solution slowly with stirring to a mixture of water (7.0 mL) and absolute ethanol (25 mL), and filtering to remove any suspended solid.

† *Tollen's reagent.* This reagent must be prepared immediately before use from the following stock solutions: *(Continued on p. 238.)*

silver mirror on the walls of the test tube, either immediately or on warming in a beaker of hot water, constitutes a positive test for an aldehyde. The silver mirror will only form if the test tube has been thoroughly cleaned.

Test for methyl ketones or compounds capable of being converted to them (iodoform reaction)

Dissolve the unknown (2–3 drops of liquid, *ca.* 50 mg of solid) in aqueous dioxan (1:1) and add 2 mL of 3 M aqueous sodium hydroxide, followed by 3 mL of iodine solution.* A positive result is indicated by the disappearance of the brown colouration and the formation of a pale yellow precipitate (mp 119°C) which has a characteristic pervasive antiseptic odour which should be detectable without the need to smell the reaction directly.

Do not smell the reaction mixture directly

If an aldehyde or ketone is found to be present, suitable derivatives to prepare are *2,4-dinitrophenylhydrazones*, *oximes* (p. 254). Other derivatives which may be prepared include *phenylhydrazones*, *4-nitrophenylhydrazones*, *semicarbozones* and *dimedone derivatives* (aldehydes only).

Esters

Esters react with hydroxylamine to produce hydroxamic acids which give a purple or deep red colouration with iron (III) chloride. Carboxylic acids and anhydrides, acyl halides and phenolic or enolic compounds may interfere with this test. These can all be ruled out, however, by their solubility in aqueous sodium hydroxide. The derivatization procedure for esters relies upon saponification to the constituent acid and alcohol, followed by separation and preparation of suitable derivatives of both of these (pp. 268–269 and 255–257).

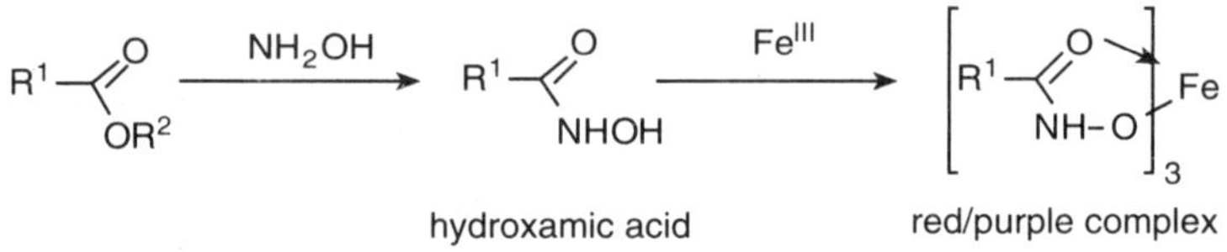

Test for esters

To the unknown (2–3 drops of liquid or *ca.* 50 mg of solid) add a saturated ethanolic solution of hydroxylamine hydrochloride (10 drops) and 20%

Cont.
silver nitrate (2.5 g) in distilled water (42 mL)—solution A,
potassium hydroxide (3.0 g) in distilled water (42 mL)—solution B,
concentrated ammonia solution (30%).
Add the concentrated ammonia solution to solution A (3 mL) until the initial brown precipitate has almost totally redissolved to give a greyish slightly cloudy solution. Add solution B (3 mL) to this and then add more concentrated ammonia solution until the mixture is almost clear again.

NOTE: excess reagent must not be stored as it decomposes on standing to yield a potentially explosive solid.

**Iodine solution*. A stock solution may be prepared by dissolving iodine (25 g) in a solution of potassium iodide (50 g) in distilled water (200 mL).

ethanolic potassium hydroxide (10 drops). Heat the mixture to boiling, acidify with 5% hydrochloric acid and to this add a 5% solution of iron (III) chloride dropwise. A deep red or purple colouration due to the formation of an iron (III) salt of the hydroxamic acid is a positive result.

Alcohols and ethers

A neutral compound containing only carbon, hydrogen and oxygen which is neither a carbonyl compound nor an ester is liable to be an alcohol or an ether. These two classes of compounds may be distinguished from each other by the use of acetyl chloride, which reacts vigorously with alcohols to form an ester and evolve hydrogen chloride, which may be detected with indicator paper. Ethers are unreactive, but adventitious water will interfere, giving a seemingly positive result. If in doubt, dry your compound and always use a dry test tube. Phenols, carboxylic acids and amines will also react with acetyl chloride but should have been ruled out due to their non-neutrality.

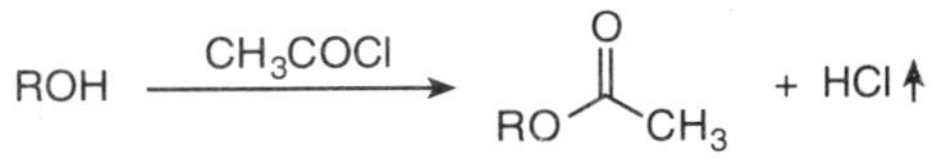

If an alcohol containing the $-CH(OH)CH_3$ group is suspected, the iodoform reaction may be applied. Primary, secondary and tertiary alcohols may be distinguished using Lucas' reagent which converts tertiary alcohols rapidly to the insoluble chloride, secondary alcohols more slowly and primary alcohols not at all.

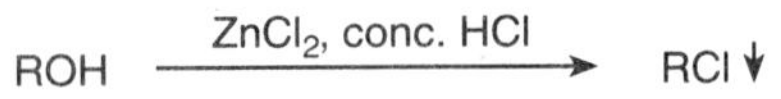

Suitable crystalline derivatives of alcohols are *urethanes* (pp. 255–256) and *3,5-dinitrobenzoates* (pp. 256–257).

Reaction with acetyl chloride

HOOD In a dry test tube place the unknown (*ca.* 0.5 mL of liquid or 500 mg of solid—most alcohols encountered will be liquid) and add acetyl chloride (0.3 mL) dropwise by pipette. A reaction, indicated by the mixture becoming warm and the evolution of hydrogen chloride, is a positive indication for an alcohol.

Differentiation between primary, secondary and tertiary alcohols (Lucas' test)

HOOD To the unknown (0.5 mL) in a test tube, add 3 mL of Lucas' reagent,* close the tube with a cork, shake for 15 s and allow to stand. Observe the mixture after 5 min when the following results may be seen.

* *Lucas' reagent.* A stock solution may be prepared by adding anhydrous zinc chloride (68 g) in portions to concentrated hydrochloric acid (45 mL) with cooling. This must be carried out in the hood.

- Solution totally clear (some darkening may occur)—*primary alcohol.*
- Solution becomes gradually cloudy (*ca.* 5–10 min)—*secondary alcohol.*
- Solution goes cloudy immediately—*tertiary alcohol.*

This test has its drawbacks, however. Allyl alcohols give results similar to secondary alcohols and the biphasic mixtures resulting from water-insoluble primary and secondary alcohols may be mistaken for a positive result for a tertiary alcohol. Preparation of derivatives is the only sure way to identify the alcohol.

Test for ethers

Ethers are difficult compounds to identify simply. However, if you think that your neutral unknown contains oxygen (e.g. by solubility in conc. H_2SO_4) and the functional group tests thus far have proved negative, it is likely to be an ether. Owing to their inertness, ethers are difficult compounds to derivatize. Symmetrical ethers can be cleaved with 3,5-dinitrobenzoyl chloride in the presence of zinc chloride and the crystalline 3,5-dinitrobenzoates can be characterized (p. 258). Unsymmetrical ethers are problematical, however, and identification in the absence of spectroscopic data relies mainly on their physical properties.

Alkenes and alkynes

Tests for unsaturated hydrocarbons are based on their ready ability to undergo electrophilic addition reactions. A simple test involves shaking with a solution of bromine water and observing whether or not the solution is decolourized. However, this test is not unequivocal as some alkenes react only very slowly with this reagent.

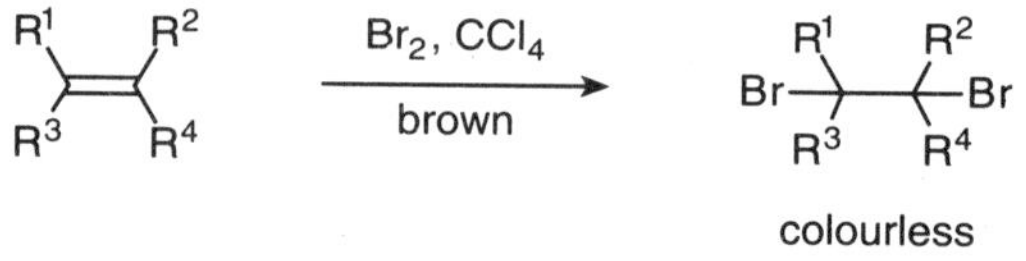

A better test is to look for decolourization of a solution of potassium permanganate (*Baeyer test*), but this test must only be carried out after determining the absence of other easily oxidized groups such as aldehydes.

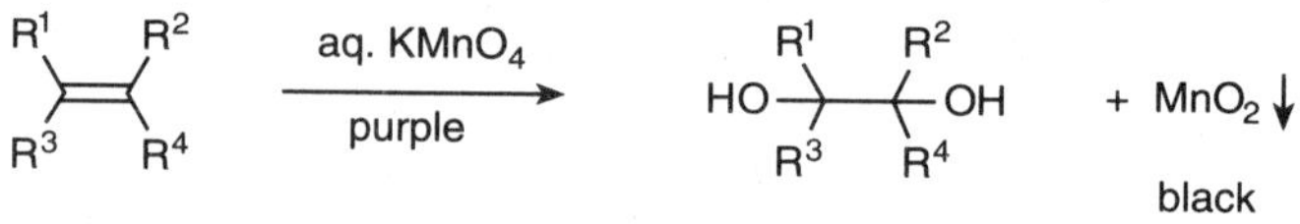

Test for unsaturation using aqueous potassium permanganate (Baeyer test)

Dissolve the unknown (2–3 drops of liquid or *ca.* 50 mg of solid) in ethanol (2 mL) and add 1 drop of a 0.1 M solution of potassium permanganate. If the purple colouration is discharged with the formation of a brown/black precipitate of manganese dioxide, continue adding the solution dropwise, counting the drops, until the purple colouration persists. Repeat this procedure with a blank solution of ethanol; a significant difference in the number of drops needed for persistence of the purple colour indicates the presence of an unsaturated hydrocarbon.

Both alkenes and alkynes may be derivatized by the formation of their crystalline addition products with 2,4-dinitrobenzenesulfenyl chloride (pp. 258–260).

Alkanes and arenes

Both alkanes and simple arenes are insoluble in concentrated sulfuric acid, whereas alkenes and alkynes undergo sulfonation to give soluble products. Although some polyalkylated aromatic compounds are also sufficiently reactive to be sulfonated and therefore dissolve, these should give a negative reaction with the test for unsaturation using bromine water. Distinction between alkanes and arenes is possible by reacting with chloroform in the presence of anhydrous aluminium chloride. Alkanes are unreactive and give little or no colour change, whereas arenes undergo a series of Friedel–Crafts alkylations resulting in colour changes which are frequently quite characteristic.

$$\text{ArH} \xrightarrow{\text{CHCl}_3,\ \text{AlCl}_3} \text{Ar}_3\text{CH}$$

Owing to the chemical inertness of aliphatic hydrocarbons there are no satisfactory derivatization procedures and so identification relies heavily on the observation of physical properties. Aromatic hydrocarbons may be nitrated or any alkyl side chains may be oxidized with alkaline potassium permanganate to give aromatic acids. In a two-step procedure, aromatic compounds may be converted to the corresponding *sulfonamide* via chlorosulfonylation (pp. 260–261) and treatment of the resultant arylsulfonyl chloride with ammonia. Another convenient means of derivatizing aromatic compounds involves the formation of the 1:1 π-complex with 1,3,5-trinitrobenzene (p. 261).

Distinction between alkanes and arenes

Dissolve the unknown (3 drops of liquid or *ca.* 100 mg of solid) in dry chloroform (1 mL) in a clean dry test tube and wet the sides of the tube by shaking vigorously. Add a spatula tip of powdered anhydrous aluminium chloride to the tube so that it clings to the wet sides. The observation of a bright colouration, ranging from red to blue, where the three components have come into contact is a positive test for an aromatic compound. These colours are often characteristic of particular classes of arene and examples are given in Table 4.2.

Neutral compounds containing a halogen

The fusion test will have shown which halogen is present in your unknown, but

Table 4.2 Colour reactions of aromatic compounds with $AlCl_3$–$CHCl_3$.

Compound class	Colour
Benzene and alkylated derivatives	Orange to red
Naphthalene	Blue
Anthracene	Green
Phenanthrene	Purple
Biphenyl	Purple

it is also possible to obtain evidence about the degree of substitution of the carbon to which the halogen is attached by reacting it with ethanolic silver nitrate. As reaction proceeds via an SN1 mechanism to give the alkyl nitrate and silver halide, tertiary halides are much more reactive than secondary halides, and these in turn are more reactive than primary halides. Benzylic and allylic halides, which ionize readily to generate resonance stabilized cations react with silver nitrate at a similar rate to tertiary halides, but halogens at sp^2 hybridized centres, such as vinyl or aryl halides, are unreactive. The rate of reaction is judged by observing the rate of formation of a precipitate of silver halide.

$$RX \xrightarrow{AgNO_3,\,EtOH} R{-}ONO_2 + AgX\downarrow$$

$X = Cl, Br, I$

white ($X = Cl$), cream ($X = Br$) or yellow ($X = I$) precipitate

If an aromatic halide is suspected, the $AlCl_3$–$CHCl_3$ test for an aromatic ring may be applied to the unknown; an orange or red colouration being a positive result for the aromatic ring. Primary and secondary aliphatic bromides and iodides may be characterized as *S*-alkylated thiouronium salts (p. 263). Chlorides react poorly but the yield can be improved by adding some potassium iodide to the reaction mixture. Tertiary halides give anomalous results, however, but you may rely on physical data to characterize these. Aromatic halides are best converted to their 2,4-dinitro derivatives which are high melting point solids (p. 264).

Ethanolic silver nitrate test for distinguishing tertiary, secondary, primary and aryl halides

Add 1 drop of the halide to a 0.1 M solution of silver nitrate in ethanol (2 mL) and leave the mixture at room temperature for 5 min. If no white or cream precipitate is observed, warm the mixture in a water bath and observe any change. Tertiary halides normally react in the cold, whereas secondary and primary halides require heating, with primary halides giving a much more slowly formed precipitate. Aromatic halides give no precipitate. Iodides are the most reactive, and bromides are more reactive than chlorides. This test may give spurious positive results if a carboxylic acid group is present, owing to the formation of an insoluble silver salt, and so should only be applied to neutral compounds. (There is a method for ruling out this possibility but a slight error in the procedure might lead to an explosive reaction. It is better just to use this test for compounds that are known to be neutral.)

Neutral compounds containing nitrogen

Three common classes of compounds fall into this category: nitriles, amides and nitro compounds. If you believe your unknown to be one of these, it is simplest to test first for the presence of a nitro group.

Nitro compounds

Both aliphatic and aromatic nitro compounds are oxidizing agents and their presence can be detected using freshly prepared iron(II) hydroxide which is oxidized to the brown iron(III) hydroxide.

$$RNO_2 \xrightarrow[\text{greenish-blue solid}]{Fe(OH)_2} RNH_2 + \underset{\text{brown precipitate}}{Fe(OH)_3 \downarrow}$$

Hydroxylamines, alkyl nitrates, alkyl nitrites and nitroso compounds also give this reaction, but are less likely to be encountered in the teaching laboratory (nitroso compounds must never be used in the laboratory as they are potent carcinogens).

Characterization of nitro compounds is a relatively lengthy procedure involving reduction to the corresponding amines (pp. 264–265) and derivatization of the amine. Aromatic compounds possessing alkyl substituents may be oxidized to the corresponding aromatic carboxylic acids if preferred.

Iron(II) hydroxide test

Add the unknown (2 drops of liquid or *ca.* 50 mg of solid) to a freshly prepared solution of 5% aqueous iron(II) ammonium sulfate (2 mL) in a test tube. Add 1 M sulfuric acid (3 drops) followed by a 2 M ethanolic solution of potassium hydroxide (1 mL), stopper the tube and shake it. If the initially formed blue precipitate turns brown within 1 min this is a positive result for the presence of a nitro group. Any slight darkening or greenish colour forming during this time does not constitute a positive test.

Nitriles and amides

Both primary amides and nitriles may be hydrolyzed to carboxylic acid salts and ammonia with aqueous sodium hydroxide. The two can usually be distinguished by the rate of hydrolysis, as nitriles are more slowly hydrolyzed than primary amides in base (amides are intermediates in the hydrolysis of nitriles). Nitriles are relatively easily hydrolyzed by warming in concentrated sulfuric acid.

$$RCONH_2 \xrightarrow{\text{aq. NaOH}} RCO_2^- + NH_3 \uparrow$$

$$RCN \xrightarrow{\text{aq. } H_2SO_4} RCO_2H + NH_4^+$$

Another aid to differentiation is that nitriles are usually liquids, whereas amides are almost invariably solids. Access to IR data would also permit ready differentiation between the two types of functionality. Characterization of primary amides and nitriles consists of hydrolysis to their corresponding acids whereas secondary and tertiary amides also necessitate identification of the amine component (pp. 271–274).

Alkaline hydrolysis

Add the unknown (4–5 drops of liquid or *ca.* 100 mg of solid) to 2 M aqueous sodium hydroxide (2 mL) and boil the mixture. Test for the evolution of ammonia with damp litmus or universal indicator paper. The rapid evolution of ammonia is indicative of a primary amide, slower evolution indicates a nitrile.

Neutral compounds possessing sulfur

No sane analysis course in a teaching laboratory will include thiols or thioethers due to their repulsive odours. Should one ever come your way, you will not need, or want, to prepare any derivatives. This is one instance when you will have no choice but to smell the compound! Sulfoxides and sulfones, however, are odourless and may well appear in a laboratory course. Generally sulfoxides are crystalline solids, whereas sulfones are liquids. Having decided that your unknown is a neutral compound that contains sulfur, it should be possible to identify it on the basis of its physical properties. Sulfoxides may be distinguished from sulfones by oxidation with potassium permanganate, but only if other easily oxidized groups are absent.

Acidic compounds in which halogens and sulfur are absent

The solubility tests using aqueous sodium bicarbonate and aqueous sodium hydroxide will have given a good indication whether or not your unknown is a phenol or a carboxylic acid. One source of confusion might come from the low rate of hydrolysis of some anhydrides. If in doubt, shake the tube containing the unknown and sodium bicarbonate, leave it for a few minutes and look for the steady evolution of small bubbles of carbon dioxide. Simple phenols (pK_a = 9–11) are weaker acids than carbonic acid ($pK_a = 6.35$) and so do not displace carbon dioxide from its salts. The few exceptions are phenols possessing electron-withdrawing groups in the 2- and 4-positions such as 2,4,6-trinitrophenol (picric acid, $pK_a = 0.38$). These tend to be brightly coloured solids, however, and should be readily recognizable.

Carboxylic acids and anhydrides

The liberation of carbon dioxide from aqueous sodium bicarbonate, coupled with the absence of halogens or sulfur, is sufficient evidence to justify proposing that your unknown is a carboxylic acid or anhydride. The two may be differentiated from each other using thionyl chloride which does not react with anhydrides, but converts carboxylic acids to acyl chlorides with the liberation of sulfur dioxide and hydrogen chloride. A positive result for a carboxylic acid is a steady, continuous evolution of gas; but remember that any moisture will react with the thionyl chloride giving a spurious result.

$$RCO_2H \xrightarrow{SOCl_2} RCOCl + HCl\uparrow + SO_2\uparrow$$

Differentiation between a carboxylic acid and an anhydride

HOOD

Place the unknown (3 drops of liquid or *ca.* 50 mg of solid) in a dry test tube. Add 3 drops of thionyl chloride using a pipette, allowing the reagent to run down the side of the test tube. Observe the mixture; a steady fizzing and evolution of gas at the point where the unknown and the thionyl chloride meet indicates a carboxylic acid is present. Any slow evolution of gas may be due to moisture present in the sample but should cease fairly rapidly.

Carboxylic acids may be derivatized by conversion into the corresponding *phenacyl esters* ($RCO_2CH_2(CO)Ar$) which are easy to prepare and highly crystalline (pp. 268–269). The 4-bromophenacyl and 4-phenylphenacyl esters are commonly prepared. Another popular derivatization procedure is the preparation of the *S-benzylisothiouronium* salt. However, this suffers from the drawback that the *S*-benzylisothiouronium chloride used to prepare the derivative decomposes to the extremely malodorous benzyl thiol if the reaction conditions are allowed to become too alkaline.

Anhydrides may be characterized by hydrolysis to the corresponding acid (pp. 269–270) (unsymmetrical anhydrides pose too many problems for simple qualitative analysis) or may be converted to *N*-phenyl amides, often referred to as *anilides*. The carboxylic acid products from hydrolysis may of course be derivatized further.

Phenols

Insolubility in aqueous sodium hydrogen carbonate but solubility in aqueous sodium hydroxide indicates a phenol. Simple phenols give moderately strong blue or purple colour reactions with iron(III) chloride whereas polyhydroxylated aromatic molecules give more varied colours, or are oxidized if the hydroxyl groups have a 1,4-relationship to each other. The colour reaction is much less strong than the intense purple colouration given by esters or 1,3-dicarbonyl compound derivatives with this reagent and can be used to distinguish between phenol and 1,3-dicarbonyl compounds which may show similar acidity.

Many phenols yield crystalline *benzoates* when reacted with benzoyl chloride in aqueous sodium hydroxide (*Schotten–Baumann reaction*, see pp. 272–273) and *3,5-dinitrobenzoates* are also commonly prepared; in this instance the reaction proceeds best in pyridine solution. An indirect derivatization procedure makes use of the high reactivity of phenols towards electrophilic aromatic substitution to prepare crystalline polybrominated derivatives using an excess of an aqueous solution of bromine (pp. 262–263). This procedure is only suited to simple phenols, however, as polyhydroxylated aromatics undergo ready oxidation and any deactivating groups on the aromatic ring inhibit reaction. Other derivatives which are often prepared are *aryloxyacetic acids* (p. 257).

Acidic compounds possessing halogen

The only monofunctional compounds which fall into this category are the acyl halides, their acidic properties being a consequence of ready hydrolysis to carboxylic acids and hydrogen chloride. They are simply distinguished from carboxylic acids possessing a halogen substituent by their vigorous reaction with water to evolve a hydrogen halide. Derivatization procedures are the same as for anhydrides.

Acidic compounds possessing sulfur

The common strongly acidic monofunctional compounds which fall into this category are the sulfonic acids and these are derivatized in very much the same manner as carboxylic acids, giving *S*-benzylisothiouronium salts (p. 268). Alternatively they may be converted via the sulfonyl chloride (pp. 274–275) to sulfonamides (pp. 273–274). Another derivative commonly prepared is the *p-toluidine salt*, obtained by reaction of the sodium salt of the sulfonic acid with 4-methylaniline (*p*-toluidine) (p. 275).

Aryl thiols are weakly acidic ($pK_a = 6–8$) and dissolve in aqueous sodium hydroxide. The presence of such a compound will manifest itself without the need for any rigorous chemical analysis, however. As previously stated, the use of any thiol as an unknown in a class experiment is really not a practical proposition due to the repulsive odours of these compounds.

Basic compounds

The basic organic compounds are all amines of one sort or another. If the unknown contains a halogen and dissolves in water to give an alkaline solution, it is a quaternary ammonium halide. These compounds are crystalline and, whilst it may be sufficient to compare the melting point of the unknown with literature values, quaternary ammonium salts are frequently hygroscopic and in such cases are not amenable to simple analysis. Aliphatic amines dissolve in water to give a strongly alkaline solution. Primary, secondary and tertiary amines may be distinguished by *Hinsberg's method* in which the amine is reacted with an arylsulfonyl chloride (pp. 273–274). Primary and secondary amines both react to give sulfonamides; those derived from primary amines possess a relatively acidic proton on the nitrogen and dissolve in aqueous alkali, whereas those derived from secondary amines are insoluble in base. Tertiary amines react to yield water-soluble salts of the arylsulfonic acid.

$$RNH_2 \xrightarrow{ArSO_2Cl} RNHSO_2Ar \xrightarrow{aq.\ NaOH} R\overset{-}{N}SO_2ArNa^+ \ \text{(soluble)}$$

$$R_2NH \xrightarrow{ArSO_2Cl} R_2NSO_2Ar \xrightarrow{aq.\ NaOH} \text{no reaction}$$

$$R_3N \xrightarrow{ArSO_2Cl} R_3\overset{+}{N}SO_2Ar\ Cl^-$$

A quicker means of distinction, involving reaction of the amine with nitrous acid, is *not* recommended as secondary amines react with this reagent to give a class of compounds called nitrosamines of which many members are potent carcinogens.

$$RNH_2 \xrightarrow[HCl]{aq.\ NaNO_2} \left[R-\overset{+}{N}\equiv N\right]\ \text{(unstable diazonium salt)} \xrightarrow{H_2O} ROH + N_2\uparrow$$

$$R_2NH \xrightarrow[HCl]{aq.\ NaNO_2} R_2N-N=O\ \text{nitrosamine (carcinogen)}$$

$$R_3N \xrightarrow[HCl]{aq.\ NaNO_2} R_3\overset{+}{N}H\ Cl^-$$

Benzoylation under *Schotten–Baumann* conditions (pp. 272–273) and acetylation with acetic anhydride (pp. 271–272) are suitable derivatization procedures for aliphatic and aromatic primary and secondary amines. Other derivatives which might be prepared include formamides, phenylthioureas and picrates. The crystalline 1 : 1 molecular complexes with picric acid are also suitable derivatives for tertiary amines (p. 274).

Reaction thin layer chromatography for ultra small-scale characterization of functional groups

Before continuing with this section or attempting any characterizations using RTLC, you should read pp. 165–175 which describe the various techniques and procedures of analysis using thin layer chromatography.

The technique of RTLC, which permits the simple and rapid characterization of several important functional groups and requires only minute quantities of material, can be traced back to the work of J.M. Miller and J.G. Kirchner in 1953. In essence, the unknown is spotted onto the baseline of a TLC plate and then over-spotted with the characterization reagent. After allowing some time for the reaction to proceed, the TLC plate is developed alongside samples of the unknown and reagent as standards, and is visualized as usual.

The technique can be considered to be a natural extension of the procedure for following the progress of a reaction by TLC. The difference in this case is that the reaction is allowed to take place on the TLC plate itself instead of in a flask. A new spot appearing in the mixed sample which does not have a counterpart in either of the two standard samples indicates reaction of the unknown with the reagent and gives a good indication of the presence of the functional group—'good indication'—but not proof.

There are perfectly good reasons why a reaction may occur on the TLC plate which does not involve the particular derivatization reaction which is being examined; hydrolysis or dehydration brought about by acid in a reagent for instance. With a little thought, however, such side reactions may be minimized and the technique can provide good experimental evidence for functionality using quantities of material which would be difficult or impossible to analyze using classic or even spectroscopic analysis. Table 4.3 shows a list of

Table 4.3 Derivatization and functionalization procedures amenable for use in RTLC.

Reaction	Reagent system
Acetylation of alcohols	Acetic anhydride Acetyl chloride
Benzoylation of alcohols	Benzoyl chloride
Dehydration	Sulfuric acid (concentrated)
Derivatization of alcohols	3,5-Dinitrobenzoyl chloride Phenyl isocyanate
Derivatization of carbonyl compounds	2,4-Dinitrophenylhydrazine
Halogenation of alkenes or phenols	Bromine
Catalytic hydrogenation	H_2/catalyst
Methylation of acids	Methanol/sulfuric acid (concentrated) Diazomethane
Nitration	Nitric acid (concentrated)
Oxidation	Chromium(VI) oxide/glacial acetic acid 30% Hydrogen peroxide Ozone Peracid
Reduction	Lithium aluminium hydride Sodium borohydride Tin(II) chloride

reactions which may be carried out using the technique. Modifications of the basic procedure such as *elatography* involve applying the reagent to the plate as a band through which the unknown passes on development. Alternatively the reagent can be included in the stationary phase or the eluting solvent. These more complex procedures have been reviewed by Beroza (1977) and those interested are directed to this article. The simple double spotting technique will be sufficient for our needs (Fig. 4.12).

Procedure

The analysis is carried out in exactly the same way as a normal TLC analysis with the one difference that a certain period of time is allowed to elapse between double spotting the reagent with the unknown and developing the TLC plate. To encourage reaction even more, the TLC plate may be warmed *gently*, but this should be avoided wherever possible, as organic compounds are highly prone to aerial oxidation when highly dispersed on the adsorbant. Incomplete reaction before development is indicated by the presence of a new spot accompanied by a spot corresponding to residual starting material. On leaving the plate for a longer period before developing or increasing the amount of reagent applied, the new spot should appear to increase at the expense of that corresponding to unreacted starting material.

As well as allowing time for the reaction to proceed, the spots must also be as dry as possible before development, otherwise the residual solvents in

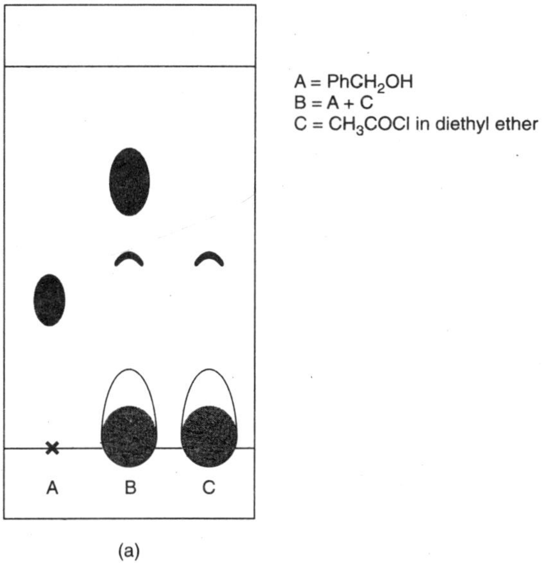

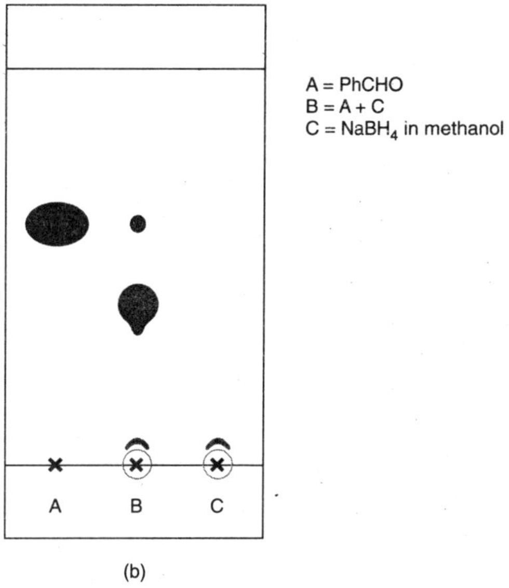

Fig. 4.12 Examples of RTLC analysis: (a) esterification of benzyl alcohol with acetyl chloride; (b) reduction of benzaldehyde with methanolic sodium borohydride (adsorbant, silica G_{254}; eluting system, diethyl ether–light petroleum 1:1; visualization, 254 mm UV light).

which the reagent was applied will interfere with the analysis. When the reagent is dissolved in a high boiling point solvent, or the unknown is a sensitive material, it is frequently advantageous to apply the reagent first, dry the plate and apply the unknown afterwards. This order of application is also worth trying when the reagent is dissolved in a polar solvent. This will avoid enlarging the unknown spot on application of the reagent, and will remove problems due to subsequent distortion of the spots on the developed chromatogram (see Fig. 3.69, p. 174). Some reagents, for example Brady's reagent, tail badly if too much is spotted onto the plate and it is advisable to find the optimum quantity of reagent to use before carrying out the analysis. In the cases where gaseous reagents are used (catalytic hydrogenation, oxidation), the unknown is spotted onto the plate and the gas is played onto the spot in a slow stream using a Pasteur pipette before development of the plate.

The solvent system should be such that the unknown has an R_f value of *ca.* 0.5, but any solvent that undergoes reaction with the derivatizing reagent is precluded. For instance, acetone cannot be used for the development of reductions using hydride reagents and likewise methanol for chromium(VI) oxide oxidations.

The use of two-dimensional TLC provides additional sophistication in searching for a compound possessing a specific functional group within a mixture of compounds (see Fig. 3.66, p. 172). The mixture is first spotted in the corner of a square TLC plate and the first development is carried out as usual. The plate is then dried and a line of reagent is applied carefully to the whole of the new baseline for the second development. After drying and reaction, the plate is developed a second time at 90° to the first. The developed plate should be compared with a two-dimensional analysis of the same mixture carried out without the intermediate *in situ* reaction.

The next paragraphs contain some practical advice for carrying out the TLC reactions listed in Table 4.3, but it is impossible to generalize the procedures. Each individual case will require optimization of eluting solvent composition and stationary phase as well as optimization of the quantities of reagent to use, and the length of time between application and development.

Acetylation and benzoylation of alcohols

All these RTLC analyses should be carried out in a hood

The acylating agents are added as 10% solutions in dry ethyl ether to the unknown, previously spotted onto the TLC plate, and the solvent is allowed to evaporate. Reactions with acetyl chloride may be developed as soon as the spot appears to be dry. Reactions with acetic anhydride and benzoyl chloride are better left for 5 min before drying the spot with a current of air and developing the plate. The ester products will be less polar than the starting alcohols in the vast majority of cases. Use of alumina TLC plates may be advantageous with acid-sensitive alcohols.

Dehydration

Apply a small quantity of neat concentrated sulfuric acid to the unknown spot. The TLC plate may be developed after 30 s. As the products may be much less polar than the starting alcohols, it is usually more practical to check for disappearance of starting material than for the appearance of new spots. Any residual starting material may have a slightly different R_f value to that of the standard due to interference by the concentrated acid on the baseline.

Derivatization of alcohols

Apply the 3,5-dinitrobenzoyl chloride or the isocyanate as 10% solutions in dry diethyl ether. Allow the solvent to evaporate and allow at least 5 min for reaction before development.

Derivatization of carbonyl compounds

Brady's reagent is spotted onto the plate first, and the spot is allowed to become almost dry, using a stream of air to encourage drying. The unknown is spotted onto the reagent and the plates are developed after 5 min. An advantage of using Brady's reagent is that the 2,4-dinitrophenyl-hydrazones are visible to the naked eye. The disadvantage of these derivatives is their relative insolubility in common solvents with the effect that it is very easy to overload TLC plates.

Bromination of unsaturated hydrocarbons

Care!

A 5% solution of bromine in acetic acid is applied to the unknown spot on the TLC plate and the acetic acid and excess bromine are removed with a current of air. Development proceeds as soon as the spot appears dry.

Catalytic hydrogenation

Care! No naked flames

A solution of the unknown in diethyl ether, in which the catalyst has been suspended, is spotted onto the plate and the solvent is allowed to evaporate. In the hood, a slow stream of hydrogen is played onto the spot for 15 min with the tip of the Pasteur pipette held 2 mm from the surface of the plate. The plate may be developed immediately after this period. Reductions of double bonds may give products with very similar R_f values to the starting material, but these frequently visualize differently with some spray reagents; it is necessary to experiment.

Methylation of carboxylic acids

A small quantity of concentrated sulfuric acid is spotted onto the plate, followed by a 5% solution of the carboxylic acid in methanol. After 5 min the plate is developed. The esters are less polar than the starting acids. The use of diazomethane for RTLC has been described but is not recommended. Although it methylates carboxylic acids instantly, its toxicity, volatility and explosive nature do not make it an easy reagent to manipulate in this manner. Above all, a micro-pipette must *never* be dipped into a solution of diazomethane as rough surfaces can catalyze an explosive decomposition.

Nitration

Phenols may be nitrated by co-spotting with concentrated nitric and then drying the plate in a current of warm air. Development of the plate proceeds as soon as the spot appears dry.

Oxidation

Care! Oxidants

Chromium(VI) oxide or peracetic acid are applied to the unknown as solutions in acetic acid, and hydrogen peroxide is applied as the 30% aqueous solution. The plates are dried in a current of warm air after 5 min and developed.

Reduction

Care! Solutions of metal hydrides are highly flammable and react vigorously with water

A freshly prepared saturated ethereal solution of lithium aluminium hydride or freshly prepared 5% methanolic sodium borohydride are spotted onto the unknown. The spots are allowed to dry and the plate is developed after 5 min. Owing to their different reducing abilities, a combination of these two systems allows the differentiation of ketones and aldehydes from esters and carboxylic acids, the latter two being unaffected by sodium borohydride; whereas all are reduced by lithium aluminium hydride.

Tin(II) chloride, applied as a solution in glacial acetic acid, may be used for the reduction of aromatic nitro compounds to anilines. The solvent is removed with gentle warming and the plate is developed after 5 min.

Further reading

The following works provide further introductions to the techniques of RTLC and contain many useful references:

M. Beroza, *Chimia (Supplement)—Column Chromatography* (ed. E.Sz. Kovatz), *Chimia*, 1977, p. 92.

K. Blau, and G.S. King, *Handbook of Derivatives for Chromatography*, Heyden, London, 1977, p. 323.

A.M. Osmam, M. El-Gorby Younes, and F.M. Ata, *J. Chem U.A.R.*, 1970, **13**, 273.

J.C. Touchstone, *Practice of Thin Layer Chromatography*, Wiley (Interscience), New York, 1983, p. 214.

Preparation of derivatives

The confirmation of which functional groups are present in your unknown, together with the knowledge of its physical properties, should enable you to narrow the range of possible candidate structures. Indeed, it is possible that the data available to you will only fit for one particular substance. However, as generic compounds having melting points or boiling points within 5°C of that obtained from your unknown must be included for consideration, it is likely that you will still have two or more structures as possible candidates. It is now time to prepare two derivatives of your unknown and compare the melting points of these with literature values. Tables of melting points of derivatives have not been included in this book as it would be impossible to provide anything like a comprehensive list for each functional group that might be encountered. Besides which, an important part of the exercise of identifying your unknown is using the chemical literature. There are many sources of such information, some more complete than others, but no single work is exhaustive. Some, such as the *CRC Handbook, Vogel's Textbook* and the *Dictionary of Organic Compounds*, are particularly useful for this kind of information and it is highly likely that the details you require will be contained somewhere within one of these works; the full details of these are given at the end of this section.

The choice of which derivative to prepare will be largely governed by the functional groups within the molecule; an extreme category being the alkanes which cannot be derivatized. Nonetheless, it is usual that you will be presented with a choice of possibilities and it is up to you to decide. Whilst convenience of preparation should be borne in mind, a paramount consideration is that the derivative should not have a melting point much lower than 50°C, as crystallization of the crude material might be difficult, causing purification problems. Even more important is the need for a derivative having a melting point sufficiently different from that of the same derivative of other candidate structures. For example, an unknown alcohol with a boiling point of 99°C might be 1-propanol (bp 97°C) or 2-butanol (bp 99°C). The respective 3,5-dinitrobenzoate esters of these alcohols have melting points of 74°C and 75°C and therefore will not permit differentiation between the two candidate structures. However, their 1-naphthylurethane derivatives have melting points of 80°C and 97°C respectively, which will permit this distinction, and so these should be prepared.

The following list of derivatization procedures is not comprehensive but has attempted to include those which are most convenient and useful. The procedures are listed by functional group, more or less in the same order as the characterizations have been described. All require filtration with suction (pp. 77–79) and small-scale recrystallization (pp. 137–138) at some stage, and some involve distillation (pp. 146–159) or periods of reflux (pp. 96–100). The level of difficulty of the procedures calls for some prior experience with basic manipulative techniques and your attention is drawn to the hazards associated with some of the reagents used. Where appropriate, suggested quantities of reagents are given in the materials section, and the smaller volumes of liquid reagents quoted may be estimated accurately enough using a simple 1 mL graduated Pasteur pipette. The derivatizations may be carried out on slightly larger or smaller scales by modifying the quantities pro rata, but if you want to change the scale by a factor of 10 or more, consult an instructor before proceeding.

Aldehydes and ketones

Preparation of dinitrophenylhydrazones

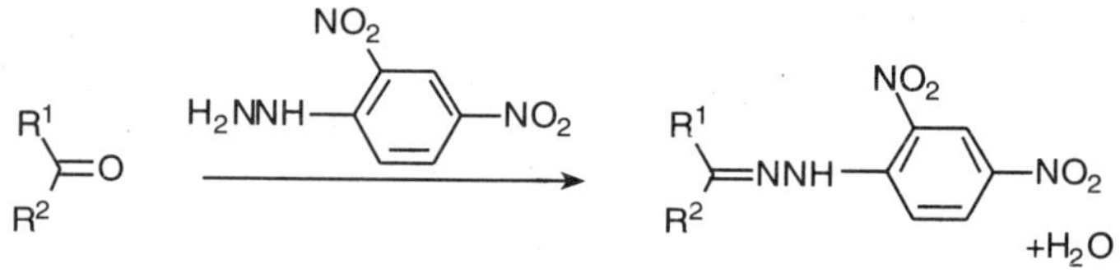

Equipment	Apparatus for filtration and recrystallization	
Materials		
unknown sample	*ca.* 0.20 g	
2,4-dinitrophenylhydrazine	0.25 g	**toxic**
sulfuric acid (98%)	0.50 mL	**corrosive, oxidizer**
ethanol		**flammable, toxic**

Procedure

Add ethanol (5 mL) to the 2,4-dinitrophenylhydrazine in a 25 mL Erlenmeyer flask and add the concentrated sulfuric acid cautiously to the suspension with constant swirling during the addition.[1] Dissolve the unknown carbonyl compound in a small volume of ethanol and to this add the clear supernatant[2] of the 2,4-dinitrophenylhydrazine reagent. Warm the mixture if no solid separates immediately, and then allow to stand for 10 min. If a precipitate still does not form, add water dropwise until precipitation occurs. Filter off the solid with suction and wash it with 1:1 aqueous methanol (5 mL). Recrystallize the solid from ethanol or ethyl acetate to constant melting point.

[1]*Care! Exothermic*

[2]*Do not transfer undissolved solid*

Preparation of oximes

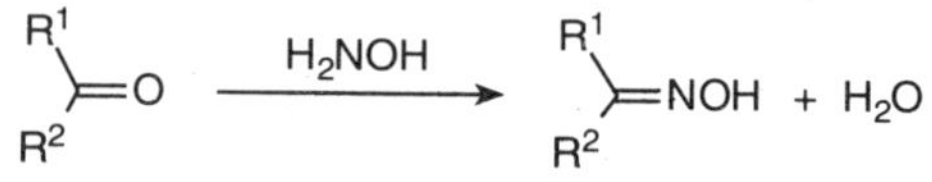

Equipment	apparatus for filtration and recrystallization	
Materials		
unknown sample	*ca.* 0.5 g	
hydroxylamine hydrochloride	1.0 g	**corrosive**
sodium acetate trihydrate	2.0 g	
ethanol		**flammable, toxic**

Procedure

Dissolve the hydroxylamine hydrochloride and sodium acetate in 5 mL of distilled water in a 25 mL Erlenmeyer flask, and to this solution add the unknown carbonyl compound. If the unknown is not soluble in the aqueous system, add ethanol dropwise until solution occurs. Swirl the mixture with warming for 10 min on a water bath and then cool in ice. Filter off the precipitated solid with suction and recrystallize to constant melting point from ethanol, ethyl acetate or aqueous ethanol. ■

Alcohols and phenols

Many of the derivatives for characterizing alcohols (3,5-dinitrobenzoates, urethanes) may be used equally successfully for phenols. Phenols may also be characterized directly as benzoate esters, by adapting the Schotten–Baumann procedure described for derivatizing amines (pp. 272–273), and as aryloxyacetic acid derivatives; they can also be characterized indirectly by bromination of the aromatic ring (pp. 262–263).

Preparation of urethanes

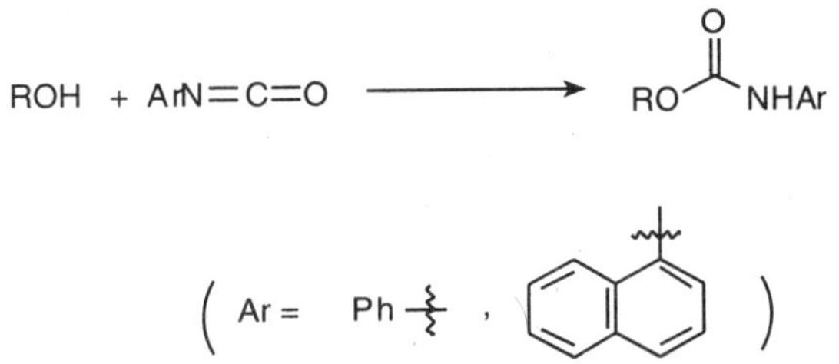

Both naphthyl and phenyl urethanes are useful derivatives of alcohols, but phenyl isocyanate used for the preparation of the latter derivatives is highly lachrymatory and is also readily decomposed by any moisture to form diphenylurea (mp 238°C) which can interfere with the derivatization. 1-Naphthyl isocyanate is more stable to hydrolysis (dinaphthylurea, mp 297°C) and is less lachrymatory, and consequently is the reagent of choice for urethane preparation. A further advantage is that the 1-naphthylurethane derivatives have higher melting points than the phenyl analogues. The procedure below is readily adapted for the preparation of phenylurethanes and may also be used for preparing urethane derivatives of phenols.

Equipment	apparatus for filtration and recrystallization	
Materials		
unknown alcohol	*ca.* 1.0 g	
1-naphthyl isocyanate	0.5 mL	**lachrymator,**
light petroleum (bp 40–60°C)		**flammable**

Procedure

HOOD

Measure the alcohol into a dry test tube and add the 1-naphthyl isocyanate to it in one portion. *Loosely* plug the mouth of the tube with cotton wool, shake to mix the contents and allow to stand for 5 min with occasional shaking. If no solid separates during this period, warm briefly on a water bath and cool the mixture in ice, scratching the sides of the tube with a glass rod to encourage crystal formation. Filter off the solid with suction and recrystallize it to constant melting point from light petroleum, after first removing any 1-naphthylurea which is insoluble in the light petroleum. If crystallization of the reaction mixture cannot be induced by the heating–scratching procedure, digest the whole mixture with light petroleum, filtering off any insoluble material, and remove the solvent on the rotary evaporator to furnish crude urethane suitable for further recrystallization.

Preparation of 3,5-dinitrobenzoates

3,5-Dinitrobenzoate esters are suitable derivatives for both alcohols and phenols for which the following general procedure is applicable. However, this is not necessary for volatile alcohols which can be derivatized simply by heating with twice the weight of 3,5-dinitrobenzoyl chloride for 10 min and cooling the mixture.

Equipment apparatus for filtration, recrystallization and extraction

Materials		
unknown alcohol or phenol	*ca.* 0.5 mL (0.5 g if solid)	
3,5-dinitrobenzoyl chloride	1.0 g	**lachrymator, corrosive**
pyridine	2.0 mL	**flammable, irritant**
diethyl ether		**flammable, irritant**
light petroleum (bp 40–60°C)		**flammable**
ethanol (alternative recrystallizing solvent to light petroleum)		**flammable, toxic**
aqueous hydrochloric acid (5%)		**corrosive**
aqueous sodium hydroxide (5%)		**corrosive**

Procedure

HOOD

Place the unknown, the 3,5-dinitrobenzoyl chloride and the pyridine in a test tube. Stopper the tube loosely with cotton wool and heat the mixture on a water bath for 15 min (30 min if the unknown is believed to be a tertiary alcohol). Allow the mixture to cool, add diethyl ether (20 mL) to the mixture and extract with dilute hydrochloric acid (3 × 25 mL) to remove pyridine. Wash the organic phase with dilute sodium hydroxide solution (25 mL) to remove any 3,5-dinitrobenzoic acid (and unreacted phenol if the unknown is phenolic) and dry over $MgSO_4$. Filter the solution and remove the solvent on the rotary evaporator. Recrystallize the residue from light petroleum or aqueous ethanol.

Phenol characterization by aryloxyacetic acid preparation

$$\mathrm{ArONa + ClCH_2CO_2Na \longrightarrow [ArOCH_2CO_2Na] \xrightarrow{H^+} ArOCH_2CO_2H}$$

Equipment apparatus for filtration, recrystallization and extraction

Materials		
unknown phenol	*ca.* 0.20 g	
chloroacetic acid	0.25 g	**corrosive, toxic**
sodium hydroxide	0.25 g	**corrosive**
diethyl ether		**flammable, irritant**
ethanol		**flammable, toxic**
aqueous hydrochloric acid (5%)		**corrosive**
aqueous sodium carbonate (5%)		**corrosive**

Procedure

HOOD

Measure the phenol and sodium hydroxide into a test tube and then add water (1 mL) and the chloroacetic acid. Heat the mixture on a steam bath and add sufficient water to render the mixture homogeneous. Continue to heat the mixture for 1 h, allow to cool and then acidify by dropwise addition of dilute hydrochloric acid. Filter off with suction any solid which precipitates and recrystallize it to constant melting point from aqueous ethanol. If no solid forms on acidification, extract the acidic solution with diethyl ether (2 × 10 mL). Wash the combined organic phases with water (2 × 10 mL) to remove excess chloroacetic acid and then with 5% aqueous sodium carbonate[1] (3 × 10 mL) to extract the aryloxyacetic acid derivative as its sodium salt. Cautiously acidify this aqueous extract,[1] filter off the precipitate with suction and recrystallize from aqueous ethanol. ■

[1] *Care CO_2 evolved*

Ethers

Owing to their lack of reactivity, ethers are difficult compounds to derivatize, particularly unsymmetrical aliphatic ethers, where it is necessary to rely on the physical constants of the unknown for characterization. However, if the ether is believed to be symmetrical it is possible to carry out a one-pot cleavage of the ether linkage and obtain the 3,5-dinitrobenzoate ester derivative of the cleavage products. If the ether is aromatic, there is scope for characterization by electrophilic substitution of the aromatic ring. Bromination is a convenient procedure and that described for derivatization of phenols may be followed (pp. 262–263).

Cleavage of an ether and derivatization of the resulting alcohol

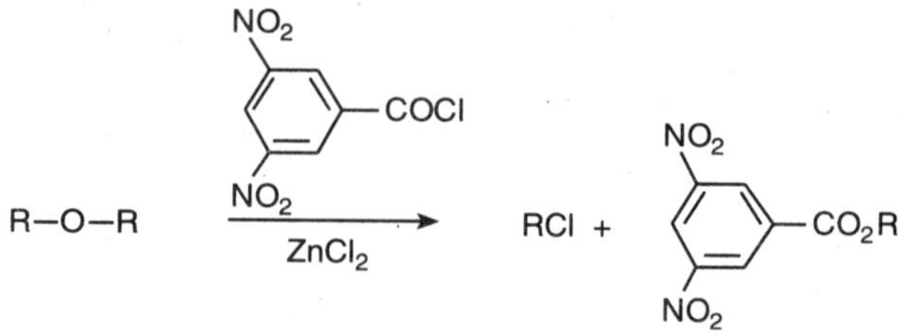

Equipment	apparatus for reflux (with protection from atmospheric moisture), filtration and recrystallization

Materials		
unknown symmetrical ether	*ca.* 2.0 mL	
3,5-dinitrobenzoyl ether	1.0 g	**lachrymator, corrosive**
anhydrous zinc chloride	0.3 g	**irritant, toxic**
ethanol		**flammable, toxic**
aqueous sodium carbonate (10%)		**corrosive**

Procedure

HOOD

Weigh out the zinc chloride rapidly, grind it to a fine powder and add this to a dry 25 mL round-bottomed flask. Add the 3,5-dinitrobenzoyl chloride followed by the ether and arrange the apparatus for reflux with protection from atmospheric moisture. Heat the mixture on a boiling water bath for 1 h and allow to cool. Dismantle the apparatus, carefully add 5 mL of aqueous sodium carbonate[1] to the residue and heat the mixture on the boiling water bath, with stirring, for 1 min. When evolution of gas subsides, add a further 5 mL and repeat the process until a total of 20 mL of sodium carbonate solution has been added. Allow the mixture to cool and filter off the solid residue with suction. Recrystallize the product to constant melting point from aqueous ethanol. ■

[1] *Care! Exothermic*

Alkenes and alkynes

Alkenes and alkynes may be characterized conveniently by preparing the crystalline adducts with 2,4-dinitrobenzenesulfenyl chloride. Moreover, as addition to the unsaturated linkage is stereospecifically *anti*, it is possible to differentiate between *E*- and *Z*-alkenes which give isomeric adducts possessing different melting points. However, owing to the lack of other suitable general derivatization procedures for alkenes and alkynes, it will be necessary also to rely on the physical constants of the unknown.

Derivatization of alkenes

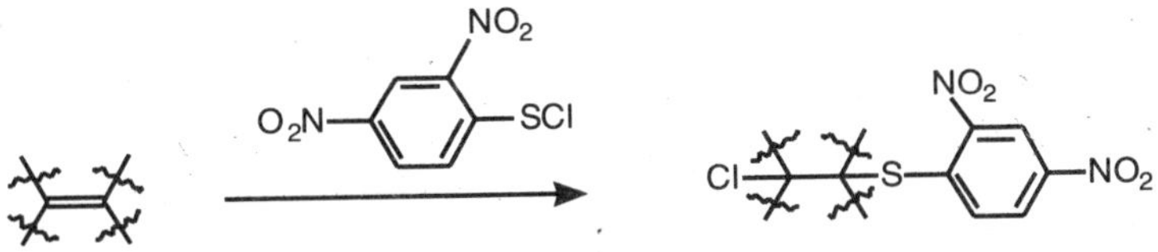

Equipment	apparatus for filtration and recrystallization	
Materials		
unknown alkene	*ca.* 0.3 g	
2,4-dinitrobenzenesulfenyl chloride	0.2 g	**lachrymator, corrosive**
glacial acetic acid	3.0 mL	**corrosive**
ethanol		**flammable, toxic**

HOOD

Procedure
Dissolve the 2,4-dinitrobenzenesulfenyl chloride and the unknown alkene in 3 mL of glacial acetic acid in a test tube and heat for 15 min on a steam bath. Allow the mixture to cool, pour onto crushed ice and stir until the precipitated product becomes solid. Filter off the crude derivative with suction and recrystallize it to constant melting point from ethanol.

Derivatization of alkynes

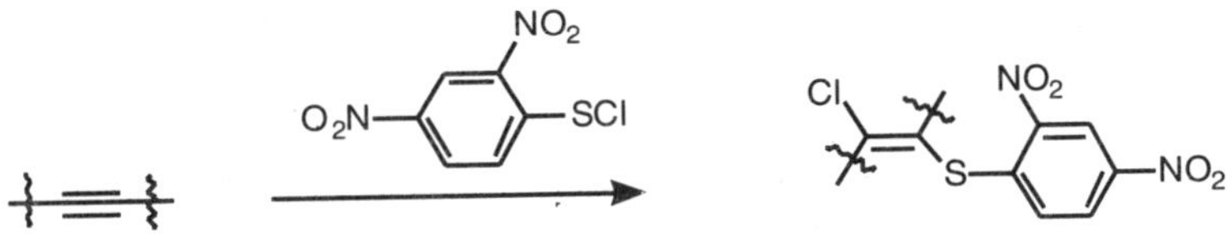

Equipment	apparatus for filtration and recrystallization	
Materials		
unknown alkyne	*ca.* 3.0 mL	
2,4-dinitrobenzenesulfenyl chloride	1.5 g	**lachrymator, corrosive**
1,2-dichloroethane	15 mL	**cancer suspect agent,**
ethanol		**flammable flammable, toxic**

HOOD

Procedure

Dissolve the 2,4-dinitrobenzenesulfenyl chloride in the 1,2-dichloroethane in a 25 mL Erlenmeyer flask, loosely stopper and cool in ice for 15 min. Add the alkyne and allow the mixture to stand at 0°C for 2 h (refrigerator) or until a crystalline product is formed. Filter off the product with suction and recrystallize it from ethanol to constant melting point. If the crude material is dark in colour, it may be helpful to decolourize with charcoal before proceeding with the recrystallization. ■

Aromatic hydrocarbons

Aromatic compounds may be converted to the corresponding sulfonamides in a two-step process by first reacting with chlorosulfonic acid followed by addition of ammonia. If the unknown is believed to possess an electron-rich aromatic ring, it is usually possible to obtain a crystalline complex with 1,3,5-trinitrobenzene, although other planar electron-poor aromatic compounds which may be used include picric acid (2,4,6-trinitrophenol) and styphnic acid (2,4,6-trinitroresorcinol). If alkyl groups are present, another option may be to degrade these oxidatively to the corresponding carboxylic acid. Other procedures involving bromination or nitration are less generally applicable for preparing crystalline derivatives. However, bromination can be used with phenols which are not readily oxidized and nitration may prove useful for indirect derivatization of aromatic halides (p. 264).

Preparation of sulfonamides

$$ArH \xrightarrow{ClSO_3H} ArSO_2Cl \xrightarrow{NH_3} ArSO_2NH_2$$

Equipment apparatus for filtration, recrystallization and extraction

Materials		
unknown aromatic sample	*ca.* 1.0 g	
chlorosulfonic acid	3.0 mL	**corrosive, toxic**
chloroform		**cancer suspect agent, toxic**
ethanol		**flammable, toxic**
aqueous ammonia (conc., 30%)	10 mL	**lachrymator, corrosive, toxic**

HOOD

[1]*Care! Corrosive*

Procedure

Dissolve the unknown in the chloroform and add the chlorosulfonic acid dropwise[1] with cooling in an ice bath. After the evolution of hydrogen chloride fumes has slowed down, allow the mixture to stand at room temperature for 30 min with periodic gentle shaking, and then pour onto crushed ice. Separate the lower chloroform layer, adding a little more chloroform if necessary, and dry the solution over $MgSO_4$. Filter off the drying agent and remove the solvent on the rotary evaporator in a 50 mL round-bottomed flask. Add the ammonia[2] to the residue and heat the mixture on a steam bath for 10 min. Add 25 mL of water to the mixture and break up any lumps of solid with a glass rod. Filter off the crude sulfonamide with suction and recrystallize to constant melting point from aqueous ethanol.

[2] ***Care! Lachrymator***

Preparation of 1,3,5-trinitrobenzene adducts

Equipment apparatus for filtration and recrystallization

Materials		
unknown aromatic sample	*ca.* 0.2 g	
1,3,5-trinitrobenzene	0.2 g	**flammable**
Note: *1,3,5-trinitrobenzene is potentially explosive. Do not heat or grind the solid and do not handle in quantities greater than recommended*		
ethanol		**flammable, toxic**

Procedure

Dissolve the unknown in 1 mL of ethanol and add this to a solution of the 1,3,5-trinitrobenzene[1] dissolved in cold ethanol (2 mL). Cool the mixture in ice, filter off the precipitate solid with suction and recrystallize it to constant melting point from ethanol.

[1] ***Do not expose to heat!***

Oxidation of side chains of aromatic substrates

Any alkyl group possessing at least one benzylic hydrogen can be degraded to the carboxylic acid group by oxidation on refluxing with alkaline potassium permanganate. However, many aromatic compounds such as phenols and anilines will not withstand such vigorous reaction conditions. Compounds possessing more than two alkyl side chains usually require inconveniently long periods of time for complete oxidation.

Equipment apparatus for filtration, recrystallization and reflux

Materials		
unknown aromatic sample	*ca.* 0.5 g	
potassium permanganate	2.0 g	**irritant, oxidizer**
sodium carbonate	0.5 g	**corrosive**
ethanol		**flammable, toxic**
aqueous sulfuric acid (5%)		**corrosive**
saturated aqueous sodium bisulfite		**irritant**

Procedure

[1]See Fig. 3.23a

Check for flammable materials in the area

Measure the unknown, potassium permanganate and sodium carbonate into a 100 mL round-bottomed flask and add 50 mL of water. Set the apparatus for reflux[1] and reflux vigorously over a microburner until the purple colour of the oxidizing agent has been replaced by a black precipitate of manganese dioxide (or 2 h whichever is the shorter period). Cool the mixture, acidify with 5% aqueous sulfuric acid and add saturated sodium bisulfite solution with shaking until the manganese dioxide has been removed. Filter the mixture with suction and recrystallize the residue to constant melting point from water or aqueous ethanol.

Bromination of phenols

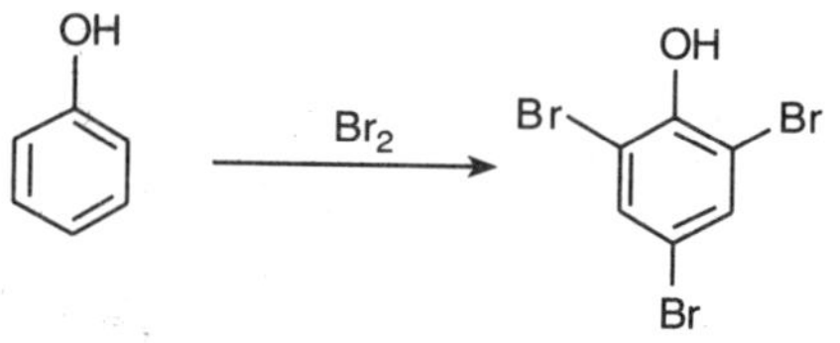

This procedure is really only suitable for phenolic compounds possessing one hydroxyl group as bromine–acetic acid will oxidize the more sensitive polyhydroxylated substrates. The number and position of the bromine atoms introduced depend on the substrate; phenol itself readily yields the 2,4,6-tribromo derivative.

Equipment apparatus for filtration and recrystallization

Materials

unknown phenol	*ca.* 0.5 g	
aqueous solution of bromine*		**corrosive**
ethanol		**flammable, toxic**
saturated aqueous sodium bisulfite		**irritant**

NOTE: ***extreme caution must be exercised when using bromine as its volatility, density and highly irritant properties make it extremely difficult to handle. Always wear gloves and manipulate bromine in the hood***

*The aqueous bromine reagent is conveniently prepared as a stock solution by dissolving potassium bromide (10 g) in water (50 mL) followed by the addition of bromine (2 mL).

Procedure

HOOD

[1]***Care! Corrosive***

Dissolve the phenol in ethanol (5 mL) and add the aqueous bromine reagent dropwise,[1] shaking the reaction mixture until a permanent yellow colouration just appears. Add water (20 mL) to this mixture and filter off the precipitate with suction. If the precipitate is yellow in colour due to residual bromine, wash it on the filter with saturated aqueous sodium bisulfite (5 mL) followed by water (3 × 15 mL). Recrystallize the crude material to constant melting point from ethanol or aqueous ethanol. ■

Halides

Halides are relatively inert compounds from the point of view of efficient derivatization, but primary and secondary halides form crystalline *S*-alkylisothiouronium salts; the normally slow reaction of chlorides is increased by adding an inorganic iodide to the reaction mixture. Tertiary halides do not give such derivatives and their characterization presents difficulties, particularly in view of their tendency towards elimination. Halides may be converted into a wide range of easily characterized compounds by first converting them into the corresponding Grignard reagent, but this procedure is sometimes difficult on a small scale. Aromatic halides may be derivatized indirectly by electrophilic substitution of the aromatic nucleus or by oxidation of any alkyl side chains (pp. 261–262).

Preparation of S*-alkylisothiouronium picrates*

Equipment apparatus for filtration, recrystallization and reflux

Materials		
unknown halide sample	*ca.* 0.2 g	
thiourea	0.2 g	**cancer suspect agent, toxic**
picric acid (2,4,6-trinitrophenol)	0.2 g	**flammable, toxic**
ethanol		**flammable, toxic**
potassium iodide (for use with alkyl chlorides)	0.2 g	

Procedure

HOOD

[1] *See Fig. 3.23a*

Place the thiourea, unknown and ethanol (10 mL) in a 25 mL round-bottomed flask and set the apparatus for reflux[1] and heat the mixture. If the unknown is a chloride, add the potassium iodide at the beginning of the reflux period, together with sufficient water to produce a homogeneous solution when the mixture is refluxing. After 30 min (primary bromides and iodides) or 2 h (chlorides or secondary bromides and iodides) at reflux, cool the mixture temporarily; add the picric acid and return to reflux until a clear solution is formed. At this point cool the mixture to obtain the crystalline picrate salt, adding several drops of water if crystallization does not occur spontaneously. Filter off the crude derivative with suction and recrystallize it to constant melting point from ethanol.

Nitration of aromatic halides

This procedure may also be used to derivatize alkylated aromatic compounds but the conditions are much too extreme for use with activated aromatic compounds.

Equipment	apparatus for filtration and recrystallization	
Materials		
unknown aromatic halide	*ca.* 0.5 g	
sulfuric acid (conc.)	3 mL	**corrosive, oxidizer**
fuming nitric acid (*ca.* 90%)	3 mL	**corrosive, oxidizer**
NOTE: ***extreme care must be exercised when handling fuming nitric acid. Always wear gloves and handle in the hood***		
ethanol		**flammable, toxic**

HOOD

[1]***Care! Highly corrosive***

Procedure

Add the unknown to the sulfuric acid in a test tube and *cautiously* add the fuming nitric acid dropwise.[1] Heat the mixture on a water bath for 15 min and then pour onto ice-water. Filter off the precipitated material with suction and recrystallize it to constant melting point from aqueous ethanol. ■

Nitro compounds

The usual derivatization procedure involves reducing the nitro compound to an amine and then characterizing the primary amine as an amide or *p*-toluidine salt. Most unknowns possessing a nitro group which are likely to appear in the teaching laboratory are aromatic nitro compounds, and so indirect methods of derivatization such as nitration (above) or oxidation of alkyl side chains (pp. 261–262) may be used.

Polynitrated aromatic compounds may be dangerously explosive. Consult an instructor before attempting such a derivatization.

Owing to the deactivating effect of the electron-withdrawing nitro group on the aromatic ring, relatively forcing conditions are needed to effect electrophilic substitution reactions.

Reduction to primary amines

$$RNO_2 \xrightarrow{\text{Sn / HCl}} RNH_2$$

The standard means of reducing nitro groups uses tin–hydrochloric acid from which the reduced product is extracted after basification.

Equipment apparatus for filtration, distillation and reflux

Materials		
unknown nitro compound	*ca.* 1.0 g	
mossy tin	3.0 g	
ethanol		**flammable, toxic**
diethyl ether		**flammable, irritant**
hydrochloric acid (10%)	30 mL	**corrosive**
aqueous sodium hydroxide (20%)		**corrosive**

HOOD

[1]*See Fig. 3.23a*

[2]***Care! Heat evolved***

Procedure

Weigh the unknown and the mossy tin into a 50 mL round-bottomed flask and arrange for reflux.[1] Add 10 mL of the hydrochloric acid down the condenser, shake thoroughly and heat this mixture on the steam bath. If the unknown is insoluble in the aqueous system, add ethanol (4 mL) to aid solution. Add the remainder of the hydrochloric acid in 10 mL portions at 10 min intervals, shaking the flask after each addition. After the final portion of acid has been added, and the mixture heated for 10 min, allow the flask to cool and decant the supernatant into 40% sodium hydroxide (10 mL) with cooling in ice.[2] If the mixture still contains solid tin salts, stir the mixture vigorously and add further 40% sodium hydroxide until any residual tin salts dissolve. Extract the alkaline mixture with diethyl ether (3 × 10 mL), combine the organic extracts and dry over $MgSO_4$. Filter and remove the solvent on the rotary evaporator to furnish the crude amine. Further derivatization should follow the procedures described on pp. 271–274. ■

Esters, amides and nitriles

Esters are considered in this section because, in common with amides and nitriles, they are characterized by hydrolysis. In the case of primary amides and nitriles, it is only necessary to characterize the acid, but with esters it is also necessary to characterize the alcohol produced on saponification. Similarly, with secondary and tertiary amides, the amine moiety must be identified. Derivatization of alcohols has already been discussed (pp. 255–257) and derivatization of acids is considered on pp. 268–269. Moreover, many acids are crystalline and can be considered as derivatives in their own right. Primary amides and esters are most efficiently hydrolyzed with aqueous base, but nitriles and substituted amides are hydrolyzed more effectively under acidic conditions.

Hydrolysis of esters

$$R^1CO_2R^2 \xrightarrow{\text{KOH}} R^2OH + R^1CO_2K \xrightarrow{H^+} R^1CO_2H$$

Equipment	apparatus for filtration, distillation and reflux		
Materials			
unknown ester		*ca.* 1 mL (1.0 g if solid)	
diethylene glycol (2-hydroxyethyl ether)		3 mL	**irritant**
potassium hydroxide		1.0 g	**corrosive**
sulfuric acid (20%)			**corrosive**

Procedure

Measure the potassium hydroxide and the diethylene glycol into a 25 mL round-bottomed flask and heat the mixture gently with a small flame until the mixture becomes homogeneous. Add the ester and a boiling stone, arrange the apparatus for reflux[1] and heat until only one liquid layer is visible (*ca.* 5 min), ignoring any solid which may remain. Allow the flask to cool and arrange for distillation.[2] Distil the alcohol from the mixture, with fairly strong heating if necessary, but do not allow the diethylene glycol to distil (bp 245°C). Note the still head temperature at which the alcohol distils to help you to make a preliminary identification and to decide which derivatives to prepare. Allow the residue containing the potassium salt of the acid to cool, add water (10 mL) and acidify with 20% sulfuric acid. If a solid precipitates, filter it off with suction, washing the residue with cold water (3 × 5 mL) and characterize the acid as appropriate. If a precipitate does not form, the aqueous phase should be made neutral to phenolphthalein and the solution of the potassium salt should be used to prepare a derivative (see pp. 268–269).

[1]*See Fig. 3.23(a)*

[2]*See Fig. 3.48*

Hydrolysis of primary amides with aqueous base

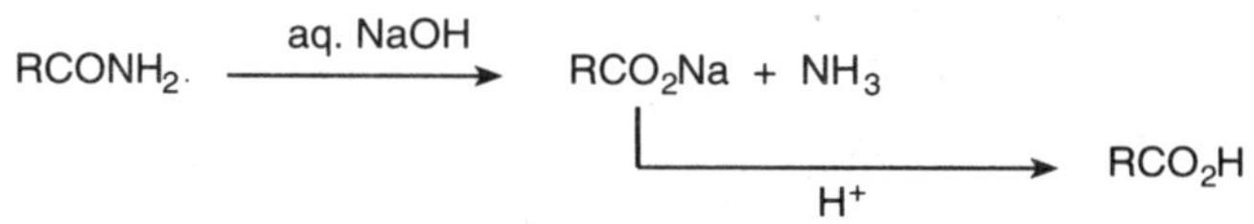

Primary amides hydrolyze efficiently under alkaline conditions, but the hydrolysis of secondary or tertiary amides is better attempted under the acidic conditions described for hydrolysis of nitriles.

Equipment	apparatus for filtration		
Materials			
unknown primary amide		*ca.* 0.5 g	
aqueous sodium hydroxide (10%)		10 mL	**corrosive**
aqueous sulfuric acid (20%)			**corrosive**

HOOD

Procedure

Measure the unknown and the aqueous sodium hydroxide into a 50 mL Erlenmeyer flask and heat the mixture on a steam bath for 30 min during which time ammonia is evolved. Acidify the residual solution, filtering off with suction any precipitated acid for derivatization. If no precipitate is formed on acidification, neutralize the mixture towards phenolphthalein and use this solution to prepare a derivative of the acid (pp. 268–269).

Acidic hydrolysis of nitriles and secondary or tertiary amides

$$RCN \xrightarrow{H_3O^+} RCO_2H + \overset{+}{N}H_4$$

$$R^1\overset{\overset{\displaystyle O}{\|}}{C}NR^2R^3 \xrightarrow{H_3O^+} R^1CO_2H + R^2R^3\overset{+}{N}H_2$$

Equipment	apparatus for filtration, extraction and reflux		
Materials			
unknown nitrile or amide		*ca.* 0.5 g	
sulfuric acid (conc.)		5.0 mL	**corrosive, oxidizer**
diethyl ether			**flammable, irritant**
aqueous sodium hydroxide (20%)			**corrosive**

Procedure

Place the unknown and the concentrated sulfuric acid in a 50 mL round-bottomed flask, attach a reflux condenser and heat to *ca.* 50°C for 30 min.[1] Allow the mixture to cool and **cautiously** add water[2] (15 mL) down the condenser. Reflux the resulting mixture for 1 h and cool in ice. Filter off with suction any acid which precipitates and characterize it. If no solid precipitates, extract the mixture with diethyl ether (3 × 10 mL), combine the organic extracts and dry them over $MgSO_4$. Filter the mixture, remove the solvent on the rotary evaporator and use the residue of crude acid directly for derivatization. If the unknown is a secondary or tertiary amide, the amine component contained in the acidic aqueous phase as a salt may be isolated. Basify the layer with aqueous sodium hydroxide and extract it with diethyl ether (3 × 10 mL). This solution can be used to prepare derivatives of the amine directly. Removal of the solvent should not be attempted as the lower homologues of primary and secondary amines are highly volatile. Some amines are extracted from water only with great difficulty and the yield of amine may be very low in such instances. ■

[1]*See Fig. 3.23(a)*

[2]***Care! Exothermic***

Carboxylic acids

Preparation of S-Benzylisothiouronium salts

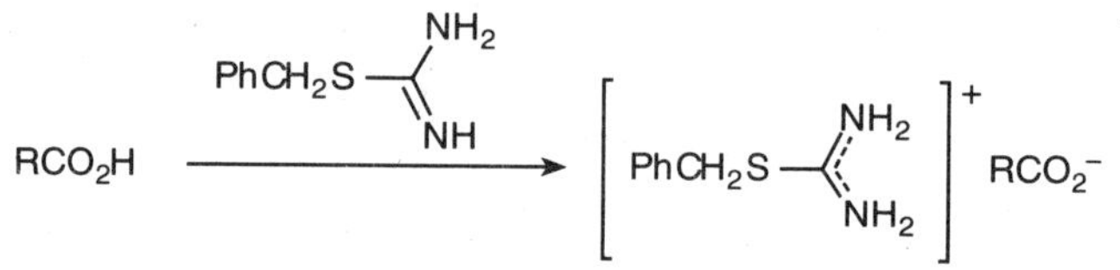

S-Benzylisothiouronium chloride reacts with the sodium salt of the acid to produce the salt. It is important not to allow the reaction medium to become too alkaline as this causes the liberation of benzyl thiol which possesses a particularly penetrating and repulsive odour. This procedure may also be used for characterizing sulfonic acids.

Equipment apparatus for filtration and recrystallization

Materials		
unknown carboxylic acid	*ca.* 0.2 g	
S-benzylisothiouronium chloride	0.8 g	**toxic**
ethanol		**flammable, toxic**
aqueous sodium hydroxide solution (5%)		**corrosive**
aqueous hydrochloric acid (1%)		**corrosive**

Procedure

HOOD

Dissolve or suspend the unknown acid in water (0.5 mL) in a test tube and add the sodium hydroxide solution until the mixture is just alkaline when tested with phenolphthalein. Neutralize the excess alkali by adding dilute hydrochloric acid—**do not proceed if the solution is alkaline.**[1] Add to this a solution of the *S*-benzylisothiouronium chloride in water (2 mL) and cool the mixture in ice until the derivative precipitates. Filter off the solid with suction and recrystallize it to constant melting point from aqueous ethanol.

[1]***Stench!***

Preparation of 4-bromophenacyl esters

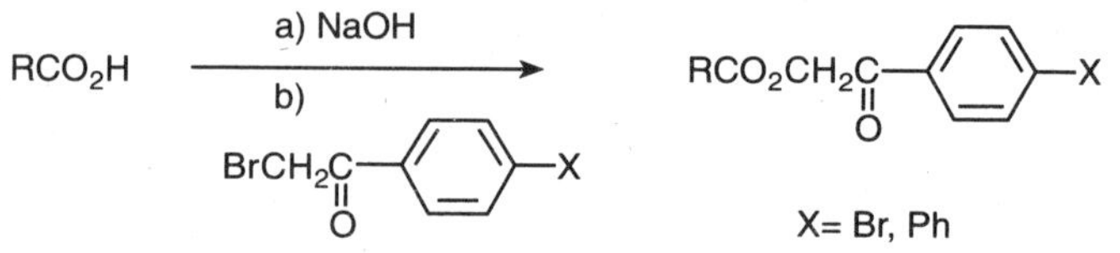

The sodium salt of the acid can also be used in the preparation of the 4-phenylphenacyl esters.

Equipment	apparatus for filtration, recrystallization and reflux	

Materials		
unknown carboxylic acid	*ca.* 0.2 g	
4′-bromophenacyl bromide (2,4′-dibromoacetophenone)	0.2 g	**lachrymator, corrosive**
aqueous sodium hydroxide (5%)		**corrosive**
aqueous hydrochloric acid (1%)		**corrosive**
ethanol		**flammable, toxic**

Procedure

HOOD

Prepare a solution of the sodium salt of the acid in a 25 mL round-bottomed flask as described on p. 268. Dissolve the 4′-bromophenacyl bromide in ethanol (5 mL), add this to the flask and reflux the mixture for 1 h.[1] Add more ethanol during the reflux period if necessary to maintain a homogeneous mixture. (If the unknown is a dicarboxylic acid it is advisable to double the reflux period.) At the end of this period, cool the solution and filter off the precipitated product with suction. Recrystallize the solid to constant melting point from aqueous ethanol. ■

[1]*See Fig. 3.23(a)*

Acid anhydrides and acid halides

Both acid anhydrides and halides are hydrolyzed to the corresponding carboxylic acids which may be characterized as such, or derivatized using the procedures outlined previously. Anhydrides and halides also react very readily with aromatic amines such as aniline or 4-methylaniline (*p*-toluidine) to furnish crystalline *anilides* (*N*-phenylamides) and *toluidides* respectively. (This derivatization is also suitable for carboxylic acids, after first being converted to acid chlorides by heating with excess thionyl chloride for 30 min, followed by removal of excess thionyl chloride.) Only symmetrical acid anhydrides are readily amenable to analysis by such procedures. Acid halides react very readily with concentrated aqueous ammonia to furnish primary amides although this procedure is less useful for anhydrides.

Hydrolysis of anhydrides and halides to carboxylic acids

Equipment	apparatus for filtration and recrystallization	

Materials		
unknown acid anhydride or halide	*ca.* 0.20 mL (0.2 g)	
aqueous sodium hydroxide (10%)		**corrosive**
aqueous hydrochloric acid (10%)		**corrosive**

Procedure

Add the unknown anhydride or halide dropwise to the aqueous sodium

[1]*Care! Exothermic*

hydroxide (3 mL) in a test tube with swirling.[1] After the initial vigorous reaction has subsided, heat the mixture on the water bath for 15 min or until the contents of the tube become homogeneous. Allow to cool, acidify the reaction mixture with hydrochloric acid and filter off the precipitate with suction. Alternatively, if no precipitate forms, the acid may be derivatized via its sodium salt (pp. 268–269) by adding aqueous sodium hydroxide until the solution is just alkaline to phenolphthalein.

Preparation of anilides and toluidides

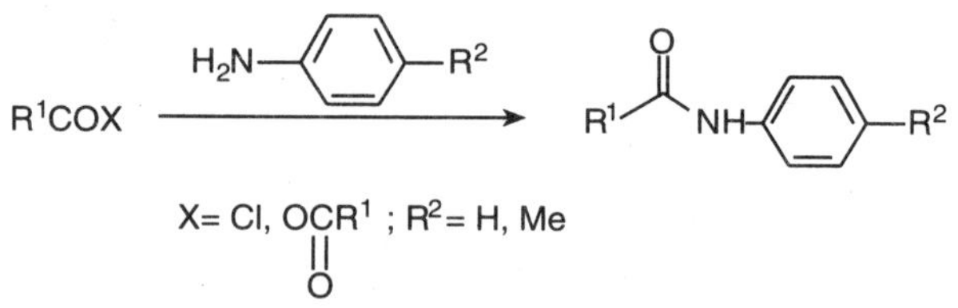

Equipment	apparatus for filtration and recrystallization		
Materials			
unknown acid anhydride or halide	*ca.* 0.2 mL		
aniline (or 4-methylaniline)	0.2 mL (0.20 g)	**cancer suspect agent, irritant, toxic**	
ethanol		**flammable, toxic**	
aqueous hydrochloric acid (5%)		**corrosive**	

HOOD

Procedure

Add the aniline (or 4-methylaniline) to the unknown acid anhydride or halide in a test tube with shaking and then heat the contents on a steam bath for 5 min. Add dilute hydrochloric acid (2 mL) to dissolve excess aromatic amine, breaking up any lumps of solid with a glass rod to ensure the thorough removal of amine. Filter the crude material with suction, washing it with water (2 × 10 mL) and recrystallize it to constant melting point from ethanol or aqueous ethanol.

Conversion of acid halides (and carboxylic acids) to primary amides

Equipment	apparatus for filtration and recrystallization	
Materials		
unknown acid halide	*ca.* 0.2 mL	
ammonia solution (conc., 30%)		**lachrymator, corrosive, toxic**
ethanol		**flammable, toxic**

HOOD

[1]*Care! Vigorous reaction*

Procedure

Add the unknown acid halide dropwise to the concentrated ammonia solution (2 mL) in a test tube.[1] Allow the reaction mixture to cool and filter off the precipitate of amide with suction, washing the residue with water (2 × 5 mL). Recrystallize the crude material to constant melting point from ethanol or aqueous ethanol.

HOOD

[2]*Care! Lachrymator*

Adaptation for derivatization of carboxylic acids. Prepare the crude acid chloride by heating a mixture of the carboxylic acid (0.2 g or 0.2 mL) and thionyl chloride (2 mL)[2] for 30 min in a thick-walled test tube. Remove the excess of thionyl chloride by attaching the test tube to a water aspirator and heating the mixture gently with continuous shaking. Use the residue for conversion to the amide as described above. This procedure is not applicable for carboxylic acids which form volatile halides. ■

Amines

Primary and secondary amines are readily acylated to form the corresponding amides with both acetic anhydride or benzoyl chloride under aqueous conditions. The reaction with benzoyl chloride in the presence of aqueous sodium hydroxide is often referred to as the *Schotten–Baumann reaction* and it is equally applicable to the preparation of benzoate esters of phenols. Primary and secondary amines react in a similar manner with arylsulfonyl chlorides to furnish sulfonamides and this reaction forms the basis of the *Hinsberg method* of distinction of primary, secondary and tertiary amines. Tertiary amines do not undergo these reactions and probably the best method for derivatizing these compounds is to form a crystalline salt with picric acid (2,4,6-trinitrophenol). Tertiary amines may also be derivatized as their quaternary ammonium salts, but these derivatives are frequently hygroscopic and difficult to handle. In addition, their preparation involves the use of the volatile and highly toxic iodomethane and this procedure is not recommended for the teaching laboratory.

Acetylation of primary and secondary amines

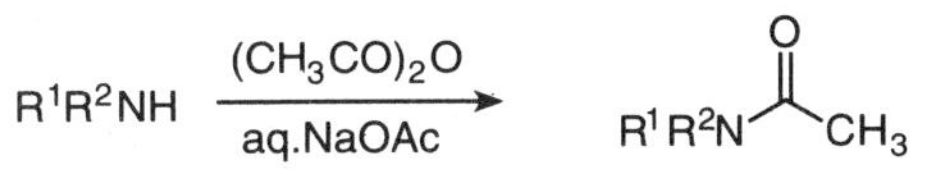

R^2 = alkyl, aryl, H

The following method involves acetylation under aqueous conditions and usually gives excellent results, even with some 2,6-disubstituted anilines which are frequently sluggish towards acylation due to steric hindrance.

Equipment	apparatus for filtration and recrystallization	
Materials		
unknown primary or secondary amine	*ca.* 0.2 mL (0.2 g)	
acetic anhydride	2 mL	**lachrymator, corrosive**
hydrated sodium acetate	2.0 g	
aqueous hydrochloric acid (10%)		**corrosive**
ethanol		**flammable, toxic**

Procedure

HOOD

Dissolve the amine in hydrochloric acid (3 mL) in a 25 mL Erlenmeyer flask, add the sodium acetate and make the solution volume up to about 10 mL with water. Add a few pieces of crushed ice followed by the acetic anhydride and swirl the mixture. Stopper and shake the flask until the ice has melted and then leave the mixture for a further 15 min, re-stoppering and shaking at 5 min intervals. Collect the solid amide by filtration with suction, wash it with water (5 mL), and recrystallize it to constant melting point from aqueous ethanol.

Benzoylation of primary and secondary amines (Schotten–Baumann reaction)

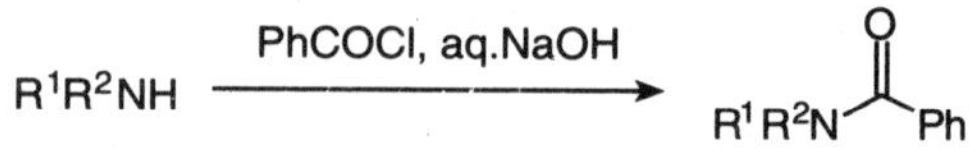

R^2 = alkyl, aryl, H

This procedure is equally applicable to the benzoylation of phenols. Failure of the reaction is generally the consequence of overgenerous use of the benzoyl chloride. Benzoyl chloride is particularly lachrymatory and, for both reasons, excesses of the reagent are to be avoided. Always handle it in the hood and destroy any residual material with concentrated ammonia solution.

Equipment	apparatus for filtration and recrystallization	
Materials		
unknown primary or secondary amine	*ca.* 0.2 mL (0.2 g)	
benzoyl chloride	0.4 mL	**lachrymator, corrosive**
aqueous sodium hydroxide (10%)		**corrosive**
ethanol		**flammable, toxic**
ammonia solution (conc., 30%)		**lachrymator, corrosive, toxic**

Procedure

HOOD

Add the amine to the aqueous sodium hydroxide (3 mL) in a 10 mL round-

[1]*Care! Lachrymator*

[2]*Care! Wear gloves*

bottomed flask capable of being tightly closed with a ground glass stopper. Add a portion of the benzoyl chloride[1] (*ca.* 0.1 mL) by pipette, stopper the flask securely, and shake vigorously for 2 min.[2] Repeat this procedure until all of the benzoyl chloride has been added and then leave the mixture to stand for 10 min. Destroy any residues of the reagent in the pipette by washing with concentrated ammonia.[1] Check the reaction mixture is still alkaline, adding more aqueous sodium hydroxide if not, and filter off the precipitated solid with suction. Wash the residue with water (10 mL) and recrystallize it to constant melting point from aqueous ethanol.

Preparation of sulfonamides from primary and secondary amines (Hinsberg's distinction)

$$R^1R^2NH \xrightarrow{ArSO_2Cl,\ base} R^1R^2NSO_2Ar$$

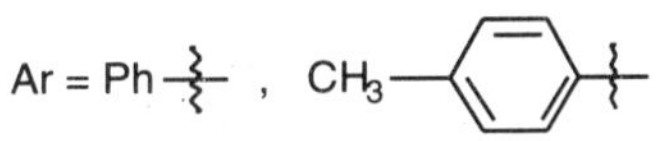

Most primary and secondary amines may be sulfonylated using an aqueous system corresponding to the Schotten–Baumann type conditions for benzoylation. To do this, substitute the same quantity of benzenesulfonyl chloride or *p*-toluenesulfonyl chloride for the benzoyl chloride and follow the instructions given in the previous procedure. However, some aromatic amines substituted with electron-withdrawing groups (for example, 2-nitroaniline) are such weak nucleophiles that the majority of the sulfonyl chloride will be hydrolyzed under aqueous conditions instead of forming the sulfonamide. For these reluctant amines the following procedure should give excellent results. Whilst it may be used for the sulfonylation of all primary and secondary amines, the simpler aqueous procedure is to be preferred for any but the least reactive substrates.

Equipment apparatus for filtration, recrystallization and reflux

Materials

unknown primary or secondary amine	*ca.* 0.5 mL (0.5 g)	
benzenesulfonyl chloride (*alternatively p-toluenesulfonyl chloride (1.0 g) may be used observing the same precautions with regard to its toxicity)*	0.7 mL	**corrosive, toxic**
pyridine	4 mL	**flammable, irritant**
ethanol		**flammable, toxic**
aqueous hydrochloric acid (5%)		**corrosive**

Procedure

HOOD

Measure the amine, sulfonyl chloride and pyridine into a 10 mL round-

[1] *See Fig. 3.23(a)*

bottomed flask, attach a reflux condenser[1] and heat the mixture on a steam bath for 30 min. Pour the hot reaction mixture into dilute hydrochloric acid (25 mL) and stir with a glass rod until the product crystallizes. Filter off the solid with suction, wash the residue with water (10 mL) and recrystallize it to constant melting point from ethanol or aqueous ethanol.

Preparation of amine–picrate complexes

Crystalline 1:1 complexes of amines with picric acid may be prepared for any class of amine, but these derivatives are most important for tertiary amines.

Equipment apparatus for filtration and recrystallization

Materials		
unknown amine	*ca.* 0.3 mL (0.3 g)	
saturated ethanolic solution of picric acid (2,4,6-trinitrophenol)	5 mL	**flammable, toxic**
ethanol		**flammable, toxic**

Procedure

Dissolve the amine in sufficient ethanol in a test tube to give a totally homogeneous solution (*ca.* 5 mL) and to this add the solution of picric acid. Heat the mixture on a hot water bath for 5 min and then allow it to cool. Filter off the precipitate with suction and recrystallize the product to constant melting point from ethanol. ■

Sulfonic acids

Sulfonic acids are frequently derivatized as sulfonamides by conversion to sulfonyl chlorides using phosphorus pentachloride followed by reaction with concentrated ammonia or an amine (pp. 273–274). The *S*-benzylisothiouronium salts may be prepared using the procedure described for carboxylic acids (p. 268), and the crystalline salts formed with *p*-toluidine are also useful derivatives.

Conversion of sulfonic acids to sulfonyl chlorides for further derivatization

Equipment apparatus for reflux

Materials		
unknown sulfonic acid	*ca.* 1.0 g	
phosphorus pentachloride	2.5 g	**corrosive**
NOTE: ***phosphorus pentachloride is readily hydrolyzed by atmospheric moisture, liberating hydrogen chloride. Always use this reagent in the hood***		
toluene	20 mL	**flammable, toxic**

HOOD

[1]*See Fig. 3.23(a)*

Procedure

Mix the sulfonic acid and phosphorus pentachloride in a dry 25 mL round-bottomed flask, attach a reflux condenser, plug the mouth of the condenser loosely with cotton wool and heat the mixture on an oil bath to 150°C for 30 min.[1] Remove the flask from the heating bath and allow to cool for 2 min. Add toluene (20 mL) down the condenser and heat the mixture to reflux for 5 min. Allow the mixture to cool to room temperature and carefully decant the supernatant liquid into a clean 25 mL round-bottomed flask and remove the toluene on the rotary evaporator. The residue of crude sulfonyl chloride may be used directly for further derivatization.

Preparation of p*-toluidine salts*

Equipment apparatus for filtration and recrystallization

Materials

unknown sulfonic acid	*ca.* 0.5 g	
4-methylaniline (*p*-toluidine)	0.3 g	**cancer suspect agent, irritant, toxic**
hydrochloric acid (conc., 36%)		**corrosive**

Procedure

Dissolve the sulfonic acid in the minimum volume of hot water and add to it a solution of *p*-toluidine in concentrated hydrochloric acid (*ca.* 1.0 mL). Heat the mixture on a steam bath and add more water if necessary to obtain a homogeneous solution. Allow the mixture to cool and filter off the precipitate with suction. Recrystallize the solid to constant melting point from water acidified with one or two drops of concentrated hydrochloric acid.

Further reading

The following references should provide the necessary data required for identification of unknowns. In addition, Furniss *et al.* (1989) provides additional derivatization procedures:

Aldrich Catalog Handbook of Fine Chemicals, Aldrich-Sigma Co. Ltd, Milwaukee, USA.

J. Buckingham and F. MacDonald (eds) *Dictionary of Organic Compounds*, Vols 1–9, 6th edn, Chapman & Hall, London, 1996.

T.J. Bruno, *CRC Handbook of Basic Tables for Chemical Analysis*, CRC Press, Boca Raton, 1989.

CRC Handbook of Chemistry and Physics, CRC Press, Boca Raton. (This extremely useful reference work is published annually but the tables of physical constants or organic compounds do not change appreciably from year to year.)

B.S. Furniss, A.J. Hannaford, V. Rogers, P.W.G. Smith and A.R. Tatchell, *Vogel's Textbook of Practical Organic Chemistry*, 5th edn, Longman, London, 1989.

Chapter 5 Spectroscopic Analysis of Organic Compounds

5.1 Absorption spectroscopy

Spectroscopic methods, introduced during the middle of the twentieth century, now play a fundamental role in the solution of many problems in organic chemistry. Of the four spectroscopic techniques most widely used by practising organic chemists—ultraviolet (UV) spectroscopy, infrared (IR) spectroscopy, nuclear magnetic resonance (NMR) and mass spectrometry (MS)—UV spectroscopy is historically the most important, having been introduced in the 1930s. The 1940s saw the advent of IR spectroscopy, and this was followed by MS and NMR in the 1950s and early 1960s. The use of these techniques, which enable recovery of the compound, has revolutionized structural organic chemistry, and their impact cannot be overstated. Although the techniques are usually used in combination, many would argue that NMR, looking as it does at carbon and hydrogen (the elements most relevant to organic chemists), has had the single greatest effect on organic chemistry.

In the following sections we will look at the four spectroscopic techniques in turn, dealing with them not in the order of historical development (i.e. UV spectroscopy first), but in the order that reflects common practice in the organic laboratory for the collection of spectroscopic data: IR spectroscopy, NMR, UV spectroscopy and MS. Many teaching laboratories now possess IR, NMR and UV spectrometers for students to use themselves; MS, however, requires expensive special instrumentation.

Of the four spectroscopic techniques, three of them (IR, NMR and UV) come under the general heading of *absorption spectroscopy*, the absorption of electromagnetic radiation by the sample under study over a range of wavelengths, while MS is fundamentally different to these in that it does not involve the absorption of radiation. Although the theory of spectroscopy will be dealt with in detail in other parts of your course, and in your lecture texts, a brief discussion of the theory behind the techniques is needed here.

Electromagnetic radiation can be specified by wavelength (λ), frequency (ν) or energy (E). Wavelength and frequency are related by the well-known equation:

$$\lambda \nu = c$$

where c is the speed of light. Hence wavelength and frequency are inversely proportional; long wavelengths corresponding to low frequencies and vice versa. Organic molecules absorb electromagnetic radiation over a wide range of wavelengths, and this absorption occurs in discrete 'packets' of energy known as *quanta*. When a molecule absorbs radiation energy it enters an energetically *excited state*, and the difference in energy (ΔE) between the ground state and the excited state is given by

$$\Delta E = h\nu$$

where ν is the frequency of the absorbed radiation and h is Planck's constant (6.626×10^{-34} Js). Promotion of a molecule to an excited state can only occur when a quantum of the correct amount of energy is supplied, that is when the electromagnetic radiation has precisely the right energy (frequency). From the above equation, high frequency radiation (short wavelength) has higher energy than low frequency radiation. The energy absorbed by an organic molecule is displayed in either mechanical or electronic motion, the nature of which depends on the energy of the radiation. The *electromagnetic spectrum* (the wavelengths, energies and associated effects) is shown in Fig. 5.1.

When a molecule absorbs low energy radiation in the radiowave region, nuclear spin transitions occur, and this is the basis of NMR spectroscopy. More energetic radiation in the microwave region causes rotation about bonds, although microwave spectroscopy is not widely used by organic chemists. IR radiation causes vibration of the molecular framework, whilst visible radiation

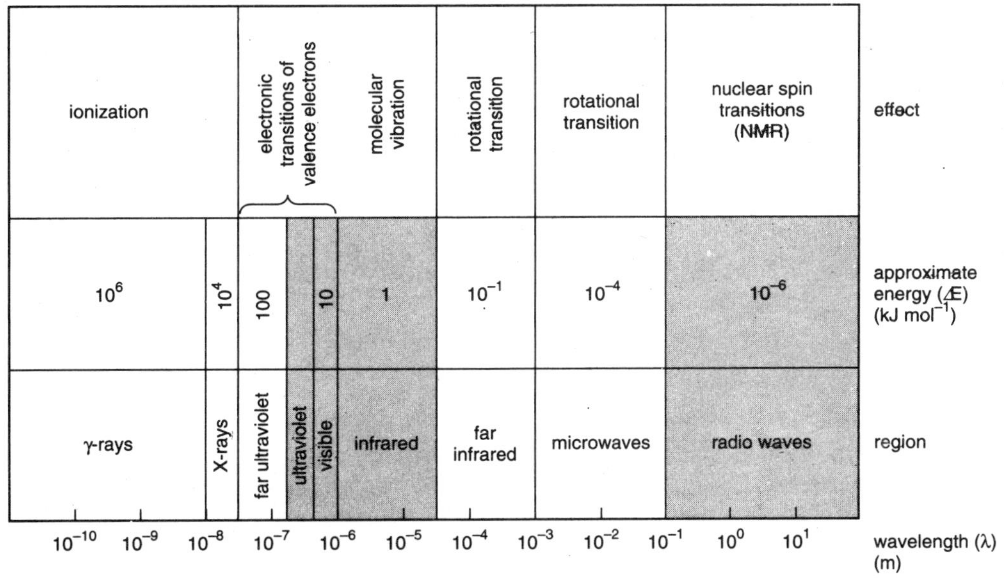

Fig. 5.1 The electromagnetic spectrum: the shaded areas represent the regions of most interest to organic chemists.

and UV radiation cause electronic transitions—the promotion of an electron from a bonding or lone pair orbital to an antibonding orbital. Radiation in the X-ray and γ-ray regions of the spectrum causes electronic transitions of core electrons and ionization. Indeed, such high energy radiation is often known as ionizing radiation, and exposure to it is highly dangerous.

In essence, absorption spectroscopy involves the irradiation of a sample, and the observation of how the absorption varies with the wavelength of the radiation. The instrument used for this is called a *spectrometer*, and is designed to look at one particular region of the electromagnetic spectrum. The output from a spectrometer is usually recorded onto calibrated paper in the form of a plot of wavelength (or frequency) against absorption of energy. This plot, simply referred to as the *spectrum*, consists of a series of peaks or bands which correspond to absorption of radiation at that particular wavelength, and which can be interpreted in terms of the molecular structure of the sample under investigation. It should also be remembered that the magnitude of the absorption is directly proportional to the amount of sample.

5.2 Infrared spectroscopy

The IR region of the electromagnetic spectrum corresponds to wavelengths in the range 2×10^{-4} to 1×10^{-6} m. Although this is outside the range visible to the human eye, IR radiation can be detected by its warming effect on the skin. The energies associated with IR radiation, in the range 4–40 kJ, cause vibrations, either of the whole molecule, or of individual bonds or functional groups within the molecule. There are several *modes of molecular vibration*, and these are often described in such terms as stretching, bending, scissoring, rocking and wagging. However, for the purposes of this brief discussion we will only consider the simple stretching of a bond X–Y. To a good approximation, such a two-atom system can be considered as two balls connected by a spring; therefore *Hooke's law* will be obeyed. Thus the frequency of vibration (stretching) of the bond X–Y is directly proportional to the strength of the bond, and inversely proportional to the masses of both X and Y. Consequently different bonds belonging to different groups within the molecule will vibrate at different frequencies and many organic functional groups can be readily identified by their IR absorption properties. The stronger the bond, the higher the vibration frequency. Hence double bonds vibrate at higher frequencies than single bonds between like pairs of atoms, and strong bonds such as O–H, N–H and C–H vibrate at higher frequencies than weaker bonds such as C–C and C–O. Also the heavier the atoms, the lower the vibration frequency of the bond between them. Hence in deuterated compounds, the C–D bonds involving the heavier isotope vibrate at lower frequency than the C–H bonds. Similarly in moving down the periodic table, S–H bonds vibrate at lower frequency than O–H bonds.

Hooke's law

The stronger the bond, the higher the vibration frequency

The heavier the atoms, the lower the vibration frequency

The position of an IR absorption peak can be specified in terms of wavelength, usually expressed in *microns* (1 μm = 10^{-6} m), or in terms of frequency. The latter is preferred since we usually talk about vibration frequencies of bonds, and nowadays IR absorptions are always measured in frequency units by *wavenumber* ($\bar{\nu}$), expressed in *reciprocal centimetres* (cm^{-1}). However, you may still see IR spectra described in microns, particularly in the older literature, and you have to be prepared to convert these into the more familiar reciprocal centimetre units. The conversion is given by:

$$\text{Wavenumber}\left(\text{cm}^{-1}\right) = \frac{1}{\text{Wavelength}\left(\text{cm}\right)} = \frac{10\,000}{\text{Wavelength}\left(\mu\text{m}\right)}$$

Remember the higher the wavenumber, the higher the frequency, and the lower the wavelength.

The majority of functional groups relevant to organic chemistry absorb radiation within a fairly narrow range of the IR region, 600–4000 cm^{-1}, and therefore most simple spectrometers operate only within this range.

The spectrometer

Most IR spectrometers operate on the double beam principle, and a typical example of such a spectrometer is shown schematically in Fig. 5.2. The source of radiation is an electrically heated glowing wire which emits throughout the whole frequency range of the instrument. Mirror optics are used to split the beam into two beams of equal intensity. One beam passes through a cell containing the sample to be examined, whilst the other passes through a reference cell containing the solvent (this may be missing altogether). After passing through the cells, a rotating segmented mirror alternately allows light from each of the two beams to enter the *monochromator*. The monochromator is a device, based on a prism or grating, which scans through the range of the instrument, usually from high to low frequency, but only allows one frequency of radiation through the slit and into the *detector* at any one time. The scan-

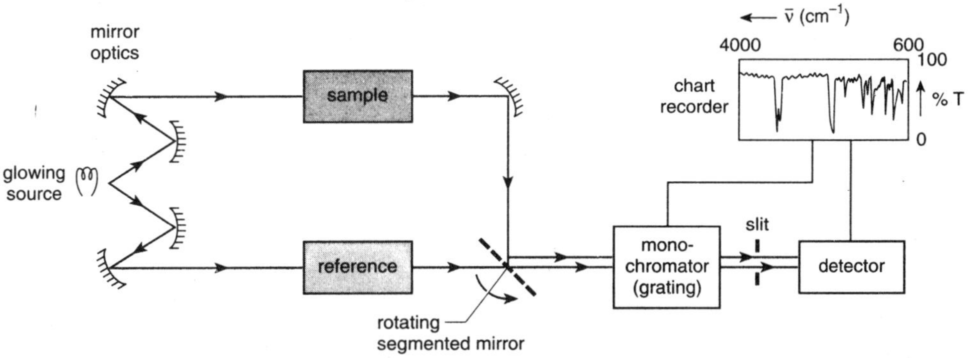

Fig. 5.2 Schematic representation of a double-beam IR spectrometer.

ning mechanism is coupled to the chart recorder and moves the pen along the frequency scale (x axis) of the paper, with high frequency (4000 cm^{-1}) at the left of the paper. It should be noted that the frequency scale on the paper may not be linear throughout the whole 4000–600 cm^{-1} range. Many spectrometers divide the range into two separate linear scales; one between 4000 and 2000 cm^{-1}, and another, more expanded scale, between 2000 and 600 cm^{-1}. The signal from the detector, which is proportional to the difference in light intensity between the sample and reference beams, is fed to the chart recorder and moves the pen along the y axis of the paper. This vertical scale on the IR spectrum is usually calibrated in *percentage transmittance* (%T), with 100% transmittance (no absorption) at the top of the paper. At the frequency at which the sample absorbs the IR radiation, the detector response is recorded as a reduction in %T, a dip, on the chart.

FTIR

In recent years a new type of IR spectroscopy, known as Fourier transform infrared (FTIR) spectroscopy, has been developed. Although the final spectrum looks almost identical to one that is obtained on a double beam instrument, the spectrometer operates on an entirely different principle. Light, often from a laser source, covering the whole range of IR frequencies, is passed through the sample. A second beam, which has travelled along a longer path length, is combined with the first beam to produce a complex interference pattern which looks nothing like a spectrum. Technology then takes over, and the on-board microcomputer performs a Fourier transformation on a series of these interference patterns to convert them into a conventional plot of absorption against frequency. FTIR has many advantages over the traditional method: sensitivity (very small samples can be examined), resolution (not dependent on optical properties of gratings, slits and prisms), time (the whole spectral range is measured in a few seconds), and the flexibility that comes with the on-board computer (allows subtraction of one spectrum from another, digital plots of data and so on).

For a further application of Fourier transforms, see section on NMR, pp. 306–356

Preparing the sample

Infrared spectra can be recorded on liquids, solids and even gases, although we will only be concerned with the first two. Spectra of liquids can be recorded on the *neat liquid*, or as *solutions* in an appropriate solvent, whereas spectra of solids can be obtained in *solution*, or in the *solid state* as a *mull* or *KBr disk*. To record the spectrum, the sample must be placed in the beam of the IR spectrometer in a suitable sample cell. Unfortunately glass is opaque to IR radiation, and therefore sample cells are usually made out of sodium chloride, which is IR transparent.

NaCl is transparent to IR

Neat liquids

The IR spectrum of a pure liquid is most easily determined as a *thin film* between two *sodium chloride plates*. The sodium chloride plates commonly used for this purpose are circular, about 20–25 mm in diameter and 5 mm

Take care with sodium chloride plates

thick, with a polished flat surface. The plates are cut from a large crystal of sodium chloride, and hence are expensive. Unfortunately they are also rather fragile, and sensitive to moisture. Exposure to moisture from wet samples, damp hands or even atmospheric moisture causes the polished surfaces of the plates to become fogged. Such fogged plates produce poor IR spectra, and should be repolished. Never attempt to polish plates yourself without first seeking expert advice. To prevent damage to plates, they should be stored, wrapped in tissue or cotton wool, in a desiccator, or in a screw-capped jar that contains some drying agent. Handle the plates only by their edges, and ensure that all your samples are free from water.

Handle plates by the edges

To record the IR spectrum of a neat liquid, place 1 or 2 drops of the liquid in the centre of a sodium chloride plate using a Pasteur pipette as shown in Fig. 5.3a. Place the second plate on top (Fig. 5.3b), and *gently* squeeze the plates together so that the liquid spreads out into a thin film. Holding the plates by their edges, mount them in a sample holder (Fig. 5.3c). Most sample holders have a top cover plate which can be *gently* screwed down to hold the plates in place. Place the sample holder in the sample beam (usually the front beam) of the IR spectrometer, and record the spectrum (see below). When recording the spectrum of a thin film, it is not necessary to put anything in the reference beam of the spectrometer. After running the spectrum, clean the plates with an anhydrous solvent, such as dichloromethane, dry them on a soft tissue, and return them to their storage jar or desiccator. If you need to recover the sample, you must wash the liquid off the plates with dichloromethane into a suitable receptacle, and then evaporate off the

Always clean plates after use

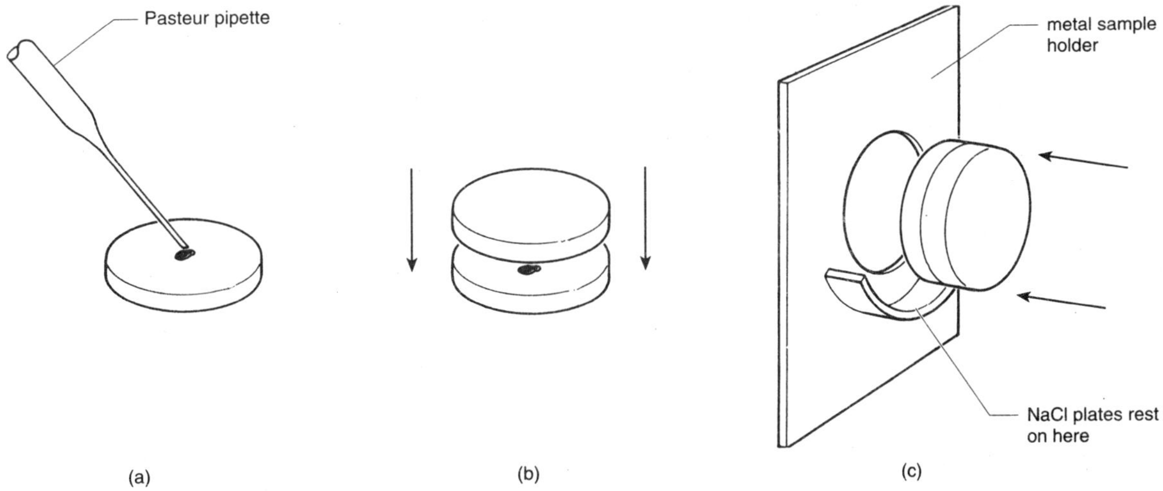

Fig. 5.3 Obtaining the IR spectrum on a neat liquid: (a) 1 or 2 drops of the liquid are placed in the centre of a sodium chloride plate; (b) a second plate is placed on top, and the plates are *gently* squeezed together; (c) the two plates are mounted in the sample holder (top cover plate omitted for clarity).

solvent. However, in these circumstances it is much better to run the IR spectrum using the solution method.

Solutions

IR spectra of both liquids and solids can be obtained in solution. The compound is dissolved in an appropriate solvent (see below), and the solution is placed in a special IR *solution cell* (Fig. 5.4a). The solution cell consists of two rectangular sodium chloride plates sealed together to give a gap of uniform and accurately known dimensions, usually in the range 0.05–0.2 mm. The sodium chloride plates are held together by two metal cover plates which incorporate two syringe ports for filling and flushing the cells. Solution cells usually come in pairs, the second cell precisely matching the first. Like the plates used for thin films, sodium chloride solution cells are fragile and moisture sensitive, and because of the precision machining required in their manufacture, they are also very expensive. Handle them with care.

Solution cells must match

The choice of solvent for solution IR spectra is quite restrictive. No solvent is ideal because all organic solvents absorb at some point in the IR spectral range. Traditionally three solvents have been recommended for IR spectroscopy: carbon tetrachloride, carbon disulfide and chloroform. All three are **toxic**, and although carbon tetrachloride occasionally could give better resolved spectra than chloroform, it is no longer commercially available due to environmental legislation and, in addition, it is rather a poor solvent for many organic compounds. Carbon disulfide is far too hazardous for general use because of its extremely low flash point; indeed, it is our opinion that

Solvents for IR

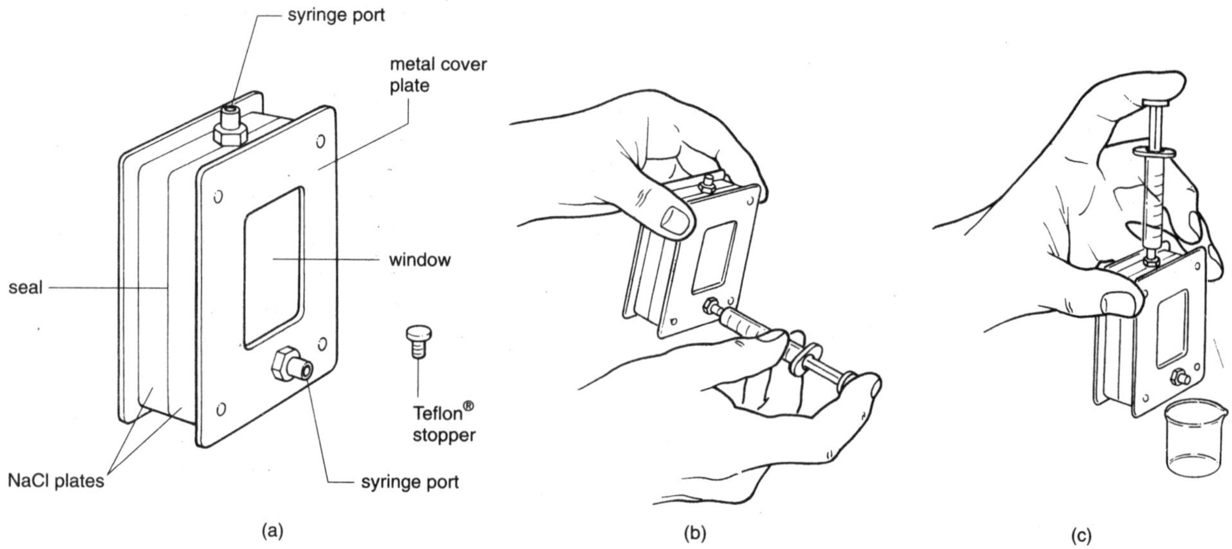

Fig. 5.4 Obtaining the IR spectrum of a solution: (a) the sodium chloride solution cell; (b) filling the cell through the lower syringe port; (c) flushing the cell after use through the top syringe port.

carbon disulfide should never be used in the teaching laboratory. That only leaves chloroform, which although a **cancer suspect agent**, can be used in the organic laboratory, **provided due regard is paid to its potential toxicity**. Commercial chloroform contains ethanol as a stabilizer, and therefore must be purified before use as a solvent for IR spectroscopy. The purification is easily and quickly accomplished by passing the solvent down a short column of alumina as described in Appendix 2. The IR spectrum of pure chloroform is shown in Fig. 5.5, and consists of two strong absorptions centred at 1216 and 759 cm^{-1}. In practice, this means that when running solution spectra in chloroform, no useful information about the absorptions of the sample can be obtained in the ranges 1200–1250 and 650–800 cm^{-1}. However, this is not a serious limitation. If chloroform is considered too toxic, use dichloromethane.

Remember, chloroform is toxic

To run a solution IR spectrum, make up a 5–10% solution of the compound in pure chloroform. The internal volume of the solution cells is quite small, so 0.2–0.5 mL of solution is plenty. If the sample is a liquid, a solution of about 10% concentration can easily be approximated by adding 1 drop of liquid to 9 drops of chloroform. If the sample is a solid, it is best to weigh it out, bearing in mind the difficulty in estimating weights by eye; dissolve 10–20 mg of solid in 0.1–0.2 mL of chloroform. To transfer the solution to the IR cell, draw it up into a 0.5 or 1.0 mL syringe, remove the needle, and holding the cell by its top edges slightly inclined from the vertical, fill the cell through the

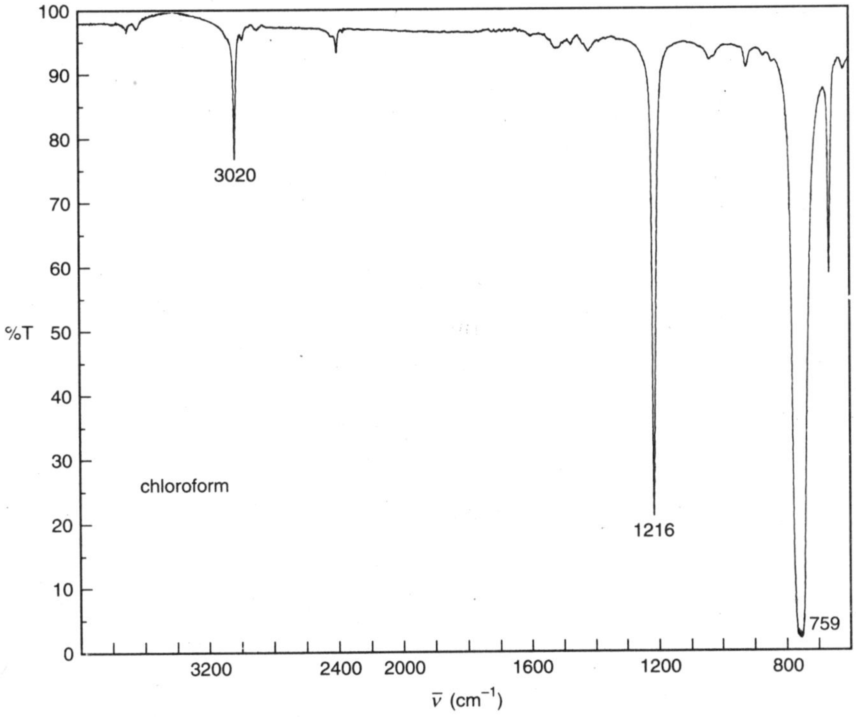

Fig. 5.5. IR spectrum of chloroform.

lower syringe port (Fig. 5.4b). As the liquid enters, air is displaced through the top port. It is important that the cell is filled beyond the top of the window, and that no air bubbles are present. Having filled the cell, gently but firmly stopper the two syringe ports with the small Teflon® stoppers. Clean out the syringe with fresh chloroform, and fill the reference cell with pure chloroform. Place the sample cell in the sample beam of the IR spectrometer, the reference cell in the reference beam, and record the spectrum. If the cells are perfectly matched, the absorptions due to solvent in the sample and reference cells will cancel each other out, and these peaks will not appear on the final spectrum. However, despite this cancelling, do not forget that you cannot obtain information about the absorption of the sample in the region where chloroform is opaque to IR radiation (see above). After running the spectrum, clean the cells out immediately by flushing with fresh chloroform as shown in Fig. 5.4c. The original solution and washings can be collected as shown, and, if necessary, the sample can be recovered by evaporation of the solvent. Dry the cells by drawing air through with either an empty syringe or by attaching the outlet to a water aspirator. Never dry solution cells by attaching them to the compressed air line; the air stream from compressors is inevitably contaminated with dirt and grease. Finally, return the clean, dry cells to a desiccator.

Mulls

Spectra obtained from samples in the solid state look different from spectra obtained on the same compound in solution

Infrared spectra of solid samples can also be recorded in the solid phase. However, it should be borne in mind that, in the solid state, intermolecular forces are particularly strong, and will affect the vibrational properties of the molecule; the IR spectrum obtained on a compound in the solid state may look quite different from that obtained in solution (see Fig. 5.14). This is particularly true for compounds containing polar functional groups that can participate in hydrogen bonding. Because of these additional complications associated with the solid state, many organic chemists prefer, as a matter of course, to run IR spectra in dilute solution.

Before you can record the IR spectrum of a solid sample, the solid must be made transparent to IR radiation. One way to do this is to prepare a *mull* by grinding the solid with an inert carrier agent. The usual carrier agent is a liquid hydrocarbon oil (paraffin oil, mineral oil); the commercial material most commonly used is known as Nujol®. Nujol® shows the characteristic absorptions associated with the C–C and C–H vibrations of hydrocarbons, and its IR spectrum is shown in Fig. 5.6. The spectrum consists of four major peaks centred at 2922, 2854, 1461 and 1377 cm^{-1}. Obviously when recording the IR spectrum of a Nujol® mull, the C–H and C–C vibrations of the sample will be obscured by those of the mulling agent. If it is important to examine the C–H vibration region (*ca.* 3000 cm^{-1}) of your sample, then hexachlorobutadiene can be used as an alternative mulling agent since, as can be seen from its IR spectrum in Fig. 5.7, it is transparent in this region.

To prepare a Nujol® (or hexachlorobutadiene) mull, place about 5 mg of

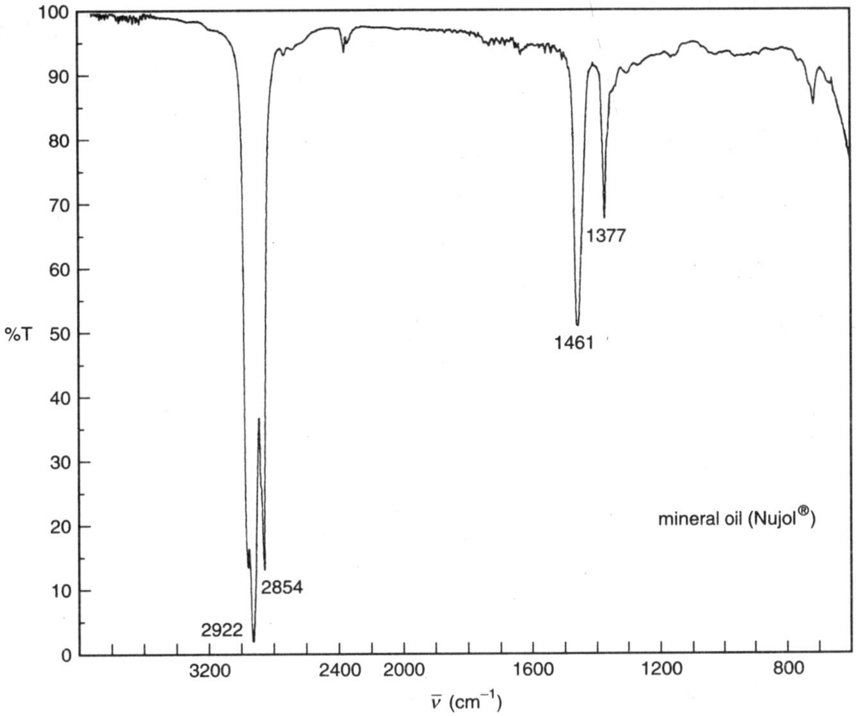

Fig. 5.6 IR spectrum of Nujol®.

Solid must be finely ground

Do not add too much Nujol®—add it 1 drop at a time

the solid in a small agate mortar, and grind it to fine powder using the agate pestle. It is very important that the solid be finely ground since large particles cause reflection and scattering of the radiation. Ideally the particle size should be less than the shortest wavelength of the radiation, in other words less than 2.5 μm (4000 cm^{-1}). Because of this requirement for finely ground samples, it is better to grind the sample *before* adding the mulling agent. Having ground the sample, add 1 small drop of Nujol®, and continue to grind the sample until the mull takes on a thick pasty consistency. If the mull is too thick, add another drop of Nujol®. Chemists very quickly develop their own technique for transferring the mull to the sodium chloride plates, but one of the best methods is to use a thin flexible piece of metal such as a razor blade (**mind your fingers!**). Spatulas are generally too thick and inflexible. Scrape the mull out of the mortar, and place it as a blob in the centre of the circular sodium chloride plate (*cf.* Fig. 5.3a) or, better, as a thin line along the plate diameter. Never attempt to spread the mull over the whole surface of the plate. Place the second plate on top, and gently but firmly squeeze the plates together to distribute the sample evenly into a thin layer between the plates, taking care not to scratch the plates with any solid that may remain in the mull. Place the plates in the sample holder in the sample beam, and with nothing in the reference beam, record the spectrum. After running the spectrum, clean the plates

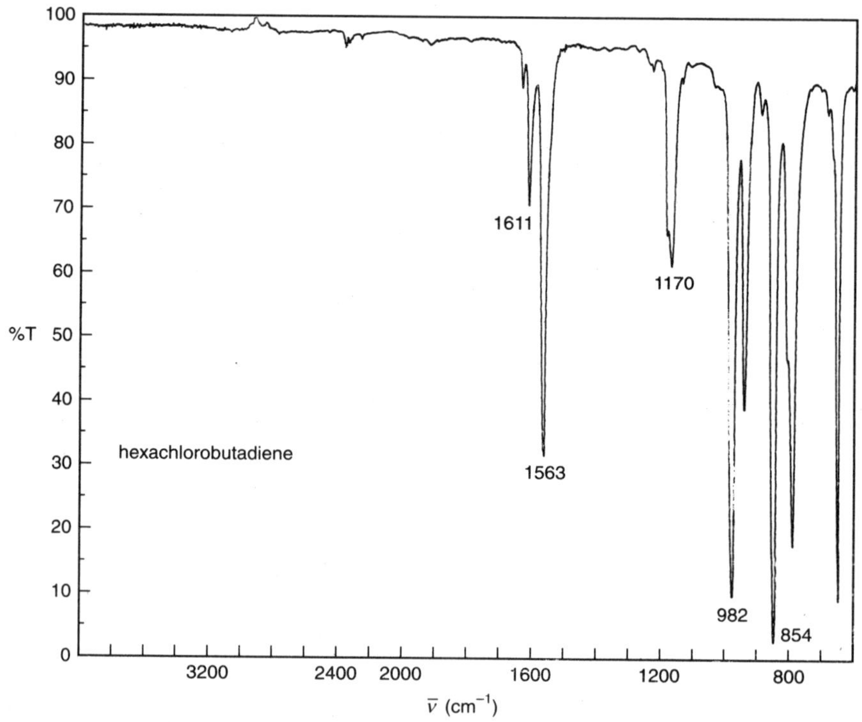

Fig. 5.7 IR spectrum of hexachlorobutadiene.

with a tissue soaked in dichloromethane, and return them to their desiccator or jar. It is not easy to recover the sample from Nujol® mulls.

KBr disks

The second way to record IR spectra of samples in the solid state is in the form of a KBr disk or wafer. Potassium bromide is completely transparent throughout the IR range, and therefore has advantages if the absorptions of the mulling agent interfere. However, special equipment in the form of a hydraulic press is needed, and this may not be available in your laboratory. To prepare a KBr disk, grind about 2 mg of sample in a small agate mortar. Add 300–400 mg of pure spectroscopic grade KBr, and mix, but *do not grind*, with the sample. Place the mixture in the die of the press, and subject it to high pressure (*ca.* 1000 bar) for a few minutes. This causes the KBr to become fluid, resulting in the formation of a very fragile translucent disk, which can be removed from the die with tweezers and placed in the sample beam of the IR spectrometer; the spectrum can then be recorded.

KBr disks are fragile: handle them carefully

The design of hydraulic press varies, but a typical example is shown in Fig. 5.8a. It consists of a hydraulic ram (which can be pumped up by hand to the required pressure) on which is placed a die of appropriate diameter, usually in the range 7–13 mm. Since KBr is hygroscopic, the die often incorporates an

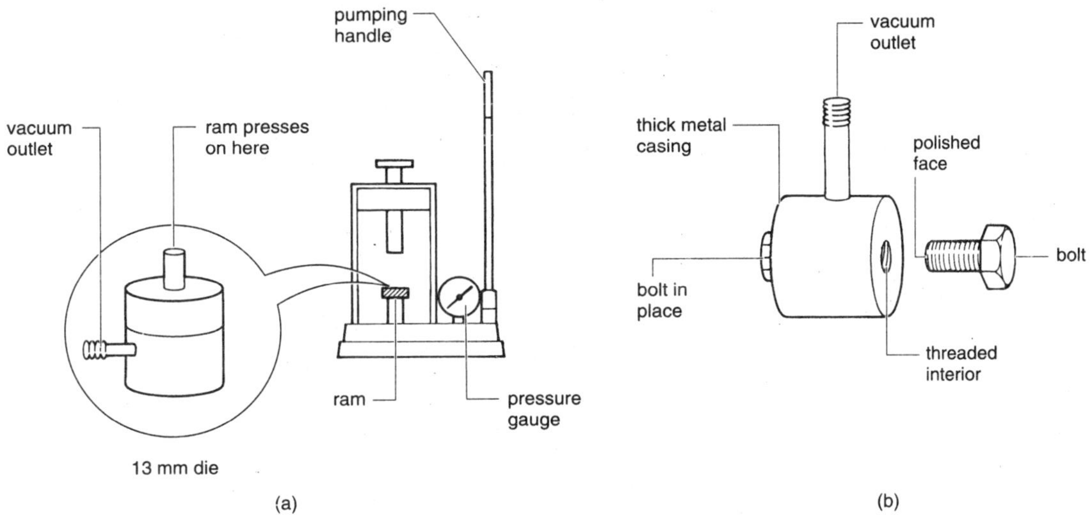

Fig. 5.8 (a) A typical hydraulic press and die for preparing KBr disks; (b) a small low cost press for preparing KBr disks.

outlet for connection to a vacuum so that the sample can be pressed in the absence of atmospheric moisture. If your laboratory does not possess a purpose-designed hydraulic press, various low cost small presses are available. One design is shown in Fig. 5.8b. The press consists of a thick metal casing with a threaded central hole, at the centre of which is a small (1 mm) diameter hole leading to a vacuum take-off. Two machined bolts with flattened polished faces complete the press. One bolt is screwed into place, the sample is placed in the press on the end of the bolt, and the second bolt is screwed down on top of it. Grip the whole assembly in a vice, and tighten the bolts with a spanner or wrench to press the disk. After a few minutes, loosen and remove the bolts. The press is designed so that is can be placed directly into the sample beam of the instrument, so that there is no need to attempt to remove the fragile disk from the press. If carefully prepared, KBr disks give excellent results. However, there are two notes of warning. Since KBr is hygroscopic, the spectra often show an O–H absorption, and before assigning this to your sample, remember that it may be due to the absorbed water in the disk. Secondly, KBr disks may give different spectra from those of the same solid obtained as a mull (see Fig. 5.14), and direct comparison of solid state spectra is not possible unless they were prepared in the same way.

KBr is hygroscopic!

Running the spectrum

One of the great advantages of IR spectroscopy is that highly satisfactory spectra can be recorded on relatively low cost instruments, thereby bringing the technique within the range of most organic laboratories. IR spectrometers usually require very little adjustment, and have relatively few controls.

Although one instrument will differ slightly from another, the general protocol for running an IR spectrum is as follows. Before starting the scan, check that the chart paper is positioned correctly with respect to the horizontal position of the pen. If not, the position of the paper must be adjusted. The only other controls that you need to worry about are the *100% control*, the scan speed/stop/start control and, occasionally, the *gain control*. Having placed your sample (and reference if necessary) in the spectrometer, adjust the vertical position of the pen to about 95%T using the 100% control. Select a scan speed; often the choice is just fast or slow, and press the scan start button. At the end of the run the scan will stop automatically. At this stage it is as well to check the calibration. Remove the sample (and reference) and replace it with a standard reference sample of polystyrene film. Back up the chart paper and superimpose a section of the reference spectrum on that of your sample. Polystyrene has a very sharp, but strong, absorption at 1602 cm^{-1}, and it is normal to record only this section of the reference spectrum. If the calibration is out, then the appropriate correction factor must be applied to all peak positions. Occasionally you should check the *gain* of the spectrometer, and this is done with no sample in the beam. Set the pen position to 90%T using the 100% control, and place your hand in the sample beam so that the pen dips to about 70%T. Quickly remove your hand, and the pen should immediately and quickly return to the 90%T mark after overshooting it by 1 or 2%. If the pen returns sluggishly or badly overshoots, the gain should be adjusted using the gain control. Some instruments have a *gain check* button, and pressing this replaces putting your hand in the beam.

Polystyrene as reference

It is rare that serious problems are encountered in using IR spectrometers, and poor spectra are usually the fault of poor samples rather than the instrument. The two most common minor problems are spectra in which the peaks are too strong, i.e. a lot of the peaks are in the 0–10%T range, and the reverse problem of spectra with very weak 70–90%T peaks. The first problem is due to too much sample, and is easily corrected if a neat liquid is being used, by squeezing the plates together to make a thinner film. If a solution is being used, dilute the sample with more solvent. If a Nujol® mull is being used, squeeze the plates together to make a thinner film, or, if that fails, remake the mull using less sample or more Nujol®. Similarly if a KBr disk is being used, remake the disk using more KBr. To deal with the problem of weak spectra, the reverse procedures apply—add more sample. The only possible problem in this respect is with neat liquids; if the liquid is volatile, it may evaporate from between the plates in the warmth of the sample beam. In such cases, the spectrum must be recorded in solution.

Interpreting the spectrum

The interpretation of IR spectra can be carried out at different levels according to why you ran the spectrum in the first place. If you know what the compound is, the interpretation may consist of confirming the presence of the characteristic peaks associated with the vibrational absorptions of certain functional groups, and confirming the absence of others. Alternatively, since every organic compound has a unique IR spectrum, the interpretation may simply involve comparing your spectrum, peak for peak, with a published spectrum of the same compound, thereby confirming its identity. However, if you do not know what the compound is, the spectrum must be analyzed much more thoroughly in order to extract the maximum amount of information from it. Although it is rarely possible to assign the complete structure of an unknown compound from its IR spectrum alone, you will be able to identify certain bond types and functional groups which, in combination with other data, will lead to the correct structure.

Initial deductions

Whatever level of interpretation is required, the analysis of IR spectra follows a few simple guidelines. These guidelines become second nature, and you will soon learn what to look for first when confronted with an IR spectrum. When analyzing an IR spectrum, always proceed as follows:

Where to look first

1 Start at the high frequency (4000 cm^{-1}) end, as many of the common functional groups of organic chemistry absorb in the high frequency half of the IR spectroscopic range.

2 Look at the largest peaks first; these are usually the most structurally significant.

3 Do not try to identify every peak; smaller peaks are often overtones (harmonics) or even 'noise'.

4 Note the absences of peaks; the absence of a strong peak in a key area of the spectrum is as equally diagnostic as the presence of peaks.

Having some idea of what peaks to look at first, you need to assign them to specific bond types or functional groups within the molecule. Fortunately these assignments are greatly facilitated by the fact that a vast body of IR spectroscopic data has been accumulated over the last 40 years. These data have been combined into *correlation tables* which link peak position with various types of functional groups; correlation tables for the major functional groups of organic chemistry are included in Appendix 3. In order to analyze your IR spectrum using the correlation tables, it is convenient to divide the IR spectroscopic range (4000–600 cm^{-1}) into smaller sections, and the key dividing point is 1500 cm^{-1}. The region to the right (lower frequencies) of this line is usually complex, consisting of many peaks, and is therefore difficult to interpret. Although some functional groups do show characteristic absorptions in this range (Table 5.1), many of the absorptions correspond to vibrations of the molecule as a whole, and since these are unique to the particular compound, this part of the spectrum is known as the *fingerprint region*. The region to the left (higher frequencies) of 1500 cm^{-1} is much more useful, since it is here that most of the common functional groups of organic chemistry absorb. For convenience, this 4000–1500 cm^{-1} region of the spectrum is further subdivided

Division of the spectroscopic range

Table 5.1 IR correlation table.

Frequency (cm^{-1})	Functional group	Comment
4000–2500 region		
3600	O–H	Free, non-H-bonded; sharp
3500–3000	O–H	H-bonded; broad peak
	N–H	Amine or amide; often broad
3300	≡C–H	Sharp
3100–2700	C–H	Variable intensity
3500–2500	COO–H	Carboxylic acids; broad
2500	S–H	Weak
2500–1900 region		
2350	CO_2	Carbon dioxide from path-length imbalance and not your sample!
2200	C≡C, C≡N	Often weak
2200–1900	X=Y=Z	Allene, isocyanate, azide, diazo groups, etc; strong
1900–1500 region		
1850–1650	C=O	Strong
1650–1500	C=C, C=N	Variable intensity
1600	C=C (aromatic)	Often weak
1550	$-NO_2$	Strong
1500–600 region (fingerprint region)		
1350	$-NO_2$	Strong
	$-SO_2-$	Strong
1300–1250	>P=O	Strong
1300–1000	C–O	Alcohol, ether, ester; strong
1150	$-SO_2-$	Strong
850–700	Aromatic C–H	*o*-, *m*-, *p*-disubstituted benzenes
800–700	C–Cl	Usually strong

into three smaller portions (4000–2500, 2500–1900 and 1900–1500 cm^{-1}), the division being based on the type of functional group which absorbs there. The various regions of the IR spectroscopic range, together with the bond and functional group types associated with them, are shown schematically in Fig. 5.9.

The information contained in this simple correlation chart is also given, in slightly more detail, in tabular form in the IR correlation table (Table 5.1). These types of correlation charts and tables form the basis of the analysis and interpretation of IR spectra, and from them you should learn to locate the important regions in the spectrum. Do not try to remember the exact vibration frequency of every functional group and bond type, but rather get to recognize the O–H/N–H, C–H and C=O regions. Use Fig. 5.9 and Table 5.1 to

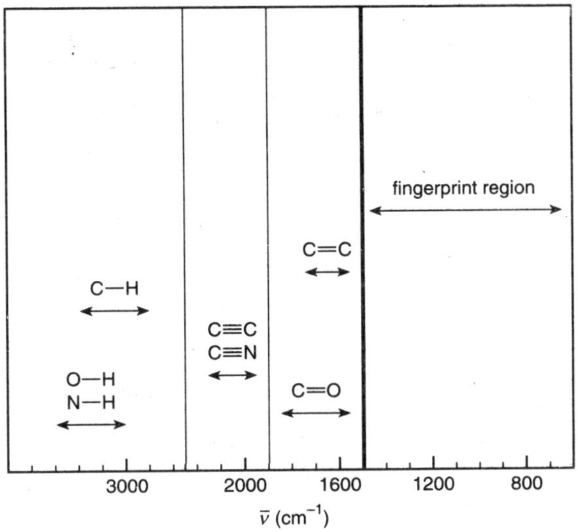

Fig. 5.9 Simple IR correlation chart showing the major regions of the spectroscopic range.

help you make your initial deductions about the presence, or absence, of certain types of groups within your molecule. Having done this, carry out a more thorough analysis of your spectrum using the more detailed correlation tables in Appendix 3. Expanded versions of these tables are widely available in standard spectroscopy texts, and most of your lecture texts will contain some IR correlation tables.

More detailed analysis

The 4000–2500 region

This is the region where bonds to hydrogen usually absorb, and hence C–H, O–H and N–H bonds all show stretching absorptions in this range. Because of the effect of atomic mass on vibration frequency, the higher frequency absorptions are the O–H and N–H absorptions. Therefore as you 'read' the spectrum from left to right, the first peaks that you might encounter around 3500 cm^{-1} are likely to be due to O–H or N–H stretching. Peaks in this region of the spectrum are highly diagnostic; if no peaks are present then the compound does not contain such functional groups. One note of warning: beware of small peaks in the 3600–3200 cm^{-1} range since these could possibly be overtones of strong carbonyl peaks in the 1800–1600 cm^{-1} range.

O–H (Appendix 3, Table A3)

The O–H group of alcohols and phenols absorbs in the range 3500–3000 cm^{-1}. It is rare to observe the absorption of the 'free' O–H group—if present it is a sharp band at about 3600 cm^{-1}—since both alcohols and phenols are usually

Hydrogen bonds

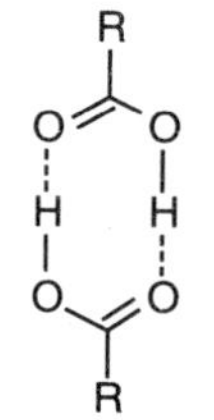

H-bonded dimer of a carboxylic acid

Intermolecular vs intramolecular hydrogen bonding: distinguish by dilution

involved in hydrogen bonding. The resulting polymeric hydrogen-bonded aggregates manifest themselves as broad peaks in the IR spectrum. The appearance of these broad peaks varies according to the type of hydrogen bonding involved. Carboxylic acids, for example, form strongly hydrogen-bonded dimers, which result in the O–H stretching absorption being extremely broad, reaching down to about 2500 cm^{-1}. The position of O–H absorptions can also depend on whether the hydrogen bond is intermolecular or intramolecular. However, you can distinguish between these possibilities by running the IR spectra in chloroform solution at different sample concentrations. In relatively concentrated solution both intermolecular and intramolecular hydrogen bonds are possible. Intramolecular hydrogen bonds are unaffected by dilution, and therefore the position of absorption remains the same. Intermolecular hydrogen bonds, on the other hand, are broken on dilution, and therefore the broad band they produce will disappear on dilution of the sample to be replaced by the sharper, higher frequency, free O–H band. In the solid state, the O–H absorption band is always broad. The positions of various types of O–H groups are given in Table A3 in Appendix 3, and some examples of IR spectra of compounds containing O–H bonds are shown in Figs 5.10–5.12.

Figure 5.10 shows the IR spectrum of a simple alcohol, 2-methylcyclohexanol (*cis/trans* mixture) run in the liquid phase. The most striking feature of the

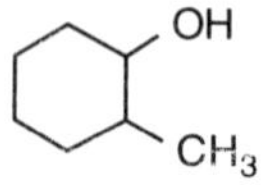

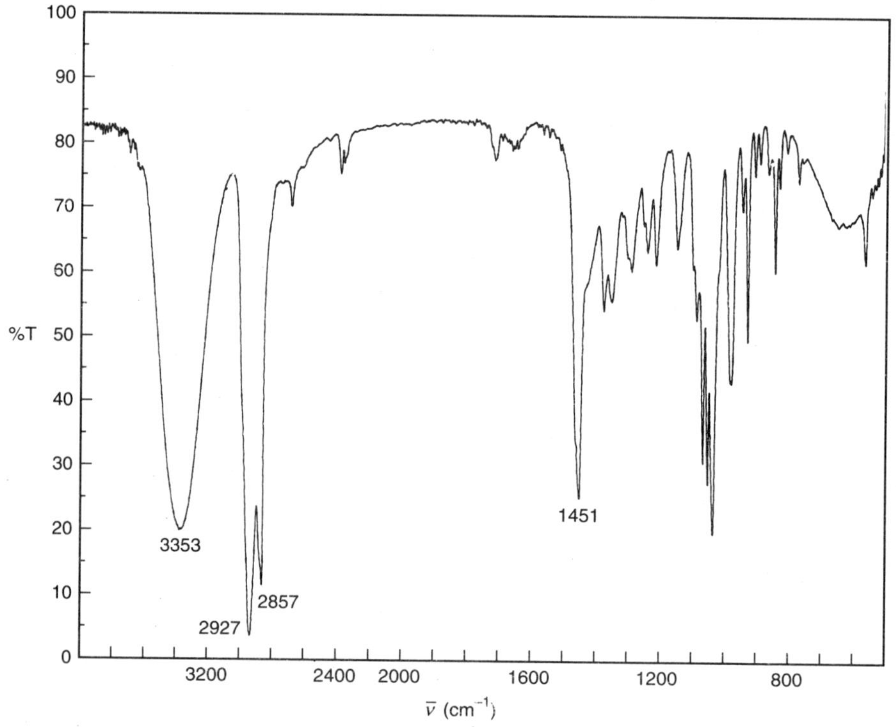

Fig. 5.10 IR spectrum of 2-methylcyclohexanol.

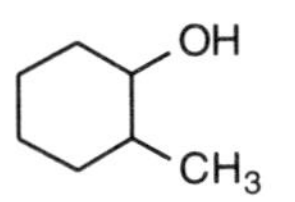

2-methylcyclohexanol

spectrum is the strong broad absorption centred at 3353 cm^{-1}, typical of the O–H stretching frequency of hydrogen-bonded alcohols. The presence of such a band in the IR spectrum of an unknown compound would be strongly indicative of an alcohol group, but since alcohols necessarily contain a C–O bond, you should immediately check for the presence of this to confirm your initial deduction. Compounds with C–O bonds (alcohols, ethers, esters) show a strong absorption due to C–O stretching in the range 1300–1000 cm^{-1}, although the unambiguous assignment of the C–O absorption is complicated by the fact that other functional groups also absorb in this region (see Table 5.1). However, the *absence* of a strong peak in this region does suggest that there is no C–O bond in your molecule, and hence your initial deduction about the alcoholic O–H group is probably wrong; the assumed O–H may in fact be N–H (see p. 295). In the example shown in Fig. 5.10 there are three strong bands around 1050 cm^{-1}, probably due to C–O stretching.

Continuing with the analysis, moving to the right of the O–H peak, there are only two more significant peaks above the fingerprint region at 2927 and 2857 cm^{-1}. These are aliphatic C–H stretching absorptions (see below and Table A5 in Appendix 3). Detailed analysis of the fingerprint region is not usually possible, although in this case the C–H bending deformation absorption at 1451 cm^{-1} is clearly seen.

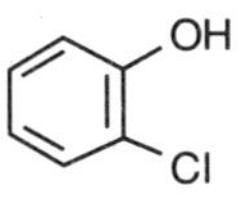

2-chlorophenol

Figure 5.11a shows the IR spectrum of a phenol, 2-chlorophenol, in the liquid phase. Starting our analysis from the 4000 cm^{-1} end, the first peak we come to is a broad peak centred at 3522 cm^{-1}. Again this would strongly suggest a hydrogen-bonded O–H group. The only other significant peak above the fingerprint region is at 1586 cm^{-1}; this is associated with the aromatic ring C=C absorptions (see also Table A8 in Appendix 3). The lack of strong C–H absorptions at about 3000 cm^{-1}, seen in the previous example, should also be noted. Aromatic C–H stretching absorptions are much weaker than aliphatic stretching absorptions.

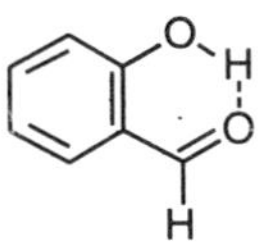

2-hydroxybenzaldehyde
(salicylaldehyde)

(intramolecular H-bond)

Figure 5.11b shows the liquid phase IR spectrum of another phenol, salicylaldehyde (2-hydroxybenzaldehyde), and nicely illustrates the effect of hydrogen bonding on the position and appearance of the O–H absorptions. As indicated by the structure, the phenolic O–H of salicylaldehyde is strongly intramolecularly hydrogen bonded to the aldehyde carbonyl. The effect of this is seen in the spectrum; the O–H peak is broader and at a lower frequency than the other phenol (Fig. 5.11a). The effect of intramolecular hydrogen bonding is also seen on the position of the C=O stretching absorption which, at 1667 cm^{-1}, is lower than expected for an aromatic aldehyde (see below). Since the O–H group is intramolecularly hydrogen bonded, dilution of the sample would have no effect on the appearance of the spectrum.

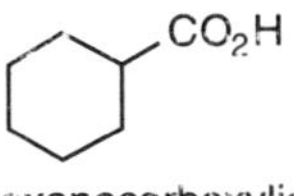

cyclohexanecarboxylic
acid

Figure 5.12 shows the IR spectrum of cyclohexanecarboxylic acid. The spectrum is dominated by the intense broad absorption from 3500 to 2500 cm^{-1} corresponding to the O–H stretch of the carboxyl group. This broad band is highly characteristic of carboxylic acids, but the assignment can be confirmed

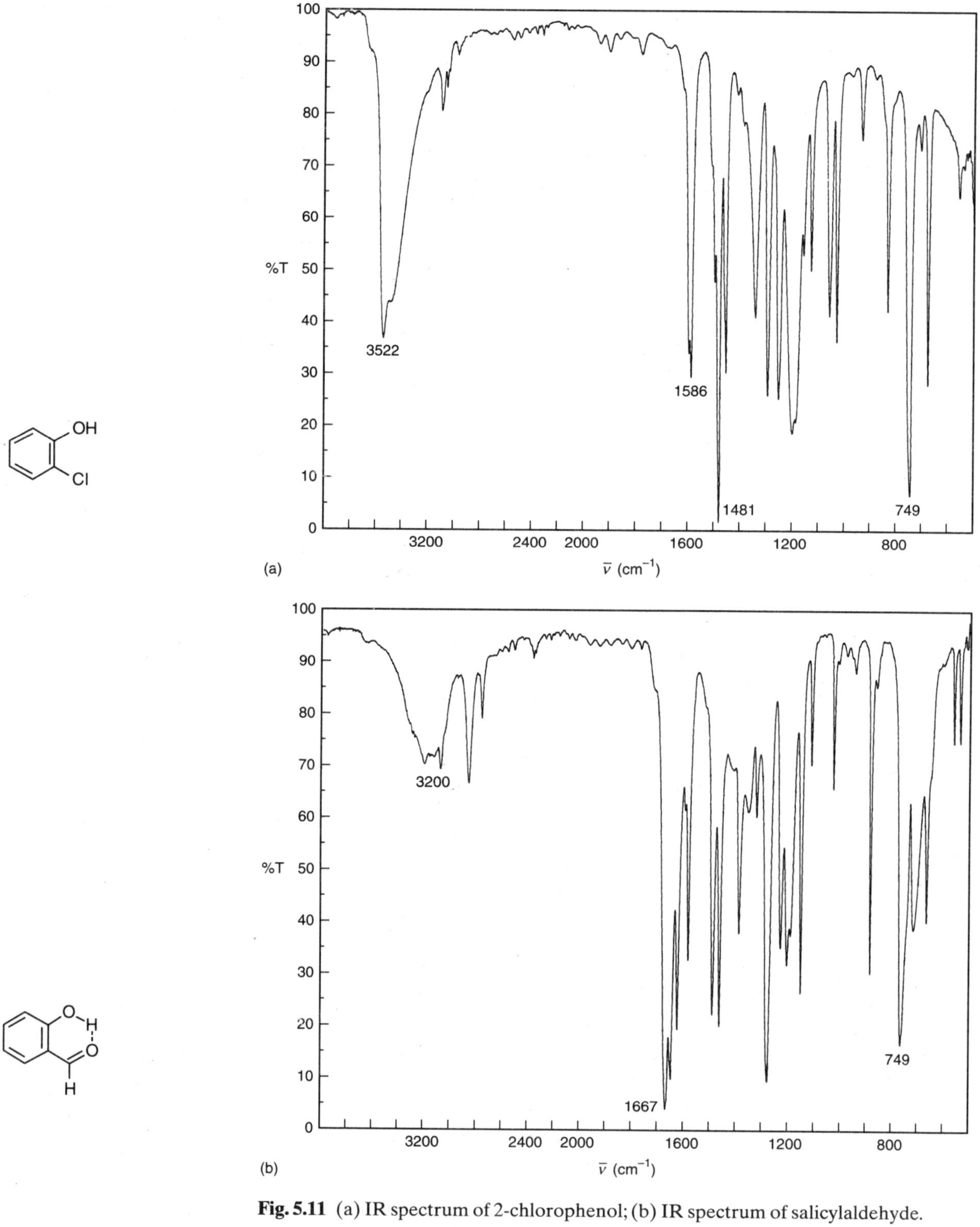

Fig. 5.11 (a) IR spectrum of 2-chlorophenol; (b) IR spectrum of salicylaldehyde.

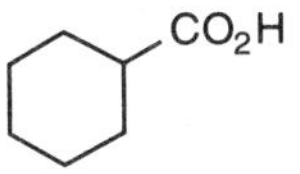

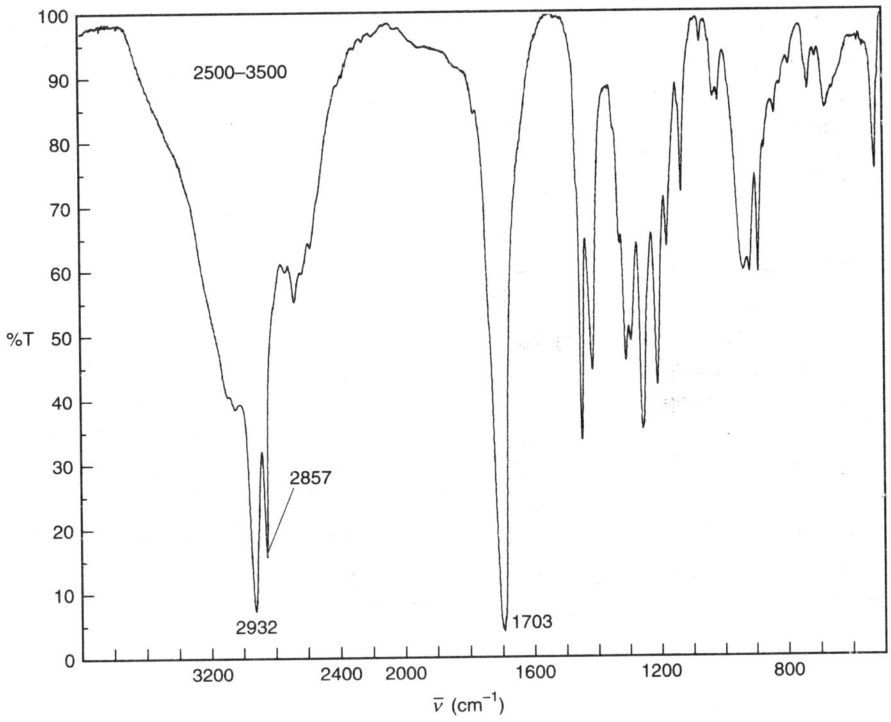

Fig. 5.12 IR spectrum of cyclohexanecarboxylic acid.

by the presence of a strong peak in the 1700 cm^{-1} region corresponding to the C=O stretching absorption—1703 cm^{-1} in the present example. It should be noted that although the COOH peak is broad and intense, the strong C–H stretching absorptions are still clearly seen at 2932 and 2857 cm^{-1}.

N–H (Appendix 3, Table A4)

O–H or N–H?

As can be seen from Fig. 5.9 and Table 5.1, the stretching frequency of N–H bonds occurs in the same region of the spectrum as that of O–H bonds. This can lead to confusion and possible misinterpretation. However, there are a number of ways in which a distinction may be made. We have already seen that the O–H stretch of alcohols and acids is *always* accompanied by a C–O and C=O stretch, respectively, thereby confirming O–H assignments in the 3500 cm^{-1} region. In addition, the N–H absorption is usually less intense than the O–H, and since N–H bonds do not participate in hydrogen bonding as readily as O–H, the peaks are usually sharper. The positions of various types of N–H absorptions are detailed in Table A4 of Appendix 3, and some examples of IR spectra of compounds containing N–H bonds are shown below.

Figure 5.13 shows the IR spectrum of a primary amine, cyclohexylamine. The spectrum was recorded on the neat liquid. The first absorption consists of

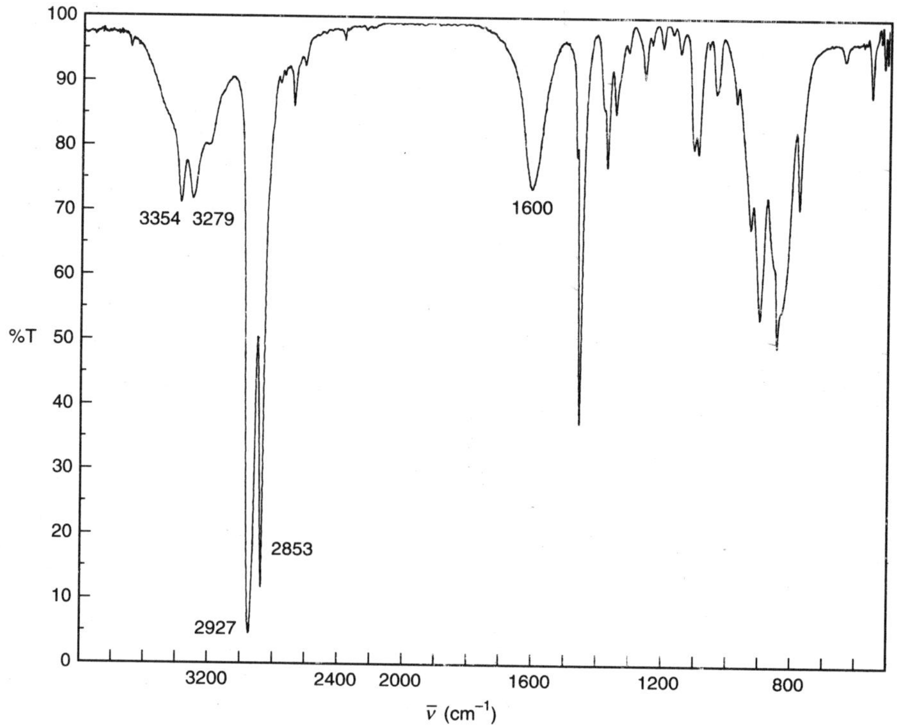

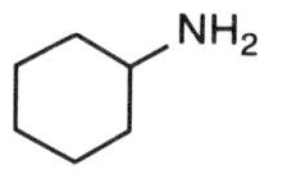

Fig. 5.13 IR spectrum of cyclohexylamine.

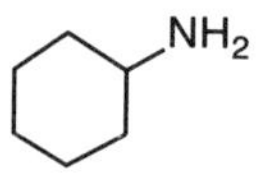

cyclohexylamine

two sharp peaks at 3354 and 3279 cm^{-1} superimposed on a broader band. These correspond to N–H stretching absorptions, the underlying broadness being due to hydrogen bonding. Primary amines always give two bands, whereas secondary amines with only one N–H bond give a single peak; tertiary amines, lacking N–H bonds, of course, are transparent in this region. Amines also show N–H bending absorptions of medium intensity in the 1650–1550 cm^{-1} region, and you should always look for this peak to confirm your initial assignment of the N–H stretching peak. In the present example, the peak is seen at 1600 cm^{-1}. The only other peaks outside the fingerprint region in the spectrum of cyclohexylamine are the by now familiar strong C–H stretching absorptions at 2927 and 2853 cm^{-1}. The C–H bending deformation at 1450 cm^{-1} is seen within the fingerprint region.

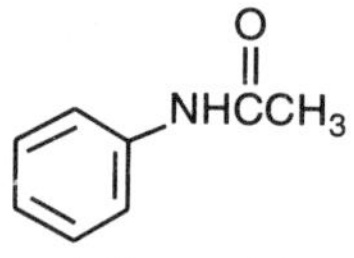

N-phenylethanamide
(acetanilide)

Primary and secondary amides also contain N–H bonds, and the IR spectrum of a typical secondary amide, *N*-phenylethanamide (acetanilide) is shown in Fig. 5.14. The example also illustrates the effect of running IR spectra with the sample in different phases; some differences between the spectra recorded in chloroform solution (Fig. 5.14a), in the solid state as a Nujol® mull (Fig. 5.14b) and as a KBr disk (Fig. 5.14c) should be immediately apparent. As usual we start our analysis from the high frequency end, and focus on the peaks in the 3300 cm^{-1} region. The solution spectrum shows two peaks at 3436

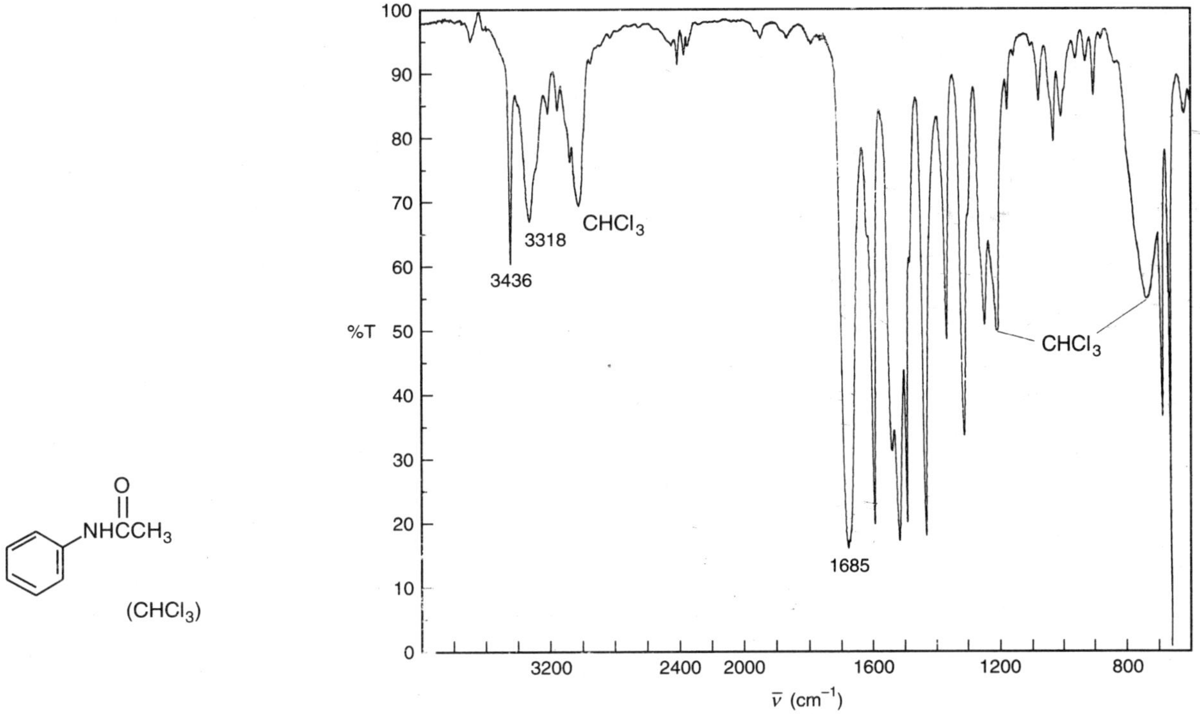

(a)

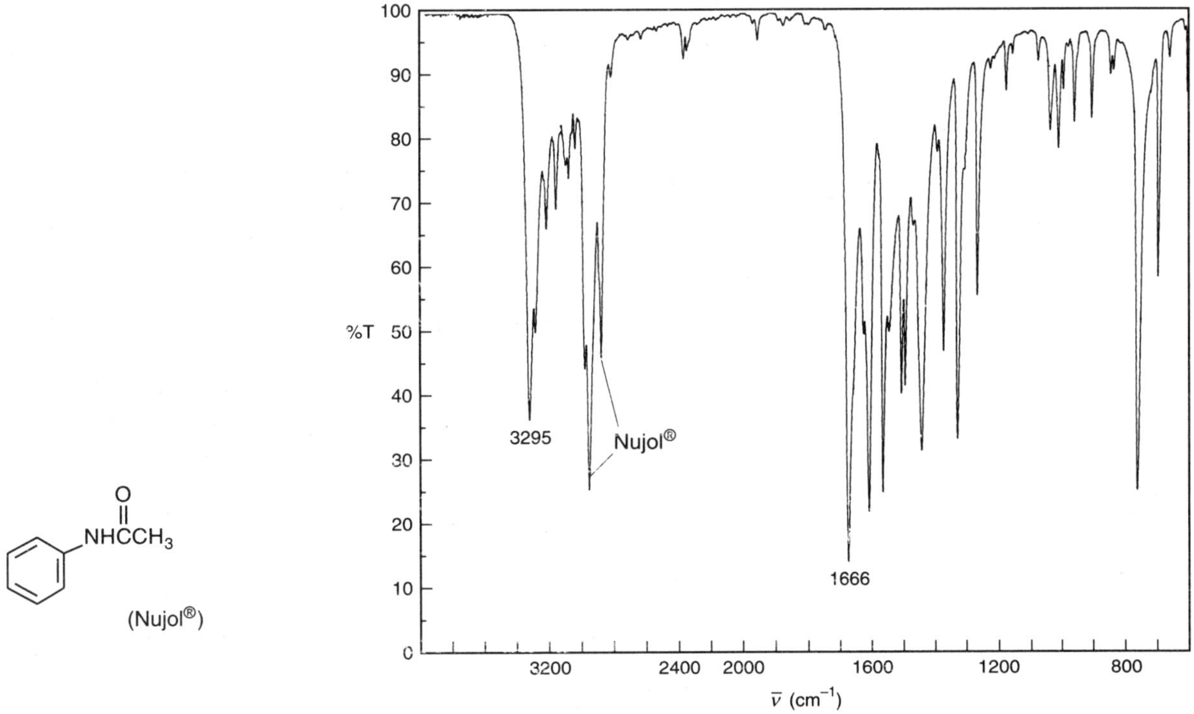

(b)

Fig. 5.14 IR spectrum of *N*-phenylethanamide (acetanilide): (a) in chloroform solution; (b) as a Nujol® mull; (c) as a KBr disk.

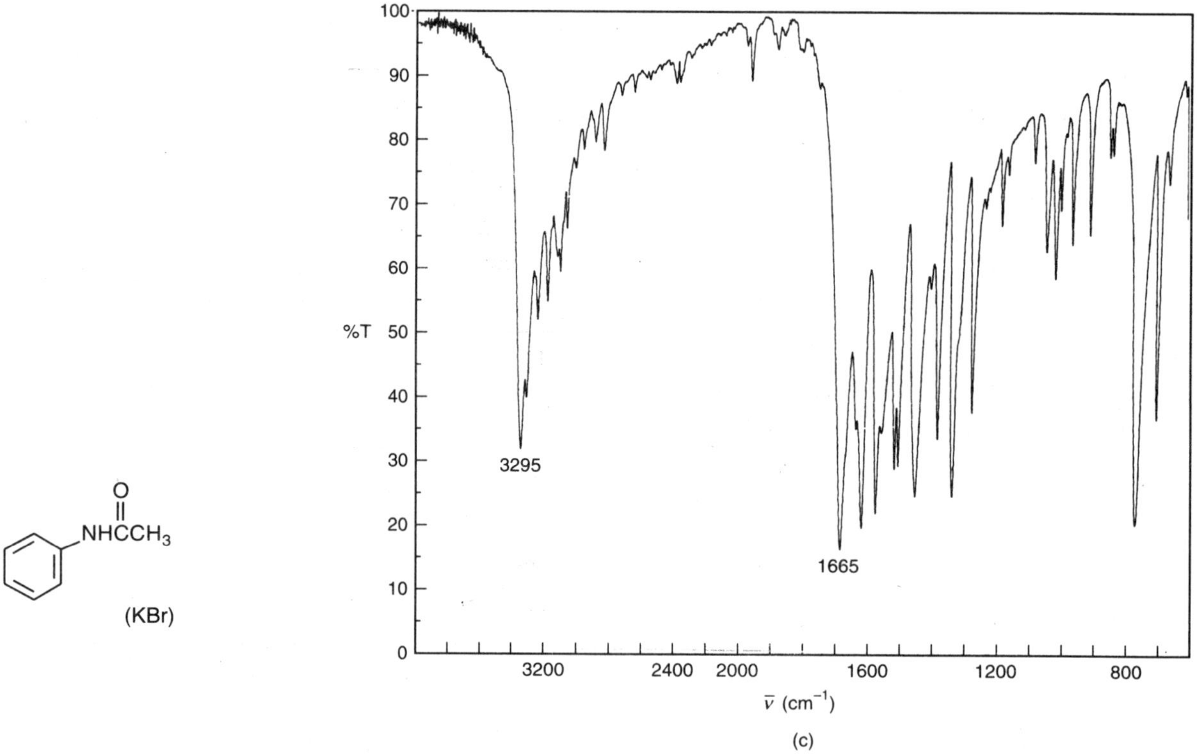

Fig. 5.14 *Continued.*

and 3318 cm^{-1} due to N–H stretching. In the solid state spectra, the N–H absorption is lowered to 3295 cm^{-1}. The tentative assignment of a peak to an amide N–H *must* be confirmed by locating the corresponding C=O stretching absorption. The relevant peaks occur in the carbonyl region of the spectrum; amides show two peaks in this range, referred to as amide I (higher frequency) and amide II. Again the positions of the peaks are dependent on the method of sample preparation, and they appear at lower frequency in the solid state. In the present example, the solution spectrum shows the amide I peak at 1685 cm^{-1}. Amide II which is usually less intense is probably the peak at 1525 cm^{-1}. In the solid state spectra, the amide I peak occurs at 1666 cm^{-1}. Other differences between the spectra that should be noted are as follows: the presence of chloroform peaks due to imperfectly matched cells in Fig. 5.14a; the presence of Nujol® peaks in Fig. 5.14b—the peaks at 1461 and 1377 cm^{-1} are hidden; the absence of Nujol® C–H peaks in the KBr spectrum; the general broadening of the N–H region up to 3500 cm^{-1} in the KBr spectrum probably due to the presence of water in the sample as KBr is hygroscopic.

C–H (Appendix 3, Table A5)

The vast majority of organic molecules contain C–H bonds, and therefore their IR spectra contain peaks due to C–H vibration absorptions. The C–H

$HC\equiv C(CH_2)_4CH_3$

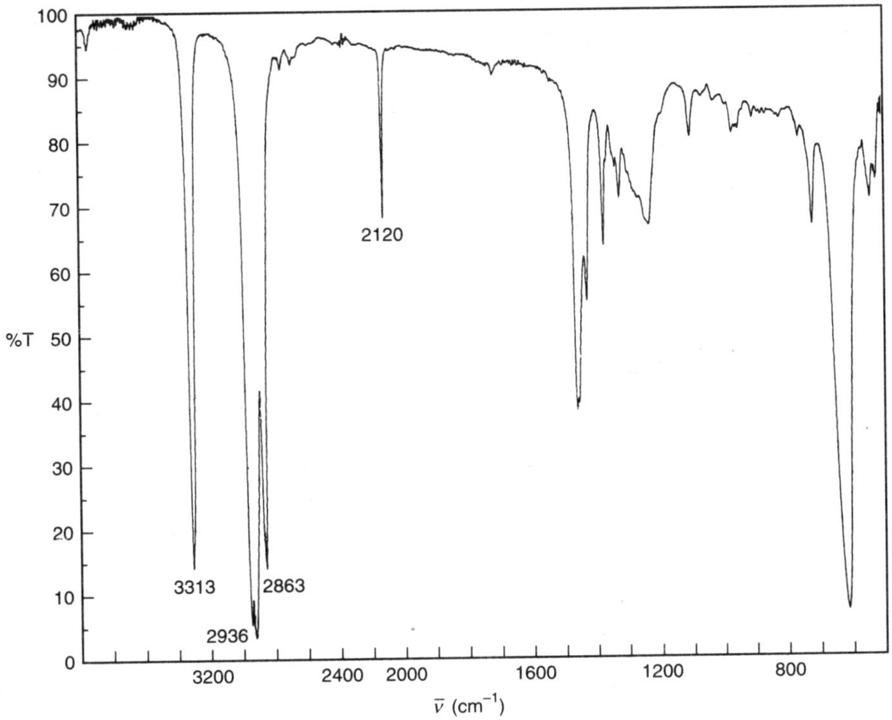

Fig. 5.15 IR spectrum of 1-heptyne.

Strength, and hence absorption frequency, of C–H bond depends on hybridization of C

$C_5H_{11}C\equiv CH$
1-heptyne

stretching absorption occurs at the high frequency end of the spectrum in the range 3300–2700 cm^{-1}, the exact position depending, amongst other things, on the strength of the C–H bond in question. Since the strength of a C–H bond depends on the hybridization of the carbon atom involved, we can use IR spectroscopy to identify different types of C–H bond. The strongest C–H bonds are those involving sp hybridized carbons, the stronger bond resulting from orbitals with a high degree of s-character. Hence the highest frequency C–H stretching absorptions are exhibited by terminal alkynes. The absorption is always sharp, usually quite intense, and occurs around 3300 cm^{-1}. Figure 5.15 shows the IR spectrum of 1-heptyne, and the acetylenic C–H is clearly seen at 3313 cm^{-1}. The presence of a terminal acetylene can be confirmed by locating the C≡C stretching absorption. This occurs in the range 2150–2100 cm^{-1} (2120 in the present example), although it is often rather weak in intensity, and may be missed. The other characteristic peaks in Fig. 5.15 are the aliphatic C–H stretching absorptions at 2936 and 2863 cm^{-1}.

C–H bonds involving sp^2 hybridized carbon atoms absorb at just above 3000 cm^{-1}, whilst as we have seen several times already (Figs 5.10, 5.12, 5.13, for example), bonds to sp^3 carbons absorb just below 3000 cm^{-1} in the range 2950–2850 cm^{-1}. In terms of peak intensity, C–H absorptions involving sp^3 carbons are usually very strong, whilst those involving sp^2 carbons are much weaker. Aromatic C–H bonds give particularly weak IR bands (Fig. 5.11a), and are often not clearly visible. The aldehyde–CHO group deserves special mention; aldehydes usually show two weak bands in the range 2900–2700 cm^{-1} due to C–H stretching, and these are visible in the spectrum of salicylaldehyde (Fig. 5.11b) at 2847 and 2752 cm^{-1}. Although these aldehyde C–H bands are not completely diagnostic, the presence of an aldehyde is easily confirmed by locating the strong C=O band.

The 2500–1900 region

This region of the spectrum is comparatively easy to interpret since, of the functional groups that you are likely to encounter, only alkynes and nitriles absorb in this region. The other functional groups which absorb here are much less common, and are of the cumulene type, X=Y=Z, such as isocyanates (RN=C=O), azides ($RN{=}\overset{+}{N}{=}\overset{-}{N}$), diazo compounds ($R_2C{=}\overset{+}{N}{=}\overset{-}{N}$), ketenes ($R_2C{=}C{=}O$), carbodiimides (RN=C=NR) and allenes ($R_2C{=}C{=}CR_2$). One very simple cumulene is carbon dioxide (O=C=O) which absorbs at about 2350 cm^{-1}. IR spectra quite often contain a small peak or pair of peaks around 2350 cm^{-1}; these may be puzzling at first sight until you remember that any slight inequalities in path length in the spectrometer will result in imperfect subtraction of sample and reference beams, and hence a peak due to atmospheric carbon dioxide will appear in the spectrum (see Fig. 5.18a).

C≡C (Appendix 3, Table A6)

As we have already seen in Fig. 5.15, terminal alkynes absorb in the range 2150–2100 cm^{-1}. In non-terminal alkynes this absorption moves to a slightly higher frequency (2250–2150 cm^{-1}), although as with terminal alkynes, the band is often weak. The intensity of the C≡C stretching absorption in both types of alkyne is increased if the triple bond is conjugated to an alkene or carbonyl. In symmetrical, or nearly symmetrical, alkynes, which have a zero or very small dipole moment, the C≡C stretching absorption is usually absent.

C≡N (Appendix 3, Table A6)

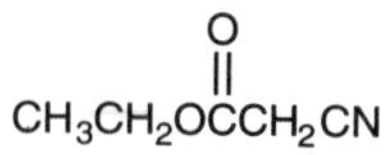
ethyl cyanoacetate

Nitriles exhibit similar triple bond stretching absorptions to alkynes, although the C≡N bond absorbs at a slightly higher frequency in the range 2270–2200 cm^{-1}. Again the absorption band is often very weak. Figure 5.16 shows the IR spectrum of ethyl cyanoacetate recorded as a thin film. Starting from the left we can interpret the spectrum as follows: the weak bands at around 3500 cm^{-1} are overtones of the strong carbonyl peak at around 1750 cm^{-1}; the two bands at 2987 and 2937 cm^{-1} are the familiar strong sp^3 C–H stretching absorptions; the nitrile peak is at 2266 cm^{-1}; the ester carbonyl has a very strong absorption at 1747 cm^{-1}; and the associated C–O stretch is probably the strong peak at 1201 cm^{-1}.

The 1900–1500 region

This is the region where double bonds absorb IR radiation, and detailed cor-

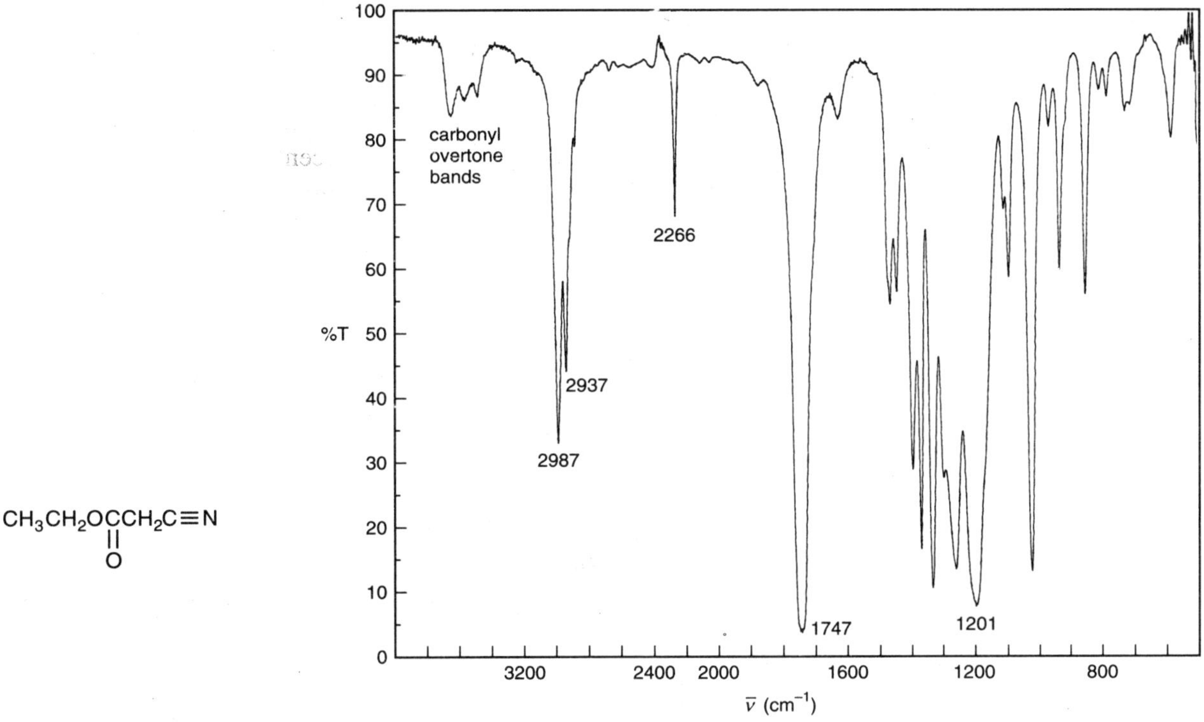

Fig. 5.16 IR spectrum of ethyl cyanoacetate.

relation tables for C=O and other double bonds are given in Tables A7 and A8 in Appendix 3. The carbonyl group has a large dipole moment, and has an intense C=O stretching absorption. Therefore the presence of a strong peak in your spectrum at around 1700 cm^{-1} is highly indicative of a carbonyl group. Indeed the absorption is so strong that the overtones can usually be seen at around 3500 cm^{-1}. Since the exact type of carbonyl group can often be inferred from the precise position of its IR absorption, careful analysis of this region of the spectrum is usually very helpful in assigning structures to unknown compounds. Carbon–carbon and carbon–nitrogen double bonds usually absorb at lower frequency than carbonyl groups.

C=O (Appendix 3, Table A7)

All carbonyl-containing compounds show a strong band corresponding to the C=O stretching absorption in the range 1800–1600 cm^{-1}. The exact position of the peak varies according to the specific functional group and its environment. For detailed correlation values see Table A7 in Appendix 3, but rather than trying to remember all these values, you may find it more useful to remember some general guidelines as to the position of the carbonyl group in various compounds. These can be summarized as follows.

Factors affecting position of C=O absorption

1 In compounds of the type RCO.X, the more electronegative the group X, the higher the frequency of the carbonyl absorption. Thus acid anhydrides (X=OCOR), acid chlorides (X=Cl) and esters (X=OR) all absorb at higher frequency than ketones (X=carbon).

2 When the carbonyl group is in a ring, the smaller the ring, and hence the greater the compression of the carbonyl bond angle, the higher the frequency; six-membered rings and larger give carbonyl absorptions similar to acyclic analogues.

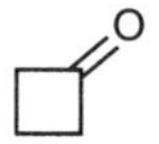

cyclobutanone
1780 cm^{-1}

3 If the carbonyl group is conjugated to a C=C bond, the carbonyl frequency is lowered by 40–15 cm^{-1} (except for amides).

4 Hydrogen bonding to the carbonyl oxygen lowers the frequency by about 50 cm^{-1}.

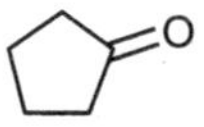

cyclopentanone
1746 cm^{-1}

Some examples of IR spectra of compounds containing carbonyl groups are shown in Figs. 5.11b, 5.12, 5.14 and 5.16–5.18. The examples are chosen to illustrate the major types of carbonyl functional group, and to exemplify the above guidelines.

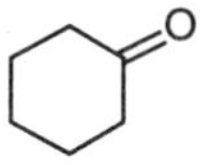

cyclohexanone
1713 cm^{-1}

Figure 5.11b shows the IR spectrum of an aromatic aldehyde, salicylaldehyde. The carbonyl absorption is at 1667 cm^{-1}; this is lower than normal for an aromatic aldehyde (1715–1695 cm^{-1}) because of the hydrogen bonding to the adjacent hydroxyl. As has already been discussed, aldehydes also show C–H absorptions in the range 2900–2700 cm^{-1}.

Figure 5.12 shows the IR spectrum of a carboxylic acid, and Fig. 5.14 shows an amide. These spectra have already been discussed, and you will find that the positions of the carbonyl peaks conform to those expected from the correlation table in Appendix 3.

The spectrum of an ester is shown in Fig. 5.16; the carbonyl peak is at 1747 cm^{-1}. Esters can usually be distinguished from ketones by the presence of the associated C–O stretch, which ketones do not possess.

Figure 5.17 shows the IR spectra of two simple cyclic ketones, cyclopentanone and cyclohexanone, and illustrates the effect of ring size on the position of the carbonyl absorption. Ring strain shifts the C=O absorption to a higher frequency, and hence in cyclopentanone the peak is at 1746 cm^{-1} (Fig. 5.17a). Cyclohexanone, a relatively unstrained ketone, shows a C=O peak at 1713 cm^{-1} (Fig. 5.17b), a value typical of an acyclic ketone. In cyclobutanone, however, the effect of increased strain is to shift the C=O absorption to about 1780 cm^{-1}. Apart from the differences in carbonyl absorption, the spectra of both ketones show weak absorptions at around 3500 cm^{-1} due to overtones of the carbonyl peak, and similar C–H absorptions in the 2970–2860 cm^{-1} range, although there are obvious differences in the fingerprint region.

$CH_3CH_2CH_2CHO$

butanal
1714 cm^{-1}

Figure 5.18a shows the IR spectrum of butanal (butyraldehyde), the analysis of which is fairly straightforward, as follows: typical strong sp^3 C–H stretching absorptions at 2962 and 2876 cm^{-1}, a small shoulder on the side of the 2876 peak which may be the aldehyde C–H stretch, and the strong carbonyl peak at 1714 cm^{-1}. Since the second aldehyde peak is obscured by the adjacent strong

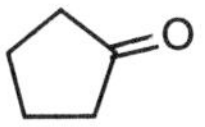

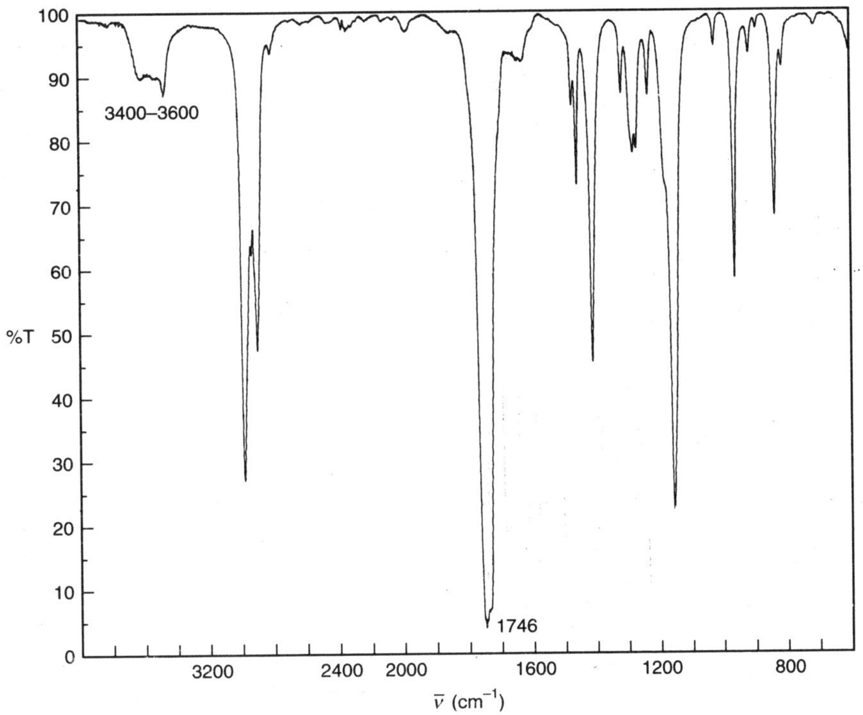

(a)

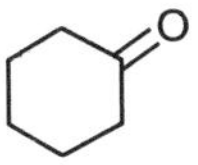

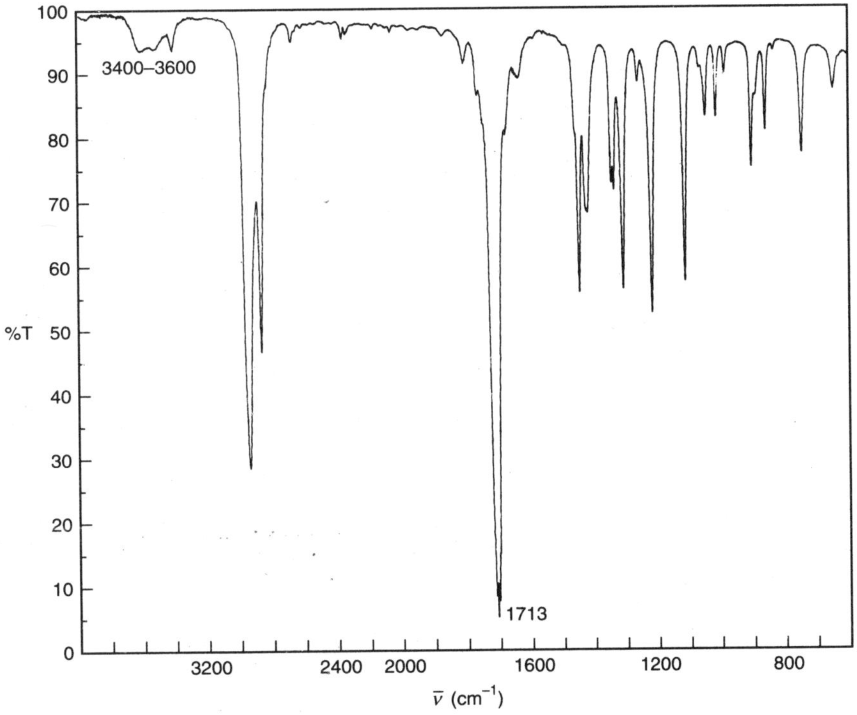

(b)

Fig. 5.17 (a) IR spectrum of cyclopentanone; (b) IR spectrum of cyclohexanone.

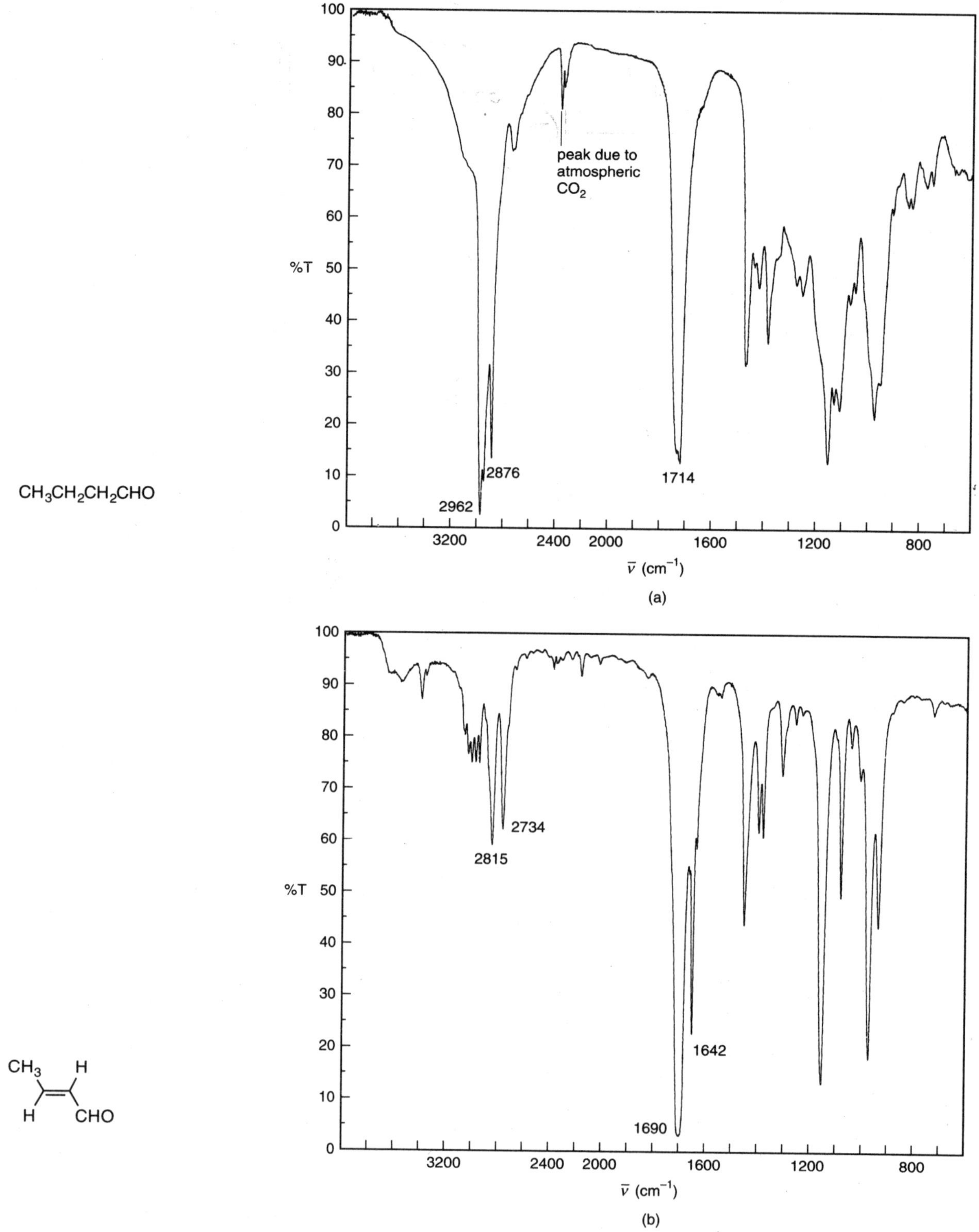

Fig. 5.18 (a) IR spectrum of butanal (butyraldehyde); (b) IR spectrum of butenal (crotonaldehyde).

C–H peak, this spectrum also illustrates the dangers of relying on small peaks for structural assignments. The pair of small peaks at about 2350 cm^{-1} is due to carbon dioxide!

$CH_3CH{=}CHCHO$
but-2-enal
1690 cm^{-1}

Figure 5.18b shows the spectrum of butenal (crotonaldehyde), and nicely illustrates the effect of conjugation on the position of the C=O absorption, which is to lower the frequency by about 25 cm^{-1} to 1690 cm^{-1}. It should also be noted that the C–H region lacks the strong C–H stretches associated with sp^3 C–H bonds, the sp^2 C–H absorptions being much weaker. Hence the two aldehyde bands are more easily seen. The strong band at 1642 cm^{-1} is due to the C=C stretching absorption.

C=C (Appendix 3, Table A8)

Conjugation increases intensity of C=C absorption

Although C–C single bond absorption is not particularly useful for structure determination, the absorptions of C=C double bonds are quite useful. Most compounds containing C=C bonds show stretching absorptions in the 1680–1500 cm^{-1} region of the spectrum. Remember that the C=C bond is weaker than the C≡C bond, and therefore absorbs at a lower frequency. Simple alkenes show a weakish absorption in the range 1680–1640 cm^{-1}. Conjugation with another double bond increases the intensity of, and lowers the frequency of, the absorption. Therefore the C=C bond in α, β-unsaturated carbonyl compounds is usually easy to pick out (1642 cm^{-1} in Fig. 5.18b), although it is weaker than the associated carbonyl peak. Conjugation of the C=C bond with a lone pair of electrons, as in enamines and enol ethers, also increases the intensity of the C=C absorption, but *increases* the frequency. Aromatic C=C bonds are a special case, and most aromatic compounds show two or three bands in the region 1600–1500 cm^{-1}. The reason that aromatic C=C bonds absorb at lower frequency than aliphatic C=C bonds is that the reduced π-overlap associated with aromatic delocalization means that the aromatic C=C bond is not a true double bond, and is therefore weaker than an alkene C=C bond. The presence of two or three bands in this region of the spectrum is often diagnostic of an aromatic compound (*cf.* Fig. 5.11), the presence of which can usually be confirmed by additional strong bands in the 850–730 cm^{-1} region of the spectrum. These bands result from out-of-plane aromatic C–H vibrations, the position of the bands being dependent on the number of adjacent aromatic protons. Hence, in principle, differently substituted aromatic compounds can be identified by the positions of these IR absorptions. For example, *ortho*-substituted benzenes with four adjacent hydrogens show a strong band in the range 770–735 cm^{-1}, and although this absorption can be seen in the spectra of the *ortho*-substituted phenols shown in Fig. 5.11, the general complexity of the fingerprint region often makes such unambiguous interpretations impossible.

The fingerprint region

By its very nature, the fingerprint region of an IR spectrum is complex, and detailed analysis is not usually possible. However, as we have seen, some useful information can be extracted from this region of the spectrum; for example, the distinction between ester and ketone carbonyls can be made by looking for the ester C–O absorption in the fingerprint region. Other functional groups of organic chemistry such as nitro- and sulfonyl also show characteristic absorptions in the fingerprint region, and the more important of these are summarized in Table A9 in Appendix 3.

Further reading

A selection of reference books that contain sections on IR spectroscopy is given below:

L.J. Bellamy, *The Infrared Spectra of Complex Molecules*, 2nd edn, Chapman & Hall, London, 1981.

L.D. Field S. Sternhell and J. Kalman, *Organic Structures from Spectra*, 2nd edn, Wiley & Sons, New York, 1995.

L.M. Harwood and T.D.W. Claridge, *Introduction to Organic Spectroscopy*, Oxford University Press, Oxford, Chapter 3, 1996.

C.J. Pouchert (ed.) *The Aldrich Library of Infrared Spectra*, 3rd edn, Aldrich Chemical Co. Inc., Milwaukee, USA, 1981.

C.J. Pouchert (ed.) *The Aldrich Library of FT-IR Spectra*, Aldrich Chemical Co. Inc., Milwaukee, USA, 1985.

R.M. Silverstein, G.C. Bassler and T.C. Morrill, *Spectrometric Identification of Organic Compounds*, 5th edn, Wiley & Sons, New York, 1991.

D.H. Williams and I. Fleming, *Spectroscopic Methods in Organic Chemistry*, 5th edn, McGraw-Hill, Maidenhead, 1995.

For a discussion of FT-IR spectroscopy, see: P.R. Griffiths and J.A. de Haseth, *Fourier Transform Infrared Spectrometry*, Wiley & Sons, New York, 1986. S.F. Johnston, *Fourier Transform Infrared: a Constantly Evolving Technology*, Ellis Horwood, Chichester, 1991.

5.3 Nuclear magnetic resonance spectroscopy

It is no exaggeration to say that the development of NMR spectroscopy has been the single largest factor contributing to the rapid progress in organic chemistry during the second half of the twentieth century. Prior to about 1955, all organic structures had to be determined by combinations of chemical tests and degradations—such as those described in Chapter 4—supplemented where possible by the small amount of information available from optical absorption measurements. As a consequence, structure determination was the major activity (at least when measured by the time spent in its performance) of organic chemists. During the pre-NMR period of chemistry it would not have been at all unusual for a complete research project for a graduate student to be the elucidation of the structure of a single natural product of only moderate complexity. The great difficulties associated with the determination of structures by chemical means naturally diverted effort away from other, perhaps more central problems of organic chemistry, such as the synthesis of complex molecules and the investigation of the intermediates and mechanisms of organic reactions.

Circumstances are quite different now, as NMR (in conjunction with the other physical methods described in this chapter) permits the straightforward determination of the structure of most small-to-medium organic molecules (say with molecular weights below 1000) in a very short time. This is especially true in synthetic work, where the range of structures to be considered is naturally restricted by the known compositions of the reactants. As a result, it becomes possible to try out new reactions on a small scale, and to discover much about what has happened during the reaction (or even what is happening as it takes place) without the lengthy purification and degradations required in earlier times. The pace of chemical experimentation and discovery can therefore be much faster.

NMR instrumentation is quite expensive, but nevertheless it is fairly common for teaching laboratories to possess at least a rudimentary spectrometer. Even if your laboratory lacks this facility, you should be provided with NMR spectra of the materials you handle. It is most important to get into the habit of examining these and trying to understand the information they contain, and especially to relate the changes in the spectra to the reactions you are doing. In this way it is easy to develop an appreciation of NMR spectroscopy suitable for everyday application to organic chemistry. Do not fall into the trap of viewing NMR as a rather disconnected, perhaps disconcertingly physical subject, remote from the thinking of organic chemists. In reality we shall see that there is a strong connection between the kinds of information contained in NMR spectra and the way in which organic structures are represented—which is of course what makes the technique so useful. The physical theory of NMR is an intriguing subject that forms a major research area in its own right, but if you find yourself attracted by this aspect there are many specialized texts available and some of these are listed at the end of this section. To understand NMR at a level useful for organic chemistry the following very simple physical model will suffice.

Nuclear 'spin'

Nuclear resonance comes about because the nuclei of at least one of the isotopes of most elements possess *magnetic moments* (in other words, they behave like small bar magnets). The magnetic moment arises because the nucleus may have 'spin', and is also charged, so that if you like you can think of it as a tiny loop of electric current (Fig. 5.19). When placed in a constant magnetic field, the energy of the nuclear magnetic moment obviously depends on the orientation of the nucleus with respect to that field (just as bar magnets attract or repel according to their relative orientation), and on the microscopic nuclear scale only certain energies are permitted (that is, the energy is quantized). Application of electromagnetic radiation at a suitable frequency can stimulate transitions between the nuclear energy levels, which as usual provides the basis for any form of spectroscopy.

NMR thus differs from other kinds of absorption spectroscopy only with

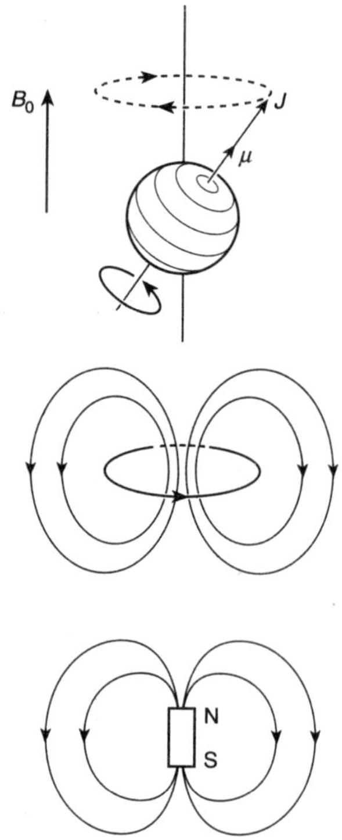

Fig. 5.19 Three ways of picturing a nucleus: as a spinning, charged ball (top), a loop of current (middle) and a bar magnet (bottom).

respect to the requirement for the sample to be subjected to an external magnetic field. So by analogy with IR, for instance, we can devise an experimental set-up to measure the resonances (Fig. 5.20).

The aim here is to find the combinations of external field and applied frequency that cause absorption of the electromagnetic energy by the sample; we may conveniently achieve this by holding one parameter static (say, the field) and varying the other (i.e. the frequency). This is the most obvious way to perform NMR, and is most likely to be the way a basic instrument, as may be found in a teaching laboratory, will work. Later we will see that there is an alternative approach that offers distinct advantages. However, in the main you will probably find it useful to keep in mind the analogy with the more 'obvious' IR or UV measurements, and imagine NMR spectra to be obtained by varying the frequency of applied electromagnetic radiation while the sample sits in a constant magnetic field. This measurement mode is known as the *continuous wave* (CW) method, with *frequency sweep*.

The fundamental properties of a nucleus of significance for NMR are clearly its spin, characterized by quantum number I that can take integral or half-integral values (for example, $0, {}^1\!/_2, 1, {}^3\!/_2 \ldots$), and the relationship between its angular momentum and its magnetic moment, a parameter known as the *gyromagnetic ratio*, often represented by γ. From our point of view, we are obviously concerned that I should not be zero, because then there is no spin and hence no magnetic moment; however, it also turns out that nuclei with $I > {}^1\!/_2$ have rather inconvenient NMR properties, so that we will, in practice, only be investigating nuclei for which $I = {}^1\!/_2$. The normal isotope of hydrogen (^{1}H) is, fortunately, such a nucleus, but we are not so lucky with the element of

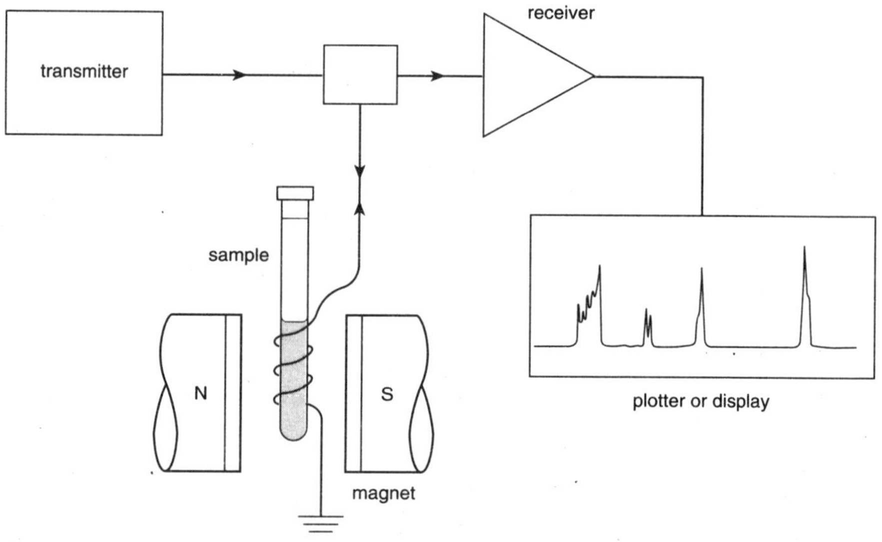

Fig. 5.20 Schematic diagram of a simple NMR spectrometer.

greatest importance to organic chemistry (carbon!) as its most abundant isotope (^{12}C) has $I = 0$, as do all nuclei with even atomic number and mass. However, natural carbon contains around 1.1% ^{13}C, which does have $I = ½$, so that NMR of carbon is possible, although with more difficulty and with significantly different information content in the resulting spectra (of which more later). The number of quantized energy states allowed for a nucleus with spin I is $2I + 1$, so that spin ½ nuclei can only be in either of two states. In the 'bar magnet' picture (Fig. 5.21) you can think of these two states as corresponding with parallel and antiparallel arrangements of the magnet relative to the static field; the lower energy (parallel) state is often labelled α, whereas that of higher energy (antiparallel) state is represented as β. The NMR resonance corresponds with a flip of the magnet from parallel to antiparallel, or in other words with transitions from α to β. We will find shortly that this rather simplistic picture helps us to understand some very important interactions that make NMR distinctively different from other kinds of spectroscopy.

The frequency at which nuclei 'resonate' depends on the applied magnetic field

For practical applied field strengths (typically in the range 1.4–14 tesla), nuclear resonances are found to occur in the radiofrequency region (for instance, protons resonate around 60 MHz at a field strength of 1.4 tesla), and the resonant frequency is directly proportional to the field (so in a 14 tesla magnet the proton frequency increases to 600 MHz). Different nuclei have

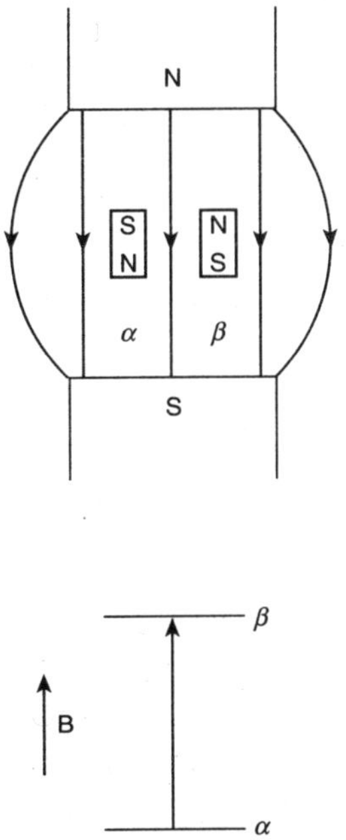

Fig. 5.21 Using the 'bar magnet' picture, we can see that the two orientations of the nuclei relative to the static field will have different energies (top). Transitions between the resulting energy levels are responsible for the NMR absorption (bottom).

different gyromagnetic ratios and hence different NMR frequencies (for example, ^{13}C resonates at about one-quarter of the frequency of ^{1}H for the same applied field). These gross changes from one nucleus to another are of practical significance in that they affect the ease with which NMR measurements can be made, but otherwise they are not relevant from the point of view of structure determination. It is the much more subtle changes in frequency depending on various aspects of the environment of the nuclei that are chemically interesting.

Preparing the sample

Before proceeding to investigate the use of NMR spectra, it is appropriate to discover how they are obtained in practice. This section covers sample preparation techniques that you will need to use yourself in your day-to-day application of NMR to routine problems.

NMR specialists are often regarded as mildly eccentric by the organic chemists who consult them, because despite having ordinary, harmless views on most topics, they seem to suffer from a highly specific form of paranoia when it comes to the preparation of NMR samples. The object is to put the sample, in solution, in a tube and you might suppose that there is not much room for error on the chemist's part. However if you reflect for a moment on the nature of the NMR experiment it should become clear that the spectroscopist's paranoia is not entirely misplaced. Throughout the discussion of coupling on pp. 326–328, frequent reference will be made to interactions that cause line splittings of 1 or 2 Hz. Now, this measurement might be made on a spectrometer with an operating frequency of 500 MHz, and so detection of a 1 Hz frequency difference is a measurement accurate to 2 parts in 10^9 (equivalent to measuring the distance between the earth and the moon to within a few centimetres). Considerable effort is required to construct and maintain instrumentation capable of measurements of this kind, so it is a shame if easily avoided problems related to sample quality are allowed to degrade performance.

High resolution NMR spectra are always obtained on samples in solution. In preparing a sample for NMR spectroscopy it is necessary to select a solvent, arrange that the solute concentration is appropriate to the measurement to be attempted, and eliminate, so far as possible, any contaminants that might affect the homogeneity of the field in the region of the sample. The third point is particularly important, and means taking care to remove solid particles that might be suspended in the solution, because these distort the static magnetic field and hence degrade the resolution of the spectrometer.

Many solvents are suitable for use in NMR spectroscopy, but it is necessary to replace any hydrogen they contain with deuterium. This is in order that the solvent proton signal does not obscure the much weaker signals from the solute, and also because, on advanced spectrometers, the NMR resonance of the deuterated solvent (^{2}H has $I = 1$) is used as a reference to stabilize the

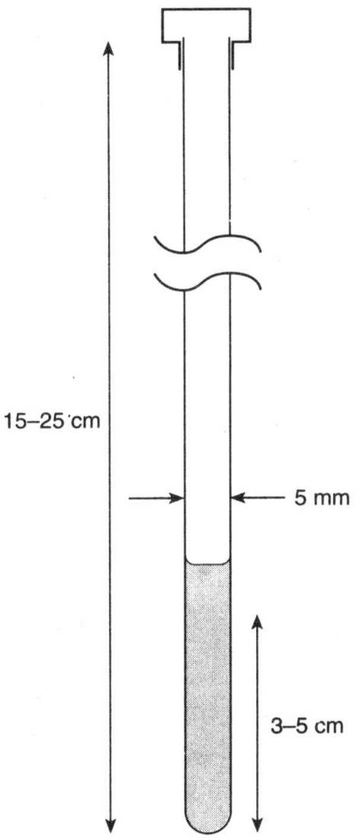

Fig. 5.22 NMR sample tube—typical dimensions.

instrument. All the usual organic solvents are available in deuterated form, although in some cases at considerable cost (Table 5.2). For routine applications of proton NMR, chloroform-*d* ($CDCl_3$) is the most versatile and economic solvent.

Samples for proton NMR are usually prepared in glass tubes of 15–25 cm length and 5 mm outside diameter, which are specially made for NMR spectroscopy (Fig. 5.22). The volume of solvent to be placed in the tube varies depending on the model of spectrometer in use, but is typically 0.4–0.7 mL. Do not make the mistake of *filling* the tube! Only a small portion of the total length (about 3–5 cm) should contain solution. On a 60 MHz CW instrument it will probably be necessary to use at least 25 mg of substance in order to obtain adequate spectra, which is far more material than is needed for other spectroscopic techniques. On a modern, high-field instrument this quantity may be reduced to less than 1 mg, but even so NMR is a method of rather low sensitivity.

In order to avoid problems with floating particles in the sample, it is good practice to prepare the solution in a small vial, and then filter it directly into the NMR tube. This can conveniently be done using a Pasteur pipette with a small plug of cotton wool pushed into the narrow section (Fig. 5.23). Take care that the sample is compatible with these materials; if it is not, glass wool can be used instead, but this does not make such an effective filter.

For dilute samples, signals due to both residual proteated solvent and dissolved water can obscure significant regions of the spectrum (see the spectra of solvents in Table A16 in Appendix 3). The latter is often the more objectionable of the two, and so it is sometimes helpful to combine the filtration of the sample with drying using sodium sulfate or alumina above the plug in the pipette. Once again you should consider whether the sample will be adversely

Table 5.2 Properties of some deuterated NMR solvents.

Solvent	Relative cost*	mp (°C)	bp (°C)	δ^1H
Acetone-d^6	10	−93	55	2.05
Acetonitrile-d^3	15	−48	81	1.95
Benzene-d^6	10	7	79	7.16
Chloroform-*d*	1	−64	61	7.27
Dichloromethane-d^2	20	−97	40	5.32
Dimethyl sulfoxide-d^6	10	18	190	2.50
Methanol-d^4	15	−98	65	3.31
Pyridine-d^5	40	−42	114	8.71, 7.55, 7.19
Tetrahydrofuran-d^8	100	−106	65	3.58, 1.73
Toluene-d^8	20	−93	110	7.1–6.9, 2.09

*The relative cost column gives approximate costs per unit weight, relative to that for chloroform-*d*.

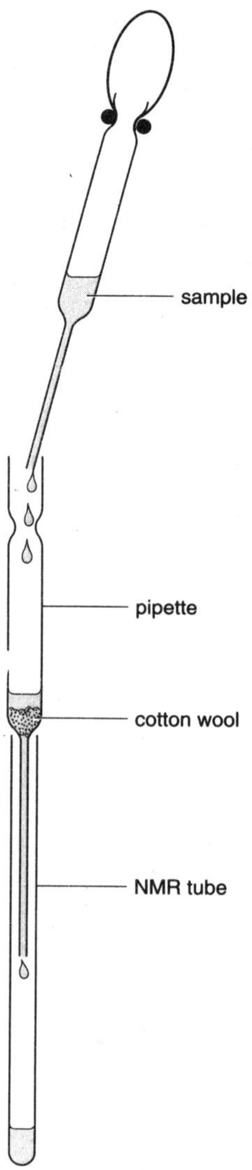

Fig. 5.23 A convenient arrangement for filtering NMR samples.

affected by any drying agent chosen. Molecular sieves are not very suitable for drying NMR samples, as they sometimes contain fine dust that is difficult to remove by filtration.

Once the sample is in the tube, the tube is sealed with a plastic cap and mounted in a turbine assembly before being placed in the spectrometer (Fig. 5.24). This is in order to allow the tube to be spun at fairly high speed (20–30 Hz) about its vertical axis, which helps to average out inhomogeneities in the magnetic field. Care should be taken to ensure that the outside of the tube and turbine assembly are clean before introducing them into the spectrometer, because contamination in the active region of the instrument is very detrimental and hard to remove. The spinning of the sample, although essential if high resolution spectra are to be obtained, sometimes introduces artefacts into the spectrum in the form of satellite lines separated from the real lines by one or two multiples of the spinning speed (Fig. 5.25). These satellites, known as *spinning sidebands*, should never be more than a few per cent of the height of the main peaks; if they are bigger, the spectrometer is in need of adjustment. Spinning sidebands can sometimes be confused with other small, genuine peaks. If this is a problem the sidebands can readily be identified by re-running the spectrum with altered spinning speed, in which case the sidebands move while the real peaks do not.

Samples for ^{13}C NMR were traditionally prepared in 10 or 15 mm outside

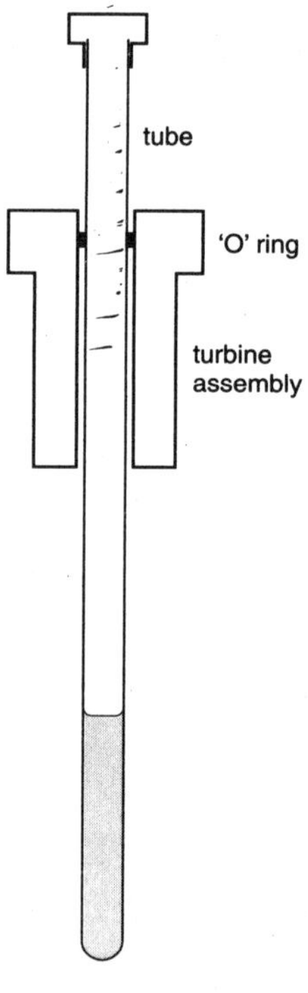

Fig. 5.24 NMR tube mounted in the turbine assembly.

diameter tubes, which require a solvent volume of 1–3 mL in order to allow the use of large amounts of substance (around 150–200 mg) to compensate for the much lower signal strength obtained with this nucleus (see pp. 341–345). However, it is now common to find 'dual purpose' spectrometers that permit the measurement of ^{1}H and ^{13}C spectra on the same sample and, for these instruments, 5 mm tubes are used in both cases. When the larger tubes are necessary, it is virtually essential to employ a plastic or glass plug known as a *vortex suppressor*, in order to prevent the spinning of the sample creating a whirlpool in the solution. The vortex suppressor is introduced after the solution, and is pushed down until it just contacts the liquid surface (Fig. 5.26). Plastic types, made from PTFE (Teflon®), are a close fit in the tube and usually have a small hole through the centre to let trapped air escape; the glass ones are looser fitting and float on the surface of the solution. Both kinds incorporate a hook or threaded hole so that they can be fished out after the experiment is finished.

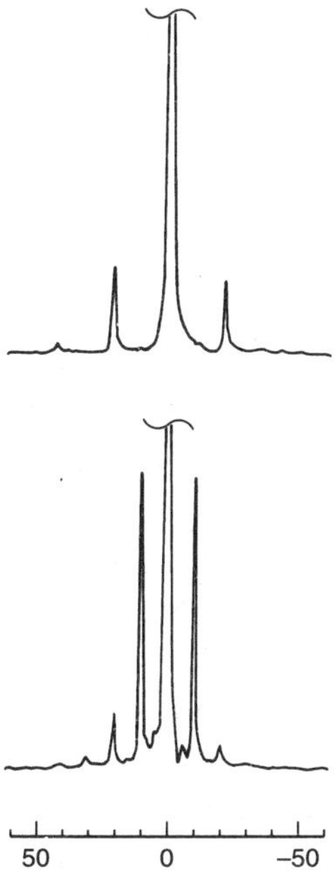

Fig. 5.25 Spinning sidebands at two different spinning speeds. With faster spinning (top) the sidebands are weaker and further from the main line.

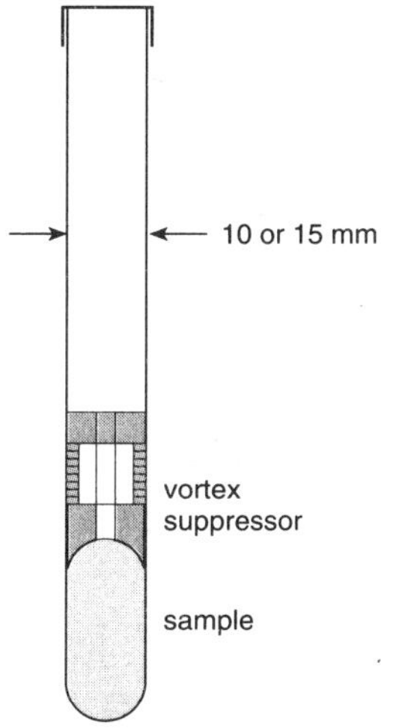

Fig. 5.26 Typical arrangement for ^{13}C NMR, using a large diameter tube, 1–3 mL of sample and a vortex suppressor.

Obtaining the spectrum

There are two kinds of NMR spectrometer in widespread use at present. In the teaching laboratory you are most likely to find CW instruments, which use permanent magnets and obtain the spectrum by sweeping either the field or the frequency as described on pp. 307–308. Operation of this kind of instrument is not substantially different from the use of an IR absorption spectrometer. The sample is introduced as described above, and the instrument sweeps through the spectroscopic region plotting out the signals as it goes. There will be controls to allow the selection of the sweep range, alteration of the sensitivity and adjustment of the magnetic field homogeneity, amongst others, but these are instrument-specific and cannot be described here.

In the research laboratory, CW spectrometers have been virtually supplanted by machines that work on an entirely different principle in order to offset a major problem with NMR that has already been mentioned: low sensitivity. The sensitivity of NMR is so low that it is unsatisfactory even when every aspect of the spectrometer has been carefully optimized. It is therefore useful to employ *signal averaging* to improve further the signal-to-noise ratio. It can be shown, by analyzing the statistical properties of the electrical noise in the NMR spectra, that by repeating the analysis and summing the results, the sensitivity increases as the square root of the number of repetitions (in other words, doing the experiment four times gives twice as good a result).

Now, this can certainly be attempted on a CW spectrometer, but unfortunately it proves to be inefficient because of the time taken to sweep through the spectrum. An alternative, and much better, approach is to measure *all* the NMR resonances simultaneously. This can be achieved by applying a short, intense pulse of radio energy to the sample, which is absorbed by all of the nuclei present. After the pulse, the sample *emits* signals for a time, while the various transitions return to their equilibrium state. The resulting signal, called a *free induction decay* (FID), consists of a superimposition of all the resonances from the sample, which have to be unscrambled in order to obtain the familiar presentation in the form of a spectrum. The unscrambling is done by an arithmetical process known as *Fourier transformation*, and so this experiment mode is referred to as *FT NMR*. The point of the exercise is to increase the speed of the measurement in order to make signal averaging efficient.

The above description will scarcely give you more than a flavour of what is involved in FT NMR, but regrettably there is insufficient space to provide more details. FT spectrometers are characterized by much higher sensitivity than equivalent CW instruments. In addition, the FT technique tends to be used on more advanced systems with high magnetic field strengths, so the effective difference is even more noticeable. Very high magnetic fields, from about 4.5 tesla upwards, are obtained using *superconducting magnets*, in which a current flows in a coil of wire immersed in a bath of liquid helium. After being established, such magnets require no power, and have very good properties with respect to stability and homogeneity of the field. Apart from differing in terms of signal-to-noise ratio and peak separation, the spectra obtained on low field CW and high field FT instruments are basically similar, the only major distinction being the appearance in CW spectra of 'ringing' patterns after the lines (Fig. 5.27). For clarity, some of the spectra in this chapter have been obtained on high field FT instruments, but the worked examples in Figs 5.54 and 5.55 were run at 60 MHz in CW mode.

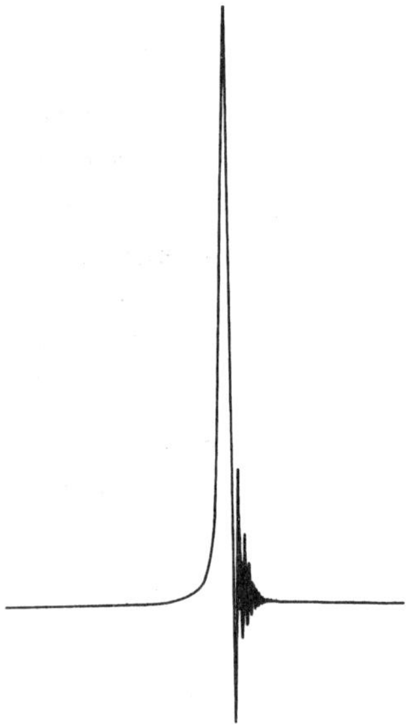

Fig. 5.27 Typical line shape obtained on a CW spectrometer. The 'wiggles' following the line are absent from spectra obtained in FT mode.

Interpreting the spectrum

Main features

Homing in on the resonances of a single nuclear species such as ^{1}H, we generally find that not all nuclei in a molecule resonate at exactly the same frequency. By scanning through the expected range within which the resonances fall (which is known from past experience), we obtain a spectrum containing peaks corresponding to the different absorption frequencies. The origin of these differences will be surveyed in the following sections, but we can quickly gain some perspective on the usefulness of NMR spectroscopy by considering three facts (until further notice, the discussion will now be concerned solely with ^{1}H NMR).

1 *Peak positions depend on chemical environment.* For instance, in benzyl acetate the methyl group contributes a signal in a different position to the benzylic CH_2 (Fig. 5.28). This variation in frequency is known as the *chemical shift*, in recognition of its link with chemical structure.

2 *Peak intensities depend on the number of contributing nuclei* (subject to certain experimental conditions, which will normally be met in ^{1}H NMR). This means that the methyl resonance of benzyl acetate will be 1.5 times stronger

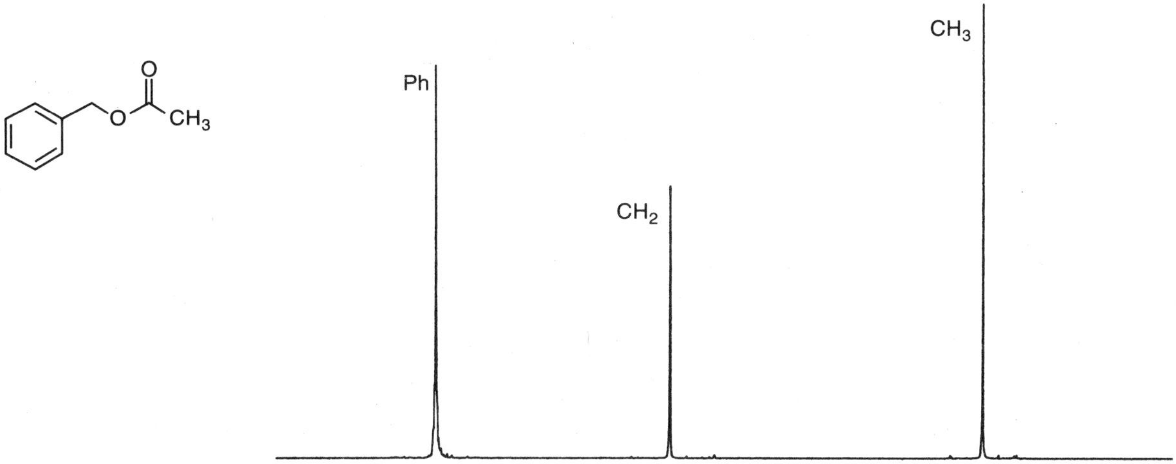

Fig. 5.28 Proton spectrum of benzyl acetate.

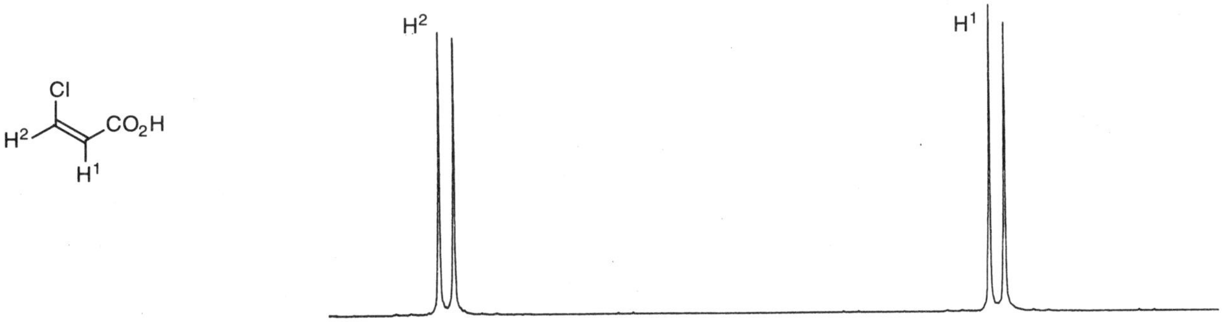

Fig. 5.29 Part of the proton spectrum of Z-3-chloropropenoic acid, showing the splitting of each alkene signal into a doublet.

than that due to the CH_2. However, you have to be careful about what is meant by 'peak intensity'; a point which is discussed later.

3 *Peaks have a fine structure related to the presence of neighbouring nuclei.* In Z-3-chloropropenoic acid (β-chloroacrylic acid) each of the two alkene protons exhibits a signal consisting of two lines of slightly different frequency (Fig. 5.29). This phenomenon, known as *coupling*, reflects the fact that each proton is in some sense 'aware' of the fact that its neighbour can be in one of two states (i.e. α or β).

These three things are all we need to understand. We will examine the significance and application of these aspects of NMR in detail, but it is quite exciting to notice immediately how the information in NMR spectra is peculiarly well suited to structure determination. The fact that chemical shifts reflect the chemical environments of nuclei is obviously useful. However, it is not so different from the observation that, for instance, certain IR bands

NMR permits elucidation of molecular 'connectivity'

reflect the presence of functional groups. What *is* different, and is unique to NMR, is the coupling interaction that reveals relationships between pairs of nuclei. We will see that coupling depends essentially on the existence of paths of *bonds* through which the interaction is relayed, and of course mapping out paths of bonds is just what structural elucidation is about. It is this feature above all that makes NMR useful in chemistry.

Measuring chemical shifts

The two spectra we have seen so far contained no indication of the separation between the various peaks, but obviously this will normally be required. Your first thought might be that the natural thing to do is to measure the exact frequency of each resonance, in a similar fashion to the presentation of IR spectra; however, although this is possible there are two reasons why it is not satisfactory. Firstly, the absolute frequency of the resonances depends on the static field, and this varies (widely) between spectrometers, comparison of spectra obtained on different instruments would be difficult and, since the use of NMR rests in part on the comparison of known spectra with that of the unknown, this is quite unacceptable. Secondly, it turns out that the variations in frequency due to chemical shifts are very small (typically less than 1000 Hz for protons at 60 MHz), so that making absolute frequency measurements to a suitable degree of accuracy and reproducibility is technically difficult. The solution to these problems is to measure shifts *relative* to a reference NMR signal, and to express them as *fractional* changes. So, if the reference signal has frequency F_{ref} and an NMR resonance is found at F, its chemical shift δ is *defined* as

Frequencies are always measured relative to a reference signal

$$\delta = \left(F - F_{ref}\right)/F_{ref}$$

Notice that this definition implies that signals at higher frequency than the reference have positive chemical shifts. This choice of 'direction' for the scale, which has now been agreed as an IUPAC convention, has not always been consistently adopted in the past, so that some care is needed when working with data from old literature (in practice this problem is mainly encountered for nuclei other than ^{1}H and ^{13}C). Another scale which may be encountered in older literature, but which is now not used, is represented as τ and is defined as $\tau = 10 - \delta$ (the historical origin of this confusion lies in the possibility of measuring NMR spectra by varying either the frequency or the field; τ is the 'field sweep' version). All chemical shifts in this book are expressed on the δ scale.

The δ scale clearly depends on the choice of a reference signal, and for both ^{1}H and ^{13}C NMR the universally agreed standard is the methyl resonance of tetramethylsilane (TMS). On rudimentary spectrometers this substance, which is conveniently inert and volatile (for subsequent ease of removal), is generally added to the sample so that the correct referencing of the spectrum can be checked directly. Whenever proton chemical shifts are quoted you can assume, in the absence of any statement to the contrary, that they are relative to TMS. Clearly, from the definition of δ the shift of TMS itself is 0. Some further rather subtle points regarding chemical shift referencing are discussed on pp. 350–351.

The range of proton shifts is of the order of hundreds of hertz at 60 MHz, as indicated above, so that the most convenient units for δ are 'parts per million' (ppm). Protons in the majority of organic structures have chemical shifts that fall within the range 0–10 ppm, although a significant minority are found outside this region in both the positive and negative directions. By convention, NMR spectra are presented so that the δ scale increases *from right to left*. We now have enough information to put a scale on the benzyl acetate spectrum (Fig. 5.30).

There is a final point of notation regarding chemical shifts which is rather confusing, as it again has its origin in the historical distinction between field and frequency sweep spectra. Regrettably, it is still in widespread use and you must be aware of it. Resonances with high (positive) chemical shifts (on the δ scale, which is a frequency scale) are often referred to as being at 'low field'. So, the left-hand end of Fig. 5.30 would commonly be described as 'the low field end', whereas the methyl resonance of benzyl acetate is found 'to high field' of that due to the CH_2. Because it is confusing, this terminology will not be used again in this book, but you will certainly encounter it in conversation and in the literature. Beware of the chaos that may result from careless use of such terms!

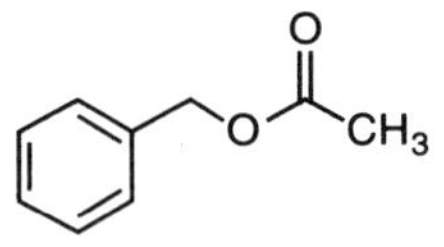

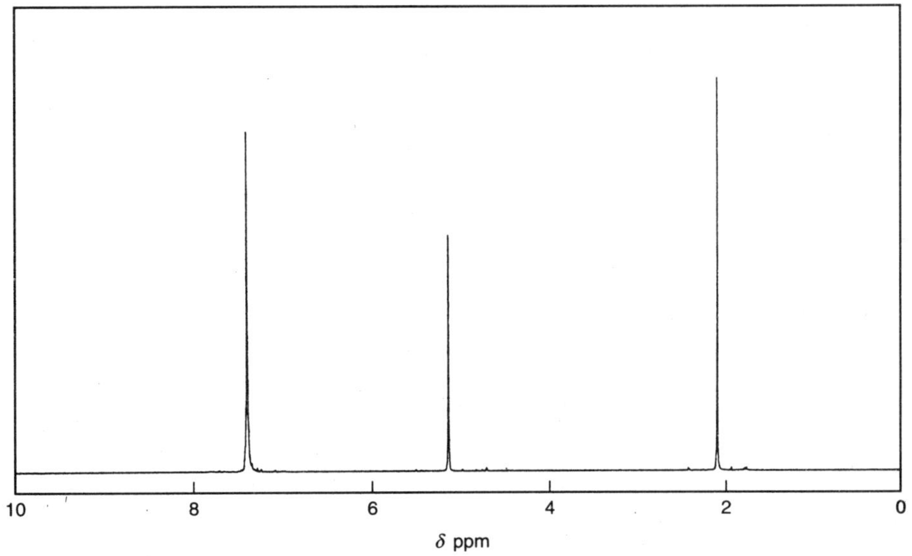

Fig. 5.30 The conventional presentation of a proton spectrum covering the range 0–10 ppm with δ increasing from right to left.

The meaning of chemical shifts

Nuclei experience 'local' magnetic fields which differ slightly from the applied magnetic field

Chemical shifts arise because of the local magnetic properties of molecules. That is, the static field at the site of each nucleus is not quite the same as the external field applied to the sample. The essential character of this effect is that the nuclei are, to a greater or lesser extent, *shielded* from the external field by the magnetic behaviour of their surrounding electrons. They therefore resonate at lower frequency than would an equivalent 'naked' nucleus. Variations in structure, and particularly those that influence the electron density in different parts of the molecule, alter the extent of this shielding and hence give rise to chemical shifts. There is a well-developed theory to explain these variations in shielding, but from the perspective of organic chemistry all that is needed is empirical information concerning the influence of different structural features on chemical shifts. This has been built up from the measurement of the spectra of many compounds of known structure, and is recorded in the form of tables of shift data (for instance, those in Appendix 3).

Data tables are the primary source of shift information, but it is neither pleasant nor desirable to spend much time poring over such collections of numbers. For the routine interpretation of proton NMR spectra it is fortunately much more important to have an appreciation of general trends than to be able to remember the exact shifts of specific compounds. It is also essential not to make the mistake of attaching too much significance to the exact values of chemical shifts. Beginners often use tables, such as Tables A10 and A11 in Appendix 3, to estimate shifts to several decimal places, and then base structural conclusions on the equality or otherwise of these predictions with the signals found in the unknown. This approach, although unfortunately common, is fundamentally wrong; the correlations do not always correspond that well. Estimated shifts should be used as a *guide*, to help you to find your way around a spectrum; other, more substantial evidence, principally derived from patterns of coupling, must be used to support suggested structures. You can best build up familiarity with the typical chemical shift ranges for different structural fragments simply by regular use of NMR spectra in conjunction with your practical work, but as a starting point the following guidelines may be helpful.

Rough chemical shifts values can be estimated by combining a knowledge of the basic areas of the spectrum in which different groups resonate, with a feel for the variations induced by substituents. We will see that the effectiveness of substituent groups in influencing chemical shifts correlates quite well with familiar chemical concepts such as electronegativity and the strength of inductive and mesomeric effects, so that the necessary categorization of groups should already be familiar to you. The essential theme that runs through all of what follows is that reduction in the electron density around a nucleus moves its chemical shift to higher frequency (i.e. more positive δ or the left of the spectrum), by virtue of increasing its exposure to the applied field (*deshielding*). (**Warning**: this is a naïve view,

Lowering the electron density around a nucleus (deshielding) causes resonance at higher frequencies

and there are many special cases and exceptions, but it works well enough to be of some value.) We will use terms such as 'shifted to high frequency', 'deshielded' or 'increased chemical shift' to indicate the displacement of peaks towards the left-hand end of the spectrum. The following discussion is not intended to be a comprehensive survey of the variation of shifts with structure, which you can readily find in texts, but rather is an overview to get you started.

Basic shift ranges

To begin with it is helpful to identify three regions within the typical 0–10 ppm range of proton chemical shifts that are particularly characteristic of different groups in the absence of modification by substituents. The majority of protons in organic structures fall into one of these three types:

0–2 ppm	Alkane protons (the aliphatic region)
5–6 ppm	Alkene protons (the olefinic region)
7–8 ppm	Arene protons (the aromatic region)

Some special cases, such as protons bound to heteroatoms, are discussed later. These basic values are then modified according to the various trends mentioned below. In following this approach it is important to keep in mind that the aim is to establish *very roughly* the region in the spectrum in which a particular type of proton might reasonably be found to resonate. Arguments based on these trends, or on the more detailed additivity rules summarized in Table A11 in Appendix 3, work best in non-rigid systems for which the influence of various substituents is averaged over a wide range of conformations. In rigid molecules, *anisotropic* (uneven) magnetic effects around certain kinds of bond or functional group can cause wide deviations from the expected shift ranges, and some examples of these will be discussed later. You should not be surprised to find protons in rigid systems resonating up to about 1 ppm away from their estimated positions, but deviations much greater than this should be treated as a cause for suspicion that the assignment or structure is wrong.

Substituent effects

The basic resonance frequencies are modified by many factors, of which the most important are the following.

1 *In aliphatic compounds, increased branching leads to increased shift* (i.e. δ *increases* in the series $CH_3 < CH_2 < CH$). For example, in 2-methylbutane, the methyl groups resonate near δ 0.9, the methylene at δ 1.2 and the methine at δ 1.45 (Fig. 5.31).

2 *Substitution by electronegative elements causes increased shift, and the degree of the shift correlates roughly with electronegativity.* So, for instance, while an aliphatic methyl group would resonate around δ 0.8, the methyl resonance of methylamine is found at δ 2.3 and that of methanol is at δ 3.3. This effect, which as you can see is quite strong for protons adjacent to the heteroatom, is also propagated with rapidly reducing intensity to more distant protons—for example, examine the shifts indicated for 1-nitropentane (Fig. 5.32).

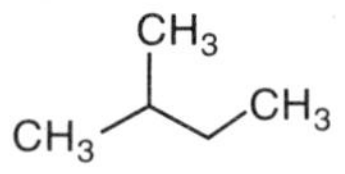

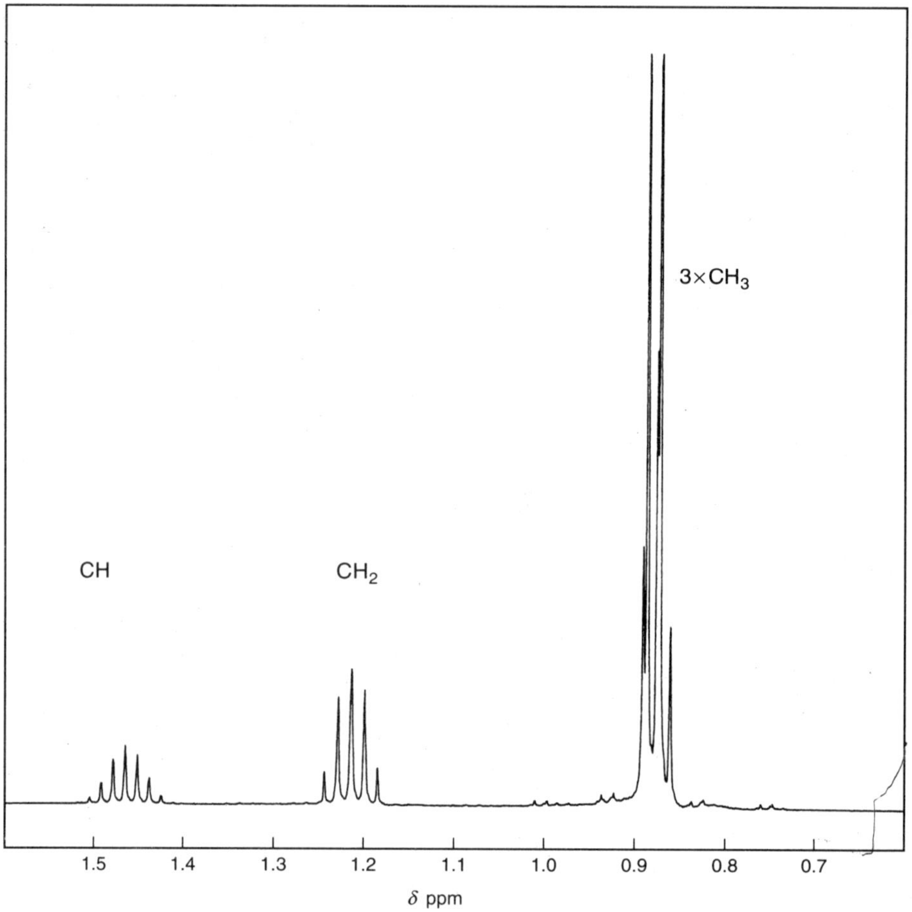

Fig. 5.31 Proton spectrum of 2-methylbutane at 500 MHz.

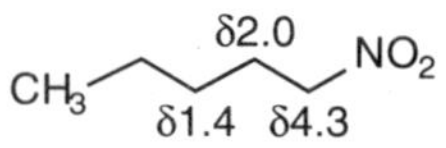

Fig. 5.32 Chemical shifts of methylene protons in 1-nitropentane at increasing distances from the electron-withdrawing substituent.

3 *Substitution by electropositive elements causes decreased shift.* This is much less commonly observed in practice, as many compounds in which carbon is bound to a more electropositive element are reactive organometallic species. It is, however, the reason that the TMS resonance occurs at lower frequency than those of most other normal organic compounds.

4 *Substitution by unsaturated groups causes increased shift.* Vinyl substitution generally produces an increase in shift of about 1 ppm (e.g. allylic methyl groups typically resonate around δ1.6) while aryl groups and carbonyls have a stronger effect (e.g. the methyl groups of toluene and acetone are both found close to δ2.2).

5 *In unsaturated compounds, mesomeric effects can also influence shifts.* The direction of the shift depends on whether the substituent has a $+M$ or $-M$ effect, and the locations at which it is most effective can be predicted by drawing resonance structures, or by 'arrow pushing'. For instance, the introduction of a methoxyl substituent on a benzene ring causes a *decrease* in the

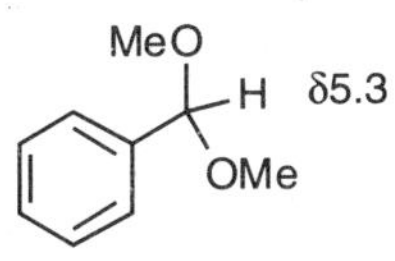

Fig. 5.33 The strongly deshielded methine proton of benzaldehyde dimethylacetal.

shift of the 2 and 4 protons by about 0.5 ppm, but has much less effect on the protons in the 3 position.

All these effects are roughly additive, so that a CH group bearing three strongly deshielding substituents such as 2 × MeO and Ph might be found straying into the 'alkene' part of the spectrum. For example, the methine proton of benzaldehyde dimethylacetal resonates at δ5.3 (Fig. 5.33).

Anisotropic effects

Certain bonds or groups are found to have characteristic effects on the shifts of nearby protons that are spatially *anisotropic*; in other words, you get different effects in different places. Because they are dependent on the relative spatial arrangement of groups, the analysis of these shifts can be particularly useful. A simple way to picture the variation in shift around such groups is to divide their surroundings into two regions, separated by a boundary in the shape of two cones with their points meeting (Fig. 5.34). Protons located on one side of this boundary will experience increased chemical shift (indicated by a + sign in the figure), while protons on the other side experience the opposite effect. *The orientation of the cones relative to the group, and the location of the + and – regions, depends on the group.* Figure 5.34 illustrates the pattern of shielding and deshielding regions for several common groups (deshielding = increased shift = +).

A common and strong effect of this kind is associated with the carbonyl group (Fig. 5.34d). As a result of lying in the strongest part of the deshielding region surrounding the C=O bond, aldehyde protons are found to resonate in

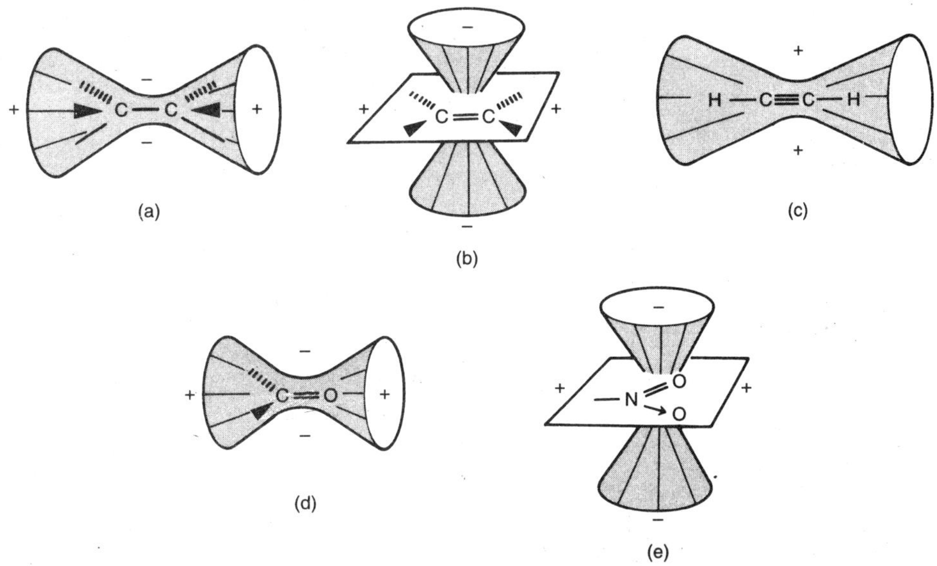

Fig. 5.34 Anisotropic magnetic fields surrounding carbon–carbon single, double and triple bonds (a)–(c) and carbonyl and nitro groups (d, e). + = regions of increased shift; – = regions of decreased shift. (Adapted from H. Günther, *NMR Spectroscopy*, 2nd edn, Wiley & Sons New York, 1995, with kind permission.)

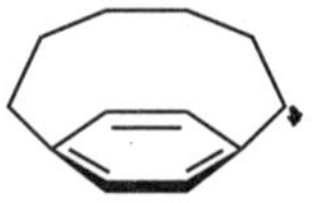
(a)

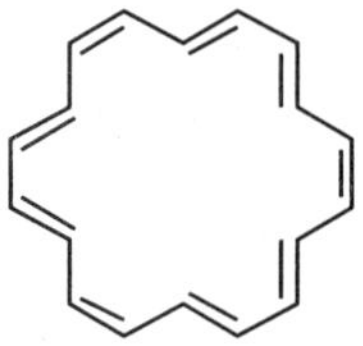
(b)

Fig. 5.35 (a) Cyclophanes, and (b) $4n+2$ electron annulenes show abnormal chemical shift positions for 'inside' and 'outside' protons.

the range 9–11 ppm (of course, it would be expected that the inductive effect of the carbonyl group would cause a shift in this direction, but not to such a great extent). Similarly, in α,β-unsaturated carbonyl compounds, β-substituents *cis* to the carbonyl are shifted to higher frequency than the equivalent *trans* substituents.

'Ring currents' in aromatic systems

Another very important anisotropic effect of this kind is associated with aromatic rings (Fig. 5.35). Here substituents around the outside edge of the ring (in particular, those directly attached to it) are in the deshielding region. This is the reason that shifts of aromatic protons are typically higher than those of alkenes. The existence of the opposite shielding region can be demonstrated with rather contrived compounds, such as cyclophanes (Fig. 5.35a), in which the protons in the middle of the methylene chain are found to resonate at abnormally low frequency. It is also evident in the astonishing difference in shift between the 'inside' (δ -- 2.99) and 'outside' (δ 9.28) protons of large aromatic systems such as [18]-annulene (Fig. 5.35b). This effect, which is found to be characteristic of cyclic conjugated π systems containing $4n + 2$ electrons, can be explained in a simple way by imagining that the external field induces a flow of the π electrons around the ring. This *ring current* then generates a local magnetic field which is in the same direction as the static field outside the ring, and in the opposite direction within it (Fig. 5.36).

Protons on heteroatoms

Protons attached directly to atoms such as nitrogen or oxygen do have characteristic shifts, but the situation here is complicated by the fact that such protons may be involved in interactions such as hydrogen bonding and chemical exchange. As a result, the shifts become strongly dependent on the precise conditions of the measurement. The values recorded in Table A13 (Appendix 3) are typical of those found under average observation conditions (i.e. without taking special precautions to exclude water, acids or bases from the sample). The following factors often alter the shift and appearance of such peaks.

1 *Hydrogen bonding causes very strong shifts to high frequency.* The degree of hydrogen bonding experienced by a proton may vary either because of intramolecular factors, or because of changes of solvent, pH or temperature.

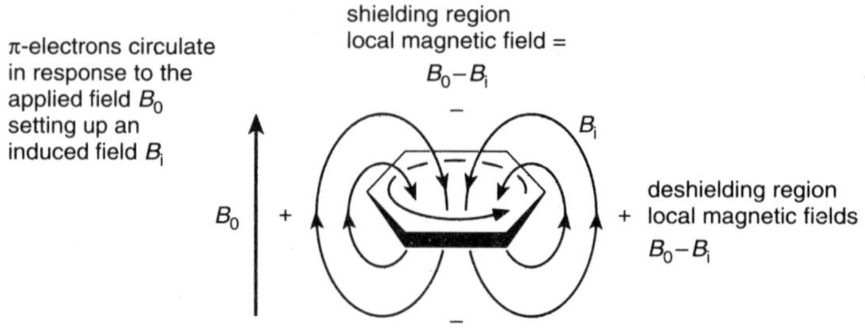

Fig. 5.36 Magnetic fields surrounding a benzene ring. B_0 represents the applied field, B_1 represents the induced field.

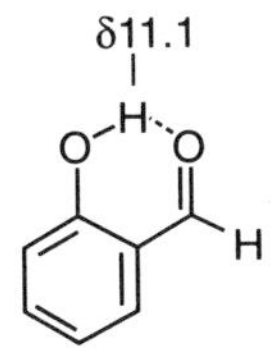

Fig. 5.37 The strongly hydrogen-bonded phenolic proton of 2-hydroxybenzaldehyde resonates at an anomalously high frequency. Also see p. 293.

For example, phenolic protons typically resonate around δ 5–6, but in 2-hydroxybenzaldehyde (salicylaldehyde) the strong hydrogen bond from the hydroxyl to the adjacent carbonyl group shifts the resonance to δ 11.1 (Fig. 5.37). Carboxylic acids commonly exist as hydrogen-bonded dimers in solutions of moderate concentration, and in this form they have resonances in the region δ 12–14; however, if the dimer can be broken up by dilution or change of solvent polarity, shifts to low frequency of many parts per million can be obtained.

2 *Chemical exchange can cause averaging of resonance positions.* The effects arising from chemical exchange are discussed in more detail later (pp. 345–347) but for the moment we need only consider the observation that, if a proton finds itself alternating between two different chemical environments at a sufficient rate, then its chemical shift becomes the average of the shifts appropriate to those environments. The two cases of interest here are exchange amongst acidic protons within a molecule (e.g. several OH or NH groups), and exchange between such protons and those of water, which is always present in NMR samples to a greater or lesser extent. The rate of this kind of exchange is strongly affected by acid or base catalysis, so that surprising variations may be found between samples containing different batches of the same compound. A highly purified substance may exhibit separate resonances for each of several hydroxyl protons, but on another occasion the presence of a trace of acid may accelerate exchange so that the peaks merge into one. Fast exchange with dissolved water, which resonates around δ 1.6 in chloroform solution, may 'pull' the shifts of acidic protons to lower frequency.

Rates of chemical exchange are sometimes accelerated by traces of acid

3 *Exchange may broaden peaks.* When exchange is not quite fast enough to achieve complete averaging, the resonances involved may be broadened (see pp. 345–347 for more details). As a general rule, OH and amino-NH resonances in average organic samples do show unusually broad lines as a result of this effect, but clearly changes in solvent, temperature or purity will influence their appearance strongly. The exchange properties of OH and NH protons can be used in a diagnostic test for their presence; this is discussed on pp. 347–348.

4 *Protons attached to nitrogen are broadened for a special reason.* While the common broadness of amino-NH protons can reasonably be attributed to the effect of chemical exchange, it is often found that *amide* protons are also broad; however, it can readily be demonstrated that amide protons are not in fast exchange in the absence of base catalysis. The reason for their broadness is that ^{14}N is an NMR-active isotope with spin 1, and a combination of coupling and the special properties of nuclei with $I > \frac{1}{2}$ leads to the broadening. It is not particularly necessary to appreciate the technicalities behind this effect, but it is important to realize that the broadness of amide protons is not normally due to exchange. An analogous broadening of ^{13}C resonances of carbon attached to nitrogen in certain functional groups can also sometimes be seen.

Some special cases

A few important groupings give rise to shifts that do not fit very well into the pattern described above. Cyclopropanes, which are often regarded in chemical terms as falling somewhere between alkanes and alkenes, do not show such behaviour with respect to their NMR signals. Cyclopropyl methylene resonances are found around δ 0.2 in the absence of deshielding substituents on the ring, and since compounds containing silicon are the only other common species that resonate in this region the observation of such a signal is quite diagnostic. This effect has also been attributed to the existence of a ring current, as in aromatic compounds, but with the difference that since the cyclopropyl protons are out of the plane of the ring they fall in the shielding region. Similar shifts to low frequency are seen in other three-membered ring compounds; contrast, for instance, the methylene resonance of oxirane (ethylene oxide, δ 2.54) with that of ethanol (δ 3.59). In four-membered rings the effect, although present, is much smaller.

Protons attached to small rings resonate at lower frequency than expected

Alkyne protons also resonate at lower frequency than might at first be expected, with monoalkyl-substituted compounds appearing around δ 1.7–1.9 (see Fig. 5.34c). As *substituents*, however, triple bonds cause the expected shifts to high frequency, leading to the rather surprising observation that in propyne the methyl group and the alkyne proton have the same shift (δ 1.8).

Peaks that should not be there

Aside from the various peaks due to your sample, you are very likely to encounter resonances in NMR spectra due to assorted impurities. Three very common types will be mentioned here; they can all be avoided by good experimental technique!

Nice crystalline solids are often assumed to be pure, but they can still contain large residues of the last solvent in which they were dissolved. Peaks of the common solvents, such as diethyl ether, ethyl acetate and acetone, are readily identified in proton NMR spectra, and as long as they are not too intense they are tolerable. However, since solvents are generally of low molecular weight, it does not require a very high percentage of solvent in mass terms to generate very strong NMR signals, and these may obscure regions of the spectrum. Impurities at this level are also unacceptable in samples intended for elemental analysis. In crystalline samples the solvent is often trapped within the crystal, and so it cannot be removed unless the sample is ground to a fine powder. Subsequent pumping under high vacuum for several hours will remove solvents with boiling points below 100°C at atmospheric pressure. Removal of solvent from viscous, liquid samples is much more difficult. The best method, if the material is sufficiently volatile, is short path distillation (pp. 154–155). Failing that, prolonged pumping under high vacuum will be needed. For the removal of spurious peaks from the proton spectrum another alternative is to evaporate solutions repeatedly in a proton-free solvent, such as carbon tetrachloride. Unfortunately, although this is very effective as a way of cleaning up the proton spectrum, it does not help to improve the accuracy of elemental analysis or the yield of your reaction!

Take care to remove solvents from your sample

A second very common impurity is also solvent-related. Some commercial solvents, particularly the various hydrocarbon fractions, contain a proportion of very involatile material. If small amounts of sample are exposed to relatively large volumes of such solvent, as may easily happen when carrying out chromatography for instance, then the involatile residue may accumulate to an unacceptable extent. These impurities, which are wax-like polymers, give rise to a broad peak in the proton spectrum around δ 1.2 and a weaker triplet at about δ 0.8. This problem can be avoided by using the solvent purification procedures described in Appendix 2.

Impure solvents leave contaminants which give broad absorptions around δ 1.2 and δ 0.8

Finally, most samples are exposed at some stage to apparatus with ground-glass joints. If these are treated with a silicone-based vacuum grease, this inevitably finds its way into the sample and gives rise to peaks at δ 0.1–0.2. To avoid this contamination, which is difficult to remove subsequently, it is best to avoid greasing joints wherever possible. Grease is not necessary on any non-moving joint in a system which will work at atmospheric pressure or will only be used under rough vacuum (e.g. for drying samples). Moving ground glass joints (stopcocks) have to be greased, but these are being superseded by more modern alternatives which use a Teflon® key.

Silicone grease causes signals at δ 0.1–0.2

Measuring peak intensities

The relative intensities of the peaks in a proton NMR spectrum reflect the number of nuclei contributing to them. This information can be used as an assignment aid, for which it is only necessary to determine the relative intensities to the nearest integer multiple, so that sets of equivalent protons can be identified. It can also be used in a more quantitative way to measure the concentrations of different species present in a solution, in which case considerable care may be necessary in order to obtain sufficiently accurate results. It is not appropriate to discuss the latter application here, except to issue a warning. The familiar use of peak intensities to count groups of equivalent protons often leads chemists to have an over optimistic view of the potential of NMR to yield quantitative results with respect to peak intensities. Many conditions, which in routinely obtained spectra are most unlikely to be met, determine whether measurements accurate to better than a few per cent can be made. It *is* possible to use NMR for accurate quantitative analysis, but special care must be taken in choosing experimental conditions.

It is difficult to measure peak intensities accurately. NMR integrations are usually for guidance only

For the former application, however, it can be assumed that routine ^1H spectra will provide adequate information. Since NMR signals may be split into several lines by coupling, and since the widths of the lines may vary for a number of reasons, it is necessary to measure areas rather than just peak heights in order to make this comparison. This can be done either by numerical analysis of the spectrum (typical on an advanced spectrometer), or by electronic summation of the signal as it is obtained (typical on a rudimentary spectrometer). Either way the result is presented in the form of an integral, which is usually plotted directly over the spectrum (Fig. 5.38). The size of the

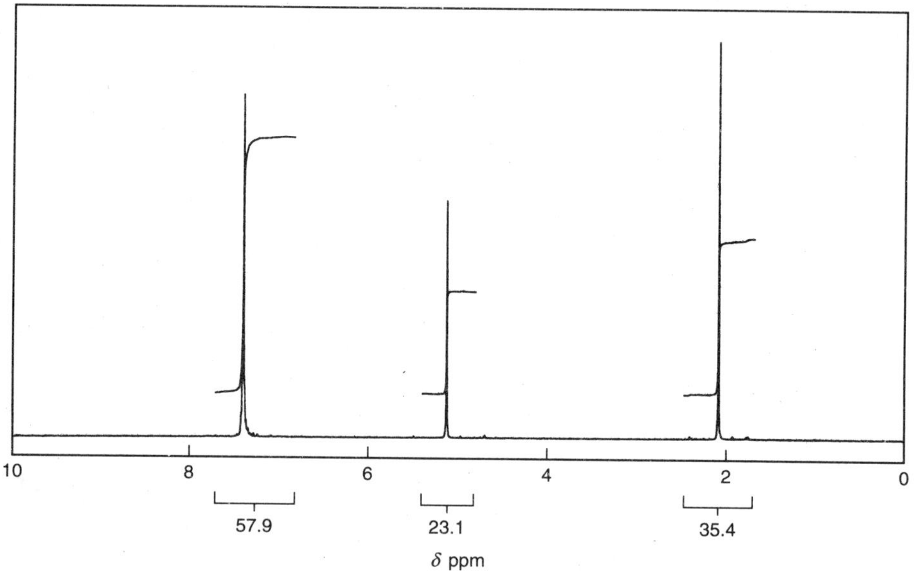

Fig. 5.38 Spectrum of benzyl acetate including the integral. The ratio of the peaks should be 5 : 2 : 3, and in fact is found to be 5.01 : 2.00 : 3.06 in this case.

integral can be measured with a ruler, counted by means of a graticule on the chart paper, or, on a modern computer-controlled spectrometer, displayed in numerical form, as in this example. The measurement will be fairly crude, with perhaps an error of up to ±10%, but should be adequate for counting groups of protons.

The origin of coupling

Imagine measuring the NMR transitions of a proton which has a neighbour. The neighbour can be in one of two states, and, viewing these states as two orientations of a magnet, there are in effect two different types of molecule whose spectra are being measured. In some molecules the neighbour proton is aligned parallel to the external field, while in others it is antiparallel. In order to understand the effect this has on the spectrum of the first proton, we need to consider two questions: how many of the neighbours are in each state, and what influence does the neighbour's state have on the magnetic field experienced by the original proton?

The first question can be answered by comparing the energies of NMR transitions, which are very low, with the general thermal energy in the sample. A Boltzmann distribution is established between the upper and lower levels of the transitions, or in other words between the two orientations of the magnets. With a very small energy difference, the difference in populations of the two states is also small, so that to all intents and purposes we can assume that half the molecules have the neighbour proton in the α-state, while for the

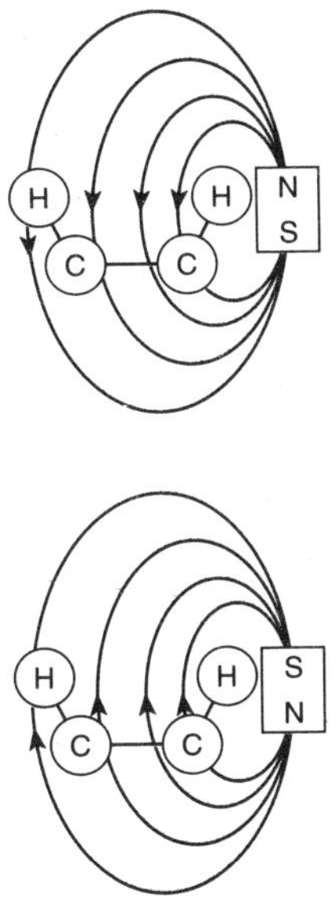

Fig. 5.39 The direct, or dipolar, interaction between two protons reverses as the nuclei change from the α- to the β-state.

Neighbouring nuclei 'couple' with each other

other half the neighbour proton is in the β-state. This is not quite true of course—otherwise it would not be possible to measure the NMR absorption at all—but the excess in the lower energy state is only of the order of 1 part in 10^5 for protons in presently available magnetic fields.

The answer to the second question proves to be slightly more subtle. The most obvious influence of one proton on the other is its direct magnetic interaction: the neighbour proton has a magnetic field, in which the first proton sits, and the direction of this field reverses between the α- and β-states (Fig. 5.39). However, since NMR spectra are measured in solution, we have to allow for the fact that the complete molecule can move freely relative to the static field. This means that the direct interaction, which is known as the *dipolar coupling*, is averaged over all possible relative orientations of the two protons, and because of the symmetry of the field surrounding each nucleus its average value is zero. In order for there to be any remaining interaction between the protons, it is therefore necessary to find a mechanism which is not affected by the molecular motion, and this is obtained by remembering that the nuclei are surrounded by electrons. The state of the neighbour proton can influence the electrons around it, which in turn can influence the field at the proton to be measured, as long as a suitable network of bonds is available to relay the information (we will see what qualifies as a 'suitable network' later). This pathway *through the bonds* leads to an effect which is not cancelled out by motion relative to the static field, and it is the origin of the coupling we observe in solution-state NMR which is known as *scalar coupling*.

Therefore half of the molecules have the neighbour proton in the α-state, and if we measure the spectrum of these molecules we obtain a resonance line for the observed proton. The other half have the neighbour proton in the β-state, and this change influences the static field at the observed proton if there is a suitable path of bonds linking the two. These molecules therefore contribute a resonance line at a different frequency, with the net result that the signal for the observed proton appears as a *doublet*, consisting of two lines of equal intensity. The argument works equally well in reverse, of course, so the signal for the neighbour proton is also split into a doublet. This is the typical pattern of *first-order* coupling, which is an approximation to reality: the resonances of a pair of coupled protons each split into two lines of equal intensity. Although it is not obvious from the preceding discussion, the nature of the coupling interaction is such that the degree of splitting of the signals of each of the coupling partners is equal. Thus the separation between the lines in either doublet can be measured to give us a parameter known as the *coupling constant J* (Fig. 5.40). This is the physical principle; the chemical application arises because of the dependence of coupling on the presence of bonds.

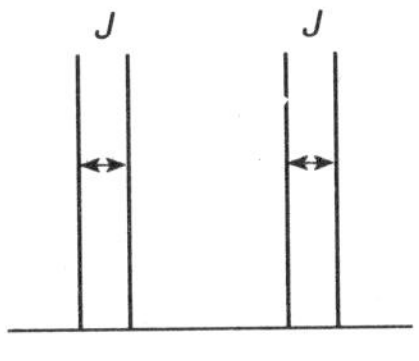

Fig. 5.40 First-order coupling. Each partner in a coupling has its signal split into two lines separated by *J* Hz.

Measuring coupling constants

Just as for chemical shifts, quantitative measurements of coupling constants are required so that they may be correlated with structural features. There is,

Coupling constants between nuclei do not depend on the applied magnetic field

however, a vital distinction. Coupling is an interaction within the molecule under consideration, and as such it is *independent of the applied field*. It is therefore essential to measure coupling constants in terms of the actual frequency differences between lines, which are typically in the range 0–20 Hz for proton–proton couplings. Line separations that arise from coupling must *never* be converted to parts per million, because the result would then vary from one spectrometer to another.

Coupling constants can be measured directly from the spectrum as line separations, *provided that the first-order approximation applies*. This requires that all the chemical shift differences between the coupled protons (measured in hertz) are much larger than all the relevant coupling constants. Guidelines for determining whether first-order analysis is applicable will be presented later. For the moment, it should be noted that increasing the static field increases frequency differences without changing coupling constants, so that first-order analysis is more likely to be possible on spectrometers with stronger magnets. This is one of several motivations for using such instruments.

Coupling constants have sign as well as size

Coupling constants vary in sign as well as in magnitude, which seems a little mysterious, but in fact has a simple physical interpretation. In the discussion so far we have argued that the state of a neighbour proton (α or β) influences the field at the observed proton, and hence causes its resonance to be split into two lines. While the magnitude of J reflects the strength of this effect, the sign of J reflects its direction. Therefore, suppose that for some particular structure it is found that resonances from molecules in which the neighbour protons are α are at higher frequency than those in which the neighbour protons are β. Then in another structure which gives rise to a coupling of opposite sign, the reverse will be true and the β-neighbours will cause resonance at higher frequency. Either circumstance may arise in practice because of the indirect way in which the interaction is relayed through the molecule. Determination of the sign of J generally requires either detailed analysis of complex coupling patterns, or special experimental techniques; therefore it is not normal to obtain this information in routine applications of NMR. However, it is necessary to appreciate that coupling constants have a sign, because substituent effects that increase the coupling constant (in the sense of making it more positive) may make its absolute value (which is what we observe) bigger or smaller according to whether the basic starting value is positive or negative.

Typical coupling patterns

'First-order' splitting patterns

So far we have only considered the interaction between a pair of protons. In realistic chemical structures much more complex patterns of coupling arise, and within the first-order approximation the resulting multiplet patterns can be derived in a straightforward way. Each additional coupling causes further splitting of the lines, so that coupling to one, two or three distinct neighbours

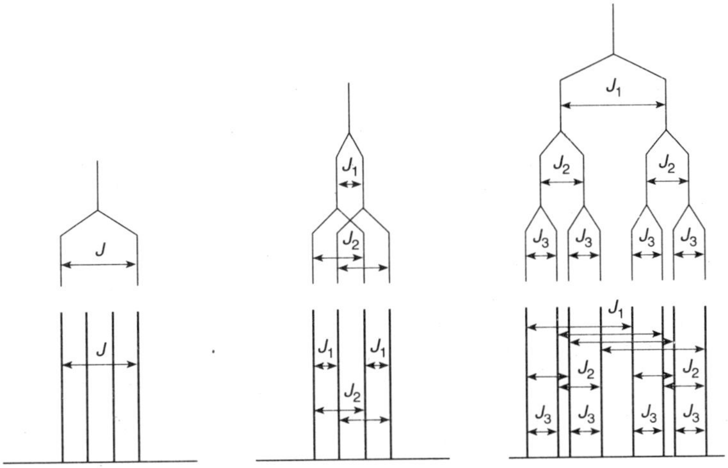

Fig. 5.41 First-order splitting patterns arising from coupling to one, two or three nuclei with distinct coupling constants J_1–J_3.

gives patterns of two, four or eight lines, respectively (Fig. 5.41), and so on for further couplings. The coupling constants can still be obtained directly from the line separations, as indicated in the figure.

The chemical shift of a proton involved in coupling is taken to be the location at which its resonance would be found in the absence of the coupling, or in other words the centre of the multiplet in these first-order cases.

Another common circumstance is equal coupling to two or more protons. This may arise due to accidental equality of certain coupling constants, or out of necessity if several protons are indistinguishable, for example the three protons of a methyl group. The same procedure can be applied to derive the multiplet pattern, but with the difference that some lines are now coincident (Fig. 5.42). There are therefore fewer lines in the multiplet than would be obtained from coupling to an equal number of non-equivalent protons, and the intensities of the lines reflect the number of degenerate transitions that contribute to them. The single coupling constant characteristic of the system is reproduced in each of the line separations.

Coupling to n *equivalent leads to multiplet with* n *+1 lines*

The result of calculating the multiplet patterns can be summarized in a simple rule: coupling to n equivalent protons leads to a multiplet with $n+1$ lines whose relative intensities are given by the $(n+1)$th row of Pascal's triangle:

1
1 1
1 2 1
1 3 3 1
1 4 6 4 1
1 5 10 10 5 1
1 6 15 20 15 6 1

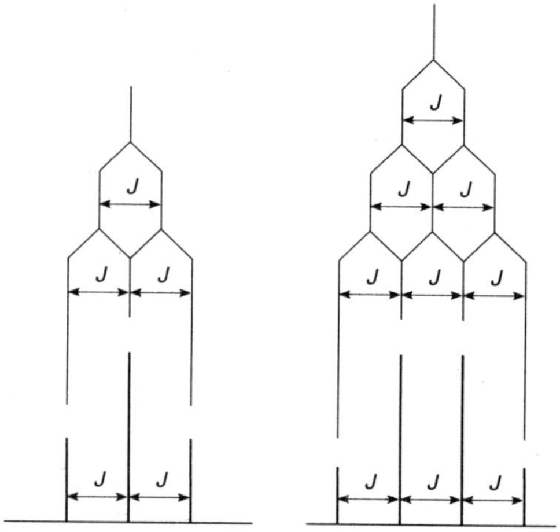

Fig. 5.42 The patterns arising from coupling to two or three equivalent nuclei.

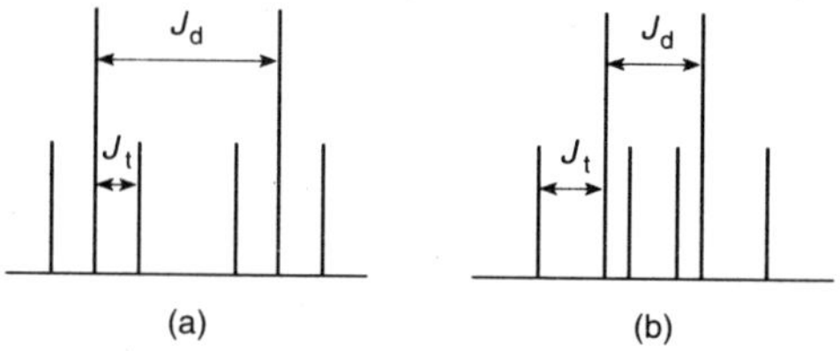

Fig. 5.43 'Double triplet' patterns with the single coupling (a) greater than and (b) less than the sum of the couplings to the two equivalent nuclei.

Cases up to $n = 6$ are easily imagined (e.g. the methine of an isopropyl group). The $n = 2$ and $n = 3$ patterns (1:2:1 triplet and 1:3:3:1 quartet) are extremely common and easily recognized, which makes the identification of ethyl groups, for instance, very straightforward.

The final extension of these ideas to a mixture of coupling of an equivalent group or groups and other non-equivalent couplings follows in a straightforward way. For instance, a proton flanked on one side by a methylene and on the other by a methine may appear as a 'double triplet', in which the disposition of the various components will depend on the relative values of the coupling constants (Fig. 5.43).

Only nuclei which are close neighbours show measurable couplings

With experience it becomes quite easy to pick out characteristic patterns of this kind even in complex spectra. Of course, the patterns presented here are idealized, and on a real spectrometer it will not necessarily be possible to resolve all the different lines expected within a multiplet.

Coupling and chemical structure

Various correlations of the magnitude of J with structural features have been obtained, but the most important fact about coupling can be summarized very simply: *it is only large over paths of two or three bonds*. 'Large' in this context means greater than about 2 Hz. The existence of such a coupling between two protons is a good indication that they are in either a *geminal* or *vicinal* relationship to one another (Fig. 5.44). However, in some circumstances such protons can show small or undetectable coupling, so that the reverse conclusion that pairs of protons which appear not to be coupled are more than three bonds apart cannot be so readily drawn. For structure determination *vicinal* couplings are particularly important, because they define a link between protons attached to two adjacent carbon atoms. Mapping out the relationship between carbon atoms obviously plays a large part in defining the structure of organic molecules.

Vicinal coupling

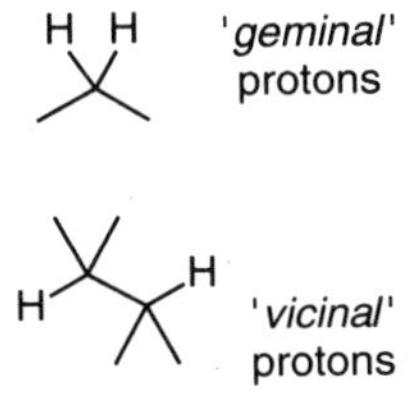

Fig. 5.44 The observation of a 'large' coupling between protons usually indicates that they are in one of these two relationships.

The average value of three-bond proton–proton coupling (^3J) in a freely rotating system (e.g. an ethyl group) is about +7 Hz. This can be modified by substituents attached to the H–C–C–H fragment, the general trend being that electronegative substituents cause a reduction in ^3J. However, this is quite a small effect in saturated systems, the change generally being less than 1 Hz. Much more interesting variations are found in rigid molecules, in which the coupling constant depends on the dihedral and valence angles (ϕ and θ, Fig. 5.45) and the C–C bond length. The dependence on the dihedral angle can be summarized in the *Karplus–Conroy* curve (Fig. 5.46), in which the key features are that the coupling is a maximum for *syn*- and *anti*-periplanar arrangements of the protons (with the latter invariably leading to larger coupling), but falls to a small value for a dihedral angle of about 90°. The H–C–C valence

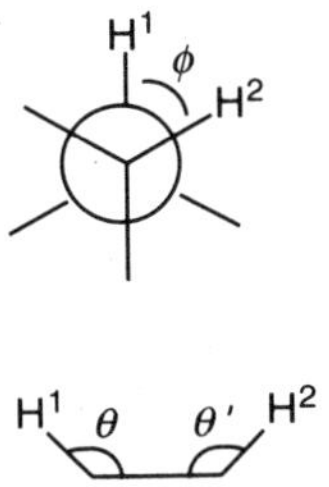

Fig. 5.45 Definition of the dihedral angle ϕ and valence angle θ.

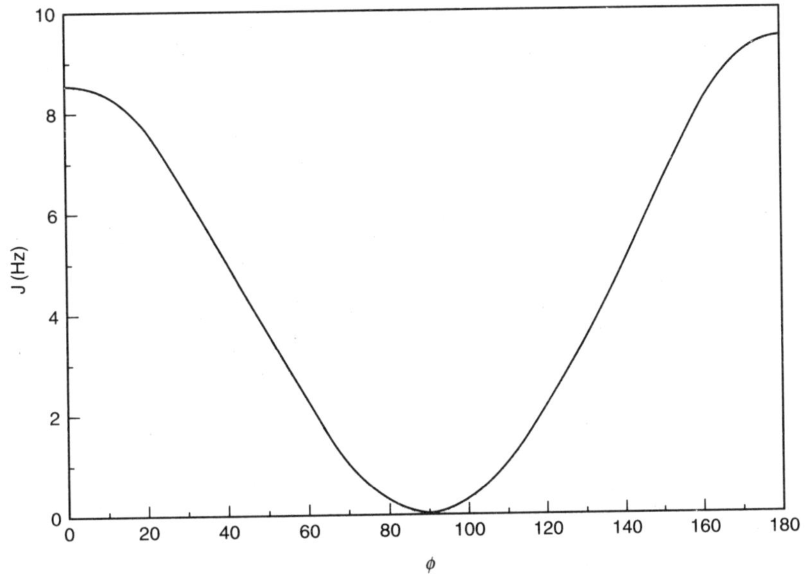

Fig. 5.46 The relationship between vicinal coupling constants and the dihedral angle ϕ. The values of J at $\phi = 0°$ and $\phi = 180°$ may be altered by substituent effects, but the shape of the curve remains the same.

angle dependence is such that larger angles lead to smaller coupling; for instance in acyclic alkenes the coupling between *cis* protons is about 10–12 Hz, whereas for cyclopropenes the widening of the H–C=C angle required by the three-membered ring reduces the coupling to about 1 Hz. An increase in the C–C bond length also leads to a decrease in ^3J.

The form of the Karplus–Conroy curve leads to some very useful applications of ^3J measurements to stereochemical problems. *Cis*- and *trans*-alkenes clearly have H–C=C–H dihedral angles of 0° and 180° respectively, so that it is predicted that the coupling should be larger in *trans* compounds. This is found to be the case in practice, with *cis* couplings typically in the range 9–12 Hz and *trans* couplings in the range 14–16 Hz. Similarly, in rigid cyclohexanes in the chair form, protons in an *axial–axial* relationship invariably show larger coupling than either *axial–equatorial* or *equatorial–equatorial* pairs. Typical values for these and other couplings are given in Table A14 (Appendix 3).

Geminal coupling

Geminal (^2J) coupling constants are found to have a wide range of values between −20 and +40 Hz. However, the most common cases observed in everyday structures are saturated methylene groups, which in the absence of the substituent effects described below, show couplings of around −12 Hz, and terminal alkenes, which show small couplings of around ±2 Hz. The main factors that contribute to the very wide variation in *geminal* coupling are hybridization, substitution by electronegative groups and substitution by π-bonds.

Change in hybridization from sp^3 to sp^2, and the addition of electronegative substituents at the carbon to which the protons are attached, both cause an increase in ^2J, that is, a change *in the positive direction*. Therefore, the *magnitude* of ^2J initially decreases from its basic value of around 12 Hz as these effects come into play, but sufficiently strong influences may eventually cause an increase in magnitude as the value passes beyond zero. For instance, in methylene imines ($RN{=}CH_2$), in which the effects of hybridization and electronegative substitution combine, the ^2J value is +16.5 Hz.

Substitution by adjacent π-bonds and by electronegative substituents β to the carbon to which the protons are attached both cause a decrease in ^2J, that is, a change *in the negative direction*. Therefore the *magnitude* of ^2J is usually increased by these effects in sp^3 hybridized systems, for which the starting value is almost always negative, but may be increased or decreased in the case of sp^2 hybridization.

Long-range coupling

Couplings over more than three bonds are usually less than 2 Hz, but, as we have seen, geminal and vicinal couplings can also fall in this region in some cases. Thus it is important to be able to spot cases in which long-range coupling is likely to occur, and fortunately these can be classified into a few structural types. In saturated systems, significant couplings over four and five bonds are most common when the path of bonds involved is held in a rigid zig-zag arrangement (Fig. 5.47). Four-bond coupling of this kind is often referred to as

Fig. 5.47 The 'W' arrangement of bonds most favourable for four-bond coupling.

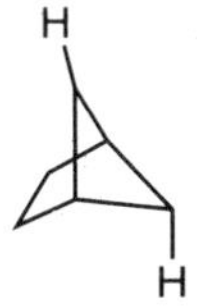

Fig. 5.48 Four-bond coupling may also be large in strained rings.

W coupling, for obvious reasons. If the path of bonds is also in a strained ring system, ^4J values can become quite large, for example around 7 Hz for the indicated protons in bicyclo[2.1.1]hexane (Fig. 5.48).

In unsaturated compounds, four-bond allylic coupling (over the path H–C=C–C–H) of around 1–2 Hz is common. Even when this does not appear as a line splitting, it is often responsible for an increase in line width for groups adjacent to alkenes or aromatic rings. coupling over more than four bonds is often found in conjugated alkenes, because such substances naturally tend to adopt the favourable 'W' arrangement.

Connecting up couplings

The interpretation of the values of coupling constants in the light of the effects described above is really a rather specialized aspect of this part of NMR. For the purposes of structure determination it is sufficient to check that the coupling under investigation is the right size to be a short-range (^2J or ^3J) effect. The problem then is to work out which signal elsewhere in the spectrum is due to the proton responsible for the coupling, so that its couplings can be examined in turn in order to continue the chain of assignments. In a simple molecule this may be a trivial question; for instance, in ethyl acetate the methyl and methylene of the ethyl group are the only participants in coupling, and this is immediately obvious from the spectrum. In general, however, connecting up the couplings is the major difficulty to be overcome in interpreting NMR spectra.

Coupled nuclei must show a common coupling constant

One obvious way to tackle this problem is to use the fact that the splittings at each end of a coupling have to be equal. Therefore if it is required to find which proton is responsible for a 6 Hz splitting in a multiplet, then the rest of the spectrum can be searched for a matching splitting. There are two limitations to this approach: it cannot be guaranteed that the other part of the coupling will give rise to a readily identifiable multiplet in a complex spectrum, and since coupling constants only have a fairly narrow range of values, the likelihood of confusion with other couplings is high. Because of these difficulties, considerable attention has been paid to the discovery of experimental methods for identifying coupling partners unambiguously. The traditional solution to this problem, known as *homonuclear decoupling* will be described here, while a more recent and extremely powerful alternative method based on *two-dimensional NMR* is introduced briefly on pp. 354–355.

The essence of the homonuclear decoupling experiment is that the coupling of one proton is 'deactivated' by continuous irradiation at its resonance frequency during the measurement of the NMR spectrum. You can think of this irradiation as bringing about constant, rapid transitions between the α- and β-states of the proton to be decoupled, so that the distinction between the two is effectively lost. All the splittings due to this proton elsewhere in the spectrum then disappear, so that comparison of the spectra obtained with and without decoupling allows the coupling partners to be identified immediately (Fig. 5.49). The limitations of this technique are that a new experiment is needed for each signal in the spectrum, and practical difficulties may be

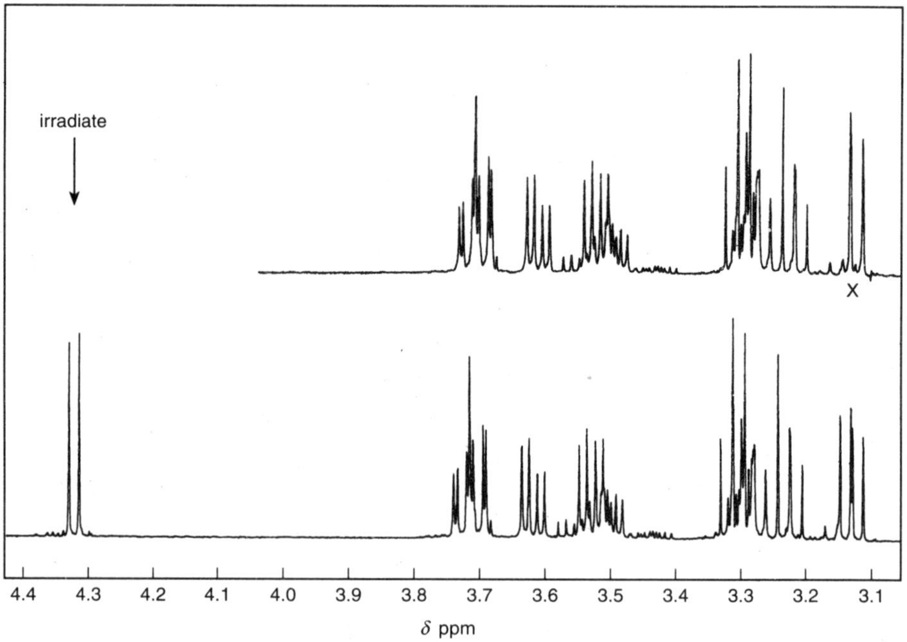

Fig. 5.49 Use of homonuclear decoupling to identify coupling partners in a complex spectrum. The lower trace is the normal spectrum, while in the top trace the doublet at δ4.32 has been irradiated during the acquisition, causing one splitting to disappear from a double doublet at δ3.13 (marked X in the top trace).

encountered in achieving selective irradiation of a signal resonance or in identifying the resulting changes in a complex spectrum. These problems are absent from the two-dimensional experiment described later.

Failure of the first-order model

The very simple model we have used to explain coupling patterns so far works well as long as all the shift differences involved in the spin system are much larger than all the coupling constants. When this ceases to be true, care is needed to avoid drawing incorrect conclusions from the appearance of multiplets. The essential character of the first-order approximation is that it attributes each line in the spectrum to a transition of a single nucleus. When the magnitude of the coupling interaction becomes comparable with chemical shift differences this is no longer true, and the lines in the spectrum arise because of transitions involving mixtures of the wave functions of all the nuclei involved in the spin system. It is not appropriate to discuss the theoretical basis of this process here, but it is essential to appreciate the important consequences of it, which are as follows.

1 *Peak intensities no longer follow the first-order rules of Pascal's triangle.*

2 *Line separations are not necessarily equal to coupling constants.*

3 *Chemical shifts are not necessarily at the centre of multiplets.*

Chemical shifts and coupling constants can still be extracted from spectra which deviate from first-order coupling, but a more detailed analysis is necessary. This can be done by hand for small spin systems, and for more complex cases computer programs are available that make the process essentially routine. However, for most straightforward chemical applications there is no particular need to extract these parameters; the essential thing is to avoid measuring line separations and calling them coupling constants when they are not. Therefore you need to be able to recognize the symptoms of deviation from first-order coupling, and these can be illustrated with a few common cases.

For first-order splitting $\Delta\delta \geqslant 10\Delta J$

The first-order model begins to fail when the smallest shift differences in a spin system are about 10 times the largest coupling constants. For instance, on a 60 MHz spectrometer, shift differences of less than about 1.5 ppm are likely to give rise to breakdown of the first-order approximation, while at 500 MHz peaks as little as 0.2 ppm apart may still show first-order coupling. As shifts fall below this point, the position, intensity and number of lines in the spectrum may change. For instance, for two coupled protons the first-order model predicts two doublets, with equal intensity for all four lines. As the shift difference between the protons falls, a quantum-mechanical calculation predicts that the inner pair of lines should grow in intensity at the expense of the outer pair, until, as the shifts coincide, the outer lines disappear completely, leaving a single resonance for the two protons (Fig. 5.50). This behaviour is confirmed in

Two-spin systems

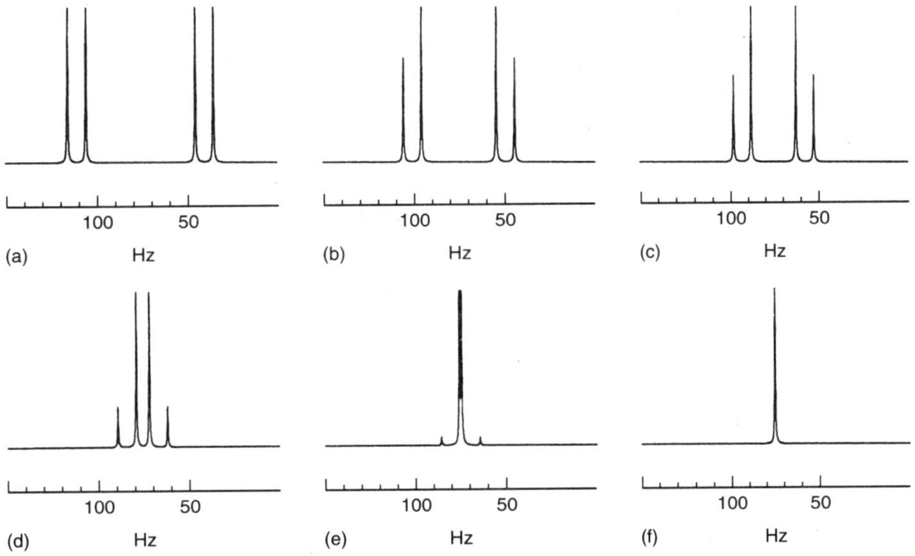

Fig. 5.50 The progressive change from an AX pattern (a), through various AB quartets, to a single line for two equivalent protons (f). The spectra were simulated with $J_{AX} = 10$ Hz and $\delta_A - \delta_B$ varied in the sequence: (a) effectively infinite (forced X approximation), (b) 50 Hz, (c) 34 Hz, (d) 14 Hz, (e) 5 Hz, (f) 0 Hz.

practice. In this simple case the line separation (between each of the outer pairs of lines) remains equal to J, but the chemical shifts move from the centre of each of the doublets to their 'centres of gravity' with respect to the unequal peak heights. The 'slope' of the multiplets towards each other, known as the *roof effect*, is quite characteristic of breakdown of the first-order model, and in addition aids in locating the coupling partner by examination of the direction of slope.

It might be supposed that limitless possibilities exist for coupling patterns once the first-order restriction has been removed. In fact, a surprising number of real cases can be related to only a few typical patterns. To aid in categorizing these patterns, a notation has been developed that expresses the character of the spin system independently of the specific values of shifts and coupling constants. In this notation, the first-order two-spin case is described as an AX system. The choice of letters at opposite ends of the alphabet indicates first-order coupling. As the first-order approximation fails, letters next to each other are selected, so the characteristic four-line pattern with the inner lines stronger than the outer lines is referred to as an AB quartet. Once the shifts coincide, the system degenerates to A_2. The disappearance of the outer lines as the system changes from AB to A_2 illustrates a general principle that equivalent nuclei cannot show any splitting due to their mutual coupling (but see the discussion of chemical and magnetic equivalence later, to find out what 'equivalent' really means).

Three-spin systems

The three-spin case in which all shift differences are small relative to the coupling constants (an ABC system) leads to rather complicated splitting patterns. However, it is very common to encounter situations in which two nuclei are close in shift, while one is substantially different: the ABX system. Figure 5.51 illustrates the variation in both the 'AB part' and the 'X part' of such a spectrum as a function of the shift difference between A and B.

An interesting feature of these spectra is the rather harmless appearance of the X signal, which in most cases looks like a simple double doublet. **Beware!** The line separations in this multiplet are not necessarily equal to coupling constants, as is clear in this case since the spectra have all been simulated with $J_{BX} = 0$. Only the top spectrum shows the patterns that would be predicted, apart from the roof effect in the AB part, by the first-order model.

Some of the AB patterns look as if each of the two protons is split by proton X (for example, spectra (b) and (c) in Fig. 5.51), but this is completely untrue. In addition, for some values of the AB shift difference, the AB part of the spectrum has rather few strong lines. In a real spectrum, in which the weak outer lines might easily be lost in noise or under other signals, such patterns can be quite confusing. This effect is referred to as *deceptive simplicity*. Clearly you must watch out for this, because it is very easy to draw false conclusions.

Beware of deceptively simple multiplets

A particularly subtle cause of failure of the first-order rules arises when protons have the same shift but still cannot be regarded as equivalent from an NMR point of view. To appreciate this, consider the difference between the

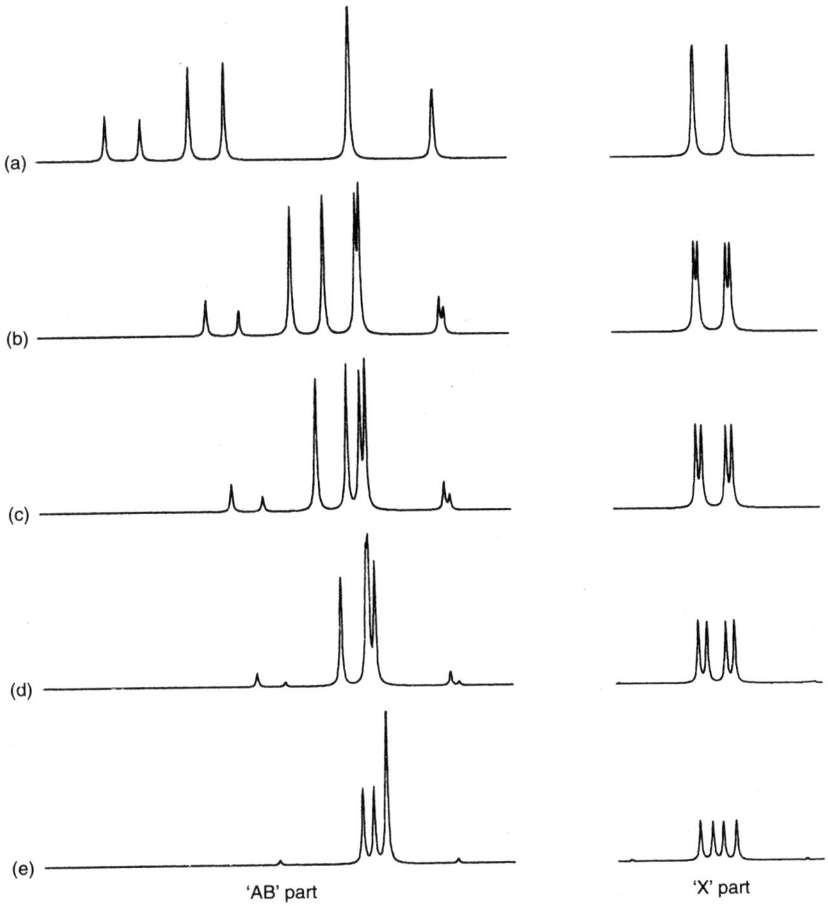

Fig. 5.51 Simulated ABX spectra with the following parameters: $J_{AB} = 16$ Hz, $J_{AX} = 7$ Hz, $J_{BX} = 0$ Hz. $\delta_A - \delta_B$ was varied in the sequence: (a) 40 Hz, (b) 20 Hz, (c) 15 Hz, (d) 10 Hz, (e) 5 Hz.

protons in a methyl group and the 2 and 6 protons of a 1,4-disubstituted benzene ring (Fig. 5.52). In both cases the chemical shifts of the groups of protons have to be the same by symmetry, so they can be described as *chemically equivalent*. However, to be *truly* equivalent, from the perspective of NMR, *all* their magnetic interactions (both shifts and couplings) have to be the same. Now, for the methyl group this will certainly be so, since any coupling experienced by one of the three protons will also be experienced by the others. The methyl protons are thus *magnetically equivalent*, and an adjacent proton widely differing in shift will be split into a quartet in accord with the first-order rules.

Chemical and magnetic equivalence

For the pair of protons on the aromatic ring the situation is quite different. Consider the interaction of the 2 and 6 protons with proton 3. For the 2 proton this is a three-bond relationship, so the coupling constant will be fairly large;

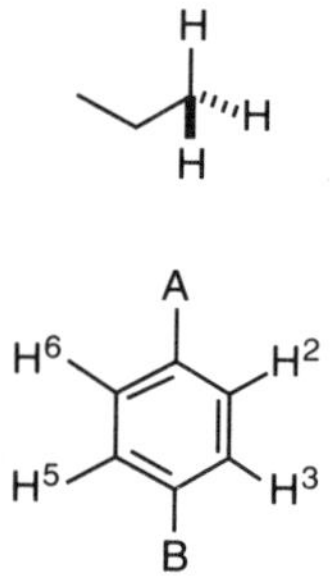

Fig. 5.52 Protons of a methyl group are both chemically and magnetically equivalent, but the protons of 1,4-disubstituted benzene rings are magnetically inequivalent, even though the chemical shifts of the pairs of protons (H_2, H_6) and (H_3, H_5) must be the same.

however, for proton 6 it is a five-bond coupling. Thus their interactions *are not identical*. The situation is not ameliorated by the fact that the 6–5 coupling must equal the 2–3 coupling; magnetic equivalence requires that *all* interactions to each other magnetic nucleus *treated individually* must be equal. In the letter notation, magnetically inequivalent protons are distinguished by use of a prime (′); therefore, assuming a large shift difference between the 2,6 and 3,5 positions, this case would be described as an AA′XX′ system. The calculated spectrum (Fig. 5.53) is radically different from that of either an A_2X_2 system (two triplets) or a pair of superimposed AX systems (two doublets), either of which might have been suggested to model this case had the magnetic inequivalence not been recognized.

The moral of this section is that care is needed to avoid false interpretation of NMR spectra. This is especially true for spectra obtained at low field, which are exactly the type that you are likely to need to interpret in your first encounters with NMR. Things become much easier with higher fields, although, of course, the complexity of the problems being tackled usually increases proportionately.

Working with ¹H NMR

Even if you nave read the previous pages assiduously, you are probably still at a loss as to how to proceed when actually faced with a spectrum for the first time. The purpose of this section is to demonstrate the analysis of proton spectra using a couple of examples. In one case we will assume that the structure is already known, so that the object of the exercise is just to assign the peaks. This is a very common requirement, for instance, when checking the spectrum of a starting material. For the second example we will try to work out the structure from the spectrum.

Figure 5.54 is the 250 MHz FT spectrum of 4-(1-methylpropyl)phenol. The

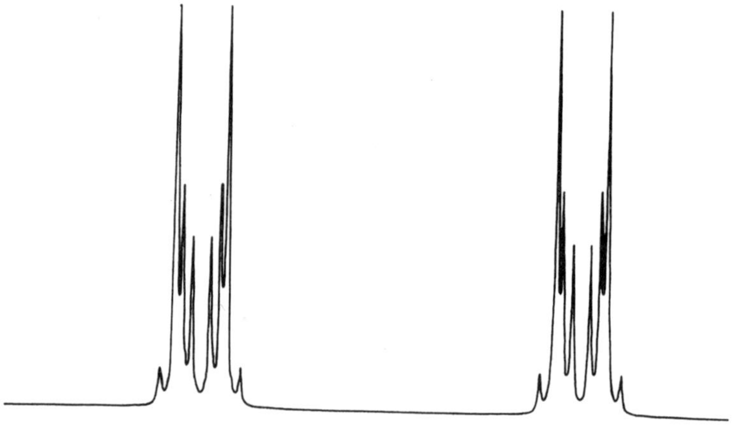

Fig. 5.53 Simulated AA′XX′ spectrum with $J_{AX} = J_{A'X'} = 7$ Hz, $J_{AA'} = J_{XX'} = 2.5$ Hz, $J_{AX'} = J_{A'X} = 1$ Hz (typical for a 1,4-disubstituted aromatic ring).

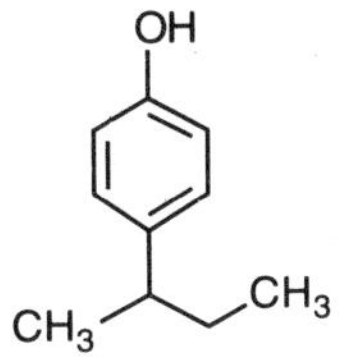

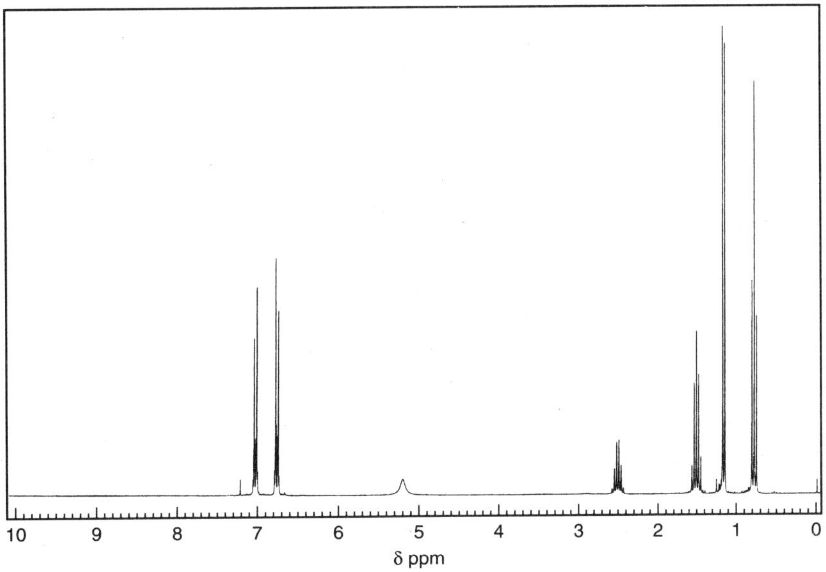

Fig. 5.54 The first example spectrum: 4-(1-methylpropyl)phenol.

first thing to do in assigning this spectrum is to split it into sections corresponding to groups of protons, either mentally or by drawing lines on the chart. The obvious groups in this case are centred on δ 6.90, 5.90, 2.55, 1.50, 1.15 and 0.80. From the integration (which is not reproduced in the figure), the number of protons contributing to each group can then be determined, as follows:

δ6.90: 4H, δ5.90: 1H, δ2.55: 1H, δ1.50: 2H, δ1.15: 3H, δ0.80: 3H

In this simple compound the assignments can be made rapidly on the basis of shifts, and then confirmed by examination of the coupling patterns. The peaks at δ 6.90 must be due to the four aromatic protons, whereas the single, broad resonance at δ 5.90 is in the typical region for phenolic hydroxyl protons. Of the remaining aliphatic resonances, the two 3H groups should presumably correspond to the methyls. Indeed they are at a low chemical shift, whereas the methine adjacent to the aromatic ring is shifted to high frequency and the methylene falls somewhere in between. It is also reasonable that the methyl nearer the aromatic ring (which must be the δ 1.15 doublet) is found to have a larger shift than that in the ethyl group.

Finally, we should examine the coupling patterns. The aromatic protons form an AA′BB′ system, which typically leads to a spectrum with four strong lines and a number of weaker ones. One of the methyl resonances is a triplet and the other a doublet, in accord with the structure. The methine is split into six lines as it is adjacent to methyl and methylene groups. The methylene resonance partly overlaps with the δ 1.15 methyl, but it is still possible to discern four of the five lines that it would be expected to show on a first-order analysis. However, there are also signs of other partially resolved splittings (e.g. the lump on the side of the second line from the left), so it is best to attribute this peak as a *multiplet*, a term which implies no commitment as to the exact pattern of coupling. If you wanted a formal record of this assignment, you might then present it like this: δ (250 MHz, $CDCl_3$) 6.90 (4H, AA′BB′, Ar), 5.90 (1H, s, br, ArO$\underline{H}$), 2.55 (1H, sext., *J* 7 Hz, $CH_3C\underline{H}CH_2$), 1.50 (2H, m, $CHC\underline{H}_2CH_3$), 1.15 (3H, d, *J* 7 Hz, $C\underline{H}_3CHCH_2$), 0.80 (3H, t, *J* 7 Hz, $CHCH_2C\underline{H}_3$). The abbreviations in the parentheses are: d, doublet; t, triplet; sext. sextet; m, multiplet; s, br, broad singlet (see pp. 403–404 for more details on the recording of NMR data in notebook form).

For the spectrum of an unknown, such as Fig. 5.55, we initially proceed in the same way and split the signals into groups. In this case there are clearly discernible multiplets centred on δ 4.20, 3.75, 3.50, 2.60 and 1.20 (once again the integration is not reproduced in the figure, but these were found to have relative intensities 1 : 1 : 1 : 1 : 3). Next, we need to decide what structural fragments might give rise to each group. The signal at δ 1.20 is most likely due to a methyl group (or groups—remember we only have the relative numbers of protons at present), while the remaining signals are probably various methylenes or methines. In addition, all the other signals have quite large shifts to high frequency, implying that these groups are adjacent to electron-withdrawing sub-

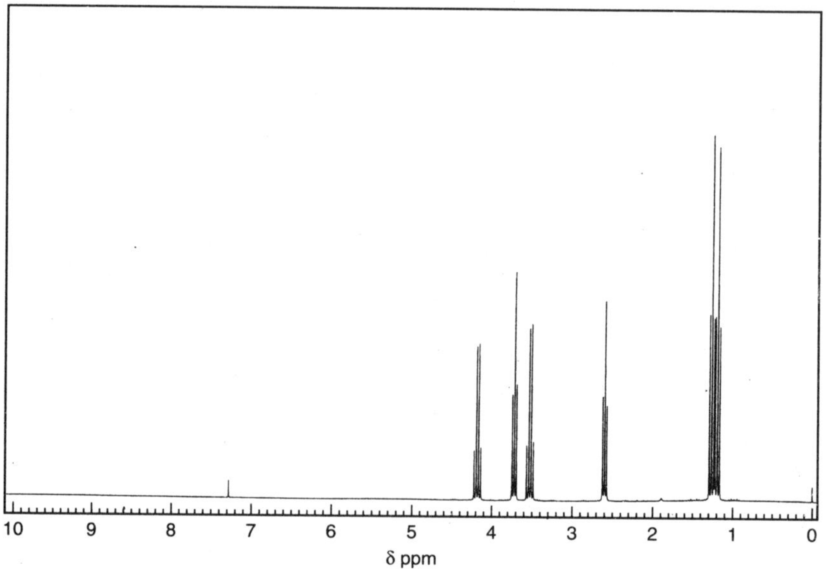

Fig. 5.55 Spectrum of an unknown compound (250 MHz).

stituents. The three groups at δ 4.20, δ 3.75 and δ 3.50 are, in fact, at such high frequency that the protons that give rise to them must almost certainly be directly adjacent to an electronegative atom such as oxygen or chlorine.

This is about as far as we can go without risking over-interpretation of the data; the next thing to do is to take account of any other available information. The formula of this compound, obtained from its mass spectrum, is $C_7H_{14}O_3$, and IR spectroscopy shows the presence of an ester carbonyl. The formula implies one double-bond equivalent, taken up by the carbonyl, so there will be no further unsaturation or rings. The formula also tells us that the actual number of protons contributing to each peak is double the relative number obtained from integration. We now have to take the plunge and come up with a possible structure. With the additional knowledge that the multiplet at δ 1.20 is due to two methyl groups we can go a little further with the identification of structural fragments. Examining the δ 1.20 resonance closely, it can be seen to consist of two overlapping triplets. Thus, we must have two ethyl fragments in the structure and we need to look for the corresponding methylene signals which are visible as quartets at δ 4.20 and δ 3.50. Given that both the ethyl CH_2 groups are at high frequency, we can assume two CH_3CH_2O– subunits in the molecule, one of which is presumably part of the ester (because there are only three oxygens in the formula altogether), giving CH_3CH_2O– and –$COOCH_2CH_3$ fragments so far. This leaves only –CH_2CH_2– to accommodate, and clearly the only way these fragments can be put together is as ethyl 3-ethoxypropanoate.

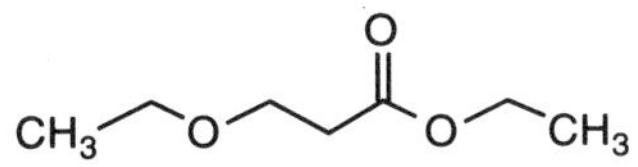

ethyl 3-ethoxypropanoate

With this structure in mind, we can make some further sense of the spectrum. The triplet at δ 2.60 must be due to the CH_2 adjacent to the carbonyl, because of its shift. The other CH_2 triplet at δ 3.75 corresponds to a CH_2 adjacent to an oxygen. This relationship also explains why the two CH_2 groups couple with each other but with no other groups. Therefore everything is quite consistent with the proposed structure. This is a very simple example, but it illustrates the three main stages of structure elucidation.

1 *Make initial inferences from the spectra (NMR, IR, UV, MS).*
2 *Assemble the fragments into candidate structures.*
3 *Check the candidates against a more detailed analysis of the spectra.*

In realistic cases the second stage is the most difficult, and it is here that the connectivity information available from the detection of coupling in NMR spectra is extremely useful. In our simple example there was only one way the fragments could fit together, but in general this will not be so, and it will be necessary to use coupling patterns to help to decide on the right combinations of fragments.

^{13}C NMR

Since only 1.1% of natural carbon consists of ^{13}C, the character of ^{13}C NMR spectroscopy is considerably different from that ^{1}H NMR. The first striking difference is that sensitivity is much lower: use of FT NMR and signal averag-

Obtaining ^{13}C NMR spectra requires more sample than for ^{1}H NMR spectra

In 'natural abundance' spectra C–C coupling is not visible

ing is essential for the detection of ^{13}C, and even then, sample quantities need to be about 10 times greater than for proton observation. The low proportion of the NMR-active isotope also means that homonuclear coupling is not observed; it certainly exists, but the probability of finding two adjacent ^{13}C nuclei is negligible. Therefore the information content of basic ^{13}C spectra is limited to carbon chemical shifts and the coupling with ^{1}H—*heteronuclear coupling*. This section surveys briefly how these can be exploited.

Coupling to protons has a major and in some ways undesirable effect on ^{13}C spectra. The ^{1}J values for directly attached protons are large (135–210 Hz), whereas ^{2}J and ^{3}J values are generally in the 0–15 Hz range. Carbon atoms in average organic structures are often within two or three bonds of a considerable number of protons, so that the heteronuclear coupling leads to extensive splitting of the carbon lines. This, in turn, complicates the spectrum, especially since the large ^{1}J couplings tend to cause multiplets to overlap, and it also degrades sensitivity. It is therefore usual to remove completely coupling with the protons by use of *broad-band proton decoupling*. This is essentially similar to the homonuclear decoupling described on pp. 333–334, but with suitable adjustments to the irradiation method to make the effect non-selective. The peaks in carbon spectra obtained under conditions of broad-band proton decoupling consist of sharp, single lines (Fig. 5.56), from which the chemical shifts can easily be determined.

Carbon chemical shifts follow very similar trends to those of protons, but the range of δ values involved is larger (about 0–200 ppm). A very useful rule

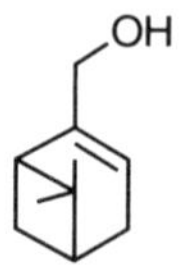

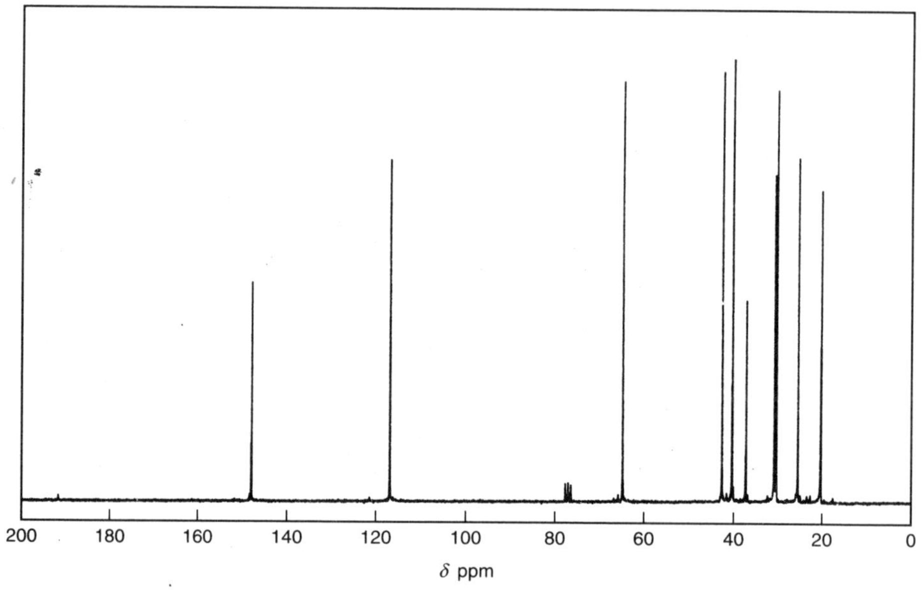

Fig. 5.56 ^{13}C spectrum (with broadband proton decoupling) of myrtenol. The small signal at δ77 is due to the solvent, $CDCl_3$; it is split into three lines because of the coupling to deuterium ($I = 1$).

$\delta^{13}C \approx 20\delta^{1}H$

of thumb to aid interpreting ^{13}C shifts is that they are about 20 times greater than the shifts of protons in analogous environments. So, for example, the alkene region of ^{1}H spectra is around δ 5, whereas in ^{13}C spectra it is in the region of δ 100. Since the relative chemical shift range is 20 times larger than that of ^{1}H, while the actual carbon frequency is only four times smaller in the same static field, the absolute shift range (in hertz) is also large. This, together with the freedom from coupling, means that even complex molecules yield well-resolved ^{13}C spectra, in which each distinct carbon site contributes a single peak to the spectrum. It is therefore often possible to use the ^{13}C spectrum to count the number of carbons in a molecule. Unfortunately, for technical reasons related to the use of signal averaging and broad-band proton decoupling, the peak intensities in ^{13}C spectra, obtained under normal conditions, do not reflect the number of contributing nuclei, so that identification of groups of equivalent nuclei is not so straightforward as in ^{1}H NMR.

Signal intensities in ^{13}C spectra do not reflect number of carbons

A very useful classification of the resonances in a ^{13}C spectrum according to the number of protons attached to each carbon can be obtained in any of several ways. A crude method identified *quaternary* carbons on the grounds that their resonances are usually weaker than those of proton-bearing nuclei; for example, the peaks at δ 148 and δ 37 in Fig. 5.56. This is clearly a rather vague criterion, but nevertheless it can be helpful in the everyday interpretation of ^{13}C spectra. More well-defined information can be obtained either by the *off-resonance decoupling* experiment, or by *spectrum editing*.

Quaternary carbons give low intensity signals

Off-resonance ^{13}C spectra show couplings to attached protons

Off-resonance decoupling was the original technique used to determine the number of protons attached to each carbon, and involves *partial* decoupling of protons, such that the two- and three-bond couplings are more or less removed, whereas the one-bond couplings are scaled down to a manageable value. Peaks then appear as singlets, doublets, triplets or quartets according to whether they are due to quaternary, methine, methylene or methyl carbons respectively (Fig. 5.57).

The sensitivity of this experiment is rather low, because of the splitting and broadening of the lines, and in complex spectra identification of the multiplicities may not be straightforward. It is also vital to realize that the line separations in an off-resonance proton-decoupled ^{13}C spectrum *do not equal* $^{1}J_{HC}$; the splittings are scaled down by some unknown factor.

In the more recently developed and vastly superior spectrum editing technique, actual subspectra containing only resonances due to methine, methylene or methyl carbons are obtained (Fig. 5.58). Quaternary carbons can be identified in the original spectrum by elimination, on assignment of all the other resonances, or by some separate technique. The mechanism of this experiment is too subtle to describe here, but the major advantage is that the spectra are obtained with broad-band decoupling, so that sensitivity and resolution are not compromised.

Because of the lack of homonuclear coupling information, ^{13}C NMR does not play such a prominent role as ^{1}H NMR in routine chemical applications.

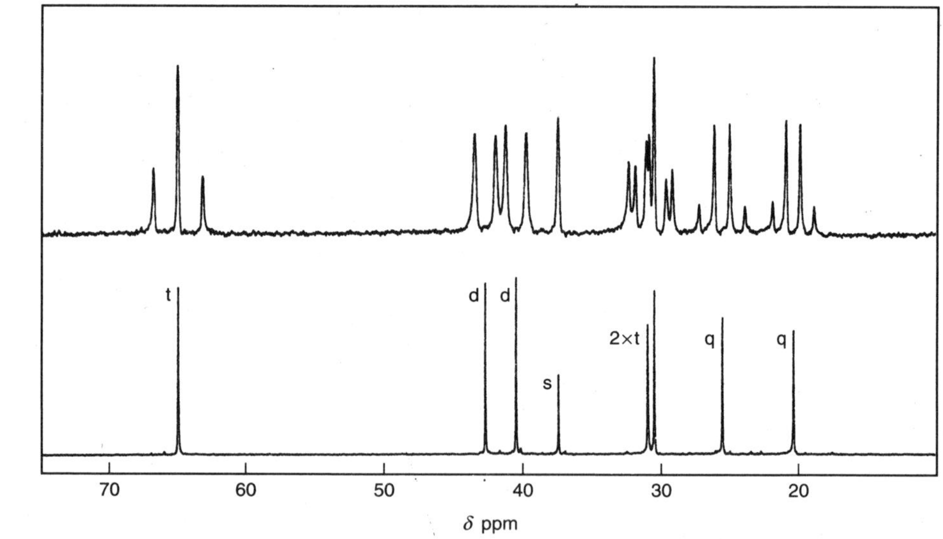

Fig. 5.57 Low frequency part of the ^{13}C spectrum of myrtenol, with broadband (bottom) and off-resonance (top) proton decoupling. The assignment of the peaks as singlets, doublets, etc. is mostly obvious, but even in this simple compound the off-resonance experiment is not totally clear. The result for the two peaks near δ31 is confused by the fact that their multiplets overlap in the off-resonance experiment, and one of the two does not appear as a clean triplet owing to a large shift difference between its attached protons.

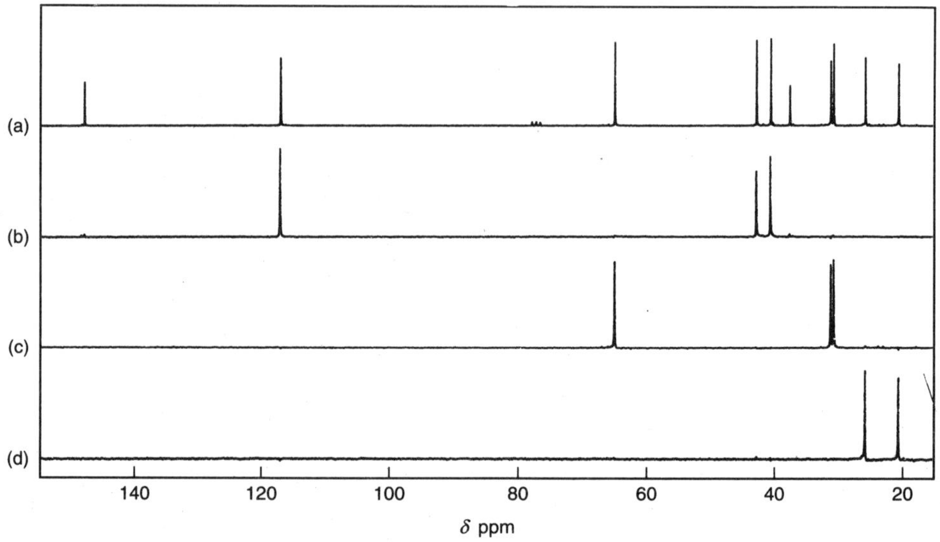

Fig. 5.58 Spectrum editing applied to the spectrum of myrtenol. (a) Normal ^{13}C spectrum acquired with broad-band proton decoupling; (b) CH carbons; (c) CH_2 carbons; (d) CH_3 carbons. Quaternary carbons (including that of the solvent $CDCl_3$, as its protons have been replaced by deuterium) do not appear in the edited spectra.

The determination of the numbers of different types of carbons is probably the most useful aspect of the technique in this area. However, in more advanced structure determination, and particularly in conjunction with two-dimensional techniques, the ability of ^{13}C NMR to resolve distinct peaks for each carbon in the majority of complex molecules becomes extremely important.

Further features of NMR

Why are the peaks in the spectrum of this amide broad?

Because the frequency differences involved in NMR are so small, some quite surprising things can happen to the spectra when nuclei do not wait around long enough for us to measure their resonances. This effect has already been mentioned briefly on p. 323 (in the discussion of protons on heteroatoms), but because it is both puzzling and useful it warrants a little further discussion. The essential principle is that to discriminate between resonances separated by F Hz, it is necessary to be able to make the measurement for at least $1/F$ s. Now, in IR spectroscopy, for instance, where the frequency differences involved are of the order of 10^{12}–10^{14} Hz (tens to thousands of cm^{-1}), this does not impose much of a condition on the length of the measurement. Things are quite different for NMR, in which it might be necessary for a nucleus to maintain exactly the same resonance frequency for a second or more in order for us to be able to make an adequate measurement.

Therefore processes with a time scale in the millisecond to second range can significantly affect NMR spectra. Most overall molecular motions (translations, rotations, etc.) occur much faster than this in solution, so that we see averaged spectra with respect to them. However, some internal motions, such as certain conformational changes and a wide variety of chemical reactions, do occur on this *NMR time scale*.

Exchanging systems — 'dynamic' NMR

It is helpful to distinguish three rate regimes in terms of their effects on the NMR spectrum. If a process interchanging a nucleus between two environments in which it has NMR frequencies differing by F Hz occurs with a rate constant k much greater than F s^{-1}, then a completely averaged spectrum is obtained and the effect of the process is concealed. Conversely, if the rate constant is much less than F, there are effectively two distinct species in the solution, each with its own characteristic signal. Once again, the existence of the exchange process is not immediately apparent from the spectrum. In between, when k and F are comparable, a kind of partial averaging arises, leading to broadening of the lines. If the rate is varied, for instance by varying the temperature, it is possible to observe the transition between the three types of spectrum (Fig. 5.59).

Analysis of the line shapes in the *intermediate exchange* regime is a very powerful method for obtaining rate constants of processes that are too fast to investigate by more conventional means, but this is too specialized an applica-

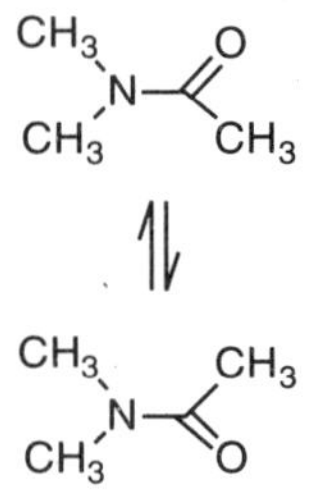

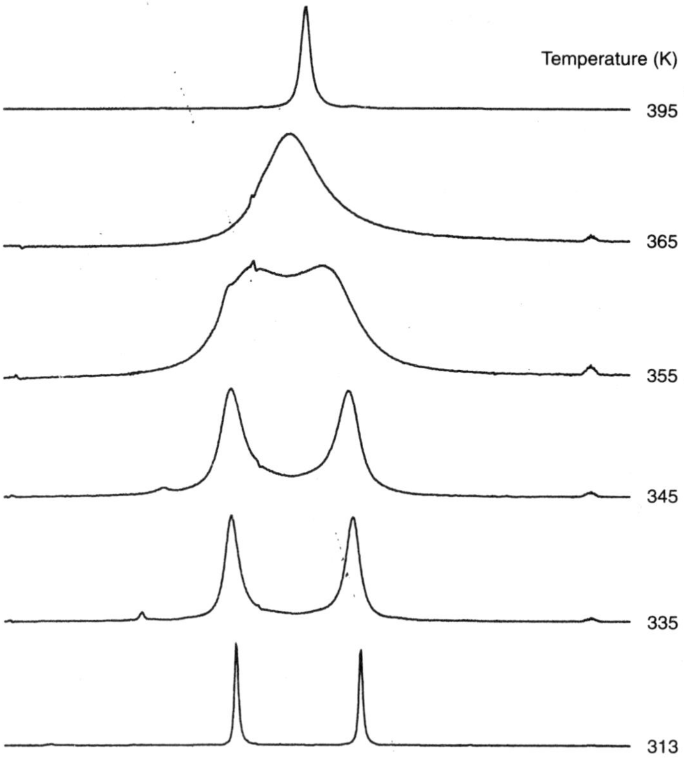

Fig. 5.59 Proton spectra of the *N*-methyl groups of *N*, *N*-dimethylacetamide. As the temperature is increased, the rate of rotation about the C–N bond becomes comparable with the frequency difference between the peaks, they gradually broaden and coalesce, and eventually an averaged spectrum is obtained.

tion to discuss here. However, you will need to be able to spot the effects of exchange and to understand how they vary according to the spectrometer field strength, sample temperature and observed nucleus. All these follow naturally from the relationship between the frequency difference between the exchanging sites, the rate of exchange and the appearance of the spectrum. So, for instance, a spectrum that appears broad on a low field spectrometer may become sharp (with double the number of peaks) at high field, because the peak separations have been increased, while the rate of the exchange process remains constant. You might like to compare this change with photography of a humming bird: with a slow film, and hence long exposure time, the wings appear blurred, but on changing to a fast film and shortening the exposure they can be photographed in the extreme positions of the wing beat.

Similarly, a compound may quite easily have a broad proton spectrum but show perfectly sharp peaks for ^{13}C, or vice versa, because the peak separations are different for the two nuclei. Some peaks in the spectrum can be doubled, some broadened and some unaffected, according to the different influences that the exchange process has on their chemical shifts. When you are not concerned with rate measurements, these broadening effects can be quite annoying, since they make the spectrum hard to interpret. They are common for acidic protons, as mentioned on p. 323. Problems may also sometimes arise as a result of conformational changes: rotations about single bonds are usually fast on the NMR time scale, but a common exception to this, which explains the title to this section, is found for amides. Here the partial double-bond character of the amide bond raises the barrier to rotation and makes the process sufficiently slow so that it often causes peak doubling or broadening in NMR spectra. If a properly resolved spectrum is required in such a case, then it is necessary to change to either slow or fast exchange (preferably the latter, because then there will only be one set of peaks in the spectrum). This can be achieved by altering the temperature, or by changing to a spectrometer of different field strength (lowering the field strength is equivalent in its effect to raising the temperature).

Exchange can also have an indirect broadening effect on nuclei via coupling. For instance, when acidic protons are broadened by exchange amongst themselves or with water in the sample, this process clearly will not affect the chemical shift of any other protons in the molecule and so will not change their line shapes directly. However, protons coupled to the exchanging proton may be influenced in a way that can be understood as follows. Imagine a proton adjacent to an OH group; its signal is split by the *vicinal* coupling into the usual kind of doublet, one line arising from molecules in which the hydroxyl proton is α and the other from molecules in which the hydroxyl proton is β. When the hydroxyl is exchanged, the replacement proton has an equal chance of being α or β, so that molecules which had been contributing to one of the doublet components may find themselves contributing to the other after the exchange. There is, in effect, an internal exchange going on between the two lines of the doublet, and if the rate constant is much greater than their separation the coupling will be lost. The rapid averaging of the α- and β- states is akin to the effect of the homonuclear decoupling experiment described on pp. 333–334, and the result is the same: the doublet collapses to a singlet. At intermediate exchange rates the lines of the doublet are broadened, and in practice it is quite common to see this effect for nuclei coupled to acidic protons.

Other useful techniques

Useful extra information can often be obtained from NMR spectra by performing simple tests or chemical reactions directly on the sample. For instance, the fact that acidic protons (e.g. those in hydroxyl or amino groups) exchange rapidly with water can be used to aid in their assignment. After obtaining a proton spectrum, a small amount of D_2O (1–2 drops) is mixed with the sample. For solvents which are not completely miscible with water the sample should be shaken vigorously and then allowed to stand for a few moments to separate. The spectrum is then re-run, and since the acidic protons will have been replaced by deuterium, their peaks should have disappeared

D_2O exchange

(Fig. 5.60). Amines, alcohols and carboxylic acids usually exchange instantly when treated in this way, while amides exchange slowly or not at all. Amide signals can be located in a further experiment, by adding a trace of base to the sample (e.g. a drop of sodium deuteroxide solution, prepared by dissolving sodium in D_2O—***care!***). A side effect of the D_2O exchange experiment is the removal of the line broadening effect due to coupling with acidic protons (described at the end of the previous section), and it may sometimes be desirable to perform the exchange solely for this reason.

Acylation

Another straightforward technique also uses the presence of hydroxyl and amino groups to aid in making assignments. After obtaining the original spectrum, the sample is treated with an excess of trifluoroacetic anhydride (**care!**—in practice a few drops should be sufficient). This reagent is highly reactive, and will usually acylate primary and secondary amines and alcohols almost instantly. In addition, it does not contribute extra resonances to the spectrum, but because of the powerful electron-withdrawing character of the

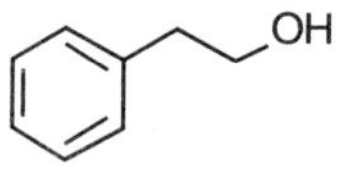

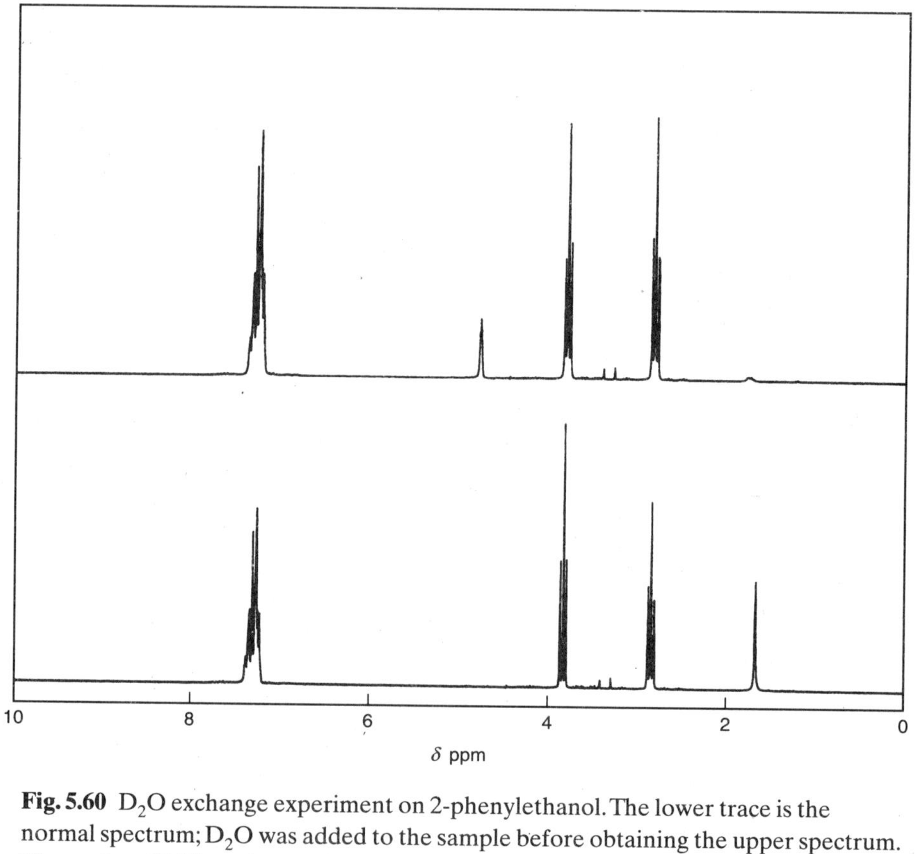

Fig. 5.60 D_2O exchange experiment on 2-phenylethanol. The lower trace is the normal spectrum; D_2O was added to the sample before obtaining the upper spectrum. The peak at δ1.7 has almost disappeared, and is therefore assigned to the hydroxyl resonance. The new peak at δ4.7 is due to residual HDO in the D_2O (note that this signal is due to *droplets* of water, and is in a different place to the typical signal obtained for water dissolved in $CDCl_3$ which occurs at δ1.57).

trifluoroacetyl group it has a strong effect on the resonances of the original compound. Resonances α- to the site (or sites) of acylation will be shifted to high δ by about 0.7–0.9 ppm, while β- and γ-protons will also show significant changes. These shifts can help in assignment of the spectrum, or they may simply be used to improve the peak separation for a compound whose basic spectrum is poorly resolved.

Manipulating chemical shifts

Changing the NMR solvent

It often happens that peaks in a proton spectrum overlap, even at high field. When faced with this problem all is not lost, because there are a number of techniques available for altering shifts. The most straightforward and highly recommended approach is to try another solvent. Any change of solvent is likely to alter shifts significantly, but particularly strong effects are found with the aromatic solvents benzene, toluene and pyridine. This is a consequence of the magnetic anisotropy typical of aromatic systems; different parts of the solute will naturally have different interactions with solvent molecules, and hence may find themselves in shielding or deshielding regions. For samples which have previously been run in $CDCl_3$, benzene is often a suitable alternative solvent, and its use can have spectacular results (Fig. 5.61). Toluene, although slightly less attractive from an NMR point of view because of its greater spread of residual solvent peaks, may sometimes be preferred on the grounds of reduced carcinogenicity. Pyridine is suitable for many more polar solutes, but it is toxic and unpleasant to handle.

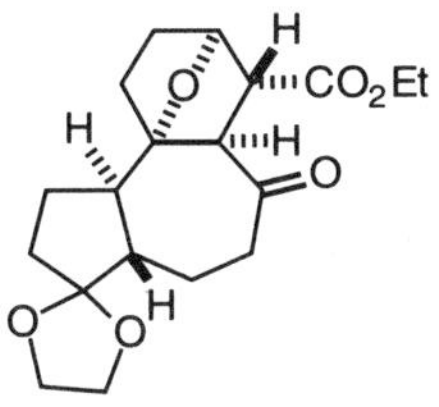

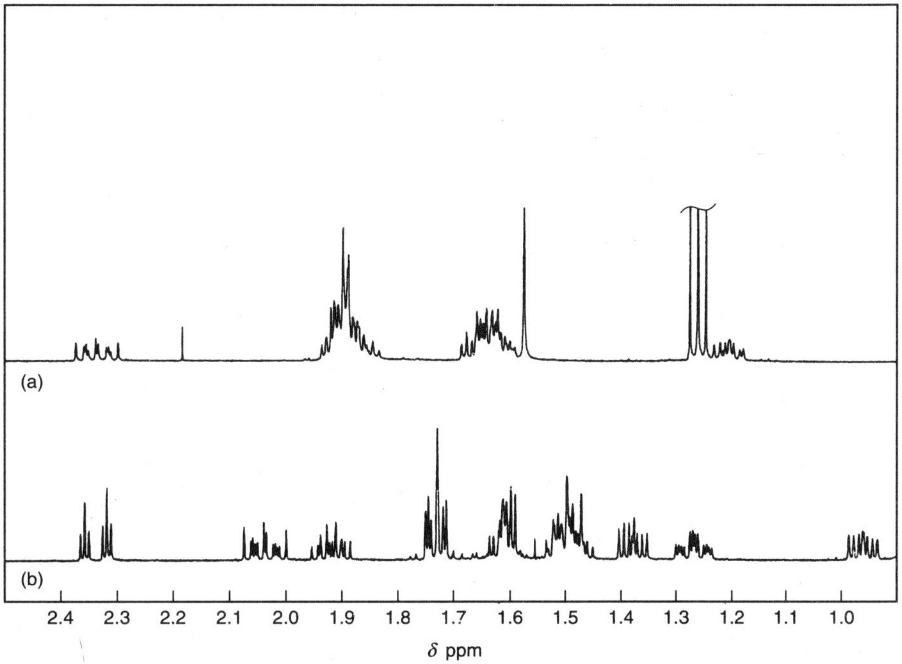

Fig. 5.61 Part of the proton spectrum of a fairly complex molecule run in (a) $CDCl_3$, and (b) benzene-d^6. The broad singlet at δ 1.57 in (a) is due to water in the $CDCl_3$. The triplet at δ 1.26 in (a) is shifted off-scale in (b).

Shift reagents

A more sophisticated approach to chemical shift control employs *shift reagents*. These are paramagnetic complexes of certain lanthanides, such as europium and ytterbium, with ligands designed to make them soluble in organic solvents. When added to NMR samples, they coordinate weakly to polar functional groups, such as esters and ketones, and create a strong local magnetic field that can produce large shift changes. There are very many shift reagents available, and you should refer to specialized literature for further information; however a useful practical hint regarding their use is to proceed with care. It is necessary to achieve a fine balance between the desired shift change and the undesirable side effect that follows from their paramagnetism: line broadening. Small incremental additions, starting with much less than one molar equivalent of the reagent, give the best results. Re-examine the spectrum after each addition, and stop as soon as the desired simplification has been achieved, or the line broadening effect becomes too strong. Problems are likely to occur with compounds containing strongly coordinating groups such as carboxylic acids, because then the shift reagent becomes too strongly bound.

Chiral shift reagents can be used to measure enantiomeric excess

Apart from their basic use in attempting to simplify unresolved spectra, shift reagents have another very important application to the study of enantiomeric purity. Shift reagents with chiral ligands are available in optically active form, and if these bind a substrate possessing an asymmetric centre, two diastereomeric complexes can be formed from its enantiomers. In principle these will exhibit different shifts and, as long as the actual difference is sufficient, the ratio of the enantiomers can be measured in a straightforward way. If this technique is to be used to estimate optical purity, it is essential to start with a racemic mixture and to establish the combination of reagent and concentration that gives the best separation of peaks. The purified enantiomers can then be assayed under the same conditions. It is hopeless to start with a substance expected to be 99% optically pure, add some chiral shift reagent and then take the absence of any new peaks as proof of purity!

Measuring chemical shifts (again!)

The basic principle behind chemical shift measurement was introduced on pp. 316–318: comparison of the observed signals with that of a reference substance. Unfortunately, things are not quite as simple as they may at first appear, and it is important that you should not have any misconceptions about the 'accuracy' of chemical shift determinations. It is not, in fact, necessary to measure shifts very accurately at all, *except* when it is required to demonstrate the identity of two substances (e.g. a natural product and its synthetic counterpart). The guidelines for estimating shifts are accurate to a few tenths of a part per million at best and so in routine structure determination the problems described in this section are inconsequential. For proof of identity, and when using literature data for exact comparison purposes (and, for that matter, when reporting your own data that others may use), more care is necessary.

The primary reference substance for proton and carbon NMR is tetramethylsilane (TMS). On low field CW spectrometers, for which the sample concentration is quite high, it is common to add this material to the sample. Referencing may then take the form of aligning the TMS peak with a chart mark, and at this level of accuracy the effects described here will rarely prove troublesome. On more advanced machines the spectrum will be stored in a computer, and referencing is then the numerical process of assigning the correct shift value to the reference line. With lower sample concentrations such as are typical on FT instruments it is convenient, and quite acceptable, to take the known shift of the residual solvent signal as the reference (but see the warning about D_2O below). Either way, this process is known as *internal referencing*, as the reference substance is in the sample. The alternative mode, known as *external referencing*, involves measuring the spectrum of the reference separately, and then comparing it somehow with that of the unknown. On a modern instrument, which has field stabilization using the deuterium resonance of the solvent, external referencing can comprise measurement of the absolute frequencies of the NMR lines and then calculation of their shifts on the basis of some previous calibration experiment.

Internal and external referencing

All these approaches are more than adequate for routine shift measurement. A computer-controlled FT spectrometer may encourage you to record and interpret shifts to higher levels of accuracy, by displaying them to hundredths of a part per million or better, but consider whether this is meaningful. All of the measurements presume that the shift of the reference substance is absolutely fixed, but clearly this is not true. For a start, there is no reason why TMS should have the same resonance frequency when dissolved in chloroform as it does in benzene. Furthermore, the shift of the reference may be altered by the presence of the sample, and vice versa. External referencing presumably avoids this problem, but still we need to define some kind of standard conditions for the reference sample. What if the sample shifts themselves are concentration dependent, as they may well be? Should we define a standard sample concentration, too? Clearly there is more to the accurate measurement of shifts than meets the eye.

So what *can* be done with chemical shifts? Those of a physical turn of mind like to convert everything to standard conditions, by introducing corrections for solvent susceptibility, extrapolating sample and reference concentrations to infinite dilution, etc. For normal organic applications, however, it is sufficient to be aware of the problem and to work round it in various ways. Obviously, comparisons can best be made when conditions are similar. Therefore it is important to try to identify the measurement conditions used to obtain data you find in the literature, and to quote the conditions when you report data. 'Conditions' should include field strength and solvent, and ideally also concentration, temperature, the reference peak used and the shift that was assigned to it (because for peaks other than that of TMS there is no absolute agreement on what shift to use). Regrettably it is not common to find the last three items reported in literature data. When you cannot discover all the details of the experiment, consider the likely accuracy of any comparisons you make, on the basis of whatever information is available. In practice, the various problems described above are not too significant for reasonably dilute samples in organic solvents, but they are much more pronounced in D_2O solution. Here the solvent shift can be strongly influenced by solute concentration, pH and temperature, so internal referencing using the residual solvent peak is unreliable. Changes in the solvent shift also affect the field stabilization of an FT spectrometer, so that external referencing may be equally invalid. Water-soluble reference compounds, such as the sodium salt of 3-(trimethylsilyl)propionic acid (TSP), are available and should be used when reproducible measurements are required. Another handy, water-soluble substance that gives a single, sharp peak and is more easily removed than TSP is 1,4-dioxan.

For proof of identity by NMR it is vital that the measurements are made under identical conditions. This is best achieved by measuring the substances to be compared in the same sample. In other words, obtain a spectrum of the authentic material, and then add an equal quantity of the comparison substance to the sample and repeat the measurement. This maximizes the chance of discovering differences between the two, for if they are identical there should be no extra peaks in the spectrum. If the sample concentration is kept constant during the addition, then the two spectra should be exactly the same.

Advanced techniques

We have already seen an NMR experiment that goes beyond the simple measurement of a spectrum: homonuclear decoupling. This is one example of a vast array of more complicated experimental techniques available in NMR spectroscopy. With the advent of FT NMR spectroscopy, some particularly exciting progress in the design of new experiments has occurred, and totally changed the way in which organic chemists use NMR. There is no space here to give you any of the theoretical background to the more advanced NMR experiments, but it seems appropriate to describe the information available from two of the most useful. One is by no means new, but technological progress has steadily made its use more practical (the nuclear Overhauser effect), while the other is the most important example of the new class of *two-dimensional* NMR experiments (COSY).

Nuclear Overhauser effect

The great thing about the nuclear Overhauser effect (NOE) is that it gives information complementary to that obtained from couplings. Couplings tell us about the bonding relationships in a structure, but the NOE is a direct, through-space effect, and helps in the determination of molecular geometry. In an NOE experiment, the *intensities* of resonances are measured after one peak in the spectrum has been irradiated for a time. Changes in intensity occur because the whole system tries to stay at thermal equilibrium: irradiating a peak reduces the population differences across its transitions to zero, so that in order to maintain the same net population difference for the system the differences for other transitions increase, and hence the corresponding peaks become stronger. The mechanism by which this happens turns out to be strongly distance dependent, so that it is generally found that only the resonances of protons fairly close to that which was irradiated change in intensity.

To clarify the intensity changes that occur during an NOE experiment, which can never be more than 50% and are more typically 1–10%, it is usual to employ *difference spectroscopy*. In this technique two spectra are recorded under identical conditions, except that in one spectrum a peak is irradiated for a time before acquiring the spectrum, while in the other it is not. Subtracting the latter 'blank' experiment from the one with irradiation generates the difference spectrum, in which only peaks that changed intensity should appear (Fig. 5.62). In this example, the stereochemistry of *E*- and *Z*-methylbutenedioic acids was determined by the observation of a much larger NOE from the methyl group to the alkene proton in the *Z*-compound. The main difficulty in using NOE measurements in practice is that, although the effect always varies with distance, it is also influenced by many extraneous factors. Thus, when examining a single effect in one compound, it is difficult to gauge whether it shoxuld be considered as 'large' or 'small'. The best circumstance is to be able to compare effects in geometrical isomers, as in the above example. It is then reasonable to take the isomer with the larger NOE as being the one in which the protons involved are closer together.

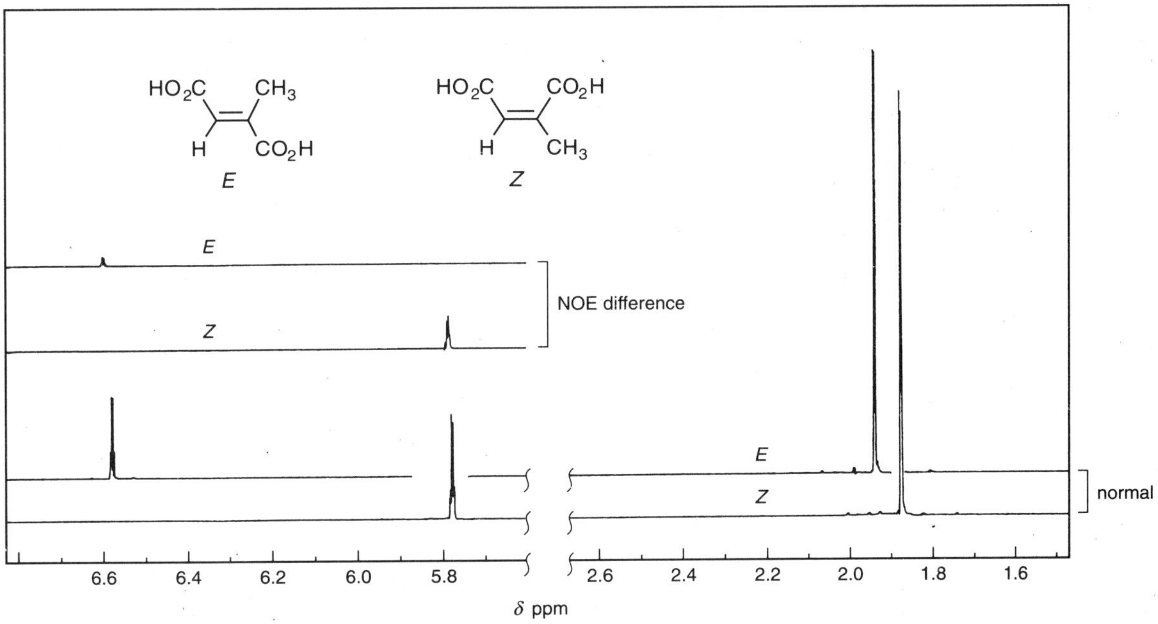

Fig. 5.62 Normal spectra of *E*- and *Z*-methylbutenedioic acid and the corresponding NOE difference spectra obtained after irradiating the methyl group in each compound. The NOE spectra are plotted to the same absolute scale so that the size of the enhancements can be compared directly.

Two-dimensional NMR

Two-dimensional NMR experiments are exclusive to FT spectrometers, and produce a kind of map rather than a simple spectrum (Fig. 5.63). The two axes of the rectangular spectrum both represent frequency, while the contours represent amplitude; so where there are contours, there are peaks. In a COSY experiment both axes correspond to proton chemical shifts (although this need not be the case in general). The idea of the two-dimensional experiment is to clarify the relationships between nuclei that are engaged in some kind of interaction, by mapping out the connections between them directly. There are two kinds of peak in Fig. 5.63: those which have the same shift in each frequency dimension and hence lie along the diagonal of the spectrum, and those with different shifts in each dimension. The latter kind, known as *cross-peaks*, are the most informative, as we shall see momentarily.

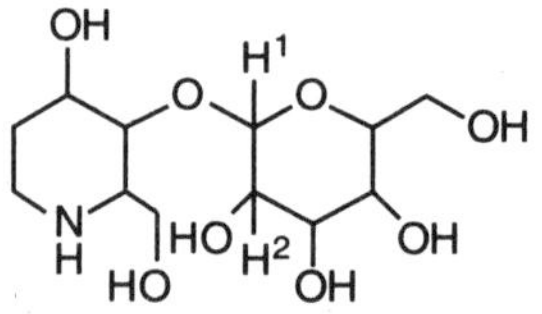

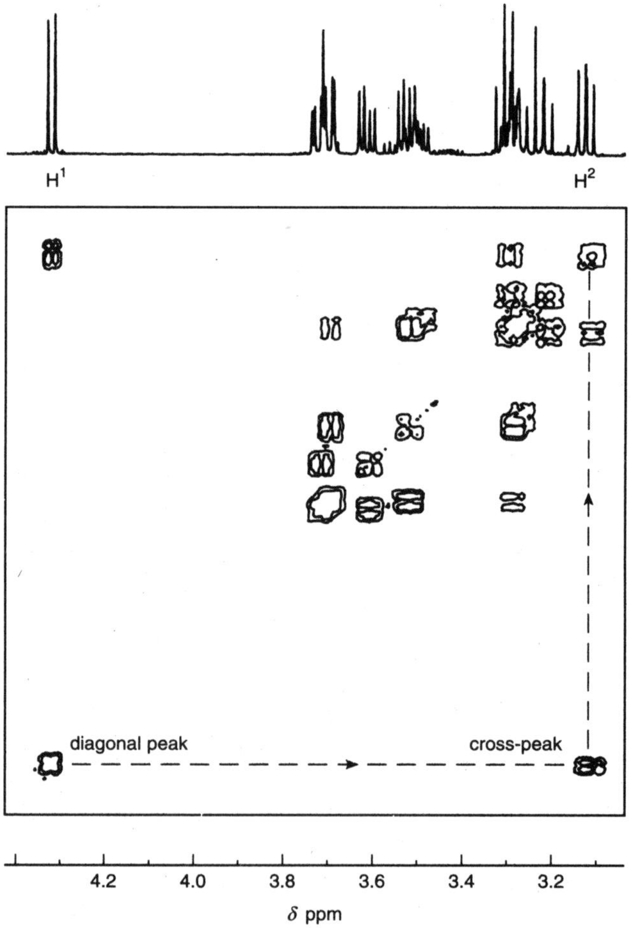

Fig. 5.63 Part of the COSY spectrum of the same compound as used for the example of homonuclear decoupling in Fig. 5.49. The connection between the doublet at δ4.33 and its partner is identified by way of the cross-peak, as indicated by the broken line drawn on the spectrum.

The diagonal peaks in a COSY spectrum correspond to the normal one-dimensional proton spectrum of the sample, and serve as a reference point for making assignments (examine the one-dimensional spectrum plotted at the top of Fig. 5.63, and see how each multiplet has a corresponding 'blob' on the diagonal of the two-dimensional plot). The cross-peaks link signals that are coupled in square patterns. Therefore, if you know the assignment of one resonance, you can trace a path through the spin system to which it belongs by alternating between diagonal and cross-peaks, as indicated in the figure. This method has several advantages over a series of homonuclear decoupling experiments, which could be considered as an alternative way of getting the same information. Decoupling requires both that the target peak can be irradiated selectively, and that the ensuing effect occurs in a tractable region of the spectrum. In a COSY experiment, even if the signals of both coupling partners are hidden in complex spectral regions, the cross-peak between them is still likely to be identifiable. Cross-peaks are generally well resolved even in spectra of large molecules, because two different shifts contribute to their location; there is much more 'space' in a COSY spectrum over which to spread the peaks. An additional advantage is that the COSY experiment requires the same time to perform regardless of the number of correlations it contains; whereas the more decouplings you need to carry out, the more time you must spend on the experiment. This is analogous to the advantage of FT over CW NMR discussed on pp. 313–314.

COSY, and a similar experiment that correlates ^{13}C shifts with those of their attached protons, have passed into standard use in research laboratories already. They make the mapping out of the vital coupling relationships in organic compounds very straightforward, and render structure elucidation of complex products even more feasible than before.

Further reading

Introductory theory

L.M. Harwood and T.D.W, Claridge, *Introduction to Organic Spectroscopy*, Oxford University Press, Oxford, 1996, Chapters 4 and 5.

Proton NMR

H. Günther, *NMR Spectroscopy*, 2nd edn, Wiley & Sons, New York, 1995.

L.M. Jackman and S. Sternhall, *Applications of Nuclear Magnetic Resonance Spectroscopy in Organic Chemistry*, 2nd edn, Pergamon, Oxford, 1969.

D.H. Williams and I. Fleming, *Spectroscopic Methods in Organic Chemistry*, 5th edn, McGraw-Hill, Maidenhead, 1995.

Carbon NMR

R.J. Abraham and P. Loftus, *Proton and Carbon-13 NMR Spectroscopy—an Integrated Approach*, 2nd edn, Heyden, London, 1988.

C.J. Pouchert and J. Behnke (eds), *The Aldrich Library of ¹³C and ¹H FT-NMR Spectra*. Aldrich Chemical Co., Milwaukee, 1992.

Data tables

E. Pretsch, J. Seibl, W. Simon and T. Clerc, *Tables of Spectral Data for Structure Determination of Organic Compounds*, 2nd edn, Springer-Verlag, Berlin, 1989.

Practical techniques

S.A. Richards, *Laboratory Guide to Proton NMR Spectroscopy*, Blackwell Scientific Publications, Oxford, 1988.

Shift reagents

R.E. Sievers (ed.) *NMR Shift Reagents*, Academic Press, New York, 1973.

Exchanging systems

J. Sandstrom, *Dynamic NMR Spectroscopy*, Academic Press, New York, 1982.

Advanced techniques

D. Canet, *Nuclear Magnetic Resonance, Concepts and Methods* (English Translation). Wiley & Sons, New York, 1996.

A.E. Derome, *Modern NMR Techniques for Chemistry Research*, Elsevier, Oxford, 1987.

H. Friebolin, *One and Two-Dimensional NMR Spectroscopy*, 2nd edn, VCH, Weinheim, 1993.

J.K.M. Sanders and B.K. Hunter, *Modern NMR Spectroscopy*, 2nd edn, Oxford University Press, Oxford, 1987.

5.4 Ultraviolet spectroscopy

UV and visible regions

Ultraviolet spectroscopy was the first method of spectroscopic analysis to make an impact on organic chemistry. The UV region of the electromagnetic spectrum comprises radiation with wavelengths from just below 10^{-7} and up to about 3.5×10^{-7} m. As can be seen from Fig. 5.1, this region borders the visible region of the spectrum, which stretches on up to about 8×10^{-7} m. Hence UV light has a shorter wavelength, higher frequency, and therefore higher energy than visible light. UV spectroscopy is usually extended into the visible region to study the absorptions which give rise to coloured organic compounds. This is not a problem from the practical point of view since both UV and visible regions can be measured on a single instrument (see later). When extended into the visible region, the technique is more correctly called ultraviolet–visible (UV–VIS) spectroscopy, although the simpler term UV spectroscopy is widely used to cover both regions. For the purposes of the present discussion we will refer simply to UV spectroscopy, and following common practice we will use *nanometres* as the units of wavelength (1 nm = 10^{-9} m).

Although the UV region of the electromagnetic spectrum stretches down to below 100 nm, we will only be concerned with wavelengths in the range 200–700 nm, the longer wavelengths (350 nm upwards) corresponding to visible light. The higher frequency, higher energy radiation below 200 nm is absorbed by oxygen molecules in the atmosphere, and therefore the study of this region of the spectrum requires special instrumentation which can operate with the sample in a vacuum. This region of the spectrum, normally called the *far UV* or, because of the experimental requirements, *vacuum UV*, is rarely used by organic chemists.

As we have already seen (pp. 276–277), the energy (E) of electromagnetic radiation is related to its frequency (v) by the equation:

$$E = hv$$

where h is Planck's constant. Since frequency is related to wavelength by the speed of light, we can derive a simple relationship between energy and wavelength by inserting a value for Planck's constant. Thus:

$$E\left(\text{kJ mol}^{-1}\right) = \frac{118\,825}{\lambda\left(\text{nm}\right)}$$

Hence the energies associated with the wavelengths of interest (200–700 nm) fall in the range 170–600 kJ mol^{-1}, and these cause electronic transitions within organic molecules. The detailed theory of electronic transitions incorporates rules, known as *selection rules*, to indicate which transitions are allowed and which are forbidden on the basis of molecular symmetry. This theory is quite complicated and is way beyond the scope of this book; you should consult your appropriate lecture text.

Electronic transitions

The electronic transitions that concern organic chemists are those involving the excitation (promotion) of an electron from a bonding or lone-pair orbital to a non-bonding or antibonding orbital. The energy, and hence the wavelength of radiation required, to cause the promotion of an electron, depend on the energy difference between the two relevant orbitals, which in turn depends on the type of electrons involved. Organic chemists are mainly interested in three types of electron: those in (single) σ-bonds, those in (double) π-bonds and lone-pair electrons. Hence, for example, a π-electron can be promoted from a bonding orbital (π) to an antibonding orbital (π^*), and in notation form this is described as a $\pi \rightarrow \pi^*$ *transition*. There are several other types of transition which are possible, and the more important ones are shown in Table 5.3, together with the wavelength of radiation required to cause the transition.

The first thing that should be apparent from Table 5.3 is that only one of the transitions (the last one) actually falls in our 200–700 nm range, and as it happens, this n $\rightarrow \pi^*$ transition of the carbonyl group is 'forbidden' and therefore gives rise to a very weak absorption. (This 'forbidden' transition can only be seen because the molecular symmetry that forbids it is broken by molecu-

Table 5.3 Common electronic transitions relevant to UV spectroscopy.

Electron type	Example	Transition notation	Approx. wavelength (nm)
σ	C–C	$\sigma \rightarrow \sigma^*$	150
π	C=C isolated	$\pi \rightarrow \pi^*$	180
Lone pair	O	$n \rightarrow \sigma^*$	185
	N	$n \rightarrow \sigma^*$	195
	C=O	$n \rightarrow \sigma^*$	190
	C=O	$n \rightarrow \pi^*$	300

Conjugation

lar vibrations.) Thus electrons in isolated systems usually require radiation well outside the UV range to excite them, and it is in the study of *conjugated* systems, such as dienes, α,β-unsaturated carbonyl compounds and aromatics, that UV spectroscopy comes into its own. The presence of an *isolated* C = C or C = O bond in a compound is much better established by NMR or IR than by UV.

Why then do organic molecules containing conjugated functional groups absorb at longer wavelengths in the observable UV range? As a simple example let us compare ethene and butadiene. In general, π-electrons are much more easily excited than σ-electrons (Table 5.3), so as far as UV spectroscopy is concerned we need only consider the π-system, and its associated molecular orbitals. The molecular orbitals of ethene comprise the HOMO, which contains the two π-electrons, and the LUMO, which is unoccupied. Therefore the simplest possible transition of a π-electron is from the HOMO to the LUMO, and this represents the $\pi \rightarrow \pi^*$ transition for ethene. The energy difference between these orbitals is about 690 kJ mol^{-1}, and therefore from the equation

$$E = \frac{118\,825}{\lambda}$$

we can calculate that, in order to effect this transition, we would need radiation with a wavelength of 172 nm, below the normal UV range. The energy levels for ethene are shown schematically in Fig. 5.64a; the σ and σ^* orbitals are below and above the π and π^* orbitals respectively, and are not shown. The much larger energy gap between the σ and σ^* orbitals means that the $\sigma \rightarrow \sigma^*$ transition would require even shorter wavelength radiation.

Butadiene, on the other hand, has four molecular orbitals associated with the π-system (Fig. 5.64b). Since the HOMO is higher in energy than that of ethene, and the LUMO is lower in energy, the energy gap between the two orbitals is only about 544 kJ mol^{-1}. Hence, less energy is needed to effect the

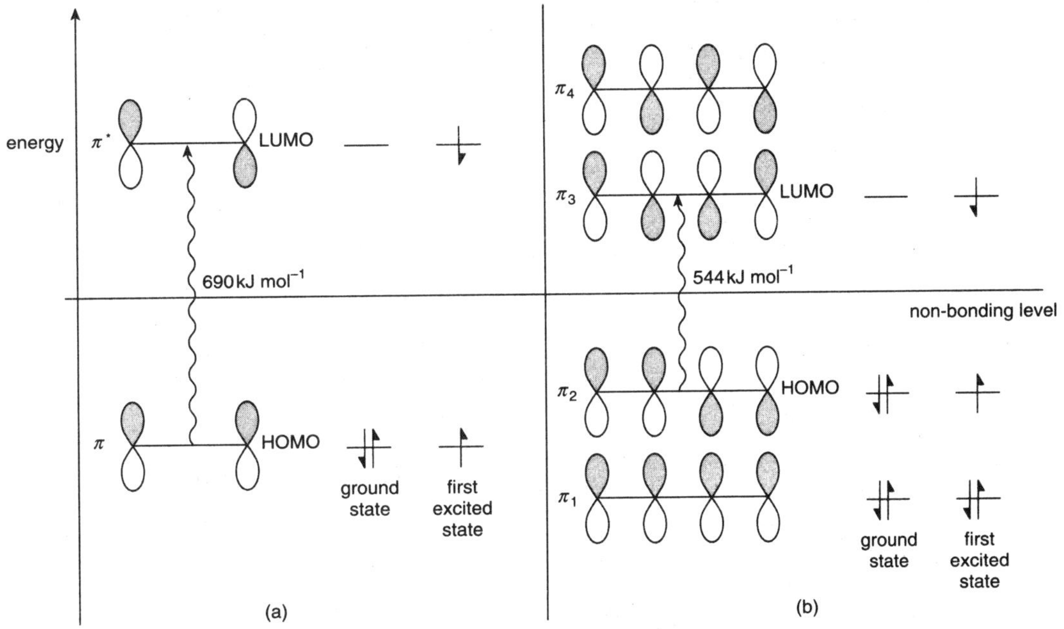

Fig. 5.64 (a) Energy levels of ethene π-orbitals; (b) energy levels of butadiene π-orbitals.

$\pi \rightarrow \pi^*$ transition in butadiene than in ethene, and the transition will occur on absorption of radiation of wavelength 218 nm, inside the normal UV range. With increasing conjugation, the HOMO LUMO energy difference progressively decreases, and therefore the wavelength of light needed to cause the $\pi \rightarrow \pi^*$ transition increases.

Chromophores

In such molecules it is the π-system that is responsible for the absorption of UV radiation, and the functional group or collection of functional groups responsible for the absorption is referred to as a *chromophore* (Greek: *chroma* = colour). Complex molecules can, of course, contain more than one chromophore. Hence, the effect of conjugation on the chromophore, often described as extending the chromophore by conjugation, is to shift the position of maximum absorption to a longer wavelength. Such shifts to longer wavelengths are often called *red shifts or bathochromic shifts*; shifts to shorter wavelengths are called *blue shifts* or *hypsochromic shifts*. However, do not let the jargon confuse you: the important point to remember is that *extending a chromophore by conjugation causes an increase in the wavelength of absorption*. This is a general rule with no exceptions; *the more double bonds there are in conjugation, the longer the wavelength of absorption.*

Red/blue shifts
Bathochromic/hypsochromic shifts

Conjugation causes an increase in the wavelength of absorption

As an extreme example of the effects of conjugation, consider lycopene, a natural product that can be isolated from tomatoes, which contains 11 conjugated C = C bonds. The absorption maximum occurs at 470 nm, well into the visible region; the compound strongly absorbs blue light and therefore appears red. Indeed such compounds are responsible for the bright orange and red colours of carrots, tomatoes, and so on. This association of molecular structure with colour is, of course, central to the chemistry of dyestuffs and photographic materials, and is vital for vision where the photoreceptors in the eye contain a pigment called *rhodopsin* which absorbs in the visible region at 498 nm.

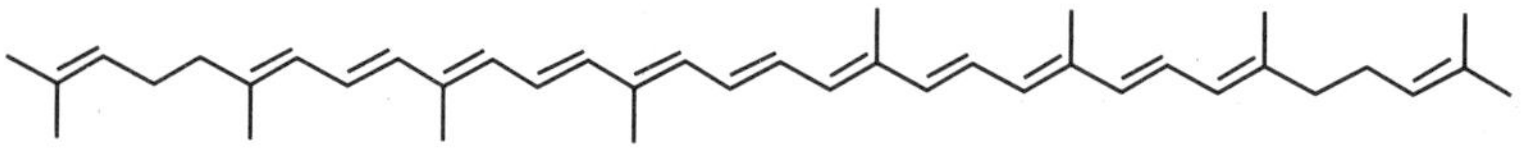

lycopene

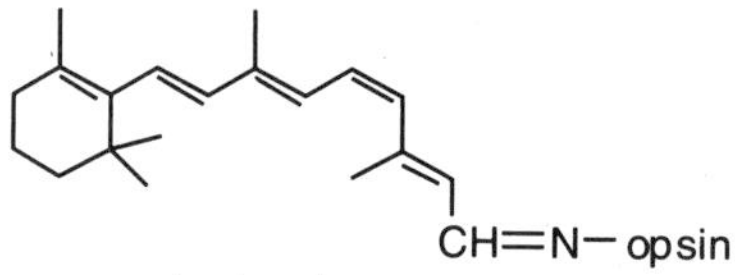

rhodopsin

So far we have restricted our discussion to the *position* of the absorption, that is, at what wavelength the chromophore absorbs. The other variable is the efficiency with which a compound absorbs light, in other words the *intensity* of absorption. Amongst other factors, this is related to the probability of the particular electronic transition occurring; this takes us back to the complex selection rules referred to earlier. The only point to note is that certain forbidden transitions, notably the $n \rightarrow \pi^*$ transition of the $C = O$ group, do have weak, but observable absorptions. However, from the *practical* point of view, there are two empirical laws which have been derived concerning absorption intensity. Individually these are known as Lambert's law and Beer's law. However, it is common practice for them to be combined into the *Beer–Lambert law* which states that the absorbance (A) of a sample at a particular wavelength is proportional to the concentration (c) of the sample (in moles per litre) and the path length (l) of the light through the sample (in centimetres). Absorbance (A), or optical density (OD) as it is sometimes called, is further defined as the logarithm of the ratio of the intensity of the incident light (I_0) to the intensity of transmitted light (I). Hence:

Absorption intensity

Beer–Lambert law

$$A = \log_{10}\left(\frac{I_0}{I}\right) = \varepsilon c l$$

The constant ε is called the *molar extinction coefficient*, and is a measure of how strongly the compound absorbs at that wavelength. In general, we find that *the longer the chromophore, the more intense the absorption* and hence the higher the value of ε. From the above equation we can see that ε has the rather meaningless units of $1000\,cm^2\,mol^{-1}$, but, by convention, these are never expressed. Provided that the concentration of the sample is known, ε is readily calculated; conversely, if the ε value for a compound is known at a given wavelength, measuring the absorbance at this wavelength permits the determination of the concentration of the sample. This is what makes UV spectroscopy such an important quantitative tool in analytical chemistry.

The instrument

Like IR spectrometers, most UV spectrometers operate on the double-beam principle, with one beam passing through the sample and the other passing through a reference cell. A typical example of such an instrument is shown schematically in Fig. 5.65. Most spectrometers use two lamps, one emitting in the UV range 200 nm to *ca.* 330 nm, and one for the visible part of the spectroscopic range *ca.* 330 nm to 700 nm. The light from the source passes through the *monochromator*. This consists essentially of a prism or a grating for breaking down the beam into its component wavelengths and allowing one wavelength at a time to pass through. The light emerging from the monochromator is then further divided into two beams of equal intensity, with one beam passing through a solution of the compound to be examined in the sample cell, and the other beam passing through the reference cell which contains pure solvent. After passing through the cells, the light arrives at the detector, which measures the ratio of the intensity of the reference beam (the incident intensity, I_0) to the intensity of the sample beam (the transmitted intensity, I). Hence the detector measures the quantity I_0/I. However, on most machines the output from the detector is automatically converted and plotted on the chart recorder *y* axis as $\log_{10}(I_0/I)$—the absorbance (A). Therefore, as the instrument scans the wavelength range, a plot—the UV spectrum—of absorbance (A) against wavelength (λ, in nanometres) is obtained. The appearance of UV spectra contrasts sharply with that of IR and NMR spectra, in that they usually consist of rather broad peaks, and often only one peak.

The absorbance scale on most spectrometers will run from 0 to 1 or from 0 to 2. In regions of the spectrum where the sample does not absorb light, $I = I_0$, $(I_0/I) = 1$, and hence $A = 0$. At the other extreme, if the sample absorbs very strongly, I is small and hence the ratio I_0/I is large. The value of the ratio that

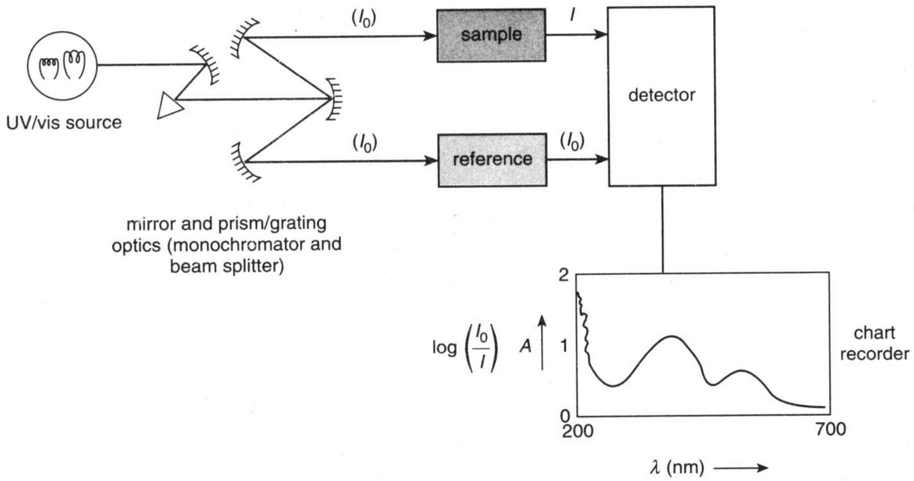

Fig. 5.65 Schematic representation of a double-beam ultraviolet spectrometer.

the instrument can tolerate is 10 ($\log_{10} 10 = 1$) or 100 ($\log_{10} 100 = 2$) depending on whether the maximum on the absorbance scale is 1 or 2. If the absorbance is too great, the chart recorder pen will move off-scale, and the only way round this is to dilute the sample.

Preparing the sample

Although spectrometers can measure the UV spectra on solid samples by reflecting light off the solid surface (reflectance spectroscopy), organic chemists routinely record UV spectra on solutions of the compound contained in a special cell. Therefore in preparing samples for UV spectroscopy, the three factors we have to consider are the *type of cell*, the *concentration* of the solution and which *solvent* to use.

Cells

Cells for UV spectroscopy are made out of quartz, glass or plastic. Whereas quartz is transparent throughout the 200–700 nm range, both glass and plastic, which 'cut-off' somewhere between 350 and 300 nm, are opaque to the shorter wavelengths, and can only be used in the visible range of the spectrum. Therefore, to study the UV part of the spectroscopic range, quartz cells have to be used. This is unfortunate since quartz cells are both fragile and much more expensive than glass or plastic cells, and they *must* be handled carefully. Plastic cells, although cheap, can only be used with certain solvents, usually water or alcohols. Whatever the material, standard UV cells are about 1 cm square and about 3 cm high (Fig. 5.66). The faces that are placed in the beam are polished, and the cell is constructed so as to give a path length of exactly 1 cm. The other two faces are often 'frosted' or of ground glass to distinguish them from the polished faces. Always handle cells by these faces to avoid putting fingerprints on the clear polished faces. Cells come in pairs, the individual cells accurately matching one another, so that there are no problems with differences in the sample and reference beams due to unmatched cells. Before running your UV spectrum, always check that you have matched cells. UV cells usually have a small stopper of some sort, often made out of Teflon®, which seals well with slight pressure—do not ram the stopper in too far. Although standard UV cells have a path length of 1 cm, cells of different path length are available.

You must use quartz cells for measurements in the UV range

Handle cells by non-polished edges

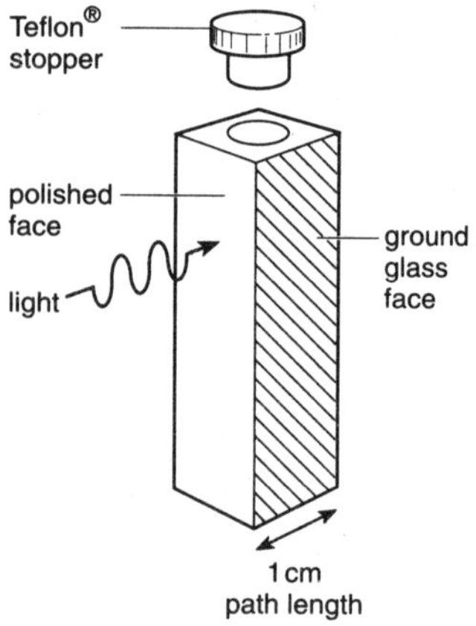

Fig. 5.66 Standard 1 cm UV cell.

Concentration

As we have already seen, the absorbance of a sample is proportional to its concentration and to the path length, and is given by

$$A = \varepsilon c l$$

If you are using a standard UV cell, $l = 1$, and hence

$$A = \varepsilon c$$

Since the maximum value of A that the spectrometer can usually cope with is 2, you need to choose a concentration that will keep within these limits. Unfortunately this requires some knowledge of the value of the extinction coefficient, ε, at the wavelength of maximum absorption—i.e. how strongly will the compound absorb? This is not as difficult to estimate as you might think, and you will soon develop a feel for how certain types of organic compounds absorb UV light. You will presumably already have some idea about what sort of compound you are dealing with, either by knowing its origin or by examining its IR and NMR spectra. For the purposes of the present discussion, suffice it to say that it is not at all uncommon for an organic compound to have an ε value of 10000 or more. Putting the values $l = 1$ and $\varepsilon = 10000$ into the Beer–Lambert law, we can see that to give an absorbance (A) of 1, we require a solution of concentration of 10^{-4} M (0.0001 M). This simple example illustrates one of the great strengths of UV spectroscopy; the fact that you can use *very dilute solutions* requiring very small quantities of compound. In the example above, if we assume a molecular weight of 200, we need only 0.2 mg of compound to make up 10 mL of solution of the required concentration. This obviously places considerable demands on the actual experimental technique in making up such solutions, and this is discussed in more detail later in this section.

One problem in obtaining UV spectra is that your compound may have two or more chromophores with widely differing extinction coefficients, a situation which is in fact quite common. For example, the compound may have a chromophore with an extinction coefficient of 10000 absorbing at 250 nm, and it may also have a much weaker intensity, 'forbidden' absorption with $\varepsilon = 100$, due to another chromophore at, say, 350 nm. If we were to run the spectrum using a solution of 0.0001 M concentration, we would see a large peak ($A = 1$) for the shorter wavelength absorption, but the second chromophore would have an absorbance of 0.01 and a very small peak that could easily be missed. The only way round this problem is to run the UV spectrum on samples of two different concentrations; a difference factor of 100 is usually appropriate. Make up the more concentrated solution first, and run the spectrum. Even though some peaks may go off-scale you will see the small ones. Then dilute the sample and re-run the spectrum; this technique was used to obtain the UV spectrum of isophorone shown in Fig. 5.67.

Use solutions of two different concentrations

Solvent

The prime requirement for a solvent for UV spectroscopy is that it should be transparent to radiation over the complete UV range. Fortunately most common organic solvents meet this requirement, the only differences between them being the point at which they 'cut-off' at the short wavelength end of the range. Since spectrometers operate on the double beam principle, any absorptions due to solvent are cancelled out at the detector. Although the solvents do not contain any chromophores, they do of course constitute effec-

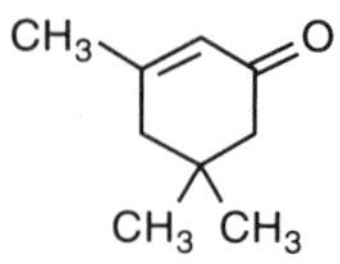

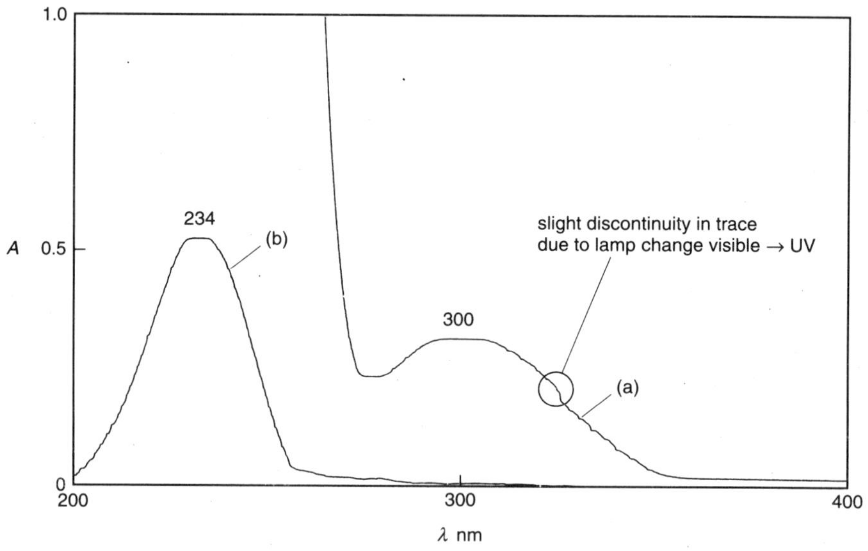

Fig. 5.67 UV spectrum of isophorone: (a) at a concentration of 6.2 mg per 10 mL; (b) diluted by a factor of 100.

Table 5.4 Cut-off points for solvents for UV spectroscopy.

Solvent	Approx. cut-off point (nm)
Water	190
Hexane	200
Ethanol	205
Dichloromethane	220
Chloroform	240

tively 100% of the sample; there comes a point at which the 1 cm path length of the solvent absorbs so strongly that no light of that particular wavelength, or shorter, will be transmitted through the sample. The cut-off points for various solvents are given in Table 5.4, and it is this which leads to the feature known as *end absorption* in UV spectra.

The most commonly used solvent for UV spectroscopy is ethanol, usually the commercially available 95% grade. Ethanol is cheap, a good solvent for a wide range of organic compounds, and is transparent down to about 205 nm. Although it is **toxic** and **flammable**, it can be handled safely, provided that due regard is paid to the potential hazards. Whatever solvent is used it must be free from impurities that might absorb in the UV region. UV spectroscopy is very sensitive and so even a tiny amount of impurity can cause problems if it has a large ε value. This is particularly true of hydrocarbon solvents which may contain aromatic impurities. To reassure chemists, many solvents are sold as 'spectroscopic grade' or 'spectrophotometric grade', the absorption proper-

Beware of UV absorbing contaminants in your solvents. In particular, never use 'absolute' ethanol

ties of which are clearly defined and guaranteed. You must never use 'absolute' or commercially dried ethanol, as this may have been dried azeotropically with benzene, traces of which remain in the ethanol and interfere with the spectrum.

The solvent also affects the wavelength of maximum absorption and the appearance of UV spectra. This is because many electronic transitions lead to an excited state which is more polar than the ground state, and therefore polar solvents, such as ethanol, will stabilize the excited state by dipole interactions to a greater extent than the ground state. Non-polar solvents, such as hexane, have little or no dipole interactions. Hence the energy difference between the two electronic states will be slightly smaller in ethanol than in hexane, and therefore the absorption maximum will be at a longer wavelength in ethanol than in hexane. This shift to longer wavelength (*bathochromic shift*) in moving from a non-polar solvent to a polar solvent can be as much as 20 nm. Solvent effects on the absorption maxima of α,β-unsaturated ketones are given in detail in Table A19 in Appendix 3. Molecules containing isolated carbonyl groups often show the reverse solvent effect; the absorption moves to a shorter wavelength on increasing the polarity of the solvent. This is because polar hydroxylic solvents, such as ethanol, form stronger hydrogen bonds to the ground state, and therefore stabilize the ground state to a greater extent than the excited state. In addition to the effects on the wavelength of absorption, non-polar solvents often lead to UV spectra which show more fine structure than those run in ethanol.

Making up the sample

The fact that UV spectra can be run on very dilute solutions is one of the great assets of the technique: however, it is also one of the potential pitfalls from the practical point of view. How do you make up such dilute solutions with accurately known concentration? The answer is by dilution.

Treat analytical balances with care

To make up solutions for UV spectroscopy, you need an accurate analytical balance reading to 0.01 mg, some volumetric flasks (preferably 10 mL) and a 1 mL pipette. Remember that the volume of standard UV cells is only about 3 mL, so there is no need to make up several hundred millilitres of solution. Weigh out *accurately* about 1 mg of your compound on the analytical balance into an appropriate container. It does not matter whether you end up with 1.27 or 0.93 mg, as long as you know exactly what the weight is. Transfer the material to a 10 mL volumetric flask, taking care to rinse it all in with portions of the solvent if necessary, and then make up the volume to 10 mL with solvent. (Alternatively, if your laboratory does not have a balance that can weigh to 0.01 mg, you should weigh out accurately about 10 mg of compound, and dissolve it in 100 mL of solvent in a 100 mL volumetric flask.) Label the flask immediately, so that you know its concentration. This solution is likely to be too concentrated, so it is as well to make up at least one, and preferably two, more solutions before going to the instrument. This is easily done by

See section on weighing on pp. 70–72

Never suck up liquids into pipettes by mouth

dilution. Pipette out exactly 1 mL from the first solution (use a pipette filler), and transfer it to a second 10 mL volumetric flask. Make up the volume to 10 mL, and label the flask. Using a clean pipette, withdraw 1 mL of the second solution and transfer it to a third 10 mL volumetric flask. Make up the volume to 10 mL, and label the flask. You now have three solutions with accurately known concentrations of approximately 1, 0.1 and 0.01 mg per 10 mL. As with all quantitative analytical work, you must take great care that no impurities are introduced, either during the weighing, or the making up of the solutions.

Avoid contamination

Running the spectrum

Ultraviolet spectrometers are quite simple to operate, and have relatively few controls. The controls usually allow you to adjust the wavelength range of the scan, the absorbance range ($A = 1$ or 2), the scan speed and the expansion along the x axis (how many centimetres of chart paper correspond to 10 nm). There will also be a baseline adjusting control, which may have been preset. If this adjustment is correct, the spectrometer will produce a nice straight line at the $A = 0$ mark when pure solvent is placed in both sample and reference cells. With the machine turned on, both the UV and visible lamps should be lit; if not, check that they are not linked to separate switches.

Using a clean Pasteur pipette fill the sample cell with the most concentrated of your solutions and, holding the cell by the edges, place it in the sample beam of the spectrometer. Fill the reference cell with pure solvent, using a clean Pasteur pipette, ensuring that you use the same batch of solvent used to make up the solution in the first place. Likewise, place the reference cell in the reference beam, holding the cell by the edges.

Most spectrometers scan from long to short wavelength. If the compound is colourless, there is no point scanning the whole of the visible range, and you should start the scan at 450 nm; however, for coloured compounds you must scan the whole range. Select the wavelength from which you want to scan, and press the start button. As the spectrometer scans to shorter wavelength there may be a slight hiccup as the lamps switch over; this switch-over point can be seen at 325 nm in the spectra shown in Figs 5.67 and 5.69.

The chances are that your first solution will be too concentrated and therefore some of the peaks will go off-scale. In this case, remove the sample cell, discard the solution, wash the cell with a little solvent, then with 1 or 2 mL of the more dilute solution; and finally refill it with the more dilute solution. There is no need to change the reference cell. In most cases one of your three solutions will give a suitable spectrum, but in exceptional cases, particularly if the compound is very strongly coloured, you may have to make extra dilutions. Do not worry if the peaks start to go off-scale below about 220 nm; this usually happens. Most organic molecules, the solvent included, start to absorb strongly below this wavelength, and this is generally referred to as *end absorption*. After running the spectrum you should calibrate the instrument by

End absorption

running a reference sample which has a sharp absorption at an accurately known wavelength. The common reference material used is *holmium glass*, which has a sharp peak at 360.8 nm.

Interpreting the spectrum

Ultraviolet spectra look relatively simple and straightforward compared with IR and NMR spectra. They consist of broad peaks, and indeed many may only be a single peak. The initial data that should be extracted from your spectrum are as follows.

1 The wavelength or wavelengths at which the absorption reaches a maximum, referred to as λ_{max}.

2 The absorbance, A, at each of the maxima.

Knowing the concentration of the solution, the molecular weight of the compound and the path length of the cell, you should then calculate the value of the extinction coefficient, ε, at each maximum. The whole process is best illustrated with an actual example. Figure 5.67 shows the UV spectrum of isophorone recorded in ethanol solution at two different concentrations in a cell of path length 1 cm. Spectrum (a) was obtained on a solution containing 6.2 mg per 10 mL; this solution was then diluted 100-fold to obtain spectrum (b). Note that the absorption at 300 nm is only visible in the spectrum of the more concentrated sample; this absorption, which is due to a 'forbidden' transition, would have been missed if the spectrum had only been recorded on the dilute solution. The 'allowed' $\pi \rightarrow \pi^*$ transition gives rise to a much stronger absorption at 234 nm. The spectrum is simple, and we can immediately read off the values of λ_{max} and the absorbance A. The molecular weight of isophorone is 138.2, and using the Beer–Lambert law

$$A = \varepsilon c l$$

we can see that for the absorption at 234 nm, $A = 0.52$, and hence

$$\varepsilon = \frac{A}{cl} = \frac{0.52 \times 138.2}{0.0062 \times 1} = 11\,590 \text{ (to four significant figures)}$$

Similarly for the absorption at 300 nm, we can calculate ε as 71.

UV spectroscopic data are usually quoted in the form: λ_{max} (solvent) (ε) nm. Alternatively, the extinction coefficient is often quoted as its logarithm (to base 10). Hence we should quote the UV data for the $\pi \rightarrow \pi^*$ transition of isophorone as λ_{max} (EtOH) 234 (ε 11 590) nm or λ_{max} (EtOH) 234 (log ε 4.06).

So far the analysis of the spectrum has simply been a matter of reading off the λ_{max} and calculating ε values for all the peaks. We now need to interpret these in terms of the structural features and functional groups of the compound under study. Nowadays despite its historical importance as the first spectroscopic method of organic chemistry, UV spectroscopy is rarely used as the prime spectroscopic tool for structure determination. Therefore by the time that you run your UV spectrum you will know exactly what your compound is, or at least have some idea about its structure. Nonetheless UV spectroscopy remains a useful confirmatory technique, and occasionally still provides the key evidence—for instance in distinguishing between α,β-unsaturated ketones and other types of unsaturated ketones.

The types of compound giving rise to characteristic UV spectra that can be interpreted in terms of distinct chromophores arising from functional groups within the molecule are those with conjugated systems: dienes, α,β-unsaturated carbonyl compounds and aromatics. Unfortunately, you cannot correlate a peak at, say, 265 nm in the UV spectrum with one particular functional group in the same way as you can correlate an IR peak at, say, 1700 cm^{-1} with a carbonyl group. However, when faced with a UV spectrum, there are some general guidelines that will help you to make some initial deductions. These are listed below.

1 Starting at the short wavelength end, ignore the end absorption. Peaks with λ_{max} of less than about 220 nm cannot usually be interpreted unambiguously.

2 If the spectrum is very simple with essentially one main peak absorbing below 300 nm with an ε value in the range 10 000–20 000, the compound probably contains a very simple conjugated system such as a diene or an enone, the $\pi \rightarrow \pi^*$ transition of which is responsible for the absorption. Less intense bands in this region (ε, 2000–10 000) may suggest an aromatic system. Obviously these possibilities would be readily distinguished by IR or NMR spectroscopy.

3 If the spectrum is more complex and extends into the visible region, the molecule contains an extended chromophore such as a polyene, an aromatic ring with conjugating substituents, or a polycyclic aromatic system.

At this stage you can abandon the analysis/interpretation of your UV spectrum, and simply say that it is consistent with certain structural features in your compound, and confirms previous assignments made from IR or NMR spectroscopy. However, it is possible to take the analysis a stage further, because there are some very useful correlations between structure and UV absorption maxima. These empirical rules, first formulated by R.B. Woodward in 1941 and subsequently modified by L.F. Fieser, are known as the *Woodward rules* or the *Woodward–Fieser rules*, and enable us to predict the λ_{max} values for conjugated dienes and α,β-unsaturated carbonyl compounds. The rules were further developed by A.I. Scott in one of the classic works on UV spectroscopy, *Interpretation of the Ultraviolet Spectra of Natural Products*, published in 1964.

Woodward rules

In effect the rules assign a λ_{max} value to the $\pi \rightarrow \pi^*$ transition of the parent chromophore, and tabulate increments for the effect of added substituents. Substituents which are not chromophores in their own right, but which alter the λ_{max} value of a chromophore, are known as *auxochromes*. The simplest types of auxochromes are alkyl groups, which cause a small (5–10 nm) bathochromic shift (to longer wavelength) when attached to a chromophore.

Auxochromes

Similarly other groups act as auxochromes: OR, OCOR, SR, NR_2 and halogen all cause bathochromic shifts. The addition of extra unsaturation in the form of another double or triple bond obviously causes a much larger shift to longer wavelength. The rules for diene absorptions are given in Table A17 in Appendix 3, and list the values for the parent chromophore according to whether the diene is acyclic or cyclic, together with the increments due to various auxochromes. The analogous rules for α,β-unsaturated ketones are given in Table A18; however, there is an additional complication here, since with carbonyl groups, the position of maximum absorption is subject to changes in solvent polarity as discussed earlier. The effects of solvent on the absorption maxima of α,β-unsaturated ketones are shown in Table A 19 in the form of the correction factors needed to 'convert' the λ_{max} to that expected in ethanol. There is no solvent effect with dienes.

The application of Woodward's rules is best illustrated with a few examples, although you must remember that the rules only predict the lowest $\pi \rightarrow \pi^*$ transition.

Example 1. Cholesta-3,5-diene

Parent (heteroannular) diene	214
Substituents:	
2–3 bond (ring residue)	5
6–7 bond (ring residue)	5
5–10 bond (ring residue)	5
Exocyclic double bond	5
Calculated λ_{max}	234 nm

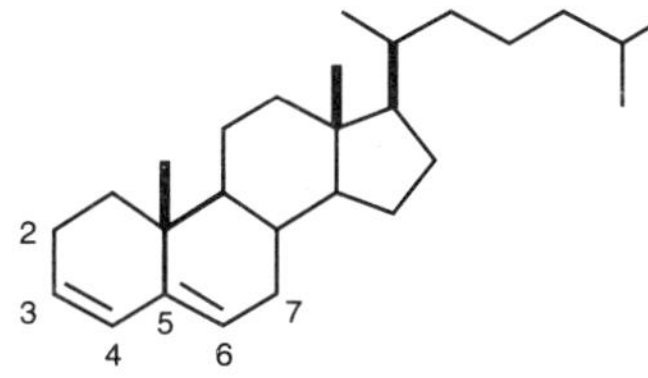

The observed value is 235 nm.

Example 2. Cholesta-5,7-diene-1,3-diol

Parent (homoannular) diene	253
Substituents:	
4–5 bond (ring residue)	5
8–9 bond (ring residue)	5
5–10 bond (ring residue)	5
8–14 bond (ring residue)	5
Calculated λ_{max}	273 nm

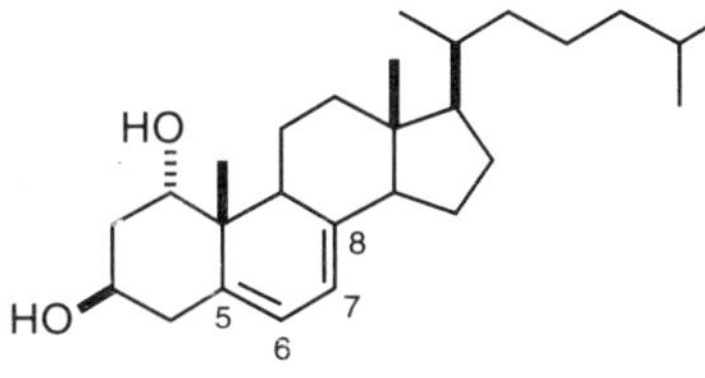

The observed value is 272 nm.

Example 3. Dihydrojasmone

Parent α,β-unsaturated five-ring ketone	202
α-Substituents: alkyl group	10
β-Substituents:	
alkyl group	12
ring residue	12
Calculated λ_{max} (EtOH)	236 nm

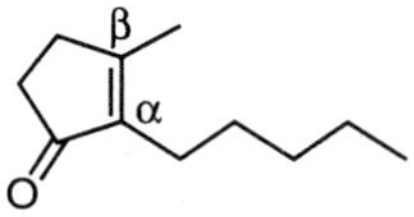

The observed value is 237 nm.

Example 4. Rotundifolene

Parent α,β-unsaturated acyclic ketone	215
α-Substituents: ring residue	10
β-Substituents: two alkyl groups	24
Exocyclic double bond	5
Calculated λ_{max} (EtOH)	254 nm

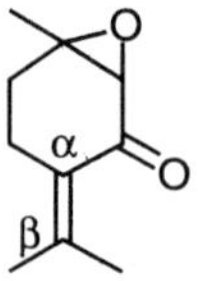

The observed value is 260 nm.

Aromatic compounds

The other types of compound that give useful UV spectra are aromatic molecules, but unfortunately simple quantitative rules for the prediction of their spectra do not exist. However, there are a number of general guidelines that will assist you in the interpretation of the UV spectra of aromatic compounds.

1 In monosubstituted benzenes, conjugating substituents, such as CH = CH or COR, which extend the chromophore increase both the wavelength and intensity of the absorption. This is, of course, the general rule that applies to all compounds.

2 Alkyl substituents have a small bathochromic effect.

3 Substituents with lone pairs of electrons also cause bathochromic shifts. The effect is a result of the interaction of the aromatic π-system with the substituent lone pair, and the magnitude of the bathochromic shift is related to the substituent's ability as a donor. Thus the effect of substituents decreases in the order: $NH_2 > OH > Cl$.

4 In polysubstituted benzenes, the combined effects of substituents may be considerably greater than that expected on the basis of the individual effect of each substituent. As an example of this consider 4-methoxybenzaldehyde (Fig. 5.68). Since the two substituents are 'complementary' with the methoxy-

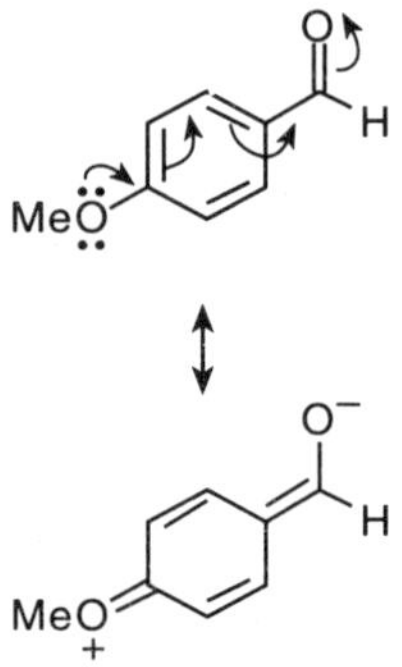

Fig. 5.68 'Complementary' substitution in 4-methoxybenzaldehyde.

releasing and the aldehyde-withdrawing electrons, and they are *para* related, we can write a resonance form in which the conjugation is considerably extended. This extends the chromophore, and the observed λ_{max} is greater than would be expected from the *individual* effects of the groups. When the groups are *meta* or *ortho* related, the effect on the chromophore is much less dramatic, and the observed λ_{max} values are much closer to those expected from the individual effects of the substituents. Similarly if the two substituents are non-complementary, in other words both are electron-releasing or electron-withdrawing, the chromophore is not affected to the same extent.

5 Bicyclic and polycyclic aromatic systems absorb at much longer wavelengths than monocyclic compounds.

Phenols and bathochromic shifts

There are two types of aromatic compound that can usually be readily identified from their UV spectra: phenols and anilines. We have already referred to the effect of interaction of the aromatic π-system with substituent lone pairs of electrons, and in comparing the long wavelength λ_{max} values for benzene, phenol and aniline, we find that they occur at 254, 270 and 280 nm, respectively. The interaction of the phenolic oxygen with the π-system increases considerably in the phenolate anion, since there are now two non-bonding pairs of electrons, and there is a large *bathochromic* shift in the absorption maximum. Hence the UV spectrum of a phenol should change dramatically if a base is added to the sample to deprotonate the phenolic OH. This effect is illustrated in Fig. 5.69, which shows the UV spectrum of 4-

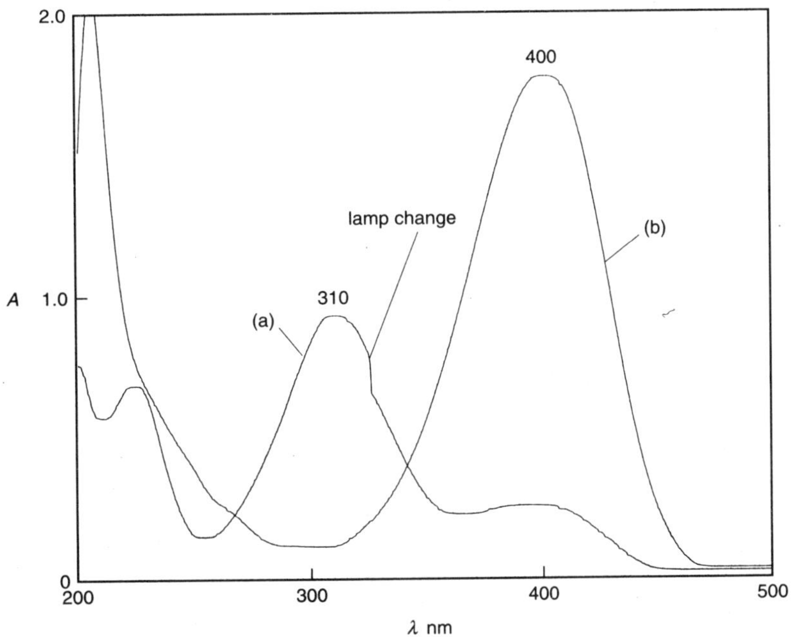

Fig. 5.69 UV spectra of 4-nitrophenol: (a) in ethanol; (b) in ethanol with added sodium hydroxide solution.

nitrophenol run in ethanol, and the changes that occur on adding sodium hydroxide to the solution. On addition of base the λ_{max} value increases from 310 to 400 nm. Note that the *intensity* of absorption also increases. In this particular case the change in absorption properties on addition of base is so dramatic as to be visible to the human eye; the original dilute ethanol solution of 4-nitrophenol is *very* faintly yellow, but the colour deepens considerably when a drop of sodium hydroxide solution is added.

Anilines and hypsochromic shifts

The reverse arguments apply with anilines. Because of the greater donor ability of nitrogen over oxygen, the nitrogen lone pair has a greater interaction with the π-system. However, we can remove this interaction by protonating the nitrogen. The resulting anilinium cation no longer has non-bonding electrons to interact with the aromatic system, and therefore shows a *hyp-*

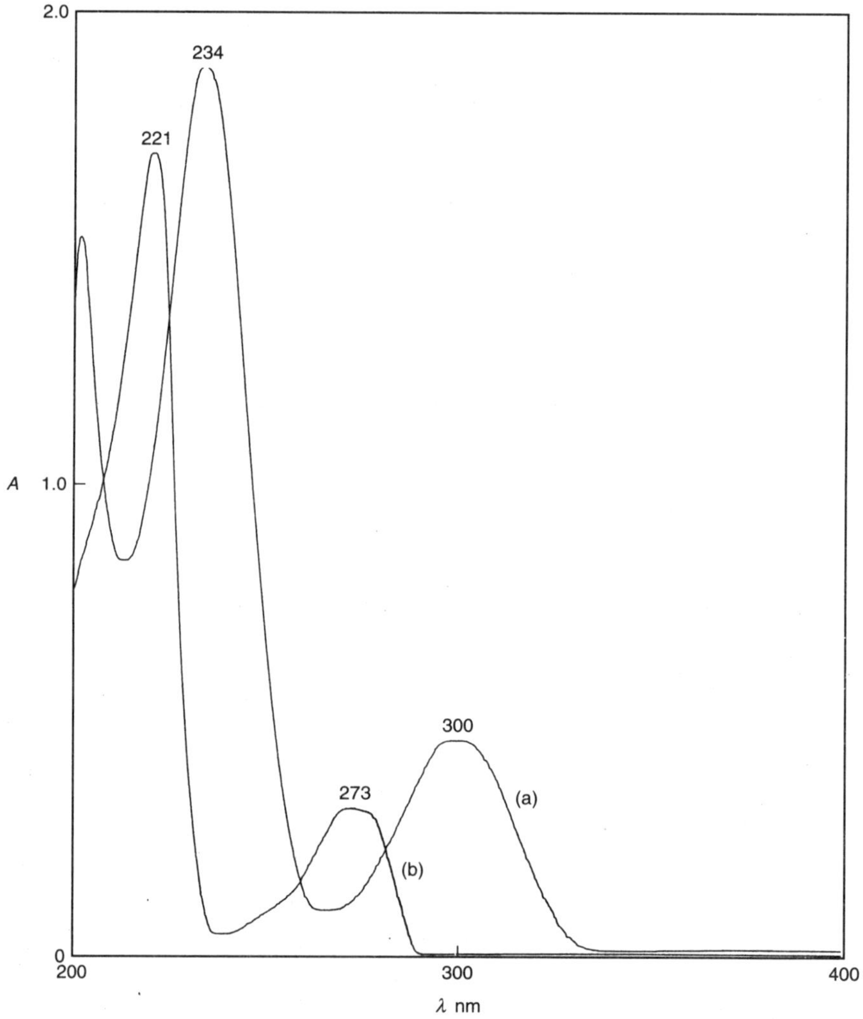

Fig. 5.70 UV spectra of 4-methoxyaniline: (a) in ethanol; (b) in ethanol with added hydrochloric acid.

sochromic shift (to shorter wavelength) in the UV spectrum. Hence the UV spectrum of an aniline should change if an acid is added to the solution to protonate the NH_2 group. This effect is illustrated in Fig. 5.70, which shows the UV spectrum of 4-methoxyaniline in ethanol and the changes which occur on addition of hydrochloric acid. The long wavelength absorption at 300 nm moves to 273 nm with a decrease in intensity on addition of the acid. Such simple experimental tricks are very useful in the identification of these functional groups.

Further reading

Organic Electronic Spectral Data, Vols 1–31, Wiley & Sons, New York, 1960–1989.
Sadtler Handbook of Ultraviolet Spectra, Sadtler, Pennsylvania, 1979.
L.M. Harwood and T.D.W. Claridge, *Introduction to Organic Spectroscopy*, Oxford University Press, Oxford, 1996, Chapter 7.
A.I. Scott, *Interpretation of the Ultraviolet Spectra of Natural Products*, Pergamon, Oxford, 1964.
R.M. Silverstein, G.C. Bassler and T.C. Morrill, *Spectrometric Identification of Organic Compounds*, 6th edn, Wiley & Sons, New York, 1998.
S. Sternhell and J. Kalman, *Organic Structures from Spectra*, 2nd edn, Wiley & Sons, New York, 1995.
D.H. Williams and I. Fleming, *Spectroscopic Methods in Organic Chemistry*, 5th edn, McGraw-Hill, Maidenhead, 1995.

5.5 Mass spectrometry

Mass spectrometry is concerned with the determination of the molecular mass of the sample in question—a particularly useful piece of information for the organic chemist which the other spectroscopic techniques cannot provide. The basic principle by which the individual molecules are 'weighed' is very simple and was first demonstrated by Wien in 1898. The sample is first converted into positive ions by being bombarded with high energy electrons which remove an electron from the molecule on impact. The positive ions are then accelerated by an electrical potential and pass through a magnetic field which causes them to be deflected from their initial straight line of flight. The degree of deviation depends on the magnetic field strength, the charge on the ion and its momentum. It is not difficult to appreciate intuitively that lighter ions will be deflected more than heavier ions for a given magnetic field strength and ionic charge, and very simple application of classic mechanics permits the following relationship to be derived.

$$\frac{m}{z} = \frac{H^2R^2}{2V}$$

where m = mass of the ion, z = charge on the ion, H = applied magnetic field strength, R = radius of arc of deflection, and V = applied accelerating voltage.

Of course, the whole procedure only works in the absence of energy exchanges resulting from intermolecular collisions; therefore the analysis has to be carried out under extremely high dilution conditions, necessitating a very high vacuum. As it examines individual species and not the bulk sample, mass spectrometry readily distinguishes between isotopes of the same element and this is also useful for the organic chemist.

In addition to giving the molecular weight of the substance under examination (the *molecular ion*), mass spectrometry enables a detailed analysis of molecular structure to be made. Under the fairly brutal conditions of electron impact ionization, the molecules tend to undergo cleavage either at weak bonds or to give particularly stable fragments in very predictable ways. Consequently, it is usually possible to infer molecular structure by analysis of the breakdown pattern in the mass spectrum of an unknown. Some molecules are so sensitive that none survive the conditions of electron impact ionization intact and therefore a molecular ion is not obtained in the mass spectrum. Naturally this can be very misleading and also deprives the chemist of the one piece of information that cannot be obtained by the other spectroscopic techniques—the molecular weight of the substance. Fortunately there are 'softer' ionization techniques available which allow the molecular ion to be observed by using lower energy electron beams or a pre-ionized gas.

Machines of higher resolving power, referred to as *double-focusing* instruments, permit the accurate measurement of molecular masses to within a few parts per million. With this precision it is possible to obtain the actual atomic constitution of the molecule by differentiation between different species which have the same integral molecular mass. Such measurements permit a very good guess at the molecular formula of even rather complex substances, and this technique provides an alternative to microanalysis for determining elemental composition—of particular importance when only small amounts (less than $500\,\mu g$) of material are available.

Mass spectrometry requires only a very small amount of sample; less than a microgram is needed for the analysis itself. The actual amount of sample required is therefore really only a function of the limitations of manipulation rather than the analysis. This makes mass spectrometry effectively a non-destructive technique.

Computers are central to mass spectrometry. An important feature of commercial machines is the computing hardware available to manage the wealth of data that can be extracted from the mass spectrum of a compound, but a discussion of such aspects is beyond the scope of this book.

The instrument

Organic chemists can thank the petroleum industry for providing the impetus to move mass spectrometry from the realm of the physicists into the organic chemistry laboratory for use as an analytical tool. Mass spectroscopic analysis proved ideal for providing rapid solutions to the problems of differentiating between members of homologous series of alkanes and alkenes. From this sprang the large range of commercial machines which are able to cope with an enormous spread of chemical structures and molecular weights.

All instruments, whatever additional sophistication they might possess, require a very high vacuum (around 10^{-6} mmHg) to operate, at the same time permitting the introduction of sample. It is this requirement, placing very stringent demands on the design, engineering and operation of a mass spectrometer, which makes these instruments extremely sensitive to misuse. For this reason, organic chemists are usually kept well clear of the machine, and its operation is left to those who have been fully trained. Mass spectrometry is very rarely available 'hands-on', although with the advent of more robust pumping systems this situation is beginning to change, at least in some research laboratories.

The resolution in the type of instrument used to obtain a standard mass spectrum of organic molecules by electron impact ionization can be achieved by the *single focusing* arrangement depicted in Fig. 5.71.

A small quantity of the sample to be analyzed is introduced through the inlet port as a vapour where it meets a beam of high energy electrons (*ca.* 70 eV). Whilst electrons of about 10 eV possess sufficient energy to cause ionization of the molecule, the higher energy electrons used can rupture bonds within the molecule, causing its fragmentation and giving a much more informative spectrum than one which just contains the molecular ion. The positive ions produced in the ionization chamber are then accelerated by a high voltage (4–8 kV) and focused into a tight beam. The collimated beam then passes through a strong magnetic field disposed at right angles to its path which causes the ions to be deflected in an arc. Lighter ions are deflected to a greater extent than heavier ions with the same charge, and the separated ion beams are collected and the intensity of each beam is measured (Fig. 5.72).

To record the entire range of molecular masses, either the accelerating potential or (more commonly) the magnetic field strength is varied, in order to focus each ion beam in turn onto the detector where the positive ions combine with electrons. This sets up a current proportional to the intensity of

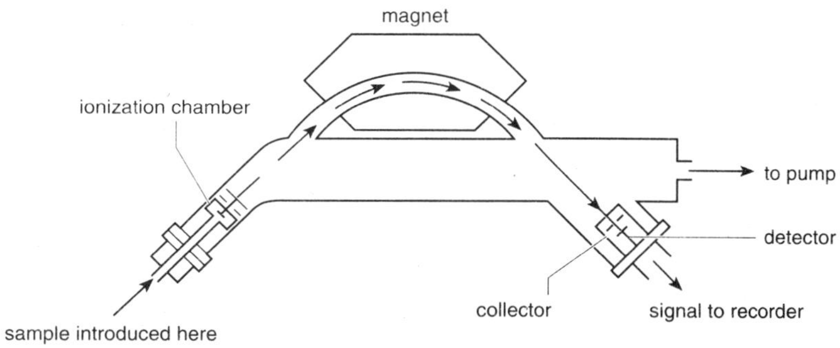

Fig. 5.71 Schematic diagram depicting the layout of a single focusing mass spectrometer.

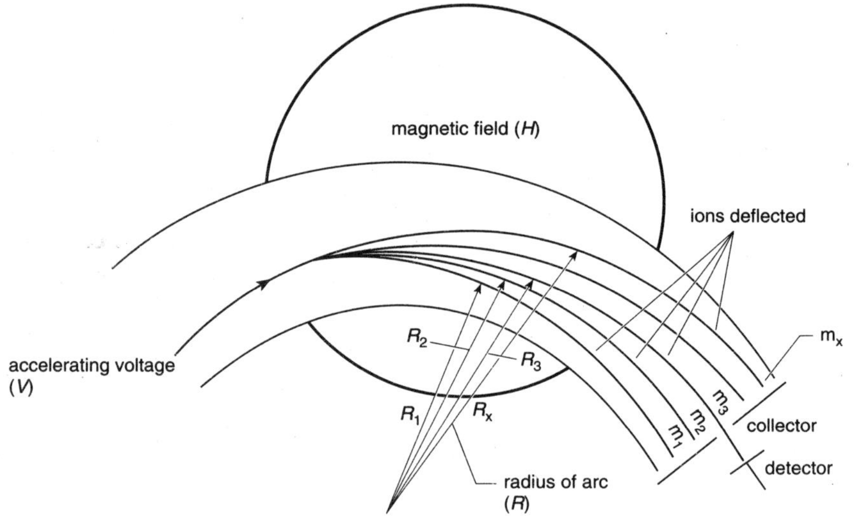

Fig. 5.72 Positively charged ions are deflected to varying degrees by an applied magnetic field according to their mass.

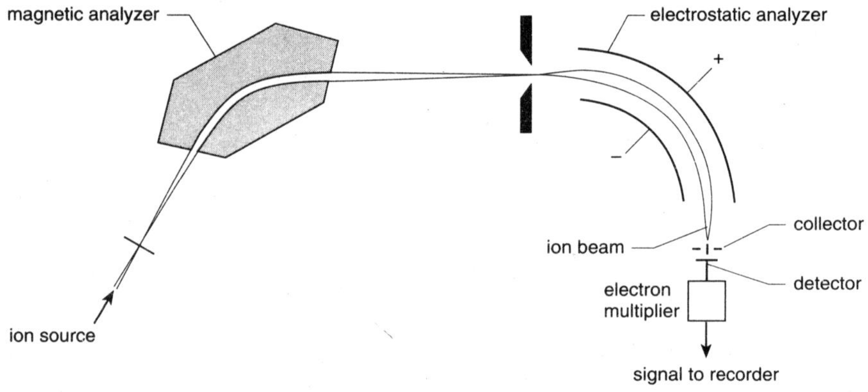

Fig. 5.73 Schematic diagram showing the principal features of a double-focusing mass spectrometer.

the ion beam and measurement of this gives the *relative abundance* of the ions produced by that particular fragmentation process. The relative abundance of each ion formed is, of course, dependent on the ease of the fragmentation process which gives rise to it, and is an important diagnostic feature of the mass spectrum of a molecule.

The construction of the *double-focusing* instrument is similar to the single-focusing system except than an additional electrostatic analyzer is placed after the magnetic analyzer (Fig. 5.73). After the ions have been sorted according to their mass by the magnetic analyzer, the electrostatic analyzer separates ions of the same mass but possessing different energy. This enhances resolution by refocusing the small energy spread that is found within each collection of ions of the same integral mass. To increase resolution further, the slits on the collector are narrower than in the single focusing instrument, enabling much greater discrimination in the analysis of the ion beams. Unfortunately, this higher selectivity is won at the cost of sensitivity because the narrower slit means that fewer ions can be sampled at any one time. The sensitivity problem is overcome by using electron multipliers in conjunction with the collector, making it possible to detect ion currents as low as 10^{-18} A.

Other means of mass analysis are also available in addition to deflection of ions by a magnetic field as just described. Other systems include *time of flight spectrometers* and *ion-cyclotron spectrometers*; however, by far the commonest alternative to magnetic sector spectrometers are those using a *quadrupole mass filter*. The advantage of this system is that it is robust and compact, making it suitable for 'hands-on' bench-top machines. In addition, its fast molecular weight scanning capability renders it ideal for use in GC–MS systems and such quadrupole instruments are rapidly gaining acceptance. However, there is insufficient space to cover these systems here and those interested in the principles governing the operation of such instruments are directed to the references at the end of this section.

A development which is proving to be a very powerful technique is *on-line GC–MS*. As its name suggests, this involves connecting the outlet from a gas chromatograph directly to the inlet of a mass spectrometer, permitting the analysis of very complex mixtures. However, the need for selective removal of the carrier gas from the effluent before introduction of the sample into the high vacuum of the mass spectrometer results in many additional technical difficulties. Several designs of GC–MS interface exist, but one commonly encountered arrangement uses a jet molecular separator in which the column effluent gas exits through a fine jet and impinges onto a sharp-edged collector nozzle (Fig. 5.74). The lighter components of the mixture diffuse more quickly to the periphery and are removed. The sharp-edged collector nozzle, a small

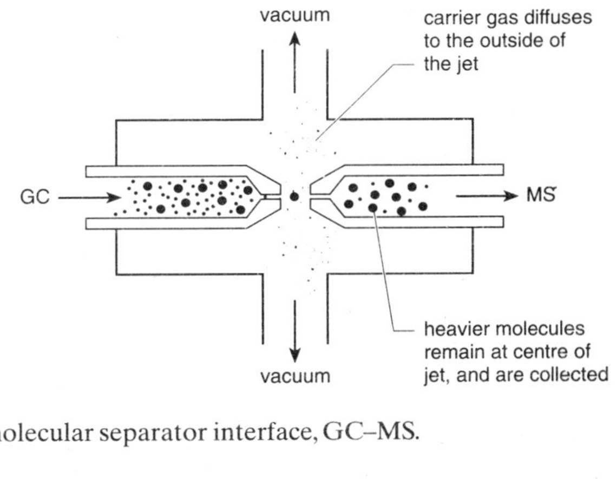

Fig. 5.74 Jet molecular separator interface, GC–MS.

distance from the jet, only permits passage of the innermost part of the jet (containing the heavier molecules) into the mass spectrometer.

In *directly coupled GC–MS* systems the use of highly efficient vacuum pumps, combined with the reduced rate of gas throughput in capillary GC, now mean that it is possible for the chromatography effluent gases to enter the mass spectrometer without the necessity for an interface.

Combined high performance liquid chromatography (HPLC)–MS instruments are also available which take the output from a liquid chromatography column directly into a mass spectrometer. The problems associated with GC–MS pale into insignificance against those encountered in the selective removal of the eluant solvents from purified components after HPLC. However, the prize of being able to analyze mixtures which are not volatile enough to be separated by vapour phase chromatography makes the additional instrumental complication all worthwhile.

It has not been possible in these paragraphs to do more than mention a few of the extensions of mass spectrometry which now make up the sophisticated analytical arsenal available to organic chemists. The limitation on the technique is the stability of molecules to conditions in which they are volatile enough to pass through the mass spectrometer. As the kinds of molecules of interest to chemists grow in complexity and sensitivity, so new techniques are developed to analyze them by mass spectrometry. Whilst many of these techniques involve extremely complex instrumentation, what is considered as 'state-of-the-art' today has a habit of becoming routine very rapidly in mass spectrometry. There is insufficient space to give procedures such as *field desorption spectrometry*, *field ionization spectrometry*, *fast atom bombardment*, *electroscopy*, *thermospray* and MALDI, even the cursory treatment which has been afforded to the basic mass spectrometric techniques in this book. The references given at the end of this section contain useful additional information.

Preparing the sample

Avoiding contamination

As far as most organic chemists are concerned, preparation of the sample simply involves placing a suitable quantity in a labelled tube and submitting it for analysis. However, the very high sensitivity of mass spectrometry underlines the need to avoid contamination of the sample at all costs. Many a pure sample has given an unacceptable or misleading mass spectrum because of thoughtlessness in preparing the sample for analysis. The problem stems from the almost ubiquitous use of additives to maintain pliability in plastics—particularly those used to make push-caps for specimen tubes. The plasticizers leach perniciously into the sample if allowed to come into contact with it, and give a whole series of spurious peaks in the mass spectrum. *Be warned! Never use push-cap tubes to submit samples for mass spectrometry*. The types of

Beware of plasticizers!

Table 5.5 Common impurity peaks encountered in mass spectra.

Contaminant	Peaks observed (m/z)
(a) Plasticizers	
n-Butyl phthalate	149, 205, 223, 278
n-Octyl phthalate	149, 167, 279
Tri-*n*-butyl acetyl citrate	129, 185, 259, 429
Tributyl phosphate	99, 155, 211
(b) Antioxidants	
2,6-Di-*t*-butyl-*p*-cresol	205, 220
(c) Stopcock grease	
Silicone grease	133, 207, 281, 355, 429
(d) Air	18 (H_2O), 28 (N_2), 32 (O_2), 40 (Ar), 44 (CO_2)

plasticizers used (Table 5.5) have molecular weights in the region 200–300, precisely the sort of region of interest to organic chemists. The best tubes to use for mass spectrometry samples are those having screw-caps with an aluminum-covered inner liner to the cap. However, plastic push-caps are not the only source of plasticizers and you should not allow your sample to come into contact with anything made of flexible polymer such as pipette bulbs or even plastic-backed TLC plates. Impurities which are frequently encountered in mass spectra of apparently rigorously purified samples are silicone grease and polymeric hydrocarbons. The usual sources of these materials are over-liberally greased stopcocks on chromatography columns or separatory funnels; however, care should also be taken when sealing flasks with commercially available paraffin film, traces of which can find their way into the sample. Hydrocarbons often give a whole series of peaks separated by 14 mass units whose intensities gradually decrease with increasing molecular weight. As these tend not to give a definite molecular ion the presence of these peaks is usually unsatisfactory rather than misleading; however, samples giving a weak molecular ion can be swamped by the background contamination. Silicone grease is a different affair, giving very distinct peaks in the mass spectrum. Finally, many plastics contain added antioxidants, usually hindered phenols, to slow down atmospheric degradation and increase their useful life. Although only present in trace amounts, these are readily leached by organic materials with which they come into contact. You should learn to recognize and distrust any peaks corresponding to those in Table 5.5.

Sample submission

Although the technique requires only a vanishingly small amount of sample for analysis, have pity on the operator and supply at least enough sample to see—this makes life much easier when trying to extract the sample from the tube! In addition, the more sample you supply the less will be the effect of any

Submit samples in a manner which makes it easy for the operator to handle them

chance contamination on the resultant spectrum. At the same time, there is no need to supply grams of material; usually a few milligrams of a crystalline solid or a little more of a viscous oil will suffice. Whenever possible, liquid samples should be supplied in containers with a conical or hemispherical bottom in which the sample accumulates for easy removal. Never forget to label your tube clearly with your name, where you can be contacted, the possible structure of your sample and any dangerous properties it may possess. Normally it will be necessary to fill in a form with all of these details and also to fill in a booking sheet. Courtesy and common sense should always be paramount with sample submission to any analytical service; once goodwill between yourself and the operator has been lost it is nearly impossible to regain it!

Always check before submitting noxious materials for analysis

Never submit noxious or toxic materials for analysis without first discussing your intentions with the operator.

Derivatizing samples for GC–MS

The common derivatization procedures for GC–MS involve the conversion of polar groups such as alcohols, amines and carboxylic acids into the silylated, acetylated or methylated derivatives, and some procedures are described on pp. 196–197. Derivatization is used in mass spectrometry, not only for rendering the material more volatile, but also to give a more abundant molecular ion peak or clearer fragmentation pattern.

Running the spectrum

Introducing the sample

The choice of method for introducing the sample into the mass spectrometer is usually dictated by the physical properties of the substance under investigation. All systems are designed to permit the material to be introduced in a controlled and measured way without destroying the vacuum within the instrument or requiring extended periods of additional evacuation.

Heated inlet

Moderately volatile samples can be introduced by a *heated inlet* in which the material diffuses into a reservoir maintained at *ca.* 10^{-2} mmHg and a temperature of up to 350°C. The reservoir is attached to the ultra-low pressure part of the mass spectrometer by a porous disk which allows the sample in the reservoir to bleed into the ionization chamber (Fig. 5.75). The drawback of this arrangement is that thermally unstable compounds may undergo decomposition on the container walls before being introduced into the ion chamber.

Direct insertion

A septum inlet may be used for liquids, but materials of low thermal stability are usually introduced into the mass spectrometer using a *direct insertion probe*. The sample is loaded onto the ceramic tip of the probe contained in a glass capillary, and this is then passed through a vacuum lock into the ioniza-

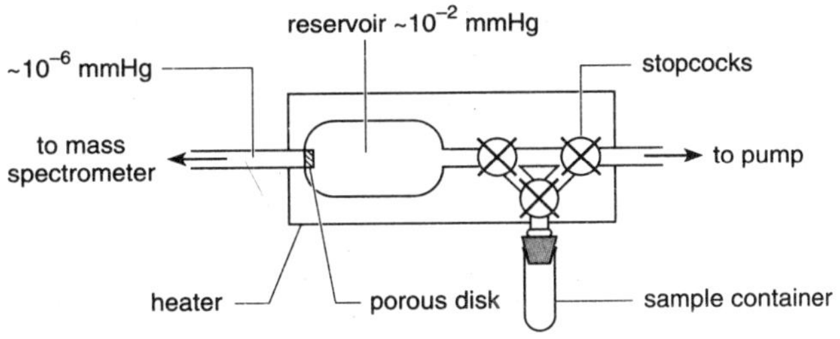

Fig. 5.75 Sample introduction by a heated inlet system.

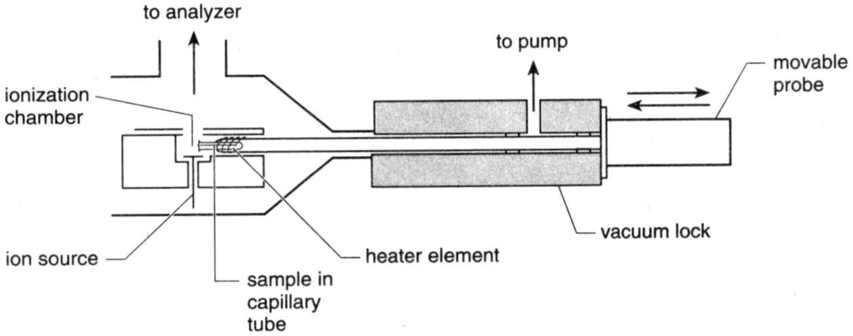

Fig. 5.76 Direct insertion probe for thermally unstable materials.

tion chamber where the sample is exposed to the electron beam (Fig. 5.76). The tip of the probe can also be heated by means of a platinum element to extend the temperature range of samples which can be analyzed.

Recording and calibrating spectra

The mass spectrum is scanned over the full range from low to high mass in the magnetic sector instrument (high to low mass with quadrupole instruments). Recording is usually stopped before the lowest ion $m/z = 12$, corresponding to $C^{+\cdot}$, is reached.

Peak counting on photographic charts

Older spectrometers produce the spectra as photographic charts which require each peak to be counted by eye. A recognizable starting point is therefore necessary. You should look for nitrogen and oxygen molecular ions at $m/z = 28$ and 32 as a pair of peaks with relative intensities of roughly 4 : 1 (see Table 5.5). Another useful calibration point is the closely spaced double peak that occurs at $m/z = 40$ due to the presence of argon and the $C_3H_4^+$ fragment ion from the introduced sample. Although the peaks on photographic charts are widely separated at low molecular mass, they close up at high mass and it becomes difficult to count them at molecular masses higher than about 300. When counting, you should not be misled by the appearance of any small peaks which appear at the mid-point between expected peaks, as these are

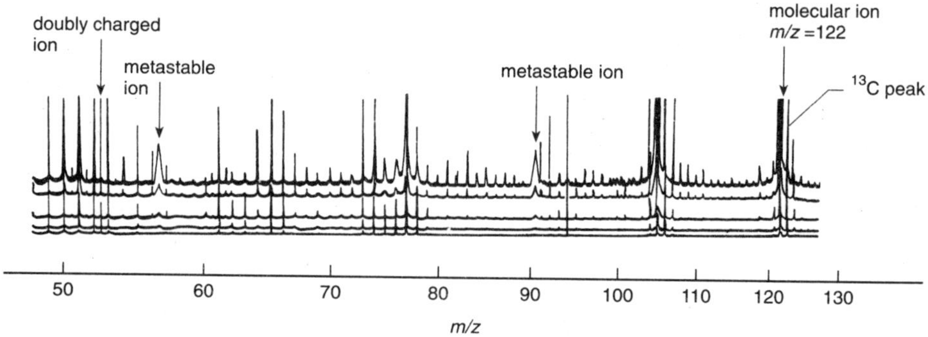

Fig. 5.77 The mass spectrum of benzoic acid presented as a photographic chart. Note the metastable peaks at $m/z = 56.47$ ($105 \rightarrow 77$) and 90.37 ($122 \rightarrow 105$) and the doubly charged ion peak at $m/z = 52.5$. The peaks close up with increasing mass and the major peaks on the top trace are off-scale and have been truncated.

due to doubly charged odd molecular weight ions ($m/2z$) which have been detected. To ease peak counting, especially in 'empty' areas in the sample spectrum, a spectrum of perfluorokerosene is often included against the unknown spectrum, or a scale of mass units may be marked on the bottom of the chart.

Perfluorokerosene contains a regular series of peaks separated by 12 or 14 mass units in a molecular weight range of 19–800 mass units. Photographic charts normally present the spectrum as a series of superimposed traces of increasing sensitivity. By this means it is usually possible to count the peaks using the most sensitive trace at the same time as identifying the major fragmentation ions (Fig. 5.77). However, it is not very easy to measure the relative abundances of the fragment peaks.

The photographic charts fade if left exposed to bright light, so always roll them up when not needed and store them in a dark place.

Bar graphs

A more convenient representation of the mass spectrum is given by a bar graph, plotting relative abundance of the ions against their mass. (This is the form in which mass spectra will be depicted in this book). The spectrum is normalized to give the most abundant ion (the *base peak*) an intensity of 100% (Fig. 5.78). One drawback to this method of presentation is that the wide variation in peak intensities in a mass spectrum can cause important peaks such as the molecular ion to be too small to be observed. This can be overcome by magnifying the high molecular weight end of the spectrum to render small but important peaks visible. Another disadvantage of this presentation is that it gives no information on any metastable peaks (pp. 388–389), as it only shows peaks occurring at integral values.

A third form of output presents the data in tabular form but, although this contains all of the necessary data, the fact that the information is not in a pictorial format makes it difficult to assimilate at a glance.

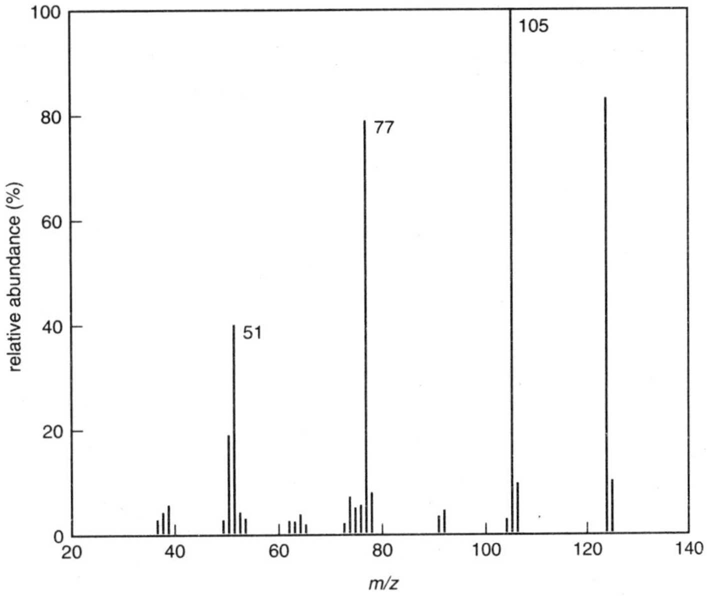

Fig. 5.78 Mass spectrum of benzoic acid represented as a bar graph.

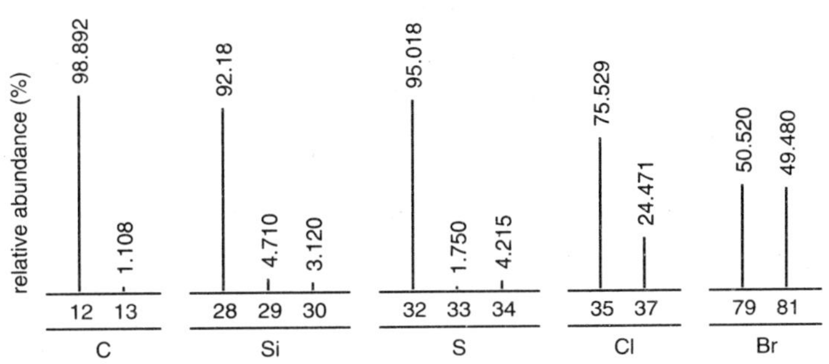

Fig. 5.79 Isotope abundances for carbon, silicon, sulfur, chlorine and bromine.

Interpretation of spectra

Isotopes

Before we can start to discuss the extraction of data from the mass spectrum of an unknown, it is necessary to consider the consequences of the isotopic constitution of the constituent elements of the sample. Of the elements likely to be encountered in your sample, only fluorine, iodine and phospho are monoisotopic. However, with the exception of the elements shown in Fig. 5.79, most others can be considered to be effectively monoisotopic due to the low abundance of their minor constituent isotopes.

Let us discuss the effect of a polyisotopic element on the appearance of the mass spectrum by considering a monobrominated compound. Bromine consists of two isotopes (^{79}Br, ^{81}Br) in roughly equal amounts, and therefore the molecular ion, or any species containing bromine, will appear in the mass spectrum as a pair of equal intensity peaks separated by two mass units (Fig. 5.80a). It is not difficult to see that a species containing two atoms of bromine will appear as three peaks (each separated by two mass units) of approximate intensity 1:2:1 (Fig. 5.80b). Likewise tribrominated species will give four peaks of intensity 1:4:4:1 (Fig. 5.80c). Parts d–f show the equivalent isotope patterns for species containing one, two and three chlorine atoms (76% ^{35}Cl, 24% ^{37}Cl).

The relative intensity of peaks resulting from the presence of atoms of an element with two isotopes in a molecule can be calculated using a binomial expansion

$$(a+b)^n$$

where a = the abundance of the light isotope, b = the abundance of the heavy isotope, and n = the number of atoms of the element.

These isotope patterns are quite useful when examining mass spectra of molecules containing chlorine or bromine. However, the 1.1% ^{13}C isotope naturally present in organic molecules can be a trap for the unwary chemist when it comes to deciding which is the molecular ion of the compound under investigation. If a molecule contains 10 carbon atoms, there is a 1.1% chance that any of them will be a ^{13}C isotope and there is a 10 × 1.1% chance that the molecule will contain one ^{13}C atom somewhere. Consequently, if we forget the possibility of other polyisotopic elements being present, the molecular ion ($M^{+\cdot}$) will be accompanied by another peak at (M + 1) of about one-tenth its intensity (see Figs 5.77 and 5.78). *Do not mistake the ^{13}C peak at M + 1 for the molecular ion.* With larger molecules this ^{13}C peak becomes more and more important and peaks due to molecules containing two or more ^{13}C isotopes start to become visible at M + 2, M + 3 and so on, complicating the situation still further. However, for the usual size of C,H,N,O-containing organic molecule encountered, the molecular ion will be the largest of the peaks at the high molecular weight limit.

Look out for the ^{13}C peak at M + 1

The molecular ion

The first, and arguably the most important, piece of information that can be obtained from the mass spectrum is the molecular ion ($M^{+\cdot}$) which corresponds to the molecular weight of the unknown. In deciding which peak actu-

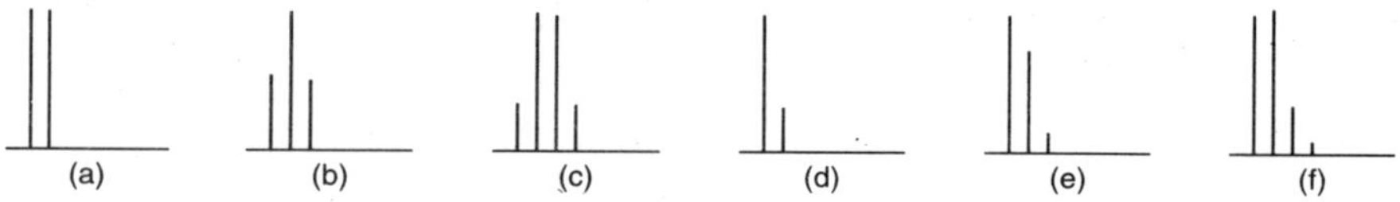

Fig. 5.80 Isotope patterns of species: (a) Br; (b) Br_2; (c) Br_3; (d) Cl; (e) Cl_2; (f) Cl_3.

ally corresponds to the molecular ion, it is important to remember the possibility of polyisotopic atoms and not to be tricked by the ^{13}C peak.

The nitrogen rule

Molecules containing odd numbers of nitrogen atoms have odd molecular weights

Most organic molecules have molecular weights that are even, with the common exceptions to this rule being those compounds which contain odd numbers of nitrogen atoms—a consequence of nitrogen having an even atomic weight and an odd valency. However, whilst the observation of an odd molecular ion in a mass spectrum run under electron impact conditions indicates the presence of nitrogen in the molecule, this need not be the situation. It may be that this highest molecular weight peak is actually a fragment ion, with the true molecular ion being too unstable to be observed. You should particularly suspect this if the 'molecular ion' loses any fragment between 3 and 14 mass units. These would correspond to highly unfavourable events, such as multiple losses of hydrogen atoms or the formation of high energy species. For this latter reason, loss of methylene (CH_2) is almost never observed, and so that appearance of a fragment ion at 14 mass units below the highest peak is clear evidence that the true molecular ion is not being observed. This can be checked by repeating the electron impact spectrum under 'softer' ionizing conditions (using lower energy electrons of, say, 20 eV) to see if the molecular ion becomes visible.

Chemical ionization

If the molecular ion is still not observed, the spectrum can be obtained using even milder *chemical ionization* conditions. This technique is carried out by introducing the sample at low pressure (10^{-4} mmHg) into the ionization chamber in the presence of excess ammonia or methane at a pressure of 1 mmHg. Electron impact causes preferential ionization of the gas which can then undergo intermolecular proton transfer under the relatively high concentrations in the ionization chamber to furnish NH_4^+ or CH_5^+. These species can protonate the sample under conditions which are sufficiently mild so that fragmentation of the resultant MH^+ *quasi-molecular ion* does not occur. With ammonia the highest peak is often at M + 18 due to the formation of the MNH_4^+ species. However, electrophilic additions are much less common with methane and any such peaks are usually small compared with MH^+.

Some molecules will self-protonate in the mass spectrometer

Some substances, particularly amines and polyols, show a tendency to carry out a similar sort of intermolecular protonation process under standard electron impact conditions. This results in a diminished molecular ion with a larger than predicted M + 1 peak, and is most noticeable when the substance itself has a molecular ion which is unstable with regard to fragmentation (Fig. 5.81).

As a general rule of thumb, aromatic compounds give strong molecular ions (exceptions are bromides, iodides, benzylic halides and aryl ketones, although these usually give easily detected molecular ions). Molecular ions which are very weak or totally absent can be expected in spectra obtained from tertiary alcohols and halides, and branched or long chain alkanes.

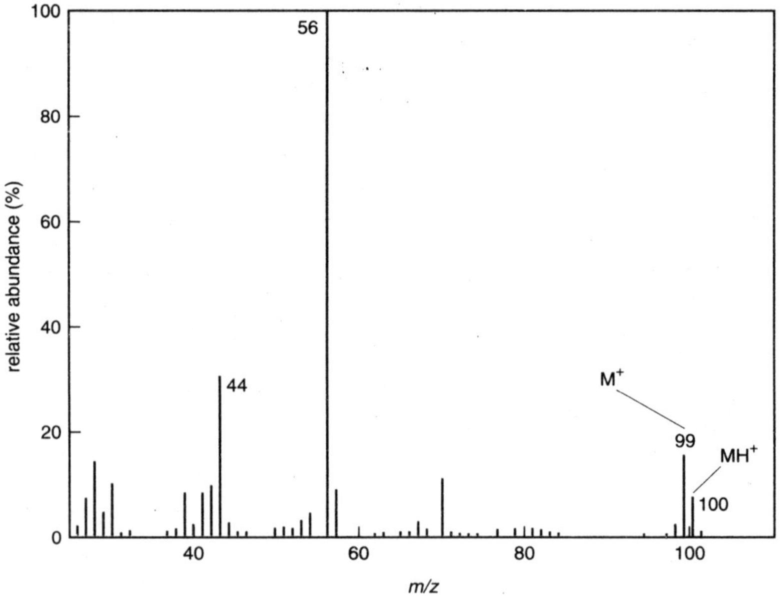

Fig. 5.81 Mass spectrum of cyclohexylamine showing an M + 1 peak due to intermolecular self-protonation.

Common fragmentation pathways

When a molecule is ionized by electron impact with 70 eV electrons, more energy can be imparted than is needed to remove an electron. In the absence of intermolecular interactions, this excess electronic energy of the excited state is transferred to ground-state vibrational energy, and can result in fragmentation of the molecule. The energy transferred in any impact can vary up to the maximum energy of the ionizing electrons. This leads to a range of different decomposition pathways, giving fragment ions which provide a characteristic fingerprint of the compound.

Fragmentation peaks are important for structural elucidation

Under any given conditions, the degree to which a particular fragmentation occurs, and hence the relative abundance of the peaks corresponding to the fragments, depends to a large extent on the facility of the cleavage process. Generally, one-bond cleavages occur more readily than those which involve simultaneous breaking of more than one bond, as the latter process imposes strict conformational constraints on the molecule. One-bond cleavages from C,H,O compounds will result in odd mass fragment ions, whereas two-bond cleavages, with the loss of a neutral molecule, will give even-mass fragments. A list of some of the more frequently encountered fragmentations is given in Appendix 3, but this is by no means exhaustive and other more complete tables may be found in the works listed on pp. 395–396. However, some particular fragmentations are so important that they deserve special mention here.

Tropylium ion = 91

Any aromatic molecule containing a benzyl group will show a very important fragment (usually the base peak) at $m/z = 91$. This corresponds to formation of the highly stabilized tropylium species, either directly or by rearrangement of the benzyl cation. Usually the tropylium peak is accompanied by a peak at $m/z = 65$ due to a second fragmentation resulting in loss of ethyne.

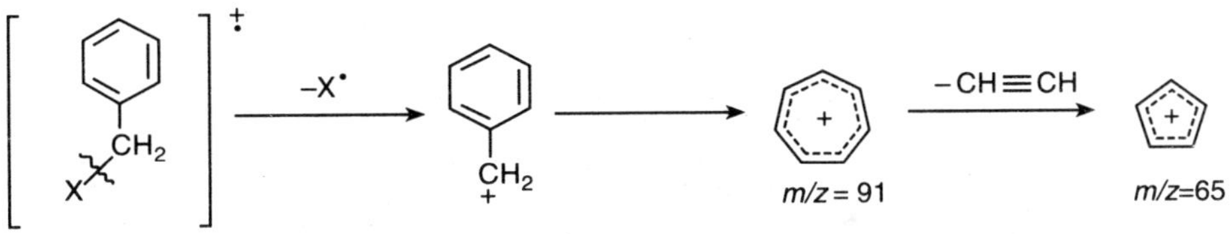

Acetyl ion = 43
Benzoyl ion = 105

Compounds possessing acyl groups will give important fragment peaks at m/z corresponding to formation of the acylium cation. For instance, acetates and methyl ketones give a strong peak at $m/z = 43$ and benzoates or phenyl ketones give an equivalent peak at $m/z = 105$. Usually these species are accompanied by peaks corresponding to loss of carbon monoxide.

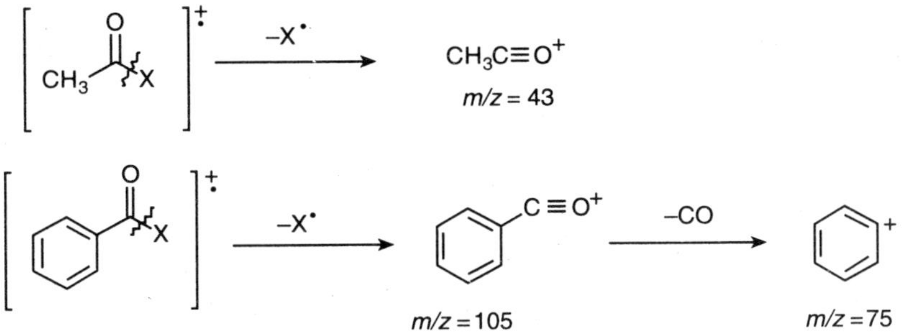

Among the two-bond fragmentation processes, one of the most documented is the *McLafferty rearrangement* which occurs with ketones and esters in which a hydrogen substituent is present γ- to the carbonyl group. The molecular ion can be considered to undergo a reverse-ene reaction, with the charge usually residing on the portion retaining the carbonyl atoms.

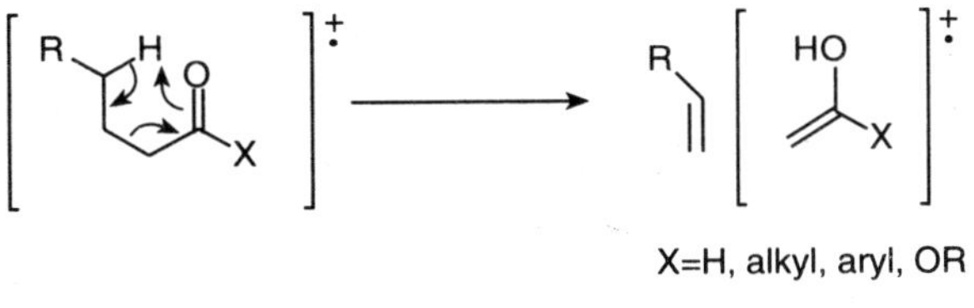

The *retro-Diels–Alder* reaction is an important fragmentation which occurs with cyclohexenes, commonly leaving the charge on the diene component.

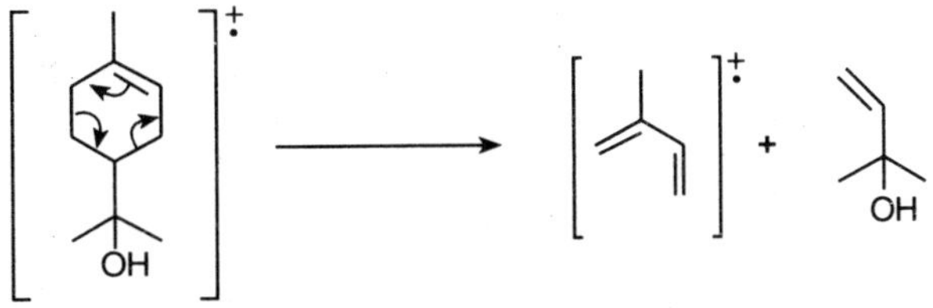

In general, if an elimination can occur to furnish a small stable neutral molecule then this will happen, particularly in molecules where one-bond cleavages are not favoured. In particular, alcohols lose water giving a peak at M – 18 and acetates lose acetic acid to give a peak at M – 60.

In fragmentation reactions it is possible to predict which fragment will be lost as the neutral moiety and which will retain the charge and be detected in the mass spectrometer. The *Stephenson–Audier rule* states that in a fragmentation reaction, the positive charge will reside on the moiety which has the lowest ionization potential. The easiest way of applying this rule is to remember the approximation that the greater possibility a fragment has for resonance stabilization, the lower its ionization potential (Fig. 5.82).

Metastable peaks

These are a special kind of fragment peak which are seen in spectra recorded on photographic chart paper. They are much less common than normal fragmentation peaks, are characteristically broad and occur at non-integral positions in the spectrum. Metastable peaks can be clearly seen at $m/z = 56.47$ and 90.37 in the spectrum of benzoic acid in Fig. 5.77.

Metastable peaks are the result of fragmentations which occur outside the ionization chamber but before the magnetic analyzer of the spectrometer. The qualitative result of such a fragmentation can be appreciated without the need for rigorous mathematical treatment. When fragmentation occurs in the field-free zone, the parent ion has already experienced a period of time within the accelerating voltage. On fragmentation, the daughter ion keeps the velocity but has a lower mass than the parent ion. This means that the daughter ion has

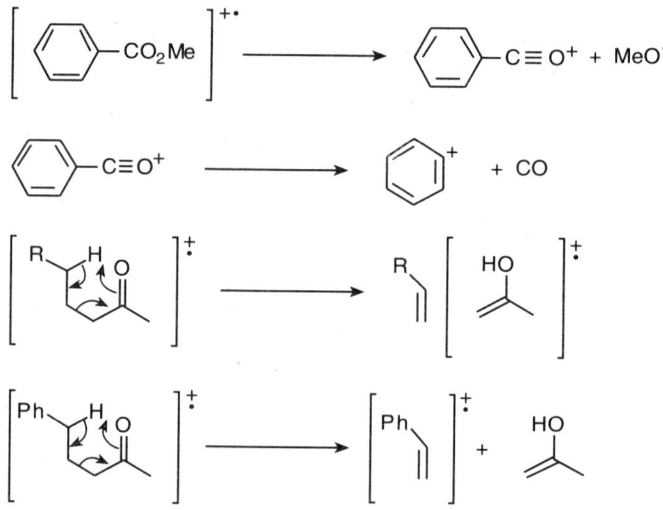

Fig. 5.82 Illustrations of the Stephenson–Audier rule.

a momentum which results in a measured mass lower than its actual mass. The actual relationship which can be derived is as follows:

$$m^* = \frac{(m_2)^2}{m_1}$$

where m_1 = the parent ion mass, m_2 = the daughter ion mass, and m^* = the metastable peak position.

The reason for the low abundance of metastable peaks can also be understood qualitatively. The rate constant for the fragmentation to furnish a metastable peak must be such as to allow the reaction to occur in the field-free region before the magnetic analyzer. If it occurs at a faster rate, the daughter ion is formed in the ionization chamber and gives a normal peak; if it occurs within the analyzer the ion peak is not transmitted to the detector. It turns out that very few ions have the type of lifetime (*ca.* 10^4–10^6) which fits the above constraints, and so only relatively few metastable peaks are recorded.

The mathematical relationship relates the position of the metastable peak to the masses of the parent and daughter ions. Unfortunately we only have one equation and two unknowns and so this has to be solved in a trial-and-error manner by inserting possible values for m_1 and m_2. However, to make life a little easier nomographs such as that shown in Fig. 5.83 have been developed, enabling values of m_1 and m_2 to be read off by placing a ruler at the value for m^*. Fortunately, the particular fragment ions m_1 and m_2 are usually abundant in the mass spectrum and this helps in choosing the likely parent and daughter ions. In addition, differences between m_1 and m_2 of less than 15 mass units can be ruled out.

High resolution mass measurement

Chemists usually quote atomic weights to no greater accuracy than one decimal place. However, using the non-integral atomic weight values based on ^{12}C = 12.000000, it is clearly possible to differentiate between atomic combinations having the same integral mass if the molecular mass can be measured with sufficient accuracy. If we consider species having an integral mass of 28, the accurate molecular mass values are as follows: CO = 27.99492; C_2H_4 = 28.03123; N_2 = 28.00616; and CH_2N = 28.01870. Consequently, it is possible to distinguish any of these from the others with a high resolution mass spectrometer. Conversely, if the mass of an unknown substance can be measured accurately (to around 1 ppm) it is possible to propose atomic combinations giving molecular mass values which agree with the measured result. This job is readily carried out using a computer, and it is frequently the case that a unique combination of elements fits the result, or all but one combination can be discarded on chemical grounds. This permits elemental

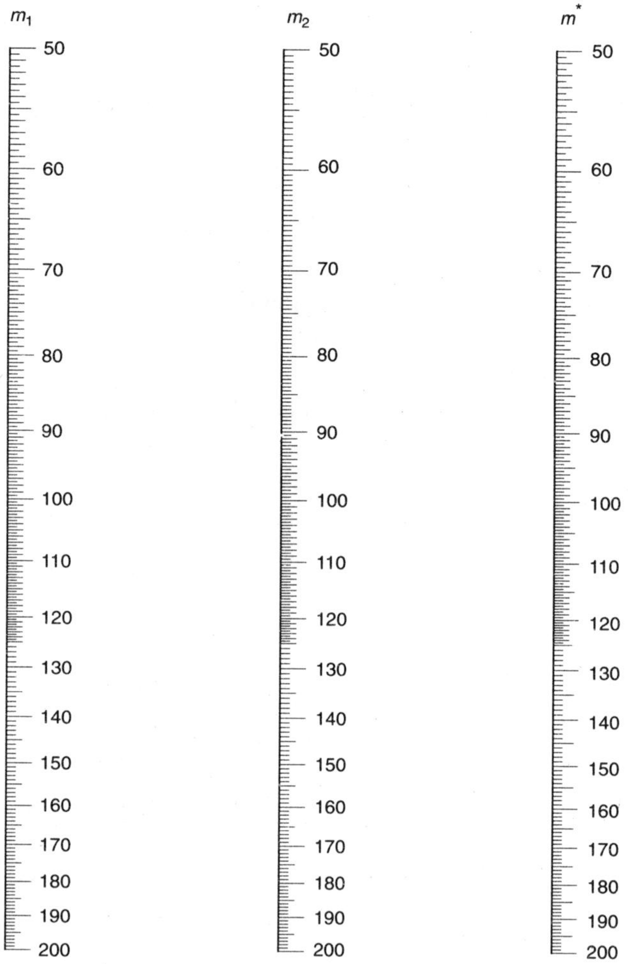

Fig. 5.83 Nomograph for relating metastable peaks to parent and daughter ions (after J.H. Benyon).

analysis by mass spectroscopy with all the attendant advantages of economy of sample.

Procedure for interpreting the spectrum of an unknown

It is impossible to give a foolproof procedure for interpreting any mass spectrum that you will encounter, and there is no substitute for experience. The flow diagram in Fig. 5.84 might help to put you on the right track, particularly with the types of compound you are liable to encounter in the early stages of your training, such as those listed below.

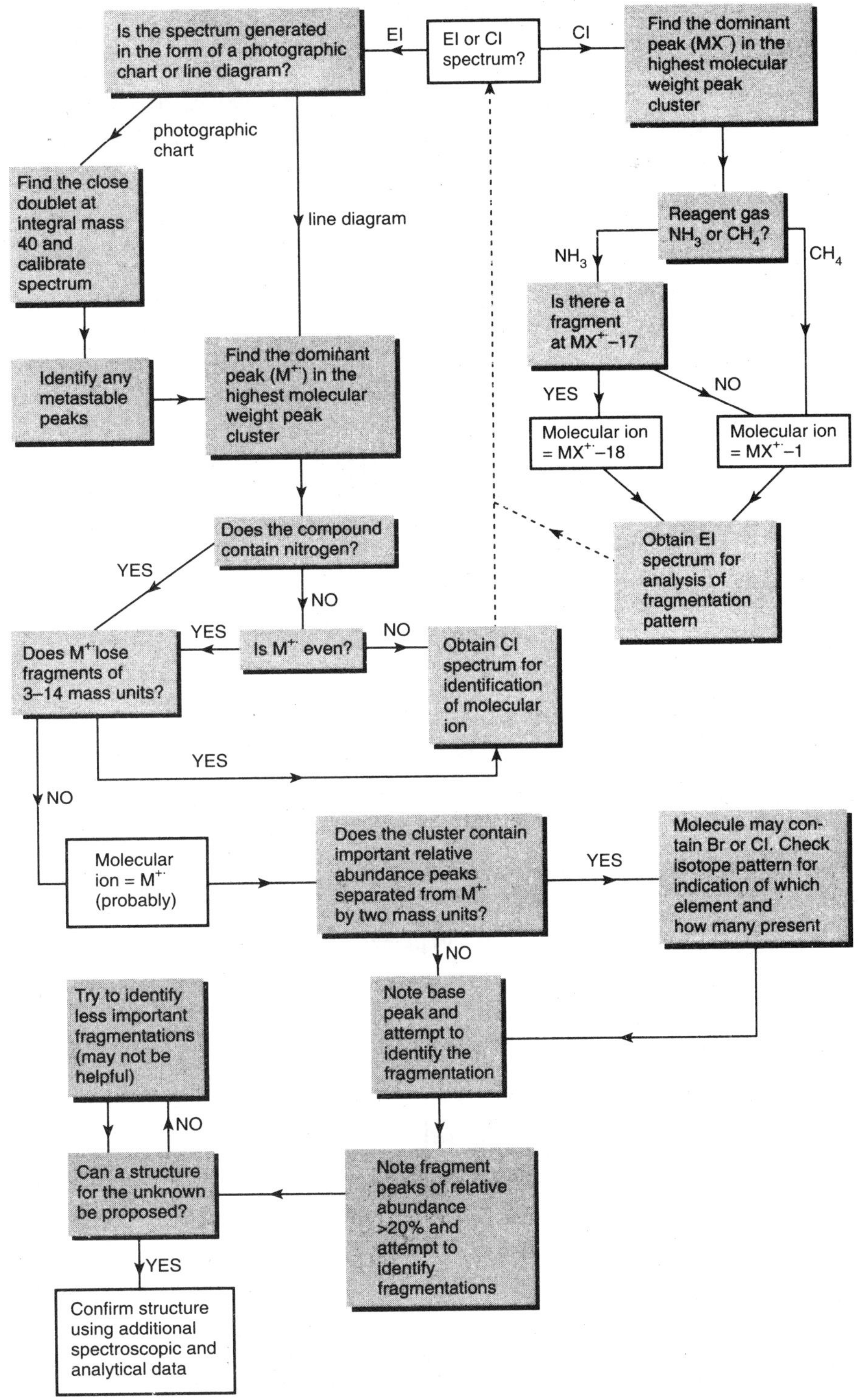

Fig. 5.84 Flow diagram of the suggested protocol for the interpretation of mass spectra. CI, chemical ionization; EI, electron impact.

Examples

2,4-Pentanedione

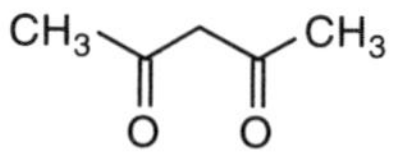

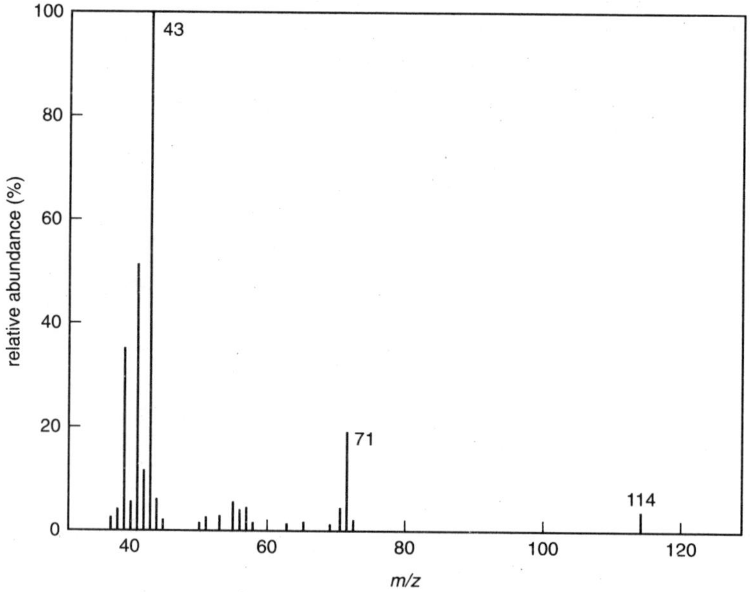

Points to note
Highest peak ($M^{+\bullet}$) = m/z 114.
Base peak = m/z 43 ($CH_3C{\equiv}O^+$).
Important fragment ions at m/z 71 ($M^{+\bullet} - 43$), 41 ($C_3H_5^+$), 39 ($C_3H_3^+$).

2-Octanone

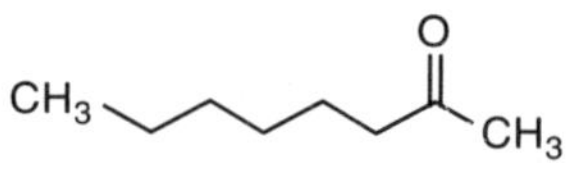

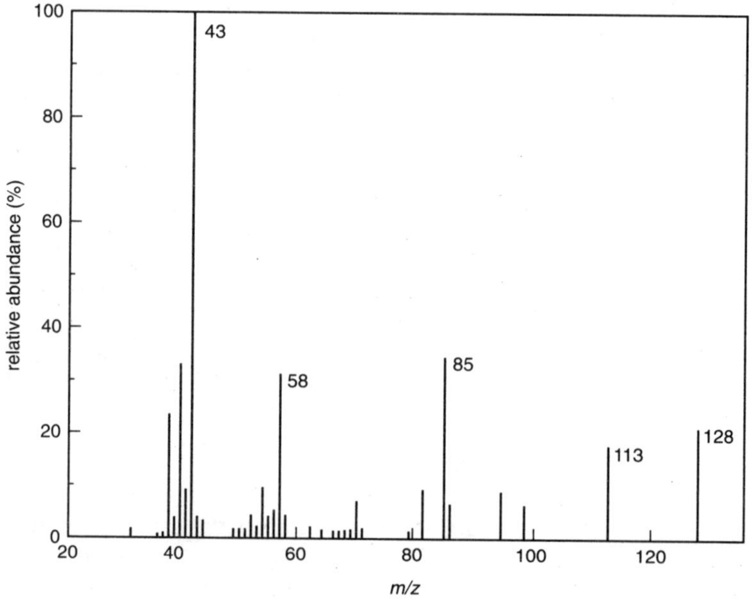

Points to note

Highest peak ($M^{+\bullet}$) = m/z 128.

Base peak = m/z 43 ($CH_3C{\equiv}O^+$).

Important fragment ions at m/z 113 ($M^{+\bullet}$ – 15), 85 ($M^{+\bullet}$ – 43), 58 $[H_2C{=}C(OH)CH_3]^{+\bullet}$ (McLafferty rearrangement).

Propanamide

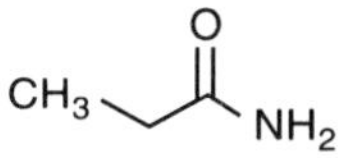

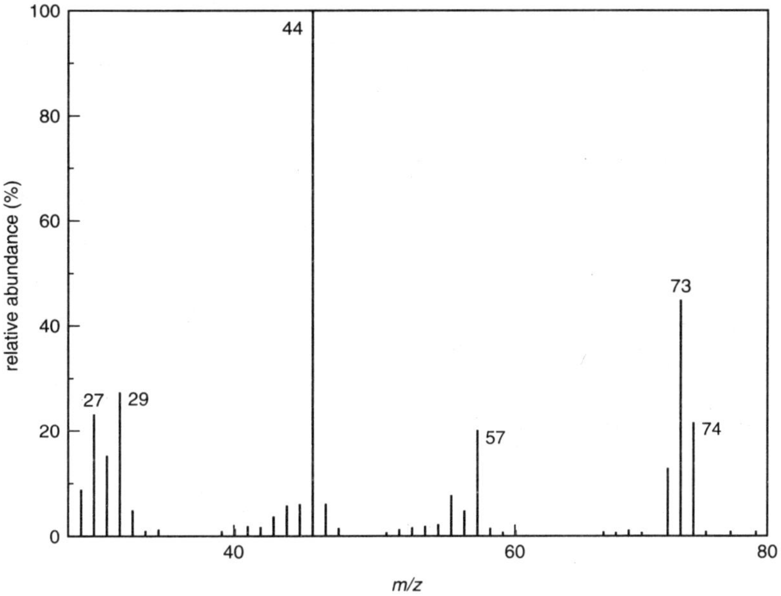

Points to note

Highest peak (MH^+) = m/z 74 due to intermolecular self-protonation. ($M^{+\bullet}$) = m/z 73 (odd molecular weight—nitrogen present).

Base peak = m/z 44 ($O{=}C{=}NH_2^+$).

Important fragment ions at m/z 57 ($M^{+\bullet}$ – $NH_2^\bullet$) (McLafferty rearrangement), 29 ($C_2H_5^+$), 27 ($C_2H_3^+$).

Benzyl acetate

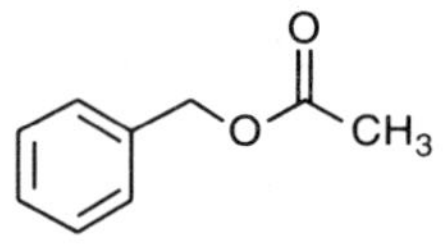

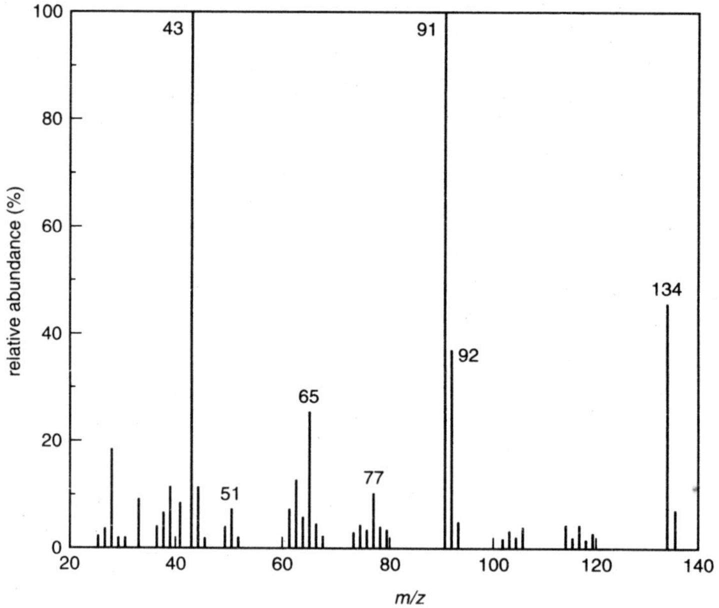

Points to note

Highest peak ($M^{+\bullet}$) = m/z 134.
Base peaks = m/z 91 (tropylium ion), 43 ($CH_3C{\equiv}O^+$).
Important fragment ions at m/z 92 (loss of $CH_2{=}C{=}O$ from molecular ion), 65 (loss of $CH{\equiv}CH$ from tropylium ion).

1,4-Dibromobenzene

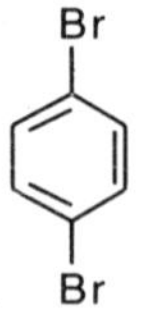

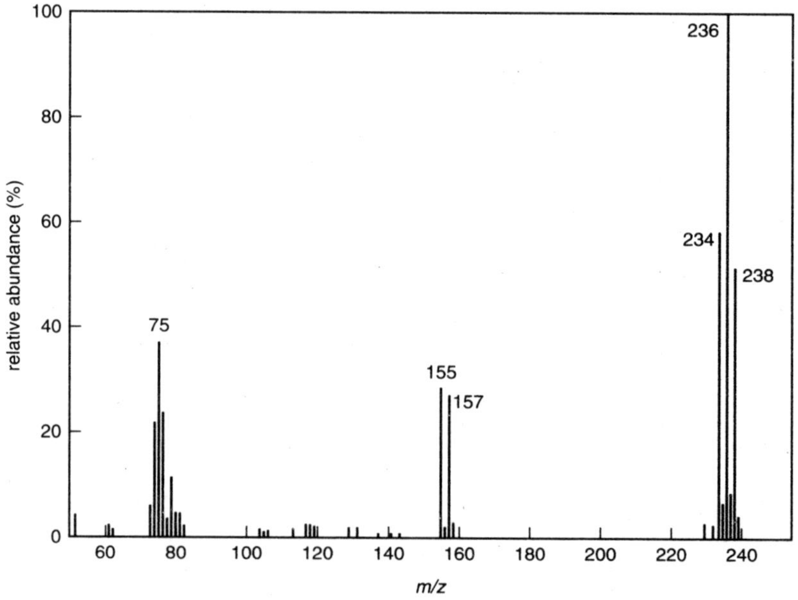

Points to note

Highest peak cluster = *m*/*z* 234/236/238.

Important fragment ions at *m*/*z* 155/157 ($C_6H_4Br^+$), 75 ($C_6H_3^+$). The appearance of the molecular ion region indicates the presence of two atoms of bromine in the molecule. The pair of roughly equal intensity fragments at *m*/*z* 155/157 indicates the presence of one atom of bromine.

1,3-Dichloro-5-nitrobenzene

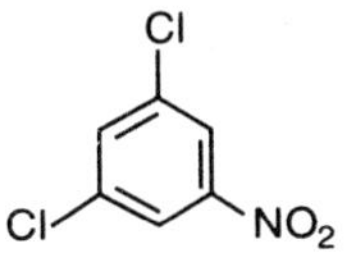

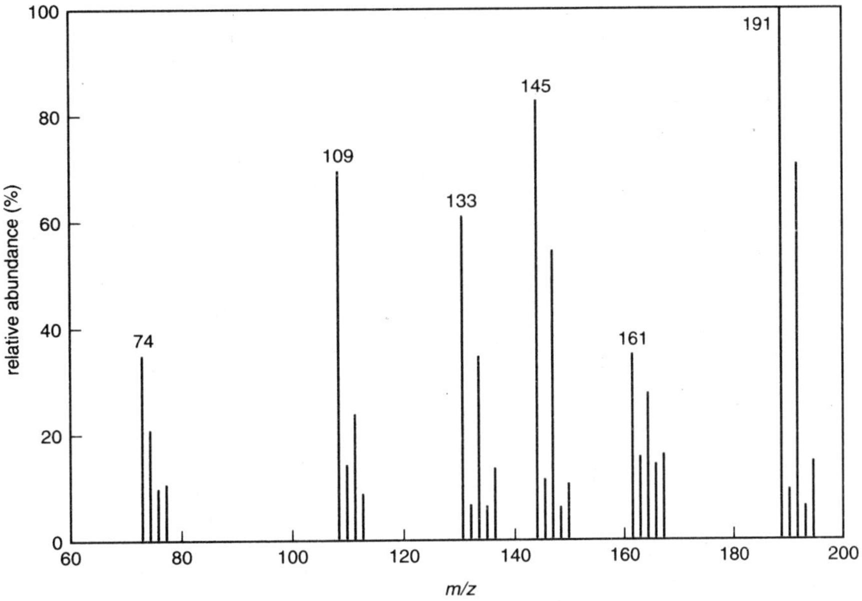

Points to note

Highest peak cluster = *m*/*z* 191/193/195 (odd molecular weight—nitrogen present).

Base peak = *m*/*z* 191 ($M^{+\bullet}$).

Important fragment ions at *m*/*z* 161/163/165 ($M^{+\bullet}$ – •NO), 145/147/149 ($M^{+\bullet}$ – •NO_2), 133/135/137, 109/111 ($M^{+\bullet}$ – •NO_2, HCl), 74 (C_6H_2•N). The appearance of the molecular ion and fragment peak clusters at *m*/*z* > 133 indicates the presence of two atoms of chlorine. The fragment peak cluster at *m*/*z* 109/111 indicates one chlorine atom to be present.

Further reading

A.J. Gordon and R.A. Ford, *The Chemist's Companion. A Handbook of Practical Data, Techniques and References*, Wiley & Sons, New York, 1973.

L.M. Harwood and T.D.W. Claridge, *Introduction to Organic Spectroscopy*, Oxford University Press, Oxford, 1996, Chapter 6.

I. Howe, D.H. Williams and R.D. Bowen, *Mass Spectrometry*, 2nd edn, McGraw-Hill, Maidenhead, 1981.

E. Pretsch, J. Seibl, W. Simon and T. Clerc, *Tables of Spectral Data for Structure Determination of Organic Compounds*, 2nd edn, Springer-Verlag, Berlin, 1989.

D.H. Williams and I. Fleming, *Spectroscopic Methods in Organic Chemistry*, 5th edn, McGraw-Hill, Maidenhead, 1995.

Further experimental aspects

J.R. Chapman, *Practical Organic Mass Spectroscopy*, Wiley & Sons, New York, 1985.

Mass spectrometry

The following specialist books discuss some of the principles and techniques for the more sophisticated developments in mass spectrometry:

H.D. Beckey, *Principles of Field Ionisation and Field Desorption Spectroscopy*, Pergamon, Oxford, 1977.

J.R. Chapman, *Practical Organic Mass Spectrometry*, 2nd edn, Wiley & Sons, New York, 1995.

R.B. Cole, *Electrospray Ionization Mass Spectrometry*, Wiley & Sons, New York, 1997.

A.G. Harrison, *Chemical Ionization Mass Spectrometry*, CRC Press, Boca Raton, 1983.

E. De Hoffmann, J. Charette and V. Strooband, *Mass Spectrometry: Principles and Application*, Wiley & Sons, New York, 1996.

GC–MS interfacing methods

F.W. Karasek and R.E. Clement, *Basic Gas Chromatography–Mass Spectrometry*, Elsevier, Amsterdam, 1991.

F.G. Kitson, B.S. Larsen and C.N. McEwan, *Gas Chromatography–Mass Spectrometry*, Academic Press, London, 1996.

R.D. Smith and H.R. Udseth, *Chem. Br.*, 1988, **24**, 350.

Computer programs

For a computer program predicting the relative intensities of peaks for any given number of isotopes, see: B. Dombek, J. Lowther and E. Carberry, *J. Chem. Educ.*, 1971, **48**, 729.

For a description of a computer program for the analysis of metastable ions, see: L.E. Brady, *J. Chem. Educ.*, 1971, **48**, 469.

Chapter 6

Keeping Records: the Laboratory Notebook and Chemical Literature

Despite what some theoreticians would have us believe, chemistry is founded on experimental work. An investigative sequence begins with a hypothesis which is tested by experiment and, on the basis of the observed results, is ratified, modified or discarded. At every stage of this process, the accurate and unbiased recording of results is crucial to success. However, whilst it is true that such rational analysis can lead the scientist towards his or her goal, this happy sequence of events occurs much less frequently than many would care to admit. Serendipity frequently plays a central role in scientific discovery, and is often put down by others to simple good fortune. This overlooks the fact that many important chance discoveries can be ascribed largely to a combination of perseverance and meticulous technique. From penicillin to polythene, accurate observations of seemingly unimportant experimental results have led to discoveries of immeasurable importance.

Discovery is only part of the story, however. Having made the all-important experimental observations, transmitting this information clearly to other workers in the field is of equal importance. The record of your observations must be made in such a manner that others as well as yourself can repeat the work at a later stage. Omission of a small detail, such as the degree of purity of a particular reagent, can often render a procedure irreproducible, invalidating your claims and leaving you exposed to criticism. The scientific community is rightly suspicious of results which can only be obtained in the hands of one particular worker!

Therefore, as an experimentalist, your laboratory notebook is your most valuable asset. In it you must record everything that you do and see in the laboratory which pertains to your work, no matter how trivial or superfluous it might seem at that moment. Time and again, results which might not have appeared to be directly relevant to the investigation *at the time* have proved to have deep significance when re-examined at a later stage.

It is sometimes difficult to consider experiments which do not give the expected or desired result to be as vital as those which do proceed in the predicted manner. Remember that there is a reason for everything, and if a reaction does not follow the expected course, then it is necessary to reconsider the premise that led to the experiment in the first place. Do not be tempted to attempt to bend the facts to fit in with some preconceived notion of what ought to happen. In this respect, it is crucial that you observe and record results impartially and without bias. Always record what you actually observe, and not what you have been told will happen, or what you expect or want to see. Above all, record your results in a way which will be clear, not only to yourself, but to others as well.

Remember—honesty, accuracy and clarity, in that order, are the three pre-requisites when undertaking and reporting experimental work.

6.1 The laboratory notebook

Style and layout

The following passages contain suggestions as to how you should record your work in the laboratory. Whilst these follow generally accepted guidelines, they may not tally completely with instructions given to you by your institution. If differences exist, always follow the rules of the establishment in which you are working. Remember, in the teaching laboratory, it is the instructor's assessment of your reports that will determine your class position at the end of the course and, in research, your notebook is a lasting record of your efforts—successful or otherwise.

Use a sturdy notebook

As your notebook has to contain a permanent record of your work, it must be made to last. The book should be bound with a strong spine that will not break under repeated opening and closing. The pages should be numbered and sewn into the spine so that they do not drop out with continued use. A good durable cover is a necessity to protect the contents from wear and tear and from any water splashes when on the laboratory bench. It is a good idea to cover the book with clear adhesive film to provide additional waterproofing.

Do not use loose sheets of papers—even for rough notes

Never record your observations on sheets of loose paper for copying into your notebook at a later stage as these are too easily lost during the course of a working day. Likewise, clip binders or spiral bound notebooks are not suitable for recording your work as the sheets may be torn out easily, either by careless handling or intentionally. Always write in ink, not in pencil which fades with time and can be erased. However, you must remember not to use water-soluble ink, otherwise your precious notes will be rapidly obliterated if you

Do not erase mistakes totally—or tear out pages

spill water onto the open book. Cross out any mistakes boldly, but in a manner which does not totally obscure what was written in the first place. Whilst desirable, the requirement for an absolutely neat notebook is secondary to the necessity for accurate reporting. *Never* tear pages out of your book; like a ship's log, whatever goes into your book must stay in. The only exceptions to this rule are notebooks fitted with duplicate pages for use with carbon paper. With this arrangement the copy may be removed for storage in a safe place. In some universities, and in all commercial enterprises, the laboratory notebook remains the property of the institution and is a legal document which can be

Your notebook is a legal document

used for evidence after an accident or to indicate prior knowledge in patent disputes—always bear this in mind.

The outside cover of the book should have your name on it, together with the general subject matter it contains and a means by which it can be returned to you if lost (for instance, the address of the department). It is convenient if your name and the contents are also written on the spine, to help in finding the book when it is stacked in a pile or on a shelf.

Write all observations directly into your notebook

Leave the first few pages of the book clear for an index of contents and then use the remaining pages consecutively. Always write your observations directly into the notebook *as they are made* and do not rely on your memory at a later stage as it is highly likely that you will forget some of the details in the intervening period. The best arrangement is to write your rough notes, weighings and any observations on the left-hand pages of the book and to write the actual report on the right-hand pages (Fig. 6.1).

The top of every page should have your name and the date entered on it, and the first page of each experiment should begin with a brief title describing its aim. Underneath the title, there should be a scheme depicting structural formulae with the molecular weight of each compound clearly noted. It helps if this scheme is emphasized by drawing a box around it. Underneath this, the quantities of compounds and reagents to be used (by weight as well as by the number of moles) together with their purity and source should be noted, together with a listing of the apparatus to be used. In this section you should include any literature references relevant to the procedure. All of these details should be put into the book *before* starting the experiment as, in this manner, you will be made to think in advance about the experiment.

Keep reports concise

Whilst your laboratory notebook should contain all information pertinent to the experiment being undertaken, keep the writing concise and avoid unnecessary verbosity. If following a set of specific instructions, it is usually unnecessary to write out the whole procedure again, a simple reference will suffice, but any variations (things rarely go exactly as laid out in the manuals) must be faithfully described. This is of particular importance if, at some later stage, you need to explain why you did not obtain the predicted result!

During the course of the experiment, keep a record of your actions, together with any observations, as rough notes on the left-hand pages. These can be transcribed into a more legible form on the right-hand pages, either when time permits during the course of the experiment, or at the end of the day. Never leave the updating of your book for another day as, by then, the details will no longer be clear in your mind. Any thin layer chromatography (TLC) analyses should be drawn faithfully into the book with shading to show the appearance of the spots, together with a note of how they have been visualized.

When recording and reporting your observations during the qualitative analysis of an unknown, it is best to employ a tabular layout as shown in

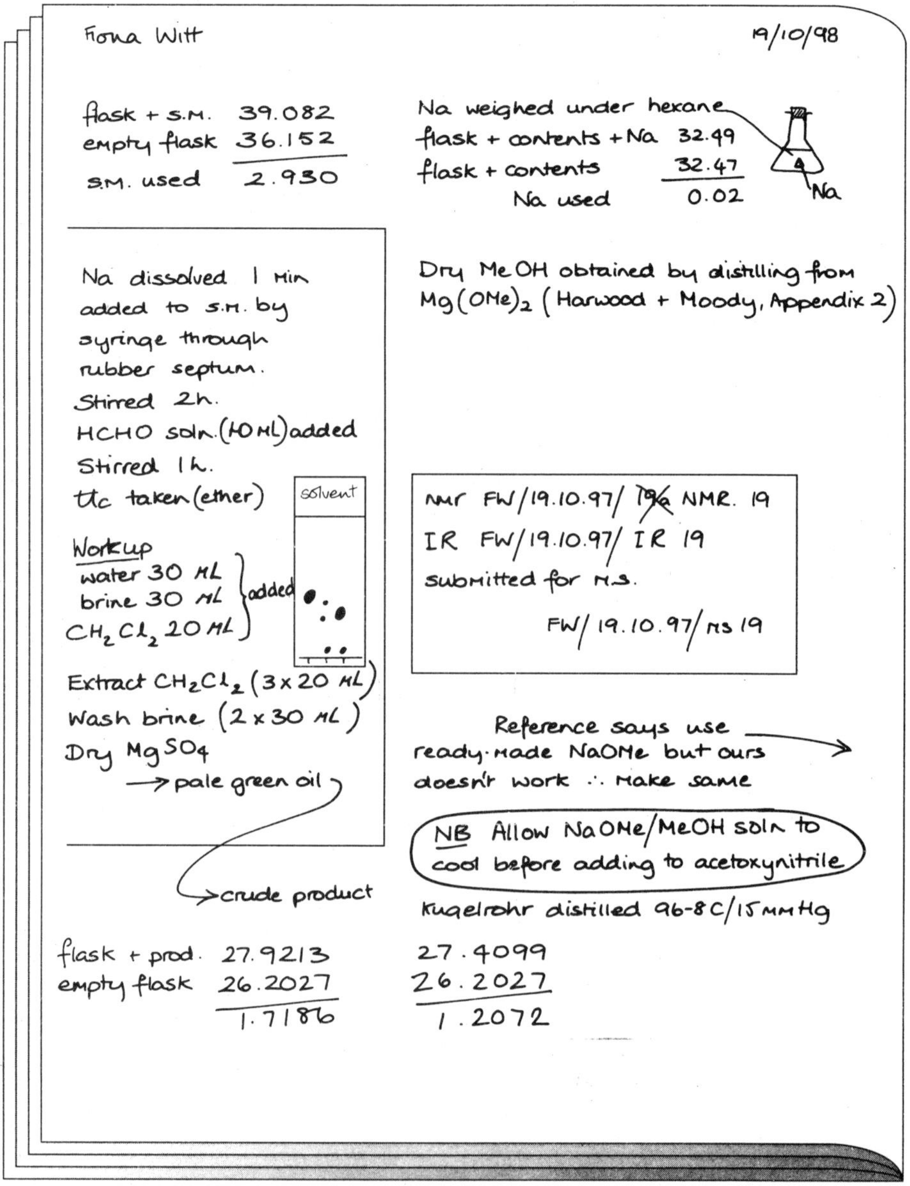

Fig. 6.1 Enter all preliminary observations on the left-hand pages of your notebook, and write the final report on the right-hand pages.

Fig. 6.2. In this manner, you will learn to fall into a set order for carrying out the tests, and this will result in more efficient use of laboratory time and make it less likely that you will forget to carry out a crucial test.

File spectra separately

Spectra should be filed in separate folders, and reference numbers for any spectra taken during the course of the experiment should be recorded in the notebook. Do not stick the spectra in your book as this will cause the spine to tear, in time; file them separately. A coding system which is concise—but at the

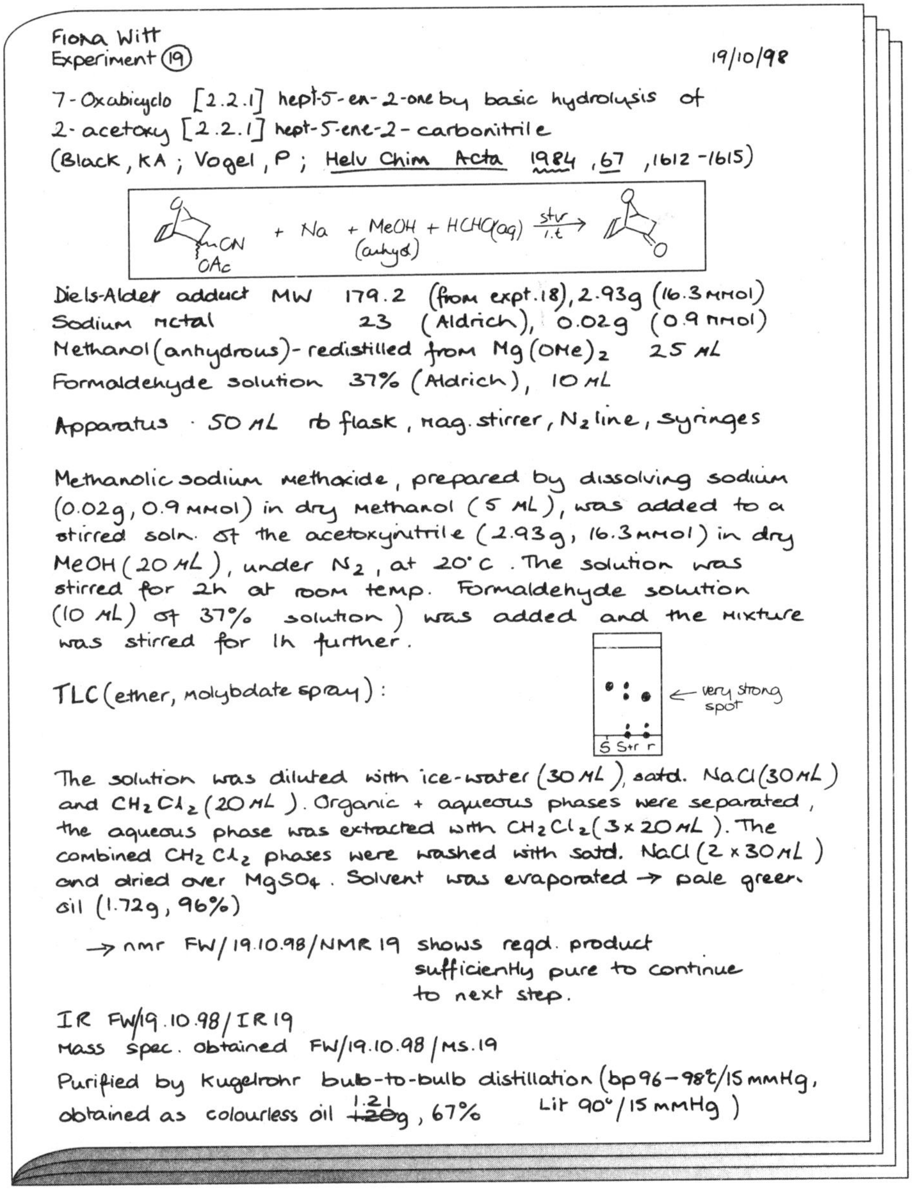

Fiona Witt
Experiment (19) 19/10/98

7-Oxabicyclo [2.2.1] hept-5-en-2-one by basic hydrolysis of
2-acetoxy [2.2.1] hept-5-ene-2-carbonitrile
(Black, KA; Vogel, P; Helv Chim Acta 1984, 67, 1612-1615)

Diels-Alder adduct MW 179.2 (from expt. 18), 2.93g (16.3 mmol)
Sodium metal 23 (Aldrich), 0.02g (0.9 mmol)
Methanol (anhydrous) - redistilled from Mg(OMe)₂ 25 mL
Formaldehyde solution 37% (Aldrich), 10 mL

Apparatus · 50 mL rb flask, mag. stirrer, N₂ line, syringes

Methanolic sodium methoxide, prepared by dissolving sodium (0.02g, 0.9 mmol) in dry methanol (5 mL), was added to a stirred soln. of the acetoxynitrile (2.93g, 16.3 mmol) in dry MeOH (20 mL), under N₂, at 20°C. The solution was stirred for 2h at room temp. Formaldehyde solution (10 mL) of 37% solution) was added and the mixture was stirred for 1h further.

TLC (ether, molybdate spray):

The solution was diluted with ice-water (30 mL), satd. NaCl (30 mL) and CH₂Cl₂ (20 mL). Organic + aqueous phases were separated, the aqueous phase was extracted with CH₂Cl₂ (3 × 20 mL). The combined CH₂Cl₂ phases were washed with satd. NaCl (2 × 30 mL) and dried over MgSO₄. Solvent was evaporated → pale green oil (1.72g, 96%)

→ nmr FW/19.10.98/NMR 19 shows reqd. product sufficiently pure to continue to next step.

IR FW/19.10.98/IR 19
Mass spec. obtained FW/19.10.98/MS.19
Purified by Kugelrohr bulb-to-bulb distillation (bp 96–98°C/15 mmHg, obtained as colourless oil ~~1.20~~ 1.21g, 67% Lit 90°/15 mmHg)

Fig. 6.1 *Continued.*

same time enables you to locate readily any spectroscopic data associated with an experiment—uses your initials, the date, the technique used and a number for the component being analyzed (for example FW/19.10.97/NMR19). This reference should enable you to find the pages in your notebook on which the experiment has been recorded as well as the position of the spectrum in its folder. All samples prepared or studied should be listed, together with their reference number, in the index at the front of the notebook against

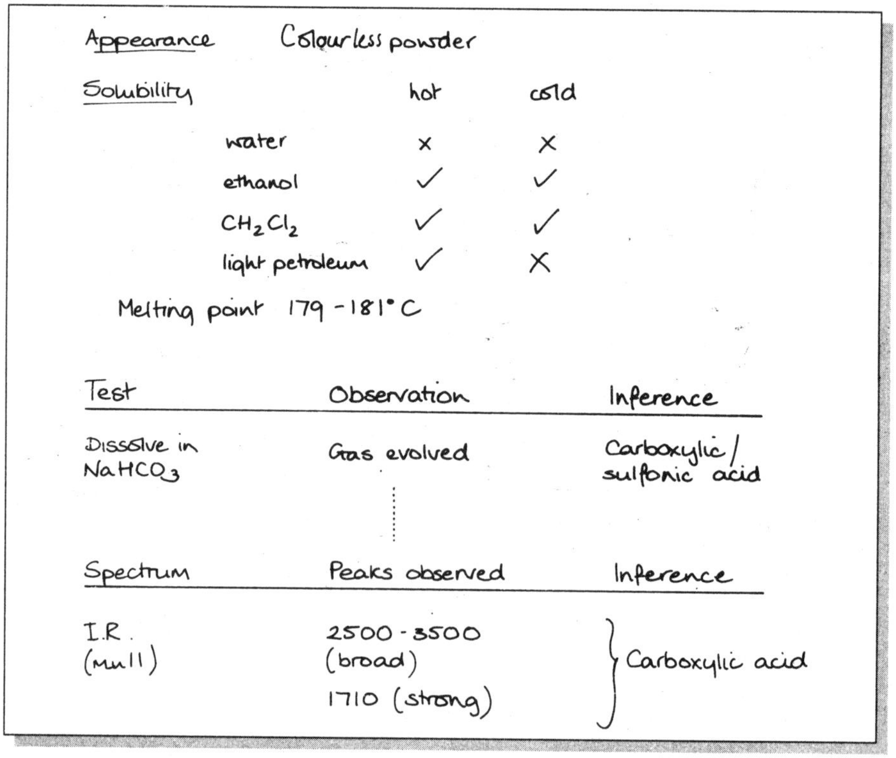

Fig. 6.2 Use a tabular format for recording results of qualitative analysis investigations.

Use a cross-referencing system to collate spectra and experiments

the page number on which the experiment is described. This cross-referencing system enables you to find a particular spectrum or experimental procedure rapidly and will become increasingly important as you progress through your teaching course and into research. Starting such a system at the very beginning will save much frustration in the long term, and will avoid the embarrassment of rummaging through a mountain of paper, looking for a particularly elusive spectrum, whilst the instructor or your research supervisor breathes down your neck impatiently!

Reporting spectroscopic and microanalytical data

The practical aspects of recording spectroscopic data on your samples are dealt with in Chapter 5. Such results are usually reported by listing the important features of each spectrum in a shorthand notation. Uniformity in presentation of these results is necessary to enable ready interpretation and to avoid ambiguity. The following formats are recommended but, once again, you must always follow the style laid down by your institute where differences of opinion occur. Please note that the preferred term is '*spectroscopic*' and not '*spectral*' which may imply that your results are ghostly! For once, do not follow the rather dubious example of the many experienced organic chemists all around the world who ought to know better.

Infrared spectra

The position of maximum absorption (ν_{max}) is quoted for sharp peaks such as those due to carbonyl absorptions. Broad peaks, for instance hydroxyl absorptions, should be quoted as a range. Peak absorption positions in IR spectra are recorded as their *wavenumber* (cm^{-1}) which, as the units indicate, is the reciprocal of the wavelength. The strength of the absorption can be indicated using the letters w (weak), m (medium) and s (strong) after the position of each peak quoted. 'Weak' usually refers to peaks having less than 10% absorbance, and 'strong' refers to those having greater than about 80% absorbance—the exact judgement is rather subjective. Remember that it is not usual practice to quote every peak in the IR spectrum, particularly in the fingerprint region. The method of preparing the sample for analysis must also be given before quoting the absorption positions. The terms 'neat' or 'thin film' are used for pure liquid samples placed between sodium chloride plates. Solids may have been obtained as a 'mull' in a specified mulling agent (Nujol® or hexachlorobutadiene), or as a KBr disk. Solution spectra can be indicated by stating the solvent used (usually $CHCl_3$). For example, an IR spectrum of 7-oxabicyclo[2.2.1]hept-5-en-2-one quoted in this manner would be written as follows:

IR, ν_{max} (thin film), 3700–3250 (m), 3020 (m), 1750 (s), 1635 (w) cm^{-1}

Nuclear magnetic resonance spectra

It is always necessary to quote the operating frequency of the instrument used (in MHz) and the solvent in which the sample was dissolved. Chemical shift values are reported using the δ-scale against tetramethylsilane (TMS) = 0.0 ppm. The relative number of protons contributing to the absorption is given to the nearest integer, together with any multiplicity of the absorption and related coupling constants.

For multiplets which show interpretable first-order splittings, the chemical shift at which the absorption would have occurred in the absence of splittings is quoted. For uninterpretable multiplets an absorption range is sufficient. The type of splitting is denoted as d (doublet), t (triplet), q (quartet), quint (quintet), sext (sextet) and m (multiplet), with additional qualifications such as dd (double doublet) and br (or broad). Peaks removable on treatment with D_2O need to be specified. The coupling constant J is quoted in hertz, and for multiplets from which several different values can be obtained these are listed progressively as J, J', J'' and so on. Thus the NMR spectrum of 7-oxabicyclo[2.2.1]hept-5-en-2-one would be reported as follows:

NMR δ_H (200 MHz, $CDCl_3$), 1.90 (1 H, d, J 16.0 Hz), 2.28 (1 H, dd, J 15 Hz, J' 5 Hz), 4.50 (1 H, s, br), 5.38 (1 H, d, br, J 5 Hz), 6.40 (1 H, dd J 5.5 Hz, J' 1.5 Hz), 6.68 (1 H, dt, J 5.5 Hz, J' 1.0 Hz)

An equivalent format applies to the recording of ^{13}C spectra which may be obtained as both 'proton coupled' or 'broadband decoupled' spectra, with the exception that coupling constants are not quoted in proton coupled ^{13}C spectra.

Mass spectra

The particular technique used to obtain the mass spectrum (electron impact (EI) or chemical ionization (CI)) must always be quoted, together with the ionizing reagent used if the spectrum was obtained under chemical ionization conditions. The peak positions are quoted as *m/z* and, wherever possible, their relative abundances should be given compared with the most abundant peak (the *base peak*). The molecular ion is denoted $M^{+\bullet}$, or if chemical ionization has been used, MH^+, MNH_4^+ or MCH_5^+, depending on the reagent system used to carry out the ionization. There is usually little point in listing peaks below about 15% relative abundance (other than the molecular ion which may be of low abundance), nor any with *m/z* less than 40.

Accurate mass measurements should be reported, together with the expected value for the molecule being examined and an estimation of the margin of error in the measurement in parts per million. Once again let us consider 7-oxabicyclo[2.2.1]hept-2-en-5-one:

m/z (EI) 110 ($M^{+\bullet}$, 4%), 68 (100%)
Accurate mass: found 110.0367, $C_6H_6O_2$ requires 110.0368 (2 ppm error)

Ultraviolet spectra

The two important pieces of information obtained from the UV spectrum of a compound are the wavelength at maximum absorption (λ_{max} (nm)) and the *extinction coefficient* which possesses the units of 1000 $cm^2 mol^{-1}$ (not surprisingly these are never expressed by convention). A peak may appear as an ill-defined maximum superimposed on a stronger absorption and the λ_{max} position is often qualified with 'sh' denoting that it is a shoulder. Obviously it is necessary to note the solvent in which the sample has been dissolved. An example of the format for quoting a UV spectrum is given in Chapter 5.

Microanalytical data

You are unlikely to be required to produce microanalytical data as proof of purity until you begin to carry out research, when it is still considered (quite rightly) to be one of the important pieces of information for total characterization of a new substance. Carbon, hydrogen and nitrogen are determined by combustion analysis, with the combustion products being estimated by gas chromatography. This technique permits estimation of these elements with an

Acceptable C, H, N analysis must have results within 0.3% of expected values

accuracy in the region of ±0.3% and an acceptable analysis therefore requires the recorded results to be within 0.3% of those expected. Estimation of oxygen requires special facilities (C, H, N combustion analysis is carried out in an atmosphere of oxygen) and is usually not undertaken. Other elements such as halogens, sulfur and phosphorus are determined titrimetrically, and the lower accuracy in their estimation means that a greater error of up to 0.5% is usually acceptable.

The style of reporting microanalytical data which is commonly adopted quotes both the required values (or calculated values if the compound has been previously reported) and the results found by the analysis to within ±0.1%. There is no point in quoting calculated values to any greater degree of precision than this as the analysis techniques do not warrant it; however, you must always calculate the values using accurate atomic weight values (±0.001) before rounding off the final result and quoting it as follows:

C_7H_8O. Calculated (or required) C, 77.7; H, 7.5%. Found C, 77.8; H, 7.3%

Calculating yields

The yield is based on the limiting reagent

The theoretical yield of a reaction is decided by the limiting reagent present. When this material is used up, the reaction necessarily stops no matter how much of the other constituents remain. Therefore a little thought is necessary here to determine which reagents are being used in excess in the reaction and which is the limiting reagent before calculating the theoretical yield. The actual yield obtained after isolation and purification of the product is calculated as a percentage of the maximum theoretical yield:

$$\text{Percentage yield} = \frac{\text{Yield of pure product}}{\text{Theoretical yield}} \times 100$$

Quoting a percentage yield permits an estimate to be made of the efficiency of the reaction which is independent of the scale on which the reaction was carried out. Yields of 50–80% are in the range of moderate to good depending on the optimism of the reporter, and yields greater than 80% are usually considered to be excellent. Yields of 100% are impossible to obtain in practice as some losses are inevitable during work-up. Thus yields which approach this figure (>99%) should be quoted as 'quantitative'. Sometimes the quoted yield is accompanied by the phrase '*accounting for recovered starting material*'. As it implies, the yield here has been calculated on the basis of material converted, rather than the amount initially placed in the reaction vessel. Although this somewhat cosmetic treatment is justified on the grounds that the recovered material can be used again, this practice has the effect of giving an impression that the reaction is more efficient than is actually the case. You must be on your guard for such statements when planning multi-step syntheses to avoid running out of material before reaching your target.

Quote percentage yields to the nearest whole number

When presenting the yield always round off the figure to the nearest whole number, as the way in which reagents are measured does not warrant greater precision—despite the fact that your calculator can give you an answer to several decimal places!

Data sheets

It is a good idea to record the full spectroscopic data for every compound you prepare on a data sheet (Fig. 6.3). Just as with writing up a notebook, record data continuously during your work. This will remove the rather arduous task of transcribing all of your data on completion of the project. This practice is worth cultivating in the teaching laboratory and it is usually obligatory for the research student.

Get into the habit of filling in data sheets regularly

The action of filling in a data sheet will make you aware of any pieces of information, such as a melting point, that still need to be obtained whilst you have material available. All too often, research workers reach the stage of writing up their thesis before realizing that some compounds are incompletely characterized: this usually necessitates the preparation of a new batch of material.

Filling in a data sheet will also make you examine your spectra carefully, and will help you to bring to light any discrepancies or interesting features which might otherwise pass unnoticed as the spectra linger in some file at the back of a drawer. In any event, the practice in interpreting your data will help you to develop your technique and, on the principle of 'never keeping all your eggs in one basket', this set of data sheets which can be kept apart from your original spectra provides a useful safeguard against loss or destruction, for instance in a laboratory fire.

References

You must always record in your notebook all references that are needed to perform the experiment. Of particular importance are the literature sources of the physical properties of known compounds. The observed values must never be simply stated without including the literature data for comparison together with the source reference.

Every detail of the reference must be quoted

When citing a reference it is important to quote it fully and not to be tempted to leave out some of the authors' names, replacing them with *et al.* If there is an error somewhere in the reference, it will be possible to track down the correct reference using the combination of authors. If just one author is cited, this job can become quite a long one, whereas there are likely to be many less references with the specific combination of authors in your reference. Styles of quoting literature mainly fall into two main categories, depending on which side of the Atlantic you are working. In the United States, the standard format follows that laid down by the American Chemical Society and is as follows:

Name of compound — Compound ref. no. FW/19.10.98/19

7-oxabicyclo[2.2.1] hept-5-en-2-one

Structure

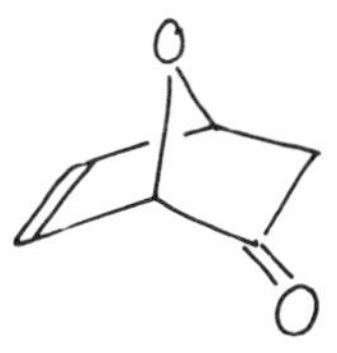

Compound description colourless oil

M.p./b.p. 96–98°C / 15 mmHg (lit 90°C, 15mmHg)

Molecular formula/weight $C_6H_6O_2$, MW 110

High resolution

Mass spectrum

Analysis:

Found: C, 65.40% H 5.40%

Requires: C, 65.45% H, 5.49%

$[\alpha]_D^{20}$ racemic

H n.m.r. 200 MHz $CDCl_3$

δ_H 6.68, 1H, dt, J 1, 5.5Hz, H6

6.40, 1H dd, J 1.5, 5.5Hz, H5

5.38, 1H, bd, J 5Hz, H4

4.50, 1H, bs, H1

2.28, 1H, dd, J 5, 15 Hz, H3 exo

1.90, 1H, d, J 16Hz, H3 endo

Infra-red spectrum (thin film)

ν_{max} 3700–3250 (m), 3020 (m), 1750 (s) C=O, 1635 (m) C=C

Mass spectrum EI/CI/IBEI/DCI/FI/FD/FAB

110 (M^+, 4%), 68 (CH=CHCH$_2$OOH$_2$, 100%)

Other data:

Fig. 6.3 A typical data sheet.

Year bold — *First and last page numbers given*

Comma separating surname and initials — *Semicolon between names and before journal*

Katsuki, K; Sharpless, K.B; *J. Am. Chem. Soc.*, **1980**, *102*, 5974–5976.

Initials after name — *Journal title italicized* — *Volume italicized*

When writing by hand, italics and bold print can be indicated by underlining with straight and wavy lines respectively.

The other common format is that adopted by the Royal Society of Chemistry in Britain. Typically, the American and British formats differ from each other in several ways!

Final author preceded by 'and' — *Comma before journal* — *Year in normal typeface*

G. Pattenden and G.M. Robertson, *Tetrahedron Lett.*, 1986, **27**, 399.

Initials before name — *Journal title italicized* — *Volume bold* — *Only first page given*

Each particular journal will demand that references conform to their 'house style' and your institution may also require you to use a particular format. If not, it is perhaps best to conform to that most popular in your particular country. A list of generally approved abbreviations for journal titles is given in Table 6.1, p. 413; however, when writing a paper for publication, always verify the abbreviations required by the journal to which you intend to send the paper. Software is now available to help you to switch reference formatting from one style to another.

6.2 The research report

At the completion of a research project it is necessary to produce a report which encapsulates precisely the aims and achievements of the work, including all experimental details. Such a report may be for the eyes of your instructor or research adviser, or it may be for publication in a journal to be read throughout the world. Whatever its target audience, the production of a clear report in the required standard format will be very much simpler if you have conscientiously noted all of your results in your notebook, and kept your data sheets up to date. There are no hard and fast rules for the format required in a report, but some general points are outlined here to cover a few of the common requirements.

The report must have a title which concisely summarizes the aims of the work and will alert readers to its contents, for instance 'Studies on the intermolecular Diels–Alder reactions of furans'. As articles are often abstracted for content by searching for '*keywords*' in the title, the correct choice of title can make the difference between your article being noticed by chemists or passing into obscurity. Most journals require a brief abstract of the work to be inserted before the main body of the text. Whilst brief, this must contain all of the salient features of the work, otherwise someone scanning the abstract may fail to realize the true contents of the paper.

Titles and abstracts are important for conveying the content of the report

The report itself should begin with a concise but complete review of all relevant work that has been carried out previously, referencing and giving due credit to work carried out by other workers. Sufficient background material should be given for someone who is not a specialist in the field to be able to grasp the problem. Frequently the area will have been the subject of reviews by others and it is often sufficient to give references to these reviews followed by the phrase 'and references cited therein'. Each citation in the body of the text is marked by a numerical superscript and the references themselves are grouped together at the end of the report or at the foot of the page containing the reference work.

Always review earlier work, giving due credit to other workers

The main body of the report contains the 'results and discussion' section, where the work is presented and conclusions are drawn, with supporting evidence. It is the presentation of this section which distinguishes between good and bad reports. Take care to use the correct terminology, without falling into the trap of using too much jargon—the aim is to inform, not mystify. The presentation should be scholarly and any arguments must be presented logically. Only reasonable conclusions should be drawn, with experimental support being given at all times. Explanations for reactions which did not go as planned are just as important as those for 'successful' reactions. What exactly constitutes a 'scholarly' presentation is difficult to define, and it is best to ask a more experienced chemist to comment on your efforts whilst in draft form, before preparing the final copy.

Present results and conclusions logically with clear reasoning

The last part of this section should contain a summary which encapsulates the final conclusions of the work and discusses implications and future aims. In a report submitted to a journal, it is usual at this point to acknowledge any financial assistance, gifts of chemicals and technical assistance given by individuals.

Experimental section

The experimental section should begin with a listing of all the instrumentation used in the recording of the spectroscopic data, the sources of the compounds used and details about any purification and analytical processes used. If a standard work-up procedure is used throughout the experiments, this can be described here and then be referred to in individual experiments as 'usual work-up' to save repetition.

The experiments should be listed in the order in which the compounds appear in the results and discussion section, even though this may not always be the order in which they were actually prepared during the project. If a series of related compounds have been prepared using the same procedure, it is acceptable to write out one general procedure and then list the individual spectroscopic and analytical data for each compound afterwards.

Styles vary between departments and from journal to journal, but the usually accepted practice is to present the experimental section in the third person, passive past tense. In other words, 'The experiment was carried out' and not 'I carried out the experiment'. This does vary, however, and some journals prefer the experimental section to be written in the present tense. In any case, it is important to read the instructions to authors which are published in the journals before submitting papers to them. Non-adherence to the required style could result in rejection of the paper.

Clear hazard warnings

Whether writing a report for an adviser or for publication in a journal, the details given in the experimental section must be sufficient for another chemist to be able to repeat your work. The names of all compounds should be written out in full and the quantity of each as weight or volume, as well as number of moles, should be given in parentheses after the name. Any dangerous properties must be highlighted by adding ***Caution!*** followed by an indication of the danger (***Toxic***, ***Explosive***). SI units should be used (although organic chemists are rather bad at this and you are still likely to see kilocalories being used instead of kilojoules) and any abbreviations must follow the SI recommendations. The yield of product quoted must be the actual yield obtained in the experiment and must give an indication of purity of the isolated material (crude, recrystallized). Chromatography supports and elution systems are required and the full physical data of the compound prepared must be presented following the formats outlined on pp. 402–405. An example of the style of reporting an experimental procedure is as follows.

Preparation of 7-oxabicyclo[2.2.1]hept-5-en-4-one (2)[12]

Methanolic sodium methoxide, prepared by dissolving sodium (0.20 g, 0.9 mmol) in freshly dried methanol (5 mL), was added via syringe to a stirred solution of the nitrile (1) (2.93 g, 16.3 mmol) in dry methanol (20 mL) at 20°C. After stirring for 2 h, formaldehyde solution (10 mL, 30%) was added and the mixture was stirred for 1 h. The mixture was cooled to 0°C using an ice-water bath, and was quenched with ice-water (30 mL). Usual work-up gave, after drying ($MgSO_4$) and removal of solvents at reduced pressure, crude (2) as a pale green oil (1.72 g, 96%). Pure material was obtained by short path distillation (1.21 g, 67%); bp 96–98°C/15 mmHg, (lit.[12] 90°C/15 mmHg).

IR ν_{max} (thin film) 3700–3250 (m), 3020 (m), 1750 (s), 1635 (w) cm^{-1}.

NMR (200 MHz, $CDCl_3$), 1.90 (1 H, d, *J* 16.0 Hz), 2.28 (1 H, dd, *J* 15 Hz, *J'* 5 Hz), 4.50 (1 H, s, br), 5.38 (1 H, d, br, *J* 5 Hz), 6.40 (1 H, dd, *J* 5.5 Hz, *J'* 1.5 Hz), 6.68 (1 H, dt, *J* 5.5 Hz, *J'* 1.0 Hz).

m/z (EI) 110 (M^+, 4%), 68 (100%).

Accurate mass: found 110.0367, $C_6H_6O_2$ requires 110.0368 (2 ppm error).

References

No research report is complete without a full listing of all pertinent literature. This should be referenced in the body of the text using numerical superscripts and then listed in numerical order at the end of the report. You must include references to all material necessary for readers to familiarize themselves with the background to your work, as well as specific details relating to your project. You should only refer to the actual articles you have used in carrying out the work and preparing the report. For instance, do not quote a reference from *Croat. Chem. Acta* if you actually gleaned your information from a summary of the article in *Chemical Abstracts*—quote both references. Likewise, if a review article was your source of information, reference the review, followed by the phrase 'and references cited therein', to alert the reader to the fact that it may be necessary to read further.

Remember whatever the details of style and format, your report must be accurate, clear and concise at all stages.

Further reading

The following books and articles contain useful hints on keeping a laboratory notebook and writing up reports:

R. Barrass, *Scientists Must Write*, Chapman & Hall, London, 1978.

B.E. Cain, *The Basics of Technical Communicating*, American Chemical Society, Washington, 1998.

J.S. Dodd (ed.) *The ACS Style Guide, a manual for Authors and Editors*, American Chemical Society, Washington, 1986.

H. Ebel, C. Bliefert and W. Russey, *The Art of Scientific Writing*, VCH, Deerfield Beach, 1987.

A. Eisenberg, Keeping a laboratory notebook, *J. Chem. Educ.*, 1982, **52**, 1045.

P.A. Ongley, Improve your English, *Chem. Br.*, 1984, **20**, 323.

J.M. Pratt, Writing a thesis, *Chem. Br.*, 1984, **20**, 1114.

R. Schoenfeld, *The Chemist's English*, VCH, Weinheim, 1986.

McGraw-Hill Dictionary of Scientific and Technical Terms, 5th edn, McGraw-Hill, New York, 1993.

The Oxford Dictionary for Scientific Writers and Editors, Oxford University Press, Oxford, 1991.

6.3 Chemical literature

The chemical literature is huge, and getting bigger. Over 500 000 papers are added to the literature of chemistry every year, to say nothing of books and patents. Much of this literature is now held on computer databases adding to the vast store of published knowledge to draw on. There will be many occasions on which you have to consult this store of knowledge, but before marching into your departmental or campus library and consulting books, journals and computer databases at random, you should attempt to plan your search of the literature in advance. This planning will save you considerable time, but to do this you need to know: (i) what type of literature is available, and (ii) what is the most appropriate for your particular problem. This short section is designed to help you to find your way through the literature of organic chemistry, by a brief discussion of points (i) and (ii) above. Some common text books (e.g. March, *Advanced Organic Chemistry*) also contain a brief overview of, and guide to, the literature of organic chemistry.

With the recent rapid developments in information technology and the advent of the Internet, an increasing amount of information that is useful to organic chemists is available on the World Wide Web in electronic form. There are a number of Internet sites that are relevant to organic chemists; these contain listings of databases and other sources of information. Most national chemical societies (e.g. the American Chemical Society and the Royal Society of Chemistry) maintain their own Internet site, as do a number of major chemistry publishers. Since all of these sites are under constant development, a discussion of this rapidly moving area is beyond the scope of this book. If you are interested in accessing such information, please consult your university Internet expert. Alternatively, just start surfing.

Primary literature

This is the place where chemists publish their original research results in the form of communications and papers. *Communications* are intended for important new advances in the subject, and are published fairly quickly, but usually without experimental detail. *Papers*, on the other hand, are intended to be detailed accounts of the research, containing a full discussion of the background to the work, the results and their significance, and *importantly* the experimental details.

Most nations that are engaged in serious chemical research have learned societies which publish chemical journals; in addition, there are a number of respected commercial publishers who also produce chemistry journals. Table 6.1 lists the major journals which are relevant to organic chemistry, although the list is by no means comprehensive. The table also shows the approved style of journal abbreviations defined in *Chemical Abstracts Service Source Index (CASSI)* and based on internationally recognized systems. Always use the approved journal abbreviation.

Use approved journal abbreviations

The primary literature is indispensable for finding precise details of how certain reactions have been carried out, and the properties of the products. However, you cannot go to the relevant reference immediately; you need another source to find the reference. This other source is either the *review literature* or one of the *major reference works*.

Review literature

There are several journals and series which contain review articles on organic chemistry. These cover such topics as classes of compounds, synthetic methods, individual reactions and so on. They are a valuable source of information and, of course, of references to the primary literature. Table 6.2 lists the major sources of reviews in organic chemistry, although again the list is not comprehensive.

Table 6.1 The primary literature of organic chemistry.

Journal title	Abbreviation
Acta Chemica Scandinavica	*Acta Chem. Scand.*
Angewandte Chemie, International Edition	*Angew. Chem. Int. Edn Engl.*
Australian Journal of Chemistry	*Aust. J. Chem.*
Bulletin of the Chemical Society of Japan	*Bull. Chem. Soc. Jpn.*
Bulletin de la Société Chimique de France	*Bull. Soc. Chim. Fr.*
Canadian Journal of Chemistry	*Can. J. Chem.*
Chemische Berichte	*Chem. Ber.*
Chemistry Letters	*Chem. Lett.*
Gazzetta Chimica Italiana	*Gazz. Chim. Ital.*
Helvetica Chimica Acta	*Helv. Chim. Acta*
Heterocycles	*Heterocycles*
Journal of the American Chemical Society	*J. Am. Chem. Soc.*
Journal of the Chemical Society, Chemical Communications	*Chem. Commun.*
Journal of the Chemical Society, Perkin Transactions 1	*J. Chem. Soc. Perkin Trans. 1*
Journal of Heterocyclic Chemistry	*J. Heterocycl. Chem.*
Journal of Medicinal Chemistry	*J. Med. Chem.*
Journal of Organic Chemistry	*J. Org. Chem.*
Journal of Organometallic Chemistry	*J. Organomet. Chem.*
Liebigs Annalen der Chemie	*Ann. Chem.*
Monatshefte für Chemie	*Monatsh. Chem.*
Recueil des Travaux Chimique des Pays-Bas	*Recl. Trav. Chim. Pays-Bas*
Synlett	*Synlett*
Synthesis	*Synthesis*
Synthetic Communications	*Synth. Commun.*
Tetrahedron	*Tetrahedron*
Tetrahedron: Asymmetry	*Tetrahedron: Asymmetry*
Tetrahedron Letters	*Tetrahedron Lett.*

Major reference works

There are a number of major reference works for organic chemistry, each running to many volumes. These are the main source of references to the primary literature, and anyone who works in chemistry eventually has to get to know their way around these works, particularly *Chemical Abstracts*. The major reference works are summarized below.

The Dictionary of Organic Compounds (DOC)

This is a useful source of data on relatively common compounds. The most recent edition (the 6th) was published in 1996, and regular supplements are issued. DOC contains information on over 170000 organic compounds,

Table 6.2 The review literature of organic chemistry.

Review title	Abbreviation
Accounts of Chemical Research	*Acc. Chem. Res.*
Advances in Heterocyclic Chemistry	*Adv. Heterocycl. Chem.*
Advances in Organometallic Chemistry	*Adv. Organomet. Chem.*
Advances in Physical Organic Chemistry	*Adv. Phys. Org. Chem.*
Annual Reports (on the Progress of Chemistry), Section B, Organic Chemistry	*Annu. Rep. Prog. Chem. Sect. B*
Chemical Reviews	*Chem. Rev.*
Chemical Society Reviews	*Chem., Soc. Rev.*
Methods of Organic Synthesis	*Meth. Org. Syn.*
Organic Reactions	*Org. React.*
Organic Reaction Mechanisms	*Org. React. Mech.*
Specialist Periodical Reports (SPR)	*Specialist Periodical Reports (SPR)*
Synthesis	*Synthesis*
Synthetic Methods of Organic Chemistry (Theilheimer)	*Synthetic Methods of Organic Chemistry (Theilheimer)*
Tetrahedron Reports	*Tetrahedron Reports*
Topics in Stereochemistry	*Top. Stereochem.*

together with a name and formula index. The information includes name, formula and structure of compound, mp or bp, rotation (if relevant), mp of simple derivatives, and references to its preparation and properties. DOC is available in electronic form on a CD-ROM.

Handbuch der Organischen Chemie (Beilstein)

This major reference work deals with individual compounds, and is indispensable for the early literature of organic chemistry. It is published in German although new editions are produced in English, in several parts:

Hauptwerk (main edition) abbreviated to	H	up to 1910
1e Erganzungswerk (1st supplement)	EI	1910–1919
2e Erganzungswerk (2nd supplement)	EII	1920–1929
3e Erganzungswerk (3rd supplement)	EIII	1930–1949
4e Erganzungswerk (4th supplement)	EIV	1950–1959
5e Erganzungswerk (5th supplement)	EV	1960–1979

Each part of the work is divided into 27 volumes ('Band') by subject areas; thus volumes 1–4 cover acyclic compounds; volumes 5–16 cover carbocyclic compounds and volumes 17–27 cover heterocyclic compounds. For some volumes, the 3rd and 4th supplements are combined. The compounds are further divided into about 5000 classifications ('Systemnummer'), so that a given compound (and very closely related ones) always appears in the same volume under the same Systemnummer. Having located the correct entry, you will find methods of preparation, physical properties and chemical reactions of the compound, together with references to the primary literature. Unfortunately many chemists are put off using Beilstein because they think it is too complicated. To remedy this the publishers have produced a small guide, *How to use Beilstein*, in English and a 2000 word German dictionary; both of these are freely available. An example of using Beilstein is given later in this section. Like *Chemical Abstracts* (see below), Beilstein is now available on-line.

Chemical Abstracts (CA)

This is the comprehensive abstracting service run by the American Chemical Society, and reckons to abstract all papers, books, patents and conference proceedings covering the whole of chemistry. *Chemical Abstracts* started in 1907, and a new issue of about 10000 abstracts appears every week. Each abstract contains key information from the primary literature source: authors, reference, brief resumé of the work (in English), and language of the original. A volume consists of 26 weekly issues, and each completed volume has associated *Author*, *Subject*, *Chemical Substance* and *Formula Indexes*. Every 5 years, a *Collective Index* covering the preceding 10 volumes, is published, and it is these *collective indexes* that are the most use in searching the literature. In the period 1947 onwards, collective indexes have appeared as follows:

5th Collective Index	1947–1956	Volumes 41–50
6th Collective Index	1957–1961	Volumes 51–55
7th Collective Index	1962–1966	Volumes 56–65
8th Collective Index	1967–1971	Volumes 66–75
9th Collective Index	1972–1976	Volumes 76–85
10th Collective Index	1977–1981	Volumes 86–95
11th Collective Index	1982–1986	Volumes 96–105
12th Collective Index	1987–1991	Volumes 106–115
13th Collective Index	1992–1996	Volumes 116–125

Chemical Abstracts is the largest single source of information relating to chemistry, and is therefore invaluable in locating the original literature on a particular problem. In recent years it has become possible to search this vast database by computer using the CAS ONLINE service, although the database is only complete from 1967 onwards. Therefore do not get used to relying on computer literature searches totally, since for earlier work you must still use the hard copy abstracts or Beilstein.

Science Citation Index (SCI)

This index, published regularly, enables you to find work in a closely related area given a reference to the original (or early) work in the field. The citation index then leads to all subsequent papers which cite the original reference. Again, this is available on-line.

In addition to the above, regularly updated, reference works, there are a number of other major reference works relevant to organic chemistry. These are encyclopedia-type works, and include the following.

Rodd's *Chemistry of Carbon Compounds* (2nd edn); over 30 volumes published from the mid-1960s to date; covers organic compounds by compound class.

Elsevier's *Encyclopedia of Organic Chemistry*; a multi-volume work, particularly useful for the literature on carbocyclic compounds with two or more rings.

Houben-Weyl's *Methoden der Organischen Chemie* (in German); published in several volumes, and deals with compound classes, with emphasis on experimental aspects.

Fieser's *Reagents for Organic Synthesis*; 17 volumes to date, lists organic reagents alphabetically, together with examples of their use, and references to the primary literature.

Comprehensive Organic Chemistry, *Comprehensive Organometallic Chemistry*, *Comprehensive Heterocyclic Chemistry (I and II)*, *Comprehensive Organic Synthesis*, *Comprehensive Organic Functional Group Transformations*, and *Encyclopedia of Reagents for Organic Synthesis* are all multi-volume works containing review chapters written by experts in the field.

Compilations of spectroscopic data, such as *The Aldrich Library of IR Spectra*, *The Aldrich Library of NMR Spectra*, the *DMS Atlas of IR Spectra*, *Organic Electronic Spectral Data* and the *Eight Peak Index of Mass Spectra* are particularly useful in finding reference spectra of fairly common compounds.

How to use the literature

To find a specific compound

The best method is to use the formula indexes of DOC, Beilstein and CA.

1 Work out the molecular formula of the compound; most indexes use the system: C, H (both in ascending order), then other elements alphabetically.

2 Consult the formula index of DOC (and latest supplements); compounds of that molecular formula will be listed. Make sure you consider all the possible names for your compound, since the indexers may not have used the same name. If the compound is present, look up the appropriate page in the appropriate volume, and retrieve the information.

For example, find the mp of 1-naphthol, and any crystalline derivatives:

Formula = $C_{10}H_8O$

Formula Index	→	1-naphthol N-00193
N-00193 (in volume 4)	→	**Answer**
		1-naphthol mp 94°C
		benzoate mp 56°C
		3,5-dinitrobenzoate mp 217.4°C

If the compound is not in the DOC, go to Beilstein for pre-1950 literature and to CA for post-1950 work.

3 Start with the formula index ('Generalformelregister') of the second supplement (EII) of Beilstein; this is cumulative for the main edition, and the 1st and 2nd supplements. Compounds of that molecular formula will be listed with their German name; make sure you recognize the German name for your compound! Turn up the appropriate pages, and obtain the information. To look up the compound in the 3rd and 4th supplements, go to the same volume (Band) number, find the part that pertains to the correct Systemnummer, and look up the formula index.

For example, find a method of preparation of *O*-benzylhydroxylamine, $C_6H_5CH_2ONH_2$:

Formula = C_7H_9NO		
EII Formelregister	→	**6**, 440; I 222 (refers to volume 6 of main work and 1st supplement)
6, 440	→	Systemnumber 528
	→	**Answer**
		Plenty of information and references
I 222	→	More information

To find more recent references, go to the formula indexes of volume 6 of the 3rd and 4th supplements that pertain to Systemnummer 528:

EIII Band 6 (Systemnummer 525–533)	→	1552 (p. 1552 in that volume) more information
EIV Band 6 (Systemnummer 524–528)	→	2562 (p. 2562 in that volume) more information

4 Go to the *Formula Index* of CA and use the collective indexes; but whether to start with the most recent and work backwards, or to start with the earliest and work forwards is a matter of choice—sometimes you intuitively feel that the most likely source of references will be in the most recent volumes. Having checked the collective indexes, do not forget to check the most recent individual volume indexes. When using the CA *Formula Index* it is essential that you consult the relevant *Index Guide*. CA has had the unfortunate habit of changing the way in which it names compounds, so you must look up the *Index Guide* to find the correct CA name for that particular period.

Having found your compound in the *Formula Index*, this will lead you to the appropriate volume of abstracts and to the abstract itself. At this point you may be able to decide whether it is worth looking up the original reference, or whether to go on to the next abstract. To be certain of obtaining all the information, you may have to look up several original references.

For example, find the preparation and properties of 7b-methyl-7b*H*-cyclopent[*cd*]indene, a recent addition to the interesting family of novel 10π-aromatic compounds:

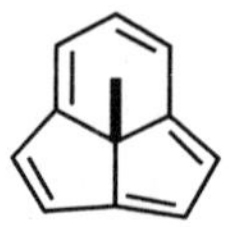

Formula = $C_{12}H_{10}$
Compound is fairly recent, so work backwards through CA.

11th Collective Index	→	9 references
10th Collective Index	→	1 reference
Volume 106 Index	→	0 references
Volume 107 Index	→	0 references
Look up Abstracts	→	**Answer**
		10 references to the primary literature

To find information on a type of compound or reaction

For this type of literature search it is best to use the review literature, or to consult one of the encyclopedia-type works.

For more recent references on such a topic, try sources such as the latest volumes of *Annual Reports*, the Royal Society of Chemistry *Specialist Periodical Reports on General and Synthetic Methods* or Fieser's *Reagents for Organic Synthesis*.

Conclusion

The purpose of this section has been to alert you to the types of literature, and to provide some guidelines as to how to search for information in the chemical literature. Further guidelines are given in the references below. No foolproof method of finding chemical information exists, and those of you who remain in chemistry will eventually develop your own system of literature searching. You may even end up having an information scientist to do the job for you, although this removes the element of serendipity, in which the adjacent paper turns out to be more interesting to you than the one the search led to!

Further reading

J. March, *Advanced Organic Chemistry*, 4th edn, Wiley & Sons, New York, 1992.
R.E. Maizell, *How to Find Chemical Information*, 3nd edn, Wiley & Sons, New York, 1998.
Y. Wolman, *Chemical Information: a Practical Guide to Utilization*, Wiley & Sons, New York, 1983.

PART 2 EXPERIMENTAL PROCEDURES

Introduction

This part of the book contains a series of experiments, some of which have microscale variants, from which it is hoped a selection can be chosen to suit the requirements of any teaching course or individual. The range of experiments is intended to cover a spectrum of difficulty from introductory to research level chemistry and has been chosen with the following aims in mind:

- To permit the practice and development of manipulative techniques commonly used in organic chemistry.
- To highlight and illustrate important chemical transformations and principles and provide first-hand experience of subjects discussed in lectures.
- To excite curiosity within the individual carrying out the experiment, and instil the desire to read further into the subject.

It is the authors' hope that the experiments contained within this book will give students an enthusiasm for organic chemistry, both practical and theoretical, and lead to the expression of latent desires to continue into research.

Before qualifying for inclusion in this book, each experiment has had to satisfy the demanding combination of criteria of repeatability, minimization of hazards, and absence of unduly long laboratory sessions. Microscale experiments are included to minimize waste disposal problems. Each experiment has been checked by independent workers. Each experimental procedure is broken down into several sections to encourage forward planning and to help in deciding whether or not a particular experiment is suitable for study and can be completed with the time and resources available. In Chapter 7, there is a relatively informal grouping according to reaction class, with the experiments being concerned with functional group inter-conversions, whilst those in Chapter 8 are broadly concerned with C–C bond-forming reactions. Chapter 9 contains a series of short projects, utilizing many of the conversions covered specifically in Experiments 1–66, and Experiments 80–86 are concerned with aspects of physical organic chemistry. The experiments are listed on pp. 424–426 and, as explained on p. 427, certain experiments can be taken together to form a longer multi-stage sequence and the subsequent experiment is indicated by a signpost symbol (➠).

In the list of experiments which immediately follows this introduction, those experiments which have both a standard and a microscale protocol described are marked with a test tube symbol (🧪). Within the experimental section itself standard-scale protocols are indicated by a flask symbol ( ) and, again, microscale protocols by a test tube symbol ( ), in the margin.

In each experiment the reaction scheme is given first, followed by some background information about the reaction and the aims of the study. The next two sections contain advance information about the experiment, which is useful for planning ahead. One of the more important pieces of information is an indication of the degree of complexity of the procedure. This has been broken down arbitrarily into four levels:

1 introductory;

2 use of more complex manipulative procedures;

3 as level 2, with emphasis upon spectroscopic analysis;

4 research level procedures involving a wide range of techniques and analysis, often on small scale.

However, it should be remembered that these levels are subjective and are guidelines only. The time required to complete the experiment has been estimated usually as a number of 3 h periods. Such a time unit seems to be the highest common denominator for teaching laboratories generally, but common sense will indicate how the experimental procedure might be adapted for longer laboratory periods. Equipment, glassware set-ups and spectroscopic instrument requirements are then given, followed by a complete listing of the chemicals and solvents needed, any hazards associated with them and the quantities of each required. The experimental section consists of the procedure, contained in the main body of text, together with warnings, suggestions, and break-points highlighted in the margin. Finally, after each experimental procedure is a section of problems designed around the experiment, followed by further reading lists. The problems and references are an important feature of the experiment and should be undertaken conscientiously to get the most out of the exercise. For further information on certain reagents we simply refer the reader to the *Encyclopedia of Reagents for Organic Synthesis* (ed. L.A. Paquette, 1995, Wiley & Sons, Chichester) by giving the relevant reference in the form: EROS, page number.

The format in which the experiments are presented requires you to have read thoroughly the first five chapters of this book, in particular Chapter 1 which deals with safety in the laboratory. In addition, it is assumed that individuals will not attempt experiments having a high difficulty rating before achieving competence at the lower levels.

Always observe general laboratory safety precautions and any special precautions associated with a particular experiment, as well as being constantly on the look out for unexpected hazards connected with your experiment or any neighbouring experiment. If in doubt, ask an instructor before doing anything.

It must be stressed that, whilst every effort has been made to ensure that the details contained in the procedures are accurate, it is inevitable that the same experiment carried out by different individuals in different laboratories will show some variation. The responsibility for the safe conduct of the experiment rests ultimately with the individual carrying it out.

The hazards associated with any particular substance are clearly shown next to its position in the 'materials' list. Whilst every effort has been made to exclude or restrict the use of unduly toxic materials such as benzene, 3-bromoprop-1-ene (allyl bromide) or iodomethane it has not been possible to avoid the use of chloroform which has been cited as a **cancer suspect agent**. However, if due regard is paid to its potential toxic properties, chloroform should be considered safe enough for use in the undergraduate laboratory. Never assume that the absence of any hazard warning means that a substance is safe; the golden rule is to treat all chemicals as toxic and pay them the respect they deserve.

Remember, the motto in the laboratory is always '**safety first**' and enjoy your chemistry!

List of Experiments

// Refers to the fact that this experiment has a microscale version, as well as a macroscale one.

Level	*Number*	*Experiment*
// 1	**1**	Preparation of 3-methyl-1-butyl ethanoate (isoamyl acetate) (pear essence)
2	**2**	Preparation of *s*-butyl but-2-enoate (*s*-butyl crotonate)
2	**3**	Preparation of *N*-methylcyclohexanecarboxamide
2	**4**	Protection of ketones as ethylene ketals (1,3-dioxolanes)
// 1	**5**	Preparation of *E*-benzaldoxime
// 1	**6**	Preparation of 4-bromoaniline (*p*-bromoaniline)
1	**7**	Hydration of alkenes: preparation of hexan-2-ol from 1-hexene
3	**8**	Stereospecific preparation of *trans*-cyclohexane-1,2-diol via bromohydrin and epoxide formation
3	**9**	Preparation of *cis*-cyclohexane-1,2-diol by the Woodward method
3	**10**	Asymmetric dihydroxylation of *trans*-1,2-diphenylethene (*trans*-stilbene)
// 2	**11**	Peracid epoxidation of cholesterol: 3β-hydroxy-5α,6α-epoxycholestane
4	**12**	The Sharpless epoxidation: asymmetric epoxidation of (*E*)-3,7-dimethyl-2,6-octadien-1-ol (geraniol)
4	**13**	Hydration of alkenes by hydroboration–oxidation: preparation of octan-1-ol from l-octene
3	**14**	Preparation of 7-trichloromethyl-8-bromo-Δ^1-*p*-menthane by free radical addition of bromotrichloromethane to β-pinene
// 1	**15**	Preparation of 1-iodobutane by SN2 displacement of bromide: the Finkelstein reaction
// 3	**16**	Preparation of 4-bromomethylbenzoic acid by radical substitution and conversion to 4-methoxymethylbenzoic acid by nucleophilic substitution
// 1	**17**	Reduction of benzophenone with sodium borohydride: preparation of diphenylmethanol
// 2	**18**	Reduction of 4-*t*-butylcyclohexanone with sodium borohydride
3	**19**	Stereospecific reduction of benzoin with sodium borohydride; determination of the stereochemistry by NMR spectroscopy
2	**20**	Chemoselectivity in the reduction of 3-nitroacetophenone
3	**21**	Reduction of diphenylacetic acid with lithium aluminium hydride
4	**22**	Reduction of *N*-methyl cyclohexanecarboxamide with lithium aluminium hydride: *N*-methyl cyclohexylmethylamine
4	**23**	Reduction of butyrolactone with di*iso*butylaluminium hydride and estimation by NMR of the relative proportions of 4-hydroxybutanal and its cyclic isomer, 2-hydroxytetrahydrofuran, in the product mixture
2	**24**	Wolff–Kishner reduction of propiophenone to *n*-propylbenzene
2	**25**	Preparation of Adams' catalyst and the heterogeneous hydrogenation of cholesterol
3	**26**	Preparation of Wilkinson's catalyst and its use in the selective homogeneous reduction of carvone to 7,8-dihydrocarvone
4	**27**	Birch reduction of 1,2-dimethylbenzene (*o*-xylene): 1,2-dimethyl-1,4-cyclohexadiene

Experiments which can be Taken in Sequence

Experiments 2 and 37
Experiments 3 and 22
Experiments 4 and 36
Experiments 5 and 66
Experiments 16 and 51
Experiments 29 and 46
Experiments 29 and 48
Experiments 34 and 62
Experiments 44 and 47
Experiments 59 and 71

Experiments which Illustrate Particular Techniques

Catalytic hydrogenation	Experiments	25,26
Ozonolysis	Experiment	73
Reactions under an inert atmosphere	Experiments	13, 23, 39, 48, 49, 52, 54, 55, 58, 63
Syringe techniques	Experiments	12, 13, 23, 39, 48, 49, 55, 58, 59
Low temperature reactions	Experiments	23, 39, 48, 55
Continuous removal of water	Experiments	2, 4, 32, 45, 46
Reactions in liquid ammonia	Experiments	27, 47
Soxhlet extraction	Experiments	67, 69
Simple distillation	Experiments	1, 7, 8, 15, 29, 31, 44, 61, 72, 73
Fractional distillation	Experiment	2
Distillation under reduced pressure	Experiments	2, 4, 30, 37, 38, 45, 46, 53, 64, 65
Short path distillation	Experiments	12, 13, 22, 23, 26, 27, 47, 54, 63, 68
Steam distillation	Experiments	59, 67, 68
Sublimation	Experiment	62
TLC	Experiments	10, 17, 33, 50, 58,
Column chromatography	Experiments	36, 58, 73
GC	Experiments	18, 27, 30, 68, 72
Refractive index measurement (as *key*-part)	Experiment	65
Optical rotation measurement	Experiments	5, 10, 11, 12, 26, 30
IR (as *key* part)	Experiments	26, 29, 41, 65, 71, 84
NMR (as *key* part)	Experiments	19, 23, 26, 32, 46, 48, 65, 71
UV (as *key* part)	Experiments	26, 41, 42, 53, 76, 80, 81, 82, 83, 85

Note: the order of techniques corresponds to the order in which they are discussed in Chapter 2–5.

Chapter 7 Functional Group Interconversions

The ability to convert one functional group into another is one of the two fundamental requirements of the practising organic chemist, the other being the ability to form carbon–carbon bonds (see Chapter 8). There can be few syntheses of organic compounds that do not involve at least one functional group interconversion at some stage in the process. Therefore an organic laboratory text should reflect the importance of functional group interconversion reactions, and the first 35 experiments in this book attempt to do just that. We have included examples of reactions involving the major functional groups of organic chemistry—alkenes, halides, alcohols, and carbonyl compounds—under headings which give some idea of the reaction type.

7.1 Simple transformations

The experiments in this section all involve aspects of the chemistry of the carbonyl group, C=O. The carbonyl group is the most versatile group in organic chemistry, and appears in a range of different compound classes: acid chlorides, aldehydes, ketones, esters, amides and carboxylic acids. Because of the highly polarized nature of the C=O bond, the carbonyl carbon is susceptible to nucleophilic attack, the reactivity of the different types of carbonyl decreasing in the order shown above. The following experiments illustrate this reactivity, and include examples of the formation of esters and amides from carboxylic acids and their derivatives, and the formation of ketals and oximes from aldehydes and ketones. The final experiment in this section introduces the concept of multi-stage reaction sequences.

Some additional examples of simple transformations involving carbonyl compounds can be found as part of longer experiments in later sections: see Experiments 36, 37, 60 and 71.

Carboxylic acid esters are usually formed by reaction of a carboxylic acid with an alcohol in the presence of a proton acid catalyst such as hydrogen chloride or sulfuric acid (often called Fischer esterification), or a Lewis acid catalyst such as boron trifluoride (usually as its complex with diethyl ether), or by the reaction of an acid derivative such as the acid chloride or anhydride with an alcohol. Esters are versatile compounds in organic chemistry and are widely used in synthesis because they are easily converted into a variety of other functional groups. The two experiments which follow illustrate the preparation of esters from acids and alcohols.

Experiment 1

Preparation of 3-methyl-1-butyl ethanoate (isoamyl acetate) (pear essence)

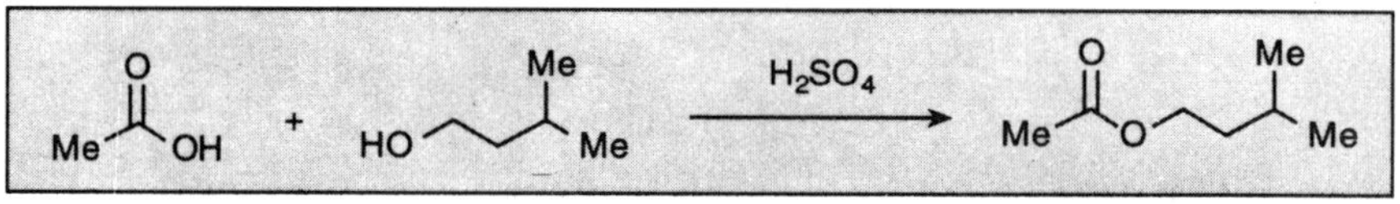

3-Methyl-1-butyl ethanoate, often known as pear essence because of its highly characteristic smell, has also been identified as one of the active constituents of the alarm pheromone of the honey bee. Cotton wool impregnated with isoamyl acetate apparently alerts and agitates the guard bees when placed near the entrance to the hive. The ester can be prepared from 3-methylbutan-1-ol (isoamyl alcohol) and ethanoic (acetic) acid by heating in the presence of sulfuric acid. Ethanoic acid is inexpensive, and is therefore used in excess to drive the reaction to completion. After extraction with diethyl ether, the ester is purified by distillation at atmospheric pressure.

Level	1
Time	3 h
Equipment	apparatus for reflux, extraction/separation, suction filtration, distillation

Materials

3-methylbutan-1-ol (isoamyl alcohol) (FW 88.2)	5.3 mL, 4.4 g (50 mmol)	**irritant**
ethanoic acid (FW 60.1)	11.5 mL, 12.0 g (200 mmol)	**corrosive**
sulfuric acid (conc.)	1 mL	**corrosive, oxidizer**
diethyl ether		**flammable, irritant**
sodium carbonate solution (5%)		**corrosive**
iron(II) sulfate solution (5%)		

Procedure

Place the 3-methylbutan-1-ol, ethanoic acid, and a few boiling stones in a 50 mL round-bottomed flask. Add the concentrated sulfuric acid, swirl to dissolve, fit a reflux condenser to the flask,[1] and heat the mixture under reflux for 1.5 h using an oil bath.[2]

Cool the flask by immersing it in cold water for a few minutes, and then pour the reaction mixture into a 100 mL beaker containing *ca.* 25 g cracked ice. Stir the mixture with a glass rod for 2 min, and then transfer it to a 100 mL separatory funnel, rinsing the reaction flask and the beaker with 2 × 10 mL diethyl ether. Add a further 25 mL of diethyl ether to the funnel, shake the funnel venting carefully and allow the layers to separate. Run off the lower, aqueous layer, and wash the organic phase with 30 mL iron(II) sulfate solution,[3] and then with 2 × 15 mL portions of the sodium carbonate solution.[4] Dry the diethyl ether layer by standing it over $MgSO_4$ for 10 min. Filter off the drying agent under gravity,[5] evaporate the filtrate on the rotary evaporator,[6] and distil the residual liquid at atmospheric pressure[7] in a 10 mL flask, collecting the product that boils at *ca.* 140–145°C. Record the exact bp and yield of your product. The IR and NMR spectra of the product are provided (see p. 432). ■

[1] *See Fig. 3.23*
[2] *During this time, get apparatus and solutions ready for extraction*
[3] *Must be freshly prepared*
[4] ***Care! Gas evolved***
[5] *See Fig. 3.5*
[6] *If not available, distil the ether off first using the distillation apparatus*
[7] *See Fig. 3.48*

MICROSCALE

Level	1
Time	3 h
Equipment	apparatus for microscale reflux, extraction/separation, pipette column filtration (Hickman still for optional distillation)

Materials		
3-methylbutan-1-ol (isoamyl alcohol) (FW 88.2)	0.53 mL, 440 mg (5 mmol)	**irritant**
ethanoic acid (FW 60.1)	1.15 mL, 1.20 g (20 mmol)	**corrosive**
sulfuric acid (conc.)	0.10 mL	**corrosive, oxidizer**
diethyl ether		**flammable, irritant**
sodium carbonate solution (5%)		**corrosive**

Procedure

Place the 3-methylbutan-1-ol, ethanoic acid and a single boiling stone in a 5 mL conical reaction vial. Add the sulfuric acid (from an adjustable or graduated pipette), mix the vial contents by drawing the mixture up into a Pasteur pipette and expelling several times, then fit a reflux condenser[1] and heat the mixture under reflux for 1.5 h.[2] Cool the flask and then transfer the contents by pipette onto *ca.* 2.5 g of cracked ice in a tapered test tube or vial. Using a Pasteur pipette, rinse the reaction flask with three successive portions of diethyl ether (0.5 mL each) transferring each in turn to the tube containing the

[1] *See Fig. 3.24*
[2] *Prepare the sodium carbonate solution and the drying column*

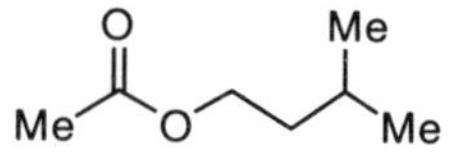

(neat)

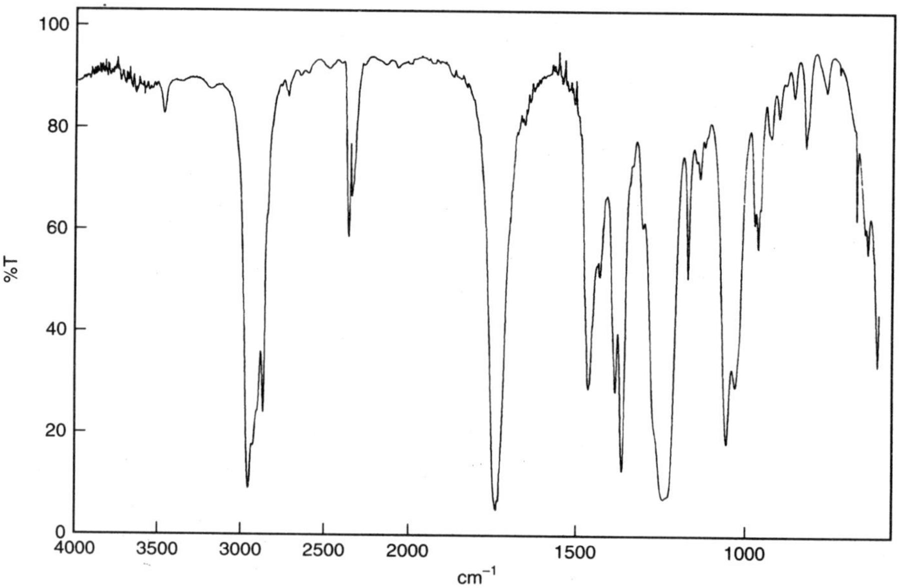

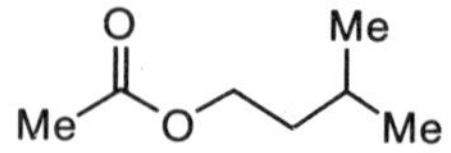

(250 MHz, $CDCl_3$)

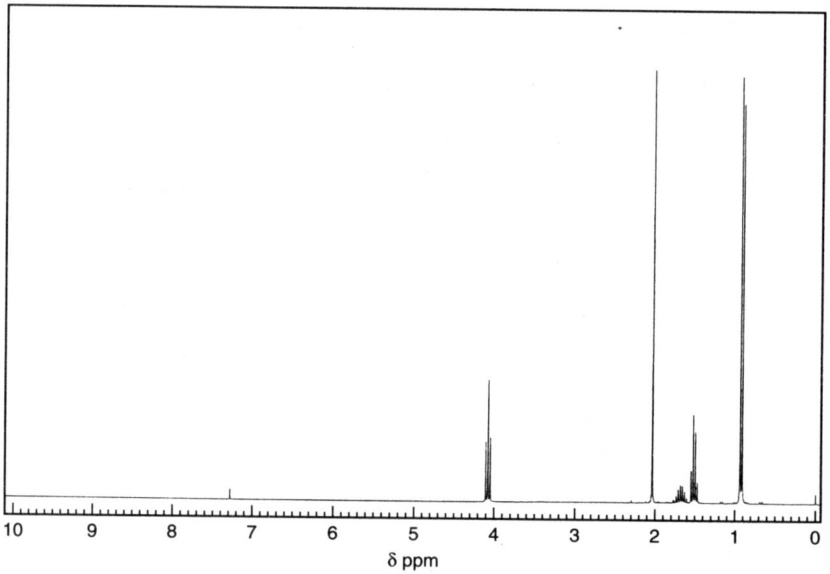

aqueous phase. Mix the aqueous and ether layers vigorously using a Pasteur pipette and then allow the layers to separate. Carefully withdraw the aqueous layer from beneath the diethyl ether and discard it. Wash the ether layer with portions of sodium carbonate solution (2 × 1.5 mL).[3] Dry the ether layer by passing it through a column of $MgSO_4$ in a plugged Pasteur pipette[4] and evaporate the solvent by passing a stream of air or nitrogen over the surface.[5] The product can be distilled using the Hickman still at atmospheric pressure.[6] Transfer the distilled product into a preweighed vial and determine the yield. Record an IR spectrum (film).

[3]*Care! Gas evolved*
[4]*See Fig. 3.9*
[5]*See Fig. 2.31*
[6]*See Fig. 3.58*

Problems

1 Diethyl ether is a hazardous solvent since, as well as being highly flammable, it can form explosive peroxides. The work-up in the standard scale experiment includes a step to remove any such peroxides. Which is this step?

2 Why is a gas evolved during the carbonate extraction? What is it?

3 Write a reaction mechanism for the esterification reaction between ethanoic acid and 3-methylbutan-1-ol. What is the role of the sulfuric acid?

4 Examine the IR spectrum of 3-methylbutyl provided. Assign the peaks which correspond to the C=O and C–O bonds in the molecule.

5 Examine the NMR spectrum of 3-methylbutyl provided. Assign peaks to each of the groups of protons within the molecule.

Experiment 2 — *Preparation of* s-*butyl but-2-enoate* (s-*butyl crotonate*)

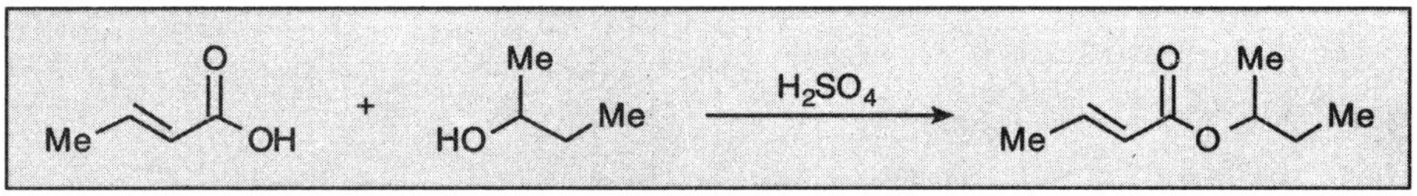

This experiment, like Experiment 1, involves an esterification reaction that is carried out in the presence of concentrated sulfuric acid. The carboxylic acid and alcohol components are the unsaturated acid but-2-enoic acid (crotonic acid) and the secondary alcohol butan-2-ol (*s*-butyl alcohol), which react to give the corresponding ester, *s*-butyl but-2-enoate. The experiment is carried out in toluene solution, and illustrates the use of a Dean and Stark apparatus for the continuous removal of water from a reaction mixture. The product ester is purified by distillation under reduced pressure, and can subsequently be used in Experiment 37 if desired.

Level	2
Time	2 × 3 h
Equipment	apparatus for reflux with water removal (Dean and Stark apparatus), extraction/separation, suction filtration, distillation under reduced pressure
Instruments	IR, NMR (optional)

Materials

but-2-enoic acid (crotonic acid) (FW 86.1)	4.3 mL (50 mmol)	**corrosive, toxic**
butan-2-ol (FW 74.1)	7.7 mL (83 mmol)	**flammable, irritant**
toluene	25 mL	**flammable, irritant**
sulfuric acid (conc.)	0.1 mL	**corrosive, oxidizer**
diethyl ether		**flammable, irritant**
sodium carbonate solution (10%)		**corrosive**

Procedure

Place the butan-2-ol in a 50 mL round-bottomed flask, add the sulfuric acid,[1] and swirl the flask until the acid dissolves. Add the but-2-enoic acid and the toluene, and swirl the flask to mix the reagents. Add a boiling stone, fit the flask with a Dean and Stark water separator and reflux condenser.[2] Heat the flask so that the toluene refluxes vigorously,[3] and the water that is formed collects in the trap. Continue to heat the mixture until no more water separates.[4] Allow the mixture to cool,[5] then transfer it to a separatory funnel. Dilute the mixture with 10 mL diethyl ether, and wash the solution with a 2 × 10 mL portion of 10% sodium carbonate solution,[6] then with 2 × 5 mL saturated sodium chloride solution, and finally dry it over $MgSO_4$.[7] Filter off the drying agent by suction, evaporate the filtrate on the rotary evaporator, and distil the residue from a 10 mL flask under reduced pressure using a water pump (*ca.* 30 mmHg) collecting the product at *ca.* 75°C.[8] Record the exact bp, yield, and the IR (film) and NMR ($CDCl_3$) spectra of your product.

[1] *Care!*

[2] *See Fig. 3.27*

[3] *Toluene should condense half-way up condenser*

[4] *Can continue the refluxing overnight if necessary—about 1 mL of water should be formed*

[5] *May be left at this stage*

[6] ***Care! CO_2 evolved***

[7] *May be left at this stage*

[8] *A purer product is obtained if a fractionating column is used—see Fig. 3.50*

See Exp. 37

Problems

1 Write a reaction mechanism for the esterification reaction.

2 Assign the IR and NMR (if recorded) spectra of s-butyl but-2-enoate. In the IR spectrum, pay particular attention to the position of the peak for the ester carbonyl stretch. Where would you expect the carbonyl peak in the IR spectrum of ethyl acetate?

Experiment 3

Preparation of N-methylcyclohexanecarboxamide

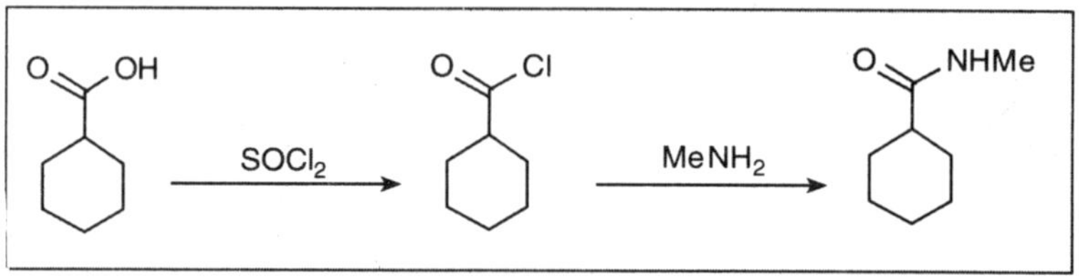

The preparation of derivatives of carboxylic acids is an important process in organic chemistry. Carboxylic acid chlorides are particularly versatile intermediates which can be converted into a variety of other functional groups. This experiment illustrates the preparation of the acid chloride from cyclohexanecarboxylic acid by refluxing the acid with thionyl chloride, and its subsequent conversion into the corresponding methyl amide by reaction with aqueous methylamine. In a more advanced follow-up experiment (Experiment 22), *N*-methylcyclohexanecarboxamide is reduced with lithium aluminium hydride to *N*-methylcyclohexylmethylamine.

Level	2
Time	2 × 3 h
Equipment	magnetic stirrer; apparatus for reflux, suction filtration, recrystallization
Instruments	IR

Materials

cyclohexanecarboxylic acid (FW 128.2)	6.4 g (50 mmol)	
thionyl chloride (FW 119.0)	5.5 mL (75 mmol)	**lachrymator, corrosive**
methylamine (40% aqueous solution) (FW 31.1)	15 mL (190 mmol)	**corrosive stench**
toluene	25 mL	**flammable, irritant**

Procedure

Place the cyclohexanecarboxylic acid and a few boiling stones in a 25 mL round-bottomed flask. Add the thionyl chloride,[1] fit the flask with a reflux condenser carrying a calcium chloride drying tube,[2] and heat the mixture under reflux for 1 h. Allow the flask to cool, transfer it to a rotary evaporator,[3] and evaporate off the excess thionyl chloride to leave the acid chloride.

Place the aqueous methylamine in a 250 mL round-bottomed flask. Cool the flask in an ice bath, and stir the solution rapidly with a magnetic stirrer. Add the acid chloride dropwise from a Pasteur pipette,[4] and continue to stir the mixture for about 30 min.[5] Collect the product by suction filtration, wash with water, and dry it with suction at the pump for a few minutes.[5] Recrystallize the product from toluene.[6] Record the yield, mp, and the IR spectrum (Nujol®) of your product after one recrystallization. Record an IR spectrum of the starting acid for comparison.

HOOD
[1]***Care! Lachrymator***
[2]*See Fig. 3.23(a); HCl and SO_2 evolved*
[3]*Preferably in the hood*
[4]***Care! Exothermic***
[5]*May be left at this stage*
[6]*If the follow-up experiment 22 is being carried out, compound need not be recrystallized*

See Exp. 22

Problems

1 Write a mechanism for the conversion of an acid into the acid chloride using thionyl chloride. What other reagents could be used for this transformation?

2 When the acid chloride is treated with aqueous methylamine, why is the amide formed by reaction with the amine, rather than the acid by reaction with the water?

3 Compare and contrast the IR spectra of the acid and the amide. What are the carbonyl frequencies of each compound?

Further reading

For the procedures on which this experiment is based, see: A.C. Cope and E. Ciganek, *Org. Synth. Coll. Vol*, **4**, 339; H.E. Baumgarten, F.A. Bower and T.T. Okamoto, *J. Am. Chem. Soc.*, 1957, **79**, 3145.

For further information on thionyl chloride as a reagent, see: EROS, 4873.

Experiment 4   *Protection of ketones as ethylene ketals (1,3-dioxolanes)*

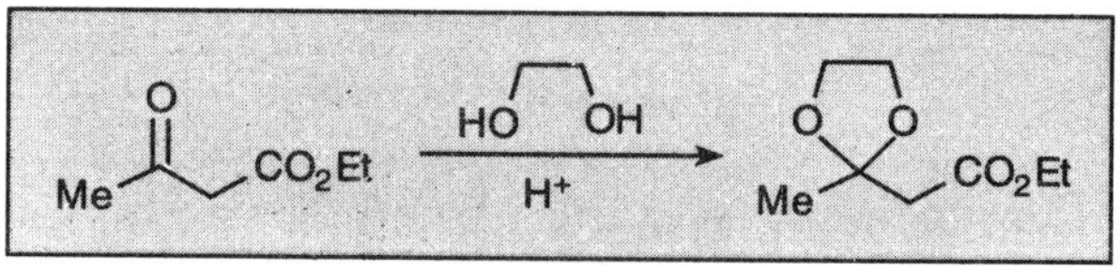

Aldehydes and ketones are extremely versatile compounds for organic synthesis, since they readily undergo nucleophilic attack (Experiments 39, 49–54) and can be deprotonated to give enolates (Experiments 48, 49). However, in polyfunctional molecules, it is often necessary to protect aldehyde and ketone carbonyl groups to stop undesirable side reactions during a synthetic sequence, and then remove the protecting group at a later stage. One common protecting group for aldehydes and ketones is the ethylene acetal or ketal (1,3-dioxolane derivative), easily prepared from the carbonyl compound and ethane-1,2-diol (ethylene glycol) in the presence of an acid catalyst. The protecting group can be removed subsequently by treatment with aqueous acid. This experiment involves the preparation of the ethylene ketal of ethyl 3-oxobutanoate (ethyl acetoacetate), by reaction of the keto ester with ethane-1,2-diol in the presence of toluene-4-sulfonic acid. The reaction is carried out in refluxing toluene, and the water that is formed is removed by azeotropic distillation using a Dean and Stark water separator. The protected ketone can then be used in Experiment 36 if desired.

Level	2
Time	2 × 3 h
Equipment	apparatus for reflux with water removal (Dean and Stark apparatus), extraction/separation, suction filtration, distillation under reduced pressure (water aspirator)
Instruments	IR, NMR

Materials

ethyl 3-oxobutanoate (ethyl acetoacetate) (FW 130.1)	12.7 mL, 13.0 g (100 mmol)	**irritant**
ethane-1,2-diol (FW 62.1)	5.8 mL, 6.5 g (105 mmol)	**irritant**
toluene-4-sulfonic acid monohydrate	0.05 g	**corrosive, toxic**
toluene	50 mL	**flammable, irritant**
sodium hydroxide solution (10%)		**corrosive**
anhydrous potassium carbonate		**corrosive, hygroscopic**

Procedure

Set up a 100 mL round-bottomed flask with a Dean and Stark water separator and reflux condenser.[1] Add the ethyl 3-oxobutanoate, toluene, ethane-1, 2-diol, toluene-4-sulfonic acid, and a few boiling stones to the flask. Heat the flask so that the toluene refluxes vigorously.[2] Continue to heat the mixture until no more water collects in the separator.[3] Cool the mixture to room temperature, transfer it to a separatory funnel, and wash the solution with 15 mL sodium hydroxide solution, followed by 2 × 20 mL portions of water. Dry the organic layer over anhydrous potassium carbonate.[4] Filter off the drying agent by suction, evaporate the filtrate on the rotary evaporator,[4] transfer the residue to a 25 mL flask and distil it under reduced pressure using a water aspirator (*ca.* 50 mmHg)[5] collecting the fraction boiling at about 135°C. Record the exact bp, yield, and the IR (film) and NMR ($CDCl_3$) spectra of your product. Record the IR (film) and NMR ($CDCl_3$) spectra of ethyl 3-oxobutanoate for comparison.

1 See Fig. 3.27 (separator arm may need lagging)
2 Vapour should condense half-way up condenser
3 Takes about 45 min
4 May be left at this stage
5 See Fig. 3.53

See Exp. 38

Problems

1 Write a reaction mechanism for the ketal formation.
2 Why does the ketone carbonyl group react in preference to the ester carbonyl?
3 Assign the IR and NMR spectra of your product and compare them with those of the starting ethyl 3-oxobutanoate.

Further reading

For the procedure on which this experiment is based, see: D.R. Paulson, A.L. Hartwig and G.F. Moran, *J. Chem. Educ.*, 1973 **50**, 216.

For a general discussion of protecting groups, see: P.J. Kocienski, *Protecting Groups*, Thieme, 1994.

Experiment 5

Preparation of E*-benzaldoxime*

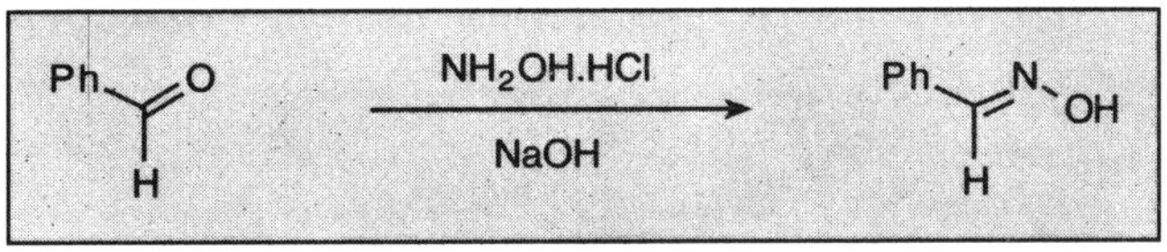

Aldehydes and ketones readily form a range of derivatives containing a C=N bond by reaction with various XNH_2 compounds as described in Chapter 4 (pp. 254–255). Thus reaction with 2,4-dinitrophenylhydrazine gives 2,4-dinitrophenylhydrazones, and reaction with hydroxylamine gives oximes. This experiment illustrates the latter process in the preparation of *E*-benzaldoxime from benzaldehyde. The *E* nomenclature refers to the geometry about the C=N bond; the oxime can be used in Experiment 66 if desired.

Level	1
Time	3 h
Equipment	magnetic stirrer; apparatus for extraction/separation
Instruments	IR (optional)

Materials		
benzaldehyde (FW 106.1)	5.1 mL, 5.2 g (50 mmol)	**irritant, toxic**
hydroxylamine hydrochloride (FW 69.5)	4.2 g (60 mmol)	**corrosive**
sodium hydroxide pellets	3.5 g (87 mmol)	**corrosive, hygroscopic**
ethanoic acid		**corrosive**
diethyl ether		**flammable, irritant**

Procedure

Dissolve the sodium hydroxide in 30 mL of water in a 100 mL Erlenmeyer flask containing a magnetic stirrer bar. Allow the solution to cool and then add *ca.* 0.5 mL of benzaldehyde followed by *ca.* 0.5 g of hydroxylamine hydrochloride. Stopper the flask and stir the mixture vigorously, briefly stop the stirring at 5 min intervals to add further portions of benzaldehyde and hydroxylamine hydrochloride until both reagents have been completely added. The reaction mixture will become warm, giving a homogeneous solution with no almond odour, indicating total consumption of the benzaldehyde.[1] Neutralize the mixture by the addition of ethanoic acid[2] and allow the mixture to cool before extracting with diethyl ether (2 × 30 mL). Separate the organic extracts, dry over $MgSO_4$, filter and remove the solvent on the rotary evaporator, and record the yield of your material. Pure *syn*-benzaldoxime has a mp of 35°C but your product will probably be an oil. Record an IR spectrum of the product, and of the benzaldehyde starting material.

[1] *Reaction mixture may remain slightly cloudy*

[2] *If a precipitate of sodium acetate forms, add more water*

See Exp. 64

MICROSCALE

Level	1
Time	3 h
Equipment	magnetic stirrer; apparatus for extraction/separation, pipette column drying

Materials		
benzaldehyde (FW 106.1)	0.204 mL, 208 mg (2 mmol)	**irritant, toxic**
hydroxylamine hydrochloride (FW 69.5)	168 mg (2.4 mmol)	**corrosive**
sodium hydroxide pellets	140 mg (3.5 mmol)	**corrosive, hygroscopic**
ethanoic acid		**corrosive**
diethyl ether		**flammable, irritant**

Procedure

Dissolve the sodium hydroxide in water (0.12 mL) in a 1 mL reaction vial containing a spin vane. Allow the solution to cool and then add *ca.* 0.02 mL of the benzaldehyde followed by *ca.* 20 mg of hydroxylamine hydrochloride. Stopper the flask and stir vigorously, briefly stopping the stirring at 5 min intervals to add further portions of benzaldehyde and hydroxylamine until both reagents have been added completely. The reaction mixture will become warm, giving a homogeneous solution with no almond odour, indicating total consumption of the benzaldehyde. Neutralize the mixture by the addition of ethanoic acid[1] and allow the mixture to cool before extracting with diethyl ether (2 × 1.2 mL). Separate the organic extracts, dry by passing through a column of $MgSO_4$,[2] into a preweighed reaction vial and remove the solvent *in vacuo*. Record the yield of product.

[1] *If a precipitate of sodium acetate forms, add more water*

[2] *See Fig. 3.9*

Problems

1 Write a mechanism for the formation of oximes from aldehydes and hydroxylamine.

2 Reaction of unsymmetrical ketones with hydroxylamine gives a mixture of oxime isomers:

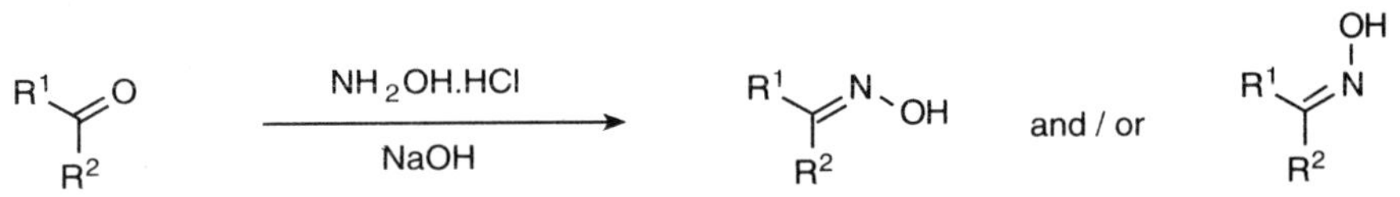

Describe how you might distinguish the two possible products.

3 Compare and contrast the IR spectra of benzaldehyde and benzaldoxine.

Further reading

For other reactions of hydroxylamine, see: EROS, 2760.

Experiment 6 *Preparation of 4-bromoaniline (p-bromoaniline)*

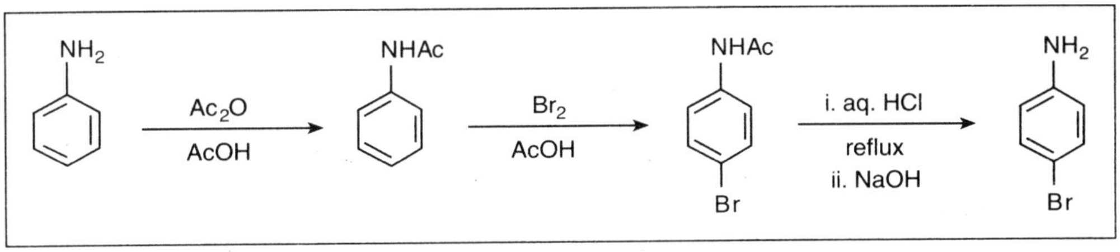

The aromatic ring of aniline is very electron rich due to the ability of the lone pair on the nitrogen to be delocalized into the π-system, and consequently aniline undergoes very ready electrophilic substitution reactions. Even with aqueous bromine in the cold, polysubstitution occurs to give 2,4,6-tribromoaniline and other more reactive reagents such as nitric acid react so vigorously that they lead to decomposition of the aniline.

However, 'tying up' the nitrogen lone pair, by derivatizing the aniline as an amide, lowers the reactivity of the system to the point where controlled mono-substitution reactions can be carried out. In amides, an important contribution towards resonance stabilization comes from delocalization of the nitrogen lone pair onto the amide oxygen, making the lone pair less available to the aromatic ring.

An additional advantage of the derivatization procedure results from the increased steric bulk of the amide group, favouring substitution at the 4-position over the 2-positions which it shields. Consequently, the advantages of increased control over the degree and position of substitution far outweigh the disadvantages of the extra steps involved in the preparation and hydrolysis of the amide—an example of a protection–deprotection sequence.

In this experiment, the aniline is first converted to *N*-phenylethanamide (acetanilide) which is then brominated in the 4-position. After bromination, the amide group is hydrolyzed back to the amine to furnish the desired 4-bromoaniline. Notice that, even with the amide group present, the aromatic ring is sufficiently electron rich to undergo aromatic substitution with bromine, without the need for a Lewis acid catalyst to be added to the reaction mixture.

Level	1
Time	2 × 3 h
Equipment	apparatus for stirring, suction filtration, reflux

Materials

1. Preparation of N-*phenylethanamide (acetanilide)*

aniline (FW 93.1)	10 mL, 10 g (0.11 mmol)	**cancer suspect agent, toxic**
ethanoic anhydride (FW 102.1)	12 mL, 12 g (0.12 mol)	**corrosive, irritant**
glacial ethanoic acid (FW 60.1)	25 mL	**corrosive, irritant**

2. Preparation of N-(4-bromophenyl)ethanamide (p-bromoacetanilide)

N-phenylethanamide (FW 135.2)	5 g (37 mmol)	

Continued

Box cont.

bromine (FW 159.8)	2.1 mL, 6 g (38 mmol)	**corrosive, toxic**
NOTE: ***bromine is highly toxic and corrosive. Its volatility combined with its density make it very difficult to handle. Always wear gloves and measure out in the hood***		
glacial ethanoic acid	2 × 25 mL	**corrosive, toxic**
sodium metabisulfite	1–2 g	**irritant**
3. Preparation of 4-bromoaniline		
N-(4-bromophenyl)ethanamide (FW 214.1)	5 g (23 mmol)	
hydrochloric acid (5 M)	50 mL	**corrosive**
sodium hydroxide solution (25%)		**corrosive**
pH indicator paper		

Procedure

HOOD

1. Preparation of N*-phenylethanamide (acetanilide)*

Place the ethanoic acid in a flask and add the aniline followed by the ethanoic anhydride.[1] Mix well and allow the solution to stand at room temperature for 5 min. Dilute with 100–200 mL of water until crystallization of the product occurs. When this is complete filter off the colourless lustrous crystals of *N*-phenylethanamide, dry in air and record the yield. Although the material is pure enough for further use, a portion should be recrystallized from aqueous ethanol and the mp of the purified material determined.

[1] ***Care! Exothermic***

HOOD

2. Preparation of N*-(4-bromophenyl)ethanamide* (p*-bromoacetanilide)*

Dissolve the *N*-phenylethanamide and bromine in separate 25 mL portions of ethanoic acid, then add the bromine solution[2] over 5 min to the acetanilide solution while stirring. The bromine colour disappears and the product may begin to crystallize out. Allow the mixture to stand at room temperature for 15 min and then pour into 300 mL of cold water.[3] Stir well, adding 1–2 g of sodium metabisulfite to remove any remaining bromine. Filter off the product by suction[4] and record the yield of crude dry material. The product is sufficiently pure for use in the final stage, but a portion should be recrystallized from aqueous ethanol and the mp determined.[5] (If a brown colouration persists at this point add a little activated charcoal during the recrystallization then filter whilst hot.)[6]

[2] ***Care! Wear gloves***

[3] *Product certainly crystallizes out now*

[4] *See Fig. 3.7*

[5] *May be left at this stage*

[6] *See Fig. 3.6*

3. Preparation of 4-bromoaniline

Place the *N*-(4-bromophenyl)ethanamide in a 100 mL round-bottomed flask and add the hydrochloric acid. Fit a reflux condenser[7] and allow the mixture to boil until all the solid dissolves and then heat for a further 10 min. Cool the solution in ice and cautiously make alkaline by the addition of sodium hydroxide (use pH paper).[8] The product separates as an oil which solidifies on

[7] *See Fig. 3.23(a)*

[8] ***Care! Exothermic***

cooling and scratching. When all has crystallized, filter by suction,[4] wash with a little water and recrystallize from a mixture of water and ethanol. Charcoal may again be used at this point to remove coloured impurities if present. The amine is susceptible to oxidation by air, particularly when wet or in solution, but the dry solid will keep indefinitely. Record the mp and yield of your purified material. ■

MICROSCALE

Level	1
Time	2 × 3 h
Equipment	apparatus for stirring, Craig tube recrystallization, reflux

Materials

1. Preparation of N-*phenylethanamide (acetanilide)*

aniline (FW 93.1)	0.20 mL, 200 mg (2.2 mmol)	**cancer suspect agent, toxic**
ethanoic anhydride (FW 102.1)	0.24 mL, 240 mg (2.4 mmol)	**corrosive, irritant**
glacial ethanoic acid (FW 60.1)	0.50 mL	**corrosive, irritant**

2. Preparation of N-*(4-bromophenyl)ethanamide* (p-*bromoacetanilide)*

N-phenylethanamide (FW 135.2)	100 mg (0.74 mmol)	
bromine (FW 159.8)	0.42 mL, 1.20 g (7.6 mmol)	**corrosive, toxic**

NOTE: ***bromine is highly toxic and corrosive. Its volatility combined with its high density make it very difficult to handle, particularly when small quantities are involved. Always wear gloves and measure out in the hood. Alternatively, make up a larger quantity than you require for a single experiment of a standard solution in glacial acetic acid by weighing accurately and using a volumetric flask***

glacial ethanoic acid (60.1)	5.5 mL	**corrosive, irritant**
sodium metabisulfite	50–100 mg	**irritant**

3. Preparation of 4-bromoaniline

N-(4-bromophenyl)ethanamide (FW 214.1)	100 mg (0.47 mmol)	
hydrochloric acid (5 M)	1 mL	**corrosive**
sodium hydroxide solution (25%)		**corrosive**
pH indicator paper		

HOOD

Procedure

1. Preparation of N-*phenylethanamide (acetanilide)*

Place the ethanoic acid in a 2 mL Craig tube and add the aniline followed by the ethanoic anhydride.[1] Mix well using a Pasteur pipette and allow to stand at room temperature. Dilute with water (0.5 mL) and leave to stand to allow

[1] *Care! Exothermic*

complete crystallization of the product. Collect the colourless crystals by centrifugation[2] and air dry. Record the yield, and recrystallize a small sample (*ca.* 30 mg) from aqueous ethanol.

[2]*See pp. 137–138*

HOOD

2. *Preparation of* N-*(4-bromophenyl)ethanamide* (p-*bromoacetanilide*)
Dissolve the acetanilide in ethanoic acid (0.5 mL) in a Craig tube containing a tiny stirrer bead, then add bromine solution[3] (0.5 mL) slowly over 5 min to the stirred solution. Allow the decolourized solution to stand at room temperature for 15 min, remove the stirrer bead with tweezers, then add cold water (1 mL) by pipette and mix thoroughly.[4] Add small portions (*ca.* 40 mg) of sodium metabisulfite to remove any remaining bromine. Filter by centrifugation[2] and air dry the product.[5]

[3]*Care! Wear gloves*

[4]*Product certainly crystallizes out now*

[5]*May be left at this stage*

3. *Preparation of 4-bromoaniline*
Place the bromoacetanilide in a 3 mL reaction vial and add the hydrochloric acid. Fit a reflux condenser[6] and heat the mixture until all the solid dissolves, then heat for a further 10 min. Transfer the hot solution to a Craig tube and allow to cool, finishing the cooling in a beaker of ice. Cautiously make the solution alkaline by the addition of sodium hydroxide solution.[7] The product separates as an oil which solidifies on cooling and scratching. When all the material has crystallized, filter by centrifugation,[2] wash the solid with a little (0.25 mL) water, recentrifuge and recrystallize the solid from aqueous ethanol. Collect the recrystallized material by centrifugation, dry the solid *in vacuo* and record the mp.

[6]*See Fig. 3.24*

[7]*Care! Exothermic*

Problems

1 Write mechanistic equations for each step in the preparation of *p*-bromoaniline from aniline. Why does bromination of acetanilide stop at the monobromo stage?

2 Predict products of bromination of the following:

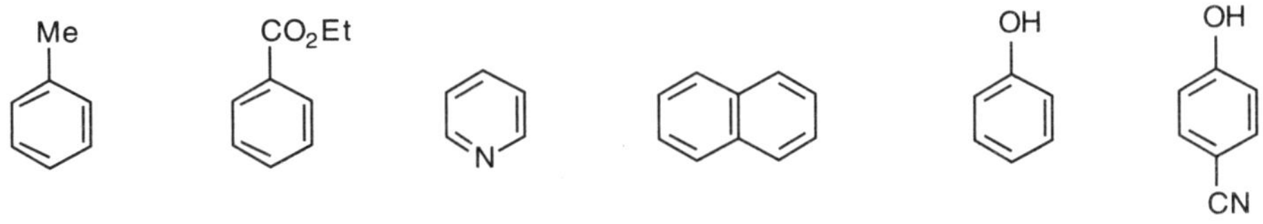

Indicate which might be expected to react with bromine in ethanoic acid ('molecular bromination') and which would need a Lewis acid catalyst.

7.2 Reactions of alkenes

The chemistry of alkenes is dominated by the properties of the C=C bond. Hence alkenes undergo a range of addition reactions which are initiated by electrophilic attack on the electron-rich double bond. For example, the addition of bromine to cyclohexene results in the formation of *trans*-1,2-dibromocyclohexane. The addition is *trans* because the cyclic bromomium cation formed in the initial electrophilic attack on the alkene subsequently undergoes nucleophilic attack with inversion.

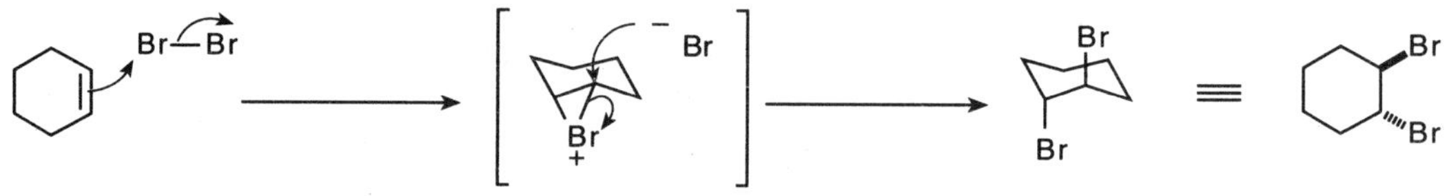

In unsymmetrical alkenes, the direction or regiochemistry of the addition is determined in the initial electrophilic step to give the more stable carbo-cation. Thus addition of HBr under ionic conditions to 1-pentene gives 2-bromopentane via the more stable secondary cation. Under free-radical conditions, the direction of addition to alkenes is often different.

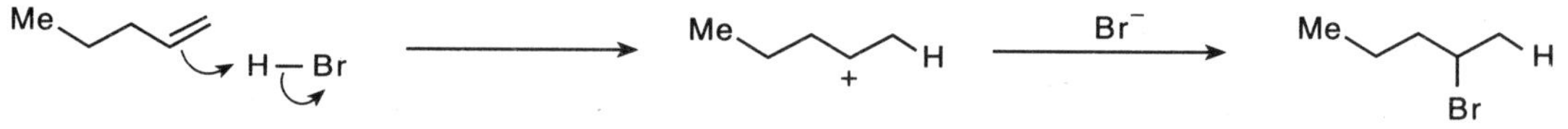

The experiments which follow illustrate the major type of addition reactions of alkenes: hydration, hydroboration, the formation of epoxides and 1,2-diols, and free-radical addition.

Experiment 7 *Hydration of alkenes; preparation of hexan-2-ol from 1-hexene*

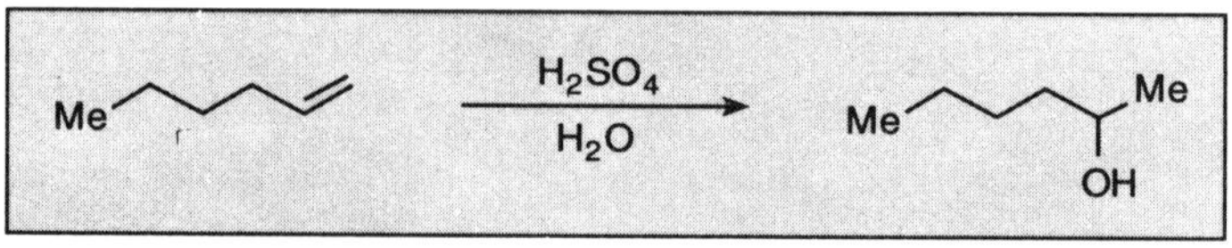

The addition of HX across the double bond is a common reaction of alkenes. The direction of the addition, which is determined in the initial protonation step to give the more stable carbo-cation, normally results in the hydrogen being added to the carbon atom which already has the most hydrogens (Markovnikov's rule). This experiment illustrates the hydration (addition of water) of an alkene in aqueous acid, an important industrial process, and involves the treatment of 1-hexene with dilute sulfuric acid at room temperature, followed by heating to 100°C. The product, hexan-2-ol, is easily isolated, and purified by distillation at atmospheric pressure.

Level	1
Time	3h
Equipment	apparatus for extraction/separation, reflux, distillation

Materials

1-hexene (FW 84.2)	10.0mL, 6.7g (80mmol)	**flammable, irritant**
sulfuric acid (conc. 98%)	7.6mL	**corrosive, oxidizer**
sodium hydroxide solution (5%)	0.5mL	**corrosive**

Procedure

Place 2.5g crushed ice in a 25mL beaker, and carefully add the concentrated sulfuric acid. Cool the acid to 20–25°C, and transfer it to a 100mL separatory funnel. Add 5.0mL 1-hexene,[1] stopper the funnel, and shake it *with frequent venting* until a homogeneous solution is obtained.[2] (If the reaction becomes too exothermic, stop shaking the funnel until the exotherm moderates.[3]) Add the remaining 5.0mL 1-hexene, and continue to shake the funnel until the mixture is again homogeneous.[4] Allow the mixture to stand for 5min, and then transfer it to a 100mL round-bottomed flask. Dilute the mixture with 35mL water, heat the solution under reflux for 5min, and then cool the flask in an ice bath. Transfer the cool mixture to a separatory funnel, and run off the lower aqueous layer.[5] Wash the upper organic layer (*ca.* 8–10mL) with 0.5mL 5% sodium hydroxide solution, and then dry it over $MgSO_4$.[6] Decant the product off the drying agent into a small round-bottomed flask, and distil it at atmospheric pressure.[7] Collect the fraction boiling at *ca.* 135°C. Record the exact bp and the yield of your product. The IR and NMR spectra are provided (see p.446).

[1] ***Care! Exothermic***
[2] *About 5 min*
[3] *If mixture does not heat up, the reaction is not proceeding*
[4] *About 3 min*
[5] *Increased yields can be obtained by extracting the mixture with 20mL ether*
[6] *May be left at this stage*
[7] *See Fig. 3.48*

Problems

1 What is the reaction mechanism for the hydration reaction? What intermediates are involved, and why is the 2-isomer formed in this case?

2 What products would you expect from the hydration of: (i) phenylethene (styrene), (ii) 1-methylcyclohexene?

3 The hydration of 1-hexene can also be carried out by reaction with aqueous mercury(II) acetate, followed by treatment with sodium borohydride. Discuss the reaction mechanism for this process, and identify any intermediates involved.

4 Examine the IR and NMR spectra of hexan-2-ol. What are the key features of each spectrum? What differences would you expect to see in the spectra of the isomeric hexan-1-ol?

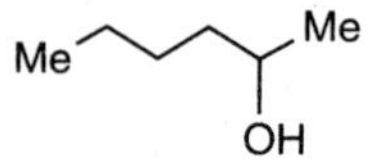

(neat)

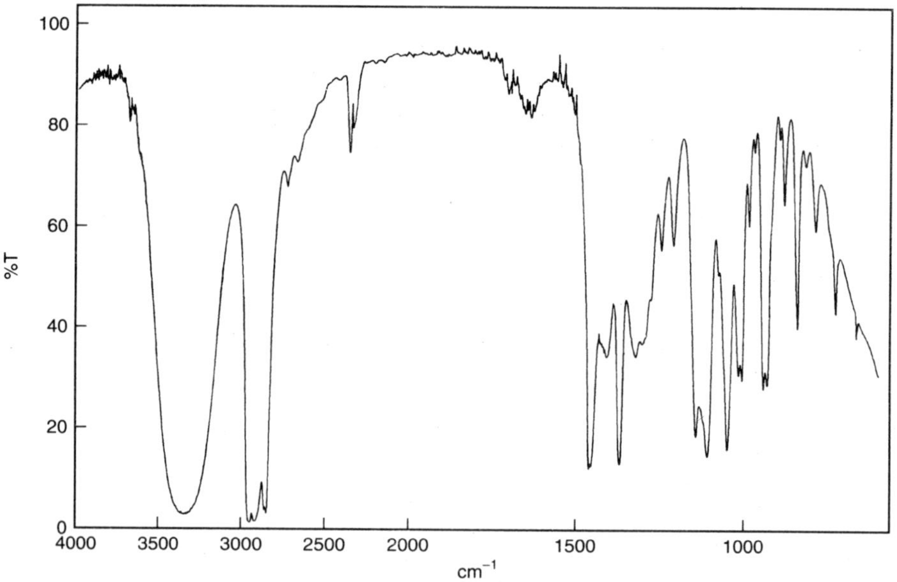

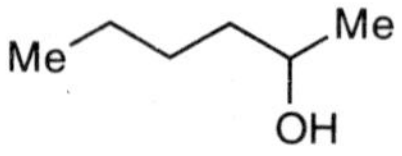

(250 MHz, $CDCl_3$)

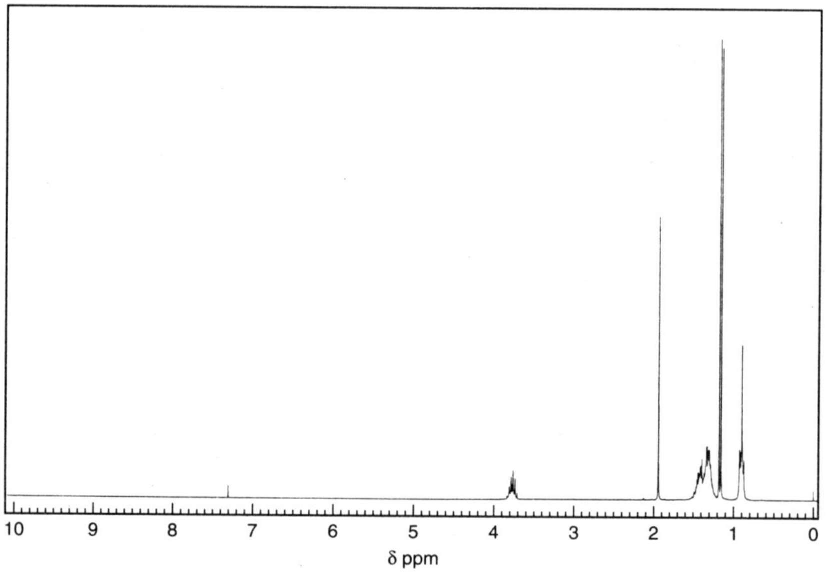

Further reading

For the procedure on which this experiment is based, see: J.R. McKee and J.M. Kauffman, *J. Chem. Educ.*, 1982, **59**, 695.

Experiment 8 — *Stereospecific preparation of* **trans-*cyclohexane-1,2-diol via bromohydrin and epoxide formation***

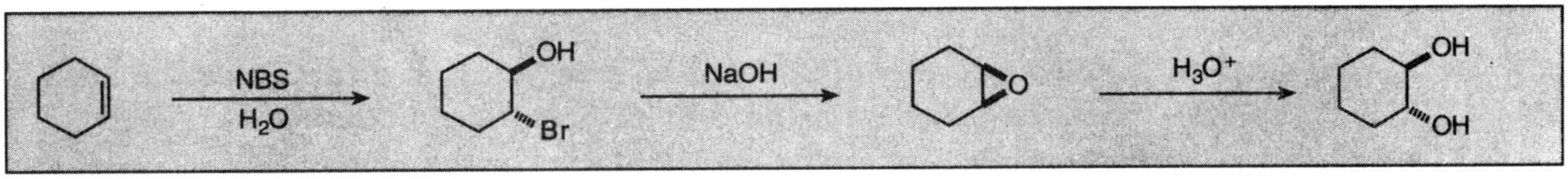

In this experiment, *trans*-cyclohexane-1,2-diol is obtained from cyclohexene by stereocontrolled preparation of *trans*-2-bromocyclohexanol followed by epoxide formation and cleavage.

The *anti*-addition of the elements of hypobromous acid (HOBr) to the double bond is achieved by reaction of the cyclohexene with *N*-bromosuccinimide in an aqueous system. The initial bromonium intermediate is trapped by water which is the most nucleophilic species present. In the experiment described here the product, which is an example of a bromohydrin, is not isolated but converted immediately to the epoxide.

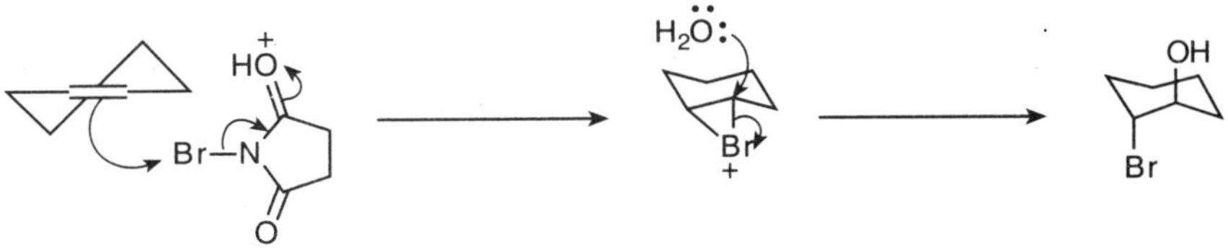

The treatment of *trans*-2-bromocyclohexanol with base produces the epoxide. Whilst this can be considered formally as a 1,3-elimination, the reaction is in fact an intramolecular SN2 process, the *anti*-relationship of the hydroxy- and bromine substituents causing the nucleophilic and the electrophilic centres to be well aligned for reaction.

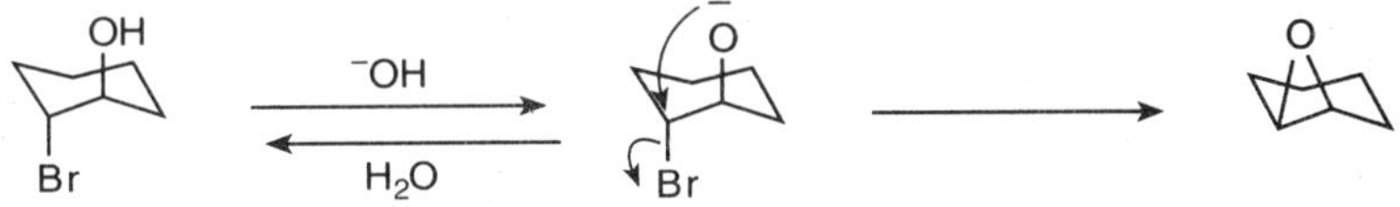

The hydrolytic opening of the cyclohexene oxide (more rigorously named 7-oxabicyclo[4.1.0]heptane) also occurs in a stereocontrolled manner despite the fact that the acidic conditions involved entail some degree of SN1 character in the reaction. Whatever the degree of initial cleavage of the C–O bond in the protonated epoxide before attack by the relatively non-nucleophilic water, the favoured axial orientation of approach of the nucleophile still results in backside attack and *anti*-opening of the epoxide.

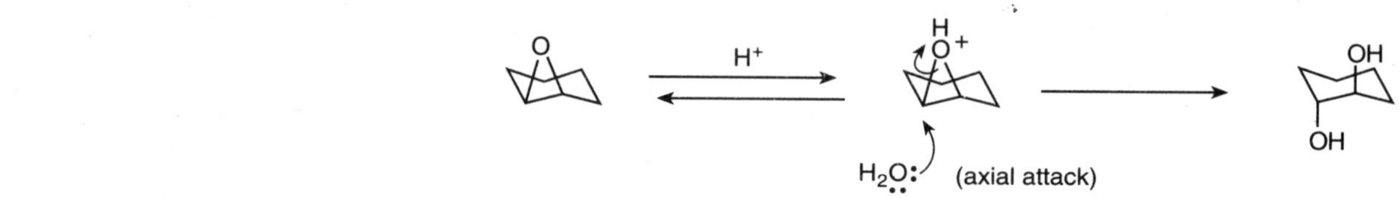

In acyclic epoxides, such conditions would lead to stereorandomization at the electrophilic carbon due to the generation of a planar carbonium ion. Epoxide opening can also be achieved under alkaline conditions when the S_N2 pathway operates. The greater reactivity of epoxides compared with other ethers towards cleavage of the C–O bond is a direct consequence of ring strain due to bond angle compression in the three-membered ring.

Level	3
Time	3 × 3 h
Equipment	magnetic stirrer, hotplate; apparatus for extraction/separation, reflux with addition, distillation
Instruments	IR, NMR

Materials

1. Preparation of cyclohexene oxide

cyclohexene (FW 82.2)	7.60 mL, 6.15 g (75 mmol)	**flammable, irritant**

NOTE: *cyclohexene is prone to peroxide formation on storage. Old samples must be washed with saturated aqueous sodium metabisulfite before use*

N-bromosuccinimide (FW 178.0)	14.7 g (82.5 mmol)	**irritant**
tetrahydrofuran		**flammable, irritant**
diethyl ether		**flammable, irritant**
aqueous sodium hydroxide (5 M)		**corrosive**
sodium hydroxide pellets		**corrosive, hygroscopic**

2. Preparation of trans-*cyclohexane-1,2-diol*

cyclohexene oxide	2.0 mL, 1.95 g (15 mmol)	
aqueous sulfuric acid (*ca.* 1 M)		**corrosive**
aqueous sodium hydroxide (*ca.* 1 M)		**corrosive**
ethyl acetate		**flammable, irritant**
pH indicator paper		

Procedure

1. Preparation of cyclohexene oxide

Measure the cyclohexene into a 100 mL Erlenmeyer flask equipped with a magnetic stirrer bar. Add 20 mL of water and 25 mL of tetrahydrofuran to the flask and arrange a thermometer such that the bulb dips into the reaction mixture but does not interfere with the stirrer bar. With an ice-water bath available, commence stirring the mixture *vigorously* and add the *N*-bromosuccinimide in 1 g portions over *ca.* 20 min, maintaining the reaction at 25–30°C by immersion in the cooling bath as necessary. After addition of the *N*-bromosuccinimide is complete, stir the flask for a further 30 min and then transfer the mixture to a 250 mL separatory funnel. Add 30 mL of diethyl ether and 30 mL of brine to the mixture, extract and separate the upper organic layer, and then re-extract the aqueous layer twice more with 20 mL portions of diethyl ether. Combine the extracts and wash them three times with 30 mL portions of brine to obtain a solution of *trans*-2-bromocyclohexanol suitable for conversion into the epoxide.[1]

Into a 250 mL round-bottomed flask equipped with a magnetic stirrer bar, add 25 mL of 5 M aqueous sodium hydroxide and fit the flask with a Claisen adapter carrying a reflux condenser and an addition funnel.[2] Commence stirring the solution, warm it to 40°C and add the diethyl ether solution of *trans*-2-bromocyclohexanol dropwise over a period of about 40 min. When all of the solution has been added, stir the mixture for 30 min and then transfer the mixture to a separatory funnel. Separate the upper organic phase and dry it over NaOH pellets with occasional swirling for 15 min. Decant the solution from the pellets into a round-bottomed flask and remove the solvent on the rotary evaporator. Distil the residue at atmospheric pressure[3] and collect the material distilling at 124–134°C.[1] Note the yield of your product based on cyclohexene and obtain the IR (thin film) and NMR ($CDCl_3$) spectra.[4]

[1] *May be left at this stage*

[2] *See Fig. 3.25b*

[3] *See Fig. 3.48*

[4] *Record these at convenient stages during part 2 of the experiment*

2. *Preparation of* trans-*cyclohexane-1,2-diol*

Place 2.0 mL (1.95 g, 15 mmol) of cyclohexene oxide in a 50 mL round-bottomed flask equipped with a magnetic stirrer bar. Add 10 mL of water and 1 mL of 1 M sulfuric acid, stopper the flask loosely with a bung and stir vigorously for 1 h.[5] During this period the mixture will become warm and a clear solution will be formed. Bring the mixture to pH 7 by the dropwise addition of aqueous sodium hydroxide, checking against indicator paper, and remove the water on the rotary evaporator using a steam or boiling water bath to furnish a white solid. Triturate the contents of the flask with 20 mL portions of boiling ethyl acetate[6] until a small insoluble residue remains, combine the extracts and reduce them to *ca.* 15 mL on the heating bath. Allow the solution to cool in an ice bath and filter off the crystals of purified diol. Note the yield and mp of your product and obtain the IR ($CHCl_3$) and NMR ($CDCl_3$) spectra. Add a few drops of D_2O to your NMR sample, shake the sample well to ensure thorough mixing, and record the spectrum again.

[5] *Record spectra from Part 1 here*

[6] ***Care! Flammable***

Problems

1 Assign the IR and NMR spectra of your products. Discuss the effect of adding D_2O to the NMR sample of *trans*-cyclohexane-1,2-diol.

2 Predict the products expected from the reaction of: (i) cyclopentene with

N-bromosuccinimide in methanol, (ii) hex-1-ene with *N*-bromosuccinimide in acetic acid.

3 Under the conditions that convert *trans*-2-bromocyclohexanol to cyclohexene oxide the *cis*-isomer is unreactive. Use of more vigorous basic conditions results in the formation of cyclohexanone. Rationalize this finding.

4 A dilute solution of *cis*-cyclopentane-1,2-diol in CCl_4 shows hydroxyl stretching frequencies at 3572 and 3633 cm^{-1} in its IR spectrum, whereas the *trans*-isomer shows only one absorption at 3620 cm^{-1}. Explain these results.

Further reading

For the procedure upon which this experiment is based, see: V. Dev, *J. Chem. Educ.*, 1970, **47**, 476.

For other uses of *N*-bromosuccinimide, see: EROS, 768.

Stereospecific syntheses of *cis*-1,2-diols from alkenes

Syn-dihydroxylation of a double bond may be achieved with a variety of reagents. Both osmium tetroxide and alkaline potassium permanganate result in addition from the least hindered side of the double bond. Osmium tetroxide forms a cyclic ester which can be isolated but is usually decomposed *in situ* to furnish the desired diol, and it is likely that alkaline potassium permanganate reacts in an analogous manner.

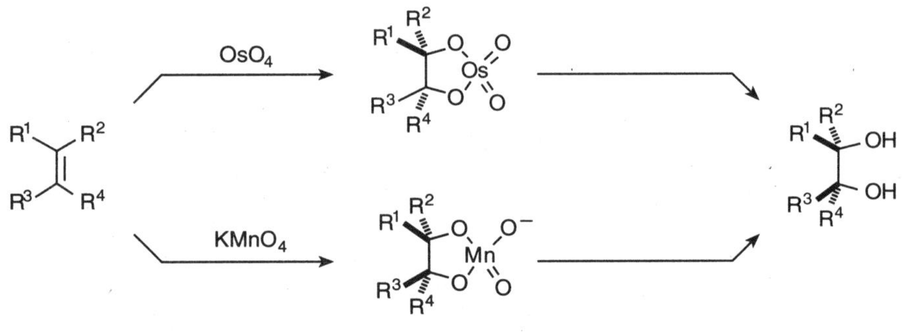

The drawbacks with osmium tetroxide are its extreme toxicity, which is compounded by its volatility, and the expense of the reagent. Potassium permanganate rarely gives good yields of diols as, even in alkaline solution, it tends to degrade the products oxidatively. However, osmium tetroxide can be used in catalytic amounts if another co-oxidant such as *N*-methylmorpholine-*N*-oxide is present. This variant allows enantioselective dihydroxylations to be carried out in the presence of a chiral quinine-based ligand, as described in Experiment 10.

A two-step process for generation of *cis*-1,2-diols has been developed by R.B. Woodward, arguably the greatest and most complete organic chemist ever, who was awarded the Nobel Prize for Chemistry in 1965 in recognition of his work in organic synthesis. In the Woodward method, an alkene is treated with iodine and silver acetate in aqueous acetic acid. Initial *anti*-addition to the alkene yields a 2-acetoxyiodide which, in the aqueous system, undergoes clean SN2 conversion to the 2-acetoxyalcohol via internal displacement of iodide by the neighbouring acetate to result in overall *syn*-addition to the double bond. Hydrolysis of the ester then generates the 1,2-diol.

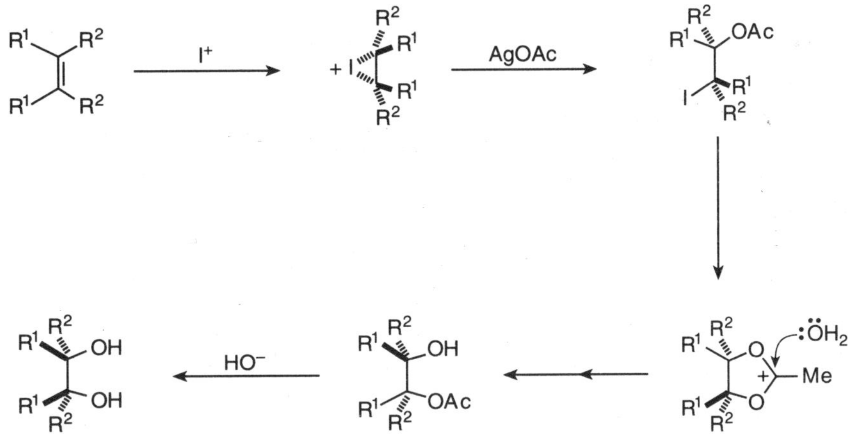

This procedure is used in the following experiment to prepare *cis*-cyclohexane-1,2-diol and provides a stereochemical complement to the preparation of *trans*-cyclohexane-1,2-diol described in Experiment 8. In addition, it should be noted that, with cyclic alkenes in which one face is sterically more hindered than the other, use of permanganate or osmium tetroxide leads to hydroxylation on the most accessible face whereas the Woodward method furnishes the more hindered diol.

Experiment 9 — *Preparation of* cis-*cyclohexane-1,2-diol by the Woodward method*

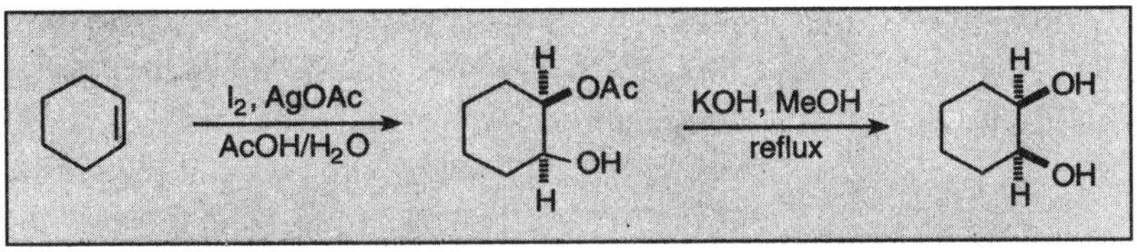

Level	3
Time	3 × 3 h
Equipment	stirrer hotplate; apparatus for stirring at reflux, extraction/separation, stirring at room temperature
Instruments	IR, NMR

Materials

1. Preparation of cis*-2-acetoxycyclohexanol*

cyclohexene (FW 82.2)	10.0 mL	**flammable, irritant**

NOTE: *cyclohexene is prone to peroxide formation on storage. Old samples must be washed with saturated aqueous sodium metabisulfite before use*

iodine (FW 253.8)	1.27 g (5 mmol)	**lachrymator, corrosive, irritant**
silver acetate (*light sensitive*) (FW 166.9)	1.67 g (10 mmol)	

NOTE: *all silver residues should be retained for future recovery, ask an instructor for the disposal procedure*

ethanoic acid		**corrosive**
diethyl ether		**flammable, irritant**
sodium bicarbonate solution (saturated)		

2. Preparation of cis*-cyclohexane-1,2-diol*

potassium carbonate (anhydrous)	2.0 g	**corrosive**
methanol		**flammable, toxic**
diethyl ether		**flammable, irritant**

Procedure

HOOD
[1]Care! Cyclohexene may form peroxides on prolonged storage. See note above
[2]Care! Toxic
[3]See Fig. 3.24
[4]Save the silver residues
[5]Care! CO_2 evolved
[6]May be left at this stage
[7]Leave analysis until the stirring period in part 2

1. Preparation of cis*-2-acetoxycyclohexanol*

Place the cyclohexene (peroxide free),[1] silver acetate, 20 mL of ethanoic acid and 1.0 mL of water in a 100 mL round-bottomed flask containing a magnetic stirrer bar. Stir the mixture vigorously and add the powdered iodine[2] to the mixture over 15 min. Arrange the apparatus for reflux and heat to reflux for 90 min with vigorous stirring.[3] Cool the mixture in an ice bath and filter off the precipitate of silver iodide with suction, washing the residue[4] with 2 mL of ethanoic acid. Remove the solvents on the rotary evaporator with gentle heating using a water bath (*ca.* 60°C), to remove all of the ethanoic acid and give the product as a yellow oil. Dissolve the oil in 30 mL of diethyl ether and wash the solution with saturated aqueous sodium bicarbonate (2 × 10 mL).[5] Separate the organic phase, dry over $MgSO_4$, filter, and evaporate the solution on the rotary evaporator to furnish crude *cis*-2-acetoxycyclohexanol.[6] Record the yield of this material, retaining a small quantity (*ca.* 50 mg) for IR ($CHCl_3$) and NMR ($CDCl_3$) analysis,[7] and use the remainder directly in the next stage.

[8]See Fig. 3.20(a)

2. Preparation of cis*-cyclohexane-1,2-diol*

Dissolve the majority of your crude product from the first stage in a mixture of 15 mL of methanol and 5 mL of water in a 100 mL Erlenmeyer flask.[8] Add the

[9]*Record the spectra of* cis-*2-acetoxycyclohexanol during this stage*

potassium carbonate and stir the mixture vigorously for 90 min.[9] Remove the solvent on the rotary evaporator and triturate the residue with diethyl ether (3 × 20 mL). Wash the combined ether extracts with 20 mL of water and dry them over $MgSO_4$.[6] Filter off the drying agent and remove the solvent on the rotary evaporator to furnish the crude product which can be recrystallized from diethyl ether/hexane. Record the yield and mp of your crude and re-crystallized products, and obtain the IR ($CHCl_3$) and NMR ($CDCl_3$) spectra. You should also obtain the NMR spectrum of your product after the addition of a few drops of D_2O to the solution in the NMR tube.

Problems

1. Assign the important absorptions in the IR and NMR spectra of your intermediate monoacetate and product diol.
2. If the water is not included in the reaction mixture for the first step, the product isolated is *trans*-1,2-diacetoxycyclohexane. Explain the reason for this stereochemical divergence between the aqueous and non-aqueous systems.
3. Make a list of reactions which involve addition to alkenes, and group them according to whether the addition is *syn*- or *anti*- (remember that such reactions include cycloadditions as well as electrophilic additions).
4. Predict the major product expected in the following transformations and explain your reasoning in each case:

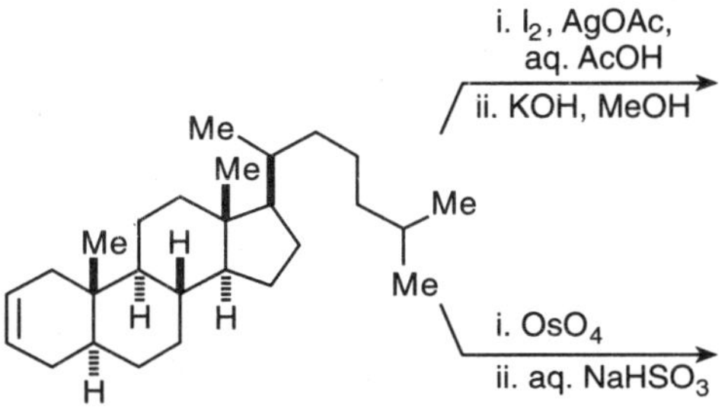

Further reading

For a summary of the awards, honours and achievements of Robert Burns Woodward (born 1917, deceased 1979), see: *Tetrahedron*, 1979, **35**, iii.

For the original description of this reaction see: R.B. Woodward and F.V. Brutcher, *J. Am. Chem. Soc.*, 1958, **80**, 209.

Experiment 10 *Asymmetric dihydroxylation of* trans-*1,2-diphenylethene* (trans-*stilbene*)

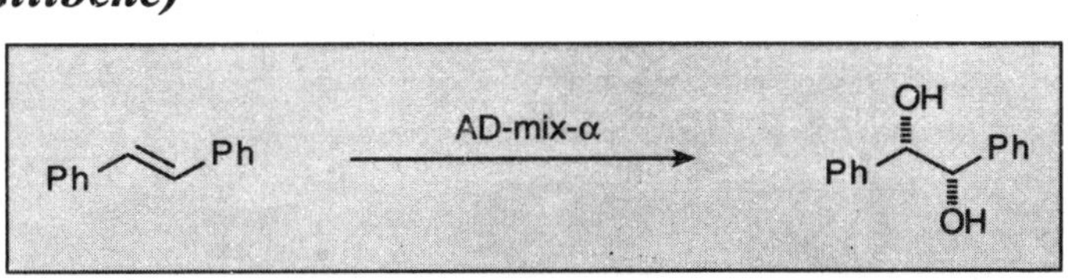

The *cis*-1,2-dihydroxylation of an alkene using osmium tetroxide has been known for many years. However, in recent years, efficient methods for the enantioselective dihydroxylation of alkenes have emerged; these methods complement the direct asymmetric epoxidation reactions such as the Sharpless epoxidation of allylic alcohols (Experiment 12). In order to effect an enantioselective reaction there must be some source of asymmetry in the reaction mixture, such as a chiral reagent or catalyst. In the osmium tetroxide dihydroxylation reactions, a chiral nitrogen-containing ligand for osmium is used. There have been several systems developed, but this experiment involves the procedure developed by Professor Barry Sharpless of the Scripps Institute, California. A catalytic amount of osmium in the form of dipotassium osmate is used together with a co-oxidant, potassium ferricyanide. The chiral ligand is based on a derivative of the naturally occurring alkaloid quinine, dihydroquinine phthalazine, $(DHQ)_2PHAL$. The whole reaction system (osmium, chiral ligand and co-oxidant) is available as a single reagent sold commercially as AD-mix-α. Not only is this extremely convenient, it avoids handling and mixing the toxic osmium reagent.

However, osmium is toxic and due regard must be paid to the safe handling of the reagent, and in particular to waste disposal. If in doubt, consult your instructor.

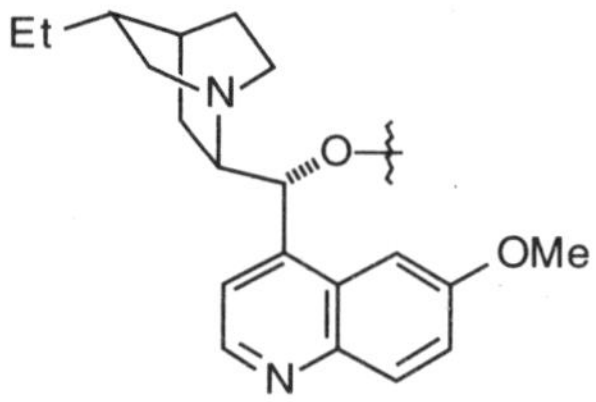

R*O

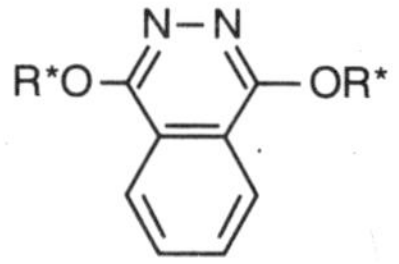

ligand $(DHQ)_2PHAL$

The experiment involves the *cis*-dihydroxylation of *trans*-1,2-diphenylethene (*trans*-stilbene); use of AD-mix-α gives the product, 1,2-diphenylethene-1,2-diol as the (*S*,*S*)-enantiomer. The reaction is carried out in the presence of one equivalent of methanesulfonamide which increases the reaction rate.

Level	3
Time	2 × 3 h (with overnight reaction in between)
Equipment	magnetic stirrer; apparatus for extraction/separation, recrystallization
Instruments	IR, polarimeter

Materials		
AD-mix-α	7 g	**hygroscopic, toxic**
t-butanol	25 mL	
methanesulfonamide (FW 95.1)	0.475 g (5 mmol)	
trans-stilbene (FW 180.2)	0.90 g (5 mmol)	
sodium sulfite	7.5 g	
dichloromethane		**irritant, toxic**
sulfuric acid (0.25 M)		**corrosive**
potassium hydroxide (2 M)		**corrosive**

Procedure

Place the AD-mix-α in a 100 ml round-bottomed flask equipped with a magnetic stirrer bar. Add 25 mL *t*-butanol and 25 mL water and stir the mixture at room temperature.[1] Add the methanesulfonamide, and cool the mixture in an ice bath.[2] Add the *trans*-stilbene, and stir the mixture vigorously at 0°C for 5 h (or until the end of the laboratory period). Continue stirring and allow the mixture to warm up to room temperature overnight. Re-cool the mixture in an ice bath, add 7.5 g solid sodium sulfite, allow the mixture to warm up to room temperature, and stir for a further hour. Extract the mixture with 4 × 40 mL portions dichloromethane, and wash the organic extracts sequentially with 2 × 30 mL portions 0.25 M sulfuric acid and 2 × 30 mL portions 2 M potassium hydroxide solution. Dry the organic solution over anhydrous $MgSO_4$. Filter off the drying agent, and remove the solvent on the rotary evaporator to give the crude product. Recrystallize the product from aqueous ethanol, and record the yield, mp and IR spectrum ($CHCl_3$ or Nujol®) of the recrystallized sample. Make up a solution of the product in ethanol of known concentration (aim for about 2 g per 100 mL or equivalent), and measure the optical rotation of the material. Hence calculate the specific rotation,[3] and calculate the enantiomeric excess of your product, given that pure (*S*,*S*)-1,2-diphenylethane-1,2-diol has a specific rotation of $[\alpha]_D$ −94 (c = 2.5, EtOH).

[1] *Two clear phases should be produced, with lower aqueous phase being bright yellow*

[2] *Some solid may precipitate*

[3] *See pp. 220–223*

Problems

1 Assign the IR spectrum of your product.

2 With reference to the original literature (see below), comment on the fact that the (*S*,*S*)-isomer is produced in this experiment.

3 Suggest other methods for the conversion of *trans*-stilbene to 1,2-diphenylethane-1,2-diol; pay particular attention to the stereochemical outcome of the methods you suggest.

Further reading

For the original procedure on which this experiment is based, see: K.B. Sharpless, W. Amberg, Y.L. Bennani, G.A. Crispino, J. Hartung, K. Jeong, H. Kwong, K. Morikawa, Z. Wang, D. Xu and X. Zhang, *J. Org. Chem.*, 1992, **57**, 2768.

For a general discussion of the use of osmium tetroxide, see: EROS, 3801.

Experiment 11 — *Peracid epoxidation of cholesterol: 3β-hydroxy-5α,6α-epoxycholestane*

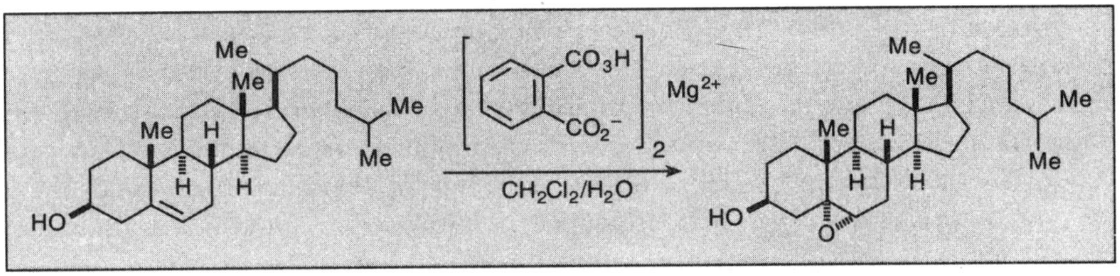

Peracids are extremely useful reagents for the epoxidation of alkenes. However, peracids such as peracetic acid often have to be made *in situ* by reaction of the corresponding carboxylic acid with hydrogen peroxide. The magnesium salt of monoperoxyphthalic acid (MMPP) on the other hand is a relatively stable, easy-to-handle crystalline solid and hence is often the reagent of choice for epoxidation reactions. This experiment illustrates the use of MMPP to epoxidize cholesterol (3β-hydroxycholestane) to give the pure α-epoxide; other reagents give appreciable amounts of the β-epoxide. Cholesterol is the most widespread steroid and is found in almost all animal tissues. High levels of cholesterol in the blood are often associated with hardening of the arteries (arteriosclerosis), and it is possible that blood cholesterol levels can be controlled by diet by avoiding cholesterol-rich foods such as eggs. However, this is a controversial subject, particularly since cholesterol is synthesized from acetylcoenzyme-A in the body anyway. Nevertheless drugs which interfere with the biosynthesis of cholesterol might prove useful in the control of arterial disease.

Level	2
Time	2 × 3 h
Equipment	magnetic stirrer; apparatus for reflux with stirring and addition, extraction/separation, suction filtration, recrystallization, TLC analysis
Instruments	IR, polarimeter (both optional)

Materials

cholesterol (FW 386.7)	1.93 g (5.0 mmol)	
magnesium monoperoxyphthalate (90%) (FW 494.7)	3.00 g (5.5 mmol)	**irritant, oxidizer**
dichloromethane		**irritant, toxic**
sodium hydroxide solution (5%)		**corrosive**
sodium sulfite solution (10%)		**irritant**
sodium bicarbonate solution (saturated)		
sodium chloride solution (saturated)		
pH indicator paper		
starch-iodide paper		

Procedure

Place the cholesterol, 20 mL dichloromethane and a magnetic stirrer bar in a 100 mL two-neck flask equipped with a reflux condenser and addition funnel.[1] Charge the addition funnel with a solution of the magnesium monoperoxyphthalate[2] in 15 mL water and add this dropwise to the *vigorously* stirred reaction at reflux.[3] When addition is complete, maintain stirring and heating for a further 90 min, maintaining the pH in the range 4.5–5.0 by adding 5% sodium hydroxide solution dropwise as necessary down the condenser.[4] After this period, allow the mixture to cool and destroy the excess peracid by adding

[1] *See Fig. 3.25(b)*

[2] ***Oxidizing agent***

[3] *About 10 min*

[4] *Remove a sample through the condenser with a glass rod*

sodium sulfite solution a few drops at a time until the mixture gives a negative starch-iodide test.[5] Transfer the mixture to a separatory funnel, and wash the organic solution with 2 × 10 mL sodium bicarbonate solution, 2 × 5 mL water, and finally 5 mL saturated sodium chloride solution. Emulsions frequently form during the extraction. This is best dealt with as follows: add a little more dichloromethane and sodium chloride solution to the emulsion. If, after shaking, the layers do not separates add more sodium chloride solution. Dry the solution over $MgSO_4$.[6] Filter off the drying agent by suction, and evaporate the filtrate to dryness on the rotary evaporator. Recrystallize the residue from 90% aqueous acetone. Record the yield and mp of your product after one recrystallization. If required, record the IR spectrum ($CHCl_3$) and optical rotation ($CHCl_3$) of both the starting material and the product. Run a TLC of your product before and after recrystallization; use a silica gel TCL plate and diethyl ether–light petroleum (1 : 1) as eluting solvent. Run the product against a sample of cholesterol to determine if all the starting material has been consumed. ■

[5] *Dip a glass rod into the mixture and test with starch-iodine paper*

[6] *May be left at this stage*

MICROSCALE

Level	2
Time	2 × 3 h
Equipment	magnetic stirrer; apparatus for reflux with stirring, extraction/separation, Pasteur pipette drying column, Craig tube recrystallization, TLC analysis

Materials		
cholesterol (FW 386.7)	97 mg (0.25 mmol)	
magnesium monoperoxyphthalate (90%) (FW 494.7)	150 mg (0.27 mmol)	**irritant, oxidizer**
dichloromethane		**irritant, toxic**
sodium hydroxide solution (5%)		**corrosive**
sodium sulfite solution (10%)		**irritant**
sodium bicarbonate solution (saturated)		
pH indicator paper		
starch-iodide paper		

Procedure

Dissolve the cholesterol in dichloromethane (1 mL) in a 5 mL reaction vial containing a spin vane. Fit a reflux condenser to the vial[1] and prepare a solution of the magnesium monoperoxyphthalate[2] in water (0.75 mL) in a vial or sample tube. Heat the solution of cholesterol to reflux with stirring and add the aqueous solution of magnesium monoperoxyphthalate dropwise down the condenser to the *vigorously* stirred mixture from a Pasteur pipette.[3] When the addition is complete, continue stirring at reflux for a further 90 min, main-

[1] *See Fig. 3.24*

[2] ***Oxidizing agent***

[3] *About 10 min*

taining the pH in the range 4.5–5.0 by the dropwise addition of dilute sodium hydroxide solution as necessary down the condenser.[4] Allow the mixture to cool and destroy the excess oxidant by adding one drop of sodium sulfite solution and testing with starch-iodide paper until the solution gives a negative test.[5] Wash the organic solution with sodium bicarbonate solution (2 × 0.5 mL), then water (2 × 0.25 mL) and saturated sodium chloride solution (0.25 mL).[6] Dry the organic layer by passing through a column of $MgSO_4$ in a plugged Pasteur pipette into a Craig tube.[7] Evaporate the solvent in a stream of air or nitrogen[8] and recrystallize the solid product from 90% aqueous acetone. Collect the crystals by centrifugation and record the yield and mp. Analyze a sample of your product by TLC, spotting cholesterol on the same plate and developing the plate in 1:3 ethyl acetate:hexane. Use sulfuric acid–methanol stain or iodine vapour to visualize the spots.[9]

4Remove a sample through the condenser with a glass capillary

5Dip a glass capillary into mixture and test with starch-iodine paper. If a positive test obtains add one drop more of sodium sulfite solution

6If separation of layers is extremely slow, add hydrochloric acid (4 drops of 5 M solution)

7See Fig. 3.9

8See Fig. 2.31

9See p. 170

Problems

1 Write a reaction mechanism for the epoxidation of an alkene with a peracid. What is the other product from the reaction?

2 Why is the α-epoxide formed as the sole (or major) product in the epoxidation of cholesterol?

3 Compare and contrast the IR spectra of cholesterol and its epoxide.

Further reading

P. Brougham, M.S. Cooper, D.A. Cummerson, H. Heaney and N. Thompson, *Synthesis*, 1987, 1015.
EROS, 3663.

Experiment 12

The Sharpless epoxidation: asymmetric epoxidation of (E)-3,7-dimethyl-2,6-octadien-1-ol (geraniol)

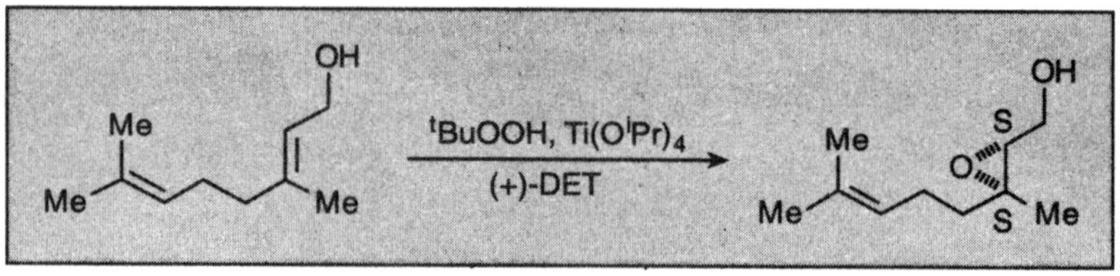

The organic chemists' attempts to carry out organic transformations enantioselectively have not always been very successful. One notable exception is the Sharpless epoxidation reaction. Sharpless began his search for a reagent that would epoxidize alkenes enantioselectively in 1970, and he was ultimately successful in January 1980 when the titanium catalyzed asymmetric epoxidation was discovered. The reaction involves the *t*-butyl hydroperoxide (TBHP) epoxidation of allylic alcohols in the presence of titanium tetraisopropoxide using diethyl tartrate as the chiral auxilliary. Although the reaction in its original form required the tartrate and the titanium reagents to be present in stoichiometric amounts, it has now been discovered that only catalytic quantities of these reagents are necessary, making the asymmetric epoxidation truly catalytic. Organic chemists have been quick to realize the importance of Sharpless' discovery, and the reaction has been widely applied, even on the industrial scale. Indeed the Sharpless epoxidation is probably one of the most important new organic chemical reactions discovered in the last 30 years. Subsequently many workers have developed other enantioselective epoxidation protocols.

This experiment illustrates the use of the catalytic variant of the Sharpless epoxidation in the TBHP epoxidation of 3,7-dimethyl-2,6-octadien-1-ol (geraniol). The reaction is run in the presence of catalytic amounts of titanium tetraisopropoxide and L-(+)-diethyl tartrate, and of powdered activated 4 Å molecular sieves. The presence of the sieves is essential for the catalytic reaction since adventitious water seems to destroy the catalyst system.

Level	4
Time	2 × 3 h for experiment, but it is necessary to allow plenty of time for preparatory operations
Equipment	magnetic stirrer, vacuum pump; apparatus for stirring with addition (3-neck flask), extraction/separation, suction filtration, short path distillation
Instruments	IR, NMR, polarimeter

Materials		
powdered activated 4 Å molecular sieves	280 mg	**irritant**
L-(+)-diethyl tartrate (FW 206.2)	0.128 mL, 154 mg (0.75 mmol)	
titanium(IV) isopropoxide (FW 284.3)	0.146 mL, 140 mg (0.49 mmol)	**flammable**
TBHP solution (*ca.* 6 M in CH_2Cl_2) (FW 90.1)	*ca.* 2.5 mL (15 mmol)	**oxidizer, toxic**
Stock solution prepared as described below:		
geraniol (FW 154.3)	1.73 mL, 1.54 g (10 mmol)	
dichloromethane		**irritant, toxic**
sodium hydroxide solution (30%)	0.7 mL	**corrosive**
powdered Celite®		

Procedure

1. Preparatory operations

Oven dry all the glassware at 125°C overnight. Distil the geraniol before use (bp 229–230°C) and dry the dichloromethane by distillation or by standing over freshly activated 3 Å molecular sieves.[1] Distil the titanium(IV) isopropoxide under reduced pressure, and store under nitrogen.[2] If a stock solution of TBHP in dichloromethane is not available, it can be prepared as

[1] *See Appendix 2*

[2] *See Fig. 3.53(a)*

follows. Shake 20 mL commercially available aqueous 70% TBHP with 20 mL dichloromethane in a separatory funnel. Transfer the lower organic phase to a 50 mL flask fitted with a heavier-than-water solvent Dean and Stark trap with condenser.[3] Heat the solution[4] under gentle reflux until no more water azeotropes out. Store the TBHP solution over activated 3 Å sieves in a refrigerator for several hours (overnight) to complete the drying process. The resulting solution should be *ca.* 6 M in TBHP, but the molarity can easily be determined with accuracy by iodometric titration as described by Sharpless.[5]

[3] *See Fig. 3.27*

[4] ***Caution—all heating of peroxides must be carried out behind a safety shield***

[5] *J. Org. Chem.*, 1986, **51**, 1922

2. *Preparation of (2S,3S)-epoxygeraniol*

Set up a three-neck flask with a thermometer, magnetic stirrer bar, nitrogen bubbler, and stopper the remaining neck with a septum.[6] Place the molecular sieves and 15 mL dichloromethane in the flask, and stir and cool the mixture to –10°C under nitrogen. Using a syringe, add the diethyl tartrate,[7] the titanium(IV) isopropoxide, and the TBHP solution[8] sequentially to the flask through the septum. Stir the mixture at *ca.* –10°C for 10 min, and then cool it to –20°C. Add the geraniol in 1 mL dichloromethane dropwise to the rapidly stirred mixture,[9] and continue to stir the mixture at –20 to –15°C for a further 45 min. Allow the mixture to warm up to 0°C over 5 min, and add 3 mL water. Allow the mixture to warm up to room temperature over 10 min whereupon it will separate into two distinct phases.[10] Add the sodium hydroxide solution saturated with sodium chloride to hydrolyze the tartrates, and continue to stir the mixture vigorously for 10 min. Separate the lower organic phase, and extract the aqueous layer with 2 × 5 mL portions of dichloromethane. Combine the dichloromethane layers, and dry them over $MgSO_4$.[11] Filter the mixture by suction through Celite®,[12] and evaporate the filtrate on the rotary evaporator. Distil the residue under reduced pressure using a vacuum pump (*ca.* 1 mmHg) and a short path distillation apparatus.[13] Record the bp, yield, optical rotation ($CHCl_3$), and the IR ($CHCl_3$) and NMR ($CDCl_3$) spectra of your product.

[6] *See Fig. 3.22*

[7] *Viscous—use wide bore needle*

[8] *15 mmol required; volume depends on molarity*

[9] ***Mild exotherm***

[10] *Emulsion may form*

[11] *May be left at this stage*

[12] *See Fig. 3.7*

[13] *See Fig. 3.54*

Problems

1 Why is only the 2,3-double bond of geraniol epoxidized under these conditions?
2 Discuss possible mechanisms for the asymmetric epoxidation reaction.
3 How would you determine the optical purity of your product?

Further reading

For the procedures on which this experiment is based, see: R.M. Hanson and K.B. Sharpless, *J. Org. Chem.*, 1986, **51**, 1922 and references therein.
For a review of the chemistry of TBHP, see: K.B. Sharpless, *Aldrichimica Acta*, 1979, **12**, 63.
For developments in enantioselective epoxidation reactions, see: P. Besse and H. Veschambre, *Tetrahedron*, 1994, **50**, 8885.
K.B. Sharpless, *Chem. Br.*, 1986, **22**, 38.

Experiment 13

Hydration of alkenes by hydroboration–oxidation: preparation of octan-1-ol from 1-octene

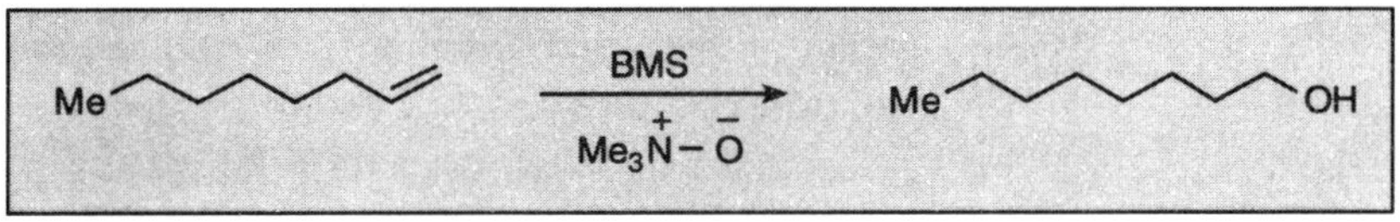

The hydroboration of alkenes, developed by H.C. Brown, is a useful reaction in organic chemistry, because the resulting organoboranes can be converted into a variety of functional groups; alcohols, carbonyl compounds and amines for example. The importance of organoboranes was recognized by the award of the 1979 Nobel Prize to Brown. One of the most useful applications of organoboron chemistry is the hydroboration–oxidation sequence which provides a method for the anti-Markovnikov hydration of alkenes (*cf.* Experiment 7). This experiment illustrates the application of this process to the preparation of octan-1-ol from 1-octene, and utilizes the relatively stable and easy-to-handle borane methylsulfide (BMS) complex as the hydroborating agent in diglyme (2-methoxyethyl ether) as solvent, and trimethylamine-*N*-oxide as the oxidant. The product 1-octanol can be purified by distillation under reduced pressure.

Level	4
Time	2 × 3 h
Equipment	magnetic stirrer; apparatus for stirring with addition under nitrogen (3-neck flask), extraction/separation, suction filtration, short path distillation
Instruments	IR, NMR

Materials

1-octene (FW 112.2)	1.57 mL, 1.12 g (10.0 mmol)	**flammable**
borane methylsulfide (FW 76.0)	0.34 mL (3.6 mmol)	**flammable, moisture sensitive**
trimethylamine-*N*-oxide dihydrate (FW 111.1)	1.11 g (10.0 mmol)	**oxidizer**
diglyme (2-methoxyethyl ether)	6 mL	
diethyl ether	10 mL	**flammable, irritant**

HOOD

Procedure

Set up a three-neck flask with a reflux condenser, nitrogen inlet and magnetic stirrer bar.[1] Place a septum in the third neck, and flush the flask with a slow stream of nitrogen. Place the 1-octene and the diglyme in the flask, stir the solution, and cool the flask in an ice bath, still maintaining the nitrogen atmos-

[1]*See Fig. 3.22, but insert a condenser between flask and bubbler*

phere. Add the borane methylsulfide by syringe through the septum, remove the ice bath, and continue to stir the reaction mixture for 1 h. Add 0.25 mL water to destroy the excess borane,[2] followed by the trimethylamine-*N*-oxide dihydrate. Replace the nitrogen inlet and the septum by stoppers, add a few boiling stones, and *slowly* heat the mixture to *gentle* reflux[2] for 1 h. When the reflux period is complete, allow the mixture to cool to room temperature,[3] and transfer it to a separatory funnel containing 10 mL diethyl ether. Wash the solution with 5 × 10 mL portions of water to remove the diglyme, and dry the ether layer over $MgSO_4$.[3] filter off the drying agent by suction,[4] evaporate the filtrate on the rotary evaporator, and distil the residue in a short path distillation apparatus[5] under reduced pressure using a water aspirator (*ca.* 25 mmHg), taking care that the product is not contaminated with diglyme (the distillate can be checked by IR spectroscopy). Record the bp, yield, and the IR ($CHCl_3$) and NMR ($CDCl_3$) spectra of your product. Record the spectra of 1-octene for comparison.

[2] ***Foaming!***

[3] *May be left at this stage*

[4] *See Fig. 3.7*

[5] *See Fig. 3.54*

Problems

1 Write a reaction mechanism for the hydroboration of alkenes. What would be the products of the hydroboration (using diborane) of: (i) phenylethene (styrene), and (ii) 2,3-dimethylbut-2-ene?

2 Write a reaction mechanism for the subsequent oxidation of the organoborane using trimethylamine-*N*-oxide. What other oxidants could be used for this transformation?

3 Compare and contrast the IR and NMR spectra of 1-octene and octan-1-ol. Is there any evidence for the formation of the isomeric alcohol, octan-2-ol?

Further reading

For the procedure on which this experiment is based, see: G.W. Kabalka and H.C. Hedgecock, *J. Chem. Educ.*, 1975, **52**, 745.

For a discussion of borane methylsulfide and related complexes, see: EROS, 634.

Experiment 14

Preparation of 7-trichloromethyl-8-bromo-Δ¹-p-menthane by free radical addition of bromotrichloromethane to β-pinene

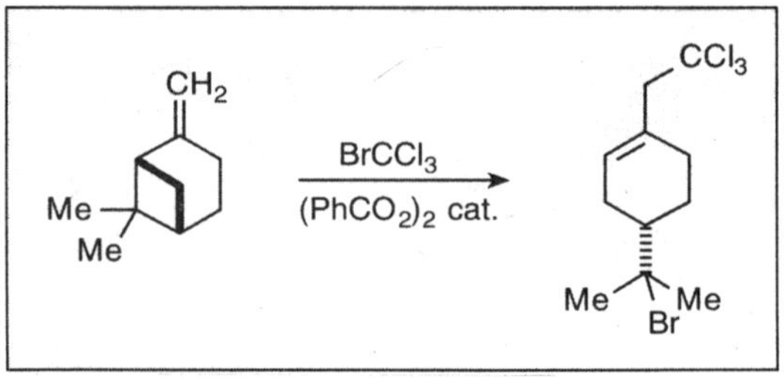

Free radical additions to alkenes are examples of chain reactions, with each cycle of addition generating more radical species. Although the reaction should be self-sustaining once initiated, continuous production of radicals is necessary to maintain the reaction due to quenching processes taking place, in which two radicals combine and are removed from the reaction sequence.

Benzoyl peroxide is used in the following experiment as the initiator of the reaction, but radical species may also be generated conveniently in the laboratory using UV light.

Radical additions to β-pinene result in cleavage of the cyclobutane ring and generation of monocyclic products. The release of steric strain resulting from the ring opening makes this reaction very favoured and thus β-pinene is a very reactive substrate for such additions. It is this reactivity which forms the basis of an old veterinary technique for sterilizing wounds in livestock in which iodine and turpentine (which is largely a mixture of α- and β-pinenes) are mixed together in the wound. The resulting violent exothermic electrophilic addition of iodine to the double bond forces excess iodine into all parts of the injury and also causes the production of purple clouds of iodine vapour. Doubtless such effects served to impress the client, but the thoughts of the patients are not recorded!

Level	3	
Time	3 h	
Equipment	apparatus for reflux, suction filtration	

Materials

β-pinene (FW 136.2)	1.2 mL, 1.02 g (7.5 mmol)	**flammable, irritant**
bromotrichloromethane (FW 198.3)	0.85 mL (8.2 mmol)	**irritant, toxic**

NOTE: *bromotrichloromethane is highly toxic. Always handle in the hood*

benzoyl peroxide (FW 242.2)	*ca.* 5 mg (catalytic quantity)	**explosive**

NOTE: *benzoyl peroxide is an oxidizing agent and liable to explode if heated or ground as the dry solid. Handle with extreme caution*

cyclohexane		**flammable**
methanol		**flammable, toxic**

Procedure

HOOD

Place the β-pinene, bromotrichloromethane and benzoyl peroxide[1] in a 100 mL three-necked flask equipped with a reflux condenser with nitrogen bubbler and a nitrogen inlet. The third neck is stoppered. Add 30 mL cyclohexane, taking care to wash down all the material that may be adhering to the walls of the flask. Heat the mixture under a nitrogen atmosphere under reflux for 40 min.[2,3] Add 5 mL of water to the mixture and remove the solvent and excess bromotrichloromethane on the rotary evaporator,[4] heating with a hot water bath. If bumping is a problem, transfer the mixture to a larger flask using a further 5 mL of water. Cool the aqueous residue in an ice bath until the oil solidifies (*ca.* 15 min), break up the solid with a spatula and filter it with suction.[5] Powder the solid on the funnel and wash it with 10 mL of water followed by three 5 mL portions of ice-cold methanol. Dry the residue with

[1] ***Care! See note above***

[2] *See Fig. 3.23(a)*

[3] ***Do not apply heat above the surface of the liquid***

[4] ***The rotary evaporator must be used in the hood***

[5] *See Fig. 3.7*

suction, and record the yield and mp of your crude product. The material is fairly pure but, if time permits, it may be recrystallized from methanol.[5] However take care not to expose the material to prolonged heating as this causes decomposition.

[5] *Recrystallization is sometimes tricky*

Problems

1 Write out the sequence of events which occur in the radical chain reaction that you have just carried out.

2 Explain which structural features of benzoyl peroxide make it a useful means of generating radicals thermally in the laboratory.

3 Halogenated hydrocarbons are used in certain types of fire fighting equipment. Apart from displacing oxygen from the vicinity of the fire due to the density of their vapour, they serve as radical quenching agents. Show how this is so and explain why this should be an advantage.

4 Predict the major products (if any) of the following reactions and explain your reasoning:

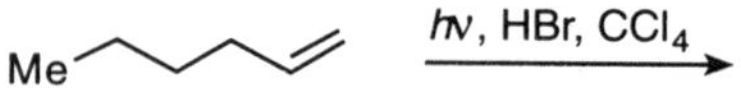

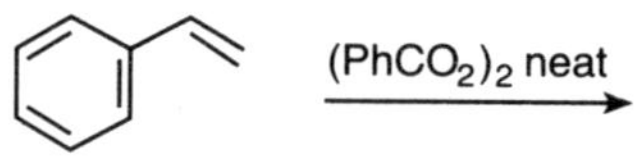

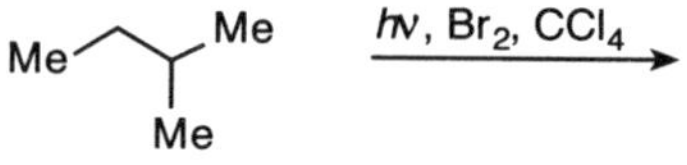

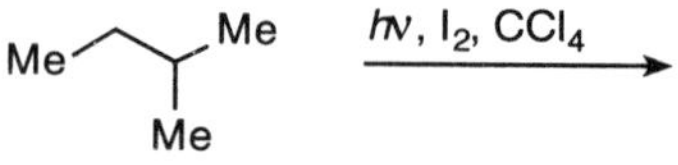

Further reading

For the procedure on which this experiment is based, see: T.A. Kaye and R.A. Odum, *J. Chem. Educ.*, 1976, **53**, 60.

7.3 Substitution

This short section includes three examples of substitution reactions—nucleophilic and free radical.

Experiment 15

Preparation of 1-iodobutane by SN2 displacement of bromide: the Finkelstein reaction

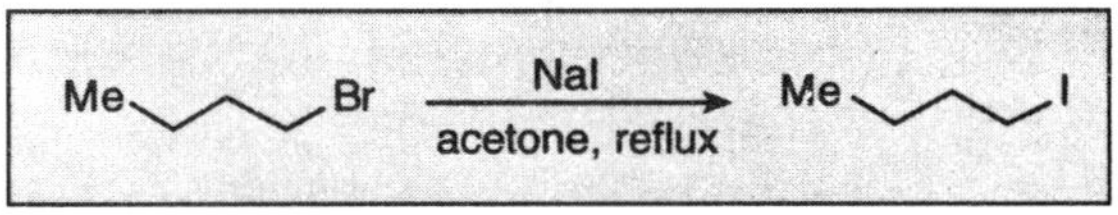

Alkyl iodides may be prepared by nucleophilic displacement from the corresponding bromide using a solution of sodium iodide in acetone. The reaction follows an SN2 mechanism and the unfavourable equilibrium position of the halide exchange is forced over to the iodide by precipitation of the sparingly soluble sodium bromide. This reaction is often referred to as the Finkelstein reaction and can be applied equally well to the preparation of iodides from chlorides but, as the mechanism is SN2, the process works more efficiently with primary halides than for secondary or tertiary halides. Care should be taken to avoid skin contact or inhalation of alkyl halides, particularly iodides, as they are rather toxic and have been implicated as possible cancer-inducing agents.

Level	1
Time	3 h
Equipment	apparatus for reflux, extraction/separation, distillation, distillation at reduced pressure (optional)
Instruments	Abbé refractometer

Materials

1-bromobutane (FW 137.0)	5.4 mL, 6.85 g (50 mmol)	**flammable, irritant**
sodium iodide (FW 149.9)	15 g (0.1 mol)	**irritant**
acetone		**flammable**
diethyl ether		**flammable, irritant**
sodium bisulfite solution (saturated)		**irritant**

Procedure

HOOD

[1]*See Fig. 3.23(a)*

[2]*See Fig. 3.48*

[3]*See Fig. 3.7*

Dissolve the sodium iodide in 80 mL acetone in a 250 mL round-bottomed flask with magnetic stirring. Add the 1-bromobutane and reflux the mixture over a water bath for 20 min.[1] Remove the flask from the heating bath and allow the mixture to cool. Set the apparatus for distillation[2] and distil off *ca.* 60 mL of acetone. Cool the residue to room temperature in an ice bath, add 50 mL of water and extract the product with 25 mL diethyl ether. Separate the organic phase and wash it with saturated aqueous sodium bisulfite (10 mL) to remove any colouration due to iodine which has been liberated during the reaction. Dry the solution over $MgSO_4$, filter with suction,[3] and remove the solvents on the rotary evaporator without any external heating. The residue of crude 1-iodobutane may be purified by distillation at atmospheric pressure,[2] collecting the fraction boiling at about 125–135°C. Decomposition during distillation can be minimized by placing a short length of bright copper wire in the distilling flask.[4] Alternatively the product may be distilled at reduced pressure using an aspirator,[5] collecting the fraction boiling at about 60–65°C. Record the weight of your material, calculate the yield and obtain the refractive index. ■

[4] *Some frothing may occur*

[5] *See Fig. 3.53*

MICROSCALE

Level	1
Time	3 h
Equipment	apparatus for reflux, downward distillation, extraction/separation, pipette drying column, Hickman still

Materials		
1-bromobutane (FW 137.0)	0.36 mL, 460 mg (3.3 mmol)	**flammable, irritant**
sodium iodide (FW 149.9)	1.00 g (6.7 mmol)	**irritant**
acetone		**flammable**
diethyl ether		**flammable, irritant**
sodium bisulfite solution (saturated)		**irritant**

Procedure

Dissolve the sodium iodide in acetone (6 mL) in a 25 mL round-bottomed flask, add the bromobutane followed by a single boiling stone, and reflux the mixture for 20 min.[1] Remove the flask from the heating bath and allow to cool. Set for downward distillation[2] and remove *ca.* 4.5 mL of the acetone. Cool the residue to room temperature, add water (3 mL) and extract with diethyl ether (1.5 mL). Remove the aqueous layer from beneath the ether layer, and wash the ether layer with saturated aqueous sodium sulfite solution (0.5 mL) to remove traces of iodine. Pass the ether layer through a Pasteur pipette column[3] of $MgSO_4$ into a 3 mL tapered vial and remove the remaining solvent *in vacuo* without heating, or using a stream of air or nitrogen. Add a small piece (1–2 mm) of bright copper wire[4] to the residue and distil into the Hickman still,[5] heating with a small Bunsen flame or hot air blower. Measure the yield and refractive index of the product.

[1] *See Fig. 3.24*

[2] *See Fig. 3.48(b)*

[3] *See Fig. 3.9*

[4] *Some frothing may occur*

[5] *See Fig. 3.58*

Problems

1 What are the characteristic features of an SN2 mechanism? How does it differ from an SN1 process?

2 How might you convert 1-butanol into 1-bromobutane?

3 How might you convert 1-butanol into 1-iodobutane without going via the bromide?

Free-radical substitution

Free-radical substitution for hydrogen in organic substrates follows the mechanism of a classic chain reaction and consists of three distinct phases, namely *initiation, propagation* and *termination*.

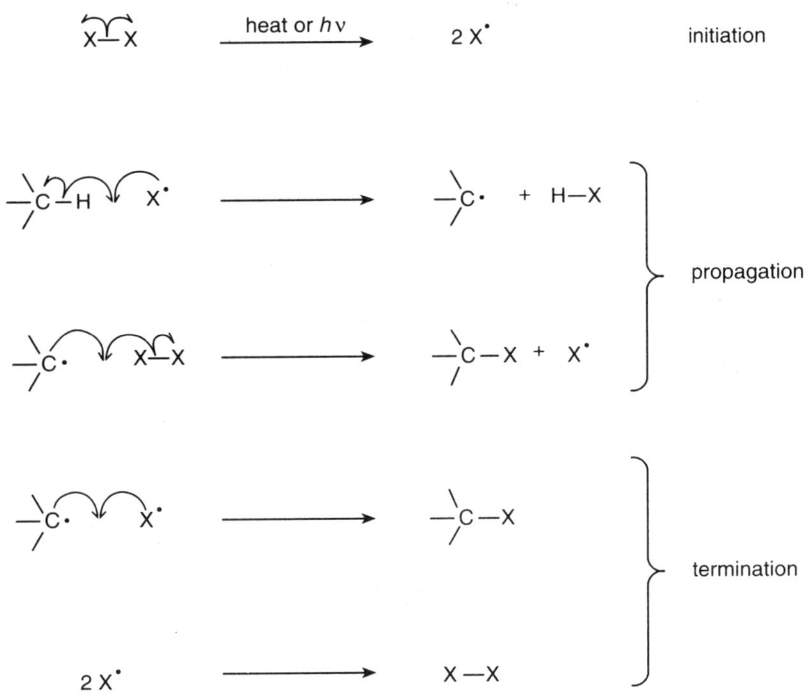

The ease of substitution at any particular position is mainly governed by the stability of the carbon radical generated on removal of a hydrogen atom and, whilst saturated hydrocarbons will undergo this reaction, the greater reactivity of the radical species needed to abstract a hydrogen atom usually results in loss of selectivity with the formation of complex reaction mixtures. Nonetheless, this reaction is important for obtaining chlorinated hydrocarbons from petroleum and natural gas feedstocks when the mixtures can be separated by efficient fractional distillation and all of the products are commercially useful. However, benzylic and allylic radicals, being stabilized by resonance, can be formed preferentially by hydrogen atom abstraction using radicals generated under relatively non-forcing conditions and such reactions are of use in the laboratory. With unsymmetrical allylic substrates there is the added complication of regiocontrol of substitution of the allyl radical generated, but this is not a problem with benzylic systems.

Experiment 16

Preparation of 4-bromomethylbenzoic acid by radical substitution and conversion to 4-methoxymethylbenzoic acid by nucleophilic substitution

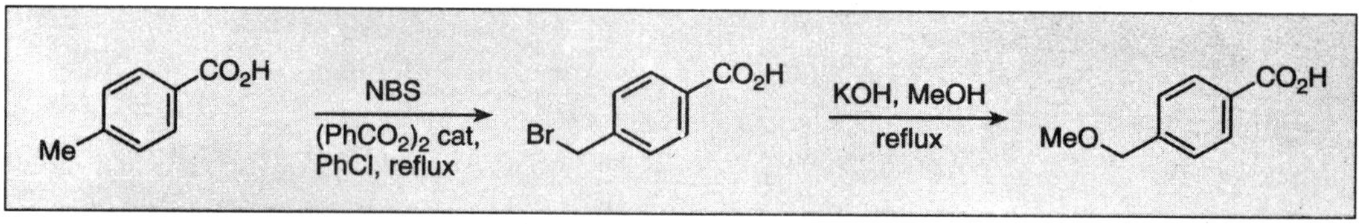

A convenient procedure for generating bromine radicals utilizes *N*-bromosuccinimide as the bromine source and benzoyl peroxide as the initiator. Heating benzoyl peroxide causes homolytic cleavage of the labile peroxide linkage, giving radicals which react with the *N*-bromosuccinimide, breaking the relatively weak N—Br bond to generate bromine radicals. The HBr generated by benzylic hydrogen atom abstraction from the 4-methylbenzoic acid reacts with more *N*-bromosuccinimide to form molecular bromine which in turn combines with the benzyl radical to furnish the product and another bromide radical. Thus, the bromine atoms function as the chain carrier in this reaction.

Unlike most benzyl halides, the 4-bromomethylbenzoic acid prepared in this experiment is not lachrymatory, making it suitable for use in a laboratory procedure. Nonetheless, the product is a potential skin irritant and due caution should be exercised in its handling.

Benzyl halides undergo ready substitution and this can be demonstrated in an optional experiment by converting the brominated product to 4-methoxymethylbenzoic acid using methanolic potassium hydroxide.

Level	3
Time	2 × 3 h
Equipment	stirrer/hotplate; apparatus for reflux (×2)
Instruments	IR, NMR

Materials

1. Preparation of 4-bromomethylbenzoic acid

4-methylbenzoic acid (*p*-toluic acid) (FW 136.2)	2.72 g (20 mmol)	**toxic**
N-bromosuccinimide (FW 178.0)	3.60 g (20 mmol)	**irritant**
benzoyl peroxide (FW 242.2)	0.20 g	**explosive**

NOTE: ***benzoyl peroxide is an oxidizing agent and liable to explode if heated or ground as the dry solid. Handle with extreme caution***

Continued

Box cont.

chlorobenzene		**flammable**
light petroleum (bp 40–60°C)		**flammable**
2. Preparation of 4-methoxymethylbenzoic acid		
methanol	25 mL	**flammable, toxic**
potassium hydroxide pellets	1.1 g (20 mmol)	**corrosive**

Procedure

1. Preparation of 4-bromomethylbenzoic acid

Place the 4-methylbenzoic acid and *N*-bromosuccinimide in a 100 mL round-bottomed flask. Add the benzoyl peroxide,[1] taking care that none sticks to the ground glass joint of the flask. Finally, add 25 mL chlorobenzene by pipette and wash down any solids which may be adhering to the sides of the flask, paying particular attention to the ground glass joint. Arrange the apparatus for reflux[2] and heat gently over a small flame for 1 h with occasional (*ca.* every 5 min) vigorous swirling[3] in order to ensure good mixing. After this period, cool the flask and contents in an ice bath (*ca.* 10 min) and filter off the precipitated products with suction.[4] Wash the residue on the funnel with light petroleum (3 × 10 mL), and transfer the solid to a beaker. Add water (50 mL), stir the slurry thoroughly to dissolve the succinimide present, and filter the mixture under suction, washing the solid residue successively with water (2 × 10 mL) and light petroleum (2 × 10 mL). Leave the product on the funnel with suction to dry as thoroughly as possible and record the yield and mp of the crude material. Obtain the IR ($CHCl_3$) and NMR ($CDCl_3$) spectra of your product. The crude material is of sufficient purity to use in the following experiment but, if time permits, may be recrystallized from ethyl acetate.

[1] *Care! Potentially explosive*

[2] *See Fig. 3.23(a)*

[3] ***Care! Chlorobenzene boils at 132°C***

[4] *See Fig. 3.7*

2. Preparation of 4-methoxymethylbenzoic acid (optional)

Place the potassium hydroxide pellets and the methanol in a 100 mL round-bottomed flask and add 1.1 g of the 4-bromomethylbenzoic acid prepared in the previous experiment. Set the apparatus for reflux with a calcium chloride guard tube and heat gently for 45 min.[5] Remove the methanol at reduced pressure on the rotary evaporator with gentle warming[6] and dissolve the alkaline residue in water (30 mL). Acidify the mixture with dilute hydrochloric acid and filter the precipitated product. Wash the solid with light petroleum (2 × 15 mL) and dry with suction on the funnel. Record the yield and mp of your crude product and then recrystallize it from water. As before, filter the precipitated product with suction, wash the crystalline solid with light petroleum (2 × 15 mL) and dry on the funnel with suction. Obtain the IR ($CHCl_3$) and NMR ($CDCl_3$) spectra of the purified product and compare its mp with that of the crude material.

[5] *See Fig. 3.23(c)*

[6] *Bumping may occur if heating is too strong*

See Exp. 51

MICROSCALE

Level	3
Time	2 × 3 h
Equipment	stirrer/hotplate; apparatus for reflux, Craig tube recrystallization

Materials

1. Preparation of 4-bromomethylbenzoic acid

4-methylbenzoic acid (*p*-toluic acid) (FW 136.2)	136 mg (1.0 mmol)	**toxic**
N-bromosuccinimide (FW 178.0)	180 mg (1 mmol)	**irritant**
benzoyl peroxide (FW 242.2)	10 mg	**explosive**

NOTE: *benzoyl peroxide is an oxidizing agent and liable to explode if heated or ground as the dry solid. Handle with extreme caution, even when using the small quantities required in this experiment*

chlorobenzene		**flammable**
light petroleum (bp 40–60°C)		**flammable**

2. Preparation of 4-methoxymethylbenzoic acid

methanol	25 mL	**flammable, toxic**
potassium hydroxide pellets	1.1 g (20 mmol)	**corrosive**

Procedure

1. Preparation of 4-bromomethylbenzoic acid

Place the toluic acid and the *N*-bromosuccinimide in a 3 mL conical reaction vial containing a spin vane. Add the dibenzoyl peroxide,[1] carefully avoiding any contact with ground glass surfaces. Add the chlorobenzene from a Pasteur pipette, using the solvent to rinse any traces of the peroxide into the base of the vial. Heat the mixture at reflux[2] for 1 h with vigorous stirring. Cool the flask in an ice bath and remove the liquid carefully using a drawn out Pasteur pipette. Wash the solid by slurrying with light petroleum ether (3 × 0.5 mL) then transfer the solid to a Craig tube. Add water (1 mL) and stir the slurry thoroughly to dissolve the succinimide. Filter by centrifugation,[3] washing the solid with water (2 × 0.5 mL), then light petroleum ether (2 × 0.5 mL), and centrifuging after each washing. Dry the solid rapidly *in vacuo*[4] and reserve a TLC sample for later use.

2. Preparation of 4-methoxymethylbenzoic acid

Prepare a solution of potassium hydroxide in methanol and transfer 1.25 mL of the solution to a 3 mL reaction vial. Add bromomethylbenzoic acid (55 mg) prepared in the previous experiment. Set the apparatus for reflux with a calcium chloride guard tube[5] and heat gently for 45 min with stirring. Remove the methanol with a gentle vacuum[6] and dissolve the residue in water (1.0–1.5 mL). Transfer the solution to a Craig tube and acidify by adding concentrated

[1] *Care! Potentially explosive*

[2] *See Fig. 3.24*

[3] *See pp. 137–138*

[4] *See Fig. 3.46*

[5] *See Fig. 3.24*

[6] *Bumping may occur if heating is too strong*

hydrochloric acid carefully one drop at a time testing the pH between drops. Filter the precipitated solid by centrifugation. Wash the solid with light petroleum ether (2 × 0.75 mL), centrifuging after each washing. Transfer the solid to a vial and dry *in vacuo*. Record the melting point and TLC against the starting material and the intermediate bromomethyl compound.

Problems

1 Assign the important absorptions in the IR spectra and interpret the NMR spectra of your products.

2 Write out the full mechanism for the radical chain reaction which is occurring in the conversion of 4-methylbenzoic acid to 4-bromomethylbenzoic acid.

3 Kerosene consists mainly of C_{11} and C_{12} hydrocarbons and finds use as a fuel for jet engines although it is not suitable for automobiles. However, catalytic cracking will convert it to shorter chain hydrocarbons. The process involves the formation of radical intermediates and results in two smaller molecules, one of which is an alkene. Write out a mechanism for the overall process below:

$$C_{11}H_{24} \xrightarrow{\text{heat, catalyst}} C_9H_{20} + C_2H_4$$

4 Suggest reaction pathways for the following transformations:

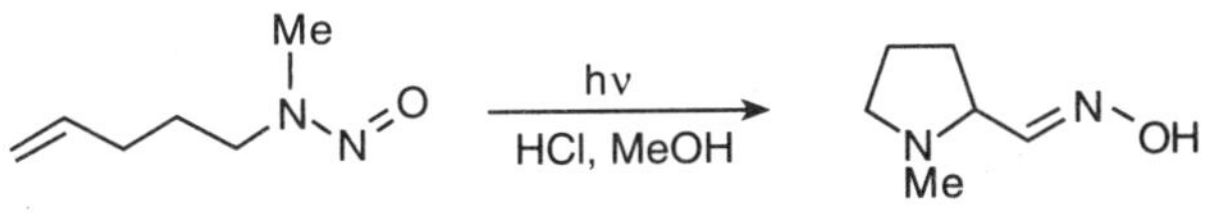

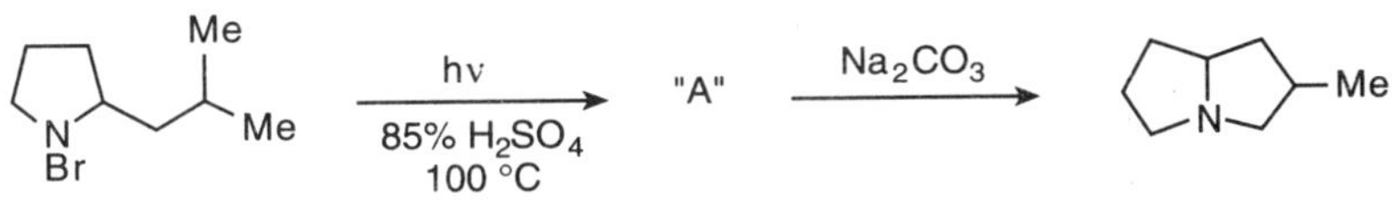

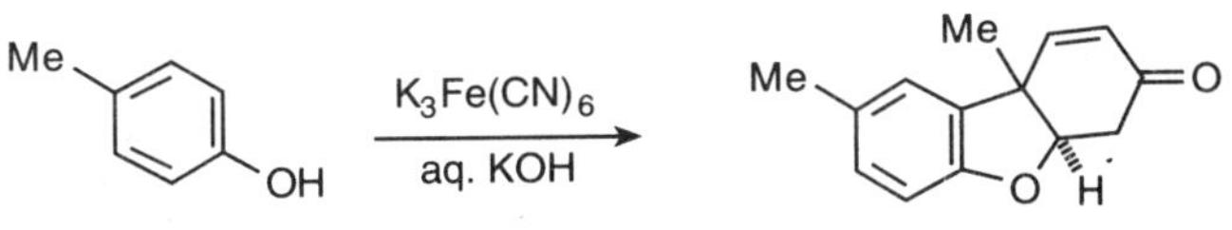

Further reading

For the procedure on which this experiment is based, see: E.S. Olson, *J. Chem. Educ.*, 1980, **57**, 157.

D.L. Tuleen and B.A. Hess, *J. Chem. Educ.*, 1971, **48**, 476.

7.4 Reduction

The reduction of an organic molecule is an extremely important general process. Reduction can involve the addition of two hydrogens across a double or triple bond, or the replacement of a functional group such as OH or halide by hydrogen. Despite the very many different sets of reaction conditions and reagents for carrying out reductions, there are only three basic processes involved.

1 The addition, or transfer, of hydride, followed by a proton, usually in the work-up. This is normally accomplished using a hydride transfer reagent, and is a common method of reducing polarized multiple bonds.

2 The addition of molecular hydrogen, catalyzed by a transition-metal compound (catalytic hydrogenation).

3 The addition of a single electron followed by a proton, a second electron, and another proton. Since a metal is the usual source of electrons in this method, the procedure is known as dissolving metal reduction.

This section includes examples of each type of reduction; other experiments which include a reduction step are 63 and 83.

Reduction with hydride transfer reagents

Hydride transfer reagents are commonly used as reducing agents in organic synthesis. The two reagents most frequently used are lithium aluminium hydride ($LiAlH_4$) and sodium borohydride ($NaBH_4$), and although both the reagents can be regarded as a source of nucleophilic hydride (or deuteride if the corresponding deuterated reagents are employed), their reducing powers are quite different. Lithium aluminium hydride is a powerful reductant and reduces most functional groups which contain a polarized multiple bond. It reacts vigorously with water and must be used in dry solvents and under anhydrous conditions. In contrast, sodium borohydride is a milder reducing agent and shows considerable selectivity and, although it reduces acid chlorides, aldehydes and ketones rapidly, esters and other functional groups are only slowly reduced or are inert under the same conditions. It is usually used in protic solvents such as methanol or ethanol. The reducing power of lithium aluminium hydride can be attentuated by replacing one or more of the hydrogen atoms by an alkoxy group, and, for example, reagents such as lithium tri-*t*-butoxyaluminium hydride ($LiAlH(Ot\text{-}Bu)_3$) exhibit increased selectivity in the reduction of functional groups. Similarly the reducing power of sodium borohydride can be modified by replacing one of the hydrogens by the electron-withdrawing cyanide group, and the resulting reagent, sodium cyanoborohydride ($NaBH_3CN$) has important differences in properties to sodium borohydride itself—in particular, enhanced stability under acidic conditions.

Another reagent which illustrates modified reactivity because of its steric bulk is diisobutylaluminium hydride (i-Bu_2AlH). Since the aluminium atom is now tri-coordinate, it acts as a Lewis acid, and therefore the first step in reductions using this reagent is coordination of the substrate to the aluminium.

The experiments which follow illustrate the use of hydride transfer reagents in the reduction of carbonyl groups, together with some of the stereochemical consequences of such reductions.

Experiment 17

Reduction of benzophenone with sodium borohydride: preparation of diphenylmethanol

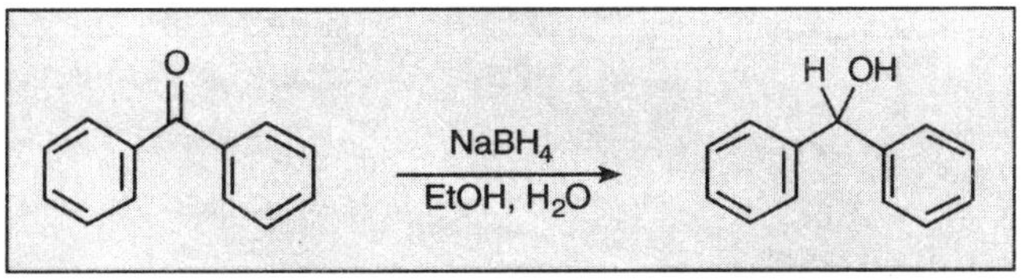

In this experiment sodium borohydride is used to reduce the aromatic ketone benzophenone to diphenylmethanol (benzhydrol). The reducing agent is used in excess to ensure complete reduction of the carbonyl group, and the reaction is carried out in aqueous ethanolic solution. The product is easily isolated, purified by crystallization, and its purity is checked using TLC. The reaction is ideal for gaining experience at working on the millimolar scale.

Level	1
Time	3 h
Equipment	magnetic stirrer; apparatus for suction filtration, TLC analysis
Instruments	IR

Materials

benzophenone (FW 182.2)	364 mg (2.0 mmol)	
sodium borohydride (FW 37.8)	84 mg (2.2 mmol)	**corrosive, flammable**
ethanol		**flammable, toxic**
light petroleum (bp 60–80°C)		**flammable**
dichloromethane		**irritant, toxic**
ethyl acetate		**flammable, irritant**
hydrochloric acid (conc.)		**corrosive**

Procedure

Dissolve the benzophenone[1] in 5 mL ethanol in a 25 mL Erlenmeyer flask, and stir the solution magnetically. In a small test tube, dissolve the sodium borohydride in 1.5 mL cold water, and add this solution one drop at a time[2] to the stirred ethanolic solution of benzophenone at room temperature. After all the sodium borohydride has been added, continue to stir the mixture for a further 40 min. Slowly pour the mixture into a 50 mL beaker containing a mixture of

[1] *Benzophenone should be finely ground*

[2] *Use a Pasteur pipette*

10 mL ice-water and 1 mL concentrated hydrochloric acid. After a few minutes collect the precipitated product by suction filtration,[3] and wash it with 2 × 5 mL portions of water. Dry the crude product by suction at the filter pump for 10 min, and then recrystallize it from the minimum amount of hot petroleum.[4] Record the yield and mp of the product. Finally record an IR (Nujol®) spectrum of your diphenylmethanol, and one of benzophenone for comparison.

To check the purity of the recrystallized diphenylmethanol by TLC,[5] dissolve *ca.* 10 mg of the product in few drops of dichloromethane, and spot this solution onto a silica gel TLC plate. Similarly spot a reference solution of the starting ketone, benzophenone, onto the same plate. Develop the plate in a mixture of petroleum and ethyl acetate (9:1). Visualize the developed plate under UV light[6] and work out the R_f values for the two compounds. ■

[3] *See Fig. 3.7*

[4] ***No flames***

[5] *For a discussion of TLC, see Chapter 3*

[6] ***Care! Eye protection***

MICROSCALE

Level	1
Time	3 h
Equipment	magnetic stirrer; apparatus for TLC analysis, Craig tube recrystallization

Materials		
benzophenone (FW 182.2)	36 mg (0.2 mmol)	
sodium borohydride (FW 37.8)	84 mg (2.2 mmol)	**corrosive, flammable**
ethanol		**flammable, toxic**
light petroleum (bp 60–80°C)		**flammable**
dichloromethane		**irritant, toxic**
ethyl acetate		**flammable, irritant**
hydrochloric acid (conc.)		**corrosive**

Procedure

Prepare a solution of sodium borohydride (84 mg) in water (1.5 mL).[1] Dissolve the benzophenone[2] in ethanol (0.5 mL) in a small test tube containing a small stirrer bead. Add the sodium borohydride solution (0.15 mL *only*) to the stirred solution of benzophenone using a drawn out Pasteur pipette.[3] After all the sodium borohydride has been added, stir for a further 40 min, following the reaction by TLC[4] and running the reaction mixture against starting ketone. When the reaction is complete, pipette the mixture into a Craig tube containing a mixture of ice-water (1 mL) and concentrated hydrochloric acid (0.1 mL). Centrifuge the tube in an upright position to compact the precipitate, then invert the tube and recentrifuge to collect the crude product.[5] Wash the solid with water (2 × 0.5 mL), dry the solid *in vacuo*[6] and recrystallize from light petroleum ether. Record the mp and compare the product to the starting material by TLC using 9:1 hexane:ethyl acetate to develop the plates and a UV lamp[7] to visualize the spots.

[1] *This fresh stock solution can be used for a number of experiments.*
[2] *Benzophenone should be ground finely*
[3] *Control is easier if the pipette is drawn out to a capillary*
[4] *For a discussion of TLC, see Chapter 3*

[5] *See pp. 137–138*

[6] *See Fig. 3.46*

[7] ***Care! Eye protection***

Problems

1 Discuss the mechanism of sodium borohydride reduction of ketones in ethanolic solution.
2 Suggest an alternative synthesis of diphenylmethanol.
3 How would you prepare deuterated diphenylmethanol, $(C_6H_5)_2$ CDOH?
4 How would deuterated diphenylmethanol differ from the protonated version in: (i) its physical properties, and (ii) its chemical reactions?
5 Compare and contrast the IR spectra of benzophenone and diphenylmethanol.

Further reading

For a discussion of sodium borohydride, see: EROS, 4522.

Experiment 18

Reduction of 4-t-butylcyclohexanone with sodium borohydride

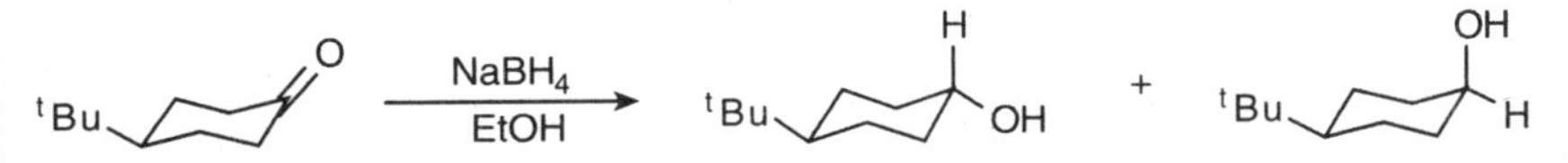

The reduction of the sp² carbonyl group in unsymmetrical ketones to an sp³ secondary alcohol creates a new asymmetric centre. The stereochemical outcome of such a reaction depends upon which side of the carbonyl group is attacked by the reagent, although the two possible directions of attack, and hence the two possible secondary alcohol products, are only distinguishable when there is another stereochemical 'marker' in the starting ketone. This experiment illustrates the reduction of 4-*t*-butylcyclohexanone with sodium borohydride (excess). The bulky *t*-butyl group remains in the equatorial position in the chair conformation of the six-membered ring, and hence the two possible alcohol products will have the OH group axial (*cis*- to the *t*-butyl group) or equatorial (*trans*- to the *t*-butyl group). As you will discover, these isomeric alcohols are formed in unequal amounts, and their ratio can be determined by gas chromatography (GC).

Level	2
Time	3 × 3 h
Equipment	magnetic stirrer; apparatus for suction filtration, recrystallization, reflux
Instruments	IR, GC. 3 m 10% Carbowax®, 150°C isotherm

Materials

4-*t*-butylcyclohexanone (FW 154.3)	3.08 g (20 mmol)	
sodium borohydride (FW 37.8)	0.38 g (10 mmol)	**corrosive, flammable**
ethanol		**flammable, toxic**
diethyl ether		**flammable, irritant**
light petroleum (bp 40–60°C)		**flammable**
hydrochloric acid (1 M)		**corrosive**

Procedure

1. *Preparation of* cis *and* trans *4-t-butylcyclohexanols*

Dissolve the 4-*t*-butylcyclohexanone in 20 mL of ethanol in a 50 mL Erlenmeyer flask. Stir the solution magnetically at room temperature, and add the sodium borohydride in small portions over 15 min. If necessary, rinse in the last traces of sodium borohydride with 5 mL of ethanol. Allow the mixture to stir at room temperature for a further 30 min, and then pour it into a 250 mL beaker containing 50 mL of ice-water. *Slowly* add 10 mL of dilute hydrochloric acid, and stir the mixture for 10 min.[1] Transfer the mixture to a 250 mL separatory funnel, and extract the product with 2 × 50 mL portions of diethyl ether. Dry the combined ether extracts over $MgSO_4$.[2] Filter, and retain 1 mL of the ether filtrate in a sample tube for analysis by GC (see below). Evaporate the remainder of the filtrate on the rotary evaporator, and recrystallize the solid residue from petroleum (bp 40–60°C).[3] Record the yield, mp and IR spectrum of the product after a single recrystallization.[3] Record an IR spectrum of the starting ketone for comparison.

[1] *May be left longer*

[2] *May be left at this stage*

[3] *Mp and IR can be recorded in the next period—**it is important to set up part 3 now***

2. *GC analysis*

Analyze the ethereal solution of the crude reaction product using a Carbowax® column.[4] Determine the ratio of *cis* to *trans* isomeric alcohols by relative peak areas. The *cis*- isomer has the shorter retention time. Run a sample of 4-*t*-butylcyclohexanone for reference to check that the reduction has gone to completion. ■

[4] *See Chapter 3 for a discussion of GC*

MICROSCALE

Level	2
Time	3 h
Equipment	magnetic stirrer; apparatus for TLC analysis, Craig tube recrystallization

Materials

4-*t*-butylcyclohexanone (FW 154.3)	308 mg (2 mmol)	
sodium borohydride (FW 37.8)	38 mg (1 mmol)	**corrosive, flammable**
ethanol		**flammable, toxic**
diethyl ether		**flammable, irritant**
light petroleum (bp 40–60°C)		**flammable**
hydrochloric acid (1 M)		**corrosive**

Procedure

Dissolve the ketone in ethanol (2 mL) in a test tube containing a small stirrer bead and stir at room temperature. Prepare a solution of the sodium borohydride in ethanol (0.5 ml) and add the solution over 15 min using a drawn out Pasteur pipette. Follow the reaction by TLC against the ketone starting material; two new spots (corresponding to the *cis* and *trans* stereoisomers) will appear, and the ketone spot will disappear.[1] When the reaction is complete,[2] pipette the tube contents into a second tube containing ice-water (5 mL). Slowly add dilute hydrochloric acid (1 mL) from a Pasteur pipette, transfer the stirrer bead using tweezers and stir the mixture for 10 min.[3] Extract the product with portions of diethyl ether (2 × 1 mL). Dry the combined ether extracts by passing through a column of $MgSO_4$ into a Craig tube.[4] Evaporate the solvent from using a stream of air or nitrogen and recrystallize the solid residue from light petroleum (bp 40–60°C). Carry out GC analysis as described earlier.

[1]*Developing solvent, 33% ethyl acetate in hexane; visualization, iodine vapour or anisaldehyde dip. See p. 170*
[2]*Add further 0.1 mL portions of borohydride solution if the ketone spot persists*
[3]*May be left longer*
[4]*See Figs 3.9, 2.31*

Problems

1 Discuss the stereochemistry of the reduction of cyclic ketones by hydride transfer reagents, and rationalize the ratio of *cis* and *trans* alcohols obtained in your experiment.

2 Compare and contrast the IR spectra of the starting ketone and the alcohol, assigning peaks to all the functional groups.

Further reading

For a related experiment see: E.L. Eliel, R.J.L. Martin and D. Nasipuri, *Org. Synth. Coll. Vol.*, **5**, 175.

For a discussion of sodium borohydride, see: EROS, 4522.

Experiment 19

Stereospecific reduction of benzoin with sodium borohydride; determination of the stereochemistry by NMR spectroscopy

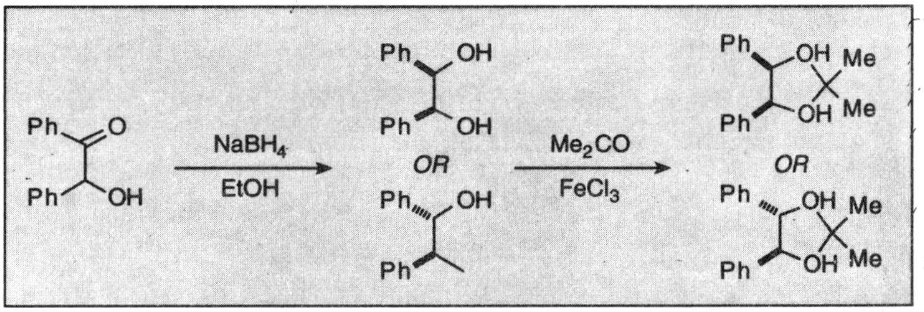

In Experiment 18 the stereoselectivity of reduction of a cyclic ketone with sodium borohydride was investigated, in which the stereochemistry was controlled by various torsional and steric effects in the transition state. The stereochemical course of ketone reductions can also be influenced by the presence of hydroxyl groups close to the carbonyl function. This experiment illustrates the stereoselective reduction of benzoin using sodium borohydride as a reducing agent, followed by the conversion of the resulting 1,2-diol into its acetonide (isopropylidene) derivative catalyzed by anhydrous iron(III) chloride, a reaction commonly used for the protection of 1,2-diols during a synthetic sequence. Nuclear magnetic resonance (NMR) spectroscopic analysis of the acetonide permits the determination of its relative stereochemistry and hence that of the diol.

Level	3
Time	2 × 3 h
Equipment	magnetic stirrer; apparatus for suction filtration, recrystallization, reflux, extraction/separation
Instruments	IR, NMR

Materials

1. Preparation of 1,2-diphenylethane-1,2-diol		
benzoin (FW 212.3)	2.00 g (9.4 mmol)	**irritant**
sodium borohydride (FW 37.8)	0.40 g (10.6 mmol)	**corrosive, flammable**
ethanol		**flammable, toxic**
light petroleum (bp 60–80°C)		**flammable**
hydrochloric acid (6 M)		**corrosive**
2. Preparation of acetonide derivative		
acetone (pure)		**flammable**
iron(III) chloride (anhydrous)	0.30 g	**corrosive, hygroscopic**
dichloromethane		**irritant, toxic**
light petroleum (bp 40–60°C)		**flammable**
potassium carbonate solution (10%)		**corrosive**

Procedure

1. Preparation of 1,2-diphenylethane-1,2-diol

Dissolve the benzoin in 20 mL of ethanol in a 100 mL Erlenmeyer flask.[1] Stir the solution magnetically, and add the sodium borohydride in small portions over 5 min using a spatula.[2] If necessary, rinse in the last traces of sodium borohydride with 5 mL of ethanol. Stir the mixture at room temperature for a further 20 min, and then cool it in an ice bath whilst adding 30 mL of water followed by 1 mL of 6 M hydrochloric acid.[3] Add a further 10 mL of water, and stir the mixture for a further 20 min. Collect the product by suction filtration,[4] and wash it thoroughly with 100 mL water. Dry the product by suction for 30 min, and record the yield. This material is sufficiently pure to be used, so set aside 1.00 g of the product to be left drying until the next period for use in the next stage. Recrystallize the remainder (*ca.* 0.50 g) from petroleum (bp 60–80°C).[5] Record the mp and IR spectrum (Nujol®) of the product after one recrystallization. Record an IR spectrum (Nujol®) of benzoin for comparison.

[1] *Warming may be necessary; solution need not be complete*

[2] ***Care! Exothermic***

[3] *Foaming may occur*

[4] *See Fig. 3.7*

[5] *Probably necessary to add a few drops of acetone for complete solution*

2. Preparation of acetonide derivative (2,2-dimethyl-4,5-diphenyl-1,3-dioxolane)

Dissolve 1.00 g of the diol in 30 mL of pure acetone, and add the anhydrous iron(III) chloride.[6] Heat the mixture under reflux with a calcium chloride guard tube for 20 min,[7] and then allow it to cool to room temperature. Pour the mixture into a 100 mL beaker containing 40 mL water, and add 10 mL potassium carbonate solution. Transfer the mixture to a 250 mL separatory funnel

[6] ***Transfer $FeCl_3$ rapidly; hygroscopic***

[7] *See Fig. 3.23(c)*

[8] *Interface may be difficult to see due to presence of iron salts*

[9] *Scratching may be necessary*

[10] *Do not delay NMR analysis; the acetonide slowly decomposes at room temperature*

and extract with 3 × 20 mL portions of dichloromethane.[8] Wash the combined organic extracts with 25 mL water, and then dry them over $MgSO_4$. Evaporate the solvent on the rotary evaporator, and purify the crude acetonide by dissolving it in 15 mL boiling petroleum (bp 40–60°C), and filtering whilst hot to remove any unreacted diol. Concentrate the filtrate to a volume of 3–5 mL, and then cool the solution in ice, whereupon the acetonide crystallizes out.[9] Collect the product by suction filtration, and wash it with a *little ice-cold* petroleum. Dry the product by suction at the filter pump for 10 min. Record the yield, mp and IR spectrum (Nujol®) of the product. Record the NMR spectrum ($CDCl_3$)[10] of your purified material for assignment of stereochemistry.

Problems

1 Discuss the NMR spectrum of the acetonide derivative; assign its stereochemistry, and hence that of the diols.

2 Discuss the mechanism and stereochemistry of the reduction of benzoin; propose a transition state for the reduction which accounts for the stereochemistry.

3 Discuss the mechanism of acetonide formation. What is the role of the $FeCl_3$?

4 Compare and contrast the IR spectra of benzoin, the diol and the acetonide, assigning peaks to all the functional groups.

Further reading

For the procedure on which this experiment is based, see: A.T. Rowland, *J. Chem. Educ.*, 1983, **60**, 1084.

For a discussion of sodium borohydride, see: EROS, 4522.

Experiment 20   *Chemoselectivity in the reduction of 3-nitroacetophenone*

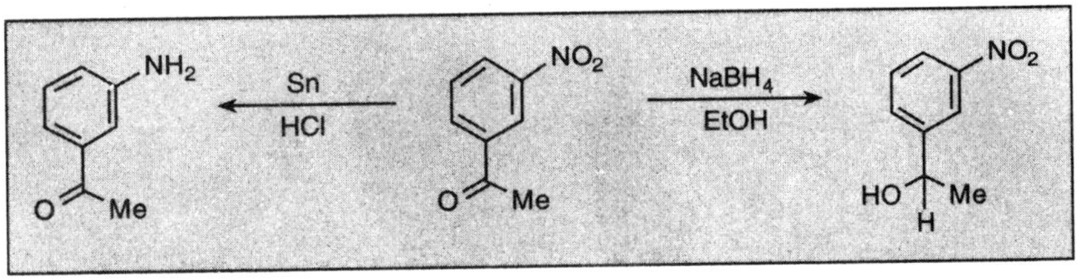

Chemoselectivity, the selective reaction at one functional group in the presence of others, is not always easy to achieve, and recourse is often made to protecting groups (*cf.* Experiment 36). However, by appropriate choice of reagent and reaction conditions, chemoselectivity can often be accomplished. This experiment, in two parts, illustrates the chemoselective reduction of 3-nitroacetophenone, a compound with two reducible groups (NO_2 and C=O). In the first part, the aromatic nitro group is reduced to an aromatic amine using tin and hydrochloric acid, a reagent commonly used for this transformation, and one that does not reduce carbonyl groups. In the second part, the ketone carbonyl is reduced using the mild hydride transfer agent, sodium borohydride.

Level	2
Time	2 × 3 h (either experiment may be carried out independently if desired)
Equipment	magnetic stirrer/hotplate: apparatus for reaction with reflux, suction filtration, recrystallization, extraction/separation
Instruments	IR

Materials

1. Reduction using tin and hydrochloric acid		
3-nitroacetophenone (FW 165.2)	1.65 g (10 mmol)	
granulated tin (FW 118.7)	3.3 g (28 mmol)	
hydrochloric acid (conc.)		**corrosive**
sodium hydroxide solution (40%)		**corrosive**
2. Reduction using sodium borohydride		
3-nitroacetophenone (FW 165.2)	1.65 g (10 mmol)	
sodium borohydride (FW 37.8)	0.45 g (12 mmol)	**corrosive, flammable**
ethanol		**flammable, toxic**
diethyl ether		**flammable, irritant**
toluene		**flammable, irritant**

Procedure

1. Reduction using tin and hydrochloric acid: 3-aminoacetophenone

Cut the tin into small pieces, and place it in a 100 mL round-bottomed flask equipped with a reflux condenser and a magnetic stirrer bar.[1] Add 1.65 g (10 mmol) 3-nitroacetophenone to the flask, followed by 24 mL water and 9 mL concentrated hydrochloric acid. Stir the mixture, and heat the flask in a boiling water bath for 1.5 h.[2] Cool the reaction mixture to room temperature, and filter it by suction.[3] Add 20 mL 40% sodium hydroxide solution to the filtrate with stirring and external cooling. Collect the resulting yellow precipitate by suction filtration,[3] and wash it thoroughly with water. Dissolve the crude product in the *minimum* volume of hot water, filter it whilst hot, and allow the filtrate to cool. Collect the crystals by suction filtration,[3] and dry them by suction.[4] Record the yield, mp, and the IR spectrum ($CHCl_3$) of your product. Record an IR spectrum of the starting nitro ketone for comparison.

[1] *See Fig. 3.24*

[2] *Record the IR of starting material during this period*

[3] *See Fig. 3.7*

[4] *May be left at this stage*

2. Reduction using sodium borohydride: 1-(3-nitrophenyl)ethanol

Dissolve 1.65 g (10 mmol) 3-nitroacetophenone in 20 mL warm ethanol in a 100 mL Erlenmeyer flask. Stir the solution magnetically, and cool the flask in an ice bath.[5] Add the sodium borohydride in small portions over 5 min, and stir the mixture at room temperature for 15 min. Add 15 mL water to the mixture, and heat it to its boiling point for 1 min. Cool the mixture to room temperature, transfer it to a 100 mL separatory funnel, and extract it with 2 × 20 mL portions of diethyl ether. Combine the ether extracts and dry them over

[5] *The ketone may form a fine precipitate at this point*

$MgSO_4$.[4] Filter off the drying agent by suction,[3] and evaporate the filtrate on the rotary evaporator. Cool the residue in ice, and scratch it until crystallization occurs.[6] Recrystallize the product from the *minimum* volume of hot toluene. Record the yield, mp, and the IR spectrum ($CHCl_3$) of your product.

Problems

1 Discuss the reaction mechanism for the reduction of a nitro group using tin and hydrochloric acid. What intermediates are involved?
2 Discuss the reduction of the ketone carbonyl with sodium borohydride.
3 What reagent(s) could be used to reduce both nitro and ketone functional groups in a single reaction?
4 Compare and contrast the IR spectra of the starting nitroketone, the aminoketone, and the nitroalcohol, assigning peaks to all the functional groups involved.

Further reading

For the procedure on which this experiment is based, see: A.G. Jones, *J. Chem. Educ.*, 1975, **52**, 668.

For further discussions of reductions using tin or sodium borohydride, see: EROS, 4888 and 4522 respectively.

Experiment 21

Reduction of diphenylacetic acid with lithium aluminium hydride

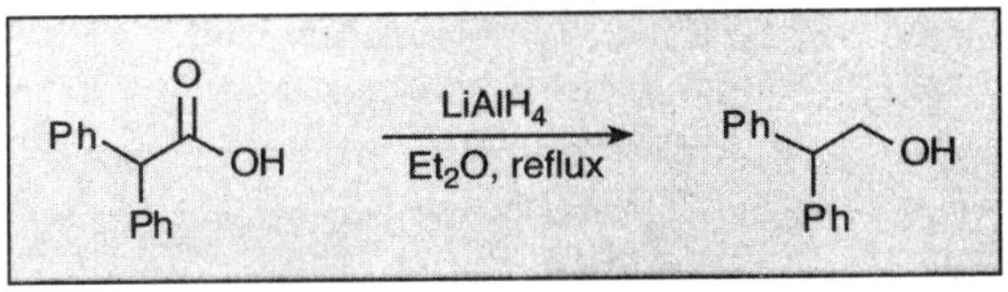

Lithium aluminium hydride, more correctly named lithium tetrahydroaluminate but almost invariably referred to by its trivial name, is an extremely powerful hydride-reducing agent which is able to reduce a wide range of functionalities. As a consequence of this greater reactivity, it is much less selective than sodium borohydride which is usually the reagent of choice if it is desired to reduce a ketone or an aldehyde to the corresponding alcohol.

Lithium aluminium hydride is prepared from the reaction of four equivalents of lithium hydride with aluminium chloride in dry diethyl ether; but high quality material is commercially available, usually taking the form of a grey powder which can inflame spontaneously in air and react extremely violently with water. All manipulations with this reagent must be carried out in rigorously dried apparatus and all reaction solvents must be anhydrous.

Any fire involving lithium aluminium hydride can only be extinguished with dry sand or a fire blanket.

Reductions are usually carried out in diethyl ether in which lithium aluminium hydride is moderately soluble, and procedures sometimes call for the use of the predissolved reagent. Frequently, however, this is not necessary and, as in the experiment described here, it is sufficient to use an ethereal suspension.

Lithium aluminium hydride finds particular application in the reduction of carboxylic acids to alcohols. As with all hydride reductions of carbonyl compounds, the key step involves transfer of hydride to the electrophilic carbonyl carbon. However, in the reduction of a carboxylic acid, the initial step is probably the formation of the salt $[RCO_2AlH_3]^- Li^+$ which then undergoes further reduction to the lithium tetra-alkoxyaluminate followed by hydrolysis to the alcohol on aqueous work-up.

Level	3
Time	3 h
Equipment	hotplate/stirrer; apparatus for reflux with protection from atmospheric moisture, extraction/separation
Instruments	IR, NMR

Materials

2,2-diphenylacetic acid (FW 212.3)	0.64 g (3 mmol)	
lithium aluminium hydride (FW 38.0)	0.39 g (10 mmol)	**flammable**

NOTE: ***great care must be taken with the disposal of lithium aluminium hydride residues, for instance residues in weighing vessels or on spatulas***

diethyl ether (both reagent grade and sodium dried)		**flammable, irritant**
light petroleum (bp 40–60°C)		**flammable**

Procedure

HOOD

All apparatus must be thoroughly dried in a hot (>120°C) oven before use. Weigh the lithium aluminium hydride into a 100 mL round-bottomed flask as rapidly as possible, and cover it with 20 mL of sodium-dried diethyl ether. Add a magnetic stirrer bar and fit the flask with a reflux condenser carrying a drying tube.[1] Weigh the 2,2-diphenylacetic acid into a 25 mL Erlenmeyer flask, dissolve it in *ca.* 10 mL of sodium-dried diethyl ether and add this solution dropwise by pipette down the condenser at such a rate that the stirred mixture refluxes gently.[2] Replace the drying tube between additions and rinse out the contents of the Erlenmeyer flask with a small amount of dry diethyl ether, adding this to the mixture as well. Reflux the mixture gently with stirring for 1 h and then allow the contents to cool. During the reflux period, prepare some 'wet' diethyl ether by shaking 50 mL of diethyl ether[3] with an equal volume of water in a separatory funnel for 5 min and retaining the upper organic layer.[4] Add *ca.* 30 mL of this wet diethyl ether dropwise to the cooled reaction mixture,[5] maintaining stirring to decompose excess hydride, but stop addition and stirring temporarily if the reaction becomes too vigorous. After addition of the wet diethyl ether, reflux the mixture for a further 10 min to

[1] *See Fig. 3.23(c)*

[2] ***If the reaction becomes too vigorous stop stirring temporarily***

[3] *Reagent grade*

[4] *Contains* ca. *7% water*

[5] ***Care!***

complete the decomposition and allow the mixture to cool once more. At this stage there should be no grey, unreacted lithium aluminium hydride remaining and the precipitate should be white. If some grey solid persists, add another 15 mL of wet diethyl ether and repeat the reflux. Transfer the mixture to a separatory funnel and slowly add 15 mL of 5% aqueous sulfuric acid, followed by thorough shaking to decompose the aluminium complex.[6] Separate the phases, collecting the upper organic phase, and re-extract the aqueous phase with a further 15 mL of diethyl ether. Dry the solution over $MgSO_4$,[7] filter and remove the solvent on the rotary evaporator to obtain your crude product which should solidify on cooling in ice. Record the yield of crude material and recrystallize it from light petroleum. Record the mp and yield of your purified product and obtain the IR ($CHCl_3$) and NMR ($CDCl_3$) spectra of both this material and the starting material.

[6] *No solid should remain*

[7] *May be left at any convenient stage*

Problems

1 Interpret and compare the IR and NMR spectra of your starting material and product, highlighting in particular the salient features of each which permit structural assignment.

2 Compare and contrast reductions with the hydride-reducing agents diborane, sodium borohydride and lithium aluminium hydride from the viewpoint of substrate and product selectivity in each instance.

3 Predict the results of the following reactions:

(i)
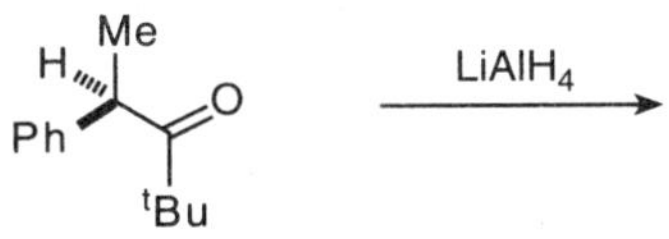

(ii)
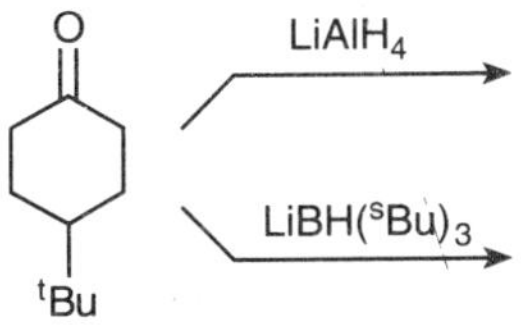

(iii)
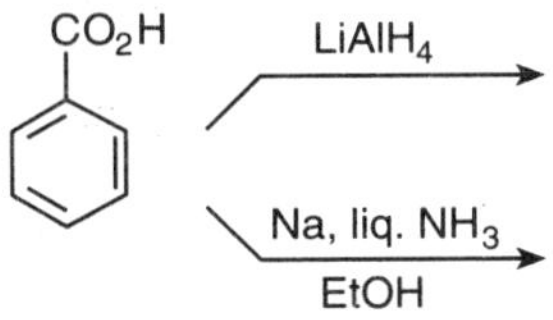

(iv)
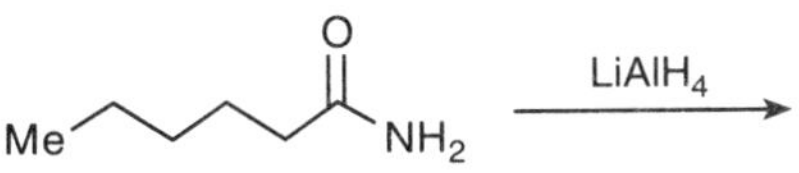

(v)
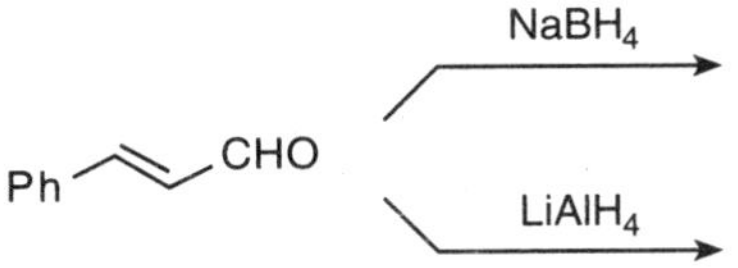

(vi)
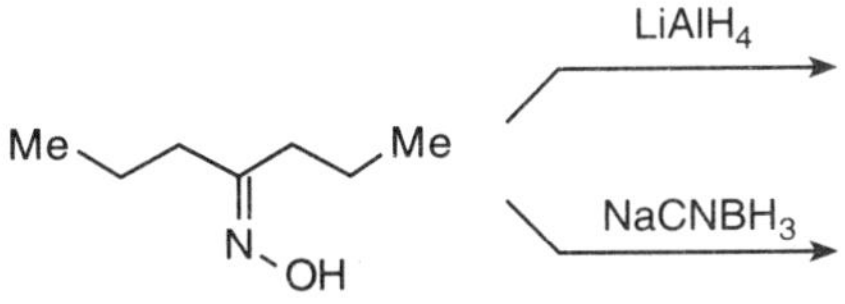

Further reading

For a discussion of the uses of lithium aluminium hydride, see: EROS, 3009.

Experiment 22

Reduction of N*-methyl cyclohexanecarboxamide with lithium aluminium hydride:* N*-methyl cyclohexylmethylamine*

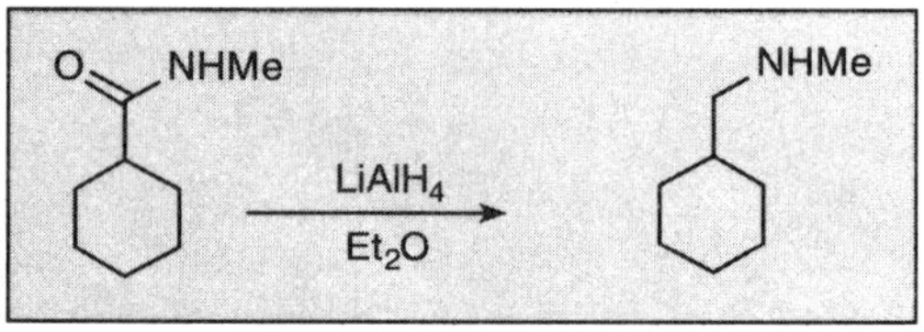

Lithium aluminium hydride reduces most polar functional groups. This experiment illustrates its use in the reduction of an amide, *N*-methyl cyclohexanecarboxamide, to an amine, *N*-methyl cyclohexylmethylamine, prepared as described in Experiment 3. The reaction is carried out under anhydrous conditions in dry diethyl ether, and the product is purified by distillation at atmospheric pressure.

Level	4
Time	2 × 3 h (with overnight reaction between)
Equipment	magnetic stirrer; apparatus for reaction with addition and reflux (3-neck flask), suction filtration, distillation (or short path distillation)
Instruments	IR, NMR

Materials

N-methyl cyclohexanecarboxamide (FW 141.2) (prepared as in Experiment 3)	2.82 g (20 mmol)	
lithium aluminium hydride (FW 38.0)	1.52 g (40 mmol)	**flammable**

NOTE: ***Great care must be taken with the disposal of lithium aluminium hydride residues, for instance residues in weighing vessels or on spatulas***

diethyl ether (anhydrous)	**flammable, irritant**
potassium carbonate (anhydrous)	**corrosive**

Procedure

HOOD

All apparatus must be thoroughly dried in a hot (>120°C) oven before use. Set up a 50 mL three-neck flask with a reflux condenser, addition funnel and magnetic stirrer bar.[1] Protect both the addition funnel and condenser with calcium chloride drying tubes, or alternatively carry out the reaction under nitrogen. Add the lithium aluminium hydride to the flask, followed by 10 mL *dry* diethyl ether.[2] Stopper the third neck of the flask, and stir the suspension. From the addition funnel, add a solution of the *N*-methyl cyclohexanecarboxamide in 15 mL *dry* diethyl ether[3] at such a rate as to maintain gentle reflux. When the addition is complete, heat the mixture under reflux for 1 h, and then allow it to stand overnight at room temperature.[4] Stir the mixture, and *cautiously* add water dropwise until the precipitated inorganic salts become granular.[5] Filter

[1] *See Fig. 3.25*

[2] *See Appendix 2*

[3] *May not be totally soluble; add 15 mL dry THF*

[4] *Can be longer*

[5] *Do not add too much water; salts become difficult to filter*

[6]See Fig. 3.7
[7]May be left at this stage
[8]See Figs 3.54, 3.58

the mixture by suction,[6] and dry the filtrate over anhydrous potassium carbonate.[7] Filter off the drying agent, evaporate the filtrate on the rotary evaporator, and distil the residue from a small (or short path[8]) distillation set at atmospheric pressure. Record the bp, yield, and the IR ($CHCl_3$) and NMR ($CDCl_3$) spectra of your product.

Problems

1 Write a reaction mechanism for the reduction of amides to amines by lithium aluminium hydride. What other reagents accomplish this transformation?
2 Suggest an alternative route to *N*-methylcyclohexylmethylamine.
3 Assign the IR and NMR spectra of your product.

Further reading

For the procedure on which this experiment is based, see: H.E. Baumgarten, F.A. Bower, and T.T. Okamoto, *J. Am. Chem. Soc.*, 1957, **79**, 3145.
For a discussion of lithium aluminium hydride, see: EROS, 3009.

Experiment 23

Reduction of butyrolactone with diïsobutylaluminium hydride and estimation by NMR of the relative proportions of 4-hydroxybutanal and its cyclic isomer, 2-hydroxytetrahydrofuran, in the product mixture

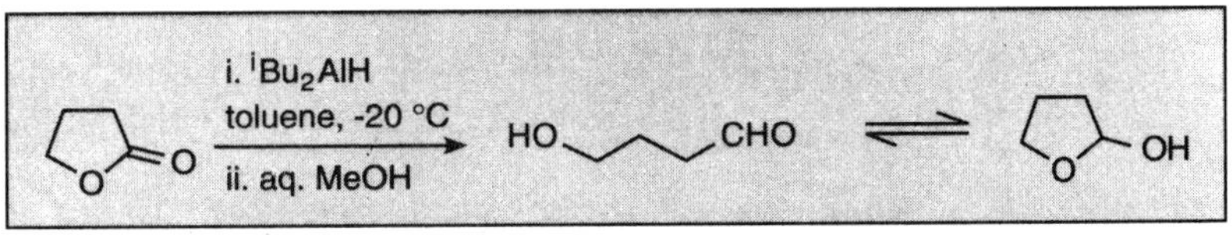

Di*iso*butylaluminium hydride (strictly named hydro*bis*(2-methylpropyl)-aluminium but usually referred to affectionately by the acronyms DIBAL or DIBAH) is an example of a hydride-reducing agent having modified activity as a consequence of its bulk. It is often used to convert esters to aldehydes and provides the chemist with a useful mid-way reagent between $LiAlH_4$, which reduces esters to the corresponding alcohols, and $NaBH_4$ which does not reduce esters at all. As with all such hydride reagents, the first step involves hydride attack at the carbonyl carbon (which, in the case of DIBAL reductions, is activated by prior coordination to the electrophilic aluminium), and formation of an aluminate salt. However, in the case of reductions with DIBAL, this intermediate is too sterically encumbered to permit a second reaction with another equivalent of DIBAL—itself a bulky reagent. Consequently, under mild conditions, the reduction stops at this stage and decomposition of the complex on work-up yields the aldehyde. Nonetheless, it must be remembered that this selectivity is simply a kinetic effect brought about by the combined steric bulk of the reagent and initial complex. DIBAL is perfectly capable of reducing a free aldehyde to the alcohol, and will also reduce esters to alcohols if care is not taken to work at low temperatures.

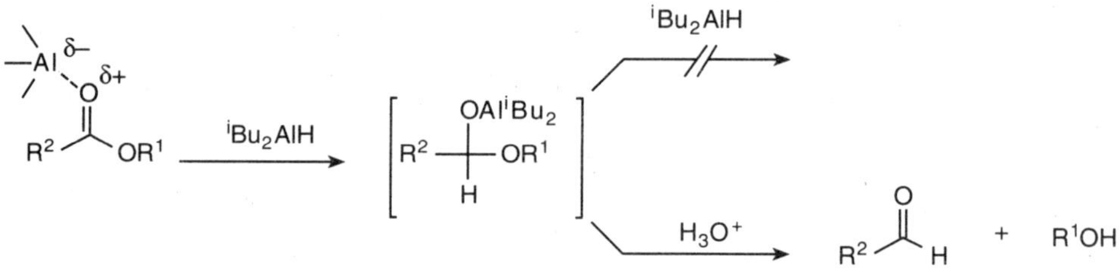

In this experiment, we are going to investigate the reduction of the cyclic ester γ-butyrolactone with DIBAL. The 4-hydroxybutanal, which is the expected product of the reaction, can also exist in equilibrium with its cyclic hemiacetal form, 2-hydroxytetrahydrofuran. This equilibrium is an illustration of the ready occurrence of many intramolecular reactions in which five- or six-membered rings are formed.

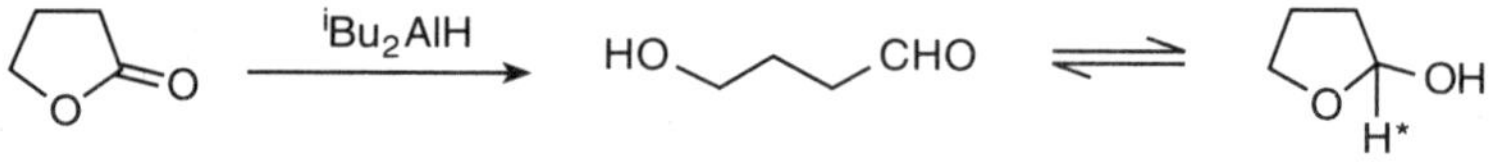

By integration of the peaks in the NMR spectrum due to the aldehyde proton of the acyclic form and the *glycosidic* or *anomeric* proton (*) of the cyclic hemiacetal, we can obtain an estimate of the relative proportions of each species in the product.

This ω-hydroxyaldehyde–cyclic hemiacetal equilibrium is of crucial importance in sugars which, although usually depicted in their cyclic forms, owe much of their reactivity to the existence of a small percentage of the open chain isomers in equilibrium. It is this equilibration which makes it impossible to specify stereochemistry at the anomeric carbon in the free sugars.

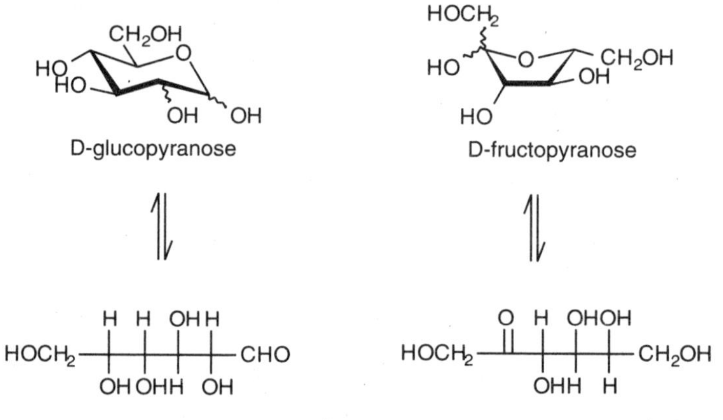

Di*iso*butylaluminium hydride is extremely air and moisture sensitive and is usually supplied as a solution in containers sealed with a septum. In the laboratory it is always transferred using a syringe and reactions are carried out under an inert atmosphere. **Extreme caution must be exercised when handling the reagent.** All manipulations must be carried out in the hood, gloves must be worn and a spare dry needle and syringe should be available in case of blockage.

Level	4
Time	reduction of γ-butyrolactone 3 h; purification and analysis 3 h
Equipment	magnetic stirrer, 2 × 20 mL syringes, needles (plus spares), solid CO_2–ethylene glycol freezing bath (–15°C); apparatus for stirring under inert atmosphere with addition by syringe, short path distillation
Instruments	IR, NMR

Materials

γ-butyrolactone (FW 86.1)	2.15 g (25 mmol)	**hygroscopic, irritant**
di*iso*butylaluminium hydride (FW 142.2; 25% solution in toluene by weight, 1.5 M)	18.4 mL (27.5 mmol) (1.1 equivalents)	**moisture sensitive, pyrophoric**
toluene (anhydrous)		**flammable, irritant**
methanol		**flammable, toxic**
diethyl ether		**flammable, irritant**

Procedure

HOOD

All apparatus must be thoroughly dried in a hot (>120°C) over before use. Weigh out the γ-butyrolactone in a pre-dried 25 mL Erlenmeyer flask, dissolve it in 15 mL of anhydrous toluene[1] and rapidly transfer it to a dry 100 mL three-necked reaction flask containing a magnetic stirrer bar and fitted with a septum, nitrogen bubbler and –100 to +30°C thermometer.[2] Rinse the Erlenmeyer flask with a further 15 mL of dry toluene and transfer these washings to the flask as well. Place the reaction flask in a solid CO_2–ethylene glycol cooling bath and stir the solution until the thermometer registers *ca.* –15°C. Add the diisobutylaluminium hydride dropwise by syringe to the stirred mixture[3] at such a rate that the temperature does not rise above –10°C and then allow the mixture to stir for 90 min at –15°C. Quench the reaction at –15°C by adding 10 mL of methanol by syringe and allow it to warm to room temperature with stirring. Add 2 mL of water and transfer the gelatinous mixture to a 1 L round-bottomed flask, rinsing several times with 5 mL portions of methanol. Remove the solvents on the rotary evaporator with gentle warming (40°C) and triturate the solid residue with five 50 mL portions of diethyl ether, warming the flask carefully in a water bath. Dry the combined extracts ($MgSO_4$),[4] filter and remove the solvent to yield the crude reduction product as an orange oil. Purify this material by short path distillation[5] at reduced pressure (32–36°C/2 mmHg, or 40–55°C/5 mmHg, or 80–95°C/20 mmHg). Record the yield and obtain the IR (film) and NMR ($CDCl_3$) spectra of your product.

[1] *See Appendix 2*

[2] *See Fig. 3.22*

[3] *See Fig. 3.15*

[4] *May be left at this stage*

[5] *See Fig. 3.54*

Problems

1 Measure the integration of the peaks due to the anomeric proton of 2-hydroxytetrahydrofuran (*ca.* δ5.6) and the aldehydic proton of 4-hydroxybutanal (*ca.* δ9.7) and estimate the relative abundance of these species in your product. The spectrum is not 'first order' at 60 MHz; what are the reasons for this?

2 What absorptions in the IR of your material support the presence of both species? Are you able to detect the presence of any residual γ-butyrolactone in the IR spectrum? Explain why δ-lactones show a carbonyl absorption at roughly the same frequency as acyclic esters but γ-lactones absorb at higher frequency.

3 List the following ω-hydroxyaldehydes in order of decreasing percentage of cyclic hemiacetal in the equilibrium mixture and explain your reasoning.

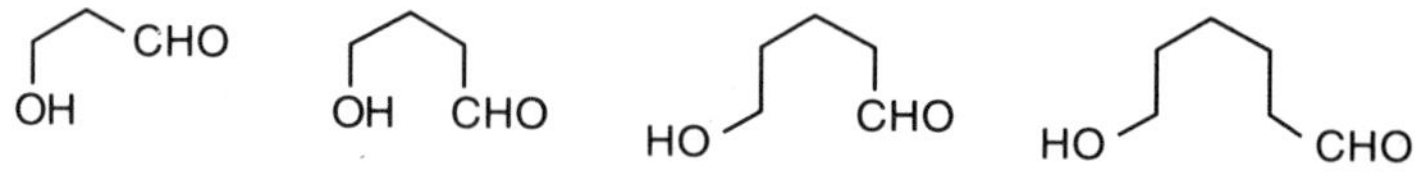

4 Complete the following reaction sequences:

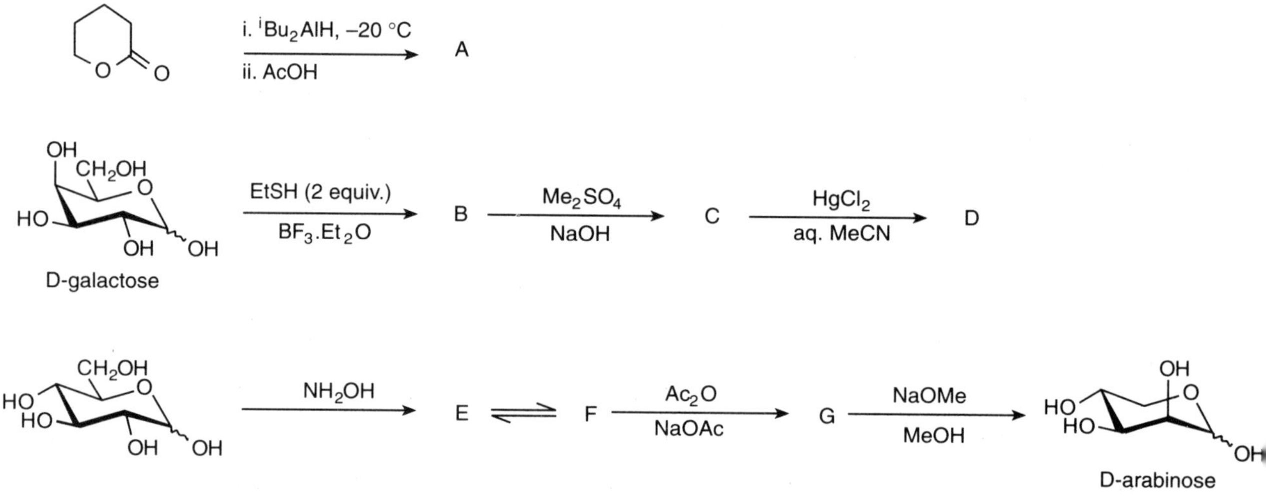

5 Suggest alternative syntheses of 4-hydroxybutanal from commercially available starting materials.

Further reading

For a discussion of the reactivity of diisobutylaluminium hydride, see: EROS, 1908.

Reduction of aldehyde or ketone carbonyl groups to methylene groups

Although not as common as the reduction to an alcohol, the *complete* reduction of an aldehyde or ketone carbonyl group (C=O) to the corresponding methylene (CH_2) compound is sometimes required. There are four general ways of achieving this transformation.

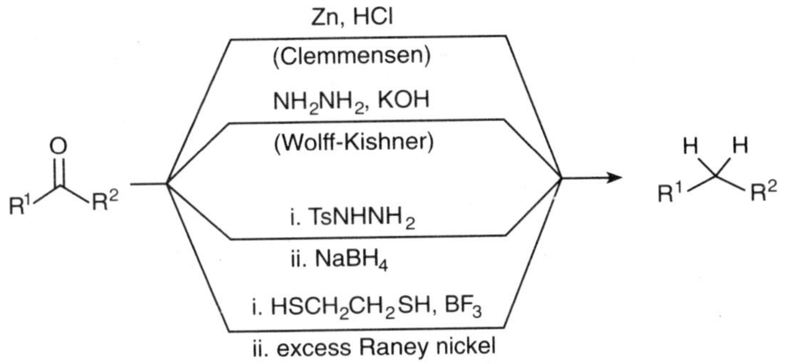

The Clemmensen and Wolff–Kishner reductions are the classic methods of effecting the transformation; the methods are complementary, one involving acidic and the other basic conditions. In the Clemmensen reduction a carbonyl compound is reduced to the corresponding methylene derivative using amalgamated zinc and hydrochloric acid. The conversion is most efficient for aromatic ketones but is unsuitable for α,β-unsaturated ketones when reduction of the double bond is usually unavoidable. High molecular weight substrates tend to react sluggishly and modified conditions are required using gaseous hydrogen chloride dissolved in a high boiling solvent. Of course, the reaction is inapplicable to acid-sensitive substrates, and the toxicity associated with the mercury salts needed to form the zinc amalgam render it unsuitable for general use. Consequently, we only include an example of the Wolff–Kishner reaction.

Experiment 24 *Wolff–Kishner reduction of propiophenone to* **n***-propylbenzene*

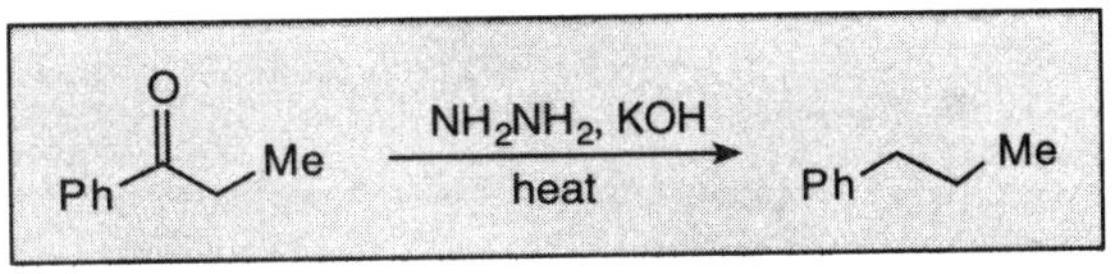

The Wolff–Kishner reduction is an excellent method for the reduction of the carbonyl group of aldehydes and ketones to a CH_2 group. However, as originally described, the method involved heating the pre-formed hydrazone or semicarbazone derivative of the carbonyl compound with sodium ethoxide in a sealed vessel at 200°C. Nowadays it is more convenient to use the Huang-Minlon modification, which involves heating a mixture of the carbonyl compound, hydrazine hydrate and potassium hydroxide in a high boiling solvent such as diethylene glycol or triethylene glycol. Despite the elevated temperatures this method gives excellent yields, although if the high temperature presents real problems, then a further modification of treating the pre-formed hydrazone with potassium *t*-butoxide in dimethyl sulfoxide or toluene may be used. This experiment illustrates the Huang–Minlon modification in the reduction of propiophenone to *n*-propylbenzene.

Level	2
Time	2 × 3 h
Equipment	apparatus for reflux, extraction/separation, distillation (or short path distillation)
Instruments	IR

Materials

propiophenone (FW 134.2)	6.7 mL, 6.7 g (50 mmol)	
triethylene glycol	50 mL	**irritant**
potassium hydroxide (FW 56.1)	6.7 g	**corrosive**
hydrazine hydrate (85%) (FW 32.1)	5 mL	**cancer suspect agent, corrosive, toxic**
diethyl ether		**flammable, irritant**
hydrochloric acid (6 M)		**corrosive**

Procedure

HOOD

Place the propiophenone, triethylene glycol and the potassium hydroxide in a 100 mL round-bottomed flask. Add the hydrazine hydrate, a few boiling stones, and fit a reflux condenser. Heat the mixture under reflux[1] for 45 min. Remove the condenser, equip the flask for distillation,[2] and distil off the low boiling material (mainly water) until the temperature of the liquid rises to 175–180°C. Re-fit the reflux condenser, and heat the mixture under reflux for a further 1 h. Combine the reaction mixture and the aqueous distillate in a separatory funnel, and extract the mixture with 2 × 20 mL portions of diethyl ether. Combine the ether extracts, and wash them with 2 × 10 mL dilute hydrochloric acid (6 M), and with 2 × 20 mL water. Dry the ether solution over $MgSO_4$,[3] filter off the drying agent, and evaporate the filtrate on the rotary evaporator. Transfer the residue to a small distillation set, and distil it at atmospheric pressure. Record the bp, yield and the IR spectrum (film) of your product. Record an IR spectrum of propiophenone for comparison.

[1] *See Fig. 3.23(a)*

[2] *See Fig. 3.48*

[3] *May be left at this stage*

Problems

1 Write a reaction mechanism for the formation of a hydrazone from a ketone.

2 Write a reaction mechanism for the Wolff–Kishner reaction (hydrazone to methylene compound).

3 What other methods are available for the transformation of C=O to CH_2?

4 Compare and contrast the IR spectra of propiophenone and *n*-propylbenzene.

Further reading

For the original references on this modification, see: Huang-Minlon, *J. Am. Chem. Soc.*, 1946, **68**, 2487; 1949, **71**, 3301.

Catalytic hydrogenation

Catalytic hydrogenation involves the reduction of multiple-bonded functional groups by the addition of molecular hydrogen gas in the presence of a transition-metal catalyst. Although it requires some special apparatus (Chapter 2), the method is extremely useful. The catalyst is usually based on a transition metal which is finely divided and often supported on powdered support such as charcoal or alumina, but is insoluble in the reaction medium (*heterogeneous catalysis*). Some catalysts, however, particularly those possessing lipophilic ligands round the metal, are soluble in organic solvents (*homogeneous catalysis*).

Experiment 25 — *Preparation of Adams' catalyst and the heterogeneous hydrogenation of cholesterol*

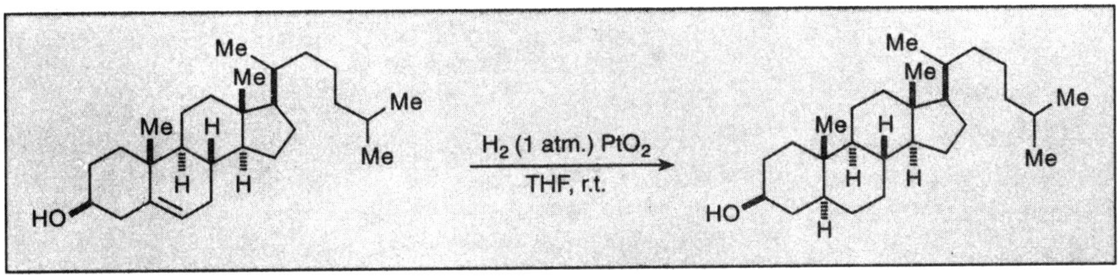

Hydrogenation of unsaturated groups such as alkenes, alkynes and nitriles, as well as nitro and carbonyl groups, can often be conveniently carried out by shaking a solution of the substrate in an inert solvent with hydrogen in the presence of a finely divided transition-metal catalyst. The activity of catalysts towards hydrogenation increases in the order Ru, Ni, Pt, Rh, Pd, although palladium catalysts sometimes promote hydrogen migration within the molecule and are to be avoided if site-specific deuteration is desired. The rate of heterogeneous hydrogenation is also dependent upon the degree of substitution of the unsaturated moiety (although not as sensitive to steric factors as homogeneous hydrogenation, see Experiment 26) and tetrasubstituted alkenes are very resistant to hydrogenation.

The catalyst used in the experiment described here is platinum(IV) oxide monohydrate, known commonly as Adams' catalyst.

Care should be taken when filtering not to suck air through the dry catalyst as it is pyrophoric. This is especially important when working-up hydrogenation mixtures when organic solvents are present. Air/hydrogen mixtures will inflame spontaneously in the presence of the dry catalyst and so the reaction flask must be first evacuated before introduction of hydrogen. Remember that hydrogen is potentially explosive (flammability limits 4–74% by volume in air). No naked flames!

Level	2
Time	3 h
Equipment	magnetic stirrer, porcelain crucible, hydrogenation burette

Materials

1. Preparation of Adams' catalyst		
hydrogen hexachloroplatinate (chloroplatinic acid)	0.40 g	**irritant, toxic**
sodium nitrate	4.0 g	**irritant, oxidizer**
2. Hydrogenation of cholesterol		
Adams' catalyst	0.1 g	**pyrophoric**
cholesterol (FW 386.7)	3.87 g (10 mmol)	
tetrahydrofuran		**flammable**
glacial ethanoic acid		**corrosive**
bromine water		**corrosive**

Procedure

HOOD

1. Preparation of Adams' catalyst

Dissolve the hydrogen hexachloroplatinate in 5 mL of water in the crucible, add the sodium nitrate and evaporate the mixture to dryness over a microburner, stirring with a glass rod. Heat the solid mass until it is molten and brown fumes of nitrogen dioxide are evolved, and continue heating strongly for 20 min.[1] Allow the melt to cool, add 10 mL of distilled water to the solid residue and bring it to the boil. After allowing the mixture to cool and settle, remove the supernatant and then wash the brown residue three times with 10 mL of distilled water by decantation. Finally, suspend the precipitate in distilled water, filter with suction[2] using a glass sinter funnel and wash with water until the precipitate starts to become colloidal. *At all times during the washing do not allow the residue to become totally dry.* Remove the excess water from the precipitate *without permitting it to become totally dry* and store the catalyst in a stoppered vial.

[1] *Commence setting up the hydrogenation experiment*

[2] *See Fig. 3.7*

FIRE HAZARD
No naked flames!

2. Hydrogenation of cholesterol

Dissolve the cholesterol in the 30 mL of tetrahydrofuran containing 4 drops of ethanoic acid in a 100 mL hydrogenation flask, add 0.1 g of Adams' catalyst and a magnetic stirrer bar. Attach the flask to the hydrogenation apparatus,[3] evacuate it using a water aspirator and introduce hydrogen. Repeat this evacuation/filling procedure three more times and finally charge the system with 1 atmosphere of hydrogen. Stir the mixture until the uptake of hydrogen ceases (this is rapid and should be complete in less than 1 h but if not, the hydrogenation can be left overnight) and then remove the catalyst by filtration with suction, washing the residue with 10 mL of tetrahydrofuran but without

[3] *See Fig. 2.32*

[4]*Pyrophoric when dry! See instructor for disposal details*

drawing air through the dry catalyst.[4] Reduce the volume of the filtrate to 10 mL on the rotary evaporator and cool in an ice bath. If crystals do not form, even after scratching, reduce the volume further to 5 mL and repeat the cooling–scratching procedure. Filter off the crystals with suction and record the yield and mp. If the mp is not sharp and further purification is necessary the product can be recrystallized from aqueous ethanol. Compare the behaviour of tetrahydrofuran solutions of the starting material and your reduced product toward bromine water.

Problems

1 Predict the major products from the following reactions:

(a)

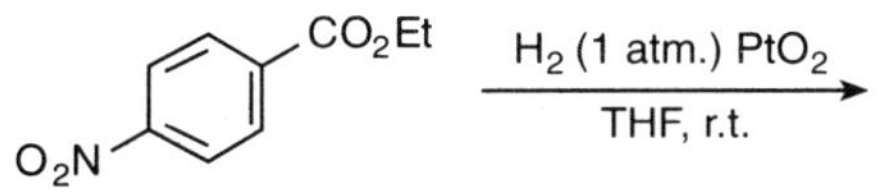

(b)

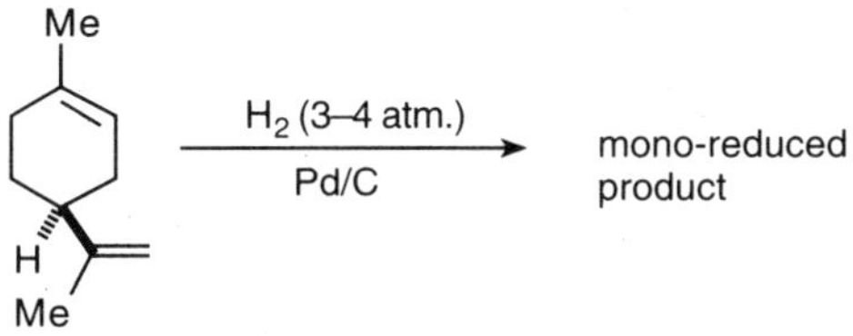

(c)

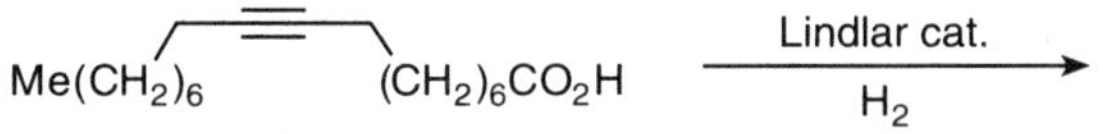

(d)

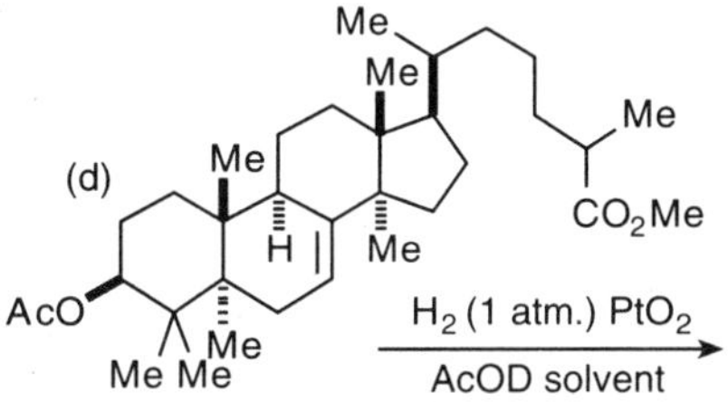

2 Despite the fact that the enthalpy of hydrogenation (ΔH) of ethene is $-137\,kJ\,mol^{-1}$, a mixture of ethene and hydrogen is indefinitely stable in the absence of a catalyst. Explain why this is so.

3 List other reagents capable of converting alkenes into alkanes.

4 From the bond energies given, calculate the enthalpy of hydrogenation of *E*-butene.

$$CH_3CH{=}CHCH_3 \rightarrow CH_3CH_2CH_2CH_3$$

C–H	$410\,kJ\,mol^{-1}$	C–C $339\,kJ\,mol^{-1}$
H–H	$431\,kJ\,mol^{-1}$	C=C $607\,kJ\,mol^{-1}$

Further reading

For a discussion of hydrogenation, see: P.N. Rylander, *Hydrogenation Methods*, Academic Press, London, 1985.

Experiment 26 — *Preparation of Wilkinson's catalyst and its use in the selective homogeneous reduction of carvone to 7,8-dihydrocarvone*

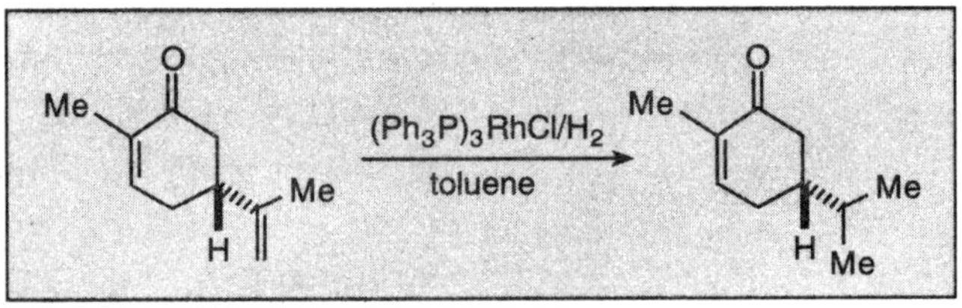

One of the most widely used homogeneous hydrogenation catalysts, *tris*(Triphenylphosphine)rhodium(I) chloride is often known as Wilkinson's catalyst after its discoverer Geoffrey Wilkinson (1921–1996). For a discussion of Wilkinson's other major contribution to chemistry see Experiment 58. Alkenes and alkynes may be reduced in the presence of other functionalities such as carbonyl, nitro and hydroxy groups and nitriles. Homogeneous catalysts are much more sensitive towards steric factors than their heterogeneous counterparts as the rate of complexation of the substrate with the transition-metal centre depends heavily upon accessibility of the point of ligation. In the case of carvone, it is the exocyclic double bond which is more readily reduced, and observation of the rate of hydrogen uptake permits the reaction to be stopped at the dihydrocarvone stage. The apparatus for quantitative measurement of hydrogen uptake and the correct procedure for its use is described in Chapter 2. The catalyst is available commercially but its preparation is straightforward and is described in the first part of the procedure.

Remember that hydrogen is potentially explosive (flammability limits 4–74% by volume in air) and there must be no naked flames in the vicinity of the experiment.

Level	3
Time	preparation of Wilkinson's catalyst 3 h; reduction of carvone 3 h; purification and analysis 3 h
Equipment	magnetic stirrer; apparatus for reflux under nitrogen, hydrogenation burette, short path distillation (optional)
Instruments	UV, IR, NMR, polarimeter (optional)

Materials

1. Preparation of Wilkinson's catalyst

triphenylphosphine (FW 262.3)	0.52 g (2 mmol)	**irritant**
rhodium(III) chloride trihydrate (FW 263.3)	0.08 g (0.3 mmol)	**hygroscopic**
ethanol		**flammable, toxic**

Continued

Box cont.

2. Selective reduction of carvone		
Wilkinson's catalyst	0.20 g	
R-(−)-carvone (FW 150.2)	1.50 g (10 mmol)	
sodium-dried toluene		**flammable, irritant**
diethyl ether		**flammable, irritant**
ethanol		**flammable, toxic**
chromatographic grade silica	20 g	**irritant dust**

Procedure

1. Preparation of Wilkinson's catalyst

Dissolve the triphenylphosphine in 20 mL of hot ethanol in a 100 mL three-necked flask and bubble nitrogen through the solution for 10 min. Meanwhile, dissolve the rhodium(III) chloride trihydrate in 4 mL of ethanol in a test tube and bubble nitrogen through this until the triphenylphosphine solution has been degassed. Add the solution in the test tube to the contents of the flask and rinse with a further 1 mL of ethanol, adding this to the flask. Set up the apparatus for reflux under nitrogen,[1] flush out the apparatus with nitrogen for 5 min and the reflux the mixture for 90 min. (During the reflux period obtain the UV (MeOH), IR (film) and NMR ($CDCl_3$) spectra of a sample of carvone for comparison with your reduced product.) After this period of time, allow the mixture to cool and filter off the crystalline precipitate with suction using a glass sinter funnel.[2] Record your yield and store the catalyst in a screw-cap vial from which the air has been displaced by nitrogen. If you have not obtained sufficient material for the second step the filtrate may be refluxed for a further period of time to obtain a second crop of crystals. However, if this is necessary it must be carried out immediately as the solution is not stable for extended periods.

[1]*See Fig. 3.23(b)*

[2]*See Fig. 3.7. Expose catalyst to air as briefly as is necessary to dry it*

2. Selective reduction of carvone

FIRE HAZARD
No naked flames!

Degas 35 mL of dry toluene by bubbling nitrogen through it for 10 min. In the meantime, weigh the carvone and 0.2 g of the Wilkinson's catalyst into a hydrogenation flask containing a magnetic stirrer bar. Add the toluene and bubble nitrogen through the mixture for a further 5 min. Attach the flask to the gas burette and evacuate the flask.[3] Flush out the system totally with hydrogen by repeated evacuation and filling (at least four times). The more care you take at this stage, the faster will be the rate of hydrogenation. Fill the apparatus with hydrogen, commence stirring and follow the uptake with time.[4] Stop the reaction when the theoretical volume has been reached (or possibly slightly exceeded due to leakage) and the reaction rate appears to plateau. Filter the solution through the silica contained in a sinter funnel and wash the residual silica with 100 mL of diethyl ether.[5] Remove the solvent on the rotary evaporator with moderate heating (*ca.* 40°C)[6] and distil the product in a short path distillation apparatus[7] under reduced pressure using a water

[3]***Air/hydrogen mixtures may ignite on the catalyst***

[4]*Plot a graph of volume against time*

[5]*Retain the residues for recovery of the rhodium*
[6]*7,8-dihydrocarvone is volatile*
[7]*See Fig. 3.54*

aspirator, collecting the fraction boiling at a bath temperature of 90–110°C. Record the yield and obtain the UV (MeOH), IR (film) and NMR spectra ($CDCl_3$) of your material. If sufficient time is available, record the specific rotation of your product (*ca.* 25 mg in 10 mL of ethanol).

Problems

1 Assign the spectra of the starting material and your reduced product. On the basis of the spectroscopic evidence justify the formulation of the reduced material as 7,8-dihydrocarvone. Highlight the features of each spectrum which support this structural assignment.
2 Discuss the means of selectively carrying out the reduction of the alternative endocyclic double bond.
3 Discuss the '18 electron rule' with regard to transition-metal complexes and show how Wilkinson's catalyst is an exception to this general rule.
4 Present a scheme showing the catalytic cycle for the reduction of an alkene using Wilkinson's catalyst. Pay particular attention to the number of valence electrons associated with the rhodium at each step of the cycle.

Further reading

For an introduction to and general discussion of the field of transition-metal complexes, see: S.G. Davies, *Organotransition Metal Chemistry: Applications to Organic Synthesis*, Pergamon, Oxford, 1982.

For a discussion of Wilkinson's catalyst, see: EROS, 1253.

Dissolving metal reduction

Dissolving metal reductions are usually used in the reduction of conjugated C=C bonds such as α,β-unsaturated carbonyl compounds and aromatic rings. The reaction involves the transfer of an electron from the metal to the substrate to give a radical anion. Since the reaction is carried out in the presence of a proton donor, the radical anion is protonated to give a radical, which accepts a second electron, furnishing an anion' which is then protonated to result in the overall addition of two hydrogens to the substrate, e.g.

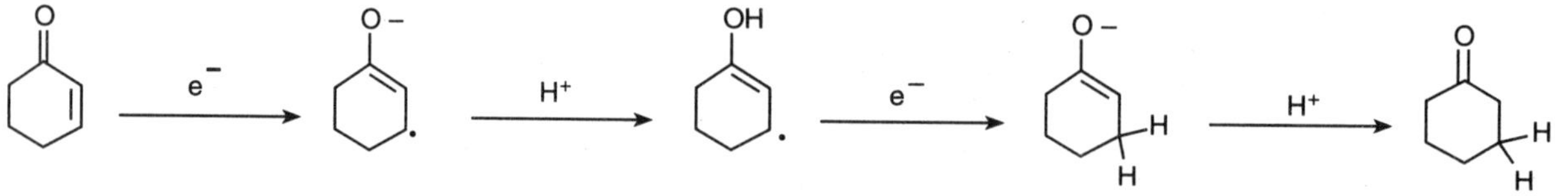

The following experiment illustrates the dissolving metal reduction of the aromatic ring of 1,2-dimethylbenzene, and Experiment 47 illustrates a variant of the enone reduction above, in which the final protonation step is replaced by an alkylation.

Experiment 27

Birch reduction of 1,2-dimethylbenzene (o-xylene): 1,2-dimethyl-1,4-cyclohexadiene

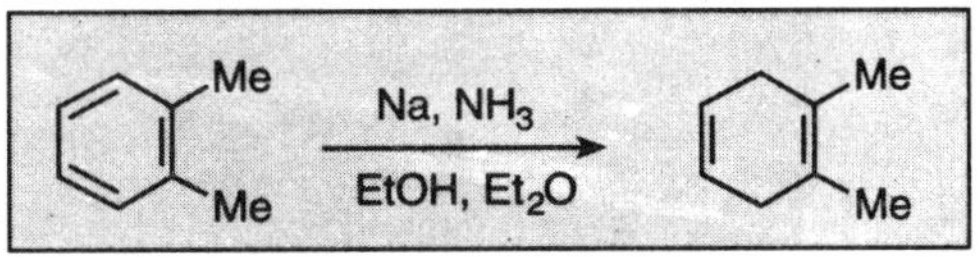

One of the consequences of aromatic stabilization is that benzene rings are substantially more resistant to catalytic hydrogenation than alkenes (Experiments 25 and 26) or alkynes. Vigorous conditions (high temperatures, high pressures of hydrogen) are required, and the reduction cannot be stopped at the intermediate cyclohexadiene or cyclohexene stage, since these are hydrogenated more readily than the starting aromatic compound itself. However, aromatic rings can be readily reduced by solutions of alkali metals in liquid ammonia, a source of solvated electrons, in the presence of a proton source such as an alcohol to give 1,4-cyclohexadienes. This reduction, usually known as the Birch reduction, has proven extremely useful in organic chemistry, because in one single, simple step it bridges the gap between aromatic and aliphatic chemistry. This experiment illustrates the Birch reduction of 1,2-dimethylbenzene (*o*-xylene) using sodium in liquid ammonia in the presence of ethanol. The product is purified by vacuum distillation, and can, if desired, be analyzed by GC. If the use of sodium is considered too dangerous, lithium may be used instead—consult your instructor.

Level	4
Time	2 × 3 h (to be carried out on two consecutive days)
Equipment	magnetic stirrer; apparatus for reaction in liquid ammonia, short path distillation
Instruments	IR, NMR, GC (optional)

Materials

liquid ammonia (see handling notes pp. 66–67)	*ca.* 10 mL	**corrosive, toxic**
1,2-dimethylbenzene (*o*-xylene) (FW 106.2)	1.18 mL (10 mmol)	**flammable, irritant**
diethyl ether (anhydrous)		**flammable, irritant**
absolute ethanol (FW 46.1)	1.95 mL (33 mmol)	**flammable, toxic**
sodium metal (FW 23.0)	0.69 g (30 mmol)	**flammable**

Procedure

HOOD

Following the procedure described on pp. 104–105, set up a 25 mL three-neck flask with a magnetic stirrer bar, small addition funnel, gas inlet and a low temperature condenser.[1] Cool the flask in an acetone–solid CO_2 bath, and con-

[1] *See Fig. 3.30*

dense about 10 mL of liquid ammonia. Replace the gas inlet with a stopper, and add 2 mL *dry* diethyl ether,[2] the absolute ethanol[2] and the *o*-xylene (both measured *accurately*) in that order from the addition funnel. Cut up the sodium into small pieces,[3] and slowly add it to the mixture through the third neck of the flask by quickly removing the stopper. The addition should take about 30–60 min. Remove the cooling bath, and allow the ammonia to evaporate overnight.[4] At the start of the next period, **cautiously** add 5 mL water to the flask,[5] and stir the mixture until all the inorganic material dissolves. Transfer the mixture to a separatory funnel with the aid of 5 mL of diethyl ether, and separate the layers. Wash the upper organic layer with 3 × 5 mL of water, and then dry it over $MgSO_4$.[6] Filter off the drying agent by suction,[7] and evaporate the filtrate on the rotary evaporator. Distil the residue under reduced pressure (water aspirator, *ca.* 50 mmHg) in a short path distillation apparatus.[8] Record the bp, yield and the IR (film) and NMR ($CDCl_3$) spectra of your product.

[2] *See Appendix 2*

[3] ***Caution***

[4] *May be left at this stage*

[5] ***Care!***

[6] *May be left at this stage*

[7] *See Fig. 3.7*

[8] *See Fig. 3.54*

If required, analyze the product by GC and hence, by comparing with a sample of *o*-xylene, determine the amount of unreacted aromatic compound present.

Problems

1 Write a reaction mechanism for the Birch reduction of *o*-xylene, clearly identifying each of the steps involved. Why is only the 1,4-cyclohexadiene formed?

2 What would be the products of the Birch reduction of: (i) methoxybenzene (anisole), (ii) naphthalene, and (iii) 1,2,3,4,-tetrahydronaphthalene?

Further reading

For the procedure on which this experiment is based, see: L.A. Paquette and J.H. Barrett, *Org. Synth. Coll. Vol.*, **5**, 467.

Biological reduction

Experiment 28

Reduction of ethyl 3-oxobutanoate using baker's yeast; asymmetric synthesis of (S)-ethyl 3-hydroxybutanoate

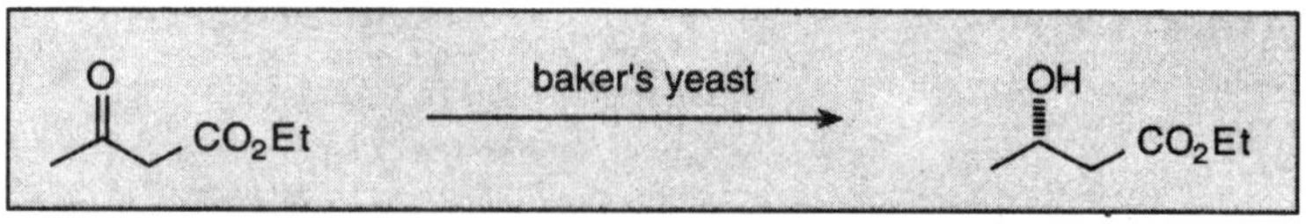

Given the central role played by the carbonyl group in much of organic chemistry, it is not surprising that asymmetric reactions of the carbonyl group have been widely studied. The two faces of an unsymmetrical ketone are *enantiotopic*, and therefore reduction with a chiral reducing agent or using a chiral catalyst can give rise to asymmetric induction and the stereoselective formation of one of the possible enantiomeric alcohol products. The development of efficient methods for the asymmetric reduction of ketones has been a major goal in recent years, and 'chiral versions' of the common boron or aluminium-based hydride reducing agents have been widely studied, as has hydrogenation over chiral catalysts. However, another approach is to use nature's catalysts, i.e. enzymes, to carry out asymmetric transformations on organic molecules. This 'biotransformation' approach has been widely investigated, and a number of efficient procedures have been developed. Either pure (or partially purified) enzymes or whole organisms can be used to effect biotransformation. This experiment uses the latter approach and illustrates the asymmetric reduction of a ketone using baker's yeast. Such reductions were amongst the earliest biotransformations reported. The ketone, ethyl 3-oxobutanoate (ethyl acetoacetate), is reduced to the corresponding alcohol with good enantioselectivity. Both baker's yeast, and the other essential ingredient, sucrose (sugar), can be obtained from your local supermarket.

Level	4
Time	3 h to set up experiment, 1 h on the next day, and then a week later 3 h to isolate product
Equipment	magnetic stirrer, constant temperature bath (30°C); apparatus for extraction/separation, short path distillation, TLC
Instruments	IR, NMR, polarimeter

Materials		
sucrose (sugar)	25 g	
baker's yeast (supermarket type)	20 g	
(or Sigma type II)	4 g	
ethyl 3-oxobutanoate (FW 130.1)	2 g (15 mmol)	**irritant**
(ethyl acetoacetate)		
sodium chloride		
ethyl acetate		**flammable, irritant**
chloroform		**cancer suspect agent, toxic**

Procedure

Equip a three-neck 500 mL round-bottomed flask with a thermometer, bubbler and magnetic stirrer bar. The third neck should be stoppered. Add 80 mL tap water to the flask, followed by 15 g sucrose and *half* (10 g of supermarket variety or 2 g of Sigma type II) of the yeast. Stir the mixture for 1 h at 30°C, during which time fermentation starts and CO_2 is evolved through the bubbler. Add *half* of the ethyl 3-oxobutanoate dropwise using a Pasteur pipette; stir the mixture at about 30°C for 24 h. The next day add the remaining sucrose dissolved in 50 mL warm (*ca.* 40°C) tap water and remaining yeast, stir the mixture for 1 h, and then add the remaining ethyl 3-oxobutanoate; continue to stir the mixture. The reaction takes a further 24–72 h to complete, and it is essential that all the starting ketone is consumed before the reaction terminates. The reaction can be followed by TLC using silica gel plates, dichloromethane as eluent, and staining the plates with vanillin solution.[1]

[1]*See p. 170*

Add 4 g Celite® to the suspension and filter the mixture through a sintered glass funnel, and wash the pad thoroughly with 20 mL water. Saturate the filtrate with solid sodium chloride, and then extract the aqueous mixture with 5 × 25 mL portions of ethyl acetate. Combine the extracts, and dry them over anhydrous $MgSO_4$. Filter off the drying agent, and evaporate the filtrate on the rotary evaporator to give a pale yellow oil. Distil the crude produce under reduced pressure using a short path distillation apparatus,[2] and collect the product (*ca.* 55–70°C at 10–12 mmHg). Record the yield, and IR and NMR spectra of the product. Make up a solution of the product in chloroform of known concentration (*ca.* 1.0 g per 100 mL or equivalent) and record the optical rotation. Hence calculate the specific rotation[3] and enantiomeric purity of your product, given that enantiomerically pure (*S*)-ethyl 3-hydroxybutanoate has $[\alpha]_D^{25} + 43.5$ ($c = 1$, $CHCl_3$).

[2]*See Fig. 3.54*

[3]*See pp. 220–223*

Problems

1 Suggest other reagents for the chemoselective reduction of a ketone in the presence of an ester.

2 The stereochemistry of yeast reductions can be predicted by Prelog's rule (S = small group, L = large group):

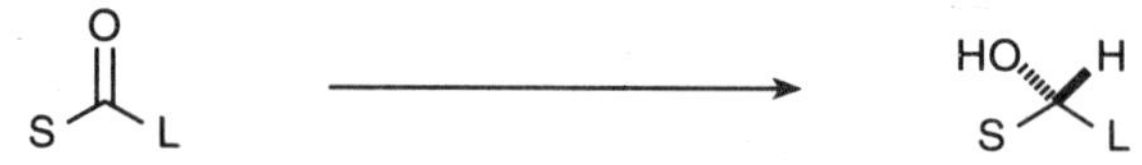

Show that the reduction of ethyl 3-oxobutanoate obeys this rule.

3 Assign the NMR and IR spectra of your product.

4 Suggest methods (other than rotation) for determining the enantiomeric purity of your product.

Further reading

For the procedure on which this experiment is based, see: D. Seebach, M.A. Sutter, R.H. Weber and M.F. Züger, *Org. Synth. Coll. Vol.*, **7**, 215.

The procedure used here is adapted from: S.M. Roberts (ed) *Preparative Biotransformations*, John Wiley, Chichester, 1992, p. 2:1.1.

For other uses of yeast in organic synthesis, see: R. Csuk and B.I. Glänzer, *Chem. Rev.*, 1991, **91**, 49.

7.5 Oxidation

Oxidation of organic molecules is complementary to, and equally as important as, their reduction. Oxidation is essentially the reverse of reduction and can involve the removal of two hydrogens, the addition of oxygen, or the replacement of hydrogen by a heteroatom functional group. Although various organic molecules can be oxidized, the reaction that is most frequently encountered is the oxidation of alcohols to carbonyl compounds.

Other experiments which involve an oxidation step are Experiments 72 and 83.

Oxidation of alcohols

The conversion of an alcohol into a carbonyl compound is a frequently encountered process in organic synthesis, and many reagents have been developed for this very important transformation. Primary alcohols are oxidized first to aldehydes, but, since aldehydes are themselves easily oxidized, the oxidation of primary alcohols often continues to the carboxylic acid stage. However, by appropriate choice of reagent, the oxidation can be controlled and stopped at the aldehyde stage (Experiments 31–33). Secondary alcohols are readily oxidized to ketones (Experiments 29 and 30), but tertiary alcohols are not usually oxidized, although under acidic oxidizing conditions, they may dehydrate to alkenes (*cf.* Experiment 36) which may themselves be subject to oxidation.

Many laboratory oxidizing agents are inorganic compounds of metals with high oxidation potentials such as Cr(VI), Mn(VII), Mn(IV), Ag(I), or Ag(II). Of these, oxidants based on Cr(VI) are the most common. One particularly useful organic reagent for the oxidation of alcohols is dimethyl sulfoxide (DMSO), used in combination with an activating agent such as dicyclohexyl carbodiimide (DCC) (Pfitzner–Moffatt oxidation) or oxalyl chloride (Swern oxidation).

Alcohols, particularly ethanol, can also be oxidized biologically. In mammalian systems, ingested ethanol is oxidized primarily in the liver by an enzyme called alcohol dehydrogenase. Overindulgence in drinking alcohol eventually overloads the system and leads to liver damage.

The experiments which follow illustrate the use of the most important and commonly employed reagents for the oxidation of primary and secondary alcohols.

Experiment 29

Oxidation of 2-methylcyclohexanol to 2-methylcyclohexanone using aqueous chromic acid

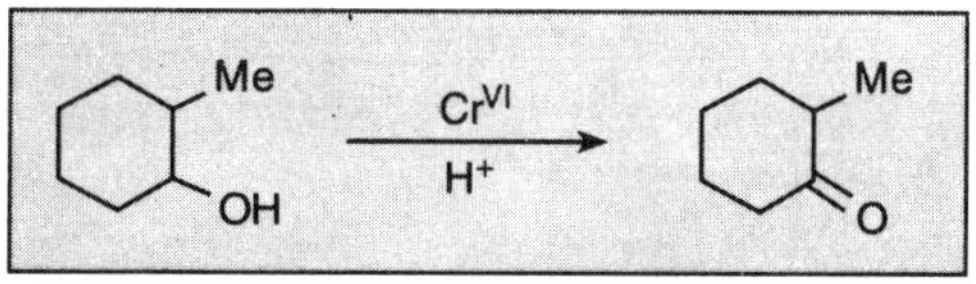

This experiment illustrates the use of aqueous chromic acid, prepared from sodium dichromate and sulfuric acid, to oxidize the secondary alcohol 2-methylcyclohexanol to the ketone 2-methylcyclohexanone. The oxidant is used in excess and the reaction is carried out in a two-phase ether–water system at 0°C. The work-up is simple, involving separation and washing of the diethyl ether layer, and the product ketone is purified by distillation at atmospheric presure.

Level	1
Time	3 h
Equipment	magnetic stirrer; apparatus for reaction with addition, extraction/separation, suction filtration, distillation

Materials		
2-methylcyclohexanol (*cis/trans*) (FW 114.2)	5.7 g (50 mmol)	
sodium dichromate dihydrate (FW 298.0)	10.0 g (33 mmol)	**cancer suspect, agent, oxidizer, toxic**
sulfuric acid (97%)	7.4 mL	**corrosive, oxidizer**
diethyl ether		**flammable, irritant**
sodium carbonate solution (5%)		**corrosive**

Procedure

Dissolve the sodium dichromate in 30 mL water in a 100 mL beaker, and stir the solution rapidly with a glass rod. Add the sulfuric acid slowly to the stirred solution,[1] and then make up the total volume of the solution to 50 mL with water. Place the beaker in an ice bath, and allow the oxidizing solution[2] to cool for about 30 min, whilst the reaction equipment is set up.

Place the 2-methylcyclohexanol and 30 mL diethyl ether in a 250 mL round-bottomed flask, add a magnetic stirrer bar, and fit an addition funnel to the flask.[3] Stir the solution and place the flask in an ice bath for 15 min. Keep the flask in the ice bath, and add about half of the ice-cold oxidizing solution *dropwise* to the rapidly stirred reaction mixture. Add the remaining oxidant slowly over about 5 min, and stir the mixture rapidly in the ice bath for a further 20 min. Stop the stirrer, and allow the layers to separate.[4] Transfer the mixture to a separatory funnel, and separate the layers.[5] Extract the lower aqueous layer with 2 × 15 mL portions diethyl ether. Combine the ether layers, and wash them with 20 mL sodium carbonate solution,[6] and then with 4 × 20 mL portions of water. Dry the ether layer over $MgSO_4$.[7] Filter off the drying agent using a fluted filter paper,[8] and evaporate the filtrate on the rotary evaporator. Transfer the residue to a 10 mL flask, and distil the liquid at atmospheric pressure,[9] collecting the product at *ca.* 160–165°C. Record the exact bp and the yield of your product. The IR spectra of 2-methylcyclohexanol and 2-methylcyclohexanone are reproduced below.

[1] ***Care! Exothermic***

[2] ***Caution — the oxidizing solution is highly corrosive***

[3] *See Fig. 3.21*

[4] *Can be left overnight*

[5] *Solution is very dark; may need a light to see interface*

[6] ***Care! CO_2 evolved***

[7] *May be left at this stage*

[8] *See Fig. 3.5*

[9] *See Fig. 3.48*

See Exps 46,48

MICROSCALE

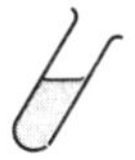

Level	1
Time	3 h
Equipment	magnetic stirrer; apparatus for TLC analysis, pipette drying column, distillation (Hickman still)

Materials		
2-methylcyclohexanol (*cis*/*trans*) (FW 114.2)	228 mg (2 mmol)	
sodium dichromate dihydrate (FW 298.0)	400 mg (1.34 mmol)	**oxidizer, toxic cancer suspect agent**
sulfuric acid (97%)	0.16 mL, 296 mg (2.2 mmol)	**corrosive, oxidizer**
diethyl ether		**flammable, irritant**
sodium carbonate solution (5%)		**corrosive**

Procedure

Dissolve the sodium dichromate in water (1.2 mL) in a 3 mL reaction vial containing a spin vane and stir the solution rapidly. Add the sulfuric acid dropwise slowly to the stirred solution[1] and make up the total volume to 2 mL with water. Cool the oxidizing solution in a ice bath for 3 min. Remove the spin vane with tweezers, rinse clean with cold water and dry. Place the clean, dry

[1]*Care! Exothermic*

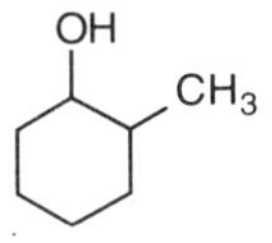

(neat)

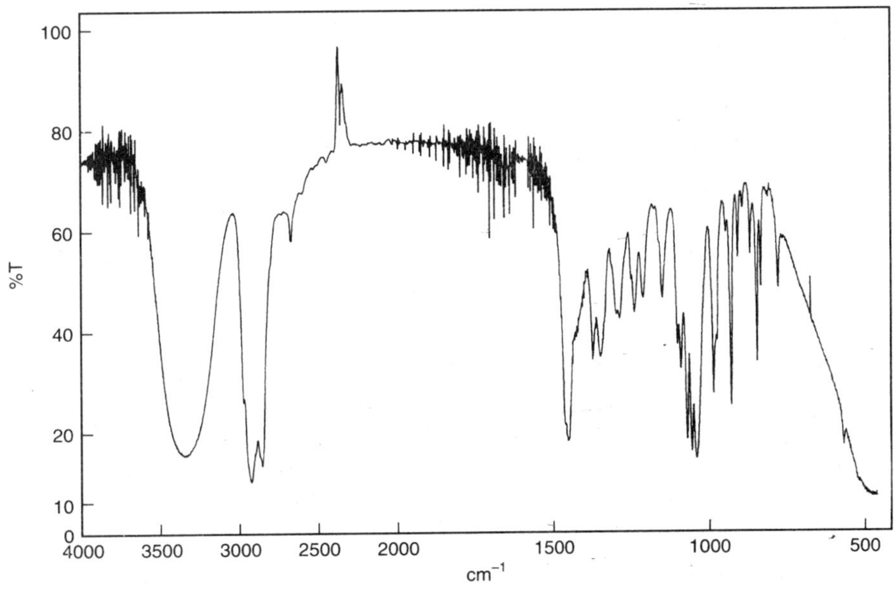

spin vane in a 5 mL reaction vial, add the 2-methylcyclohexanol and diethyl ether (1.2 mL) and cool the stirred solution in an ice bath for 5 min. Add about one-half (1 mL) of the ice-cold oxidizing solution[2] to the rapidly stirred reaction mixture. Add the remaining oxidant slowly over 5 min and stir the mixture rapidly with ice-bath cooling for a further 20 min. Stop the stirrer and allow the layers to separate.[3] Transfer the lower aqueous layer to a test tube and leave the upper ether layer in the vial.[4] Extract the transferred aqueous layer with diethyl ether (2 × 0.6 mL) and combine the two extracts with the original ether layer. Wash the combined organic extracts with sodium carbonate solution[5] (0.8 mL) and water (4 × 0.8 mL). Dry the ether layer by passing through a column of $MgSO_4$,[6] into a 3 mL reaction vial or tapered tube and remove the diethyl ether using a stream of air or nitrogen, or a gentle vacuum.[7] Distil the residue using a Hickman still[8] and record your yield and an IR spectrum.

[2] ***Caution — the oxidizing solution is highly corrosive***

[3] *Can be left overnight*

[4] *Solution is very dark; may need a light to see the interface*

[5] ***Care! CO_2 evolved***

[6] *See Fig. 3.9*

[7] *See Fig. 2.31*

[8] *See Fig. 3.58*

Problems

1 Write a balanced equation for the dichromate oxidation of a secondary alcohol to a ketone. How many mols of alcohol are oxidized by 1 mol of dichromate? What is the chromium-containing by-product?

2 Write a reaction mechanism for the oxidation of 2-methylcyclohexanol. Identify any intermediates that might be involved.

3 Compare and contrast the IR spectra of 2-methylcyclohexanol and 2-methylcyclohexanone which are provided. What are the major differences?

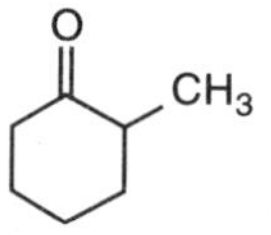

(neat)

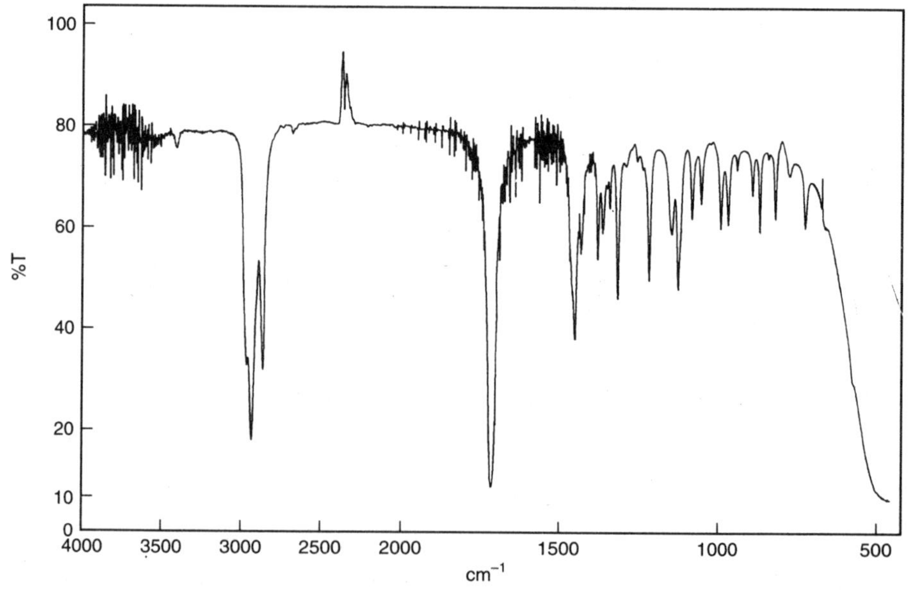

Further reading

For the procedure on which this experiment is based, see: S. Krishnamurthy, T.W. Nylund, M. Ravindranathan and K.L. Thompson, *J. Chem. Educ.*, 1979, **56**, 203.

For a discussion of chromium oxidants, see: A.H. Haines, *Methods for the Oxidation of Organic Compounds*, Academic Press, London, 1988.

Experiment 30

Oxidation of menthol to menthone using aqueous chromic acid

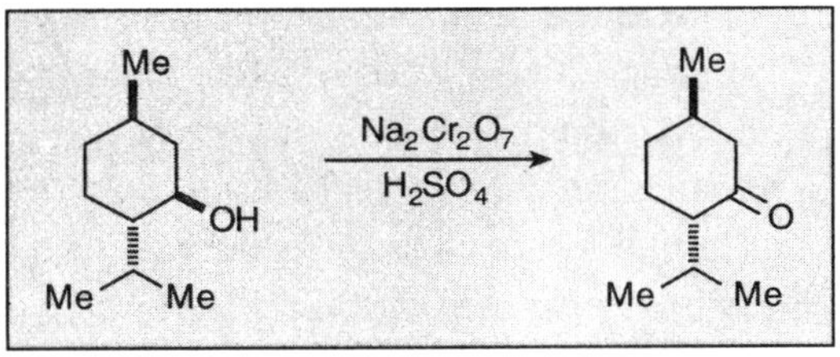

This experiment illustrates the use of aqueous chromic acid to oxidize the naturally occurring secondary alcohol, menthol into the ketone menthone. The chromic acid is prepared from sodium dichromate and sulfuric acid, and the reaction is carried out in a two-phase system of diethyl ether and water, which is useful in preventing both over-oxidation, and possible isomerization of the product into isomenthone. Gas chromatography (GC) is used to analyze the final product and to determine the amounts of unreacted menthol and isomenthone present (if any). The menthone may be purified by distillation under reduced pressure.

Level	2
Time	2 × 3 h
Equipment	overhead stirrer motor; apparatus for addition with overhead stirring, extraction/separation, suction filtration, distillation under reduced pressure (or short path distillation)
Instruments	GC with 3 m 10% Carbowax® column, 120°C isotherm, IR, polarimeter (optional)

Materials

sodium dichromate dihydrate (FW 298.0)	1.2 g (4 mmol)	**cancer suspect agent, oxidizer, toxic**
sulfuric acid (conc.)	1.5 mL	**corrosive, oxidizer**
(–) (1*R*, 2*S*, 5*R*) menthol (FW 156.3)	1.56 g (10 mmol)	**irritant**
diethyl ether		**flammable, irritant**
sodium bicarbonate solution (saturated)		

Procedure

1. Oxidation of (–)-menthol

[1] ***Care***

[2] *See Fig. 3.21*

[3] *Watch the temperature!*

[4] *Leave here*

[5] *Start part 2*

[6] ***Care! CO_2 evolved***

[7] *See Fig. 3.7*

[8] *See Fig. 3.53*

[9] *See Fig. 3.54*

Dissolve the sodium dichromate in the sulfuric acid,[1] and dilute the solution with 12 mL water. Set up the 50 mL two- or three-neck flask with a thermometer, addition funnel and overhead stirrer.[2] Place the menthol in the flask and add 15 mL diethyl ether. Stir the solution rapidly and cool the flask in an ice–salt bath. Place the acidic dichromate solution in the addition funnel, and add it *dropwise* to the stirred menthol solution at such a rate that the *internal* temperature is maintained in the range -3 to 0°C.[3] The addition should take about 15–20 min. Continue to stir the solution rapidly for about 2 h, maintaining the temperature at about 0°C. Stop the stirrer, and allow the reaction mixture to stand overnight (or until the next period) to allow the layers to separate.[4] Transfer the mixture to the separatory funnel and separate the layers.[5] Wash the aqueous layer with 2 × 5 mL portions of diethyl ether. Combine the ether solutions, wash them with 2 × 5 mL portions of sodium bicarbonate solution,[6] and dry them over $MgSO_4$. Filter off the drying agent by suction[7] and put aside 0.5 mL of the filtrate for GC analysis (see below). Evaporate the rest of the filtrate on the rotary evaporator, and distil the residue under reduced pressure under water aspirator vacuum using a small distillation set[8] or a short path distillation apparatus.[9] Record the bp, yield and IR spectrum ($CHCl_3$) of your product, along with an IR spectrum of menthol for comparison. Finally, if required, measure the optical rotation of your menthone product, either neat or in ethanol solution.

2. GC analysis

[10] *See Chapter 3 for a discussion of GC*

Analyze the ether solution of the product on the gas chromatograph using a Carbowax® column.[10] Run a standard sample of menthol for reference, and determine the ratio of product (menthone) to starting material (menthol) (if present). Also determine the amount of isomenthone present (if any): this will appear as a small peak or shoulder immediately after the menthone peak.

Problems

1 Write a balanced equation for the dichromate oxidation of a secondary alcohol (R_2CHOH) to a ketone ($R_2C{=}O$).

2 Write a mechanism for the oxidation of alcohols using chromium(VI) oxidants, clearly identifying any intermediates involved.

3 Discuss the mechanism of the isomerization of menthone to isomenthone under acidic conditions.

4 Compare and contrast the IR spectrum of your product ketone with that of the starting alcohol.

Further reading

For the procedure on which this experiment is based, see: H.C. Brown and C.P. Garg,

J.Am.Chem. Soc., 1961, **83**, 2952.
For a discussion of chromium oxidants, see: EROS, 1261.

Experiment 31

Oxidation of 1-heptanol to heptanal using pyridinium chlorochromate

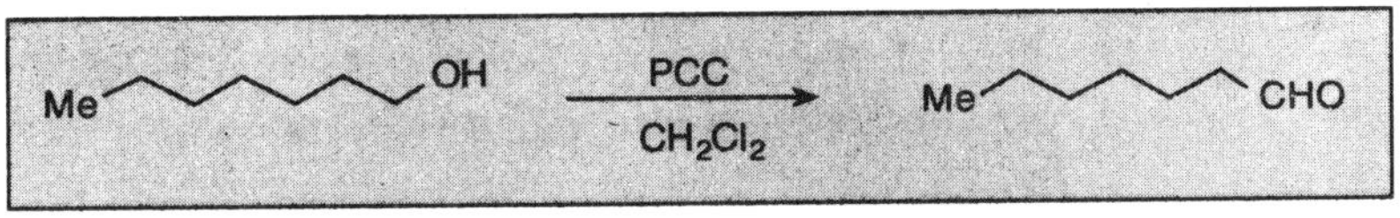

The oxidation of primary alcohols to aldehydes is often complicated by further oxidation of the aldehyde to the corresponding carboxylic acid. Indeed this is one of the major drawbacks in using aqueous chromic acid for the oxidation of *primary* alcohols, compared with the successful oxidation of *secondary* alcohols with this reagent (Experiments 29 and 30). Various solutions to the over-oxidation problem have been developed, and several of these involve the combination of a chromium(VI) oxidant with pyridine. These systems are less powerful oxidants than aqueous chromic acid, and two particularly useful reagents of this type are pyridinium chlorochromate (PCC) and pyridinium dichromate (PDC), both of which were popularized by E.J. Corey of Harvard University, who received the 1990 Nobel Prize for his contribution to organic chemistry. This experiment illustrates the preparation of PCC, a relatively stable orange solid, and its use in the oxidation of the primary alcohol 1-heptanol to the aldehyde heptanal. The reagent is prepared by adding pyridine to chromium(VI) oxide dissolved in hydrochloric acid, and the oxidation reactions are carried out by stirring the alcohol with a suspension of PCC in dichloromethane. Product isolation simply involves filtration of the spent reagent, and purification of the product by distillation.

Level	2
Time	2 × 3 h
Equipment	magnetic stirrer; apparatus for suction filtration, reflux, distillation
Instruments	IR

Materials

1. *Preparation of pyridinium chlorochromate (PCC)*

hydrochloric acid (6 M)	18.4 mL (0.11 mol)	**corrosive**
chromium(VI) oxide (FW 100.0)	10.00 g (0.1 mol)	**cancer suspect agent, oxidizer, toxic**
pyridine (FW 79.1)	7.7 mL, 7.91 g (0.1 mol)	**flammable, toxic irritant, stench**

Continued on p. 508

Box cont.

2. *Oxidation of 1-heptanol with PCC*		
1-heptanol (FW 116.2)	5.81 g (50 mmol)	**toxic**
pyridinium chlorochromate (FW 215.6)	16.2 g (75 mmol)	**cancer suspect agent, oxidizer, toxic**
dichloromethane		**irritant, toxic**
diethyl ether		**flammable, irritant**
Florisil® or silica gel (TLC grade)	ca. 5 g	**irritant dust**

Procedure

1. Preparation of pyridinium chlorochromate (PCC)[1]

Place the 6 M hydrochloric acid in a 100 mL Erlenmeyer flask, add a magnetic stirrer bar, and stir the acid rapidly. Add the chromium(VI) oxide to the acid, and stir the mixture for 5 min at room temperature. Cool the solution to 0°C in an ice bath, and add the pyridine dropwise over 10 min with the cooling bath in place.[2] Re-cool the solution to 0°C and collect the orange-yellow solid by suction filtration. Dry the solid under vacuum over phosphorus pentoxide for at least 1 h.[3] Record the yield of your product.

HOOD
[1]***Cancer suspect agent***
[2]*Mixture warms up during addition*
[3]*May be left at this stage*

2. Oxidation of 1-heptanol with PCC

Suspend 16.2 g (75 mmol) PCC in 100 mL dry dichloromethane[4] in a 250 mL round-bottomed flask fitted with a reflux condenser and a magnetic stirrer bar.[5] Stir the solution magnetically and add a solution of the 1-heptanol in 10 mL dichloromethane through the condenser in one portion. Stir the mixture at room temperature for 1.5 h. Dilute the mixture with 100 mL dry diethyl ether,[4] stop the stirrer, and decant the supernatant liquid from the black gum. Wash the black residue thoroughly with 3 × 25 mL portions of warm diethyl ether, and combine the ether washings with the previous organic layer. Filter the organic solution through a short pad of Florisil® or silica gel with suction,[6] and evaporate the filtrate on the rotary evaporator.[3] Transfer the residual liquid to a 10 or 25 mL flask, and distil it at atmospheric pressure,[7] collecting the product at about 150°C. Record the exact bp, yield and the IR spectrum (film) of your product. Record an IR spectrum (film) of the starting alcohol for comparison. ■

[4]*See Appendix 2*
[5]*See Fig. 3.24*
[6]*See Fig. 3.74*
[7]*See Fig. 3.48; better yields are obtained if liquid is heated quickly*

MICROSCALE

Level	1
Time	3 h
Equipment	magnetic stirrer; apparatus for TLC analysis, desiccator, distillation (Hickman still)

Continued

Box cont.

Materials		
1. Preparation of pyridinium chlorochromate		
hydrochloric acid (6 M)	0.92 mL (5.5 mmol)	**corrosive**
chromium(VI) oxide (FW 100.0)	500 mg (5 mmol)	**cancer suspect agent, oxidizer, toxic**
pyridine (FW 79.1)	0.39 mL, 400 mg (5 mmol)	**flammable, toxic irritant, stench**
2. Oxidation of 1-heptanol with PCC		
1-heptanol (FW 116.2)	116 mg (1 mmol)	**toxic**
pyridinium chlorochromate (FW 215.6)	324 mg (1.5 mmol)	**cancer suspect agent, oxidizer, toxic**
dichloromethane		**irritant, toxic**
diethyl ether		**flammable, irritant**
Florisil® or silica gel (TLC grade)	*ca.* 100 mg	**irritant dust**

Procedure

1. Preparation of pyridinium chlorochromate[1]

HOOD

[1] *Cancer suspect agent*

Place the 6 M hydrochloric acid in a test tube containing a small stirrer bead and stir rapidly. Add the chromium(VI) oxide and stir for 5 min at room temperature. Cool to 0°C and add the pyridine dropwise over 10 min from a drawn out Pasteur pipette with the cooling bath in place.[2] Re-cool to 0°C and collect the yellow-orange solid at the pump using a micro-Hirsch funnel and dry *in vacuo* over phosphorus pentoxide for at least 1 h.[3] Record the yield of your product.

[2] *Mixture warms up during addition*

[3] *May be left at this stage*

2. Oxidation of 1-heptanol with PCC

Suspend the pyridinium chlorochromate in dry dichloromethane[4] (2.5 mL) in a 10 mL round-bottomed flask containing a small stirrer bead. Stir the suspension and add a solution of heptanol in dry dichloromethane (2.5 mL) in one portion from a Pasteur pipette. Stir the mixture at room temperature for 1.5 h, following the reaction by TLC.[5] When the reaction is complete, dilute the mixture with dry diethyl ether (2.5 mL), stop the stirrer and decant (and keep) the supernatant liquid from the black gummy residue. Wash the gummy residue with warm diethyl ether (3 × 0.5 mL) and combine the washings with the original supernatant. Filter the solution through a short pad of Florisil® or silica[6] with suction (use a micro-Hirsch funnel) and remove the solvent carefully using a rotary evaporator and a cold water bath. Alternatively distil off most of the solvent, transfer the residue (*ca.* 0.3 mL) to a conical vial and distil using the Hickman still[7] allowing the diethyl ether to distil off directly. Collect the aldehyde product while heating rapidly[8] with a small bunsen flame or heat gun. Record your yield and an IR spectrum of your product.

[4] *See Appendix 2*

[5] *Use 30% diethyl ether in hexane to develop your TLC plate*

[6] *See Fig. 3.74*

[7] *See Fig. 3.58*

[8] *Better yields are obtained if liquid is heated quickly*

Problem

1 What is the structure of PCC? Suggest why it is a milder reagent than CrO_3.

Further reading

For the original report of PCC, see: E.J. Corey and J.W. Suggs, *Tetrahedron Lett.*, 1975, vol 2647.

For a review, see: G. Piancatelli, A. Scettri and M.D'Auria, *Synthesis*, 1982, vol 245; EROS, 4356.

Experiment 32

Preparation of 'active' manganese dioxide and the oxidation of E*-3-phenyl-2-propenol (cinnamyl alcohol) to* E*-3-phenyl-2-propenal (cinnamaldehyde)*

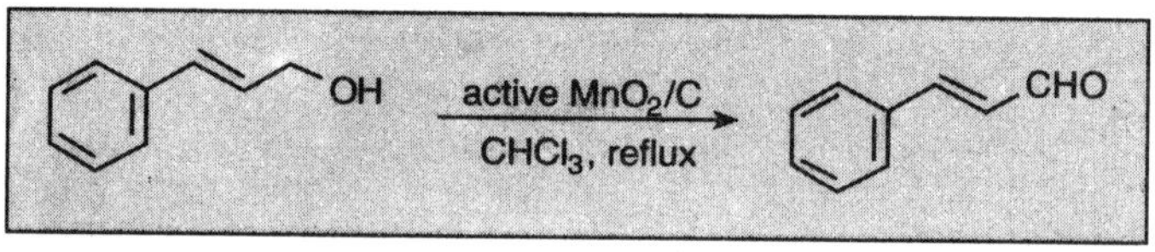

Activated manganese dioxide is an extremely mild oxidizing agent which demonstrates good chemoselectivity for allylic and benzylic alcohols as well as related substrates such as propargylic alcohols and cyclopropylcarbinols. Primary and secondary alcohols are usually oxidized much more slowly by this reagent, if at all. Other oxidizable moieties such as thiols and thioethers do react with this reagent but selectivity is not difficult to achieve. The reagent is effectively neutral and so its use is compatible with a wide range of acid- and base-sensitive functionalities and *E*/*Z*-isomerization or oxidative rearrangement of allylic alcohols does not occur. More than this, oxidation of the initially produced α,β-unsaturated aldehydes is usually appreciably slower than the rate of oxidation of their primary alcohol precursors, permitting aldehydes to be isolated readily. This combination of mildness and chemoselectivity makes activated manganese dioxide an extremely important reagent in the research laboratory.

The reagent most frequently used in the laboratory is prepared by a procedure described by Attenburrow and is composed essentially of manganese dioxide with about 5% water of hydration. The one drawback to this reagent is the tedious nature of its preparation, as anyone who has had to prepare it will testify! A later reagent described by Carpino consists of active manganese dioxide supported on activated carbon and is prepared by the oxidation of charcoal with potassium permanganate. This reagent contains approximately 20% carbon and possesses all of the chemical advantages of the Attenburrow reagent with the additional bonus of being simple to prepare. Whilst the preparation and use of the Carpino reagent will be described here, the oxidation reaction can be carried out with a little modification using commercially available Attenburrow reagent.

Level	3
Time	preparation of activated manganese dioxide 3 h; preparation of *E*-3-phenyl-2-propenal 3 h; analysis and derivatization of product 3 h
Equipment	magnetic stirrer/hotplate; apparatus for azeotropic removal of water with a Dean and Stark set-up, reflux, small-scale recrystallization
Instruments	NMR, IR, UV

Materials

1. Preparation of activated manganese dioxide on carbon

potassium permanganate (FW 158.0)	24 g (*ca.* 0.15 mol)	**irritant, oxidizer**
activated carbon, Darco® G-60	7.5 g	
toluene		**flammable, irritant**

2. Preparation of E*-3-phenyl-2-propenal (cinnamaldehyde)*

activated manganese dioxide	15 g	**oxidizer**
E-3-phenyl-2-propenol (cinnamyl alcohol) (FW 134.2)	670 mg, 642 μL (5 mmol)	
Brady's reagent		**corrosive, toxic**
chloroform		**cancer suspect agent, toxic**
ethanol		**flammable, toxic**

Procedure

HOOD

1. *Preparation of activated manganese dioxide on carbon*

Dissolve the potassium permanganate with magnetic stirring in 300 mL of boiling water in a 1 L beaker. Remove the beaker from the hotplate[1] and add the activated carbon portionwise to the solution over a period of 10 min, **allowing the vigorous frothing to subside between additions**. After all of the carbon has been added, return the beaker to the hotplate and boil the mixture with stirring for a further 5 min to discharge the purple colouration completely. Allow the mixture to cool for 15 min[2] and then filter with suction through a Büchner funnel. Wash the residue four times with 50 mL portions of water, stopping the vacuum each time and carefully stirring the residue into a thick slurry before filtering off the washings with suction. Dry the residue with suction for 5 min, transfer the cake to a 250 mL round-bottomed flask of the Dean and Stark set-up, add 150 mL toluene and reflux the mixture until no more water is seen passing into the receiver and the refluxing toluene appears clear and not milky. Allow the flask contents to cool[3] and filter the mixture with suction, drying the cake on the Büchner funnel. Remove final traces of toluene on the rotary evaporator with a boiling water bath[4] after transfering the product to a preweighed 500 mL round-bottomed flask. When the powder appears dry and relatively free-running, record the weight of your reagent.

[1] *Care! Wear gloves*

[2] *Assemble the Dean and Stark set-up now: see Fig. 3.27*

[3] *May be left at this stage*

[4] *Care! Bumping can be troublesome*

2. *Preparation of E-3-phenyl-2-propenal (cinnamaldehyde)*

Dissolve the *E*-3-phenyl-2-propenol in 60 mL chloroform in a 250 mL round-bottomed flask, add 15 g of the activated manganese dioxide reagent and reflux the mixture for 2 h.[5] Allow the mixture to cool and filter off the solid with suction, washing the residual cake with 10 mL of ethanol.[6] Remove the solvent on the rotary evaporator and weigh your crude product. Obtain the NMR ($CDCl_3$), IR (thin film) and UV (MeOH) spectra of this material. From 100 mg of your product, prepare the DNP derivative, recrystallizing to constant mp from aqueous ethanol.

[5] *See Fig. 3.23(a)*

[6] *May be left at this stage*

Problems

1 Compare your NMR spectrum with that below, assigning the peaks due to the product aldehyde and any due to unoxidized starting material. Assign the stereochemistry of the double bond in your product. Rationalize the fact that the characteristic chemical shift for aldehyde protons is *ca.* 10 ppm.

2 Assign the important absorptions in the IR and UV spectra. Explain why the DNP derivative of your product is red whereas DNP derivatives of aliphatic aldehydes are yellow.

3 Why would there be no point in attempting to purify your crude material by distillation? What purification procedures would be most suitable for small (*ca.* 100 mg) and large quantities (*ca.* 1 kg) of your crude product?

4 Give an example of a natural source from which *E*-3-phenyl-2-propenal might be obtained.

Further reading

For articles and reviews covering the use and range of reactivity of activated manganese dioxide, see: J.S. Pizey, *Synthetic Reagents*, vol. II, Ellis Horwood (Wiley), 1974, p. 143.

For a general discussion of manganese dioxide, see: EROS, 3229.

For the Attenburrow reagent, see: J. Attenburrow, A.F.B. Cameron, J.H. Chapman, R.M. Evans, B.A. Hems, A.B.A. Jansen and T. Walker, *J. Chem. Soc.*, 1952, 1094.

For the Carpino reagent, see: L.A. Carpino, *J. Org. Chem.*, 1970, **35**, 3971.

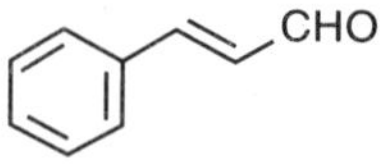

(250 MHz, $CDCl_3$)

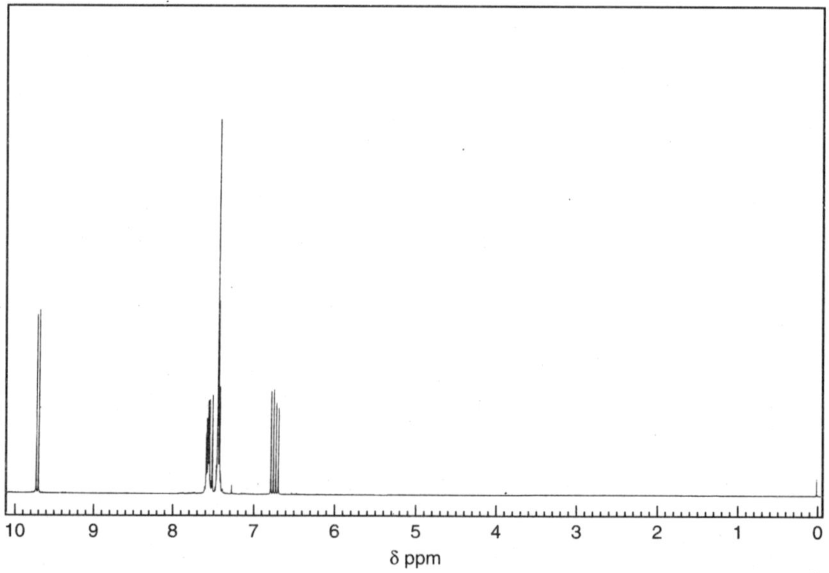

Experiment 33

Organic supported reagents: oxidations with silver(I) carbonate on Celite® (Fetizon's reagent)

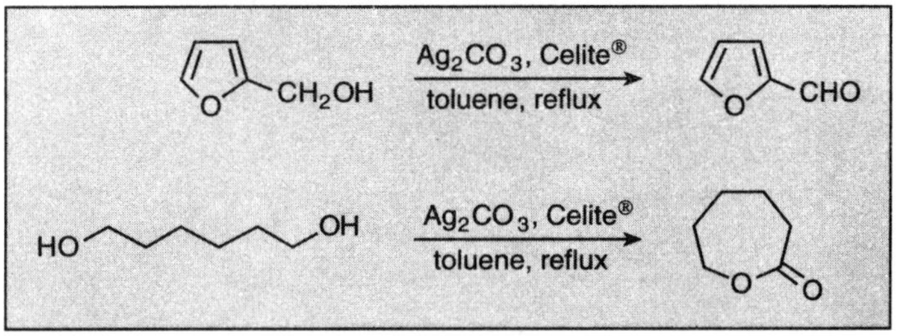

Inorganic reagents when absorbed onto inert solid supports often result in reactions with greatly simplified work-up procedures: the inorganic by-products remain bound to the support, and the organic product is isolated in solution by simple filtration. One such reagent system is silver carbonate on Celite® (Fetizon's reagent). It has been known for a long time that silver carbonate is a useful oxidant for alcohols. However, Fetizon and co-workers noticed that while freshly prepared silver carbonate, precipitated by reaction of sodium carbonate with silver nitrate was a highly effective oxidant, it was difficult to filter, wash and handle, and consequently the reproducibility of the oxidations was often poor. Fetizon discovered that these problems could be averted by precipitating the reagent in the presence of Celite®. The resulting reagent is a versatile and useful oxidant, and is probably the most widely used supported reagent in organic synthesis. This experiment illustrates the preparation of Fetizon's reagent, and two examples of its use, either or both of which may be selected. The first involves the oxidation of 2-furanmethanol (furfuryl alcohol) to 2-furaldehyde (furfural). This transformation, which is difficult to effect with normal oxidants because of the extreme sensitivity of the furan ring to acid, highlights the use of Fetizon's reagent for the oxidation of alcohols containing sensitive groups. As with PCC oxidations, there is no over-oxidation of primary alcohols. The second example illustrates one of the most valuable uses of Fetizon's reagent, the direct oxidation of α,ω-diols to lactones, in this case the oxidation of hexane-1,6-diol to ε-caprolactone. Both reactions are carried out in refluxing toluene, and employ an excess of reagent. Work-up is simple, and the products are generally isolated in a pure state.

Level	4
Time	4 × 3 h (plus overnight drying time after washing off Celite®)
Equipment	mechanical stirrer; apparatus for overhead stirring, suction filtration, reflux, TLC
Instruments	IR, NMR

Continued on p. 514

Box cont.

Materials

1. Preparation of Fetizon's reagent		
Celite®	25 g	
silver nitrate (FW 169.9)	17.0 g (0.1 mol)	**oxidizer, toxic**
methanol		**flammable, toxic**
hydrochloric acid (conc.)		**corrosive**
sodium carbonate decahydrate (FW 286.2)	15.0 g (53 mmol)	**irritant**
2. Oxidation of 2-furanmethanol		
2-furanmethanol (FW 98.1)	87 μL, 98 mg (1 mmol)	**irritant, toxic**
3. Oxidation of hexane-1,6-diol		
hexane-1,6-diol (FW 118.2)	118 mg (1 mmol)	**irritant**
toluene		**flammable, irritant**
dichloromethane		**irritant, toxic**

Procedure

1. Preparation of silver carbonate on Celite® (Fetizon's reagent)

Place the Celite® in a filter funnel, and wash it thoroughly with a mixture of 50 mL methanol and 5 mL concentrated hydrochloric acid, and then with distilled water until the washings are neutral. Dry the purified Celite® in an oven at 120°C.[1]

[1] *May be left at this stage*

Dissolve the silver nitrate in 100 mL distilled water, and stir the solution mechanically with an overhead stirrer. Add 15 g purified Celite®, and continue to stir the mixture rapidly whilst adding dropwise a solution of the sodium carbonate in 150 mL distilled water. After the addition is completed, continue to stir the mixture for 10 min, and then collect the greenish-yellow precipitate by suction filtration. Transfer the solid to a round-bottomed flask, and dry it on a rotary evaporator for about 2 h.[1] The reagent contains about 2 mmol silver carbonate per gram, and if required the last traces of water can be removed by azeotropic distillation with toluene.[2]

[2] *See Fig. 3.27*

HOOD

2. Oxidation of 2-furanmethanol

Suspend 3.5 g (*ca.* 7 mmol) Fetizon's reagent in 25 mL dry toluene in a 50 mL round-bottomed flask fitted with a reflux condenser.[3] Add the 2-furanmethanol by syringe, and heat the mixture under reflux for 6 h.[4] Filter the suspension, and wash the solid with 3 × 5 mL dichloromethane. Evaporate the combined filtrate and washings on the rotary evaporator. Check the purity of the residue by TLC, and record the yield and the IR ($CHCl_3$) and NMR ($CDCl_3$) spectra of your product.

[3] *See Fig. 3.23(a)*

[4] *Set up part 3 now*

HOOD

3. Conversion of hexane-1,6-diol into caprolactone

Suspend 13.1 g (23 mmol) Fetizon's reagent in 50 mL dry toluene in a 100 mL

[5] *See Fig. 3.23(a)*

round-bottomed flask fitted with a reflux condenser.[5] Add the hexane-1,6-diol dissolved in a few drops of toluene, and heat the mixture under reflux for 2.5 h. Filter the suspension, and wash the solid with 3 × 5 mL dichloromethane. Evaporate the combined filtrate and washings on the rotary evaporator. Check the purity of the residue by TLC, and record the yield and the IR ($CHCl_3$) and NMR ($CDCl_3$) spectra of your product.

Problems

1 Write a mechanism for the oxidation of a primary alcohol to an aldehyde with silver(I) carbonate.

2 Why are furans sensitive to acid? What is the product when furan itself is treated with aqueous acid?

3 Write a mechanism for the conversion of hexane-1,6-diol into ε-caprolactone.

4 Assign the IR and NMR spectra of your products.

Further reading

For the original reports of Fetizon's reagent, see: M. Fetizon, M. Golfier and J.-M. Louis, *Tetrahedron*, 1975, **31**, 171; M. Fetizon, F. Gomez-Parra and J.-M. Louis, *J. Heterocycl. Chem.*, 1976, **13**, 525.

For a general discussion, see: EROS, 4448.

For a review of solid supported reagents, see: A. McKillop and D.W. Young, *Synthesis*, 1979, 401.

7.6 Rearrangements

The term *rearrangement* covers a multitude of processes in organic chemistry. However, although many of these rearrangements have different names and operate on different substrates, and on the face of it appear unrelated, almost all of them involve the migration of an atom (often hydrogen) or an alkyl or aryl group to an electron-deficient centre. The rearrangement experiments included here are no exception, and illustrate rearrangement by migration to electron-deficient nitrogen and carbon centres.

Experiment 34 — *Preparation of 2-aminobenzoic acid (anthranilic acid) by Hofmann rearrangement of phthalimide*

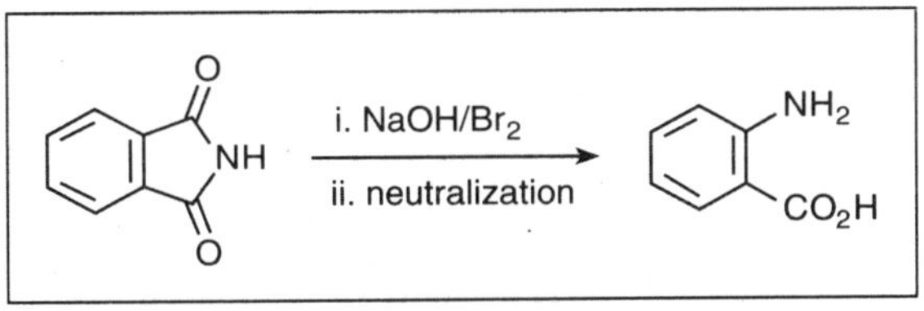

The Hofmann rearrangement of an amide to an amine with loss of carbon dioxide is a member of that class of reactions involving migration of an alkyl or aryl group to an electron-deficient nitrogen. Other examples include the closely related group of Curtius, Lossen and Schmidt rearrangements in which a carboxylic acid is converted initially to an isocyanate via an acyl azide, and also the Beckmann rearrangement of oximes to amides (Experiment 35).

In the Hofmann rearrangement, the amide is submitted to oxidation with hypobromite to form an intermediate *N*-bromoamide. In the presence of alkali this undergoes deprotonation followed by alkyl migration to the nitrogen centre with concomitant loss of bromide to produce an isocyanate. Under the reaction conditions, hydrolysis of the isocyanate occurs to liberate carbon dioxide and form the amine containing one carbon less than the starting amide.

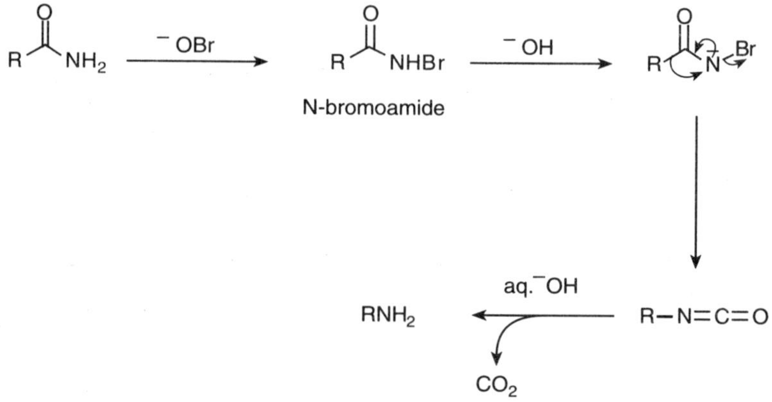

This conversion finds particular use for the preparation of aromatic amines and in the following experiment will be applied to the synthesis of 2-aminobenzoic acid, itself an important precursor for the preparation of the reactive intermediate *benzyne* (Experiment 62).

Level	1
Time	3 h
Equipment	magnetic stirrer; apparatus for stirring, suction filtration

Materials

phthalimide (FW 147.1)	5.9 g (40 mmol)	
bromine (FW 159.8)	2.1 mL, 6.5 g (41 mmol)	**oxidizer, toxic**

NOTE: ***bromine is highly toxic and corrosive. Its volatility combined with its density make it very difficult to handle. Always wear gloves and measure out in the hood***

Continued

Box cont.

sodium hydroxide pellets	**corrosive, hygroscopic**
hydrochloric acid (conc.)	**corrosive**
glacial ethanoic acid	**corrosive**
pH indicator paper	

HOOD

[1]*Care!*

[2]*Look for disappearance of brown colouration*

[3]*Foaming occurs in the next stage*

[4]*See Fig. 3.7*

Procedure

Dissolve 8.0 g of sodium hydroxide in 30 mL of distilled water in a 100 mL Erlenmeyer flask containing a magnetic stirrer bar and cool the solution with stirring in an ice bath. Add the bromine[1] in one portion and stir the mixture vigorously until all of the bromine has reacted[2] and the mixture has cooled to *ca.* 0°C. Continue vigorous stirring and add the finely powdered phthalimide to the solution, followed by a solution of a further 5.5 g of sodium hydroxide in 20 mL of water. Remove the ice bath, allow the temperature of the mixture to rise spontaneously to *ca.* 70°C and continue stirring for a further 10 min. Cool the clear solution in an ice bath with stirring (if the mixture is cloudy, filter under gravity before cooling), and add concentrated hydrochloric acid dropwise with a pipette until the solution is just neutral when a drop is spotted onto universal indicator paper (*ca.* 15 mL should be necessary). If too much acid is added, the mixture may be brought back to neutrality by adding further quantities of sodium hydroxide solution, but it is better to avoid this by careful addition of acid in the first instance. Transfer the mixture to a 500 mL beaker[3] and precipitate the 2-aminobenzoic acid by addition of glacial ethanoic acid (*ca.* 5 mL). Filter off the precipitate with suction,[4] wash the residue with 10 mL of cold water and dissolve it in the minimum quantity of boiling water containing a little activated charcoal. Filter the hot solution to remove the charcoal and cool the filtrate in ice. Filter off the pure acid with suction, dry the residue with suction on the filter for 5 min and complete the drying to constant weight in an oven at 100–120°C. Record the mp of your purified product and the yield based upon the amount of phthalimide used.

See Exp. 62

Problems

1 Explain why it is necessary to carry out a careful neutralization of the reaction mixture in order to isolate your product efficiently.

2 An important class of natural products are the amino acids which are the basic building blocks of proteins. Although organic molecules, the amino acids are typically very soluble in water, insoluble in organic solvents and have high (>200°C) melting points. Explain why this should be so.

3 Write out the mechanisms of the Curtius and Beckmann rearrangements and discuss how these are related to the Hofmann rearrangement.

4 A compound **(1)** ($C_6H_{13}Br$), on reaction with magnesium turnings in diethyl ether followed by carbon dioxide, furnished **(2)** ($C_7H_{14}O_2$) on work-up. Product **(2)** reacted with excess ammonia in methanol to yield **(3)** ($C_7H_{15}NO$) which was degraded by alkaline sodium hypobromite to **(4)** ($C_6H_{15}N$) with the evolution of carbon dioxide. Treatment of **(4)** with excess iodomethane in diethyl ether gave a crystalline solid **(5)** which, on heating

with moist silver(II) oxide, furnished 1-hexene. Identify substances **(1)** through **(5)** and rationalize the conversions taking place.

Further reading

L.M. Harwood, *Polar Rearrangements*, Oxford University Press, Oxford, 1992.

Experiment 35 *Investigation into the stereoselectivity of the Beckmann rearrangement of the oxime derived from 4-bromoacetophenone*

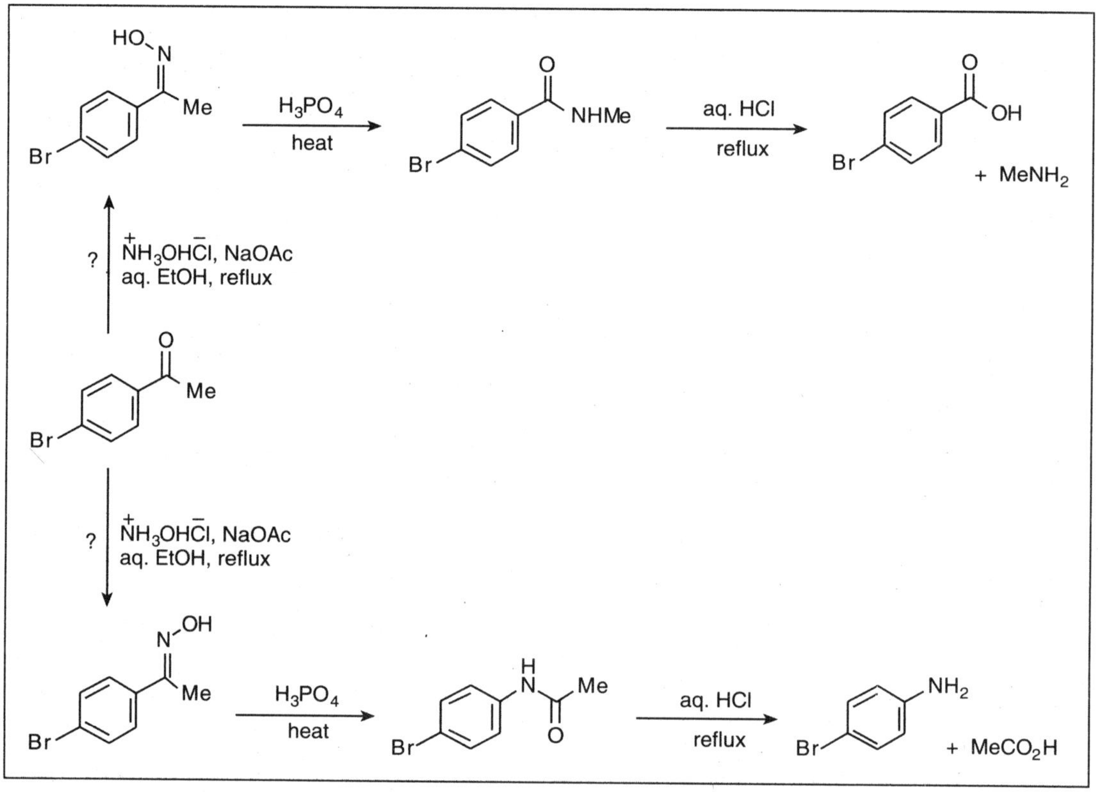

In the Beckmann rearrangement, an oxime is converted to an amide by treatment with one of a variety of Brønsted or Lewis acids. The reaction involves migration of group to the electron-deficient nitrogen centre, and significant insight into the mechanism comes from the fact that it is the alkyl group *anti*- to the hydroxyl group of the oxime which migrates. This result is explained by invoking concerted migration of the alkyl group with heterolytic cleavage of the N–O bond. The resulting nitrilium ion is then quenched by addition of a nucleophile (usually water) followed by tautomerization to the amide product (see p. 519).

Unfortunately, examples of stereospecific Beckmann rearrangements are rare, due to the stereochemical lability of oximes under the reaction conditions. Frequently, prior interconversion between *E*- and *Z*-oximes occurs under the acidic conditions used for the rearrangement and any stereochemical information is therefore lost. In the following example, not only is the

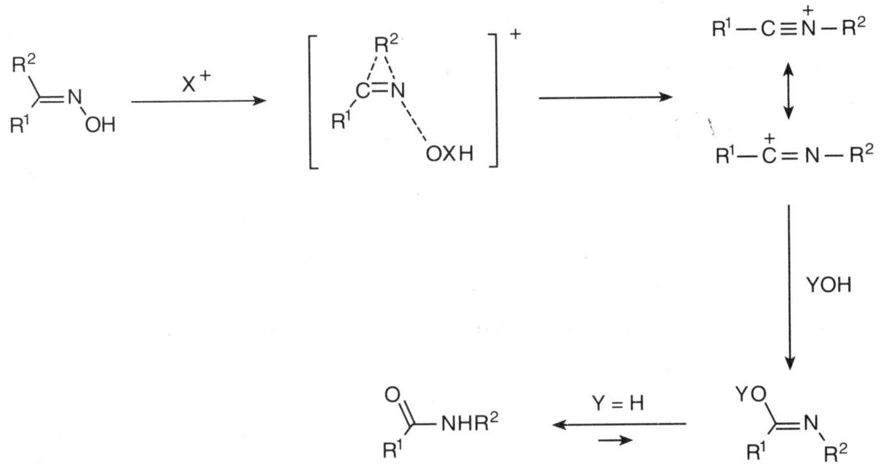

initial oxime formed with a high degree of stereoselectivity, but the rearrangement leads very cleanly to one amide, thus permitting identification of the initial oxime stereochemistry. Analysis of the amide is carried out by identification of the products obtained after hydrolysis. Experiment 5 also describes the preparation of a simple oxime.

Level	2
Time	2 × 3 h
Equipment	apparatus for reflux

Materials

1. Conversion of 4-bromoacetophenone to the oxime

4-bromoacetophenone (FW 199.1)	8.0 g (40 mmol)	**irritant**
hydroxylamine hydrochloride (FW 69.5)	4.9 g (70 mmol)	**corrosive, hygroscopic**
ethanol		**flammable, toxic**
sodium acetate trihydrate (FW 136.1)	5.5 g (40 mmol)	

2. Beckmann rearrangement of the oxime

polyphosphoric acid	*ca.* 50 g	**corrosive, hygroscopic**

NOTE: ***take great care when handling polyphosphoric acid. Use of this highly corrosive reagent is made worse by its syrupy consistency***

ethanol	**flammable, toxic**

3. Hydrolysis of the amide

hydrochloric acid (conc.)	**corrosive**
ammonia solution (conc.)	**corrosive, irritant**

Procedure

1. Conversion of 4-bromoacetophenone to the oxime

Dissolve the 4-bromoacetophenone in 20 mL of ethanol in a 50 mL round-bottomed flask and add the hydroxylamine hydrochloride and sodium acetate dissolved in 15 mL of warm water. Heat the mixture to reflux[1] on a water bath for 20 min and then filter the hot solution rapidly through a fluted filter paper.[2] Cool the filtrate in an ice bath and collect the crystalline oxime by filtration under suction.[3] Wash the crystals with a little cold 50% ethanol and dry them on the filter with suction. Record the yield and mp[4] of your product.

[1] *See Fig. 3.23(a)*

[2] *See Fig. 3.5*

[3] *See Fig. 3.7*

[4] *Do this during part 3*

2. Beckmann rearrangement of the oxime

Roughly weigh out the polyphosphoric acid[5] into a 100 mL Erlenmeyer flask, to this add 5.0 g of your oxime from the first step and heat the mixture on a boiling water bath for 10 min, stirring continuously with a glass rod. **Carefully**[6] pour the hot mixture onto *ca.* 100 g of crushed ice and stir with the glass rod until the viscous mass has dispersed, leaving behind a suspension of the amide. Filter off the product with suction and wash the residue with cold water until the washings are no longer acidic. Dry the solid as thoroughly as possible with suction and note the yield of crude product.[7] Recrystallize a portion from ethanol and obtain the mp of the purified material. Consult the literature and use this to make a provisional structural assignment for the amide.

[5] ***Care! Corrosive***

[6] ***Care! Wear gloves***

[7] *The crude material can be used in part 3*

HOOD

3. Hydrolysis of the amide

Place 2.15 g (10 mmol) of your crude amide in a 50 mL round-bottomed flask, add 12 mL concentrated hydrochloric acid and reflux the mixture over a small flame for 30 min.[8] At the end of this period, add 20 mL of water to the contents of the flask and pour the mixture slowly[9] into 20 mL of concentrated ammonia with cooling in an ice bath. Cool the alkaline mixture to 0°C and scratch the walls of the flask if the precipitated product is reluctant to solidify. Filter the mixture with suction,[3] wash the solid with a little cold water and dry as thoroughly as possible with suction on the filter funnel. Note the crude yield of your product, recrystallize all of it from aqueous ethanol, and record the mp of this material.

[8] ***HCl fumes evolved***

[9] ***Care! Exothermic***

Problems

1 Carry out a literature search for the melting points of all the possible products in the sequence that you have just carried out. From the melting points of the amide from the Beckmann rearrangement and the amine from the hydrolysis reaction, propose structures for these materials and hence derive the initial stereochemistry of the oxime.

2 Assuming no initial stereorandomization of the starting oxime, what would be the expected products from the following reactions (a) to (d):

(a)

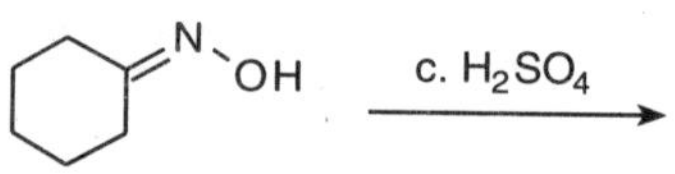

(b)
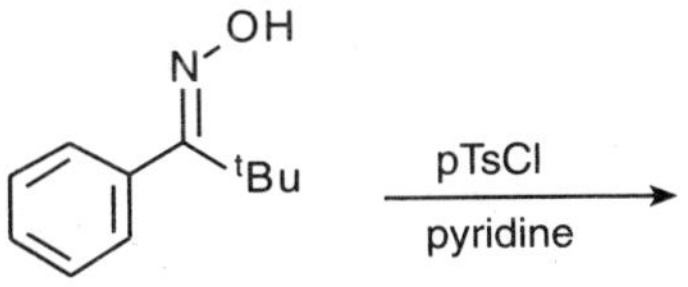

(c)
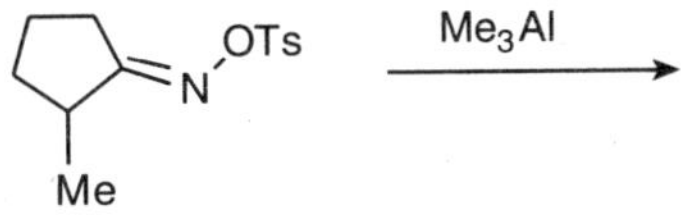

(d)
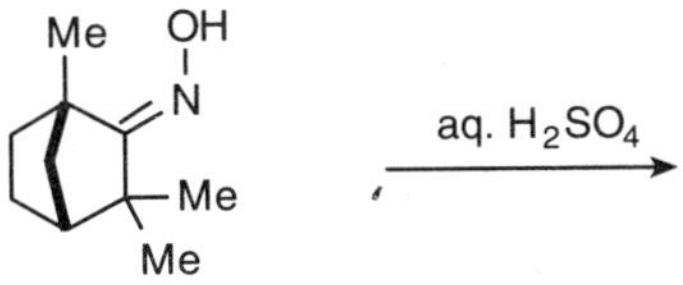

Further reading

For the procedure on which this experiment is based, see: R.M. Southam, *J. Chem. Educ.*, 1976, **53**, 34.

For a general discussion of rearrangement reactions, see: L.M. Harwood, *Polar Rearrangements*, Oxford University Press, Oxford, 1992.

Chapter 8 Carbon–Carbon Bond-Forming Reactions

Organic chemistry is based on compounds containing carbon–carbon bonds, and therefore the formation of these bonds is fundamental to the experimentalist. If one considers a carbon–carbon single bond which contains two electrons, there are only two ways in which the bond can be formed: from the reaction of two fragments supplying one electron each (a free-radical reaction), or from the reaction of an electron-rich species (a nucleophile) with an electron-deficient species (an electrophile). Although recently we have seen rapid advances in the use of free radicals, many of the useful laboratory and industrial reactions for the formation of carbon–carbon bonds still fall into the second category, that is the reaction of a nucleophilic carbon species with an electrophilic one.

There are many organic compounds that contain an electrophilic carbon atom: halides, sulfonates, epoxides, aldehydes, ketones, esters and nitriles to name but a few. However, compounds that contain a nucleophilic carbon atom useful for forming carbon–carbon bonds essentially fall into two groups: organometallic compounds, R_3C–Metal, which contain a formal carbon–metal bond heavily polarized as $R_3C^{\delta-}$–$Metal^{\delta+}$, and carbanions, R_3C^-, formed by deprotonation of the corresponding R_3CH with an appropriate base.

This chapter focuses on the formation of carbon–carbon bonds, and is organized according to the carbon nucleophile, organometallic reagent or carbanion involved, although for convenience the carbanions are divided into two groups: those which are stabilized by an adjacent carbonyl group (enolate anions) and those which are stabilized by an adjacent heteroatom.

Also included are experiments on aromatic electrophilic substitution, which can also lead to new carbon–carbon bonds, and experiments on pericyclic reactions.

8.1 Grignard and organolithium reagents

Although organometallic reagents involving many different metals have found application in organic synthesis, those based on magnesium and lithium have probably found the widest use. Organomagnesium reagents, more commonly known as Grignard reagents after their discoverer the Frenchman Victor Grignard, who received the Nobel Prize in 1912, are particularly suited for use in the organic laboratory since they are easily prepared by reaction of an alkyl or aryl halide with magnesium metal in a dry ether solvent. Organolithium compounds on the other hand are more difficult to handle, requiring the use of rigorously anhydrous solvents under an inert atmosphere. They are made by the reaction of halides with lithium metal, although many organolithium reagents are commercially available as stock solutions in inert solvents. Whilst for practical purposes the structures of organometallic compounds can be regarded as monomeric, in actual fact the structures are much more complicated, and involve aggregated species.

As well as this section, other examples of Grignard reagents in use can be found in Experiments 72 and 73.

Experiment 36 *Grignard reagents: addition of phenylmagnesium bromide to ethyl 3-oxobutanoate ethylene ketal*

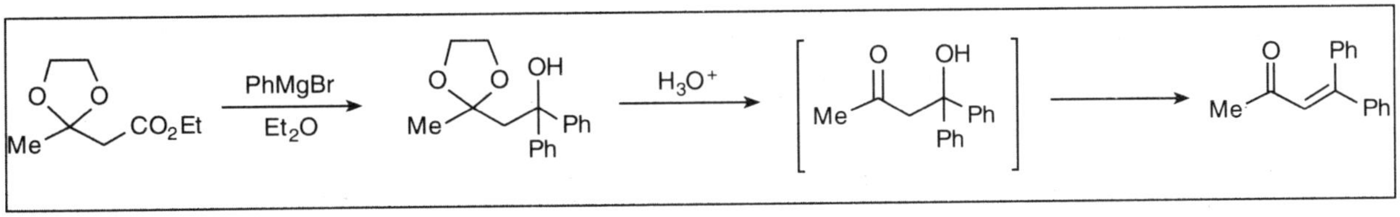

Esters react readily with an excess of a Grignard reagent to give tertiary alcohols. This experiment illustrates the addition of phenylmagnesium bromide, prepared from bromobenzene and magnesium turnings, to the ethylene ketal of ethyl 3-oxobutanoate, prepared as described in Experiment 4. It is essential for the reactive ketone group of ethyl 3-oxobutanoate to be protected from reaction with the Grignard reagent. In a second, optional step, the ketal-protecting group is removed by acid hydrolysis, to give the keto tertiary alcohol which spontaneously dehydrates under the acidic conditions to the α,β-unsaturated ketone 4,4-diphenylbut-3-en-2-one. The final product can be purified by column chromatography if desired.

Level	3
Time	2 × 3 h (plus 3 h for the hydrolysis–elimination step)
Equipment	magnetic stirrer/hotplate; apparatus for addition with reflux, extraction/separation, suction filtration, recrystallization, reflux, column chromatography
Instruments	IR, NMR

Materials

1. Preparation and reaction of the Grignard reagent		
magnesium turnings (FW 24.3)	1.34 g (55 mmol)	**flammable**
diethyl ether (dry)		**flammable, irritant**
iodine	1–2 crystals	**lachrymator, corrosive**
bromobenzene (FW 157.0)	7.85 g (50 mmol)	**irritant**
ethyl 3-oxobutanoate ketal (FW 174.2) (prepared as in Experiment 4)	4.35 g (25 mmol)	**irritant**
light petroleum (bp 60–80°C)		**flammable**
2. Hydrolysis of the ketal		
hydrochloric acid (conc.)		**corrosive**
acetone		**flammable**
diethyl ether		**flammable, irritant**
sodium bicarbonate solution (saturated)		
silica gel		**irritant dust**

Procedure

All apparatus must be thoroughly dried in a hot (>120°C) oven before use.

1. Preparation and reaction of the Grignard reagent

Set up a 100 mL round-bottomed flask with an addition funnel, magnetic stirrer bar and reflux condenser carrying a calcium chloride guard tube.[1] Add the magnesium turnings, 10 mL *dry* diethyl ether[2] and a crystal of iodine to the flask. Place 10 mL *dry* diethyl ether and the bromobenzene in the addition funnel, and add a few drops of this solution to the magnesium. Start the stirrer, and wait until the formation of the Grignard reagent starts.[3] Add the remaining bromobenzene solution diluted with an extra 20 mL diethyl ether at such a rate as to maintain gentle reflux. After the addition is complete, reflux the mixture with stirring on a hot water bath for about 10 min. Cool the flask in an ice bath, and then add a solution of the ethyl 3-oxobutanoate ketal in 10 mL *dry* diethyl ether dropwise. After the addition is complete, stir the mixture for a further 30 min at room temperature, and then add 20 mL ice-water to the flask.[4] When the ice has melted, add a further 10 mL diethyl ether, and stir the mixture until the gummy solid dissolves.[5] Transfer the mixture to a separatory funnel, and separate the layers. Extract the aqueous layer with 10 mL diethyl ether, combine the ether layers, wash them with 10 mL water, and dry them over $MgSO_4$.[6] Filter off the drying agent by suction,[7] and evaporate the filtrate

[1] *See Fig. 3.25(a)*

[2] *See Appendix 2*

[3] *The start of the reaction will be apparent; the diethyl ether starts to reflux, and takes on a grey-brown appearance*

[4] *May be left at this stage*

[5] *Extra diethyl ether may be needed*

[6] *May be left at this stage*

[7] *See Fig. 3.7*

on the rotary evaporator to leave a yellow-orange oil which crystallizes on cooling.[6] Recrystallize the crude product from diethyl ether. Record the yield, mp and the IR (Nujol®) and NMR ($CDCl_3$) spectra of your product.

2. *Hydrolysis of the ketal: 4,4-diphenylbut-3-en-2-one (optional)*

Place 2.84 g (10 mmol) of the above tertiary alcohol, 1 mL concentrated hydrochloric acid, 25 mL acetone and 1.5 mL water in a 50 mL round-bottomed flask. Fit a condenser, and heat the mixture under reflux for 1 h.[8] Transfer the cooled mixture to a separatory funnel, add 25 mL water, and extract it with 2 × 15 mL diethyl ether. Combine the ether layers, wash them with 15 mL saturated sodium bicarbonate solution,[9] 15 mL water, and dry them over $MgSO_4$.[6] Filter off the drying agent by suction, and evaporate the filtrate on the rotary evaporator to leave the crude product. Purify a small sample of the product by column chromatography on silica gel using toluene as the eluant.[10] Record the yield, and the IR ($CHCl_3$) and NMR ($CDCl_3$) spectra of your chromatographed product.

[8] *See Fig. 3.23(a)*

[9] ***Care! CO_2 evolved***

[10] *See Chapter 3*

Problems

1. Write a reaction mechanism for the acid hydrolysis of the ketal-protecting group, and the subsequent dehydration of the resulting keto alcohol.
2. Assign the spectroscopic data for your product(s).
3. Suggest an alternative synthesis of 4,4-diphenylbut-3-en-2-one.

Further reading

For the procedure on which this experiment is based, see: D.R. Paulson, A.L. Hartwig and G.F. Moran, *J. Chem. Educ.*, 1973, **50**, 216.

Experiment 37

Conjugate addition of a Grignard reagent to s*-butyl but-2-enoate (*s*-butyl crotonate): preparation and saponification of* s*-butyl 3-methylheptanoate*

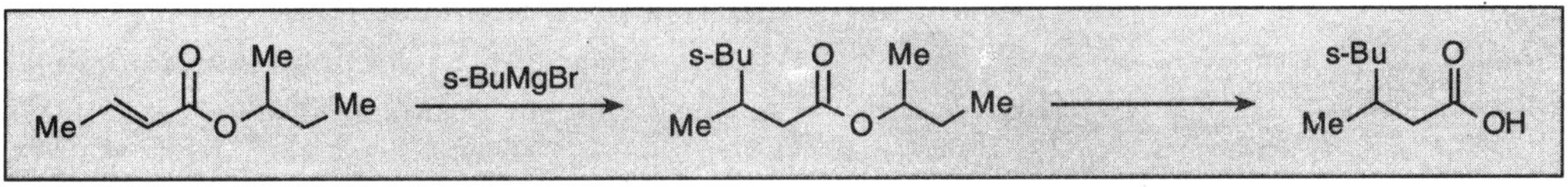

α,β-Unsaturated carbonyl compounds can either undergo direct nucleophilic attack at the carbonyl group (often called *1,2-addition*) or conjugate addition at the β-carbon (often called *Michael* or *1,4-addition*). The site of attack is dependent on the nature of the α,β-unsaturated carbonyl compound and on the attacking nucleophile. When Grignard reagents are used as nucleophiles, the site of addition is not always easy to predict, and both 1,2- and 1,4-addition products can be formed. This experiment illustrates the conjugate addition of butylmagnesium bromide to the α,β-unsaturated ester *s*-butyl but-2-enoate, prepared as described in Experiment 2, to give *s*-butyl 3-methylheptanoate. In this case, conjugate addition is favoured by having a bulky secondary ester, and by using a large excess of Grignard reagent with a slow addition of the ester. In a second optional step, the product ester can be hydrolyzed to the corresponding acid, 3-methylheptanoic acid.

Level	3
Time	2 × 3 h (plus 3 h for optional hydrolysis)
Equipment	magnetic stirrer/hotplate, vacuum pump; apparatus for reflux with addition (2- or 3-neck flask), extraction/separation, suction filtration, distillation under reduced pressure, reflux, short path distillation
Instruments	IR, NMR

Materials

1. Preparation of s-*butyl 3-methylheptanoate*		
magnesium turnings (FW 24.3)	1.88 g (77 mmol)	**flammable**
1-bromobutane (FW 137.0)	10.5 mL (98 mmol)	**flammable, irritant**
s-butyl but-2-enoate (FW 142.2) (Experiment 2)	4.27 g (30 mmol)	**irritant**
diethyl ether		**flammable, irritant**
hydrochloric acid (conc.)		**corrosive**
sodium bicarbonate solution (saturated)		
2. Preparation of 3-methylheptamoic acid		
ethanol		**flammable, toxic**
potassium hydroxide (FW 56.1)	0.93 g (17 mmol)	**corrosive**
sodium chloride solution (saturated)		

Procedure

All apparatus must be thoroughly dried in a hot (>120°C) oven before use.

HOOD

1. Preparation of s*-butyl 3-methylheptanoate*

Place the magnesium turnings in a 250 mL two- or three-neck flask fitted with a reflux condenser carrying a calcium chloride guard tube, a 50 mL addition funnel, and a stirrer bar.[1] Stopper the third neck, and place the flask in a water bath on a magnetic stirrer/hotplate. Place a solution of the 2-bromobutane in 25 mL *dry* diethyl ether[2] in the addition funnel. Add 2 mL of the bromobutane solution to the flask, heat the reaction mixture to reflux for a few minutes in a hot water bath, and start the stirrer. The formation of the Grignard reagent should start almost immediately.[3] Add the remainder of the bromobutane solution at such a rate as to maintain the diethyl ether at gentle reflux.[4] After the addition has been completed, heat the solution under reflux for a further 10 min, and then cool the flask in an ice bath for 10 min. In the meantime, place a solution of the *s*-butyl but-2-enoate in 30 mL diethyl ether in the addition funnel; add this dropwise to the stirred ice-cooled reaction mixture.[5] After the

[1] *See Fig. 3.24*

[2] *See Appendix 2*

[3] *If not, consult the instructor*

[4] *Addition should take about 15 min*

[5] *Addition should take about 20 min*

addition of the ester is complete, stir the mixture for a further 10 min in the ice bath, and then at room temperature for 30 min.[6] Place 8 mL concentrated hydrochloric acid, 10 mL diethyl ether and 50 g crushed ice in a 250 mL beaker. Stir the mixture vigorously, and slowly pour the Grignard reaction mixture into the beaker, adding more ice if necessary to keep the temperature at about 0°C. Transfer the mixture to a separatory funnel and separate the layers. Retain the ether layer, and extract the aqueous layer with 3 × 10 mL diethyl ether. Combine all the ether layers and wash them with 10 mL saturated sodium bicarbonate solution,[7] then with 10 mL water, and dry them over $MgSO_4$.[6] Filter off the drying agent with suction,[8] evaporate the filtrate on the rotary evaporator, and distil the residue[9] from a 10 mL flask under reduced pressure (*ca.* 9 mmHg) using a vacuum pump, collecting the product at *ca.* 90°C. Record the exact bp, yield and the IR ($CHCl_3$) and NMR ($CDCl_3$) spectra of your product.

[6]*May be left at this stage*

[7]***Care! CO_2 evolved***

[8]*See Fig. 3.7*

[9]*See Fig. 3.53*

2. *Preparation of 3-methylheptanoic acid (optional)*

Place a mixture of 2.0 g *s*-butyl 3-methylheptanoate, 0.93 g potassium hydroxide, 5 mL ethanol and 1 mL water in a 25 mL round-bottomed flask. Fit a reflux condenser, and heat the mixture under reflux for 30 min.[10] Cool the mixture to room temperature, dilute it with 10 mL water, and acidify it by the addition of 3 mL concentrated hydrochloric acid.[11] Transfer the mixture to a separatory funnel, and extract the product with 3 × 5 mL diethyl ether. Combine the ether layers, wash them with 5 mL saturated sodium chloride solution, and dry them over $MgSO_4$.[6] Filter off the drying agent with suction,[7] evaporate the filtrate on the rotary evaporator, and distil the residue under reduced pressure in the short path distillation apparatus[12] (*ca.* 10 mmHg) using a vacuum pump, collecting the product at *ca.* 115°C. Record the exact bp, yield and the IR ($CHCl_3$) and NMR ($CHCl_3$) spectra of your product.

[10]*See Fig. 3.23*

[11]***Care! Exothermic***

[12]*See Fig. 3.54*

Problems

1 Discuss in detail the factors affecting the 1,2- or 1,4-addition of nucleophiles to α,β-unsaturated carbonyl compounds. In the present experiment, what product would you expect if butyllithium were used in place of butylmagnesium bromide?

2 Suggest an alternative synthesis of 3-methylheptanoic acid.

3 Compare and contrast the IR spectra of *s*-butyl 3-methylheptanoate and 3-methylheptanoic acid.

4 Assign as fully as possible the NMR spectra of your products, paying particular attention to the spin–spin splitting patterns.

Further reading

For the procedure on which this experiment is based, see: J. Munch-Petersen, *Org. Synth. Coll. Vol.*, **5**, 762.

Experiment 38 — *Acetylide anions: preparation of ethyl phenylpropynoate (ethyl phenylpropiolate)*

$$PhC\equiv CH \xrightarrow[\text{ii. ClCO}_2\text{Et}]{\text{i. Na, Et}_2\text{O}} PhC\equiv CCO_2Et$$

One of the characteristic properties of alkynes is that terminal acetylenes are weakly acidic, and the acetylenic sp proton can be removed by an appropriate base to give an acetylide anion. This major difference between alkynes and alkenes is due to the enhanced stability of the *sp* acetylide anion, with its high degree of s-character, over the sp^2 alkene anion. The difference is reflected in the pK_a values: ethyne pK_a 25; ethene pK_a 44. The acidity of terminal acetylenes can be exploited in synthesis because, once formed, the nucleophilic acetylide reacts with a range of electrophilic compounds such as alkyl halides, acylating agents and carbonyl compounds. This experiment involves the formation and acylation of the anion derived from phenylacetylene, which is commercially available. The anion is generated by reaction of the alkyne with sodium metal in dry ether, and is subsequently treated with ethyl chloroformate to give ethyl phenylpropynoate. The conjugated triple bond in ethyl phenylpropynoate is highly susceptible to attack by nucleophiles in a Michael-type reaction.

Level	3
Time	2 × 3 h (with overnight stirring in between)
Equipment	magnetic stirrer/hotplate; apparatus for reaction with addition and reflux (3-neck flask), extraction/separation, suction filtration, distillation under reduced pressure or short path distillation
Instruments	IR, NMR

Materials

phenylacetylene (FW 102.1)	11.0 mL, 10.2 g (0.1 mmol)	**flammable, irritant**
ethyl chloroformate (FW 108.5)	9.5 mL, 10.8 g (0.1 mol)	**lachrymator, flammable, toxic**
sodium (FW 23.0)	2.3 g (0.1 mol)	**flammable**
diethyl ether (dry)		**flammable, irritant**
hydrochloric acid (10%)		**corrosive**
sodium bicarbonate solution (saturated)		

Procedure

HOOD

All apparatus must be thoroughly dried in a hot (>120°C) oven before use. Equip a 250 mL two- or three-neck flask with a magnetic stirrer bar, addition funnel, and reflux condenser protected with a calcium chloride guard tube.[1]

[1]*See Fig. 3.25*

[2]*See Appendix 2*
[3]***Caution***

Place 50 mL *dry* diethyl ether[2] in the flask. Cut up the sodium metal into *small* pieces,[3] and add them directly to the diethyl ether in the flask. Stopper the third neck of the flask, start the stirrer, and then slowly add a solution of the phenylacetylene in 20 mL *dry* diethyl ether from the addition funnel. Continue to stir the mixture until all the pieces of sodium dissolve, and a slurry of the acetylide anion is formed. If any sodium metal remains after stirring for 1 h, heat the mixture under reflux, with stirring, using a warm water bath. When formation of the acetylide is complete (it is important to ensure that no sodium remains unreacted), add a solution of the ethyl chloroformate in 15 mL *dry* diethyl ether, and stir the reaction mixture overnight at room temperature. Carefully add ethanol (1–2 mL), then some ice, followed by 25 mL dilute hydrochloric acid, to the reaction mixture and, after stirring for a few minutes, transfer the mixture to a separatory funnel. Separate the layers, and wash the ether layer with 25 mL saturated sodium bicarbonate solution and with 25 mL water. Dry the ether extract over $MgSO_4$.[4] Filter off the drying agent with suction[5] and evaporate the filtrate on the rotary evaporator. Transfer the residue to a small distillation set and distil it under reduced pressure at *ca.* 20 mmHg using a water aspirator.[6] Collect a fore-run of unreacted phenylacetylene, followed by the product at *ca.* 150–160°C. Record the exact bp, yield and the IR ($CHCl_3$) and NMR ($CDCl_3$) spectra of your product. Record the spectra of phenylacetylene for comparison.

[4]*May be left at this stage*
[5]*See Fig. 3.7*
[6]*See Fig. 3.53*

Problems

1 Apart from the acidity of the acetylenic proton, discuss other differences in the chemistry of alkynes and alkenes.
2 Suggest an alternative synthesis of ethyl phenylpropynoate.
3 How would ethyl phenylpropynoate react with: (i) aniline, and (ii) cyclopentadiene?
4 Compare and contrast the IR and NMR spectra of phenylacetylene and ethyl phenylpropynoate. What features of the IR spectra are characteristic of the different types of triple bond? Comment on the chemical shift of the acetylenic proton in the NMR spectrum of phenylacetylene.

Further reading

For the procedure on which this experiment is based, see: J.M. Woollard, *J. Chem. Educ.*, 1984, **61**, 648.

Experiment 39

Generation and estimation of a solution of t*-butyl-lithium and preparation of the highly branched alcohol tri-*t*-butylcarbinol (3-(1, 1-dimethyl)ethyl-2,2,4,4-tetramethylpentan-3-ol)*

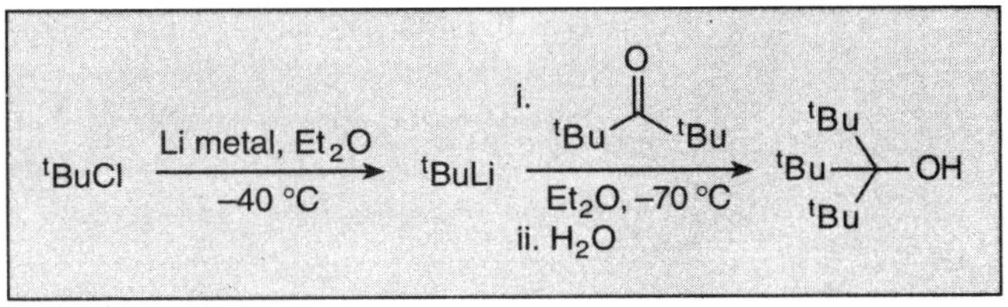

In this experiment the highly reactive *t*-butyllithium will be generated and used to prepare a highly branched molecule by condensation with 2,2,4,4-tetramethylpentan-3-one (hexamethylacetone). The usual reactivity of *t*-butyllithium is that of an extremely powerful base (the pK_a of the *t*-butyl carbanion is difficult to measure but has been estimated as >51) but, in the absence of any readily removable protons as with the substrate used here, nucleophilic addition to the carbonyl carbon occurs to yield a highly sterically hindered alcohol.

The lithium reagent is prepared by reacting *t*-butyl chloride with finely divided lithium metal containing about 1% of sodium to aid initiation of the reaction; other forms of lithium are ineffective. The reagent is not isolated, but reacted *in situ* with the requisite quantity of ketone, after first estimating the amount of alkyl lithium present by titrating against 2,5-dimethoxybenzyl alcohol. Due to the highly reactive nature of the reagent and intermediates, the experiment cannot be left at any stage before quenching with water and extracting the condensation product into ether. If circumstances do not permit an uninterrupted 6 h laboratory session, the titration of *t*-butyllithium solution and preparation of the alcohol can be carried out using commercially available reagent.

Level	4
Time	drying of solvents and preparation of glassware 3 h; generation of *t*-BuLi, titration and preparation of tri-*t*-butylcarbinol 6 h; purification and spectroscopic analysis 3 h
Equipment	2 × 10 mL syringes and needles, 20 mL syringe and needle, 2 × 5 mL syringes and needles; apparatus for stirring under inert atmosphere at reduced temperature with addition by syringe, –78°C cooling bath
Instruments	IR, NMR

Materials

1. Preparation of t*-butyl-lithium*

lithium metal powder or shot (sodium content 1%) (FW 6.9)	*ca.* 0.35 g (50 mmol)	**flammable, moisture sensitive**

NOTE: ***lithium metal of this form is extremely pyrophoric and moisture sensitive, and is usually supplied as a dispersion in mineral oil. With this reagent it is sufficient to weigh out the corresponding quantity of dispersion (taking into account the percentage of lithium present by weight) into a weighed flask and reweigh the flask and contents after removal of the mineral oil. The quantity of 2-chloro-2-methylpropane used can then be adjusted to the actual weight of lithium transferred. Great care must be exercised in its handling, particularly when free of mineral oil***

Continued

Box cont.

2-chloro-2-methylpropane (*t*-butyl chloride) (FW 92.6), redistilled	*ca.* 4.65 g (50 mmol)	**flammable**
diethyl ether (anhydrous)		**flammable, irritant**
ethanol (anhydrous)		**flammable, toxic**
2. *Titration of* t-*butyl-lithium solution*		
2,5-dimethoxybenzyl alcohol (FW 168.2)	*ca.* 0.4 g	
diethyl ether (anhydrous)		**flammable, irritant**
3. *Preparation of tri-*t-*butylcarbinol*		
t-butyl-lithium solution		
2,2,4,4-tetramethyl-3-pentanone (hexamethylacetone) (FW 142.2)	2.15 g (15 mmol)	**flammable**

Procedure

The diethyl ether must be dried and distilled according to the procedure in Appendix 2. The 2-chloro-2-methylpropane must be distilled before use. All apparatus must be thoroughly dried in a hot (>120°C) oven before use. This preparative work will require about 3 h. Once the preparation of the t-*butyl-lithium reagent has been commenced the experiment must be continued without a break at least until the tri-*t-*butylcarbinol experiment has been quenched and the solution of crude product is drying over* $MgSO_4$*. This stage should not be started unless it is possible to continue to this break point should delays occur.*

HOOD

1. *Preparation of* t-*butyl-lithium*

Equip a 100 mL three-neck flask with two stoppers and a septum and weigh it. Rapidly weigh into it the required amount of lithium powder or shot dispersed in mineral oil.[1] Replace one stopper with a gas bubbler, clamp the flask over the stirrer and flush it with argon for 5 min. Add 10 mL of *dry* diethyl ether by syringe to the flask through the septum, stir to disperse the lithium powder or shot and then allow the dispersion to settle. With a second syringe, draw off the supernatant liquid and dispose of this liquid by adding to 50 mL of anhydrous ethanol contained in a 250 mL beaker.[2] Repeat the procedure two more times, keeping one syringe for the addition of solvent and one syringe for the removal of supernatant. At the end of this procedure, dismantle the syringe used for removal of supernatant and place the barrel, plunger and needle in the beaker containing ethanol to destroy any lithium residues.[2] With the argon supply passing rapidly, warm the residue in the flask gently, using a hot air gun to remove any residual diethyl ether. Allow to cool, replace the gas inlet with the original stopper and rapidly reweigh the flask and contents to obtain the weight of lithium powder present. Return the flask to the magnetic stirrer, replace the stoppers with the gas inlet and a low temperature thermometer[3] and allow argon to pass for 5 min. Add 40 mL of *dry* diethyl ether to the residue of oil-free lithium, stir the mixture vigorously and cool to –40°C in a solid CO_2–acetone cooling bath. Add dropwise by syringe, a solu-

[1] ***Care! Flammable; wear gloves***

[2] ***Care!***

[3] *See Fig. 3.22*

tion of *t*-butyl chloride (equivalent to the amount of lithium present) in 10 mL of *dry* diethyl ether, taking care to maintain the temperature of the reaction flask between –30 and –40°C. When addition is complete, allow the mixture to stir below –40°C and commence setting up the apparatus for the estimation of the strength of this solution.

2. *Titration of* t*-butyl-lithium solution*

Weigh accurately (±1 mg) *ca.* 0.4 g of 2,5-dimethoxybenzyl alcohol into a 25 mL round-bottomed flask containing a small magnetic stirrer bar and close the flask with a septum. Flush out the flask with argon via a needle, add 10 mL of *dry* diethyl ether and stir the mixture. Remove about 4 mL of the prepared *t*-butyl-lithium solution by syringe, note the initial volume of solution in the syringe, and add it dropwise to the stirred solution of 2,5-dimethoxybenzyl alcohol at room temperature until a permanent red-brown colouration indicates the onset of dianion formation. Note the final volume of solution remaining in the syringe and hence calculate the concentration of the *t*-butyl-lithium solution you have prepared. Destroy the remaining solution remaining in the syringe by adding it to the titration flask and then adding anhydrous ethanol by syringe through the septum, maintaining the inert atmosphere.

3. *Preparation of tri-*t*-butylcarbinol*

Equip a 100 mL three-necked flask containing a magnetic stirrer bar with a gas inlet and bubbler, low temperature thermometer and a septum.[3] Add the 2,2,4,4-tetramethyl-3-pentanone and 20 mL of *dry* diethyl ether and flush out the apparatus with argon whilst the stirred solution is cooled to below –70°C using a solid CO_2–acetone cooling bath. Transfer 20 mmol of the *t*-butyl-lithium reagent to the cooled solution by syringe, adding it dropwise at such a rate that the temperature of the reaction does not exceed –60°C. After addition is complete, stir at this temperature for 1 h,[4] then add 10 mL of water to the mixture to quench the reaction and allow the contents of the flask to warm to room temperature with stirring. Separate the lower aqueous phase and wash the organic solution with a further two 50 mL portions of water and dry it over $MgSO_4$.[5] Filter the dry solution and remove the solvent on the rotary evaporator to furnish the crude alcohol. Recrystallize this material by dissolving in the minimum amount of cold ethanol and then adding an equal volume of water. Filter off the solid precipitate, drying with suction, and record the yield, mp, IR ($CHCl_3$) and NMR ($CDCl_3$) spectra of your purified material, and the IR ($CHCl_3$) and NMR ($CDCl_3$) spectra of the starting ketone.

[4] *Record spectra of starting material during this period*

[5] *May be left at this stage*

Problems

1 Assign the IR and NMR spectra that you have obtained on the starting ketone and product alcohol. Explain the salient features of each.

2 As well as 2,5-dimethoxybenzyl alcohol, another method for determining the strength of solutions of alkyl-lithium reagents uses titration against diphenylacetic acid. Describe the processes which are occurring in the titrations of these reagents.

Further reading

For tables of pK_a values and a discussion of base strength, see: J. March, *Advanced Organic Chemistry*, 4th edn, Wiley & Sons, New York, 1992, Chapter 8.

For the original method from which this procedure is adapted, see: P.D. Bartlett and E.B. Lefferts, *J. Am. Chem. Soc.*, 1955, **77**, 2804.

For further discussion of organolithium reagents, see: B.J. Wakefield, *Organolithium Methods*, Academic Press, London, 1988.

W.G. Kofron and L.M. Baclawski, *J. Org. Chem.*, 1976, **41**, 1879.

8.2 Enolate anions

Carbanions which are stabilized by an adjacent carbonyl group are known as *enolate anions*. The enolate anion is a particularly versatile intermediate in organic synthesis, since it is easily formed and reacts with a variety of electrophilic carbon species to give compounds with new carbon–carbon bonds. The ease of enolate anion formation depends on the acidity (pK_a) of the protons adjacent to the carbonyl group, and some pK_a values for typical carbonyl compounds are given below. It is important to have a rough idea of the acidity of protons adjacent to carbonyl groups, because this will influence the choice of base used to carry out the anion formation.

This section includes several examples of enolate anions in action. The experiments range from simple condensation reactions using a weak base, to those involving strong bases and requiring advanced syringe techniques.

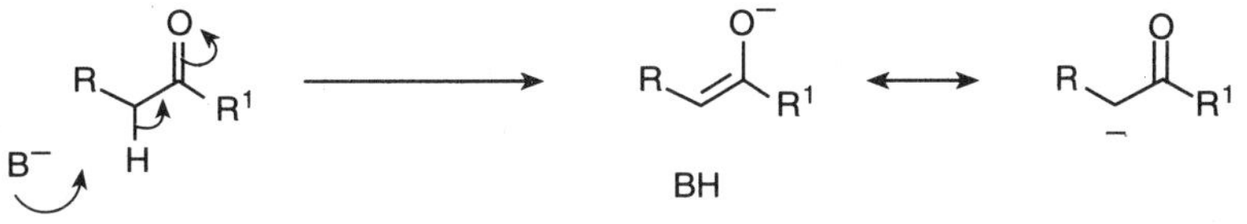

Compound	pK_a
$CH_2(COCH_3)_2$	9
$CH_3COCH_2CO_2CH_3$	11
$CH_2(CO_2C_2H_5)_2$	13
$C_6H_5COCH_3$	19
CH_3COCH_3	20

Additions of enolate anions to carbonyl compounds

A compound possessing an active methylene group may undergo base catalyzed addition to a carbonyl group, followed by subsequent dehydration of the initial adduct. This general reaction is referred to as the *aldol condensation* after the structure of the initial adduct in the archetypal self-condensation reaction of ethanal (acetaldehyde).

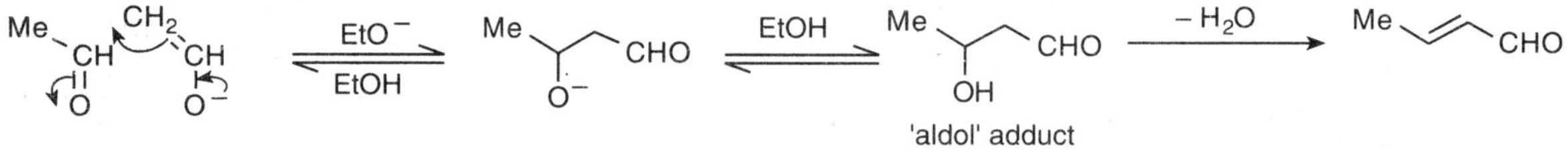

Whilst the carbanion stabilizing functionality of the nucleophile is frequently a carbonyl group, other moieties capable of resonance withdrawal of electrons (e.g. nitro, nitrile, triarylphosphonium, dimethylsulfonium and trialkylsilyl groups) are also effective. In addition, the electrophilic component may be the β-position of an α,β-unsubstituted carbonyl compound and this whole class of reactions has provided the chemist with a wealth of carbon–carbon bond-forming procedures.

The reaction is not without potential synthetic pitfalls, however. Both the addition and elimination are equilibrium steps but, as dehydration furnishes an α,β-unsaturated carbonyl compound, this can be used to drive the reaction over to completion. Nonetheless, the reverse process is possible and should always be borne in mind. In the reaction between two different carbonyl-containing substrates, self-condensation will compete with the desired cross-condensation. However, if precautions are taken to ensure that the component destined to be the nucleophile has been previously deprotonated or the electrophile is an aldehyde (usually aromatic) lacking α-hydrogens, very good yields of cross-condensation products can be obtained.

If the nucleophile is the enolate of a ketone, there are problems of regiocontrol in the generation of the desired enolate anion, but frequently the formation of one enolate can be favoured by the use of kinetic or thermodynamic deprotonation conditions.

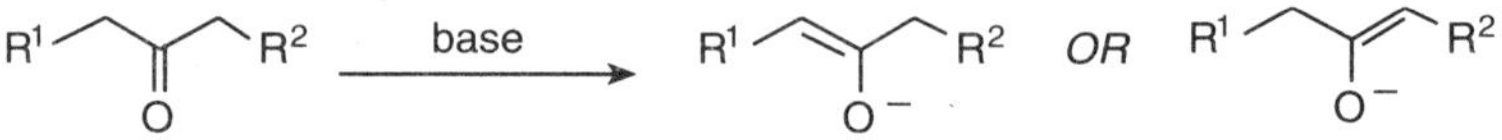

Finally, the aldol adducts generated from the enolate of an α-substituted carbonyl compound are usually formed as a mixture of diastereoisomers, although with care this problem can be overcome despite the fact that one of the asymmetric centres is at an epimerizable carbon.

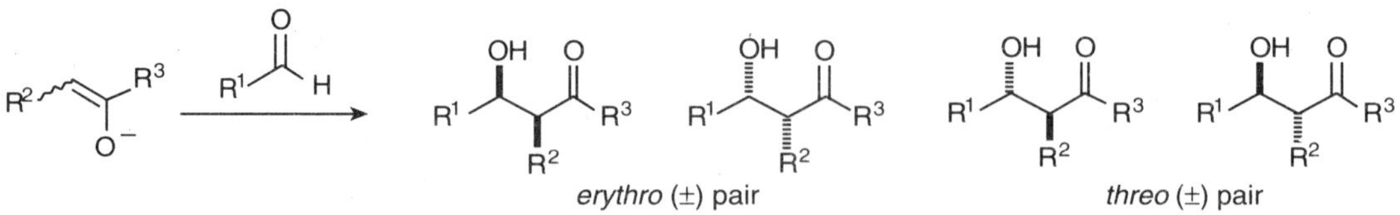

The following experiments will attempt to illustrate some of the variants of the basic aldol condensation which have been developed with the express intention of circumventing the difficulties alluded to above.

Further reading

For some of the many reviews of the aldol condensation, see: A.T. Nielsen and W.J. Houlihan, *Org. React.*, 1968, **16**, 1; C.H. Heathcock, *Science* (*Washington DC*), 1981, **214**, 395; D.A. Evans, J.V. Nelson and T.R. Taber, *Top. Stereochem.*, 1982, **13**, 1; A.S. Franklin and I. Paterson, *Contemp. Org. Synth.*, 1994, **1**, 317.

The Knoevenagel reaction

In the Knoevenagel reaction, an aldehyde without α-hydrogens is condensed with a doubly stabilized carbanion. The frequently employed enolate precursor for such reactions is propanedioic acid (malonic acid) and the condensation is accompanied by concomitant decarboxylation to yield an α,β-unsaturated acid. In the example below, a mixture of pyridine and piperidine is used as the base system. This also conveniently acts as the reaction solvent, permitting the reaction mixture to be heated to facilitate decarboxylation.

Experiment 40 — *Preparation of* E*-3-phenylpropenoic acid (cinnamic acid)*

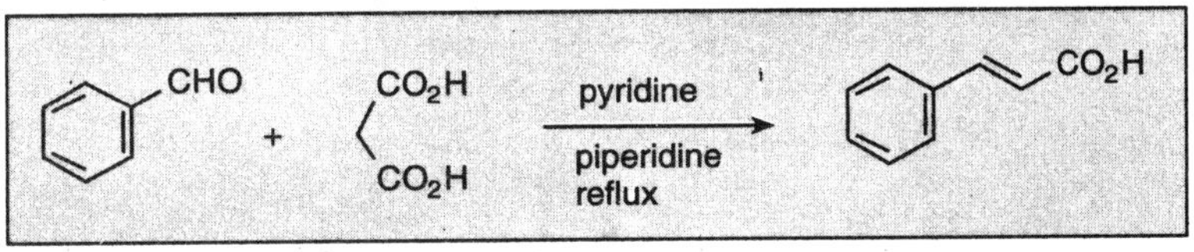

Level	1
Time	3 h
Equipment	apparatus for suction filtration

Materials

benzaldehyde (FW 106.1)	*ca.* 5 mL	**flammable, toxic**

NOTE: ***if benzaldehyde which has been freshly freed of benzoic acid is used, the purification procedure described below may be omitted and only 3 mL (3.2 g, 30 mmol) of benzaldehyde will be required***

propanedioic acid (malonic acid) (FW 104.1)	3.1 g (30 mmol)	**irritant**
pyridine	5 mL	**flammable, irritant, stench**
piperidine	*ca.* 10 drops	**corrosive, flammable, stench**
light petroleum (bp 40–60°C)		**flammable**
potassium carbonate	8.0 g	**corrosive**
hydrochloric acid (2 M)		**corrosive**

Procedure

HOOD

Weigh the potassium carbonate into a 100 mL Erlenmeyer flask and add 20 mL water and the benzaldehyde. Swirl the mixture vigorously, pour it into a test tube and allow the two phases to separate over 30 min when the upper layer of benzaldehyde should be clear.[1] Meanwhile weigh the propanedioic

[1] This procedure removes any benzoic acid present and may be omitted if pure benzaldehyde is available

acid into a second 100 mL conical flask and dissolve it in the pyridine with gentle warming on a hot water bath. From the test tube remove 3 mL of the upper layer carefully, using a graduated pipette, and add it to the solution of propanedioic acid in pyridine. Heat the resultant mixture on the water bath and add a catalytic quantity of piperidine (10 drops). Reaction is indicated by evolution of bubbles of carbon dioxide as the decarboxylation proceeds. Continue heating until the rate of appearance of bubbles becomes very slow (*ca.* 30 min). Make the volume up to 50 mL with 2 M hydrochloric acid and filter off the resultant solid with suction.[2] Triturate the solid on the funnel sequentially with 20 mL 2 M hydrochloric acid, 20 mL water and 20 mL light petroleum, drying with suction between washings. Tip the crystals into a preweighed 100 mL beaker and dry them to constant weight in an 80°C oven. Record the weight, yield and mp of your product.

[2]*See Fig. 3.7*

MICROSCALE

Level	1
Time	3 h
Equipment	apparatus for suction filtration, Craig tube recrystallization

Materials		
benzaldehyde (freshly distilled) (FW 106.1)	0.10 mL (1 mmol)	**flammable, toxic**
propanedioic acid (malonic acid) (FW 104.1)	104 mg (1 mmol)	**irritant**
pyridine	0.2 mL	**flammable, irritant**
piperidine	0.01 mL	**corrosive, flammable**
light petroleum (bp 40–60°C)		**flammable**
potassium carbonate	270 mg	**corrosive**
hydrochloric acid (2 M)		**corrosive**
hydrochloric acid (conc.)		**corrosive**

Procedure

Dissolve the malonic acid in the pyridine in a small test tube and add the benzaldehyde followed by the piperidine catalyst and warm the tube carefully in a water bath until gas evolution commences. Continue heating until the rate of gas evolution becomes very slow. Dilute to a total volume of *ca.* 1.7 mL with 2 M hydrochloric acid followed by 1 drop of concentrated hydrochloric acid and collect the solid at the pump using a micro-Hirsch funnel.[1] Wash the solid at the pump with 2 M hydrochloric acid (0.6 mL), water (0.6 mL) and light petroleum (0.6 mL), then suck dry, transfer to a vial and weigh. Dry *in vacuo* to constant weight and record the melting point and calculate the yield.

[1]*See Fig. 3.7*

Problems

1 Propose a reaction mechanism for the formation of *E*-3-phenylpropenoic acid. Why is the *E*-isomer formed in preference to the *Z*-isomer under the reaction conditions employed?

2 Suggest starting materials and reaction conditions for preparation of the following products:

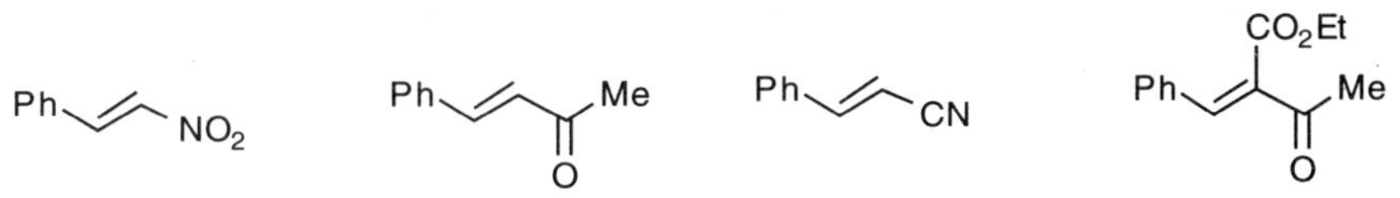

3 List the following compounds in order of their ease of deprotonation:

Further reading

For a review of the Knoevenagel reaction, see: G. Jones, *Org. React.*, 1967, **15**, 204.

Experiment 41 *Condensation of benzaldehyde with acetone: the Claisen–Schmidt reaction*

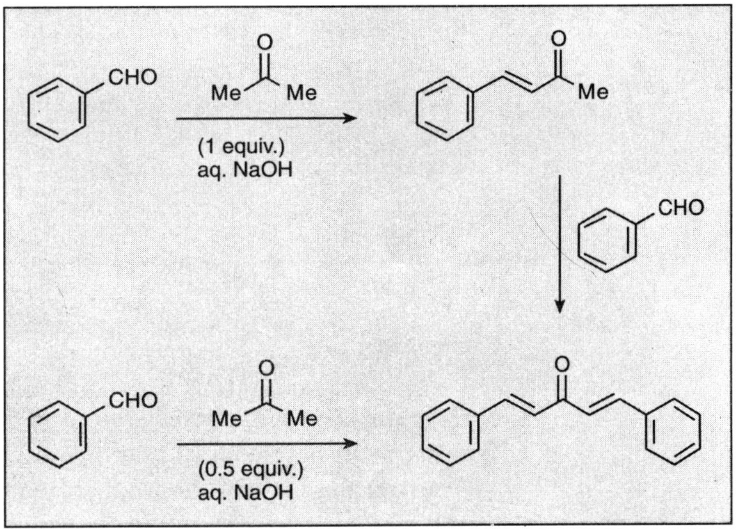

The *Claisen–Schmidt reaction* refers specifically to the synthesis of α,β-unsaturated ketones by the condensation of an aromatic aldehyde with a ketone. As the aromatic aldehyde possesses no hydrogens α- to the carbonyl group, it cannot undergo self-condensation but reacts readily with the ketone present. The initial aldol adduct cannot be isolated as it dehydrates spontaneously under the reaction conditions but the α,β-unsaturated ketone so produced also possesses activated hydrogens and may condense with a further molecule of benzaldehyde. In the following experiments, conditions will be chosen to optimize formation of the mono- and *bis*-adducts respectively, and they will be differentiated by their physical and spectroscopic properties. In the first experiment the acetone is used in a large excess in order to minimize the second condensation step. In the second experiment the benzaldehyde is present in twofold excess and sufficient ethanol is added to the reaction mixture to keep the initial condensation product in solution long enough to react with a second molecule of benzaldehyde.

Level	2
Time	preparation and isolation 3 h; purification and analysis 3 h (both parts may be run concurrently)
Equipment	magnetic stirrer; apparatus for reduced pressure distillation
Instruments	UV, IR, NMR

Materials

1. Preparation of E*-4-phenylbut-3-en-2-one*

benzaldehyde (FW 106.1)	8.0 mL, 8.4 g (80 mmol)	**flammable, toxic**
acetone (FW 58.1)	16.0 mL, 12.7 g (0.22 mol)	**flammable**
sodium hydroxide (2.5 M)	2.0 mL	**corrosive**
diethyl ether		**flammable, irritant**
light petroleum (bp 40–60°C)		**flammable**

*2. Preparation of 1,5-diphenyl-(*E,E*)-1-4-pentadien-3-one*

benzaldehyde (FW 106.1)	2.5 mL, 2.6 g (25 mmol)	**flammable, toxic**
acetone (FW 58.1)	0.9 mL, 0.75 g (13 mmol)	**flammable**
sodium hydroxide pellets	2.5 g	**corrosive, hygroscopic**
ethanol	20 mL	**flammable, toxic**
ethyl acetate		**flammable, irritant**

Procedure

HOOD

1. Preparation of* E*-4-phenylbut-3-en-2-one (benzylideneacetone)

Weight out the benzaldehyde in a 100 mL Erlenmeyer flask containing a magnetic stirrer bar and add to it the acetone followed by the aqueous sodium hydroxide. Place the flask in a water bath at 25–30°C and stir the reaction for 90 min (alternatively the flask may be shaken at frequent intervals).[1] At the end of this time, add dilute hydrochloric acid slowly until the solution is just acid to litmus and transfer the mixture to a separatory funnel, rinsing the conical flask with 15 mL diethyl ether. Separate the phases and extract the lower aqueous phase with a second volume of diethyl ether. Combine the organic extracts, wash with 15 mL water and dry them over $MgSO_4$.[2] Filter the solution, washing the desiccant with 5 mL diethyl ether and remove the

[1] *Commence Part 2 at this stage*

[2] *May be left at this stage*

[3]See Fig. 3.53

solvent on the rotary evaporator. Distil the crude product at reduced pressure (water aspirator)[3] and collect the fraction distilling at 130–145°C. Record the yield of the product which should solidify on standing. If crystallization does not occur spontaneously, scratch the walls of the flask with a glass rod or seed with a small crystal of pure material. Record the mp of this material and recrystallize a portion (*ca.* 1 g) of the solid from light petroleum. Record the mp of the colourless crystals obtained and obtain the UV spectrum (EtOH) and NMR spectrum ($CDCl_3$).

2. *Preparation of 1,5-diphenyl-(E,E)-1,4-pentadien-3-one (dibenzylideneacetone)*

Dissolve the sodium hydroxide pellets in 25 mL water, add the ethanol and cool the mixture under running water. Weigh the benzaldehyde into a 100 mL Erlenmeyer flask and add the acetone from a graduated pipette followed by the alkaline ethanolic solution. Stir the mixture for 15 min at 20–25°C (this may require some external cooling) and filter off the precipitate with suction,[4] washing thoroughly with cold water to remove any alkali. Allow the product to dry at room temperature on filter paper.[5] Record the yield and mp of the crude material, recrystallize it from ethyl acetate (*ca.* 2.5 mL g^{-1}) and record the yield and mp of the purified product. Obtain the IR spectrum (Nujol®) and NMR spectrum ($CDCl_3$).

[4]See Fig. 3.7

[5]Return to Part 1

Problems

1 Note the absorption maxima in the UV spectrum of the mono-condensation product and calculate the extinction coefficients. What is the chromophore in the molecule?

2 Compare the IR spectrum of the bis-condensation product with that of benzaldehyde (*Aldrich* FT-IR **1** (2) 104A). What are the important distinguishing features of each? Assign the important absorptions of the product spectrum.

3 Assign all of the absorptions in the NMR spectra of the mono-condensation product. Justify the assignment of the *E*-stereochemistry to the double bond. Compare the NMR spectra of the two condensation products.

4 Make a list of named reactions which proceed by related pathways. A major drawback of the aldol condensation is the possibility of self-condensation as well as cross-condensation. What two synthetically useful reagents are utilized to overcome this?

5 Aromatic aldehydes may also undergo a disproportionation reaction in the presence of aqueous alkali. What is the mechanism of this reaction and what are the products?

Further reading

For the procedure upon which this experiment is based, see: B.L. Hawbecker, D.W. Kurtz, T.D. Putnam, P.A. Ahlers and G.D. Gerber, *J. Chem. Educ.*, 1978, **55**, 540.

Experiment 42 *Synthesis of 5,5-dimethylcyclohexane-1,3-dione (dimedone)*

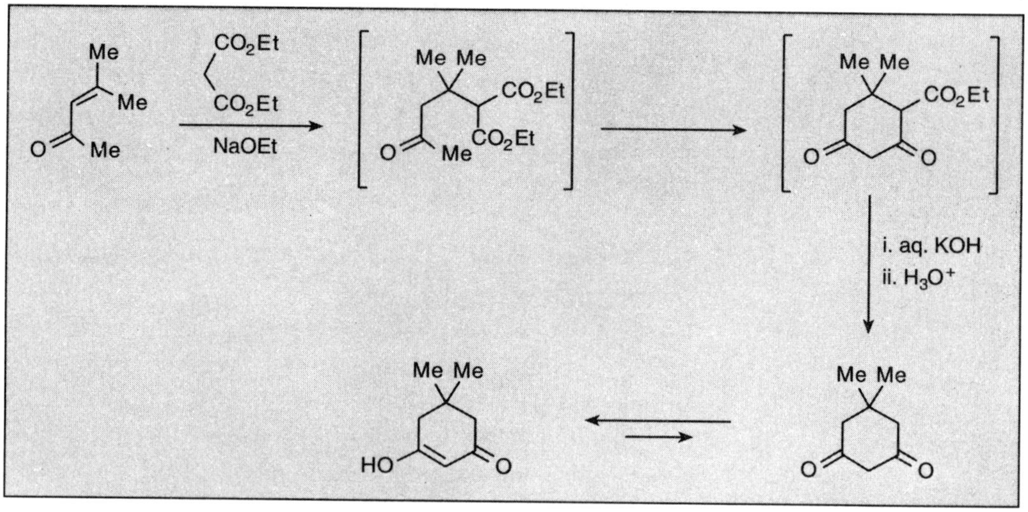

The base catalyzed conjugate addition (*Michael addition*) of diethyl propanedioate (diethyl malonate) to 4-methylpent-3-en-2-one (mesityl oxide) yields an intermediate which undergoes concomitant intramolecular aldol condensation under the reaction conditions. The cyclized material, on hydrolysis, undergoes ready decarboxylation to furnish 5,5-dimethylcyclohexane-1,3-dione which exists largely as its enol tautomer. The procedure given below is adapted from one kindly supplied by Dr C.I.F. Watt of the University of Manchester, UK.

Level	2
Time	preparation 3 h; isolation, purification and analysis 3 h
Equipment	apparatus for reflux, distillation at atmospheric pressure, extraction/separation, suction filtration
Instruments	UV, NMR

Materials

sodium **Caution**	1.15 g (50 mmol)	**corrosive, flammable**
diethyl propanedioate (FW 160.2)	8.5 mL, 8.0 g (50 mmol)	
4-methylpent-3-en-2-one (FW 98.2)	6.0 mL, 4.9 g (50 mmol)	**lachrymator, flammable, toxic**

NOTE: ***all manipulations of 4-methylpent-3-en-2-one must be carried out in the hood***

absolute ethanol		**flammable, toxic**
light petroleum (bp 60–80°C)		**flammable**
diethyl ether		**flammable, irritant**
acetone		**flammable**
potassium hydroxide pellets	6.3 g	**corrosive, hygroscopic**
hydrochloric acid (conc.)		**corrosive**

HOOD

[1]*Wear gloves*

[2]*See Fig. 3.25(b)*

[3]*After the first few pieces have been added, reaction rate slows. Rate of addition may then be increased*

[4]*Care!*

[5]*May be left at this stage*

[6]*See Fig. 3.48*

[7]*See Fig. 3.23(a)*

[8]*Complete precipitation of the product may take anything from 1 to 24 h; mixture best left overnight before filtration*

[9]*See Fig. 3.7*

Procedure

All apparatus must be thoroughly dried in a hot (>120°C) oven before use. Place the sodium in a 100 mL beaker under *ca.* 50 mL petroleum and cut it up *carefully* with a sharp blade and tweezers to pieces the size of a small pea.[1] Place 30 mL absolute ethanol in a 100 mL flask fitted with a magnetic stirrer bar, a Claisen adapter, a reflux condenser carrying a $CaCl_2$ guard tube, and an addition funnel.[2] Add the sodium piece by piece down the condenser to the ethanol with gentle stirring at such a rate that the mixture boils.[3] Replace the guard tube after each addition. Ensure that no more than two pieces of sodium accumulate in the flask at one time and verify that no pieces become lodged in the condenser (if this happens, **carefully** push the sodium into the flask with a glass rod).[4] When all the sodium has dissolved, add the diethyl propanedioate from the addition funnel over 5 min followed by 5 mL absolute ethanol. Similarly add the 4-methylpent-3-en-2-one over 5 min, followed by 5 mL absolute ethanol, and then reflux the stirred mixture gently for 45 min. After this time, dissolve the potassium hydroxide in 25 mL water, add this through the addition funnel and continue refluxing for a further 45 min. Allow the mixture to cool,[5] remove the adapter, reflux condenser and addition funnel and arrange the apparatus for distillation.[6] Distil off *ca.* 35 mL of the ethanol–water mixture, cool the residue in ice and extract with 25 mL diethyl ether, *retaining the aqueous layer.* Return the aqueous layer to the reaction flask, acidify it to pH 1 with concentrated hydrochloric acid and reflux[7] for 15 min. Allow the mixture to cool in an ice bath until crystallization is complete,[8] before filtering off the crude product under suction.[9] Triturate the crude product on the sinter with 25 mL water and 25 mL light petroleum, drying the product with suction after each washing. Record the yield of crude material and recrystallize *ca.* 1 g from aqueous acetone. Record the mp of the recrystallized material, and obtain the NMR spectrum ($CDCl_3$; some warming may be required to obtain a sufficiently strong solution) and the UV spectrum (EtOH) before and after addition of 1 drop of aqueous sodium hydroxide.

Problems

1 Note the absorption maxima in the UV spectrum of the product before and after the addition of base and explain the observed changes. Suggest another class of compound which behaves similarly.

2 Assign the peaks in the NMR spectrum. What information does this spectrum give you on the degree of enolization of the product?

3 5,5-Dimethylcyclohexane-1,3-dione forms highly crystalline derivatives with aldehydes RCHO and can be used for purposes of aldehyde identification. The derivatives formed have the general formula shown below. Suggest a mechanistic pathway for their formation.

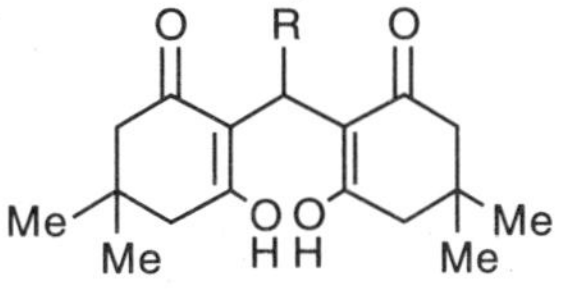

4 If 5,5-dimethylcyclohexane-1,3-dione is treated sequentially with sodium ethoxide and bromoethane, two isomeric monoalkylated products are formed. What are their structures and what is the reason for their formation?

Experiment 43 *Reactions of indole: the Mannich and Vilsmeier reactions*

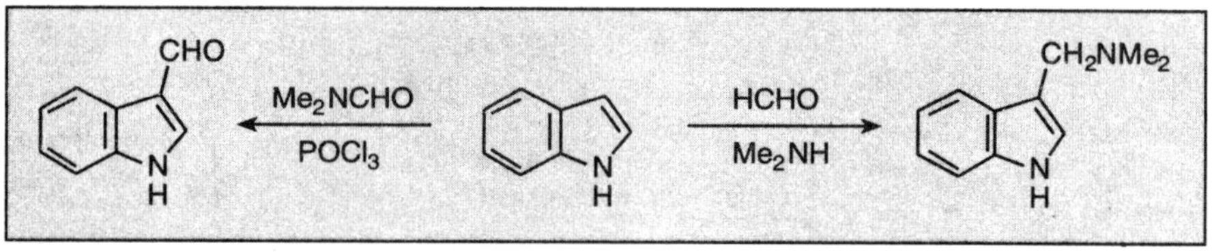

Indole is arguably one of the most important heteroaromatic compounds; such heterocyclic systems are aromatic by virtue of having [4n + 2] delocalizable π-electrons. Indoles are widely distributed in nature; the essential amino acid tryptophan is a constituent of most proteins, and is one of nature's building block for the *indole alkaloids*, a large range of structurally diverse natural products, many of which exhibit powerful biological activity. Examples include lysergic acid and vinblastine (see p. 613). Synthetic indole derivatives are widely studied in the pharmaceutical industry; a recent example is Sumatriptan, developed for the treatment of migraine.

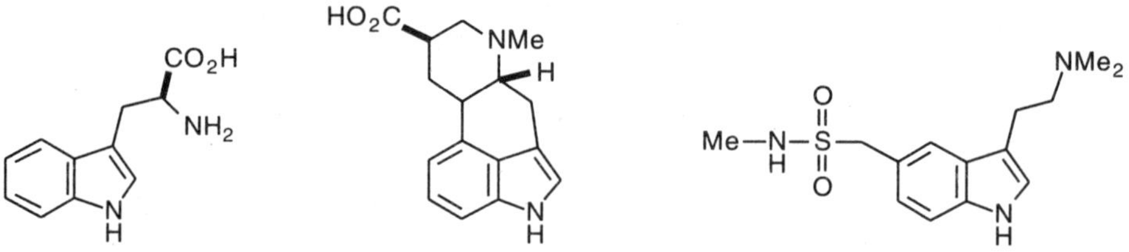

L-tryptophan lysergic acid Sumatriptan

The chemistry of indole is dominated by facile electrophilic substitution reactions at the 3-position. The indole ring is a sufficiently reactive nucleophile to react with iminium ions, intermediates generated from carbonyl compounds. This experiment illustrates two examples of this process, both of which result in the formation of new carbon–carbon bonds: the Mannich reaction to give gramine, a simple naturally occurring indole found in barley, and the Vilsmeier reaction to give indole-3-carboxaldehyde, a useful synthetic intermediate for the preparation of other indoles.

The Mannich reaction involves the combination of a nucleophile, an aldehyde or ketone, and a primary or secondary amine. In this case the components are indole, formaldehyde and dimethylamine which react to give 3-(*N,N*-dimethylaminomethyl)indole (gramine). The Vilsmeier, or Vilsmeier–Haack, reaction involves the generation of an electrophilic iminium species by reaction of dimethylformamide (DMF) with phosphoryl chloride. Again electrophilic substitution occurs at the indole-3-position, and the intermediate is hydrolyzed to the product by brief heating with aqueous sodium hydroxide.

Level	2
Time	2 × 3 h (extra for recrystallization)
Equipment	apparatus for suction filtration, stirring with addition, recrystallization
Instruments	IR, TLC

Materials

1. Preparation of gramine		
indole (FW 117.1)	1.0 g (8.6 mmol)	**stench, toxic**
dimethylamine (40% solution in water) (FW 45.1)	3.0 mL	**corrosive, stench**
formaldehyde (35% aqueous solution) (FW 30.0)	2.0 mL	**cancer suspect agent, toxic**
glacial ethanoic acid		**corrosive**
acetone		**flammable**
sodium hydroxide solution (30%)		**corrosive**
2. Preparation of indole-3-carboxaldehyde		
dimethylformamide (FW 73.1)	5 mL (67 mmol)	**irritant**
phosphoryl chloride (FW 153.3)	1.7 g (11 mmol)	**corrosive, irritant, toxic**
indole (FW 117.1)	1.17 g (10 mmol)	**stench, toxic**
sodium hydroxide (60%)		**corrosive**
methanol		**flammable, toxic**

Procedure

1. Preparation of gramine

HOOD

Dissolve the indole in 20 mL ethanoic acid in a small beaker or flask and add the dimethylamine. There will be some fumes at this point and the solution will become quite warm. Cool the mixture so that its temperature is around 30°C, add the formaldehyde solution with stirring and allow the mixture to stand for 60 min. Pour the solution onto about 100 g of crushed ice and, stirring vigorously all the time, make the mixture alkaline by the careful addition of *ca.* 45 mL of 30% sodium hydroxide solution. It is important that, in this last operation, the solution is never allowed to heat up. There must at all times be excess ice present, otherwise the gramine will be precipitated as a gummy solid. When precipitation is complete, allow the remaining ice to melt, and filter the gramine with suction[1] and wash with distilled water until the washings are neutral. Dry the product as thoroughly as possible with suction, and complete the drying process in a desiccator. Record the yield of your product.

[1] *See Fig. 3.7*

Gramine is not easy to recrystallize but can be obtained as needles from acetone. Take a portion of your product, and recrystallize it from the minimum volume of hot acetone. Record the mp of the recrystallized product, and its IR spectrum (Nujol®) if desired.

HOOD

2. *Preparation of indole-3-carboxaldehyde*

Place 4 mL dimethylformamide in a dry 50 mL three-necked round-bottomed flask equipped with a drying tube, addition funnel, thermometer and magnetic stirrer bar. Start the stirrer, cool the flask in an ice–salt bath, and add the phosphoryl chloride dropwise from the addition funnel, ensuring that the temperature does not rise above 10°C.[2] When the addition is complete, add a solution of the indole in 1 mL dimethylformamide dropwise to the stirred mixture, again ensuring that the temperature is below 10°C.[3] Replace the ice bath with a warm (*ca.* 35–40°C) water bath and stir the mixture for 1 h.[4] Add 5 g ice and then slowly add 8 mL of 60% sodium hydroxide solution. Rapidly heat the mixture to boiling for 2 min,[5] and then set it aside to cool. Leave the mixture in ice until all the product crystallizes out.[6] Filter off the product with suction, wash it with cold water, and dry it. Record the yield and mp of your product. If required, the product can be recrystallized from methanol. Record the yield, mp and IR spectrum of the recrystallized material. Analyse by TLC (silica, dichloromethane) to check the purity of the product.

[2] Takes 10–20 min

[3] Takes 10–15 min

[4] The solution may turn opaque

[5] If flames are permitted in the laboratory, this can be carried out using a burner. Otherwise use a heating mantle or heat gun

[6] Can be left in a refrigerator overnight

Problems

1 Write out the steps involved in the following Mannich reactions indicating intermediates which may be formed:

(a) $CH_2O + NH_4Cl + CH_3COCH_3 \longrightarrow CH_3COCH_2CH_2NH_2$

(b)
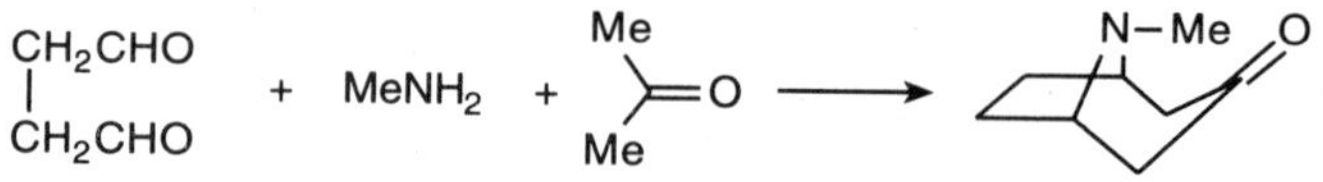

(c) $PhCH_2CHO + NH_3 + CN^- \xrightarrow[\text{aq. alkali}]{} PhCH_2CH(NH_2)COOH$

2 Discuss the mechanism of the Vilsmeier reaction.

3 Explain why electrophilic substitution in indole occurs at C-3.

Further reading

For reviews of the Mannich reaction, see: M. Tramontini, *Tetrahedron*, 1990, **46**, 1791; H. Heaney, *Comprehensive Organic Synthesis*, Vol. 2 (eds B.M. Trost and I. Fleming), Pergamon, Oxford, 1991, p. 953.

For a review of the Vilsmeier reaction, see: O. Meth-Cohn and S.P. Stanforth, *Comprehensive Organic Synthesis*, Vol. 2 (eds B.M. Trost and I. Fleming), Pergamon, Oxford, 1991, p. 771.

The preparation of indole-3-carboxaldehyde is based on the procedure described in: P.N. James and H.R. Synder, *Org. Synth. Coll.*, **4**, 539.

Experiment 44 — *Preparation of 3-methylcyclohex-2-enone*

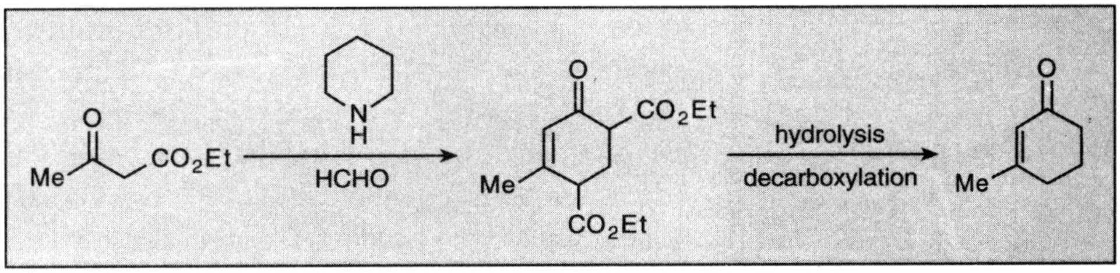

This experiment illustrates the base-catalyzed condensation of two molecules of ethyl 3-oxobutanoate with formaldehyde to give 4,6-diethoxycarbonyl-3-methylcyclohex-2-enone, which is subsequently hydrolyzed and decarboxylated to give 3-methylcyclohex-2-enone. The product can be used in Experiment 47.

Level	2
Time	2 × 3 h (with 5 h reaction in between)
Equipment	steam bath; apparatus for reaction with reflux, extraction/separation, suction filtration, small-scale distillation or short path distillation
Instruments	IR, NMR (optional)

Materials

ethyl 3-oxobutanoate (FW 130.1)	12.7 mL, 13.0 g (100 mmol)	**flammable, irritant**
paraformaldehyde (FW $[30.0]_n$)	1.5 g (50 mmol)	**irritant**
piperidine (FW 85.2)	0.5 g	**corrosive, flammable**
glacial ethanoic acid		**corrosive**
diethyl ether		**flammable, irritant**
sulfuric acid (conc.)		**corrosive, oxidizer**
sodium hydroxide	2.6 g	**corrosive**

HOOD

Procedure

Grind the paraformaldehyde to a fine powder and place it in a 250 mL round-bottomed flask.[1] Add the ethyl 3-oxobutanoate and the piperidine to the flask. After a short period, the reaction will start and the contents of the flask will heat up rapidly, and the solid paraformaldehyde will dissolve. If necessary, moderate the reaction by cooling the flask in an ice bath.[2] As soon as the initial reaction is over and the mixture is homogeneous,[3] heat the mixture on a steam bath for 1 h. (At this stage, the flask contains crude 4,6-diethoxycarbonyl-3-methylcyclohex-2-enone which is used without purification.)

Dissolve 30 mL glacial ethanoic acid in 20 mL water, and **carefully** add 3 mL concentrated sulfuric acid. Add this acid solution to the reaction flask, fit

[1] *Get an ice bath ready—see below*

[2] ***Ice may be needed!***

[3] *Takes about 20 min*

[4] *See Fig. 3.23(a). Can be left longer; leave overnight or use time switch*
[5] *Cooling may be needed*
[6] *May be left at this stage*
[7] *See Fig. 3.7*
[8] *See Fig. 3.48*

a reflux condenser, and heat the mixture under reflux for about 5 h.[4] Cool the mixture to room temperature, and **carefully** add a solution of the sodium hydroxide in 70 mL water.[5] Transfer the mixture to a separatory funnel and extract the product with 3 × 20 mL portions of diethyl ether. Combine the ether extracts and dry them over $MgSO_4$.[6] Filter off the drying agent by suction,[7] and evaporate the filtrate on the rotary evaporator. Transfer the residue to a small distillation set, and distil it at atmospheric pressure,[8] collecting the fraction boiling at about 200°C. Record the exact bp, yield and the IR (film) spectrum of your product. If required, record the NMR ($CDCl_3$) spectrum of the product.

See Exp. 46

Problems

1 Write a reaction mechanism for the reaction of ethyl acetoacetate with formaldehyde to give 4,6-diethoxycarbonyl-3-methylcyclohex-2-enone. What is the role of the piperidine?
2 Why does the corresponding dicarboxylic acid, obtained by acidic hydrolysis of the diester, decarboxylate so easily?
3 Assign the IR spectrum of your product. What particular feature proves the presence of a conjugated ketone group?

Further reading

For a procedure on which this experiment is based, see: L. Spiegler and J.M. Tinker, *J. Am. Chem. Soc.*, 1939, **61**, 1001.

Experiment 45 — *Enamines: acetylation of cyclohexanone via its pyrrolidine enamine*

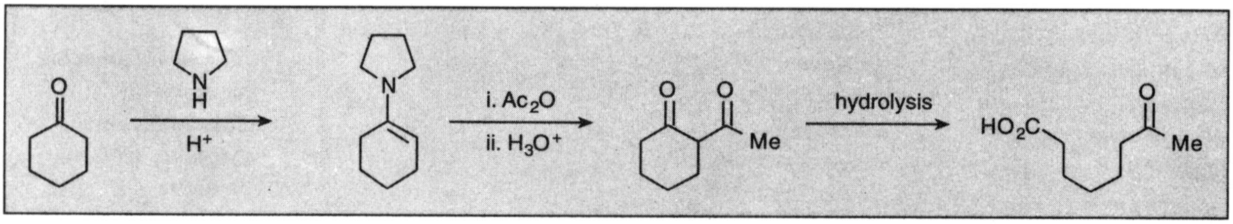

Organometallic compounds and carbanions are not the only type of species that possess a nucleophilic carbon atom. The β-carbon atom of an enamine has nucleophilic character, and can be alkylated or acylated with appropriate electrophilic reagents. This reactivity of enamines, which are readily prepared from carbonyl compounds, is due to delocalization of the nitrogen lone pair through the double bond to the β-carbon. Alkylation (or acylation) of an enamine leads to an iminium ion, which on hydrolysis is reconverted to a carbonyl compound.

This experiment illustrates the acetylation of cyclohexanone via its pyrrolidine enamine. In the first stage, cyclohexanone is converted into the enamine, 1-pyrrolidinocyclohexene, by reaction with pyrrolidine in the presence of an acid catalyst in boiling toluene using a Dean and Stark apparatus to remove the water that is formed. The enamine is not isolated but is reacted immediately with ethamoic anhydride to effect the acetylation. Aqueous work-up hydrolyzes the material to 2-acetylcyclohexanone, which is purified by vacuum distillation. 2-Acetylcyclohexanone, a β-diketone, exists in a mixture of keto and enol forms, and the percentage enol content can be estimated from the NMR spectrum. Finally, in an optional step, 2-acetylcyclohexanone may be converted into 7-oxo-octanoic acid by hydrolysis, an example of a general route to keto-fatty acids.

Level	3
Time	2 × 3 h (with 24 h standing period in between, plus 3 h for optional hydrolysis step)
Equipment	steam bath, vacuum pump (for part 2); apparatus for reflux with water removal, distillation, extraction/separation, suction filtration, distillation under reduced pressure, short path distillation (for part 2)
Instruments	IR, NMR

Materials

1. Preparation of 2-acetylcyclohexanone

cyclohexanone (FW 98.2)	5.0 mL, 4.7 g (48 mmol)	**irritant, toxic**
pyrrolidine (FW 71.1)	4.0 mL, 3.4 g (48 mmol)	**corrosive, flammable, stench**
toluene-4-sulfonic acid	0.1 g	**corrosive**
ethanoic anhydride (FW 102.1)	4.5 mL (48 mmol)	**lachrymator, corrosive, hygroscopic**
toluene		**flammable, irritant**
hydrochloric acid (3 M)		**corrosive**

2. Preparation of 7-oxo-octanoic acid

diethyl ether	**flammable, irritant**
chloroform	**cancer suspect agent, toxic**
potassium hydroxide solution (60%)	**corrosive**
hydrochloric acid (conc.)	**corrosive**

Procedure

HOOD

1. Preparation of 2-acetylcyclohexanone

Place the cyclohexanone, pyrrolidine, toluene-4-sulfonic acid, a boiling stone, and 40 mL toluene in a 100 mL round-bottomed flask. Fit the Dean and Stark apparatus to the flask, and fit the reflux condenser (protected with a calcium chloride drying tube) to the top the apparatus.[1] Heat the flask so that the toluene refluxes vigorously,[2] and the water that is formed in the reaction collects in the trap. Maintain the solution at reflux for 1 h. (During this period, prepare a solution of the ethanoic anhydride in 10 mL toluene for use later.) Allow the solution to cool somewhat, remove the Dean and Stark apparatus, fit the still head and thermometer, and reassemble the condenser with a receiver and receiving flask for distillation.[3] Continue to heat the flask and distil off the remaining pyrrolidine and water. Continue the distillation until the temperature at the still head reaches 108–110°C. Remove the heat and allow the flask, which contains a toluene solution of the enamine, to cool to room temperature. Remove the still head, etc., and add the ethanoic anhydride solution. Stopper the flask[4] and allow it to stand at room temperature for at least 24 h.[5] Add 5 mL water to the flask, fit a reflux condenser, and heat the mixture under reflux for 30 min.[6] Cool the mixture to room temperature, and transfer it to a 50 mL separatory funnel containing 10 mL water. Shake the funnel, separate the layers, and wash the organic layer with 3 × 10 mL hydrochloric acid (3 M), and with 10 mL water, and then dry it over $MgSO_4$.[7] Filter off the drying agent, and concentrate the filtrate on the rotary evaporator. Transfer the residue to a small distillation set, and distil the material under reduced pressure (*ca.* 15 mmHg) using a water aspirator or vacuum pump.[8] Record the bp, yield and IR (film) and NMR ($CDCl_3$) spectra of your product.

[1] *See Fig. 3.27*
[2] *Vapour should condense well up the condenser*
[3] *See Fig. 3.48*
[4] *Must get to here in period 1*
[5] *Can be longer*
[6] *See Fig. 3.23*
[7] *May be left at this stage*
[8] *See Fig. 3.53*

2. *Preparation of 7-oxo-octanoic acid (optional)*

Place 1.40 g (10 mmol) 2-acetylcyclohexanone in a 50 mL round-bottomed flask, add 3 mL potassium hydroxide solution,[9] and heat the mixture on a boiling water (steam) bath for 15 min. After cooling the mixture,[10] add 30 mL water, and concentrated hydrochloric acid dropwise to the solution until it just remains alkaline (*ca.* pH 7–8).[11] Transfer the solution to a separatory funnel, and extract it with 2 × 5 mL diethyl ether. Discard the ether extracts, and make the aqueous phase strongly acidic (pH 1) with concentrated hydrochloric acid. Extract the product with 3 × 10 mL chloroform,[12] and dry the combined chloroform extracts over $MgSO_4$.[7] Filter off the drying agent, and evaporate the filtrate on the rotary evaporator. If desired, distil the product in a short path distillation apparatus under vacuum (*ca.* 4 mmHg).[13] Record the bp, yield and the IR ($CHCl_3$) and NMR ($CDCl_3$) spectra of your product.

[9] ***Care! Very corrosive***
[10] *May go solid on cooling*
[11] *Use pH paper*
[12] ***Toxic!***
[13] *See Fig. 3.54*

Problems

1 Assign the IR and NMR spectra of 2-acetylcyclohexanone. From the NMR spectrum, estimate the percentage of enol form present.

2 Write a reaction mechanism for the conversion of 2-acetylcyclohexanone into 7-oxo-octanoic acid.

3 Assign the IR and NMR spectra of the 7-oxo-octanoic acid.

Experiment 46

Enol derivatives: preparation of the enol acetate, trimethylsilyl enol ether, and the pyrrolidine enamine from 2-methylcyclohexanone

The problems associated with the reaction of unsymmetrical ketones have already been referred to. One approach to the regiochemical problem of unsymmetrical ketones is to prepare specific enol derivatives of known structure. This experiment involves the preparation of three derivatives of 2-methylcyclohexanone, an unsymmetrical cyclic ketone which is commercially available or is prepared by oxidation of the corresponding alcohol as described in Experiment 29. In the first part of the experiment, the ketone is reacted with ethanoic anhydride in the presence of an acid catalyst to give the enol acetate derivative. Under these conditions, only one of the two possible enol acetates is formed, and its structure can easily be assigned from its NMR spectrum.

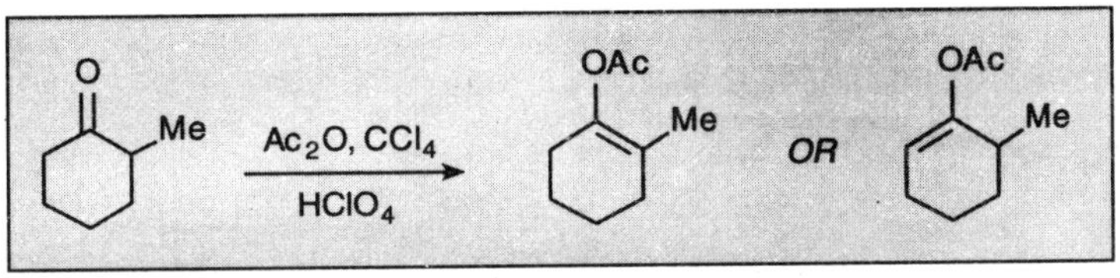

In the second part of the experiment, the ketone is converted into its trimethylsilyl (TMS) enol ether derivative by reaction with chlorotrimethylsilane and triethylamine in hot dimethylformamide (DMF). In this case both of the possible enol derivatives are formed, although one isomer predominates. The structure of the major TMS enol ether, and the isomeric ratio, can be ascertained by NMR spectroscopy.

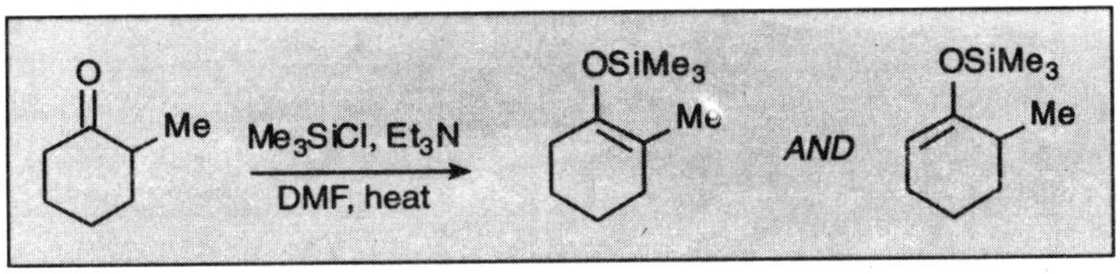

Both enol acetates and, particularly, TMS enol ethers are easily hydrolyzed back to their starting ketones, but can be converted directly into the corresponding lithium enolate by reaction with methyl-lithium. (TMS enol ethers can also be converted into tetra-alkylammonium enolates by reaction with tetraalkylammonium fluoride.) Hence this use of structurally specific enol derivatives represents a way of generating specific enolates from unsymmetrical ketones.

Scheme continued on p. 550

Cont.

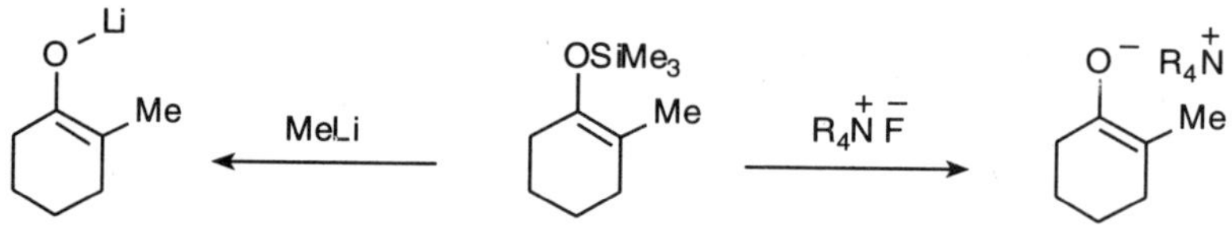

The nitrogen analogues of enol derivatives are enamines, and we have already seen the use of the pyrrolidine enamine of cyclohexanone in the previous experiment. However unsymmetrical ketones such as 2-methylcyclohexanone can form two enamines, although as with the enol derivatives above, one isomer usually predominates. The third part of this experiment involves the conversion of 2-methylcyclohexanone into the pyrrolidine enamine using the method previously described for cyclohexanone itself (Experiment 45). Both enamines are in fact formed in the reaction, and the structure of the major enamine, and the isomeric ratio, can be determined by NMR spectroscopy.

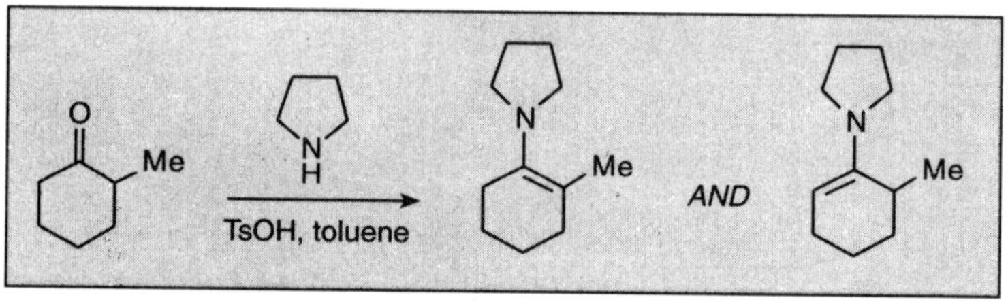

Level	4
Time	preparation of enol 2 × 3 h (with overnight reaction in between); preparation of trimethylsilyl enol ether 2 × 3 h (with overnight reaction in between); preparation of pyrrolidine enamine 2 × 3 h (any of the parts may be carried out independently)
Equipment	magnetic stirrer/hotplate, high temperature heating bath; apparatus for extraction/separation, suction filtration, short path distillation, reflux, reflux with water removal (Dean and Stark trap)
Instruments	NMR

Materials

1. Preparation of enol acetate

2-methylcyclohexanone (FW 112.2)	2.5 mL, 2.3 g (20 mmol)	**irritant**
ethanoic anhydride (FW 102.1)	10 mL (0.11 mol)	**corrosive, irritant**
chloroform		**cancer suspect agent, toxic**
pentane		**flammable**
perchloric acid (70%)	1 drop	**corrosive, oxidizer**

NOTE: ***perchloric acid and all perchlorates are potentially explosive. Consult an instructor***

Continued

Box cont.

sodium bicarbonate solution (saturated)		
sodium bicarbonate	15 g	
2. Preparation of trimethylsilyl enol ether		
2-methylcyclohexanone (FW 112.2)	2.5 mL, 2.3 g (20 mmol)	**irritant**
chlorotrimethylsilane (FW 108.6)	3.0 mL, 2.6 g (24 mmol)	**corrosive, flammable**
triethylamine (FW 101.2)	6.7 mL, 4.9 g (48 mmol)	**corrosive, flammable**
dimethylformamide (DMF)		**irritant**
pentane		**flammable**
sodium bicarbonate solution (saturated)		
3. Preparation of pyrrolidine enamine		
2-methylcyclohexanone (FW 112.2)	2.5 mL, 2.3 g (20 mmol)	**irritant**
pyrrolidine (FW 71.1)	1.7 mL, 1.45 g (20 mmol)	**corrosive, flammable, stench**
toluene-4-sulfonic acid	0.1 g	**corrosive**
toluene (sodium dried)		**flammable, irritant**

Procedure

1. Preparation of the enol acetate of 2-methylcyclohexanone

Place 25 mL chloroform, the ethanoic anhydride and the 2-methylcyclohexanone in a 50 mL Erlenmeyer flask. **Carefully**[1] add 1 drop of 70% perchloric acid, stopper the flask and swirl it to ensure complete mixing of the reagents. Set the flask aside at room temperature for 3 h.[2] Whilst the reaction is proceeding, place 15 mL saturated sodium bicarbonate solution and 15 mL pentane in a 250 mL Erlenmeyer flask, and cool the flask to 0–5°C in a refrigerator or an ice bath. At the end of the reaction period, pour the reaction mixture into the cool bicarbonate/pentane with thorough mixing.[3] Maintain the whole mixture at 0–5°C, and add the solid sodium bicarbonate in small portions, with constant swirling.[3] At the end of the sodium bicarbonate addition, the mixture should be slightly basic.[4] Transfer the mixture to a separatory funnel, remove the lower organic layer, and extract the aqueous phase with 3 × 10 mL portions of pentane. Combine all the organic solutions and dry them over $MgSO_4$.[5] Filter off the drying agent with suction,[6] and evaporate the filtrate on the rotary evaporator.[7] Distil the residue under reduced pressure in a short path distillation apparatus[8] using a water pump (*ca.* 20 mmHg). Record the bp, yield and the NMR ($CDCl_3$) spectrum of your product. From the NMR spectrum, determine the structure of the enol acetate.

[1]*Care! See note above*

[2]*Can be left longer*

[3]***Care!*** CO_2 ***evolved***

[4]*About pH 8. Check!*

[5]*May be left at this stage*

[6]*See Fig. 3.7*

[7]*Bath temperature below 35°C*

[8]*See Fig. 3.54*

2. *Preparation of the trimethylsilyl enol ether of 2-methylcyclohexanone*

Place 10 mL DMF, the triethylamine and the chlorotrimethylsilane in a 50 mL round-bottomed flask. Add the 2-methylcyclohexanone, fit a reflux condenser, and heat the mixture under reflux with stirring for about 48 h using a heating bath on a stirrer/hotplate.[9] Allow the mixture to cool to room temperature, and dilute it with 20 mL pentane. Transfer the mixture to a separatory funnel, and wash it with 3 × 25 mL portions of saturated sodium bicarbonate solution. Dry the organic layer over $MgSO_4$.[10] Filter off the drying agent by suction and evaporate the filtrate on the rotary evaporator.[11] Distil the residue in a short path distillation apparatus[8] under reduced pressure using a water aspirator (*ca.* 20 mmHg). Record the bp, yield and the NMR ($CDCl_3$) spectrum of your product. From the NMR spectrum, determine the structure of the major TMS enol ether, and the ratio of isomers.

[9]*See Fig. 3.24*

[10]*May be left at this stage*

[11]*Below 40°C*

3. *Preparation of the pyrrolidine enamine of 2-methylcyclohexanone*

Place 20 mL dry toluene, 2-methylcyclohexanone, pyrrolidine, toluene-4-sulfonic acid and a boiling stone in a 50 mL round-bottomed flask. Fit the Dean and Stark apparatus to the flask, and fit the reflux condenser (protected with a calcium chloride drying tube) to the top of the apparatus.[12] Heat the flask so that the toluene refluxes vigorously,[13] and the water that is formed in the reaction collects in the trap.[14] Maintain the solution at reflux for 1 h. Allow the solution to cool,[10] transfer the flask to a rotary evaporator, and concentrate the mixture under reduced pressure.[10] Transfer the residue to a short path distillation apparatus,[8] and distil it under reduced pressure using a water aspirator (*ca.* 15 mmHg).[15] Record the bp, yield and the NMR ($CDCl_3$) spectrum of your product. From the NMR spectrum, determine the structure of the major enamine and the ratio of isomers.

[12]*See Fig. 3.27*

[13]*Vapour should condense well up condenser*

[14]*Check that water does form and collect in trap*

[15]*If time is short, record the NMR spectrum of the crude product before distillation, and estimate the ratio of enamines from this spectrum*

Problems

1. What is the structure of the enol acetate formed from 2-methylcyclohexanone? Account for the formation of this isomer on mechanistic grounds.
2. What is the structure of the major TMS enol ether?
3. What is the structure of the major pyrrolidine enamine? Why is this particular isomer favoured? What is the mechanism for the formation of an enamine from a ketone and a secondary amine? How do primary amines react with ketones?
4. How would you convert 2-methylcyclohexanone into: (i) 2-benzyl-2-methylcyclohexanone, (ii) 2-acetyl-6-methylcyclohexanone, and (iii) 6,6-dimethyl-1-trimethylsiloxycyclohexene?

Further reading

For the procedures on which this experiment is based, see: M. Gall and H.O. House, *Org. Synth.*, 1972, **52**, 39.

H.O. House, L.J. Czuba, M. Gall and H.D. Olmstead, *J. Org. Chem.*, 1969, **34**, 2324.

W.D. Gurowitz and M.A. Joseph, *J. Org. Chem.*, 1967, **32**, 3289.

Experiment 47

Reductive alkylation of enones: 2-(prop-2-enyl)-3-methylcyclohexanone

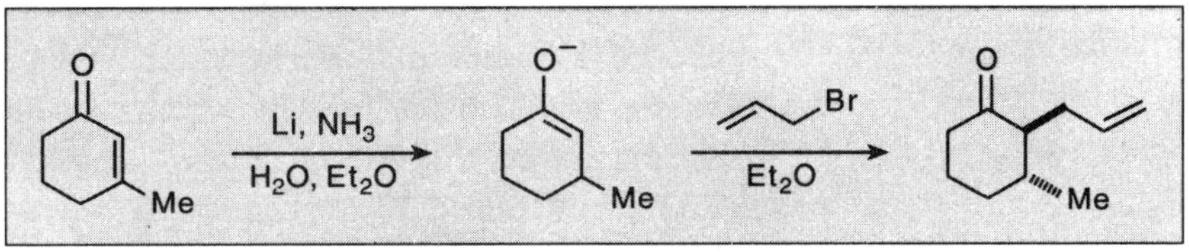

Alkali metals in liquid ammonia not only reduce aromatic rings, but also reduce other conjugated systems such as α,β-unsaturated carbonyl compounds. Indeed metal–ammonia reductions are often the method of choice for the selective reduction of the C=C bond in such systems. This experiment involves the reduction of 3-methylcyclohex-2-enone (which is commercially available or can be prepared as described in Experiment 44) using lithium metal in liquid ammonia in the presence of water as a proton source. However, the initial product of the reduction, the lithium enolate of 3-methylcyclohexanone, is not isolated, but is alkylated *in situ* using 3-bromoprop-1-ene (allyl bromide), thereby illustrating a useful variant on dissolving metal reductions. This enone reduction–alkylation sequence was originally developed by Professor Gilbert Stork at Columbia University, and has proved useful in the alkylation of relatively inaccessible α-positions of unsymmetrical ketones. In the present case, the 2-(prop-2-enyl)-3-methylcyclohexanone is formed as a mixture of *trans*- and *cis*- isomers, in which the *trans*- isomer predominates. The ratio of isomers can be determined by GC analysis, the *trans*-isomer having the shorter retention time.

Level	4
Time	2 × 3 h
Equipment	magnetic stirrer; apparatus for reaction in liquid ammonia, extraction/separation, suction filtration, short path distillation
Instruments	IR, NMR, GC

Materials

3-methylcyclohex-2-enone (FW 110.2)	2.20 g (20 mmol)	**irritant**
3-bromoprop-1-ene (allyl bromide) (FW 121.0)	5.20 mL (60 mmol)	**flamable, toxic lachrymator, flammable, irritant**
diethyl ether (anhydrous)		
liquid ammonia	*ca.* 100 mL	
Care (*see handling notes pp. 66–67*)		**corrosive, toxic**
lithium wire (FW 6.9)	0.30 g (43 mmol)	**caution, flammable**
ammonium chloride	3.00 g	
hydrochloric acid (5%)		**corrosive**
sodium chloride solution (saturated)		

Procedure

HOOD

All apparatus must be thoroughly dried in a hot (>120°C) oven before use. Set up a 250 mL three-neck flask with a magnetic stirrer bar, addition funnel, gas inlet and a low temperature condenser.[1] Surround the flask with a bowl of cork chips, and condense about 100 mL liquid ammonia. Stir the liquid ammonia and add the lithium wire in small pieces. Whilst the lithium is dissolving, place a solution of the 3-methylcyclohex-2-enone, 40 mL *dry* diethyl ether[2] and 0.36 mL (20 mmol) water (*measured accurately*) in the addition funnel. As soon as the lithium has dissolved,[3] add the enone solution *dropwise* over about 40 min.[4] After the addition, allow the mixture to stir for 10 min, and then *rapidly* add a solution of the 3-bromoprop-1-ene in 15 mL *dry* diethyl ether from the addition funnel.[5] Stir the mixture for 5 min, and then rapidly add the solid ammonium chloride. Stop the stirrer, remove the low temperature condenser, and allow the ammonia to evaporate.[6] Add a mixture of 30 mL diethyl ether and 30 mL water to the flask, swirl to dissolve all the material, and transfer the mixture to a separatory funnel. Separate the layers and saturate the aqueous layer with sodium chloride. Extract the water layer with 2 × 10 mL diethyl ether, and combine all the ether layers. Wash the combined ether extracts with 10 mL dilute hydrochloric acid, 10 mL saturated sodium chloride solution, and dry them over $MgSO_4$.[6] Filter off the spent drying agent by suction,[7] and evaporate the filtrate on the rotary evaporator. Transfer the residue to a short path distillation apparatus,[8] and distil the product under reduced pressure using a water aspirator (*ca.* 14 mmHg), collecting the product at about 100°C. Record the exact bp, yield and the IR ($CHCl_3$) and NMR ($CDCl_3$) spectra of your product. Analyze the product by GC, and hence determine the ratio of *trans-* to *cis-* isomers; the *trans-* isomer has the shorter retention time. Run samples of 3-methylcyclohex-2-enone and, if available, 3-methylcyclohexanone for comparison.

[1] *See Fig. 3.30*

[2] *See Appendix 2*

[3] *About 20 min*

[4] *The enone solution **must** be homogeneous*

[5] *Ammonia may boil vigorously*

[6] *May be left at this stage*

[7] *See Fig. 3.7*

[8] *See Fig. 3.54*

Problems

1 Write a reaction mechanism for the reductive alkylation reaction, clearly identifying all the steps involved.

2 What is the ratio of isomers formed in your experiment? Why does the *trans-* isomer predominate?

3 Is there any 3-methylcyclohexanone present in your sample? How is this formed?

4 Assign the IR and the NMR spectra of 2-allyl-3-methylcyclohexanone.

5 Suggest an alternative synthesis of 2-allyl-3-methylcyclohexanone.

Further reading

For the procedure on which this experiment is based, see: D. Caine, S.T. Chao and H.A. Smith, *Org. Synth.*, 1977, **56**, 52.

Experiment 48

Lithium diisopropylamide as base: regioselectivity and stereoselectivity in enolate formation

In order to convert a ketone into its enolate anion, a base is needed. The position of the equilibrium of the reaction between a ketone and a base is dependent on the acidity of the ketone and the strength of the base.

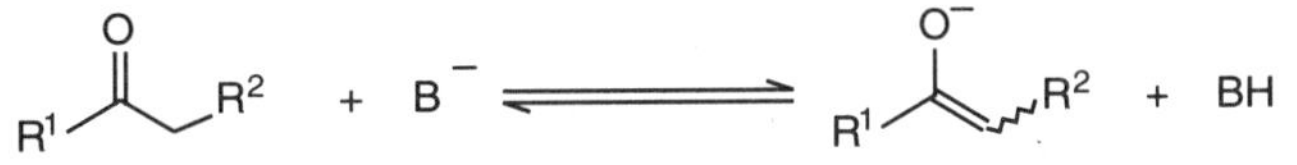

For synthetic purposes a high concentration of the enolate is usually desirable, and therefore bases which are capable of rapid and essentially complete deprotonation of the ketone are often used. One of the most commonly used modern bases is lithium diisopropylamide (LDA), generated by the action of *n*-butyllithium on diisopropylamine. It is a very strong base, but is sufficiently bulky to be relatively non-nucleophilic—an important feature. The steric bulk of the base also usually ensures that in unsymmetrical ketones the more sterically accessible proton is removed faster (*kinetic control* of deprotonation), to give what is referred to as the *kinetic enolate*. The composition of an enolate or enolate mixture can be determined by allowing it to react with chlorotrimethylsilane to give the corresponding trimethylsilyl enol ether(s) which can be analyzed by NMR.

This whole experiment is designed around the use of LDA, a vital reagent for modern synthetic organic chemistry, in the deprotonation of ketones. Two ketones are suggested, each of which illustrates a different point; either or both of them may be selected for study. The first part involves the deprotonation of 2-methylcyclohexanone, as an example of an unsymmetrical ketone (*cf.* Experiment 46). Two enolates are possible, although the use of LDA as base should ensure the exclusive formation of the kinetic enolate, trapped as its TMS enol ether. This method of making TMS enol ethers contrasts with that described in Experiment 46 which gives largely the *thermodynamic enol* derivative.

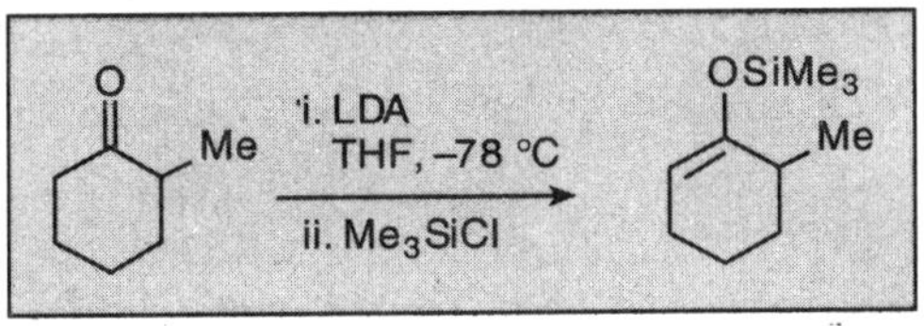

Although the regiochemistry of enolate formation (kinetic versus thermodynamic enolates) is reasonably predictable, the stereochemistry of enolate formation is less well understood. The deprotonation of an acyclic ketone can lead to a *Z*- or *E*-enolate (or a mixture), and although in simple reactions, for example alkylation, the geometry of the enolates does not matter, in reactions such as the aldol condensation, enolate geometry has a pronounced effect on the outcome. In general, Z-enolates are thought to be more stable, and the second part of the experiment examines this question of enolate geometry. Ethyl phenyl ketone (propiophenone), is deprotonated with LDA, the enolates trapped as their TMS enol ethers, and the ratio of geometric isomers obtained by NMR analysis. Clearly in this ketone there is no problem of regiochemistry since it only possesses one type of α-proton.

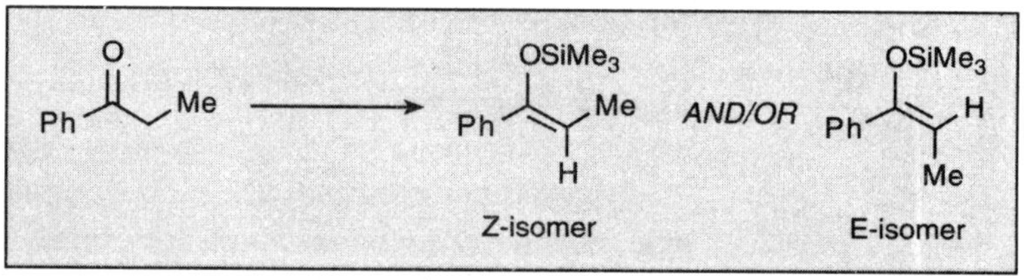

Level	4
Time	2 × 3 h for each ketone
Equipment	magnetic stirrer; apparatus for stirring at reduced temperature with addition by syringe under an inert atmosphere, extraction/separation, suction filtration
Instruments	NMR

Materials

For each reaction:

ketone (see below)	(5.0 mmol)	
tetrahydrofuran (dry)	20 mL	**flammable, irritant**
di*iso*propylamine (FW 101.2) (distilled)	0.77 mL (5.5 mmol)	**corrosive, flammable, stench**
n-butyl-lithium (FW 64.1) (1.6 M in hexane)	3.45 mL (5.5 mmol)	**flammable, moisture sensitive**
chlorotrimethylsilane (FW 108.6)	0.70 mL (5.5 mmol)	**corrosive, flammable**
sodium bicarbonate solution (saturated)	10 mL	
pentane	20 mL	**flammable**

Ketones:

2-methylcyclohexanone (FW 112.2)	0.61 mL, 560 mg (5.0 mmol)	**irritant**
ethyl phenyl ketone (propiophenone) (FW 134.2)	0.66 mL, 670 mg (5.0 mmol)	**flammable**

Procedure

All apparatus must be thoroughly dried in a hot (>120 °C) oven before use. This is the general method for the deprotonation of ketones with LDA, and trapping of enolates with chlorotrimethylsilane.

HOOD

1. Formation of lithium diisopropylamide

Equip an oven-dried 50 mL round-bottomed flask with a magnetic stirrer bar, flush the flask with dry nitrogen (or argon), and fit a septum. Insert a needle attached via a bubbler to the nitrogen supply through the septum.[1] Using appropriate-sized syringes, add 20 mL *dry* THF[2] to the flask, followed by the *dry* di*iso*propylamine.[2] Start the stirrer, and cool the flask in an ice bath. Add 5.5 mmol of the hexane solution of *n*-butyl-lithium dropwise using a syringe,[3] and stir the mixture at 0°C for 10 min.

[1]*See Fig. 3.22*
[2]*See Appendix 2*
[3]***Caution!***

HOOD

2. *Deprotonation and chlorotrimethylsilane quench*

Replace the ice bath with a solid CO_2–acetone bath, and allow the solution of LDA to cool. Add 5.0 mmol of the ketone[4] dropwise by syringe, and stir the mixture at low temperature for a further 20 min. Add the chlorotrimethylsilane by syringe and allow the solution to warm up slowly to room temperature.[5] Stir the mixture at room temperature for about 30–45 min, and then quench it by the addition of the saturated sodium bicarbonate solution. Transfer the mixture to a separatory funnel and extract it with 20 mL pentane. Dry the pentane extract over $MgSO_4$.[6] Filter off the drying agent by suction,[7] and evaporate the filtrate on the rotary evaporator.[8] Record the yield and the NMR ($CDCl_3$) spectrum of your product. From the NMR spectrum of the crude product, determine the structure of the major TMS enol ether present.

[4]*See list above*
[5]*Over about 30 min*
[6]*May be left at this stage*
[7]*See Fig. 3.7*
[8]*Bath temperature below 30°C*

Problems

1 For each of the ketones you used, discuss the results of the experiment in terms of the regio- and stereochemistry of enolate formation.
2 Why is it desirable that a base should be non-nucleophilic?

Further reading

For the procedures on which this experiment is based, see: C.H. Heathcock, C.T. Buse, W.A. Kleschick, M.C. Pirrung, J.E. Sohn and J. Lampe, *J. Org. Chem.*, 1980, **45**, 1066; H.O. House, L.J. Czuba, M. Gall and H.D. Olmstead, *J. Org. Chem.*, 1969, **34**, 2324.
For a wider discussion on the uses of LDA, see: EROS, 3096.

Experiment 49

Dianions: aldol condensation of the dianion from ethyl 3-oxobutanoate (ethyl acetoacetate) with benzophenone

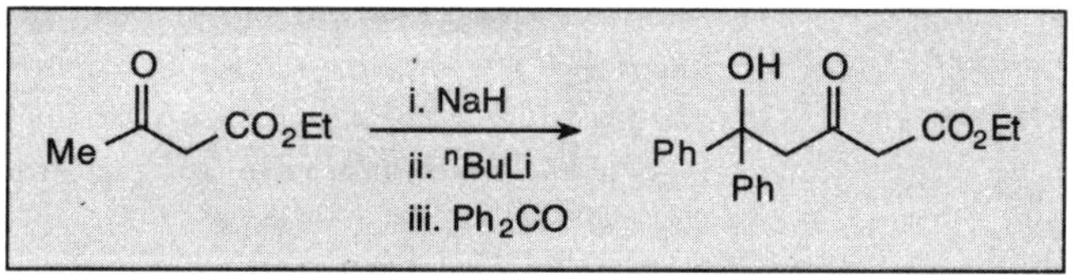

The widespread use of β-dicarbonyl compounds in synthesis is a result of the favoured deprotonation of the CH_2 (or CH) group (pK_a *ca.* 10) between the two carbonyl functions. However in the presence of a very strong base, β-dicarbonyl compounds can be converted into dianions by sequential deprotonation. For example, reaction of ethyl acetoacetate with sodium hydride gives the expected sodium enolate. If this monoanion is then treated with a mole of a stronger base such as *n*-butyl-lithium, the dianion is formed. Subsequent reactions of the dianion, such as alkylation with a halide RX, occur exclusively at the more basic enolate centre, and this technique therefore allows selectivity in the alkylation of β-keto esters.

This experiment illustrates the formation of the dianion from ethyl 3-oxobutanoate, using the conditions described above, and its subsequent aldol condensation with benzophenone to give ethyl 5-hydroxy-3-oxo-5,5-diphenylpentanoate, which is best purified by column chromatography.

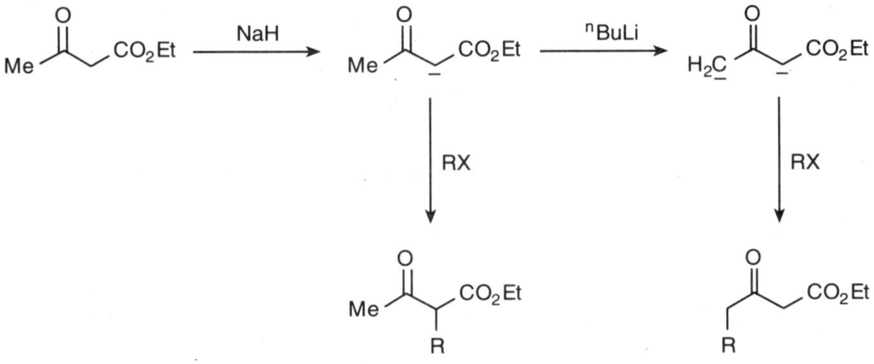

Level	4
Time	2 × 3 h (plus 3 h if product is to be purified by chromatography)
Equipment	magnetic stirrer, nitrogen (or argon) supply; apparatus for stirring at reduced temperature under inert atmosphere, addition by syringe, extraction/separation, suction filtration, column chromatography
Instruments	IR, NMR

Materials

ethyl 3-oxobutanoate (ethyl acetoacetate) (FW 130.1)	1.27 mL (10 mmol)	**irritant**
benzophenone (FW 182.2)	2.00 g (11 mmol)	
sodium hydride (FW 24.0) (60% in oil)	0.44 g (11 mmol)	**flammable**

NOTE: ***sodium hydride reacts violently with moisture to liberate hydrogen with the risk of fire. As a dispersion in oil, the reagent is safer to handle and store than the dry solid, when it is intensely pyrophoric. All apparatus and solvents must be rigorously dried before use. Take special care when quenching reactions involving the use of sodium hydride***

n-butyl-lithium (FW 64.1) (1.6 M in hexane)	6.6 mL (10.5 mmol)	**flammable, moisture sensitive**
light petroleum (dry)		**flammable**
tetrahydrofuran (dry)		**flammable, irritant**
diethyl ether		**flammable, irritant**
ammonium chloride solution (saturated)		
brine		

HOOD

[1]*Caution!*

[2]*See Fig. 3.22*

[3]*See Appendix 2*

[4]*May be left longer*

[5]*May be left at this stage*

[6]*See Fig. 3.7*

Procedure

All apparatus must be thoroughly dried in a hot (>120°C) oven before use. Transfer the sodium hydride[1] to an oven-dried 100 mL two- or three-neck round-bottomed flask, add a magnetic stirrer bar, nitrogen inlet and thermometer.[2] Flush the flask with dry nitrogen (or argon), and close it with a septum. Add 5 mL *dry* light petroleum to the flask by syringe. Swirl the flask, allow the sodium hydride to settle, and then carefully remove the supernatant liquid by syringe. Repeat this washing procedure, and then add 25 mL *dry* THF[3] to the flask by syringe, start the stirrer, and cool the flask in an ice bath. Add the ethyl 3-oxobutanoate dropwise by syringe, and stir the mixture at 0°C for 10 min. Add 10.5 mmol of the hexane solution of *n*-butyl-lithium dropwise by syringe, and stir the mixture for a further 10 min at 0°C. Dissolve the benzophenone in 5 mL *dry* THF, and add this solution dropwise by syringe to the stirred reaction mixture at 0°C. Continue to stir the reaction mixture at 0°C for 10 min,[4] and then quench it by adding the saturated ammonium chloride. Pour the reaction mixture into a beaker containing 15 mL water and 30 mL diethyl ether. Transfer the mixture to a separatory funnel, separate the layers, and further extract the aqueous layer with 2 × 30 mL portions of diethyl ether. Combine the organic extracts, wash them with 4 × 15 mL saturated sodium chloride solution, and dry them over $MgSO_4$.[5] Filter off the drying agent by suction,[6] and evaporate the filtrate on the rotary evaporator. Dissolve the residue in the minimum volume of cyclohexane and add a few drops of methanol. Collect the resulting precipitate by suction filtration and dry it by suction for a few minutes. If crystallization does not commence on cooling in ice and scratching the sides of the flask with a glass rod, this may be due to the presence of unreacted benzophenone. In this instance it is best to purify the mixture by chromatography on silica eluting with light petroleum–ether (1 : 1). The benzophenone is eluted before your product and it will be necessary to allow a further 3 h period for the chromatography. Record the yield, mp and the IR ($CHCl_3$) and NMR ($CDCl_3$) spectra of your product.

Problems

1 Why is such a strong base (*n*-butyl-lithium) needed to remove the second proton in ethyl 3-oxobutanoate?

2 Why do reactions of ethyl 3-oxobutanoate dianion occur exclusively at the terminal anion?

3 What would you expect to happen if the product from the reaction with benzophenone was subsequently treated with acid?

4 Fully assign the IR and NMR spectra of your product.

Further reading

For the procedure on which this experiment is based, see: S.N. Huckin and L. Weiler, *Can. J. Chem.*, 1974, **52**, 2157 and references therein.

For a review on dianions, see: E.M. Kaiser, J.D. Petty and P.L.A. Knutson, *Synthesis*, 1977, 509.

8.3 Heteroatom-stabilized carbanions

The series of mechanistically related reactions to be considered in this section covers the condensation of carbonyl compounds with carbanions generated adjacent to a triarylphosphonium group (Wittig reaction), a phosphonate ester (Wadsworth–Emmons reaction) and a sulfonium group. The carbanionic species generated from phosphonium and sulfonium salts possess no net charge overall and are termed *ylids*. The sequences utilizing the phosphorus and silicon reagents are condensation reactions which result in the conversion of carbonyl compounds into alkenes. However, in the sulfonium ylid reaction, epoxides are produced, corresponding to the overall insertion of a methylene group into the carbonyl double bond.

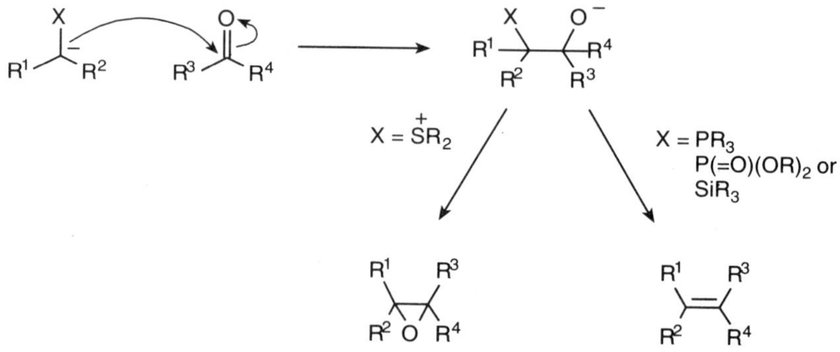

The Wittig reaction

This reaction is named after its discoverer Georg Wittig who was awarded the Nobel Prize in 1979 in recognition of his fundamental contributions to organic chemistry. The hydrogens on the α-carbons of phosphonium salts are acidic due to the potential for resonance stabilization of the carbanionic species by back-donation into the unoccupied 3*d*-orbitals of the phosphorus.

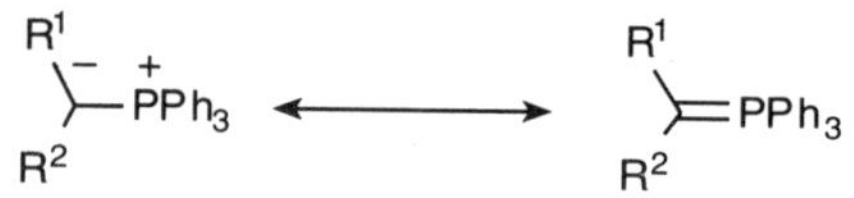

The phosphonium salts are prepared by the reaction of trisubstituted phosphines (commonly triphenylphosphine) with alkyl halides. The deprotonation normally requires strongly basic conditions, although ylids in which the carbon bearing the phosphonium substituent possesses another group capable of withdrawing elections by resonance (*stabilized ylids*) can be generated under mildly basic conditions and are more stable.

The reaction may be considered to involve nucleophilic attack on a carbonyl group to yield a dipolar *betaine* followed by loss of triphenylphosphine oxide and the formation of an alkene. A cyclic *oxaphosphetane* is implicated in this fragmentation and such an intermediate may be considered formally to be the 2 + 2 cycloaddition product of the ylid with the carbonyl group.

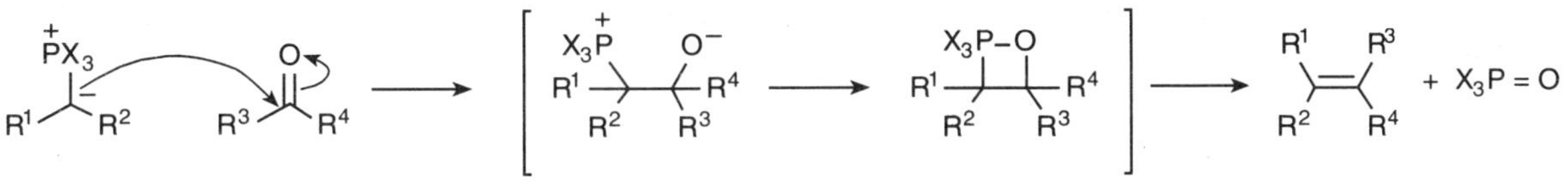

Due to the strength of the P=O bond, the final extrusion step is thermodynamically very favourable and permits the synthesis of alkenes not available by other approaches, such as strained, deconjugated or terminal alkenes.

Further reading

For a discussion of the Wittig and related reactions, see: S. Warren, *Chem. Ind. (London)*, 1980, **20**, 824; W.J. Stec, *Acc. Chem. Res.*, 1983, **16**, 411; M. Julia, *Pure Appl. Chem.*, 1985, **57**, 763; B.E. Maryanoff and A.B. Reitz, *Chem. Rev.*, 1989, **89**, 863; J.M.J. Williams (ed.) *Preparation of Alkenes: A Practical Approach*, Oxford University, Press, Oxford, 1996.

Experiment 50 *Preparation of* E*-diphenylethene (stilbene) with ylid generation under phase transfer conditions*

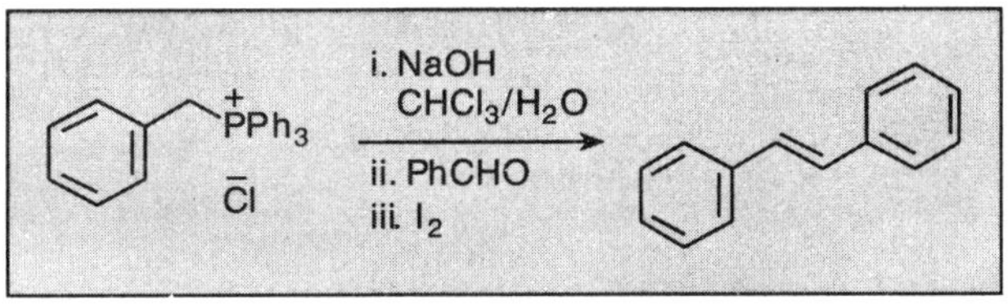

Generation of non-stabilized ylids from phosphonium salts generally requires strong bases such as *n*-butyl-lithium, and the ylids, once formed, require protection from water and oxygen with which they react. However, use of a two-phase system permits the simpler procedure described here which utilizes aqueous sodium hydroxide and does not require manipulation under an inert atmosphere. The phosphonium salt acts as a phase transfer catalyst and hydroxide ions in the aqueous phase can be exchanged for chloride ions. The deprotonation of the phosphonium salt occurs in the organic solvent where, in the absence of an aqueous solvation sphere, the hydroxide ion is a much stronger base than in water. This is an interesting example of phase transfer catalysis where the catalyst is also the substrate!

Although the preparation of alkyltriphenylphosphonium halides used in the Wittig reaction is generally not complicated, the particular procedure in this case would require benzyl chloride which is highly lachrymatory. Thus, use of commercially available benzyltriphenylphosphonium chloride is recommended here. The Wittig reaction in this example is not totally stereoselective but treatment of the product mixture with a trace of iodine causes isomerization of the Z-1,2-diphenylethene to the sterically preferred E-isomer.

Level	3
Time	preparation and isolation 3 h; purification and analysis 3 h
Equipment	magnetic stirrer; apparatus for extraction/separation, reflux, TLC
Instruments	UV, NMR

Materials

benzaldehyde (FW 106.1)	*ca.* 5 mL	**flammable, toxic**
If benzaldehyde, which has been freshly freed of benzoic acid, is used, the purification procedure described below may be omitted and only 2 mL (2.10 g, 20 mmol) of benzaldehyde will be required		
benzyltriphenylphosphonium chloride (FW 388.9)	7.78 g (20 mmol)	**hygroscopic, irritant**
dichloromethane		**irritant, toxic**
light petroleum (40–60°C)		**flammable**
methanol		**flammable, toxic**
ethanol		**flammable, toxic**
ethyl acetate		**flammable, irritant**
sodium hydroxide	50 g	**corrosive, hygroscopic**
potassium carbonate solution (10%)		**corrosive**
sodium metabisulfite solution (25%)		

Procedure

Into a 100 mL Erlenmeyer flask measure benzaldehyde (5 mL) and to this add 30 mL of 10% potassium carbonate solution with vigorous swirling for 1 min.[1] Decant the mixture into a test tube and allow the layers to separate. Meanwhile, suspend the benzyltriphenylphosphonium chloride in dichloromethane (15 mL) in an Erlenmeyer flask containing a magnetic stirrer bar. Dissolve the sodium hydroxide in cold distilled water (75 mL) in a 250 mL Erlenmeyer flask and, whilst this solution is cooling, carefully remove the purified benzaldehyde (top layer) from the aqueous potassium carbonate. Add 2.0 mL of the benzaldehyde to the reaction mixture, followed by the aqueous sodium hydroxide. Clamp the flask securely, plug the neck with cotton wool and stir the yellow mixture vigorously for 30 min.[2] Decant the mixture into a separatory funnel through a small filter funnel and rinse the reaction flask and stirrer bar with dichloromethane (2 × 20 mL) and water (15 mL). Separate the two phases (due to the density of the aqueous base used, the dichloromethane should be the upper layer—check before discarding any of the phases),[3] dry the dichloromethane solution over $MgSO_4$,[4] and filter the clear solution. Save a small volume of this solution for TLC investigation and remove the remainder of the solvent from the sample on the rotary evaporator. Triturate the

[1] *See note above*

[2] *Vigorous stirring is essential; some heating may occur*

[3] *Vent the funnel*

[4] *May be left here or at any convenient stage*

residue repeatedly with hot petroleum (25 mL portions) until no further material is extracted. (This can be verified by looking for the absence of oily streaks on the ground glass after decanting the petroleum.) Save a second sample and concentrate the remainder of the solution to 25 mL on the rotary evaporator. Add a crystal of iodine, reflux the solution[5] for 30 min to effect isomerization and allow to cool. Decolourize the mixture with 25% sodium metabisulfite solution (10 mL), remove the lower aqueous phase, and add methanol (25 mL) to the organic phase remaining in the separatory funnel. If two phases do not form, add water dropwise until this occurs. Separate the upper layer of petroleum, dry over $MgSO_4$, filter and remove the solvent on the rotary evaporator in a preweighed flask. Record the yield and mp of the crystalline product and recrystallize from ethanol. Carry out TLC analysis[6] of the two aliquots obtained during the course of the experiment and the final sample. Use a TLC plate pre-coated with silica, elute with light petroleum and observe the developed plate under UV light[7] and, after standing over iodine, noting the R_f value. Obtain the NMR ($CDCl_3$) and UV (EtOH) spectra.

[5] *See Fig. 3.23(a)*

[6] *See Chapter 3*

[7] ***Care! Eye protection***

Problems

1 Discuss the mode of action of phase transfer catalysts, particularly with regard to this experiment.

2 From the TLC and spectroscopic evidence, comment upon the purity or otherwise of your material. what purpose is served by trituration of the initial reaction material with petroleum? Which is the major isomer of 1,2-diphenylethene formed in the reaction.

3 *E*-1,2-diphenylethene demonstrates very weak oestrogenic activity. The related *E*-1,2-di(4-hydroxyphenyl)ethene is much more active in this respect and is also called stilboestrol. The *Z*-isomers of these compounds are inactive. Suggest a reason for this activity.

Further reading

The authors thank Dr D.C.C. Smith, University of Manchester, for supplying details upon which this experiment is based.

For a review of the Wittig reaction, see the references given on p. 561.

For reviews and monographs of phase transfer catalysis, see: E.V. Dehmlow and S.S. Dehmlow, *Phase Transfer Catalysis*, 2nd edn, Verlag Chemie, Deerfield Beach, Florida, 1983; J.M. McIntosh, *J. Chem. Educ.*, 1978, **55**, 235; E.V. Dehmlow, *Angew. Chem. Int. Ed. Engl.*, 1977, **16**, 493.

Experiment 51

Preparation of 4-vinylbenzoic acid by a Wittig reaction in aqueous medium

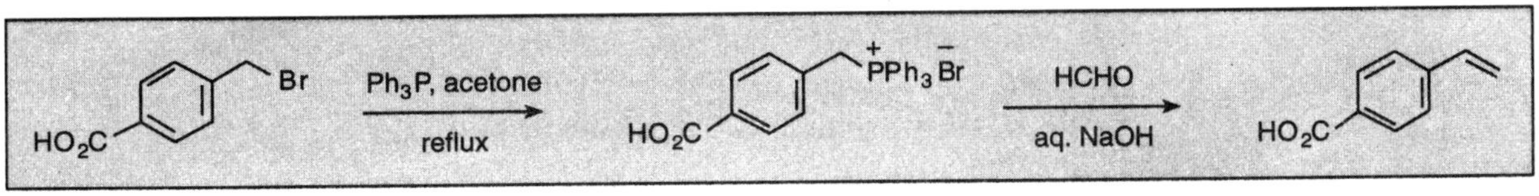

In this second example of an aqueous Wittig reaction, the ylid is generated in the presence of a large excess of a reactive aldehyde. The ylid is stabilized by virtue of the electron-withdrawing carboxylic acid group on the aromatic ring and is resistant to hydrolysis. The phosphonium salt is prepared from 4-bromomethylbenzoic acid which, being non-volatile, is relatively safe to handle, although it still has irritant properties. This starting material may be prepared according to the procedure described in Experiment 16; it is also available commercially.

Level	1
Time	3 h
Equipment	magnetic stirrer; apparatus for suction filtration, reflux, TLC

Materials

1. Preparation of phosphonium salt		
4-bromomethylbenzoic acid (FW 215.1)	4.30 g (20 mmol)	**lachrymator, irritant**
triphenylphosphine (FW 262.3)	5.20 g (20 mmol)	**irritant**
acetone		**flammable**
diethyl ether		**flammable, irritant**
2. Preparation of 4-vinylbenzoic acid		
formaldehyde (37% aqueous solution) (FW 30.0)	32 mL	**cancer suspect agent, toxic**
This represents a large excess of formaldehyde		
4-carboxybenzyltriphenyl-phosphonium bromide	3.76 g (8 mmol)	**irritant**
sodium hydroxide pellets	2.5 g	**corrosive, hygroscopic**
ethanol		**flammable, toxic**
hydrochloric acid (conc.)		**corrosive**

Procedure

HOOD

[1] ***Wear gloves***

[2] *See Fig. 3.23(a)*

[3] *See Fig. 3.7*

[4] *This can be done during Part 2*

1. Preparation of 4-carboxybenzyltriphenylphosphonium bromide

Dissolve the bromomethylbenzoic acid[1] and the triphenylphosphine in 60 mL acetone in a 100 mL round-bottomed flask and reflux the mixture[2] for 45 min. After this time, cool the reaction mixture and filter off the precipitated phosphonium salt with suction.[3] Wash the solid with diethyl ether (2×20 mL) on the sinter and dry it with suction. Record the yield and mp[4] of the product, which is sufficiently pure to use directly in the next stage.

HOOD

2. Preparation of 4-vinylbenzoic acid

Place the 4-carboxybenzyltriphenylphosphonium bromide (3.76 g, 8 mmol), aqueous formaldehyde and 15 mL water in a 250 mL Erlenmeyer flask equipped with a magnetic stirrer bar. Clamp the flask, stir vigorously and add a solution of the sodium hydroxide in 15 mL water over *ca.* 10 min. Stir the mixture for an additional 45 min and filter off the precipitate with suction,[3] washing it with water. Acidify the combined filtrate and washings with concentrated hydrochloric acid and filter off the resultant precipitate of crude product with suction.[3] Recrystallize the product from aqueous ethanol and record the yield and mp of the material obtained. Record an IR (Nujol®) spectrum of the purified material, and run a TLC of the product (silica gel, dichloromethane–ethyl acetate (1:1)) and compare its R_f with that of the starting material. ■

MICROSCALE

Level	1
Time	3 h
Equipment	magnetic stirrer; apparatus for suction filtration (micro-Hirsch and side arm tube), Craig tube recrystallization

Materials

1. Preparation of phosphonium salt		
4-bromomethylbenzoic acid (FW 215.1)	108 mg (0.5 mmol)	**lachrymator, irritant**
triphenylphosphine (FW 262.3)	130 mg (0.5 mmol)	**irritant**
acetone		**flammable**
diethyl ether		**flammable, irritant**
2. Preparation of 4-vinylbenzoic acid		
formaldehyde (37% aqueous solution) (FW 30.0)	0.8 mL	**cancer suspect agent, toxic**
This represents a large excess of formaldehyde		
4-carboxybenzyltriphenylphosphonium bromide	94 mg (0.25 mmol)	**irritant**
sodium hydroxide (16.7% w/v)	0.375 mL	**corrosive, hygroscopic**
ethanol		**flammable, toxic**
hydrochloric acid (conc.)		**corrosive**
Celite® or Hyflo®	*ca.* 100 mg	**irritant dust**

Procedure

HOOD

1. Preparation of 4-carboxybenzyltriphenylphosphonium bromide

Dissolve the 4-bromomethylbenzoic acid[1] and the triphenylphosphine in the acetone in a 3 mL reaction vial and reflux the mixture[2] for 45 min. After this time, cool the reaction mixture and collect the precipitated phosphonium salt at the pump using a micro-Hirsch funnel.[3] Wash the solid at the pump with diethyl ether (2 × 0.5 mL) and suck dry. Record the yield and mp.[4]

[1] ***Wear gloves***

[2] *See Fig. 3.24*

[3] *See Fig. 3.7*

[4] *This can be done during Part 2*

HOOD

2. Preparation of 4-vinylbenzoic acid

Place the phosphonium salt (94 mg, 0.25 mmol), the aqueous formaldehyde and water (0.375 mL) in a small test tube containing a small stirrer bead, and add the sodium hydroxide solution. Stir the solution for an additional 45 min, then remove the precipitate by filtration through a short plug of Celite®,[5]

[5] *See Fig. 3.9*

washing the filter bed with water (2 × 0.2 mL). Collect the filtrate and the washings in a 2 mL Craig tube. Acidify the tube contents with concentrated hydrochloric acid and collect the precipitated product by centrifugation.[6] Recrystallize the crude product from aqueous ethanol in a Craig tube and record the yield and mp.

[6]See pp. 137–138

Problems

1 Assign the main absorptions in the IR spectrum of 4-vinylbenzoic acid.

2 Explain why it is possible to generate the ylid with aqueous sodium hydroxide in this example.

3 If an aldehyde other than formaldehyde were to be used, what would be the geometry of the double bond in the major product and why?

Experiment 52

A Wittig reaction involving preparation and isolation of a stabilized ylid: conversion of 1-bromobutyrolactone to α-methylenebutyrolactone

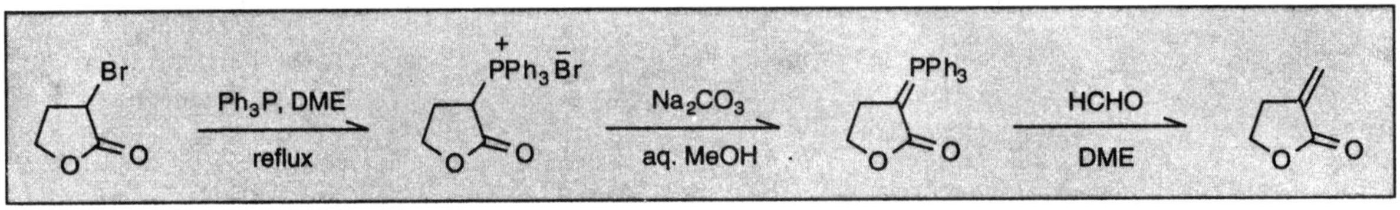

In the following experiment it is possible to isolate the intermediate ylid after its generation with aqueous sodium carbonate. The mildness of the reaction conditions and the relative stability of the phosphorane are a reflection of the presence of an electron-withdrawing group (the lactone moiety) on the carbon α- to the phosphorus, which permits additional resonance delocalization of the carbanion.

Wittig reactions of stabilized ylids with aldehydes (other than formaldehyde of course) favour the thermodynamically more stable *E*-product. This is considered to be a consequence of reversibility of the initial nucleophilic addition step, with one betaine selectively collapsing to products and the other betaine reverting to starting materials.

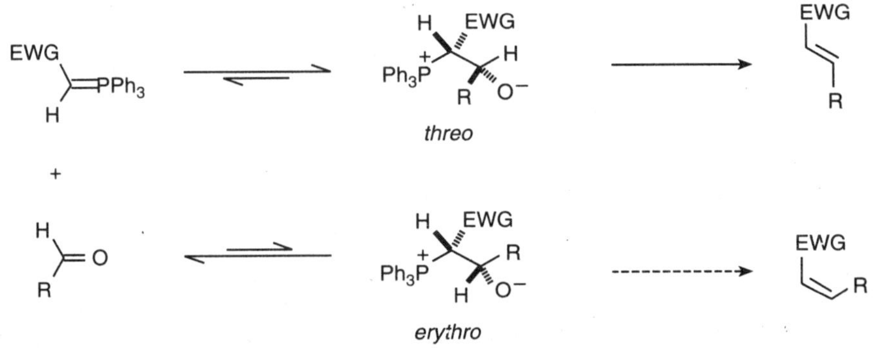

The α-methylenebutyrolactone moiety is a structural unit found in a wide range of terpenoids, many of which possess interesting physiological activities, particularly those of tumour inhibition (e.g. vernolepin). α-Methylenebutyrolactone itself has been isolated from tulips (from which it derives its trivial name tulipalin A) and has been shown to possess fungicidal properties.

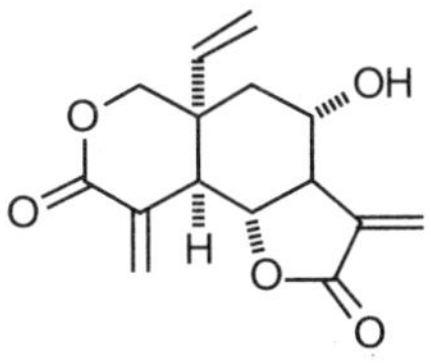

vernolepin

Level	3
Time	4 × 3 h (5 × 3 h if both Wittig condensations are attempted)
Equipment	apparatus for reflux, reflux under nitrogen
Instruments	IR, NMR

Materials

1. Preparation of phosphonium salt		
1-bromobutyrolactone (FW 165.0)	16.5 g (0.1 mol)	**irritant**
triphenylphosphine (FW 262.3)	26.2 g (0.1 mol)	**irritant**
1,2-dimethoxyethane		**flammable**
methanol		**flammable, toxic**
ethyl acetate		**flammable, irritant**
2. Preparation and isolation of 1-butyrolactonylidene triphenylphosphorane		
aqueous methanol (30%)		**toxic**
aqueous sodium carbonate (5%)		**corrosive**
dimethylformamide		**irritant**
3. Preparation of α-methylenebutyrolactone		
paraformaldehyde (FW $[30.0]_n$)	1.20 g (40 mmol)	**irritant**
1,2-dimethoxyethane		**flammable**
light petroleum (bp 60–80°C)		**flammable**
diethyl ether		**flammable, irritant**
TLC grade silica gel		**irritant dust**

Procedure

HOOD

1. Preparation of 1-butyrolactonyltriphenylphosphonium bromide

Dissolve the 1-bromobutyrolactone and triphenylphosphine in 40 mL 1,2-dimethoxyethane and reflux for 2 h.[1] After cooling in an ice bath for 10 min, filter off the crystalline precipitate. Redissolve the phosphonium bromide in methanol (*ca.* 50 mL) with warming and then reprecipitate the salt with ethyl acetate.[2] Record the mp[3] and yield of the product.

[1] *See Fig. 3.23(a)*

[2] *May be left here*

[3] *Leave this until end of Part 2*

HOOD

2. *Preparation and isolation of 1-butyrolactonylidene triphenylphosphorane*

Dissolve 9.0 g of purified phosphonium salt from the previous preparation in 150 mL 30% aqueous methanol in a 250 mL Erlenmeyer flask, add 60 mL 5% aqueous sodium carbonate and allow the mixture to stand for 10 min. Filter off the fine white precipitate of the phosphorane and dry it on the filter with suction. Recrystallize the product from dimethylformamide and record the yield of the purified material. Determine its mp and that of the phosphonium bromide prepared in part 1.

HOOD

3. *Preparation of α-methylenebutyrolactone*

Heat to gentle reflux a suspension of the recrystallized phosphorane (3.46 g, 10 mmol) and 1.2 g paraformaldehyde in 100 mL 1,2-dimethoxyethane under an atmosphere of nitrogen for 1.5 h.[4] Cool the mixture and remove the solvent on the rotary evaporator with *slight* (<40°C) warming until the mixture is reduced to one-half of its original volume. Add 50 mL light petroleum and filter the mixture with suction through a 2–3 cm pad of TLC silica contained in a cylindrical sinter funnel (4.5 cm diameter).[5] Wash the silica with 50 mL 1:4 ether–light petroleum and remove the solvent from the combined filtrates on the rotary evaporator.[6] Note the yield of the colourless oil obtained and record the IR (film) spectrum and NMR ($CDCl_3$) spectrum. Purify further by short path distillation (optional).[7] Set the bath temperature to *ca.* 120°C if carrying out the distillation under water aspirator vacuum (*ca.* 16 mmHg) or *ca.* 85°C if using an oil pump (*ca.* 2 mmHg).

[4] *See Fig. 3.23(b)*

[5] *See Fig. 3.74*

[6] *May be left at this stage*

[7] *See Fig. 3.54*

Problems

1 Assign the important absorptions in the IR spectra of the product lactone(s). Compare the spectra with that of α-bromobutyrolactone (*Aldrich* FTIR, **1** (1), 699D).

2 Assign the peaks in the NMR spectra of the products. In the case of α-ethylidenebutyrolactone, estimate the product isomer ratio. Taking into account the mechanism of the Wittig reaction of stabilized ylids, suggest the structure of the major product.

3 Suggest mechanisms and products for the reaction of α-methylenebutyrolactone with: (i) thiophenol in the presence of piperidine, (ii) cyclopentadiene, and (iii) sodium methoxide in methanol.

Further reading

For reviews of syntheses of α-methylenebutyrolactones, see: P.A. Grieco, *Synthesis*, 1975, 67; J.C. Sarma and R.P. Sharma, *Heterocycles*, 1986, **24**, 441.

The Wadsworth–Emmons reaction

In the Wadsworth–Emmons variant of the Wittig reaction, the nucleophile is generated by deprotonation of a phosphonate ester. The starting phosphonates are readily available via the *Michaelis–Arbusov reaction* of trialkylphosphites with alkyl halides.

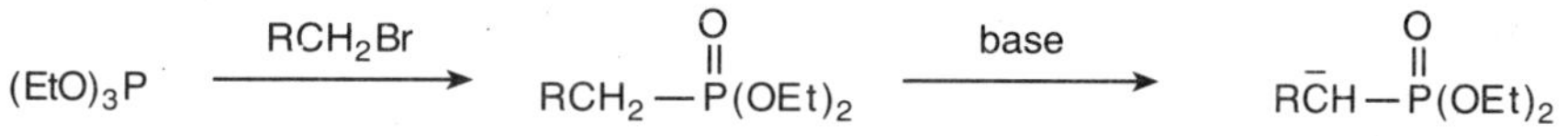

Michaelis–Arbusov reaction

This procedure has several advantages over the Wittig reaction. The phosphonate anions are more reactive than the neutral ylids derived from phosphonium salts and give more consistent results with ketones which are frequently unreactive under standard Wittig reaction conditions. Another practical advantage of the procedure is that a water-soluble phosphate by-product is formed which simplifies the work-up procedure.

Experiment 53 *Preparation of* E,E-*1,4-diphenyl-1,3-butadiene*

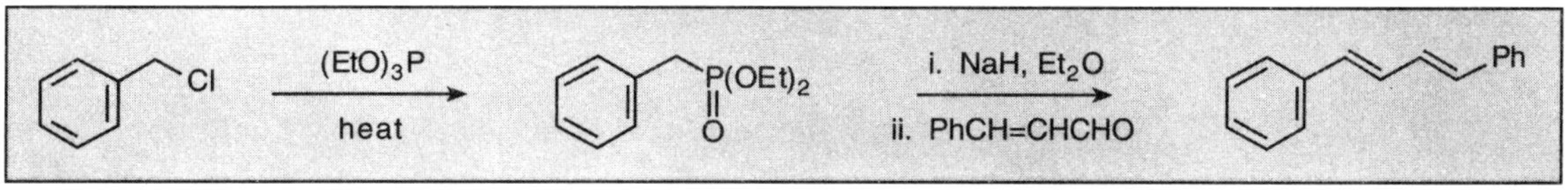

The first part of this experiment, in which diethyl benzyl phosphonate is prepared by the *Michaelis–Arbuzov reaction* of benzyl chloride with triethyl phosphite, is optional. Benzyl chloride is intensely lachrymatory and triethyl phosphite is highly toxic with a disagreeable odour.

All manipulations with these reagents must be carried out in the hood.

Alternatively, commercially available diethyl benzyl phosphonate may be used, thus avoiding use of these toxic materials.

Level	3
Time	preparation of diethyl benzyl phosphonate 3 h; preparation and isolation of *E,E*-1,4-diphenyl-1,3-butadiene 3 h; purification and spectroscopic analysis 3 h
Equipment	magnetic stirrer; apparatus for: reflux, reduced pressure distillation, reflux with simultaneous addition and stirring, extraction/separation, recrystallization
Instruments	UV, IR, NMR

Materials

1. Preparation of diethyl benzyl phosphonate

benzyl chloride (FW 126.6)	5.0 mL, 4.55 g (36 mmol)	**cancer suspect agent, lachrymator, corrosive**
triethyl phosphite (FW 166.2)	8.3 mL, 8.00 g (48 mmol)	**irritant**

Continued on p. 570

Box cont.

2. *Preparation of* E,E-*1,4-diphenyl-1,3-butadiene*		
E-3-phenylpropenal (cinnamaldehyde) (FW 132.2)	1.3 mL, 1.30 g (10 mmol)	**irritant**
sodium hydride (60% dispersion in oil)	0.45 g (*ca.* 10 mmol)	**flammable, moisture sensitive**
NOTE: ***sodium hydride reacts violently with moisture to liberate hydrogen with the risk of fire. As a dispersion in oil, the reagent is safer to handle and store than the dry solid, when it is intensely pyrophoric. All apparatus and solvents must be rigorously dried before use. Take special care when quenching reactions involving the use of sodium hydride***		
diethyl ether (sodium dried)		**flammable, irritant**
ethanol (anhydrous)		**flammable, toxic**
2-propanol		**flammable, toxic**
methanol		**flammable, toxic**

Procedure

All apparatus must be thoroughly dried in a hot (>120°C) oven before use.

HOOD

[1]*Wear gloves*

[2]*See Fig. 3.23(a)*

[3]*See Fig. 3.53*

1. *Preparation of diethyl benzyl phosphonate*

Place the benzyl chloride[1] and triethyl phosphite in a 50 mL round-bottomed flask and reflux vigorously for 1 h.[2] Allow the flask to cool, set up the apparatus for reduced pressure distillation[3] and distil the residue slowly. After a forerun of unreacted material, collect the diethyl benzyl phosphonate (160–165°C/14 mmHg or 105–10°C/1 mmHg). Record the yield and obtain the NMR spectrum ($CDCl_3$) of your product.

HOOD

[4]*Care!*

[5]*See Fig. 3.25(a)*

[6]*See Appendix 2*

2. *Preparation of* E,E-*1,4-diphenyl-1,3-butadiene*

Quickly weigh out the sodium hydride[4] and transfer it to a 100 mL round-bottomed flask equipped for reflux and addition with protection from atmospheric moisture.[5] Add 15 mL *dry* diethyl ether[6] and stir the suspension gently for 1 min. Stop stirring, allow the mixture to settle, and then *quickly but carefully* remove most of the supernatant with a pipette.[4] (Destroy any sodium hydride that might have been removed with the supernatant by adding the diethyl ether to 50 mL of 2-propanol in a 250 mL beaker.) Repeat this procedure twice more and then add a final 15 mL portion of diethyl ether to cover the sodium hydride. Stir the mixture gently and to the suspension add a solution of 2.28 g diethyl benzyl phosphonate in 10 mL *dry* diethyl ether dropwise over *ca.* 5 min. To ensure complete reaction, stop the addition after adding half of the phosphonate solution, add 3 drops of dry ethanol down the condenser and warm the mixture. When the hydrogen evolution becomes vigorous, remove the heating and add the remainder of the solution. Rinse the funnel with a further 5 mL of diethyl ether and add it to the reaction mixture in order to transfer the last traces of the phosphonate into the flask. After the addition, stir the mixture at room temperature until hydrogen evolution is no longer apparent (*ca.* 45 min). During this time, charge the addition funnel with a solution of the *E*-3-phenylpropenal in *dry* diethyl ether (10 mL). At the end of the stirring period, add this solution dropwise at such a rate that the resultant exothermic reaction maintains a gentle reflux. Stir the reaction for a further 15 min at room temperature after addition and then cautiously add ethanol (*ca.* 1 mL). After another 2 min follow this with water (30 mL) and transfer the mixture to a separatory funnel, washing the reaction flask with diethyl ether (15 mL). Separate the lower aqueous layer, wash the organic phase with water (20 mL) and dry the ethereal solution over $MgSO_4$.[7] Remove the solvent on the rotary evaporator and recrystallize the pale yellow, semicrystalline mass from methanol. Record the yield and mp of the recrystallized product and obtain the UV (MeOH), IR ($CHCl_3$) and NMR ($CDCl_3$) spectra of your material.

[7] *May be left at this stage*

Problems

1 Calculate the extinction coefficients for the absorption maxima in the UV spectrum of the diene. Describe, in qualitative terms, the changes expected in the UV spectra of a series of related conjugated polyenes as the conjugation is progressively increased. What physical property would such extended conjugation confer upon the molecules? Suggest a class of natural products in which this phenomenon exists.

2 Assign the important absorptions in the IR spectrum of the product diene and compare the spectrum with that of the starting aldehyde (*Aldrich* FT IR, **1**(2), 102A).

3 Assign the peaks in the diene NMR spectrum. At 60 MHz the spectrum is relatively uninformative; why do you think this is so?

4 Explain the mechanistic reasoning behind the fact that stabilized ylids favour formation of *E*-alkenes.

Further reading

For reviews of the Michaelis–Arbuzov reaction, see: B.A. Arbuzov, *Pure Appl. Chem.*, 1964, **9**, 307; R.G. Harvey and E.R. DeSombre, *Top. Phosphorus Stereochem.*, 1964, **1**, 57.

For a discussion of the Wadsworth–Emmons reaction with a comprehensive list of examples, see: W.S. Wadsworth, *Org. React.*, 1977, **25**, 73; J.M.J. Williams (ed.), *Preparation of Alkenes: a Practical Approach*, Oxford University Press, Oxford, 1996.

Sulfur ylids

Sulfur ylids, in contrast to phosphorus ylids (Experiments 50–52), do not give alkenes on reaction with carbonyl compounds.

The initial step in the reaction of sulfur ylids with carbonyl compounds follows the usual nucleophilic addition to the carbonyl carbon. However, collapse of this adduct occurs to liberate a neutral sulfur moiety and generate an epoxide. Such a 1,3-elimination is directly analogous to the reaction of halohydrins on treatment with base and means that sulfur ylids can be considered to be carbene equivalents which insert into the carbonyl double bond. Hence the reaction constitutes a useful way of making epoxides, and complements the more usual route to epoxides from alkenes either directly (Experiments 11 and 12) or via the halohydrin (Experiment 8).

The ylids generated from dimethyl sulfide and dimethyl sulfoxide by sequential methylation and base treatment both provide a means of inserting a methylene into a carbonyl group; they also show a fascinating divergence of stereoselectivity towards carbonyl groups having facial bias. The smaller, more reactive dimethylsulfonium methylide favours axial attack on cyclohexanones, whereas the larger, less reactive dimethylsulfoxonium methylide yields equatorial insertion products with high stereoselectivity. Consequently, this latter reagent provides an important stereochemical alternative to epoxidation of double bonds.

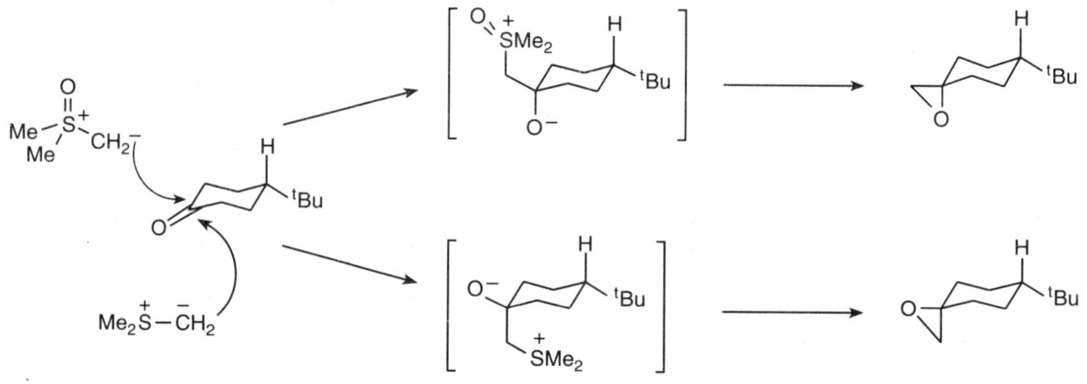

Experiment 54 *Sulfur ylids: preparation of methylenecyclohexane oxide (1-oxaspiro[5.2]octane)*

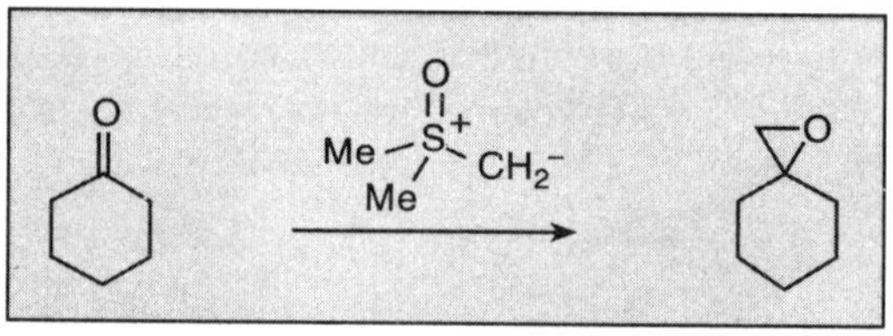

This experiment illustrates the reaction of the sulfur ylid, dimethylsulfoxonium methylide, with cyclohexanone to give the spiro-epoxide methylenecyclohexane oxide (1-oxaspirol[5.2]octane). The ylid is generated from the sulfoxonium salt, trimethylsulfoxonium iodide, using sodium hydride in dry dimethyl sulfoxide as solvent under anhydrous conditions. Addition of the ketone, followed by an aqueous work-up, gives the epoxide which is purified by short path distillation under reduced pressure. The use of commercial trimethylsulfoxonium iodide is strongly recommended.

Level	4
Time	2×3h
Equipment	magnetic stirrer/hotplate, oil bath; apparatus for stirring with addition under inert atmosphere, solid addition tube, separation/extraction, suction filtration, short path distillation under reduced pressure
Instruments	refractometer, IR, NMR

Materials

1. Preparation of dimethylsulfoxonium methylide

dimethyl sulfoxide (dry)	25 mL	**hygroscopic, irritant**
trimethylsulfoxonium iodide (FW 220.1)	5.06 g (23 mmol)	**irritant**
sodium hydride (*ca.* 60% oil dispersion) (FW 24.0)	0.88 g (22 mmol)	**flammable**

NOTE: ***Sodium hydride reacts violently with moisture to liberate hydrogen with the risk of fire. As a dispersion in oil, the reagent is safer to handle and store than the dry solid, when it is intensely pyrophoric. All apparatus and solvents must be rigorously dried before use. Take special care when quenching reactions involving the use of sodium hydride***

light petroleum (bp 40–60°C)		**flammable**

2. Preparation of methylenecyclohexane oxide

cyclohexanone (FW 98.2)	2.0 mL (20 mmol)	**irritant, toxic**
diethyl ether		**flammable, irritant**
sodium chloride solution (saturated)		

Procedure

All apparatus must be thoroughly dried in a hot (>120°C) oven before use.

HOOD

1. Preparation of dimethylsulfoxonium methylide

Set up a 100 mL three-neck flask with a nitrogen bubbler, a solid addition tube[1] containing the trimethylsulfoxonium iodide, a pressure-equalizing addition funnel, and a magnetic stirrer bar. Connect the supply of dry nitrogen, and under a nitrogen atmosphere, flame dry the flask. The rest of the experiment is then carried out under a gentle stream of nitrogen. Place the sodium hydride and the 15 mL dry petroleum[2] in the flask, and start the stirrer. Stir the suspension for 2–3 min, and then allow it to settle. Remove the supernatant petroleum layer using a pipette, add 25 mL *dry* dimethyl sulfoxide[3] from the addition funnel, and stir the mixture. Add the trimethylsulfoxonium iodide in small portions[4] over 15 min, and then stir the mixture for an additional 30 min to complete the formation of the ylid.[5]

[1] *See Fig. 3.18*

[2] *See Appendix 2*

[3] *Use distilled dimethyl sulfoxide, see Appendix 2*

[4] *Mild exotherm*

[5] *Hydrogen evolved*

HOOD

2. Preparation of methylenecyclohexane oxide

Place the cyclohexanone in the addition funnel and add it to the reaction mixture dropwise over 5 min. If necessary rinse in the last traces of cyclohexanone with a few drops of *dry* dimethyl sulfoxide. Stir the mixture for 15 min at room temperature, and then at 55–60°C for 30 min, heating the flask with an oil bath.[6] Disconnect the nitrogen line, and pour the mixture into a 100 mL separatory funnel containing 50 mL cold water. Extract the product with 3 × 10 mL portions of diethyl ether. Combine the ether extracts, wash them with 10 mL water and then 5 mL saturated sodium chloride solution, and dry them over $MgSO_4$.[7] Filter off the drying agent by suction, and concentrate the filtrate on the rotary evaporator (whilst cooling the evaporating flask) in ice[8] to leave an almost colourless residue.[7] Distil the residue in the short path distillation apparatus[9] under a water aspirator vacuum (*ca.* 40 mmHg) to give the product. Record the bp, yield, refractive index, and the IR (film) and NMR ($CDCl_3$) spectra of your product.

[6] *Mixture can be left at room temperature at this stage, before work-up*

[7] *May be left at this stage*

[8] *Product is volatile!*

[9] *See Fig. 3.54*

Problems

1 Assign the IR and NMR spectra of the product.

2 Suggest an alternative route to methylenecyclohexane oxide from cyclohexanone.

Further reading

For the procedure on which this experiment is based, see: E.J. Corey and M. Chaykovski, *Org. Synth. Coll. Vol.*, **5**, 755.

Umpolung of reactivity

A large proportion of the synthetically useful carbon–carbon bond-forming reactions are polar in nature; that is, they involve the combination of two centres, one of which has δ –ve character and the other δ +ve character. Whilst free carbanions or carbo-cations may be involved, a great number of processes rely upon the slight bond polarization in molecules resulting from the presence of either an electron-donating or -withdrawing substituent (for instance SN2 reactions or nucleophilic additions to carbonyl groups).

When designing a synthesis, it is logical to attempt conversions which profit from this inherent polarization of the substrate molecules, as such an approach is more likely to lead to a successful reaction. However, the construction of complex synthetic targets frequently presents the chemist with certain constraints which close such avenues to him or her and, at this point, it may be necessary to seek connective processes which apparently flout the

nucleophilic substitution

nucleophilic addition

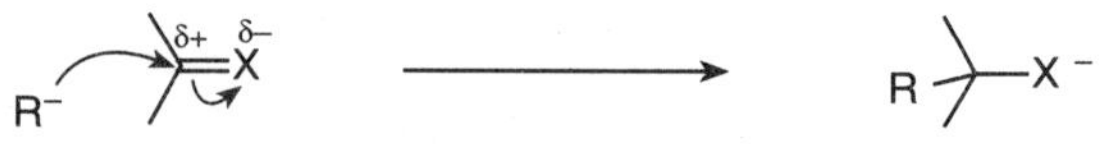

inbuilt polarity of the reactants. This can often be achieved by some reversible modification of the substrate structure which, after the conversion has been carried out, can be returned to the original functionality. This procedure is commonly referred to as *umpolung* (literally 'polarity reversal') and, in this context, it is useful to consider the idea of a *synthetic equivalent* and the concept of the *synthon*.

Although frequently not distinguished from each other by organic chemists, the two latter terms actually refer to very distinct entities. A synthetic equivalent is any compound capable of being used in a particular conversion and then converted to another functionality at the end of the process; a synthetic equivalent is a real molecule. In contrast, a synthon is the imaginary molecular building block, with all its requisite charges, which is formally introduced by the above procedure. In the case of the umpolung, the charges on the synthon are the inverse of what would be expected from the natural polarity of that part molecule. The whole thing is most easily understood by consideration of what is possibly the archetypal example of umpolung: the conversion of an aldehyde to its thioacetal followed by base treatment.

The π-cloud of the carbonyl group of an aldehyde or ketone is polarized such as to render the carbon atom $\delta+$ ve and the oxygen atom $\delta-$ ve, making the electrophilic carbon a potential receptor site and the nucleophilic oxygen a potential donor. Indeed, this alternating donor/acceptor property is propagated down the carbon chain of the aldehyde (although in the absence of conjugation it is not demonstrated to any utilizable extent further than the α-position) and is expressed in the relatively high acidity of protons on the α-carbons of ketones and aldehydes which turn out to be donor positions.

Nucleophilic attack on the aldehyde, for instance with a Grignard reagent, furnishes a secondary alcohol which may in turn be oxidized to a ketone. In these conversions, the aldehyde can be considered to be acting as two synthons; namely an α-cation of a primary alcohol or an acylium cation. Conversely, the Grignard reagent is an alkyl anion synthon.

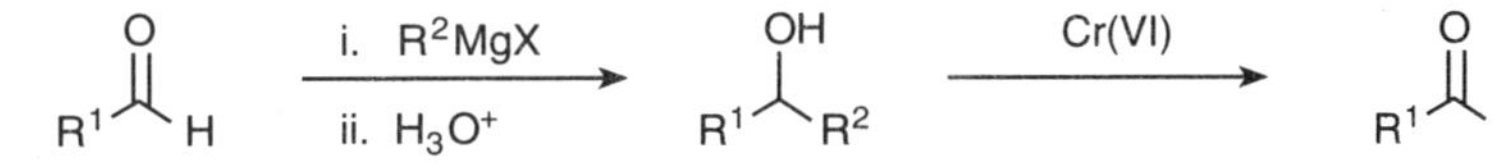

so overall

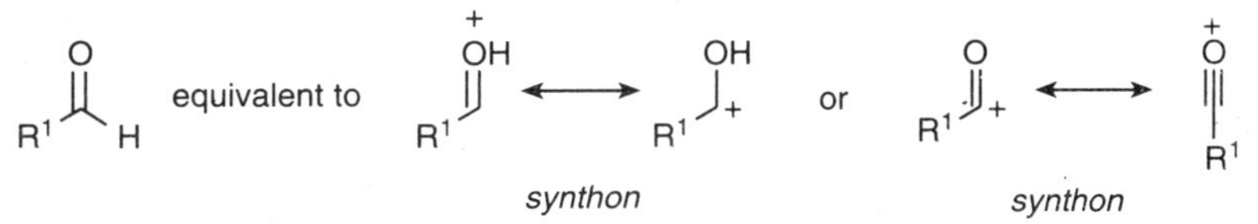

However, converting an aldehyde to its thioacetal, now renders the methine proton liable to abstraction by a strong base, as the carbanionic centre generated may be stabilized by the strong inductive electron-withdrawing effect of the two sulfur atoms through the C–S σ-bonds. Thus, what was the accepting site of the aldehydic carbonyl group has now become a donor centre, in other words—umpolung. Such a carbanion may be alkylated in the usual way and the thioacetal group may be removed to liberate the carbonyl group once more, with the overall result of alkylating the carbonyl carbon via a process where it acted as a nucleophilic centre. The synthon that this thioacetal anion can be considered to represent is thus an acyl anion, which is at odds with the inherent polarization of a carbonyl group. Note that if we choose to desulfurize the alkylated thioacetal in a reductive way to furnish an alkane, the thioacetal moiety is now acting as an alkyl anion synthon.

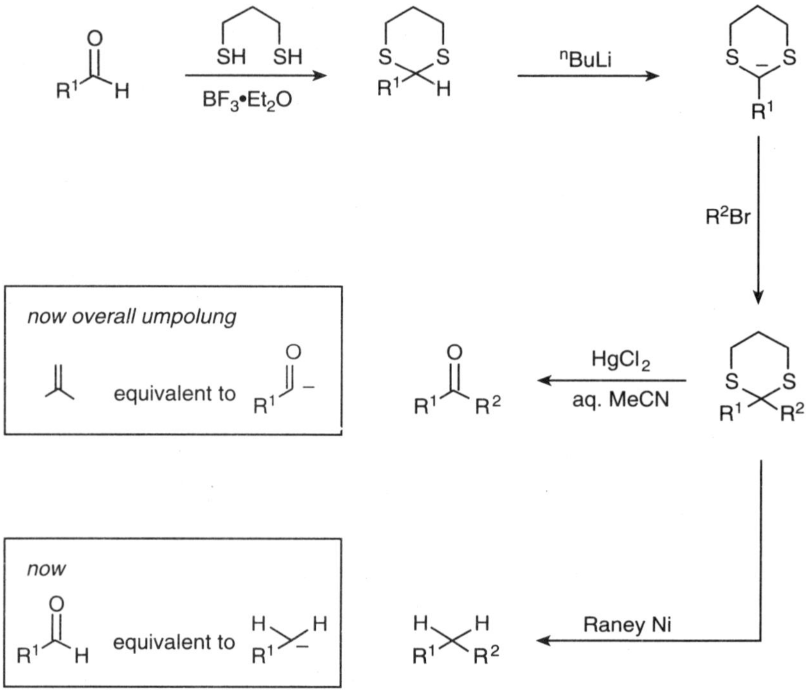

Experiment 55 *Illustration of 'umpolung' in organic synthesis: synthesis of ethyl phenylpyruvate via alkylation of ethyl 1,3-dithiane-2-carboxylate, followed by oxidative hydrolysis with* N*-bromosuccinimide*

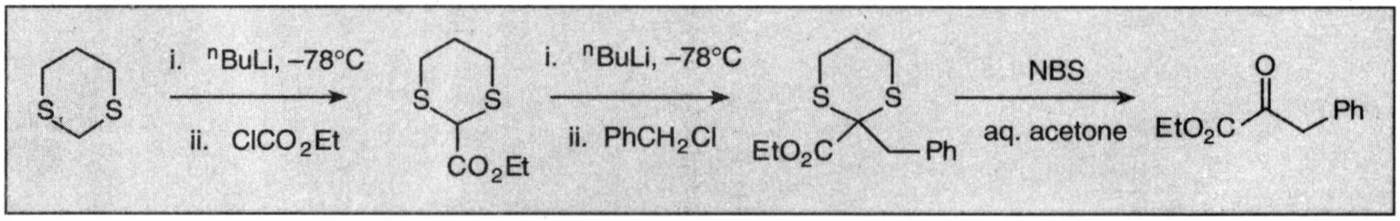

In the experiment described here, we will investigate the alkylation of a dithiane derivative followed by deprotection, in order to appreciate the utility of thioacetals for carbonyl group umpolung. A major synthetic drawback to the use of thioacetals to achieve umpolung of the carbonyl group is that, unlike their oxygen analogues, there are no really general procedures for the deprotection of thioacetals (this can be judged from the enormous number of procedures which have been developed in attempts to overcome this problem), and actually regenerating the carbonyl group at the end of the sequence can often be quite tricky. Another factor which is not inconsequential is that thiols are extremely smelly and the experimentalist must never forget this. (Thiols are also highly toxic but their smell usually makes it impossible to ignore their presence before harmful concentrations accumulate in the air.) Always work in the fume hood when carrying out any work using, or liable to generate, thiols, and soak all apparatus in hypochlorite bleach after use before bringing it into the open laboratory in order to oxidize any thiols adhering to it. The penalty for sloppy work or ignoring this precaution is instant unpopularity, and the all-pervading smell of a thiol clings to the body for some period of time.

In the particular example chosen here, the deprotonation of ethyl 1,3-dithiane-2-carboxylate is further aided by the presence of the ester substituent. This substrate is commercially available.

Level	4
Time	preparation of ethyl 2-benzyl-1,3-dithiane-2-carboxylate 2 × 3 h; preparation of ethyl phenylpyruvate 3 h
Equipment	magnetic stirrer, vacuum pump, acetone–solid CO_2 cooling bath; apparatus for stirring at reduced temperature with addition by syringe, extraction/separation, short path distillation, stirring at room temperature
Instruments	IR, NMR

Materials

1. Preparation of ethyl 2-benzyl-1,3-dithiane-2-carboxylate

ethyl 1,3-dithiane-2-carboxylate (FW 192.3)	1.64 mL, 2.00 g (10.5 mmol)	
benzyl chloride (FW 126.6)	1.05 mL, 1.25 g (10 mmol)	**cancer suspect agent, lachrymator, corrosive**
n-butyl-lithium (1.6 M solution in hexane)	6.9 mL (11 mmol)	**flammable, moisture sensitive**

NOTE: *other concentrations of reagent of similar strengths (1.0–2.5 M) are equally acceptable and may be used with corresponding adjustments of solution volumes*

tetrahydrofuran (anhydrous)		**flammable, irritant**
diethyl ether		**flammable, irritant**
ammonium chloride (saturated)		

continued on p. 578

Box cont.

2. *Preparation of ethyl phenylpyruvate*		
ethyl 2-benzyl-1,3-dithiane-2-carboxylate (FW 270.4)	0.54 g (2 mmol)	
N-bromosuccinimide (FW 178.0)	2.85 (16 mmol)	**irritant, moisture sensitive**
acetone		**flammable**
dichloromethane		**irritant, toxic**
light petroleum (bp 40–60°C)		**flammable**
aqueous sodium bicarbonate (5%)		

Procedure

All apparatus must be thoroughly dried in a hot (>120°C) oven before use.

HOOD
Wear gloves

1. Preparation of ethyl 2-benzyl-1,3-dithiane-2-carboxylate

Measure the ethyl 1,3-dithiane-2-carboxylate into a 100 mL three-necked flask containing a magnetic stirrer bar and equip it with a gas bubbler, a septum and a low temperature thermometer.[1] Introduce a nitrogen atmosphere to the flask, add 30 mL anhydrous tetrahydrofuran[2] and cool the solution to –78°C with stirring. Add the solution of *n*-butyl-lithium dropwise by syringe[3] and then allow the temperature of the mixture to reach 0°C by raising the flask almost totally out of the cooling bath. Stir at this temperature for 1 h and then lower the flask back into the cooling bath to return the temperature of the reaction mixture to –78°C. Add the benzyl chloride[4] dropwise by syringe and again raise the temperature of the reaction to 0°C. After stirring for 20 min at this temperature, quench the reaction by adding 20 mL of saturated aqueous ammonium chloride. Separate the organic phase and re-extract the aqueous phase with 25 mL of diethyl ether. Dry the combined organic extracts with $MgSO_4$,[5] filter and remove the solvents on the rotary evaporator with gentle heating. Purify the residue by short path distillation[6] at reduced pressure (bath temperature *ca.* 160–200°C/0.1 mmHg) and record the yield of your purified product. Obtain the IR (film) and NMR ($CDCl_3$) spectra of this material and the starting thioacetal.

[1] *See Fig. 3.22*

[2] *See Appendix 2*

[3] ***Care!***

[4] ***Toxic***

[5] *May be left at this stage*

[6] *See Fig. 3.54*

2. Preparation of ethyl phenylpyruvate

Dissovle the *N*-bromosuccinimide in 50 mL of water contained in a 100 mL round-bottomed flask containing a magnetic stirrer bar. Add 1.5 mL of acetone, stir the mixture, and then cool to –5°C in an ice–salt cooling bath. Whilst the mixture is cooling, prepare a solution of the ethyl 2-benzyl-1,3-dithiane-2-carboxylate in 10 mL of acetone and add it in one amount to the reaction flask with vigorous stirring. After 5 min pour the reaction into a mixture of 10 mL of dichloromethane, 10 mL of light petroleum and 10 mL of 5% aqueous sodium bicarbonate contained in a 250 mL Erlenmeyer flask, and stir the mixture vigorously for a further 5 min. Allow the mixture to settle and separate the organic phase, re-extracting the aqueous phase with a further

15 mL of diethyl ether. Wash the combined organic phases with 15 mL of water and dry over $MgSO_4$.[7] Filter the solution and remove the solvents on the rotary evaporator to furnish the crude product, which may be purified by short path distillation[6] at reduced pressure[8] (bath temperature *ca.* 150–200°C at water aspirator pressure). Record the yield of crude and distilled product and obtain the IR (film) and NMR ($CDCl_3$) data for your purified material.

[7] *May be left at this stage*

[8] *Extensive decomposition may occur on distillation*

Problems

1 Interpret the IR and NMR spectra of your starting material and products, highlighting significant diagnostic features in each case.

2 In the following conversions, identify the synthon attributable to the starting material under the conditions shown and say whether or not the process involves umpolung.

(i)

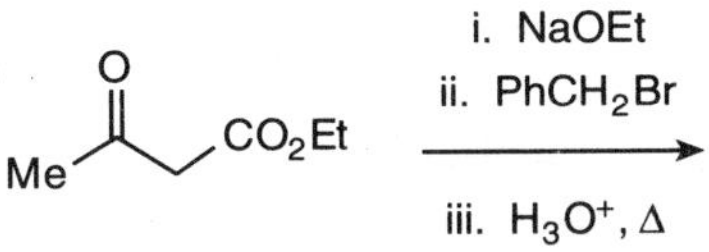

(ii)

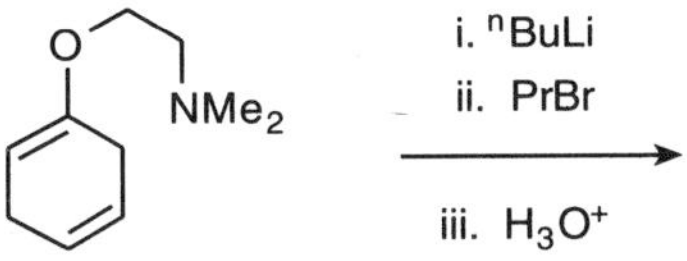

(iii)

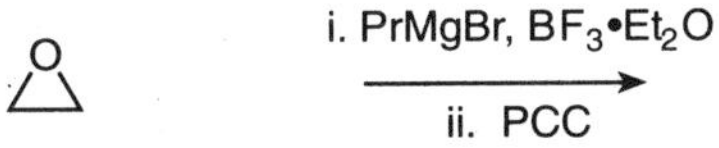

(iv)

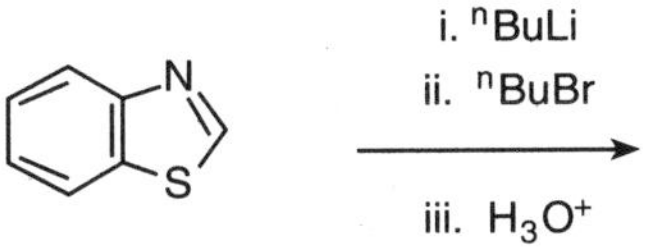

(v)

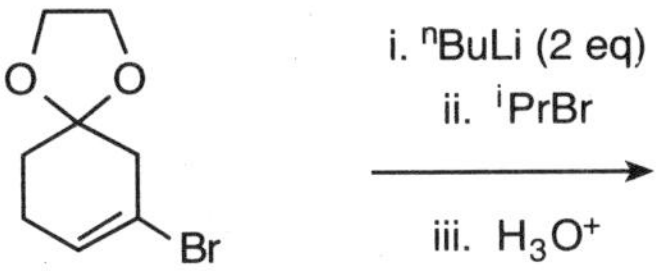

3 Describe how the following compounds might be synthesized starting from 1,3-dithiane and any other organic materials you require (full experimental details are not necessary).

(i) 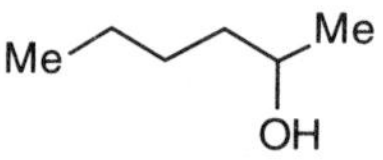

(ii) 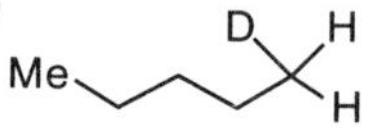

(iii) 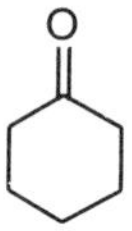

(iv) PhCDO

(v) 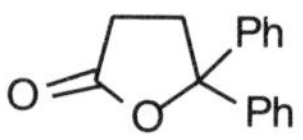

(vi) 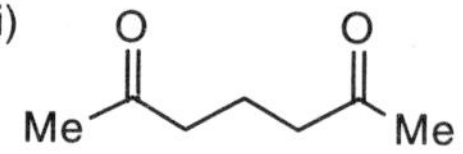

(vii) 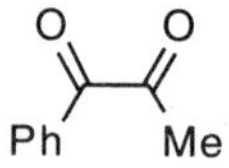

4 Make a list of methods for converting thioacetals and thioketals back into carbonyl compounds.

Further reading

The term 'umpolung' is attributable to G. Wittig, P. Davis and G. Koenig, *Chem. Ber.*, 1951, **84**, 627. For a review of the concept, see: D. Seebach, *Angew. Chem. Int. Edn Engl.*, 1979, **18**, 239.

For the term 'synthon', see: E.J. Corey, *Pure Appl. Chem.*, 1967, **14**, 19; *Quart. Rev.*, 1971, **25**, 455. For treatments of the basis of the use of synthons in retrosynthetic analysis, see: D. Lednicer, *Adv. Org. Chem.*, 1972, **8**, 179; S. Warren, *Organic Synthesis: the Disconnection Approach*, Wiley, Chichester, 1982.

For a review of the use of ethyl 1,3-dithiane-2-carboxylate in the synthesis of α-ketoesters, see: D. Seebach, *Synthesis*, 1969, 17.

8.4 Aromatic electrophilic substitution

Almost all aromatic electrophilic substitutions proceed by initial π-complex formation, followed by conversion to an intermediate σ-complex or arenium ion, with subsequent loss of a positively charged species (usually a proton) to furnish the product.

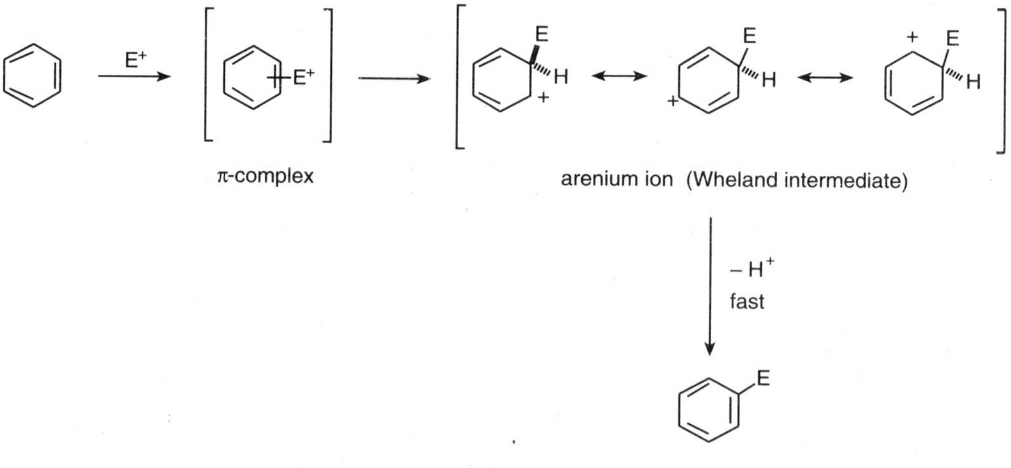

The intermediate arenium ion, also referred to as the Wheland intermediate, benefits from resonance stabilization even though it has lost the very important stabilization associated with the six π-electrons of the aromatic system. The second elimination step regenerates the aromatic ring with all of its associated stabilization and is therefore a very rapid and usually irreversible process. Thus, such substitutions are under kinetic control with the initial electrophilic addition to form the arenium ion being the rate-determining step. An exception to this general irreversibility of aromatic substitutions is sulfonation, but generally substituents present on the aromatic nucleus can exert a strong controlling influence on both the reactivity of the substrate and the orientation of substitution.

As a general fact, any substituent which is electron donating activates the nucleus towards electrophilic attack; whereas electron-withdrawing groups deactivate the ring. Additionally, substituents can be classified according to three types:

1 activating, *ortho-*, *para-* directing (e.g. –OMe, –Ar, –Alk);
2 deactivating, *meta-* directing (e.g. $-NO_2$, $-CO_2H$);
3 deactivating, *ortho-*, *para-* directing (e.g. –Hal, $-CF_3$, $-CH{=}CHCO_2H$).

Although the common explanation offered for these effects considers stabilization of the various Wheland intermediates, a truer picture is obtained by considering the electron density at the positions around the ring of the substrate. Substituents in class 1 increase electron density throughout the ring, but more so at the *ortho-* and *para-* relative to the *meta-* sites of the substrate. This not only increases the overall rate of electrophilic substitution at all centres but favours *ortho-* and *para-* attack. In contrast, substituents in class 2 decrease electron density in the aromatic ring, with the effect being least at the *meta-* positions. Thus, reactivity is lowered, with *meta-*substitution being less disfavoured than *ortho-* or *para-* substitution. The situation is less clear cut with substituents in category 3 which deactivate by virtue of their inductive withdrawing power, but favour *ortho-* and *para-* attack due to resonance stabilization of intermediates resulting from *ortho-* or *para-* attack.

Unfortunately such simplistic formalisms frequently break down with polysubstituted benzene rings when the electronic effects of the various substituents may buttress or counteract each other.

Experiment 56 *Nitration of methyl benzoate*

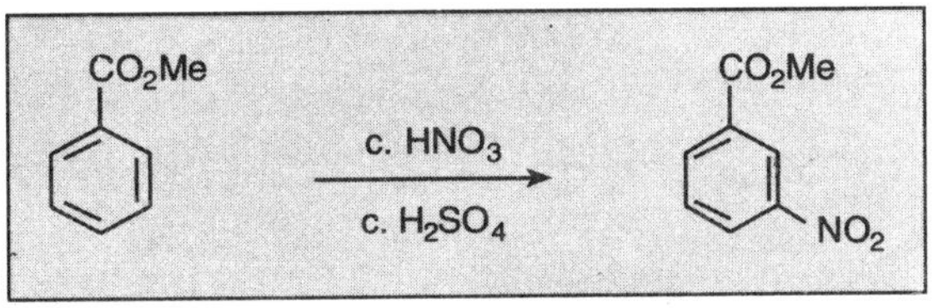

The introduction of a nitro group into an aromatic ring by means of nitric and sulfuric acids, is an example of aromatic electrophilic substitution by the nitronium ion, NO_2^+. The carbomethoxy group of methyl benzoate deactivates the ring and directs substitution to the *meta*- position.

Level	1		
Time	3 h		
Equipment	apparatus for suction filtration		
Materials			
methyl benzoate (FW 136.2)	1.8 mL, 2.0 g (15 mmol)	**irritant**	
sulfuric acid (conc.) (FW 98.1)	5.5 mL, 10.1 g (103 mmol)	**corrosive, oxidizer**	
nitric acid (conc.) (FW 63.0)	1.5 mL, 2.2 g (35 mmol)	**corrosive, oxidizer**	

Procedure

Place the methyl benzoate in a 25 mL Erlenmeyer flask and add 4 mL of the concentrated sulfuric acid[1] with shaking, and cool the mixture in an ice bath. In another flask place the nitric acid[1] and add the remaining 1.5 mL of sulfuric acid, shaking and cooling in ice. Using a Pasteur pipette, add the nitric acid solution to the methyl benzoate solution with shaking, maintaining the temperature between 0 and 10°C by means of the ice bath.[2] The addition takes about 30 min and after this allow the solution to stand for a further 10 min at room temperature. Pour the solution onto ice and stir until the precipitate becomes granular. Filter the methyl 3-nitrobenzoate with suction[3] and wash well with water. Recrystallize from ethanol to obtain an almost colourless solid. Record the yield and mp of your product. ■

[1] ***Wear gloves when handling concentrated acids***

[2] *It is important to maintain temperature between 0 and 10°C*

[3] *See Fig. 3.7*

MICROSCALE

Level	1		
Time	3 h		
Equipment	magnetic stirrer; apparatus for Craig tube recrystallization		
Materials			
methyl benzoate (FW 136.2)	0.09 mL, 100 mg (0.75 mmol)	**irritant**	
sulfuric acid (conc.) (FW 98.1)	0.275 mL, 506 mg (5.2 mmol)	**corrosive, oxidizer**	
nitric acid (conc.) (FW 63.0)	0.075 mL, 110 mg (1.75 mmol)	**corrosive, oxidizer**	

Procedure

Place the methyl benzoate in a small test tube containing a small stirrer bead and add concentrated sulfuric acid (0.15 mL), cooling the tube in a beaker of ice.[1] In a pre-chilled small test tube or vial, place the nitric acid and the remaining concentrated sulfuric acid (0.125 mL). Using a drawn out Pasteur pipette, add the nitration mixture to the cold stirred methyl benzoate/sulfuric

[1] ***Wear gloves when handling concentrated acids***

acid mixture. The temperature must stay below 10°C. The addition should take *ca.* 30 min; at the end of the addition allow the mixture to stand for 10 min. Add the mixture by pipette into ice (1 g) in a 2 mL Craig tube and stir until the precipitate becomes granular. Collect the solid by centrifugation[2] and wash with water. Recrystallize from ethanol to obtain an almost colourless solid and record the yield and mp of your product.

[2] *See Fig. 137–138*

Problems

1 Write a mechanistic equation for the nitration of toluene by nitric/sulfuric acids.

2 Predict the position(s) of nitration of the following compounds and also estimate the rate relative to that of benzene.

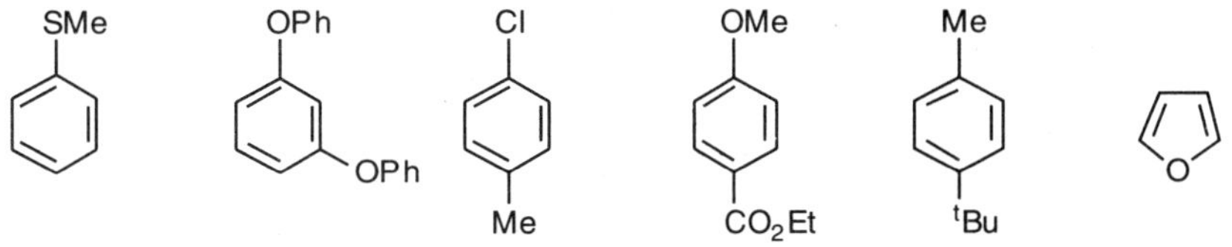

The Friedel–Crafts reaction

In its most general form, the *Friedel–Crafts reaction* refers to the acylation or alkylation of an aromatic substrate in the presence of an acidic catalyst. Most frequently the reaction involves the use of acyl chlorides in the presence of Lewis acids (typically aluminium chloride) to furnish aromatic ketones. However, a wide range of alkylating and acylating agents can be used, includ-

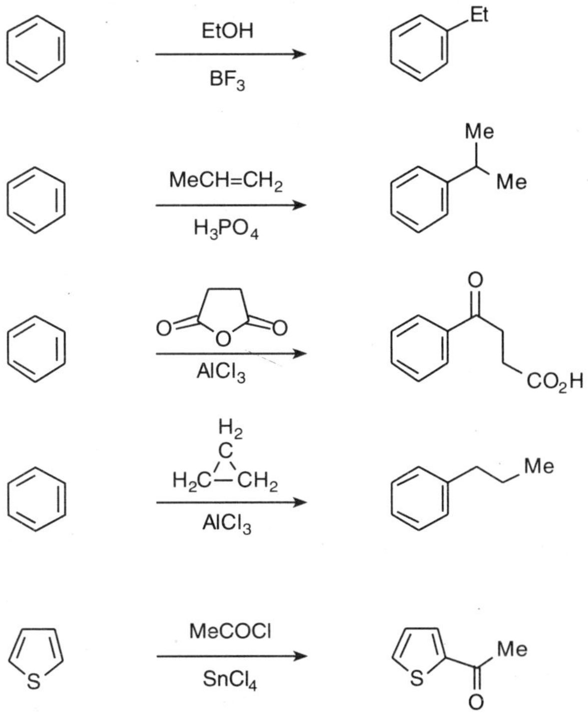

ing alcohols, anhydrides, alkenes and even cyclopropanes and the catalyst might be any of a whole range of Lewis or Brønsted acids. Likewise, the aromatic substrates can include heterocyclic and fused aromatics as well as benzene derivatives. Some of these modifications are illustrated above.

The Friedel–Crafts reaction is usually only of limited use for alkylation as, being an electrophilic substitution, it is promoted by the presence of electron-donating groups on the ring. Thus, the initial alkylation product is more reactive than the precursor and preferentially alkylates to give an even more reactive dialkylated product. Consequently, alkylations are frequently uncontrollable and produce complex mixtures of polyalkylated products. Another feature of Friedel–Crafts alkylations includes the propensity for the most stable carbo-cation to be formed regardless of the structure of the initial alkylating agent.

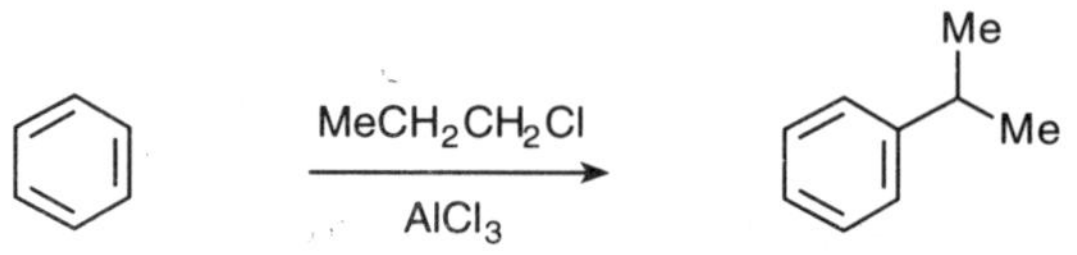

As a result, poor yields of straight chain alkylated aromatics are obtained by this procedure and usually the indirect course of acylation, followed by reduction of the carbonyl group, is used for the preparation of alkyl benzenes.

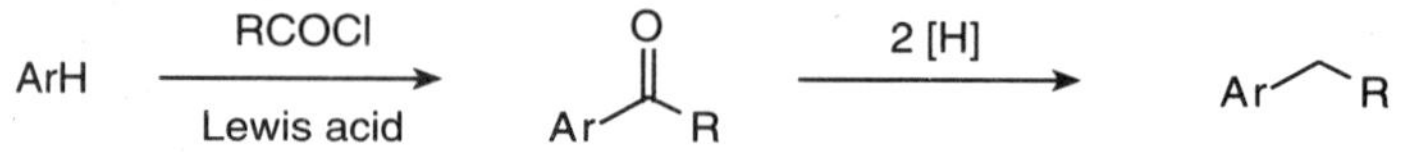

The reaction first involves generation of the electrophilic species by an interaction between the catalyst and the halide, which then attacks the aromatic nucleus in the usual manner. With acid halides or anhydrides, the attacking species can be considered formally to be the acylium ion; whereas with alkyl halides the carbo-cation can be considered to be the electrophile.

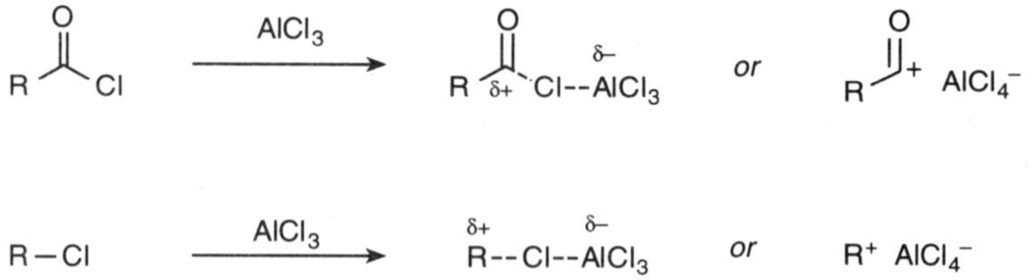

Experiment 57 *4-Bromobenzophenone by the Friedel–Crafts reaction*

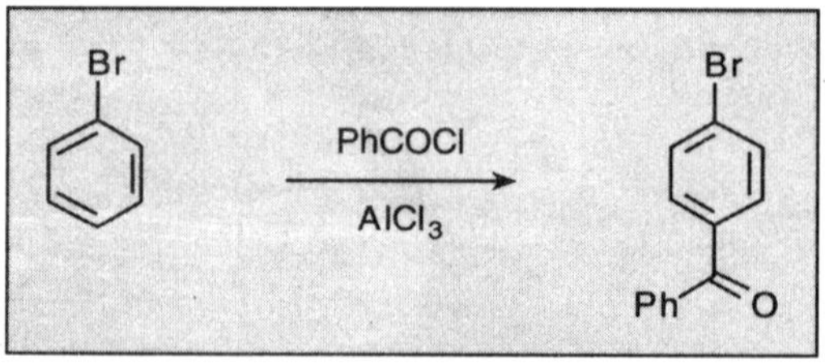

The introduction of an acyl group into an aromatic ring is accomplished by an electrophilic substitution by the acylium ion ($RC{\equiv}O^+$) generated by the reaction between an acyl halide and aluminium chloride. In bromobenzene, the bromine is a deactivating and *ortho-*,*para-* directing substituent, although this reaction gives mainly the *para-* isomer; presumably *ortho-* substitution, which might also be expected, is sterically less favoured.

Level	2
Time	3 h
Equipment	steam (or hot water) bath; apparatus for extraction/separation, recrystallization

Materials

bromobenzene (FW 157.0)	2.0 mL, 3.0 g (19 mmol)	**irritant**
benzoyl chloride (FW 140.6)	3.3 mL, 4.0 g (30 mmol)	**lachrymator, corrosive**
anhydrous aluminium chloride (FW 133.3)	4.0 g (30 mmol)	**corrosive, moisture sensitive**
sodium hydroxide (10%)		**corrosive**
diethyl ether		**flammable, irritant**
light petroleum (bp 60–80°C)		**flammable**
pH indicator paper		

Procedure

HOOD

Place the bromobenzene and benzoyl chloride in a 50 mL Erlenmeyer flask. Add the aluminium chloride in three portions, shaking or stirring in between additions, and then heat the flask on a boiling water bath for 20 min. Cool, and pour the dark-red liquid onto ice[1] and wash out the remaining contents by careful addition of 10% NaOH to the flask. Make the combined solutions alkaline[2] by the addition of 10% sodium hydroxide solution to dissolve any benzoic acid present as well as the aluminium salts. Extract with 2 × 25 mL of diethyl ether, dry the organic extracts over $MgSO_4$ and remove the diethyl ether on the rotary evaporator. 4-Bromobenzophenone remains and may be recrystallized from light petroleum[3] to give a colourless solid. Record the yield and mp of your product.

[1] *Caution! Vigorous reaction*

[2] *Use pH paper*

[3] *Requires a large volume of solvent*

Problem

1 Suggest syntheses of the following from benzene:

(a)
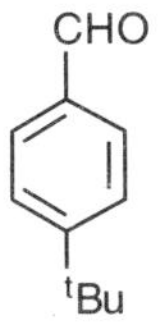

(b)
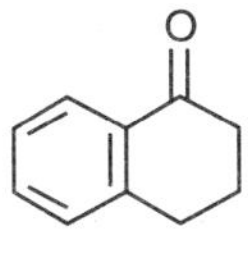

(c)
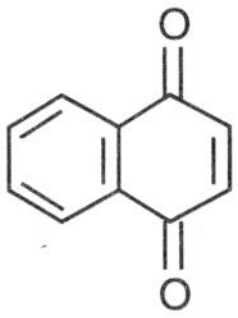

Experiment 58 *Friedel–Crafts acetylation of ferrocene using different Lewis acid catalysts and identification of the products by NMR*

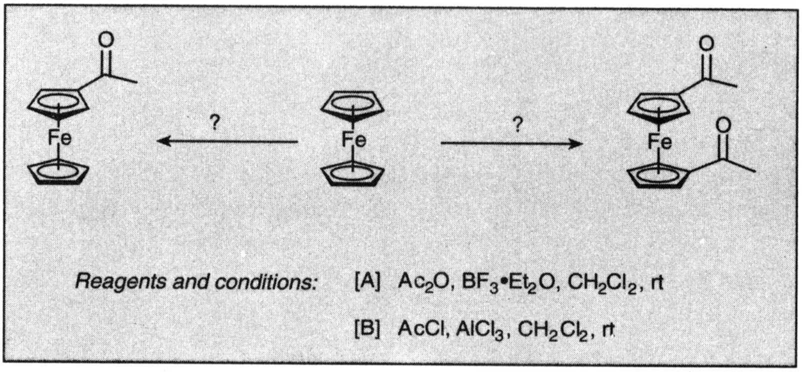

Ferrocene is the most well known example of a *sandwich compound* in which the iron atom is enclosed between two cyclopentadienylide rings. Its discovery in 1951 by Kealy and Pauson and subsequent structure elucidation by Wilkinson who shared the 1973 Nobel Prize with Fischer, heralded a new dawn in organotransition-metal chemistry. The complex is very stable, being chemically unaffected by heating to 400°C. In this stable complex, the one s-orbital, five d-orbitals and three p-orbitals of the iron valence shells are filled, achieving an inert gas electronic configuration. The 18 electrons required to do this come from an overall bonding combination of the eight available valence electrons on the iron (0) and two sets of five electrons from the cyclopentadienylide ligands. With a few exceptions, this requirement for 18 electrons in nine orbitals is a constant feature in stable organometallics and is often referred to as the *18-electron rule.*

Ferrocene is conveniently prepared by the reaction of two cyclopentadienyl anions with an iron(II) salt and behaves as an electron-rich aromatic system, undergoing electrophilic substitution readily.

A feature of Friedel–Crafts acylations of ferrocene is that the mono-adducts may still undergo a second substitution in the second cyclopentadienylide ring despite the electron-withdrawing and deactivating effect of the acyl group on the first ring. The formation of mono- or bis-acylated materials as the major products depends upon the reaction conditions used, particularly the Lewis acid catalyst. The following experiment (adapted from one developed by Dr J.M. Brown of the Dyson Perrins Laboratory, Oxford) will investigate the effect of boron trifluoride and aluminium chloride upon the course of acetylation of ferrocene in separate experiments, which can be carried out in parallel by two workers or consecutively by a single worker. The identification of the major product in each case is amenable to NMR analysis.

Level	3
Time	2 × 3 h
Equipment	magnetic stirrer; apparatus for stirring under nitrogen with addition by syringe, TLC, extraction/separation, column chromatography (chromatography may not be necessary)
Instruments	NMR

Materials

1. Boron trifluoride catalyzed acetylation of ferrocene

ferrocene (FW 186.0)	0.56 g (3 mmol)	
boron trifluoride etherate (distilled) (FW 141.9)	1.25 mL, 1.42 g (10 mmol)	**corrosive, moisture sensitive**
acetic anhydride (FW 102.1)	0.85 mL, 0.92 g (9 mmol)	**lachrymator, corrosive**
dichloromethane		**irritant, toxic**
hexane		**flammable**
chloroform containing 1% volume of methanol for TLC analysis		**cancer suspect agent, toxic**
silica gel	50 g	**irritant dust**

2. Aluminium chloride catalyzed acetylation of ferrocene

ferrocene (FW 186.0)	0.56 g (3 mmol)	
anhydrous aluminium chloride (FW 133.3)	1.33 g (10 mmol)	**corrosive, moisture sensitive**
acetyl chloride (FW 78.50)	0.70 mL, 0.78 g (10 mmol)	**corrosive, flammable**
dichloromethane		**irritant, toxic**
hexane		**flammable**
chloroform containing 1% volume of methanol for TLC analysis		**cancer suspect agent, toxic**
silica gel	50 g	**irritant dust**

Procedure

HOOD

1. Boron trifluoride catalyzed acetylation of ferrocene

Place the ferrocene, acetic anhydride and 15 mL of dichloromethane in a dry 100 mL three-necked flask containing a magnetic stirrer bar and fitted with a nitrogen inlet, bubbler and septum.[1] Fit the reaction flask to a source of nitrogen and flush the flask with nitrogen, allowing nitrogen to flow through the system for several minutes. Stir the solution and add the boron trifluoride etherate dropwise by syringe.[2] After stirring for 30 min, remove a small sample of the reaction mixture using a fresh syringe and compare it with the starting material by TLC on silica,[3] eluting with 1% methanol in chloroform

[1] *See Fig. 3.21*

[2] ***Care! Clean syringe immediately after use with methanol***

[3] *See Chapter 3*

and examining the developed plate under UV light.[4] If starting material is still present, stir for a further 15 min and analyze a fresh sample, repeating this procedure until the starting material is no longer demonstrable by TLC. Disconnect the nitrogen supply, add a further 10 mL of dichloromethane, and quench the reaction by *cautious* dropwise addition of water (50 mL).[5] Separate the deep-red organic phase, washing it three times with water (10 mL), dry over $MgSO_4$, filter and reduce the volume of the solution to 5 mL on the rotary evaporator without external heating. To the residual solution add 10 mL of hexane and induce crystallization by cooling in ice and scratching the walls of the flask with a glass rod if necessary. Filter off the solid with suction, wash with 10 mL of hexane and dry it on the funnel, continuing the suction. If crystallization cannot be induced, the reaction mixture may be chromatographed on silica (50 g),[3] eluting firstly with 4 : 1 hexane–dichloromethane (50 mL) followed by a 1 : 1 mixture (2 × 50 mL) and, finally, neat dichloromethane. Record the yield and mp of your product and obtain the NMR spectrum ($CDCl_3$).

[4] *Use special eye protection*

[5] *Care! Exothermic*

HOOD

2. *Aluminium chloride catalyzed acetylation of ferrocene*

Weigh the aluminium chloride as quickly as possible into a dry 100 mL three-necked flask containing a magnetic stirrer bar and fitted with a gas bubbler, and a septum.[1] To this add 25 mL of dichloromethane and the ferrocene. Connect the flask to a nitrogen supply and allow the flask to be flushed with nitrogen for several minutes. Add the acetyl chloride dropwise by syringe[6] to the stirred mixture and continue stirring for 30 min. Carry out TLC analysis of the mixture as described in the previous procedure and, when no more starting material can be detected, quench and work-up in the same manner as before, except that 35 mL of hexane should be used at the crystallization stage. If crystallization does not occur after cooling and scratching, purify the product by chromatography as previously described. Record the yield and mp of this material and obtain the NMR spectrum ($CDCl_3$).

[6] *Clean syringe immediately after use with methanol*

Problems

1 Assign structures to the products on the basis of the NMR data you have obtained.

2 Explain why the reactivity of ferrocene towards electrophilic substitution is about 10^5 times higher than that of benzene.

3 Ferrocene will undergo sulfonation with the pyridine–sulfur trioxide complex but not with concentrated sulfuric acid. Likewise, ferrocene does not undergo electrophilic substitution with nitric acid or bromine. Explain the reasons for this reactivity.

4 Compare and contrast the chemical and physical properties of ferrocene with cyclopentadienyl sodium and explain how the differences reflect the nature of the bonding in each organometallic compound.

Further reading

For the report of the discovery of ferrocene, see: T.J. Kealy and P.L. Pauson, *Nature (London)*, 1951, **168**, 1039.

For structure elucidation, see: G. Wilkinson, M. Rosenblum, M.C. Whiting and R.B. Woodward, *J. Am. Chem. Soc.*, 1952, **74**, 2125; E.O. Fisher and W. Pfab, *Z. Naturforsch. B*, 1952, **7B**, 377.

For similar experiments, see: J.S. Gilbert and S.A. Monti, *J. Chem. Educ.*, 1973, **50**, 369; H.T. McKone, *J. Chem. Educ.*, 1980, **57**, 380.

Experiment 59 — *Fries rearrangement of phenyl acetate: preparation of 2-hydroxyacetophenone*

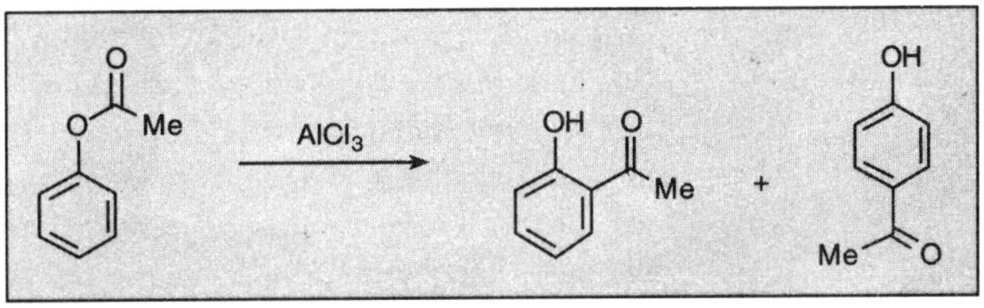

When heated in the presence of aluminium chloride, phenyl acetate is converted into a mixture of 2- and 4-hydroxyacetophenones in a reaction known as the *Fries rearrangement*. The two isomers are then separated by virtue of the fact that the desired 2-hydroxyacetophenone has an internal hydrogen bond and is volatile in steam. The 4-hydroxy- isomer remains in the flask after the steam distillation, and can be isolated if required. 2-Hydroxyacetophenone can be used subsequently as the starting material for the synthesis of flavone (Experiment 71).

Level	2
Time	2 × 3 h (plus 3 h for the optional isolation of 4-hydroxyacetophenone)
Equipment	steam bath; apparatus for reflux with air condenser, extraction/separation, suction filtration, steam distillation, distillation under reduced pressure, recrystallization
Instruments	IR, NMR (optional)

Materials		
phenyl acetate (FW 136.2)	13.6 g (0.1 mol)	
aluminium chloride	*ca.* 18 g	**corrosive, moisture sensitive**
diethyl ether		**flammable, irritant**
hydrochloric acid (conc.)		**corrosive**
sodium hydroxide solution (2 M)		**corrosive**

Procedure

HOOD

1. *Preparation of 2-hydroxyacetophenone*

Place the phenyl acetate in a 250 mL round-bottomed flask. Weigh out the aluminium chloride, *rapidly* powder it in a pestle and mortar and add it to the phenyl acetate. Fit an air condenser carrying a calcium chloride guard tube,[1] and swirl the flask in order to mix the materials. As soon as the initial evolution of HCl subsides, heat the flask on the steam bath for 1 h. Cool the flask to

[1] *See Fig. 3.23(c)*

room temperature, add about 100 g crushed ice and 15 mL concentrated hydrochloric acid. Heat the flask on the steam bath for 5 min, cool it in ice, and extract the mixture with 3 × 25 mL diethyl ether. Combine the ether extracts,[2] and extract the phenolic materials with 2 × 50 mL 2 M sodium hydroxide solution. Combine the alkaline extracts and acidify them by the dropwise addition of concentrated hydrochloric acid.[3] Transfer the mixture to a 500 mL round-bottomed flask which is set up for steam distillation.[4] Start the steam distillation and collect *ca.* 250 mL of distillate which contains oily droplets at the start but becomes clear towards the end of the process. *Retain the dark residue in the distillation flask for subsequent isolation of the steam involatile 4-hydroxyacetophenone if required.* Extract the distillate with 2 × 20 mL diethyl ether. Combine the ether extracts and dry them over $MgSO_4$.[2] Filter off the drying agent by suction[5] and evaporate the filtrate on the rotary evaporator. Distil the residue from a 10 mL flask under reduced pressure[6] using a water aspirator. Collect a fore-run (contaminated with phenol) and then, when the temperature stabilizes, the product. Record the bp, yield and the IR ($CHCl_3$) and NMR ($CDCl_3$) (optional) spectra of your product.

[2] *May be left at this stage*

[3] ***Care! Exothermic***

[4] *See Fig. 3.55*

[5] *See Fig. 3.7*

[6] *See Fig. 3.53*

2. *Isolation of the 4-hydroxyacetophenone (optional)*

Extract the distillation pot residue from above with 3 × 25 mL diethyl ether. Combine the ether extracts and dry them over $MgSO_4$. Filter off the drying agent by suction and evaporate the filtrate on the rotary evaporator. Recrystallize the residue from diethyl ether/light petroleum (bp 40–60°C). Record the yield, mp and IR ($CHCl_3$) spectrum of the product after one recrystallization.

See Exp. 7

Problems

1 Discuss the reaction mechanism of the Fries rearrangement.

2 Assign the IR (and NMR) spectra of your 2-hydroxyacetophenone. Is there any evidence of the internal hydrogen bond in the molecule?

8.5 Pericyclic reactions

Pericyclic reactions are governed by orbital symmetry, the principles of which were first delineated by R.B. Woodward and R. Hoffmann in the 1960s, and therefore are often known as the *Woodward–Hoffmann rules*. Hoffmann was awarded a share in the Nobel Prize in 1981 for his contribution to theoretical organic chemistry; unfortunately Woodward's untimely death in 1979 may have prevented him from collecting his second Nobel Prize. The best known pericyclic reaction is the *Diels–Alder reaction*, whose discoverers, Otto Diels and Kurt Alder, were awarded the Nobel Prize in 1950. The reaction involves the reaction of a diene (the 4π-electron component) with a dienophile (the 2π-component), and proceeds through a 6-centre transition state, e.g:

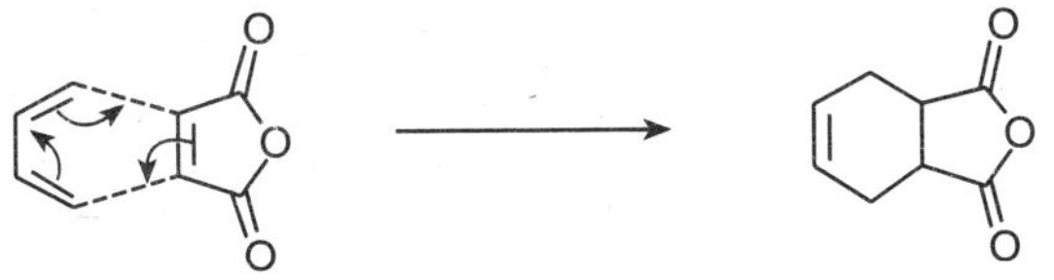

However, the Diels–Alder reaction is not the only pericyclic reaction to have found use in organic chemistry and this section includes experiments which illustrate other important pericyclic reactions such as [2+2]-cycloadditions, [3,3]-sigmatropic rearrangements, and 1,3-dipolar cycloadditions.

Experiment 60

Diels–Alder preparation of cis-*cyclohex-4-ene-1,2-dicarboxylic acid*

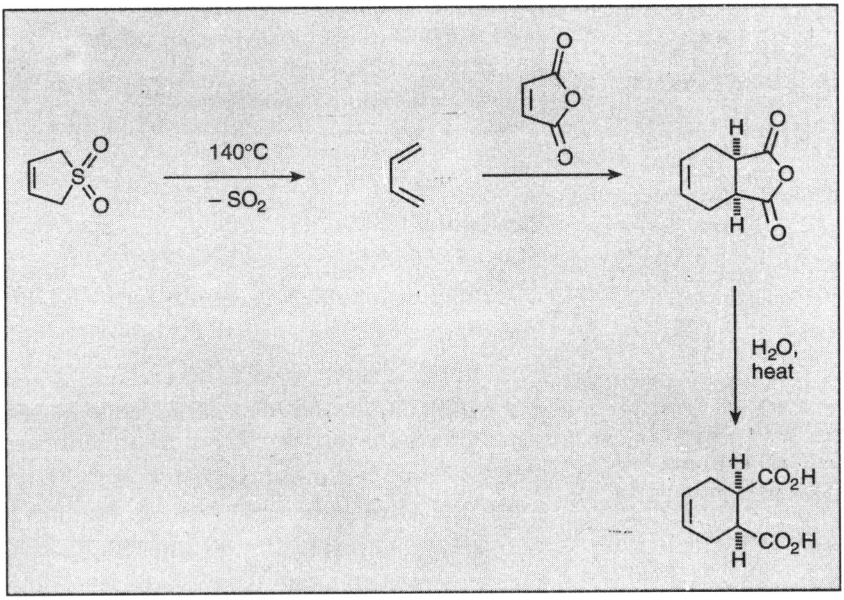

The simplest diene substrate for the Diels–Alder reaction, 1,3-butadiene, is a gas at room temperature and pressure (bp –4.5°C) and consequently its handling requires specialized procedures. However, it can be generated readily *in situ* by means of cheletropic extrusion of sulfur dioxide from 2,5-dihydrothiophene-1,1-dioxide (frequently referred to as butadiene sulfone or sulfolene) which is a stable solid at room temperature. It is prepared by the addition of sulfur dioxide to butadiene under the effect of heat and pressure; the addition and elimination reactions are simply the reverse of one another.

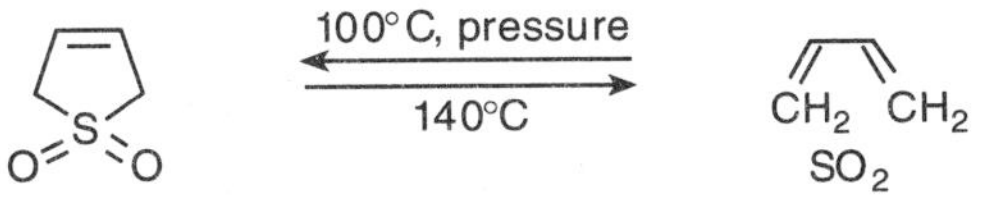

Heating 2,5-dihydrothiophene-1,1-dioxide to *ca.* 140°C results in the dissociation reaction and presents us with an experimentally convenient laboratory source of butadiene which can be trapped, as it is generated, by reactive dienophiles, such as butenedioic anhydride (maleic anhydride). The Diels–Alder adduct formed in this instance can be hydrolyzed readily to the dicarboxylic acid by heating with water.

Level	1	
Time	3 h	
Equipment	apparatus for suction filtration, recrystallization	

Materials		
2,5-dihydrothiophene-1,1-dioxide (butadiene sulfone, sulfolene) (FW 118.2)	2.4 g (20 mmol)	**irritant**
butenedioic anhydride (maleic anhydride) (FW 98.1)	2.0 g (20 mmol)	**corrosive**
bis(2-methoxyethyl)ether (diglyme)	2 mL	

Procedure

HOOD

1. *Preparation of* cis-*cyclohex-4-ene-1,2-dicarboxylic anhydride*

Into a large test tube weigh the 2,5-dihydrothiophene-1,1-dioxide and butenedioic anhydride and add the bis(2-methoxyethyl)ether. Stir the mixture with a 360°C thermometer and clamp the tube vertically with the thermometer remaining in the mixture. Warm the mixture *gently* with a small flame,[1] stirring constantly with the thermometer and observe the temperature. At about 140°C the mixture begins to evolve bubbles of sulfur dioxide; at this point, stop heating and allow the exothermic reaction to continue. When the reaction begins to moderate, as evidenced by a drop in temperature, maintain the temperature at 150–160°C with intermittent heating until the evolution of bubbles finally subsides (*ca.* 5 min). Cool the reaction by placing the end of the test tube in a water bath and stir the contents with the thermometer to induce partial crystallization. Add cold water (*ca.* 25 mL), stir the mixture and filter it with suction,[2] washing the crystals with two further 25 mL portions of water. Leave the crystals on the funnel and continue suction for several minutes to remove as much excess moisture as possible. Weigh the slightly moist product, remove 1.0 g for the hydrolysis experiment, and dry the remainder of the product in a vacuum desiccator over P_2O_5.[3] Record the weight of the dried product and calculate the percentage yield, knowing the initial weight of total moist product and accounting for the fact that 1.0 g of damp product has been removed. Record the mp of your product.

[1] ***Check for flammable solvents before lighting burner; alternatively use a heat gun***

[2] *See Fig. 3.7*

[3] *Commence the next experiment*

2. *Hydrolysis of initial anhydride adduct to* cis-*cyclohex-4-ene-1,2-dicarboxylic acid*

Place the 1.0 g portion of moist adduct in a large test tube, add a boiling stone and water (10 mL), and boil the mixture over a small flame until the crystals of the adduct have totally dissolved. Remove the boiling chip with a spatula and cool the test tube in an ice bath (5 min). Filter off the crystals with suction, wash them with a small volume (*ca.* 5 mL) of chilled water, and dry with suction until excess moisture has been removed. Finally, dry the crystals in a vacuum desiccator over P_2O_5. Record the mp and calculate the yield of product based upon the actual amount of starting material contained in the moist material used for the hydrolysis (calculate this from your weights of material before and after drying in the first experiment). ■

MICROSCALE

Level	1
Time	3 h
Equipment	apparatus for suction filtration

Materials		
2,5-dihydrothiophene-1,1-dioxide (butadiene sulfone, sulfolene) (FW 118.2)	120 mg (1 mmol)	**irritant**
butenedioic anhydride (maleic anhydride) (FW 98.1)	100 mg (1 mmol)	**corrosive**
bis(2-methoxyethyl)ether (diglyme)	0.2 mL	

Procedure

Weigh the 2,5-dihydrothiophene-1,1-dioxide and maleic anhydride into a test tube and add the diglyme. Stir the mixture with a 360°C thermometer and clamp the tube vertically with the thermometer remaining in the mixture. Warm the mixture gently with a small flame[1] or hot air blower, stirring constantly with the thermometer and observe the temperature. At about 140°C the mixture begins to evolve bubbles of sulfur dioxide; at this point, stop heating and allow the exothermic reaction to continue. When the reaction begins to moderate, as evinced by a drop in temperature, maintain the temperature at 150–160°C with intermittent heating until the evolution of bubbles ceases finally (*ca.* 5 min). Cool the reaction by placing the end of the test tube in a water bath and stir the contents with the thermometer to allow partial crystallization. Add cold water (*ca.* 1.5 mL), stir the mixture and filter at the pump using a micro-Hirsch funnel,[2] washing the crystals with portions of water (2 × 1 mL). Suck the crystals as dry as possible and dry in a vacuum dessicator over phosphorus pentoxide.[3] Weigh the dried product and record the mp and yield of the dry product.

[1] ***Check for flammable solvents before lighting burner***

[2] *See Fig. 3.7*

[3] *See Fig. 3.45*

Problems

1 What conformation must be adopted by the diene for cycloaddition of a dienophilic component to occur? Explain why this accounts for the unreactivity of 2*Z*,4*Z*-hexadiene in the Diels–Alder reaction.

2 In the Diels–Alder reaction of cyclopentadiene with butenedioic anhydride, what are the two possible stereochemistries of the adduct? Which of the two products would you predict to be the most stable? Explain why it is the *least* stable adduct which is formed preferentially in this reaction.

3 What diene and dienophile would be required as starting materials for the eventual synthesis of the following compounds via Diels–Alder cycloaddition?

4 What are the ultimate organic products when the following dienes are heated strongly with diethyl butynedioate (diethyl acetylenedicarboxylate)?

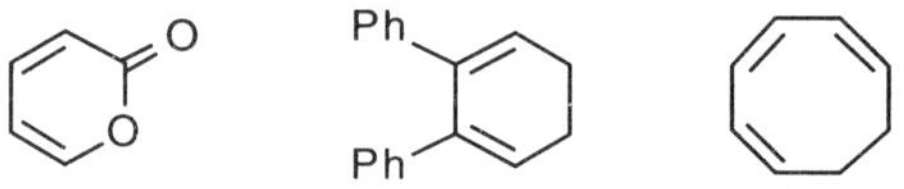

Experiment 61

Preparation of 2,3-dimethyl-1,3-butadiene and its Diels–Alder reaction with butenedioic anhydride (maleic anhydride)

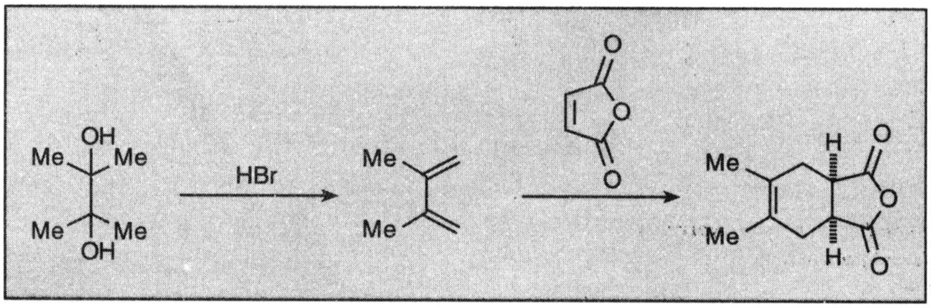

In this experiment the diene required for the Diels–Alder reaction is prepared by acid-catalyzed elimination of two molecules of water from 2,3-dimethylbutan-2,3-diol (pinacol). A by-product of this reaction is 3,3-dimethylbutane-2-one (pinacolone) formed by an acid-catalyzed 1,2-alkyl migration of the diol, but this does not interfere with the Diels–Alder reaction. (This competing reaction, known as the *pinacol–pinacolone rearrangement* is the archetype of a whole class of such migrations called *Wagner–Merwein shifts*.) The rearrangement pathway predominates over the desired elimination reaction but redistillation of the crude product provides enough material in sufficient purity to carry out the Diels–Alder reaction, albeit in poor yield.

The reaction between the diene and butenedioic anhydride (maleic anhydride) occurs very readily and results in a brief but dramatic exothermic reaction. The ease of this Diels–Alder reaction is a consequence of the 2,3-dimethyl-1,3-butadiene being a relatively electron-rich diene and the dienophile electron poor. In addition, steric repulsion between the 2,3-dimethyl groups on the diene preferentially stabilizes the *s-cis* conformation over the *s-trans* conformation making it a more reactive diene than butadiene itself.

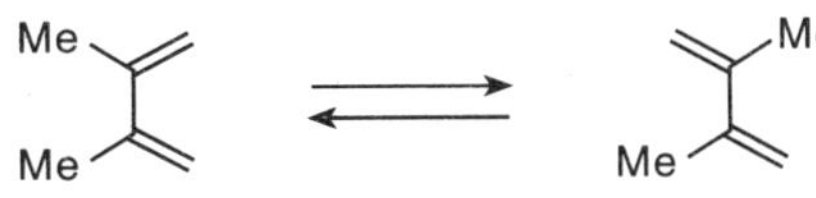

Level	2
Time	2 × 3 h
Equipment	magnetic stirrer; apparatus for stirring at room temperature, extraction/separation, distillation at atmospheric pressure

Materials		
1. Preparation of 2,3-dimethyl-1,3-butadiene		
2,3-dimethylbutane-2,3-diol (pinacol) (FW 118.2)	11.8 g (0.1 mol)	**irritant**
hydrobromic acid (conc. *ca.* 48%)	1.5 mL	**corrosive**
2. Diels–Alder reaction		
butenedioic anhydride (maleic anhydride) (FW 98.1)	0.3 g (3 mmol)	**corrosive**
hexane		**flammable**

Procedure

1. Preparation of 2,3-dimethyl-1,3-butadiene

Weigh the 2,3-dimethylbutane-2,3-diol into a 25 mL round-bottomed flask containing a magnetic stirrer, add the hydrobromic acid[1] and stir the mixture for 1 h. If the diol dissolves slowly, this can be speeded up by *gentle* heating[1] After this time, remove the stirrer bar and equip the flask for distillation[2] with a -10 to 110°C range thermometer. Distil the mixture *slowly* and collect the product which distils, until the temperature recorded by the thermometer reaches 95°C. Transfer the distillate, which consists of two phases, to a 25 mL separatory funnel. Remove the lower aqueous layer, wash the organic layer twice more with 3 mL portions of water, and dry the organic phase for 5–10 min over $MgSO_4$.[3] Filter the mixture into a 10 mL round-bottomed

[1] ***Care! Corrosive***

[2] *See Fig. 3.48*

[3] *Set up the next distillation during the drying time*

flask through a small filter funnel plugged lightly with glass wool. Set the apparatus for distillation as before and distil *slowly*, collecting two fractions with boiling ranges of 65–75°C and 75–100°C. The first fraction is 65–90% pure diene, whilst the second fraction is about 65% pure.[4] The major impurity in both fractions is 3,3-dimethylbutan-2-one. Record the quantity of each fraction.

[4] *May be left at this stage*

HOOD

2. *Diels–Alder reaction*

Place the butenedioic anhydride in a test tube, powder it finely with a glass rod and clamp the tube vertically. Add 0.5 mL of fraction 1 of redistilled 2,3-dimethyl-1,3-butadiene[5] and heat the mixture to 50°C in a water bath, stirring with a 0–250°C thermometer. After a short period of time (*ca.* 30 s) an exothermic reaction begins and the temperature should rise to *ca.* 100°C in several seconds, causing excess diene to boil off. When the reaction has subsided, remove the test tube from the heating bath and allow the mixture to cool to about 40°C. Add 15 mL hexane to the pasty product, warm the mixture in a hot water bath and stir until no more solid dissolves. Remove the thermometer, allow the test tube to stand undisturbed for 1 min, and transfer the clear supernatant *carefully* to a 10 mL Erlenmeyer flask with a pipette, making sure to leave the insoluble residue of unreacted butenedioic anhydride behind. Leave the solution to cool for 10 min and filter off the crystals of the adduct with suction,[6] washing them with a small quantity (*ca.* 2 mL) of cold hexane, and dry them with suction. Record the mp of your product and calculate the yield based on the quantity of butenedioic anhydride used.

[5] *Use fraction 2 if fraction 1 is insufficient*

[6] *See Fig. 3.7*

Problems

1 What is the structure of the major by-product of the elimination reaction in the first step? Write a mechanism to explain its formation.

2 Place the following dienes in order of their Diels–Alder reactivity:

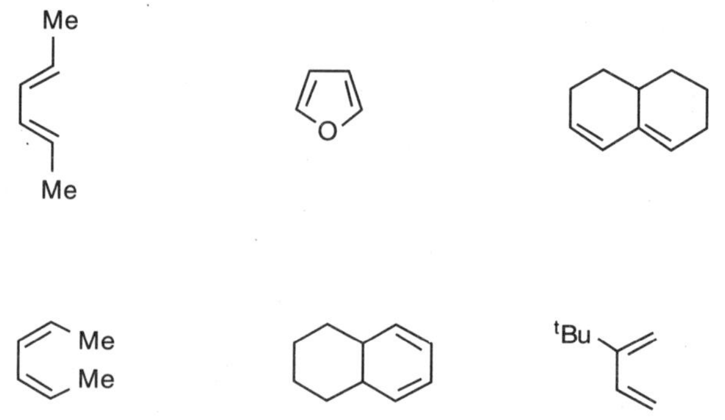

3 Explain why the major products in the following Diels–Alder reaction are dependent upon reaction conditions. Why does furan behave differently from the majority of dienes in the Diels–Alder reaction?

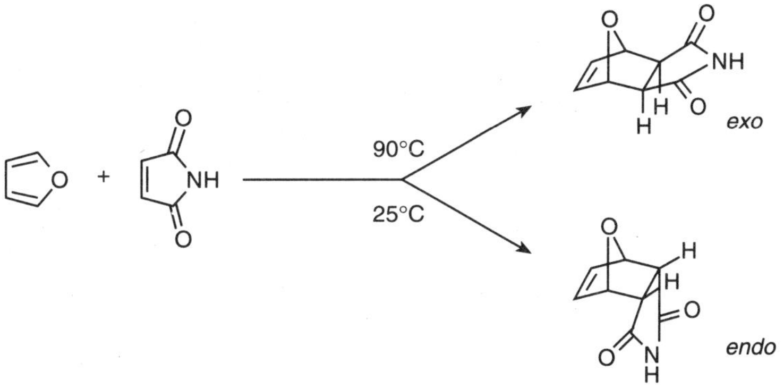

4 Arrange the following in order of increasing dienophilicity:

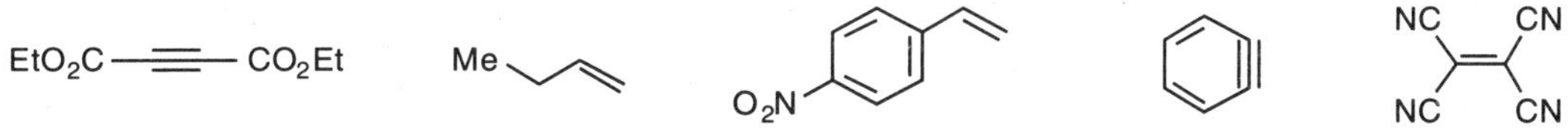

Experiment 62 *Benzyne: Diels–Alder reaction with furan*

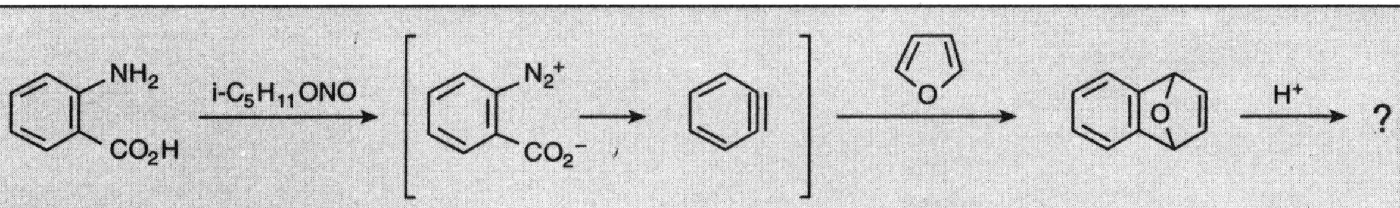

The reactive intermediate benzyne (1,2-didehydrobenzene) is implicated in certain nucleophilic aromatic substitution reactions. It can be generated by the reaction of halobenzenes with strong bases, by diazotization of anthranilic acid, or by the oxidation of 1-aminobenzotriazole. As a result of its electronic structure (which despite the usual triple bond representation is not like that of an alkyne with sp carbons but has the 'third bond' formed by geometrically unfavourable side-to-side overlap of two sp^2 orbitals) benzyne is a highly reactive intermediate. However, this high reactivity—as an electrophile and in cycloaddition reactions—can be exploited in synthesis. This experiment illustrates the reactivity of benzyne as a dienophile in the Diels–Alder reaction with furan as the diene. The benzyne is generated in the presence of furan by diazotization of anthranilic acid (commercially available or prepared as described in Experiment 34) under aprotic conditions using isoamyl nitrite in 1,2-dimethoxyethane as solvent. The intermediate benzenediazonium-2-carboxylate eliminates N_2 and CO_2 to generate benzyne, which immediately undergoes reaction with furan to give the Diels–Alder adduct, 1,4-dihydronaphthalene-1,4-endoxide. In a subsequent optional step, the endoxide may be treated with aqueous acid, which causes an isomerization to occur. The structure of the rearrangement product can be deduced from the IR and NMR spectra provided.

Level	3
Time	2 × 3 h (plus 3 h for optional step)
Equipment	steam bath; apparatus for reflux, extraction/separation, suction filtration, recrystallization, sublimation (optional)

Materials

1. Preparation of 1,4-dihydronaphthalene-1,4-endoxide		
furan (FW 68.1)	10 mL, 9.4 g (0.14 mmol)	**flammable**
isoamyl nitrite (FW 117.2)	4 mL (30 mmol)	**heart stimulant, flammable, irritant**
anthranilic acid (FW 137.1)	2.74 g (20 mmol)	**irritant**
1,2-dimethoxyethane		**flammable**
light petroleum (bp 40–60°C)		**flammable**
sodium hydroxide	0.50 g	**corrosive, hygroscopic**
2. Treatment of 1,4-dihydronaphthalene-1,4-endoxide with acid (optional)		
ethanol		**flammable, toxic**
diethyl ether		**flammable, irritant**
hydrochloric acid (conc.)		**corrosive**

Procedure

HOOD

1. Preparation of 1,4-dihydronaphthalene-1,4-endoxide

Place the furan, a few boiling stones, and 10 mL 1,2-dimethoxyethane (DME) in a 100 mL round-bottomed flask. Fit an efficient reflux condenser to the flask,[1] and heat the solution to reflux on a steam (or boiling water) bath. In two separate 25 mL Erlenmeyer flasks, make up a solution of the isoamyl nitrite in 10 mL DME, and a solution of the anthranilic acid in 10 mL DME. At 8–10 min intervals, add 2 mL of each of these solutions *simultaneously* to the flask through the condenser, using two separate Pasteur pipettes. When the additions are complete, heat the mixture under reflux for a further 30 min. During this period, prepare a solution of the sodium hydroxide in 25 mL water. Allow the brown reaction mixture to cool to room temperature, and add the sodium hydroxide solution.[2] Transfer the mixture to a 100 mL separatory funnel, and extract the product with 3 × 15 mL light petroleum. Wash the organic layer with 6 × 15 mL portions of water, and then dry it over $MgSO_4$.[3] Filter off the drying agent by suction,[4] and evaporate the filtrate on the rotary evaporator to leave an almost colourless crystalline solid. Slurry the crystals with a *very small* quantity of *ice-cold* light petroleum, and rapidly filter them by suction through a *pre-cooled* filter funnel.[5] Dry the crystals by suction for a few minutes. Record the yield and mp of your product.

[1]*See Fig. 3.23*

[2]*Check solution is basic*

[3]*May be left at this stage; if solution is very dark, it can be decolourized with charcoal*

[4]*See Fig.3.7*

[5]*Crystallization is tricky; compound can also be purified by sublimation*

2. *Treatment of 1,4-dihydronaphthalene-1,4-endoxide with acid (optional)*

Dissolve 432 mg (3 mmol) of 1,4-dihydronaphthalene-1,4-endoxide in 10 mL ethanol in a 25 mL Erlenmeyer flask. Add 5 mL concentrated hydrochloric acid, swirl the mixture, and allow it to stand at room temperature for 1 h. Transfer the mixture to a separatory funnel, and add 20 mL diethyl ether and 15 mL water. Shake the funnel, separate the ether layer, and wash it with 2 × 5 mL water, then dry it over $MgSO_4$.[6] Filter off the drying agent by suction, and evaporate the filtrate on the rotary evaporator at room temperature. Purify the solid residue by recrystallization from light petroleum or by vacuum sublimation,[7] and record the yield and mp of your product. The IR (Nujol®) and NMR spectra (p. 600) of the rearrangement product are provided.

[6] *May be left at this stage*

[7] *See Fig. 3.59*

Problems

1 What would be the products of the reaction of benzyne with: (i) water; (ii) ammonia; and (iii) tetraphenylcyclopentadienone?

2 In the absence of reactants, benzyne forms a dimer; what is its structure?

3 By reference to its IR and NMR spectra, what is the structure of the compound formed by treatment of the endoxide with acid? Confirm your assignment by comparing the mp with the literature value. Write a mechanism for its formation.

Further reading

For the procedure on which this experiment is based, see: L.F. Fieser and M.J. Haddadin, *Can. J. Chem.*, 1965, **43**, 1599.

For a discussion of aryne intermediates, see: C.J. Moody and G.H. Whitham, *Reactive Intermediates*, Oxford University Press, Oxford, 1992.

Rearrangement product (Nujol ®)

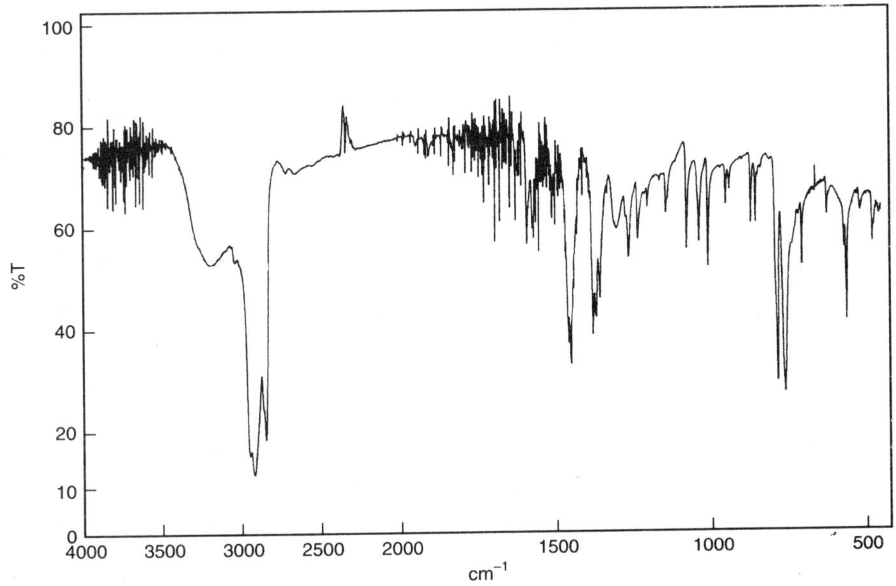

Rearrangement product
(250 MHz $CDCl_3$)

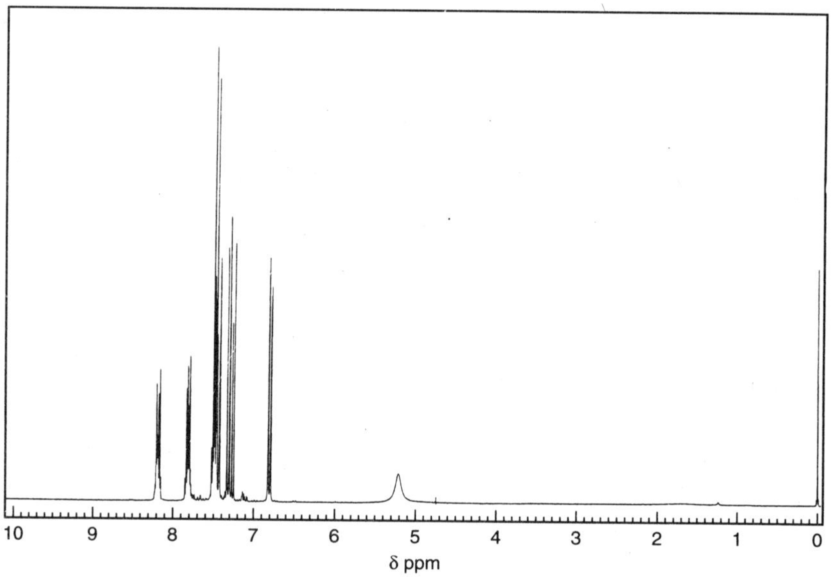

Experiment 63 *[2 + 2]-Cycloaddition of cyclopentadiene to dichloroketene: 7,7-dichlorobicyclo[3.2.0]hept-2-en-6-one*

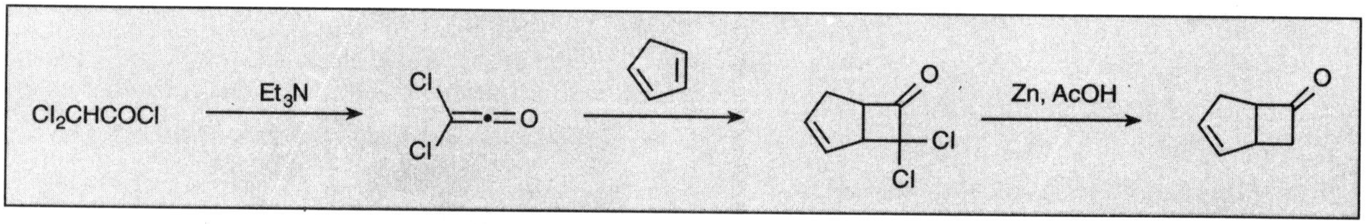

Although the [2 + 2]-cycloaddition of an alkene to another alkene under thermal conditions is disallowed according to the rules of orbital symmetry (Woodward–Hoffmann rules), it does occur under photochemical conditions. Cumulenes (allenes, ketenes, carbodiimides, etc.), however, because of their unique electronic structure, possess additional orbitals which allow them to participate in [2 + 2]-cycloadditions under thermal conditions. This experiment illustrates the cycloaddition of dichloroketene (generated by elimination of HCl from dichloroacetyl chloride with triethylamine) to cyclopentadiene, to give the 4–5 fused ring system, 7,7-dichlorobicyclo[3.2.0]hept-2-en-6-one. In a third, optional step, the dichlorobicyclic ketone is dechlorinated by treatment with zinc dust in ethanoic acid to give bicyclo[3.2.0]hept-2-en-6-one, a useful intermediate in the synthesis of the natural product *cis*-jasmone and of pharmacologically important prostaglandins.

Level	4
Time	Preparation of cyclopentadiene 4 × 3 h; preparation of 7,7-dichlorobicyclo[3.2.0]hept-2-en-6-one 2 × 3 h (with overnight reaction); preparation of bicyclo[3.2.0]hept-2-en-6-one 2 × 3 h
Equipment	magnetic stirrer/hotplate, vacuum pump; apparatus for distillation, reaction with addition under an inert atmosphere, suction filtration, short path distillation, extraction/separation, TLC (optional)
Instruments	IR, NMR

Materials

1. Preparation of cyclopentadiene from dicyclopentadiene

dicyclopentadiene (FW 132.2) (bp 60–80°C)	*ca.* 10 mL	**flammable, toxic**

2. Preparation of 7,7-dichlorobicyclo[3.2.0]hept-2-en-6-one

dichloroacetyl chloride (FW 147.4)	2.95 g (20 mmol)	**lachrymator, corrosive, hygroscopic**
triethylamine (FW 101.2)	2.8 mL (20 mmol)	**corrosive, flammable,**
hexane (or light petroleum bp 60–80°C)		**flammable**

3. Preparation of bicyclo[3.2.0]hept-2-en-6-one

zinc dust (FW 65.4)	3.95 g (61 mmol)	**flammable**
ethanoic acid (glacial)		**corrosive**
diethyl ether		**flammable, irritant**
sodium carbonate solution (saturated)		**corrosive**

Procedure

1. *Preparation of cyclopentadiene from dicyclopentadiene*

HOOD

Cyclo-pentadiene is prepared by 'cracking' the dimer by heat.[1] Place the dicyclo-pentadiene in a round-bottomed flask, fit a short fractionating column, a still head with thermometer, condenser and receiver.[2] Cool the receiving flask in ice, and heat the distillation flask until the dicyclopentadiene starts to boil gently (bp 170°C). At this point, cyclopentadiene monomer is formed and will distil over (bp 40°C). Collect the cyclopentadiene in the cooled receiving flask. The cyclopentadiene should be used immediately, otherwise it reverts to the dimer. It can, however, be stored for short periods in the freezer.

[1] *May be performed on a larger scale*

[2] *See Fig. 3.50*

HOOD

[3]*Stench*

[4]*See Appendix 2*

[5]*See Fig. 3.11, but replace septum with addition funnel*

2. *Preparation of 7,7-dichlorobicyclo[3.2.0]hept-2-en-6-one*

Dissolve 2.64 g (40 mmol) of *freshly distilled* cyclopentadiene[3] and the dichloroacetyl chloride in 20 mL *dry* hexane[4] in a 100 mL three-neck flask fitted with an addition funnel and nitrogen bubbler.[5] Stir the solution *vigorously* with a magnetic stirrer under a nitrogen atmosphere, and add a solution of the triethylamine in 20 mL *dry* hexane in small portions over a period of 1.5 h. Continue to stir the mixture under nitrogen for about 15 h (overnight) or until the next period.[6] Filter the mixture by suction,[7] wash the solid well with 3 × 10 mL hexane and evaporate the combined filtrate and washings on the rotary evaporator.[6] Distil the residue under reduced pressure using a vacuum pump (range 0.5–5.0 mmHg) and the short path distillation apparatus.[8] Record the bp, yield and the IR ($CHCl_3$) and NMR ($CDCl_3$) spectra of your product.

[6]*May be left at this stage*

[7]See Fig. 3.7. *Start part 3*

[8]*See Fig. 3.54*

3. *Preparation of bicyclo[3.2.0]hept-2-en-6-one (optional)*

Suspend the zinc dust in 5 mL ethanoic acid in a 25 mL round-bottomed flask, and stir the mixture *vigorously* at room temperature. Add a solution of 1.77 g (10 mmol) 7,7-dichlorobicyclo[3.2.0]hept-2-en-6-one in 3 mL ethanoic acid dropwise to the stirred zinc suspension. As soon as the addition is complete, raise the temperature of the reaction to 70°C by heating the flask in an oil bath. Maintain the temperature at 70°C for about 40 min, by which time TLC should indicate that no starting material remains. Cool the mixture and transfer it to a separatory funnel containing 20 mL diethyl ether. Wash the ether solution with 3 × 5 mL portions of saturated sodium carbonate solution to remove the ethanoic acid. Wash the solution with brine, and then dry it over $MgSO_4$.[6] Filter off the drying agent by suction and evaporate the filtrate on the rotary evaporator, cooling the evaporating flask in ice.[9] Distil the residue under reduced pressure (*ca.* 15 mmHg) using the short path distillation apparatus.[8] Record the bp, yield and the IR ($CHCl_3$) and NMR ($CDCl_3$) spectra of your product.

[9]*Product is volatile*

Problems

1 Discuss the mechanism of the addition of dichloroketene to cyclopentadiene. Why does cyclopentadiene not function as a diene and undergo Diels–Alder addition in this case?

2 Why are halogen atoms adjacent to carbonyl groups easily removed by reduction with metals?

3 Compare and contrast the IR and NMR spectra of 7,7-dichlorobicyclo[3.2.0]hept-2-en-6-one and the dechlorinated ketone.

Further reading

For the procedure on which this experiment is based, see: P.A. Grieco, *J. Org. Chem.*, 1972, **37**, 2363.

For the use of the final product in prostaglandin synthesis, see: J. Davies, S.M. Roberts, D.P. Reynolds and R.F. Newton, *J. Chem. Soc. Perkin Trans.*, 1981, 1317.

Experiment 64

Generation of dichlorocarbene and addition to styrene: preparation of (2,2-dichlorocyclopropyl)benzene

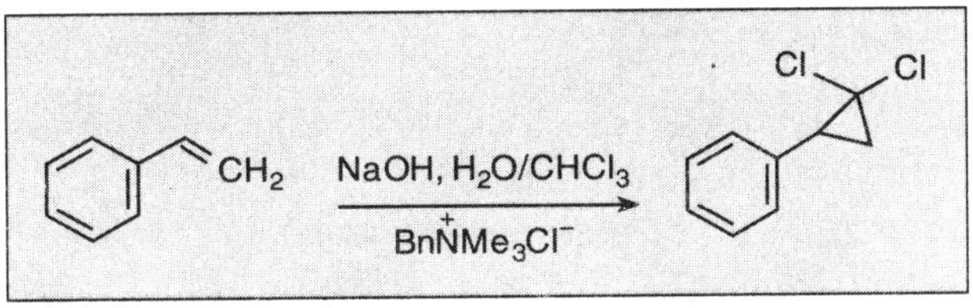

Carbenes are neutral divalent carbon species in which the carbon, being surrounded by a sextet of electrons, is electron deficient. Carbenes may exist either in the singlet or triplet states depending on whether the two non-bonded electrons are in the same molecular orbital with paired spins or in two equal energy orbitals with parallel spins.

singlet *triplet*

Carbenes may be generated in numerous ways, including thermolytic or photolytic decomposition of diazoalkanes, sulfonylhydrazone salts, diazirines and epoxides.

Another approach towards the generation of such reactive intermediates is via 1,1-elimination of alkyl halides. Such eliminations are more difficult to achieve than 1,2-eliminations and so this procedure is only efficient if there are no hydrogens β- to the halogen substituent.

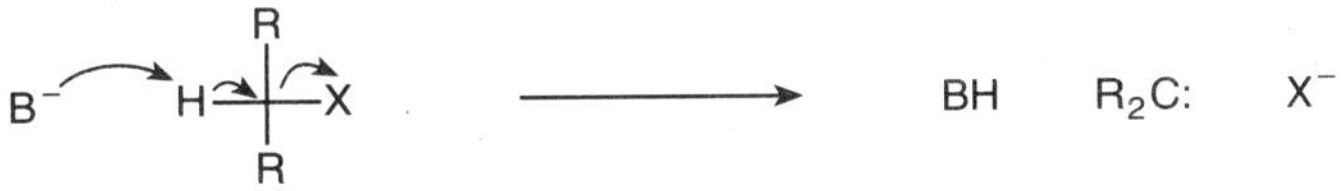

Particularly useful precursors for this method of generation are chloroform, dichloromethane and benzyl halides, and the strong base frequently used is potassium *t*-butoxide. However, by the use of phase transfer catalysis, it is possible to generate dichlorocarbene in an experimentally very convenient manner using a biphasic mixture of chloroform and aqueous sodium hydroxide. Without the added phase transfer catalyst, the formation of dichlorocarbene is very inefficient as the hydroxide ion acts as a trap for the dichlorocarbene, resulting in its hydrolysis to formate. Under phase transfer conditions however, the initial CCl_3^- ion formed at the interface is transported into the organic phase by the quaternary ammonium salt before breaking down to dichlorocarbene, which can then be trapped in a synthetically useful manner. In the experiment described here, the trapping agent is an alkene and the procedure provides us with a convenient means of preparing cyclopropanes.

Level	3
Time	2×3 h
Equipment	magnetic stirrer; apparatus for extraction/separation, small-scale reduced-pressure distillation or short path distillation
Instruments	NMR

Materials

styrene (vinylbenzene) (FW 104.2)	5.25 mL, 5.2 g (50 mmol)	**flammable, irritant**
benzyltrimethylammonium chloride	0.2 g (catalyst)	**corrosive, hygroscopic**
chloroform (FW 119.4)	8.0 mL, 12.0 g (0.1 mol)	**cancer suspect agent, toxic**
hydrochloric acid (5%)		**corrosive**
sodium hydroxide	20 g	**corrosive, hygroscopic**
diethyl ether		**flammable, irritant**

Procedure

HOOD

Place the sodium hydroxide in a 100 mL Erlenmeyer flask containing a magnetic stirrer bar, add 20 mL of water cautiously[1] and stir gently until solution is complete. Add the styrene followed by the chloroform[2] and the phase transfer catalyst and fit the flask loosely with a cork stopper or a plug of glass wool. Clamp the flask on the magnetic stirrer within a beaker or crystallizing dish (to stop spillage in the event of the stirrer bar breaking the walls of the flask) and stir the mixture vigorously for 2.5 h.[3] The success of the experiment depends upon the intimate mixing of the two phases and therefore the stirring should be as vigorous as possible without causing the mixture to leak through the stopper. At the end of the stirring period, add 40 mL of diethyl ether and separate the upper organic phase, taking care not to cause emulsification by over-vigorous shaking. Wash the organic phase with 20 mL of 5% aqueous hydrochloric acid followed by 20 mL of water, and dry over $MgSO_4$.[4] Filter the solution and remove solvents and unreacted starting materials on the rotary evaporator using a hot (*ca.* 60°C) water bath. Distil the residue under reduced pressure using a small-scale distillation apparatus or short path distillation apparatus[5] and collect the material boiling at 110–130°C/water aspirator/ (80–95°C/2 mmHg). Record the yield of your distilled product and obtain the NMR ($CDCl_3$) spectrum to compare with that of styrene.

[1] *Care!*

[2] *Toxic!*

[3] *Record the NMR ($CDCl_3$) spectrum of styrene during this period*

[4] *May be left at this stage*

[5] *See Fig. 3.53 and 3.54*

Problems

1 Assign the peaks in the NMR spectra of styrene and your product.

2 What are the two modes by which a carbene might add to an alkene? How would you design an experiment to decide which pathway was operating in the reaction of monochlorocarbene with an alkene?

3 Chloroform is stored in dark glass containers and frequently sold with about 1% ethanol added. What are the reasons for this and why do you think this practice came about?

4 Complete the reaction mechanisms and show the structures of the products for the following reactions:

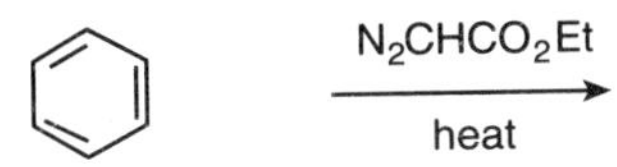

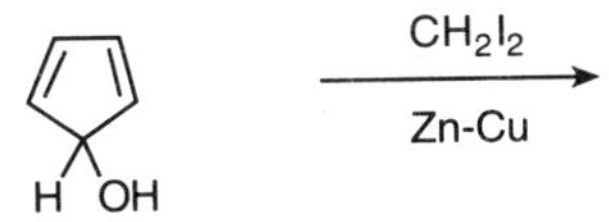

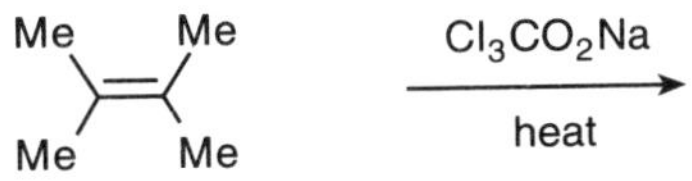

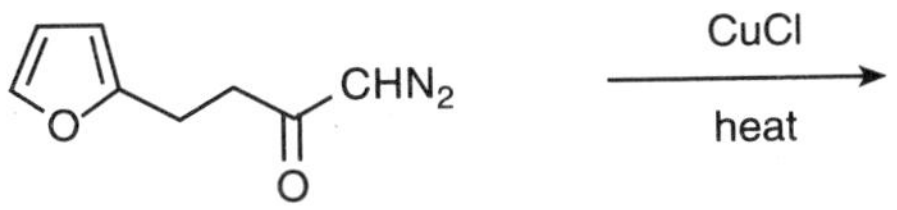

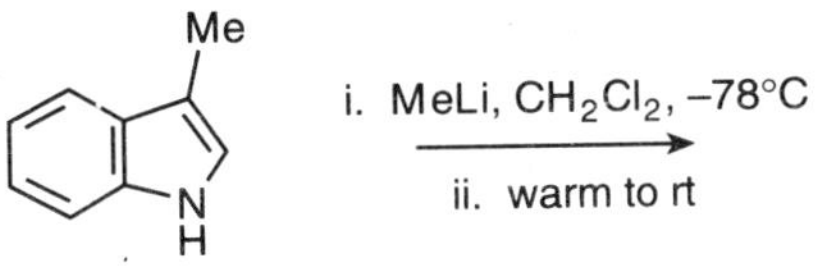

Further reading

For a discussion of carbene intermediates, see: C.J. Moody and G.H. Whitham, *Reactive Intermediates*, Oxford University Press, Oxford, 1992.

Experiment 65 *Claisen rearrangement of 2-propenyloxybenzene (allyl phenyl ether): preparation and reactions of 2-allylphenol*

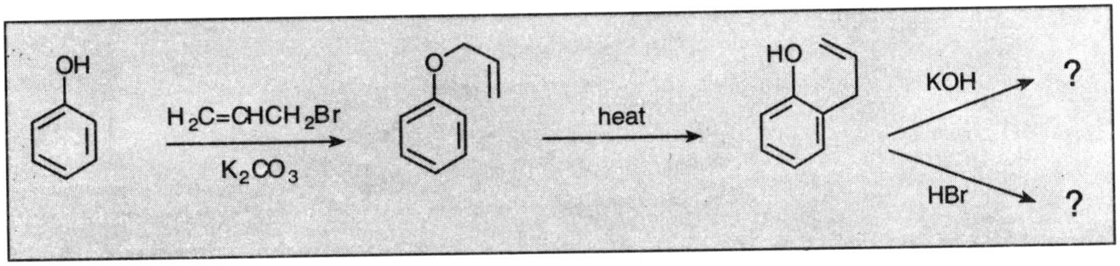

The rearrangement of allyl aryl ethers, discovered by Claisen in 1912, is an example of a general class of rearrangements known as [3,3]-sigmatropic reactions, and as such is closely related to other pericyclic processes such as the Cope rearrangement. This experiment illustrates the Claisen rearrangement of allyl phenyl ether, prepared by reaction of phenol with 3-bromoprop-1-ene (allyl bromide) in the presence of potassium carbonate in acetone. Under these conditions the product is almost entirely allyl phenyl ether, that is the product of *O*-allylation, although under other conditions products of *C*-allylation may result. When heated to its boiling point, allyl phenyl ether undergoes Claisen rearrangement to 2-allylphenol. Finally in two optional exercises, 2-allylphenol is treated separately with potassium hydroxide and with hydrobromic acid. The structure of the products of these subsequent reactions can easily be assigned from their IR and NMR spectra.

Level	2
Time	3 × 3 h (plus 2 × 3 h for optional stages)
Equipment	apparatus for reflux, extraction/separation, suction filtration, distillation under reduced pressure, reflux with air condenser, distillation, recrystallization, Abbé refractometer
Instruments	refractometer, IR, NMR (for optional exercises)

Materials

1. Preparation of allyl phenyl ether		
phenol (FW 94.1)	4.70 g (50 mmol)	**highly toxic, corrosive, toxic**
3-bromoprop-1-ene (allyl bromide) (FW 121.0)	4.3 mL (50 mmol)	**lachrymator, flammable, hygroscopic**
potassium carbonate (anhydrous) (FW 138.2)	6.91 g (50 mmol) + *ca.* 1 g	**corrosive**
acetone		**flammable**
diethyl ether		**flammable, irritant**
sodium hydroxide solution (2 M)		**corrosive**
2. Claisen rearrangement		
light petroleum (bp 40–60°C)		**flammable**
sodium hydroxide solution (5 M)		**corrosive**
hydrochloric acid (6 M)		**corrosive**
3. Reaction with KOH		
methanolic potassium hydroxide (saturated)		**corrosive, flammable**
light petroleum (bp 60–80°C)		**flammable**
4. Reaction with HBr		
glacial ethanoic acid		**corrosive**
hydrobromic acid (conc.)		**corrosive**

Procedure

HOOD

1. Preparation of allyl phenyl ether

Place the phenol, 3-bromoprop-1-ene, 6.91 g potassium carbonate and 10 mL acetone in a 50 mL round-bottomed flask. Fit a reflux condenser,[1] and heat the mixture under reflux in a mantle for about 2–3 h.[2] After cooling, pour the mixture into a 100 mL separatory funnel containing 50 mL water. Extract the product with 3 × 5 mL portions of diethyl ether. Combine the ether extracts, wash them with 3 × 5 mL sodium hydroxide (2 M), and then dry them over anhydrous potassium carbonate.[2] Filter off the drying agent by suction,[3] and

[1] *See Fig. 3.23(a)*

[2] *May be left at this stage*

[3] *See Fig. 3.7*

evaporate the filtrate on the rotary evaporator. Distil the residue in a small apparatus under reduced pressure[4] (water aspirator, *ca*. 20 mmHg). Record the bp, yield and IR spectrum (film) of your product.

[4] *See Fig. 3.53*

2. *Preparation of 2-allylphenol*

Place 5.37 g (40 mmol) allyl phenyl ether in a 10 mL round-bottomed flask. Add a boiling stone, fit an air reflux condenser,[5] and heat the material under reflux for about 3 h. The rearrangement can be conveniently followed by measuring the refractive index of the mixture at 30 min intervals; the reaction is complete when the refractive index has risen from 1.520 to 1.544. After cooling,[2] dissolve the product in 10 mL sodium hydroxide solution (5 M), and extract the solution with 2 × 5 mL portions of light petroleum.[6] Acidify the aqueous solution with hydrochloric acid (6 M), and extract the product with 3 × 5 mL diethyl ether. Dry the combined ether extracts over $MgSO_4$.[2] Filter off the drying agent by suction, and evaporate the filtrate on the rotary evaporator. Distil the residue at atmospheric pressure in a small distillation set.[7] Record the bp, yield and IR spectrum (film) of your product.

[5] *See Fig. 3.23(c)*

[6] *Petrol removes any by-product*

[7] *See Fig. 3.48*

3. *Treatment of 2-allylphenol with KOH (optional)*

Dissolve 1.34 g (10 mmol) 2-allylphenol in 5 mL saturated methanolic potassium hydroxide solution in a 10 mL round-bottomed flask. Heat the solution, allowing the methanol to distil out, until the temperature of the liquid reaches 110°C. Fit a reflux condenser, and heat the mixture under reflux for 1.5 h.[1] Acidify the mixture with hydrochloric acid (6 M), and extract the product with 3 × 5 mL diethyl ether. Dry the ether solution over $MgSO_4$,[2] filter off the drying agent by suction,[3] and evaporate the filtrate on the rotary evaporator. Distil the residue in a small set at atmospheric pressure, and record the bp of the product. The distillate should crystallize in the receiver, and can be further purified by recrystallization from light petroleum (bp 60–80°C). Record the mp and yield of the product. The IR (film) and NMR spectra of the product are reproduced below.

HOOD

4. *Treatment of 2-allylphenol with HBr (optional)*

Dissolve 1.34 g (10 mmol) 2-allylphenol in 6 mL glacial ethanoic acid in a 10 mL round-bottomed flask. Add 3 mL hydrobromic acid, a boiling stone, and heat the mixture under reflux for 20 min.[1] Cool the mixture, transfer it to a separatory funnel containing 25 mL water, and extract the product with 3 × 5 mL diethyl ether. Combine the ether extracts, wash them with 5 mL sodium hydroxide solution (2 M), and dry them over $MgSO_4$.[2] Filter off the drying agent by suction,[3] evaporate the filtrate on the rotary evaporator, and distil the residue at atmospheric pressure. Record the bp yield, and the IR (film) and NMR ($CDCl_3$) spectra of the product.

Product from KOH, treatment (neat)

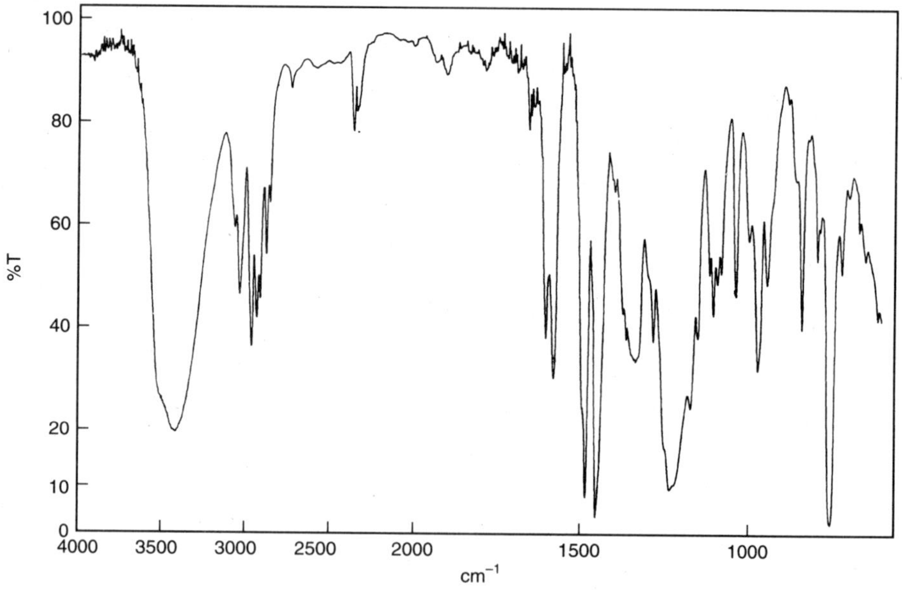

Product from KOH treatment (250 MHz $CDCl_3$)

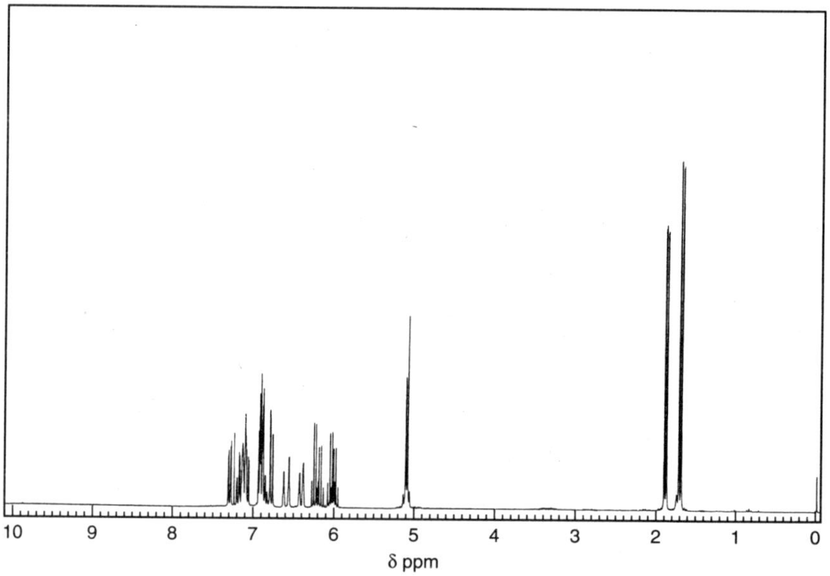

Problems

1 Write a mechanism for the Claisen rearrangement of allyl phenyl ether.

2 Assign the IR spectra of allyl phenyl ether and 2-allylphenol.

3 By consideration of the IR and NMR spectra (provided) of the product of part 3, assign a structure to this product, and write a mechanism for its formation.

4 Assign a structure for the product of part 4 based on its IR and NMR spectra, and write a mechanism for its formation.

Further reading

For a review of the Claisen rearrangement, see: S.J. Rhoads and N.R. Raulins, *Org. Reactions*, 1975, **22**, 1.

Experiment 66 — *Preparation of 3,5-diphenylisoxazoline by a 1,3-dipolar cycloaddition*

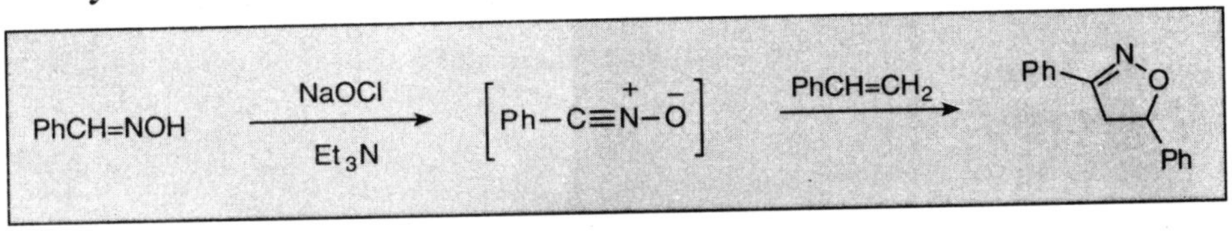

The Diels–Alder reaction is a thermally favourable cycloaddition which involves six π-electrons—four from the diene component and two associated with the dienophile. An analogous concerted thermal cycloaddition can occur between *1,3-dipolar species* and alkenes; with the 1,3-dipole contributing four electrons. In such reactions the product is a five-membered ring instead of the six-membered ring formed in the Diels–Alder reaction.

Diels-Alder reaction

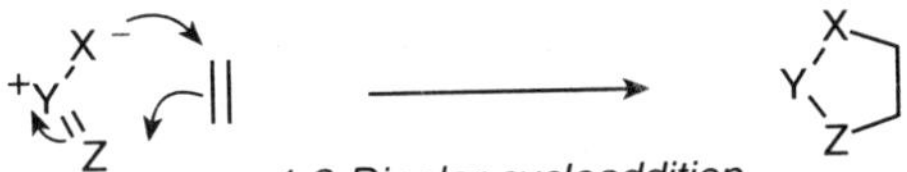

1,3-Dipolar cycloaddition

Nitrile oxides are typical 1,3-dipoles and react readily with an alkene (the *dipolarophile*) to generate heterocyclic products called *isoxazolines*. In the following experiment the nitrile oxide is generated *in situ* by oxidation of an oxime. The oxime used in this case is *syn*-benzaldoxine; this is commercially available or can be prepared as described in Experiment 5.

Level	1
Time	3 h
Equipment	magnetic stirrer; apparatus for extraction/separation, recrystallization

Materials

styrene (FW 104.2)	2.9 mL, 2.6 g (25 mmol)	**flammable, irritant**
triethylamine (FW 101.2)	0.3 mL, 0.2 g (2 mmol)	**corrosive, flammable, stench**
dichloromethane		**irritant, toxic**
sodium hypochlorite (*ca.* 10% available chlorine)	25 mL	**corrosive, oxidizer**
benzaldoxime (FW 121.1)	2.5 g (21 mmol)	**irritant**

Procedure

HOOD

Dissolve the styrene and triethylamine in 15 mL of dichloromethane in a 100 mL Erlenmeyer flask containing a magnetic stirrer bar. Add the sodium hypochlorite solution to the flask and cool the mixture in ice with stirring. Maintain stirring in the ice bath and add 2.5 g of the *syn*-benzaldoxime dropwise from a Pasteur pipette over 15 min to the mixture. When addition is complete, allow the reaction to stir in the ice bath for a further 45 min. Separate the lower organic phase and extract the aqueous layer with another 15 mL of dichloromethane. Combine the organic extracts, dry over $MgSO_4$, filter and remove the solvent on the rotary evaporator. Record the weight of your crude product and recrystallize from ethanol. Record the mp and yield of your recrystallized material.

MICROSCALE

Level	1
Time	3 h
Equipment	magnetic stirrer; apparatus for extraction/separation, pipette column drying, Craig tube recrystallization

Materials		
styrene (FW 104.2)	0.116 mL, 104 mg (1 mmol)	**flammable, irritant**
triethylamine (FW 101.2)	12 µL, 8 mg (0.08 mmol)	**corrosive, flammable, stench**
dichloromethane		**irritant, toxic**
sodium hypochlorite (ca. 10% available chlorine)	1 mL	**corrosive, oxidizer**
benzaldoxime (FW 121.1)	100 mg (0.83 mmol)	**irritant**

HOOD

Dissolve the styrene and triethylamine in dichloromethane (0.6 mL) in a 3 mL reaction vial containing a spin vane. Add the sodium hypochlorite solution to the flask and cool the mixture in ice with stirring. Maintain stirring in the ice bath and add 100 mg of the *syn*-benzaldoxime in 10 mg portions to the mixture over 15 min. When addition is complete, allow the reaction to stir in an ice bath for a further 45 min. Separate the lower organic phase and extract the aqueous layer with another portion of dichloromethane (0.6 mL). Combine the organic extracts, and dry by passing them through a column of $MgSO_4$ into a Craig tube.[1] Blow down the solution to dryness,[2] record the yield of crude product and recrystallize from ethanol. Record the yield and mp of the pure product.

[1] *See pp. 137–138*
[2] *See Fig. 2.31*

Problems

1 The following reagents are known to act as 1,3-dipoles: (i) azides, (ii) diazomethane, (iii) nitrones, and (iv) ozone. Draw out these structures, showing their extreme resonance canonical forms, to indicate why each of these is capable of acting as a 1,3-dipole.

2 Predict the products which would be obtained from the reaction of each of the reagents listed in (1) with styrene.

Further reading

For the procedure on which this experiment is based, see: G.A. Lee, *Synthesis*, 1982, 508.

Chapter 9 Projects

This chapter contains 20 experiments which are loosely described as projects. These experiments are either multi-stage syntheses or involve the preparation, or isolation, of compounds with interesting properties. The final section illustrates some aspects of physical organic chemistry.

9.1 Natural product isolation and identification

Natural product extraction as a technique has its roots in antiquity. By infusion or distillation, humankind has attempted to concentrate various constituents of both plants and animals in order to accentuate and standardize their properties. Whilst curative powers were the commonest goal of such efforts, properties such as the possession of a particular colour, odour or flavour, were the usual reasons for initial interest. As a consequence, many plant parts, or their extracts, have found use both in the kitchen and as components of medicaments whose origin lies in folklore. Although wildly exaggerated claims were frequently made for many such potions, the scientific community does recognize that within many herbal remedies lies a kernel of truth. As a consequence, much effort is directed towards the identification of the physiologically active components of natural extracts claimed to have properties such as pain killing, hallucinatory, contraceptive or abortive activities. From the ubiquitous oral analgesic aspirin, to the antineoplastic agent vinblastine, used in the treatment of Hodgkin's disease and other lymphomas, the wealth and variety of natural products provides many leads for drug design and development in pharmaceutical research; the potential seems boundless.

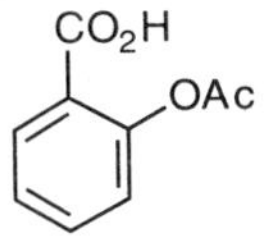

aspirin

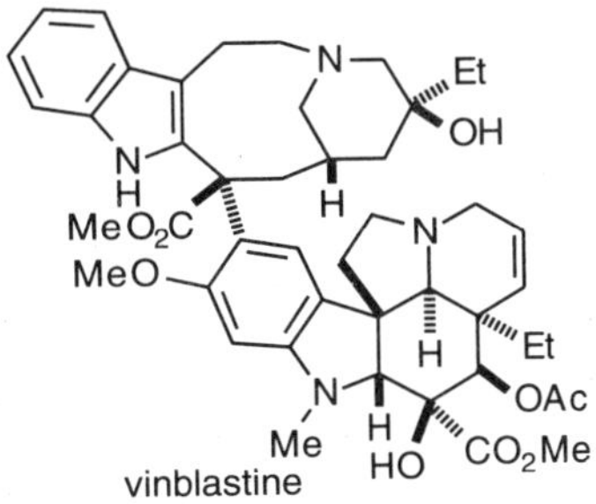

vinblastine

Experiment 67

Isolation of eugenol, the fragrant component of cloves, and lycopene, a colouring component of tomatoes

Many natural products are not suitable for a laboratory extraction experiment for various reasons such as their presence in trace amounts, toxicity, instability, complex structure, non-availability of their source or combinations of these. The following experiment describes extractions of a component of a material which is widely available due to its widespread culinary use.

Cloves are the dried flower buds of the evergreen tropical tree *Eugenia aromatica*, a native of South East Asia, and are known to have been used in cooking by the Chinese over 2000 years ago, being valued for inhibiting putrefaction of meat with which they were cooked. This property and their pungent odour are due largely to a single component, eugenol, which makes up the bulk of the 'oil of cloves' that is obtained by steam distillation of the flower buds. Other applications for eugenol include its use in dental preparations, perfumery and as an insect attractant.

The compounds responsible for the bright orange and red colours of carrots and tomatoes are known as *carotenoids*: C_{40} compounds which occur widely in nature. Lycopene, $C_{40}H_{56}$, is the bright-red compound responsible for the colour of ripe tomatoes. Its highly unsaturated structure containing 11 conjugated double bonds means that it absorbs light in the visible region of the electromagnetic spectrum as described in the section on UV spectroscopy in Chapter 5. Lycopene is readily extracted from tomatoes but since 1 kg of fruit only yields about 0.02 g lycopene, it is much more convenient to use concentrated tomato paste. The experiment must be started at the beginning of the laboratory period since lycopene does not store well. The experiment also illustrates the use of dry flash chromatography.

Level	3
Time	isolation of eugenol 3 h; isolation of lycopene 3 h; detailed spectroscopic analysis 3 h

Continued on p. 614

Box cont.

Equipment	apparatus for distillation at atmospheric pressure, extraction, separation, suction filtration, reflux, dry flash chromatography, TLC		
Instruments	UV, IR, NMR		
Materials			
1. Isolation of eugenol			
cloves		*ca.* 30 g	
dichloromethane			**irritant, toxic**
sodium hydroxide solution (3 M)			**corrosive**
hydrochloric acid (conc.)			**corrosive**
bromine water			**corrosive, irritant**
pH paper (pH 7–12)			
2. Isolation of lycopene			
tomato paste		10 g	
methanol			**flammable, toxic**
dichloromethane			**irritant, toxic**
sodium chloride solution (saturated)			
silica gel			**irritant dust**
light petroleum (bp 49–60°C)			**flammable**
toluene			**flammable**

Procedure

1. Isolation of eugenol

Place the cloves in a 500 mL round-bottomed flask containing 300 mL of water and distil the mixture vigorously over a flame until *ca.* 200 mL of distillate has been collected, being careful not to boil the residue to dryness.[1] Transfer the oily distillate to a separatory funnel, extract with 2 × 30 mL dichloromethane and wash the combined organic layers with 100 mL of water. Extract the dichloromethane with 2 × 50 mL 3 M sodium hydroxide, add concentrated hydrochloric acid dropwise[2] to the alkaline aqueous extract to lower it to pH 9, and extract the milky aqueous mixture with 2 × 30 mL dichloromethane. Dry these organic extracts over $MgSO_4$,[3] filter into a preweighed flask and remove the solvent on the rotary evaporator. Record your yield of product and obtain the UV (95% EtOH), IR (film) and NMR ($CDCl_3$) spectra of this material. Check the purity of your product by TLC (diethylether–light petroleum (2:1) on silica plates), staining the plate with iodine. Test the acidity of your product by observing the solubility of 1 or 2 drops in aqueous sodium hydroxide and aqueous sodium bicarbonate. Check for unsaturation by observing whether the aqueous layer is decolourized when a few drops of bromine water are added to the pure material. You may be able to recognize the characteristic odour of your product as that in many proprietary brands of dental preparations and throat and cough medicines.

[1] *See Fig. 3.57*

[2] ***Care! Exothermic***

[3] *May be left at this stage if necessary*

2. *Isolation of lycopene*

Heat a mixture of 10g tomato paste, 25mL methanol and 50mL dichloromethane under reflux for 5min in a 250mL round-bottomed flask using a steam bath,[4] swirling it at frequent intervals. Filter the mixture with suction,[5] and transfer the filtrate to a separatory funnel. Wash the solution with 3 × 150mL portions of saturated sodium chloride solution, and then dry the organic layer over anhydrous $MgSO_4$. Filter off the drying agent and evaporate the filtrate to dryness on the rotary evaporator.[6]

[4]*See Fig. 3.23(a)*
[5]*See Fig. 3.7*
[6]*Evaporate at 40–50°C maximum*

Set up the apparatus for dry flash chromatography using 40g of TLC grade silica gel.[7] **This step must be carried out in a hood owing to the hazardous dust**. Dissolve the crude red material in 5mL light petroleum and carefully transfer this solution to the top of the silica gel using a Pasteur pipette. Elute the column using a mixture of light petroleum and toluene (5:1) in 50mL portions. A yellow band elutes first (*ca.* 70–80mL of solvent) followed by the orange lycopene (*ca.* a further 200mL of solvent). Combine the fractions containing the orange lycopene in a preweighed flask and evaporate them to dryness on the rotary evaporator.[8] Reweigh the flask to obtain the yield of lycopene. Record the UV spectrum (in hexane) of the lycopene, and check its purity by TLC (silica gel and light petroleum–toluene, 5:1). Dispose of the used silica gel following a procedure approved by your instructor, or the method described on pp. 179–180.

[7]*See pp. 184–187*
[8]*Evaporate at 60°C (or slightly higher) to remove all the toluene*

Problems

1. From your spectroscopic and chemical information, and the mass spectrum provided, propose reasonable structures for eugenol. Suggest a synthesis of one of your suggested structures.
2. By what biosynthetic pathway do you think eugenol and lycopene are formed? Suggest labelling experiments to test your hypothesis (experimental details are not required).
3. Pure lycopene has absorptions at λ_{max} 444, 470 and 501nm. Common impurities include phytofluene (λ_{max} 331, 348 and 368nm) and zeta-carotene (λ_{max} 378, 398 and 424nm). Analyze your UV spectrum to ascertain the presence (or otherwise) of impurities.
4. Using the correlation table (Table A17, Appendix 3) calculate the λ_{max} for lycopene, and compare it with the experimental value.

Further reading

Merck Index, 11th edn, Merck and Co., Rahway, 1989; eugenol, p. 612 no. 3855; lycopene, p. 884 no. 5492.

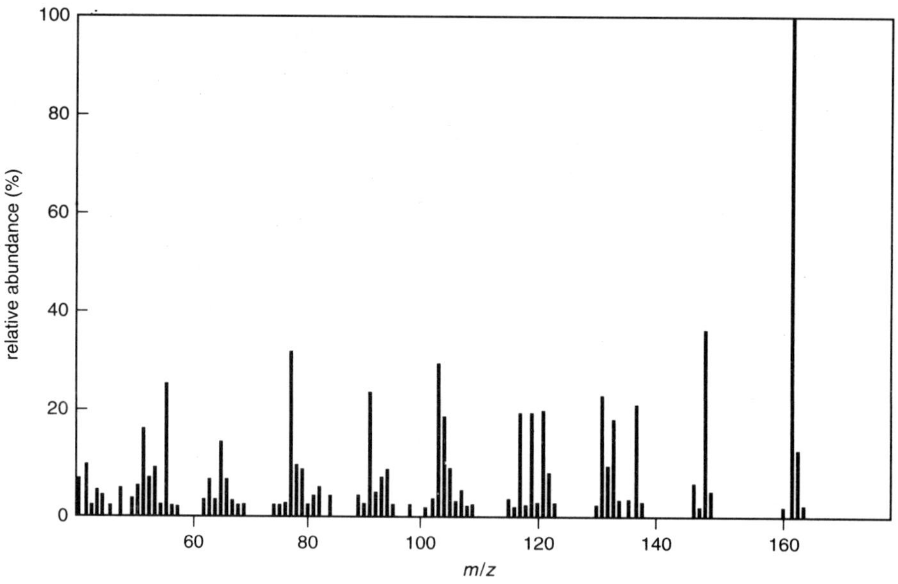

Mass spectrum of clove oil.

Experiment 68

Isolation and characterization of limonene; the major component of the essential oil of citrus fruit

Limonene belongs to the enormous family of terpenoids which are formed by the linking together of a series of five carbon fragments, formally derived from isoprene.

This generic trait was first recognized by Ruzicka, who formulated the *isoprene rule* in 1953, and the whole family is now subdivided by the number of C-5 fragments in the molecule.

No. of C-5 units	*Class of terpene*
2	monoterpene
3	sesquiterpene
4	diterpene
6	triterpene

The units are often linked in a regular head-to-tail manner, but head-to-head and head-to-middle connections also occur and this, coupled with the fact that much additional functionalization, cyclization and loss of carbon fragments can take place, often obscures the biosynthetic origin of these compounds.

The lower members of the class (the monoterpenes and sesquiterpenes) are characteristically volatile oils with pleasant odours and are much used in the perfumery and flavouring industries. Isoprene-derived materials are widespread throughout the animal and plant kingdoms and provide us with a wealth of compounds possessing varied properties ranging from the odorous

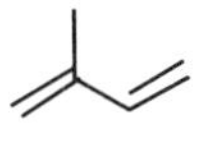

isoprene

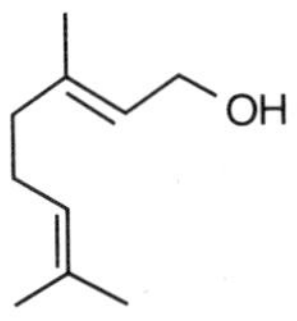

geraniol

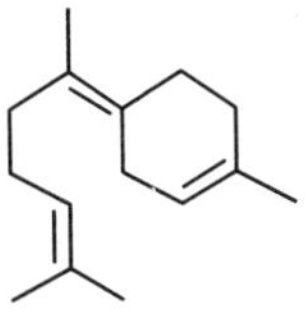

γ-bisabolene

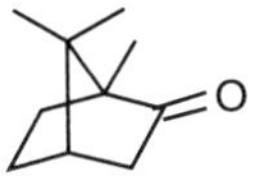

camphor

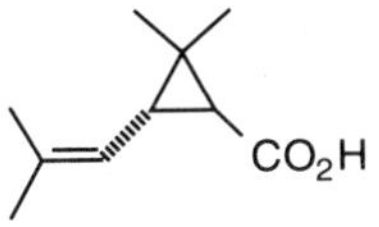

trans-chrysanthemic acid

α-pinene

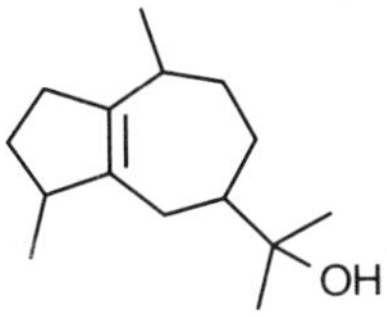

guajol

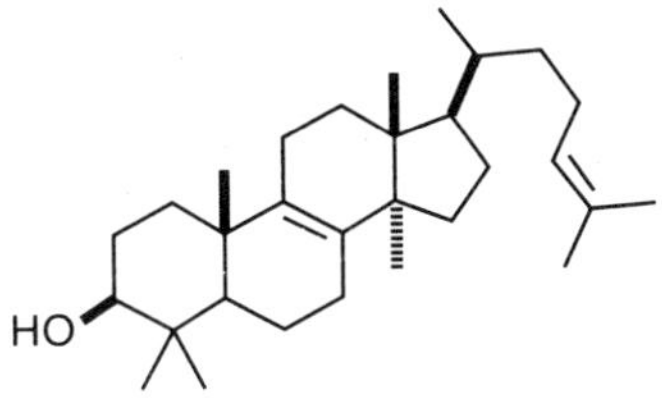

lanosterol

monoterpenes which include limonene, through diterpenes such as the daphnanes (arrow tip poisons, fish poisons—potential antitumur drugs) to triterpenes such as the steroids.

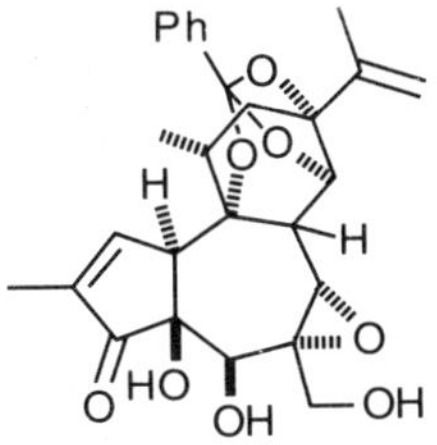

daphnetoxin

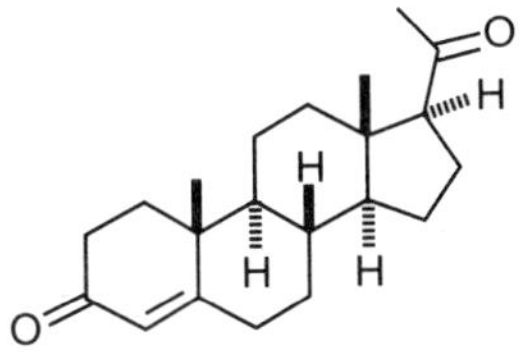

progesterone

The incredible diversity of the terpenes appears to present the organic chemist with an apparently inexhaustible supply of problems in structure elucidation, biogenesis and total synthesis. However, knowing that a natural product belongs to a particular family often enables us to rule out certain postulated structures which are not compatible with the biogenetic sequence.

The characteristic odour of citrus fruit is mainly due to one aptly named component, limonene, which is by far the major constituent. Its simple isolation in a pure state is due to this fact (the essential oil of sweet oranges consists of about 95% (R)-limonene, whilst lemon peel contains the (S)-isomer) and also to its volatility, which makes possible an isolation by steam distillation.

Limonene is a member of the class of regular monoterpenes and, with this knowledge, we can attempt to establish its structure after isolation and purification. ■

Level	3
Time	isolation and purification 3 h; analysis 3 h
Equipment	apparatus for distillation, extraction/separation, short path distillation under reduced pressure
Instruments	IR, NMR (a mass spectrum of the material is provided), GC (suggested system, 10% Carbowax®; 100–200°C/20°C min^{-1})

Materials

oranges (3 thick-skinned or 5 thin-skinned)

dichloromethane — **irritant, toxic**

Procedure

Peel the oranges, weigh the peel (only the outer, orange part is needed, the pith can be discarded) and break it into pieces small enough to fit through the neck of 500 mL round-bottomed flask. Add 250 mL of water to the flask containing the peel and set the apparatus for distillation.[1] Boil the mixture vigorously and collect the distillate until no more oily drops can be seen passing over. More water should be added if necessary to avoid charring of the flask contents. Extract the distillate with two 50 mL portions of dichloromethane, combine the extracts, dry them over $MgSO_4$,[2] and remove the solvent on the rotary evaporator without external heating. Obtain the weight of the crude material thus obtained. Save one drop of this product if it is intended to carry out GC analysis[3] and purify the remainder by short path distillation at reduced pressure (bp 55 ± 10°C/10 mmHg, or 71 ± 10°C/20 mmHg, or 25 ± 10°C/27 mmHg, or 87 ± 15°C/40 mmHg, or 175–185°C/760 mmHg)[4] collecting material within the range stated. Record the yield of purified product, calculate the yield based upon the weight of peel used and obtain the IR (film) and NMR ($CDCl_3$) spectra. If possible, compare the purity of the initially obtained crude and distilled materials by gas chromatography. A suggested system for this analysis is a 10% Carbowax® column with a temperature programme of 100–200°C at 20°C min^{-1} or equivalent.

[1]*See Fig. 3.57*

[2]*May be left at this stage*

[3]*Analyze during distillation*

[4]*See Fig. 3.54*

Problems

1 Limonene is a regular monoterpene, 1 mol of which reacts with 2 mols of hydrogen in the presence of a platinum catalyst. From these facts and your spectroscopic data, derive a structure for limonene, justifying your structure by assigning the NMR spectrum, and the important absorptions in the IR and fragment ions in the mass spectrum.

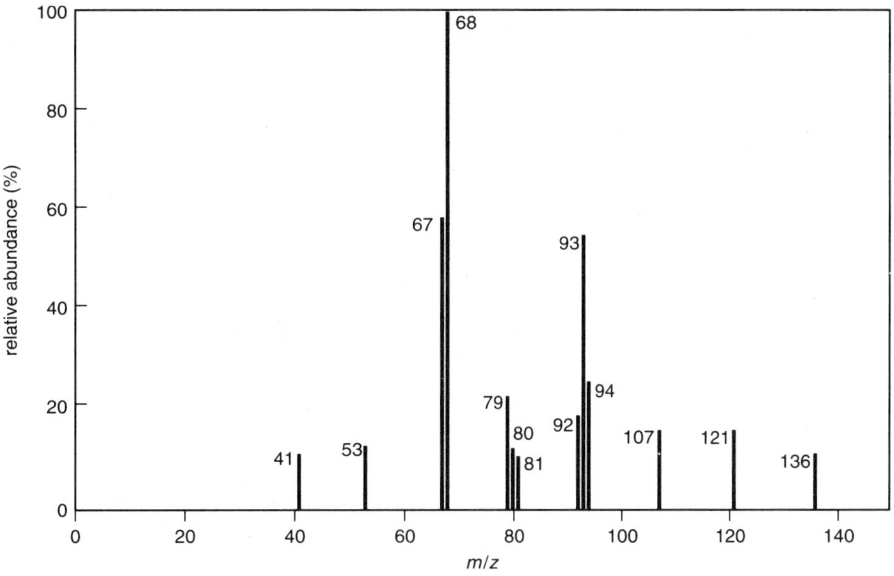

Mass spectrum of limonene (only peaks of relative abundance >10% shown)

2 Discuss the biogenesis of limonene from two C-5 subunits, considering any intermediates to exist formally as cationic species.

3 Describe how you might synthesize limonene in one step from a 5-carbon precursor in the laboratory (*hint*: look at the fragmentation pattern in the mass spectrum).

Further reading

For discussions of terpene biogenesis, see: J. Mann, *Secondary Metabolism*, 2nd edn, Oxford University Press, 1987, Oxford, chapter 3.

Experiment 69 — *Isolation of caffeine from tea and theobromine from cocoa*

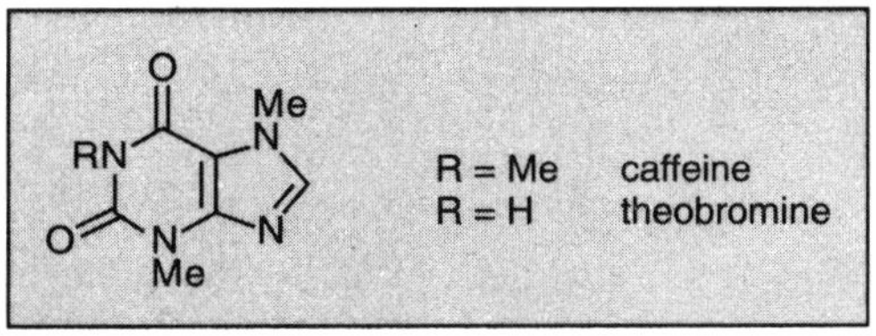

The popularity of tea and coffee as beverages stems from their mildly stimulant activity which is mainly due to the presence of the purine alkaloid caffeine. Caffeine acts as a stimulant for the central nervous system and relaxes the smooth muscle of bronchi as well as having diuretic properties. Theobromine is another active principle of coffee but differs from caffeine in that the nitrogen at position 1 is lacking a methyl substituent. It is a less active stimulant than caffeine but is a stronger diuretic. Whilst it co-occurs with caffeine in tea leaves and coffee beans, a better source of this product is the cocoa bean, in which it is the principal alkaloid. Theobromine, reported to be highly toxic orally, is obtained in large quantities as a by-product in the preparation of chocolate and cocoa and is usually converted to the more pharmaceutically useful caffeine. The following experiments describe the extraction of both purines. Either or both extractions may be carried out by a single worker or by working in a team. ■

Level	3
Time	2 × 3 h
Equipment	apparatus for Soxhlet extraction, extraction/separation, reflux
Instruments	IR

Materials

1. Isolation of caffeine		
tea (finely ground)	25 g	
magnesium oxide	13 g	
ethanol (95%)		**flammable, toxic**
chloroform		**cancer suspect agent, toxic**
sulfuric acid (10%)		**corrosive, oxidizer**
sodium hydroxide solution (1%)		**corrosive**
2. Isolation of theobromine		
cocoa	20 g	
magnesium oxide	6 g	
methanol		**flammable, toxic**
chloroform		**cancer suspect agent, toxic**
diethyl ether		**flammable, irritant**

Procedure

HOOD

1. Isolation of caffeine

Place the finely ground tea leaves in the thimble of the Soxhlet extractor and arrange the apparatus for continuous extraction for 1 h with 100 mL ethanol.[1] Transfer the extract to a 1 L round-bottomed flask containing the magnesium oxide and evaporate to dryness on the rotary evaporator, heating with a warm water bath.[2] Extract the solid residue with boiling water (4 × 50 mL), and filter the slurry with suction whilst hot in each instance. Add 12 mL of 10% sulfuric acid to the filtrate and reduce it to *ca.* one-third of its original volume on the rotary evaporator with heating on a steam or boiling water bath. If a flocculent precipitate forms at this stage, it should be filtered off whilst the solution is still hot and the solution allowed to cool, before extracting four times with 15 mL portions of chloroform. The yellow organic extracts can be decolourized by shaking with a few millilitres of 1% aqueous sodium hydroxide followed by washing with the same volume of water. Remove the solvent on the rotary evaporator and recrystallize the residue of crude caffeine from the minimum quantity of boiling water (<1 mL). Record the weight and mp of your product and obtain the IR spectrum ($CHCl_3$).

[1] *See Fig. 3.40*

[2] *Bumping may be a problem with a smaller flask*

HOOD

2. *Isolation of theobromine*

Mix the cocoa and magnesium oxide in a 250 mL beaker containing 20 mL methanol and 40 mL of water.[3] Heat this slurry on the steam bath with constant stirring until a crumbly, semi-solid mass forms (*ca.* 45 min). Transfer this to a 500 mL round-bottomed flask, add 150 mL of chloroform[4] and reflux the mixture for 30 min.[5] Filter the hot mixture through a large Büchner funnel, washing the residue with 25 mL of hot chloroform,[6] and remove the majority of the solvent on the rotary evaporator until *ca.* 10 mL remain. Allow the residue to cool and then add 600 mL of diethyl ether to the flask. Stopper the flask tightly and allow to stand overnight or until the next laboratory session.[7] Filter off the resultant precipitate by filtration under gravity using a fine porosity filter paper to avoid loss of product or blocking of the filter. Record the weight and IR (Nujol®) of your material and observe what occurs on attempting to obtain its mp. The sample may be recrystallized if desired from *ca.* 40 mL of boiling water using a little decolourizing charcoal.

[3] ***Wear gloves***

[4] ***Toxic***

[5] *See Fig. 3.23(a)*

[6] *If the solvent cools, product may be lost*

[7] *Leave at this stage*

Problems

1 Assign the important absorptions in the IR spectrum of your product.

2 Caffeine is a basic compound, forming salts with acids; whereas theobromine is amphoteric and is freely soluble in basic as well as acidic solutions. Comment on the structural features of each molecule which confer these properties.

3 Theobromine is only sparingly soluble in most solvents. However, its NMR spectrum may be obtained in D_2O/NaOD, although only seven of the eight protons are visible. Which proton is missing and why should this be so?

4 Both caffeine and theobromine are purine bases. List other purine derivatives found in living systems and comment upon their importance for processes such as the control of heredity, energy storage, methylation, and fatty acid biosynthesis.

Further reading

For the procedure on which this experiment is based, see: D.L. Pavia, *J. Chem. Educ.*, 1973, **50**, 791; *Merck Index*, 11th edn, Merck and Co., Rahway, 1983, p. 248, no. 1635 and p. 1460, no. 9209.

9.2 Synthetic projects

The experiments in this section involve the synthesis of compounds with interesting properties: natural products, including insect pheromones, macrocyclic metal-chelating compounds, chemiluminescent, photochromic and piezochromic compounds, and compounds of theoretical interest. The experiments vary in length and complexity, but for the most part are based on techniques and reactions discussed in earlier chapters.

Experiment 70 *Dyes: preparation and use of indigo*

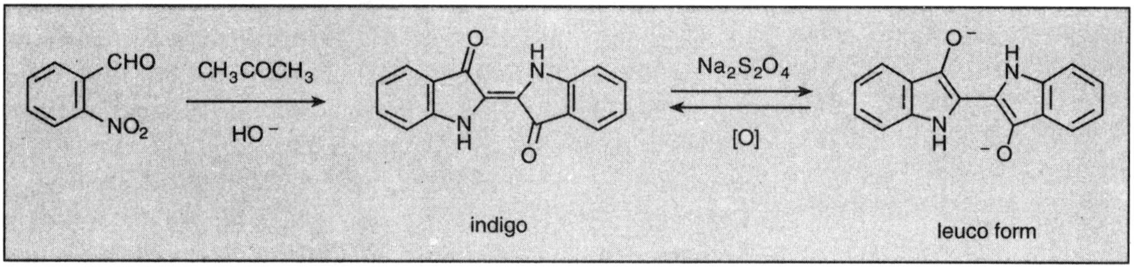

Dyes, coloured organic compounds which are used to impart colour to fabrics, have been known to humans for thousands of years. Tyrian purple, obtained from the mollusc *Murex brandaris* found near the city of Tyre, was used in ancient Rome to dye the togas of the emperors; alizarin, extracted from the roots of the madder plant, has long been used as a red dye, particularly in the eighteenth and nineteenth centuries for the red coats of the British army; but the oldest known dye of all is indigo, which was used by the ancient Egyptians. The 6,6′-dibromo derivative of indigo is in fact responsible for the colour of Tyrian purple. More recently indigo was used to dye the blue coats supplied by the French to the Americans during the American Revolution, and in modern times to produce large quantities of blue denim. Although ancient dyes were entirely of natural origin, most modern dyes are synthetic and, in order to be useful, a dye must be fast (i.e. remain in the fabric during washing). To do this, the dye must be bonded to the fabric in some way, and the easiest fabrics to dye (cotton, wool, silk) contain polar functional groups which can interact with dye molecules. Dyes are classified into three groups according to how they are applied to the fabric: vat dyes, mordant dyes and direct dyes.

Indigo is an example of a vat dye and was originally obtained by fermentation of the woad plant (*Isatis tinctoria*), hence its use as the 'woad' of the ancient Britons, and from plants of the *Indigofera* species. Both plants contain a glucoside which can be hydrolyzed to indoxyl, the colourless precursor of indigo, the structure of which was elucidated by Baeyer in 1883. In the vat dying process, the dye is applied to the fabric in a vat in a soluble form and is subsequently allowed to undergo chemical reaction to an insoluble form. Indigo is applied in the reduced and soluble *leuco* form which, on exposure to air, is reoxidized to the insoluble blue dye. Nowadays indigo is produced synthetically and is reduced to the leuco form using sodium hydrosulfite (sodium dithionite). This project illustrates a one-step preparation of indigo from 2-nitrobenzaldehyde. The vat dying process is then simply carried out by reducing the indigo with sodium hydrosulfite, soaking a piece of cotton in the resulting solution, and exposing the dyed fabric to air.

Level	1
Time	3 h (plus 3 h for the dying)
Equipment	magnetic stirrer (optional), hot plate or steam bath; apparatus for suction filtration

Materials		
2-nitrobenzaldehyde (FW 151.2)	1.0 g (6.6 mmol)	**irritant**
acetone		**flammable**
ethanol		**flammable, toxic**
sodium hydroxide (2 M)		**corrosive, hygroscopic**
sodium hydrosulfite	0.3 g	**hygroscopic**
prewashed cotton	*ca.* 2 g	
soap solution (0.5%)		

Procedure

1. *Preparation of indigo*

Dissolve the 2-nitrobenzaldehyde in 20 mL acetone in a 100 mL beaker, and dilute the solution with 35 mL of water. Stir the solution *vigorously* using a magnetic stirrer, or more simply with a glass rod, whilst adding 5 mL 2 M sodium hydroxide solution. The solution turns deep yellow, then darker, and within 20 s a dark precipitate of indigo will appear. Continue to stir the mixture for 5 min, and then collect the purple-blue precipitate by suction filtration.[1] Wash the product with water until the washings are colourless (*ca.* 100 mL needed), then with 20 mL ethanol. Dry the solid with suction for 5–10 min, and then at 100–120°C for 30–40 min.[2] Record the yield of your product.

[1] *See Fig. 3.7*

[2] *Prepare for Part 2 now*

2. *Vat dying of cotton*

Place 100–200 mg of indigo on a watch glass, add a few drops of ethanol, and make a paste by rubbing the mixture with a glass rod. Suspend the paste in 1 mL water in a 100 mL beaker, and add 3 mL sodium hydroxide solution (2 M). Make up a solution of the sodium hydrosulfite in 20 mL water, and add this to the mixture in the beaker. Heat the mixture up to 50°C on a steam bath, and as soon as a clear yellow solution is obtained, add 40 mL of water.[3] Immerse the cotton in the 'vat', and leave for 1 h at 50°C, occasionally moving the fabric to ensure even dyeing. Remove the cotton, squeeze it dry, and hang it in the air for 30 min to develop the colour.[4] In order to 'brighten' the colour, immerse the dyed fabric in 50 mL soap solution in a 100 mL beaker, and heat it on a steam bath for 15 min. Rinse the fabric with water and hang it to dry.

[3] *If substantial amounts of blue–purple solid remain, the solution should be decanted at this point*

[4] *May be left at this stage; 'brightening' is optional*

Problems

1. Indigo can exist in two isomeric forms: what are these? What is this sort of isomerism called?
2. The mechanism of indigo formation is complex. How would you establish the origin of the ring carbon atom between the O and N atoms?

Further reading
For other uses of sodium hydrosulfite as a reducing agent, see: EROS, 4554.

Experiment 71 *Synthesis of flavone*

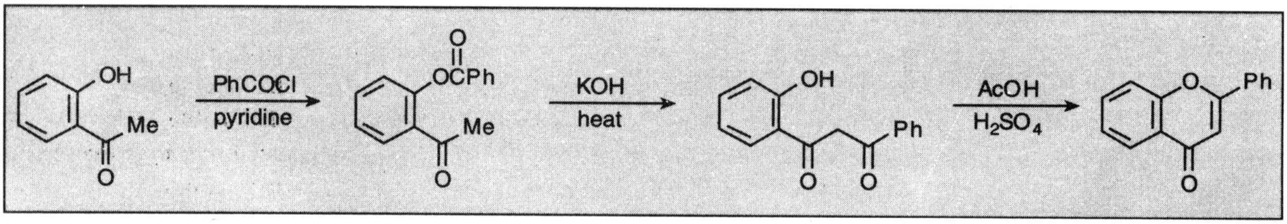

Nature abounds with bright colours. Although some, such as those of peacock feathers, arise by light diffraction by the unique complex structure of the feathers, most colours in nature arise by the absorption of certain wavelengths of visible light by organic compounds.

Most red and blue flowers contain coloured glucosides called *anthocyanins*. The colour imparted by an anthocyanin is pH dependent; for example, the red colour of roses and the blue of cornflowers are due to the same compound, *cyanin*, which in its phenol form is red, and in its anionic form is blue. The non-sugar part of the glucoside is a type of *flavylium salt*. This term comes from the parent compound *flavone*, itself colourless, although the 3-hydroxy derivative, called flavonol, is yellow in colour (Latin *flavus* = yellow).

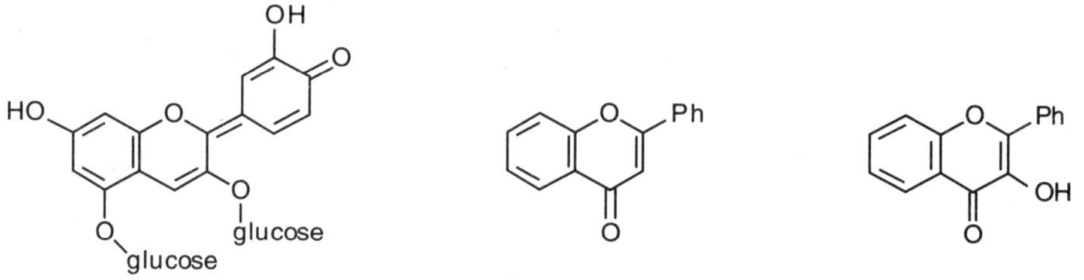

cyanin flavone flavonol

This project involves the three-step synthesis of flavone from 2-hydroxyacetophenone, which is commercially available or can be prepared as described in Experiment 59. The first stage is the benzoylation of the phenolic OH group with benzoyl chloride in pyridine to give 2-benzoyloxyacetophenone, which on heating in the presence of potassium hydroxide undergoes the Baker–Venkataraman rearrangement to give *ortho*-hydroxydibenzoylmethane in the second step. The final step involves cyclization of the *ortho*-hydroxydibenzoylmethane to flavone in the presence of ethanoic and sulfuric acids. After recrystallization, the flavone is obtained as colourless needles.

Level	2
Time	2 × 3 h (plus 3 h for full spectroscopic characterization)
Equipment	steam bath; apparatus for suction filtration, reflux, recrystallization
Instruments	IR, NMR (both optional)

Materials

1. Preparation of 2-benzoyloxyacetophenone		
2-hydroxyacetophenone (FW 136.2)	2.46 mL, 2.72 g (20 mmol)	**corrosive, irritant**
benzoyl chloride (FW 140.6)	3.48 mL, 4.22 g (30 mmol)	**lachrymator, hygroscopic, toxic**
pyridine (FW 79.1)	5 mL	**flammable, irritant, toxic, stench**
hydrochloric acid (3%)		**corrosive**
methanol		**flammable, toxic**
2. Preparation of 2-hydroxydibenzoylmethane		
potassium hydroxide	0.85 g	**corrosive, hygroscopic**
pyridine	8 mL	**flammable, irritant, toxic, stench**
acetic acid solution (10%)	15 mL	**corrosive**
3. Preparation of flavone		
glacial acetic acid	7 mL	**corrosive**
sulfuric acid (conc.)	0.25 mL	**corrosive, oxidizer**
light petroleum (bp 60–80°C)		**flammable**

Procedure

1. Preparation of 2-benzoyloxyacetophenone

HOOD

[1]*Use pyridine that has been dried over KOH. See Appendix 2*

[2]*See Fig. 3.7*

Dissolve the 2-hydroxyacetophenone in 5 mL pyridine[1] in a 25 mL round-bottomed flask. Add the benzoyl chloride, fit the flask with a calcium chloride guard tube, and swirl the flask to ensure mixing of the reagents. The temperature of the reaction mixture rises spontaneously. Leave the reaction mixture for about 20 min or until no further heat is evolved, and then pour it into a 250 mL beaker containing 120 mL hydrochloric acid (3%) and 40 g crushed ice with good stirring. Collect the product by suction filtration,[2] and wash it with 4 mL *cold* methanol and then 5 mL water. Dry the product by suction at the filter pump for 20 min, and then recrystallize it from *ca.* 5 mL methanol. Record the yield, mp and, if required, the IR ($CHCl_3$) and NMR ($CDCl_3$)

spectra[3] of the product after one recrystallization. Record an IR spectrum of the starting 2-hydroxyacetophenone for comparison.

[3]Spectra can be recorded in a subsequent period

HOOD

2. *Preparation of 2-hydroxydibenzoylmethane*

Dissolve 2.40 g (10 mmol) of the 2-benzoyloxyacetophenone in 8 mL pyridine[1] in a 50 mL beaker, and warm the solution to 50°C on a steam or hot water bath. Add the finely powdered potassium hydroxide,[4] and stir the mixture for 15 min using a glass rod. During this time a yellow precipitate of the potassium salt of the product forms. Cool the mixture to room temperature and add 15 mL of 10% acetic acid solution. Collect the product by suction filtration, and dry it by suction at the filter pump for a few minutes.[5] Record the yield and mp of the product, which is sufficiently pure for use in the next stage.

[4]Pulverize the KOH rapidly in mortar preheated to 100°C

[5]May be left at this stage

3. *Preparation of flavone*

Dissolve 1.20 g (5 mmol) of the 2-hydroxydibenzoylmethane in 7 mL glacial acetic acid in a 25 mL round-bottomed flask. Swirl the solution and add 0.25 mL concentrated sulfuric acid. Fit the flask with a reflux condenser,[6] and heat it on the steam bath for 1 h, carefully shaking it occasionally. Pour the reaction mixture onto 40 g crushed ice contained in a 100 mL beaker with rapid stirring using a glass rod.[7] When all the ice has melted, collect the crude product by suction filtration, and wash it with *ca.* 80 mL water until free from acid. Dry the product by suction at the filter pump, and then at 50°C.[7] Recrystallize the crude flavone from *ca.* 40 mL petroleum. Record the yield, mp and, if required, the IR (Nujol®) and NMR ($CDCl_3$) spectra[3] of the product after one recrystallization. The IR and NMR spectra of flavone are reproduced below.

[6]See Fig. 3.23(a)

[7]Care!

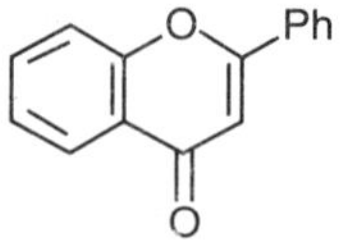

(Nujol®)

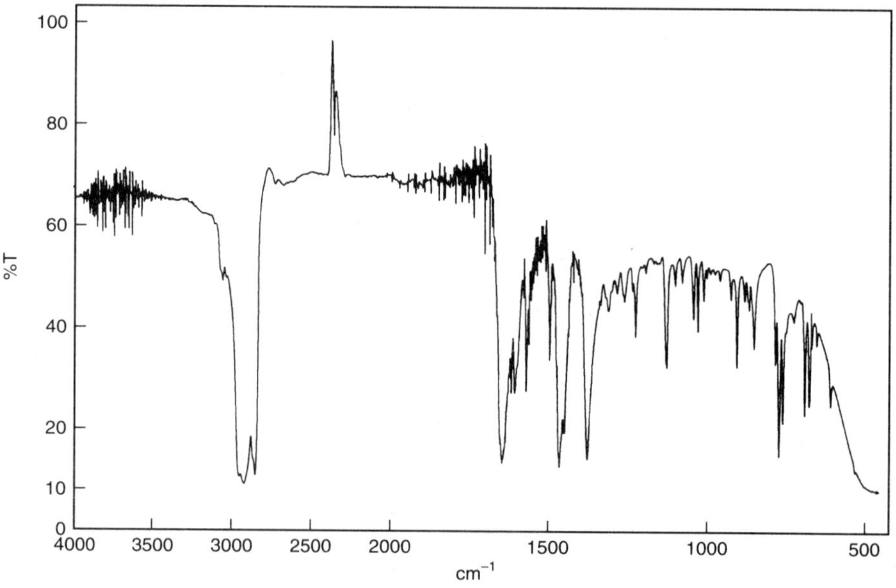

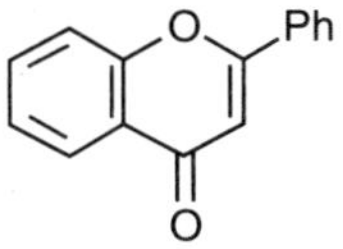

(250 MHz, $CDCl_3$)

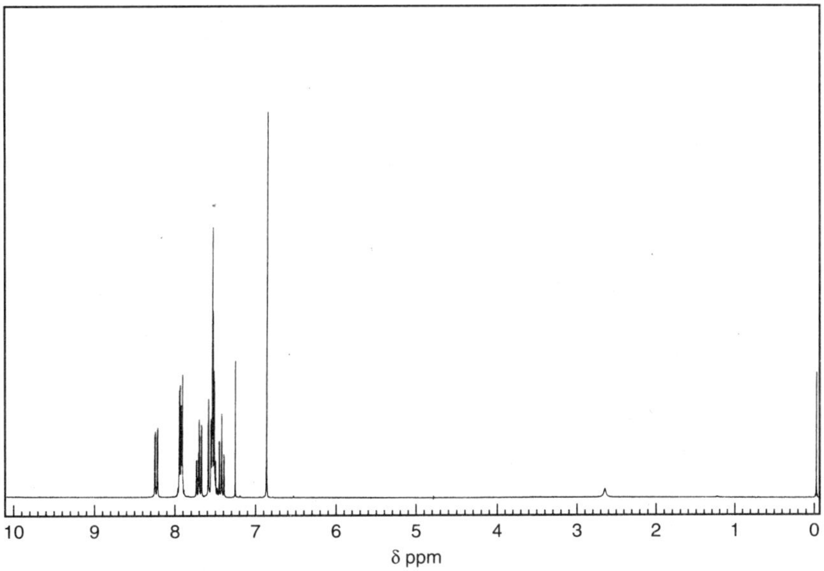

Problems

1 Discuss the mechanism of the Baker–Venkataraman rearrangement.

2 Assign the spectroscopic data for the starting 2-hydroxyacetophenone, its benzoylated derivative, and for flavone. Compare your spectra of flavone with those provided.

Further reading

For the procedures on which this experiment is based, see: R.M. Letcher, *J. Chem. Educ.*, 1980, **57**, 220; T.S. Wheeler, *Org. Synth. Coll. Vol.*, **4**, 478.

Syntheses of pheromones

Many animal and insect species communicate with one another by means of chemical signals. These substances, known as *pheromones*, serve as sex attractants and for alarm, trail and aggregation purposes. Many pheromones are structurally quite simple substances: isoamyl acetate (Experiment 1) is the alarm pheromone of the honey bee, and valeric acid is a sex attractant for the male sugar-beet wireworm, although other pheromones are more complex. The target molecules are of varying structural complexity, and illustrate a number of important reactions and experimental techniques.

Experiment 72 *Insect pheromones: synthesis of 4-methylheptan-3-ol and 4-methylheptan-3-one*

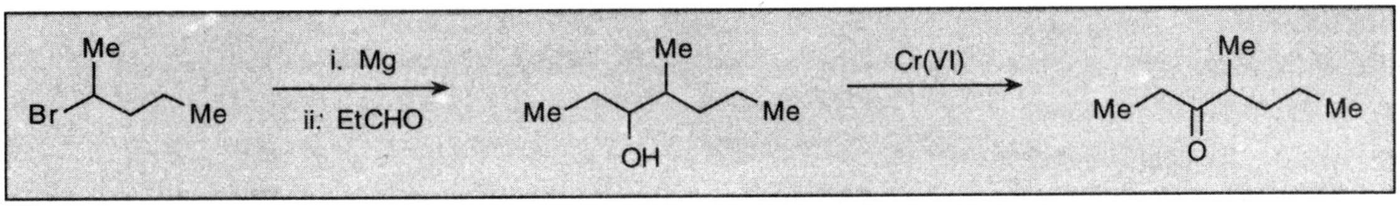

The alcohol, 4-methylheptan-3-ol, is one of the three known aggregation pheromones of the European elm beetle, *Scolytus multistriatus*, an insect which is largely responsible for the spread of Dutch elm disease. The pheromone is easily prepared by the addition of the Grignard reagent derived from 2-bromopentane to propanal. The corresponding ketone, 4-methylheptan-3-one prepared by chromium(VI) oxidation of the secondary alcohol, also functions as a pheromone: it is the alarm pheromone for several ant species such as the harvest ant, *Pogonomyrmex barbatus*, and the Texas leaf cutting ant, *Atta texana*.

Level	2
Time	3–4 × 3 h
Equipment	magnetic stirrer; apparatus for reflux with addition (3-neck flask), extraction/separation, suction filtration, distillation
Instruments	IR, GC (optional)

Materials

1. Preparation of 4-methylheptan-3-ol		
2-bromopentane (FW 151.1)	6.2 mL (50 mmol)	**flammable, irritant**
propanal (FW 58.1) (propionaldehyde)	3.6 mL (50 mmol)	**flammable**
diethyl ether (dry)		**flammable, irritant**
diethyl ether		**flammable, irritant**
magnesium (FW 24.3)	1.83 g (75 mmol)	**flammable**
hydrochloric acid (10%)		**corrosive**
sodium hydroxide solution (5%)	10 mL	**corrosive**
2. Preparation of 4-methylheptan-3-one		
sulfuric acid (concentrated)	3.5 mL	**corrosive, oxidizer**
sodium dichromate dihydrate (FW 298.0)	8.0 g (27 mmol)	**cancer suspect agent, oxidizer, toxic**
diethyl ether		**flammable, irritant**
sodium hydroxide solution (5%)		**corrosive**

Procedure

All glassware must be thoroughly dried in a hot (<120 °C) oven before use.

HOOD

1. Preparation of 4-methylheptan-3-ol

Set up a 100 mL three-neck flask with a 25 mL addition funnel, a reflux condenser protected with a calcium chloride guard tube, and a magnetic stirrer bar.[1] Add the magnesium and 15 mL *dry* diethyl ether[2] to the flask, and stopper the third neck of the flask. Place a solution of the 2-bromopentane in 15 mL *dry* diethyl ether in the addition funnel, add a few drops of this solution to the magnesium, and start the stirrer. The formation of the organometallic

[1] *See Fig. 3.25*
[2] *See Appendix 2*

[3]If reaction does not start, a crystal of iodine may be added. The start of the reaction is indicated by the diethyl ether starting to reflux and taking on a grey–brown appearance

[4]Can be left longer

[5]May be left at this stage

[6]See Fig. 3.7

[7]See Fig. 3.48

reagent should start fairly quickly.[3] Continue to stir the mixture, and add the remaining bromide solution dropwise over 15 min. When the addition is complete, stir the mixture for a further 10 min. During this time, make up a solution of the propanal in 10 mL *dry* diethyl ether, and place it in the addition funnel. Add this solution *dropwise* to the stirred Grignard solution, and continue the stirring for a further 15 min after the addition is completed.[4] Add 10 mL water *dropwise* to the reaction mixture. Follow this by adding 10 mL dilute hydrochloric acid (10%) until all the inorganic salts dissolve. Decant the mixture from any remaining magnesium into a separatory funnel, and separate the ether layer. Wash the diethyl ether solution with 10 mL 5% sodium hydroxide solution, separate the ether layer, and dry it over $MgSO_4$.[5] Filter off the drying agent by suction,[6] and evaporate the filtrate on the rotary evaporator. Transfer the residue to a small distillation set,[7] and distil it at atmospheric pressure, collecting the fraction boiling in the range 150–165°C. Record the yield and the IR spectrum (film) of your product.

2. *Preparation of 4-methylheptan-3-one*

HOOD

[8]Care!

Place 35 mL distilled water and a magnetic stirrer bar in a 100 mL Erlenmeyer flask. Clamp the flask in an ice bath, start the stirrer, and add the concentrated sulfuric acid.[8] Add the sodium dichromate, and stir the mixture until a clear orange solution is obtained. Continue to stir the solution, and add 5.0 g (38 mmol) of your 4-methylheptan-3-ol in small portions over about 10 min; the colour of the reaction mixture should gradually change to green. Stir the mixture for a further 10 min, and then transfer it to a 100 mL separatory funnel. Add 200 mL diethyl ether, shake the funnel, and separate the organic layer. Wash the ether layer with 3 × 20 mL portions of 5% sodium hydroxide solution, and dry it over $MgSO_4$.[5] Filter off the drying agent, evaporate the filtrate on the rotary evaporator, and distil the residue from a small distillation set[7] at atmospheric pressure, collecting the product in the range 155–160°C. Record the yield and the IR spectrum (film) of your product. If required, the product can be analyzed by GC, and the amount, if any, of unreacted alcohol present can be determined.

Problems

1 Discuss the reaction mechanism for the addition of a Grignard reagent to a ketone.
2 Discuss the oxidation of secondary alcohols using chromium(VI) compounds. What other reagents could be used to effect the oxidation?
3 Compare and contrast the IR spectra of the alcohol and the ketone.
4 Suggest an alternative synthesis of 4-methylheptan-3-one.

Further reading

For the procedure on which this experiment is based, see: R.M. Einterz, J.W. Ponder and R.S. Leno, *J. Chem. Educ.*, 1977, **54**, 382.

For a discussion of chromium oxidants, see Experiments 29–31.

Experiment 73 — *Insect pheromones: methyl 9-oxodec-2-enoate; the queen bee pheromone*

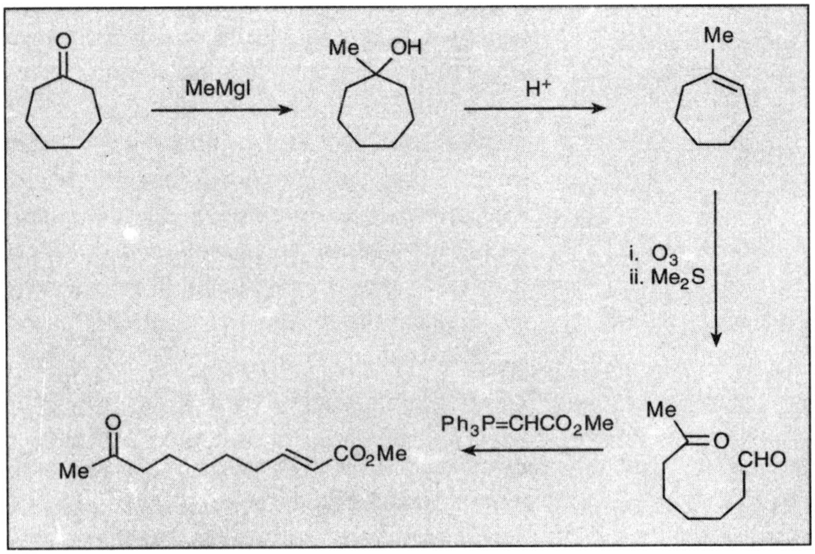

This multi-step experiment involves a synthesis of the methyl ester of the compound secreted by the queen bee during mating flights to attract the drone bees, which have high and specific sensitivity to the compound. The synthesis is in four sequential steps: (1) addition of a Grignard reagent to a ketone; (2) acid-catalyzed dehydration of a tertiary alcohol; (3) ozonolysis of an alkene; and (4) a Wittig reaction using the stabilized ylid, methyl (triphenylphorphoranylidene) acetate, which is commercially available or can be prepared as described in part 5. Hydrolysis of the ester to the pheromone itself is not described.

Level	3
Time	4 × 3 h (plus 3 h for preparation of the Wittig reagent)
Equipment	magnetic stirrer, ozonizer; apparatus for reflux with addition (2- or 3-neck flask), extraction/separation, reflux, distillation, ozonolysis, TLC, column chromatography
Instruments	IR, NMR

Materials

1. Preparation of 1-methylcycloheptanol

magnesium turnings (FW 24.3)	2.5 g (104 mmol)	**flammable**
iodomethane (FW 141.9)	6.6 mL (106 mmol)	**cancer suspect agent, toxic**

NOTE: ***the toxicity of iodomethane coupled with its volatility require rigorous precautions against inhalation. Always handle in the hood under supervision***

Continued

Box cont.

diethyl ether (anhydrous)		**flammable, irritant**
cycloheptanone (FW 112.2)	11.6 mL (98 mmol)	
hydrochloric acid (2 M)		**corrosive**
sodium bicarbonate solution (saturated)		
2. Preparation of 1-methylcycloheptene		
potassium bisulfate (FW 136.2)	25 g (0.18 mol)	**hygroscopic, irritant**
3. Preparation of 7-oxo-octanal		
dichloromethane	75 mL	**irritant, toxic**
dimethyl sulfide (FW 62.1)	7.5 mL (102 mmol)	**flammable, stench**
starch-iodide paper		
4. Preparation of queen bee pheromone methyl ester		
methyl (triphenylphosphoranylidene) acetate(FW 334.4) (commercial or prepared as in part 5)		
acetonitrile		**lachrymator, flammable**
hexane		**flammable**
silica for flash chromatography		**irritant dust**
5. Preparation of methyl (triphenylphosphoranylidene)acetate		
triphenylphosphine (FW 262.3)	10 g (38 mmol)	**irritant**
methyl chloroacetate (FW 108.5)	4.1 g (38 mmol)	**corrosive**
toluene		**lachrymator, flammable, irritant**

Procedure

All glassware must be thoroughly dried in a hot (>120°C) oven before use.

HOOD

1. Preparation of 1-methylcycloheptanol

Place the magnesium turnings in two-necked round-bottomed flask fitted with condenser, magnetic stirrer bar and addition funnel,[1] and ad about 50 mL of the anhydrous diethyl ether[2] and a small crystal of iodine. Place the iodomethane[3] in 20 mL of diethyl ether in the addition funnel and add it dropwise to the flask over 0.5 h. The mixture should reflux gently under its own heat of reaction. After the reaction has ceased, a dark solution should result and nearly all the magnesium will have dissolved. Add the cycloheptanone dissolved in 10 mL diethyl ether through the funnel over 20 min, stirring during the addition. When all has been added, stir for 10 min, and acidify by the addition of 2 M hydrochloric acid. Separate the ether layer, wash with sodium bicarbonate solution,[4] dry over $MgSO_4$, filter, and remove the solvent on the rotary evaporator. The product is a dark oil but need not be purified at this stage. Record the yield and IR spectrum (film) of the product.

[1] *See Fig. 3.25*

[2] *See Appendix 2*

[3] ***Toxic!***

[4] ***Care!*** **CO_2** ***evolved***

2. *Preparation of 1-methylcycloheptene*

HOOD

[5]*See Fig. 3.23*

[6]*See Fig. 3.48*

To the product of part 1 contained in a 100mL round-bottomed flask, add the anhydrous potassium bisulfate. Fit a reflux condenser[5] and heat in an oil bath at *ca.* 150°C until the liquid is refluxing gently. Continue to reflux for 30min and then set the apparatus for distillation.[6] Distil out the olefinic product boiling in the range 125–135°C. Record the yield, which should be *ca.* 10g (90%), and retain for the next part of the sequence. Record the IR (film) and NMR ($CDCl_3$) spectra of the distilled product.

3. *Preparation of 7-oxo-octanal*

HOOD

[7]*See Fig. 2.33*

[8]*Time required depends on scale of experiment, and on output of ozonizer*

[9]***Stench!***

Dissolve all the 1-methylcycloheptene obtained in part 2 in 75mL dichloromethane and place the solution in the apparatus for ozonolysis.[7] Cool to −70°C by immersing in a solid CO_2–acetone cooling bath, and pass in ozone/oxygen from the ozonizer. Monitor the gas which emerges, testing with damp starch-iodide paper and continue to pass in ozone until the paper immediately turns dark blue.[8] Add the dimethyl sulfide[9] and allow the mixture to warm to room temperature. Remove the solvent on the rotary evaporator and weigh the 7-oxo-octanal which remains. Record the yield and IR (film) and NMR ($CDCl_3$) spectra of the product.

4. *Preparation of methyl 9-oxodec-2-enoate (queen bee pheromone methyl ester)*

HOOD

[10]*See Chapter 3*

[11]***Care! Eye protection***

To the 7-oxo-octanal obtained in part 3, add an equivalent amount of methyl (triphenylphosphoranylidene)acetate in a round-bottomed flask set up for reflux.[5] For each gram of the 7-oxo-octanal, add 2.35g of phosphorane and sufficient acetonitrile (5–10mL) to dissolve the solid. Reflux the solution and analyze the mixture by TLC,[10] using silica plates eluting with hexane–diethyl ether (1:1), at 30min intervals. Observe the developed plates under UV light.[11] A new product spot should become apparent after 30min and the reaction should be completed after 1h. Cool, add hexane, which will precipitate triphenylphosphine oxide, and filter this off. Concentrate the filtrate on the rotary evaporator, and purify the residue by dry flash chromatography[10] on silica gel, eluting with hexane–ether (1:1). Remove the solvents by rotary evaporation to leave a sample of queen bee pheromone methyl ester. Record the yield, and IR ($CHCl_3$) and NMR ($CDCl_3$) spectra of the product.

HOOD

5. *Preparation of methyl (triphenylphosphoranylidene) acetate (optional)*

Dissolve the triphenylphosphine in 25 mL of toluene and add the methyl chloroacetate. Heat the mixture under reflux[5] for 30 min. Allow the mixture to cool, and then filter the white precipitate of the phosphonium salt by suction. After drying in the air, suspend the solid, with stirring, in 100 mL of water, and add 2 M sodium hydroxide solution. Filter the ylid which precipitates and allow to dry in the air.

Problems

1 Assign all the IR and NMR spectra of the compounds you prepared.
2 What is the double bond geometry in the final product?
3 Suggest an alternative route to 7-oxo-octanal.

Further reading

For a further discussion of the Wittig reaction, see Exps 50–52.
For the uses of ozone, see: EROS, 3837.
M. Barbier, E. Lederer and T. Nomura, *Compt. Rend.*, 1960, **251**, 1133.
H.J. Bestmann, R. Kunstmann and H. Schulz, *Liebigs Ann. Chem.*, 1966, **699**, 33.

Experiment 74 *Synthesis of 6-nitrosaccharin*

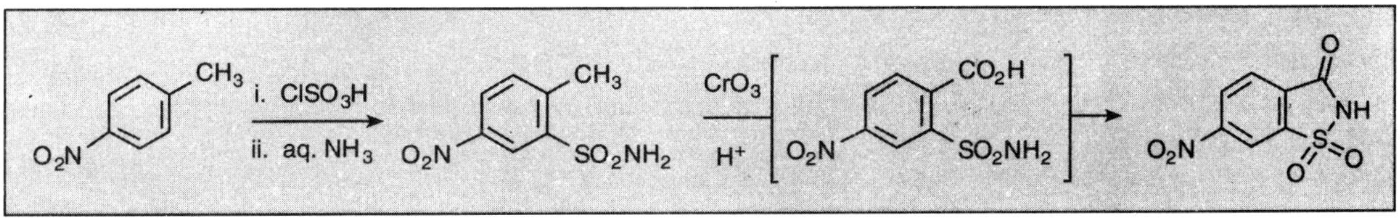

The sweetness in foodstuffs is either due to natural sugars or to added artificial sweeteners. The natural sugars such as sucrose have excellent taste qualities, but have a number of disadvantages, particularly their very high energy content, and the need to use high concentrations in processed and convenience foods. Consequently, artificial (non-nutritive) sweeteners, which are often many hundreds of times sweeter than sucrose, find wide application. Artificial sweeteners have various chemical structures, and the controversy that has surrounded cyclamate (now banned) and saccharin (banned in certain countries) has led to the development of new sweeteners such as Aspartame® and Acesulpham®.

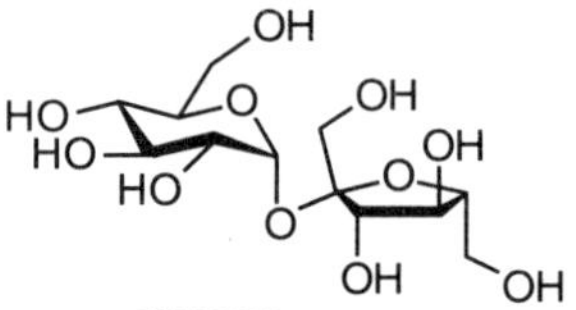

sucrose

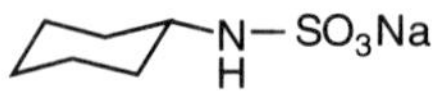

cyclamate (Na salt)

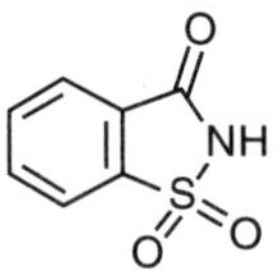

saccharin

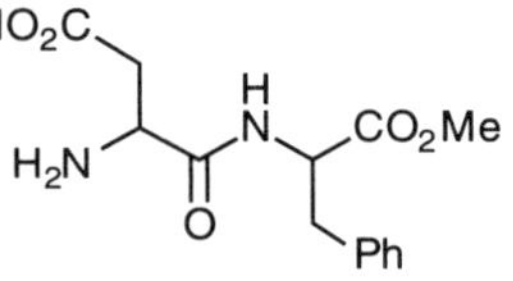

aspartame®

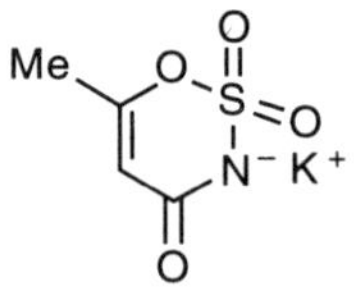

acesulpham®

This project involves the preparation of the 6-nitro derivative of saccharin from 4-nitrotoluene, and illustrates a number of important features of the chemistry of aromatic compounds. The first stage involves the chlorosulfonation of 4-nitrotoluene to give 4-nitrotoluene-2-sulfonyl chloride, which is converted into the corresponding sulfonamide by reaction with aqueous ammonia. Oxidation of the toluene methyl group with chromium(VI) oxide in sulfuric acid gives the *ortho*-sulfonamidobenzoic acid which spontaneously cyclizes to 6-nitrosaccharin.

Level	2
Time	3 × 3 h
Equipment	steam bath; apparatus for reflux, suction filtration, recrystallization

Materials

1. Preparation of 4-nitrotoluene-2-sulfonamide

chlorosulfonic acid (FW 116.5)	12.0 mL, 21.0 g (0.18 mol)	**corrosive, toxic**
4-nitrotoluene (FW 137.4)	6.85 g (50 mmol)	**irritant, toxic**
diethyl ether		**flammable, irritant**
ammonia solution (conc.)		**corrosive, toxic**

2. Preparation of 6-nitrosaccharin

sulfuric acid (conc.)		**corrosive, oxidizer**
chromium(VI) oxide (FW 100.0)	3.0 g (30 mmol)	**cancer suspect agent, oxidizer, toxic**

Procedure

HOOD

1. *Preparation of 4-nitrotoluene-2-sulfonamide*

Place the 4-nitrotoluene in a 25 mL round-bottomed flask, and carefully add the chlorosulfonic acid. Fit a reflux condenser,[1] and heat the flask on a steam bath (or equivalent) for 30 min. Cool the flask in an ice bath, and then carefully pour the reaction mixture into a beaker containing *ca.* 100 g ice,[2] stirring the mixture vigorously with a glass rod. Transfer the mixture to a separatory funnel, and extract it with 2 × 20 mL diethyl ether. Combine the ether extracts and transfer them to a 250 mL beaker. Stir the diethyl ether solution *rapidly*, and slowly add 20 mL ammonia solution.[3] Continue to stir the mixture until a light-brown solid forms. Collect the solid by suction filtration,[4] and wash it well with 20 mL cold diethyl ether, then 40 mL cold water. Dry the solid by suction at the pump for a few minutes, and then recrystallize it from hot water.[5] Record the yield and mp of the product after one recrystallization.

[1] *See Fig. 3.23*

[2] ***Care! Vigorous reaction on quenching with water***

[3] *Heat of reaction will cause diethyl ether to boil*

[4] *See Fig. 3.7*

[5] *Compound is not particularly soluble in hot water; a large volume is required*

2. *Preparation of 6-nitrosaccharin*

Place 12 mL concentrated sulfuric acid in a 100 mL beaker, and add 2.15 g (10 mmol) of *dry* 4-nitrotoluene-2-sulfonamide. Heat the mixture to 65°C on a steam bath (or equivalent), stirring it gently. Add the chromium(VI) oxide in small portions to the stirred solution at such a rate that the temperature is maintained between 65 and 70°C.[6] Do not add the oxidant unless the temperature is at least 65°C. The addition should take 15–30 min, during which time the mixture becomes green and viscous. When the addition is complete, stir the mixture for a further 10 min at 65–70°C, and then cool it in an ice bath. Pour the reaction mixture into a beaker containing 50 mL cold water, and stir for a few minutes until a solid forms. Collect the solid by suction filtration,[4] wash it well with cold water, and dry it by suction at the pump for a few minutes. Recrystallize the product from hot water. Record the yield and mp of your product.

[6] *May be necessary to heat or cool the mixture to maintain the temperature*

Problems

1 Discuss the chlorosulfonation of 4-nitrotoluene. Why is the 2-isomer formed?

2 Write reaction mechanisms for the reaction of the sulfonyl chloride with ammonia, and for the cyclization of the *o*-sulfonamidobenzoic acid.

3 Why are aromatic methyl groups oxidized much more readily than aliphatic methyl groups?

Further reading

For the procedure on which this experiment is based, see: N.C. Rose and S. Rome, *J. Chem. Educ.*, 1970, **47**, 649.

Macrocyclic compounds

Experiment 75 *Preparation of copper phthalocyanine*

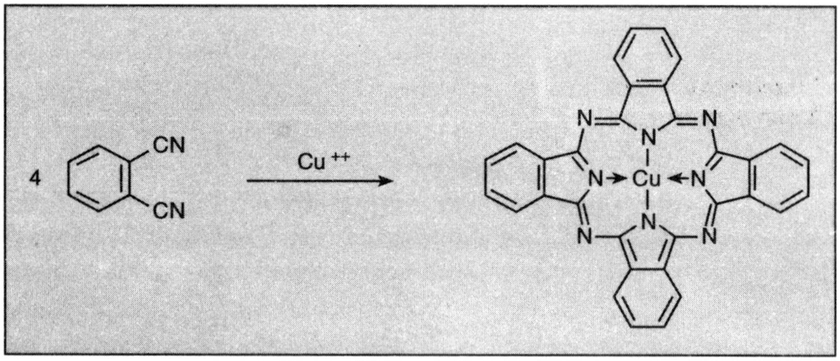

Phthalocyanines, which may contain a variety of coordinated metals, are a class of extremely stable blue pigments. The copper compound in particular is used extensively for the blue colouring of paints and printing inks. The complex ring system is an analogue of the naturally occurring porphyrins (see Experiment 76) of which haem and chlorophyll are examples. Copper phthalocyanine is very simply synthesized from four molecules of phthalonitrile in the presence of the metal salt.

Level	1		
Time	2 × 3 h		
Equipment	apparatus for reflux, suction filtration		
Materials			
phthalonitrile (FW 128.1)		3.2 g (25 mmol)	**irritant, toxic**
anhydrous copper(II) chloride (FW 134.5)		2.0 g (16 mmol)	**irritant, toxic**
1,5-diazabicyclo[4.3.0]non-5-ene (DBN) (FW 124.2)		2.5 g (20 mmol)	**corrosive**
2-methoxyethyl ether (diglyme)		10 mL	

Procedure

[1]*See Fig. 3.23(a)*

Place all the materials in a 100 mL round-bottomed flask[1] and heat until the solvent boils (*ca.* 160°C). Continue to reflux for about 2 h, then cool and pour the contents into water. Bring the water to the boil briefly in order to dissolve unreacted copper compounds, then cool, acidify to remove the base, and filter the copper phthalocyanine. Dry the blue powder in the air. If the copper phthalocyanine is obtained as a brown solid it can be purified as follows: dissolve the finely ground product in concentrated sulfuric acid[2] (*ca.* 5 mL acid per 1 g product). Leave for about 30 min, and then **carefully** pour the acid solution onto 100 g of crushed ice in a beaker. Allow the blue flocculent precipitate

[2]***Care!***

[3] *Often needs 1–2 h*
[4] *See Fig. 3.7*

to coalesce,[3] and collect it by suction filtration.[4] Finally, wash the product thoroughly with hot water, and dry it at 100°C.

Problems

1 Why is the copper complex so stable?
2 Outline the reaction mechanism for the formation of the phthalocyanine.

Further reading

For a series of classic papers on the phthalocyanins by R.P. Linstead and co-workers, see: *J. Chem. Soc.*, 1934, 1016; 1017; 1022; 1027; 1031; 1033.
For a review, see: P. Sayer, M. Gonterman and C.R. Connell, *Acc. Chem. Res.*, 1982, **15**, 73.

Experiment 76 *Synthesis of tetraphenylporphin and its copper complex*

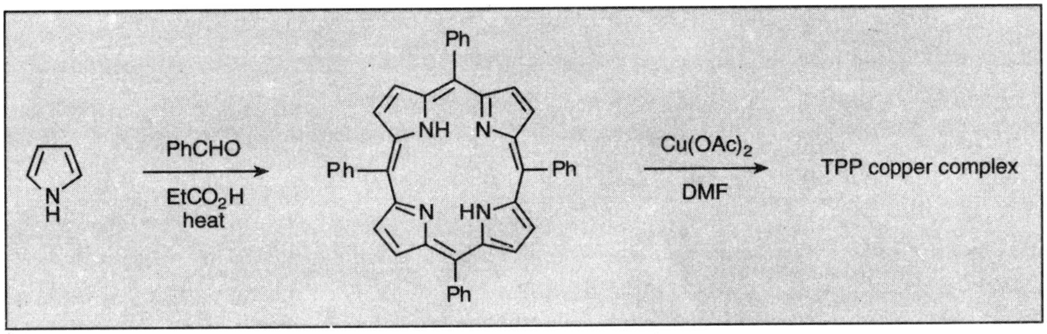

In vertebrates, two proteins, myoglobin and haemoglobin, function as oxygen carriers. Myoglobin is located in muscles where it stores oxygen and releases it as necessary. Haemoglobin is present in red blood cells and is responsible for oxygen transport. Although these natural compounds are complex proteins,

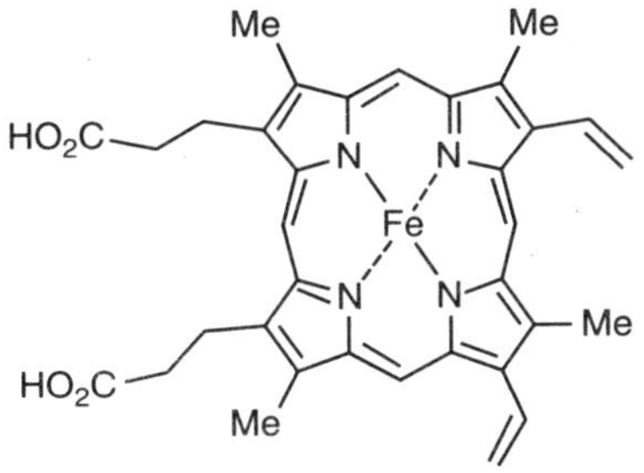

haem

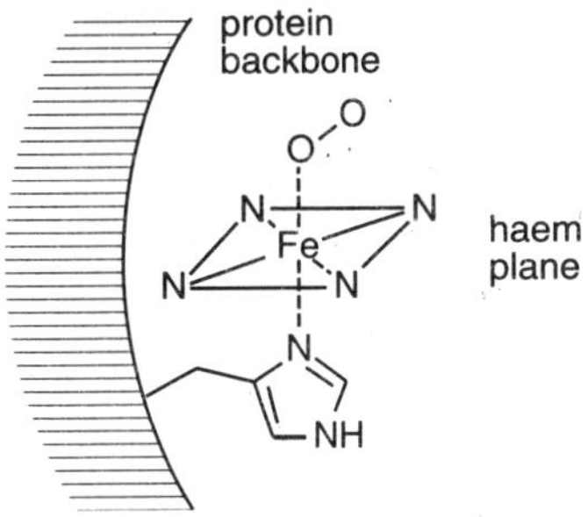

haemoglobin (schematic)

the secret of their oxygen-carrying ability lies in the non-protein part of the molecule, the so-called haem unit. Haem is a planar macrocyclic organic molecule made up of four linked pyrrole rings surrounding an iron atom. Although the iron is associated with four nitrogens it can accommodate two additional ligands, one above and one below the plane of the ring. In haemoglobin one of these ligands is the imidazole ring of a histidine residue in the protein chain, and, more importantly, the other ligand is molecular oxygen.

Haem is an example of a general class of biologically important macrocyclic nitrogen-containing pigments known as *porphyrins*. All porphyrins have the ability to complex metal ions and the simplest, unsubstituted porphyrin is known as porphin. The ring system is planar, contains 18 delocalizable π-electrons, and on the basis of the Hückel $[4n + 2]$ rule, can be considered as an aromatic compound. This project illustrates a simple laboratory preparation of a porphyrin derivative, 5,10,15,20-tetraphenylporphin (*meso*-tetraphenylporphyrin or TPP, for short), and its copper(II) complex. The preparation involves the condensation of benzaldehyde with pyrrole in boiling propanoic acid. Both TPP and its copper complex are deeply coloured solids with interesting UV/visible spectra.

Level	2
Time	2 × 3 h
Equipment	hotplate; apparatus for reflux, suction filtration
Instruments	UV

Materials

1. Preparation of meso-*tetraphenylporphin*		
pyrrole (FW 67.1)	1.4 mL, 1.35 g (20 mmol)	**flammable**
benzaldehyde (FW 106.1)	2.0 mL, 2.1 g (20 mmol)	**irritant, toxic**
propanoic acid	75 mL	**corrosive, toxic**
methanol	*ca.* 50 mL	**flammable, toxic**
2. Preparation of copper complex		
dimethylformamide	10 mL	**irritant, toxic**
copper(II) acetate monohydrate (FW 199.7)	40 mg (0.2 mmol)	**irritant**

Procedure

HOOD

1. Preparation of meso-*tetraphenylporphin*

Place the propanoic acid in a 250 mL round-bottomed flask, fit a reflux condenser,[1] add some boiling stones, and bring the acid to reflux. Simultaneously add the pyrrole[2] and the benzaldehyde to the refluxing propanoic acid down through the condenser using two Pasteur pipettes. Continue to heat the mixture under reflux for 30 min. Cool the mixture to room temperature,[3] and collect the deeply coloured product by suction filtration.[4] Wash the product thoroughly with methanol until the methanol washings are colourless. Dry the product by suction for a few minutes. Record the yield and the UV spectrum ($CHCl_3$) of your product.

[1] *See Fig. 3.23*

[2] *Best if freshly distilled*

[3] *May be left at this stage*

[4] *See Fig. 3.7*

HOOD

2. Preparation of TPP copper complex (5,10,15,20-tetraphenylporphyrinatocopper(II))

Place the dimethylformamide in a 25 mL Erlenmeyer flask, add a few boiling stones, and heat the flask on a hotplate until the solvent begins to boil gently. Add 100 mg (0.16 mmol) TPP to the hot dimethylformamide, and allow it to dissolve. Add the copper(II) acetate, and continue to heat the solvent at its boiling point for 5 min. Cool the flask in an ice bath for about 15 min, and then dilute the mixture with 10 mL distilled water. Collect the solid product by suction filtration,[4] wash it well with water, and dry by suction. Record the yield and the UV spectrum ($CHCl_3$) of your product. If required, the product can be purified by column chromatography on alumina,[5] eluting with chloroform.[6]

[5] *See Chapter 3*

[6] ***Toxic!***

Problems

1 Suggest a reaction mechanism for the reaction of pyrrole with benzaldehyde.
2 Compare and contrast the UV spectra of TPP and its copper complex.
3 Which other metals might form complexes with TPP?

Further reading

For the procedures on which this experiment is based, see: A.D. Adler, F.R. Longo, J.D. Finarelli, J. Goldmacher, J. Assour and L. Korsakoff, *J. Org. Chem.*, 1967, **32**, 476.
A.D. Adler, F.R. Longo and V. Varadi, *Inorg. Synth.*, 1975, **16**, 213.

Chemiluminescence

Most exothermic reactions give out their energy in the form of heat and, if the rate of production is great enough, this can lead to light being evolved as incandescence. However, a small group of reactions have the fascinating property of dissipating the excess energy in the form of 'cold' light, referred to as *chemiluminescence*.

This somewhat eerie phenomenon finds application in providing emergency lighting, particularly on occasions where the risk of explosion is high, and chemiluminescence is also useful in a wide range of analytical procedures. However, nature pre-dates humans by hundreds of millions of years for finding uses for *bioluminescence*. Otherwise unremarkable insects such as the firefly (*Lampyridae*) attract their mates by sending vivid pulsed messages to each other at night. The various species of aptly named angler fish, living in the endless dark of the deep ocean, use luminescent lures dangling over cavernous mouths to attract their prey, and other fish such as *Argyropelecus* have developed defence mechanisms based upon breaking up the body outline, whilst the crustacean *Cypridina* distracts potential predators with sudden bursts of light. With this head start over people, it is not surprising that bioluminescence provides us with the most efficient systems. The firefly, with its enzymic process powered by ATP, still holds the record for the most efficient chemiluminescent reaction, with a quantum yield of 88% for the isolated system, whereas few manmade systems approach 30%.

Whilst *incandescence* from hot bodies is the result of emission from vibrationally excited molecules, *fluorescence* and *chemiluminescence* are derived from electronically excited species. In fluorescence, the excited species is produced by the initial absorption of a quantum of light; whereas chemiluminescence, as its name suggests, generates the excited species by chemical means. A chemiluminescent reaction generally consists of three stages, as exemplified below for the peroxyoxalate system. In the first step, an energetic species (in this case dioxetane) is generated chemically. The chemical energy contained in this intermediate is then converted into excitation energy, usually by transfer to a *fluorescer* (also termed a *sensitizer*), and finally, the fluorescer in the singlet excited state returns to its electronic ground state by emitting a quantum of light. As the wavelength of light emitted is dependent upon the fluorescer, the peroxyoxalate system may be modified to produce differently coloured chemiluminescent systems.

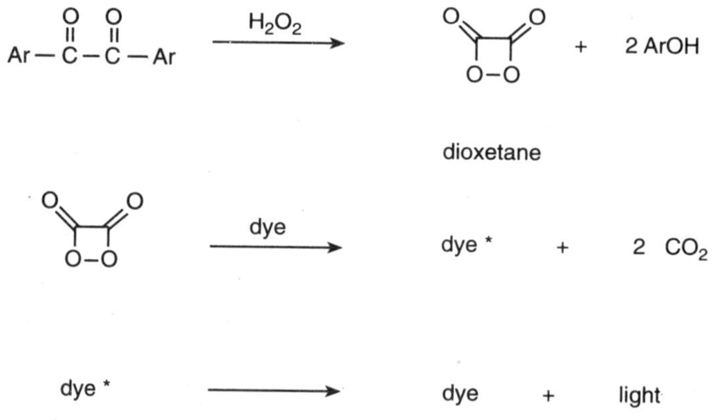

Experiment 77 Observation of sensitized fluorescence in an alumina-supported oxalate system

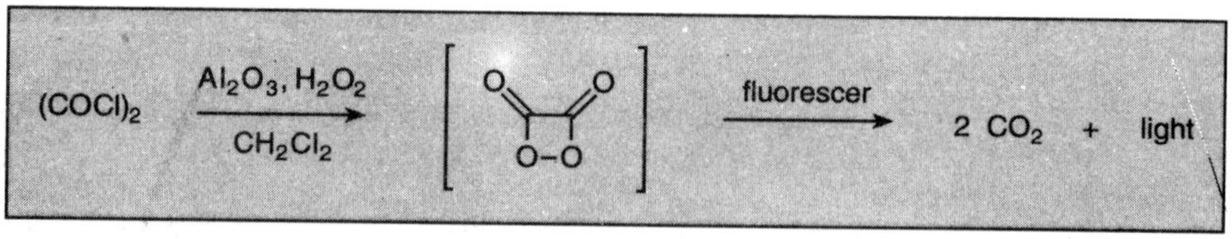

This procedure permits the simple preparation of a chemiluminescent system based upon the dioxetane system. The reaction is known to be base catalyzed and, as the effect is observed upon the surface of the alumina in the three-phase system, it seems likely that the first step involves reaction of the oxalyl chloride with free hydroxyl groups on the alumina. The colour of the emitted light depends upon the nature of the added fluorescer.

Level	1
Time	1 h

Materials

oxalyl chloride (FW 126.9)	*ca.* 0.5 mL (20 drops)	**lachrymator, corrosive**

NOTE: *oxalyl chloride reacts violently with moisture, producing hydrogen chloride, carbon monoxide and carbon dioxide. All manipulations with this reagent must be carried out in the hood and gloves should be worn*

perylene (FW 252.3)	*ca.* 40 mg	
9,10-diphenylanthracene (FW 330.4)	*ca.* 40 mg	
chromatographic grade alumina		**irritant dust**
dichloromethane		**irritant, toxic**
hydrogen peroxide (3%, '10 volume') (H_2O_2, FW 34.0)		**corrosive, oxidizer**

Procedure

HOOD

Take two 250 mL Erlenmeyer flasks with ground glass stoppers and in each of them prepare a slurry consisting of 4 g of chromatographic grade alumina, 25 mL of dichloromethane and 5 mL of 3% hydrogen peroxide. To one of the flasks add the perylene and to the other add the 9,10-diphenylanthracene, swirl both mixtures thoroughly, mark the flasks, stopper and set them aside. Meanwhile, prepare a solution of the oxalyl chloride[1] in 10 mL of dichloromethane in a 50 mL Erlenmeyer flask and stopper this flask. In subdued light, transfer approximately 2 mL of the oxalyl chloride solution with a pipette to the slurry in the flask containing the perylene sensitizer. Loosely stopper the flask,[2] and gently swirl the contents, observing the colour of the light evolved and the exact site of evolution (aqueous phase, dichloromethane or alumina surface). Repeat the procedure and observations with the slurry in the flask containing the 9,10-diphenylanthracene. In each case, the luminescence may be renewed by adding a fresh quantity of oxalyl chloride solution. Be sure that all the oxalyl chloride has reacted (no more luminescence) before attempting to dispose of the reaction mixture.

[1] ***Care! Wear gloves***

[2] ***Caution! Do not permit pressure to build up***

Further reading

For reviews of chemiluminescence, see: M.M. Rauhut, *Acc. Chem. Res.*, 1969, **2**, 80; F. McCapra, *Acc. Chem. Res.*, 1976, **9**, 201; S.K. Gill, *Aldrichimica Acta*, 1983, **16**, 59; W. Adam, W.J. Baader, C. Babatsikos and E. Schmidt, *Bull. Soc. Chim. Belg.*, 1984, **93**, 605.

For an article listing examples of bioluminescence, see: F. McCapra, *Biochem. Soc. Trans.*, 1979, **7**, 1239.

Photochromism and piezochromism

Experiment 78 looks at an example of a photochromic compound, but the phenomenon of piezochromism, in which a substance changes colour under the influence of applied pressure, is a rarer physical property. Some compounds thought to show this property are actually thermochromic compounds responding to the heat generated on grinding, but the 'piezochromic dimer' of White and Sonnenberg which will be prepared in Experiment 79 is an example of the genuine article. This pressure sensitivity is due to a C-4 linked dimer obtained by the oxidative coupling of two units of 2,4,5-triphenylimidazole (lophine), itself simply prepared from a condensation of benzil, benzaldehyde and ammonia. This colourless C-4 linked dimer can be converted into the purple free radical by homolytic cleavage of the bridging bond as a result of the shear forces generated on grinding. This cleavage also occurs on dissolving in organic solvents or exposure to light, but on storing the purple solutions in the dark, the colour is lost due to radical recombination to form a second dimeric species. This species also demonstrates photochromism and the purple–colourless cycle can be repeated almost indefinitely. Bubbling air through the solvent discharges the colour rapidly, as does the addition of a free-radical scavenger such as hydroquinone.

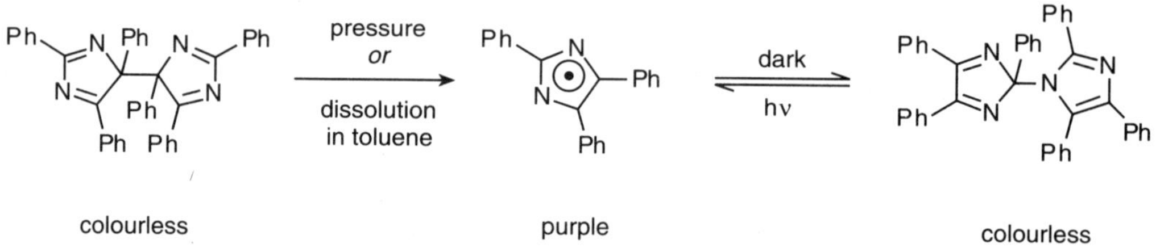

Experiment 78 *Synthesis of 2-[(2,4-dinitrophenyl)methyl]pyridine; a reversibly photochromic compound*

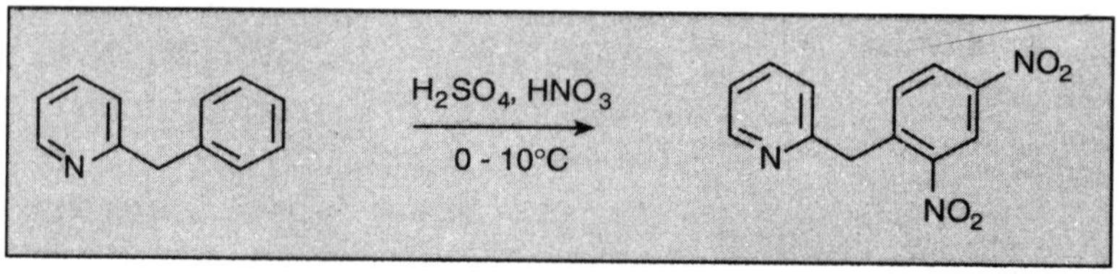

The title compound exhibits the unusual property of photochromism as both the solid and in solution. In the absence of light, the crystals are tan in colour but, on exposure to bright sunlight, they turn a deep blue within a few minutes. In the dark, the crystals regain their tan colouration over a period of a day and the interconversion is apparently indefinitely reversible. The ability of a molecule to be switched reversibly between two forms has aroused much interest in the area of information storage and retrieval; although the stringent requirements for rapid and repeatable interconversion, coupled with stability in the absence of the switching impulse, drastically limit the number of potential candidates. The probable source of the photochromic behaviour of 2-[(2,4-dinitrophenyl)methyl]pyridine is the interconversion between two tautomeric forms. Evidence in support of this is the lack of activity in the analogous 2-[(4-nitrophenyl)methyl]pyridine.

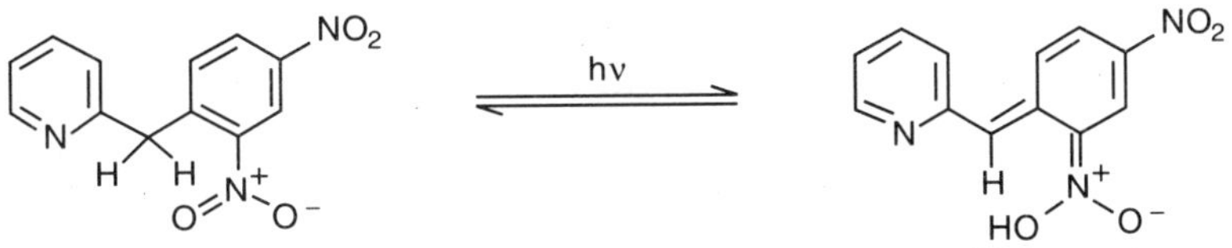

tan   blue

The photochromic material can be obtained readily by dinitration of 2-benzylpyridine. Relatively forcing conditions are necessary due to the deactivating effect of the first nitro-substituent. Substitution of the pyridine nucleus is very unfavoured as it is almost totally protonated under the highly acidic reaction conditions and therefore highly resistant to electrophilic attack. **Extreme care should be exercised when using 2-benzylpyridine as it is reported to be a severe poison.** It has a melting point below room temperature under most conditions (mp 8–10°C). Being more easily handled as a liquid, any solid samples should be first carefully liquefied by standing the container in a bath of slightly warm water (*ca.* 30°C) in the hood.

Level	2
Time	3 h
Equipment	stirrer/hotplate; apparatus for extraction/separation, recrystallization

Materials		
2-benzylpyridine (FW 169.2)	1.60 mL (1.7 g, 10 mmol)	**irritant, toxic**
sulfuric acid (conc.)	10.0 mL	**corrosive, oxidizer**
fuming nitric acid (*ca.* 90%)	2.0 mL	**corrosive, oxidizer**
sodium hydroxide solution (2 M)		**corrosive**
diethyl ether		**flammable, irritant**
ethanol (95%)		**flammable, toxic**

HOOD

Procedure

Place the sulfuric acid in a 25 mL Erlenmeyer flask containing a magnetic stirrer bar and cool it to below 5°C in an ice–salt bath on the stirrer/hotplate.[1] Clamp the flask securely, stir gently and add the 2-benzylpyridine dropwise from a Pasteur pipette at such a rate that the temperature remains below 10°C. Similarly add the fuming nitric acid,[2] keeping the temperature below 10°C at all times during the addition.[3] Remove the ice bath, replacing it with a water bath and heat the mixture to 80°C with stirring. After 20 min at this temperature, pour the contents onto 100 g of crushed ice in a 500 mL Erlenmeyer flask,[4] rinsing the reaction flask with ice-water (*ca.* 20 mL). Place the flask in an ice bath, replace the bar magnet with one of a larger size, stir gently, and add the sodium hydroxide solution carefully from an addition funnel until the mixture is strongly alkaline (*ca.* pH 11).[5] Add 150 mL of diethyl ether to the resulting milky yellow mixture and continue stirring for a further 15 min to extract the product into the organic phase. Separate the ether layer, dry it over

[1] *See Fig. 3.20(a)*

[2] ***Care! Wear gloves***

[3] *The reaction becomes dark brown initially but lightens as the acid is added*

[4] ***Care!***

[5] *Do not add the base too quickly to avoid the mixture becoming hot*

$MgSO_4$, filter into a 250 mL round-bottomed flask[6] and reduce the volume to 30 mL on the rotary evaporator without external heating. Cool the flask in ice to complete crystallization, collect the precipitated crystalline material by filtration with suction[7] and recrystallize from 95% ethanol (*ca.* 10 mL g^{-1}) using a little decolourizing charcoal if the crude product appears dark.[8] Record the yield, appearance and mp of your purified product. Observe the effect of sunlight on a few crystals.

[6] *In a smaller flask bumping may be a problem*

[7] *See Fig. 3.7*

[8] *Avoid prolonged exposure to light during the recrystallization*

Problems

1 Predict the major products of aromatic chlorination of the following: (i) chlorobenzene, (ii) 1,2-dichlorobenzene, (iii) 1,3-dimethylbenzene (*m*-xylene), and (iv) trichloromethylbenzene.

2 Define the electrophilic reagent in the following aromatic substitution reactions: (i) nitration, (ii) chlorination, (iii) sulfonation, (iv) acetylation, (v) alkylation with 2-chlorobutane, and (vi) alkylation with 2-methylpropene (isobutene).

3 Classify each of the following substituents as *ortho-*, *meta-* or *para-* directing and say if it is activating or deactivating.

(a)
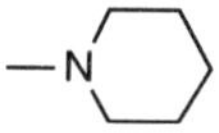

(b)
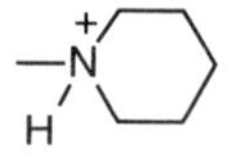

(c)
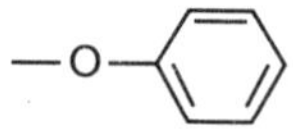

(d)
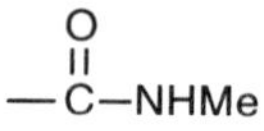

(e)
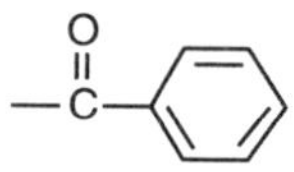

(f)
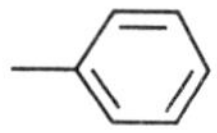

(g)
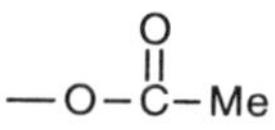

(h)
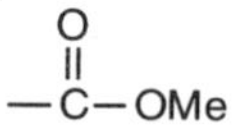

(i)
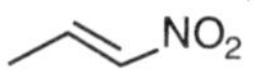

4 Account for the following monochlorination relative rate ratios: benzene, 1; methylbenzene, 344; 1,4-dimethylbenzene, 2100; 1,3-dimethylbenzene, 180 000.

Further reading

A.L. Bluhm, J. Weinstein and J.A. Sousa, *J. Org. Chem.*, 1963, **28**, 1989.

Experiment 79

Preparation of 2,4,5-triphenylimidazole (lophine) and conversion into its piezochromic and photochromic dimers

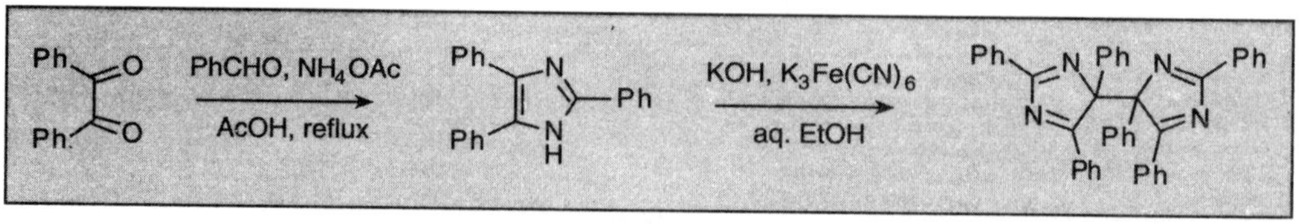

The preparation of 2,4,5-triphenylimidazole is simply carried out by refluxing a solution of benzil, benzaldehyde and ammonium acetate in ethanoic acid to give the condensation product. The oxidative dimerization has been described using either sodium hypochlorite or potassium ferricyanide and use of the latter oxidant is described here.

Level	2
Time	2 × 3 h
Equipment	stirrer/hotplate, pestle and mortar; apparatus for reflux, recrystallization

Materials

1. Preparation of 2,4,5-triphenylimidazole

benzaldehyde (FW 106.1)	2.65 g, 2.5 mL (25 mmol)	**toxic**
benzil (FW 210.2)	5.25 g (25 mmol)	**irritant**
ammonium ethanoate (FW 77.1)	*ca.* 10 g (130 mmol)	
glacial ethanoic acid (100%)		**corrosive**
ethanol (95%)		**flammable, toxic**
ammonium hydroxide (*ca.* 30% NH_3)		**corrosive, irritant**

2. Preparation of piezochromic and photochromic dimers

2,4,5-triphenylimidazole (from part 1) (FW 296.4)	1.5 g (5 mmol)	
potassium ferricyanide	4.5 g	
potassium hydroxide pellets	12.0 g	**corrosive, hygroscopic**
ethanol (95%)		**flammable, toxic**
light petroleum (bp 40–60°C)		**flammable**
toluene		**flammable**

Procedure

1. Preparation of 2,4,5-triphenylimidazole

HOOD

Dissolve the benzil, benzaldehyde and ammonium ethanoate in 100 mL ethanoic acid in a 250 mL round-bottomed flask containing a magnetic stirrer bar, and heat the mixture to reflux in an oil bath for 1 h with stirring.[1] After this time, cool the mixture to room temperature and filter to remove any precipitate which may be present. Add 300 mL of water to the filtrate and collect the precipitate by filtration with suction.[2] Neutralize the filtrate with ammonium hydroxide and collect the second crop of solid. Combine the two crops of precipitate and recrystallize from aqueous ethanol. Record the yield and mp of your purified material.

[1] *See Fig. 3.24*

[2] *See Fig. 3.7*

2. Preparation of piezochromic and photochromic dimers

Dissolve the potassium hydroxide in 100 mL of 95% ethanol with heating and to this add 1.5 g of 2,4,5-triphenylimidazole. When fully dissolved add the mixture to a 1 L beaker containing a large magnetic stirrer bar and cool to 5°C in an ice-water bath with stirring. Prepare a solution of the potassium ferricyanide in 450 mL of water and place this in an addition funnel clamped securely over the beaker. Add the potassium ferricyanide solution to the vigorously stirred ethanolic mixture at such a rate that the temperature of the reaction does not exceed 10°C.[3] (This should require about 1 h.) In the initial stages of the addition, a violet colouration develops to be replaced by a light-grey precipitate. After addition is complete, filter off the precipitate with suction, washing thoroughly with water (5 × 50 mL). Dry the precipitate on the filter by rapid washing with *cold* 50% ethanol (10 mL) followed by light petroleum (2 × 25 mL). Record the yield, appearance and mp of your material and store it in the dark.[4] Place a small quantity of your product in a mortar, grind it and observe the colour change. Dissolve 20 mg of the material in 30 mL of toluene, stopper and store the mixture in the dark. After the solution has become colourless or nearly so, stand the solution in strong sunlight or irradiate it with a bright tungsten light and note the effect. Return the solution to the dark and observe it after a day or so.

[3] *Higher temperatures lead to several products*

[4] *May be left at this stage*

Problems

1 Write out a reasonable mechanism for the formation of 2,4,5-triphenylimidazole.
2 Discuss any chemical or physical method that might be used to demonstrate that the violet colouration is caused by radical species.
3 Suggest a mechanism by which the oxidative coupling of two molecules of 2,4,5-triphenylimidazole occurs.
4 What features of the radical favour its formation? Give other examples of relatively long-lived radical species.

Further reading

For spurious piezochromism of dianthraquinone, see: A. Schönberg and E. Singer, *Tetrahedron Lett.*, 1975, 1925.
For the procedures on which this experiment is based, see: D.M. White and J. Sonnenberg, *J. Am. Chem. Soc.*, 1966, **88**, 3825; M. Pickering, *J. Chem. Educ.*, 1980, **57**, 833.
For other uses of potassium ferricyanide as oxidant, see: EROS, 4218.

9.3 Aspects of physical organic chemistry

The investigation of organic chemistry by the techniques of physical chemistry has been a fruitful area of study for many years. Physical organic chemistry, as this part of the subject is known, is concerned with the details of reaction mechanism, and involves the measurement of reaction rates, equilibrium constants, heats of reactions, and other similar 'physical' parameters. This section reflects some aspects of physical organic chemistry, and leads you, the student, to think in quantitative terms about some simple organic reactions.

Experiment 80 — *Preparation and properties of the stabilized carbo-cations triphenylmethyl fluoborate and tropylium fluoborate*

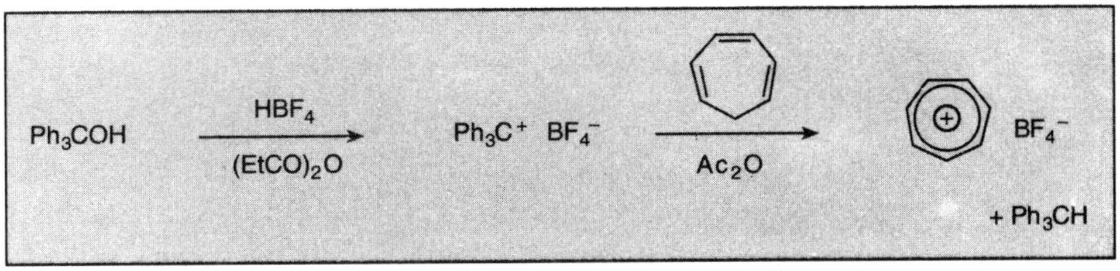

The triphenylmethyl cation is one of the few examples of a carbo-cation whose salts are sufficiently stable to permit isolation. Nonetheless, it is highly electrophilic and its preparation must be carried out under anhydrous conditions in order to prevent reaction with any water present. The preparation described here is carried out using propanoic anhydride as the reaction solvent, as this combines selectively with the water formed during the course of the reaction. The effect of adding pyridine to the fluoborate salt of the cation will be studied, and the salt can also be used to generate another stabilized carbo-cation, the tropylium ion. Triphenylmethyl fluoborate is capable of abstracting a hydride ion from cycloheptatriene to form this aromatic 6π-electron species which is stable enough to be stored and handled in air.

Level	3
Time	3 h (both experiments can be carried out in this time)
Equipment	magnetic stirrer; apparatus for stirring under nitrogen with addition by syringe and cooling, 5 mL syringe and needle, vacuum desiccator, solid CO_2–acetone cooling bath
Instruments	UV

Materials

1. Preparation of triphenylmethyl fluoborate

triphenylmethanol (FW 260.3)	2.60 g (10 mmol)	
propanoic anhydride	25 mL	**lachrymator, corrosive**
fluoboric acid (FW 87.8) (60% aqueous solution)	2.0 mL (13.7 mmol)	**corrosive, toxic**

NOTE: ***great care must be taken when handling fluoboric acid. Always wear gloves and seek immediate treatment if any is splashed onto the skin***

diethyl ether (sodium dried)	**flammable, irritant**
dichloromethane	**irritant, toxic**
pyridine	**flammable, irritant, stench**

Continued on p. 648

Box cont.

2. *Preparation of tropylium fluoborate*		
triphenylmethyl fluoborate (from part 1)	1.0 g (3 mmol)	**hygroscopic, toxic**
cycloheptatriene (FW 92.1)	0.5 mL, 0.45 g (5 mmol)	**flammable, toxic**
ethanoic anhydride		**lachrymator, corrosive**
diethyl ether		**flammable, irritant**
ethanol (absolute)		**flammable, toxic**

Procedure

All apparatus must be thoroughly dried in a hot (>120°C) oven before use.

1. Preparation of triphenylmethyl fluoborate

Set up a 100 mL three-necked flask containing a magnetic stirrer bar with a −10 to 110°C thermometer, nitrogen bubbler and septum.[1] Connect the apparatus to the nitrogen source and add the triphenylmethanol and propanoic anhydride to the flask. Warm the contents to 45°C using a water bath with stirring until all of the solid has dissolved and then cool the contents to *ca.* 0°C by partially immersing the flask in a −20°C cooling bath. Add the fluoboric acid dropwise to the stirred solution by syringe,[2] keeping the temperature of the reaction mixture below 10°C, and then allow the mixture to cool to *ca.* 0°C for 15 min. Filter off the orange precipitate on a sinter funnel with suction[3] and wash the residue with sodium-dried diethyl ether[4] *as rapidly as possible* until the washings are colourless. Dry the crystals briefly by suction and then transfer them rapidly to the vacuum desiccator. *Avoid prolonged contact of the product with the atmosphere.* Record the yield and obtain the UV spectrum of the salt in dichloromethane.[5] Prepare a solution by dissolving *ca.* 5 mg of your product in 10 mL of solvent and then further dilute 1 mL of this solution to 10 mL. After recording the UV spectrum, add 1 drop of pyridine, shake the solution and immediately re-run the spectrum.

[1] *See Fig. 3.22*

[2] ***Care!***

[3] *See Fig. 3.7*

[4] *See Appendix 2*

[5] *May be left until convenient, bearing in mind the lability of the salt*

2. Preparation of tropylium fluoborate

Dissolve the triphenylmethyl fluoborate in 25 mL ethanoic anhydride in a predried 100 mL Erlenmeyer flask containing a magnetic stirrer bar and add the cycloheptatriene with stirring. Note any colour changes and then add 100 mL of diethyl ether and filter off the white precipitate on a sinter with suction. Wash the solid on the sinter with diethyl ether and dry briefly in a vacuum desiccator. Record the yield of your material and obtain the UV spectrum in dry ethanol.

Problems

1 Comment upon the changes noted in the UV spectra of triphenylmethyl fluoborate before and after the addition of pyridine. Why is the salt coloured?

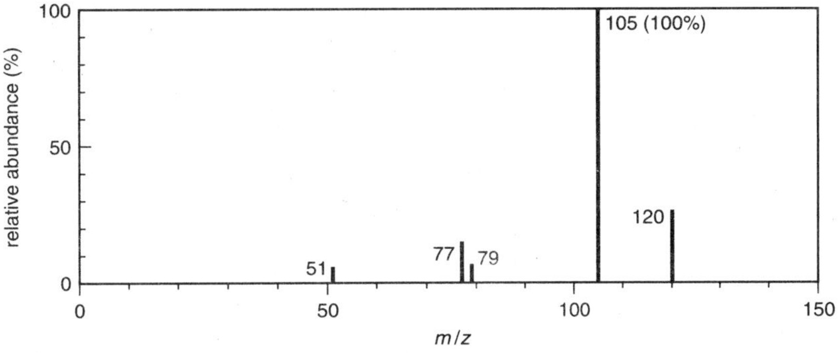

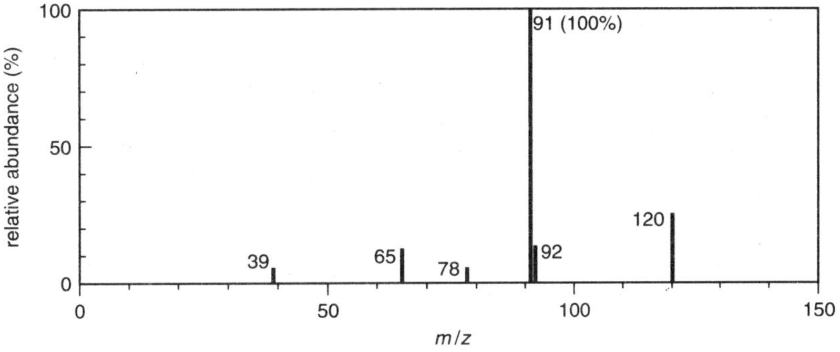

2 Comment upon the wavelengths of absorptions in the UV spectrum of tropylium fluoborate. What other spectroscopic evidence points to the aromaticity of the tropylium ion?

3 The cyclooctatetraene cation may be easily formed by protonation of cyclooctatetraene. The chemical shifts of H[a] and H[b] are as shown. Suggest a reason for the relative stability of this cation.

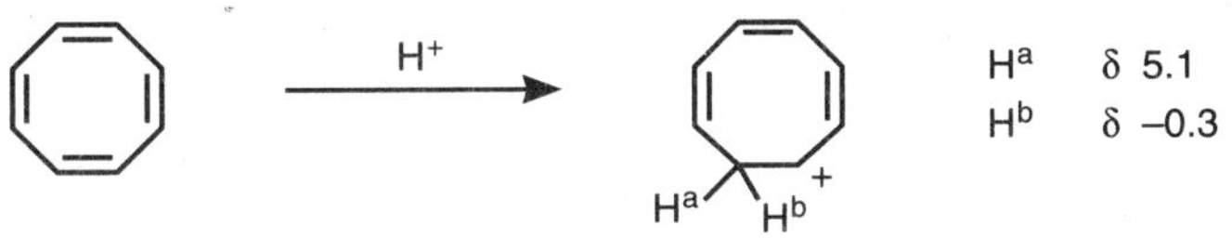

4 An aromatic compound has been identified by combustion analysis as either propylbenzene or (1-methyl)ethylbenzene. On the basis of the mass spectrum shown below propose which of the two isomers corresponds to the unknown and explain your reasoning.

5 The 'trityl' (triphenylmethyl) group is a useful protecting group, and has found particular use in peptide synthesis for terminal amine protection. What are the advantages and disadvantages of such a protecting group.

Experiment 81 — *Measurement of acid dissociation constants of phenols: demonstration of a linear free-energy relationship*

$$\mathrm{ArOH} + \mathrm{OH} \underset{}{\overset{K_a}{\rightleftharpoons}} \mathrm{ArO^-} + \mathrm{H_2O}$$

Phenols are more acidic than alcohols (pK_A values lie in the range 8–10) and are capable of dissociation in aqueous alkali. The extent of dissociation may be assumed to be 0% in acidic solution and 100% in 0.1 M sodium hydroxide (pH = 12) and these extremes may be characterized by different values of absorbance at some wavelength, λ, in their ultraviolet spectra. The extent of dissociation at some intermediate pH can also be estimated by absorption at the same wavelength and, if the pH is known, can permit the estimation of the pK_A of the phenol.

If the pK_A values of a series of substituted phenols are measured, a *Hammett plot* (pK_A against *substituent constants*, σ) can be made and the susceptibility of the acidity of phenols to substituents (the *reaction constant*, ρ) can be estimated.

Level	3
Time	2 × 3 h (for measurements on three or four phenols)
Equipment	volumetric glassware
Instruments	UV

Materials

Very small quantities (0.1 g each) of a range of phenols such as:

phenol, 3-cresol, 4-cresol	
3-chlorophenol, 4-chlorophenol, 3-nitrophenol	
4-methoxyphenol, 4-hydroxyacetophenone	**All phenols are corrosive**
borax buffer solution (pH = 9.00) (sodium tetraborate decahydrate (FW 381.4), 9.535 g made up to 1 L in distilled water and to this, 92 mL 0.1 M HCl added)	
hydrochloric acid (2 M)	**corrosive**
sodium hydroxide (2 M)	**corrosive**

Procedure

Prepare a solution of a phenol in the pH 9 buffer solution[1] such that its absorption in the ultraviolet spectrum is near the middle of the absorbance scale. This may conveniently be done by placing a little of the phenol (about 0.05 g) in a conical flask and adding 100 mL of buffer solution. Shake or stir the solution and then run its ultraviolet spectrum between 350 and 250 nm, observing the maximum in that region. Dilute with buffer solution, or add more phenol as necessary until the main absorption maximum at about 270 nm is around half-way on the absorbance scale (*ca.* $A = 1$). Decant or filter the clear solution free of any remaining undissolved phenol into a clean flask. This will be the stock solution of the phenol, and its concentration will be around 10^{-4} M although this need not be known. Now transfer by pipette[2] 20 mL of stock solution into each of three 25 mL volumetric flasks and make up to the mark, respectively, with 2 M HCl, buffer solution and 2 M sodium hydroxide. The three solutions will then contain the same concentration of phenol in undissociated, partially dissociated (at pH 9.00), and completely dissociated forms respectively. Record the UV spectra of these three solutions and determine the absorbances of each at a chosen wavelength, either that of the maximum for the dissociated or the undissociated form.[3] The former is usually

[1] *Using pH9 buffer gives satisfactory results for phenols with pK_A values in the range 8–10*

[2] *Use a pipette filler*

[3] *The absorbances of the three solutions must be measured at the same wavelength*

the more satisfactory since the difference is greater. Repeat the experiment for a series of substituted phenols. Note that the wavelength at which you carry out the measurements will not necessarily be the same for each compound. It must be selected in order to give a satisfactory difference in absorbance between dissociated and undissociated forms.

Calculation

If the absorbances of the solutions in acidic, buffered and basic media are A_a, A and A_b, respectively,

$$A = xA_b + (1 - x)A_a$$

in which x is the mole fraction of the dissociated (phenolate) form.

The mole fraction, x, is defined as:

$$x = [ArO^-]/[ArO^-] + [ArOH]$$

hence

$$x = (A - A_a)/(A_b - A_a)$$

and the indicator ratio, I, = $[ArOH]/[ArO^-] = (1 - x)/x$, since

$$pK_A = pH + \log I$$

$$pK_A = pH + \log[(1 - x)/x)]$$

from which the pK_A of the phenol may be calculated.

Linear free-energy relationship

Substituent effects, defined with reference to the dissociations of benzoic acids by the Hammett equation,

$$\log K_X/K_H = \sigma$$

(where K_X, K_H are dissociation constants of X-substituted benzoic acid and benzoic acid itself, respectively) would be expected to be paralleled by their effects on phenol acidity. Plot your values of pK_A of the phenols against substituent constants, σ. The following values may be used:

Substituent	σ-*meta*	σ-*para*
H	0.00	0.00
Me	–0.06	–0.17
Cl	0.37	0.22
OMe	0.11	–0.28
Ac	0.38	0.48
NO_2	0.71	0.78

Calculate the best (least-squares) slope of the plot which is the value of the reaction constant, ρ. Interpret this value.

Problems

1 The following table sets out values of the pK_A of halogen-substituted benzoic acids and phenols.

	Benzoic acid, 4.76			Phenol, 10.00		
	o-	*m*-	*p*-	*o*-	*m*-	*p*-
F	3.83	4.42	4.70	8.70	9.21	9.91
Cl	3.48	4.39	4.53	8.53	9.13	9.42
Br	3.41	4.37	4.49	8.54	9.03	9.36
I	3.42	4.41	4.46	8.51	9.06	9.30

Construct Hammett plots from these values and examine the fit for *ortho*-, *meta*- and *para*-series. Calculate the reaction constant, ρ, and comment upon its magnitude.

2 What approximate value of σ would you expect to obtain for the following substituents (positive or negative, large or small)?

a	b	c	d	e
–OEt	$-SO_2Et$	–CN	–SEt	$-NHCOCH_3$

Experiment 82 *Measurement of solvent polarity*

The term *polarity* refers to the ability of a solvent to associate with (*solvate*) ionic and dipolar substances. The attractive forces between the solvent and solute molecules are mainly electrostatic, but hydrogen bonding also contributes. Most organic chemists develop an 'intuitive feel' for how polar or non-polar certain solvents are, but occasionally intuition lets you down and there is a need to put the concept of solvent polarity on a firm experimental quantitative basis. Several attempts have been made to quantify solvent polarity; one way is to measure the rate of chemical reaction which proceeds from electronically neutral starting materials to a charged transition state or to a transition state in which there is considerable charge separation. Since polar solvents will stabilize a polar transition state (lower its energy) by solvation, the rate of the reaction will be faster in polar solvents than in non-polar ones. Hence the rate of reaction gives a quantitative measure of solvent polarity. One such reaction is the SN1 solvolysis of a tertiary halide, and Grunwald and Winstein used the solvolysis of *t*-butyl chloride to establish a definition of solvent polarity. This polarity scale is known as the *Y-scale*, and *Y-values* for a range of solvents have been measured. A second measure of solvent polarity is based on *solvatochromic dyes*, and it is this method that is illustrated in this experiment.

The effect of solvent polarity on the UV absorption maxima of organic compounds was discussed on pp. 365, 693. Hence the absorption maximum of an appropriate organic compound can be used as a measure of solvent polarity, and compounds which absorb at markedly different wavelengths in different solvents are described as *solvatochromic*. One compound which exhibits a remarkable degree of solvatochromism over the whole of the visible region of the spectroscopic range is 2,6-diphenyl-4-(2,4,6-triphenylpyridinio) phenolate, usually known as Dimroth's dye or Reichardt's dye. The dye is commercially available and, although it is expensive, only a very small amount is needed.

The experiment consists of measuring the absorption maxima of the dye in a range of solvents, and thereby constructing a quantitative measure of solvent polarity. The scale of solvent polarity obtained by this method is called the *E_T scale* (E_T stands for transition energy), and the E_T value for a solvent is given by:

$$E_T\left(\text{in kcal mol}^{-1}\right) = \frac{28\,591}{\lambda(\text{nm})}$$

where λ is the measured wavelength of absorption. Since the method is based on *precise* spectroscopic measurements, the E_T scale of solvent polarity is generally thought to be the most useful. This experiment is an ideal introduction to the technique of UV spectroscopy.

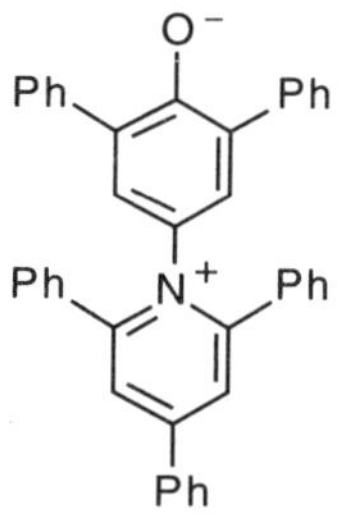

Dimroth's or Reichardt's dye

Level	2		
Time	2 × 3 h		
Instruments	UV		
Materials			
Reichardt's dye (FW 551.7)		2 mg per solvent studied	**irritant**
various solvents		5 mL of each	

Procedure

The following solvents[1] are suggested: water, methanol, ethanol, propan-2-ol, dioxan, acetone, tetrahydrofuran, dichloromethane, and toluene.[2] Other solvents may be suggested by your instructor.

Pipette 5 mL of solvent[3] into a small Erlenmeyer flask, sample vial or test tube. Add 1–2 mg (tip of a micro-spatula) of the dye to the flask, and swirl the

[1] *See Appendix 1*

[2] ***Some are toxic or flammable***

[3] *Use a pipette filler*

flask until the dye dissolves. The amount of dye need not be weighed since although the absolute concentration affects the *intensity* of UV absorption, it does not affect the *wavelength*. Using a Pasteur pipette, transfer 2–3 mL of solution to a UV cell, place it in the spectrometer, and measure the position of maximum absorption in the visible region. Hence from the measured value of λ, calculate the E_T value for that particular solvent. Repeat the experiment with as many different solvents as your instructor requires. Arrange the solvents in order of polarity as given by their E_T values.

Problems

1 Comment on the order of solvent polarity established by your experiment. Does this fit in with your intuitive ideas about polarity?

2 Which of the following reactions would you expect to exhibit a rate which is dependent on the polarity of the solvent? Why?

(a) $CH_3Cl + HO^- \longrightarrow CH_3OH + Cl^-$

(b) $CH_3Br + NEt_3 \longrightarrow CH_3\overset{+}{N}Et_3\ Br^-$

(c) 

(d) $Me_4\overset{+}{N}\ OH^- \longrightarrow Me_3N + MeOH$

(e) 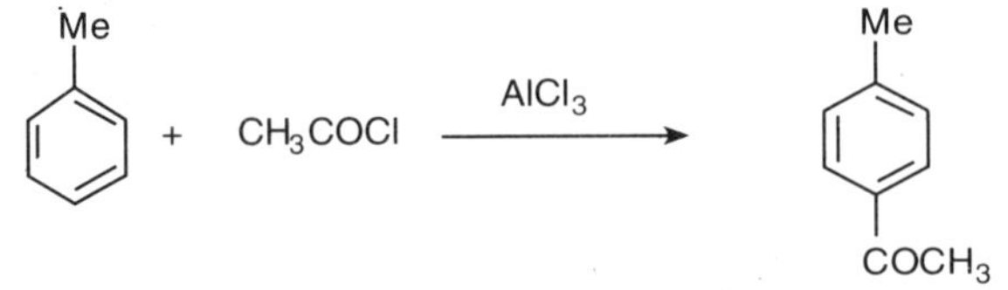

Further reading

K. Dimroth and C. Reichardt, *Z. Anal. Chem.*, 1966, **215**, 344.
B.P. Johnson, M.G. Khaledi and J.G. Dorsey, *Anal. Chem.*, 1986, **58**, 2354.

Experiment 83

Preparation of 1-deuterio-1-phenylethanol and measurement of a kinetic isotope effect in the oxidation to acetophenone

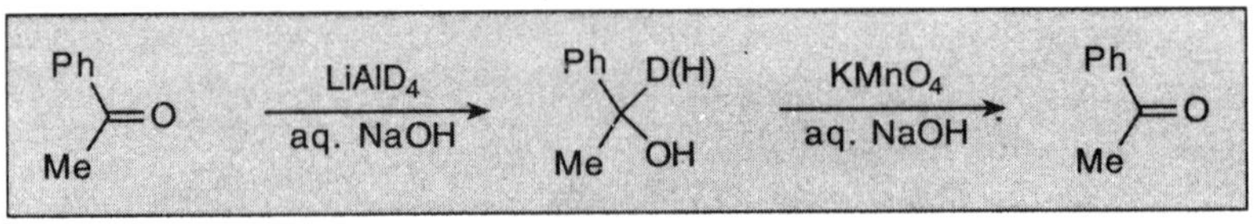

The bond dissociation energies of bonds to isotopically distinct atoms differ, with that to the heavier isotope being the stronger. Therefore a C–D bond needs more energy to dissociate it than a C–H bond and, other things being equal, will break more slowly than that of the corresponding C–H bond.

Therefore, a reaction of a compound with a C–D bond will be observed to proceed more slowly than the isotopic species with a C–H bond, provided that the rate-determining step is fission of that bond. The difference in rate between reactions of isotopic species is known as a *kinetic isotope effect* (a primary effect or PKIE in this case), expressed as k_H/k_D, which can have a value up to about 8 at room temperature. The observation of a PKIE is diagnostic of C–H bond fission occurring in the rate-determining step of the reaction and hence is a test used extensively to establish reaction mechanisms. The reaction to be studied in this experiment is the oxidation of a secondary alcohol to the ketone.

Level	4
Time	2 × 3 h
Equipment	apparatus for reflux with addition, short path distillation, volumetric glassware
Instruments	UV

Materials

1. Preparation of 1-deuterio-1-phenylethanol

lithium aluminium deuteride (FW 42.0)	0.1 g (23.8 mmol)	**flammable**
acetophenone (FW 120.2)	1.0 mL, 1 g (8.3 mmol)	**irritant**
diethyl ether (anhydrous)		**flammable, irritant**
hydrochloric acid (10%)		**corrosive**

2. Measurement of kinetic isotope effect

1-phenylethanol (FW 122.2)	0.5 g (4 mmol)	**irritant, toxic**
1-phenylethanol-1-*d* (FW 123.2)	0.5 g (4 mmol)	**irritant, toxic**
potassium permanganate (analytical grade) (FW 158.0)		**irritant, oxidizer**
aqueous sodium hydroxide (0.005 M)		**corrosive**

NOTE: water for all solutions should be distilled rather than purified by passage through an ion-exchange column since the latter may contain traces of organic matter which can be oxidized by the permanganate solution and lead to spurious results. For the same reason, all glassware should be really clean and free from surface organic materials and dried thoroughly

To minimize loss of deuterium by reaction of the lithium aluminium deuteride with water contained in the acetophenone, this should be distilled (bp 202 °C) or, at least, heated to about 150 °C to expel any water. The diethyl ether used in the reduction step must be rigorously dried as described in Appendix 2, p. 677

Procedure

1. *Preparation of 1-deuterio-1-phenylethanol*

Place 10mL of diethyl ether in a 50mL flask fitted with a Claisen adapter, condenser and addition funnel[1] and add the lithium aluminium deuteride. Stir magnetically and add the acetophenone dropwise, cooling if the reaction becomes too vigorous. When all has been added, stir for a further 5min, then add water dropwise[2] into the solution and acidify with 10% hydrochloric acid. Separate the ether layer, wash with water, dry over $MgSO_4$[3] and remove the diethyl ether on the rotary evaporator. Finally, purify the 1-deuterio-1-phenylethanol by short path distillation at reduced pressure (bp 100°C at 20mmHg).[4]

[1] *See Fig. 3.25*

[2] ***Care!***

[3] *May be left at this stage*

[4] *See Fig. 3.54*

2. *Measurement of kinetic isotope effect*

Make up a standard solution of potassium permanganate as follows; weigh accurately (±0.5mg) 20mg of potassium permanganate into a 100mL volumetric flask. Make up to the mark with 0.005 M sodium hydroxide solution to give a deep-pink solution. Transfer some of this solution to a glass or plastic 1cm UV cell, place the cell in the UV spectrometer, set the spectrometer wavelength to 520nm, and measure the absorbance (A) of the sample. A solution of this concentration should give an absorbance of about 2, that is a full-scale reading. From the measured absorbance (A), calculate the extinction coefficient (ε) for potassium permanganate at 520nm using the Beer–Lambert Law (p. 360).

Weigh accurately (±0.5mg) into a 25mL volumetric flask, approximately 100mg of 1-phenylethanol and make up to the mark with 0.005 M sodium hydroxide solution. This will give a solution whose concentration is about 3.3×10^{-2} M and is accurately known. Allow all solutions to come to ambient temperature and try to keep the temperature as constant as possible throughout the course of the experiment. Pipette 5.0mL of the 1-phenylethanol solution into a 25mL volumetric flask, make up to the mark with the permanganate solution, mix well and immediately transfer to the spectrophotometer cuvette. Start the chart recorder or begin taking readings of absorbance at 520nm at regular time intervals and continue until the absorbance ceases to fall appreciably (*ca.* 10min). It may subsequently increase but this is due to precipitation of MnO_2 and should be ignored. The purple solution will be found to have been replaced by a green colour due to manganate. Repeat the experiment so that you have duplicate results for assessment of reproducibility.

Make up a solution of 1-deuterio-1-phenylethanol similar in concentration and repeat the kinetic runs with this solution.

From your data calculate the specific rate coefficients from each kinetic run, using the Guggenheim method.[5]

[5] *For a discussion, see the references given or any other standard work on physical chemistry or chemical kinetics*

$$R_2CHOH + M_nO_4^- + OH^- \longrightarrow R_2C{=}O + HM_nO_4^{2-} + H_2O$$

The oxidation is third order, first order in each of hydroxide, permanganate and alcohol. Of these, the concentrations of hydroxide and of alcohol are essentially constant (in large excess) so that the disappearance of the permanganate follows a first-order rate law (pseudo-first order). This makes the determination of the rate constants easy and the Guggenheim method is most conveniently used as this requires no 'infinity' value. A small correction needs to be applied since the molar quantities of the alcohol and the deuterated alcohol are not likely to be equal.

If k_H', k_D' are calculated rate constants and m_H, m_D are the weights of the 1-phenylethanol and 1-deuterio-1-phenylethanol, respectively, then the kinetic isotope effect is given by:

$$k_H/k_D = k_H'/k_D' \cdot m_D/m_H$$

Decide whether or not the α-hydrogen of the alcohol is removed in the rate-determining step of the oxidation.

Problem

1 Explain in terms of mechanism why the following isotope effects are observed (isotopic atoms are shown in red).

(a) 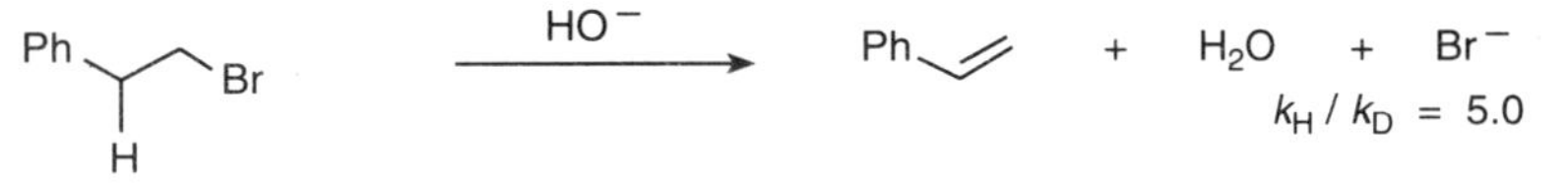

(b) 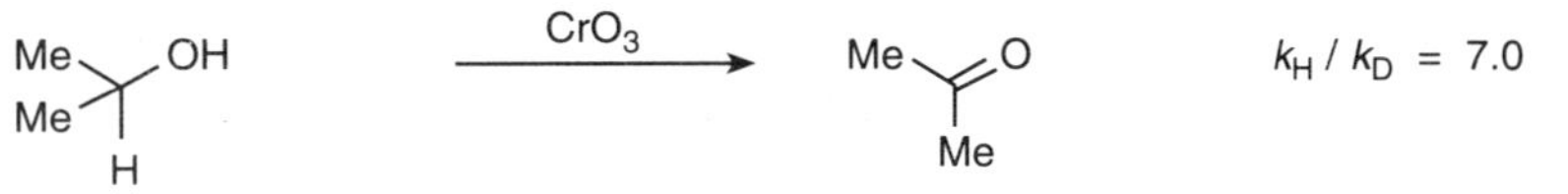

(c) 

(d) 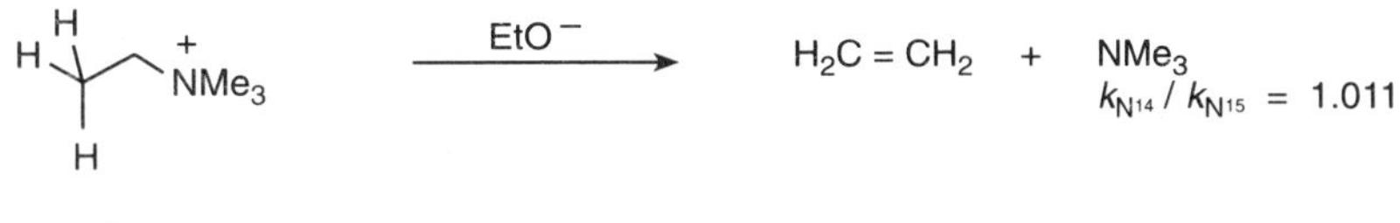

Further reading

K. Denbigh, *The Principles of Chemical Equilibrium*, 4th edn, Cambridge University Press, Cambridge, 1981.

D.P. Shoemaker, C.W. Garland, J.I. Steinfeld and J.W. Nibler, *Experiments in Physical Chemistry*, 4th edn, McGraw-Hill, New York, 1981.

Experiment 84 *Tautomeric systems*

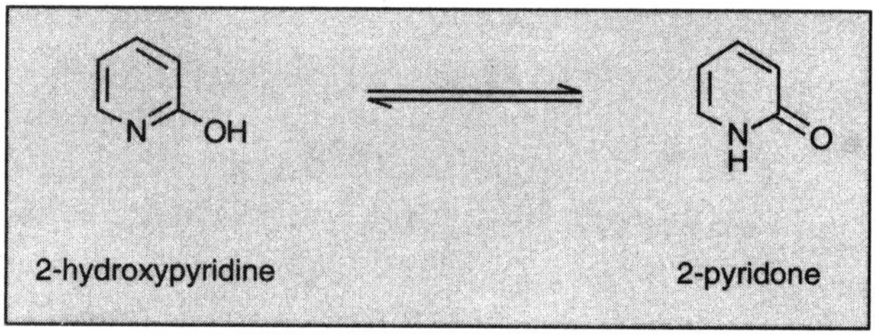

Tautomerism is the equilibrium between two isomeric structures of a compound which differ in the location of a hydrogen and a double bond. The most commonly discussed example is the interconversion between the keto and enol forms of a carbonyl compound.

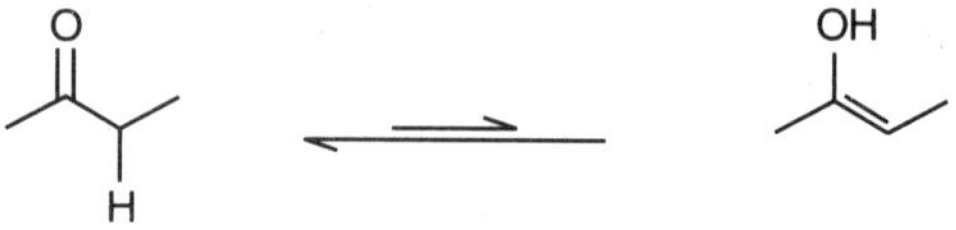

Direct observation of the above equilibrium is usually difficult since the enol form is frequently only present in a minute amount. In the example below the enolic form is more stable in the gas phase, but the keto form is stabilized by polar solvents on account of its higher dipole moment and the availability of carbonyl oxygen and ring nitrogen to form hydrogen bonds. The two forms can be differentiated by IR spectroscopy and the experiment is an ideal example of the use of this particular spectroscopic technique.

Level	1
Time	3 h
Instrument	IR

Materials

2-hydroxypyridine (FW 95.1)	*ca.* 1 g	**irritant**
selection of solvents for spectroscopy such as:		
hexane		**flammable, irritant, toxic**
chloroform		**cancer suspect agent, toxic**
dichloromethane		**irritant, toxic**
acetonitrile		**flammable, toxic**

Procedure

Run the IR spectrum of 2-hydroxypyridine in each of the four solvents in turn. For each spectrum locate the O–H absorption of the enol form at around 3200 cm^{-1}, and the C=O absorption of the keto form at about 1700 cm^{-1}. Estimate the relative areas of each of these two absorptions in each spectrum. This can be done by considering the peaks as triangles, and calculating the area, or by tracing or photocopying the peaks, and cutting them out and weighing. The relative areas of the keto and enol peaks are approximately proportional to the relative amounts of each tautomer present in that particular solvent.

For comparison run the IR spectrum of 2-hydroxypyridine in the solid state as a Nujol® mull.

Problems

1 Tabulate the relative proportions of keto and enol forms versus the solvent. Comment on how the ratio of the two forms changes with changes in the solvent. Do the changes fit in with your ideas about the relative polarity of the solvents involved?

2 What is the relative proportion of keto and enol forms in the solid state, as determined by the IR spectrum of the Nujol® mull? Is this difference between the solid and liquid states what you would expect?

Experiment 85

Kinetic versus thermodynamic control of reaction pathways: study of the competitive semicarbazone formation from cyclohexanone and 2-furaldehyde (furfural)

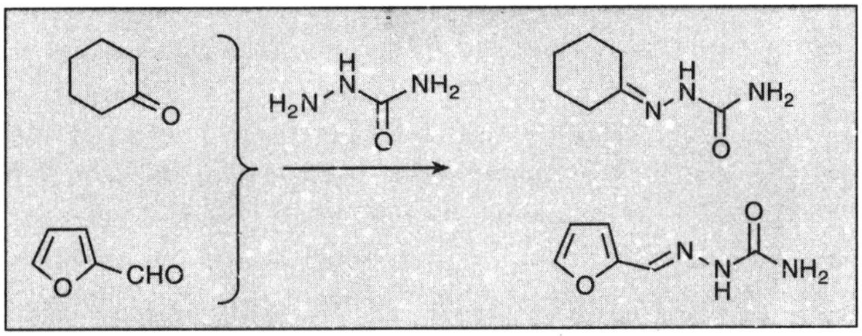

When a choice of reaction pathways exists to form different products, they usually occur at different rates. Under conditions where the back reaction to starting materials is not possible, the dominant product is the one that is formed at the fastest rate. Such a reaction is said to be under *kinetic control* and the favoured product is referred to as the *kinetic product*. However, organic reactions are frequently equilibrium processes, with significant back reaction occurring. In these cases, given time to reach equilibrium, the reaction will result in accumulation of the most stable material as the favoured product and this *thermodynamic product* is frequently different to the kinetic product. A diagram (Fig. 9.1) of the free-energy profile of such competing kinetic and thermodynamic pathways enables us to appreciate that the kinetic product is formed more quickly due to the lower activation energy barrier ($\Delta G^{\ddagger}_{kp}$) for its formation; whereas in the equilibrium system the more stable thermodynamic product predominates.

Thermodynamic conditions are usually achieved by heating up the reaction mixture (to increase both forward and back reactions) or by leaving the reaction for a long period of time. Conversely, kinetic conditions require the use of low temperature (commonly down to –80°C or lower) and short reac-

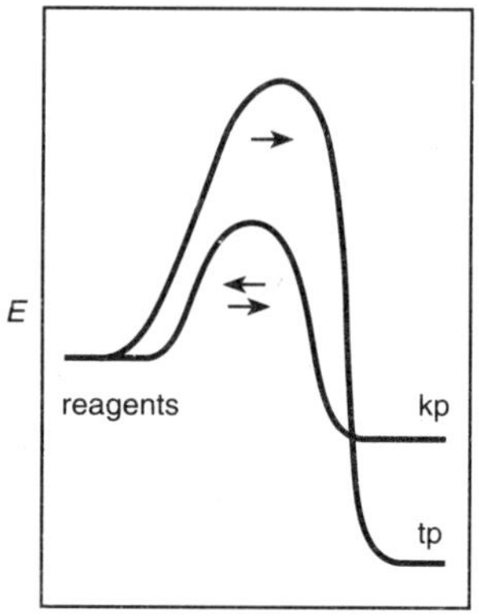

Fig. 9.1 The free-energy profile of competing kinetic and thermodynamic pathways.

tion times. Examples of reactions in which the product compositions are determined by judicious use of kinetic or thermodynamic conditions can be found in Experiments 46 and 48, but high selectivity is often difficult to achieve experimentally.

In the following experiment we will look at the competitive formation of semicarbazones of cyclohexanone and 2-furaldehyde (see pp. 254–255 for comments on other crystalline derivatives of carbonyl compounds). The condensation reaction of a carbonyl compound with semicarbazide is a reversible process, the molecule of water produced serving to cause hydrolysis back to starting materials. The particular carbonyl compounds in this experiment have been chosen for their different rates of reaction with semicarbazide and the different stabilities of the product semicarbazones. The experiment involves initial preparation of both semicarbazones as pure materials and an observation of their relative rates of formation, followed by competitive experiments carried out under kinetic and thermodynamic conditions and identification of major components of the product mixtures. This identification can be carried out by comparison of the melting points of the crude products with those of the pure semicarbazones. However, an optional part of the experiment uses UV spectroscopy to estimate the product compositions. This procedure is simplified because each material has an absorption maximum at a region of the spectrum where the other is effectively transparent and the formula weights of the two semicarbazones are very similar.

Level	1 (2 if the UV spectroscopic determination is carried out)
Time	2×3 h (with at least 24 h between the two work periods) (another 3 h period is required for optional spectroscopy)

Continued

Box cont.

Equipment	wristwatch or stopclock for timing reactions, volumetric glassware (for optional UV estimation); apparatus for suction filtration
Instruments	UV (optional)

Materials

cyclohexanone (FW 98.2)	*ca.* 6 mL (60 mmol)	**irritant**
2-furaldehyde (furfural, FW 96.1)	*ca.* 6 mL (60 mmol)	**irritant, toxic**
semicarbazide hydrochloride (FW 98.2)	*ca.* 8 g (80 mmol)	**cancer suspect agent, irritant, toxic**
aqueous sodium bicarbonate (saturated)		

Procedure

1. Preparation of the pure semicarbazones of cyclohexanone and 2-furaldehyde and observation of precipitation times

Place *ca.* 2.0 g of semicarbazide hydrochloride in a 100 mL Erlenmeyer flask, add 50 mL of saturated aqueous sodium bicarbonate, and swirl the flask until solution is complete. (Alternatively, a stirrer bar can be placed in the flask, and the mixture stirred magnetically.) Commence timing and *immediately* add 2 mL of cyclohexanone to the mixture in one amount with swirling. Note the times at which formation of a precipitate just commences and when precipitation appears complete (±1 s). Filter the precipitate with suction[1] and recrystallize it from water. Dry the purified material in a desiccator[2] and record the yield and mp.

[1] *See Fig. 3.7*

[2] *See Chapter 3*

Repeat the procedure using 2.0 mL of 2-furaldehyde and the same quantities of the other reagents, timing the beginning and end of precipitation as before. Recrystallize the product from water, dry in a desiccator and record the yield and mp of the purified material.

2. Competitive semicarbazone formation from cyclohexanone and 2-furaldehyde under thermodynamic control

Add a mixture of 1 mL of cyclohexanone and 1 mL of 2-furaldehyde to a solution of 2.0 g of semicarbazide hydrochloride in 50 mL of saturated aqueous sodium bicarbonate in a 50 mL Erlenmeyer flash. Stopper the flask and store it in your laboratory bench for at least 24 h. Filter off the resultant precipitate with suction, dry the material in a desiccator and record the mp.

3. Competitive semicarbazone formation from cyclohexanone and 2-furaldehyde under kinetic control

Repeat the competitive experiment, but this time filter off the crystals 30 s after crystallization begins, ignoring any material which crystallizes out of the filtrate afterwards. Dry and record the mp of this material.

4. *Estimation of composition of the kinetic and thermodynamic product mixtures by UV spectroscopy (optional)*

Make accurately known concentration solutions of each of the pure semicarbazones by dissolving *ca.* 50 mg in methanol in a 50 mL graduated flask. Transfer 1 mL of this solution to a 100 mL graduated flask and make up to 100 mL with methanol to give a solution with an accurately known concentration of *ca.* 0.01 mg mL^{-1}. Use these solutions to record the quantitative UV spectra of the pure semicarbazones and record the wavelength of maximum absorbance (λ_{max}) and the extinction coefficient (ε) in each case. Similarly record the quantitative UV spectra for the kinetic and thermodynamic reaction product mixtures. The proportion of major semicarbazone in each material can be estimated by comparing the extinction coefficient at maximum absorption of each UV spectrum with that of the pure material to which the spectrum bears the greatest likeness. For the determination of the extinction coefficient of the mixed products, assume a formula weight of 156.

Problem

1 Which of the two semicarbazones is formed as the kinetic product and which as the thermodynamic product? What is the evidence for your conclusion and what structural features of the products and starting materials might explain this result?

Experiment 86 *The determination of an equilibrium constant by NMR spectroscopy*

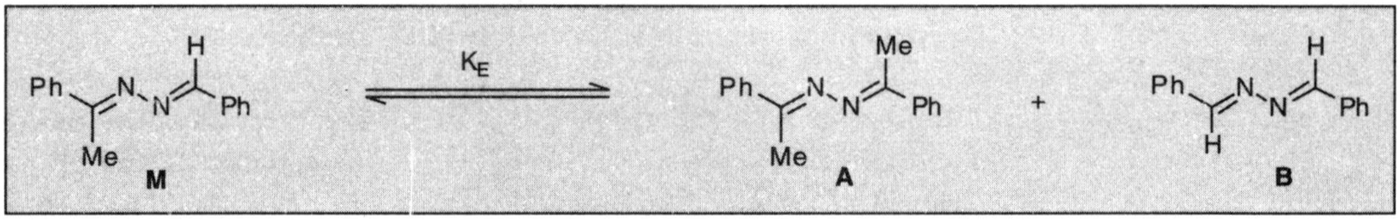

When left to stand in solution, unsymmetrical azines, R^{1}CH=N–N=CHR^2, disproportionate, and an equilibrium mixture is reached which contains the original unsymmetrical azine, and the two symmetrical azines, R^{1}CH=N–N–CHR^1 and R^{2}CH=N–N=CHR^2. This experiment illustrates the use of NMR spectroscopy to determine the equilibrium constant, K_E, for the disproportionation of the unsymmetrical azine of benzaldehyde and acetophenone, **M**, into the symmetrical azines **A** and **B** of acetophenone and benzaldehyde.

The equilibrium constant for the process is given by:

$$K_E = \frac{[A][B]}{[M]^2}$$

where [A], [B] and [M] are the concentrations of **A**, **B** and **M** respectively at equilibrium. The reaction is set up in an NMR tube, and NMR spectroscopy is used to determine the concentrations of the various compounds in the equilibrium mixture.

Since the equilibrium can be reached from either direction, the experiment can be conducted in several ways:

- you can prepare a sample of the mixed azine, **M**, and then observe its disproportionation by NMR spectroscopy;
- you can prepare *both* single azines, **A** and **B**, make an equimolar mixture of the two, and observe the formation of the mixed azine, **M**, by NMR spectroscopy;
- you can prepare *one* of the single azines, **A**, and then make an equimolar mixture with the single azine, **B**, which has been prepared by a fellow student.

The final part of the experiment (the NMR spectroscopy) can be performed in pairs. Ascertain from your instructor which way the experiment is to be conducted.

The symmetrical azines **A** and **B** are synthesized from hydrazine hydrate and acetophenone and benzaldehyde, respectively. The reaction involving benzaldehyde proceeds readily, although the acetophenone reaction requires the presence of an acid. The preparation of the mixed unsymmetrical azine **M** is slightly more time consuming.

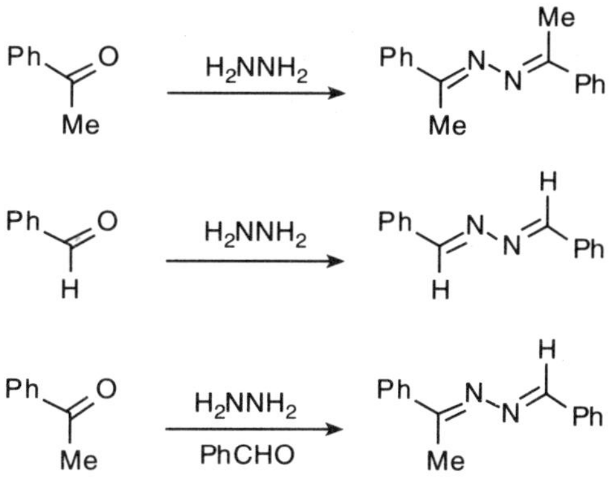

Level	2
Time	2 × 3 h
Equipment	apparatus for recrystallization, extraction/separation, suction filtration
Instruments	NMR

Materials

1. Preparation of acetophenone azine

acetophenone (FW 120.1)	6 mL, 6.2 g (51 mmol)	**irritant**
hydrazine hydrate (FW 32.0)	1 mL (*ca.* 20 mmol)	**cancer suspect agent, toxic, corrosive**

Continued on p. 664

Box cont.

ethanol		**flammable, toxic**
hydrochloric acid (conc.)		**corrosive**
2. *Preparation of benzaldehyde azine*		
benzaldehyde (FW 106.1)	5 mL, 5.2 g (49 mmol)	**irritant, toxic**
hydrazine hydrate (FW 32.0)	1 mL (*ca.* 20 mmol)	**cancer suspect agent, toxic, corrosive**
ethanol		**flammable, toxic**
3. *Preparation of mixed acetophenone benzaldehyde azine*		
acetophenone (FW 120.1)	3 mL, 3.1 g (25 mmol)	**irritant**
ethanoic acid (glacial)		**corrosive**
hydrazine hydrate (FW 32.0)	2.5 mL (*ca.* 50 mmol)	**cancer suspect agent, toxic, corrosive**
diethyl ether		**flammable, irritant**
benzaldehyde (FW 106.1)	2.5 mL, 2.6 g (25 mmol)	**irritant, toxic**
ethanol		**flammable, toxic**

Procedure

1. Preparation of acetophenone azine

Dissolve the hydrazine hydrate in 7 mL ethanol in a 25 mL Erlenmeyer flask. Add 1 mL concentrated hydrochloric acid, swirl the flask, and add the acetophenone dropwise from a Pasteur pipette. Heat the mixture on a steam bath for 15 min. Filter off the yellow product with suction,[1] and recrystallize it from 95% ethanol. Record the yield and mp of your product.

[1]*See Fig. 3.7*

2. Preparation of benzaldehyde azine

Dissolve the hydrazine hydrate in 7 mL ethanol in a 25 mL Erlenmeyer flask. Swirl the flask, and add the benzaldehyde dropwise from a Pasteur pipette. Cool the mixture in ice, collect the product by suction filtration,[1] and recrystallize it from 95% ethanol. Record the yield and mp of your product.

3. Preparation of mixed acetophenone benzaldehyde azine

Place the hydrazine hydrate in a 25 mL Erlenmeyer flask. In another vessel, dissolve the acetophenone in a mixture of 0.5 mL glacial ethanol acid and 1 mL ethanol, and add this mixture dropwise to the hydrazine hydrate. Heat the mixture for 10 min on a steam bath, and after cooling, dissolve the mixture in 30 mL diethyl ether. Transfer the ether solution to a separatory funnel and wash it with 2 × 10 mL portions of water. Dry the ether layer over anhydrous $MgSO_4$, and filter off the spent drying agent. Transfer the filtrate to a 50 mL round-bottomed flask, and add the benzaldehyde dropwise from a Pasteur pipette. Allow the mixture to stand for 10 min at room temperature (during which time it may become cloudy), and then evaporate to dryness on the rotary evaporator. Recrystallize the residue from 95% ethanol. Record the yield and mp of your product.

4. Equilibration studies and determination of K_E by NMR spectroscopy

Make up the solution for the NMR studies as follows:

1 Weigh out exactly equimolar (*ca.* 0.1 mmol) quantities of acetophenone azine and benzaldehyde azine, mix them and dissolve in *ca.* 0.6 mL deuterochloroform. *OR*

2 Weigh out about 40 mg (*ca.* 0.2 mmol) of the mixed azine, and dissolve it in *ca.* 0.6 mL deuterochloroform.

As soon as the relevant NMR solution has been prepared, transfer it to an NMR tube, and record the NMR spectrum immediately. Set the mixture in the NMR tube aside, ideally until next week's laboratory period, to allow the reaction to reach equilibrium. If a full week is not available, then the equilibration can be achieved in 2–3 h by the addition of 1 drop glacial ethanoic acid to the NMR tube. Occasionally the reaction mixture remains essentially unchanged even after a week; to preclude this, a drop of acid can be added at the start so that equilibrium is achieved quickly. Record a second NMR spectrum once the mixture has equilibrated.

The spectrum of the mixed azine, **M**, shows singlets for the methyl and methine hydrogens at about δ2.6 and 8.4, respectively. The spectrum of acetophenone azine, **A**, shows a singlet for its methyl group at about δ2.4, whereas the benzaldehyde azine, **B**, shows a singlet at about δ8.7 for the methine. The areas of these peaks (obtained by integration) is proportional to the number of protons and the concentration of compound responsible for the signal. Hence the relative concentrations of each species at equilibrium can be determined, and hence the equilibrium constant calculated.

Problems

1 What is the mechanism of azine formation from acetophenone and hydrazine?

2 What product would you expect if acetophenone was reacted with an excess of hydrazine?

Further reading

For the procedure on which this experiment is based, see: D.H. Kenny, *J. Chem Educ.*, 1980, **57**, 462.

APPENDICES

Appendix 1 Hazardous Properties of Chemicals

The hazardous properties of some 100 commonly encountered laboratory solvents, reagents and chemicals are described in tabular form. The table contains information under the following headings.

Name: the common name for the chemical.

Warnings: the standard hazard warnings: flammable, corrosive, etc.

Handling: precautions required in handling the chemicals (see pp. 5–11): **S** refers to standard precautions, i.e. avoid breathing the vapour, avoid contact with skin and eyes, avoid breathing the dust; **C** refers to suspected carcinogen.

Effects: effects immediately apparent: **E**, eyes; **S**, skin; **RS**, respiratory system; **N**, nausea; **D**, dizziness or drowsiness.

First aid: immediate treatment required in the event of an accident involving the chemical (see pp. 12–13): **S** refers to standard treatment, i.e. flush affected eyes or skin with copious amounts of cold water, remove any contaminated clothing, and summon medical assistance for eye injuries.

Water: reaction of compound with water: **R**, reacts; **VR**, violent reaction; **M**, miscible or soluble; **I**, immiscible or insoluble.

Special: any special hazards or precautions not noted elsewhere.

Name	Warnings	Handling	Effects	First aid	Water	Special
Acetic acid	Flammable Highly corrosive	S	E, S, RS	S	M	
Acetic anhydride	Flammable Corrosive Lachrymator	S	E, S, RS	S	R	
Acetone	Highly flammable Irritant	S	E, D	S	M	
Acetyl chloride	Highly flammable Corrosive	S	E, S, RS	S	VR	
Allyl bromide (or chloride)	Highly flammable Extremely toxic Irritant, lachrymator	S	E, S, RS, D	S	I	
Alumina	Irritant	S	RS	S	I	
Aluminium chloride	Corrosive	S, keep dry	E, S	S	VR	Moisture sensitive
Ammonia gas	Flammable Toxic Corrosive	S	E, RS	S	M	Liquefied gas
Ammonium hydroxide	Corrosive Toxic	S	E, S, RS	S	M	
Aniline (and aromatic amines)	Extremely toxic Cancer suspect agent	S, C	S, D	S	I	
Benzaldehyde	Irritant Toxic	S	E	S	I	Easily oxidized
Benzene	Highly flammable Extremely toxic Cancer suspect agent	S, C	E, S, D	S	I	
Benzoyl chloride (and aroyl chlorides)	Corrosive Lachrymator	S	E, S, RS	S	R	
Benzyl bromide (and chloride)	Corrosive Lachrymator	S	E, RS	S	I	
Biphenyl	Irritant	S	RS, E	S	I	
Bromine	Extremely toxic Highly corrosive Oxidizer	S	E, S, RS	S	Slightly soluble	Reacts with many organic materials
Bromobenzene	Flammable Irritant	S	D	S	I	

Continued

Appendix 1 cont.

Name	Warnings	Handling	Effects	First aid	Water	Special
Bromoethane	Flammable Irritant Cancer suspect agent	SC	E, RS, D	S	I	
N-Bromosuccinimide	Cancer suspect agent, corrosive Irritant	S, keep dry	E, S, RS	S	I	Moisture sensitive
t-Butanol	Highly flammable Irritant	S	E, RS	S	M	
Butyl-lithium (in hexane)	Flammable Pyrophoric	S, keep dry	E, S	S	VR	Work under inert atmosphere
Carbon tetrachloride	Extremely toxic Cancer suspect agent	S, C	E, RS, S D, N	S	I	
Chlorobenzene	Flammable Irritant	S	D, S	S	I	
Chloroform	Extremely toxic Cancer suspect agent	S, C	E, D, N	S	I	
3-Chloroperbenzoic acid	Oxidizer Irritant	S	RS, S	S	I	Explosion risk
Chromium (VI) oxide	Oxidizer Corrosive Cancer suspect agent	S, C	RS, S	S	M	
Copper salts	Toxic Irritant	S	E, RS	S	M	
Cyanides	Extremely toxic	Not for general use	Fatal	Antidote needed	M	
Cyclohexane	Highly flammable Irritant	S	E, S, RS	S	I	
Cyclohexanone	Flammable Harmful	S	E, S, RS	S	I	
Cyclopentadiene (dicyclopentadiene)	Highly flammable Harmful, stench	S	RS	S	I	Exothermic dimerization
Dichloromethane	Toxic Irritant	S	E, RS	S	I	
Dicyclohexylcarbodiimide	Toxic Irritant	S, keep dry	E, S	S	R	Causes skin reactions

Continued on p. 672

Cont.

Name	Warnings	Handling	Effects	First aid	Water	Special
Diethyl ether	Highly flammable Irritant	S	D, RS	S	I	Forms explosive peroxides
Diethyl malonate	Harmful	S	E, RS	S	I	
Diisopropylamine	Highly flammable Corrosive	S	E, RS, S	S	M	
Dimethylformamide	Harmful Irritant	S	E, S, RS	S	M	
Dimethylsulfoxide	Harmful Irritant	S	E, S	S	M	Hygroscopic; absorbed through skin
2,4-Dinitrophenylhydrazine	Harmful Flammable	S	S	S	I	Explosion risk
Dioxan	Highly flammable Cancer suspect agent	S, C	E, D	S	M	Forms explosive peroxides
Ethane-1,2-diol	Harmful	S	RS	S	M	Hygroscopic
Ethanol	Highly flammable Toxic	S	Well known	S	M	
Ethyl ethanoate	Highly flammable Irritant	S	E, RS	S	I	
Ethyl 3-oxobutanoate	Irritant	S	E, RS	S	I	
Ethyl chloroethanoate acetate	Toxic Lachrymator	S	E, RS, S	S	I	
Ethyl chloroformate	Highly flammable Toxic Irritant	S	E, RS	S	I	
Ferric chloride	Irritant Corrosive	S	E, S	S	M	
Formaldehyde (aqueous solution)	Toxic Cancer suspect agent	S, C	E, RS	S	M	
Hexane (and light petroleum)	Highly flammable Irritant Toxic	S	RS	S	I	
Hydrazine hydrate	Flammable Corrosive Cancer suspect agent	S, C	E, S	S	M	

Continued

Appendix 1 cont.

Name	Warnings	Handling	Effects	First aid	Water	Special
Hydrochloric acid	Corrosive Toxic	S	E, RS, S	S	M	
Hydrogen	Highly flammable	Special	Asphyxiant	S	I	Forms explosive mixtures with air; compressed gas
Hydrogen peroxide	Oxidizer Corrosive	S	E, S	S	M	Reacts with many organic materials
Hydroxylamine hydrochloride	Corrosive Irritant	S	E, S	S	M	Explodes when heated
Iodine	Corrosive	S	E, RS, S	S	I	Reacts with many organic materials
Iodomethane	Extremely toxic Cancer suspect agent	S, C	D, E, S	S	I	Very volatile
Lead salts	Toxic	S	N	S	M/I	
Lithium	Reacts violently with water	S, keep dry	S	S	VR	
Lithium aluminium hydride	Reacts violently with water Flammable	S, keep dry	S	S	VR	
Magnesium	Highly flammable	S	S	S	R (slow)	Explosion risk
Magnesium sulfate	Irritant	S	RS	S	M	Hygroscopic
Maleic anhydride	Harmful Irritant	S	E, RS, S	S	R	Moisture sensitive
Manganese dioxide	Oxidizer Irritant	S	RS	S	I	
Mercury	Extremely toxic	S	N	S	I	High vapour pressure
Mercury salts	Extremely toxic	S	E, N	S	M/I	
Methanol	Highly flammable Extremely toxic	S	D, E, RS	S	M	
Methylamine (solutions)	Flammable Corrosive	S	E, RS, S	S	M	

Continued on p. 674

Cont.

Name	Warnings	Handling	Effects	First aid	Water	Special
Nitric acid	Highly corrosive Oxidizer	S	E, S, RS	S	M	
Perchloric acid (and perchlorates)	Corrosive Oxidizer Explosive	S	E,S, RS	S	M	Explosion risk
Peroxides and peracids	Oxidizer	S	RS, S	S	M/I	Explosion risk
Petroleum ether (light petroleum)	Highly flammable	S	E, RS	S	I	
Phenol (and substituted phenols)	Extremely toxic Highly corrosive	S	E, S, RS	S	M	Absorbed through the skin
Phosphoryl chloride (phosphorus oxychloride)	Corrosive Irritant	S	E, S, RS	S	R	Moisture sensitive
Phthalic anhydride	Irritant	S	E, RS	S	R	Moisture sensitive
Picric acid (and other polynitro aromatics)	Toxic Explosive	S	S	S	M	Explosion risk
Piperidine	Highly flammable Toxic Corrosive	S	E, RS, S	S	M	
Potassium	Reacts violently with water	S, keep dry	S	S	VR	
Potassium hydroxide	Highly corrosive Toxic	S	E, S	S	M	
Potassium permanganate	Oxidizer Corrosive	S	S	S	M	Explosion risk
Pyridine	Highly flammable Harmful	S	E, D, N, RS	S	M	Stench
Pyrrolidine	Highly flammable Corrosive Irritant	S	RS, S	S	M	
Semicarbazide hydrochloride	Cancer suspect agent	S, C	S	S	M	
Silica gel	Irritant	S	RS	S	I	
Silver nitrate	Corrosive Toxic Oxidizer	S	E, S	S	M	

Continued

Appendix 1 cont.

Name	Warnings	Handling	Effects	First aid	Water	Special
Sodium	Reacts explosively with water	S	S	S	VR	
Sodium borohydride	Flammable Harmful	S	RS	S	R	Evolves H_2 with acids
Sodium carbonate	Corrosive	S	S	S	M	
Sodium hydride	Reacts violently with water	S	S	S	VR	
Sodium hydroxide	Corrosive Toxic	S	E, S	S	M	
Sodium hypochlorite (bleach)	Oxidizer Corrosive	S	E, S	S	M	Can liberate Cl_2
Sodium iodide	Irritant	S	S	S	M	Liberates I_2 with oxidizers
Sodium nitrite	Toxic Oxidizer	S	E, S	S	M	Liberates nitrous fumes with acids
Sodium sulfate	Irritant	S	S	S	M	Hygroscopic
Styrene	Flammable Toxic	S	E, RS	S	I	
Sulfuric acid	Highly corrosive Oxidizer	S	E, S	S	M	
Tetrahydrofuran	Highly flammable Irritant	S	D, E, RS	S	M	Forms explosive peroxides
Thionyl chloride	Corrosive Irritant Lachrymator	S	E, RS, S	S	VR	
Toluene	Highly flammable Irritant	S	D, E, RS, S	S	I	
Toluene-4-sulfonic acid	Corrosive Toxic	S	E, S	S	M	
Toluene-4-sulfonyl chloride	Corrosive	S	E, S	S	R	Moisture sensitive
Triethylamine	Highly flammable Corrosive	S	E, RS, S	S	M	

Continued on p. 676

Cont.

Name	Warnings	Handling	Effects	First aid	Water	Special
Trimethylchlorosilane	Highly flammable Corrosive Irritant	S	E, S, RS	S	VR	
Triphenylphosphine	Irritant	S	RS	S	I	
Xylene	Flammable Toxic	S	E, RS	S	I	
Zinc (dust)	Flammable	S	RS	S	I	Liberates H_2 with acids

Appendix 2 Organic Solvents

Table A1 Properties of common laboratory solvents.

Solvent*	Bp (760 mmHg) (°C)	Mp (°C)	Flashpoint (°C)	Density, d^{20} (g mL^{-1})	Refractive index, n_D	Dielectric constant, ε	Toxicity, TLV† (ppm)	Hazards
Acetone	56.2	–95.3	–30	0.790	1.3588	20.7	1000	Flammable
Acetonitrile (methyl cyanide)	81.6	–45.2	5	0.786	1.3442	37.5	40	Flammable Lachrymator
Benzene‡	80.1	5.5	–11	0.874	1.5011	2.3	8	Carcinogen Flammable
1-Butanol (*n*-butyl alcohol)	117.3	–89.5	35	0.810	1.3993	17.5	100	Flammable Irritant
2-Butanol (*s*-butyl alcohol)	99.5	–114.7	26	0.808	1.3978	16.6	100	Flammable Irritant
Carbon tetrachloride	76.5	–22.9	None	1.594	1.4601	2.2	10	Carcinogen Highly toxic
Chloroform	61.7	–63.5	None	1.483	1.4460	4.8	10	Carcinogen Photosensitive
Cyclohexane	80.7	6.6	–18	0.779	1.4266	2.0	300	Flammable Irritant
1,2-Dichloroethane (ethylene dichloride)	83.5	–35.4	15	1.235	1.4448	10.4	20	Carcinogen Flammable
Dichloromethane (methylene chloride)	39.8	–95.1	None	1.327	1.4242	8.9	200	Toxic Irritant
Diethyl ether	34.5	–116.2	–40	0.714	1.3526	4.3	400	Flammable Irritant Forms peroxides
Dimethoxyethane (glyme, ethylene glycol dimethyl ether)	83.0	–58.0	0	0.863	1.3796	7.2		Flammable Forms peroxides
N,*N*-Dimethyl-formamide	157.0	–60.5	57	0.949	1.4305	36.7	20	Irritant

Continued on p. 678

Table A1 *Cont.*

Solvent*	Bp (760 mmHg) (°C)	Mp (°C)	Flashpoint (°C)	Density, d^{20} (g mL^{-1})	Refractive index, n_D	Dielectric constant, ε	Toxicity, TLV† (ppm)	Hazards
Dimethylsulfoxide	189.0	18.5	95	1.101	1.4770	46.7		Irritant Readily adsorbed
1,4-Dioxan	101.3	11.8	12	1.034	1.4224	2.2	50	Carcinogen Flammable
Ethanoic acid	117.9	16.6		1.049	1.3716	6.2	10	Corrosive
Ethanol (ethyl alcohol)	78.5	−117.3	8	0.789	1.3611	24.6	1000	Flammable Toxic
Ethyl ethanoate	77.1	−83.6	−3	0.900	1.3723	6.0	400	Flammable Irritant
n-Hexane	69.0	−95.0	−23	0.660	1.3751	1.9	50	Flammable Irritant Toxic
Methanol (methyl alcohol)	65.0	−93.9	11	0.791	1.3288	32.7	200	Flammable Toxic
2-Methyl-2-propanol (*t*-butyl alcohol)	82.2	25.5	4	0.789	1.3878	12.7	100	Flammable
n-Pentane	36.1	−129.7	−49	0.626	1.3575	1.8	600	Flammable
1-Propanol (*n*-propyl alcohol)	97.4	−126.5	15	0.804	1.3850	20.3	200	Flammable Irritant
2-Propanol (isopropyl alcohol)	82.4	−89.5	22	0.786	1.3776	19.9	400	Flammable Irritant
Pyridine	115.5	−41.6	20	0.982	1.5095	12.4	5	Flammable Irritant
Tetrahydrofuran	67.0	−108.6	−17	0.889	1.4050	7.6	200	Flammable Irritant Forms peroxides
Toluene	110.6	−95.0	4	0.867	1.4961	2.4	200	Flammable Irritant
Xylene (isomers)	138–144	<−45	~25	~0.87	~1.50	2.4	200	Flammable Irritant

* Purification procedures are described (see Table A2).
† Threshold limit value: time-weighted average concentration for a normal 8 h working day to which nearly all workers may be repeatedly exposed without adverse effects. Absence of a quoted value must not be interpreted as absence of toxicity.
‡ Benzene has been proved to be a causative agent for leukaemia and its use should be avoided whenever possible. In particular, the use of benzene as a solvent is proscribed and toluene should be substituted, with due modification, in any procedure calling for benzene solvent.
For further information, see: I.M. Smallwood, *Handbook of Organic Solvent Properties*, Arnold, London, 1996; A. Collings and S.G. Luxon (eds), *Safe Use of Solvents*, Academic Press, New York, 1982.

Table A2 Purification procedures for commonly used laboratory solvents.

Solvent	Purification procedure	Hazards, boiling range, comments
(a) Aliphatic hydrocarbons		
Cyclohexane Hexane Light petroleum Pentane	If contaminated with olefins (particularly light petroleum) shake with concentrated sulfuric acid (1/10 volume of solvent), separate and wash with water. Dry ($MgSO_4$) and distil, discarding the initial fore-run which contains water	**Flammable** Hexane is toxic Cyclohexane: 79–82°C Hexane: 67–71°C Light petroleum: collect fraction distilling below 60°C Pentane: 35–37°C Light petroleum must always be distilled before use Distilled hydrocarbons may be stored in dark bottles more or less indefinitely without special precautions
(b) Aromatic hydrocarbons		
Benzene Toluene Xylene	Distil, rejecting milky fore-run (*ca.* 5%).	**Benzene is carcinogenic** **Flammable** Benzene: 79–81°C Toluene: 109–111°C Xylene: *ortho*- 143–146°C *meta*- 138–140°C *para*- 137–139°C Store as aliphatic hydrocarbons Use toluene in place of benzene wherever possible
(c) Chlorinated hydrocarbons		
Chloroform 1,2-Dichloroethane Dichloromethane	Distil, discarding wet fore-run (*ca.* 5%). Chloroform required for IR analyses should be passed through Activity I alumina immediately before use (25 g alumina : 500 mL chloroform).	**Chloroform and 1,2-dichloroethane are possible carcinogens** **Never treat halogenated solvents with sodium as an explosion will result** Chloroform is decomposed by light forming phosgene and rendering the solvent acidic Store as aliphatic hydrocarbons Chloroform should only be kept for limited periods in dark glass containers
(d) Ethers		
Diethyl ether	Test for peroxides by shaking for 1 min with acidified	**Flammable**

Continued on p. 680

Cont.

Solvent	Purification procedure	Hazards, boiling range, comments
Dimethoxyethane 1,4-Dioxan Tetrahydrofuran	10% aqueous potassium iodide. If positive (yellow colour) shake with 1/5 volume 5% aqueous sodium bisulfite until test for peroxides is negative. Small volumes may then be purified by passage through Activity I alumina. Dry by standing over potassium hydroxide pellets overnight and then over sodium wire. Very dry ethers are obtained by refluxing the sodium-dried material (1 L) over sodium (3 g) and benzophenone (1 g) until the mixture develops the deep purple colour of the sodium benzophenone ketyl. Distil and use immediately. Never distil to dryness. Never distil without verifying absence of peroxides	**Readily form explosive peroxides on storage** Diethyl ether: 33–35°C 1,2-Dimethoxymethane: 82–85°C Tetrahydrofuran: 64–66°C Diethyl ether may be kept over sodium wire. Ultra-dry solvents should be used immediately Always check for peroxides before distillation—distrust old or partially filled bottles in particular Such distillations need care and attention, and should only be carried out by experienced personnel
(e) Alcohols		
Ethanol Methanol	Add magnesium (5 g) to 50 mL alcohol in a 2 L round-bottomed flask. Add 0.5 g of iodine and heat to reflux until the iodine colour has disappeared. Be ready to remove the flask from the source of heat if the reaction becomes too vigorous. Make up the mixture to 1 L with alcohol and reflux for 0.5 h with protection from the atmosphere. Distil and use the dry alcohol immediately	**Flammable** Ethanol: 77–79°C Methanol: 63–66°C Use ultra-dry alcohols immediately
1-Butanol 2-Butanol	Distil, discarding initial fore-run (*ca.*10%) which contains water. Very dry material may be obtained by refluxing over and distilling from calcium hydride	1-Butanol: 115–119°C 2-Butanol: 98–101°C Use ultra-dry alcohols immediately
2-Methyl-2-propanol (*t*-butyl alcohol)	As for butanols, except that care must be taken to avoid blocking the condenser	2-Methyl-2-propanol: 81–83°C If the alcohol solidifies in cold weather, it should be melted by standing in warm (*ca.* 40°C) water. Do not heat the container more strongly
1-Propanol 2-Propanol	Distil, discarding initial fore-run (*ca.*10%) which contains water. Very dry material may be obtained by using the magnesium alkoxide method described for methanol and ethanol	1-Propanol: 96–98°C 2-Propanol: 81–84°C Use ultra-dry alcohols immediately

Continued

Table A2 *Cont.*

Solvent	Purification procedure	Hazards, boiling range, comments
(f) Miscellaneous		
Acetone	Dry over anhydrous calcium sulfate. Distil	**Flammable** Acetone: 55–57°C
Acetic acid	Add 5% acetic anhydride and 2% chromium (VI) oxide. Reflux and fractionate	**Corrosive** Ethanoic acid: 117–119°C Store in a screw-capped bottle
Acetonitrile	Dry over anhydrous potassium carbonate. Small quantities may be purified by passage through Activity I alumina. Larger quantities can be distilled from phosphorus pentoxide	**Flammable** **Lachrymator** Acetonitrile: 80–83°C Small volumes may be stored for short periods over 3Å molecular sieves. Seal the stopper with paraffin film
Dimethylformamide Dimethylsulfoxide	Stir over calcium hydride and distil *in vacuo*. Do not distil at atmospheric pressure as these solvents decompose	**Irritant** **Toxic by skin absorption** **Hygroscopic** Dimethylformamide: 41–43°C/10 mmHg, 53–56°C/20 mmHg Dimethylsulfoxide: 83–86°C/12 mmHg, 49–51°C/20 mmHg Dried solvent should be used immediately
Ethyl ethanoate	Stir over anhydrous potassium carbonate. Filter and distil	**Flammable** Ethyl acetate: 76–78°C Store over 5 Å sieves in screw-capped bottles
Pyridine Diisopropylamine	Dry for 24 h over potassium hydroxide pellets. Decant and distil from barium oxide or calcium hydride	**Flammable** **Hygroscopic** Pyridine: 114–117°C Diisopropylamine: 82–85°C Store over 5 Å sieves in screw-capped bottles

Note: This table contains guidelines for purification procedures. Further details may be found in the references below. The purification of certain solvents such as benzene, carbon disulfide and hexamethylphosphoramide should only be attempted by experienced workers, and only then after taking into account the very special hazardous properties associated with these solvents (procedures for purifying the latter two solvents are not given in this appendix).

With the exception of light petroleum, it is usually unnecessary to carry out extensive purification of solvents intended for extraction purposes. However, solvents intended for use in chromatography or recrystallization procedures require distillation before use. Owing to the presence of an appreciable proportion of high boiling residues in light petroleum, this solvent must always be distilled. Solvents for use with moisture-sensitive reagents require rigorous drying and distillation just prior to use.

All purifications involving reflux over a reagent followed by distillation, are most conveniently carried out using a solvent still expressly designed for such procedures (see Fig. 3.49).

References

For full details of purification procedures of these and other laboratory solvents, see: A.J. Gordon and R.A. Ford, *The Chemists' Companion*, Wiley (Interscience), New York, 1972, pp. 430–436;

D.D. Perrin and W.L.F. Armarego, *Purification of Laboratory Chemicals*, 3rd edn, Pergamon, New York, 1988.

Appendix 3 Spectroscopic Correlation Tables

IR correlation tables

Table A3	O–H bonds
Table A4	N–H bonds
Table A5	C–H bonds
Table A6	X≡Y bonds
Table A7	C=O bonds
Table A8	C=C bonds
Table A9	Other functional groups

NMR correlation tables

Table A10	Approximate proton chemical shifts of methyl groups CH_3–X
Table A11	Incremental rules for estimating the proton shifts of methylene and methine groups
Table A12	Incremental rules for estimating the chemical shifts of alkene protons
Table A13	Chemical shifts of some acidic protons
Table A14	Some proton–proton coupling constants
Table A15	^{13}C chemical shift ranges
Table A16	Residual proton signals of common deuterated NMR solvents

UV correlation tables

Table A17	Woodward rules for UV absorption maxima of dienes
Table A18	Woodward rules for UV absorption maxima of α,β-unsaturated ketones in ethanol
Table A19	Solvent correction for UV absorption maxima of α,β-unsaturated ketones

MS correlation tables

Table A20	One-bond cleavage processes associated with common functional groups
Table A21	Common fragmentations
Table A22	Common fragment ions

IR correlation tables

Table A3 O–H bonds.

Group	Frequency (cm^{-1})	Appearance	Comment
Free O–H	3600	Sharp	Usually only seen in dilute solution
Alcohol or phenol O–H (intermolecularly H-bonded)	3500–3100	Broad, strong	Sharpens on dilution of solution; look for alcohol C–O band (1300–1000)
Alcohol or phenol O–H (intramolecularly H-bonded)	3400–2500	Broad	Unaffected by dilution of solution
Carboxylic acid COO–H	3500–2500	Very broad	Always accompanied by strong C=O band (1730–1680)

Table A4 N–H bonds.

Group	Frequency (cm^{-1})	Appearance	Comment
Amine N–H	3500–3000	Usually sharper and weaker than O–H	Two bands for primary amines; secondary amines much weaker; look for N–H bending band (1650–1550)
Amide $CONH_2$	3500–3300	Two bands (sharp)	In solid state occur at lower frequency; always accompanied by strong C=O bands (1700–1510)
Amide CONH (and lactams)	3450–3300	Two bands	As above; only one band for lactams
Amine salts NH_3^+	3200–3000	Broad	Also show strong N–H bending (1600)

Table A5 C–H bonds.

Group	Frequency (cm^{-1})	Appearance	Comment
–C≡C–H	3300	Sharp, quite intense	C–H stretch; look for triple bond absorption (2150–2100)
C=C–H	3100–3000	Weak	C–H stretch; easily obscured by stronger bands; look for C=C bands (1680–1500)
	1000–850	Strong	C–H out-of-plane deformation
Aromatic C–H	3050–3000	Weak	Often obscured; look for aromatic C=C peaks (1600–1500)
	850–730	Strong	C–H out-of-plane deformations; can often distinguish between *o*-, *m*- and *p*-substituted benzenes
sp^3C–H	2980–2840	Strong	Two bands; C–H stretch
	1480–1420	Strong	C–H deformations
Aldehyde C–H	2900–2700	Often weak	Two bands; always accompanied by strong C=O peak (1740–1680)

Table A6 X≡Y bonds.

Group	Frequency (cm^{-1})	Appearance	Comment
Non-terminal alkynes	2250–2150	Often weak	Intensity increased by conjugation; absent if alkyne is symmetrical or nearly symmetrical
Terminal alkynes	2150–2100	Often weak	Intensity increased by conjugation; look for the sharp C–H stretch (3300)
Nitriles	2270–2200	Often weak	

Table A7 C=O bonds.

Group	Frequency (cm^{-1})	Appearance	Comment
Acid anhydrides	1850–1800 and 1790–1740	Strong	Two bands separated by about 60 cm^{-1}; lowered by 20 cm^{-1} on conjugation
Acid chlorides	1815–1790	Strong	Lowered by 40–25 cm^{-1} on conjugation
Esters	1750–1730	Strong	Lowered by about 20 cm^{-1} on conjugation; look for strong C–O band (1300–1000)
Lactones: six-ring	1750–1730	Strong	And larger rings
Lactones: five-ring	1780–1760	Strong	Four-ring at 1830–1810
Aldehydes	1740–1695	Strong	Lowered by conjugation and H-bonding; look for C–H stretch (2900–2700)
Ketones: saturated	1730–1700	Strong	All classes lowered by H-bonding
Ketones: unsaturated	1700–1670	Strong	
Ketones: six-ring	1730–1700	Strong	And larger rings
Ketones: five-ring	1750–1740	Strong	Four-ring at 1790–1770
Carboxylic acids	1730–1700	Strong	Lowered by 20 cm^{-1} on conjugation; always accompanied by broad O–H stretch (3500–2500)
Amides: primary	1690 and 1600	Strong; two bands	Values given are for solution; lowered in solid state; amide II less intense; look for N–H stretch (3500–3000); amide carbonyls are not lowered by conjugation
Amides: secondary	1700–1670 and 1550–1500	Strong; two bands	Lowered in solid state; amide II less intense; look for N–H stretch
Amides: tertiary	1670–1630	Strong	No N–H stretch!
Lactams: six-ring	1670	Strong	And larger rings
Lactams: five-ring	1700	Strong	Four-ring at 1760–1740

Table A8 C=C bonds.

Group	Frequency (cm^{-1})	Appearance	Comment
Alkene C=C	1680–1640	Often weak	Absent in symmetrical alkenes
Diene C=C	1650–1600	Strong; two bands	Intensity increased by conjugation
Alkene C=C conjugated to aromatic ring	1640–1620	Medium intensity	
Alkene C=C conjugated to C=O	1650–1590	Strong	Intensity increased by conjugation; always accompanied by stronger C=O peak
Alkene C=C conjugated to lone pair of electrons (enamines, enol ethers)	1700–1650	Strong	Intensity increased by conjugation
Aromatic C=C	1600–1500	Two or three bands of medium intensity	Look for stronger C–H deformations (850–730)

Table A9 Other functional groups.

Group	Frequency (cm^{-1})	Appearance	Comment
S–H	2500	Weak	
C=N	1700–1620	Often strong	Difficult to distinguish from C=C and (sometimes) C=O
$-NO_2$	1550 and 1350	Strong	
$-SO_2-$	1350 and 1150	Strong	
C–O	1300–1000	Strong	Esters (look for associated C=O), ethers, alcohols (look for associated O–H)
≡P=O	1300–1250	Strong	
$-SiMe_3$	1270	Strong	
C=S	1250–1050	Strong	
C–Cl	800–700	Strong	

NMR correlation tables

Table A10 Approximate proton chemical shifts of methyl groups CH_3–X.

X	δ	X	δ
Alkyl	0.90	OH	3.40
C=C	1.70	OR	3.25
C≡C	1.80	OAr	3.75
Ar	2.35	OAc	3.70
F	4.30	OCOAr	3.90
Cl	3.05	COR	2.10
Br	2.70	COAr	2.60
I	2.15	CHO	2.20
SH	2.00	CO_2H	2.10
SR	2.10	CO_2R	2.00
NH_2	2.50	CN	2.00
NHAc	2.70	$CONH_2$	2.00
NO_2	4.30		

Table A11 Incremental rules for estimating the proton shifts of methylene and methine groups (after E. Pretsch, T. Clerc, J. Seibl and W. Simon, *Tables of Spectral Data for the Structure Determination of Organic Compounds*, 2nd edn. Springer–Verlag, Berlin, 1989).

$\delta CH_2R_1R_2 = 1.25 + \Delta_1 + \Delta_2$;
$\delta CHR_1R_2R_3 = 1.50 + \Delta_1 + \Delta_2 + \Delta_3$

R	Δ	R	Δ
Alkyl	0.0	NR_2	1.0
C=C	0.8	NO_2	3.0
C≡C	0.9	SR	1.0
Ar	1.3	COR	1.2
OH	1.7	CO_2H	0.8
OR	1.5	CO_2R	0.7
OAr	2.3	Cl	2.0
OAc	2.7	Br	1.9
OCOAr	2.9	I	1.4
CN	1.2		

Note: these estimates are much more reliable for methylene groups than for methines.

Table A12 Incremental rules for estimating the chemical shifts of alkene protons (from U.E. Matter, C. Pascual, E. Pretsch, A. Pross, W. Simon and S. Sternhell, *Tetrahedron*, 1969, **25**, 691).

$\delta C{=}CH = 5.25 + \Delta_{gem} = \Delta_{cis} = \Delta_{trans}$

R	Δ_{gem}	Δ_{cis}	Δ_{trans}
Alkyl	0.45	–0.22	–0.28
Alkyl (ring)	0.69	–0.25	0.28
CH_2OR	0.64	–0.01	–0.02
CH_2Hal	0.70	0.11	–0.04
CH_2CN, CH_2COR	0.69	–0.08	–0.06
CH_2Ar	1.05	–0.29	–0.32
CH_2NR_2	0.58	–0.10	–0.08
C=C (isol.)	1.00	–0.09	–0.23
C=C (conj.)	1.24	0.02	–0.05
C≡C	0.47	0.38	0.12
Ar	1.38	0.36	–0.07
CN	0.27	0.75	0.55
COR (isol.)	1.10	1.12	0.87
COR (conj.)	1.06	0.91	0.74
CO_2H (isol.)	0.97	1.41	0.71
CO_2H (conj.)	0.80	0.98	0.32
CO_2R (isol.)	0.80	1.18	0.55
CO_2R (conj.)	0.78	1.01	0.46
CHO	1.02	0.95	1.17
$CONR_2$	1.37	0.98	0.46
OR	1.22	–1.07	–1.21
OAr, OC=C	1.21	–0.60	–1.00
OCOR	2.11	–0.35	–0.64
Cl	1.08	0.18	0.13
Br	1.07	0.45	0.55
I	1.14	0.81	0.88
NR_2	0.80	–1.26	–1.21
NRCOR	2.08	–0.57	–0.72
SR	1.11	–0.29	–0.13
SO_2	1.55	1.16	0.93

Note: the values designated 'conj.' are used when either the alkene or the substituent is involved in further conjugation. The values 'Alkyl (ring)' are used when the alkene and the alkyl group are both part of the same five- or six-membered ring.

Table A13 Chemical shifts of some acidic protons (very variable according to conditions).

	δ		δ
RCO_2H	8–14	RCONHR	5–12
ROH	0.5–4.5	ArOH	5–7
RNHR	1–5	ArNHR	3–6
RSH	1–2	ArSH	3–4
Oxime	9–12		

Table A14 Some proton–proton coupling constants.

	$\lvert J\rvert$ (typical range) (Hz)
H–C–H (*geminal*)	10–15
H–C–C–H (*vicinal*, free rotation)	≈7
C=Ch–CH	5–7
C=CH–Ch=C	10–13
HC=CH (*cis*)	9–12
HC=CH (*trans*)	14–16
C=CHH (*geminal*)	1–2
Cyclohexane, three-bond, *ax–ax*	10–13
Cyclohexane, *ax–eq* and *eq–eq*	2–5
Phenyl, 1,2	7–8
Phenyl, 1,3	1–2
Phenyl, 1,4	0–1
CH=C–CH (allylic)	1–2
CH≡C–CH	2–3
CH–C≡C–CH	0–1

Table A15 ^{13}C chemical shift ranges.

	δ		δ
Alkanes	0–50	Ketone C=O	190–220
Alkenes	100–140	Aldehyde C=O	185–205
Alkynes	75–105	Acid C=O	165–185
Arenes	115–145	Ester C=O	155–180
$\underline{C}H_3$–C=C	5–30	Amide C=O	155–180
CH_3–O	50–60	C≡N	110–125
CH_3–(Cl,Br)	10–25	CH_3–I	–21
CH_3–N	15–45	CH_3–F	75
$R\underline{C}H_2$–C=C	25–55	$R_2\underline{C}H$–C=C	35–65
RCH_2–O	35–75	R_2CH–O	65–90
RCH_2–N	40–60	R_2CH–N	50–70
RCH_2–S	25–45	R_2CH–S	55–65
$R_3\underline{C}$–C=C	30–50	R_3C–O	75–85
$R_3\underline{C}$–N	65–75	R_3C–S	55–75

Table A16 Residual proton signals of common deuterated NMR solvents.

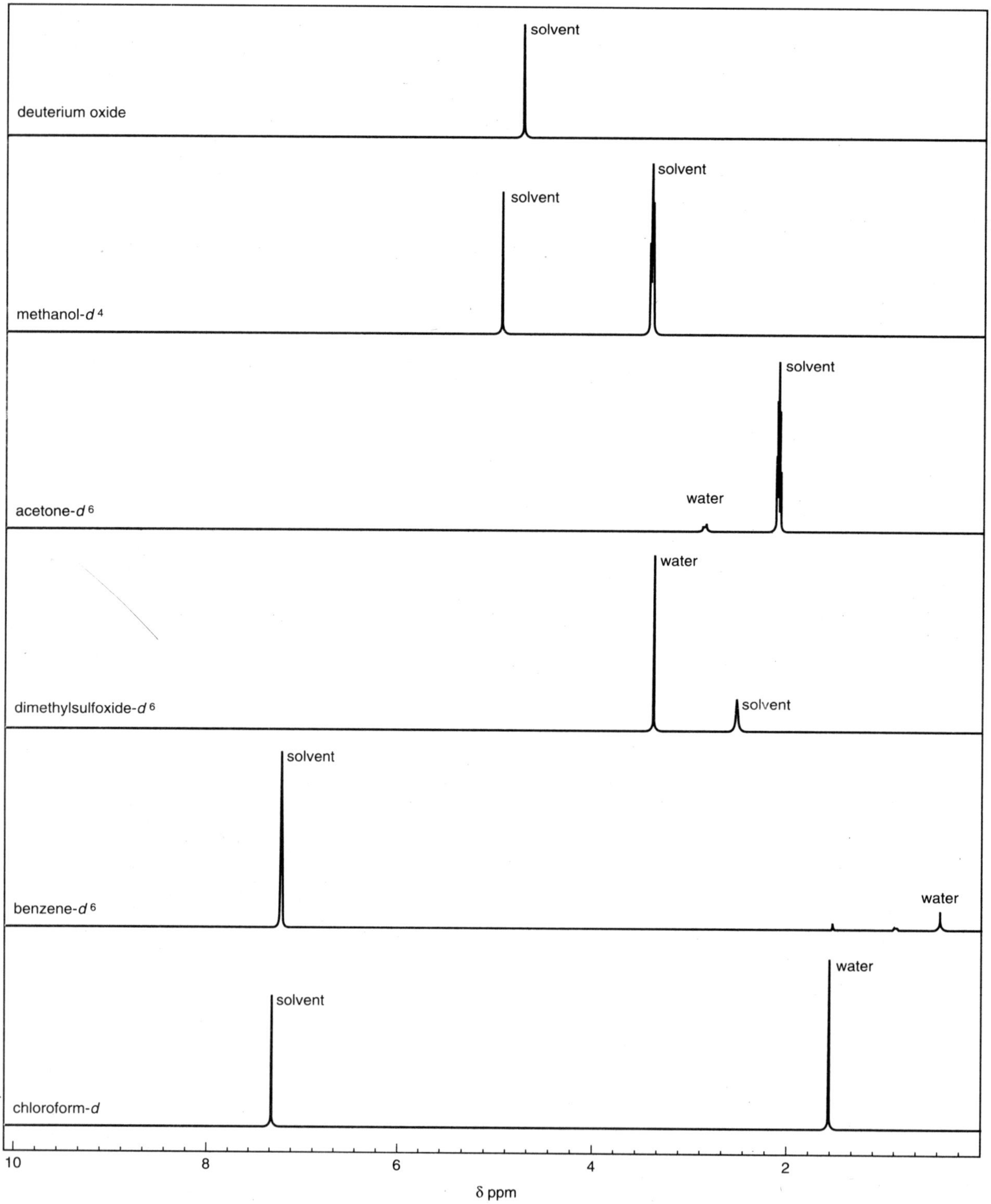

UV correlation tables

Table A17 Woodward rules for the UV absorption maxima of dienes.

Acyclic diene e.g.	Heteroannular diene e.g.	Homoannular diene e.g.
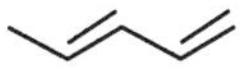	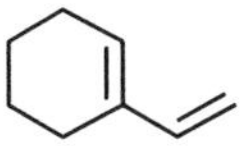	

Value for parent acyclic diene	214 nm
Value for parent heteroannular diene	214
Value for parent homoannular diene	253
Increments to be added	
If an additional double bond extends conjugation	30
If one of the diene double bonds is exocyclic	5
Increments to be added for substituents (auxochromes)	
Alkyl group	5
Ring residue	5
Halogen (Cl, Br)	5
Alkoxy group (OR)	6
Acyloxy group (OCOR)	0
Alkylthio group (SR)	30
Dialkylamino group (NR_2)	60

Table A18 Woodward rules for the UV absorption maxima of α,β-unsaturated ketones in ethanol.*

Acyclic	Six-ring	Five-ring
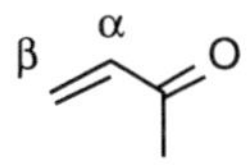	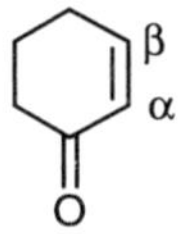	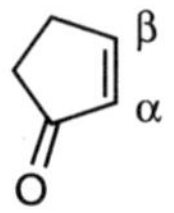

Value for parent acyclic α,β-unsaturated ketone	215 nm
Value for parent six-ring α,β-unsaturated ketone	215
Value for parent five-ring α,β-unsaturated ketone	202
Increments to be added	
If an additional double bond extends conjugation	30
If one of the double bond is exocyclic	5
Increments to be added for α-substituents (auxochromes)	
Alkyl group	10
Ring residue	10
Hydroxyl group (OH)	35
Alkoxy group (OR)	35
Acyloxy group (OCOR)	6
Chloro group (Cl)	15
Bromo group (Br)	25
Increments to be added for β-substituents (auxochromes)	
Alkyl group	12
Ring residue	12
Hydroxyl group (OH)	30
Alkoxy group (OR)	30
Acyloxy group (OCOR)	6
Chloro group (Cl)	12
Bromo group (Br)	30
Alkylthio group (SR)	85
Dialkylamino group (NR_2)	95

* For values in other solvents a solvent correction must be applied (see Table A19).

Table A19 Solvent correction for UV absorption maxima of α,β-unsaturated ketones.

The rules for the absorption maxima of α,β-unsaturated ketones apply to spectra that are run in ethanol. To calculate the expected λ_{max} in other solvents, proceed as follows:

1 using Table A18, calculate the expected λ_{max} in ethanol;

2 subtract the solvent correction factor given below

Solvent	Correction (nm)
Water	–8
Methanol	0
Hexane	11
Chloroform	1

MS correlation tables

Table A20 One-bond cleavage processes associated with common functional groups.

Functional group	Fragmentation
Alcohol	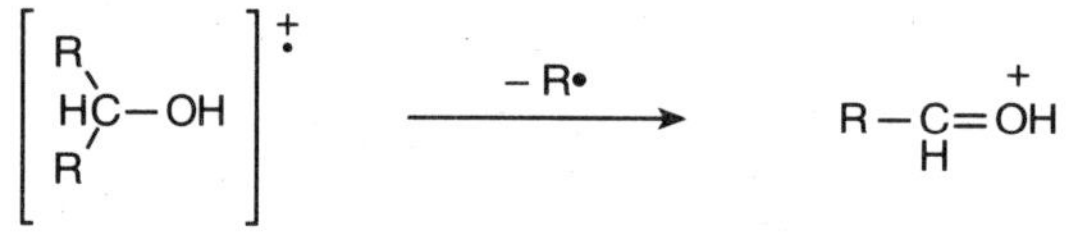
Amine	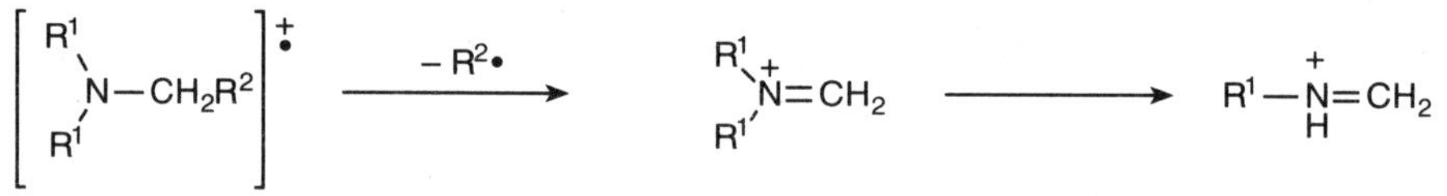
Ester	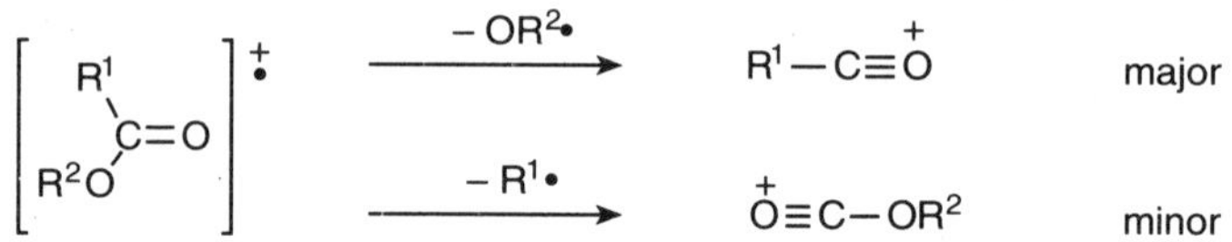
Ether	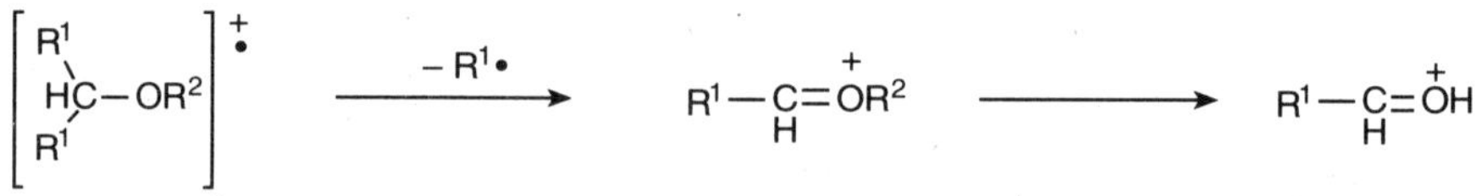
Halide	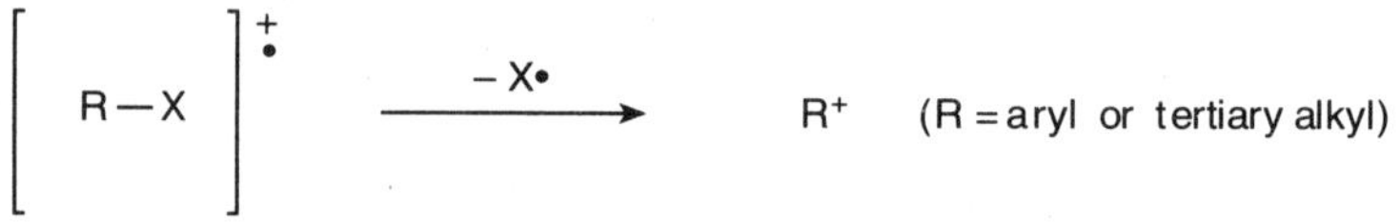
	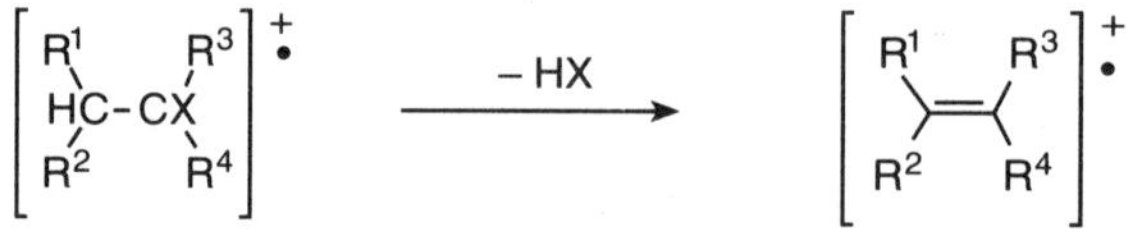
Ketal	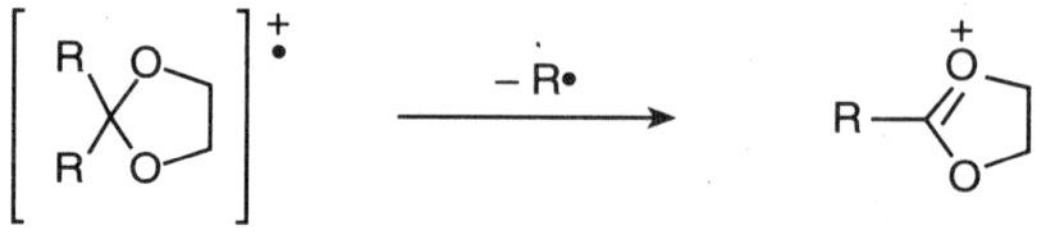

Table A21 Common fragmentations.

m/z	Possible fragment lost and conclusion
M − 1, M − 2	H, H_2
M − 14	M is not the molecular ion. Loss of CH_2 disfavoured
M − 15	CH_3
M − 17	OH, NH_3
M − 18	H_2O loss from alcohol, aldehyde, ketone
M − 26	CN, C_2H_2
M − 28	CO, C_2H_4, N_2
M − 29	C_2H_5, CHO
M − 30	NO, C_2H_6
M − 31	CH_3O
M − 35	Cl
M − 42	CH_2CO loss from methyl ketone or aromatic acetate
	C_3H_6
M − 43	CH_3CO loss from methyl ketone
	C_3H_7
M − 44	CO_2
M − 45	C_2H_5O, CO_2H
M − 46	NO_2
M − 55	C_4H_7 from butyl ester
M − 60	CH_3CO_2H loss from acetate, HCO_2CH_3 from tertiary esters, CH_2NO_2
M − 77	C_6H_5
M − 79	Br
M − 81	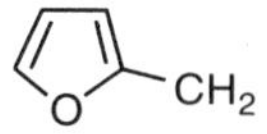
M − 91	$PhCH_2$ (tropylium), C_6H_5N
M − 93	CH_2Br
M − 105	PhCO
M − 127	I

Table A22 Common fragment ions.

m/z	Possible fragment and conclusion
15	CH_3^+
18	$H_2O^{+\cdot}$
26	$C_2H_2^{+\cdot}$
28	$CO^{+\cdot}$, $C_2H_4^{+\cdot}$, $N_2^{+\cdot}$, $CH_2N^{+\cdot}$
29	CHO^+, $C_2H_5^+$
30	$CH_2{=}NH_2^+$ (primary amine)
31	$CH_2{=}OH^+$ (primary alcohol)
36/38	$HCl^{+\cdot}$
40	$Ar^{+\cdot}$, $C_3H_4^+$ (useful reference peak)
43	CH_3CO^+, $C_3H_7^+$
44	$O{=}C{=}NH_2^+$ (primary amide), $CO_2^{+\cdot}$ $CH_2{=}CHOH^{+\cdot}$ (aldehyde)
45	$CH_2{=}OCH_3^+$, $CH_3CH{=}OH^+$ (ether or alcohol)
49/51	CH_2Cl^+
58	$CH_2{=}C(OH)CH_3^{+\cdot}$ (methyl ketone)
59	$CO_2CH_3^+$ (methyl ester), $CH_2{=}C(OH)NH_2^+$ (primary amide), $CH_2{=}OC_2H_5^+$
65	C_5H_5 (fragmentation from tropylium ion—$PhCH_2X$)
73	$(CH_3)_3Si^+$
77	$C_6H_5^+$
79/81	Br^+
80/81	HBr^+
81	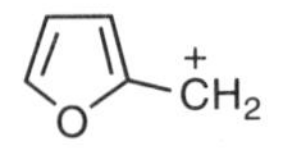
85	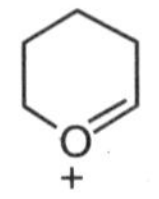 (tetrahydropyranyl ether)
91	Tropylium ion ($PhCH_2X$)
93/95	CH_2Br^+
127	I^+
128	$HI^{+\cdot}$
149	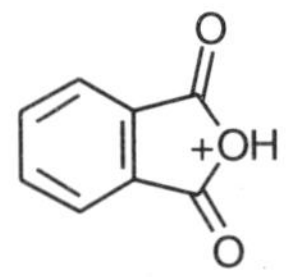 (from plasticizer contaminating sample)

The Periodic Table A23

Key to chart: atomic number — 50; symbol — Sn; 1995 atomic weight — 118.710; oxidation states — +2 +4; electron configuration — −13–18–4

Group labels: new notation; previous IUPAC form; CAS version

new notation	1	2	3	4	5	6	7	8	9	10	11	12	13	14	15	16	17	18	Shell
previous IUPAC form	Group IA	IIA	IIIA	IVA	VA	VIA	VIIA	VIIIA	VIIIA	VIIIA	IB	IIB	IIIB	IVB	VB	VIB	VIIB		
CAS version			IIIB	IVB	VB	VIB	VIIB	VIII	VIII	VIII	IB	IIB	IIIA	IVA	VA	VIA	VIIA	VIIIA	
	1 H +1 −1 1.00794 1																	2 He 0 4.002602 2	K
	3 Li + 6.941 2–1	4 Be +2 9.012182 2–2											5 B +3 10.811 2–3	6 C +2 +4 −4 12.0107 2–4	7 N +1 +2 +3 +4 +5 −1 −2 −3 14.00674 2–5	8 O −2 15.9994 2–6	9 F −1 18.9934032 2–7	10 Ne 0 20.1791 2–8	K–L
	11 Na +1 22.919770 2–2–1	12 Mg +2 24.3050 2–8–2											13 Al +3 26.981538 2–8–3	14 Si +2 +4 −4 28.0855 2–8–4	15 P +3 +5 −3 30.971761 2–8–5	16 S +4 +6 −2 32.066 2–8–6	17 Cl +1 +5 +7 −1 33.4527 2–8–7	18 Ar 0 39.918 2–8–8	K–L–M
	19 K +1 39.0983 −8–8–1	20 Ca +2 40.078 −8–8–2	21 Sc +3 44.955910 −8–9–2	22 Ti +2 +3 +4 47.867 −8–10–2	23 V +2 +3 +4 +5 50.9415 −8–11–2	24 Cr +2 +3 +6 51.9961 −8–13–1	25 Mn +1 +3 +4 +7 54.938049 −8–13–2	26 Fe +2 +3 55.845 −8–13–2	27 Co +2 +3 58.933200 −8–15–2	28 Ni +2 +3 58.6934 −8–16–2	29 Cu +1 +2 63.546 −8–18–1	30 Zn +2 65.39 −8–18–2	31 Ga +3 69.723 −8–18–3	32 Ge +2 +4 72.61 −8–18–4	33 As +3 +5 −3 74.92160 −8–18–5	34 Se +4 +6 −2 78.96 −8–18–6	35 Br +1 +5 −1 79.904 −8–18–7	36 Kr 0 83.80 −8–18–8	–L–M–N
	37 Rb +1 85.4678 −18–8–1	38 Sr +2 87.62 −18–8–2	39 Y +3 88.90585 −18–9–2	40 Zr +4 91.224 −18–20–2	41 Nb +3 +5 92.90638 −18–12–1	42 Mo +6 95.94 −18–13–1	43 Tc +4 +6 +7 (98) −18–13–2	44 Ru +3 101.07 −18–15–1	45 Rh +3 102.90550 −18–16–1	46 Pd +2 +3 106.42 −18–18–0	47 Ag +1 107.8682 −18–18–1	48 Cd +2 112.411 −18–18–2	49 In +3 114.818 −18–18–3	50 Sn +2 +4 118.710 −18–18–4	51 Sb +3 +5 −3 121.760 −18–18–5	52 Te +4 +6 −2 127.60 −18–18–6	53 I +1 +5 +7 −1 126.90447 −18–18–7	54 Xe 0 131.29 −18–18–8	–M–N–O
	55 Cs +1 132.90545 −18–8–1	56 Ba +2 137.327 −18–8–2	57* La +3 138.9055 18–9–2	72 Hf +4 178.49 −32–10–2	73 Ta +5 180.5479 −32–11–2	74 W +6 183.84 −32–12–2	75 Re +4 +6 +7 186.307 −32–13–2	76 Os +3 +4 190.23 −32–14–2	77 Ir +3 +4 191.217 −32–15–2	78 Pt +2 +4 195.078 −32–18–1	79 Au +1 +3 196.96655 −32–18–1	80 Hg +1 +2 200.59 −32–18–2	81 Tl +1 +3 204.3833 −32–18–3	82 Pb +2 +4 207.2 −32–18–4	83 Bi +3 +5 208.98038 −32–18–5	84 Po +2 +4 (209) −32–18–6	85 At (210) −32–18–7	86 Rn 0 (222) −32–18–8	–N–O–P
	87 Fr +1 (223) −18–8–1	88 Ra +2 (226) −18–8–2	89** Ac +3 (227) −18–9–2	104 Unq +4 (261) −32–10–2	105 Unp (262) −32–11–2	106 Unb (263) −32–12–2	107 Uns (262) −32–13–2	108 Uno (265) −32–14–2	109 Une (266) −32–15–2	110 Uun (269) −32–16–2									–O–P–Q

															Shell
*Lanthanides	58 Ce +3 +4 140.116 −19–8–2	59 Pr +3 140.90765 −21–8–2	60 Nd +3 144.24 −22–8–2	61 Pm +3 (237) −23–8–2	62 Sm +2 +3 150.36 −24–8–2	63 Eu +2 +3 151.964 −23–8–2	64 Gd +3 157.25 −25–9–2	65 Tb +3 158.92534 −27–8–2	66 Dy +3 162.50 −28–8–2	67 Ho +3 164.93032 −29–8–2	68 Er +3 167.26 −30–8–2	69 Tm +3 168.93421 −31–8–2	70 Yb +2 +3 173.04 −32–8–2	71 Lu +3 174.967 −32–9–2	–N–O–P
**Actinides	90 Th +4 232.0381 −18–10–2	91 Pa +5 +4 231.03588 −20–9–2	92 U +3 +4 +5 +6 218.0289 −21–9–2	93 Np +3 +4 +5 +6 (237) −22–9–2	94 Pu ++3 +4 +5 +6 (241) −24–8–2	95 Am +3 +4 +5 +6 (243) −25–8–2	96 Cm +3 (247) −25–9–2	97 Bk +3 +4 (247) −27–8–2	98 Cf +3 (251) −28–8–2	99 Es +3 (252) −29–8–2	100 Fm +3 (257) −30–8–2	101 Md +2 +3 (258) −31–8–2	102 No +2 +3 (259) −32–8–2	103 Lr +3 (262) −32–9–2	–O–P–Q

The new IUPAC format numbers the groups from 1 to 18. The previous IUPAC numbering system and the system used by Chemical Abstracts Service (CAS) are also shown. For radioactive elements that do not occur in nature, the mass number of the most stable isotope is given in parentheses.

References 1. G. I. Leigh. Editor, *Nomenclature of Inorganic Chemistry*, Blackwell Science Publications, Oxford, 1990.

2. *Chemical and Engineering News*, 63(5), 27, 1985.

3. Atomic Weights of the Elements, 1995. *Pure & Appl. Chem.*, 68, 2339, 1996.

Index of Chemicals

General Index

Please note: page references to figures appear in *italic* type and those for tables appear in **bold** type.